MW01194102

A CAMPAIGN OF GIANTS

The BATTLE for PETERSBURG

CIVIL WAR AMERICA

Gary W. Gallagher, Caroline E. Janney, and
Aaron Sheehan-Dean, editors

This landmark series interprets broadly the history and culture
of the Civil War era through the long nineteenth century and
beyond. Drawing on diverse approaches and methods, the
series publishes historical works that explore all aspects of
the war, biographies of leading commanders, and tactical and
campaign studies, along with select editions of primary sources.
Together, these books shed new light on an era that remains
central to our understanding of American and world history.

A complete list of books published in Civil War America is
available at https://uncpress.org/series/civil-war-america.

launched counterattacks that claimed a heavy Union toll—particularly in prisoners of war—including an engagement in August against an isolated Federal corps at Reams' Station, eight miles south of Petersburg. A daring cavalry raid in September yielded enough beef to feed the hungry Rebel army for a month. Still, Lee's offensive capacity diminished as his available forces shrank. Despite losing many fewer men than the Federals, the Confederates found it increasingly difficult to replace battlefield casualties. In contrast, fresh levies poured into Union ranks, although veteran commanders initially found the recruits and draftees of dubious value.

This does not suggest that Grant indulged in some grim game of human arithmetic. The Union general-in-chief wisely adapted his operations during the late summer and autumn of 1864. Gone were the bloody frontal attacks designed to bull their way through Rebel defenses. Instead, Grant exploited his numerical advantage by sending powerful detachments west, targeting Petersburg's supply lines, while at the same time threatening Richmond. The Army of Northern Virginia bent but did not break. The fate of Sheridan's forces in the Shenandoah Valley was never far from Grant's thinking. Each one of the Petersburg offensives addressed in these pages was designed to support Sheridan. The simultaneous attacks against Richmond's defenses and Petersburg's communications were intended, in part, to prevent Lee from reinforcing Early's small Confederate army in the Valley. Sheridan's victories there in September and October were a direct byproduct of this strategy.

The contest for Petersburg and its larger neighbor, the Confederate capital at Richmond, consumed 292 days in 1864 and 1865. The soldiers involved, as well as subsequent students of their ordeal, often refer to the operations around Petersburg as a siege. "Neither army can be relied on to storm works," Union staff officer Hazard Stevens explained in July 1864. "Now expect a second siege of Yorktown, slow tedious operations but little loss of life."[1] How wrong he proved to be, as the sanguinary battles described in these pages demonstrate. The struggle for Petersburg fails to meet either of the usual definitions of a siege. The defending Confederates were never encircled, nor did Grant undertake formal siege operations, such as those he conducted the previous year at Vicksburg. Rather, the battle for Petersburg entailed as a series of separate Union offensives resulting in major engagements, a handful of Confederate initiatives, and several prominent cavalry raids, all combining to form the longest sustained military operation of the Civil War.

In this, the second of three volumes focusing on the Petersburg Campaign, events between August 1 and the end of October take center stage. This period includes the Fourth, Fifth, and Sixth Petersburg Offensives, all entailing

PREFACE

The likelihood of Confederate independence diminished substantially between the first of August and the end of October 1864. The period began with a Rebel army firmly established in Virginia's Shenandoah Valley, fresh from a raid to the very gates of Washington, D.C. In Georgia John Bell Hood's Army of Tennessee, despite a series of failed offensives, still defended Atlanta, the elusive goal of William Tecumseh Sherman's powerful army group. The port of Mobile, Alabama, remained open to Confederate commerce, guarded by its twin bastions, Forts Morgan and Gaines. Sterling Price poised to lead reinvigorated Southern legions north into Missouri, aiming to redeem that border state for the Confederacy. Three months later, however, Philip H. Sheridan had all but destroyed Jubal A. Early's Valley Army, Sherman was master of Atlanta and completing preparations to march to the sea, David Farragut's fleet and its accompanying infantry had closed access to Mobile, and the pitiful remains of Price's divisions limped toward Texas, no longer recognizable as an army.

Only on the Petersburg-Richmond front had grayclad soldiers held their own. Robert E. Lee and his outnumbered Army of Northern Virginia—abetted by troops reporting to P. G. T. Beauregard and Richard S. Ewell—met three sustained Union offensives, each executed simultaneously north of the James River and south of Petersburg. Ulysses S. Grant's two armies—George G. Meade's Army of the Potomac and Benjamin F. Butler's Army of the James—seized territory but failed to capture Richmond or completely isolate Petersburg from its sources of supply. Yet the Federals did achieve material gains. Butler established a permanent presence in Henrico County, southeast of Richmond, that would require Lee to maintain a force there adequate to protect the capital. At Petersburg, Meade cut the Weldon Railroad, one of Lee's primary lifelines, and extended Union fortifications far to the west. By the end of October, the opposing armies stretched some thirty-five miles, a front Lee struggled to cover with his dwindling manpower.

Grant's accomplishments came at great cost. During each Petersburg offensive—one each in August, September, and October—the Confederates

MAPS

CONTENTS

To the memory of

RICHARD J. SOMMERS

(1942–2019),

generous scholar,

consummate gentleman,

and a most valued friend, whose

mastery of the Petersburg Campaign

(or, siege, as Dick preferred)

inspired my work

Designed by Jamison Cockerham
Set in Arno, Brothers, Fell DW Pica, Ashwood Extra Bold, Scala Sans
by codeMantra

Manufactured in the United States of America

Cover art: (*bottom*) Outer lines of Confederate fortifications, Petersburg, Virginia, June 15, 1864; (*left*) Gen. Robert E. Lee, 1864; (*right*) Gen. Ulysses S. Grant, ca. 1865, all courtesy of Library of Congress Prints and Photographs Collection, Washington, D.C.

LIBRARY OF CONGRESS CATALOGING-IN-PUBLICATION DATA
Names: Greene, A. Wilson, author.
Title: A campaign of giants : the battle for Petersburg / A. Wilson Greene.
Other titles: Battle for Petersburg | Civil War America (Series)
Description: Chapel Hill : The University of North Carolina Press, [2018]– |
Series: Civil War America Contents: Volume 2. From the Crater's aftermath to
the Battle of Burgess Mill | Includes bibliographical references and index.
Identifiers: LCCN 2017053873| ISBN 9781469684819 (cloth : alk. paper) |
ISBN 9781469683812 (epub) | ISBN 9781469684826 (pdf)
Subjects: LCSH: Petersburg (Va.)—History—Siege, 1864–1865. | Petersburg
Crater, Battle of, Va., 1864. | United States—History—Civil War, 1861–1865—
Campaigns. | Virginia—History—Civil War, 1861–1865.
Classification: LCC E476.93 .G73 2018 | DDC 973.7/37—dc23
LC record available at https://lccn.loc.gov/2017053873

A CAMPAIGN OF GIANTS

The BATTLE for PETERSBURG

VOLUME TWO

*From the Crater's Aftermath
to the Battle of Burgess Mill*

A. WILSON GREENE

THE UNIVERSITY OF NORTH CAROLINA PRESS

Chapel Hill

concurrent efforts south of the Appomattox River and north of the James River. August also witnessed one of the war's greatest acts of sabotage, while in September the Confederate cavalry conducted a spectacular raid behind Union lines.

The major engagements in August, September, and October consumed only sixteen days. The men in the ranks spent the rest of those three months engaged in the daily activities of an active campaign. Life on the picket lines elicited reams of comment in soldier correspondence, as well as claiming a deadly toll. Sometimes the proximity of the two armies created mini-engagements of their own—such as September's Battle of the Chimneys—along with multiple trench raids. The cavalry at times waged a seemingly separate war, somewhat removed from overall operations.

U.S. Colored Troops saw their most extensive combat action of the entire war during the late summer and early autumn of 1864. Black divisions in both Meade's and Butler's armies participated in the Union offensives. General Butler, in particular, emerged as a champion of these troops, relying on them for crucial attacks in several cases. The racial animus so vividly revealed at the Battle of the Crater in July persisted between Confederates and Black Union soldiers, while White Federals began to evince a grudging respect for their African American comrades.

The expansion of the military infrastructure around Petersburg claimed a great deal of soldier attention. Fortifications continued to lengthen, more than doubling the volume of earthworks between August and October. Elaborate defensive preparations on both sides elevated military engineering to its most intricate and ambitious level during the war. The Federals constructed a military railroad that linked their expanding front lines with the increasingly complex logistical center at City Point. Along the James, General Butler continued work on a canal at Dutch Gap designed to bypass the formidable Confederate defenses guarding a narrow stretch of the river known as Trent's Reach.

And, of course, the residents of Petersburg, Virginia's second-most-populous city and one of the largest urban centers in the Confederacy, suffered the malicious effects of being caught in the crucible of war.

Adj. William H. McLaurin of the Eighteenth North Carolina, in a postwar sketch of his regiment, wrote, "The story of Petersburg will never be written; volumes would be required to contain it, and even those who went through the trying ordeal, can not recall a satisfactory outline of the weird and graphic occurrences of that stormy period."[2] He may be correct, but I have done my best to do this epic story the justice it deserves.

A CAMPAIGN OF
GIANTS

The BATTLE *for* PETERSBURG

one

THIS IS A HARD AND BLOODY CAMPAIGN AND GOD ONLY KNOWS WHEN IT WILL END

August 2, 1864, promised to be another scorching day in the scarred landscape south of Petersburg, Virginia, with high humidity suggesting the likelihood of an afternoon thunderstorm. At ten o'clock that morning, four prominent Union officers assembled at the headquarters of the Second Corps, Army of the Potomac. The corps commander, Maj. Gen. Winfield S. Hancock, presided at this gathering, which included Brig. Gen. Romeyn B. Ayres, Brig. Gen. Nelson A. Miles, and Col. Edmund Schriver.[1]

These men had been summoned the previous day by the army's commander, Maj. Gen. George G. Meade, at the behest of General-in-Chief Ulysses S. Grant. Three days earlier Grant's forces had experienced what he called a "miserable failure" in his latest attempt to capture Petersburg. "So fair an opportunity will probably never occur again for carrying fortifications," wrote Grant of the events of July 30, and "I think there will have to be an investigation of the matter." Meade responded promptly, charging a handpicked "board of officers" to "examine and report upon the facts and circumstances attending the unsuccessful assault on the enemy's position in front of Petersburg" and to "report whether in their judgment any party or parties are censurable for the failure of the troops to carry into successful execution the orders issued for the occasion."[2]

There was just one problem. Hancock's board, styled a court of inquiry, had no statutory authority to act as instructed without the imprimatur of the president of the United States. Hancock, sensitive to protocol, so informed Meade and promptly adjourned the meeting. Meade conveyed this decision to Grant,

1

and at 9:30 that evening, Grant wired the U.S. Army's chief of staff, Maj. Gen. Henry W. Halleck, requesting that President Abraham Lincoln rubber stamp the composition and mission of Meade's court. Lincoln acceded the following day, and the court convened on August 8.[3]

The event that triggered this tribunal, the Battle of the Crater, had been Grant's third failed offensive at Petersburg in six weeks, and the culmination of an almost continuous campaign that had begun in early May, more than 100 miles to the northwest. Grant's victories in the western theater at Vicksburg, Mississippi, and Chattanooga, Tennessee, in 1863 had earned him promotion to lieutenant general and command of all Union armies. The new general-in-chief had arrived in Washington on March 8, 1864, and met President Lincoln for the first time, initiating what would evolve into a relationship of mutual respect and trust. He then traveled to Meade's command post near Brandy Station, Virginia. After discussions with the Pennsylvanian, Grant elected to retain him at the head of the Army of the Potomac. Rather than run the war from the capital, however, Grant would make his headquarters with Meade's army, creating a potentially problematical command arrangement.

Grant then returned to Washington, assigned Halleck, his predecessor, to the post of chief of staff, and boarded a train for Nashville, Tennessee, where he met with Maj. Gen. William T. Sherman, his favorite subordinate and the officer who would replace him as commander in the West. Here, Grant articulated his grand strategy for winning the war: simultaneous offensives across the map. One army would focus on Mobile, Alabama, the primary functioning Confederate port on the Gulf Coast. Sherman would personally lead three armies into North Georgia with the goal of capturing the Rebel transportation and industrial hub at Atlanta. In Virginia, Meade would operate against the main Confederate force there, Gen. Robert E. Lee's Army of Northern Virginia. Two additional Virginia offensives would complement Meade's efforts. Maj. Gen. Franz Sigel would spearhead a thrust up the Shenandoah Valley—a valuable source of supplies for Lee—while Maj. Gen. Benjamin F. Butler's Army of the James advanced up its namesake river from Hampton Roads to rendezvous with Meade near Richmond. Such pressure would prevent the outnumbered Confederates from shifting soldiers to meet isolated threats while degrading both Southern manpower and logistical resources.[4]

Meade's army consisted of three infantry corps—the Second, Fifth, and Sixth—plus the Cavalry Corps and an artillery component numbering some 264 guns, a force of 98,260 men present for duty. Maj. Gen. Ambrose E. Burnside led an independent corps, the Ninth, which added 18,408 more bayonets. Of the total number, however, barely half were veterans, the rest consisting of new conscripts or bounty men, whose motivation for serving and lack of field experience gave their officers pause. In reality, Burnside and Meade could count on only 70,000 thoroughly dependable soldiers.[5]

The Second Corps was the army's elite organization, and its commander was widely considered Meade's best subordinate. One of Meade's aides described General Hancock, a forty-year-old native of southeastern Pennsylvania, as "one of the handsomest men I ever saw, one of those rare combinations of the animal with the intellectual that impress you by their weight. He has the face of one of the Dutch generals of Van Dyke or . . . Rembrandt—that combination of energy, courage, intellect and obstinacy, that is determined to go through everything." Hancock stood more than six feet tall and weighed in excess of 200 pounds. "His splendid personal appearance attracts attention wherever he is seen and doubtless this is one of the adjuncts which gives him such thorough command over troops," thought another observer. He possessed a colorful vocabulary, "swearing like a trooper at some unfortunate fellow who has incurred his displeasure, the next [moment] as affable and polite as though he had been brought up exclusively in a drawing room." According to the general's former staffer and postwar biographer, Lt. Col. Francis A. Walker, Hancock could lift his troops "to the level of his impetuous valor when his men could see him in open battle." His performance on the battlefield at Williamsburg, Virginia, in 1862 had earned him the sobriquet, "Hancock the Superb."[6]

Not everyone intimately associated with Hancock admired him. Capt. Edward P. "Ned" Brownson, a Second Corps staff officer, considered him clannish and "a man with but one talent—for military affairs. He is nothing intellectually. He has risen too fast, received too much adulation, and grows more arrogant daily. He is cross as a bear, selfish and hoggish to an extreme in his manner and acts." Perhaps that ill temper sprang from the painful wound he had received during the Battle of Gettysburg in July 1863. This injury continued to plague him, at times compelling the general to travel in a wagon or entirely incapacitating him. Hancock began the campaign leading the four divisions of Brig. Gen. Francis C. Barlow, Brig. Gen. John Gibbon, Brig. Gen. Gershom Mott, and Maj. Gen. David B. Birney.[7]

Maj. Gen. Gouverneur K. Warren presided over Meade's Fifth Corps. Just thirty-four years of age at Petersburg, Warren had compiled a brilliant record as a cadet at the U.S. Military Academy, and rose quickly in the Army of the Potomac to become its chief engineer. At Gettysburg his keen eye and prompt action earned him credit as the savior of Little Round Top, the key terrain on the battle's second day. Warren subsequently assumed temporary corps command in place of the wounded Hancock, and upon that general's return to duty, he took charge of the Fifth Corps.[8]

Charles Bolton, a delegate of the Christian Commission, described Warren as "a tall slim man, with the eyes of a hawk which pierce [the] way for his commands and compel obedience. I judge him to be one of General Alcohol's Aids." Excessive drinking never compromised Warren's effectiveness, but other personality traits did. "He was egotistical," thought a newspaper correspondent. "His caution was excessive. His distrust of every one's judgment which ran counter to his own was universal." Indeed, Warren's penchant for challenging orders and providing unsolicited advice rankled Meade, who on more than one occasion considered relieving him. Warren's division commanders at the outset of the campaign included Charles Griffin, John C. Robinson, Samuel W. Crawford, and James S. Wadsworth, all brigadier generals, although neither Robinson nor Wadsworth would be present at Petersburg.[9]

The popular if unspectacular Maj. Gen. John Sedgwick led the Sixth Corps, but during the campaign's first week, he fell victim to a sharpshooter. Maj. Gen. Horatio G. Wright replaced him. Wright, like Warren, had graduated second in his class at West Point and compiled a creditable record as a prewar military engineer. His tenure in corps command during the spring campaign to Petersburg proved undistinguished. Unrelated to any of Wright's shortcomings, he and his corps found themselves transferred to the Shenandoah Valley in early July and thus were absent at Petersburg until December.[10]

Burnside's Ninth Corps was the army's odd man out. General Burnside, a West Point graduate who would celebrate his fortieth birthday during the third week of Grant's campaign, had risen to command of the entire army in November 1862. Popular and self-effacing, he led his troops to a bloody debacle at the Battle of Fredericksburg in December and the following month fell victim to the weather while attempting to redeem that defeat. Lincoln replaced him but refused to accept his resignation. Instead, the president reassigned Burnside and his corps to service in the western theater. He and his men returned east in the spring of 1864, reporting directly to Grant in an awkward organizational arrangement precipitated by Burnside's seniority to Meade. Grant would correct this flaw in late May with the humble Burnside's cheerful acquiescence.[11]

Like Warren, Burnside would test the patience of both Meade and Grant and eventually earn the former's irredeemable disdain. His corps always seemed to generate disappointing results on the battlefield. Haunted by the aroma of incompetence at Fredericksburg and earlier at the Battle of Antietam, Burnside skated on thin ice from the very outset of his service with Meade. Nevertheless, according to one Ninth Corps officer, despite "the two disasters associated with his name, his old soldiers kept faith in him, and believed that the fault lay with others, who failed to carry out his plans, rather than with him." "He was one of the noblest and best of men," testified another. "No other general in the Union army so completely won the deep and sincere love and admiration of the men under his immediate command." The loyalty of his troops, however, would provide Burnside scant protection from his increasingly toxic relationship with Meade, a dynamic that would reach its denouement at the court of inquiry. By the time the Ninth Corps reached Petersburg, its divisions were led by Brig. Gen. James H. Ledlie, Brig. Gen. Robert B. Potter, Brig. Gen. Orlando B. Willcox, and Brig. Gen. Edward Ferrero. Ferrero commanded two brigades of U.S. Colored Troops (USCT), the only African American soldiers in the Army of the Potomac.[12]

Grant handpicked a new commander for Meade's cavalry corps. Maj. Gen. Philip H. Sheridan first attracted Grant's attention in November 1863 at Chattanooga, when, while commanding an infantry division, Sheridan displayed singular initiative during the conquest of Missionary Ridge. He became one of only a handful of officers Grant brought with him from the West. "Following Sheridan in his military career is like perusing an exciting romance, which at every change of scene grows brighter and more fascinating," thought one observer. Only thirty-three years old when he arrived in Virginia, Sheridan began the war as a quartermaster, then rose to colonel of the Second Michigan Cavalry. He eventually took charge of an infantry division and fought with competence and élan at Perryville, Kentucky; Murfreesboro, Tennessee; and Chickamauga, Georgia, before Grant recognized his unusual penchant for relentless warfare. Lt. Col. Theodore Lyman of Meade's staff described the brash Irishman from Ohio as "a small broad shouldered, squat man, with black hair & a square head. He is of Irish parents, but looks very much like a Piedmontese." A prominent New Yorker commented that "with a forehead of no promise and hair so short that it looks like a coat of paint, of all our chieftains he alone has displayed the capacity of handling men in [the] actual shock of battle." Grant placed complete confidence in Sheridan and allowed him almost free rein to operate independently of Meade's infantry—another irritant for the army commander. The cavalry division heads under Sheridan included another Grant favorite, Brig. Gen. James H. Wilson, along with Brig. Gen. Alfred T. A. Torbert and Brig. Gen. David M. Gregg.[13]

Brig. Gen. Henry J. Hunt directed Meade's artillery, which, like the infantry and cavalry branches of the Army of the Potomac, outnumbered its grayclad counterpart in the Army of Northern Virginia, and that formidable Confederate army was still led by General Lee. By the spring of 1864, Lee was universally acknowledged as the premier soldier in the Confederacy. "Every man in that army believed Robert E. Lee was the greatest man alive," averred a one-time cadet at the Virginia Military Institute. "No man on this continent or any other now fills so large and important a place to so many people," wrote the ranking military physician in Petersburg. "I verily believe, under God, our whole cause is in his hands; and if he goes down the hope of the nation is extinct." At age fifty-seven Lee retained the vigor and acuity of a much younger man, although the effects of two heart attacks the previous year and recurring digestive problems began to take their toll. "He hardly looks as I expected," thought an Alabama lieutenant, "not so handsome but what anyone would call a fine looking warrior."[14]

The Army of Northern Virginia began the 1864 spring campaign with what historian Gary W. Gallagher describes as "a strong sense of optimism." Despite supply problems and sagging morale on the home front, most of Lee's soldiers believed that under the direction of "Marse Robert," they would dominate Grant as they had all previous Federal commanders. The army numbered roughly 65,000 effectives at the outset of the campaign, divided into three corps of infantry, associated artillery, and the Cavalry Corps. The leadership of these units, in place since the army's reorganization the previous spring, would suffer crippling attrition en route to Petersburg, including the men at the top of Lee's table of organization.[15]

Lt. Gen. James Longstreet, fresh from a disappointing venture in independent command in East Tennessee, returned to Virginia in the spring of 1864 at the head of Lee's First Corps. The forty-three-year-old Longstreet was, according to the colonel of the Twenty-First South Carolina, "a very stout man" with "as fine a face as I ever saw." Lee once referred to him as "my old war horse," and despite the fundamental disparity between his and Lee's strategic visions, the army commander placed implicit trust in his senior subordinate. Longstreet's serious wounding on May 6—a victim of friendly fire—imposed a grievous loss on Lee's inner circle. Lt. Gen. Richard H. Anderson, a forty-two-year-old South Carolinian of modest ability, would replace Longstreet until his return to active duty in October.[16]

Beginning the campaign at the head of the Second Corps was Lt. Gen. Richard S. Ewell. Despite losing a leg in battle in 1862, Ewell received promotion to corps command following the death of Lt. Gen. Thomas J. "Stonewall" Jackson the following May. One of Ewell's subordinates considered him "the most unique personality I have ever known. He was a compound of anomalies, the oddest, most eccentric genius in the Confederate army." The forty-seven-year-old Ewell lacked Jackson's aggressive inclinations and struggled under the strain of his heightened responsibilities. Within three weeks of the Overland Campaign's commencement, Lee found it necessary to relieve Ewell, eventually reassigning him to lead the relatively quiet Department of Richmond. Lee

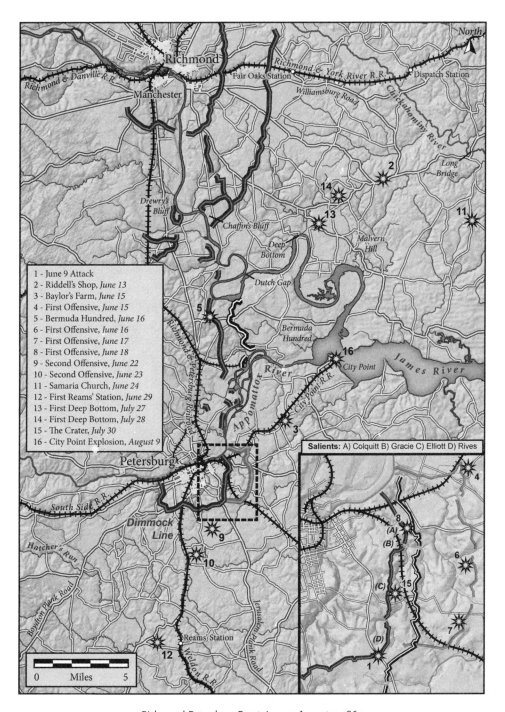

1 - June 9 Attack
2 - Riddell's Shop, *June 13*
3 - Baylor's Farm, *June 15*
4 - First Offensive, *June 15*
5 - Bermuda Hundred, *June 16*
6 - First Offensive, *June 16*
7 - First Offensive, *June 17*
8 - First Offensive, *June 18*
9 - Second Offensive, *June 22*
10 - Second Offensive, *June 23*
11 - Samaria Church, *June 24*
12 - First Reams' Station, *June 29*
13 - First Deep Bottom, *July 27*
14 - First Deep Bottom, *July 28*
15 - The Crater, *July 30*
16 - City Point Explosion, *August 9*

Salients: A) Colquitt B) Gracie C) Elliott D) Rives

0   Miles   5

Richmond-Petersburg Front, June 9–August 9, 1864

tapped Lt. Gen. Jubal A. Early as Ewell's replacement, and would send Early to the Shenandoah Valley at the head of his corps in mid-June, reducing his own army's infantry strength around Richmond and Petersburg by a third.[17]

Lt. Gen. Ambrose Powell Hill was another relative newcomer to Lee's pantheon of corps commanders. Hill had earned a reputation as the army's best division chief earlier in the war, despite clashes with Jackson, and upon Stonewall's death Hill assumed command of a new corps, styled the Third. A Virginia chaplain described him as "a small man . . . scarcely more than 5 ft 8 in. high nor . . . more than 125 or 130 lbs." A West Point graduate and thirty-eight years old, Hill, like Ewell, proved something of a disappointment in his elevated role. He frequently succumbed to incapacitation, perhaps as a result of venereal disease contracted as a younger man, often leaving the Third Corps in the hands of temporary leaders for extended periods.[18]

The campaign began with Maj. Gen. James Ewell Brown Stuart leading the Army of Northern Virginia's stellar cavalry. Although the advantage the Southerners had always enjoyed over their blueclad opponents had diminished, Stuart's horsemen exercised more parity with their Union counterparts than any other branch of the service. That calculus changed abruptly on May 11 when Stuart suffered a mortal wound in a clash with Sheridan's cavalry a few miles north of Richmond. Lee would take months to name his replacement, instructing division commanders Maj. Gen. Wade Hampton, Maj. Gen. Fitzhugh Lee, and Maj. Gen. William H. F. "Rooney" Lee, the army commander's son, to report directly to him.[19]

The armies first clashed on May 5, 1864, initiating more than five weeks of near-constant combat. A brutal two-day battle in the Wilderness of Spotsylvania and Orange Counties transitioned into nearly two weeks of fighting around Spotsylvania Court House. Meade and Grant continually maneuvered their forces southeast, maintaining supply lines via Virginia's tidal rivers and compelling Lee to withdraw ever closer to Richmond, the industrial, logistical, administrative, and symbolic center of the Southern war effort. The armies sparred again along the North Anna River in late May, yielding indecisive results. The Federals' next attempt to vanquish Lee's army and capture Richmond unfolded around an obscure crossroads known as Old Cold Harbor. Here, on June 3, the Unionists suffered a lopsided defeat, in the process persuading Grant that further operations north of the James River would be futile. Instead, he planned to focus on Petersburg, twenty-three miles south of Richmond and a railroad nexus critical to Confederate supply.[20]

Petersburg's founding predated the Civil War by more than 200 years. Situated at the head of navigation along the Appomattox River, the city exploited its natural advantages to become a thriving port, boasting an impressive U.S. Customs House, completed in 1859. A canal initially linked Petersburg with its upstream hinterlands, but in the 1830s railroads began to supplant waterborne commerce. By 1858, five separate lines connected Petersburg with all points of the compass. These transportation assets led to the development of a robust industrial economy, making it one of the South's leading manufacturing centers. Iron, cotton, and particularly tobacco processing provided employment for hundreds, including many African Americans, both enslaved and free. In 1860 3,244 of the 12,586 free persons in Petersburg were African American, the highest such proportion of any major Southern city. Voters there, like many urban Southerners, embraced conservative politics, preferring John Bell, the Constitutional Unionist candidate for president in 1860. Their delegate to Virginia's first state convention joined the majority in rejecting immediate secession. But following Lincoln's requisition of troops to suppress armed rebellion, precipitated by the firing on Fort Sumter, South Carolina, in April 1861, Virginia voted to leave the Union. Petersburg citizens enthusiastically agreed, eventually sending ten companies of infantry, two companies of cavalry, and three artillery batteries to the Confederate army.[21]

Petersburg had faced the threat of attack several times prior to Grant's impending initiative. During the campaign from Fort Monroe up the Virginia Peninsula two springs earlier, Union forces occupied City Point, the hamlet at the confluence of the Appomattox and James Rivers, then functioning as Petersburg's deep-water port. From there they launched a naval thrust designed to sever the railroad connecting Petersburg and Richmond, which failed, as did Maj. Gen. George B. McClellan's associated offensive against Richmond. McClellan subsequently proposed crossing the James to operate against an almost defenseless Petersburg, but the War Department rejected his suggestion. At last recognizing that city's vulnerability and its critical strategic relationship with Richmond, Confederate authorities approved the construction of a ten-mile defensive perimeter around the city, called the Dimmock Line. Featuring fifty-five artillery redans connected by an infantry curtain, these works anchored on the Appomattox River both downstream and up. By June 1864, the Dimmock Line remained Petersburg's sole means of defense, although time had somewhat eroded its earthen walls.[22]

More than the ravages of time and neglect, a lack of manpower left Petersburg ripe for swift capture. Gen. P. G. T. Beauregard, commander of the Department of North Carolina and Southern Virginia, bore direct responsibility for the city's defense. His vast area of authority—independent of Lee's control—extended from the mouth of southeastern North Carolina's Cape Fear River to the south bank of the James, spreading thin his limited forces. The Army of the James steamed up its namesake river in May, in keeping with Grant's grand strategy, and menaced Petersburg. Butler might have easily captured the city but for a series of events that distracted his attention. On June 9 he finally attacked Petersburg, failing through a combination of ineptitude and the heroics of a contingent of local old men and young boys who manned the Dimmock Line until Beauregard's regulars arrived. Still, as both Butler and Meade approached the city on June 15, Beauregard could count on fewer than 4,000 defenders, including a sizable body of untrained militia, to face the combined Union multitudes.[23]

Grant's plan to move from Cold Harbor to the James River was brilliantly conceived and almost flawlessly implemented. While Maj. Gen. William F. Smith's Eighteenth Corps of Butler's army, which had been temporarily attached to the Army of the Potomac at Cold Harbor, traveled up the river toward City Point, Meade's four corps followed primitive roads south, confusing Lee as to their whereabouts and intentions. By June 14, Smith was poised to move against Petersburg, while Hancock's divisions began crossing the James well downstream from City Point, evading Confederate detection. Smith, whom Grant had entrusted with responsibility for breaching Beauregard's defenses, launched his belated assault on the evening of June 15. He easily captured a large segment of the Dimmock Line east of Petersburg, while poor communications, faulty maps, and enervating heat conspired to delay Hancock's arrival until dark. Smith and Hancock opted not to push forward, while Beauregard rushed reinforcements to Petersburg from north of the city. Lee, still uncertain of Federal intentions, only incrementally released troops from north of the James. Meade arrived before Petersburg on the sixteenth and superintended substantial but uncoordinated attacks for three days, as the entire Army of the Potomac eventually spread out before Beauregard's beleaguered defenders. The Confederates resisted gamely, falling back to a new line of works closer to the city. Lee, at last informed of Grant's comprehensive presence before Petersburg, sent the remainder of the Army of Northern Virginia to the Cockade City early on the morning of the eighteenth in time to blunt Meade's final attacks. These four days of fighting, Grant's First Petersburg Offensive, claimed some 13,000 Union casualties while inflicting about 2,500 losses on the Rebels.[24]

Grant had remained at his new City Point headquarters, strangely aloof from events at the front. He reassured Meade that he was "perfectly satisfied that all has been done that could be done. . . . Now we will rest the men and use the spade for their protection until a new vein can be struck." Contrary to this promise of a respite from active operations, on June 20 Grant ordered the commencement of his Second Petersburg Offensive. This initiative involved a two-corps advance to the west designed to cut both the Weldon and South Side Railroads, a large cavalry raid far to the southwest, and the establishment of a bridgehead north of the James at a landing called Deep Bottom.[25]

Only the last of these initiatives succeeded. On the night of June 20, a brigade from Butler's army ferried across the James and secured the opposite bank, while engineers completed a pontoon bridge to the south shore the following day. Meanwhile, the Second and Sixth Corps pushed west across Jerusalem Plank Road, quickly losing contact with one another, and halting well short of their railroad objectives. On June 22, Confederate infantry led by Brig. Gen. William Mahone unleashed a devastating attack on the Second Corps, under the temporary command of General Birney. The next day Mahone's brigades hit the Sixth Corps near the Weldon Railroad, exploiting the gap between Birney and Wright, sending the Federals in retreat back to Jerusalem Plank Road. The Union army sustained heavy losses, including more than 2,200 men taken prisoner, a steep price for extending their trench lines a few hundred yards.[26]

The Second Offensive's cavalry component also fell to grief. Led by General Wilson and Butler's cavalry chief, Brig. Gen. August V. Kautz, the blueclad horsemen ranged through ten Virginia counties, ripping up tracks and burning depots, water tanks, and rolling stock on three railroads. Harassed by pursuing Southern cavalry and thwarted by a collection of untrained militia and convalescent veterans at a critical bridge over the Staunton River, Wilson and Kautz turned back to Union lines only to enter a trap at Reams' Station, a few miles south of Petersburg. Most of the Federals managed to escape, but they left behind all their artillery and the plunder they had accumulated during the raid. Wilson and Kautz lost at least 900 men during several engagements, and Confederate crews soon repaired the damaged tracks.[27]

"This is a hard & bloody campaign & god only knows when it will end," wrote Pvt. Harvey A. Marckres of the First Vermont Cavalry. "It is the most desperate & determined of anything we have had yet." In addition to absorbing tens of thousands of casualties to this point, the Army of the Potomac had suffered catastrophic attrition at the command level. Of the army's forty-one brigades, only eleven had the same commander on June 30 as they had on May 4. The turnover at the regimental level was even greater. A New York soldier told an upstate newspaper, "We thought Bull Run, Antietam and Fredericksburg hard battles, but they were mere feints compared to what we have to go through . . . in front of Petersburgh." Despite the failures of June and their calamitous consequences on manpower and leadership, Grant remained undeterred in his quest to conquer Petersburg and Richmond.[28]

The Third Petersburg Offensive began a pattern in which the Federals would strike simultaneously north of the James River and either directly against or around Petersburg's defenses. Grant's primary effort in July relied on exploiting his bridgehead at Deep Bottom. He directed Meade to send Hancock and the bulk of Sheridan's cavalry across the James to reinforce Butler's foothold on the river's left bank. Grant hoped that while Hancock pinned Richmond's defenders in place, Sheridan could ride north of the Confederate capital unhindered to wreak havoc on the railroads connecting it with the Piedmont and the Shenandoah Valley. The Unionists, after managing significant logistical problems, crossed the James on the morning of July 27 and engaged the Rebels along New Market Road. Sheridan's troopers experienced delay in moving into position, preventing the rapid ride northwest required to reach their objectives. Instead, the cavalry reinforced Hancock's attempt to find a way around the grayclad defenders, who had been heavily reinforced by brigades sent from Petersburg. Serious fighting on July 28 failed to gain the Federals an advantage, and by the next day, Hancock and Sheridan had begun to withdraw, ending the engagement that became known as First Deep Bottom.[29]

Although the foray across the James ended in failure, it did draw all but three Confederate infantry divisions from Petersburg. Lee's thinned defenses south of the Appomattox lent prominence to what, until the failure at Deep Bottom, had been something of an afterthought in Grant's strategic thinking.

Lt. Col. Henry Pleasants, a brigade commander in the Ninth Corps and a prewar engineer, had overseen construction of a mine targeting a prominent Confederate fort known as Pegram's or Elliott's Salient. Such an endeavor became feasible because Burnside's troops had gained a position opposite this point during the fighting on June 18. Hidden by the sheltering valley of Poor Creek, the Federals began their work in secrecy on June 25, and by July 27 the mine, some 510 feet in length, terminated precisely below the Confederate fort. Soldiers from the Forty-Eighth Pennsylvania, the regiment responsible for excavating the shaft, loaded the mine with 8,000 pounds of black powder and ran fuses back 98 feet to detonate the explosion. Over time the Confederates had grown suspicious and sunk several countermines, none of which plunged deep enough to intercept the Union tunnel.[30]

Meade's headquarters had been skeptical of excavating such a long shaft undetected and with adequate ventilation, and the army commander doubted the efficacy of any assault that would follow an explosion. Meade, in truth, questioned any endeavor undertaken by Burnside and indulged rather than encouraged the project. Yet with the diminution of enemy forces occasioned by the fighting north of the James and that gambit's failure, Burnside's completed mine suddenly gained not only credibility but also preeminence in Grant's plans. The general-in-chief and Meade ordered its detonation and a subsequent attack for the predawn hours of July 30.[31]

General Burnside had prepared to exploit the mine for weeks. His three White divisions had been bled badly during the initial assaults at Petersburg, so he tapped his eager but untested Black brigades to lead the charge. They received instruction for their very first combat assignment, although the extent of that training remains in doubt. Following the explosion, General Ferrero's troops were to skirt the edges of the resultant crater and head straight for high ground called Cemetery Hill, from which they could command the Confederate line. The remainder of Burnside's men would follow, widening the breach and then reinforcing the African American soldiers on Cemetery Hill.

These sensible plans collapsed on July 28 when Meade informed Burnside that the Black brigades could not lead the assault. They were too inexperienced for such an assignment, he explained, and moreover, should the attack fail, the political price for sacrificing Black soldiers in a risky offensive would be too high. Burnside protested, but Grant sustained Meade's eleventh-hour interference.[32]

Up until then, Burnside had managed the entire operation masterfully, but rather than assign either Potter's or Willcox's well-led divisions to spearhead the attack, he left the decision to chance. All three of his White division commanders drew lots to determine who would receive the assignment, and Ledlie emerged with the "short straw." This officer had demonstrated his penchant for drunkenness on two previous combat occasions, and no division commander in Meade's army exceeded his incompetence. "The lot fell on Judas Ledlie, a poor drunken imbecile," lamented Brig. Gen. Simon G. Griffin of the Ninth Corps. "That was the great mistake of Burnside's." Ledlie would have less than twenty-four hours to develop and articulate his plans, and he bungled them badly. Instead of instructing his brigade commanders to charge directly for Cemetery Hill, Ledlie ordered them to hold the ground around the Crater, relying on subsequent divisions to seize the key terrain.[33]

At 4:44 A.M. on July 30, "the ground . . . burst asunder as if a volcano [erupted]," sending earth, cannon, debris, and human bodies skyward, "showing an unsightly pile of ruins where once was a splendid fort." Three hundred and fifty-two South Carolina infantrymen and Virginia cannoneers became instant victims, buried alive or blown beyond recognition. Ledlie's men climbed out of their advanced trenches to witness an unprecedented scene of horror while their commander huddled in a rear-area bombproof, seeking comfort from a bottle. Shocked by the results of the blast, immobilized by their orders to remain around the breach, and deprived of leadership, Ledlie's men aimlessly milled around long enough for the Confederates to seal the shoulders of a 500-yard gap in their defenses. Confederates on either side of the Crater began to pour fire into the stationary Federals, while Southern artillery lobbed shells and mortar rounds into the nearly defenseless bluecoats.

Under Meade's instructions, Burnside committed his other divisions, turning the Union front into a chaotic mob scene devoid of command or control. Ferrero's troops charged last and advanced farther than most of the White troops. But by then, General Mahone had marshaled two of his brigades from the far end of the Confederate line and launched them in a counterattack that paralyzed the Union soldiers, who sought shelter in the shattered Confederate works or in the Crater itself. "Bullets came in amongst us like hail stones," testified an officer in the Nineteenth USCT. "Men were getting killed and wounded on all sides of me. . . . Soldiers were groaning and crying for water which if one undertook to give him would be most sure to get shot."[34]

Early in the afternoon, Mahone dispatched a second wave that reached the exhausted Union survivors. Some desperate bluecoats attempted to run the gauntlet back to the main Union lines, often with fatal results. The remaining White troops were allowed to surrender, but the Rebels showed no mercy to Ferrero's African American soldiers, massacring them without remorse. "Some of the men that was in the fight tell me that they were all right together every fellow killing all he could," related a South Carolinian. "The enemy charged with *niggers* in front," explained a soldier from the Fourteenth South Carolina. "But our brave boys soon rallied and drove the sable sons of Africa back in great confusion and in their retreat were run right into the excavation made by the explosion and the poor devils were butchered right and left." By 2:00 P.M., the Crater and all the ground around it returned to Confederate control. "They came hollowing no quarters," wrote a Mississippi soldier, "our men gave them the bayonet and [the Federals] did not make a hole big a naught to hold the ded." A New York captain declared the Battle of the Crater "the most disastrous of the campaigns for us," while Pvt. Joseph Cross of the Eleventh New Hampshire succinctly summarized the affair in a letter to his wife: "There has been another hard battle fought & we got the worst of it. It was a complete failure."[35]

When the battle smoke cleared and the firing ceased, the scene that greeted the triumphant Confederates shocked the senses. "In our front and almost under our noses, lay the bloated festering bodies of their dead, exposed to the scorching rays of a July sun," testified a North Carolinian. A Rebel engineer reported that "there were in the bottom of the Crater 133 of the enemy's dead and dying men, negroes, Indians, and whites and very few dead Confederates were in sight."[36]

This Is a Hard and Bloody Campaign

The Southerners reshaped and then reoccupied their shattered fortifications, maintaining a desultory fire for the remainder of the day. Grant briefly considered renewing the offensive but quickly canceled this ill-conceived notion upon learning that many of the Confederates who had marched north of the James were returning to the Petersburg lines. Instead, the Federals braced for a possible assault, something Lee did not even consider. The Southerners spent the remainder of the day and most of July 31 perfecting their makeshift defenses around the Crater and burying their dead.[37]

These activities did not include treating the wounded Union troops lying in the no-man's-land between the lines or tending to the increasingly putrefying corpses of the Federal dead. "The ground was yet dotted with the slain, nearly all blacks, swollen by the hot sun to an enormous size, and rotted with corruption," remembered a Mississippian. "One poor fellow lay weltering in his gore; while swarms of flies hovered and buzzed around him, filling him with their larvae." The colonel of the Sixty-First Virginia of Mahone's command saw an African American survivor missing both of his legs "drag himself with his hands to the outside of our earthworks, and by sticking three muskets with bayonets in the ground and throwing a small piece of tent cloth over them, improvise a shelter to protect his head from the blistering sun. A pitiful scene!"[38]

Burnside requested permission on the thirty-first to seek a flag of truce to provide succor to the wounded, but Meade hesitated, citing the Confederates' refusal to grant a ceasefire following the carnage on June 18. Eventually, with Grant's acquiescence, Meade authorized Burnside to negotiate an informal arrangement to suspend hostilities long enough to recover the Union wounded and bury the dead, thus avoiding the admission of defeat inherent in soliciting a formal ceasefire. What followed bestowed neither honor nor humanity on the Confederate commanders. The Rebels refused to acknowledge any informal truce, so Burnside forwarded Meade's official request for a suspension of hostilities. General Lee declined to consider the petition. Instead, he passed it to Beauregard, whose troops technically bore responsibility for that portion of the line, even though by then, Beauregard was no longer an independent commander. This petty pretention of protocol consumed precious hours, and by the time Beauregard received and approved the request, it was too late to effect a truce on the thirty-first. The Creole general informed Meade that hostilities would cease at 5:00 A.M. on August 1, some thirty-nine hours after combat at the Crater had ended.[39]

"Southern malice had done its worst for all who were left on the field," growled a Union soldier. "Those who were not already dead were in such a condition that human aid could avail them nothing." A Pennsylvanian reported that "some of the dead were so much torn up they had to use shovels or spades to gather them on stretchers. It was a hard looking spectacle." The relatively few Black soldiers taken prisoner emerged from the Confederate lines and joined men from the Thirty-Fifth Massachusetts and one of Ferrero's regiments to dig burial trenches in which to dump the mangled human remains. Meanwhile, soldiers and officers from both sides took advantage of the truce to emerge from their trenches and socialize amid this macabre scene. The enemies exchanged refreshments and "commenced their usual contraband traffic the Yankees exchanging jack knives canteens coffee &c for the great Rebel staple—tobacco." The Southerners allowed the ceasefire to continue beyond the designated time in order to allow the workers to finish their grim task, which resulted in recovering fewer than twenty survivors.[40]

Despite sprinkling a large quantity of lime over the burials, the Crater would remain a horrible place for weeks. "Our chief discomfort arose from the sickening & offensive smell of the dead bodies . . . buried close around us," wrote Col. Fitz William McMaster of the Seventeenth South Carolina. "A stream of water running down the hole from the crater bore a rank smell." One Confederate rode through the damp ground, and the stench that attached to his horse's hoofs caused him to vomit. Occasionally, body parts would emerge from the shallow graves. "Such . . . scenes make us think that truth is more terrible than fiction," admitted McMaster. "Man's inhumanity to man makes countless thousands mourn."[41]

"The affair of Saturday was one of awful destruction—wanton on the part of the enemy & very vindictive on our part," summarized Brig. Gen. Henry A. Wise, Beauregard's nominal garrison commander in Petersburg. "Our losses I fear were not less than 1000 and the enemy at least 5000." Meade would report some 4,400 casualties on July 30, a disproportionate number of them African American. Burnside's units lost no fewer than nineteen regimental colors. The Confederates suffered 1,622 casualties, both in the explosion and during Mahone's counterattacks. Combined with the failure at First Deep Bottom, Grant's Third Offensive had been the worst debacle of the Petersburg Campaign. "Never before or after, in the history of the Potomac army, was such an exhibition made of official incapacity and personal cowardice," concluded a staff officer.[42]

"Matters are quiet around Petersburg since the failure of Grant as a miner," wrote a Virginia trooper in early August. "I presume he will continue to blast however at the rate of 5000 men to the mine." Other Confederates expressed similar confidence. "Grant your course is ruin," a South Carolinian confided to his diary. "You go the way of your predecessors." Pvt. Paul M. Higginbotham of the Nineteenth Virginia agreed. "Grant, great as he is thought to be by the

This Is a Hard and Bloody Campaign

Northern Fanatics, is no more a match for our Noble Lee, than an Ethiopian." No lesser an observer than General Beauregard believed that the failures of Grant's Third Offensive portended ultimate Confederate success. "My conclusion is, that well commanded and well led this army cannot be whipped."[43]

William Mahone had as much to do with generating this optimism as anyone. During the week following the battle, the general issued a congratulatory address to the three brigades that executed the victorious counterattacks on July 30. "With the tread of veterans and the determination of men, you charged the works upon which [the enemy] had planted the hated flag," he wrote. "The integrity of the whole line was, by your valor, promptly reestablished." William Cameron, a leading Petersburg businessman, sent Mahone a box of fine spirits to express the gratitude of the city's residents, while Lee and Confederate president Jefferson Davis bestowed a more valued gift, promotion to major general. Mahone's corps commander, A. P. Hill, joined the chorus of praise in a general order issued on August 4.[44]

Some Confederates could not resist ridiculing the defeated Federals and their vaunted chieftain. "Richmond still stands in defiance of the largest army ever martialled on the continent of America, lead on by the hero of the West," boasted a sarcastic Alabaman. "It is a well-established fact that no one had in this war seen a Yankee who had been wounded twice," chuckled Lt. Col. Samuel W. Melton, a Richmond staff officer. "One wound settles them. They go home and stay. So that a wounding of a Yankee is almost as good as killing him."[45]

No one exceeded the vitriol toward Grant expressed by a Georgian from the Troup Artillery. "When he saw those vandals running pell mell to their works and the 'Rebel' battle flag proudly floating above the fallen breastworks . . . we can well imagine how he fretted, grieved, vexed, mortified . . . at this failure," wrote the gunner to a Georgia newspaper. "When he returned to his tent and imbibed another 'soaker' of that burning water, the forms of McClellan, Pope, Burnside, Hooker appeared before him. He . . . imagined he heard the rattling of that gold medal . . . Congress presented him. . . . Just then some poor wounded negro appears at his door, and by his 'peculiar scent' arouses him from these drunken dreams. He remembers the mine, takes another drink, and swears that 'somebody' shall suffer for this."[46]

Indeed, someone would be held responsible for this monumental failure, and the candidates were many. Grant was not immune. "A good deal is said about who was to blame in the fight of Saturday," wrote Pvt. John Tidd of the 109th New York. "It is my opinion that if any Gen is to blame, it is no one but Gen Grant himself." Another critic, thought to be former Union general Gustave Paul Cluseret, asserted that "the mountain of idiocy represented by our

Lieutenant-General, has at last brought forth ... a terrible disaster, the paternity of which cannot be doubtful." Even Gideon Welles, Lincoln's secretary of the navy, expressed doubt as to Grant's fitness for the army's top spot. The general-in-chief's detractors sometimes dredged up old accusations of drunkenness to explain his failures, while others simply pointed to his complicity in Meade's malign influence on the operation. "I believe Grant is nonplussed," asserted Pvt. Warren S. Gurney of the 56th Massachusetts. "The question in my mind is Grant going to raise the siege and fall back a whipped man. I am afraid he is."[47]

Secretary Welles's skepticism about Grant paled in comparison to his blatant distrust of the Army of the Potomac's commander. "If [Grant] has ability, I think he needs a better second in command, a more competent executive officer than General Meade," wrote the cabinet official a few days after the Crater. "I do not consider him adequate to his high position." Some would cite Meade's last-minute rejection of Burnside's plans as the cause of the debacle. "General Burnside was permitted no discretion," asserted a sympathetic biographer. "Meade has made another terrible blunder," wrote a Pennsylvania cavalryman. "Had our troops been managed properly at the time Grant blew up one of their forts we could have taken Petersburg in tact." The most damning indictments came from Ninth Corps soldiers, who saw the army commander's bias against Burnside as the root cause of their defeat. "We generally lay the blame of our failure in not taking Petersburg to Mead being jealous of Burnside and not supporting him," thought a man from the Thirty-Fifth Massachusetts. Sgt. Leander O. Merriam of the Thirty-First Maine was even more explicit. "It is hard to resist the belief that Gen. Meade deliberately preferred to destroy the Ninth Corps rather than help Burnside."[48]

Naturally, many in the army held the Ninth Corps commander responsible for the miscarriage of an operation that had been his from the outset. "Accounts agree that yesterday's assault failed by the incapacity of Gen. Burnside," wrote New Hampshire captain George F. Towle. "Burnside is to blame I think," echoed Lt. John Randolph Paxton of the 140th Pennsylvania. "If someone hadn't blundered, we would have driven the Johnnies straight into the Appomattox." General Warren and Eighteenth Corps commander Maj. Gen. Edward O. C. Ord laid the blame on Burnside, as did Lt. Col. Cyrus Comstock and Lt. Col. Adam Badeau, members of Grant's staff. "Burnside seems to have had no idea whatever what to do," intoned Badeau. "He is not competent to command a corps," agreed Comstock. Predictably, Meade remained the general's harshest detractor. "The affair was very badly managed by Burnside, and has produced a great deal of irritation and bad feeling," he confided to his wife. "I have applied to have him relieved."[49]

This Is a Hard and Bloody Campaign

Burnside had his defenders, who gazed down the table of organization as well as up. "I think him much less at fault than both his superiors and inferiors," believed Capt. Charles J. Mills, a Ninth Corps staff officer. Division commander Willcox and brigade commander Col. Zenas R. Bliss pointed the finger at General Ledlie, whom Grant likewise called "an inefficient man."[50]

In addition to his overall incompetence, some critics referenced Ledlie's fondness for his cups. "The General who was to make the charge was drunk," a soldier from the 117th New York stated unequivocally. Pvt. Austin J. Kendall, also from the 117th, alleged that Brig. Gen. Joseph B. Carr, whose Eighteenth Corps division supported Burnside's attack, "was so drunk that he did not know what end he stood on." Other accusers were less specific. "Some say our officers were drunk," Private Gurney told his uncle in a letter the night of the battle. "Whiskey is a great enemy of our army." A correspondent from the 32nd Massachusetts explained the failure to his hometown newspaper by reporting, "I will use the expression of the minister, the time the son of Neptune entered the church with a full cargo of whiskey on board, that there was always something to spoil good preaching."[51]

Some of the rank and file adopted a more generic condemnation of the officer ranks, such as Sgt. Thomas F. Walter of the Ninety-First Pennsylvania, who blamed the "sickening and villainous affair" on "the neglect and stupidity of the high officers of our army." Brig. Gen. Alfred H. Terry, who commanded a division in Butler's Tenth Corps, wrote on August 2 that he considered the general officers in the Army of the Potomac "humbugs." Butler himself told his wife that on July 30 there were "too many men, too few generals." Pvt. Lyman A. Barton of the Eighth Connecticut thought that "jealously between the Generalls" undermined the Union attack, and Lt. Harrison Montague of the Tenth New York Heavy Artillery predicted that "the affair . . . will be very likely to result in the downfall of some shoulder strapped gentlemen."[52]

The Ninth Corps itself came in for its share of opprobrium. "Never did I meet with anything quite so incomprehensible as the 9th Corps in this whole affair," grumbled Col. Charles Wainwright, the Fifth Corps chief of artillery. Another cannoneer, who had only heard about the fiasco at the Crater, wrote home, "It's too bad to see a corps lose its reputation and a strong position foolishly through pure cowardice." An officer in the 1st Delaware believed that if his corps, the Second, had made the attack, "we would have gone to Petersburg with little loss." Conversely, Ninth Corps participants blamed the supporting troops for their defeat. "I think and I always shall that if the rest of the army had gone in with any wheres near the spirit that the ninth corps did," averred Pvt. Alonzo D. Lewis of the 109th New York, "that it would have swept everything before it." His division commander, General Willcox, cited the prejudice harbored by other units against Burnside's corps as the source of undue criticism. "The 9th Corps has been considered not an integral part of the old army of the Potomac," he wrote, "& there are . . . those in the other corps that are glad to get a kick at the brave old dog now he is down."[53]

At least one Union soldier remained unsure of where to assign the blame. "Whether the true cause will ever be shown is a matter of some doubt in my mind," he admitted. Yet the majority of those who analyzed the cause of the failure felt sure they knew the culprits' identity. "You know the cause of that defeat by this time," Pvt. Newton Spencer of the 179th New York assured his hometown newspaper. "The abolition mania for employing 'nigger' soldiers has culminated in the worst disaster of the whole campaign and discouraged and nearly demoralized a whole army." Spencer disparaged Ferrero's soldiers as "a division of raw and worthless black poltroons." Lt. Charles Kline of the 115th New York expressed similar racial animus. "All we had gained was lost by the cowardice of the black scorpions who are called human. But for them I might now be writing in Petersburg." Snarled another New Yorker, "I say put the niggers out of our corps."[54]

Many White Union soldiers cited the panicked retreat of Ferrero's men as the cause of their defeat, criticism replete with explicit racial overtones. "We were . . . greatly surprised & dismayed to behold the field suddenly filled with niggers on the full run for the rear like a flock of sheep & apparently without reason or cause & almost every man of them having thrown away his gun," a Connecticut captain informed his family. "Burnside's nigers mad a charge a fiew dayes a go and thay got Scart and run like sheep," wrote semiliterate Pvt. Elisha Clark of the Seventeenth U.S. Infantry. "I guess old Birnsides wont think so much of his tar foots after this." Pvt. Edwin Paddock of the Nineteenth Wisconsin compared the retreating Black troops to dogs rather than sheep, but the common theme of all similar critics is that Ferrero's men precipitated the Union withdrawal that created chaos and prevented the defenders from holding their ground. "Niggers . . . skedadled and created a panic," summarized Cpl. Alonzo Rich of the Thirty-Sixth Massachusetts. "If it hadn't been for them we should have occupied Petersburg."[55]

A Fifth Corps soldier laid blame on the incapacity of the Black soldiers' White commanders. "You know how the nigger regiments are furnished with officers & they are not apt to be the best & bravest men," he explained to a friend. "It is said that the officers of the Negro soldiers were all drunk at the time and I believe it," wrote Sgt. Joseph Barlow of the Twenty-Third Massachusetts. Another soldier simply called the White officers in Black units "cowardly."[56]

This Is a Hard and Bloody Campaign

Even the Confederates credited their victory at the Crater to the participation of Black troops. "If the attack had been made in full force and with vigor the Confederacy would have fallen that day," believed Lt. Col. William Willis Blackford. "But Grant put his negro troops at the head of the attacking column and of course they wilted." Arch secessionist Edmund Ruffin, who spent the war years in and around Petersburg, thought it "incomprehensible" that "negro troops should have been trusted for such important service when there were plenty of white veteran troops at hand."[57]

Such disparagement of Black soldiers, although widespread, was not universal. Some rank-and-file Federals thought that Ferrero's men fought competently or at least deserved less than full blame for the humiliation. "I think that the Niggers did as well as any troops could have done under the circumstances," wrote Sgt. Sam Putnam of the 25th Massachusetts, using language echoed by a soldier in the 50th New York Engineers. "A great deal of opposition to colored troops grows out of unfounded prejudice," he explained. Surgeon Charles Mead of the 112th New York informed his brother: "There is disposition to give the colored troops the whole blame. This I do not think is just. That their behavior was shameful is true but they are not alone to blame." A Maine trooper took note that none of the Ninth Corps troops held the African Americans accountable for their defeat. General Butler remained a particular champion of Black soldiers. "They ought to bear all their share of the odium which attaches to the failure," he wrote Grant, "but no more." Nevertheless, the Battle of the Crater underscored the racial bias that had always existed in the Union army. "I wish to god that nigers were all out of the country for it is nothing but niger all the time niger for breakfast and niger for dinner and niger for supper," barked Sergeant Barlow. "For my part I do not care how many are in the army but put them by themselves. . . . They ought not to be with white soldiers."[58]

Regardless of popular opinions as to the cause of the defeat at the Crater, many in the Union army expressed a newfound discouragement and enhanced pessimism about the course of the campaign. Brigade commander Col. J. Howard Kitching reported that "everybody has been *blue* since our terrible 'fiasco' on the 30th." The colonel of the Sixth New Hampshire admitted that his men "felt depressed over our failure, and we could not help thinking of our dead that lay a few rods in front of us." Lt. Col. Theodore Bowers, an integral member of Grant's inner circle, admitted: "As the evidences of the disgraceful conduct of all concerned develop and thicken," even Grant "grows sicker at heart. . . . All men who understand the whole matter are paralized and pettrified." Such sentiments sapped the will of some soldiers to continue to fight. "Proceedings are not carried on here as they are represented to the people at Home," explained Pvt. Thomas J. Kessler of the First Michigan Sharpshooters. "It is just calling young men from home and bringing them here for slaughter and fast as they can kill them off call for more." Cpl. Henry Snow of the Twenty-First Connecticut confided to his mother, "I do not believe there is a man in the hole north that is sicker of the war than the soldier."[59]

Discouragement turned to despair for some, who saw the setback on July 30 as an omen of ultimate defeat without some fundamental change. "It is certain we cannot whip the rebels with what forces we have in the field," wrote Capt. Josiah Jones of the Sixth New Hampshire in a plea for additional troops. Meade's provost marshal, Brig. Gen. Marsena R. Patrick, believed that the time for winning the campaign by assault had passed, "and all that we can do now is to begin a regular system of works around" Petersburg and Richmond. Col. Louis P. di Cesnola, the commander of the Fourth New York Cavalry, called for the most drastic of adjustments: the replacement of Meade with former army commander Maj. Gen. George McClellan. "Everybody seems confident here that nothing can be done and even the black republican officers begin to see the necessity of having General McClellan at the head of this army once again," the colonel wrote two days after the Crater. "Rumor says that Meade has been or is going to be relieved. God grant it be so."[60]

But General Grant, as disappointed as he was in an operation he called "the saddest affair I have witnessed in this war," did not let the defeat diminish his determination. "We will peg away . . . and end this matter, if our people will but be true to themselves," he wrote. The *New York Times* assured its readers that Grant "retains an unswerving faith in his ability to take Richmond." Another newspaper correspondent reported that despite initial demoralization, the soldiers began to see that "the Rebels were no stronger and we scarcely weaker for the one unlucky day's work." "Grant . . . holds on with tenacity of iron," observed a Keystone State trooper, "& success will crown his efforts here in time as they did at Vicksburg." By August 10, Uberto A. Burnham, the quartermaster of the Seventy-Sixth New York, felt able to assure his father: "The unfortunate affair of July 30th . . . don't affect us at all here. It was a small matter compared to some battles we have had this summer. It has weakened the army only a little and discouraged it not at all." Burnham admitted that the Battle of the Crater was "very discreditable" and "who was really at fault only a court of inquiry can determine."[61]

That court's opening session on August 8 stimulated rampant speculation throughout the army. "The failure at the mine explosion of July 30th is still the theme of conversation among the officers," wrote the surgeon of the 57th New York, "but no one seems to know just where the responsibility therefore rests."

This Is a Hard and Bloody Campaign

"The truth is no one knows as yet who is responsible," agreed Cpl. George S. Youngs of the 126th New York, although Capt. William Brooke Rawle of the 3rd Pennsylvania Cavalry was sure that "some big bug will go up the spout for the lamentable failure." Youngs knew one thing for certain, "there will be a large quantity of liquor consumed in the process at all events, whether the truth is arrived at or not."[62]

A clue could be found in Meade's August 3 request to Grant that Burnside be sacked. "The whole course of that officer on the 30th ultimo, and subsequently, has been of such a character that it is impossible I can properly command this army if he continues in command," he argued. Meade not only held the Ninth Corps commander responsible for the Crater debacle but also complained of his insubordination in the hours and days that followed. The army commander's staff knew well their chief's antipathy toward Burnside, prompting Lt. Col. James C. Biddle to inform his wife that the court of inquiry would hold Burnside to account, "and then I presume Genl Meade will prefer charges against him." General Ord also recognized Burnside's partial culpability, writing his wife, "Genl Burnside is quite ready to assume—perhaps more than his share" of the blame. "He wishes his division commanders to be screened." Ned Brownson, the Second Corps staff officer, predicted that the court would "kill Burnside," while Colonel Wainwright believed that "the causes of failure are so patent & thoroughly known throughout the army that the finding of the Board is well known before hand." Captain Jones felt less sure about the court's ultimate decision, but he hoped that "the guilty party will suffer. The sacrifice of 5000 men for nothing should be properly investigated."[63]

Burnside began to defend himself even before the court convened, starting with challenging its composition. "Whilst I have the greatest respect for the officers composing the court," he wrote Secretary of War Edwin M. Stanton, "I feel I have a right to ask that it be made by officers not in this army and not selected by General Meade." Stanton dismissed this request, assuring Burnside that General Hancock and his officers composing the court would act impartially and merely forward their findings for Lincoln's consideration.[64]

Meade took the stand first and quickly moved to the attack, fixing the blame squarely on Burnside's shoulders. He ducked any responsibility for refusing to let the general lead with Ferrero's division, calling attention to Grant's approval of that decision. Meade also focused on the flurry of correspondence between himself and Burnside that reflected badly on the Ninth Corps commander. Burnside attempted to strike from the record anything that occurred after the battle, realizing that his language would be considered disrespectful at best. The court denied this request.[65]

Resuming his testimony on August 10, Meade submitted to pointed questions from Burnside aimed at refuting the army commander's version of events. Later that day Burnside himself began what by now amounted to his defense, giving testimony that spanned three days and provided a lengthy description of the mine's construction, the planning for the attack, and the course of the battle. An impartial analysis favors the corps commander's point of view, although once the battle was joined, Burnside's lack of communication with Meade did him no credit.[66]

Meade informed his wife that he thought that "active operations will interrupt [the] proceedings," and he was right. The court adjourned on its sixth day, reconvening on August 29 at the Jones house, Hancock's headquarters. Nearly thirty officers, including Grant, offered testimony over the course of the next eleven days. On September 9 the court issued its findings, and not surprisingly, it came down hard on Burnside. An "injudicious formation of the troops going forward . . . the halting of the troops in the crater instead of going forward to the crest . . . no proper employment of engineer officers," poor leadership of the assaulting column, and "the want of a competent common head at the scene of the assault" composed the indictments. Ledlie, and to a lesser extent Ferrero, Bliss, and Willcox, also received the court's condemnation for their roles in the aforementioned failures.[67]

A case can certainly be made that justice served Burnside badly during these proceedings—in fact, a subsequent investigation would bear this out—but the court's findings meant only one thing: Burnside must go. On August 13 Grant authorized Burnside to take a thirty-day leave of absence after rejecting his offer to resign for, as General Willcox quipped, "the 40-eleventh time." Meade took satisfaction at his subordinate's departure and vowed that he would "never return whilst I am here. I don't care where he goes so as he is not in my army." Burnside wrote Grant on August 25 from the White Mountains of New Hampshire inquiring if he should make plans to return to Petersburg, inquiring similarly on August 31. Grant merely responded that he should "await orders where you are." The verdict of the court ten days later sealed the general's fate. Burnside took "all his staff, both Corps & personal," reported Lieutenant Colonel Biddle, and "it is known he will never return to the command of the Corps." He was right—Burnside's military career had ended. Maj. Gen. John G. Parke, Burnside's chief of staff, replaced him at the head of the Ninth Corps on August 14. Ledlie departed on sick leave even before the court convened, also never to return to the army, but Ferrero, Bliss, and Willcox retained their positions.[68]

The soldiers of the Ninth Corps regretted the banishment of their beloved leader. A Massachusetts officer insisted that the entire corps held Burnside "in

This Is a Hard and Bloody Campaign

great esteem and affection." Augustus Woodbury, a regimental chaplain and the general's first biographer, received scores of letters from members of the corps that "contained the warmest expressions of affectionate esteem for their former commander." There were those at the time who considered Burnside a scapegoat. Even his most formidable antagonist, General Meade, expressed a form of sympathy for his disgraced subordinate. "I feel sorry for Burnside," Meade confessed to his wife, "because I really believe the man half the time don't know what he is about and is hardly responsible for his acts."[69]

President Lincoln did his part to move the army and the country beyond the defeat at the Crater by declaring August 4 a day of national fasting, humiliation, and prayer. Meade encouraged his officers to issue general orders to hold religious services in their camps whenever possible. "Today is fast day, and we are going to have some chaplains here at headquarters and some preaching," reported J. Franklin Dyer, chief surgeon in one of Hancock's divisions. Col. Alvin C. Voris of the Sixty-Seventh Ohio observed what he called the "President's Fast day. I am keeping it in the style it ought to be kept . . . by taking my ordinary meals with a thankful heart that it is no worse with us than it is."[70]

While the Federals suffered depression and sought redemption and accountability for their failure at the Crater, the Confederates planned their own subterranean surprise. The explosion on July 30 triggered anxiety bordering on paranoia in both armies over further mining. "It is very curious how soldiers become so familiar with one kind of danger . . . as to disregard it almost entirely," observed Lieutenant Colonel Blackford, "and yet become demoralized when danger in a new form presents itself. . . . To have the very ground on which they stood blown up under them, without a chance for life or a chance to retaliate, was something so new and so terrible that the bravest turned pale." Capt. John Sloan of the Twenty-Seventh North Carolina confirmed that "we were in daily and nightly apprehension of being transported to realms unknown." In early August a private in the Twenty-Third Georgia confided in his diary that "the topic of the day is mining," adding that "the boys are all rather suspicious of being blown up since Grant has begun springing his mines."[71]

A junior officer in Sloan's regiment, however, professed to be "not much frightened about being blown up, but would rather be a little farther off" from Union lines. A South Carolinian expressed confidence in his generals, who looked with "indifference" on rumored Union mining, while John L. G. Wood, regimental drummer of the Fifty-Third Georgia, hoped that the Federals would try it again, though only "if it pays out to us like their late one."[72]

Union concerns about Confederate mines focused on two specific locations. The first encompassed a huge installation along Jerusalem Plank Road. Known as Redoubt G, the Eighteen-Gun Battery, or Fort Tilton (later renamed Fort Sedgwick), this work earned the moniker "Fort Hell" for the volume of fire it attracted from nearby Confederate artillery. Completed on July 11, this bastion came under Fifth Corps jurisdiction. On August 2 Warren visited the fort and heard a distinct and constant sound of picking. He ordered pits sunk to discover if the Confederates were, in fact, trying to undermine the position. He also had his troops construct an interior line in case an explosion destroyed the fort's outer walls, removed most of the guns, and relocated the garrison to adjacent fortifications. "Ever since the springing of the mine on the 30th of July stories have been afloat that the rebels were undermining this fort and there appears to be some foundation to them, for Gen. Warren has caused shafts to be sunk . . . and subterranean passages running in such directions as to intercept any such attempt," explained a Massachusetts private to his diary. Sgt. Charles T. Bowen of the 12th U.S. Infantry testified that a deserter showed him and some officers exactly where the Confederates were mining, a report that the Federals tried to confirm by placing an officer in a shallow trench in front of the alleged target "with a drum before him on which were placed some beans. The slightest jarring of the earth made by digging would communicate its motion to the beans on the drumhead." At least one Yankee was eager for the Rebels to try their hand at mining. "We say: 'Go in John Williams!'" wrote Lt. George P. McClelland of the 155th Pennsylvania. "Blow away! We are prepared to give them a warm reception."[73]

McClelland would get his wish on August 5. The other Confederate mining target lay on high ground, Hare's Hill, defended by elements of Butler's Eighteenth Corps and opposite two Rebel strongpoints known as Gracie's Salient and Colquitt's Salient. Southern engineers, responding to widespread rumors of Union mining at several locations, had begun countermines here prior to July 30. On the thirty-first Col. Walter H. Stevens, chief engineer of the Army of Northern Virginia, authorized engineer Capt. Hugh Thomas Douglas to charge the countermine at Gracie's in order to destroy a suspected Federal gallery. By the morning of August 1, Douglas had loaded each of two countermines with 225 pounds of black powder contained in four barrels. The miners readied for the blast, but the powder failed to ignite due to defective fuses. Douglas then cleared the mine of its combustibles and began to extend one of the shafts closer to the Union lines. Work also continued on the tunnel from Colquitt's Salient.[74]

By August 4, the Gracie's Salient mine stretched farther toward the Federal works and was charged with 850 pounds of explosives. But according to

This Is a Hard and Bloody Campaign

Lieutenant Colonel Blackford, the mine followed too high an ascending angle to reach the main Union line before emerging from the ground. The Confederates decided to ignite it anyway, hoping to at least destroy a Federal sap, or approach trench, that protruded from the enemy lines on Hare's Hill. They would detonate the mine on August 5.[75]

Unlike the unsuspecting Confederates at the Crater, Union forces knew of the Rebel mine. As early as August 2, multiple deserters reported the excavations, intelligence that quickly scaled the chain of command from division commanders Hiram Burnham and Adelbert Ames, both brigadier generals, to corps commander Ord, and up to army chieftains Meade and Butler. Federal soldiers confirmed these reports with audible evidence. The Twenty-Third Massachusetts occupied the portion of the line at which the mine was aimed. "We were therefore fully prepared," testified the regimental historian.[76]

That preparation included several expedients. "It seems our commander knowing all about the mining operation of the enemy had removed all the cannon and forces from the fort—planted wooden guns there and massed our forces behind the line of works ready to repel the expected charge," explained Cpl. James Parley Coburn of the 141st Pennsylvania. The Federals had as many as three new installations constructed a short distance behind, on the flanks, and out of sight of the one they assumed was targeted. "We had all the guns out of it and had bilt a [masked] fort back of the one they had undermined and put wooden guns in so that they did not know we had found it out," confirmed Pvt. Elias S. Buterbaugh of the Signal Corps. Various witnesses counted from two to four "Quaker guns" in the embrasures of the presumably mined fort. One Pennsylvanian claimed, rather dubiously, that "our men had put up a white canvass in front of the fort and had painted port holes showing the muzzles of heavy guns" rather than mounting wooden tubes.[77]

Several Federals made the equally questionable claim that once the mine had been discovered, Union soldiers used a countermine to intercept the Confederate shaft and remove the powder placed within. Lt. Henry S. Graves of the 118th New York, for example, wrote his wife that they had anticipated the mining "and had counter mined and taken out the powder and then waited for them to come on." Capt. Henry Falls Young of the 7th Wisconsin added the detail that the Union diggers had left "just enough [powder] to make an explosion without injuring the fort."[78]

In any event, enough powder remained in the mine to create "a deep heavy rumbling explosion [that] saw clouds & masses of earth ascend above the trees & as suddenly descend." The blast, detonated sometime between 5:00 and 6:30 P.M., fell between forty feet and forty yards short of any Union fort, merely "throwing trees and dirt quite a distance in the air." "Not a gabion or sap-roller was displaced, nor much of a crater formed," reported Maj. Gen. Bushrod R. Johnson, whose troops held the Confederate lines behind the tunnel. "The mine must have been badly tamped, as the gallery was destroyed as far back as the shaft. Our picket line was partially filled up, but again dug out." Lt. Philip McKay of the Fifty-Ninth Alabama in Archibald Gracie's brigade admitted to his brother: "Our tunnel . . . did not amount to very much. It did not extend far enough to do much damage to the enemy's breast works."[79]

Nevertheless, numerous Confederates found satisfaction, fabricated or otherwise, in the effects of the blast on their enemies. "When the ground bursted they all run for life," wrote Pvt. Thomas W. G. Inglet of the Twenty-Eighth Georgia. "We stood in our works and had fun a shooting them." Sgt. James J. Kirkpatrick of the Sixteenth Mississippi recorded in his diary: "An experimental mine was sprung and some fighting done. The Yankees took a fright and ran out of their works. Our line fired on them going and returning." A Virginia private gloated that the mine explosion scared "the 'blue bellies' or 'cerulean abdomens' very badly." "We scared them badly at all events," agreed Lt. Col. Rufus A. Barrier of the Eighth North Carolina, "and showed them plainly that two can play at the game of tunneling."[80]

From the point of view of many Confederates, the explosion marked a triumphant test. General Beauregard reported to Richmond: "An experimental mine was fired successfully . . . in front of Gracie's line. Enemy appeared much alarmed." Engineer Fred Harris agreed: "We sprang a mine . . . near the Yankee works intended more as an experiment than anything else which created a considerable excitement for a while." An Alabama soldier informed the *Montgomery Daily Mail* that "the experimental mine of General Beauregard will probably cause [the Federals] to abandon their underground works entirely, as it gives them a wholesome scare, and has awakened them from their fancied security, by revealing . . . that our own picks and spades are not idle." Lt. R. Lee Barfield of the Eighth Georgia Cavalry celebrated the destruction of a Union countermine. "Gen. Lee did not expect to do more than destroy their mine & keep them from invading our battery," he explained. A Virginia cannoneer merely asserted that "we accomplished all that was intended and therefore made no further demonstration."[81]

Federal accounts agreed with their opponents on the nature of the explosion, but their descriptions of the aftermath proved markedly different. "About 6 P.M. they blew up a small mine in front of the 18th Corps," explained Lieutenant Colonel Lyman. "I don't know what they did it for exactly as it exploded some 40 yards in front of our works. Some think they miscalculated, others that it

This Is a Hard and Bloody Campaign

was to blow in one of our mines (which had no existence.)" The chaplain of the 100th Pennsylvania credited the mine with "blowing two or three trees and some earth between the lines" but affecting no portion of the Union works."[82]

General Ames commanded the division in Ord's corps targeted by the Confederate mine. The high command of this unit agreed that the Confederates failed to launch a serious assault following the detonation. Ord had been conducting an inspection of his lines when the explosion occurred. "When turning towards the sound I saw a cloud of dust and smoke rising high in the air and knew it was a mine," he told his wife. "It was followed by volleys of musketry and a brisk cannonade from both sides and as no cheers or continuation of the musketry came to my ear I thought the rebels had not assaulted which proved to be the case." Ames reported that following the blast, the Confederates "delivered a volley of musketry toward the breast-works," eliciting return fire from rifles and artillery for about thirty minutes before "everything became quiet." General Butler informed the War Department that the Confederates "did not make an assault" and that casualties were light.[83]

Soldiers from the Twenty-Third Massachusetts and other regiments in Ames's First Brigade corroborated their officers' accounts. Sergeant Barlow reported that the Rebels "had their men all ready to charge as soon as they had blowed us up but they were doomed to a disappointment they did not advance but a short distance and turned back." A noncommissioned officer from Company A agreed that "the enemy, seeing their mine a failure, satisfied themselves with rising behind their works and pouring in heavy musketry, mostly on Ames's front." A soldier correspondent from the Twenty-Third admitted that the "rebs opened a heavy fire with artillery and musketry, the shells bursting uncomfortably near sometimes," but that they failed to charge the works. A New York soldier from the same brigade expressed disappointment at the Confederates' behavior. "We were on our feet to meet them in less than a minute," he wrote a friend. "I fairly ached to have them charge us for we would have swept them like grass before the scythe." "For about half an hour it was a pretty lively time," explained Lt. Frank L. Smith of the Twenty-Fifth Massachusetts, "but then all quiet again & we laid down to sleep."[84]

These eyewitness accounts no doubt accurately reflect the nature of the fighting following the explosion. It is noteworthy, however, that numerous Union soldiers, many from the Ninth Corps, described an entirely different and apocryphal scenario. Cpl. William Boston of the Twentieth Michigan in Burnside's command wrote his aunt that the Confederates charged "five line[s] deep and when they got about two thirds of the way our forces opened on them front and flank with musketry and grape. They soon had to fall back with heavy loss." The Twentieth's Addison S. Boyce, a musician, wrote home that the Rebels came within five rods of the Union line when the bluecoats opened on them, leaving the ground "covered with their dead and wounded." A veteran of the Seventeenth Michigan characterized the phantom Rebel assault as "a feast of death" and described the attackers reaching close to the Union lines before "a storm of iron hail . . . swept their ranks as with the 'besom of destruction.'" Two Second Corps soldiers reported the capture of 700–800 prisoners, a Pennsylvanian repeated the rumor that "800 were killed 400 prisoners taken," while a New York cavalryman boasted with unmatched hyperbole that the Confederates "lost some 15,000 men" in the assault. Perhaps these capricious accounts stemmed from the desire of those who suffered defeat and humiliation on July 30 to level the score, even if doing so required outright fabrication. "After this they will not laugh so loudly at our failure of last week," hoped a Massachusetts surgeon.[85]

Confederate losses went unreported but were undoubtedly negligible. Ord listed thirty Union casualties, the most serious of which was Col. Griffin A. Stedman, commander of Ames's Second Brigade, a soldier General Ord called "one of the finest officers of this corps." Stedman, a twenty-six-year-old native of Hartford, Connecticut, practiced law before the war. A volunteer officer in the Fifth Connecticut, he rose to become the commander of the Eleventh Connecticut and assumed brigade command during the 1864 spring campaign. A fellow Nutmegger thought the colonel among the worthiest men in the army striving for promotion to general. Stedman earned a reputation for bravery that bordered at times on recklessness. Members of his old regiment thought that he "sheltered his men but was prodigal of his own life."[86]

Prior to the explosion, Stedman had responded to increased fire from Confederate pickets by examining the advanced line of trenches at which the fusillades were aimed. Ignoring the wounding of a nearby soldier, the colonel calmly told a staff officer that he hoped he would not be shot in the same place. Sometime later, General Ames joined Stedman at the front while in the process of conducting his own reconnaissance. During their conversation, a minié ball struck Stedman in the chest, carrying a part of his handkerchief into the wound. Stretcher-bearers brought the wounded officer to the rear, where several surgeons examined him, fearing the injury was fatal. Suffering great pain, Stedman expressed regret that he should be shot in so insignificant a skirmish. He died the next day. Both Butler and Ord requested his promotion to brigadier general posthumously, an honor bestowed by the War Department on August 7.[87]

Although there would be no more mining detonations at Petersburg in 1864, concern about such activity and its potential results remained integral to army life. The Confederates expressed particular worry about the possibility of being

This Is a Hard and Bloody Campaign

blown sky-high, given their unhappy experience on July 30. "We do not know at what minute the Yankees will spring another mine," confessed Pvt. John Lane Stuart of the Forty-Ninth North Carolina. "It is believed that Grant is hard at work on other parts of the line," one South Carolinian fretted, "and if he should spring several of these mines at the same time and charge the whole line there is no telling what the result would be." Pvt. John H. Walters of a Virginia artillery battery admitted that he had become "terribly demoralized at the thought of finding myself going up some fine morning or other," fearing "being buried alive and dying in that condition, while the panorama of my last life passed before my eyes. . . . This thought is terrible and almost unmans me."[88]

The Federals recognized that their enemies might assail them underground but in general professed much less anxiety about that possibility. They continued to suspect that Fort Sedgwick and the works on Hare's Hill—both places where the lines lay perilously close together—presented the most likely Confederate targets. Yet unlike their counterparts, most Unionists welcomed the possibility of another Confederate explosion. "Has any discovery been made of the points where the enemy seemed to be mining?" Grant asked Meade. "If it can be ascertained nearly where they are running their mines I think it would be well to let them run on without countermining, in hopes of having them attack us." Precautions such as excavating protective ditches around vulnerable locations left men such as Lt. James B. Thomas of the 107th Pennsylvania unfazed. "We have no fear of their blowing us up," he assured his father. Lt. Joseph J. Scroggs of the 5th USCT hoped that the Rebels would try again to detonate a mine in front of Hare's Hill, promising a deadly surprise for the attackers. "Come on Johnny!" he urged. Still, men such as John Tidd regretted that "it has got to a great pass, trying to blow one another up [and] bury them alive. . . . A warfare fit only for uncivilized nations."[89]

Federal speculation was correct. The Confederates were mining opposite Hare's Hill as well as toward Fort Sedgwick from an adjacent strongpoint called Rives Salient. Maj. Giles B. Cooke, Beauregard's assistant adjutant general, visited Colquitt's Salient on August 17 and examined two galleries, advancing 156 feet through one of them. A more elaborate shaft extended some 1,100 feet at Rives Salient, passing under Jerusalem Plank Road and ventilated by two chimneys. Additionally, Rebel engineers dug several countermines intended to intercept Federal tunnels. A Virginian praised this effort: "We found General Lee wide awake for the vile blue belly miscreants." One relieved Maryland Confederate noted, "After the first few weeks our system of countermines and galleries were in such a complete condition that we had no more fear of mining on the part of our opponents."[90]

Their experience at the Crater motivated Union engineers to confine their mining to strictly defensive measures. This activity proved particularly brisk between August 14 and 22, with much of the work occurring at Fort Sedgwick. "Our countermines run the entire front of that fort," explained Capt. Charles Francis Adams of the First Massachusetts Cavalry, "down to within eighteen inches of water." A Pennsylvanian wrote a relative, "Our men are sinking a shaft in the center of the fort for the purpose of stopping their fun." This must have worked because the Rebels made no further attempt to detonate their mines.[91]

That is not to say that the Confederates abandoned all efforts at combustion. A Kentuckian named Zedekiah McDaniel had been experimenting with explosive devices since 1862. He applied his knowledge to facilitate the sinking of the Union ironclad *Cairo* in Mississippi's Yazoo River late that year. By February 1864, his talents had earned him authority to enlist a company of up to fifty men to use explosives against the Union war effort. Dubbed "Captain McDaniel's Secret Service," this outfit included one John Maxwell.[92]

A Scottish-born Virginian, Maxwell had experience with sabotage. He and his secret-service associates had destroyed a Federal lighthouse and cut an underwater telegraph line in Chesapeake Bay earlier in the war as well as seizing a number of merchant vessels. McDaniel described Maxwell as "a bold operator and well calculated for such exploits," recruiting him for his organization. In the summer of 1864, he assigned Maxwell the mission of attacking Union shipping on the James River, employing a new device he called a "horological torpedo," essentially a primitive time bomb.[93]

On July 26 Maxwell left Richmond in the company of R. K. Dillard, a civilian intimately familiar with the geography and military situation along the James and willing, according to Maxwell, to "go anywhere I led, no matter what the danger might be." The two saboteurs reached Isle of Wight County a week later and learned of the "immense supplies of stores" stockpiled at City Point. They at once determined to use their horological torpedo against this tempting target. Traveling by night to avoid detection, Maxwell and Dillard reached City Point before dawn on August 9, crawling on hands and knees to pass undetected through the Union picket line. Maxwell instructed Dillard to stay behind as he approached the wharves carrying his contraption, a simple candle box containing twelve pounds of powder and his timing device, "arranged by means of a lever to explode a cap at a time indicated by a dial."[94]

Noticing that the skipper of the *J. E. Kendrick*, a supply barge loaded with ammunition, had left his vessel, Maxwell seized his opportunity. As he approached

This Is a Hard and Bloody Campaign

the wharf, a sentry halted him. The guard spoke only German, and Maxwell used the language barrier to his advantage, remonstrating in his broadest Scots accent and eventually persuading the confused man to let him pass. Once on board, Maxwell summoned a nearby Black man, explaining that the captain had ordered him to take the deadly box on board, which the credulous fellow allowed without question. Maxwell set the timer and calmly left the dock, rejoining Dillard to watch the results of his deception. In about an hour, around 11:30 A.M., the device detonated.[95]

Dozens of witnesses left vivid accounts of the explosion. B. H. Hibbard, a U.S. Christian Commission agent stationed at City Point, described the blast as causing "the most terrific disaster that I have ever witnessed in my whole life." Hibbard reported that the "fearful explosion" was "so strong" that "the concussion . . . made the earth tremble in our camp about ½ miles from the explosion." Samuel Jayne of the U.S. Sanitary Commission stood a mile away when the explosion "penetrated my ear so sharply as to make it ring," sending "shot and shells of every kind and description . . . whizzing through the air in every direction." Grant's adjutant general, Lieutenant Colonel Bowers, declared, "The crash made me think the foundations of the world had given way" as it sent "shot, shell, and ammunition of every kind . . . as thick as hail in every direction." The blast was so loud that it was heard as far away as Richmond and all along the Confederate defenses southwest of Petersburg, while it sent "up a huge column of white smoke wreathing and curling into fantastic shapes."[96]

Once that smoke cleared, the extent of the damage caused by the explosion shocked even the most veteran soldiers. A correspondent from the 117th New York ventured down to the docks and witnessed a scene of catastrophe. "Houses, docks, boats, tents [were] in a state of perfect wreck," he wrote. The historian of the 13th New Hampshire recalled that "the ground about the wharf and for a long distance back was covered with debris," including the office of the provost marshal. "As near as I could ascertain some acres of ground were covered with the debris—grape shot, round shot, shell and canister, muskets, saddles, pieces of timber, etc," wrote an Ohio hospital steward. Ordnance officer Lt. Morris Schaff gazed at the scene of destruction from the bluff overlooking the confluence of the James and Appomattox Rivers. "There lay before me a staggering scene, a mass of overthrown buildings, their timbers tangled into almost impenetrable heaps. In the water were wrecked and sunken barges, while out among the shipping . . . there was hurrying back and forth on the decks to weigh anchor, for all seemed to think that something more would happen." One soldier the next day saw a pile of twenty tons of soap, candles, and flour that the intense heat of the sun had melted into "one immense mass of dough." Two ships, the *General Meade* and the *Campbell*, sank along with the unfortunate *Kendrick*, while a number of vessels used by the Sanitary Commission sustained considerable damage. Some 180 feet of the new Ordnance Wharf lay in ruins as did an adjacent 600-foot warehouse filled with commissary stores and housing the Adams Express office. Railroad cars lay shattered, and rows of buildings along the waterfront, including many sutlers' establishments and "soda-water shanties," were damaged or obliterated. Some estimates placed the wreckage at 2 million dollars, while Maxwell guessed twice as much property had been destroyed.[97]

The human toll proved infinitely more disturbing than the material damage. "The millions of property destroyed was but little thought of in the midst of the immense loss of life," confirmed Thomas M. Chester, an African American newspaper correspondent. Black dockworkers and other civilian laborers composed the bulk of those killed or injured. A Richmond newspaper reporting on the aftermath believed that "mostly colored laborers" were blown into the river, and "hands and feet and scalps of colored men were rained about the town." Surgeon James Otis Moore of the Twenty-Second USCT was one of the initial responders. "The first object which met our eyes was a man lying flat on his back dead on top of one of the cars," wrote Moore. "We went a little further . . . & there lay the lower half of the trunk and about half of the thighs of a man. We proceeded up the hill where our hospital used to be & all along the road we saw detached portions of the human body. A foot, hand, pieces of the scalp—large pieces of muscle & flesh lay scattered around." Moore found a clavicle "with the muscles all detached as cleanly as if done by the dissection knife."[98]

In addition, "a large number of traders, sutlers, commissaries &c were killed or wounded," reported Capt. Solon Carter, an Eighteenth Corps staff officer. "Arms, heads and entrails are scattered all over the point." A newspaper correspondent described "fragments of flesh, hands, feet, and other parts of human bodies, literally gathered by the basketful." A drummer boy saw "bodies . . . lying in every direction, blackened and many without heads, arms, or legs." Some of these body fragments were blown a great distance from the wharf and had to be shoveled into carts.[99]

The explosion mutilated most victims beyond recognition, but a few of the identifiable casualties warranted special mention. Pvt. Solomon Leonard of the 179th New York had been wounded at the Battle of the Crater and sent to City Point for treatment. On August 9 he completed his recovery and boarded a train to return to his unit when the explosion launched a piece of lumber that struck his head, killing him instantly. A bizarre fate claimed the life of a popular vendor known as the "lemonade man," the only authorized purveyor of "pop-syrups and lemonade" at City Point. This entrepreneur was engaged in "a thriving business under a tent-fly surrounded by mule drivers, white and black, soldiers, civilians, and swarms of flies" when the blast catapulted a saddle that struck the man in the stomach, dispatching him on the spot.[100]

Naturally, a fear developed that the explosive chaos had reached General Grant, which indeed it had. "Our camp was deluged with" all manner of projectiles, reported Lieutenant Colonel Bowers. Various missiles claimed the lives of as many as three headquarters orderlies and wounded others, including Lt. Col. Orville Babcock, an aide on Grant's staff. "Sticks of [the] heaviest timber fell among our tents," added Bowers. All manner of debris surrounded Grant, but miraculously he emerged uninjured. He immediately sent a telegram to General Halleck in Washington reporting the calamity, promising "as soon as the smoke clears away I will ascertain [the damage] and telegraph you." Lt. Col. Michael R. Morgan, the army's chief commissary of subsistence, saw Grant "at his usual gait walking up from his tent toward the adjutant general's tent, taking things coolly, and seemingly not thinking anything out of the ordinary was taking place." Lieutenant Colonel Lyman thought that Grant's unflappable demeanor "shows his kind of character very well."[101]

The day following the explosion, the chief quartermaster, Brig. Gen. Rufus Ingalls, reported that 33 men had been killed by the blast and another 75 wounded. On August 11 Grant modified that count, listing among the killed 12 enlisted men, 2 citizen employees, 1 citizen not employed by the government, and 28 Black laborers. The wounded included 3 officers, 4 enlisted men, 15 civilian employees, and 86 Black workers. Eighteen others "not belonging about the wharf" added to the count.[102] These figures, however, are as suspect as the standard tally of postbattle casualties. The chronically lax accounting of the number and identity of the Black stevedores, in addition to the horrific dismemberment of so many victims, complicated any assessment. Contemporary witnesses claimed that between 250 and 400 men were killed and wounded, but brigade commander Col. Joseph R. Hawley was unpersuaded: "We are told that between 50 and 100 lives were lost, precisely how many will never be known."[103]

Volunteers rushed to the scene to rescue victims, and members of the Sanitary Commission provided first aid. A tugboat, the Lewis, ran up to the wharf and applied a firehose, extinguishing some of the flames and thereby sparing lives and property. But almost immediately thereafter, the quest to determine the cause of the blast occupied Federal officials.[104]

General Ingalls initially reported, " It is probable we shall never know how the accident occurred," a position supported on August 9 by a soldier in the Seventeenth Michigan: "How it happened will forever remain a mystery, as not one that was on board lives to tell the tale." Chaplain Henry M. Turner of the First USCT wrote to the *Christian Recorder* that "speculations are rife" regarding the cause of the blast, "but what interpretation to give it no one knows." Col. Robert McAllister, a Second Corps brigade commander, wrote his family the day after the explosion that "it is not known, nor never will be what caused the explosion," adding that "the report of a negro dropping a shell is mear supposition."[105]

The notion that a careless Black laborer caused the accident circulated widely in the hours and days following the explosion. "It was all done through the carelessness of a niger who dropped a box of caped shell into the hold of the barge," concluded Joseph Barlow. One of the sergeant's comrades in the Twenty-Third Massachusetts agreed, attributing the blast to "one of the men at work unloading one of the barges that was loaded with ammunition. It seems he was carrying a box of percussion shells, when he let the box fall." Capt. George Naylor Julian of the Thirteenth New Hampshire wrote home on the tenth with an almost identical explanation, suggesting that this narrative had spread throughout the army. The story circulated in Confederate circles as well, thanks in part to the report of a young Black boy who allegedly fled Union lines. "It is stated that a soldier accidentally dropped a percussion shell, which burst and ignited the ammunition lying around," asserted an article in the *Richmond Daily Dispatch*. Some simply ascribed the disaster to an unspecified mishap. "It was probably done accidentally and the one that done it was blown up with the rest," summarized Lieutenant Graves.[106]

Still, there were those who suspected something more nefarious than the clumsiness of a careless laborer. John Daniel Follmer, the quartermaster sergeant of the Sixteenth Pennsylvania Cavalry, recorded in his diary on August 9: "A transport loaded with powder and some shore magazines were blown up. Rebel treachery is suspected as being the cause." A Fifth Corps soldier confirmed that "some of the boys believe it was the work of a rebel spy," as did Pvt. Robert G. Carter of the Twenty-Second Massachusetts: "This was believed to be the act of somebody in the employ of the enemy." The speculation of Lieutenant Colonel Blackford possessed more insight than that of any of the Federals. "The mighty explosion we heard was the blowing up of a powder ship at City Point," Blackford wrote his wife on August 10. "It is said to have been done by a Captain Z. McDaniel, of the secret service, with some kind of infernal machine."[107]

On August 15 Grant named Lt. Col. Horace Porter, an aide on his staff, to head a commission "to investigate the cause and circumstances attending the explosion of ordnance stores at City Point." Capt. Daniel D. Wiley, a commissary officer, and Capt. Henry B. Blood, a quartermaster, served with Porter. The commissioners spent several days taking testimony from everyone they could find who had witnessed the explosion and, according to Porter, "used every possible means to probe the matter." But they uncovered no definitive evidence and so endorsed the prevailing theory that careless handling of ammunition by the laborers unloading the barge precipitated the blast. Not until June 1865 did Federal authorities find Maxwell's report to McDaniel outlining the operation. General Halleck shared the report with Secretary of War Stanton, who kept the truth of the matter secret. Porter would learn that truth in 1872 when, in the service of now President Grant, he met with Maxwell, who voiced complaints about his treatment by the commissioner of patents. While establishing his bona fides as an inventor, Maxwell revealed that he had developed the device responsible for the explosion at City Point.[108]

Grant almost missed the excitement of August 9 because he had returned to his City Point headquarters only the previous night. The situation in the lower Shenandoah Valley had prompted his absence. The general-in-chief had hoped that the small army he had assigned to the Valley at the outset of the spring campaign would occupy Confederate forces there, disrupt the Confederate supply and transportation links connecting the region with Richmond, and perhaps draw troops from Lee's army, thus weakening his primary opponent. General Sigel, however, met defeat at New Market on May 15. His replacement, Maj. Gen. David Hunter, redeemed that loss with a victory at Piedmont on June 5, then moved across the Blue Ridge Mountains intending to link with Grant's forces around Richmond. It had been Hunter's threat that prompted Lee in mid-June to detach Early's Second Corps. Early succeeded, turning back Hunter around Lynchburg and then, in keeping with Lee's orders, launching an offensive down the Valley and across the Potomac River that peaked at the outskirts of Washington the second week of July. Grant responded by sending the Sixth Corps and some dismounted cavalry to Washington, which arrived in time to man the capital's defenses. The Confederates afterward drifted back into northern Virginia, still in position to menace Maryland and Pennsylvania.[109]

Assistant Secretary of War Charles Anderson Dana wrote Grant on July 12, painting a grim picture of the Federal military situation along the Potomac. "Nothing can possibly be done here toward pursuing or cutting off the enemy for want of a commander," he warned. "There is no head to the whole, and it seems indispensable that you should at once appoint one." Dana was right. Four separate commanders operated around Washington, each looking to the War Department for guidance, which Halleck proved unable or unwilling to provide. "Until you direct positively and explicitly what is to be done," added Dana, "everything will go on in the deplorable and fatal way." As if to underscore the assistant secretary's assessment, Early defeated two Union forces in the lower Shenandoah Valley, one at Cool Spring on July 18, the other at Kernstown six days later.[110]

These problems prevented the return of the Sixth Corps to Meade's army. They also prompted Grant to redirect reinforcements from the Gulf to augment the motley collection of units around the capital. To command this aggregation, Grant first suggested Maj. Gen. William B. Franklin, an odd choice as Franklin had a checkered combat record and had earned a reputation for political intrigue. When the administration vetoed this, Grant offered Meade as a candidate. Lincoln nixed this idea as well, fearing that reassigning Meade, a Democrat, would be perceived as a rebuke to the hero of Gettysburg and thus hurt the president's standing with War Democrats in an election year. The situation only grew worse as elements of Early's cavalry torched the southern Pennsylvania city of Chambersburg on July 30, making a clean getaway back to Virginia. By then, Lincoln had requested a meeting with Grant at Fort Monroe to resolve this embarrassing turn of events, which gave credence to the idea that the war was unwinnable and threatened the president's chance for reelection.[111]

The wounded at the Crater still broiled in the sun as Grant boarded an early boat for the trip down the James on July 31. He and Lincoln conferred for five hours, but no one recorded the specifics of a discussion that must have been tense. No doubt the main topic of conversation revolved around what to do about a unified command in the Valley. Ultimately, the general-in-chief suggested Meade's cavalry commander, Phil Sheridan, for the post, and the president agreed. Grant returned to City Point and on August 1 informed Halleck, "I want Sheridan put in command of all the troops in the field [in the Valley], with instructions to put himself south of the enemy and follow him to the death." Lincoln replied that he thought these instructions were "exactly right" but urged his general-in-chief to take a personal interest in seeing that his orders were executed.[112]

Special Orders No. 68 on August 2 relieved Sheridan from his duties with Meade's Cavalry Corps and directed him and his staff to Washington to receive instructions for his new responsibilities. "General Sheridan left us to take charge of the operations against General Early in the Valley," reported a Pennsylvania military musician. "On parting with headquarters he appeared to be as happy as a boy going to see a circus, instead of showing any concern as to the serious responsibility he was about to assume." Grant told Sheridan to act with vigor and determination and to not worry about any officer's claim to higher rank. When Sheridan arrived in Washington on August 3, Grant promised, "I feel every confidence that you will do the best, and will leave you as far as possible to act on your own judgment, and not embarrass you with orders and instructions."[113]

Few in the army expressed reservations about Sheridan's fitness for his expanded responsibilities, although Lincoln, Halleck, and Stanton retained doubts about the young officer's seasoning for such an important assignment. "He is a Major-General, and is an energetic and very brave officer," wrote Lieutenant Colonel Lyman. "I have little doubt, that, for field-service, he is superior to any other officer" around Washington. "Sheridan is a good officer," agreed Capt. Walter Wallace Smith of the Second U.S. Sharpshooters, "& will soon hunt [Early] out of the northern states." General Meade, however, felt that by appointing Sheridan instead of himself, the general-in-chief had betrayed him. "I at once went to Grant," Meade wrote his wife on August 3, and "demanded to know the reason I had not been accepted." Grant had, in fact, informed Meade that he would nominate the Pennsylvanian for the command in the Valley, to which Meade merely expressed his willingness to serve wherever ordered. This apparent indifference and Lincoln's concern that transferring the general would be interpreted as a slight led Grant to suggest Sheridan.[114]

On August 4 Grant traveled north to Monocacy Junction to meet with General Hunter, who still held department command in Sheridan's new arena. When informed that Grant intended to place Sheridan in command of his field forces, Hunter graciously resigned, eliminating any potential acrimony. After conveying to Sheridan his instructions to practice aggressive warfare, Grant hurried back to City Point in time to experience Maxwell's handiwork. Meade continued to simmer privately at what he considered an insult and double-cross by his superior. "Grant has been back two days, and has not vouchsafed one word in explanation," he confided to his wife, "and I have avoided going to see him, from a sense of self-respect, and from the fear that I should not be able to restrain the indignation I hold to be natural at the duplicity some one has practiced." Meade considered resigning in protest but decided to swallow the "bitter pill & quietly bide my time." Grant and Meade had enjoyed a functional and mutually cooperative relationship during the campaign. The issue of Sheridan's promotion upset that equilibrium but, as events would demonstrate, only temporarily.[115]

After Sheridan consulted with Grant at Monocacy Junction, he took stock of his new command, the Middle Military Division, and its field force, the Army of the Shenandoah. That army consisted of Meade's old Sixth Corps, still under General Wright; the Eighth Corps (or the Army of West Virginia) led by Brig. Gen. George Crook; and thirty-five regiments of the Nineteenth Corps from the Gulf. These troops had sailed from Louisiana, slated to reinforce Butler. Instead, the crisis around Washington diverted them north under the direction of Brig. Gen. William H. Emory. Sheridan inherited Crook's cavalry division, led by Maj. Gen. William Woods Averell, but Grant saw the need for more mounted troops in the Valley. He directed two of Meade's three mounted divisions to embark from City Point to join Sheridan's Valley command.[116]

Torbert's division was the first to depart, along with its horse-artillery batteries. Hampered by limited transportation, the troopers began embarking on August 1, but not until three days later did Brig. Gen. George Armstrong Custer's Michigan Brigade board its vessels. Around noon on August 4, Grant told Meade to send Sheridan a second cavalry division, later designating Wilson's two brigades for this assignment. This left only David Gregg's Second Division still operating with Meade, although Grant ordered Butler to make Kautz's troopers available to the Army of the Potomac while Torbert and Wilson were absent. It took time to ship these forces north. "The embarkation was tedious and laborious," explained Chaplain Louis N. Beaudry of the Fifth New York Cavalry. "Every horse had to be unsaddled and his pack, saddle, and equipment tied to a blanket." Persuading their mounts to climb aboard the dark hulls of the transports frustrated the troopers. But by the second week of August, Sheridan had assembled most of his new army, which numbered roughly 40,000 soldiers.[117]

Sheridan's opponent could count only 14,000 muskets in his little Valley army. The three divisions of Early's Second Corps—led capably by Maj. Gen. Robert E. Rodes, Maj. Gen. John B. Gordon, and Maj. Gen. Stephen Dodson Ramseur—represented the heart of the Confederate force. Maj. Gen. John C. Breckinridge, a former U.S. vice president and commander of the troops originally assigned to the Valley, rounded out the Rebel infantry. Early's mounted arm numbered between 3,500 and 4,000 men, much inferior to their bluec-lad counterparts not only in number but also in quality of men, horses, and equipment.[118]

Lee had taken notice of the shifting of waterborne troops toward Washington and deduced that they were likely headed to confront Early. "I fear that this force . . . when added to that already opposed to [Early] may be more than he can manage," Lee explained to Jefferson Davis. He told the president that the most he could send to the Valley were the divisions of Maj. Gen. Joseph B. Kershaw and Maj. Gen. Charles W. Field, though doing so "would leave not a man out of the trenches for any emergency that might arise." Lee ultimately decided to detach only Kershaw's infantry, augmented by Fitzhugh Lee's cavalry division and an artillery battalion, raising Early's strength to about 19,000 men. Some Southerners believed the shift from Petersburg to the Valley would change the calculus of the entire campaign. "I am confident large reinforcements have left this army of infantry, cavalry, etc. for Genl Early or to threaten Washington," explained Lt. Hugh Randolph Crichton of the Forty-Seventh North Carolina, "which will necessitate the withdrawal of Genl Grant from this place." Edmund Ruffin was not quite as sanguine but did predict that the transfer would reduce the campaigning around Petersburg and Richmond to "a mere blockade by gunboats, & by the fortified camps & garrisons of the enemy." Although neither of these predictions came to pass, military fortunes in the Shenandoah Valley would exercise an influence on operations at Petersburg through the autumn.[119]

hile Grant and Meade concerned themselves with command issues in the Shenandoah Valley, the head of the Army of the James, Ben Butler, began an ambitious engineering project. Butler cast a huge shadow in the Federal effort to capture Petersburg and Richmond, his several failures from May through July notwithstanding. Described by historian Mark Grimsley as "shrewd, imposing, articulate, and energetic," Butler's appearance and character garnered fewer flattering assessments. The humorist Mark Twain noted that "the forward part of his bald skull, looks raised like a water blister. . . . [He] is dismally & drearily homely & when he smiles it is like the breaking of a hard winter." Another remorseless observer referred to the general as "the hideous front of hell's blackest imp . . . the unclean product of Massachusetts civilization . . . that baggy faced fruit of perdition." Colonel Hawley considered his army commander "a very bad man, a demagogue, selfish, reckless of life, loving notoriety & trying to stroll on the military stage like Napoleon."[120]

Despite his flaws of morality and physiognomy, Butler proved to be a survivor. His political clout as a War Democrat, mated with undeniable acumen, helped him avert Grant's attempt to consign him to an administrative post in July, even though the general-in-chief questioned his ability to lead troops in battle.

Butler's latest scheme intended to avoid combat, or at least to reduce it, on an important stretch of the James River. That tidal waterway twisted and turned from its head of navigation at Richmond twenty miles southeast to its confluence with the Appomattox River at City Point, where it widened and straightened considerably. One of the bends, a few miles upstream from the Federal bridgehead at Deep Bottom, defined a peninsula named Farrar's Island, formed by a six-mile loop of the river. The Confederates had heavily fortified the south bank along the straight stretch of this segment called Trent's Reach, presenting an imposing barrier to any Union warship hoping to menace Richmond.

The downstream portion of this bend was separated from its upstream counterpart by a narrow finger of land some 174 yards long. Butler proposed to dig
a canal at this point, known as Dutch Gap, to bypass the Confederate guns and
facilitate a naval approach to the Confederate capital. He explored the feasibility
of such a project with naval captain Melancton Smith and in late July escorted
Grant and his chief engineer, Brig. Gen. John G. Barnard, over the terrain. "We
came to the conclusion that to dig the canal was a very desirable thing to do,"
wrote Butler, "and General Grant directed me to undertake it."[121]

In anticipation of Grant's approval, Butler sent his own acting chief engineer,
Lt. Peter S. Michie, to Dutch Gap to develop a plan for the excavation. Michie
determined that a ditch about 500 feet long, 15 feet deep, 85 feet wide at the
water line, and 40 feet wide at the bottom would require the removal of 50,000
cubic yards of material. Butler estimated that the work would take about three
weeks if he could recruit a labor force of 1,000–1,200 men. On August 6 he called
on the commanders of the Tenth and Eighteenth Corps to provide volunteers,
promising seven-and-a half-hour shifts for twenty days. Workers who avoided
"laziness or inattention to duty" would receive bonus pay of eight cents per hour
and a daily ration of a half gill of whiskey. These incentives proved enticing, and
volunteers in great numbers enrolled for the job. Work began on August 9. But
Butler's enthusiasm did not extend to Meade's headquarters. The acerbic Lieutenant Colonel Lyman considered his plan "a humorous idea" and predicted
that "when B gets his canal cleverly through he will find fresh batteries ready to
rake it and plenty more above it on the river."[122]

The work began with encouraging results, as the first night's labor proved
deceptively productive. "The light [top] soil yielded easily, and the progress
was plain enough to be seen," reported Col. John W. Ames of the Sixth USCT.
But then "a layer . . . of an indurated clay and sand not easily moved by the pick"
slowed progress. Even more disruptive, the Confederates caught wind of the
project and began lobbing shells at the laborers, albeit at first blindly and on
speculation. General Lee ordered his heavy guns at the large battery near the
Howlett house to open fire, and the Confederate navy soon joined in. On August 13 half a dozen vessels moved to within 4,000 feet of the nascent canal and
shelled the workers every twenty minutes for twelve hours. Casualties among
the laborers were light as the Federals returned fire, but this harassing bombardment would gradually take its toll, the military labor force eventually dwindling
in favor of civilian workers, most of them African Americans. By then, however,
the next Federal offensive had run its course, including a spirited engagement
on the north side of the James.[123]

This Is a Hard and Bloody Campaign

two

THE MOST DESTRUCTION I HAVE SEEN FOR THE TIME IT TOOK

Second Deep Bottom, August 13–20

Charles Field was concerned. The thirty-six-year-old Kentuckian commanded seven brigades of Lee's Army of Northern Virginia stationed on the north side of the James River and charged with guarding the approaches to Richmond from the southeast. He deployed the five brigades of his own division, along with two others from Hill's Third Corps, from Chaffin's Bluff on the James, east along the base of a modest ridge called New Market Heights, and then north up the slope. The line terminated by Mitchell Fussell's saw and gristmill, near the headwaters of Bailey's Creek. "Covering so great a line . . . with the comparatively few troops at my disposal, weak everywhere, the men being in extended single rank, and in many places there being none at all," left Major General Field feeling uneasy.[1]

Field boasted a distinguished military pedigree. A graduate of the U.S. Military Academy with extensive experience on the frontier in the Second U.S. Cavalry, Field was teaching cavalry tactics at West Point when he offered his sword to the new Confederacy. He began this service commanding a mounted regiment but soon led an infantry brigade in A. P. Hill's Light Division with marked competence. "His gallant bearing and soldierly qualities gave him unbounded influence over his men," reported Hill, "and they were ever ready to follow where he led." A Virginia subordinate considered Field "one of the finest gentlemen I ever had the good fortune to meet. He is courteous and affable to every one. But a strict disciplinarian." Wounded in 1862 at Second Manassas, Field returned to active duty in the winter of 1864, receiving command of John Bell Hood's old division in Longstreet's First Corps.[2]

Field's brigades had lengthy experience with the army, although they had all suffered significant battle attrition. Brig. Gen. George "Tige" Anderson led one of Field's two Georgia organizations, and Col. Dudley M. DuBose commanded the other, in place of Brig. Gen. Henry L. "Rock" Benning, wounded at the Wilderness. Brig. Gen. John Bratton's South Carolina brigade, Evander M. Law's Alabamans, and the famed Texas Brigade rounded out Field's Division. General Law had also been wounded during the Overland Campaign, so Col. William F. Perry commanded in his stead. Brig. Gen. John Gregg had charge of the Texas Brigade, but as Field bore overall responsibility for Lee's troops north of the James, he named Gregg acting division commander. Col. Frederick S. Bass of the First Texas, a graduate of the Virginia Military Institute with prewar teaching experience in Petersburg, served as acting commander of the Texas Brigade.[3]

Field's command arrived on the north side of the James on the morning of July 29 as a part of Lee's response to the Federals' First Deep Bottom offensive. Two of Maj. Gen. Cadmus M. Wilcox's brigades were there to greet them. James Lane's North Carolinians and Samuel McGowan's South Carolinians had been in Henrico County since the end of June, and both functioned under temporary commanders. Col. William M. Barbour led the Tar Heels—Lane, like Law, had been wounded at Cold Harbor. Brig. Gen. James Conner not only commanded the South Carolinians—McGowan being absent with his Spotsylvania wound—but also exercised authority over Barbour's brigade as a demi-division chief. Field's entire force numbered about 7,700 men and occupied a front nearly seven miles long.[4]

There were other Confederate troops in the neighborhood independent of Field's authority. The Department of Richmond consisted of a gaggle of mostly second-line troops, including the artillerists who manned the guns in the capital's permanent defenses. Two veteran brigades buttressed these amateurs, numbering in all about 5,500 men. General Ewell led the department as his consolation prize after Lee relieved him as head of the Army of Northern Virginia's Second Corps. Ewell chafed at what could only be deemed a demotion, but like the good soldier he had always been, he discharged his new responsibilities with professionalism. He could count on a small but battle-hardened Tennessee infantry brigade of about 300 soldiers that had formerly been Bushrod Johnson's but was now led by Col. John M. Hughs. Brig. Gen. Martin W. Gary led Ewell's cavalry contingent—an experienced brigade of three regiments, including the Seventh South Carolina Cavalry, the Hampton Legion Cavalry, and the Twenty-Fourth Virginia Cavalry. Ewell's artillery chief was none other than Lt. Col. John C. Pemberton, once a lieutenant general in command of the entire Confederate army at Vicksburg but now loyally serving in a much-reduced role. Although Ewell and Field exercised separate commands, this potentially problematic arrangement would have little material effect on the upcoming operations.[5]

Field's adversaries in early August were not yet the source of his angst. They consisted of merely one brigade headed by a thirty-year-old former Indiana tinsmith named Robert Sanford Foster. Despite his lack of military training, Foster proved to be a capable commander, successively promoted to brigadier general in the Tenth Corps. "Gen. Foster was a model of an [excellent] appearing officer," wrote a lieutenant from the 100th New York, one of his regiments. "He attracted universal attention by his faultless military bearing; and he was as brave in battle as he was imposing in appearance on review." Foster's command—the 10th Connecticut, 11th Maine, 1st Maryland Cavalry (dismounted), and 24th Massachusetts, in addition to the New Yorkers—had established a bridgehead north of the James on June 20, remaining there after Grant recalled the rest of the forces engaged in late July's failed First Deep Bottom operations. Foster's five regiments numbered about 1,400 muskets.[6]

Deep Bottom, a boat landing on the left bank of the James about twelve miles downstream from Richmond, lay opposite a swampy peninsula called Jones Neck, a jungle of thick grass infested with poisonous serpents that occasionally struck with deadly results. Here, at a narrow bend of the river, the Federals maintained a pontoon bridge that connected Foster's brigade, well protected by defensive works, with the Union forces at Bermuda Hundred.[7]

Although artillery exchanges along the James, particularly those focused on the canal activity at Dutch Gap, garnered attention at headquarters, Grant fretted more about the evolving situation in the Shenandoah Valley. Word arrived at City Point that Lee had sent three divisions of infantry and one of cavalry to reinforce Early, raising the Confederate strength in the Valley to as many as 40,000 troops. This significantly exaggerated Lee's actual detachment, but it sparked in Grant the desire to protect Sheridan by undertaking a new offensive designed to draw those reinforcements back from the Valley. Improving Sheridan's odds was but one of Grant's objectives. Just as in July, the general-in-chief hoped that sending a large force north of the James would compel Lee to siphon troops away from Petersburg and thus create an opportunity to capture the Weldon Railroad, a cherished objective since June. Hancock's Second Corps would provide the backbone of such a force, perhaps because of its familiarity with the terrain from its foray across the river in July. A third objective would task David Gregg's cavalry division with targeting the Virginia Central Railroad, severing the iron link between Richmond and the Valley. Grant asked Butler to support this operation. Butler ordered David Birney, recently promoted to command of the Tenth Corps, to contribute two divisions to Hancock's strike force. Birney, of course, had been a division commander under Hancock and worked well with his former superior. Counting Foster's brigade and the artillery of the Second and Tenth Corps, some 28,000 Federals would challenge less than half as many Rebels under Field and Ewell.[8]

Shortly before noon on August 12, Grant sent Hancock instructions to launch the offensive. The Second Corps infantry would march to City Point as soon as possible, while Gregg's cavalry and Hancock's artillery would secretly cross the Appomattox River and join Birney's divisions in marching through Bermuda Hundred and Jones Neck to the bridgehead at Deep Bottom. Transports would be waiting at City Point for the three divisions of the Second Corps, and officers and enlisted men alike would be persuaded that they were bound for Washington. Grant assigned Hancock overall command of the operation. That evening Meade explained to Hancock that Grant's orders for the First Deep Bottom offensive would also apply to the current operation. The infantry would threaten Richmond, pin down the Confederates, compel the recall of Lee's Valley-bound units, and draw troops to the north side of the James from Petersburg, all while the cavalry executed its raid against the railroad.[9]

Hancock immediately adjourned the Crater court of inquiry and issued instructions to division commanders Barlow, Mott, and Col. Thomas A. Smyth to march to City Point that afternoon. Between 2:00 and 3:00 P.M., all three divisions hit the road. Few of Hancock's men failed to comment on the difficulty of that nine-to-twelve-mile trek. "Clouds of dust would rise around us so thick that you could not recognize a man five feet from you and as the weather was very warm we sweat considerable so you can imagine how pleasant it was, dust choking you at every step (almost) and sweat blinding you," explained Sgt. Samuel B. Pierce of New York. The mercury reached ninety-nine degrees, exacting a toll on both officers and men. "We march as though the 'old boy' himself was after us," wrote Sgt. Daniel G. Crotty of the 3rd Michigan. "Not a rest or a halt." Maj. Joel B. Baker of the 8th New York Heavy Artillery described the "horrors of that march" to his parents: "Men dropped in the ranks and the column marches on over them. Men lay beside the road dead, others screaming and writhing in the agonies of death . . . but like hard hearted wretches we press on." Perhaps as many as two dozen men from Barlow's First Division perished from sunstroke. "Owing to the extreme heat and dust," testified a soldier in the 140th Pennsylvania, "it was 'nip and tuck' with many of us."[10]

Most marchers were buoyed by the belief that they were leaving Petersburg for more congenial destinations. Grant's deception convinced them that Washington would be the first, if not the ultimate, stop on their journey. "Happiness enthused the men over the idea of seeing the capital again," reported a soldier in the 108th New York, "as they were not permitted to see it as often as Congressmen, though enacting more stalwart business for the perpetuity of the government." The prevailing opinion was that from Washington the troops would join the Sixth Corps and Sheridan in the Shenandoah Valley.[11]

"Thousands of rumors were afloat," admitted Lieutenant Paxton of the 140th Pennsylvania. "That the 2nd Corps was to embark on transports for Washington City was a conceded point." But from there, some men predicted that authorities would send them to Mobile, the Carolinas, Texas, or even Chicago to maintain order during the Democrats' upcoming presidential convention. Others, such as Colonel McAllister of Mott's division, confessed uncertainty. "All is as yet in the dark," he told his wife. A soldier in the 120th New York agreed, declaring that a "profound mystery shrouded the whole movement and was a delightful feature of it." Pvt. Dave Kelly of the 110th Pennsylvania simply concluded, "We was going to get a ride," which was all anyone knew.[12]

Hancock's weary troops stumbled into makeshift bivouacs near City Point between 8:00 and 11:00 that evening. Rations were distributed, and the men settled in for the night. The Second U.S. Sharpshooters, a part of Brig. Gen. Regis de Trobriand's Third Division brigade, found themselves assigned a campground in the rear of an earthwork. "The ground was covered with night soil left there by the garrison of the fort to their officer's disgrace," reported Sgt. Wyman S. White. "We were obliged to lay down in that vile place or stand up all night." White's utter exhaustion overcame his disgust, and he placed his rubber blanket "on the smeared ground" and fell asleep "as if in a field of roses." The next morning the regiment made its way to the river to cleanse their blankets in the James. The Twentieth Massachusetts enjoyed a more pleasant surprise when their former commander, Col. George N. Macy, greeted them. Macy had been badly wounded in the Wilderness and had just reported for duty, assigned command of the First Brigade of Smyth's Second Division.[13]

Saturday, August 13, dawned clear and muggy, foreshadowing another scorching summer day as plans for the movement to the north side solidified. Butler assumed responsibility for rebuilding a second, lower bridge at Deep Bottom to facilitate Gregg's cavalry. Birney's infantry would utilize the existing upper bridge to join Foster, while Hancock's troops would disembark directly from transports at the wharves at Tilghman's Landing near the lower bridge. Grant felt so confident in these preparations that he dismissed Meade's suggestion to meet with Hancock to review the operation.[14]

Hancock was not so optimistic. The corps commander, members of his staff, and Brigadier General Ingalls, the army's chief quartermaster, clambered aboard a tugboat and steamed to Deep Bottom to examine their designated landing spot. As he feared, the river's shallow depth there and the nature of the bank would make it impossible to unload troops via a gangplank connected to the shore. Moreover, the existing wharves at the landing were in poor condition and needed to be lengthened in order to facilitate an efficient disembarkation. Hancock ordered materials and workmen to repair and modify these docks and accelerated the departure from midnight to 10:00 P.M. in order to provide more time for the unavoidably arduous challenge of putting the men ashore.[15]

In the meantime, Second Corps headquarters issued instructions to the division commanders for boarding their men. Maj. William G. Mitchell, an aide on Hancock's staff, oversaw the loading of troops by divisions—Mott's first, then Smyth's and Barlow's. The process would begin at 11:00 A.M., and "the organization of brigades and regiments will be preserved, both in embarking and when on the boat, so that the troops may be in hand at all times."[16]

Instructions circulated alerting the men to prepare to move. Until those orders arrived, many soldiers indulged in a bath in the Appomattox River, the first such cleansing some had enjoyed in eight weeks. Later that morning officers marshaled their units to march to the docks and begin boarding the transports. This makeshift fleet consisted of "all kinds of craft," thought a soldier in the 124th New York, "from trim Hudson River steamboats which could make at least twenty miles an hour, to old turtle shape and scow-bottom ferry-boats that could hardly make eight." At least sixteen vessels waited at the piers, although some soldiers recalled as many as thirty-two.[17]

De Trobriand's brigade boarded first, around noon. The exercise continued for the rest of the Second Corps until 7:30 P.M., when, near sunset, "the vessels, crowded with troops and gaily bedecked with fluttering banners, swung out one after the other in midstream, and with music and song and hearty cheers—for all the bands were playing and all the troops were in exultant mood—moved slowly and majestically down the river." Despite the heat and crowded conditions on the decks, "laughter and happiness prevailed to an extent altogether beyond reason . . . general hilarity and wild delight took possession of every one." The veterans cheered and sang, "greatly elated at the prospect of getting out of this desolate and dusty country" and anticipating "the greater pleasure of ice cream and oysters" in Washington.[18]

The fleet moved downstream for a few miles, anchoring opposite Windmill Point, near where the corps had first crossed the James two months earlier. Various explanations for the halt circulated among the troops, including the need to load the corps artillery or that all the ships must gather together before proceeding farther "as there was danger of being fired upon by the rebs." The men battled swarms of mosquitoes, which were "distressingly thick," while some of the boys from the 140th Pennsylvania took a swim in the James. At 10:00 P.M. a steam tugboat drew up alongside the assembled vessels, an officer asked for the various captains, and many soldiers heard the orders to turn about and head for Deep Bottom.[19]

This news rocked the men like a cannon blast. "In five minutes every man knew that it was Deep Bottom and a fight in the morning," recalled the regimental historian of the 116th Pennsylvania. "The singing quickly died away. . . . The silence of disappointed hope settled over the men." Chaplain Lafayette Church of the 26th Michigan, the man who salivated at the prospect of devouring delectables in Washington, now realized that "instead of ease and ice cream—it is more hard marches, more dust, and more fighting—such is soldiering."[20]

The fleet proceeded upstream in the dark, except for one transport that carried 1,200 troops of Lt. Col. K. Oscar Broady's brigade of Barlow's division; it ran aground. De Trobriand's vessels maintained the lead and reached Deep Bottom about 1:00 A.M. on August 14. The entire fleet dropped anchor over the course of the next three hours as the tedious business of unloading the troops commenced.[21]

Mott was aboard one of the first boats to arrive and immediately improved the landing facility by combining a spare canal boat with trestle work. His troops began disembarking at 2:00 A.M., an enterprise that continued for six or seven hours. Most of the corps managed to land by dawn, the operation hampered by low tide, the availability of only three wharves, and the general unsuitability of many of the vessels. "Engineers or quartermasters or somebody else had forgotten that it would not be the proper thing for soldiers to jump into the James river and swim ashore," a Maine soldier sarcastically observed. Most of the men had spent the hot night on the open upper decks of their boats and could only descend one or two at a time to lower decks in order to disembark. One of the smaller steamers ran close to the bank and was used as a bridge to connect the larger boats with the wharves, which underwent modifications even as the unloading progressed. "Some one should be punished in this matter," fumed Major Mitchell as the disembarkation ground on, hours behind schedule.[22]

While Hancock's men plied the James and struggled to reach land, David Birney led five brigades from their Bermuda Hundred trenches toward the upper bridge leading from Jones Neck to Foster's enclave at Deep Bottom. Birney had been in command of the Tenth Corps for barely three weeks, having served capably under Hancock since the army's reorganization in the spring. His father, James, had been one of the nation's foremost abolitionists and twice a presidential candidate under the Liberty Party banner. The thirty-nine-year-old general was of medium height and possessed of a smile and "gentle expression

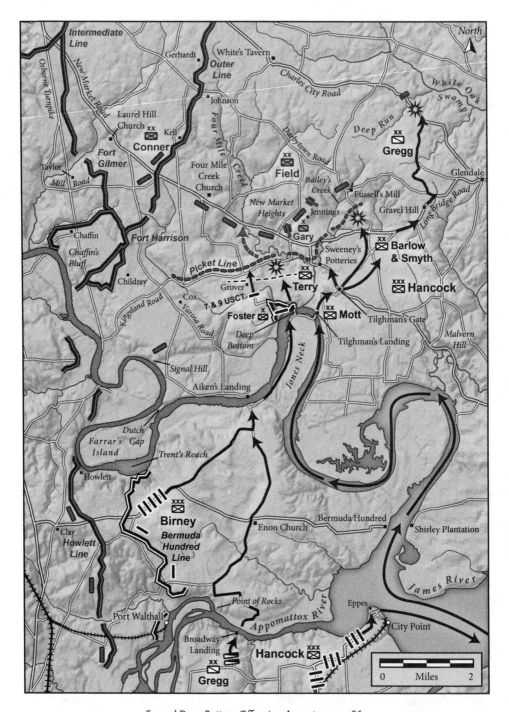

Second Deep Bottom Offensive, August 12–14, 1864

of his countenance" that, as one observer put it, "will be forgotten by few who knew him." Another thought Birney had a "striking presence, intellectual, forceful and rather austere." Meade's opinionated staff officer Lieutenant Colonel Lyman admitted that Birney cultivated his share of detractors, including Silas Edward Mead of the Tenth Connecticut, who told a friend that he did not much admire his corps commander. "To be plain, I think he is a puke," wrote the blunt private. Lyman recognized that Birney's undisguised ambition, which had helped achieve his promotion despite a lack of formal military training, combined with a "demeanor of immovable coldness" explained his unpopularity but allowed, "We had few officers who could command 10,000 men as well as he."[23]

Birney's contingent included Terry's division, two brigades of Brig. Gen. John Turner's division, and a newly arrived U.S. Colored Troops brigade commanded by Birney's older brother, William. Turner remained at Bermuda Hundred to command the units left to guard that line, much to his dismay, so William Birney inherited control of Turner's brigades as well as his own.[24]

Butler granted Birney discretion regarding the composition of his force, but once across the James, he told him to take Foster's brigade under his wing and report to Hancock. Later on the thirteenth, Birney instructed his division chiefs to "hold their commands in readiness to move at a moment's notice." He subsequently named 11:00 P.M. as the time to commence the march to Deep Bottom, the infantry to be joined by five batteries of artillery and the men provided three days' cooked rations.[25]

An hour before midnight, Terry's division, with brigades under Colonel Hawley and Col. Francis B. Pond, set off for the upper pontoon bridge at Jones Neck. The Tenth Corps artillery brigade, led by Lt. Col. Freeman McGilvery, joined the foot soldiers. After a "very dirty" march of five to nine miles, the troops began crossing the James, reaching Foster's lines between 2:00 and 3:00 A.M. August 14. Straggling marred the operation, particularly among a number of men who roused themselves from the sick list to join their healthy comrades. Just as with Hancock's soldiers, many of Birney's boys, including those unfit for service, believed their destination was Bermuda Hundred Landing, where transports would ship them to Washington. Those who belonged in bed did not want to squander their chance to escape the Petersburg front. When the actual destination became obvious, a number of soldiers, through incapacity or simple disappointment, fell by the wayside. Terry's men passed some of Gregg's cavalry on the road and, when they reached the river, observed Hancock's fleet and the Second Corps efforts to reach terra firma. William Birney's three brigades, including Turner's two, led by Lt. Col. William B. Coan and Col. Francis A. Osborn, followed Terry and gained the left bank about daybreak.[26]

David McMurtrie Gregg, a thirty-one-year-old Pennsylvanian and first cousin to the Keystone State's wartime governor, enjoyed a sterling reputation. A West Point graduate and veteran of antebellum frontier duty, Gregg rose from leading the Eighth Pennsylvania Cavalry to the command of a division by February 1863. Fellow division chief James Wilson considered Gregg "the best all-'round cavalry officer that ever commanded a division in either army." His quiet demeanor, absolute modesty, and disdain for newspaper correspondents deprived him of the popular renown warranted by his skill.[27]

Gregg led eleven regiments, perhaps 4,000 troopers, divided into two brigades commanded by his cousin, Col. J. Irvin Gregg, and Col. William Stedman, standing in for Brig. Gen. Henry E. Davies, who was on leave. The division was encamped around Prince George Court House, when on the morning of August 13, orders arrived to prepare to move at 4:00 P.M. Like the other Union troops, many of Gregg's men guessed that they were bound for Washington and then to the Valley to rejoin the rest of Sheridan's cavalry corps, a deception intentionally circulated by Meade's orders the previous day. The column departed on schedule, but by 5:00 P.M., when the troopers began to cross the Appomattox instead of heading for the City Point docks, it became apparent that they were to reprise their July offensive north of the James. "Consoling ourselves with the idea that what had been endured once could be borne again," the horsemen traveled all night, a march "as disagreeable as any in the history of the regiment," thought a man in the First Pennsylvania Cavalry. The column reached the newly constructed lower bridge well before dawn and, between 2:00 and 4:00 A.M., joined the vanguard of Hancock's soldiers on the north side.[28]

Hancock circulated his specific instructions for the offensive on August 13. Once across the James, Mott's division was to proceed west on New Market Road and drive the Confederates into their entrenchments behind Bailey's Creek, with Gregg covering his right flank. Barlow, in command of his own and Smyth's divisions, would follow, attacking the Confederates farther north toward a dwelling called the Jennings house, with Gregg shifting again to protect the infantry's right. If successful, Barlow would pivot to his left and drive south, uncovering Mott's front, allowing him to proceed farther west on New Market Road. These maneuvers would free Gregg to commence his raid toward the Virginia Central Railroad. Birney's troops at Deep Bottom would attack in concert with Mott's advance, targeting the Confederates behind Four Mile Creek, and then push westward to Varina Road and on to Mill Road as far as its intersection with Osborne Turnpike, in position to threaten the Confederate strongpoint at Chaffin's Bluff. The operation was to begin at dawn, a schedule that the delay in offloading the Second Corps would render obsolete.[29]

Foster's men on the brigade picket line at Deep Bottom listened in the pre-dawn darkness as the transports disgorged their human contents and Birney and Gregg moved across the bridges. A man from the Eleventh Maine testified, "We could distinctly hear the rumble of the artillery and the tramping of the horses of Gregg's cavalry" as they crossed the lower bridge, along with the "screeching of steamboat whistles" from the various transports. "If we heard it, and our suspicions were aroused by it, then our contiguous friends, the enemy . . . could hear it as well [and] must have been forewarned of what was coming in the morning." This soldier's regiment, along with Foster's Tenth Connecticut, occupied a picket line more than a mile long just south of Kingsland Road, extending from the Grover house on the left to Bailey's Creek on the right. On the other side of that thoroughfare the Confederates established their advanced picket line, held by Bratton's South Carolinians. "Our men [were] in pleasant relations with the then inoffensive Johnnies," reported Chaplain Henry Clay Trumbull of the Tenth Connecticut, "exchanging papers and proposing terms for the swap of coffee, tobacco and jack knives." With the first hints of daylight, all that was about to change.[30]

The delay in his disembarkation prompted Hancock to instruct Birney to suspend his half of the coordinated attack pending further orders. Perhaps Birney failed to receive these instructions or, as historian Bryce Suderow suggests, ignored them in order to win laurels in his new role as a corps commander. In any event, Birney sent Foster forward at 5:10 A.M. In addition to the 10th Connecticut and the 11th Maine, the 1st Maryland Cavalry (dismounted) and the 100th New York formed the brigade front. Foster's 24th Massachusetts deployed in support, while Pond's and Hawley's men waited in reserve. Their attack quickly overwhelmed the Rebel vedettes but then encountered the main Confederate picket line, where this premature advance stalled. "Men dropped dead in our lines, or were carried bleeding and mangled to the rear," reported Trumbull. "The rebels stood their ground so well for a time that our skirmishers could only maintain their own position and keep up a determined fire without material progress." This stalemate persisted for more than an hour until Colonel Pond advanced about 7:30 A.M. in concert with Terry's summons to the 24th Massachusetts to form for a charge. Terry addressed the men from the Bay State, reminding them of their good service on the South Carolina coast, and then turned to the regimental commander, saying, "Capt. put em in." Pond, whose four regiments moved to the left of Foster, gave the order to "charge with a yell," and the bluecoats sprang forward. "The yell and the charge had been too much for the nerves of our friends in gray," remembered Trumbull, "and, almost without another shot, they had turned, and made the best of their way to the rear," leaving as many as eighty of their comrades as prisoners of war. "Our picket line was finally driven in, pretty badly mutilated," admitted Bratton. The Confederates retired to their main line of entrenchments along New Market Road, where, with the support of artillery on the heights and a clear field of fire, the Union advance again halted. The Federal victory had not been bloodless: Foster's brigade suffered eighteen killed and 102 wounded.[31]

By then, Mott's division had formed on the left bank and begun its portion of the operation. De Trobriand's brigade assumed the lead at 7:45 A.M., and two of his regiments expelled a few Rebel outposts at the edge of some woods near Tilghman's Gate. Gaining New Market Road, the Federals wheeled left and advanced as far as an abandoned industrial site known as Sweeney's Potteries. "These potteries had been used to manufacture stone ware, jugs, crocks etc. and there were two large open cellars where the bad or broken pieces of ware had been thrown," observed Capt. Erasmus C. Gilbreath of the Twentieth Indiana. Elements of Gary's cavalry provided what little resistance the Confederates offered here, and they quickly withdrew to their main defenses west of Bailey's Creek. De Trobriand halted, and as the Richmond Howitzers began to rain fire on his troops from a redoubt on the heights, he established his own line, anchoring his left flank on Four Mile Creek. By this time, Hancock had learned that Birney's prisoners of war originated from both Wilcox's and Field's Divisions, suggesting that he suspend further offensive action until his entire corps could be engaged.[32]

This pause facilitated the movement of Barlow and Gregg into the positions specified in Hancock's plan, albeit hours behind schedule. By then, the unrelenting sun began to take its toll. "The temperature of the day . . . was something dreadful," reported Hancock's adjutant, Lieutenant Colonel Walker. "The columns, moving from the landing, literally passed between men lying on both sides, dead from sunstroke. . . . The rays of the August sun smote the heads of the weary soldiers with blows as palpable as if they had been given with a club." The suffocating air dropped members of the 152nd New York, "the froth foaming from the mouth, many dying in convulsion." Those not entirely prostrated by the heat often broke ranks to search for water, "the woods being very handy for stragglers who filling their canteens in many cases failed to report again to their Regts," lamented Capt. John Buttrick Noyes, an officer on the First Brigade staff.[33]

As Gregg's cavalry moved across Long Bridge Road, they disbursed a few of Gary's horsemen and continued northwest on Darbytown Road, where Gary deployed on the far left end of the Confederate line, the blue troopers remaining on their infantry's right as ordered. That infantry, Barlow's and Smyth's divisions, began their mission of moving to Mott's right preliminary to turning the Rebels' left flank. Because Smyth was a mere colonel and only in temporary command of his division, Hancock gave Barlow authority over Smyth in addition to his own three brigades. This was an unfortunate decision.[34]

Not yet thirty years old, Barlow grew up near Boston and finished first in his class at Harvard. Like many graduates of that ancient institution, Barlow considered himself a natural leader and dismissed most men as intellectual inferiors. He was practicing law in New York before volunteering for service at the outbreak of the war and within a few months rose to command of the Sixty-First New York. Wounded at Antietam in 1862, Barlow returned to active duty the following year in charge of a brigade and then a division in the Eleventh Corps. Wounded again at Gettysburg, upon his recovery, Barlow was Hancock's choice to lead the First Division, Second Corps. While Hancock would remain Barlow's biggest booster, Lyman also considered him to be "one of the most daring men in the army." Others held an unfavorable opinion of the young general. Many in his unit thought him reckless, rude, and overbearing. But on August 14 his health proved more of an impediment than his unpopularity; within seventy-two hours, he would be consigned to a hospital. So, between the debilitating heat and his poor physical condition, it is hardly surprising that Barlow's performance left much to be desired.[35]

Contrary to his usual aggressiveness, Barlow took the morning and most of the afternoon to deploy his six brigades. "We were belly-ached around till 3 P.M.," groused Lt. George E. Albee of the Thirty-Sixth Wisconsin. Between 4:00 and 5:00 P.M., Barlow and Smyth finally completed their alignment parallel to Long Bridge Road. Nelson Miles's First Brigade of Barlow's division occupied the left, linking with de Trobriand's right. The Consolidated Brigade, led by Col. Levin C. Crandell, took position on Miles's right, while Broady's Fourth Brigade, at last on the scene after their interrupted voyage, remained in reserve. Smyth's troops went into line on Barlow's right, Macy's brigade in front and Col. Mathew Murphy's and Lt. Col. Francis E. Pierce's commands in support.[36]

Tenth Corps troops were also on the move. Terry directed Foster to shift his 100th New York and the 6th Connecticut of Hawley's brigade to the right to close the gap between Birney's line and de Trobriand's left flank. In doing this, they came across four eight-inch siege howitzers that had been abandoned during Birney's morning assault, a sacrifice one Georgian blamed on "the generalship of Pemberton." Coan's brigade moved up on Foster's left, with Pond, Hawley, and Osborn extending to the west in that order. William Birney's African Americans advanced from their reserve position and deployed on the far left of David Birney's formation.[37]

Of course, all of this activity did not go unnoticed by the Confederates. General Field knew only too well the vulnerability of his left flank, where now just two of Gary's dismounted cavalry regiments—the Seventh South Carolina and the Twenty-Fourth Virginia—faced off against Barlow's two divisions. Gary positioned these men in the works along Darbytown Road just south of Fussell's Mill and its six-acre millpond. Field himself headed for the danger point, at the head of a portion of Anderson's Brigade and two pieces of artillery from the Third Company Richmond Howitzers, whose arrival bolstered the outgunned cavalry.[38]

Barlow did show some initiative when he ordered the Second New York Heavy Artillery, 320 strong, to assault the Confederate works 900 yards in their front while the rest of Miles's brigade filed into position. The regimental commander, Maj. George Hogg, managed to take some advanced rifle pits before artillery fire and the certainty of being enfiladed compelled him to halt. "The 2d N.Y. of the first Brig suffered badly," reported one of Miles's officers, but this did not mollify Barlow. "This regiment failed entirely to execute my orders," he fumed. "The commanding officer of this regiment . . . showed himself utterly unfit for command, and the regiment did not behave with credit to itself." Barlow then called on Maj. John W. Byron of the Eighty-Eighth New York. Byron commanded seventeen skeleton companies of the famous but now depleted Irish Brigade—252 men—in what was called the Third Provisional Regiment of the Consolidated Brigade. Barlow assured the major that only a skirmish line guarded the Confederate works and told him to charge with fixed bayonets. But like the New Yorkers, Byron's men halted at the advance rifle pits after encountering artillery and small-arms fire. "I am compelled to say that these troops behaved disgracefully and failed to execute my orders," reported Barlow in an unfair echo of his assessment of Hogg's performance. Hancock informed Grant at 3:20 P.M. that Barlow had taken "the first line of rifle-pits . . . but failed to take the second and third lines, though attempting it twice. He is now about to try it again."[39]

For his third effort, Barlow called on Broady's Fourth Brigade to shuffle half a mile to the north and in position, he hoped, to turn the left flank of the stubborn graycoats. Because so many of Broady's men had straggled from the heat, fewer than 900 gathered for the attack. These soldiers advanced into a cornfield and immediately endured a severe artillery fire that claimed eighty victims and arrested their advance in minutes. Broady's men then broke without firing a shot, a retreat the frustrated Barlow attributed to "timidity and demoralization."[40]

It was now after 5:00 P.M., and Barlow had time for one more attempt to overwhelm the Rebel works that he insisted were "occupied only by a very thin line of the enemy" despite three failed assaults. He called on Colonel Smyth to devote two of his brigades for this purpose. Accordingly, Smyth moved Murphy's troops astride Long Bridge Road, while Macy's nine regiments crossed that thoroughfare to the right of Darbytown Road and into the same cornfield where lay the prone survivors of Broady's aborted advance. Macy started the day with more than 1,300 men, but straggling had reduced his command to about 1,000. The twenty-six-year-old native of Nantucket had earned the respect of his men throughout a wartime career in the Twentieth Massachusetts, distinguished by heroics at Ball's Bluff in 1861, Fredericksburg in 1862, and Gettysburg in 1863, where, in the process of defending Cemetery Ridge during the legendary "Pickett's Charge," he was wounded, necessitating the amputation of his left arm. He returned to duty in time to be shot in both legs at the Wilderness. A vacancy in Smyth's division provided the recuperated colonel the opportunity to lead a brigade for the first time.[41]

Macy deployed in two lines, with the 19th Maine, 1st Minnesota, and 152nd New York in front. Although the allegedly vulnerable Confederate works lay less than a half-mile distant, the intervening ground would present as much of a challenge as Southern rifles and cannon. The Federals deployed on a ridge southeast of Fussell's Mill and millpond, which lay in a depression some fifty feet deep, festooned with "the entangling meshes of the wait-a-bit vine" and other dense vegetation, through which ran the millpond outflow of Bailey's Creek. A soldier in the 19th Maine remembered that the "thicket of underbrush [was] so dense that a single man could not penetrate [it] without difficulty." The ground then rose sharply to another cleared ridgeline, on which the Confederates had prepared their defenses.[42]

As Macy deployed for his assault, Gary's dismounted cavalry prepared for battle. The Twenty-Fourth Virginia Cavalry was then in the process of retiring to its horses to respond to news that Gregg's troopers were moving west along Charles City Road, north of Fussell's Mill. This left only the Seventh South Carolina Cavalry and a portion of the Hampton Legion Cavalry in the trenches. But help was on the way. General Field was urging two more of Tige Anderson's Georgia regiments, the Eighth and the Fifty-Ninth, together numbering 419 muskets, to shift northward to meet Barlow's impending threat.[43]

The Federals advanced about 5:30 P.M. As soon as they appeared on the open high ground and began to descend into the ravine, the Confederates unleashed a bruising fire that immediately claimed multiple victims. "We soon formed in line of battle & . . . charged out into a cornfield with a hill before us but in such a position as to be raked . . . before we got fairly started," explained Sgt. Samuel Ripley of the Thirty-Sixth Wisconsin, a unit in Macy's second line. Macy and his officers went into the attack mounted, and a Rebel bullet quickly disabled the colonel's horse. He returned to the staging ground and appealed directly to Barlow for a new mount. The general at first objected, but Macy argued that his men would view him as cowardly if he continued the charge on foot. Persuaded by this questionable logic, Barlow offered his own black steed, and the colonel returned to the fray. Almost immediately, a Confederate projectile found this horse as well. The wounded animal lurched, its hind legs entangled in some branches, throwing Macy hard to the ground. Shaking loose, the horse landed flush on Macy, badly bruising the colonel's chest and abdomen. The determined brigade commander managed to extricate himself and attempted to go forward, only to collapse and lose consciousness. Stretcher-bearers transported him to the rear, his battle at an end.[44]

By then, Field arrived at the head of the two Georgia regiments, and Gary had recalled his Virginians. The Georgians poured fire on the Federal left while the cavalrymen pounded the right. "Our forces allowed them [to come] near the breastworks before firing when they then were slaughtered," asserted a Rebel. The Thirty-Sixth Wisconsin suffered particularly harshly, losing both its colonel and major to serious wounds among nearly three dozen casualties. Nevertheless, elements of the first and second waves managed to reach the Rebel entrenchments, where for twenty minutes the fighting was "furious." A Richmond newspaper gloated, with obvious exaggeration, that eventually "the enemy was repulsed and driven back and every man of them who reached the road was either killed or captured."[45]

When the blue crest receded, nearly 300 Federals had been killed or wounded or were missing. Confederate casualties were a fraction of this total. Macy's survivors huddled in the ravine until darkness allowed them to withdraw. "His brigade moved forward in good order," Smyth reported, "but meeting with a ditch very difficult to cross and one portion of the column coming across a mill-pond, the attack did not succeed." Pvt. David Coon of the Thirty-Sixth Wisconsin assessed the situation less charitably: "We was put into another charge which as usual amounted to get a lot of men wounded." Barlow proved an even harsher critic, reporting that the enemy line "could have been easily carried had the troops advanced with reasonable vigor and courage," although he did praise "the great gallantry and good behavior" of Colonel Macy, who eventually received a brevet to brigadier general for his actions this day.[46]

Thus ended the combat for Barlow's infantry, but the day would conclude with two smaller engagements. David Gregg's cavalry had faithfully discharged its responsibility of screening the infantry's right. In the morning Stedman's brigade had scattered a few of Gary's vedettes at Gravel Hill on Long Bridge Road and then moved north to Charles City Road. These troopers spent the bulk of the day roaming the neighborhood between New Market Road, Malvern Hill, and the Glendale crossroads, convincing Sgt. Edward P. Tobie of the First Maine Cavalry that "they were in a great country for by roads."[47]

In the afternoon scouting reports suggested that a portion of Gary's Hampton Legion Cavalry occupied some old Confederate trenches on Charles City Road near its crossing of Deep Run, a short distance northwest of Glendale. Col. J. I. Gregg assigned two of his regiments, the Second and Eighth Pennsylvania Cavalry, to approach the Rebels directly, while his other two units, the First Maine Cavalry and Thirteenth Pennsylvania Cavalry, employed a woodland road to flank the Confederate left. The troopers trotted off about 5:00 P.M., just as Macy formed for his ill-fated attack. The flanking regiments followed "the crookedest kind of road" single file, but before reaching their target, they heard firing on Charles City Road. A squadron of the Eighth Pennsylvania Cavalry had charged the Confederate position there, an assignment that Capt. John W. Haseltine of the Second Pennsylvania Cavalry considered "a kind of feint movement to allow ourselves to be slaughtered and attract their attention" while the flanking party went into position. To Haseltine's delight, the attack succeeded, only to come under fire from the two flanking Union regiments, which mistook them for the enemy. "I was obliged to ride out in full face of their fire and yell out that we were the 2nd Penna Cav," wrote Haseltine. "They then cheered us and came up." By this time, the Confederates—they numbered nothing more than a picket reserve—had fled, leaving behind a handful of prisoners and some cooked rations that the Yankee troopers consumed with "great gusto." Sgt. Nathan Webb of the First Maine Cavalry considered the fight "a spirited little affair" that cost the Federals only one man killed and four others wounded. The Confederates retired across White Oak Swamp, while General Gregg, reporting that his horses had not been watered since the previous evening, fell back to tend to his mounts.[48]

The third Union advance to commence around 5:00 P.M. on August 14 occurred at the far left end of the Federal battle front. Seven companies of the Seventh USCT, supported by a portion of the Ninth USCT, formed at the edge of some woods opposite works that the Federals had captured during the morning attack, then voluntarily abandoned, only to see them reoccupied by the Confederates. The Black soldiers moved across a cornfield, and, according to Capt. Lewis L. Weld of the Seventh USCT, "charged the works with a yell & took them in splendid style." The African Americans then advanced toward a second Confederate line but met such a severe fire that they withdrew to the captured works, enduring "a hot fire for over an hour" but holding their ground.

This engagement, which the soldiers called the "action of Kingsland Road," cost the Seventh two men killed and thirty-three wounded and the Ninth one man killed and ten others wounded.[49]

This small victory ended a disappointing day that cost the Federals about 600 casualties, three times that of the Confederates. The delay in disembarking Hancock's troops, a product of poor planning, meant that rather than marching into position at early dawn, the men had to contend with the debilitating heat in their trek toward the Confederate left, leaving hundreds of soldiers temporarily disabled. Barlow's incremental attacks failed to turn Field's left flank, while Mott's division remained stymied on the east side of Bailey's Creek. The Tenth Corps discharged its initial duty well, but then Birney remained idle for most of the day. This lassitude allowed Field to shift Anderson's Brigade to the left to help blunt Macy's attack, Barlow's most determined assault of the day. Gary's contribution to the Confederate defense cannot be overstated—Field called the cavalry's performance "very judicious and gallant." His small brigade stood alone on the Rebel left most of the day, holding its ground against overwhelming odds. Hancock exercised little influence on either Barlow or Birney, due, as Adjutant Walker explained, to "the wide extent of the country covered by the movements of the day and the density of the woods." Be that as it may, August 14 was not Winfield Hancock's shining moment.[50]

Grant explained the one tangible result of the day's fighting in messages to Chief of Staff Halleck in Washington. "The move to the north side of the James to-day developed the presence of Field's division of Longstreet's corps, which I supposed had gone to the Valley," he wrote. "This leaves but one division of infantry to have gone to the Valley. . . . Please forward this to Sheridan." Thus, one of the operation's goals, compelling the recall of reinforcements from Lee's army to the Valley, appeared at least partially moot. The day's failures also rendered the cavalry raid against the Virginia Central Railroad highly unlikely. But the third objective, drawing Lee's Petersburg troops north of the James to open an opportunity for Meade to threaten the Weldon Railroad, was still viable. Grant encouraged Meade to evaluate the potential for such a movement, even granting him authority to call on Butler's Eighteenth Corps for assistance.[51]

In fact, Lee acted as Grant intended. He recalled Wade Hampton and his cavalry division, now led by Brig. Gen. Matthew C. Butler, from its ride toward the Valley. Lee also ordered Rooney Lee's two cavalry brigades and Brig. Gen. John C. C. Sanders's and Brig. Gen. Victor Girardey's infantry brigades from Mahone's Third Corps division to reinforce Field from their positions on the Petersburg front. All four of these units began their journey to the north side before dark on the fourteenth. Field was also on the move. By day's end, he

Second Deep Bottom, August 13–20

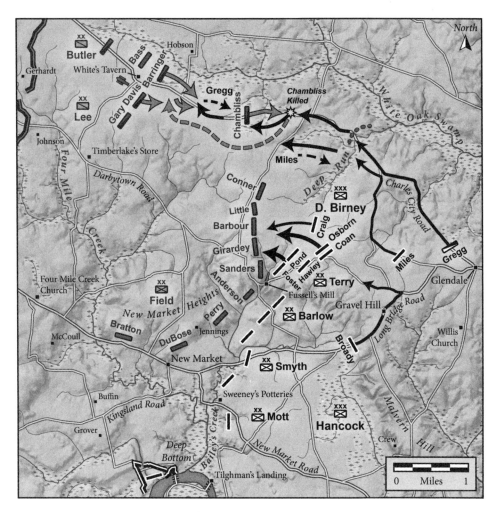

Second Deep Bottom, August 16, 1864

had reinforced Anderson and Gary with Gregg's Texas Brigade, while DuBose, Perry, and Bratton extended in a thin line opposite the Federal deployment.[52]

Those dispositions underwent a major change overnight. Hancock ordered Birney to move to the east side of Bailey's Creek by 3:00 A.M. on the fifteenth. After a short rest, the Tenth Corps would then resume its march across New Market Road and up Darbytown Road, poised to turn Field's left flank. Failing that, Birney would "attack the enemy's position with his whole force" if he thought it "practicable," while the Second Corps pressed forward in support. Gregg, as usual, bore responsibility for covering the army's right.[53]

Orders began circulating shortly after 7:00 P.M., directing the Tenth Corps to prepare for their trek to the east. Most of Birney's regiments departed two or three hours later, while Col. George Dandy and his 100th New York, along with the 39th Illinois and elements of the 85th Pennsylvania and 7th USCT, maintained the picket line until 1:00 A.M. Birney assigned the 8th USCT and 29th Connecticut to remain behind, defending the lines at Deep Bottom. The skies opened about dark, drenching the soldiers as they commenced their march. Some of the regiments crossed the upper bridge to Jones Neck, then recrossed on the lower bridge in what one officer described as "the most wearisome night marching—moving a few rods at a time and then halting for troops ahead to get out of the way . . . straggling out into the darkness, stumbling and groping along the rough road, and all the time the rain coming down." Nevertheless, Birney's men began filing onto New Market Road beyond Deep Bottom an hour after midnight and going into bivouac.[54]

Foster's brigade, the Eleventh Maine in the lead, led the Tenth Corps north, departing about 7:00 A.M. on August 15. The Federals gained Long Bridge Road, then followed several routes until reaching Darbytown Road on the right of the Second Corps, some three or four miles from their overnight camps. The staggered departures continued all morning, the Third New Hampshire among the last to leave at around noon.[55]

Virginia's unrelenting summer climate again claimed a serious toll. "During the march a great many men were obliged to fall out in consequence of the heat," reported a soldier in the 48th New York. "The idea of marching a distance of four miles with knapsacks and three days' rations, in sweltering sun, was beyond the strength of the men." Untold scores collapsed from exhaustion or sunstroke. "The army of stragglers soon became larger than the army of operations," estimated an officer in the 100th New York. "The men were falling to the ground, from heat, foaming at the mouth, shivering like dead men." Regiments had hemorrhaged great numbers by the time they reached their destinations, the 7th Connecticut, for example, counting only 161 present for duty at the end of the march. Some of Birney's troops lay down in an open field in range of Confederate artillery, which lobbed shells at them but inflicted few casualties. The 3rd New Hampshire retired into some woods and continued to endure the bombardment, happy to avail the shade, "for we preferred the shells of the enemy (and got them too) rather than the rays of old Sol." Some Tenth Corps troops joined their Second Corps comrades on the picket line.[56]

Those Second Corps soldiers had orders on August 15 to maintain a "strong line of skirmishers, well supported" and "mass the remainder of their commands to support their own lines or move to the support of others." In order to distract

Confederate attention from Birney's intended attack, Hancock would conduct noisy demonstrations. The 17th Maine set the standard. "Our picket line was upon the crest of a hill, running parallel to the enemy's works," explained the regimental historian. "Just in rear of the picket line, we gave loud commands to imaginary battalions, to give the enemy the idea that we were forming troops, preparatory to an attack. Then at a command given in a loud tone, the skirmishers advanced, with yells and shouts, and delivered one or two volleys and fell back." The Union navy got into the act, firing "a number of monstrous shells" toward the Confederates. Pvt. John W. Haley of the 17th Maine recorded that the gunboats "had such a range on the Rebel lines that they would drop a shell just where they wanted and every discharge was followed by a yell which we regarded as evidence that someone was knocked down and dragged out." Capt. Charles Weygant of the 124th New York harbored a less exalted opinion of the navy's aim, recalling that some of the projectiles "came short of their intended destination just enough to fall on the plain along our line. They were almost as large as nail kegs and the noise they made was most hideous." Fortunately, none of the New Yorkers were injured, "but several had their feelings badly wounded."[57]

Hancock provided Birney more direct support at 10:00 A.M. by ordering Mott's Second Brigade, led by Col. Calvin A. Craig, to reinforce the Tenth Corps on the army's new right flank. Craig's presence was intended to bolster the firepower of Birney's attack, but the agonizing march of the Tenth Corps undermined those plans. Instead, Craig's troops received orders to reconnoiter toward Charles City Road, where Gregg's cavalry had been engaged since early morning. In the words of a New York cavalryman, "it proved to be a bang-up day for the fighting business."[58]

Their opponents would be Rooney Lee's two cavalry brigades, led by Brig. Gen. John R. Chambliss and Brig. Gen. Rufus Barringer. Responding to R. E. Lee's orders, these seven mounted regiments left their encampments southwest of Petersburg and reached the city after dark on August 14. "We . . . marched all night, except for a half of an hour about midnight, and crossed the James on the pontoon bridge about daybreak," remembered Pvt. William A. Curtis of Barringer's Second North Carolina Cavalry. On the north side Chambliss's troopers took the lead, and his Ninth Virginia Cavalry had pushed back the Federals on Charles City Road by the time Barringer arrived about 9:00 A.M.[59]

Colonel Gregg's brigade had trotted west that morning on Charles City Road, adhering to its mission to protect the Union infantry's right. Gregg's Eighth and Thirteenth Pennsylvania Cavalry Regiments had been left on picket duty, and they were the unfortunate Federals assailed by Chambliss. When

Barringer's Tar Heels arrived, Rooney Lee ordered them to attack. The North Carolinians dismounted and charged, scattering the Pennsylvanians and driving them some two miles. The grayclad troopers maintained their pressure until all of Gregg's horsemen had withdrawn beyond Deep Run.[60]

In the meantime, Craig's brigade, with the First U.S. Sharpshooters leading as skirmishers, advanced in line of battle and struck the Rebels on their right flank below Charles City Road. "Theirs was a heavy line of infantry, ours only a skirmish line of dismounted cavalry," explained Private Curtis. According to Col. John Pulford of Craig's Fifth Michigan, the Unionists "completely routed" their grayclad opponents after an engagement of "short duration," pursuing them to Charles City Road. By this time, Gregg had rallied his troopers and joined the fray, while Miles's infantry brigade hoofed it north to provide support. The outgunned Confederates withdrew about four miles, and the Federals halted, content with redeeming the morning's defeat. Craig's brigade retired to Birney's lines after dark. The casualties were not insignificant in what the soldiers would call the Battle of Deep Run. Curtis reported losing twenty-seven killed and wounded in the Second North Carolina Cavalry alone. Craig lost thirty-nine men, while Gregg's casualties went unreported. An aborted advance by the Seventh and Ninth USCT exchanged fire, not with the Rebels, but with elements of Osborn's Tenth Corps brigade, an unfortunate circumstance that added more than a dozen names to the day's casualty list.[61]

Meanwhile to the south, Birney notified Hancock at 6:40 P.M. that although he had located the Confederate line, he felt unwilling to risk a night attack but, with Hancock's permission, "will make a vigorous one at daylight." "Another day thus passed without accomplishing anything commensurate with my wishes," groused an exasperated Hancock. Although debilitating temperatures certainly compromised Birney's plans, conservative generalship also contributed to the day's disappointments. That night Hancock circulated orders for what he hoped would, at last, be a decisive assault early on August 16. Miles would replicate Craig's approach toward Charles City Road, while the cavalry once again advanced on that highway at 4:00 A.M. These forces would attempt to turn the Confederate left. Birney's mission would be identical to the one he failed to execute on the fifteenth. Advancing between Darbytown and Charles City Roads, he would hope to help outflank the Rebels, but if failing that, he would seek a favorable opportunity to attack them in their works. Once again the three Second Corps divisions would remain ready to support Birney's success while ensuring that their skirmishers entertained the Confederates in their front.[62]

Although these orders almost directly mirrored those for the unrealized August 15 offensive, the situation along the Confederate front had changed dramatically in the intervening twenty-four hours. Not only had Rooney Lee's cavalry division arrived on the north side, but several new infantry brigades now bolstered the Confederate works on either side of Darbytown Road.

General Conner shifted both of his Carolina brigades from their positions as far west as Chaffin's Bluff to a point near Fussell's Mill, reaching there on the afternoon of the fifteenth. The men went immediately to work strengthening the trenches they now occupied. Sanders's Alabamans and Girardey's Georgians responded promptly to Lee's summons. Leaving their positions on the Petersburg lines early in the afternoon of the fourteenth during a heavy rainstorm, the men marched through the city and across the Appomattox River to Dunlop's Station on the Richmond & Petersburg Railroad, the farthest south trains could run "without danger of being knocked to pieces by Yankee shells." Detraining about 9:00 P.M., the troops marched to the pontoon bridges spanning the James a short distance upriver from Drewry's Bluff. Once on the north side at Chaffin's Bluff, these weary soldiers tramped across the sodden ground until 4:00 A.M., when they collapsed by the roadside. "Last night's march was one of the worst I ever tried," confessed Pvt. William E. Fielding of Sanders's Ninth Alabama. "We are all completely broken down. I feel as if I was 100 years old." Yet after only a short rest, the brigades resumed their journey, reaching the vicinity of Fussell's Mill around ten o'clock on the morning of the fifteenth. "Not more than ⅓ or ½ the men and officers of the line had been able to keep up," wrote Assistant Surgeon Charles W. Trueheart of the Eighth Alabama. "10 o'clock a.m. found them still stretched along the road for many a mile fast asleep."[63]

Major General Hampton, with Butler's cavalry division, left Beaver Dam Station, thirty-seven miles northwest of Richmond, on the morning of August 15, about the same time that General Lee departed his headquarters at Violet Bank, a home on high ground opposite Petersburg. Joined by most of his staff, the Confederate commander reached Chaffin's Bluff before noon and soon embarked on an inspection of Field's line. Stopping along Bratton's portion of the defenses near the Rebel right, he failed to impress Capt. John William McLure of the Palmetto Sharpshooters. "Monday morning General Lee himself came over to look after affairs," McLure wrote in an August 17 letter. "I saw him passing along the road riding in his ambulance accompanied by some other officers & followed by a courier looking more like a plain old citizen than a great Genl, dressed in plain clothes & straw hat."[64]

The Texas Brigade was also on the move, shifting farther left on the evening of the fifteenth and eventually taking position in support of the cavalry on Charles City Road. Bratton, Perry, and DuBose continued to guard New Market Heights. Ewell's men protected Lee's temporary headquarters at Chaffin's Bluff.

Field now commanded at least 15,000 troops, not counting Ewell's forces, on a line nearly nine miles long, still greatly overmatched by Hancock's two corps of infantry and Gregg's cavalry division. The stage was now set for a decisive test of arms.[65]

August 16, the fiercest and bloodiest day of the Second Deep Bottom operations, would see multiple scenes of combat north of the James River. The first fighting erupted along Charles City Road. In accordance with Hancock's instructions, Irvin Gregg's cavalry brigade was in the saddle by 4:00 A.M. and within the hour began advancing toward its picket line along Deep Run, held by the 2nd Pennsylvania Cavalry. To its left, along the same unnamed byway Craig's brigade had used the day before, the 26th Michigan, 140th Pennsylvania, and 5th New Hampshire of Miles's brigade advanced in concert with Gregg's troopers. Waiting for them in breastworks on the far side of Deep Run, the 13th Virginia Cavalry of Chambliss's Brigade watched the gradually lightening sky, anticipating another scorching Virginia day.[66]

Suddenly, a blue wave engulfed the unsuspecting Virginians. The Fourth Pennsylvania Cavalry joined Gregg's pickets in splashing across Deep Run, all the troopers advancing on foot. Almost immediately, the Sixteenth Pennsylvania Cavalry and First Maine Cavalry charged up Charles City Road, these mounted men joining their comrades in sending the Confederates flying. "We made them get away in a hurry," boasted Pvt. Porter Phipps of the Sixteenth. Colonel Gregg called this attack "gallant," while Sergeant Webb thought their charge "a very spirited little thing." The colonel made his way to the front of the column as the Confederates disappeared in great haste one-half mile up the road.[67]

These fugitives halted in the thick woods along the highway and then took position behind a hasty barricade blocking the thoroughfare. An unidentified Virginian pulled his trigger, sending a ball into the right wrist of Colonel Gregg, a painful and disabling wound. "His loss at that time was keenly felt," testified his adjutant general, Maj. John B. Maitland, "not only by the members of his staff, but by the entire brigade, as his place could not be well filled, he having the whole plan of battle well matured." The brigade's ranking regimental commander, Col. Charles H. Smith of the First Maine Cavalry, was absent, so Col. Michael Kerwin, the Irish-born commander of the Thirteenth Pennsylvania Cavalry, replaced the wounded Gregg. Before he left the field, Gregg enjoined Lt. Samuel Cormany of the Sixteenth Pennsylvania Cavalry to avenge his wound, something Cormany would soon accomplish.[68]

General Chambliss promptly learned of the setback along his picket line. He immediately called for his other two regiments, the Ninth and Tenth Virginia

Cavalry, to hasten to the front. Not waiting for these troopers to join him, Chambliss quickly rode east on Charles City Road to the scene of action, accompanied by his staff and the balance of the Thirteenth Virginia Cavalry. A thirty-one-year-old native of Southside Virginia, Chambliss had graduated from the U.S. Military Academy in 1853 but resigned his commission a year later to return to his father's large plantation in Greensville County. Active in the prewar state militia, Chambliss took command of the Thirteenth Virginia Cavalry soon after the outbreak of the war and led that regiment until he replaced the wounded Rooney Lee in brigade command after the 1863 battle at Brandy Station. He had earned the respect of his men and accolades from cavalry commanders "Jeb" Stuart and Wade Hampton.

As Chambliss approached a straight stretch of Charles City Road east of White's Tavern, he encouraged his men to make a stand until the reinforcements arrived. Two hundred yards away, a detachment of the Sixteenth Pennsylvania Cavalry led by Lieutenant Cormany spotted this "splendid looking officer" and called on him to halt. Chambliss wheeled about in an attempt to escape as Cormany ordered his men to fire. "He reeled to the left of the road—fell from his horse" fatally wounded by two rounds from the Pennsylvanians' Spencer carbines. Cormany's men approached the fallen officer and relieved him of his sword, belt, and a pipe. Later the Federals recovered a map of the Richmond fortifications from Chambliss's effects.[69]

Division commander David Gregg had been at West Point with Chambliss and recognized his fallen foe. When Gregg reported Chambliss's death, Hancock ordered the body removed and buried on New Market Road near the Potteries, "putting up a head-board by which the grave could be recognized." The general's remains were taken to Second Corps lines, where McAllister's men prepared the grave and placed Chambliss in a wooden coffin, respectfully identified. The next day Rooney Lee requested the body be returned, and Hancock so authorized under truce that afternoon. R. E. Lee would write that Chambliss's death would "be felt throughout the army," and General Gregg found time to send a letter of condolence to Chambliss's wife, enclosing her husband's West Point ring. Col. J. Lucius Davis of the Tenth Virginia Cavalry assumed command of Chambliss's Brigade.[70]

By then, most of Davis's regiment had arrived on the scene, with the Ninth Virginia Cavalry close behind, initially delayed in responding to Chambliss's summons because many of its men had scattered to fill their canteens. But now the lead elements of Miles's infantry appeared at the Deep Run crossing, the Twenty-Sixth Michigan aligned on the south side of Charles City Road and the Fifth New Hampshire supporting its left. The mounted Union troopers joined

Miles in a charge. The Confederates withdrew, at first only a few hundred yards and later a mile or more from where Chambliss fell. There, Rooney Lee ordered the brigade to halt and erect a barricade across the road, commencing an hour-long lull in the hostilities.[71]

During this interval, the Confederates brought up substantial reinforcements. Barringer's Brigade was the first to arrive, the First North Carolina Cavalry in the lead. Col. William P. Roberts, commanding the Second North Carolina Cavalry, recalled that the brigade went forward at a gallop. Reaching the Virginians' position, the Tar Heels dismounted and deployed on the north side of Charles City Road just east of White's Tavern. Davis's troopers shifted to the south side of the highway, where soon Gary's intrepid brigade formed on their right. Capt. William M. McGregor's horse artillery unlimbered behind the cavalry. About 10:00 A.M. Hampton, with a portion of Matthew Butler's Division, arrived and dismounted in support of Lee. Finally, Colonel Bass and the Texas Brigade, "having no Yanks of importance in our front," moved north and deployed along Charles City Road behind Barringer. The battle's trajectory was about to change.[72]

David Gregg, now on the scene as the ranking officer, recognized the increased Confederate strength and, because his primary mission had been to support an infantry attack to the south, thought he had gone as far west as necessary. Miles agreed, and Hancock ordered the infantry general to support Birney should he hear "heavy and continuous firing" from around Fussell's Mill. Hancock acted on that contingency shortly after noon, telling Gregg to dispatch Miles to "protect the roads leading into General Birney's right and rear while you hold strongly to the front," as Birney had broken through the Confederate line and needed help. Miles fell back, although not in the orderly fashion envisioned by the Federal high command—his brigade had become the target of a Confederate counterattack.[73]

"I never saw the enemy more beautifully driven back in my life," declared Pvt. Edmond A. Hatcher of the Ninth Virginia Cavalry. "Our men seemed determined and resolute." With a pistol shot as the signal, Rooney Lee ordered his division forward about 1:00 P.M., with Gary's and Butler's cavalry and the Texas Brigade behind them, moving fast. "A fierce yell bursts from our right," wrote a Virginia trooper, "a brigade of infantry leaps from the road, joins our line, and sweeps out across the field, carrying the enemy's line before them in the wildest disorder and confusion." This reasonably coordinated advance of four Confederate brigades bore down on Miles and Kerwin. The Federals fired a volley and then commenced a hasty retreat as the Confederates raised the Rebel Yell and, in the words of a North Carolinian, "commenced a hot pursuit." "That field was

Second Deep Bottom, August 13–20

just alive with rebels, yelling like demons, and pouring a cross-fire into us that was telling fearfully," exclaimed a Maine trooper.[74]

Gregg and Miles halted at various intervals, attempting to make a stand, but each time the superior Rebel firepower drove them eastward. "We retired the whole distance to Deep Creek under fire by forming a line of battle of about one half of our forces, which would give the enemy a rough reception when he came up to it," testified Hancock's aide Major Mitchell. "In the meantime the remaining troops would retire about half a mile and form line, when they would permit the front line to pass by them and check the enemy in their turn, until finally we reached the banks of Deep Creek and refused to go farther." During one of those brief stands, a Confederate minié ball hit Colonel Kerwin in the chest. The ball embedded in a pocket diary, thus sparing the colonel's life. Still, "the shock . . . was sufficiently severe to disable him from further service." Some of the fleeing Federal troopers veered off the road and into the quagmire of White Oak Swamp, where the marshy terrain immobilized many of their horses, making their riders easy targets. "Dying horses and men were mixed in a confused, struggling, inextricable mass, the living trampling the dying in the mud in their wild haste to reach the bank and shelter," remembered Captain Haseltine. "Of those who plunged into the swamp, a few escaped capture," admitted a Texan, "but none a submersion, head and ears, in the foul-smelling ooze into which they and their steeds sank." So many Federals fled on foot, remembered another Texan, "that it quite transformed our Brig into cavalry, nearly every other soldier being in possession of a horse."[75]

By the time Gregg's cavalry reached the banks of Deep Run, about 3:00 P.M., Miles had broken off to aid Birney. "It was unfortunate that General Miles left me," complained Gregg, but by then the Confederate pursuit had run its course, and relative quiet reigned along Charles City Road. Gregg's First Brigade moved up to relieve Kerwin's enervated troopers at sunset, allowing them to return to the camp they had left before dawn. The victorious Confederates were tired as well. "We lost several men by sun stroke," recorded Sgt. Edward Crockett of the Fourth Texas. "When night came we were all nearly exhausted." The Gregg-Kerwin brigade reported 225 casualties during the Deep Bottom operations, the bulk of the losses occurring on the sixteenth. Miles lost 274 at Deep Bottom, many of these sustained while fighting alongside the cavalry. There is no way to determine the human toll on the Confederate side. Private Curtis remembered that twenty-seven members of the Second North Carolina Cavalry fell. Cpl. Joseph B. Polley claimed that the only casualties in the Texas Brigade resulted from sunstroke. "D.B.R.," a correspondent for the *Richmond Enquirer*, simply reported, "The victory . . . cost us many valuable lives."[76]

As dramatic as the day's action along Charles City Road had been for those who participated, that engagement proved to be a sideshow to what unfolded a short distance to the south and east. The infantry clash near Fussell's Mill would be the defining action at Second Deep Bottom. As one Union soldier phrased it, "the 16th . . . was to prove the most trying period of all the regiment's time of service."[77]

At 3:30 A.M. General Terry received a summons to meet with his immediate superior, David Birney. A few hours earlier Birney had informed Terry that the Second Corps on his left and the USCT regiments on his right would launch an attack the next morning. But when Terry arrived at Birney's headquarters, the Tenth Corps commander ordered his division to make the assault instead and to do so shortly after sunrise. Birney assigned Craig's brigade of Mott's division to bolster Terry's firepower. The attack would target the Confederates in front of Colonel Hawley's position. Foster's men would be in direct support, while Pond's and Craig's units deployed in reserve.

Terry, along with Hawley and Lt. Col. Josiah I. Plimpton, commander of the Third New Hampshire, set off to examine the point of attack. Crawling up to within 250 yards of the Confederate works in the predawn gloom, the officers spotted the deep ravine that contained the waters of Fussell's millpond. Evidently, the corrugated terrain and thick vegetation in the neighborhood had disguised the presence of this major terrain feature, which rendered Terry's attack plan impractical. "It would have been madness to attack there," admitted the division commander, who reported the situation to Birney. Birney therefore directed Terry to refocus his attack about half a mile to the north, beyond the upper boundaries of the watery obstacle, prompting a realignment of his attack formation. Foster's brigade, supported by Craig, would now lead the charge, with Pond in support and Hawley in reserve.[78]

Most of Terry's soldiers were also awake at 3:30 that morning. In fact, Hawley had his men building breastworks as early as 3:00 A.M. Several Yankees remembered seeing Grant, Hancock, and Birney riding by with their staffs. Lt. Daniel Eldredge of the Third New Hampshire thought that Grant might have gone unnoticed "had not the three stars discovered his generalship." Grant was wearing a common soldier's blouse, "a slouched hat without cord or ornament, and a very cheap strap which came over in front as though the blouse pocket had been filled with apples or hard tack." Hancock presented quite a contrast, "being a large powerful man and rather superior looking." In any case, the appearance of these officers satisfied Eldredge "that it meant battle."[79]

"The ground upon which we now moved was very difficult, covered with dense woods & intersected with innumerable ravines with marshy bottoms,"

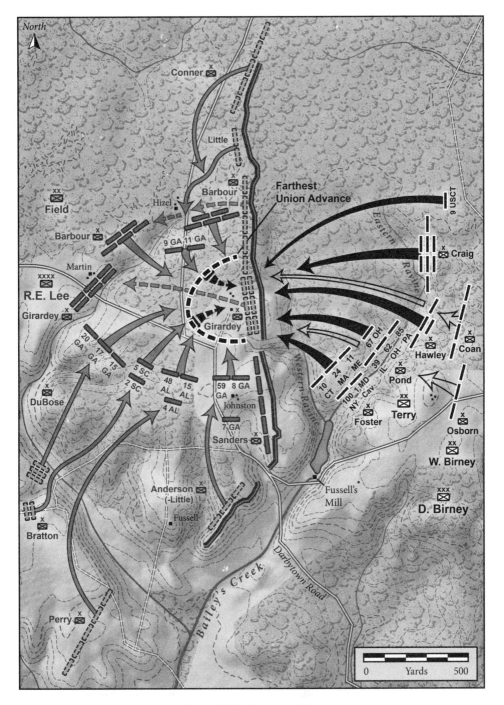

North

Conner

Little

Barbour

Hizel

Field

Barbour

9 GA 11 GA

Martin

R.E. Lee

Girardey

Girardey

Farthest
Union Advance

Eastern Ravine

9 USCT

Craig

20 GA
17 GA
15 GA

DuBose

5 SC
2 SC

48 AL
15 AL

4 AL

59 GA
8 GA

Johnston

7 GA

Sanders

10 CT
24 MA
11 ME
67 OH
39 IL
62 OH
85 PA
100 NY
1 MD
Cav.

Western Ravine

Hawley

Coan

Pond

Foster

Terry

Osborn

W. Birney

Bratton

Anderson
(-Little)

Fussell

Fussell's
Mill

D. Birney

Perry

Bailey's Creek

Darbytown Road

0   Yards   500

Fussell's Mill, August 16, 1864

Terry explained. Some of the Tenth Corps skirmishers became lost in this track-less terrain, and an officer in the Tenth Connecticut went out to find them. "It was a blind search," recalled Capt. Henry W. Camp. "I moved rapidly to where the line should have been . . . through thicket, over fallen trees, across swamps, until I came to a ravine. . . . No sound; the woods were as quiet and apparently as tenantless as if I were in the wilderness beyond the Rocky Mountains." To make matters worse, the dawn brought a renewal of the inevitable skirmish fire, some of which claimed victims as the Federals shifted to the north beyond the borders of the millpond.[80]

Eventually, Foster's men reached their designated jump-off point, advancing skirmishers while the bulk of the soldiers poised for their orders to attack. Foster placed the 11th Maine on his right, the 24th Massachusetts in the center, and the 10th Connecticut on the left of his front line. The 100th New York and 1st Maryland Cavalry (dismounted) lay down behind them as brigade reserve. Craig's soldiers stumbled into position on Foster's right, with the 1st U.S. Sharpshooters and the 5th Michigan deployed as flank protection, while the rest of the brigade formed line of battle to the rear. Hawley's and Pond's brigades did not reach their reserve positions until about 9:00 A.M. The Confederates maintained a spirited skirmish fire all the while. "If a man has nerves they are soon in a quiver," explained a Maine volunteer, "and if he has not known he had any before, he learns that he is not made quite of iron after all."[81]

That annoying fire emanated from a Confederate line that had been adjusted earlier that morning. In the evolving quest to safeguard his left flank, Field sent General Conner's two brigades even farther north at dawn in response to reports of the Federal shift. "About sunrise on the 16th, we were ordered to prepare to move, and, before many minutes, were put upon the march," wrote Adj. James Fitz James Caldwell of Conner's South Carolina unit. "Our course was northward, in rear of, and parallel with, the breastworks." Barbour's North Carolinians joined them, leaving the Georgians of Girardey's brigade to sidle left and occupy the breastworks the Tar Heels had worked so hard to improve. The South Carolinians extended to the far left of the expanded Confederate line, joined on their right by the Ninth and Eleventh Georgia of Anderson's Brigade under Col. Francis H. Little, with Barbour's men to their immediate right. Girardey's Georgians posted on Barbour's right, followed by Sanders's Alabama Brigade and then the balance of Tige Anderson's Georgians. Those deadly skirmishers took position in front of the main line, on which every Rebel had labored diligently. The Confederates, their numbers stretched over this expanded space, stood in a single rank.[82]

Second Deep Bottom, August 13–20

General Field considered the portion of his line opposite Foster's brigade the weakest segment of his entire defense. "The ground was irregular, and what was of much more consequence, there was a dense forest of oak and pines . . . which we had only had time to cut away for a few yards (about fifty) in front of our works," he recalled. Such a limited field of fire would permit an attacker to approach virtually unseen to within point-blank range of the main Confederate works. In order to compensate for this vulnerability, Field had advanced a line of vedettes on the ridge that separated the two watery ravines that fed into the millpond. A more formal picket line rested in advance of a tangle of abatis that fronted the tiny field of fire, beyond which Girardey's Georgians and the right end of Barbour's North Carolinians waited behind their barrier of logs and earth.[83]

Wright's Brigade had been under the command of Brig. Gen. Victor Jean Baptiste Girardey for about two weeks. The twenty-seven-year-old Frenchman served as a captain on Mahone's staff when, at the Battle of the Crater on July 30, he had greatly distinguished himself. General Wright had been too ill to participate in that engagement, and his temporary replacement proved unworthy of continued command. Mahone saw to the almost unparalleled promotion of Girardey from his staff position to brigadier general and placed him at the head of Wright's Georgia veterans. Pvt. Alva B. Spencer of the Third Georgia considered Girardey "truly a brave and gallant soldier" despite his brief tenure with the brigade. An ersatz commander also led the North Carolinians on Girardey's left. William Barbour, a lawyer from Wilkesboro, North Carolina, had commanded the Thirty-Seventh North Carolina for more than two years. Wounded at Fredericksburg in 1862 and at Chancellorsville in 1863, Barbour had been captured at Spotsylvania in May 1864 and exchanged on August 3. He then replaced the wounded James Lane at the head of his five Tar Heel regiments.[84]

Terry informed Birney that shortly after 9:00 A.M., Foster had positioned his line of skirmishers within 200 yards of the Confederate vedettes. A few minutes later Birney advised Hancock, "Foster will commence driving them within the next five minutes." It would take a bit longer, actually, but at 10:00 A.M. Foster's five regiments began their attack. "It was hot to suffocation" already, reported Captain Towle of Terry's staff. "The dense woods made the air close, but gave no shelter from the fierce August sun." The brigade leapt up with a cheer, loud enough to make "the woods of secessia ring with Union echoes." "Quickly we arose to our feet, and rushed forward with a wild cry which seems as necessary to a charging force as the breath with which they give it," remembered Lt. Albert Maxfield of the Eleventh Maine. "Almost immediately we were subjected to the most severe fire we were ever under."[85]

Although the labyrinthine vegetation disordered their line of battle, the Federals plunged into the eastern ravine and up the opposite side, easily scattering the Confederate vedettes. As the charge continued into the western ravine, both the 10th Connecticut on the left and the 11th Maine on the right reported a lack of flank protection. Foster rushed the 100th New York forward to assist the Nutmeggers and sent the 1st Maryland Cavalry to support the right of the 11th Maine. He then rode into the ranks of his front line and urged his men to continue the assault, regardless of their exposed flanks. "We dashed ahead . . . under a heavy fire poured on us from their main line," wrote Maxfield, and into the primary Confederate pickets and their abatis. The Federals scooped up a number of prisoners as their own casualties began to mount. "There were single enlisted men stricken down who were worth more to the country than every substitute sent to the war by the Hartford shirks," lamented Chaplain Trumbull. On the left Col. John L. Otis, commander of the 10th Connecticut, reported that his troops were so far separated from their support on the left that the Confederates had sliced in behind them and began to gobble up prisoners. "Our lines had now become so weak, by constantly extending to the left to prevent being flanked, that for several hundred yards," Otis noted, "we had only a weak line of skirmishers with very little support." On the opposite end of Foster's line, the 11th Maine found itself isolated when the 1st Maryland Cavalry failed to move forward. "This delay and hesitation caused the failure of the charge at this time," fumed the regimental commander. "The opportune moment was lost." Foster's initial attack sputtered to a halt.[86]

Terry kept Birney apprised of the situation, the corps commander responding that he was thus far satisfied with Terry's progress. But he also told Terry to "push your movement with alacrity and . . . use your entire division if, in your opinion, advisable." Terry took immediate steps to do so. He ordered Pond's brigade to move up on Foster's right, about 900 yards north of Fussell's Mill and barely 100 yards from the Confederate works, shielded by the thick woods that had so concerned General Field. Pond deployed the Sixty-Seventh Ohio in his front and the rest of the brigade behind in line of battle. Hawley's brigade advanced to a position behind and to the right of Pond. "We passed over the abandoned rifle-pits of our enemy," wrote Lieutenant Eldredge, "in which were some of the guns so recently fired at our forces, and not yet cooled. On and on, we passed, through briar and brake, through brush and over logs and fallen trees, through bush and tangled brush, tearing our clothes, scratching our faces and hands, ruffling our tempers, with the excitement each moment increasing, as each of said moments brought us nearer the foe." Terry accompanied Hawley's advance. Jokingly, he advised the officers of the Seventh Connecticut to find what cover they could until the attack orders arrived, while "he himself set the example by shielding his slim figure behind a tree about eight inches through." Craig's troops remained on the right of a formation that now included four brigades.[87]

Terry could not know that just a few hundred yards to his west, the two ranking Confederate generals were now on the scene. Major General Field and his staff had arrived behind Girardey's men after conducting a thorough examination of the defensive preparations that morning. He had informed General Lee of the unfolding situation on his front and along Charles City Road, prompting the commanding general to leave his headquarters at Chaffin's Bluff and ride east, stopping behind Sanders's Brigade. As luck would have it, both Field and Lee would soon be swept up in the most serious combat at Second Deep Bottom.[88]

Birney began his renewed attack with an artillery bombardment about noon, followed almost immediately by the infantry assault. Pond's "Western Brigade" led the charge, with Foster's Eleventh Maine and Twenty-Fourth Massachusetts on their left, the remainder of that brigade temporarily impeded by the mill-pond. Led by the skirmishers of the Sixty-Seventh Ohio, Pond's men advanced in a narrow but deep formation of as many as five distinct lines. "As the skirmish line emerged from the thick woods into the abatis of the enemy in front of their works my skirmishers delivered a deadly fire at the head of the rebels as they stood behind their earth-works," reported Colonel Voris, the Sixty-Seventh's commander, "at the same time receiving a heavy volley from them." The Thirty-Ninth Illinois, on the left of Pond's formation, also absorbed this blow, but undaunted, they gave forth "a regular Western yell," advancing "on the full jump, over logs, tree-tops and stumps thrown about in inextricable confusion." Dead and dying men littered the ground as the Illinoisans "made directly for the rebel breastworks bristling with bayonets and alive with men."[89]

Cpl. Ransom Bedell of the Thirty-Ninth Illinois explained that the Unionists "rushed on the enemy like an avalanche knocking them over with our guns—as we mounted over their high bank." Colonel Pond reported that this was "the first time I ever saw this brigade fighting hand to hand, bayonet to bayonet, over the breast-works." Various Federals estimated the duration of this close-quarters combat from two to fifteen minutes, but all agreed that the Confederates claimed a mighty toll. Colonel Voris testified that some 250 men of the brigade fell during the attack. A soldier in the Thirty-Ninth Illinois counted sixty-four of his comrades down. Fifteen out of thirty-one soldiers in one company of the Eighty-Fifth Pennsylvania were either killed outright or desperately wounded.[90]

Despite these losses, the Federal attack succeeded. It had struck that particularly vulnerable portion of the line defended by Girardey's Georgians and Barbour's right flank. General Field heard the commotion and assumed that the veterans in his front would remain masters of the field. His adjutant, Maj. Willis F. Jones, exclaimed in an excited tone, "General, they are breaking." Field expressed satisfaction, thinking Jones referenced the Federals, but the staff officer quickly disabused him of that idea. "But General, it's our men." Field leapt to his feet and witnessed what he considered "the most appalling, disheartening sight of my life," the disordered retreat of the Georgians and North Carolinians.[91]

Field and members of his staff hurriedly mounted and rode toward the chaos, hoping to rally the men. Although the "air was alive with Minie balls, the ground torn up by shells and cannon balls," Capt. Richard W. Corbin joined his chief, attempting to inspirit the retreating Georgians: "By entreaties and by menaces, and with pistols drawn we threatened to shoot them if they did not go back." At the front General Girardey exhorted his brigade to stand firm, the flag of the Sixty-Fourth Georgia in his hands. A soldier in the Sixty-Seventh Ohio aimed his rifle at this conspicuous target and launched a bullet into Girardey's forehead, killing him instantly. The Yankees scooped up the fallen colors, one of three regimental banners captured from the brigade that day.[92]

The Georgians' withdrawal exposed Barbour's right and compelled him to order his men to fall back as well, with less panic than their Georgia comrades but no less haste. "These two brigades for a time at least seemed to dissolve," thought Field. "At this time not only the day but Richmond seemed to be gone." Birney gleefully reported the situation to Hancock, who passed the news on to Meade and Grant. "He has carried one line," explained Hancock, and "will go forward again."[93]

Even though Field felt "that nothing but a miracle could save us," he took immediate steps to realize such an outcome. He ordered John Gregg, acting commander of Field's Division, "to bring me every available man he had, to leave only a skirmish line to hold his works, and to come quickly." Corbin dashed down the line to summon Perry's and DuBose's men, while word also reached Conner and the Ninth and Eleventh Georgia on the far Confederate left to move down toward the breakthrough. When General Lee, awaiting word behind Sanders's front, learned of the collapse a few hundred yards up the line, he employed his personal gravitas to redeem the situation. A Union prisoner thought the gray chieftain was "cool and collected." In fact, the Alabama boys changed front and fired into Foster's left, subjecting the Eleventh Maine and Twenty-Fourth Massachusetts to "a heavy flank fire." Barbour managed to re-form most of his brigade on the opposite side of Darbytown Road, limiting the northward extent of the Federal penetration.[94]

The Federals were not content with the status quo. Moments before Pond's regiments reached the Confederate works, Colonel Hawley gave the command, "Forward, Second Brigade," and his New Englanders charged across the western ravine and through the obstructions. Once on the parapet, Hawley's men tangled briefly with the more stalwart Rebels who had not yet succumbed to Pond's assault. "A few surrendered," wrote a soldier from the Sixth Connecticut, "while the main body skedaddled through a corn field into a piece of woods." Lieutenant Eldredge thought that the Confederates acted quite pliantly, throwing down their guns and with their knapsacks falling into line quite readily, "as though not entirely displeased at their changed condition." Lt. Ferdinand Davis of the Seventh New Hampshire considered the scene "an awful sight—the ground was strewn with the dead and dying." On the right of Birney's formation, Craig's brigade joined the attack, reaching the Confederate works, "roll[ing] them up right smart for awhile," and capturing seventy-five men and two commissioned officers. At the opposite end of the line, the remainder of Foster's units shifted north to skirt the upper end of the millpond, but the difficult terrain and Sanders's flanking fire thwarted their attempt to reach the Confederate works. Now, about 12:30 P.M., the high point of the Union attack had arrived.[95]

Lt. Wiley Roy Mason Jr. served as an aide-de-camp to his brother-in-law, General Field. Responding to the breakthrough as had Field and other members of his staff, Mason fell wounded in the liver at the hands of the Eighty-Fifth Pennsylvania and became a prisoner. Lt. Col. Edward Campbell, in charge of the Eighty-Fifth, interrogated Mason, who told him, with perhaps calculated exaggeration, that 15,000 fresh troops were even then bearing down on the Union left. Campbell informed Terry of this alarming intelligence, and the division commander instructed the colonel to find Birney and request reinforcements.[96]

David Birney responded with alacrity. The two White brigades of William Birney's provisional division, numbering 1,600–1,700 men, answered the call. Osborn and Coan had been resting in the rear near Tenth Corps headquarters when the summons arrived. They started toward the front, with Osborn's troops in the lead. A spent bullet struck the colonel in the back of the neck, disabling him, while another ball felled his second in command. Maj. Ezra L. Walrath of the 115th New York then took charge as the brigade navigated the tangled terrain and abatis to reach the captured Confederate line. "Forming as well as possible in these reversed Rebel lines, the half-mile run having been made in heavy marching order, the men carrying knapsacks were well winded," confessed Lt.

Nicholas De Graff of the 115th. Coan's men followed, traversing a narrow woods road, then dashing nearly half a mile "amid a shower of bullets" to and through the obstructions to join Walrath's troops on the front line.[97]

Major General Birney now called on Hancock for additional assistance. The Second Corps commander gave him Broady's brigade and sent word to David Gregg to release Miles's infantrymen as soon as possible. Broady's troops faced a long march and would not arrive for several hours, while Gregg could not immediately detach Miles, as he was at that time engaged with the Confederate counterattack along Charles City Road. The most noteworthy reinforcement, at least from the Confederate perspective, was William Birney's Ninth USCT, which would eventually take position on the right of the Tenth Corps line.[98]

Mason may have overstated the number of Confederate troops committed to reclaiming the captured works, but Field had indeed marshaled a powerful counterattack. His targets were the Federals now occupying a horseshoe-shaped position a short distance west of the conquered Confederate breastworks, with both flanks bent back to rest on those trenches. The Rebels would apply nearly simultaneous pressure on both sides of this salient.

Nine grayclad regiments descended on the scene from their positions along New Market Heights. Bratton contributed two from his South Carolina brigade, DuBose sent three Peach State units, Perry dispatched two of his Alabama regiments, and Anderson released his remaining pair of regiments deployed south of the breakthrough. At the other end of the line, Anderson's Ninth and Eleventh Georgia, along with Conner's South Carolinians, moved toward the Federal right, inspiring many of Barbour's North Carolinians to fall in as well. This Rebel counterattack struck between 12:45 and 1:00 P.M.

Colonel Little, with his two Georgia regiments, led the advance against the Union right, targeting the ground held by the Eighty-Fifth Pennsylvania. "Frankly, I did not like the job," Little admitted, but joined by Conner's Carolinians, the Georgians moved through some woods toward the Federal position. The Seventh New Hampshire shifted to assist the Pennsylvanians but to no avail, as the Yankees fell back in the face of this determined thrust. Fierce fighting ensued as the rest of Hawley's brigade eventually joined the fray. The Twelfth South Carolina managed to recapture a portion of the lost works, only to be expelled as the casualties mounted, including Colonel Barbour, who was wounded in the right leg.[99]

The left, or southern, side of the Federal horseshoe also faced intense pressure. Foster's Maine and Massachusetts regiments, the Western Brigade, most of Craig's men, and finally Hawley's troops took position from the captured Confederate line northwest to the apex of the advanced Federal position. The first Confederate challenge came from the Eighth and Fifty-Ninth Georgia, joined by Col. Alexander A. Lowther at the head of eight companies of his Fifteenth Alabama, and about 100 men from the Forty-Eighth Alabama. General Anderson assumed informal command of these four units, whose combined strength numbered perhaps 1,000 bayonets.[100]

The Confederate approach quickly claimed Colonel Lowther, whose wound elevated Col. William C. Oates to command of the Alabamans. With the Georgians on their right, Oates led his men forward against the position held by Craig's brigade. The combat decimated the Alabama officers, including Oates, who was shot in the right arm. On the Union side a bullet slammed into Craig's skull just as he ordered a charge, inflicting a mortal wound and leaving Colonel Pulford in brigade command. Craig died at 3:00 A.M. the next morning. "Colonel Craig was a man that was beloved & respected by all who knew him," wrote Lt. Tilton C. Reynolds of the 105th Pennsylvania. "He was brave & generous always having a kind word & a pleasant smile for everyone. In his death the country has lost a devoted patriot."[101]

As the Confederates battered their way into the Federal position, Walrath's men arrived, re-forming along the Confederate works. At the same time, the Fifth South Carolina and DuBose's three Georgia regiments joined the battle to the left of the Alabamans. General Lee, who refrained from issuing formal orders, appeared behind the Carolinians, offering an excited invitation to "charge 'em boys with a hearty shout." Anderson's two Georgia units shifted left and, along with their Peach State comrades, attacked Hawley's troops, driving them back "with greater speed than we cared to travel that day," admitted a Connecticut soldier. Both Hawley and Pond, overcome by exhaustion exacerbated by the relentless heat, relinquished control of their brigades to their senior regimental commanders, leaving four of Birney's brigades under temporary leaders. Walrath, one of those substitutes, led his troops in a charge that resulted in his wounding as well as that of his successor. "The rebels were continually firing at us and yelling like Indians," remembered Sgt. John Reardon of the 115th New York. "The Yank line advanced but we gave it to them so heavily that they retired," confirmed a South Carolina private. These bluecoats staggered back to the trenches and then trickled to the rear, hors de combat. Combined with the pressure exerted by Barbour, Conner, and Little on the north end of the Federal incursion, the temporary Union success now teetered on the brink of collapse. The remaining Unionists all withdrew to the captured Confederate trenches, where they made frantic efforts to reverse the works and make a stand.[102]

By then, Coan's reinforcements arrived, replacing Walrath's vanquished troops, with their division commander, William Birney, now on the scene.

"The position of . . . Birney's provisional division was one of critical peril," recalled a man from the Ninety-Seventh Pennsylvania. The last of Birney's fresh units, the Ninth USCT, filed into the right of the Union line shortly after 2:00 P.M. The contracted Federal position now covered barely a quarter mile of the former Confederate works, as the last of the Southern reinforcements—the Seventh Georgia, Fourth Alabama, and Second South Carolina Rifles—joined the Confederate perimeter, an exterior line that overlapped the shrunken Union formation. As the South Carolinians deployed, Field's acting division commander, John Gregg, inquired as to their identity. When told who they were, Gregg exclaimed, "Ah, that is a good regiment. I know you will do." Although Lt. Augustus A. Dean appreciated the praise, he admitted, "I knew what that meant—there was some fighting to be done and we must do it." The scene was now set for the final redemptive Rebel assault.[103]

That action commenced about 3:00 P.M., starting against the Union left, still held by Foster's stubborn soldiers. Sanders's men joined their comrades from Perry's brigade in ousting Foster's troops, who had run low on ammunition and were deprived of their two best regimental commanders, victims of a wound and sunstroke. The Rebel wave rolled up the Union line, exploiting a gap on Coan's left and compelling his brigade to withdraw, sustaining fire from its front and both flanks. Coan's departure exposed the left flank of the Ninth USCT as Conner and Little assailed them in front. The Black troops gradually fell back, displaying discipline and courage while losing more than eighty men in their short time under fire. By then, the entire Confederate line had advanced, regaining all of the ground lost in the noontime attack, as the defeated Federals retreated a quarter of a mile into the shelter of the thick woods and the eastern ravine.[104]

Content with reclaiming all their lost real estate, the Confederates, themselves badly bloodied and feeling the effects of the weather, did not pursue. This afforded David Birney the chance to reorganize his shattered brigades, which were soon joined by Miles from the north and Broady from the south. This respite, combined with the arrival of two fresh brigades, emboldened the Tenth Corps commander. "I propose to attack at 5 o'clock," he informed Hancock. Birney placed Miles on his right, protecting against any threat from Charles City Road, and advanced Broady's men in a skirmish line, trading fire with the Confederates in their front. This lively exchange left no doubt that the Rebels remained there in force. Birney took stock of his veterans—tired, hungry, short of ammunition, and deprived of many field and line officers. Shortly before 6:00 P.M., he canceled the attack. The battle at Fussell's Mill had ended.[105]

Historian John Horn, in the most recent and careful analysis of the losses on August 16, asserts that the Federals suffered nearly 2,000 casualties on August

16, including 500 prisoners, representing some 27 percent of the troops engaged. The Confederates sustained about half as many losses. Men on both sides commented on the carnage. Colonel Voris, who had assumed command of his brigade when Pond left the field, thought the battle "was a terrible thing—the most destruction I have seen for the time it took." Pvt. William C. Jordan of the Fifteenth Alabama remembered the fight as "the most terrific battle I was ever in, in proportion to the time engaged and the number that participated. It was more disastrous on the officers than any other engagement that I ever participated in." At least one Federal held David Birney responsible for the defeat. "At 12 PM we had their main front line, at 3 PM we were whipped at all points, driven in confusion and defeat from the Rebel entrenchments that it had cost a thousand lives to capture," snarled Lieutenant De Graff, "and all lost because Brig. [*sic*] Genl. Birney, who ordered the fatal advance, was not satisfied to make sure of holding what we had, but must rush troops already exhausted on a fool charge for a forlorn hope." In contrast, a Richmond newspaper published a soldier's account of the fighting, in which the author gave Charles Field "great credit for the judicious disposition of and able manner in which he handled the troops," acknowledging "the confidence which General Lee reposed in leaving the management of this formidable advance upon our capital in his hands."[106]

Although the Ninth USCT was the only African American unit to participate in the battle, and then only for a relatively short time, its presence elicited an outsized volume of comments from the Confederates. "This was the first time our brigade encountered the negro troops," Capt. William Aiken Kelly of the First South Carolina recorded in his diary. "I saw the first negro prisoners that I have seen." Sgt. D. G. Fleming of the Eighth Georgia told his sister, "I was then convinced and never before believed that there were black colored Yankees in Grant's army." Pvt. John Hamil of the Ninth Georgia and a few companions "decided we wanted to see how Negroe Soldiers looked. We had never come in contact with them before." The men went in front of their lines and examined some of the corpses.[107]

Some Confederates greatly exaggerated the role of the Black soldiers. "Negroes broke Wright's line," wrote Pvt. John Lafayette Oxford of the Ninth Georgia. Pvt. William Andrew Mauney of the Twenty-Eighth North Carolina believed "a great part of the enemy" were "negroes." Capt. Samuel L. Dorroh of the Fourteenth South Carolina considered the African Americans "the blackest ruffest set of dogs I ever saw" and boasted, "We killed a good many negroes & took a few prisoners which I am opposed to doing." In this sentiment he was not alone; apparently, Black prisoners were indeed few. "Three or four hundred prisoners were secured," reported a soldier correspondent to Georgia's

Savannah Republican, "of which strange to say only two of the misguided ne-groes remained among them to reach Libby." Pvt. Martin Hood of the Twenti-eth Georgia was less opaque in a letter to his brother. "A portion of our brigade encountered some negro troops but few of them taken any prisoners. Most of them were killed." Staff officer James Henry Hammond of Conner's brigade confirmed this grim admission. "It is the first time we fought negroes and I am sorry to say no quarter was shown them." Cpl. John W. Lokey of the Twentieth Georgia provided some insight as to the origin of the merciless attitude toward Black troops evinced by so many Confederates. "After I got back to the trenches I saw a dead Yank lying in front of the breastworks and a dead nigger lying on top of him. I said to one of the boys, 'That Yank is right where he ought to be, any man who will equalize himself with a negro ought to be at the bottom.'"[108]

Beyond the detachment of Miles, Craig, and Broady to Birney's front, the Second Corps contributed little on August 16. "General Mott felt the enemy's line at intervals during the afternoon," reported Hancock, "to prevent them from sending reinforcements to our front," an expedient that clearly failed. Mott claimed that "these demonstrations were made frequently during the day," the most serious of which involved the Eighth New Jersey and Eleventh Massachu-setts of McAllister's command. As a result, Colonel McAllister concluded that the Confederates in his front were weak, "yet it was found that his works were too strong to be surprised by a small force." The Federals withdrew after sus-taining moderate casualties. Colonel Smyth committed the Seventh Michigan and Fifty-Ninth New York to a similar exercise with equally minimal results.[109]

General Bratton had taken charge of the Confederate troops that remained from New Market Heights to Chaffin's Bluff, while regiment after regiment moved northeast to confront Birney's incursion. "My already attenuated line was depleted to furnish [these] forces," Bratton explained, "a position that made me sweat and took all the rest out of me." The South Carolinian managed the units from Lee's army alongside those from Ewell's Department of Richmond to thwart these tepid Federal probes. Ben Butler orchestrated the only Union suc-cess in the neighborhood, albeit too late to have any salutary effect on Birney's efforts. At 5:00 P.M. 950 of his men boarded the steamer *Mount Washington* at Dutch Gap. They disembarked at Aiken's Landing, upstream from Deep Bot-tom, and with minimal loss captured a portion of the Confederate line at Signal Hill on the Cox farm. When Grant learned of this initiative, he told Butler that because Hancock was "at a stand still" and that "it is now getting late" he should "use caution about advancing." With that, all the fighting on August 16 came to an end. "At dusk each side finds itself about where it was in the morning," ob-served Private Haley. "We had hoped the distance between us and Richmond would be shortened by several miles today, but this hope, like everything else since this campaign began, proved to be a disappointment."[110]

Perhaps the most meaningful accomplishment amid the Federal futility this long, hot day came, ironically, in the form of additional Confederate troops. Remembering that one of Grant's objectives was to strip forces from the Petersburg front, the detachment of Brig. Gen. Nathaniel H. Harris's Mississippi brigade along with a contingent from Maj. Gen. George Pickett's Division represented a material achievement. The Mississippians were the third of Mahone's five brigades to be transferred north across the James. About 4:00 P.M. on the sixteenth, Harris's men left their Petersburg trenches and marched into the Cockade City and across the Appomattox River, where they boarded trains for the capital. They reached Richmond at midnight and before dawn embarked on steamboats bound for Chaffin's Bluff. Once Harris's men were ashore, Lee sent them to Field's front near Fussell's Mill, where the Mississippi general assumed control of a demi-division consisting of his, Sanders's, and Girardey's brigades. Three regiments from Pickett's command—the First, Eleventh, and Nineteenth Virginia, all under Lt. Col. Francis Langley of the First—arrived at Chaffin's Bluff on the night of the sixteenth. The Virginians and Mississippians added nearly 1,200 additional infantry to Confederate manpower north of the James.[111]

That night Grant reprised his waterborne misdirection, intending to induce a Confederate attack. He sent a noisy fleet of steamers to the landings near Deep Bottom, hoping to persuade the Rebels that Hancock's men were retreating and thus vulnerable. Field did not take the bait. In fact, August 17 witnessed little serious combat. Hancock reported that the Confederates had strengthened their works overnight, so Grant sent Barnard and Comstock to ascertain if an assault could be launched from the ground Butler had taken around Signal Hill and Aiken's Landing. These two officers reported that "no benefit can arise from an advance from the works carried by General Butler last evening," so Grant told Butler to abandon the area and return to Dutch Gap. That decision became easier when three Confederate ironclads steamed down the James and bombarded Butler's position.[112]

Brisk skirmishing along the lines did keep soldiers on both sides busy on the seventeenth. Col. Daniel Chaplin of the First Maine Heavy Artillery visited the front, only to fall with a sharpshooter's bullet in his lung. Chaplin's regiment had suffered the largest loss of any unit in the entire war during an attack at Petersburg two months earlier. His brigade commander, General de Trobriand, thought that surviving that holocaust made the colonel a doomed man, the victim of "a melancholy discouragement." "Colonel Chaplin was very much beloved and highly respected by all the officers and men," wrote the regimental historian. "They regarded him as a sort of father of the Regiment." Chaplin died four days later. Hancock lost another ranking officer on the seventeenth. Francis Barlow had battled chronic diarrhea for weeks while suffering the lingering effects of wounds received earlier in the war. During the Deep Bottom operations, Colonel Walker believed Barlow "had been more like a dead man than a living man." The death of his wife from typhus in late July debilitated Barlow mentally as well. Special Orders No. 212 sent the young general to the corps hospital at City Point. Miles stepped up to take charge of the First Division.[113]

That Wednesday proved to be another hot day, with high humidity and the promise of rain—miserable conditions for any wounded still on the field and conducive to the rapid deterioration of corpses. Birney beseeched Hancock to request a ceasefire to recover the wounded and bury the dead. The corps commander responded by dispatching Major Mitchell with a flag of truce at 12:30 P.M. Despite this display of nonbelligerence, some Confederates fired at him, fortunately missing the Union emissary. The Confederates agreed to a ceasefire between 4:00 and 6:00 P.M. By then, the Southerners had removed all the Union wounded, so the details focused solely on the slain. The Federals were appalled to discover that many of the dead had been stripped naked, their uniforms appropriated by ill-clad Rebels. Clothed or not, the remains had already degraded into "a dreadful condition," and maggots swarmed in open wounds. To add to the horror, the skies unleashed a powerful summer thunderstorm, drenching the men engaged in their grim duty.[114]

As frequently happened during such occasions, officers and men wandered out between the lines to socialize with their enemies. Colonel Campbell engaged Colonel Little in conversation rather than in the mortal combat they had waged against each other the previous day. Little, joined by General Gary, also talked with Col. Samuel Armstrong, the commander of the Ninth USCT. "They were very gentlemanly," averred Armstrong, "and we had a delightful chat, or rather argument, of two hours." The topic turned to the South's "peculiar institution," the Confederate officers extolling its virtues and Armstrong allowing that his entire reason for fighting was to seek freedom for the enslaved. Gary respected Armstrong's motivation, considering that cause more just than "to fight merely to restore a Union which was only a compact and to which they were not morally bound."[115]

Meanwhile, Grant acknowledged that his offensive north of the James would result in neither the capture of Richmond nor a raid against the Virginia Central Railroad. He did, however, see the advantages achieved by drawing so many Confederates away from Petersburg and as potential reinforcements for Early in the Valley. He informed Sheridan of this happy circumstance and prepared to exploit the situation by targeting the Weldon Railroad. He advised both Hancock and Butler to watch their fronts carefully and to "take advantage of anything you can" should Lee return troops south of the river.[116]

Lee may not have been fooled into thinking the Federals were in retreat, but he retained his offensive instincts and acted on them on August 17. That night he scheduled an advance led by Hampton's cavalry on his left to turn the Federal right, supported by Field with an infantry assault that might roll the Yankees back, north to south, all the way to the James. This ambitious plan, executed on August 18, faltered immediately, as the cavalry assault, beginning at 5:00 P.M., had been delayed for six hours. M. C. Butler's horsemen descended upon the Federal cavalry at the Glendale intersection, while Rooney Lee's troopers advanced eastward on Charles City Road. Both elements at first bested their Northern opponents, prompting Hancock to once again send Miles to reinforce the beleaguered cavalry. Eventually, however, Gregg's men rallied and the Southerners fell back, having inflicted measurable losses on their opponents.[117]

As envisioned, once the cavalry attack was underway, Confederate infantry on the left of Field's line sprang into action. Brig. Gen. Samuel McGowan had returned in command of his South Carolinians, so General Conner took over for the wounded Barbour in charge of Lane's Brigade. They were joined by the newly arrived Mississippians of Harris's Brigade. All three units lurched ahead, targeting Foster's troops, ensconced in the reversed rifle pits overrun on the sixteenth. "Moving but a short distance through the woods, and driving in the skirmishers of the enemy [we] soon encountered him," reported General Harris, "in heavy force, in his entrenchments."[118]

Most Union accounts dismiss this Confederate assault in few words. Captain Towle's description was typical: "Quiet all day till 6 P.M. . . . At that hour the enemy attacked. After a sharp fight he retired. We were going to leave anyhow but we had no intention of letting them kick us out." General Foster admitted that the Rebels "drove in my pickets" but added that they "were easily repulsed by my main line." Sgt. Samuel H. Root of the 24th Massachusetts recorded that "a few volleys aided by a few shots from some well served pieces of artillery repulsed them." Other participants described a much more serious clash. Pvt. William Willoughby of the 10th Connecticut characterized the attack as creating "a consternation on the whole line." According to the 11th Maine's breathless Lieutenant Maxfield, the Union pickets fled into the makeshift Federal works as "every man [was] loading and firing for his life . . . the heavy columns of the enemy . . . yelling and firing wildly . . . until it seemed as if the pandemonium of shrieking, rushing demons would roll over our works by sheer weight of numbers, in spite of the fire mowing their front lines down." The 100th New York and

1st Maryland Cavalry temporarily broke "in the most cowardly and shameful manner and ran to the rear," complained a soldier from the 24th Massachusetts, which "stood firm . . . New England Yankees, every man." The 10th Connecticut was in reserve and by all accounts moved forward and contributed to the Confederate repulse. Col. Joshua B. Howell had returned to the command of the brigade temporarily led by Colonel Pond and was "in his element. Moving up and down the lines in the highest spirits, with a lively and encouraging word for all, he inspired the troops with his own high-toned and ardent courage to a degree that bid triumphant defiance to the whole rebel army," gushed Colonel Campbell. According to a soldier in the 11th Maine, the attack lasted twenty minutes.[119]

General Harris, to the contrary, reported that the Southerners held their ground until dark, when they retreated under orders to their main works. General Lee merely informed the secretary of war that "the left of our line . . . advanced against the enemy's right to discover his strength and position . . . and finding him strongly entrenched, withdrew." Whether a successful reconnaissance or a failed offensive, the Confederate attacks ended as darkness enveloped the rainy landscape. So, too, did Grant's ambitions north of the James. That morning the general-in-chief ordered Butler to move the bridge at Deep Bottom closer to the lower bridge "for Hancock's use by dark to-night," telling the Second Corps commander, in turn, that if he could maintain the defensive "with a division less than you have, send one division to-night, starting as soon as you can get it off, to report to General Meade." Hancock logically chose Mott's division, as it was closest to the bridges, and issued the appropriate orders at 8:00 P.M., after gaining Grant's permission to shorten his lines to compensate for the unit's departure. Two hours later Mott's troops crossed the lower bridge to Bermuda Hundred.[120]

The occupation of the Weldon Railroad by the Fifth Corps precipitated Mott's departure, as Grant now hoped to exploit Warren's success by devoting additional troops to the operation. The next several days witnessed a stream of blue and gray recrossing the James to focus on this new flashpoint southwest of Petersburg. When Lee learned of Mott's departure, he ordered Mahone's three brigades, along with Pickett's men, to follow suit. Both sides shifted cavalry to the south side on the nineteenth, Lee sending his son's two brigades and Gregg releasing Stedman's troopers. Hancock's artillery crossed the pontoon bridge that day as well. Lee wired Ewell that the brigade of local militia he had activated could return to their homes. Grant did encourage Hancock to exploit any weakness created by the diminution of Rebel troops in his front at Deep Bottom. The Pennsylvanian diligently examined the lines and thought that he might achieve some success, testing the ground "a little to the left of where General Barlow had failed on the 15th." He confessed, however, that he saw little advantage in achieving a breakthrough there, and Grant vetoed the attempt.[121]

Another sign of the operation's termination arrived via General Orders No. 25. Birney circulated this fulsome commendation among the Tenth Corps for having "proved itself worthy of its old Wagner and Sumter renown," referencing service in 1863 on the South Carolina coast. Significantly, Birney reserved special praise for his brother's African American troops "for their uniform good conduct and soldierly bearing, setting a good example to our veterans by the entire absence of straggling on the march," oddly omitting any reference to their bravery and sacrifice on the battlefield.[122]

On the morning of August 20, Grant authorized Hancock to evacuate the north side of the James. The two remaining Second Corps divisions and their associated batteries would depart first, followed by the Tenth Corps and Gregg. Foster's men would remain as guardians of the Deep Bottom bridgehead. The withdrawal began after dark, as rain continued to complicate marching conditions. "Away we skedadled to the rear with the mud to our knees," wrote Lt. Joseph H. Prime of the Seventh USCT. The Thirty-Sixth Wisconsin's Private Coon informed his family that the march took them through thick woods "and O, how dark, muddy, and slippery it was." Coon witnessed a wagon that had slipped off the narrow road, crashing into the James. "This equals any march I ever made for a continuation of disagreeables—woods, brush & two columns moving side by side on a rough uneven track scarce wide enough for one," complained Lt. Joshua H. Dearborn of the Seventh USCT. Despite these hardships, all the Union troops reached their destinations in a timely manner, Birney's men halting at Bermuda Hundred, while Hancock and the cavalry crossed the Appomattox and returned to the Petersburg lines. "It was refreshing to get back to the old spot after such experiences as we have had during the past week," reflected Capt. James M. Nichols of the Forty-Eighth New York.[123]

Lee learned of the empty Federal trenches on the morning of the twenty-first and directed most of his forces still north of the James to return to the Petersburg front. "We have been all morning assuring ourselves that the main body of the Yanks has gone back across the river," General Bratton informed his wife that morning. "Their lines are now pretty much as they were before any disturbance of that quiet that we were enjoying here." The Carolinians under Generals Conner and McGowan departed later that day as did M. C. Butler's cavalry, leaving only Gary's horsemen as a mounted presence on the north side. Anderson's, Bratton's, and Perry's brigades followed the next day. Lee decided to leave the Texas Brigade and DuBose's Georgians to reinforce Ewell's troops, retaining some 7,000 men to guard the capital. General Lee himself returned to Violet Bank on August 21.[124]

The Second Deep Bottom operations, spanning eight days commencing on August 13, claimed a heavy toll on both armies. Official Union casualty figures tallied 2,901 losses of all kinds. The Tenth Corps absorbed nearly 58 percent of those casualties, Hancock's corps one-third, and Gregg's two brigades the balance. Almost one-quarter of all the Union losses were men captured or missing. Terry's division accounted for the bulk of Birney's losses, while a brigade from each of Hancock's divisions—Miles's of Barlow's First, Macy's of Smyth's Second, and Craig's of Mott's Third—suffered far more than other Second Corps units.[125]

There is no equivalent published summary of Confederate casualties at Second Deep Bottom, but historian John Horn has carefully estimated that about 1,250 grayclads were either killed, wounded, or missing during that sanguinary week north of the James. Horn counted 415 casualties in Mahone's three brigades, 315 in Field's Division, and 215 in the Carolina brigades led by Conner. Butler and Rooney Lee left nearly 300 troopers on the field along Charles City Road.[126]

The sacrifice of these 4,000 soldiers changed little regarding the operational situation north of the James. The Confederates still held all of their defensive positions southeast of Richmond, and the Federals retained their toehold at the Deep Bottom bridgehead. Tactically, Second Deep Bottom proved far less ambiguous. Most Union attacks, particularly the fighting around Fussell's Mill on August 16, failed while entailing losses approaching twice those of the Confederates. Captain Corbin summarized events for his mother: "Our achievement was a very brilliant one, for with a handful of men . . . we drove back three of the enemy's largest corps." An article in a Richmond newspaper characterized the fighting as "one of Grant's most hopeful and determined efforts to capture Richmond," featuring "all the military genius of [Grant's] splendidly appointed army," including "the great Ulysses himself. . . . Beaten and humiliated he has again retired his force to their entrenchments around Petersburg." Ruffin Thomson, an officer in the Confederate Marines, reminded his father that Grant "promised to fight it out on this line if it took all summer. The summer is nearly gone over & I suppose he will consider his promise fulfilled & go to some other line & fight it out all winter." As was typical of Lee's generalship, the Confederate commander left the tactical conduct on the battlefield to Field, Hampton, and his son while funneling reinforcements to the front and providing personal inspiration to the rank and file.[127]

Captain Towle of Terry's staff agreed with Confederate observers that the fighting at Second Deep Bottom represented a terrible failure. "If anything was done or any advantage gained I never heard of it," he wrote. "In this way we lost thousands of men through the incapacity of our generals and yet Grant is called 'a great soldier.'" There can be little doubt that the Federal leadership committed a number of errors during the operation. The failure to ensure a smooth disembarkation at Tilghman's Landing, Barlow's piecemeal attacks on August 14, and the almost inexplicable failure to identify the existence of Fussell's millpond, which delayed the offensive on the sixteenth, are among the more egregious. Clearly, Grant, who played a more active role than he had in earlier battles at Petersburg, failed to achieve two of his goals in crossing the James: he neither captured nor severely threatened Richmond or disrupted the Virginia Central Railroad. Yet in one sense, Second Deep Bottom proved to be a resounding success for Union arms. The offensive prevented the detachment of additional Confederate troops to the Shenandoah Valley, thus providing Sheridan with the opportunity to defeat Early—something he would begin to do in a few weeks. Capt. Ansell White of the Nineteenth Maine discerned an even more immediate benefit. "I presume our move across the James was only intended to draw the rebs' attention," he wrote on August 22, "that way the 5th Corps took the R. Road."[128] Indeed, by then one of the most significant engagements of the entire Petersburg Campaign had concluded in Union victory, thanks in part to the diminished Rebel force guarding Petersburg.

three

A MOST SOUL-HARROWING DILEMMA

The Battle of Weldon Railroad, August 18–19

Petersburg's strategic importance rested almost exclusively on its several railroads that connected the city to all points of the compass. The oldest of those lines, the Petersburg Railroad, began operating in 1830 and by 1833 joined the Cockade City with Weldon, North Carolina, sixty-five miles to the south. Petersburg residents, and later soldiers from both armies, routinely referred to this route as the Weldon Railroad. From that North Carolina town, the Wilmington & Weldon Railroad ran southeast to its namesake city on the Cape Fear River, which by August 1864 was the only functioning Confederate port on the Atlantic seaboard. Because the Richmond & Petersburg Railroad covered the twenty-three miles to the Confederate capital, the iron link between Petersburg and Weldon provided the intermediate segment of communications and commerce between Richmond and the outside world.[1]

The Union high command well understood the importance of severing this connection, and doing so had been integral to General Grant's strategic thinking since his initial failure to capture the city. Success would depend in large measure on the strength and position of Confederate forces capable of contesting such an effort. He had tried and failed to break the line during his Second Offensive in the third week of June 1864. Weakening the defensive forces at the railroad by luring them north of the James River provided one of Grant's rationales for the Second Deep Bottom initiative.

The Fifth Corps, led by Maj. Gen. Gouverneur K. Warren, would bear primary responsibility for the next attempt to break or possibly occupy the Weldon

Railroad. Warren's four divisions held the far left of the Union lines south of Petersburg, a short distance east of the railroad. Early on the afternoon of August 13, as the Second and Tenth Corps made their way toward Deep Bottom, Meade issued orders to Warren to prepare "to move at short notice." The Fifth Corps commander was to gather sufficient supplies to sustain a lengthy offensive but to conceal such preparations from his troops. Identical instructions arrived at Ninth Corps headquarters, the units positioned on Warren's right, then led by Brig. Gen. Orlando Willcox in the temporary absence of Maj. Gen. John G. Parke, the new corps chief. Warren received these orders enthusiastically. "I was exceedingly pleased with my instructions," he informed his wife. "I have shown them to some of my division commanders and all alike are pleased."[2]

Meade clarified his intentions late that evening, explaining that any offensive toward the railroad would be dependent upon "the almost entire abandonment of the enemy's entrenchments in our front" as a result of Hancock's initiative north of the James. In such an event, Warren would move across the railroad, while the Ninth Corps would sidle west to occupy Warren's sector of the lines. The Eighteenth Corps would replace the Ninth. On the evening of August 14, Meade began to shift the Fifth Corps outside of the entrenchments and in position to move rapidly west if the Confederates weakened their forces around Petersburg. By the next morning, the Ninth Corps had tacked west to man Warren's works, enduring a torrential rainstorm that afternoon that flooded the trenches, even drowning several soldiers.[3]

The four Confederate divisions defending Petersburg suffered similar discomforts from the storm. Bushrod Johnson's and Maj. Gen. Robert F. Hoke's Divisions of Beauregard's command filled the works from the Appomattox River south and west to Jerusalem Plank Road. Maj. Gen. Henry Heth's Division of A. P. Hill's corps extended the line westward, connecting with Mahone's Division on the far Confederate right. Cavalry patrolled the ground south and west of the infantry. Clearly, the Rebels faced heavy odds around Petersburg, leading General Lee to doubt that he could hold the Weldon Railroad indefinitely. As early as June 21, the Confederate commander predicted that "it will be almost impossible to preserve the connection between [Petersburg] and Weldon." A cavalry raid days later temporarily broke the line, underscoring Lee's concern. At best the general hoped to maintain its functionality until the fall harvest farther south could be transported to his army, but Lee was skeptical even of this. He urged the government to repair and strengthen the Richmond & Danville Railroad, which bypassed Petersburg en route from central North Carolina to the capital. Understanding the railroad's importance and vulnerability, it came as no surprise to Lee when President Davis forwarded speculative intelligence on August 11 that "a movement against the Weldon Railroad by infantry is proposed."[4]

Confederate pessimism notwithstanding, Grant and Meade remained cautious, wishing to confirm the reduction of Lee's Petersburg defenders before unleashing Warren. That depletion began on the fourteenth, when Sanders's and Girardey's brigades, along with Rooney Lee's cavalry division, started for the north side of the James. Meade confirmed their presence on Hancock's front by noon on the sixteenth and so reported to Grant. This temporarily satisfied the general-in-chief that the time had arrived to launch Warren toward the railroad. Meade accurately reported the Confederate units remaining at Petersburg that night and, under Grant's direction, would order the Fifth Corps to advance "at early daylight or before," although he revealed the dichotomy between his conservative instincts and his chief's typical aggressiveness. "I do not think myself he [Warren] will have much chance of success unless we get more definite information of the enemy having sent away more troops than we have now," Meade advised. Still, the army commander obediently sent orders to Warren at 9:20 that evening to move at 3:00 the next morning and break the Weldon Railroad near its crossing of Vaughan Road. An hour later, however, Grant took heed of Meade's counsel and ordered him to suspend Warren's advance "until we are assured of further movements of the enemy." This exchange succinctly captured the functional and mutually respectful command relationship between Grant and Meade despite fundamentally differing operational philosophies.[5]

Such assurance arrived the next day. Based on the identity of prisoners taken north of the James, Grant was now convinced that an operation targeting the Weldon Railroad could succeed. But the lieutenant general still believed that sufficient Confederate strength remained to limit Warren's mission to a reconnaissance-in-force designed to do no more than destroy a few miles of track. Grant cautioned Meade to prevent Warren from engaging in a serious battle and expressed his primary hope that this initiative, combined with the actions on the north side, would compel Lee "to withdraw a portion of his troops from the Valley, so that Sheridan can strike a blow against the balance." Sheridan's success thus animated both facets of Grant's Fourth Petersburg Offensive.[6]

Meade acknowledged these orders on the afternoon of the seventeenth and wrote Grant that he would instruct Warren, supported by General Kautz's small brigade of cavalry, to commence his operation on August 18 at 4:00 A.M. "I anticipate no difficulty in General Warren making a lodgment on the railroad," Meade affirmed, "but I think the enemy will send out all his available reserves to endeavor to check the work of destruction." Warren's orders would direct him to work his way south, wrecking the railroad "till recalled, or forced away by the

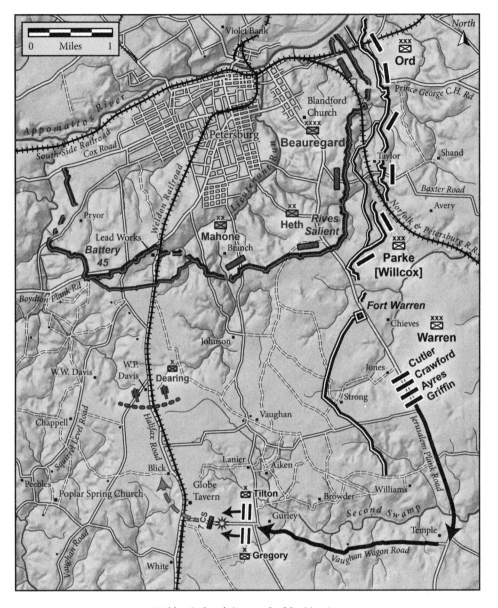

Weldon Railroad, August 18, 1864, Morning

enemy's operations." Meade promptly conveyed these instructions to the Fifth Corps commander, echoing Grant's admonition that the Fifth Corps would be on its own, as the Ninth and Eighteenth Corps would be confined to guarding the permanent lines east and south of Petersburg. Meade emphasized that Warren was to avoid fighting under any disadvantage and refrain from attacking fortifications, underscoring the highly conservative nature of this mission as no more than a raid. He forwarded 440 sets of tools for destroying the tracks.[7]

At 10:00 that night, Grant altered the plans that had evolved over the previous seventy-two hours. Believing falsely that Mahone had shifted his entire division across the James, the general-in-chief now told Meade that "Warren may find an opportunity to do more than I had expected." Meade immediately informed Warren of this change of heart. Now Warren was to strike the tracks as close to the Confederate lines as possible and, if he detected a weakness, attack the Rebel works. This sudden and unexpected escalation delighted Warren. The Fifth Corps commander craved an opportunity to operate independently and demonstrate his capabilities without the usual confining instructions from superiors. He quickly issued a circular to his division commanders, enjoining them to commence their march toward the railroad at 4:00 A.M. Charles Griffin's division would take the lead, followed by Romeyn Ayres's, Samuel Crawford's, and Brig. Gen. Lysander Cutler's divisions. The stage was now set for one of the most consequential engagements of the Petersburg Campaign.[8]

The Fifth Corps camps stirred with activity in the predawn darkness of August 18. "We were awoke from our sound slumbers by an unwonted reveille," explained a soldier in the Thirty-Second Massachusetts, "being nothing less than the roar of our artillery, which seemed to be at work all along our lines, throwing their destructive missiles over among the sleeping chivalry of the South." As the rudely roused men prepared for the march ahead, Warren began his day by sending a buoyant message to Meade's headquarters, echoing the sentiments he had expressed to his spouse. "I was exceedingly pleased with my instructions," he beamed. "I have shown them to some of my division commanders and all alike are pleased." Warren pledged to do the best he could and to accept full responsibility for the impending operation. Griffin's leading brigade, his First, under Col. William S. Tilton, was on the move by 5:00 A.M. under "an oppressive warm rain" that soon turned the unsurfaced roads to mire. Their route led them south from the Chieves house on Jerusalem Plank Road near Fort Warren. "Oh, the glorious uncertainty of a soldier's life," recorded Tilton in his diary. "No one knows our objective point, or anything else, more than that we are on an expedition, and that a fighting one." A soldier in the Twentieth Maine also apprehended that heavy combat lay ahead, but he confessed that

The Battle of Weldon Railroad, August 18–19

"we enjoyed the change from life behind the breastworks . . . and with cheerful hearts we pressed on."[9]

The column proceeded for about two and a half miles, reaching the Temple house and a byway styled Vaughan Wagon Road. Here, Griffin's troops turned west and marched two miles through thick woods, around 7:00 A.M. reaching a clearing surrounding the large two-story Gurley house about a mile east of the railroad. The mercury had already climbed beyond human comfort, and some soldiers, as had their comrades north of the James, fell out of line, suffering from exhaustion or sunstroke.[10]

By the time Griffin reached the Gurley clearing, he had deployed his leading brigades into line of battle astride Vaughan Wagon Road. Tilton formed in two lines north of the road, while Col. Edgar M. Gregory's brigade assumed a similar disposition on Tilton's left. The 150th Pennsylvania and 32nd Massachusetts advanced as skirmishers. They soon encountered a scattered fire from the pickets of the 7th Confederate Cavalry, a part of Brig. Gen. James Dearing's small brigade, the only Rebel cavalry remaining around Petersburg. Aided by troopers from the 3rd New York Cavalry, Griffin's men routed the gray horsemen, capturing fifteen or twenty of the less fleet and wounding two others. According to corps artillery chief Charles Wainwright, "this amounted to nothing & did not detain us save for the time necessary for [Griffin's] first brigade to get into line of battle."[11]

Griffin's men reached the railroad about 9:00 A.M. near a dilapidated hostelry named Globe Tavern, near the intersection of Vaughan Wagon Road and an old highway, Halifax Road, that ran west of and parallel to the tracks. Theodore Lyman described this building as "not in condition to furnish lodging either for man or for beast. All the windows were out, the lower floors torn up, and the plastering, where not peeled off was embellished with charcoal frescoes by artists in the southern cavalry." Dearing learned of the Federals' presence from the commander of his scattered vedettes. He promptly reported to General Beauregard, the ranking officer at Petersburg while Lee superintended affairs north of the James, that the "enemy has driven in my pickets and reserve in front of Yellow House," another name for Globe Tavern. Beauregard passed this news to Lee, inquiring, "Can any cavalry re-enforcements be sent him? I have none here." Beauregard also informed A. P. Hill of Dearing's setback and ordered the Third Corps commander to "send without delay a brigade from Maj. Gen. Mahone's Division, or any other which can be best spared to the support of Gen. Dearing."[12]

It would take Beauregard time to muster resistance to the Federal offensive, and Griffin would use the interlude to begin dismantling the railroad. Tilton positioned some of his regiments facing west and north, while the remainder

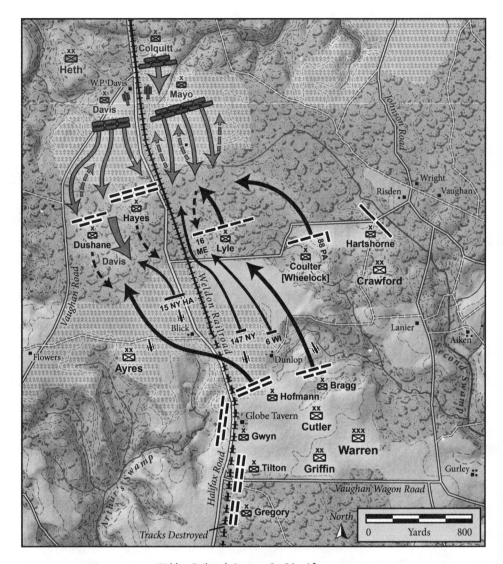

Weldon Railroad, August 18, 1864, Afternoon

of his brigade began their work of destruction. Gregory's men soon arrived, and some of them started preparing fortifications. "The use of rifle pits was full appreciated by the men and every one at once began gathering up something to make a pile to protect us from the bullets of Sir Johnny," explained a member of the 155th Pennsylvania.[13]

By this time, Warren's Second Division, commanded by thirty-eight-year-old Romeyn Beck Ayres, had arrived. A New York native, Ayres graduated from the U.S. Military Academy in 1847 and spent his subsequent days in the army. He passed the first year of the war in the artillery before being assigned to the Fifth Corps as a brigade commander, eventually rising to lead the Second Division. Although rejected by William Sherman as a possible addition to his command—Sherman called Ayres "a growler"—most of the army considered Ayres competent, one staff member commenting on his doting indulgence as a father.[14]

The Second Division had followed Griffin's men down Jerusalem Plank Road, some of Ayres's troops succumbing to sunstroke before reaching the railroad. The First Brigade, under Brig. Gen. Joseph Hayes, led the way. This unit included the army's contingent of U.S. Regulars, leavened by three veteran New York regiments. "We marched toward the left, halted on the road, and received forty rounds of extra cartridges," reported one of the Regulars. "We knew by past experience what that meant, and as our march was toward the Weldon Railroad we expected to have lively times."[15]

Ayres's troops reached the railroad by 10:00 A.M., relieving Griffin's men of their defensive deployment and allowing the work of destruction to progress in earnest. Tilton's brigade aligned along the tracks, "and at the word of command, every man took hold of the rails and lifted the track, ties and all, bodily from the road-bed," according to a soldier in the 121st Pennsylvania. "While the troops on the right rolled the huge ladder in one direction, those on the left rolled it in the opposite direction, forming an immense screw, until finally it was forced to pieces, when the ties were gathered together in piles short distances apart, and the rails laid crosswise on top, and fire applied, and the destruction was complete." The workers often removed the rails, red hot in the middle, and twisted them around a telegraph pole or convenient tree. This technique, dubbed "Sherman's neckties" in the West, rendered the rails unusable.[16]

Warren had pledged to send frequent messages to army headquarters, and he was as good as his word. "I have two divisions up and nearly formed," he informed Meade at 10:00 A.M. "Marching to-day is very slow, and there are a great many cases of sunstroke. . . . As soon as I am prepared, will move up the railroad." Ayres's division would fulfill this promise. About 11:00 A.M. Hayes's brigade advanced opposite a brick dwelling called the Blick house, located west of both the railroad and Halifax Road and hard by a farm lane leading to Vaughan Road, a substantial country byway. This route ran southwest to northeast, intersecting the railroad a long mile north of the Blick house. Hayes deployed in two lines of battle across the railroad, with the 12th U.S. Infantry and a portion of the 140th New York advanced as skirmishers. The Second Brigade, composed entirely of Maryland troops and led by Col. Nathan T. Dushane, supported Hayes on his left, the Marylanders' left flank in the air. The outsized 15th New York Heavy Artillery, representing the entirety of Ayres's Third Brigade, remained in reserve.[17]

As Ayres began to move forward into thick woods, Warren informed Meade that both Crawford's and Cutler's divisions had reached the railroad and that the Confederates had positioned some cavalry and a battery about three-quarters of a mile north of the Blick house. He reiterated the debilitating impact of the heat on his troops. "The men give out fearfully in the sun and compel us to move slowly to keep them in the ranks."[18]

Dearing had, in fact, positioned a picket line at the edge of a ripening cornfield south of the W. P. Davis house, an attractive dwelling located in a handsome grove near the intersection of Halifax and Vaughan Roads. Two cannons unlimbered on a slight rise nearby and began shelling Ayres, even before Hayes and Dushane had commenced their advance, triggering a response from a Massachusetts battery positioned near the Blick house. This resistance worried General Hayes, who now feared that his men were about to bite off more than they could chew.[19]

After moving through the tangled stretch of forest about 1:00 P.M., Hayes emerged into the Davis cornfield and began to engage Dearing's skirmishers as an intermittent drizzle became a downpour. Aided by the Bay State gunners, who had advanced their cannons in tandem with the infantry, Hayes drove the cavalrymen beyond the Davis house and compelled the annoying two-gun battery to displace as well.[20]

By this time, Crawford and his Third Division had advanced on Ayres's right, east of the railroad. Crawford's three brigades, numbering some 3,000 men, had reached the railroad about noon. "It was awful hot and we were glad to get a rest," admitted Sgt. George E. Fowle of the 39th Massachusetts. Within an hour, however, Warren ordered Crawford to support Ayres. "The ground in my immediate front was low, and in front ended in a dense and almost impenetrable thicket which ran along the whole line from right to left," reported Crawford. "The thicket was cut up with swampy grounds, and was almost impassable." He positioned Col. Peter Lyle's First Brigade on his left, with the 16th Maine adjacent to the east side of the tracks; Col. Richard Coulter's Second Brigade on Lyle's right; and Col. William R. Hartshorne's Third Brigade in support on

The Battle of Weldon Railroad, August 18–19

Coulter's right. A gap of about 150 yards separated Lyle's left from Hayes's right. The 107th Pennsylvania advanced as skirmishers. "Clouds had gathered and the rain poured down in torrents so that we all who half an hour before were reeking with perspiration were in a few moments drenched with rain," recorded Pvt. Julius Frederick Ramsdell of the 39th Massachusetts. "All who had knapsacks on could not get along owing to the thickness of the trees and underbrush and were obliged to throw them away."[21]

Ayres and Crawford were not the only ones on the move that early afternoon. The alarmed Beauregard now issued Hill orders to provide two brigades to confront this developing threat. Hill turned to division commander Heth, who selected the Mississippi–North Carolina brigade of Brig. Gen. Joseph R. Davis and a consolidated brigade of Virginians, Tennesseans, Marylanders, and Alabamans led by Col. Robert M. Mayo. To accompany the infantry, Heth sent the four Napoleon smoothbores of Capt. Thomas A. Brander's Letcher Artillery, a part of Lt. Col. William J. Pegram's Battalion. In short order Beauregard also instructed Brig. Gen. Alfred H. Colquitt's Georgia brigade of Hoke's Division to fall in behind Davis and Mayo. About one-third of Davis's men continued to work on the fortifications and failed to join their comrades. Although the exact strength of Beauregard's response went unrecorded, it numbered only a fraction of the two Union divisions it was about to confront.[22]

Heth led Davis and Mayo west and then south two or three miles to the woods north of the Davis house. He quietly deployed Davis's regiments west of the tracks and Mayo's to the east, with their respective left and right flanks resting on the railroad, a line of skirmishers in advance. Brander's guns unlimbered near the center of the infantry line. Colquitt's Georgians followed in support. About 2:00 P.M. Heth ordered the attack.[23]

The Confederates first encountered the thin array of Union skirmishers, who by then had advanced just beyond the Davis house. As the grayclad infantry burst into the clearing, the shocked Federals fled without firing a shot, dashing past the dwelling and through the cornfield into the sheltering woods beyond. Davis's troops pursued "at double-quick" through rain-soaked cornstalks and into the woods, where Hayes and Dushane awaited them. The Mississippians on Davis's right used Vaughan Road to gain the exposed left of Dushane's Maryland Brigade. The Marylanders responded nobly, firing several volleys and forcing the Confederates to seek shelter. At the same time, the Confederates hit a gap separating Hayes's left from Dushane's right while also plunging through the unguarded ground east of the tracks separating Hayes from Crawford. Thus threatened on both of his flanks, Hayes gave way. "At this critical moment it was ascertained that the troops on our right were falling back," reported Col.

Samuel A. Graham of Dushane's Purnell Legion, "of which . . . the enemy at once took advantage, rallying his men and pushing vigorously on our unprotected flanks." Dushane ordered his brigade to withdraw, a retreat that "was executed in considerable confusion, owing to the density of the woods and proximity of the enemy," explained Graham.[24]

The situation proved equally grim for Crawford. Lyle's brigade had forged ahead of the rest of the Third Division, and the general detailed a staff officer to locate the right flank of Ayres's division, as Crawford reported, "to insure a firm connection with it on my left. This was thoroughly affected by the Sixteenth Maine Regiment." That regiment's adjutant, however, challenged Crawford's assertion. "We were supposed to connect with the right of Ayres' division; but we didn't, whatever the official records may say to the contrary," he protested. The 239 officers and men of the Sixteenth Maine were the first of Lyle's regiments to take position when the Confederates struck.[25]

While Davis assailed Hayes and Dushane, Mayo's troops advanced astride and to the east of the railroad. A soldier in Mayo's 2nd Maryland Battalion remembered that "during the advance . . . the Battalion passed through a watermelon patch, and almost every one availed himself of the opportunity to 'freeze on' to a melon," apparently with little effect on the momentum of their attack. "The order being given to fire, we began and into the woods and at them we went. At our first fire the poor devils broke and ran in every direction." Col. Charles W. Tilden, commanding the 16th Maine, blamed this reversal on the collapse of Hayes's brigade on his left. "We, however, held the enemy for some minutes, when I discovered that he was close on my flank and rear, causing my men to retire to save capture." The 107th Pennsylvania, whose skirmish line had covered only a fraction of Lyle's arriving brigade, was swept up in the retreat along with the 39th Massachusetts and 19th Pennsylvania, which had just arrived on Tilden's right, although a number of Federals were captured. "Those of my command who succeeded in making their escape were rallied and formed on the left of the One hundred and fourth New York Volunteers," reported Tilden.[26]

By this time, the Second Brigade had pushed through the woods, encountering Lyle's men as they fell back under Mayo's pressure. Richard Coulter, a thirty-six-year-old lawyer, banker, and businessman from western Pennsylvania, rose to command the Eleventh Pennsylvania and at various times had acted as a brigade and division commander before receiving permanent charge of his brigade at the Wilderness. On May 18 near Spotsylvania Court House, a Rebel bullet struck him in his left breast, deflected off a rib, and coursed around his body before exiting through his back. Coulter recuperated for nearly three months before returning to the field on August 15, but now the oppressive heat had sapped his still-diminished strength. He relinquished brigade command to his senior regimental commander, Col. Charles Wheelock of the Ninety-Seventh New York. Wheelock quickly advanced a skirmish line and deployed his four regiments on the right of Lyle's rallying brigade, the Eighty-Eighth Pennsylvania refusing his right flank. Mayo's attack had run its course.[27]

West of the railroad, Hayes and Dushane rallied on the division's Third Brigade, the Fifteenth New York Heavy Artillery under Lt. Col. Michael Wiedrich. The heavies, now in their third month serving as infantry, deployed at Ayres's direction near the southern edge of the woods north of Globe Tavern, while Hayes aligned on their right and the Marylanders on their left. Ayres now called on Cutler for assistance, and the Fourth Division commander released his Second Brigade, led by Col. J. William Hofmann, to assist their beleaguered comrades.[28]

Hofmann's regiments had straggled into the Globe Tavern clearing over a period of three hours, beginning at noon. "The march was a very fatiguing one on account of the heat of the day," reported the colonel, who admitted that only half of his roughly 1,200 men arrived in an organized body. But by 3:30 P.M., the brigade was intact, and Hofmann advanced it to the northern edge of the open ground east of the railroad, sending the 147th New York ahead as skirmishers. Thirty minutes later the call to reinforce Ayres arrived, and Hofmann led the balance of his brigade across the tracks. The 4th Delaware, under Lt. Col. Charles E. LaMotte, and the 56th Pennsylvania immediately relieved the battered Maryland Brigade.[29]

"Genl Ayres . . . was glad to see me," wrote LaMotte. "I was laughing and in fine spirits. . . . My two regts drove the rebs from Genl Ayres' front & piled up dead rebs in considerable number by our well-directed fire." Within fifteen or twenty minutes, Davis's tired Mississippians and North Carolinians fell back. "The volley the enemy poured into our ranks appeared to be a veritable sheet of flame," testified Adj. Charles M. Cooke of the Fifty-Fifth North Carolina. "The enemy succeeded in turning our right and putting the lead into our right side as well as the front," confirmed Pvt. William Henry Bachman of the Forty-Second Mississippi. "This move we had not agreed to and consequently [we] became a little bit restless under this infilade firing but were soon told to get out which order we were obeying promptly and with some degree of alacrity when a bullet . . . pierced my right thigh felling me to the ground." By this time, Colonel Wainwright had unlimbered twenty-four guns that belched forth a punishing fire, silencing the Letcher Artillery, then turning their attention to the Confederate infantry.[30]

Warren continued to apprise army headquarters of events. "The falling back of General Ayres' division has deranged my plans considerably," he confessed in a 4:00 P.M. message, "and I am getting things in order again. . . . I have ordered

Ayres and Crawford to advance again, the former supported by General Cutler's division." Heth now understood that his two brigades "had done all that could be expected of them," and he remained content to hold the position to which he had retreated following Hofmann's counterattack. Warren's hope that Ayres and Hofmann would press their advantage would not be realized. The continued presence of the stubborn Confederates prompted Ayres to consider the fighting on his front at an end. He established a skirmish line and began to entrench in the thick woods south of the Davis cornfield. "In this position the command remained during the afternoon and night of the 18th," explained the commander of the Fifth New York. Hayes positioned his troops just east of the tracks, with the Fifteenth New York Heavy Artillery to their left west of the railroad, supported on their left by Hofmann and the reinvigorated Maryland Brigade.[31]

East of the railroad, events remained a bit livelier. While Hofmann's brigade, minus the 147th New York, dashed west of the tracks, Warren told Cutler to send his First Brigade to cover the gap between Ayres and Crawford created by Mayo's attack. Brig. Gen. Edward S. Bragg led this unit, comprising primarily the remnants of the once-proud Iron Brigade. These Midwesterners from Indiana, Michigan, and Wisconsin had compiled a distinguished combat record beginning in August 1862, a history that had severely diminished their ranks. Bragg directed the 6th Wisconsin to advance as skirmishers. These Badgers soon caught up with the 147th New York, and together they pressed forward through the thick woods under the direction of Lt. Col. George Harney of the 147th. Warren also called on Col. James Gwyn's brigade of Griffin's division for support, although as it turned out, they would not be engaged.[32]

Harney's two regiments, preceded by fifty volunteers serving as skirmishers and supported by the bulk of Crawford's division, drove Mayo's tired soldiers from two lines of hastily prepared works, an action that Harney described as "a determined stand." "We were in close proximity to the rebels, who blazed away at us to the best of their ability," confirmed Sgt. Grove H. Dutton of the 147th New York. Harney's ad hoc aggregation swept forward about half a mile until it encountered a strong line of works at the northern end of Davis's cornfield, where Mayo had been joined by Colquitt's Brigade. This position, admitted Bragg, "was too strong to be carried by a skirmish line." By then, Wheelock had arrived with Coulter's brigade just as the Confederates unleashed a volley at a range of one hundred yards. "I gave the order to lie down, which was very fortunate, for at that moment we received the fire from the enemy's whole line, doing but little harm, the fire mostly passing over us," reported Wheelock. Lyle's brigade then appeared, and the Federals entrenched. One of the more dramatic casualties of the fight entered the fray on four legs. As General Warren rode forward with

Bragg's advance, a Rebel sharpshooter placed a bullet squarely between the eyes of Warren's bay mount. Horse and rider went down. "I was not hurt, and the ball glanced down to the throat instead of the brain, and the horse may get well," Warren wrote his wife. "We are all well. Don't be alarmed about us."[33]

As the sun began its descent, the combat along the Weldon Railroad diminished into a desultory exchange of picket fire. Meade instructed Warren that if he felt unable to accomplish more that day, he should "intrench as close to the enemy's works as you can get, with your left well westward of the Weldon Railroad, and remain there." Warren responded at 7:00 P.M. that he had approached the Confederate line as closely as possible and that he intended to "make myself as strong here as I can, hold on till I am forced to leave and destroy the railroad as much as possible."[34]

The fighting on August 18 claimed its fair share of casualties. Warren reported a loss of 936 men—66 killed, 478 wounded, and 392 captured or missing—the bulk coming from Ayres's division. The 5th New York, for example, entered the battle with 210 officers and men and lost 73 of them, nearly 35 percent. Col. Frederick Winthrop, its commanding officer, did not escape unscathed. "I am not quite dead yet, although I have had a small piece of my little finger taken off & was slightly wounded in my left leg in two places," he wrote to a kinsman. "I have four holes in my coat . . . & two holes in my pantaloons. My sword was shot & badly bent spraining my wrist. . . . Two horses were shot under me." Winthrop's sister regiment, the 140th New York, saw 51 of its soldiers marched off as prisoners. Dushane's brigade lost 173 men.[35]

The Confederates suffered approximately 350 casualties during the afternoon's engagement. Davis's Brigade bore the bulk of those losses. "We fought a great[ly] superior force," General Davis explained to his uncle, the Confederate president. "I lost at least 30 per cent of my Brigade." Adjutant Cooke recalled that at least half of the 130 men of his regiment who went into the battle were either killed or wounded.[36]

Warren confirmed that he had established his line "as close to the enemy as I can and made arrangements for intrenching it." He stretched his picket line to the east toward a connection with the Ninth Corps. "I think I can hold on here for a hard fight if I can keep up the communication with the Ninth Corps," he added. The new Union line rested one and three-quarter miles south of the permanent Confederate defenses. Crawford's division occupied Warren's right, with Ayres on his left and Cutler on the right and rear in support of Ayres. Griffin took position below the left flank of the corps.[37]

The men began fortifying their advanced positions in the growing darkness and under a renewed rain. "We were ordered to throw breastworks up where

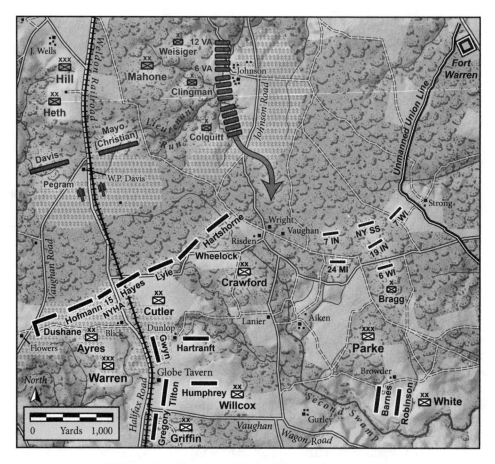

Weldon Railroad, August 19, 1864: Confederates Prepare to Attack

we were," wrote Private Ramsdell. "This we did with no other tools but our bayonets and tin plates. By working all night however we succeeded in throwing up quite a good breastwork." Other soldiers dug for a different purpose. "The night was spent burying our dead," remembered Lt. John F. Huntingdon of the 140th New York.[38]

Warren's report that his right connected with General Parke's left proved more apparent than real. Parke informed Meade at 6:30 that evening that a mile or a mile and a half separated his left flank from the developing right of the Fifth Corps. Such a gap invited the sort of slicing attack that had disordered the Federals' last attempt to control the Weldon Railroad and could not be allowed to remain. The Ninth Corps would have to slide west to close on Warren. In order to do so, Grant authorized Mott's division to recross the James that night and occupy a portion of Parke's position in the Union works, allowing the Ninth

The Battle of Weldon Railroad, August 18–19

Corps to close on Warren. General Ord would contribute 1,500 men of his Eighteenth Corps in advance of Mott's arrival, allowing Parke to send Warren a like number of troops from Willcox's division during the night. The rest of the Ninth Corps would join the Fifth Corps once Mott appeared.[39]

The Confederates were also on the move that night. Beauregard informed Lee at 7:00 P.M. of the day's events and current disposition: "Heth desires re-enforcements to complete his success. He has already all I can spare, three brigades [of] infantry, which must return to vicinity of [our] lines during [the] night," which they would do. Lee responded by authorizing Rooney Lee's cavalry division and the three brigades of Mahone's Division that had journeyed north of the James to return to the Petersburg lines. After an all-night march, the infantry arrived at 4:00 A.M. on the nineteenth, with the cavalry arriving afterward. Although General Lee had expressed doubt about his ability to maintain control of the Weldon Railroad, he was not going to relinquish it without a fight.[40]

Lieutenant General Grant was not insensible to such a probability. "Tell Warren if the enemy comes out and attacks him in the morning not to hesitate about taking out every man he has to repel it," he instructed Meade shortly before midnight. "We certainly ought to be satisfied, when we can get the enemy to attack us." Crawford's vulnerable right flank offered the most likely location for such a venture.[41]

At 8:30 P.M. Ayres informed Warren, "I can dispense entirely with Bragg's brigade," making the Iron Brigade the unit destined to protect the eastern end of Crawford's line. Edward Stuyvesant Bragg, a native New Yorker and antebellum lawyer, had moved to Fond du Lac, Wisconsin, where he became active in Democrat politics. At the outbreak of hostilities, he raised a company that became part of the Sixth Wisconsin, which he commanded as its colonel beginning in the spring of 1863. He earned his star in June 1864. "In politics and law, Edward S. Bragg stood among the first men in his state," thought Capt. Rufus Dawes of the Sixth in the spring of 1861, "but in military matters" he had much to learn. Bragg had learned well—Dawes considered him the brightest man in the regiment—and he was a highly respected officer.[42]

Bragg reported to Crawford sometime between 2:00 and 4:00 A.M. This rather large discrepancy in timing is but one of several controversies that would swirl around the brigadier's fateful experience on August 19. The once-powerful Iron Brigade had been reduced to sixty officers and about 700 enlisted men, including the attached First Battalion of New York Sharpshooters. Crawford personally ordered Bragg "to proceed to my right flank and take position there until further orders," sending a staff officer, Capt. Walter T. Chester, to direct him to the proper position. Bragg deployed about daylight in a steady rain, characterized by Colonel Wainwright as a "fine northeaster," and assigned the First Battalion, New York Sharpshooters and a portion of the Seventh Indiana to relieve the Eighty-Eighth Pennsylvania of Coulter's brigade on the picket line. He positioned the rest of his brigade about 100 yards to the rear.[43]

Warren, however, had an additional task in mind for Bragg's small command. He wished the troops to "establish a connection on the shortest line, with skirmishers, between my right and the pickets near Jerusalem Plank Road." Doing so would be awfully difficult, as the distance between these points measured nearly two and a half miles, most of it through thick woods. Capt. Emmor B. Cope, an aide on Warren's staff, reported to Crawford's headquarters before dawn, carrying these instructions for Bragg. Maj. Washington A. Roebling, another of Warren's aides, also went out to find Bragg and help him deploy to Warren's specifications. By this time, Captain Chester had returned, so Crawford told him and Lt. James B. Mead, an assistant commissary of musters on his staff, to lead Cope to Bragg's position. With Chester's help, Cope found Bragg readily enough and instructed him to "commence at the right of General Crawford's line and push out a line of skirmishers by the flank a few degrees north of east, until they met the enemy; then to fall to the rear a short distance and push on by the flank as close to the enemy as could be and join the pickets of the Ninth Corps." He grossly underestimated the distance involved as one-half to three-quarters of a mile.[44]

Bragg, who noted that he received these instructions at 7:00 A.M., considered his orders "a hazardous undertaking . . . not knowing where they were going and what was in their front," according to Cope. The brigadier claimed that Cope told him the Ninth Corps pickets were near the Aiken house, to the southeast about one and a half miles in rear of his refused right flank. Roebling would state that "the left of the 9th Corps picket-line was then near the Williams house, half way between it and Aikens' house." Bragg declined to probe toward the Confederates and instead promptly marched off through "a dense tangled thicket," finding the western end of the skirmish line of the Ninth Corps as Cope had described it. Crawford personally confirmed that by 8:00 A.M., Bragg had achieved the desired connection. Bragg then rode northeast more than a mile until he reached the works previously constructed by the Second Corps near the Strong house. He determined that this was where he could "make the shortest and most feasible line if I was not checked by the enemy" and ordered his brigade to move up to that point. "This movement was attended with great difficulty," admitted Bragg. "The nature of the wood, the pelting storm, and the extended line encumbered and seriously embarrassed the whole operation." In fact, Roebling finally found him wandering lost in the woods about 1:30 P.M. "I found he had been working at random all the morning without a compass, had lost his horse and orderly and was completely played out." It took until 2:30 P.M. to complete the deployment that achieved one of Warren's objectives—using Bragg to connect Crawford with the picket line of the Ninth Corps. Yet once Bragg shifted his brigade northeast, he not only lost contact with the Fifth Corps pickets on his left but also with the elements of the Ninth Corps, now to his rear. Moreover, the men stood ten paces apart, each soldier hunkered down behind a tree, maybe seeing one comrade on either side and no doubt feeling lonely. "The picket-line in itself was good enough there," thought Roebling, "but at no point could they see more than 20 feet around them."[45]

Most significantly, Bragg's maneuvers had opened a gap a mile to the right and rear of Crawford's right flank. Warren reported that this dangerous flaw resulted from Bragg's failure to support the Third Division as he had intended. "From what I can learn by Major Roebling, you have not got connection with the Ninth Corps at all where I wanted it," the corps commander admonished Crawford. But Bragg would protest that unnamed staff officers—presumably Chester and Mead—instructed him to form the line that he did. "I obeyed all the instructions given me . . . and posted the line as near as possible in conformity with such instructions," the general explained. He later added that his deployment was based on a conversation he heard between Captains Cope and Chester. Chester confirmed that he accompanied Bragg on his reconnaissance to the Strong house and that he saw him begin to shift his brigade in that direction before returning to Crawford's headquarters. Lieutenant Mead agreed with Chester's version of events, affirming that he also witnessed Bragg's movement to the northeast from the Aiken house vicinity. Bragg's movements would yield profound consequences later that day, but the evidence suggests that he deployed his brigade under the observation and with the approval of Crawford's emissaries. Warren had simply assigned him an impossible task, as the emaciated Iron Brigade could not possibly directly support Crawford, connect with the Ninth Corps skirmishers around the Aiken house, and extend eastward toward Jerusalem Plank Road.[46]

Bragg's brigade was not the only Union unit in transit that soggy morning. Brig. Gen. Charles J. Paine's two small Eighteenth Corps brigades of U.S. Colored Troops began relieving Willcox's division as anticipated between 2:00 and 3:00 A.M. "At 3:30 o'clock on the morning of the 19th of August, in obedience to instructions received from Maj. Gen. John G. Parke, I withdrew my command (Third Division, Ninth Army Corps) from the position it then occupied . . . near the Taylor house, marched to the . . . Yellow Tavern, on Weldon railroad, where I arrived at 7:30 A.M.," reported General Willcox. The march covered about seven miles and coursed well south of Bragg's problematical position. Willcox reported to Warren, who told him to make camp in a field east of the tavern, with the left flank of Brig. Gen. John F. Hartranft's brigade about 400 yards east of the railroad. Willcox's two brigades deployed in two lines, Hartranft's men 500 yards south of Crawford's position and Col. William Humphrey's brigade behind Hartranft. These soldiers then rested and prepared rations in a steady downpour.[47]

The situation below Globe Tavern seemed under control. Col. Samuel P. Spear's cavalry brigade rode south before dawn and drove scattered elements of Dearing's troopers southward as far as Reams' Station, picketing all the roads leading to the left and rear of Warren's position.[48]

Meanwhile, Ayres's men had been busy through the night preparing works, an endeavor that continued past dawn. Small squads crept forward sporadically during the morning, collecting the dead and wounded from the previous day's battle. Periodically, picket fire erupted along the lines, defining the northern extent such endeavors could safely operate. By midday, the picket fire grew less frequent as the men tried to make themselves comfortable under a warm rain that turned their rifle pits into slime.[49]

East of the railroad, Lyle's troops struggled to keep their rifles in firing condition during the downpours. They, too, embarked on burial duty. "Here we saw a sight while it sent a shudder of horror over us, at the same time planted deep in our bosoms the desire for revenge," recorded Julius Ramsdell. "All our dead which lay in their lines through the night were stripped of every article of clothing in many cases treated with the greatest indecency and disrespect, and left to be bleached by the rain which fell in torrents upon their uncovered bodies." The skirmish line was strengthened and earthworks constructed "somewhat in the form of a horseshoe, with the outerside to the enemy," according to a soldier in the Eighty-Eighth Pennsylvania.[50]

Meanwhile, Mott's Second Corps division completed its march from Deep Bottom to the Ninth Corps entrenchments at Petersburg. Mott received his orders for the move at 8:40 on the evening of the eighteenth and, leaving McAllister's brigade to guard the pontoon bridges, began crossing the James at 10:00 P.M. He halted his troops on the south bank at Jones Neck to wait for McAllister to catch up, during which time many of his tired troops collapsed. "In five minutes each man was sleeping just where he fell, too weary to unfold a blanket and thankful to have a chance to doze unmolested, something we hadn't done for several nights," wrote Private Haley of the Seventeenth Maine. Mott prodded his men forward again around 1:00 A.M. They crossed the Appomattox River two hours later and reported to Meade's headquarters at 7:00 that morning, prompting orders to relieve the Ninth Corps in their trenches.[51]

The Battle of Weldon Railroad, August 18–19

By then, of course, Willcox was well on his way to Warren's front, leaving Mott the responsibility of replacing the divisions of Brig. Gen. Julius White and Brig. Gen. Robert Potter. Mott's arrival spurred a flurry of correspondence between Meade and Grant. The army commander informed the general-in-chief that Mott had arrived and that Paine had replaced Willcox in the works, allowing that Ninth Corps division to reenforce Warren. Grant's response revealed a great deal about his strategic priorities. He indicated that he intended to leave the rest of the troops engaged in the Deep Bottom operations north of the James in order to pin down Confederate forces there. "It . . . seems to be a sensitive point with the enemy," he explained. "I am anxious to force the enemy to withdraw from the Valley the reenforcements he has sent to Early, and I think the best way to do this is to threaten as long a line as possible." Meade replied that he would confer with Warren to determine if Parke's additional forces would satisfy the Fifth Corps chieftain. Parke had reported that Potter's and White's divisions numbered a combined 4,000 men. Meade then told his chief of staff, Maj. Gen. Andrew Atkinson Humphreys, to inquire of Warren if, in his opinion, the Ninth Corps reinforcements would be enough to "at all hazards maintain his hold on the Weldon railroad."[52]

Warren promptly replied, "With the force you are sending me it will be safe to trust me to hold on to the railroad." Furthermore, he added, he suspected that the Rebels were withdrawing to their Petersburg lines. Such optimism spurred Meade to alter Warren's original mission. "As it is now determined to maintain our lodgment on the railroad, its destruction becomes a matter of secondary importance," he wrote. Warren's operation was no longer a raid—it was now a matter of retaining permanent control of Lee's southern lifeline. Meade, however, warned that the remainder of Parke's troops would be delayed in arriving. The covered ways that provided safe passage out of the forward trenches had been flooded waist deep by the heavy rain, so the Ninth Corps reinforcements would be withdrawing much more slowly and, in some cases, forced to leave the protection of their works and expose themselves to enemy fire. It would take Mott and Parke hours to effect the exchange of positions; White's division would not begin its march westward until midafternoon. Thus, as events stood on the morning of August 19, Grant had determined to maintain pressure north of the James to induce the recall of Lee's troops from the Valley, while Meade, leaving Mott and Ord to guard the permanent fortifications south and east of Petersburg, had decided to hold the Weldon Railroad with Warren and Parke.[53]

Shortly after noon, Meade informed Grant that he was on his way to confer with Warren. "We went slop, slop, woefully through mud and puddles," groused Lyman. The headquarters party stumbled upon a brigade of Potter's division, and Meade told Lyman to get them moving. Proceeding via the familiar route passing the Williams house, the general and his entourage reached Globe Tavern at 1:45 P.M., where the army commander met with Warren. Lyman took the opportunity to examine the deployment of the Fifth Corps. He noticed the line of troops that paralleled the tracks west of the railroad and extended at least one-third of a mile south of Globe Tavern. To the north the line turned east and was strongly entrenched, but across the railroad "the right was in the air, and only continued by a picket line." This struck Lyman as worrisome, but he hesitated to make waves. He rejoined Meade around 3:30 P.M., riding back toward army headquarters the way they had come. Lyman would not be the only officer to discern the vulnerability of Warren's right.[54]

William Mahone had established his headquarters at the Branch house overlooking the deep ravine of Lieutenant Run, a tributary of the Appomattox. This sheltering drainage had afforded him cover during his devastating June 22 attack against the Second Corps, and Mahone saw an opportunity to use it again, this time against Warren. The idea germinated on the afternoon of the eighteenth during a conversation with Capt. Richard Henry Toler Adams, an officer on Hill's staff. Mahone told Adams that "the proper thing to be done was to move a column of attack up the deep ravine west of the Branch house . . . in the direction of the Johnson house, and keeping the column out of the enemy's sight by the ravine and the intervening woods . . . and reaching his vidette line . . . plunge through this line to the right flank and rear" of Warren's corps. "This view of the situation was subsequently ascertained to be precisely correct," Mahone immodestly asserted in postwar commentary. The only variation from his version of events comes from General Heth, who credited Lee with ordering the movement on the ground; but Lee was still north of the James, thus invalidating Heth's recollection. Mahone had claimed credit for devising previous Confederate counterattacks, including those in June and July, so it is reasonable that Beauregard and Hill also assumed that a gap had likely opened between Warren and the permanent Union line to the east. Nevertheless, Mahone deserves accolades for recognizing the opportunity and, as August 19 unfolded, exploiting it.[55]

Mahone would need help if Beauregard approved his plan of attack. His three detached brigades—Harris's, Girardey's, and Sanders's—staggered into the Petersburg lines that morning, the men much too enervated to undertake another march, let alone execute an assault. Only the tiny Florida Brigade and Mahone's old Virginia command, once again led by Brig. Gen. David A. Weisiger (now recovered from his Crater wound), filled the trenches from Rives Salient on Jerusalem Plank Road to Lieutenant Run.[56]

While Mahone's exhausted new arrivals sought rest and rations, Beauregard informed Lee that he intended to renew the attempt to drive the Yankees from

The Battle of Weldon Railroad, August 18–19

the railroad. "I will endeavor to-day to dislodge him with four brigades of our infantry and the division of cavalry you have promised," adding, "result would be more certain with a stronger force of infantry." The identity of the four brigades Beauregard referenced is unclear, nor did he explain to Lee how he proposed to make his attack. He did send orders on the eighteenth to Brig. Gen. Johnson Hagood to take command of the reserve brigade of Bushrod Johnson's Division and report to headquarters, identifying one of the units in his plan. Major Cooke of Beauregard's staff, who had been detailed to assist Hill, found Hagood at Johnson's headquarters near Petersburg about 2:30 A.M. Hagood explained that the 625 men he had been ordered to lead "were perfectly unorganized" and thus unfit to participate in Beauregard's counteroffensive. "This representation was made to Genl. Beauregard by Genls. Hill and Hagood," wrote Cooke, "and the consequence was that Hagood was ordered back to the trenches to relieve [Brig. Gen. Thomas L.] Clingman, who was ordered to the support of Genl. Hill at once." Beauregard informed Hill of this change and confirmed that Hill would remain in command of Colquitt's Brigade.[57]

A new wrinkle briefly complicated Beauregard's planning as he developed his strike force. A Union prisoner informed his captors that the actual goal of Warren's operation was to draw Rebel troops to the Fifth Corps front, opening an opportunity to exploit the weakened Confederate lines elsewhere around Petersburg. Beauregard advised Lee of this intelligence but decided that "the fire of our batteries this morning must have disconcerted enemy's plans." His attack around Warren's right would proceed.[58]

Sometime that morning Beauregard settled on the outlines of his initiative, offering some discretion to Hill. The Creole general told the Virginian "to adopt such measures as will insure the immediate dislodgement of the enemy from the Petersburg and Weldon R.R. by fighting him, if not too strongly entrenched, or by maneuvering." He confirmed that Hill could use both Colquitt and Clingman to achieve his objective. He also told him that "one division of Cavalry will soon be here from the North side of James River, and on its arrival it will be ordered to report to you." That division was Rooney Lee's, but his troopers would arrive too late to participate in the attack. Mahone then learned from Hill that Beauregard had ordered him to "attack the enemy at Yellow Tavern according to the plan I had explained to his staff-officer [Adams], that General Beauregard would send me two brigades [Colquitt's and Clingman's] from Hoke's Division and that I should take one of my own brigades to make up the attacking force." Not surprisingly, Mahone selected Weisiger's veteran Virginians. But Mahone protested that "troops always fought better under their own commander than under a stranger . . . and it would be best for General Hoke to take charge of the attacking force." It is unclear whether Hill or Beauregard rejected Mahone's suggestion, but in either case, "Little Billy" would spearhead the assault. Hill would also call on Davis and Mayo to reprise the previous day's path of attack to complement Mahone, an exercise Heth characterized as "a diversion." Willie Pegram would add elements of three batteries to the operation.[59]

Mahone readily accepted his leadership role but believed that the force assigned him was inadequate to the task. Lt. Col. William H. Stewart, in charge of the Sixty-First Virginia in Weisiger's brigade, agreed that "it was plain to be seen that the success of the enterprise could not be pushed ... against such odds." But Beauregard declined to release more troops from the already thin lines wrapping around Petersburg, so Mahone would have to make do with the three brigades provided. Nowhere is the strength of this force quantified, but it could not have numbered as many as 4,000 men.[60]

Orders for Mahone's assault circulated around noon. "We started and left ... about 12 o'clock," reported Capt. Washington L. Dunn of Colquitt's Twenty-Seventh Georgia. Pvt. William H. Smith of the Twenty-Third Georgia confirmed this: "soon we had orders to be ready to march and reports said the Yankees were still in possession of the R.R. and we knew what was up." Mahone assembled his units, formed them behind the works, and then moved forward about 2:00 P.M. Colquitt's Georgians led the column, followed by Clingman's Tar Heels, with the Virginians in the rear, the Sixth Virginia in front and Petersburg's own Twelfth Virginia at the back of the brigade's column. Mahone told Weisiger to support either flank of Colquitt and Clingman when those units formed line of battle as circumstances dictated. The Lieutenant Run ravine concealed the graycoats until they emerged into the forest near the Johnson house. "I remember how disagreeable it was to the troops as they made their way through the thick undergrowth in the woods southeast of the Johnson house," wrote Colonel Stewart, "but they pressed on, as they did so, hastily gathering whortleberries that abounded."[61]

Meanwhile along Heth's line, Mayo's and Davis's brigades waited for instructions "in a state of uncertainty." But as Mahone's force moved out, Hill and his staff appeared, ordering Heth forward. "We took the same route as the day before," wrote a soldier in the Second Maryland Battalion, "on the railroad track. While on the march we were pretty thoroughly drenched by a heavy thunderstorm; our only protection our oil and India rubber cloths thrown over our shoulders." The men carried their rifles under their armpits "with trailing muzzles and locks" in an attempt to keep them dry. The brigades reached the woods north of the Davis house and formed a line of battle "just as it had been on the 18th, and upon nearly the same ground." The soldiers recognized that the previous day's battlefield offered great potential for defense, and assumed

The Battle of Weldon Railroad, August 18–19

that the Federals would have improved their breastworks significantly during the intervening hours. "It was apparent to all that the day was to see some hard fighting, with but little prospect that success would crown the Confederate arms," remembered a pessimistic Marylander. "Some of the men tried to appear cheerful," wrote another soldier, describing a comrade who had indulged in "too much 'pine-top'" ridiculing the men who had not seen action on the eighteenth. Most, however, "were engaged in quiet thought; many thinking of the quiet circle far away, when they enjoyed peaceful times and wondering whether they would ever participate in such scenes again." Pegram unlimbered six of his guns west of the railroad and two more east of the tracks.[62]

After Heth placed Pegram's cannon, he rode forward to the Davis house to be certain that the occupants had fled. To his surprise, he found a young woman inside. "I told her to get out of the house," recalled Heth. "She seemed in no hurry to do so." The presence of the Confederate guns soon elicited fire from Union artillery, a shell striking the dwelling and shattering a copse of small pines that surrounded it. As the Federal fire intensified—Heth insisted that he had never experienced a more intense bombardment—the general managed to persuade the woman to leave the house. "I told her to run, and pointed out the direction she should take in order to get out of the line of fire. She stopped and with her arms akimbo said, 'I will die before I run.'" She then stood for a full minute shaking her fist in the direction of the Yankees and "then deliberately walked in the direction I had indicated. She escaped unhurt."[63]

While Mahone and Heth readied their attacks, General Bragg, joined by Major Roebling, sat down to enjoy a repast near the modest homes of Richard Vaughan and John Wright. The Seventh Wisconsin occupied Bragg's right closest to the Strong house, with the Nineteenth Indiana and the Twenty-Fourth Michigan to their left. The First Battalion, New York Sharpshooters and Seventh Indiana were advanced as vedettes, while the Sixth Wisconsin waited in reserve. "Everything was perfectly still at this time," wrote Roebling, as little campfires warmed the delayed midday meal for many of Bragg's men.[64]

Roebling continued to urge Bragg to secure a connection with Hartshorne's skirmish line, so, after gulping down his dinner, Bragg, accompanied by Lieutenant Mead and two other members of Crawford's staff—Lt. Luke Clarke and Lt. Samuel K. Herr—rode west to investigate the situation. "While there heavy firing was heard to the left center of General Bragg's line," wrote Mead. Mahone's attack had commenced. Some witnesses marked the beginning of the assault at 3:00 P.M., but more set it between 4:15 and 4:30 P.M.[65]

The graycoats brushed aside the Federal skirmishers, first penetrating the Nineteenth Indiana's portion of the line. The heavy woods had concealed

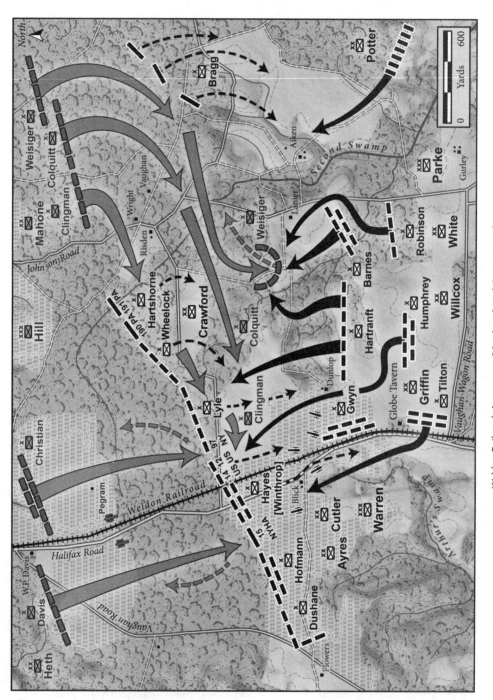

Weldon Railroad, August 19, 1864: Attack and Counterattack

Clingman and Colquitt until they were within seventy-five yards of the Hoosiers. The Confederates pressed forward in columns of fours, coming as a complete surprise. The Indianans fled, some into the ranks of the Twenty-Fourth Michigan and others to the rear. "As I was returning along the rear of my line, when opposite the Nineteenth Indiana Regiment . . . I met the men from that regiment," reported General Crawford. "I asked why they had left the front. They replied they had been driven back by the enemy." Crawford collared a second lieutenant, who seemed to be in command of this rabble, and told him to re-form the line, restoring their connection on both flanks—a futile directive. He also sent a messenger to Bragg, who with the members of Crawford's staff was still on the left of the line, and ordered him to send his reserves to bolster the disordered Nineteenth.[66]

The brigade commander required no such instruction to spring into action. "Heavy firing was heard on the left center of General Bragg's line," wrote Mead. "He immediately gave orders for the Sixth Wisconsin Volunteers, who were in reserve, and numbering seventy-four men, to be thrown to the point, and the regiment at once got in motion." Bragg, Mead, Clarke, and Herr all rode along with the tiny band of Badgers, who according to Mead, "bravely endeavored to check the enemy." The Rebel contagion also infected the Twenty-Fourth Michigan, in position just west of the Hoosiers. Its commander, Lt. Col. Albert M. Edwards, shifted his men to the right in an attempt to fill the void created by their departed comrades. But their small numbers, the tangled terrain, and the relentless Confederate pressure disordered Edwards's men. and they fell back as well. "This was more than our boys bargained for," wrote Elmer D. Wallace, a hospital steward attached to the Wolverines. "They were compelled to face about and thread their way through as best they could. In doing so they became scattered so that it is impossible to tell how many have been killed, wounded or taken prisoners. The survivors fled south to rally around the Aiken house."[67]

"The enemy had reached the open field near the old mill before my reserve could gain it," wrote Bragg, "and thus cut off the battalion of New York Sharpshooters and the detachment of the Seventh Indiana Volunteers. . . . These were captured entire." This left only the Seventh Wisconsin, Bragg's rightmost regiment, on the line. As fugitives from the Nineteenth Indiana swarmed into their sector, Lt. Col. Mark Finnicum, the unit commander, met with Captain Chester, explaining the nature of the unfolding disaster and that he expected to be attacked momentarily. Chester informed him that breastworks in his rear were now occupied by elements of Mott's division and that if he was pressed too hard or flanked, he should fall back to that refuge. That is precisely what Finnicum did, thus sparing his regiment significant harm.[68]

By then, the Sixth Wisconsin was also on the run. They had arrived in time to see the sharpshooters swept away "like chaff... who being armed with heavy telescope rifles, after their first volley, were helpless against a charge." The diminutive regiment—evidence of the hard campaigning experienced by the Iron Brigade—did its best to slow the Confederate momentum. Virtually surrounded by hostile fire, the Sixth Wisconsin retreated to a fence "with a ditch on each side of it, and the dirt from each had been thrown together and stakes driven in to which a couple of boards had been nailed." Here, General Bragg, whose "coolness and bravery . . . were eminently displayed," ordered them to halt and make a stand. "Our fellows opened fire and bothered Mahone's rebels some," recalled Sgt. James P. Sullivan, "but the Johnnies in front, who had swept away the thin skirmish line in front of them, came up on our left and rear and gave a volley to our flanks." Bragg realized that to remain behind that fence would doom the already diminished Sixth Wisconsin and shouted for every man to break for a nearby barn. What was left of the regiment rallied there and again fired at the Rebels, "but one might as well try to dam the Mississippi with a chip," concluded Sullivan. Bragg now ordered the Badgers to hotfoot it toward Globe Tavern, where they eventually found refuge.[69]

The Iron Brigade, in the words of one historian, "had crumpled like paper in a matter of minutes." Lieutenant Colonel Lyman disdainfully thought that Mahone's attack was "one of those disgraceful surprises which we have in such perfection." Bragg's brigade suffered 217 casualties, more than 25 percent of its strength. Prisoners accounted for nearly three-fourths of those losses. The two units on the advance line—the First Battalion of New York Sharpshooters and the Seventh Indiana—lost 4 men killed or wounded but 133 captured. The Sixth Wisconsin suffered more from battle wounds than any of Bragg's other regiments.[70]

Historian John Horn points out that Meade and his staff were passing the Aiken house when Mahone struck. "Had Mahone swung a quarter mile wider to his left, he might have taken prisoner the commander of the Army of the Potomac," he writes. The Rebels may have missed Meade, but they did not miss the chance to wolf down some of the victuals abandoned by the routed Federals.[71]

Meanwhile, nearer the railroad, occasional skirmishing throughout the morning, particularly against Crawford's troops east of the tracks, yielded no alteration to the opposing fronts. "Whenever our skirmishers attempted to advance, they met with firm resistance," reported General Hayes. When the firing suddenly ceased shortly after noon, Ayres ascribed the respite to the enemy's desire "to allow us to bury theirs and our dead. I ordered that done and a list of the numbers sent in." Colonel Wainwright took advantage of one of the lulls to ride toward the Davis house, where he found an opportunity to examine the Union defenses. "The place is an ugly one," thought the artillery commander, "nor should I see why Warren would want to get his line out there." Wainwright had unlimbered some guns along the latitude of the Blick house and thought that if the object was to hold the railroad, the Union works should be established there. On the other hand, if Warren's mission was to "envelop Petersburg," the lines "should be pushed forward quite through the woods to the large opening we see beyond & within sight of their main line of works."[72]

The Federals had spent much of the night adjusting their entrenchments, labor that continued throughout the sodden morning. The soldiers built as many as three shallow lines in advance of their main fortifications, which were in places fronted by an abatis some thirty yards in width. Seven brigades formed Warren's front. Crawford's three rested east of the railroad, with Hartshorne's on his right, followed by Coulter's (still under Colonel Wheelock), then Lyle's. Hayes's men straddled the railroad, with the Fifteenth New York Heavy Artillery (technically Ayres's Third Brigade) on Hayes's left, west of the tracks. Hofmann's troops of Cutler's division were next, and Dushane's Maryland Brigade formed on the left with its flank refused. "Where Ayres was the trees were sparse, so that he could see & maneuver his men," noted Wainwright. "Crawford on the contrary was in the densest kind of small pine & scrub oak where it was impossible to move in line or to see 20 yds." The colonel also fretted that if Warren's line should be attacked, those troops might be subject to his own friendly artillery fire. "Warren told me that he did not like the place, but his orders were to hold as far forward as possible & that should Crawford not be able to hold his position he had directed him to move out of it by his flanks so as to uncover the fire of my batts."[73]

The Fifth Corps executed some adjustments to their alignment in the afternoon that did nothing to alleviate the potential for such friendly fire. Hartshorne's little command, consisting of the 190th and 191st Pennsylvania and comprised of reenlisted veterans from the old Pennsylvania Reserve regiments, had recalled its pickets and contracted its line eastward, creating a gap on their left. This compelled Wheelock to shift to the right and Lyle, in turn, to sidle eastward to cover Wheelock's void. Hayes then summoned two of his small Regular Army regiments, the 12th and 14th Infantry, to occupy the ground formerly held by Lyle. The 12th U.S. Infantry rested its right on Lyle's left flank, with the 14th U.S. Infantry to its west, its left anchored on the railroad.[74]

At 2:30 P.M. Hayes informed Ayres that his pickets had spotted "heavy columns" of the enemy moving westward across the railroad. Thirty minutes later Hayes reported that Lyle had seen a mass of Confederates east of the tracks. No doubt they had spotted Heth's two brigades as they prepared for their attack. As on the previous day, Heth positioned Davis's Mississippians and Fifty-Fifth North Carolina west of the railroad, opposite the Fifteenth New York Heavy Artillery and Hofmann's brigade. Mayo's brigade, now under Col. William S. Christian of the Fifty-Fifth Virginia, as Mayo was ill, deployed east of the tracks facing Hayes's Regulars and Lyle. At roughly 4:00 P.M., Heth unleashed his assault. Major Roebling, noting that Mahone and Heth advanced at the same time, referred to the action as "a concerted attack." Capt. Charles H. Porter of the Thirty-Ninth Massachusetts believed that Heth and Mahone had agreed upon the mutual hour of attack, while historian John Horn believes that Heth began his advance when Mahone's attack became audible. In any event, as Pegram's guns roared behind them, "with a cheer, the Confederate troops bounded forward."[75]

Davis's attack first encountered the pickets from the Fifteenth New York Heavy Artillery and the Fourth Delaware of Hofmann's brigade. These bluecoats put up a stiff fight, gradually withdrawing through three lines of shallow works before stopping behind their main entrenchments. Here, the Rebel momentum ground to a halt. Adjutant Cooke testified that members of the Fifty-Fifth North Carolina who had been detailed on the eighteenth returned to the ranks, compensating for the regiment's losses suffered that day. "Our regiment charged over the same ground as the day before," wrote Cooke, "and it was repulsed at just about the same point, and with very nearly as great losses." Ayres laconically reported, "The division which attacked my front was repulsed," magnifying the strength of his opponents and adding that "a color [was] captured." That flag belonged to the Fifty-Fifth North Carolina and was taken by Pvt. James T. Jennings of the Fifty-Sixth Pennsylvania, earning him the Medal of Honor.[76]

The situation east of the railroad proved a bit dicier for the Federals. "We charged over the field and met the enemy in the edge of the woods and drove them back," reported a soldier in Christian's Second Maryland Battalion. "They had three feeble lines of works and a main line," testified another Marylander. "We drove them to the main work and occupying their second line poured in a fire." But the thick pine woods disordered the Confederates. The left-most units occupied the Federals' third skirmish line, "while from some gross mismanagement the right was held back, not even up to the first line of works." The problem seemed to rest with the acting brigade commander. "Col. Christian assumed command, but showed his inability by first ordering the men to the rear at the suggestion of a lieutenant, and immediately ordering them back at the command of a private," griped one of his troops. "The men were all mixed up."[77]

Lyle's and Wheelock's troops hunkered down behind their primary works and exchanged fire with the Confederates, some of whom were but thirty yards distant on the opposite side of the abatis. "The bullets were whistling in every direction," Private Ramsdell recorded in his diary. Just as across the tracks, the Federal line held, but here the Confederates had not withdrawn. Pinned down by the pressure to their front, Crawford's division suddenly started taking fire on their right flank and rear. Mahone's men had arrived.[78]

This was no spontaneous charge. Mahone had gathered his brigadiers together and carefully explained the nature of the terrain that lay before them, the location of Yellow Tavern, and the position occupied by the Federals squaring off against Heth. Clingman inquired about the security of their rear as they moved westward, fearful that the enemy might approach them from their works near Jerusalem Plank Road, an eminently reasonable concern. "My reply was 'that is my look-out, general, your duty is in the front,'" asserted Mahone. He aligned Clingman's Brigade on his right, placed Colquitt's on his left, and retained Weisiger's brigade in reserve behind Colquitt. "Magnificently and with steady step," the three brigades moved west.[79]

Their first target would be Hartshorne's Pennsylvanians on the east end of Crawford's line, now exposed following Bragg's dispersal. Christian's pressure had not extended as far as Hartshorne's position, so his men apprehended no immediate threat. "Sometime in the afternoon word was passed along our line that we would be relieved at 4 o'clock and that we would move directly to the rear when our relief should come," recalled Pvt. Silas Crocker of the 191st Pennsylvania. "We were posted in thick woods and could not see men very far, so when at last I believed to be about the time for our relief I heard quite a racket, as of men marching and shouting in the bushes over on my right." Nearby, Sgt. Thomas W. Springer of the 191st had gone toward the rear to fetch some ammunition and, more importantly to his tired comrades, some coffee. In a short time Springer returned, remembered a fellow soldier, "with blanched face to inform us that we were completely surrounded, that the enemy was in our rear, and for every man to look out for himself." Crocker gathered his knapsack and prepared to make a getaway when he was greeted by a Confederate with a demand to "throw down your gun and fall in here!" The private admitted: "I caught on without waiting for a second invitation, and believing that especially just then 'discretion was the better part of valor' did as directed. Nearly the whole line was received in the same manner." Colonel Hartshorne was numbered among the prisoners, seized by an unarmed courier, Robert R. Henry, of Mahone's staff. Some members of the brigade destroyed their treasured repeating rifles by smashing them against trees before giving themselves up.[80]

Warren and Wainwright had ridden to the Dunlop house, a frame home amid a small grove about half a mile north of Globe Tavern, hoping to discern the source of the ruckus unfolding in their front but obscured from view by the thick woods. Not many minutes passed, however, before a column of troops appeared just south of the wood line, heading toward the railroad. At first Warren's artillery chief assumed them to be Crawford's men, although Lt. Richard Milton of the Ninth Massachusetts Battery, his position providing Wainwright's vantage point, insisted they were Rebels. "As they moved across our front more & more of their men were crowded out of the wood by the difficulty of marching through it until there must have been a couple hundred at least, by the time they got within a short distance of the R.R.," wrote Wainwright. "At this time too one of their battle flags came in view & . . . there was no doubt now as to what the troops in my front were, though I could not imagine what had become of Crawford's men." Wainwright recalled that Crawford had been told to retreat by the flanks should his position become untenable in order to unmask the Union artillery's fire. "As the enemy were unmistakably in our front, within 400 yards of the batteries, having to all appearances driven our men to the left, I no longer hesitated to turn all the guns of that front on them."[81]

Wainwright had seen the left flank of Colquitt's Brigade as it moved westward, the remainder of the Georgians and Clingman's North Carolinians still hidden in the forest. The next Federal brigade in line belonged to Colonel Wheelock, whose position was nearly opposite Wainwright's targets. "It was discovered that the enemy had gained our rear from the right," reported Capt. Delos E. Hall of Wheelock's Ninety-Seventh New York. "This with the shell from our own batteries caused some excitement." Colonel Wheelock noted, "Our own batteries were shelling every part of the woods and with great accuracy, striking our line of works." He dispatched his adjutant, Capt. Joseph H. Smith, to find Crawford and warn the division commander about this friendly fire. Through the mistaken orders of another staff officer, Wheelock's left-most regiment, the Ninety-Seventh New York, vacated the trenches and fled to the rear, where the Confederates gobbled them up. Wheelock managed to move the rest of his regiments to the opposite side of their works, trusting that Christian's attackers had been neutralized and thus obtaining some protection from Wainwright's projectiles. "We jumped over on the other side of the works & laid low," wrote a soldier in the Eighty-Eighth Pennsylvania. "And they gave us a perfect hail of cannon balls & shells. . . . Balls to the right of us—balls to the left of us—Balls to the front of us & in short balls all around us . . . throwing up the dirt—bursting—& tearing around generally in a fearful style." One of the Federal projectiles exploded in an adjacent regiment, "& the way the limbs & muskets & things flew was appalling, mingled with the noise & screeching of the shells was the piteous cries of the wounded men. It was fearful."[82]

Chaos reigned amid Wheelock's troops. "All who tried to get off by going to the rear were taken prisoners," wrote Lt. Charles McKnight of the Eighty-Eighth Pennsylvania. "Our men and theirs were so mixed up in the woods that we dare not fire, and I suppose the rebs did not fire for the same reason. . . . Oh it was a pretty kettle of fish." Chaplain William H. Locke of the Eleventh Pennsylvania thought that "it was a moment when confusion worse confounded had come again, threatening not only the loss of our hold on the railroad, but of most of the corps."[83]

Had Locke known the situation immediately to his west in Lyle's brigade, his pessimism would have only increased. The friendly fire from Wainwright's guns had as great an effect on Lyle's men as it was having on Wheelock's. "The shells did us as much harm as they did the Rebels," admitted a member of the 39th Massachusetts. Unlike the situation on Wheelock's front, Christian's troops continued to pose a threat to Lyle's brigade, and as the right flank of Colquitt's Brigade approached their rear, Lyle's men panicked, being caught between two hostile forces and absorbing a shelling from their own artillery. "This was beyond endurance," wrote Cpl. Andrew R. Linscott of the 39th Massachusetts, "and we made a grand rush and got out the best we could." For many members of the brigade, their best merely succeeded in making them prisoners of war. "The regiment was surprised and surrounded," recalled a member of the 104th New York, "and after a few minutes sharp fighting, every commissioned officer and nearly every enlisted man were captured and sent into rebel lines, where many of them died in rebel prisons." A soldier in Lyle's 107th Pennsylvania made it out safe, one of four men left in his company. "Our regiment is nearly all captured by the rebels," he informed a correspondent. "The rebels made a gallant charge on our line and drove our right wing back then came in our rear and took our men nearly all prisoners." Lt. James Thomas of the 107th Pennsylvania informed his father that the entire division was beginning to retreat, but "what was their surprise when getting 50 yds to the rear to find the woods full of Rebs. They turned to the right and found the same thing, to the left & the same, Johnnies every where, no avenue of escape left at all."[84]

The two small Regular Army regiments of Hayes's brigade that remained east of the railroad were the next Union dominoes to fall. The Twelfth U.S. Infantry had adjoined Lyle's left, the Ninety-Seventh New York, which had disappeared. "The whole force on my right abandoned the breastworks and fell back precipitately," complained Capt. Philip W. Stanhope, commander of the Twelfth, "leaving my right flank entirely exposed." Like his sister regiments to the east, Stanhope's Regulars came under fire from Wainwright's cannon. "I ordered a retreat and forced my way through the enemy's line with the bayonet and butts of muskets bringing in some ten or twelve prisoners," wrote the captain, while losing three of his officers and "a large number of my enlisted men."[85]

The Fourteenth U.S. Infantry began the engagement with its left flank on the railroad and its right connecting with the Twelfth. Its commander, Lt. J. Chester White, reported that he maintained his position "until the whole Third Division had retreated." When the Twelfth U.S. broke, "deeming it folly to remain longer," the lieutenant ordered his regiment to withdraw. "In attempting to retreat we found ourselves completely cut off," wrote White, who fell captive along with many of his men. The Confederates also seized the division commander himself, who had returned to the left of his line, but General Crawford managed to escape "almost miraculously."[86]

General Hayes watched as the right flank of his brigade collapsed. He started toward the railroad to rally Stanhope and White, but "it was soon apparent that all the troops on my right had given way." Hayes now headed for the rear to re-form his command "when hearing the call 'Halt,' I looked in that direction and beheld at a distance of a few yards a body of Rebels standing in line with their muskets at 'aim.'" Hayes attempted to escape, relying on the cover of the woods, and had progressed to a road in some open ground when a second group of Confederates appeared. "They rushed forward and surrounded me," recalled Hayes. "The game was up. I was a prisoner of war." Lt. George K. Brady of the Fourteenth U.S., acting as Hayes's assistant adjutant general, had accompanied his boss and was captured alongside him. They were escorted to Colquitt's command post by Sgt. Richard H. Powell of the Sixth Georgia.[87]

The bulk of Hayes's troops, west of the railroad, managed to withdraw relatively unscathed, falling back under orders and re-forming about 700 yards to the rear under the cover of Wainwright's smoking artillery. Colonel Winthrop assumed command of the brigade in place of its captured general. Winthrop described the heroics of his men, who had wrested the captured colors of the Twelfth U.S. from a Confederate officer, and informed his brother that "no disgrace is or can be attached to the affair" despite the number of prisoners now in Confederate hands.[88]

Although the progress of Mahone's attack seems linear and methodical, the reality was much more complex. Most of the fighting occurred in the low, dense woods, which disordered formations and hampered command and control, reminiscent of the combat in the Wilderness three months earlier. A drummer in Clingman's 8th North Carolina admitted Mahone's entire command "became scattered in the charge and some of the men were captured; some captured and recaptured twice. It was a thorough mixture in the woods. Front and rear seemed to be on all sides. The bullets came from every direction." An officer in Clingman's

51st North Carolina characterized the assault as "a regular woods scramble, it being impossible to preserve anything like a line of battle on account of the density of the woods." He added, "We captured a large number of prisoners, and suffered considerable loss ourselves, some of our men being captured and recaptured several times." Perceptions were similar among the Federals. "Nobody could tell where the rear was, the Johnnies being as much perplexed as were our boys," confessed the 107th Pennsylvania's Lieutenant Thomas. "Here was a squad of blue coats with a squad of gray backs as prisoners hunting their way out. They would be met by a larger party of Rebs who would release their men & make prisoners of ours. They would not go far before the tables would be turned again & so it went." Lt. John H. Dusseault of the 39th Massachusetts summed up the situation succinctly. "The men on both sides were now pretty generally mixed up in the woods," he wrote. "One squad, whichever was the bigger, would capture the other."[89]

As historian John Horn has phrased it, "chaos prevailed in the 500-yard-wide belt of woods between the Globe Tavern clearing and the Davis farm." The huge number of Yankee prisoners added to the confusion and helped arrest Mahone's progress. Colquitt and Clingman collected an unwieldy body of captives, herding them north out of the woods along Halifax Road and Johnson Road toward General Hill's headquarters. Pegram's two guns stationed east of the tracks saw this brigade-sized body of bluecoats headed their way and almost opened fire, avoiding a tragedy only at the last moment. Heth unfairly blamed the pause in the Confederate momentum on "the commander of the flanking column [who] saw that he could withdraw without fighting having picked up in the woods some 1500 or 1800 fugitives."[90]

In truth, there were several factors that contributed to Colquitt's and Clingman's failure to cross to the west side of the railroad and complete the utter devastation of Warren's line, among them the loss of General Clingman. The North Carolinian had been wounded in the leg and borne off the field early in the fighting, depriving half of Mahone's front line of its experienced leadership. Colonel Hector M. McKethan of the Fifty-First North Carolina, a carriage-maker from Wilmington, assumed command of Clingman's Brigade.[91]

Up until then, Weisiger's Virginians had remained in reserve the entire afternoon and had not been seriously engaged. Mahone now hoped to use his trusted brigade to charge toward Globe Tavern and extend the gains made by Colquitt and Clingman. "It was now that we had arrived at that point in the enterprise when its consummation was capable of completeness," wrote one of Mahone's officers. But this was not to be—the Ninth Corps would see to that.[92]

Willcox's division had been resting north of Globe Tavern since early morning. Late that afternoon one of his units, the Fiftieth Pennsylvania, received a ration of salted mackerel. Commissary Sgt. Lewis Crater and other members of the regiment began dipping the dried fish into the pools of water created by the day's rain when they heard "the old familiar yell, which told us that the rebels were in our immediate front. The drum beat and cry of 'fall in' ran along the lines, hence our mackerel was left," wrote the disappointed sergeant.[93]

Indeed, the sound of Crawford's battle sparked Willcox into action. With the help of Major Roebling, Willcox launched his closest brigade, Hartranft's First, to proceed immediately to the aid of the beleaguered Fifth Corps. John Frederick Hartranft—the soldiers called him "Hardtack"—was a thirty-three-year-old Pennsylvanian. A civil engineer and lawyer in civilian life, he had been colonel of a militia unit that was among the first to muster in to service at the outbreak of the war. He then organized the Fifty-First Pennsylvania, which participated in all the adventures of the Ninth Corps. A member of his staff described Hartranft as "a thorough gentleman and an admirable soldier. . . . He is a fine looking man . . . very quiet, very hard working no humbug about him whatever." Hartranft earned his star for service at Spotsylvania in May and on August 19 would prove that he deserved his promotion.[94]

Hartranft's 1,100 men headed straight for Crawford's lines "to go in where the fire was heaviest." They had scarcely formed in line of battle before discovering "that the enemy had completely turned the right flank of Warren," according to Capt. William V. Richards, Willcox's assistant adjutant general. "All seemed lost to the eyes of many; but the old story was soon to be told again." Hartranft's seven regiments—all greatly diminished due to the previous month's disaster at the Crater—advanced across the open ground and halted 150 yards short of the wood line, where some of Colquitt's men had deployed. Hartranft's three regiments on the right—the 109th New York, 8th Michigan, and his old 51st Pennsylvania—were concealed in the woods and managed to capture fifty or sixty Rebels. The four left regiments also advanced, driving their opponents into the pines, only to meet a counterattack near the edge of the forest. The two sides exchanged fire at a range of 75 yards before, once again, the Confederates retired.[95]

Hartranft then pushed ahead toward the forsaken Union earthworks, now occupied by some of Christian's men. "The enemy came on in heavy force, with bayonets fixed and not firing a shot," according to a Rebel of the 2nd Maryland Battalion. "The battalion poured a heavy fire into them, which staggered them for an instant, but they still pressed on." For a moment, the combatants clashed hand to hand, "the Confederates on the inside trying to retain, and the Federals on the outside trying to regain possession" of the works. Some of the Federals even hurled their guns, with bayonets fixed, over into the Rebel ranks. "But this unequal contest could not continue," remembered the Marylander, "for the Federals soon swarmed into the works . . . the survivors trying to fight their way out." His battalion lost at least one-third of its men. "I never saw so many dead rebs in one space in my life," wrote Sgt. Alexander S. Patten of the 109th New York, "the battle did not last over ten minutes."[96]

Willcox's Second Brigade, led by Colonel Humphrey, had followed Hartranft forward. Lt. Col. Byron M. Cutcheon, commander of Humphrey's Twentieth Michigan, lost sight of his sister brigade as it entered the woods. "Presently out of the thick growth of pine came the 8th Michigan," wrote Cutcheon, "broken, demoralized." This unit of Hartranft's command had received a heavy fire and lost about thirty men killed or wounded, including the regiment's commander, Maj. Horatio Belcher, who was shot three times, suggesting that Hartranft's brigade had struggled more than its commander would report.[97]

Warren told Willcox to send Humphrey's 1,200 soldiers to the left, toward the railroad and Ayres's segment of the line, and recapture the lost fortifications. Humphrey promptly obeyed but, once in the woods, advanced cautiously until within sight of the Confederates occupying Hayes's captured works. "At the word we went forward through the woods . . . yelling to the best of our ability," recalled Lieutenant Colonel Cutcheon. "When we arrived at the pits a hand to hand contest took place," wrote Sergeant Crater, "bayonets, swords, and butts of muskets were used freely, finally we succeeded in capturing the pits and quite a number of the enemy, nearly all belonging to the 47th Virginia." Sgt. Charles E. Brown of the Fiftieth Pennsylvania snatched up the regimental flag of the unfortunate Virginians. "We . . . never fired a gun until we got in the pits," boasted Sgt. David S. Munroe of the Twentieth Michigan. "They said they never seen a breastwork taken at right shoulder shift." The Rebels made several attempts to regain the lost ground, all of which failed.[98]

By this time, the First Division of the Ninth Corps was on the field. Mott's troops had finally managed to relieve General White's two brigades at 3:00 P.M. White immediately marched south on Jerusalem Plank Road, then turned west past the Williams house toward Globe Tavern. The brigadier was approaching his forty-eighth birthday and had a checkered record thus far in the war. He first saw service in the Trans-Mississippi, then was the officer who surrendered the Harpers Ferry garrison to Stonewall Jackson in September 1862. Following a stint overseeing a draft rendezvous, he landed in the Ninth Corps and served Burnside poorly as his acting chief of staff at the Crater. When the First Division's commander was relieved after that fiasco, White stepped in. Lyman called him "little bald-headed White. . . . He is no soldier, but always ready to fight; a trait that goes far in war!" On August 19 White would sustain his reputation for aggressiveness. "The roads, owing to the rain, were exceedingly bad," he explained, "and the column moved slowly; it was, in consequence, about 5 P.M. when it reached the Aiken house, shortly after passing which musketry was heard to our right and front." White dispatched an officer to obtain instructions from Warren, then "moved forward at the double-quick in the direction of the firing."[99]

White deployed his First Brigade, led by its new commander, Lt. Col. Joseph H. Barnes, with its right resting on Johnson Road. His staff officer then returned with orders from Willcox, who enjoyed temporary authority over the First Division, to make a connection with his own division's right. Barnes's 521 men began to shift as directed, while Lt. Col. Gilbert P. Robinson, leading White's Second Brigade, moved up to replace Barnes. "I now received the order to advance," reported White, who sat astride his horse, waving his felt hat and shouting encouragement to the cheers of his men.[100]

That advance brought them in contact with Weisiger's brigade. The Virginians had marched into a clearing northeast of Globe Tavern, joined by perhaps 150 of Colquitt's men but isolated from any further support. Mahone had dispatched two members of his staff to request that Hill order Heth to extend to the east to support Weisiger. Neither of these men completed this mission, which was a fool's errand in any event, as Heth's two brigades had all they could do to deal with Willcox. Mahone then rode to Hill's headquarters as Weisiger found his men threatened from three directions. "This body of the enemy . . . was so large that my brigade, which had been very much depleted in the recent battle of the Crater, was overlapped on both flanks," wrote Weisiger. Barnes was now directly south of the Virginians, Robinson to their east, and Hartranft, who had shifted to within seventy-five yards of Barnes's left, to the west.[101]

Weisiger arranged his men, some of whom were standing in a ditch up to their knees in water, in a horseshoe-shaped deployment. "We soon became heavily engaged with this large force of the enemy," wrote the brigade commander. "The position of things was so serious that there was fear that the enemy would charge and capture the whole command." The compact Confederate formation stretched only seventy-four yards across. "The speedy capture of the whole of Mahone's old brigade never seemed so apparent to the rank and file of his command," remembered the color-bearer of the Twelfth Virginia. To make matters worse, some of the men kneeled or sat in the watery ditch to shield themselves from Union fire, ruining their ammunition. The hard-pressed Weisiger now dispatched a staff officer to inform Mahone that he was practically surrounded. That officer, mounted on Weisiger's own horse, encountered one of Mahone's staff, who mercifully conveyed the division commander's permission

The Battle of Weldon Railroad, August 18–19

to withdraw. Taking advantage of a temporary lull in the fire, Weisiger quietly pulled back into the piney woods, regretfully abandoning his dead and wounded and leaving sixty prisoners in Federal hands. "General Weisiger handled his brigade with great skill in its exceptionally critical position," wrote an admiring member of the brigade.[102]

With Mahone's provisional division in retreat and Christian's brigade driven back by Hartranft, the only Confederates still on the field belonged to Davis, whose men still clung to the works that Hayes had abandoned astride the railroad. Colonel Winthrop received orders to re-form his men and "move forward rapidly and endeavor to retake our old line of works." The brigade pushed ahead on both sides of the tracks and succeeded in recapturing their lines, Winthrop losing a horse and more of his men in the process. "After I had retaken the works I rode along the line [apparently on a new mount] with my staff & the entire command rose up waived their hats & gave three cheers for Colonel Winthrop," he informed his brother. "It was the highest compliment I ever rec'd."[103]

Winthrop's self-satisfaction proved short lived. Heth resumed the offensive, possibly as a stratagem to cover the withdrawal of Colquitt and Clingman, whose massive captures slowed their progress back toward the permanent Confederate works. "About 7:30 P.M. the enemy attacked my line on the right of the railroad, but were handsomely repulsed," reported Winthrop. "Again they attempted to force my position, but with no better success." Despite their ability to hold the line, Winthrop's men suffered additional losses and grew exhausted as the gathering gloom darkened the battlefield. "I sent for reinforcements to make sure of my position," the colonel admitted.[104]

Charles Griffin answered this call. He dispatched his First and Third Brigades, led by Colonels Tilton and Gwyn respectively. Gwyn's troops never became engaged, but the 187th Pennsylvania, some 500 strong, led Tilton's reinforcements to the front. The Pennsylvanians filed in on the right of the 5th New York in "magnificent style" and helped blunt the third and final assault by Heth's battle-worn veterans, a contest that lasted half an hour. "At 8:30 P.M. the enemy withdrew and quiet reigned along my lines," wrote Winthrop. Ninety minutes later he withdrew all his troops east of the tracks, their place taken by the rest of Tilton's brigade. Winthrop left the 140th and 146th New York in the trenches on the railroad's west side.[105]

Meanwhile, the last of Parke's divisions arrived on the field. Robert Potter's two brigades had been relieved by Mott during the morning, but the challenge of swapping places in the flooded works and the sloppy roads that had similarly inhibited White's movement greatly delayed their progress. "The rain poured in torrents nearly all day," complained a soldier in the 36th

Massachusetts, "and the men were thoroughly drenched. The route was circuitous, and we marched nearly six miles over very bad roads." Potter's troops finally arrived near the Aiken house just before Mahone's men began their withdrawal. Major Roebling had ridden to a point where he could see the hard-pressed Virginians and thought they looked "pretty demoralized." He urged Potter to marshal his two brigades for an immediate attack, but the division commander "did not seem inclined to believe it." Only after dark did Potter move up to close the gap between White and the Union works to his right. "Owing to the storm, the darkness, and the low, dense undergrowth, we were unable to advance beyond a short distance," wrote one of Potter's soldiers, "and remained through the night in this position, widely deployed in the dense wood without intrenchments or fires. . . . It proved to be one of those cheerless, dismal nights, of which we had experienced so many." Hartranft advanced to close a gap on Crawford's right, and after dark White connected with Hartranft. During the night, the troops strengthened the earthworks and received fresh supplies of ammunition. "Our men lay all night on their arms and a continual fire between the pickets was kept up all evening," wrote Doctor Silas Stevenson of the 100th Pennsylvania. Over on Crawford's front, some of the men cut small poles and used them as beds to avoid sleeping on the swampy ground. "The tediousness of this dark, dreary night, was enlivened by a man from each alternate company firing every ten minutes," remembered a member of the 97th New York.[106]

Meade had not visited the battlefield since his afternoon excursion, but Warren apprised him of the Confederate breakthrough and the subsequent counterattack. "I am delighted to hear the good news you send," replied Meade, "and most heartily congratulate you [and] your brave officers and men on your success. It will serve greatly to inspirit the whole army, and proves that we only want a fair chance to show our capacity to defeat the enemy." Meade dutifully passed along the news to General Grant, who remained at his City Point headquarters that day. "I am pleased to see the promptness with which General Warren attacked the enemy when he came out," Grant replied. "I hope he will not hesitate in such cases to abandon his line and take every man to fight every battle, and trust to regaining them afterward." This muted criticism found its origin in Warren's habitual caution—a tendency he exhibited on August 19 by retaining Griffin's and Willcox's divisions in reserve most of the day. Meade answered with a prediction that Warren would be attacked again in the morning. The lieutenant general then suggested reinforcing Warren and Parke with Mott's division, reasoning that the only initiative the Confederates were likely to venture would be an attempt "to dislodge our troops from the railroad. I will bring Hancock back to-morrow night, and then the Tenth Corps will relieve the Eighteenth, giving us more troops foot-loose." Meade objected, explaining that removing Mott would leave only Parke's division of U.S. Colored Troops, whom Meade distrusted, to guard critical portions of the line. "Warren, with his own corps and the two divisions of the Ninth Corps, [Meade strangely ignored Potter's arrival] ought . . . not only [be able to] maintain his lodgment on the railroad, but should be able to drive the enemy into his fortifications." He had proposed this idea to Warren but decided to allow the Fifth Corps commander to exercise his own judgment "dependent on the temper of his men." Meade also advised Grant that it would be better to send the Tenth Corps to relieve Mott because the Eighteenth Corps was familiar with the ground they currently occupied. This correspondence underscored Grant's practice of providing Meade significant discretion in positioning and employing his troops.[107]

Confederate forces were also active that night. Rooney Lee's cavalry division crossed the pontoon bridge at Chaffin's Bluff, stopping for a rest along Swift Creek, about four miles north of Petersburg. "Considerable rain fell during the evening and through the night, and having no tents we were soaked and made very uncomfortable," recalled Private Curtis of the Second North Carolina Cavalry. Beauregard ordered Hill to place the arriving cavalry in the trenches "and use your infantry thus relieved to aid you in your effort to dislodge the enemy from his position on the railroad. The prompt dislodgment of the enemy is of the highest importance."[108]

Thus, both sides prepared to assume the offensive on the morning of August 20. In the meantime, Union officers began compiling reports documenting the human toll exacted by the day's engagement, while their counterparts in gray formulated their own estimates. Warren tallied a grand total of 2,900 losses for the day, of which 2,518 were missing and assumed captured. These numbers did not include casualties in Willcox's division. Humphrey counted 53 losses in his brigade. Hartranft did not report his casualties, but a diarist from the Thirty-Seventh Wisconsin recorded 10 of the regiment's men killed or wounded and 50 taken prisoner. If that number is representative of losses throughout the brigade, Hartranft's total would approach 300. It is safe to say that the Army of the Potomac suffered in excess of 3,000 casualties on August 19.[109]

The Confederates failed to compile a comprehensive casualty list for August 19, but the leading expert on the battle, John Horn, has carefully estimated that fewer than 600 Rebels were killed, wounded, or captured that day. Many sources, however, boasted about the huge volume of prisoners seized by Heth and Mahone. "The enemy was severely chastised," crowed a Georgia newspaper, "losing two thousand two hundred prisoners and a large number of killed and wounded. . . . Vast quantities of knapsacks, oil cloths, small arms, and plunder of all kinds were thrown away by the Yankees, much of which fell into the hands of our men." Beauregard and others more accurately tallied the number of Union captives as between 2,700 and 3,000.[110]

Capt. Francis Marion Coker, a Georgia artillerist, was in Petersburg as the Union prisoners began filing into town. "I looked out & concluded Grant's army was in reality entering Petersburg," he wrote his wife, "and so it proved at least a big hunk of it, but they were under rebel bayonets. The street was full for ¾ of a mile. . . . The number of prisoners taken was greater than the number of men we had engaged." Repeating a common Confederate trope, Coker believed that many of the captives were, in fact, deserters and "were mostly foreigners and nearly all drunk."[111]

An entirely sober captive from Hartshorne's brigade remembered being ushered into an open field near Petersburg, where the prisoners were searched for anything of value "such as watches, knives, razors, shelter tents, and wearing apparel," being told that if they were not relieved of these items there, they would be confiscated once the men reached prison. On August 20 these unfortunates were marched through Petersburg to reach trains that would take them to Richmond. Pvt. Charles B. Golden of the 191st Pennsylvania reported: "We were cursed and abused to such an extent we could hardly stand it. The women and little boys ran along and threw stones at us." Private Crocker described being sent to an island in the Appomattox River and relieved of all valuables, then marched on the turnpike toward the Confederate capital. "It was raining hard at this time, and we went 'on to Richmond' in a style that was anything but pleasant to me. It soon became the darkest night and muddiest road I had ever contended with. . . . Virginia mud was the stickiest substance I ever tried to walk through, but this road did beat all."[112]

Those soldiers engaged on August 19 who survived the fighting without injury or incarceration rested uneasily that sodden night, while their commanders planned the morning's operations. The outcome of Grant's Fourth Petersburg Offensive remained very much in doubt.

　　　　　The Battle of Weldon Railroad, August 18–19

four

A PRETTIER FIGHT
I NEVER SAW

The Battle of Weldon Railroad, August 20–21

The August 19 combat along the Weldon Railroad had barely subsided when Gouverneur Warren described the day's results in a message to George Meade. "I find my losses in prisoners have been very considerable," wrote the Fifth Corps commander. "Nearly all the Pennsylvania Reserves are missing and a great many in the other brigades of General Crawford. Ayres has lost very heavily and General Hayes is missing." Warren mitigated such grim news by assuring the army commander: "We have possession of all the ground fought over, numerous prisoners, and two stands of colors. . . . The enemy fell back from our attack to-night in confusion, and if the troops had only held against the flank attack they could have stood it." Meade relayed to Ulysses Grant an earlier report from Warren that outlined the recapture of the lost ground, prompting the general-in-chief to wire Henry Halleck in Washington. "A heavy fight took place, resulting in the re-establishment of our lines and the capture of a good many prisoners," explained Grant to the army chief of staff. "We also lost considerably in prisoners."[1]

The Northern press, which closely followed events in the Virginia Theater, also acknowledged the huge volume of casualties sustained by Crawford's and Ayres's divisions but generally applied a positive spin to the day's engagement. "Our losses at the fight at the Weldon Railroad on Friday afternoon, were greater than heretofore reported," admitted the *New York Times*. "The enemy, however, suffered worse than we did . . . his men lying thick over the field." The Ninth Corps participants harbored no mixed feelings about the battle. General White issued General Orders No. 43, praising his division for its "steadiness and gallantry" when moving forward to the attack after a fatiguing march. Captain Richards of General Willcox's staff thought that his division's performance on August 19 compensated for the criticism it had received following the Battle of the Crater. "We covered ourselves with glory and wiped off for the whole corps any stain of the 30th," he wrote.[2]

Soldiers from the Fifth Corps were not nearly as enthusiastic. Col. Thomas F. McCoy of the 107th Pennsylvania, for example, deemed the fighting on August 19 "disastrous" and confessed that "there was controversy, inquiry, and no little swearing amongst superior officers in reference to this disaster." Those officers included Colonel Comstock of Grant's staff, who characterized the day's outcome as "disheartening & disgusting. The enemy do not attack strongly and yet it seems as if we were worse, feebler than they."[3]

Warren unveiled his candid analysis and emotions in a letter to his wife on August 20. "The command being taken in rear gave up easily and in the woods as they were[,] commands could not be given in [time]. We fought them heavily for about two hours and drove them all back but I have been unhappy ever since at the loss. . . . I feel so dissatisfied with the result and yet I find no special fault with my command." Others, however, did find ample room for criticism. "The position was faulty," wrote Theodore Lyman. "Warren should have corrected it, and Meade should have known it." Cpl. Isaac Hall of the Ninety-Seventh New York blamed Crawford for the huge volume of casualties suffered by his division. "Thus was lost from Crawford's division nearly 2,000 prisoners and a considerable number from General Ayres's . . . for the want at the front of a commanding officer with a clear head who could have momentarily devised a plan for the entire division, or the right wing of it to act in concert in carrying out an order similar to that inaugurated by Colonel Wheelock, and the escape of Mahone's command would simply have been impossible." Hall accused Crawford of being "insensible through the influence of liquor," although no one else ascribed his lapses to drink.[4]

Confederate assessments of the day's events were mixed. "The result of the attack is highly satisfactory to the officers in command," reported the *Richmond Daily Dispatch*, "and is viewed in the most favorable light. The enemy . . . is demoralized by his defeat . . . his prestige is gone, and he will not offer the front he has shown during the last few days." Georgia's *Athens Southern Banner* agreed that "the enemy was severely chastised" but admitted that the battle "resulted in no material advantage as far as position was concerned." Sgt. Maj. Joseph E. Folkes of Weisiger's Forty-First Virginia concurred. "The Brigade goes back to its place on the line of battle the same night, having accomplished nothing in my judgment."[5]

Rebel critics frequently cited a lack of manpower to explain the barren results of August 19. "This was but one of many occasions where a telling blow was not given for the want of a few brigades at the right time," thought Colonel Stewart of the Sixty-First Virginia, "and no one regretted more than Mahone the loss of this splendid opportunity." Pvt. D. Ridgeley Howard of the Second Maryland Battalion saw things the same way. "The Confederates captured over two thousand and seven hundred prisoners, but had not the force to support or push the advantage gained," he wrote. "Grant's 'process of attrition' had begun to tell." There were some recriminations among the Confederates. General Weisiger believed that if his brigade "had not checked and finally halted the advance of all the Federal forces that attacked it the damage would have been very serious to all of us, as Colquitt's and Clingman's brigades were disorganized," primarily due to the volume of Union captives for which they were responsible. Capt. Eugene Burnett of Colquitt's staff found fault with Clingman's North Carolinians, whom he charged with "lending but little assistance," and with Heth's brigades, who failed "to come up in time."[6]

Tactically, there can be little doubt that the Confederates accomplished a remarkable feat. Five undersized brigades faced thirteen Union brigades and inflicted casualties in a ratio of five to one. Mahone, Heth, Hill, and Beauregard all deserve credit for the conception and execution of such an achievement. But mistakes made by Union commanders contributed to this outcome, perhaps decisively. As General Humphreys would write in his campaign history, "the necessity of remaining stationary, even a single day, in a dense wood like that in which the greater part of General Warren's troops were posted, subjects a command to having some part of it taken suddenly in flank or rear, broken, thrown into confusion, and many of them captured." In fairness to Warren, his instructions directed him to entrench as close to the Confederate line as possible, which he did. Unfortunately for the Fifth Corps, their commander chose to obey his orders by locating his works in thick vegetation, which greatly limited his men's ability to discern or react to an attack. Both Heth and Mahone approached the Federal entrenchments without being detected.[7]

Moreover, Meade and Grant assigned Warren a multiplicity of objectives on August 19. They wanted the Fifth Corps to maintain its hold on the railroad, push forward against the Confederate defenses, and establish an unbroken connection with the Ninth Corps on its right. Although Warren and Crawford failed to position the Iron Brigade in the best position to achieve the desired linkage, the literal accomplishment of that task was beyond the capability of Bragg's small brigade due to the great distance between Crawford's right and the permanent Union works. Warren did err in failing to move Griffin's division forward in support of Ayres and Crawford, particularly after Willcox arrived early that morning to replace it as corps reserve. Willcox did good work when he was finally engaged, but it took too long for his two brigades to join the fray once Mahone made his appearance. Flooded trenches and bad roads delayed the arrival of White's and Potter's divisions. As for Mahone, in hindsight his decision to withhold Weisiger's experienced brigade from the initial attack seems ill conceived. Had the Virginians joined Colquitt and Clingman from the start, perhaps the Confederate sledgehammer might have landed west of the railroad as well, with even more devastating results for Ayres's division. As it was, Weisiger added relatively little to the offensive, his contribution limited to good work covering Mahone's retreat. Colonel Stewart wrote that "with the force of a division at his command no doubt [Mahone] would [have] captured Warren and all his twenty-thousand troops and repossessed the Weldon railroad." This overstates the case, but doubtless, the Rebel attack simply lacked the manpower to accomplish much more than it did. Perhaps Beauregard should have provided Mahone and Heth with additional brigades, but no one on the Confederate side argued that he could have further diminished the thin line of troops guarding the Petersburg defenses without undue risk.[8]

Captain Porter of the Thirty-Ninth Massachusetts aptly summarized the aftermath of the fighting on August 19. "All was joy in the Confederate camp," he wrote. "The Federals had not been driven from the railroad, but a division had been annihilated and another partly destroyed, and Mahone, marching into the lines at Petersburg, was able to present his commander nearly three thousand prisoners . . . and determined that he would attack again . . . and drive the enemy from the place. On our side, our generals were not disposed to loosen their grip upon the road but to hold it at all hazards, and thus, while the one was planning how to retake, the other was strengthening his hold upon the road." Indeed, those were exactly the intentions pursued by Beauregard and Warren on the night of August 19–20.[9]

Yet Warren's two superiors, Grant and Meade, articulated different priorities for August 20. The general-in-chief remained fixated on the primary objective of his Fourth Petersburg Offensive: to weaken the Confederates in the Shenandoah Valley by compelling the return of troops sent there from Petersburg and by preventing further reinforcements for General Early from Lee's army. On the night of the nineteenth, he told Hancock, who was still north of the James with the Tenth Corps and most of his own Second Corps, to keep the enemy there "so occupied that he cannot send off any of his forces." At the same time, Meade sought a knockout blow at Petersburg, encouraging Warren to resume the offensive and drive the Confederates back into their works, with the hope of accomplishing more. But Warren discouraged any notion of attacking and even doubted that he could maintain his position. "I do not think with our present force we can hold a line across where I established the picket-line yesterday," he informed Meade, even though he guessed that the Rebels had retired into their permanent fortifications, leaving only a picket line in his front. This was vintage Warren. At 11:30 A.M. a disappointed and frustrated Meade relayed this message to Grant, "from which you will see all hopes of any offensive movements on his part are at an end."[10]

Grant responded ninety minutes later, apprising Meade that based on Hancock's judgment, which was every bit as risk averse as Warren's, he had given up on any further initiatives north of the James and had ordered Hancock to return to the Petersburg front that night. He also embraced a defensive posture along the Weldon Railroad, telling him that once Hancock crossed the Appomattox, the army commander could summon the Second Corps to support Warren. "If the enemy comes out to attack," explained Grant, "we will have the advantage of position. If they hold their lines only and persist in sending more troops to the Valley we can extend still further." Grant also abandoned the goal of occupying the railroad that he had endorsed the day before. "I am not so particular about holding the Weldon road permanently as I am to destroy it effectually, and to force the enemy to attack us, with advantages on our side," he wrote. To pursue that goal, he ordered 200 railroad workers to report to Warren, men who would "destroy more railroad in a day than a division of troops." Grant's preference for a defensive posture marked a dramatic departure from the offensive mindset he had embraced thus far in the campaign. It would, however, be short lived.[11]

The Confederate high command had no intention of sending more troops west of the Blue Ridge but instead hoped to launch renewed attacks to regain the Weldon Railroad. "General Hill reports enemy still occupying part of the railroad where he is fortifying," Beauregard wrote Lee early on the morning of August 20. "Am endeavoring to make necessary arrangements to dislodge him to-day, if practicable." Apparently, Lee urged Beauregard to employ as much manpower as possible, implicitly recognizing that tactical achievements such as the one just accomplished would not be sufficient to drive the Yankees off the tracks.[12]

Beauregard had already started to marshal additional forces on the night of the nineteenth. He sent orders to Johnson Hagood, commanding a South Carolina brigade in Hoke's Division, to relinquish control to his senior officer and report to A. P. Hill with a brigade from Bushrod Johnson's Division, which defended the trenches on Hagood's left. Johnson was in the habit of relieving a single regiment from each of his four brigades to rest in the rear rather than rotating out an entire brigade. These mixed units were the ones that Johnson sent to Hagood, the heterogeneous commands arriving about 11:30 P.M. at the designated rendezvous near the Lead Works on Petersburg's southwestern fringe. Hagood worked through the night to effect some semblance of brigade organization, then reported to Hill before dawn, awakening the corps commander, who was sleeping in an ambulance. When Hill learned of the makeshift nature of these reinforcements, he told Hagood to return them to their respective brigades, ending Beauregard's hope of using these fresh troops in a renewed offensive.[13]

A single brigade would have been insufficient to resume the attack at dawn, even had Johnson provided one of his cohesive organizations. Hill recognized this and sent orders to Rooney Lee to move to the Davis house before sunrise, in hopes that "we will then be in position to push them again . . . if we can get more troops." Beauregard went about obtaining those soldiers on the morning of the twentieth. He dispatched his aide, Giles Cooke, to Hoke's headquarters with instructions for Hagood's own brigade to report to Hill, its place in the line to be filled by Clingman's bloodied North Carolinians. Major Cooke then proceeded to Johnson's command post with instructions for that division commander to release Ransom's North Carolina Brigade, led by Lt. Col. John L. Harris of the Twenty-Fourth North Carolina, replacing them in the trenches with Colquitt's exhausted Georgians. It took more time than Beauregard anticipated to complete these transfers, Clingman not reporting to Hoke until midafternoon. It was now obvious to him that the opportunity to renew the attack on August 20 had evaporated. "Shall try to attack in the morning with all the force I can spare," he informed Lee.[14]

The Louisiana general spent the rest of the day assembling the nine brigades he would employ on the twenty-first. The remaining three brigades engaged on the nineteenth all swapped places with troops manning the trenches. Weisiger's Virginians replaced Mahone's Florida Brigade, and Heth's two battle-worn units filed into the works held by his other two brigades, the Tar Heels of Brig. Gen. William MacRae and Brig. Gen. John R. Cooke. Brig. Gen. William Kirkland's command of Hoke's Division joined Hagood and Harris on the march. The three brigades of Mahone's Division that arrived from the north side would also participate in the assault. Nathaniel Harris was too sick to lead his Mississippians, so Col. Joseph M. Jayne, commander of the Forty-Eighth Mississippi and the antebellum chairman of the Mississippi Democratic Party, replaced him. The Georgians of Wright's Brigade advanced under the temporary leadership of Col. William Gibson. Sanders's Alabamans rounded out the division's fresh manpower. "Expect to attack early in the morning," Beauregard assured Lee that evening. "No available force shall be left behind." The units occupying the fortifications east and south of Petersburg stretched out to cover any gaps created by the departure of this new strike force. Efforts also began to call on all able-bodied reserves and militia to report to the front.[15]

Beauregard and Hill organized this patchwork aggregation into provisional divisions. Heth retained control of Cooke's and MacRae's troops and added Ransom's of Johnson's command and Kirkland's of Hoke's Division. Two four-gun batteries from Pegram's Battalion would join Heth. Mahone resumed command of his four brigades—Gibson's, Sanders's, Jayne's, and Brig. Gen. Joseph Finegan's Floridians—as well as Hagood's South Carolinians of Hoke's Division. Pegram supplied Mahone with a dozen guns.[16]

Hagood's South Carolinians pulled out of their trenches in midafternoon of the twentieth and marched through Petersburg amid a pouring rain. They bivouacked beyond Battery 45, where the old Dimmock Line entrenchments turned from west to north. These 740 officers and men had spent more than two months confined to the trenches, and their commander considered them "sickly and enfeebled" as a result. He obtained a promise from Hill that his men "should not be used in the next day's work, if it could be avoided." Yet once the brigade reached its campground, Hagood noticed a marked difference in their condition and demeanor. "The change from the cramped and noisome trench to the freedom of the bivouac, and the call upon the men for action, instead of endurance, aroused their spirits wonderfully," he thought. The South Carolinians would be ready and able for combat after all. The three brigades of Mahone's Division that returned from the north side of the James River headed southwest around 2:30 P.M. for a bivouac near the Lead Works, a camp sufficiently comfortable to afford Pvt. David Holt of the Sixteenth Mississippi with "a good night's sleep in the open." The Florida Brigade would follow after dark.[17]

Ransom's, MacRae's, Kirkland's, and Cooke's brigades all pulled out of the entrenchments after sunset, maintaining a brisk pace toward the Davis house, scene of such sustained fighting the previous two days. Sgt. Jacob Bartlett of MacRae's Eleventh North Carolina, like Hagood's men, was glad to leave the fetid trenches near the Crater. "After remaining in that place of torment for 14 days we were relieved . . . and started on the march, to we knew not where, it being night time and very dark." But William A. Day, a private in Ransom's Forty-Ninth North Carolina, had a markedly different attitude toward the trek that night. "This was something we didn't like," he explained. "We were perfectly willing to stay in the trenches and fight every day—we were used to that—but to be relieved by troops . . . and sent out to fight what we considered their battle went strongly against the grain." When Day's regiment finally reached the Davis farm, the men formed a picket line at the edge of a swamp and with their bayonets dug rifle pits, each large enough to hold four men.[18]

The final components of Beauregard's strike force came, at Lee's sugges-tion, from the Third Corps division of Cadmus Wilcox. Once James Lane's and Samuel McGowan's brigades sloshed into the Petersburg works from north of the James, Wilcox released Brig. Gen. Alfred Scales's North Carolinians and a detachment from Brig. Gen. Edward L. Thomas's Georgians to enhance Be-auregard's firepower.[19]

The Confederates devised their plan for the morning assault based on in-formation provided by a distinctly colorful figure. Roger Atkinson Pryor was one of antebellum Petersburg's leading citizens. Boasting a law degree from the University of Virginia, Pryor edited a Petersburg newspaper and gained election to the U.S. House of Representatives in 1859 as an outspoken states' rights Democrat. He resigned his seat in Washington after Lincoln's election and returned to Petersburg, advocating for Virginia's secession. Shortly after the Old Dominion voted to leave the Union, the thirty-three-year-old Pryor received command of the Third Virginia Infantry, only to resign to take a seat in the Confederate Congress. He remained in the legislature for less than a year before accepting a brigadier general's commission, leading a brigade in Lee's army with no more than average competence. When his unit disbanded in 1863, Pryor resigned in disgust, only to volunteer as a courier without formal rank. By the summer of 1864, he spent his time as a scout, and Beauregard utilized him in that capacity on August 20. Pryor, who knew the countryside intimately, scaled a tall tree behind Confederate lines and surveyed the Union deployment. He discerned that the Federal left was vulnerable—being refused, he thought, for only a short distance. Mahone, to whom Beauregard and Hill entrusted the impending assault's tactical details, quickly decided that this was the position he would assail. Heth would, once again, move his troops down the railroad in what he considered an attack "subordinate" to Mahone's. As it turned out, Pryor's intelligence was grossly inaccurate, and the Confederates would pay the price for not verifying his faulty report.[20]

Rain persisted throughout the evening hours of August 19, soaking Union soldiers who remained in the positions they had occupied at the close of com-bat. "A more disagreeable night than last night could hardly be imagined. It rained [and] stormed and the thunder and lightning were terrible," testified Sergeant Crater. On the morning of the twentieth, "the boys were all worn-out, cold, wet, and hungry," wrote a soldier in the Fourteenth U.S. Infantry. "The pits are full of mud and water," conditions that the brief appearance of the sun shortly after dawn did little to alleviate. To make matters worse, some of the Confederate dead had not yet been buried, "not a pleasant sight, especially when one realizes how soon they will share the same fate." One of the slain Rebels

The Battle of Weldon Railroad, August 20–21

had on a "splendid pair of shoes," remembered this Regular, who needed new footgear very badly but could not "muster courage enough to take them from him. My term of service is too short for me to 'step into a dead man's shoes,'" he decided.[21]

There were also live Rebels in front of the skirmish line held by Colonel Dushane's brigade. The Marylanders launched a surprise assault that dispersed these Confederates, also from Maryland, in a brief hand-to-hand contest. Otherwise, only a constant and annoying picket fire broke the morning silence. The working party Grant sent to Warren arrived along with William Stedman's brigade of Gregg's cavalry division. Early in the afternoon, Grant told Meade to send them both south along the tracks, the former to destroy the railroad and the latter to protect the workers, while Kautz's cavalry brigade, under Colonel Spear, ranged south and west on the lookout for grayclad counterparts. Once again Grant altered his objectives, now telling Meade, "I want to hold the Weldon road . . . permanently if easily done." But he was counting on its thorough destruction if it could not be controlled.[22]

The Federals adjusted their lines that morning to improve the likelihood of maintaining their positions. Potter and White moved their divisions forward to create an unbroken front from Willcox's right to the remnants of Bragg's brigade, still clinging to the works near the Strong house. Hartranft advanced a swarm of skirmishers about 200 yards north of the ground they had recaptured the day before and halted when they saw the Confederate picket line. In the meantime, Colonel Humphrey dispatched a detail to gather up the arms and accoutrements that remained on the battlefield. Some were found where Crawford's men had left them, neatly stacked with cartridge boxes, cap boxes, and canteens hanging over the muzzles. The Twentieth Michigan had already scooped up many of these abandoned weapons and stood along the line, each man with as many as six loaded rifles at the ready.[23]

General Warren spent part of the morning making a thorough inspection of the Federal dispositions and concluded, wisely, that despite the adjustments, the current configuration could not be safely maintained. At 10:00 A.M. he ordered his engineers to lay out a new line of entrenchments in the open, closer to Globe Tavern, with clear fields of fire for his infantry and artillery. He would make sure that his right firmly connected with Mott's division and refused his left to thwart any assault emanating from the west. The new works east of the railroad would follow a slight crest running east to west from the Dunlop house to the Lanier house, some 300 yards north of Globe Tavern, and then link snugly with Mott. Warren may have rejected offensive action that day, but these steps demonstrated that he knew how to correct the previous day's faulty deployment.[24]

The Ninth Corps, General Parke once again present and in command, withdrew to this new latitude around noon, the first to do so. Sgt. Stephen Rogers of Potter's Thirty-Sixth Massachusetts had just completed a letter to his parents when the order to realign began to circulate. "I have just finished throwing up breastworks," he wrote the home folks. "This is the third one I have thrown up since five o'clock last night and had to leave them . . . and the prospect is now that we shall have to leave this one." Potter's brigades remained on the right, where in the morning they had connected with Bragg's two isolated regiments, the Seventh Indiana and Seventh Wisconsin. White formed on Potter's left, with Willcox on White's left, Hartranft's brigade some 400 yards east of the railroad. Parke left a strong force on the entrenched picket line in front of the corps.[25]

The Fifth Corps was also on the move. The skeletal remains of Crawford's division began the day east of the railroad, with Lyle's brigade snuggling up against Willcox. They fell back to the fields surrounding some of Wainwright's guns and built a line of works that a soldier in the Thirty-Ninth Massachusetts considered "heavily made and quite impracticable for an assault in front." Lyle's brigade remained on the right of Wheelock's. Hartshorne's brigade, which had suffered so severely in prisoners on the nineteenth, ceased to exist as an operational organization.[26]

Another brigade disappeared from the table of organization that morning. Ayres's Third Brigade, the Fifteenth New York Heavy Artillery, was consolidated into the First Brigade, still under the direction of Colonel Winthrop. The First Brigade and Dushane's Maryland Brigade remained on the front line west of the tracks until evening, when they withdrew about 700 yards to the crest of a gentle slope in a large open field northwest of Globe Tavern. Dushane remained on the left of Winthrop in this new position.[27]

Before Ayres's men retired, they received help on their left from Bragg's brigade. The Westerners vacated their positions east of the railroad—including the two regiments stranded to the right of the Ninth Corps—and crossed the tracks, digging a line of works that refused Ayres's left flank. Hofmann's brigade formed on the left of Bragg, thus reuniting Cutler's division, the two brigades abutting one another near the Blick house.[28]

William Tilton's brigade of Griffin's First Division withdrew from the front lines around noon, the men joining the rest of their comrades west of the tracks in the positions they had occupied on the eighteenth. Like so many others, they had been soaked to the skin, and some of the soldiers took advantage of their new location to dry their clothes, although they, too, provided a detail of men for picket duty near Vaughan Road.[29]

The rest of Griffin's division extended their trenches farther south to a point well below Globe Tavern. The north end of these west-facing works rested several hundred yards behind Cutler's line, slightly overlapping the Fourth Division's left flank about one-quarter mile west of the tracks; it was this line that Pryor failed to detect. All the Union soldiers praised the strength of their new works, which now offered no exposed flanks or gaps such as the ones exploited by Mahone the previous day. The Federal defenders enjoyed large fields of fire and plenty of artillery support. In many places a slashing of abatis, enhanced with tripwires fabricated from vandalized telegraph lines, fronted the trenches. Although the pickets remained in their entrenched positions after dark, the Federals destroyed the rest of their old fortifications to deny them to the Confederates.[30]

The rain, which had been intermittent during the day, continued into the evening, leaving the Federals wet and miserable, even if much more secure from Rebel attacks. "Rain Rain Rain," read Tilton's diary. A few members of the Iron Brigade somehow managed to obtain a supply of whiskey and assuaged their unhappy condition by getting thoroughly drunk. "I hope there will not be much of it get into the ranks," growled Sgt. William R. Ray of the Seventh Wisconsin, "for if we have to fight tomorrow we want all [to be] sober."[31]

And fight they would, Beauregard would see to that. The Louisianan remained in overall command of the impending Confederate offensive, establishing his command post near the Lead Works, while Hill would coordinate the two provisional divisions of Heth and Mahone. General Lee arrived from the north side to observe the action from the vicinity of the Davis house, although as was the case a few days earlier at Fussell's Mill, he would exercise no specific influence on the conduct of the battle.[32]

General Hagood aroused his brigade at 2:00 A.M. August 21 and had them on the march ninety minutes later. The South Carolinians followed Halifax Road south to its intersection with Squirrel Level Road, which coursed a bit west of south until it intersected an east–west byway that led to a country meetinghouse called Poplar Spring Church. The rain that had plagued the soldiers during the previous days finally eased as Hagood's soggy soldiers halted to await the arrival of Mahone's brigades. The members of those units also awoke well before dawn. They traversed Halifax Road to its junction with Vaughan Road near the Davis house. Like Squirrel Level Road farther west, Vaughan Road ran southwest, though much closer to the railroad.[33]

Private Holt was upset that the march began before he could consume his breakfast of "mush and a little drink of sassafras tea." Nevertheless, he described

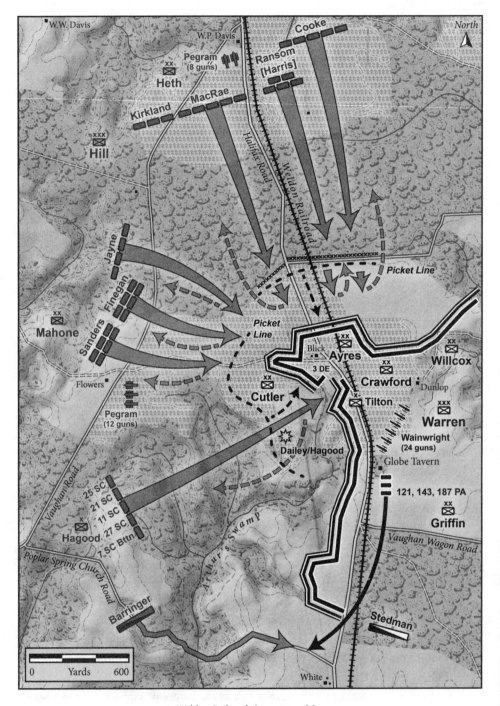

Weldon Railroad, August 21, 1864

his company of only twenty-one men as "a cheerful lot of ragged dirty, wild ruffians." Some 900 soldiers of the Mississippi brigade remained on picket duty either north of the James or outside the Petersburg trenches, which helps explain the company's reduced size, a handicap common to all of Jayne's depleted regiments this day. "Where do you think we are going?" asked one of the Mississippians. "We are going down the creek on a fish fry," a sarcastic comrade responded. "General Lee, as a mark of esteem, is giving us a little outing." Instead of attending a picnic, the brigade received orders to halt and lie down along the side of the road, where the mud further soiled their well-worn uniforms, causing one of Jayne's men to suggest that the middle of the byway would have been a drier place to rest. "He was told to apply for the job of instructing Lee and was assured of being able to put Lee wise to some of the tricks the general never knew," Holt wryly observed.[34]

Another member of the Sixteenth Mississippi, Pvt. Thomas T. Roche, remembered, "After having formed we moved forward under the guidance of an ex-general, who was at that time acting as an independent scout," clearly a reference to Roger Pryor. "It was said that he knew every foot of ground in the vicinity, and also the position occupied by the enemy." Soon enough, no scout would be required to locate Warren's men, waiting in their new entrenchments.[35]

Heth's provisional division faced a shorter trek to its jump-off positions astride the railroad near the Davis house. Thus, it was not until sunrise that his four brigades began their approach. They all followed Halifax Road adjacent to the railroad, Cooke's Brigade covering about two miles, while Colonel Harris with Ransom's Brigade traversed a shorter distance. These men, too, endured the heavy morning rain that left behind a blanket of dense fog. By 7:00 A.M., MacRae's North Carolinians had formed on the west side of the railroad along with Kirkland's brigade, while Harris deployed east of the tracks, with Cooke's men in support on his left and rear.[36]

Rufus Barringer's troopers of Rooney Lee's division were in the saddle by 3:00 A.M. and trotted down Vaughan Road to take position on Mahone's right. Pegram also followed that well-trod roadway, dropping off eight of his guns around the Davis house and continuing south to unlimber the remaining dozen pieces near the Flowers house in support of Mahone. The Confederates now waited until the fog cleared to begin their attacks.[37]

Warren arose early on August 21, firing off messages to army headquarters confirming the casualties on August 19 and describing the arrangements he had completed before daybreak. "Yesterday I disposed my command on three sides of a parallelogram with a view to prevent the possibility of being turned," he informed Meade. "The whole command is about here in the space of a little over a square mile." He then indulged his penchant for offering unsolicited advice by suggesting how best to position the two divisions of the Second Corps en route from Deep Bottom, whom Lyman admiringly called "Hancock's cavalry." Warren proposed that these welcome reinforcements march to a point "a little northeast of the Aiken house." Meanwhile, Major Roebling passed the early morning hours riding casually along Potter's line, helping Warren locate the optimum connection between Parke and Hancock. "Everything bid fair for a quiet day in the morning," thought Roebling, while even then, Pegram's guns roared into action.[38]

The eight pieces near the Davis house fired first, triggered by the fog's dissipation, which permitted the gunners a view toward the Federal lines. Private Walters of Grandy's Virginia Battery, one of the units unlimbered around the Flowers house, wrote that his battery received orders "to listen for the sounds of battle and open on our line at the same time," leading to a period of anxious waiting until "about nine o'clock, when the rumble of artillery on our left told that the issue was being joined. We immediately opened with a heavy fire." Pegram, who superintended the eruption of these batteries along Vaughan Road, ordered the cannoneers to cut their fuses to one second, testifying to the proximity of their guns to the Union lines.[39]

General Ayres's pickets had been driven in by Heth's skirmishers just prior to the bombardment. So severe was the artillery fire that Ayres estimated he faced forty Confederate cannons. Colonel Wainwright's belief that merely twenty-four guns opposed him was more accurate, but he admitted that whatever the number, "a very ugly cross-fire" was the result. "Our guns at once opened in reply," wrote the artillery chief. Some of Pegram's fuses failed to ignite, turning shells into solid shot, a less effective antipersonnel round. Nevertheless, enough explosions occurred to persuade the troops on the east side of the tracks, including Willcox's men, to avoid the incoming projectiles by hopscotching across their works to the opposite side. "Had the enemy thrown shell their bombardment would have been murderous," thought a man in the Thirty-Fifth Massachusetts, not realizing that Pegram intended just that. As it was, many rounds bounced and rolled without igniting, creating some grim amusement for soldiers in White's division. These men could see the cannonballs as they hurtled toward them, leading to "some remarkable dodging . . . and more than one roar of laughter arose at some quick movement on the part of an officer or man to escape the cold iron." Wainwright took perverse pleasure in observing the discomfiture of the habitual skulkers, who fled from peril whenever possible. "This time they were fairly caught, for the provost guard kept them on the plain, while the shot coming in three directions prevented every cover from being perfectly safe. . . . I saw lots of them actually lying half buried in the mud," he wrote. Roebling neither showed the white feather nor played a game of dodgeball but found himself exercising "the utmost agility" to avoid being struck by a projectile, the air "seeming alive with cannon balls." A gunner in the Ninth Massachusetts Battery admitted that his battery was "catching it from the front, on our left, and almost in our rear so you can imagine what a tough place we were in."[40]

Most Federals, of course, found the bombardment less than entertaining. Capt. George Breck of Battery L, First New York Light Artillery called the engagement "one of the hottest and severest" he had ever experienced. "How [his battery] escaped with so few casualties when it was exposed to a terrible fire from rebel batteries on all sides, is a wonder." One of his gunners, Pvt. Alfred Wood, fell dead when a shell fragment struck him in the back of the head. Another shot exploded at the foot of Pvt. Henry W. Sherman, the concussion alone disabling him, while a fragment of the same round claimed an eye from Pvt. Charles Brown. Colonel Dushane was the most prominent victim, decapitated by a solid shot "whilst in the active discharge of his duties." Colonel Graham assumed command of the Maryland Brigade.[41]

Both sides found it difficult to shift their ordnance into more advantageous positions as the fire and counterfire found their targets. With each discharge, the gun carriages sank a little deeper into the "sacred soil" of Virginia, saturated as the ground had become from the recent rains. "Orders were given to commanders, if obliged to fall back, to spike their guns, as it would be impossible to move" them, wrote a Massachusetts man. The sound of this iron duel reached Meade's headquarters, prompting him to wire Warren: "We hear heavy firing in your direction. What is the condition of affairs?" The general replied thirty minutes later, explaining that his pickets had been driven and that the Confederates had "opened with artillery, but his firing is from points where he cannot see." Apparently, this message failed to reach the army commander, who dispatched another missive at 9:30 A.M. "What is going on?" Meade demanded. The cannonading was audible as far as City Point. Grant sent Meade a note inquiring if what he was hearing came from Warren's front. If so, he characteristically suggested that other corps along the line probe the Confederate works to search for a weakness.[42]

Before any such orders could be transmitted, Mahone launched his attack. He assigned three of his own brigades for the task, with the Floridians and Alabamans in front and Jayne's Mississippi brigade in support behind Finegan's left. Mahone aligned his front to face northeast, believing that by doing so he would strike the Federal left flank, "crossing their T" and gaining their rear. The

Rebels, arrayed in multiple lines of battle, pushed through the woods that had concealed their deployment and burst out of the trees into the clear, facing a ripening field of corn. This revealed for the first time that the flank they expected to hit did not exist. Unfazed, Mahone adjusted his troops with a slight right wheel and directed the charge to proceed. He realized now that the Federal left must be farther south, so once he had realigned the attackers, he galloped off to find Hagood in hopes the South Carolinians would locate and turn the true Union left, thus leaving Hill to oversee the main assault.[43]

Finegan, at the head of about 800 men, would be the first to test the Federal defense. His target would be Cutler's two brigades, Bragg's on the right and Hofmann's on the left, both facing west. Two regiments of Graham's Marylanders buttressed the Iron Brigade. Col. David Lang, a native Georgian and prewar surveyor in Suwanee County, Florida, led a consolidated regiment consisting of the Second, Fifth, and Eighth Florida, while Col. Theodore W. Brevard advanced at the head of the Eleventh Florida. They pushed through the cornfield, having dispersed the Federal pickets and enduring a brutal fire from Bragg, Hofmann, and Capt. Patrick Hart's Fifteenth New York Battery. "At 9 A.M. the enemy advanced to attack our works," wrote Colonel Hofmann. "Their line of battle emerged from the wood, about 400 yards in our front, and moved steadily forward through a field of corn to within fifty feet of the works, when it broke." The Floridians, unable to stand such a fierce fire, fled to the rear, hastily passing through the ranks of Jayne's men, who now moved up to continue the assault.[44]

In the meantime, Sanders and his Alabama veterans had gone forward on Finegan's right and engaged the Yankees shortly after the Floridians reached their high-water mark. John Caldwell Calhoun Sanders hailed from Tuscaloosa and had been a student at the University of Alabama at the outbreak of the war. An admiring biographer wrote, "As a son, he was dutiful to an unusual degree; as a boy, self-reliant and manly; as a college student, fruitful and successful." Sanders enlisted in the Eleventh Alabama and in June 1861 was elected captain of Company E. Wounded early the next year and again at Sharpsburg, Maryland, in September, he returned to duty as the colonel of the Eleventh, only to be struck a third time at Gettysburg. Following his recuperation, he assumed command of the brigade formerly led by Abner Perrin and received promotion to brigadier general in May 1864, shortly after his twenty-fourth birthday. Sanders gained universal admiration in the army and is numbered among the best of the "boy generals" in the Civil War.[45]

The Alabamans also forced their way through the head-high corn, reaching to within about 100 yards of the Union works. "The fire poured on our ranks was the most severe of the war," thought Capt. William Fagan of the 8th Alabama.

"The enemy were in three lines, strongly fortified, with scores of guns in position." Lieutenant Colonel Harney of the 147th New York reported "the fire from our works was well directed and delivered rapidly," and the Alabamans wavered before it. General Sanders began walking down his stalled battle line to urge his men forward when a minié ball plowed into his upper thigh, severing his femoral artery. Capt. George Clark, his adjutant general, heard the bullet strike his commander. "As I was close to him I saw him reel, and grasping him around the waist I held him up and asked him if I should go on." Sanders replied, "no, stay with me," and then lapsed into unconsciousness.[46]

Clark corralled two nearby soldiers to assist in removing the general to a place of safety. They managed to carry Sanders about 100 yards to the rear and laid him down beneath a tree under cover of a small streambank. In moments the loss of blood claimed the young general's life. Clark attempted to conceal his demise, knowing that such news would demoralize the men, but the word soon circulated among his troops, who, like the Florida Brigade before them, retreated precipitately for the shelter of the woods, more from the unrelenting Federal fire than from grief over the loss of their commander.[47]

Sanders's body was taken to the home of Bernard Todd in Petersburg, "where it received every attention from the family and other citizens of the place." The next day the remains traveled to Richmond and were buried in a vault at Hollywood Cemetery. Sanders's death did have a profound effect on the men he had commanded. "We had our general killed dead on the field," wrote Pvt. William P. Robuck of the Eleventh Alabama. "We all morne his loss very mutch. I don't think we ever can git another sutch general." The lieutenant colonel of the Forty-First Alabama, Theodore G. Trimmier, wrote home: "John fell gallantly leading his brigade onward. . . . The loss to his friends will be deeply felt & all who knew him are deeply sympathetic with the family. He was a gallant and good officer and our army has lost one of its brightest ornaments." Col. J. Horace King of the Ninth Alabama now assumed command of the brigade. Meanwhile, General Finegan attempted to rally both his own troops and King's to no avail, much to the discomfort of Jayne's brigade, which was now engaged with Cutler's immovable division.[48]

Jayne's 450 men had rushed forward as soon as the Floridians halted and passed among their panic-stricken comrades as they approached the Union line. The Mississippians charged ahead against "a perfect blizzard of lead and iron hail," trying to cover the open ground as quickly as possible. "The hiss of the canister and minies," wrote Private Roche, "with the whir of the grape, as it went tearing, slashing, and cutting through the cornfield, carrying death and agony in its path, made it a perfect hell spot." The battered brigade, now even more reduced in number, reached a small ditch close to the Union works, where the survivors found temporary shelter from the deadly fusillade. Col. Edward C. Councell, commanding officer of the Sixteenth Mississippi, asked one of his men if any reinforcements were heading their way. "We looked over the cornfield," remembered Private Holt. "Not a stalk of corn was standing, and our batteries had ceased firing. We told the colonel that no relief was in sight." Councell, who had sustained a wound that would prove mortal, ordered the display of a white flag. "One of the men possessed a pair of drawers that had a faint resemblance to white," wrote Holt. "Placing them on the muzzle of his gun, he raised it up. Instantly all firing ceased, and the Yanks came pouring over the breastworks." The two regiments on Jayne's left, the Twelfth and Sixteenth Mississippi, were nearly all captured, even as the rest of the brigade attempted to escape. Both regiments lost their treasured battle flags. The brigade suffered 56 percent casualties.[49]

Lieutenant Colonel LaMotte of the Fourth Delaware described the engagement in a fashion emulated by many members of Cutler's division. "On the morning of the 21st the rebels advanced in force on our front & we fired grandly, repulsing them with awful loss to them & capturing several colors & 300 men," he wrote his father. "The field in our front is covered with dead rebels, we removed their wounded." Sergeant Ray summarized matters more succinctly. "We, our division, smashed up the Rebel division pretty well. We have half of them inside our lines." Lt. Col. Richard N. Bowerman of the Fourth Maryland, one of Ayres's units that participated in the fight, remembered the battle similarly, albeit tinged with a Reconciliationist overtone, typical of its postwar pedigree. "Again and again [the Confederates] reformed and pressed gallantly forward to within 30 yards of the works," he wrote. "But bone, flesh and muscle, supported by the most heroic bravery and indomitable courage, were of no avail, and each time they were repulsed with immense slaughter."[50]

Private Roche remembered that as his brigade closed on the Federal works, it came under a crossfire. "They were . . . not only mowing us down from the front, but also pouring a murderous enfilade down both flanks," he wrote. The pressure on their right came from elements of Griffin's division, posted en echelon behind Cutler's left flank. "They evidently supposed that they had struck our extreme left and came confidently on," observed Capt. William Fowler of Griffin's staff. "But they found themselves fearfully mistaken, for a terrible fire of infantry and artillery poured upon them. . . . In five minutes they broke and . . . raised white flags." When some of the Rebels tried to escape once the firing ceased, Cutler's men stopped most of them. "We bagged five or six hundred men and thirty or forty officers, ranking from colonel down," estimated the elated captain, "inflicting a heavy loss in killed and wounded. Our casualties are small. A prettier fight I never saw. . . . I have seldom been so excited, and would not have missed the action for anything."[51]

By this time, Heth had advanced three of his four brigades. "As soon as Mahone opened, I ordered our attack which was made by MacRae, Harris (Ransom's Brigade) and Cooke's in gallant style," he reported. A Georgia newspaper informed its readers that the Confederate battle line spanned both sides of the railroad and "moved forward in beautiful order, and the finest of spirits to the work before them." The men in MacRae's column considered Heth's endeavor merely a demonstration in favor of the "real attack . . . made by a larger force under General Mahone." Nevertheless, they guided along Halifax Road with determination, advancing a wave of sharpshooters to clear out the Union skirmishers, while Pegram's guns continued to fire over their heads.[52]

"After a pretty sharp skirmish," MacRae's sharpshooters scattered the Federal pickets from Dushane's Purnell Legion and Winthrop's 146th New York. As these bluecoats scampered back toward their main line, many of them suddenly tumbled to the ground, victims of the telegraph tripwires strung by their comrades. They quickly recovered and managed to pick their way more carefully to safety, being "greeted with laughter as they approached" the shelter of Ayres's new works. "They, however, were in no mood to enjoy this merriment."[53]

The relatively easy conquest of the Union picket line suggested to MacRae's Tar Heels that they had overrun the primary Union position. On they went through the woods south of the Davis cornfield, but in an instant the Union artillery massed in their front opened a punishing fire. At first the Confederates forged ahead, but soon enough Wainwright's shells took a frightful toll, and the North Carolinians withdrew to the north end of the wood lot, where they remained under cover, fending off a subsequent effort to dislodge them until darkness could shield their withdrawal. "The brigade found itself alone in front of the works," wrote Capt. Louis G. Young, MacRae's adjutant, "too weak to go on and too near to retreat."[54]

Ransom's Brigade, on the east side of the tracks, experienced similar results from its attack. These Carolinians advanced in a double line of battle, the five regiments maintaining intervals that corresponded to their regimental strength. They emerged from the woods and charged forward toward the Federal pickets, who remained in position behind a line of entrenchments. "We threw our guns to a trail and, with our well-known yell, made a dash for their works," remembered Private Day. "Still they stood and looked at us. We knew what it meant; they had the 'white-of-the-eye' order, which meant, 'Don't fire a shot until you can see the white in their eyes.'" The resolute Rebels closed to within twenty-five or thirty yards when the Federal line erupted. "Just as they stooped to fire we dropped as one man, and the whole volley went over our heads," Day continued. "As we fell as one man, we arose as one man, and before they could reload we were in the works among them." Some of the bluecoats surrendered, while others fled to the rear, negotiating a thick line of abatis that remained between the skirmish line and the primary Union entrenchments.[55]

The Tar Heels had more trouble negotiating the abatis than did the retreating Federal pickets. "We then without falt[er]ing crossed the work, and charged through a very bad blockaded way the undergrowth being cut down," wrote Pvt. Garland S. Ferguson of the Twenty-Fifth North Carolina. "The men had to pick their way through the interlaced timbers and advance without regard to company or regimental formations," recalled an officer in the Thirty-Fifth North Carolina. The Confederate momentum ground to a halt as the men became entangled in the obstructions. The color-bearer of the Forty-Ninth North Carolina was among those fighting their way through the tangle of limbs, allegedly prompting the comment from General Lee that "he had often heard of men straggling to the rear, but he had never before seen men straggle to the attack."[56]

Once the North Carolinians conquered the abatis, they sprang into the open ground in the face of the massed Federal guns. "Then it was [that] our brigade suffered so severely," wrote Capt. William H. S. Burgwyn. "It was the hottest place our brigade has ever been," agreed John Lane Stuart of the Forty-Ninth North Carolina. Capt. Robert Graham of the Fifty-Sixth North Carolina offered a colorful account of what happened next. "Now in the face of the foe . . . our line of battle, under the severe punishment it is receiving at short range, staggers and writhes like a monster serpent, mortally wounded, and as if about to snap at every vertibra." The brigade commander, Colonel Harris, understood that remaining in this position risked the very existence of his unit and shouted orders to retreat. In the chaos of the moment, however, only a portion of his men heard those instructions. To make matters worse, Pegram's guns temporarily mistook the withdrawing Carolinians for charging Yankees and claimed a few victims with friendly fire. Like MacRae's troops on their right, Harris's survivors withdrew to the first line of captured Union breastworks to wait out the day.[57]

By the time Cooke's Brigade advanced, the Union pickets had decamped, leaving behind "tent flies, blankets, meat, and even their cooked breakfast," according to Lt. Thomas Jackson Strayhorn of the Twenty-Seventh North Carolina. Cooke's men rounded up some 300 Federals who had surrendered rather than run the gauntlet through their abatis under fire. "As we made the charge, we were exposed to the most galling fire of shells and grape shot I have ever yet experienced," reported Lt. Ignatius W. Brock of the Forty-Sixth North Carolina.

Lieutenant Strayhorn believed that Cooke's men suffered more than Harris's from the Union gunnery, as many of the shells passed over the heads of Harris's men and landed among Cooke's. "I hope I may never be called on to go through just such another firing ordeal while I live," he wrote his sister. "Just at the time I was on top of the works, right and left front and rear were lying the dead and dying, which had been stricken down at the twinkling of an eye and only a few moments before were the very pictures of health." Cooke's survivors, like Mac-Rae's and Harris's before them, retreated. The brigade adjutant, Henry A. Butler, explained the defeat of Heth's attack as a product of the strong Union position, "having had two days to fortify and bring up reinforcements."[58]

A large number of Harris's and Cooke's men joined those in Mahone's attack as prisoners of war. "It was amusing to see the rebels coming running out of the woods after the firing was over, waving improvised white handkerchiefs as a token of surrender," wrote Cpl. Andrew Linscott. As these Rebels capitulated, a contest ensued between Crawford's men and those in Willcox's division as to who would have the honor of bringing them in. "We got the most of them," boasted a sergeant in Crawford's Thirty-Ninth Massachusetts. Those Confederates felled by Union fire made an even greater impression than did the prisoners. "The ground was strewn with their dead and wounded," reported Colonel McCoy. "Within a space of an acre I counted twenty-six dead rebels," explained Pvt. Warren Hapgood Freeman of the Thirty-Ninth Massachusetts. "I went over the field & think next to Gettysburg and Antietam I never saw so many of their dead in the same space," echoed Lieutenant Thomas.[59]

Many of Heth's wounded obtained some manner of transportation to the hospitals in Petersburg. Musician J. Edward Peterson of the Twenty-Sixth North Carolina in MacRae's Brigade was on duty at one of those facilities and was shocked at what he encountered. "The more I see of these horrible sights, the more detestable this war appears to me," he wrote. The case of Pvt. Elbert R. Richardson, in particular, prompted these sentiments. Richardson and his brother, Sgt. Brinkly J. Richardson, both in Peterson's regiment, fell victim to a single Union shell, which killed the sergeant and left his brother with a gruesome head wound. The private was taken to the hospital where Peterson served, and the young musician watched as the doctors "cut his scalp open, & examined his skull & I saw it was full of cracks, like ice will crack if you throw a stone on it." Capt. Henry A. Chambers of the Forty-Ninth North Carolina was on court-martial duty in Petersburg and thus missed the battle. He found an opportunity to visit his injured comrades later that day and thought it "a ghastly sight. Men were lying around wounded in every conceivable form," he confided to his diary. "The wounds being principally caused by shell, were unusually severe." Private Stuart ably summarized the experience of Heth's three brigades on August 21. "We went up before a Yankee battery and they just mowed us down. Some men was all torn to pieces. . . . It looks like we will all be killed and wounded before this war will end."[60]

But the mayhem of August 21—never mind the war—was not over yet. Hagood's Brigade was on the move. These South Carolinians in five units—the Eleventh, Twenty-First, Twenty-Fifth, and Twenty-Seventh South Carolina Regiments and the Seventh South Carolina Battalion—made their way from their reserve position to Vaughan Road, under the direction of a courier sent by A. P. Hill. They marched at double-quick, halting in a field roughly opposite Globe Tavern and screened by a 100-yard belt of woods spanning a swampy streamlet. As the opposing artillery continued their mutual firing over the heads of the Carolinians, Mahone appeared and announced himself to General Hagood. The Virginian personally directed the brigade to a position facing the woods and parallel to the railroad beyond. "Now, you are upon the flank and rear of the enemy," explained Mahone. "I have five brigades fighting them in front and they are driving them. I want you to go in and press them all you can. When you have crossed the branch swamp you will come upon a clearing in which some 300 yards further is the enemy's line, and they are not entrenched." Heeding the Virginian's admonition to act promptly, Hagood gave the order to advance.[61]

Thirty-five-year-old Johnson Hagood had compiled an enviable record thus far in the war. An 1847 graduate of the South Carolina Military Academy—now The Citadel—and an antebellum attorney, Hagood parlayed his generalship in the state militia into an appointment as colonel of the First South Carolina at the outbreak of hostilities. He participated in the bombardment of Fort Sumter in April 1861, was present at First Manassas that July, and a year to the day later, received his promotion to brigadier general. After service in his native state, in the spring of 1864, Hagood led his brigade to Virginia, where in June it played a decisive role in blunting the first Federal effort to capture Petersburg. Giles Cooke considered Hagood "to be not only very brave but very modest at the same time," and the South Carolinian was admired by the men he commanded.[62]

Hagood aligned his brigade with the Twenty-Fifth South Carolina on the left, followed by the Twenty-First, Eleventh, and Twenty-Seventh Regiments, with the Seventh South Carolina Battalion on the formation's right. The Carolinians plunged into the woods that sloped down to the marshy rivulet—a branch of Arthur's Swamp—and emerged into a clearing at the edge of the same cornfield encountered by Finegan, Sanders, and Jayne a few hundred yards to the north. The little valley created by the stream combined with the trees prevented

Hagood from seeing the Federal line in his front. Before entering the open field, the general halted and positioned himself in the center of his troops, who had been disordered by navigating through the forest, as the Federals had felled some of the timber to create an obstruction. While Hagood reorganized his units for the impending attack, a line of skirmishers advanced to the top of the rise. Word filtered back that the Federals occupied mere rifle pits, comporting with Mahone's assurance that the attack would meet limited resistance. Hagood dismounted and led his men forward, moving with members of his staff behind the Twenty-First South Carolina near the brigade's left.[63]

They immediately came under a rapid fire of musketry, prompting the attackers to forge ahead at quick time, gratified to see their assailants fleeing to the rear. The Carolinians shrieked the Rebel Yell and sprinted in pursuit, only to realize that they had merely displaced a lightly defended entrenched skirmish line. The imposing raw earth of the main Federal fortifications now came into view, and much to their dismay, not a man of the five friendly brigades Mahone had referenced was to be seen. Hagood's two left regiments continued forward, aiming for the gap that separated Hofmann's brigade in front from Tilton's brigade positioned en echelon to the left and rear of Cutler's division. Hagood now realized that instead of hitting the Yankee flank, his men were charging a re-entrant angle, meaning that they would be subject to flanking fire on both ends of their line in addition to the relentless hail of iron belching forth from Wainwright's cannons. "We moved off at double quick, running low down and where we charged we moved under a terrible front and flank fire," remembered Pvt. Frederick W. Dantzler, color-bearer of the Twenty-Fifth South Carolina. "I thought the quicker we reached the works the better, but when within thirty yards of the works . . . I saw that everybody behind me was down, so I stuck the flag staff in the ground and dropped to my knees to shoot." A soldier in the Seventh South Carolina Battalion recalled, "The enemy's artillery from the front, right, and left were playing upon us, killing and wounding our men, tearing off the tree tops over our heads and cutting down the corn in front."[64]

The 3rd Delaware, on Hofmann's left flank, had refused its line and thus took dead aim on the 21st and 25th South Carolina as they entered the angle between Cutler's and Griffin's divisions. "Although the 4th Division kept up a murderous fire on them from the time they left the woods while our batteries sent shot and shell ploughing through their ranks they kept right on," wrote Sgt. Charles A. Frey of Tilton's 150th Pennsylvania, "never wavering until they were almost in rear of the 4th Division. . . . But now they found themselves between two fires. Our brigade holding the second line had reserved their fire but now they opened, pouring deadly volleys into the exposed ranks of the enemy."[65]

Hagood now realized that his attack was a forlorn hope and shouted at the top of his lungs for the brigade to halt, but the cacophony of musketry and cannon fire bursting from the Union lines and the furious screaming of both his own men and their opponents drowned out his pleas. With no honorable choice but to share the fate of his troops, Hagood started forward, accompanied by his aide-de-camp, Lt. Ben Martin; his assistant adjutant general, Capt. P. K. Maloney; and his orderly, Pvt. J. Dwight Stoney. The four men had not gone fifty yards before Martin fell, shot in the leg. Moments later Captain Maloney sustained a mortal head wound, and Stoney took a minié ball in the shoulder, continuing to stumble alongside his unscathed chief.[66]

By this time, the brigade's remnants had advanced to within thirty paces of the Union works, but the unceasing hail of musketry halted them in their tracks. The brigade "had been so fearfully cut to pieces that it appeared too weak to advance further with any hope of success and appeared to pause for a few moments." Hagood remained on the left of his broken formation, immediately behind the Twenty-First Regiment, which was seventy-five to one hundred yards north of the remainder of the brigade, still encouraging them and the Twenty-Fifth to maintain the struggle. The general then glanced to his right and saw a mounted Federal officer amid the soldiers of the Twenty-Seventh and Eleventh South Carolina, holding a Confederate banner in his hands.[67]

That officer was Capt. Dennis B. Dailey, the commander of the Wisconsin Independent Battalion, which served as the provost guard for Cutler's division. Dailey, an Irish immigrant, had enlisted in the Second Wisconsin and rose through the ranks to obtain his commission. The twenty-seven-year-old officer saw the paralysis that had overcome the South Carolinians and bravely rode out of the works, snatching a regimental flag from a compliant Rebel color-bearer. Hagood saw this affront to his unit's honor and shouted for the surrounding Carolinians to shoot this brazen Yankee. His troops either could not hear the order or, "bewildered by the surrender of part of their number, failed to obey."[68]

Hagood considered the situation critical and feared that acquiescing in the capture of a treasured symbol of the regiment's history and sacrifice would lead to the wholesale capitulation of that portion of his brigade. The general "hurried like a raging lion" over to Dailey, somehow escaping the continuing Federal fire not thirty yards distant, and demanded that the captain release the flag, promising that his men would not fire upon him if he would agree and return to his own lines. Dailey refused, pointing out that even then Union soldiers were moving behind the South Carolinians, sealing off their avenue of escape. Hagood repeated his demand, which Dailey firmly declined for a second time. At that point in the drama, Hagood, who had drawn his pistol, fired a single round, the

The Battle of Weldon Railroad, August 20–21

bullet entering the right side of Dailey's chest and lodging in a vertebra. Dailey reeled in the saddle, and Hagood leapt upon his horse, Orderly Stoney seizing the flag and tearing it from its staff as the wounded Badger fell.[69]

Hagood now raced to the rear on his newly won mount, urging the remaining soldiers of his brigade to follow him in retreat. The Carolinians rushed through the thin line of Federals who tried to block their withdrawal and made for the cover of the little valley and its sheltering arbor. A piece of shrapnel pierced Hagood's (formerly Dailey's) horse, throwing the general unhurt to the ground but knocking silly an officer from the Seventh South Carolina Battalion.[70]

It was widely assumed that Dailey's wound was mortal, and Northern newspapers characterized Hagood's act as a shameless case of murder. But the captain received prompt medical treatment after being removed from the field and was then sent to Philadelphia to recuperate from an injury that proved debilitating, not fatal. When his survival became a matter of record, Dailey was hailed as a hero and his defiance of the Rebel general deemed "one of the bravest acts of the war in both the North and South!" In an interesting postscript to this celebrated story, Dailey, who practiced law in Council Bluffs, Iowa, after the war, wrote Hagood in August 1879 seeking verification of his wound in support of his application for a disability pension. Hagood was only too glad to oblige, confirming the event and calling Dailey's act "one of the bravest recorded in the annals of war." These two old foes maintained a friendly correspondence for the remainder of their lives, dying within ten days of one another in 1898.[71]

Although the contretemps between Dailey and Hagood provided the most dramatic episode of the South Carolinians' failed assault, for the soldiers in blue and gray locked in that combat, it had little immediate relevance. Hagood's two left regiments had entered the fatal "kink" in the line between Hofmann and Tilton and paid a terrible price for their mistake. "The 25th South Carolina was in our front and was almost annihilated," wrote Capt. Henry Gawthrop of the Fourth Delaware. "But one officer of that regiment survived and he came over the works and surrendered his sword." Colonel Hofmann reported that these two regiments "halted for a moment in the ravine to the left and about 150 yards in rear of our works. Then about one-half of them attempted to retreat." That triggered a renewed volley from the Federals on three sides of the unlucky Carolinians. "I think that of the number that came forward not more than one-fourth regained the woods from whence they had emerged," wrote Hofmann. The conflicting behavior among those Confederates wishing to surrender, those continuing to fight, and those trying to retreat persuaded many of the defenders to hold their fire, unsure of the disposition of the shattered masses before them. "The whole brigade would have been destroyed or captured had not our fire been stopped under the impression they had surrendered," claimed Wainwright.[72]

As it was, the casualties in Hagood's Brigade were enormous. "Of the 59 officers and 681 men who went into action in the brigade, only 18 officers and 274 men came out of it unhurt," wrote Hagood. Union losses were minimal, as the bluecoats fought from behind their works. "Never was an assault more completely repulsed, nor a column of troops more thoroughly shattered," thought one Federal. "The chivalry got sadly used on that day," the quartermaster of the Seventy-Sixth New York informed his parents. "We hope they keep on attacking us," wrote the Sixteenth Michigan's Capt. Charles H. Salter, "for at this rate they will soon use up their army. . . . We feel confident Lee's entire army could not drive us" from the railroad.[73]

Mahone had sent four of his brigades forward during the morning, all of them failing to threaten, much less eliminate, the Union stranglehold on the Weldon Railroad. Undaunted by his defeat, the pugnacious Virginian reexamined the Federal defenses, then approached General Lee, who had observed the debacle from near the Davis house. He appealed to the commanding general for two fresh brigades with which, he assured Lee, he could drive the Yankees away. Lee, who understood that both the immediate danger to Richmond and the opportunity to inflict significant harm to Union forces north of the James had disappeared with Hancock's departure from Henrico County, sent word to Major General Field to forward his remaining brigades from across the river. Beauregard dispatched Major Cooke north of the Appomattox River to Dunlop's Station on the Richmond & Petersburg Railroad to direct these reinforcements to the point of contact. Yet the last of Field's troops would not arrive until 8:00 P.M., and Lee was unwilling to permit Mahone to retest the Federal line without them.[74]

The final spasm of this disastrous Confederate offensive involved the cavalry of Barringer's North Carolina Brigade. Earlier in the day Colonel Spear's Federal troopers had ranged south and west of Warren's position and spotted Barringer's cavalry along Vaughan Road near a home styled "Col. Wyatt's," about two miles south of Globe Tavern. Realizing that he was probably outgunned, Spear rode southeast toward Reams' Station. Barringer took advantage of the opposing cavalry's absence—Stedman's brigade spent the morning guarding the men destroying the railroad south of Globe Tavern—and at midday the Tar Heel horsemen trotted toward the railroad north of Reams' Station. They quickly overran a few Union skirmishers ensconced behind earthworks and charged ahead toward the railroad, the Third and Fifth North Carolina Cavalry in the lead.[75]

The attackers met with a rude shock as they neared the tracks. Three of Tilton's regiments—the 121st, 143rd, and 187th Pennsylvania—had been rushed south after dispensing with Hagood's assault, arriving in time to prepare hasty works near White's farm. "Toward noon I was ordered in a great hurry with three regiments to the left of the 2nd Brigade (Col. Gregory)," recorded Colonel Tilton. "I got into position and entrenched near the RR." The historian of the 121st Pennsylvania recalled, "The regiment was hurried off at a 'double quick' to a point . . . to the left where the enemy were making an effort to get around that flank, but did not persist [up]on finding Union troops already in position behind breastworks." Barringer, seeing the Federal infantry dug in before him and "finding the attack had failed on the part of the infantry," withdrew "under a severe fire & with heavy loss." The Carolinians checked a nominal probe by the Federals and remained out of range until nightfall concealed their retreat toward Confederate lines.[76]

This minor engagement provided something of an anticlimax to the infantry combat that concluded between 10:30 and 11:00 A.M. Warren informed Meade at that hour that he had "just repulsed an attack of Mahone's division from the west of the railroad," adding, "whipped easily." By then, Edward Ferrero's Ninth Corps division of U.S. Colored Troops had arrived to bolster Warren's position, and the two divisions of Hancock's corps from north of the James continued to move in his direction, exhausted as they were by their overnight trek. Grant was, of course, pleased to learn of Warren's success. The general-in-chief, his brief flirtation with defensive strategy at an end, had been urging offensive movements all morning, and at 11:20 A.M. he wired Meade from City Point. "It is hard to say what ought to be done without being on the field," Grant admitted, "but it seems to me that when the enemy comes out of his works and attacks and is repulsed he ought to be followed vigorously to the last minute with every man. Holding a line is of no importance whilst troops are operating in front of it." Meade, agreed, having earlier written Grant that he thought Warren should "punish the enemy severely . . . if we could only get our troops to act with the audacity the enemy show."[77]

Meade then informed his superior: "Warren reports the enemy moving to his left. I have sent him your dispatch, having previously advised him the way to stop the enemy's flanking was to assume the offensive and make him look out for his flanks." The army commander then explained that the poor condition of the roads made it impossible for Warren to move his artillery, accounting for the corps commander's reluctance to assume the offensive. But Meade expressed conditional confidence that Warren's growing force could retain its position "unless the enemy should bring so superior a force as to turn his flank, in which case we cannot get our men to stand. They don't mind [that is, obey] any orders when they find themselves outflanked, but move off bodily to the rear in spite of orders."[78]

Grant, bridling at Meade's apparent unwillingness to order Warren forward, not to mention his expressed lack of trust in the tenacity of his own troops, responded quickly. "If the enemy are moving to turn Warren's left, why cannot he move out and attack between them and Petersburg, and either cut their force in two, or get in rear of it?" he asked, thus invoking the very same tactics employed by the Confederates on August 19. "If the roads are impassable for our artillery it must be so for the enemy's, and it becomes an infantry fight." Meade understood. "Instructions have gone to Warren embodying the spirit of your suggestions," he replied, "that is, to assume the offensive." It took the Fifth Corps commander two hours to answer his boss, acknowledging receipt of the dispatches from Grant and Meade "for my information and guidance"—tellingly, failing to consider them orders. Now, some four hours after the conclusion of Mahone's assaults, Warren still worried about a renewal of the Confederate offensive. "If the enemy attacks me so as to get a crushing repulse, I will take every advantage of it," he promised, limiting any potential aggression to a counterattack. "I believe I have fought against the army opposed to me to know pretty well what to do here on the field. General Parke is now here. He ranks me."[79]

This message captured the essence of Gouverneur K. Warren's combat philosophy as well as his leadership personality. The Fifth Corps commander habitually substituted his own judgment for that of his superiors and frequently failed to attack when circumstances clearly warranted doing so. He had acted similarly as recently as July 30, when he decided against launching a supporting assault in favor of the Ninth Corps. The pique he felt at being prodded to advance against a Confederate force that he had thoroughly defeated is evident in his choice of words. Abdicating responsibility to Parke when every indication from Meade confirmed that the Fifth Corps commander remained in immediate control of events along the Weldon Railroad adds to the indictment of Warren's rhetoric. There would be no Federal attack on August 21, the absence of which greatly distressed the general-in-chief. "I never saw Grant so intensely anxious to do something," wrote Theodore Bowers, a member of Grant's staff. "The failure to take advantage of opportunities pain and chafe him beyond anything that I have ever before known him to manifest." But like Lee, Grant opted not to take a personal role in the conduct of the battle, leaving its direction to his subordinates.[80]

Nevertheless, Warren and the Fifth Corps had achieved a major victory. The rank and file of the corps shared none of the high command's disappointment in their leader's failure to exploit his defensive accomplishment and saw only the acumen of their respected commander. "In the midst of all this fray—there was Genl Warren riding around as cool as if he was inspecting a wheat field," thought one admiring soldier. "He rode as leisurely and calmly as if nothing was the matter, while the shells were knocking stacked muskets sky-high, tearing off legs and arms, and smashing the bodies of the unfortunate victims into unrecognizable masses of blood, flesh, and bones." Another Pennsylvanian thought that Warren had rebounded well from the shellacking he had received on the nineteenth. "He had managed the Weldon Railroad fight with his usual skill, secured almost incalculable advantage, and rendering his holding unassailable," he wrote.[81]

Had Warren and his superiors known the precarious situation prevailing in the Confederate works, they might have tested their luck somewhere along the lines that afternoon. "We have in the trenches now almost every man it has been possible temporarily to place there," explained Pvt. George S. Bernard of the Twelfth Virginia, "the Petersburg Militia, City battalion, men of all sorts and all stragglers that could be brought up." By nightfall, however, the danger had passed. "During the night . . . my troops were withdrawn from the works they had captured, and took position behind our lines defending Petersburg," reported Heth. The battlefield they left behind them made quite an impression. "Major Roebling, who went out . . . in the afternoon, says he never saw anything equal to it," wrote Wainwright, "the whole ground being ploughed up by our shot, while hardly a tree is struck higher up than he could reach on foot."[82]

The human toll exceeded that inflicted on nature. The Confederates suffered some 1,400 casualties on August 21, including more than 500 men captured. "Our loss was principally in Hagood's Brigade," reported General Lee, "which mounted [the] enemy's entrenchments. Supports failing, many were captured." The Forty-Ninth North Carolina's Private Stuart carefully counted 239 losses in Ransom's Brigade, similar to the tally suffered by Jayne's Mississippians. Warren reported 302 Federal casualties during the day, of whom 103 were prisoners. Ayres's and Griffin's divisions accounted for most of those losses. Hartranft suffered 76 casualties, mostly men captured during Heth's attack along the picket line.[83]

It did not take long for various Southern voices to locate the causes of this singular defeat. "Today for the first time in the history of the campaign of the Army of Northern Virginia, the Confederate arms have suffered a check and repulse," opined the *Richmond Daily Dispatch*. The editor went on to explain the origin of this "unprecedented" catastrophe. "In the first place, the enemy were present in overwhelmingly strong force when compared with our numbers. In the second place, they were admirably posted and very strongly fortified. . . . In the third place, to the eternal discredit of one of our brigades, be it said that they broke and ran, and refused to be rallied by their gallant commander, though he did all that a man could do," a veiled reference to the Florida Brigade. Perhaps worst of all, the Confederate intent to attack and the identity of its targets were allegedly known "even to the very urchins of Petersburg. Whose fault it was that these matters leaked out, I do not know," admitted the writer, "but I know that eighteen hours before, the time, place, and character of the fight were on the lips of all, soldiers and citizens."[84]

An Alabama newspaper published a soldier's letter offering a different explanation. "It is plain that there has been mismanagement somewhere," wrote "Muscogee," placing the blame on Robert E. Lee for sending so many troops north of the James. "The bad management consisted in drawing all the forces from the Weldon Road, and leaving it unprotected. Had any other General committed so great a blunder, the whole country would be clamorous against him [but] nobody has ought to say about it, and not a particle of blame is attached to any one."[85]

The Twenty-Fifth South Carolina's adjutant, George H. Moffett, found the cause of the defeat in the failure of Mahone's brigade commanders to support Hagood's attack. "One Brigade goes into a fight as they are ordered & are cut to pieces simply because those who were ordered to move forward with them fail to obey.... Napoleon or Wellington would have shot four Brigade Commanders had either of them been in command of our army on the 21st of Aug." Apparently, Moffett was unaware that the Floridians, Mississippians, and Alabamans had suffered a repulse prior to Hagood's advance. In a memoir written after the war, he modified his views while still believing that the performance of Mahone's attackers "was shameful. The great error was in misunderstanding the position of the enemy." Hagood subscribed to this analysis and assigned responsibility to Hill and Mahone. "A week afterwards, in a conversation in General Lee's presence, General A. P. Hill stated to Hagood that on the morning of the 21st he was informed by his scouts as to the position and condition of the enemy's works, believing that the point upon which Hagood was sent was the left of their line, and that they had no further works down the railroad.... General Mahone also said to General Hagood that he shared the same misapprehension." Hagood was gratified that "these two distinguished officers took the blame of the blunder upon themselves," thus relieving the South Carolinian of responsibility for the worst of the day's disasters. In fact, Beauregard would address a letter to Jefferson Davis, through General Lee, recommending Hagood for promotion, particularly for the celebrated rescue of the captured battle flag. Extolling the general's "act of gallantry," Beauregard declared that such "devotion to one's flag reflects the highest credit on the officer who performed it, and should be held up to the army as worthy of imitation under similar circumstances."[86]

The significance of the August 21 setback also generated diverse opinions. Many Confederates viewed the battle as an abject defeat. "The enemy still hold the road and we have gained nothing by the fight," wrote Pvt. Hall T. McGee, one of Hagood's aides. Edward Peterson, the hospital attendant, heard from the wounded men he interviewed that the battle was a desperate one, but "not any thing accomplished at that, a complete failure." Captain Fagan viewed the outcome more darkly. "Our loss was between 12 and 1800 men," he wrote. "We accomplished nothing. . . . Such 'brilliant' movements as these will so deplete our army that Grant will soon take Richmond." Pvt. Robert C. Mabry of the Sixth Virginia judged affairs in a similar way. "I see no chance to get the enemy off the Road," he told his wife, "as they have a force on the entire line in our front and I much fear Grant will be able to make his lines too long for Lee." Three days later he further explained, "Many lives have been lost in the battles around Petersburg which seems to have resulted in but little good to us . . . and I am one of the few who believe that Grant will if sustained by the Administration at Washington take Richmond." A Texas officer shared Mabry's sensitivity to the battle's influence on Northern politics. "We did not succeed in driving the enemy from off the Weldon R.R & I fear that our losses have been great," wrote Capt. Tacitus T. Clay of the Fifth Texas. "I dislike this at all times but particularly at this junction of affairs—by our successes we are making a peace party at the North and the success of that party is greatly to be desired at this time by all parties at the South."[87]

Other Rebels, however, judged the battle's outcome less gloomily. Lt. John Elmore Hall of the Fifty-Ninth Alabama informed his father that he considered the loss of the railroad to be of no particular consequence, "as I believe Lee fully able to prevent Grant from extending his line further around the city." Lt. Thomas Jewett Goree, an aide to General Longstreet, was in Lynchburg in August tending to his wounded brother. In a wide-ranging letter to his mother, Goree explained that the Federal capture of the Weldon Railroad left Grant "no nearer the capture of Petersburg and Richmond. . . . He will be more exposed to a flank movement from our side, and his line will be so much extended that it may be in our power to break through them and possibly cut off a large portion [of his army] from their base on James River." Likewise, Virginia artillerist Maj. Francis W. Smith wrote his bride the day after the battle: "I argue nothing from Grant's holding the road. We are not dependent on it for supplies and by keeping a force there he so weakens his line that Lee may cut it & do him great harm."

A Richmond newspaper agreed. "The enemy still hold the road, but it will avail them very little," explained the editor. "It may yet be to them a very Pandora's box of evils. At least, so let us hope."[88]

Lieutenant Brock felt that the army "accomplished all that was expected and cannot be blamed" but like other Confederates he understood that "it is important to us that we regain the line of the Weldon Road." A fellow Carolinian, Lieutenant Strayhorn, agreed but understood doing so would be difficult. "I fear it will be some time and at a considerable cost of life before we get them away from it." These officers would have been disappointed had they been privy to Lee's message to Davis the day after the battle. "As I informed Your Excellency when we first reached Petersburg, I was doubtful of our ability to hold the Weldon road so as to use it," he reminded the president. "The proximity of the enemy and his superiority of numbers rendered it possible for him to break the road at any time, and even if we could drive him from the position he now holds, we could not prevent him from returning to it or to some other point, as our strength is inadequate to guard the whole road. These considerations induced me to abandon the prosecution of the effort to dislodge the enemy."[89]

Union reaction to the combat on August 21 revealed none of the ambiguity expressed by Confederates. "We have had a love of a fight today," wrote Wainwright. "For once it was all on our side, everything was well managed, and Lee got a lesson which I guess will keep him from attempting this place again." A soldier in the 140th New York agreed: "It is the best thrashing that they have received in a long time. . . . I think that we have got the place where it will take Lee's entire army to drive us out, and then they can't do it." Cpl. Peleg G. Jones of the 7th Rhode Island summarized the outcome of the day's events in a diary entry. "The rebs fought hard not liking to lose the Weldon Rail Road but they lost it after all & it is a heavy blow for them, as it cut them short of supplies."[90]

Thus ended the Battle of Weldon Railroad and, with it, Grant's Fourth Petersburg Offensive. The casualties during the four days from August 18 through 21 proved staggering. Union losses totaled 4,279 men, all but 610 of them in the Fifth Corps. The First Division was spared serious depletion, Griffin's three brigades losing only 144 men. Bragg and Hofmann lost modestly as well, some 419 soldiers between them, but Ayres and Crawford were not so fortunate. The Second Division sacrificed 1,133 soldiers, the Hayes/Winthrop brigade accounting for 720 of that total. The Third Division suffered most of all. More than 1,900 soldiers of Crawford's command were either killed, wounded, or captured. Lyle's brigade, so badly handled on August 19, lost 857 men, the greatest casualty count among any brigade on either side. Willcox's division accounted for more

The Battle of Weldon Railroad, August 20–21

than half of the 593 Ninth Corps casualties. More than two-thirds of all Union losses at the Weldon Railroad were prisoners.[91]

No such detailed figures exist for Confederate losses. The National Park Service estimates that about 1,500 Rebels were either killed or wounded, while some 800 more became prisoners of war. Historian John Horn bumps up the total to approximately 2,400 men. During the three days of intense combat, the Confederates committed fifteen infantry brigades, some more than once. The Federals engaged the same number of brigades throughout the fight, demonstrating that the Union defeat on August 19 proved more costly in human capital than did the Confederate debacle two days later.[92]

General Grant took stock of the operational situation on the morning of August 22 and wired Meade that he no longer expected Warren to assume the offensive now that the Confederates had returned to their permanent lines. "It is my desire to hold the Weldon road," he reiterated, "and to thoroughly destroy it as far south as possible." The lieutenant general also canceled a planned advance by the Tenth Corps at Bermuda Hundred based on Major General Birney's assessment that such an attack would probably fail.[93]

General Lee also employed the telegraph to apprise Confederate officials of the consequences stemming from the loss of this valuable means of supply. "Under these circumstances, we should use every effort to maintain ourselves by our remaining line of communications," he advised Secretary of War James A. Seddon. "I shall do all in my power to procure some supplies by the Weldon road, bringing them by rail to Stony Creek, and thence by wagons," he assured President Davis. But he urged the government to employ all its energies to ensure that the Richmond & Danville Railroad—this line bypassed Petersburg on its way to the Confederate capital—could be operated at maximum capacity, superintended by "the best officers of the Quartermaster Department." The army's stockpile of corn was exhausted by August 22, and Lee implored the administration to address this urgent problem immediately.[94]

Lee also discerned the change in Union strategy implicit in the Fourth Petersburg Offensive—as such, it was a turning point in the campaign. "I think it evident that the enemy has abandoned the effort to drive us from our present position by force, and that his purpose now is to compel us to evacuate it by cutting off our supplies," he accurately informed Seddon. The general also correctly characterized, at least in part, Grant's recent operations north of the James. "I think his intention . . . was not only to cause the removal of troops from Petersburg, but also to try to break through to Richmond."[95]

The Confederate commander's analysis missed only one aspect of Grant's strategic vision—his overriding concern for Sheridan's prospects in the

Shenandoah Valley. Lee understood that Hancock's and Birney's foray across the James intended to lure substantial forces away from Petersburg and that Grant hoped that the operations at Second Deep Bottom might result in a break-through to Richmond. Similarly, he grasped Grant's intention to inflict sufficient damage to the Weldon Railroad to compromise its function as a source of sup-ply. But Hancock's and Warren's initiatives shared the common goal of reducing Early's capability to oppose Sheridan's campaign, which in mid-August had been paralyzed by the prospect of reinforcements arriving from Lee's army. As the fighting along the Weldon Railroad concluded, Sheridan completed a hasty retreat that left him occupying an entrenched position just outside Harpers Ferry, the very foot of the valley he was supposed to conquer. Thus, the Fourth Petersburg Offensive should be understood, at least in part, as a holding action in favor of events 160 miles to the northwest.[96]

That is not to say that Grant rejected the hope of driving the Confederates away from either Petersburg or Richmond. His correspondence with Meade throughout the entire conflict bristled with suggestions to find and exploit a weakness in Lee's armor. But they were just that—suggestions, not orders. As he had done throughout the campaign, the general-in-chief relied on George Meade to render the ultimate judgment regarding the conduct of affairs in the field. In turn, Meade provided Warren with almost complete discretion, a li-cense the Fifth Corps commander exercised to remain on the defensive after his arrival on the railroad. Warren's refusal to take the battle to the enemy drove one more nail into the New Yorker's professional coffin, a casket that Grant would eventually seal—but not just yet. Warren compensated for his ill fate on August 19 by moving deftly to an unassailable new position two days later, which led to one of the Army of the Potomac's most lopsided tactical triumphs. It requires no particular martial genius to fight a stationary battle behind fortifications, but still, Warren's divisions—aided by the solid contributions of the Ninth Corps—acquitted themselves well on August 21, resulting in a serious tactical and logistical setback for the Army of Northern Virginia.

And Robert E. Lee saw it that way. The gray commander ascribed the failure at the Weldon Railroad to one factor—lack of manpower. As he explained to the secretary of war on August 22, "the enemy's superiority of numbers has enabled him to effect a lodgment on the Weldon Railroad. Two attacks were made upon him when he first approached the road, in both of which he was worsted, but the smallness of the attacking force prevented it from dislodging him." Like Grant, Lee delegated conduct of the fight along the Weldon Railroad to his primary subordinate, P. G. T. Beauregard. Clearly, Beauregard's attacks on August 18 and 19 lacked enough force to drive the Federals from the tracks,

The Battle of Weldon Railroad, August 20–21

tactical success notwithstanding. The Louisianan felt unable to devote more of the army to those offensives without denuding the Petersburg defenses to a dangerous degree. What might have occurred had Beauregard taken such a risk can only be imagined.[97]

Heth's contributions to the combat on August 19 and 21 should be understood as secondary. Mahone once again played the starring role in these Confederate initiatives. After all, this combative Virginian had performed brilliantly in similar circumstances during the last two Union offensives. His were the shock troops of the Confederate army. Mahone's flanking movement on August 19 resulted in a spectacular disparity between Federal casualties and his own, but two-thirds of his force were foreign to him, and he probably did not employ his old brigade as advantageously as the stakes required. Poor intelligence on the twenty-first, the proximate fault of Roger Pryor, doomed Mahone's second effort to outflank the Federals, but both he and A. P. Hill deserve a share of the responsibility for failing to confirm what Pryor asserted.

Lee scrawled a frank warning to Secretary Seddon on August 23. "Unless some measures can be devised to replace our losses, the consequences may be disastrous. . . . Without some increase of strength, I cannot see how we are to escape the natural military consequences of the enemy's numerical superiority." Would the Army of Northern Virginia now be compelled to burrow down in its trenches to await the inevitable?[98]

Sgt. Zerah Coston Monks of the 155th Pennsylvania did not think so. "They will make an attempt some place along here to drive us from the road," he predicted in a letter home. Twelve miles northeast of this Pennsylvania prophet, Grant perused a collection of Richmond newspapers, a common source of information the general-in-chief routinely consulted. "Richmond papers of yesterday show great despondency over the affair on the Weldon road," he informed Meade on August 24. "They say, however, we have not seen the end of that affair yet." In twenty-four hours Grant would know the truth of that prediction.[99]

five

ONE OF THE MOST TERRIBLE BATTLES I EVER SEEN

Second Reams' Station, August 22–25

The Union victory on the morning of August 21 stirred the fighting blood of the Federal general-in-chief. Because Gouverneur Warren's reluctance to exploit his defensive triumph would frustrate Grant, the Union commander looked elsewhere for an offensive strike. Early that afternoon he ordered Benjamin Butler to test the lines along the southern portion of the Bermuda Hundred front, thinking that the Confederates might have stripped their manpower there in favor of the effort to regain the Weldon Railroad. Butler responded by instructing Major General Birney, now returned from Deep Bottom, to launch an assault at early dawn. "Let the troops take nothing but their canteens filled and cartridge-boxes," wrote the army commander. But late that night Butler's confidence in the proposed attack wavered. "From what you have learned, what is your opinion as to the feasibility of the movement?" he asked Birney. The Tenth Corps commander answered promptly. "I dislike to abandon the movement, but regard it as . . . a doubtful one as to success." Butler passed this message to Grant, who rescinded his order. The general-in-chief had also spurred E. O. C. Ord to advance his Eighteenth Corps to test the Confederate defenses east of Jerusalem Plank Road or to shift west to relive Gershom Mott's Second Corps division, which could then reinforce the hesitant Warren, but Ord also demurred. The Army of the James would not be moved.[1]

Grant now hoped that the last two Second Corps divisions to complete the trek from north of the James River would facilitate his offensive inclinations. They reached the Petersburg front on the morning of August 21, enduring a march that Winfield Hancock considered "one of the most fatiguing and difficult performed by the troops during the campaign, owing to the wretched condition of the roads." The men halted before noon and downed a hasty meal, the first they had tasted in sixteen hours. They had rested only briefly when new orders arrived to march west to reinforce Warren, with the evident intention of assuming the offensive either themselves or by releasing the Fifth Corps to do so. Between 3:00 and 5:00 P.M., Hancock's bedraggled troops stumbled into camp near the Gurley house, diminished in strength by straggling and thoroughly enervated by their ordeal. "Hancock's men are so exhausted with their long march that nothing can be expected of them this afternoon," George Meade informed Grant. Not only would there be no further fighting on the twenty-first, but Meade wrote Grant after dark that he "found it impracticable to arrange any offensive movement for to-morrow. Warren expressed every confidence in his command defending itself against any attack, but advised against attacking. Hancock's men are completely exhausted with their march, and nearly a third behind on the road. Parke's people will be working all night on the connecting lines." With this discouraging report in hand, Grant finally relented. "I do not expect offensive operations to-morrow," he conceded, but he would focus once again on the physical destruction of the Weldon Railroad.[2]

General Lee also declined to renew hostilities, having explained to Richmond the near impossibility of regaining control of the railroad. But while the infantry rested, the grayclad cavalry remained active south and west of Petersburg. Those horsemen now served officially under Maj. Gen. Wade Hampton. The forty-six-year-old South Carolinian was the senior division commander in the Cavalry Corps, but like his peers—Maj. Gen. Fitzhugh Lee and Maj. Gen. Rooney Lee—he had reported directly to the army commander following Maj. Gen. Jeb Stuart's death in May. Lee found it difficult to envision any of these division leaders as a replacement for the lamented Stuart, but events demonstrated that he must decide. On July 2 he wrote to President Davis that despite his fear that Hampton did not possess "that activity and endurance so necessary in a cavalry commander," he considered the South Carolinian the best choice to lead the Cavalry Corps. His recommendation remained in limbo for six weeks, but on August 11 Special Orders No. 189 named Hampton head of Lee's mounted arm. Brig. Gen. Matthew Calbraith Butler assumed control of Hampton's Division, while Col. John Dunovant of the Fifth South Carolina Cavalry replaced Butler in brigade command.[3]

Hampton would prove worthy of his promotion. Born into immense wealth—the Hamptons were among the largest slaveowners in the South—Hampton accumulated vast land holdings while serving in the legislature of his native state. Although not numbered among the fire-eaters of South Carolina, he volunteered for military service shortly after his state's secession. Based solely on his name and reputation—he had no formal military training—he received a colonel's commission and quickly recruited a unit known as the Hampton Legion. In 1862, now a brigadier general, Hampton switched to the cavalry and served as Stuart's senior brigade commander. Wounded multiple times, Hampton demonstrated his acumen in the saddle in numerous battles and raids, and his promotion to corps command came despite the Virginia-centric bias that had characterized Lee's mounted arm throughout Stuart's tenure. "He was as dauntless as Stuart . . . and his fearlessness in action so conspicuous, that no man ever excited more enthusiasm," thought one knowledgeable observer.[4]

With Fitzhugh Lee's Division in the Shenandoah Valley, Hampton had Butler's and Rooney Lee's divisions under his control, some 5,000 troopers in five brigades. Rooney contracted a case of poison oak so severe that his eyes were almost swollen shut, so Rufus Barringer temporarily filled his place. Col. William H. Cheek, the twenty-nine-year-old commander of the First North Carolina Cavalry, assumed control of Barringer's Brigade. Col. J. Lucius Davis took over for the slain John Chambliss in Lee's other brigade. Col. Gilbert J. Wright of Cobb's Georgia Legion temporarily led Pierce M. B. Young's Brigade, and Brig. Gen. Thomas S. Rosser returned to active duty at the head of the famed Laurel Brigade, although he had not yet fully recovered from a wound received in June. "His return was welcomed all along our lines with a sincere and unpremeditated burst of enthusiasm," wrote one admiring trooper. Wright and Rosser joined the newly promoted Dunovant as commanders of Butler's three brigades.[5]

These Rebel riders would spend the days immediately following the battles around Globe Tavern engaging their Union counterparts, although portions of Butler's Division suffered from a lack of forage for their hungry mounts. Two Federal brigades—Colonel Spear's of the Army of the James and Stedman's of the Army of the Potomac—had been involved on the margins of the recent victory. By the night of August 21, the other half of David Gregg's division, Charles H. Smith's brigade, joined their mounted comrades along the Weldon Railroad.[6]

On the morning of August 22, Colonel Spear expected to be relieved of scouting and picket duty along the railroad now that Gregg's veterans were available to screen the infantry and keep the Confederate horsemen at bay. Once Gregg's men replaced Spear's command on the picket line, the colonel reported to Warren's headquarters at Globe Tavern, where he found a bevy of senior officers, including Meade and his chief of staff, corps commanders Parke and Warren, and several brigadiers. Instead of returning him to quiet duty with the rest of the Army of the James's cavalry, the officers instructed Spear to report to General Gregg and "proceed and attack Lee's cavalry" beyond the left flank of Warren's infantry. The diligent colonel did as directed. That afternoon he encountered 300–400 Confederate troopers some two miles southwest of Globe Tavern near the elderly "Col. Wyatt's" prosperous plantation home on Lower Church Road. In an engagement that spanned about forty-five minutes, Spear routed the graycoats at a cost of one man killed and six wounded, the Confederates covering their retreat by burning a bridge over a branch of Arthur's Swamp. Just before dark, Gregg sent a reconnaissance party to Reams' Station with orders to expel any enemy cavalry guarding the place. The troopers found the area unoccupied but learned that Confederates were present a few miles to the south. This was the Laurel Brigade, which had encamped along the substantial southeast-flowing Rowanty Creek. Davis's brigade was also in the neighborhood, encamped southwest of Reams' Station near Tabernacle Church.[7]

The opposing cavalry would engage in a more serious encounter on August 23, but in the meantime, the Federals began implementing the railroad destruction mandated by General Grant. Hancock's First Division, still under the temporary leadership of Brig. Gen. Nelson Miles, received orders to cease fatigue duty and march to the railroad to assist in dismantling it.[8]

The working party sent two days earlier from City Point had, in General Meade's words, become "alarmed and mostly deserted the work," leaving the job to Miles. Supplied with the necessary tools by Warren, his soldiers proceeded to the Perkins house, hard by the railroad about a mile south of Globe Tavern, and commenced the work of destruction. Half the division remained under arms, with skirmishers advanced, to guard against surprise from the enemy's cavalry, while the remainder exercised what had become a well-practiced ritual of ruination. First, a detail from each brigade removed the spikes from their assigned portion of the tracks. Then the brigade lined up beside the rails, and at the order "lay hold" or "heave," the men stooped in unison and lifted a section of rails as long as 400 yards. Another detail then collected the ties and placed them in in hollow squares, often supplemented with brush and other combustibles, across which others laid the dislocated rails. Once set afire, the middle sections of the iron rails would melt, causing the ends to droop, leaving a mélange of twisted iron that could not be reused without rehabilitation at a rolling mill. Occasionally, the soldiers would twist a length of molten rail around a convenient tree. The troops also leveled the railroad's embankments and filled its cuts.[9]

"It was not the first experience of the regiment in this line of business," explained the historian of the 116th Pennsylvania, "and when the fatigue of Deep Bottom wore off the men rather enjoyed the work. It was certainly better than building breast-works with the [enemy] sharpshooters cracking at the workers,

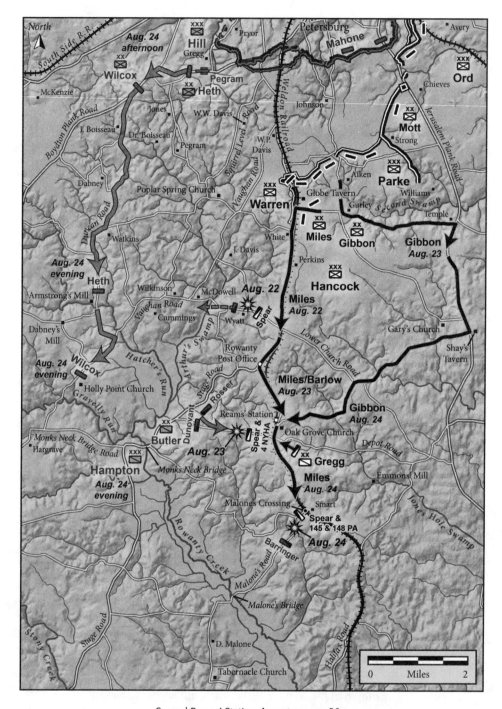

Second Reams' Station, August 22–24, 1864

and the roaring fires of the railroad ties at intervals along the line . . . looked cheerful and gave the boys a chance to dry their clothes." Indeed, a relentless rain continued to soak the soldiers, who managed to keep the fires blazing despite the precipitation. The work continued until dark, black smoke rising in spires visible for a mile. When at last Miles's men laid down their tools, they had managed to dislodge about two miles of track, half the distance from the Perkins house to Reams' Station. Fields filled with corn surrounded their makeshift bivouacs that night, and the soldiers collected and roasted the ears over sputtering campfires. "We are in an abundant country—hitherto unvisited with the ravages of war," explained Lt. Frederick Lockley of the Seventh New York Heavy Artillery. "The way the men fill themselves with this delicious succulent vegetable is a caution."[10]

The soldiers, their stomachs sated with purloined maize, endured another night of rain so heavy that only the most developed roads could support wagon traffic or allow the division's artillery to move. These conditions raised alarms at Meade's headquarters. At 10:30 on the morning of the twenty-third, the army commander sought guidance from Grant regarding how far south Miles should extend his railroad destruction. Meade reminded his superior that Miles had only about 4,000 infantry along with a single brigade of cavalry, and reports suggested the Confederates were concentrating forces from both the Petersburg front and from the south to augment their two cavalry divisions already in the neighborhood. "In my judgment . . . Miles ought not to go beyond support from Warren's position, say Rowanty Creek, some ten miles, which point he will probably reach to day," explained Meade. But should Warren believe that his position was secure, Meade would be willing to order Hancock's Second Division, once again led by Brig. Gen. John Gibbon, to reinforce Miles.[11]

This message failed to reach the general-in-chief because Grant had boarded a steamer at City Point that morning and traveled down the James to Fort Powhatan. Receiving no response from his superior, the army commander drafted an update at noon, relating that Warren now confirmed his ability to hold his position without assistance from the Second Corps. Meade explained, however, that the condition of the roads would force the use of pack mules to ferry supplies to any Second Corps troops south of Globe Tavern, "the question therefore of supplying any large force at a distance from the main army . . . enters into the expediency of movements." His concerns reached Grant at 1:15 P.M., at which time the lieutenant general agreed that "it would be imprudent to send Gen. Miles with his small force beyond the support of the main army to destroy the RR." Grant would order the Tenth Corps to relieve the Eighteenth Corps along the Petersburg front and then dispatch Ord's command to continue the destruction of the railroad all the way to Hicksford, more than forty miles below Petersburg. Doing this would so greatly lengthen a wagon haul to Petersburg that the Weldon Railroad would be practically useless to Lee.[12]

While the top brass hammered out their strategy, Miles's men arose at dawn on August 23 to resume their labors, pleased that the persistent rain had finally abated. By 11:00 A.M., the troops had torn away the tracks to within a mile of Reams' Station, at which time Francis Barlow appeared and resumed command of his division, with Miles returning to his brigade. Barlow learned that Reams' Station had not been occupied and ordered Miles to do so immediately. Miles selected Col. James C. Lynch to lead two regiments south to the site of the destroyed railroad depot. Lynch chose his own command, the 183rd Pennsylvania, and the 81st Pennsylvania for the march south. These two regiments promptly reached their destination and occupied the place without incident. About 1:00 P.M. the rest of Miles's First Brigade arrived, having destroyed the tracks all the way to the tiny hamlet.[13]

In the meantime, General Gregg sought direction from Meade as to the proper use of the three cavalry brigades now under his command. Army headquarters replied that he should assign Spear to accompany Barlow and Miles in their railroad demolition, while his own division secured the connection between the left of the Fifth Corps and Barlow, "ready to operate as circumstances require." At 11:00 A.M. Meade modified these orders, telling Gregg to concentrate his troopers at Reams' Station while merely picketing the ground between there and Warren. The army commander also hinted that additional infantry might be dispatched to Reams' Station. That infantry, Gibbon's division, would eventually embark for the little village, though not before the cavalry would participate in a spirited engagement.[14]

When Spear reported to Miles at Reams' Station, the general ordered him to conduct a reconnaissance to the west. Two oversized companies of the Fourth New York Heavy Artillery, an unbrigaded regiment that had accompanied Miles, reinforced the cavalrymen. The Federals moved west on Depot Road, driving pickets from Barringer's North Carolina regiments back to a span over Rowanty Creek called Monk's Neck Bridge. Around 2:00 P.M. two fresh companies of the Fourth New York Heavy Artillery relieved their comrades as the skirmishing continued. By then, however, Butler's grayclad cavalry division had arrived, triggering much more serious combat.[15]

Butler deployed the Virginians of the Laurel Brigade on his left along Stage Road and Dunovant's South Carolinians to his right on Depot Road. The Laurel Brigade then advanced, pushing Spear's skirmishers eastward until they encountered the riflemen from the Fourth New York Heavy Artillery, who halted the Rebels' push and forced them to fall back. As Dunovant rode eastward on Depot Road, Spear unleashed his troopers, who engaged in such close-quarters fighting that pistols and sabers became the preferred weapons. The South Carolinians retreated a short distance before Butler ordered a counterattack that forced Spear, in turn, to withdraw.[16]

Spear reported to Warren at 3:00 P.M. that he had clashed with Hampton's cavalry, combat that cost him forty men while inflicting 184 casualties on his opponents, who outnumbered him ten to one. These gross exaggerations notwithstanding, Spear needed help, but appeals to Gregg were unavailing, and Miles only agreed to send him 100 additional men. "I can do great execution and rout them if I have one or two regiments of infantry," averred the undeterred cavalry colonel. "No one seems to assist me; can I not get it from General Warren?" Spear admitted that his men were exhausted but would continue to hold their position "at all hazards," emphasizing that Gregg and Miles faced no opposition near Reams' Station and should therefore be free to assist him.[17]

Warren replied that Spear was so far southwest that he would be unable to provide him succor. But Gregg, having learned of the seriousness of Spear's engagement, dispatched two regiments of Pennsylvania cavalry, the Second and Sixteenth of Smith's brigade, to investigate the situation, with orders to engage the enemy if possible and call on the remainder of the division if necessary. Gregg accompanied these Pennsylvanians, who advanced about a mile and a half west on Depot Road. They spotted the dismounted Confederates in what Gregg estimated to be division strength. The Rebels moved ahead about 5:00 P.M., prompting Gregg to summon the remaining regiments of his division to join the fray. As these reinforcements arrived on the scene, he had them dismount. By 7:00 P.M., all of his regiments were present, only one of them remaining "to horse" and prepared to respond to a Confederate mounted attack. Both sides erected hasty fieldworks of rails and logs as the battle continued past dusk and into the darkness. By then, Barlow had positioned his infantry in the old earthworks around Reams' Station constructed by the Sixth Corps in June, prepared to meet the Rebels should they break through Gregg's troopers. But their participation would not be required. Butler called off the action between 8:30 and 9:00 P.M., ending a battle some participants called "the fight by moonlight."[18]

Losses during this engagement were not insignificant. Between Spear, Gregg, and the Fourth New York Heavy Artillery, some 130 bluecoats lay dead or wounded. Confederate casualties, contrary to Spear's inflated estimate, numbered 136. The battle may have been tactically indecisive, but it provided Hampton, who arrived after the most heated fighting had ended, with invaluable information that would profoundly inform Confederate operations.[19]

While the opposing cavalry traded saber blows and pistol shots, General Meade ordered Hancock to dispatch an additional division "to aid in covering the party destroying the railroad and at the same time to destroy the railroad." Hancock replied to this directive, vowing mistakenly to send Miles to comply with the order. The First Division, of course, was already engaged in its work of destruction, so the Second Corps commander clearly meant to designate his Second Division, Gibbon's, for the job. Although Hancock conveyed this promise to Meade at 12:10 P.M., it would take nearly six hours for Gibbon's three brigades to commence their march.[20]

About sunset Col. Thomas Smyth, once again a brigade commander, led his troops from their camps around the Aiken house to Jerusalem Plank Road. Hancock chose this longer route over the direct link to Reams' Station via Halifax Road because of the rain-soaked condition of all the secondary thoroughfares. "The country through which we passed had not been devastated by war and the crops were growing and the farms and plantations were in good order," remembered a soldier from Smyth's Fourteenth Connecticut. "Scarcely a white man was to be seen. . . . If any plundering was done it was by stragglers or deserters, but occasionally a wandering pig or an innocent calf or an unsuspecting lamb or a simple minded goose found its way into the soldiers' camp kettles." Gibbon's troops, like their First Division comrades, feasted on green corn along with apples and garden vegetables they scarfed along the march. The brigades of Mathew Murphy and Lt. Col. Horace P. Rugg followed Smyth down the plank road.[21]

Four artillery units accompanied Gibbon. The Tenth Massachusetts Battery; the Twelfth New York Battery; Battery C, Third New Jersey Artillery; and the consolidated Batteries A and B, First Rhode Island Artillery all headed south, with orders to remove the corps and state insignias from their caps and clothing; their commanders did not wish to reveal their identities should any of the gunners become prisoners of war. These 461 cannoneers supplemented the approximately 2,000 infantry marching with Gibbon.[22]

Reaching Jerusalem Plank Road proved troublesome, as the headquarters wagons repeatedly bogged down in the sticky roadway. Once the column gained the highway, however, progress improved, and the men tramped south about two miles until orders arrived to halt after dark and bivouac in the fields beside the road, with instructions to be back on the move by 3:00 A.M. The men received rations and were up well before dawn. They continued south until reaching a byway at Shay's Tavern, where they turned west. The column began arriving at Reams' Station four hours later.[23]

Reams' Station received its name from a local family from Winzingen in the Rhine Palatinate area of Germany, who originally spelled their name "Riehm." They had first settled in Pennsylvania, and at least one member of the family fought in the Revolutionary War. Sometime later they relocated to the area south of Petersburg and resumed their occupation as farmers. The whistle stop on the Weldon Railroad that now bore their Anglicized name had already seen military action in late June 1864 and was now destined to host an even larger conflict.[24]

But Francis Barlow would not be present for that fight. Early on the morning of August 24, Special Orders No. 228 granted the First Division commander twenty days' leave "on surgeon's certificate of disability." Hancock reported that "General Barlow was again obliged to relinquish command of his division to General Miles on account of sickness." Lynch resumed control of Miles's brigade. Barlow would be missed by the members of his division. "He was a fearless officer, perfectly reckless as regarded his own person and in spite of wounds and disease stuck to the work, and remained in command long after a man with less force of character would have given up the struggle," wrote an admiring member of the 116th Pennsylvania. Barlow would never regain sufficient strength to take the field, his departure on August 24 marking the end of his military career.[25]

Gibbon's arrival freed Miles to resume the First Division's railroad destruction. His troops worked their way south toward Rowanty Creek, some five or six miles below Reams' Station. He dispatched Lynch's command, Levin Crandell's Consolidated Brigade, and the Fourth New York Heavy Artillery to continue wrecking the tracks, while Oscar Broady's Fourth Brigade provided flank protection. Gibbon contributed 500 men from Rugg's command and three regiments of Smyth's to augment Miles's despoilers. Thus, several thousand men reprised the successful techniques they had employed the previous day. The brigades hopscotched their way south, lifting the rails, stacking the ties— supplemented by fence rails, boards, and posts—and placing the rails atop the blazing pyres, melting and warping them into an unusable condition. The men of the Fourteenth Connecticut expressed disappointment that they were unable to twist the red-hot iron into the shape of their corps badge—the trefoil—as the Fifth Corps had done earlier with their Maltese Cross.[26]

"A long line of smoking fires were soon seen up and down the road," recalled a soldier in the 14th Connecticut, a spectacle that Cpl. Henry C. Metzger of the 184th Pennsylvania considered "a pretty sight." The soldiers continued to revel in the relative abundance of the neighboring fields. "As the country here was not too much traveled, green corn, apples, and new potatoes were the unusual luxuries of the weary soldier," wrote a New Hampshire man. The troops utilized the heated coals of their rail pyres to roast ears of corn and boil the soldiers' tonic—coffee. "This refreshment gave a zest to our work," thought one New Yorker. During breaks from their labors, the men would gather around these makeshift campfires, "enjoying the usual smoke and chat."[27]

Spear's cavalry trotted ahead of the workers, their advance running into some of Barringer's patrols between a point on the railroad called Malone's Crossing and Rowanty Creek. Miles sent two Pennsylvania regiments from Broady's brigade, the 145th and 148th, to reinforce Spear, who managed to push the Rebel horsemen south. Gregg's cavalry was also busy this day. Stedman's brigade patrolled west from Reams' Station along Depot Road, while Smith's troopers spread out, picketing the ground between Hancock and Warren and between Reams' Station and Jerusalem Plank Road.[28]

In the meantime, the rest of Gibbon's men, along with the newly arrived artillery, took position in the works that surrounded the burned depot at Reams' Station. These fortifications covered three sides of a rectangle, facing north, west, and south, the open end toward Jerusalem Plank Road, three miles to the east. The west face of the line ran north to south for about 700 yards, several hundred feet west of and parallel to the railroad. The northern end of these works terminated only a few yards west of the railbed. As this line coursed south, it diverged slightly westward, ending about 45 yards from the ruined tracks. These badly eroded fortifications were little more than shallow rifle pits, rising three feet above the ground and consisting of fence rails banked with earth. Just south of the depot ruins at the northern end of the west face, the line bent east for 800 yards, covering the road to Shay's Tavern and the modest Oak Grove Church. These new works—the northern return—contained embrasures for artillery and were high enough to protect gunners working their pieces. At the south end of the west face, the fortifications also turned east and terminated at the railroad. An opening allowed Depot Road to penetrate the west face about halfway down its length. The railroad ran through a gap in the northern return. Halifax Road paralleled the tracks to the east.[29]

In addition to the relative weakness of the engineering, this line suffered from its compact size. Enemy artillery could affect an enfilade fire from practically anywhere outside of the works. Moreover, the ground immediately behind the northern portion of the west face fell as much as thirteen feet into a deep cut of the railroad, while to the south, a high embankment rose behind the works. Both of these features would make it difficult to ferry ammunition from the rear to the front, not to mention the impediment they presented in case of the need to withdraw. To make matters even worse, thick pine woods approached portions of the west face as close as thirty yards, leaving some of the defenders with practically no field of fire. In the words of one soldier, "the position was a death-trap."[30]

Gibbon's regiments not engaged in railroad work remained near Reams' Station. The Nineteenth Massachusetts deployed westward as skirmishers, while the First and Second Delaware formed on their left in advance of the works. The remainder of Smyth's brigade anchored its left on Halifax Road and occupied a portion of the west face, while the rest of Rugg's and Murphy's brigades filled the works from the northern half of the west face around to the northern return.[31]

The artillery unlimbered along the works, the Rhode Island batteries on the left of the line, with the Tenth Massachusetts Battery's four three-inch rifles to their right, west of the railroad in the interval between Rugg's and Smyth's brigades. The Twelfth New York Battery placed its four three-inch rifles some 300 yards west of Oak Grove Church near the angle of the northern return, with the Third New Jersey Light Artillery's four guns on the New Yorkers' right. Lt. George K. Dauchy, in command of the Twelfth New York Battery, remembered that his gunners "had been listlessly lying around in the woods, in which were placed our limbers, caissons, ambulance, etc., enjoying the luxuries of 'roasting ears' which we found in the field in the rear of the woods. We did not think the enemy would send a force large enough to attack us so far from his lines and, in fact, considered the excursion rather in the light of a picnic." Cpl. John D. Billings of the Tenth Massachusetts Battery agreed. "We remember the day as an extremely pleasant one, both in respect of the weather and our enjoyment of the surroundings," he wrote. "It seemed very holiday-like to us as we lounged about the guns." The acting chief of Hancock's artillery at Reams' Station, Capt. A. Judson Clark, reported simply that "everything was quiet while the troops were engaged in tearing up the railroad."[32]

Shortly before dark, Hancock's marauders began returning to Reams' Station. They had managed to destroy the tracks southward to a point below Malone's Crossing. The soldiers also found time to burn a machine shop and a blacksmith shop, dismantle a water tank, and tear down telegraph poles. They felled trees across the railroad bed and filled the cuts with debris. "It was another fine day," recalled a soldier in the Seventh New York Heavy Artillery, "and the demolition work progressed nicely—by four o'clock that afternoon, another three miles of track was either ablaze or smoldering." A citizen writing to the *Petersburg Express* on August 26 described "truly a sad scene" along the railroad south of Reams' Station. "On both sides of the track, the enemy have swept fences and crops, leaving scarcely a vestige remaining. The crops, consisting chiefly of corn and sorghum, have been fed to men and horses, and the leaves piled up in the railroad sills to assist in the burning." Spear's weary cavalry-men continued to picket that night, deploying near the Smart house just above Malone's Crossing, covering all the roads leading north toward Reams' Station. While some of the gunners improved the works around their batteries, others spread their blankets on the warm ground to enjoy a night's sleep undisturbed by labor they and their commanders deemed unnecessary.[33]

General Hancock allowed all of his troops to rest that night. He confessed to Meade: "My men are much fatigued. . . . They have not recovered from the fatigue of their late marches." This explains—but does not justify—the corps commander's failure to insist on improving his vulnerable position around Reams' Station. Hancock told Gibbon that his division would relieve Miles's exhausted soldiers on the twenty-fifth and continue wrecking the railroad south to Rowanty Creek, with little thought of defense beyond countering the annoy-ing and omnipresent enemy cavalry.[34]

Grant telegraphed Halleck in Washington late on the twenty-fourth, report-ing the progress of Hancock's wrecking crews and promising to continue the work the next day. The general-in-chief had been in communication with Ben Butler regarding the threat of a Confederate attack against Ord near Petersburg. Butler promised to dispatch a division of the Tenth Corps to relieve Ord's anxi-ety. Grant's intention to send the Eighteenth Corps to continue the destruction of the railroad fell victim to these concerns. Hancock's two overworked divi-sions would bear that responsibility alone.[35]

Hancock informed Meade at 8:00 P.M. that Confederate cavalry still lurked around the intersection of Depot and Stage Roads, about two miles west of Reams' Station, but that they had done no more than observe the Federal dispo-sitions. Three hours later Hancock received a dispatch from Meade's headquar-ters of momentous importance. "Signal officers report large bodies of infantry passing south from their intrenchments by the Halifax and Vaughan roads. They are probably destined to operate against General Warren or yourself—most probably against your operations. The commanding general cautions you to look out for them." Hancock promptly replied, inquiring as to the strength of this Confederate movement and suggesting, with obvious logic, that if that number was large, it would be unwise to separate Gibbon's division from Miles's down the railroad. Headquarters responded that some 8,000–10,000 Rebels were on the move and had left their works around sunset.[36]

Warren also received word of this ominous movement but dismissed it as only the reinforcement of labor parties developing a new line of works, as re-ported to him by Confederate prisoners. "I feel certain that if they have gone out it is to interfere with General Hancock," he added. "They cannot do anything with me here." Hancock directed Gregg to send a patrol at daylight on the twenty-fifth "to see how strongly the enemy hold the Vaughan road." Remarkably, despite this explicit warning that a force greater than his own might be poised to attack him, Hancock took no other precautions to meet such a potential threat. At least one Union soldier inferred the danger that his corps commander seemed to ignore. "I don't trust it right here," wrote Corporal Metzger, "something seemes to tell me that every thing is not right here. We have only two Divisions of our Corps and one of cavalry and a few Batterys of Artillery here." Events would soon validate Metzger's concern.[37]

Those events originated with Hampton's analysis of the operational situation. The cavalry chief had reached the field near the conclusion of the fighting around Monk's Neck Bridge on the evening of the twenty-third. He carefully examined the ground and evaluated reports received from Barringer and Butler, learning that only a single infantry division and one division of cavalry occupied the area around Reams' Station and had no artillery present. Of course, Gibbon, along with four batteries of guns, would arrive early the next morning, rendering this intelligence obsolete. But based on his knowledge at the time, the South Carolinian sent a message to General Lee asserting that if his troopers were reinforced with infantry, he could drive the Yankees off the railroad.[38]

Lee replied that while he appreciated Hampton's suggestion, he "thought it inadvisable to send any portion of the Infty so far from the main lines." The next day, August 24, with this rejection in mind, Hampton rode toward army headquarters to discuss the situation with his superior. He encountered a courier en route who delivered Lee's approval of his proposed offensive. Evidently, Hampton and Lee exchanged messages after this, although the contents of Hampton's half of the correspondence is uncertain, other than it was sent at 2:30 P.M. Lee replied fifteen minutes later—if accurate, it means that Hampton had ridden almost all the way to Petersburg—stating, "General Heth's division will also move down the railroad and General Hill will go in command." This implies that the message delivered by the unnamed courier specified the initial composition of Hill's force. Lee instructed his chief of cavalry to report to Hill and encouraged Hampton to "do all in your power to punish the enemy."[39]

Although the rationale for Lee's change of heart can only be inferred, the gray commander doubtless hoped to arrest the destruction of the Weldon Railroad as far north as possible to shorten the wagon haul now necessary to transport supplies to Petersburg from a new railhead south of the city. Historian Douglas Southall Freeman suggests that Lee also calculated that a Union defeat near Petersburg would undermine Lincoln and the Republicans in the upcoming fall elections, while historian John Horn points out that the Federals, if allowed to remain at Reams' Station, could threaten Dinwiddie Court House. A Union force at that village on Boydton Plank Road would severely complicate Lee's ability to use wagons to ferry supplies into Petersburg and even threaten the South Side Railroad. Lacking the manpower to extend his defenses that far southwest, he opted instead to risk an attack against Reams' Station.[40]

Lee would minimize that gamble by committing the maximum firepower to his offensive consistent with defending Petersburg. He had seen how understrength attacks ultimately failed on August 18 and 19 and sought to avoid replicating that mistake.

Orders to prepare for action circulated among Wilcox's Division on the morning of the twenty-fourth. These men had been laboring on the permanent fortifications guarding the southern approaches to Petersburg, but at 10:00 A.M. word arrived to prepare to march. About four hours later Wilcox led three of his four brigades southwest on Boydton Plank Road. Samuel McGowan, recently returned to active duty, led his South Carolina brigade, joined by Scales's North Carolinians. Lane's Tar Heels, still under the command of James Conner, was also part of the column. One of Field's units, the Georgians of Tige Anderson's Brigade, fell in under Wilcox's authority. Thomas's Georgians remained behind in the fortifications.[41]

Heth selected his two North Carolina brigades to bolster Wilcox. MacRae's and Cooke's Carolinians left the trenches about 4:00 P.M., tramping southwest on Boydton Plank Road in the footsteps of Wilcox's provisional division. MacRae had been in command of his brigade for only a short time. A member of his staff considered him "exceedingly plain in appearance, but . . . a model officer & gentleman." The last of the Confederate infantry to join the march came from Mahone's Division. The Virginians of Weisiger's Brigade and Sanders's Alabamans, still under Colonel King, received orders to prepare to move early in the afternoon, and they followed Heth's Tar Heels a few hours later. Thus, eight veteran infantry brigades headed southwest to join Hampton's cavalry, intent on punishing Hancock's two divisions.[42]

No doubt, the foot soldiers took heart when they learned that as many as seventeen pieces of artillery rumbled along the plank road in their wake. Willie Pegram led this makeshift battalion, which included two of his own Virginia batteries, the Letcher Artillery and the Purcell Battery. Capt. Hugh M. Ross's Battery A of the Sumter (Georgia) Artillery joined the procession, along with a section each from Capt. William B. Hurt's Hardaway (Alabama) Battery and Capt. Valentine J. Clutter's Virginia cannoneers.[43]

The rank and file, as usual, possessed little notion of their destination or their mission. Dame Rumor was busy, however, suggesting that the column would be guarding a wagon train traveling north from Stony Creek, the new railhead on the Weldon Railroad. Lt. Lemuel J. Hoyle of the Eleventh North Carolina admitted that he had no idea "wither we are going nor what was the object of the expedition." Doctor Robert Powel Page, a Virginia physician assigned to the Poplar Lawn Hospital in Petersburg, informed his wife on the twenty-fourth that "rumor has it that there will be tomorrow a grand combined attack . . . by Lee's army." He confessed that he did not know exactly when or where such an assault would occur, "but I hope and trust it will be soon and successful. One thing is very certain," he asserted, the Yankees could not be allowed to remain astride the railroad. "The use of the road is considered essential to the support of the army."[44]

Wilcox's troops followed Boydton Plank Road for several miles, then turned left on a country lane called Duncan Road. "The evening was hot; the march rapid," wrote Pvt. William D. Alexander of the Thirty-Seventh North Carolina. "I think we marched through some of the darkest swamp that I ever passed." The column continued in the gloom, crossing Hatcher's Run at Armstrong's Mill, then following Vaughan Road for about two and a half miles to a rural sanctuary called Holly Point Church, hard by Gravelly Run and just north of Monk's Neck Bridge Road. Here they bivouacked for the night.[45]

Members of Heth's Division reported that they followed "a circuitous route" that evening, "our generals leading us by country roads and by-paths, taking first one and then another point of the compass to deceive the enemy . . . and if possible to keep them in the same blissful state of ignorance [as us]," according to Lieutenant Hoyle. Heth's men halted around Armstrong's Mill.

The supply wagons could not keep pace with the infantry, so despite the rigors of the march, some of MacRae's Brigade retained enough energy to raid a nearby cornfield, much as the Federals had done on their march to Reams' Station. "When the troops first halted, there was a thriving crop of corn growing in the ground," wrote Capt. Benjamin Wesley Justice of the Forty-Seventh North Carolina. "Next morning not a ear, not a stalk, scarcely a blade was to be seen. The men had eaten the corn & fed the stalks to the horses. Such is war, crushing & blighting all in its path." Mahone's two brigades, bringing up the rear of Hill's column, followed Duncan Road, "coming by Joe Boisseau's & through the darkest woods we have encountered for a long while, the road in these woods being very swampy," according to a member of the Twelfth Virginia. They, too, encamped near Armstrong's Mill.[46]

Cavalry led the infantry southward. Hampton personally escorted General Hill, as the Virginian was unfamiliar with the geography this far southwest of Petersburg. The two officers halted near Monk's Neck Bridge and made camp.

Soon thereafter, Hill, Hampton, and perhaps Matthew Butler held a council of war to discuss their impending attack. Hill deferred to Hampton's local knowledge of the road network, terrain, and position of the enemy forces. The cavalry commander proposed to leave one of his regiments with the infantry and send one of his divisions across Rowanty Creek at Malone's Bridge, while the other division crossed the stream farther south on Halifax Road, dispersing Spear's pickets in the process. Then he would unite his two divisions and attack Hancock's left flank while Hill, with the infantry, charged from the west. The Third Corps commander approved this plan and circulated orders to his brigade commanders to be ready to march into position for their attack at 4:00 A.M.[47]

Robert E. Lee, in keeping with his usual command style, remained aloof from the ruminations of Hill and Hampton. He did, however, order Maj. Gen. George Pickett to launch a demonstration near Ware Bottom Church on the Bermuda Hundred front in order to distract Federal attention from Reams' Station. Pickett would enjoy initial success early on the morning of the twenty-fifth, capturing a portion of the Federal picket line and postponing Ben Butler's departure to probate his brother's will. By noon, however, the Tenth Corps had regained the lost ground in this minor affair, which had no discernible effect on events south of Petersburg. A diversion along the Petersburg lines might have pinned down prospective reinforcements for Hancock, but Lee had so stripped his defenses in favor of Hill's gambit that a feint there would have risked a disastrous Union counterattack.[48]

"Boots and Saddle" sounded around midnight August 24–25 in the Confederate cavalry camps near Monk's Neck Bridge. "Sleepy and hungry, we rose from our damp couches," wrote Lt. George W. Beale of the Ninth Virginia Cavalry. "Ere the hour for breakfast had arrived we had passed our outpost pickets and . . . deployed in close proximity to the enemy." Beale's regiment, along with the rest of Davis's troopers, rode southeast, headed for Malone's Road and Malone's Crossing on the railroad. Butler followed the Virginians with two of his brigades, Wright's and most of Rosser's Laurel Brigade. Colonel Cheek at the head of Barringer's own North Carolina troopers trotted farther east to Halifax Road. All four brigades would unite at Malone's Crossing and together move north against Hancock's left. Hampton rode with Butler, leaving Dunovant's brigade and the Seventh Virginia Cavalry of Rosser's command to screen Hill's infantry. Hampton's troopers were in position before 9:00 A.M., waiting for Hill to deploy.[49]

The infantry, however, were not early risers this morning. Exhausted by their long march the previous night, it was 8:00 A.M. before Wilcox had his men up and ready to move. From his advanced position at Holly Point Church, Wilcox crossed Monk's Neck Bridge, bore slowly left on Stage Road, then due east on

Depot Road, halting after only covering about a mile. He cautiously deployed on the south side of Depot Road, still nearly two miles west of Reams' Station. Hampton's battle plan was already tardy, as he and Hill had scheduled their mutual assaults for 9:00 A.M.[50]

In the meantime, Gregg's troopers embarked on their assignment to ascertain whether Confederate infantry actually was in the neighborhood. Hancock told the general to "drive away the enemy's cavalry, in order to give us earlier information should any considerable force advance." The Second Corps commander promised to provide "a good brigade of infantry" to support Gregg in case he needed help and indicated that he would meet with him by 7:15 A.M. to review the mission. Hancock suspended his previous order to Gibbon to pursue destruction of the railroad toward Malone's Bridge pending the results of Gregg's reconnaissance.[51]

Gregg sent out small patrols, described by Hancock as "squadrons," and reported that he reached Vaughan Road in two places without seeing any infantry. Obviously, those places did not include Holly Point Church, where the Union horsemen would have seen Wilcox's camps, and they evidently left Depot Road before Wilcox advanced. Although Hill's late start ironically worked to his advantage by masking his presence a few hours longer, it is hard not to fault Gregg for failing to detect the Rebel infantry. He must have sent his troopers north of Hatcher's Run to a portion of Vaughan Road that, in the early morning hours of August 25, was indeed devoid of anything more than a few stray Rebel cavalrymen. Yet the camps of Heth's and Mahone's four brigades were a short distance from Vaughan Road near Armstrong's Mill. Gregg is strangely silent about his activities early that morning, and only Hancock's 9:00 A.M. message to Meade documents the results of the cavalry probes. Either this was an uncharacteristically sloppy piece of scouting by a usually careful officer, or Hancock's understanding of Gregg's report was flawed. In any event, the apparent absence of any imminent threat prompted Hancock to release Gibbon for his march south to resume tearing up the tracks.[52]

Smyth's brigade, accordingly, left its position in a corn-and-sorghum field east of the railroad and headed south on Halifax Road, followed by Rugg's brigade and later Murphy's. Smyth prudently sent the 1st Delaware and the 108th New York ahead as skirmishers to guard against surprises. Some of his men believed they would destroy the railroad all the way to Stony Creek that day, while others presciently apprehended that some Confederates were likely to intervene, preventing them from completing their work.[53]

Gibbon's departure prompted Miles to adjust the regiments of his division along the Reams' Station works. Colonel Lynch moved his brigade to the northern return, with his left flank, the 81st Pennsylvania, resting on the railroad and the 140th Pennsylvania anchoring his right, all facing northeast. The Consolidated Brigade was unofficially divided into its component parts that morning, while Colonel Crandell assumed responsibility for some 700 men along Miles's picket line west of the railroad. The old Third Brigade fell under the temporary command of Capt. Nelson Penfield of the 125th New York, while John Byron of the 88th New York exercised command of the old Second Brigade. Byron deployed his men on Lynch's left along the west face of the works, with his right, the 88th New York, on the northern gap through which ran the railbed. Penfield lined up on Byron's left, with his own left, the 7th New York, resting on that ten-yard gap that allowed Depot Road to enter the works. Byron's men enjoyed a line of abatis about thirty feet wide that fronted their portion of the breastworks before giving way to a piney woods, while Penfield's portion of the line faced an open field. Broady's Fourth Brigade, along with the 4th New York Heavy Artillery, occupied the trenches to the left of Penfield. Broady contributed several of his regiments to the picket force, weakening the manpower available to cover the west face south of Depot Road. Some of Broady's men began to scratch out a line running east from Halifax Road to form a southern return, but most lounged about, comfortable in their respite from railroad duty and insensible to the looming danger. "The battle-flags were set up and the courage of the men seemed high," recalled a New Hampshire volunteer. This calm reverie was about to be broken.[54]

About 9:00 A.M. shots rang out near Malone's Crossing as Spear's vedettes spied a line of Confederate cavalry heading their way. The blueclad troopers quickly fell back on their supports while projectiles fired from Hampton's horse artillery whizzed overhead, followed quickly by Davis's dismounted Virginians. The Ninth Virginia Cavalry charged through a swamp, "our steps impeded by briers, miry places, dead timber, thick underbrush and huckleberry bushes," according to Lieutenant Beale. But perceiving that few Federals blocked their direct path, the graycoats advanced, swinging around from left to right and endangering the Union rear. The Yankees recognized their perilous situation and withdrew rapidly. "As the enemy ran, you may know, we let them have it," Beale recalled. "Several killed and more wounded fell at this point, and about a company were taken prisoners." The Confederates pursued a short distance but could not catch any more of the retreating Unionists.[55]

Spear personally assessed the threat, stemming not only from Davis's approach but also from Barringer, who had maneuvered east of Halifax Road heading northwest, and from his right, where the Sixth South Carolina Cavalry, screening the Rebel infantry, pressed the Thirteenth Pennsylvania Cavalry back

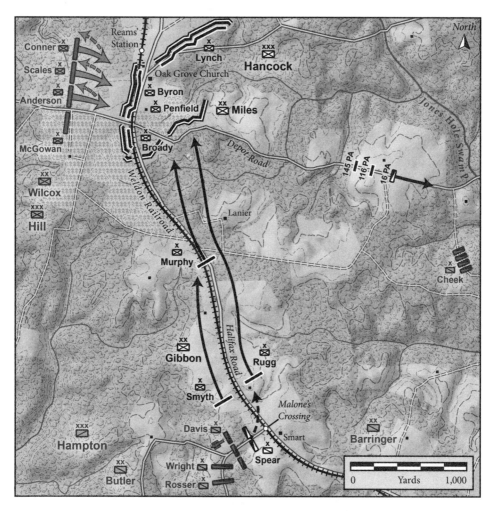

Second Reams' Station, August 25, 1864, Morning to Afternoon

along Depot Road. "I . . . found the enemy advancing in force from three directions," wrote Spear, and "sent my aide, Lieutenant [John W.] Ford, to report the same to headquarters." Hancock received this intelligence and quickly notified Gibbon to suspend plans to wreck the railroad long enough to help Spear neutralize what the corps commander believed was merely another annoying cavalry attack.[56]

Gibbon's division had progressed less than a mile from its camps when Hancock's orders arrived. Smyth, at the head of this column, received orders to deploy one of his best regiments, supported by another, west of the railroad to act as skirmishers. He was to advance them in hopes of retrieving the entrenching tools left by the First Division the day before and to try to capture the enemy then occupying that ground. Smyth selected his old regiment, the First Delaware, supported by the Twelfth New Jersey. These two units pressed ahead, pushing the Rebel cavalry back into a patch of woods, the retrieval of picks and shovels now forgotten amid the surprisingly robust resistance. A New Jerseyan considered this to be one of the "hottest places that I was ever in. . . . We were close enough to the enemy to hear their guns snap, and hear the officers giving their commands." Unable to proceed farther, Smyth called up the Fourteenth Connecticut and Tenth New York, but his brigade remained stymied, while Capt. William H. Hawley of Smyth's staff was felled by a Rebel shot. "I charged again to the swamp," reported Smyth, "and found it impossible to cross under the heavy fire."[57]

Rugg now moved up on the east side of the railbed, advancing the Seventh Michigan and Fifty-Ninth New York as skirmishers, with the remainder of his brigade advancing in support. Captain McGregor's horse artillery had accompanied Cheek's North Carolinians, and their guns played with some effect on Gibbon's soldiers along both sides of the railroad. In response, Capt. J. Henry Sleeper, in charge of the Tenth Massachusetts Battery, ordered Lt. Henry H. Granger to take a section of guns—two three-inch ordnance rifles—to the scene of action. Granger's longer-range cannon had the advantage over the smaller-caliber Confederate pieces and, after firing forty-eight rounds, silenced the Rebel guns.[58]

At some point during this exchange of artillery fire, Hampton and Hill traded communications. Hampton informed the Virginian that he was engaged with Union infantry and suggested that the time was right for Hill to advance. The Third Corps commander replied that his job would be easier if Hampton could lure his opponents farther from Hill's target at Reams' Station, allowing the Southern troops to attack Hancock's rear. Elements of Cheek's brigade attempted to do this, succeeding in drawing a portion of the 16th Pennsylvania Cavalry and two of Broady's regiments, the 116th and 145th Pennsylvania, to the far Union left. These units, however, blocked Cheek's attempt to turn Hancock's left and reach his rear via Jerusalem Plank Road and the byways leading from there to Reams' Station. Shortly after 11:00 A.M. the situation south of Reams' Station stabilized.[59]

Meanwhile, Confederate prisoners reported that Hill's Corps, reinforced by two brigades from Field's Division, had accompanied Hampton and were poised to attack. Hancock thought it "prudent" to recall Gibbon's infantry and Granger's guns to Reams' Station in light of this disturbing intelligence, despite Gregg's failure to verify the presence of Confederate infantry. Gibbon immediately ordered Rugg's and Murphy's brigades to march north and told Smyth to hold his ground until the rest of the division disengaged. Smyth would remain detached from the rest of his division until 2:00 P.M.[60]

Granger's two guns returned to Sleeper's Battery along the southern end of the west face. Murphy's brigade replaced the portion of Broady's forces that had been building the southern return, permitting Broady to move his regiments to the west face between the 10th Massachusetts Battery and Depot Road. This allowed the Consolidated Brigade to shift to the right and create a more compact line along the northern half of the west face. Rugg's units filed in on Murphy's left along the developing southern return, which now extended nearly 1,000 yards northeast of the railroad. Rugg left the 7th Michigan and 59th New York out as pickets, while Broady advanced the 116th Pennsylvania and 64th New York west of the entrenchments.[61]

Samuel Cormany of the Sixteenth Pennsylvania Cavalry had enjoyed a quiet morning on picket duty with his regiment west of Reams' Station. "I took a good bath and put on 'clean duds,'" wrote the lieutenant. Light skirmishing occupied these troopers until near noon, when elements of Dunovant's Brigade engaged them in spirited combat. The Confederates eventually retired, leaving the Pennsylvanians still unaware of the Rebel infantry that was finally on the scene.[62]

No one could accuse A. P. Hill that morning of enhancing his reputation for impetuosity. Despite his agreement to engage the Federals from the west while Hampton assailed them from the south, the cavalry had been fighting for nearly three hours before Hill's vanguard, Wilcox's four brigades, arrived within striking distance of the Reams' Station defenses. Wilcox had remained stationary just beyond Monk's Neck Bridge for two hours before countermarching on Stage Road, then moving "somewhat leisurely" east on Depot Road behind Dunovant's sheltering troopers. Wilcox halted his men about three-quarters of a mile west of the railroad and reconnoitered ahead, spotting rifle pits occupied by Federal skirmishers and beyond that a pine forest. Powder smoke from Union cannon could be seen farther east, marking what he assumed was the main enemy line.[63]

Wilcox deployed McGowan's Carolinians in the woods south of Depot Road, while sending Scales and Conner north of the road, also concealed in the trees. He then shook out the sharpshooter battalions of his division with the mission of expelling the Union skirmishers from their advanced rifle pits. Scales's sharpshooters, under Maj. John D. Young, were the first to advance. As soon as McGowan was in place, his sharpshooters, commanded by Maj. William S. Dunlop, moved forward on Young's right, and Conner's sharpshooters followed. The Confederates rousted out the Federal vedettes and then charged ahead, driving back the pickets and sending the bluecoats dashing for safety behind their main line of entrenchments. Rapid volleys from the Federal works—Major Dunlop characterized the Union fire as "a blizzard"—compelled the Rebels to halt and withdraw about a quarter mile to a slight ridge, the Federals defending the west face of the defenses still within range of the Confederate marksmen.[64]

Hancock reacted promptly to the loss of his advanced positions. He ordered Rugg to move from the left of the southern return to a supporting position behind the Consolidated Brigade along the west face. Smyth received orders to retire north and replace Rugg, while Gregg posted cavalry on the left of the southern return. Broady led his own command and a portion of the Consolidated Brigade in an attempt to regain the picket posts. "The signal for the advance was a general volley along our line," recalled Capt. James F. Weaver of the 148th Pennsylvania. "Before the smoke had time to disappear, the boys leaped the works," advancing some distance "with loud cheers in accordance with orders from Colonel Broady." But fire from McGowan and the sharpshooters sent them scurrying back to their fortifications.[65]

Hancock had been in regular contact with army headquarters all morning, first by dispatching a courier to the telegraph station near Globe Tavern, and later from a new terminal near Reams' Station. Shortly before noon the Second Corps commander informed Meade of the combat around Malone's Crossing, reiterating his earlier message that only cavalry threatened his position. Nevertheless, the army commander authorized him to retreat to Jerusalem Plank Road, "or farther if necessary," should the enemy "interpose with overpowering force between you and Warren." At 1:00 P.M. Meade acknowledged Hancock's most recent communication and informed him that he had directed two brigades of Mott's division—Brig. Gen. Byron Pierce's and Robert McAllister's, some 2,000 strong—a company of cavalry, and six Parrott Rifles from a Ninth Corps battery to march south on the plank road to reinforce him. "I think, from all the information I can obtain, that the enemy are about assuming the offensive, and will either attack you or interpose between you and Warren," he warned. Meade also relieved Hancock of any further obligation to destroy the railroad and granted him full discretion to retire to Warren's left and rear "or any other position . . . based on the knowledge of the country your recent operations may have given you." Meade has been criticized for failing to reinforce Hancock earlier and for allowing such a relatively small force to become so far separated from its closest supports. Yet he sensed trouble, even as Hancock dismissed the nearby enemy as nothing more than cavalry. "I was never in the habit of asking for reinforcements," Hancock explained, "especially when in communication with the Commander of the Army. I always thought it likely that there might be other operations as important as mine." Both generals were poised to learn the truth about their grayclad opponents.[66]

Once the Federal skirmishers fell back to the works and Broady's half-hearted attempt to redeem the situation failed, Wilcox conducted a personal reconnaissance, approaching under cover of the piney woods to within 350 yards of Hancock's position. Although trees and high brush somewhat obscured his view, the general correctly judged the Federal entrenchments to be weak but mistakenly determined that the Yankees were about to retreat. He decided to strike them a blow before they could get away. The division commander returned to McGowan's Brigade, now advanced slightly into a ripened cornfield south of Depot Road. Although the South Carolinians were no more than a quarter mile from the Union works, a wrinkle in the topography and the tall corn shielded them from view. Wilcox ordered McGowan to refrain from making an actual attack but rather to engage the Federals as a diversion.

On the north side of Depot Road, Anderson's, Scales's, and Conner's troops waited in the pines. Wilcox ordered Anderson and Scales to assail the enemy, with the Georgians on the right. When General Scales reported that the enemy extended beyond his left, Wilcox directed two of Conner's regiments to expand Scales's northern flank. McGowan opened fire, attracting a response from the Union artillery, and Wilcox ordered the Georgians and Carolinians to charge. It was almost 2:00 P.M.[67]

The Confederates burst out of the woods and into the brushy field, heading for the point where the left of the Consolidated Brigade joined Broady's right. Broady, however, was no longer in charge. Col. James A. Beaver, the brigade's former commander, had been grievously wounded on June 16 in an attack by the Second Corps during the First Petersburg Offensive. Beaver remained disabled until July 29, when he returned to the army so prematurely that he quickly returned home to resume his rehabilitation. He once again arrived at the Petersburg front on August 24 and, learning that the corps was deployed at Reams' Station, boarded an ambulance on the twenty-fifth and reported to Hancock on the very cusp of Wilcox's attack. "You are just in time," the corps commander explained, "your Brigade needs you today." Borrowing a horse, the colonel rode to the front, relieved Broady, and dismounted, even this short jaunt sapping his strength. He was about to review the disposition of his troops when a bullet slammed into his right leg. Dragged out of harm's way, stretcher-bearers removed the wounded officer from the front as Wilcox's graycoats came dashing toward the Union works. Beaver left the field in the same ambulance in which he arrived not sixty minutes earlier.[68]

As soon as the Confederates left the shelter of the timber, Union artillery blasted them with shell and canister. Although Anderson's men were at first reluctant to go forward, Wilcox's personal encouragement emboldened the Georgians to burst into the open field with a cheer. "The enemy let them get within 200 yards when they fired a volley of musketry at them, which made them retire at once," Wilcox reported. When Scales's rightmost regiment saw the Georgians flee, it, too, broke for the rear, soon followed by the rest of the Carolinians, though in better order than their chastened Georgia comrades.[69]

"The storming party came resolutely on, led by a gallant officer, who placed his cap on the point of his saber to wave them on," remembered a soldier in the Seventh New York Heavy Artillery. "They approached in extended line, yelling like demons." A Pennsylvanian recalled that as the attackers reached to within ten rods of the Union line, they let loose a Rebel Yell, which he described as "a womanlike scream." Another New Yorker reported, "Our whole line sent in a volley of lead; the result was terrible; they were mowed down as if by a scythe." Other Federals reported similar results, while Wilcox underplayed his casualties, noting only that Colonel Little of the Eleventh Georgia, the only field officer present in Anderson's entire brigade, fell badly wounded.[70]

As the Confederates returned to the cover of the pine forest, General Hill turned active direction of the infantry over to Wilcox. Hill had not been well for several days, suffering from the residual effects of a venereal disease contracted years earlier. The pain in his kidneys and his prostate gland, exacerbated by the heat of the August sun, had incapacitated him. Wilcox, unfazed by the repulse, determined to try the Federals again.[71]

The nature of this subsequent assault remains a bit murky. Hancock wrote that "a second and more vigorous attack followed at a short interval and was likewise repulsed, some of the enemy falling within a few yards of the breastwork." Major Mitchell of his staff reported that this charge lasted "only four or five minutes; enemy repulsed, with severe loss." Wilcox, however, stated that Hill, despite his incapacitation, ordered him to suspend another effort until Heth's brigades could be employed. "I thought it best to renew the attack at once," admitted Wilcox, who had intended to use Conner and McGowan in his second attempt, when Heth appeared, placing his two brigades under Wilcox's command. Either the Confederate high command conspired to mute any mention of a failed follow-up to their unsuccessful first assault, or Union witnesses mistook a second lunge by Anderson and Scales as an entirely separate effort. In either case, the opposing armies now merely exchanged random fire, neither side advancing.[72]

Hancock maintained active communications with Meade during the Confederate assault and immediately afterward. Both officers expressed concern that the Rebels would interpose in the nearly four-mile gap along the ruined railroad between Warren's position around Globe Tavern and Reams' Station. At 2:45 P.M. Hancock observed that, considering that his mission of extending the destruction of the railroad had now ended, "there is no great necessity of my remaining here," allowing that he should close on Warren's left. But Wilcox's failed attack convinced the Second Corps commander that trying to disengage with the aggressive Confederates in such proximity would be too risky, adding, "I think it will be well to withdraw to-night, if I am not forced to do so before." Hancock expressed optimism that his position was secure but confessed that he could not intercede if the Rebels inserted themselves between his troops and the Fifth Corps. "Warren had better be watchful until I can make a practicable connection with him," he advised. Meade continued to be less sanguine about Hancock's situation. He ordered Willcox's Ninth Corps division and some artillery to join Mott's troops on a trek south along Jerusalem Plank Road to further reinforce the isolated Second Corps. If both officers feared that Hill and Hampton would gain a position between Globe Tavern and Reams' Station, it is curious that Meade decided not to direct these reinforcements down Halifax Road, where they might contest any such Confederate initiative. That route entailed a five-mile march, while using the plank road meant traveling more than twice that distance. Meade's emissary, Capt. William W. Sanders, had returned to headquarters by riding north on Halifax Road, proof that it remained open at least through midafternoon.[73]

The Confederates, in fact, did nothing to interdict Halifax Road north of Reams' Station following Wilcox's initial assault, limiting their aggression to spirited fire from their advanced sharpshooters. These marksmen positioned themselves 400 yards from the Federal works, shielded by a small crest behind which they maintained a steady fire, "a perfect sheet of lead," according to Major Dunlop. The Federals responded in kind, but as the afternoon progressed, the defenders grew less eager to expose themselves above the works. "The sharpshooters mounted the crest and with unerring aim proceeded to split the scalp of every mother's son that dared to lift his head above the breastworks," wrote Dunlop. Deprived of human targets, the marksmen focused their fire on the artillery horses. "The rebel sharpshooters, from their position in the corn-field had full range of the horses attached to our limbers and rapidly shot them down until not one remained unhurt on either limber, many receiving five or six bullets before they fell," reported Lieutenant Granger, who had assumed command of the Tenth Massachusetts Battery following the wounding of Captain Sleeper. The battery's historian recalled that of its thirty animals visible to the enemy, only two remained standing, and even they were wounded. All told, 134 horses fell victim to Confederate marksmanship.[74]

The Federal gunners had expended so much ammunition trying to suppress this deadly fire that their limber chests were nearly empty. Attrition of the battery horses and both the deep cut and high embankment of the railbed that separated the cannon west of the railroad from their reserve ammunition to the east made resupplying the ordnance a difficult and dangerous task. "The only way to get a supply is for cannoneers to creep along inside the works, and reaching a point less exposed, run the gauntlet to the rear and provide themselves with a few rounds. One man from each piece makes the trip," explained a gunner. The infantry also slackened their fire to preserve its cartridges, all in response to the work of a few hundred Rebel riflemen. Dunlop found "the tenacity with which the gentlemen in blue hugged the trenches . . . amusing." According to historian Earl Hess, "at Reams Station . . . the sharpshooters of Lee's army had their finest day of the war."[75]

Hancock informed Meade at 3:40 P.M. that "the enemy just assaulted Miles's front in two lines, but were repulsed," evidently repeating the account of the Anderson-Scales 2:00 P.M. attack, as there is no unimpeachable evidence of a separate Southern advance. Within the next hour, Hancock wired the army commander thrice more, assuring Meade that his right flank was secure but allowing that the Confederates had blocked the roads to Stony Creek to the south and Dinwiddie Court House to the west. He also sought clear instructions as to whether he should retire from Reams' Station during the night and expressed disappointment that Willcox had not tried to join him by marching down Halifax Road. Hancock then communicated via courier with Mott's approaching reinforcements, under the overall command of Colonel McAllister, and with Willcox. McAllister's contingent arrived at Shay's Tavern and the road leading west to Reams' Station about 5:00 P.M., halting across the plank road and sending two couriers to Hancock announcing his presence and seeking orders. Before these emissaries returned, General Meade himself appeared and directed McAllister to advance a short distance south and "take up a good position for defence." Barringer's earlier foray toward the plank road caused the army commander to fear an attack against Hancock's rear more than against his front, which may explain why he did not make the short ride to consult with Hancock personally.[76]

Meanwhile, Wilcox and Heth approached Hill—who was evidently well enough to issue orders but not sufficiently hearty to take the field—proposing that combined, their forces could attack the Federals successfully. Hill had been wary of allowing Wilcox to exercise his desire to renew the assaults, considering how easily the Yankees had repelled his initial effort. But the recommendation of both his division commanders, backed by the opinions of Heth's two respected brigade leaders, convinced the lieutenant general to approve another attempt. This effort would be buttressed by artillery, Pegram and his seventeen guns having been on the scene since about 3:00 P.M.[77]

Hill's first instinct was to limit the attack to just Cooke's and MacRae's fresh brigades. Wilcox objected, renewing the argument that all of his units should join Heth's in the assault. Hill relented. Heth and Wilcox then conducted a brief reconnaissance that convinced them both that Conner and Scales should reinforce Heth's two brigades. Pegram's artillery would precede the infantry assault with a bombardment. Cooke's and Conner's Carolinians were to form the first line, while Scales and MacRae would deploy in support. Heth, who was senior to Wilcox, assumed tactical authority over the operation. He departed to deploy Pegram's batteries, while Wilcox positioned Cooke on his right and Conner to the left, both concealed by the piney woods. Scales deployed his Tar Heels behind and slightly to the north of Conner, and MacRae positioned his five regiments to Cooke's rear, extending south of Depot Road beyond Cooke's southern flank. Heth placed Pegram's batteries in a field to the right and rear of MacRae in position to enfilade the Union line, not more than 500 yards distant. By then, Mahone's two brigades had arrived. Hill ordered Weisiger and King to provide flank protection on the left of the formation, while Anderson's and McGowan's Brigades did the same on the right.[78]

Wilcox and Heth finished positioning their troops at 5:00 P.M. The sun grew lower behind them, and the grayclad generals knew that they would enjoy only enough daylight for this one final attack. Heth, who stationed himself with Pegram, instructed the cannoneer to open fire. "His young face aglow with the light of battle," Pegram gave the signal that unleashed the fury of his seventeen guns. "About five o'clock we received the order to commence firing, and it was done with a vim scarcely equaled in any battle," boasted an Alabama artillery-man. "We have had the honor to be in all the general engagements of this army since July 1861, but never before saw artillery so beautifully served." The excited cannoneers wielded rammers and lanyards so rapidly that their captain feared they would burst their pieces. Most of the projectiles overshot the west face of the works and landed amid Miles's troops in the northern return, taking them in reverse. An officer in the Twentieth Massachusetts recalled that "in some places men jumped on the outside of the earthwork for safety, preferring bullets to shells." A New York soldier reported that Pegram's fire "completely paralyzed

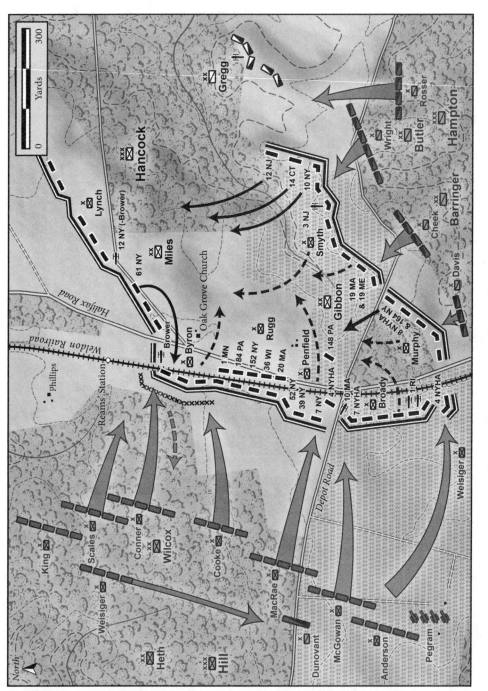

Second Reams' Station, August 25, 1864, Late Afternoon to Evening

our men with the deafening roar and terrible shrieking of shells." The firing was so intense that Cpl. Jacob Bechtel of the Fifty-Ninth New York overestimated its duration by a factor of six. Union artillery responded, but most of its shells flew harmlessly over Pegram's position. After fifteen minutes the Confederate guns fell silent. Now it was up to the infantry.[79]

Conner's men on the left of the attack formation would have to negotiate the woods that sheltered them from sight, then traverse a substantial tangle of abatis before reaching the Federal works. Most of Cooke's Brigade faced the same challenge, but MacRae's men, now virtually on the front line, had no such obstacles to overcome. Because of the impediments they faced, Conner's and Cooke's troops were to move first, followed by MacRae, with the intent that all three brigades reach the Union works simultaneously. These 1,730 battle-hardened veterans waited expectantly for the signal to advance. Giving that signal possessed no little drama. General Heth decided to trigger the attack himself by moving to the front of MacRae's formation and waving the flag of the Twenty-Sixth North Carolina. The regimental color-bearer, however, declined Heth's request to relinquish his banner and then refused Heth's order a second time. The general, submitting no doubt with unspoken admiration, then took the obstinate private, Thomas M. Minton, by the arm, saying, "Come on then, we will carry the colors together." The two men hoisted the treasured symbol, eliciting what Cpl. Joseph Mullen of Cooke's Twenty-Seventh North Carolina called a "signal whoop," and the Carolinians of Conner and Cooke moved ahead. "We had orders as soon as one loud holloa was given to all holloa and rush forward as fast as we could," wrote Mullen.[80]

Conner's brigade aimed for the right half of the Consolidated Brigade and the gap in the line on that unit's right. "After advancing about 200 yards, we reached the edge of the wood, in front of which the enemy built strong earthworks and an almost impenetrable abatis," reported Capt. James G. Harris of the Seventh North Carolina on the brigade's far left. "At this point the enemy poured a destructive fire of musketry and artillery into our front and flank, which at first caused some confusion, but owing to the exertion of the officers, order was soon restored and the men stood firmly and returned the fire of the enemy for over fifteen minutes exposed to the most galling fire they had ever been under." Col. William H. Asbury Speer, commanding Harris's regiment, fell with a mortal head wound, and his men withdrew about 300 yards, finding shelter in a small ravine.[81]

The balance of Conner's Tar Heels also suffered from the intense Union fire. "The enemy poured volley after volley into us, and their 12-pounder Napoleons literally mowed the bushes and seemed to belch forth right in our faces," wrote

Capt. Edward J. Hale, the brigade adjutant. Many of Conner's survivors joined Speer's men in retreating to a point of safety. Only the Eighteenth North Carolina on the right of the brigade formation managed to remain at the front. Pvt. Thomas M. Hanna of the Thirty-Seventh North Carolina was among those who withdrew unharmed from the relentless fire, although a bullet aimed at his chest lodged halfway through the pocket Bible in his jacket.[82]

Many of Cooke's troops charged along on the right of Conner's men, while a portion of the brigade remained concealed in the forest. "We were ordered to move forward, which we did as good as troops ever did," wrote Corporal Mullen. He and his comrades had advanced about 150 yards when they emerged from the trees to spot the Union works some 75 yards to their front. "But the ground over which we had to go was a dreadful place," thought Mullen. "They had cut down the thick undergrowth which was matted with briers and it made an almost insurmountable abatis.... They poured a volley into our ranks which thinned them very much." The Fifteenth and Forty-Sixth North Carolina retreated under this pressure.[83]

Despite this impasse, both Conner and Cooke had easily overwhelmed the Federal skirmishers from three New York regiments—the 111th, 125th, and 126th—who, in the words of General Miles, "made feeble resistance." The troops inside the works had to hold their fire until these skirmishers cleared their front, then they opened up. The men in the Consolidated Brigade and the Fourth Brigade to their left, once again under Colonel Broady, rammed cartridges down the barrels of their rifles as fast as humanly possible. Lynch's men, ensconced behind the works in the northern return, managed to fire obliquely at Conner, while the 4th New York Heavy Artillery enjoyed the same advantage against Cooke from its position on Broady's left. "Although [the Confederates] pushed forward with determination [they] were repulsed at several points and [their] organization greatly broken up by [the] severity of the fire and the obstacles in his front," reported Miles. The First Division commander had placed one gun of the 12th New York Battery at the gap where the railroad penetrated the works between the west face and the northern return. This piece, along with other Union cannon, gave the Rebels "their whole attention, using shell and shrapnel until within short range, when they fired rapidly with canister." At this point, Heth's attack looked to be as forlorn as the one Wilcox had superintended three hours earlier.[84]

General MacRae had withheld his five regiments while Conner and Cooke attacked a few hundred yards to his left. Unlike those brigades, MacRae's men did not confront a line of abatis, meaning that they would be able to reach the Union works more quickly than their comrades. Charging too soon might allow the Federals to concentrate their resistance against MacRae's troops alone. The general thought it best to wait until Conner and Cooke had progressed through the obstructions before starting his assault.

MacRae had been in charge of his brigade for less than two months, his predecessor, General Kirkland, having been wounded in June at Cold Harbor. Not yet thirty years old, the young brigadier had been a civil engineer before the war, surveying railroad lines in the South. He rose through the ranks of the Fifteenth North Carolina in Cooke's Brigade, distinguishing himself in numerous engagements. "His voice was like that of a woman," wrote one observer. "He was small in person, and quick in action. He could place his command in position quicker and infuse more of his fighting qualities into his men, than any officer I ever saw. His presence with his troops seemed to dispel all fear, and to inspire every one with a desire for the fray."[85]

And eager for the fray they were. MacRae ordered his adjutant, Louis Young, to take command of the brigade's left-most regiments. "He instructed me to walk down my portion of the line, and say to the men, that beyond the wood was an open field over which they must pass before reaching the enemy," wrote Captain Young. "That while advancing through the wood they must be quiet; but when the field was reached, the charge would begin, and then every man must yell as though he was a division in himself, dash for the enemy's works, and not fire until there. As I looked into the eyes of the men while giving them these unusual instructions, it was easy to see that the works would be taken." The intervening woods hid Conner's fate from MacRae's observation, but Cooke's hesitation and partial repulse was plain to see. "I shall wait no longer for orders," MacRae told Young as he signaled his brigade to charge.[86]

"When the order was given to advance, the men threw themselves forward at a double-quick in a line as straight and unbroken as they presented when on parade," wrote an officer in the Forty-Fourth North Carolina. Although their instructions to remain quiet were obeyed in the breach, the men did withhold their fire as they dashed across the open ground toward the seam between the Consolidated Brigade and the right flank of Broady's command. Cooke's men, seeing the progress made on their right by their North Carolina comrades, renewed their assault.[87]

At the far left flank of the Consolidated Brigade, the Seventh New York saw the gray onslaught heading straight at them. Some 600 men of this regiment, composed largely of German immigrants, had only recently joined the army and had not yet "seen the elephant." Their unsoiled uniforms and shiny new rifles betrayed their status as combat neophytes. A soldier in the Seventh New York Heavy Artillery, on Broady's immediate right, thought that the charging

Confederates, recognizing these men as newcomers, focused their attack at them. Although such a calculation amid a headlong charge seems highly unlikely, MacRae's men slammed into the inexperienced New Yorkers. The regiment broke almost immediately, carrying the Thirty-Ninth New York and the Fifty-Second New York on their right with them. "The victory was in our own hands," recalled General Miles bitterly, "and it was the fault of a few dutch cowards that we did not win a glorious victory." Pvt. Charles Lee of the Thirty-Ninth New York summarized the desperate situation succinctly: "They drove us and gave us a regular Bull Run panic."[88]

When the troops on their left broke, the 125th, 126th and 111th New York were outflanked, and they, too, collapsed. These regiments had been weakened by providing troops to the vanquished skirmish line and were thus especially vulnerable. The 148th Pennsylvania had been placed behind the Consolidated Brigade as a near support, but when the frontline regiments gave way, these Pennsylvanians became more of a hindrance than a help. Soon the North Carolinians were swarming around the unfortunate Federals, many of whom surrendered as grayclad infantry blocked their avenues of escape.[89]

The collapse of the Consolidated Brigade exposed the right flank of Broady's men to enfilade fire. Colonel Broady fell wounded, and the Swedish immigrant was assisted to a field hospital by Pvt. George B. Smith of the 53rd Pennsylvania. "In front of a portion of the brigade the rebs threw down their arms & were surrendering, but on the right they came in on the railroad, which passed through the works & got in the rear of the right of our Brigade," explained Capt. John Noyes. Some of MacRae's men also penetrated the gap in the line where Depot Road entered the works. "The victorious enemy poured through the opening, capturing flags, guns, and prisoners," wrote Col. St. Clair A. Mulholland of the 116th Pennsylvania. "Hancock and Miles were everywhere, cheering, rallying and urging the men, but the break was too great to repair and the line was forced back." Some stubborn Federals remained at the works, engaging the Confederates with clubbed muskets, but as Lieutenant Lockely recalled of the Rebels, "they seemed to swarm everywhere." The 10th Massachusetts Battery ran low on ammunition and was threatened by the Southerners, some of the cannoneers declining "the touching invitations of the 'Johnnies,' who tell us to 'come in,' or they'll shoot us," according to the battery's historian. "But we are not quite ready to respond to their appeal for their society, even when coupled with such a compulsory proposition, and make for the bushes in rear of Battery B ... where we separate, each taking the course that seemed best to him, and no one knowing whether exit from the field was then possible."[90]

Men from all three Rebel brigades claimed to be the first to plant their colors on the Union works, but all agreed that the Federals either "fled in great confusion" or "threw down their guns & came to us in droves." "No guard was required to accompany prisoners to the rear for they rushed along in crowds," wrote Captain Justice. "One officer said that he thought the hurrying crowd of prisoners was a successful charge of the enemy." Some of the victorious graycoats reversed the captured artillery and fired what ammunition they could find at the retreating enemy. "The scene was most brilliant," exclaimed Maj. William J. Baker of MacRae's staff, "and the men now think they can whip a[ny] number of Yankees."[91]

The near-total collapse of the west-face works prompted Miles to call on the reserves posted behind the deteriorating line in the railroad cut and on the embankment to the east. These reserves belonged to Rugg's brigade of the Second Division, earlier assigned to bolster Miles. Prior to Heth's attack, Rugg and a portion of his command received orders to move to the left in support of Colonel Murphy's brigade in the southern return. In doing so, he left the 20th Massachusetts and the 36th Wisconsin in position behind the west face. Sometime later, however, Rugg's 152nd New York, 184th Pennsylvania, and 1st Minnesota Battalion were sent back in support of Miles. "I looked for Lieutenant-Colonel Rugg, but not at the moment seeing him I directed his brigade to rush into the gap and commence firing," reported Miles. "Not a minute's time was lost before giving this order, but instead of executing it they either lay on their faces or got up and ran to the rear."[92]

Miles's judgment might be too harsh, as Rugg's men had almost no time to react to the sudden emergency. "The first intimation the 36th had that anything was wrong was that [a] regiment came tumbling down on them, as they were in the railroad cut, and the yelling johnnies right after them," wrote Pvt. Walter Osgood Hart of the Thirty-Sixth Wisconsin. "The reserves could do nothing," testified another Badger, "as the First Division, apparently panic-stricken, were passing to the rear and over our men, which made it impossible for them to fire on the enemy." The Confederates poured into the railroad cut, nearly surrounding Rugg's soldiers. "A few men cut their way out at great risk," recalled Lt. Col. Clement E. Warner, commanding the Thirty-Sixth Wisconsin, while the rest of the troops were compelled to surrender.[93]

The relentless Rebel attackers now threatened the rear of Lynch's brigade, posted in the northern return. "The enemy, having made a successful assault on the work on my left, broke through and attacked my left and rear with vigor, causing considerable confusion," admitted Colonel Lynch. A brief hand-to-hand fight ensued, but the Federals "had to retire in doublequick time," being overwhelmed from multiple directions. Their departure isolated the Twelfth New York Battery. Lt. Henry D. Brower commanded the gun covering the gap in the line between the northern return and the right end of the west face. Elements of Cooke's Brigade, along with the Eighteenth North Carolina of Conner's command, fired at Brower and his cannoneers, killing the lieutenant and capturing the gun. Crews from the battery's remaining three cannons attempted to save their pieces, but Rebel bullets felled many of the battery horses, compelling the gunners to abandon their ordnance.[94]

"Affairs at this juncture were in a critical condition," wrote Hancock, as the position along the northern return disintegrated. He sent a message to Willcox to hurry along a brigade which, if in time, "could save the day." "The panic had become somewhat general," admitted Miles, "and it was with the greatest difficulty that any line could be formed." The general noticed that his old regiment, the Sixty-First New York, was still "fighting with determination . . . and contesting every foot of ground gained by the enemy." He gathered a motley collection of soldiers from various regiments, forming them on the stalwart New Yorkers. The thick battle smoke that hung in the air this humid summer afternoon partially concealed this developing battle line from Confederate view. When Miles ordered these men to advance with a cheer, "it swept the enemy from the entire north face of the works, recapturing the three guns of the Twelfth New York Battery and driving the enemy into the railroad cut." Volunteers from several regiments hauled these cannons off the field. Maj. James E. Larkin, commanding the Fifth New Hampshire, claimed credit for recapturing them.[95]

It was now nearly 6:00 P.M., and Heth decided to commit a portion of McGowan's Brigade to his attack. Capt. Langdon Cheves Haskell, the brigade adjutant, led these Palmetto State men toward the gap in the works along Depot Road. Here, the remaining cannoneers of the Tenth Massachusetts Battery defended the line, supported on their right by the Fourth New York Heavy Artillery. To the left, Batteries A and B of the First Rhode Island Light Artillery joined the Bay State gunners in ramming home their remaining rounds of double canister aimed at MacRae's and now McGowan's graycoats. The pressure proved too much for the heavies, who, "at this critical juncture [were] unable to honor the draft the situation made on their courage and manhood" and started for the rear, even as the Massachusetts gunners called them cowards, "with all the choice adjectives prefixed that we can summon from our vocabulary." Pvt. William A. Templeton of the Twelfth South Carolina agreed with this assessment: "They maid a very poor resistance in our front of our brigade. They gest fierd one voley and then gave up." The noise of battle muted the orders to retreat, and the First Battalion of the heavies, on the left of their line, fell captive en masse. The Rhode Islanders exhausted their ammunition and attempted to flee, but all their officers became prisoners and the Rebels claimed their guns as trophies. Likewise, the Tenth Massachusetts Battery fell into Southern hands. "As to the fight, I can only say that we did all we could and had our infantry support been other than rank cowards, we should not have been taken," lamented the battery's Pvt. William E. Endicott. The South Carolinians seized some 400 Yankees between the cannoneers and their infantry supports.[96]

General Hancock did all he could to redeem this dire situation. His adjutant general, Colonel Walker—he would soon be captured—stated that the general "exposed himself more conspicuously than any private soldier, in his efforts to restore the fortunes of the day." Hancock's mount was shot from under him, and the corps flag "was pierced by five balls," its staff shattered. Undaunted, the Second Corps commander now ordered Gibbon to mount a counterattack to regain the works along the west face.[97]

Gibbon's division occupied the southern return, with Murphy's brigade on the right and the Nineteenth Maine and Nineteenth Massachusetts of Rugg's command, which had not been sent to Miles, to Murphy's left. Smyth's brigade, which was the last unit to return to the defenses that afternoon, was on Gibbon's far left, busily improving their works. The Confederate breakthrough had compelled Gibbon to move his troops to the opposite side of their fortifications when Hancock's attack order arrived.[98]

Gibbon promptly responded. Smyth's entire brigade arose and turned toward the Confederate breakthrough, with Rugg's two regiments to their left and the 164th New York and 8th New York Heavy Artillery of Murphy's brigade on the formation's far left. In the chaos occasioned by this tactical emergency, Gibbon's men charged straight ahead rather than wheeling toward the west face. This exposed Murphy's and Rugg's regiments to an enfilade fire that staggered them, leading Gibbon to condemn their performance as "a very feeble effort." Not all of Smyth's men distinguished themselves either, their commander ascribing their lack of "promptness and alacrity which usually characterizes the movements of the troops of my command" to their odd position on the opposite side of their trenches and "their exhausted condition after the active operations of the previous part of the day."[99]

But not all of Smyth's brigade deserved such opprobrium. The three units now on the right of his reversed alignment—the Twelfth New Jersey, Fourteenth Connecticut, and three companies of the Tenth New York—withstood the rain of Confederate lead and fought their way across the interior of the Federal horseshoe, joining some of Miles's men around the recaptured pieces of the Twelfth New York Battery. Lt. Col. George Hopper of the Tenth New York believed that his men "did not seem to know what fear was." Some of his soldiers fired fifty rounds while at the front, an unprecedented volume. The Fourteenth Connecticut dashed across the base of the Union position, "exposed to a heavy fire of both musketry and artillery," while Capt. Henry F. Chew of the Twelfth New Jersey led his regiment on the charge "in gallant style," accompanied by Ned Brownson of Hancock's staff. The Garden State men reached the recaptured guns, but Captain Brownson was killed before gaining the works. All three of these units suffered severe losses.[100]

The bulk of Gibbon's timid attackers returned to the reverse side of the southern return, only to begin receiving fire from their rear. These shots came from Hampton's cavalry, which now reentered the battle. Hampton had deployed his two divisions astride the railroad near Malone's Crossing, waiting for Hill to start his attack. When the sound of Pegram's artillery reached his ears, Hampton ordered his men forward, Butler's Division west of the railroad and Barringer's to the east. The Second North Carolina Cavalry, under Col. William P. Roberts, and a portion of the Ninth Virginia Cavalry rode ahead as skirmishers, while the rest of the Virginians followed on foot. After going about a mile, the mounted Rebels came across the Seventh Michigan and Fifty-Ninth New York of Rugg's brigade, still serving as skirmishers. Roberts charged, "sweeping the enemy before them in the wildest confusion" and rounding up five or six dozen prisoners.[101]

Once the dismounted troopers arrived, Hampton renewed his northward advance. He progressed far enough to see that the infantry had captured the Union works along the west face—so, to avoid confusion, he shifted Butler's Division east of the railroad. Davis's brigade of Barringer's division now formed Hampton's left, their left flank hugging the railbed. Cheek's North Carolinians deployed in the center, and Wright's brigade of Butler's Division formed on the right. Rosser's Laurel Brigade provided a supporting line. All four brigades advanced primarily dismounted, although some troopers remained on their horses to respond to an emergency. Hampton pivoted, keeping his left along the railroad, while the right swung wide enough to overlap the Union position, poised to gain its rear. This would be no easy feat, as elements of Smyth's brigade had refused Gibbon's left almost all the way behind Oak Grove Church. A lone three-inch rifle unlimbered to support the impending attack.[102]

After his troopers had deployed as directed, Hampton gave the signal to advance. It was now nearly sunset. The Confederates marched into a patch of woods and flushed out a few Federal skirmishers. Soon, they encountered a line of abatis, the dismounted cavalrymen "clambering through the branches and over the trunks of fallen timber." When the Rebels came within view, Gibbon's remaining men, many of whom had remained on the outside of the works along the southern return, hopped back to the inside, caught between the charging dismounted cavalry and the Carolina infantry along the captured west face. They laid down a prodigious fire which, as Hampton admitted, "for a few moments checked our advance." But in the words of another South Carolinian, the troopers "pushed forward with a spirit entitling them to march shoulder to shoulder with the infantry of the Army of Northern Virginia, and there is no higher praise than this."[103]

One of Davis's Virginians recalled, "After passing up and down several hills, through much upright and felled timber and one boggy ravine ... [we] began ascending ground that rose gently from the base of the hill, tearing ourselves as best we could through the thick abattis of fallen trees and bushes, till we came in full view of the enemy's earthworks ... scarcely fifty yards off." To their right Barringer's Tar Heels reached the clearing in front of the works and charged with a yell. On Cheek's right Colonel Wright's brigade came under artillery fire, emanating, unknown to them, from the pieces captured by the Confederate infantry and now aimed at Gibbon's line. This mixed outfit of Georgians and Alabamans hit the ground, trying to avoid the incoming shells. Wright saw what he thought were his men acting in a cowardly fashion and "indulged in uncomplimentary and uncalled for strictures." A lieutenant in Cobb's Legion Cavalry resented his commander's insinuation and challenged the colonel to personal combat. Fortunately, the bombardment ceased before these officers came to blows, and Wright's line arose and started forward. This delay allowed the Twelfth Virginia Cavalry of Rosser's command to advance on Wright's right flank. These troopers were shocked to find the Twelfth Virginia Infantry in their midst. Hill had unleashed Weisiger's Brigade to support MacRae's right, and the two Old Dominion units exchanged "salutations" and commenced a contest to see which of the Twelfths would breach the Union line first.[104]

The cavalry allegedly won this race, but in truth Confederates from many units rushed simultaneously over the works. Weisiger's men had earlier cleared out the remaining Federals near the western end of the southern return, allowing Davis to gain the right flank of Gibbon's remaining defenders. Those Federals turned to fire at the Virginians, who found shelter behind a sturdy traverse. Cheek's Carolinians endured "a perfect hailstorm of bullets" as they crested the works. Captain McGregor, accompanied by six or eight men from his battery, joined the Tar Heels and, according to a member of Barringer's staff, "charged ahead of every one and leaped his horse over the Yankee works, right in the midst of them." A Union officer fired, missing McGregor but wounding his horse. "You —— scoundrel you have shot Bolivar," screamed McGregor, who promptly put a bullet into his antagonist. On the right Colonel Wright "hesitated not to lead into the jaws of death with all the furious ferocity of a maddened tiger," as his men cleared the works. Lt. Wiley C. Howard of Cobb's Legion Cavalry claimed that Roger Pryor joined their attack, in partial atonement for his faulty reconnaissance four days earlier. "His presence, coolness and courage amid the roar of artillery and the din of battle, were an inspiration to all as he moved and fought with rank and file."[105]

Gibbon's situation had become hopeless. "The men soon gave way in great confusion and gave up the breast works almost without resistance," he reported. In reality, of course, his beleaguered soldiers had put up a respectable fight until Hampton's men penetrated their line. Colonel Murphy averred that some of his troops crossed and recrossed the works four times, "being forced by the enemy's fire, which at one time would come from the rear and then change again to the front." His brigade held its position "until the advance of the enemy on our front and flank made the capture of the greater part of the command very probable." Lieutenant Colonel Hopper wrote that "the firing was so uncertain coming from all sides," calling the engagement "one of the most terrible battles I ever seen." Murphy's and Smyth's troops abandoned the southern return and fell back to some woods, where they attempted to form a new line. Those elements of Rugg's brigade still fighting also retreated, leaving "on the double-quick to save their own heads," according to a Michigander. "The enemy had by this time turned the left of the lines and came pouring in," remembered a soldier in the Nineteenth Massachusetts, "the fire at this moment coming from three points—front, rear and left flank. . . . This command was withdrawn at dusk, being the last to leave the field."[106]

Gregg's cavalry, posted on Gibbon's far left, performed yeoman duty protecting the infantry's retreat. Assisted by a section of the Third New Jersey Battery, this "dismounted cavalry, together with about 100 infantry of different regiments collected in my vicinity, maintained a telling fire upon the enemy until after they had possession of the works on my right," wrote Gregg. "Our men were cool and behaved well," boasted Quartermaster Sgt. John Daniel Follmer of the Sixteenth Pennsylvania Cavalry. Eventually, Gregg ordered his troopers to retire, forming on Gibbon's survivors, some of the cavalry maintaining resistance until well after dark. "I have never seen anything half so beautiful as the night fighting," wrote Capt. Thomas J. Gregg of the Sixteenth Pennsylvania Cavalry. "We held their cavalry and infantry for four hours." The New Jersey cannoneers also stood firm after sunset, absorbing severe punishment for their trouble. "We fought till dark," confirmed Pvt. James Mitchell, and "out of twenty-eight cannoneers we lost twelve, all shot by rifle balls but one man who got half of his head blown off with a shell[;] the same shell knocked us all down that were around the gun."[107]

General Hancock, supposedly mortified beyond consolation at the collapse of his once-proud corps, is widely quoted as wishing to die on the field rather than face the humiliation of such a shameful defeat. Events cast doubt on this hoary characterization of his sentiments. While Gibbon's line retreated and Gregg made a last-stand defense, Miles, at the other end of the Union position, proposed a counterattack to regain everything his division had surrendered. "In going to the front I could hear the enemy's men calling out their regiments, and I felt confident his loss was much heavier than ours, that his confusion was equal, and that I could retake all my line." Miles sent a staff officer to Hancock proposing this eleventh-hour counteroffensive. Hancock consulted Gregg, who agreed to "retake the works entire," but Gibbon demurred. Without the willing participation of the Second Division, Hancock had little choice but to order a wholesale retreat.[108]

The Second Corps commander then rode rapidly east along the road to Shay's Tavern "to meet Wil[l]cox for the purpose of establishing a line of battle through which the 'Reams Station' troops could pass or form upon in case the enemy should attack." He encountered the general and his division, or what was present of it, about a mile and a half from the battlefield. Willcox asked Hancock how the battle had gone. "Licked like hell" was his reply. Willcox had been doing his best to corral the fugitives who had fled the field and explained that he had only about 900 of his own men with him, the rest straggling along the plank road. That was good enough for Hancock, who ordered him to establish a rallying point, considering the location "as good a position as I could see." Miles formed the rear guard of the withdrawing Federals, entrusting the work to the Sixty-First New York, until reaching Willcox's welcome reinforcements.[109]

By then, the heavens had unleashed a prodigious thunderstorm. "The sky was black as a thundercloud & in one hour you could not distinguish a person at two paces distance & the flashes of lightning only made it still darker," wrote one of Willcox's men. The rain added to the misery that permeated Hancock's ranks. "We . . . made a regular ski-daddle," admitted a surgeon from the Fifth New Hampshire. "On we go, faint, hungry, and drenched to the skin . . . staggering into ruts and mud holes," wrote a Pennsylvanian. Hancock's bedraggled veterans stumbled five or six miles into a wet bivouac near the Williams house, along Jerusalem Plank Road, between midnight and 2:30 A.M.[110]

During the triumphant Confederate assaults and while Hancock executed his retreat, Meade, who had returned to his command post, sent a series of messages to Reams' Station, first providing Hancock the option to withdraw and then ordering it. By 10:30 that evening, he understood that Hancock had been dislodged and now ordered both Crawford's and White's divisions to march from Warren's front to Hancock's relief. Thirty minutes later the army commander learned fully of Hancock's disaster and sent a message of condolence, laced with a justification as to why he had not reinforced the Second Corps sooner. "No one sympathizes with you more than I do in the misfortunes of this evening," wrote Meade. "If I had any doubt of your ability to hold your lines from a direct attack, I would have sent Willcox with others down the railroad, but my anxiety was about your rear, and my apprehension that they would either move around your left or interpose between you and Warren." He further explained that he had withheld the rest of the Ninth Corps as well as the entire Fifth Corps around Globe Tavern: "I thought it likely after trying you they might attack Warren, and wanted to leave him till the last moment some reserves." This rationale must have provided Hancock cold comfort.[111]

Gregg left behind two regiments, the First Maine Cavalry and Sixteenth Pennsylvania Cavalry, to keep an eye on the victorious Confederates. Although they could not know it, Hill and Hampton had no intention of pursuing their defeated enemy. Not only were the Rebels exhausted, but the thunderstorm, with "lurid streaks of lightning so vivid, so fierce, that the eyes would blind . . . while thunder rattled and rolled, peal after peal, that made the very earth shake," had made a night attack unthinkable. Squads helped remove wounded comrades and bury the dead. The battlefield was a charnel house. "In the track of the shot from guns, men were seen torn to pieces—heads, arms, and legs scattered around, and bodies horribly mangled." Col. Richard H. Dulany of the Seventh Virginia Cavalry saw Oak Grove Church filled with the dead and wounded along with 150 corpses that lay about the trenches unburied. Members of Hurt's Battery labored to strip the harness from dead horses to use them on mules, brought up from the wagon train eight miles in the rear, to remove the captured artillery. They worked amid flashes of lightning that "would impress whatever object we were looking towards at the time on the retina for at least several minutes." This was no pleasant task, given the concentration of mutilated animals near where the Federals had positioned their batteries. "The number of the enemy's horses killed was unusually large," wrote a correspondent to the *Petersburg Express*. "We counted sixty-one of their muzzles piled up lying around on about a quarter acre of ground."[112]

Between ten o'clock and midnight, most of the Rebel infantry departed the battlefield, marching four or five miles west and bivouacking on the far side of Rowanty Creek. The sharpshooters and a portion of McGowan's Brigade supported seven of Hampton's regiments, which remained on the sodden field until the next morning. They continued policing the battlefield, gathering small arms and accoutrements, and completed the interments that had begun during the night. Early on the twenty-sixth, a Federal messenger arrived under flag of truce seeking permission to send a party forward to attend to the Union casualties. Hampton declined the request, explaining that the wounded had been removed and the dead already buried. The gravediggers saved themselves some labor by rolling bodies into the ditch fronting the captured Union works, "thus offering a melancholy illustration of how often brave men in making works for their protection literally dig their own graves." By 6:30 A.M., it was apparent that the Federals had no intention of reappearing, so Hampton, leaving a few troopers behind as observers, also trotted away. By nightfall on August 26, all of the Rebels had returned to their former positions in the Petersburg works.[113]

Casualty counts at Second Reams' Station reflect the magnitude of the Confederate victory. Union losses totaled 2,742 men, including 2,073 prisoners. The Federals lost nine cannon, ten caissons, and 3,100 small arms. Hill reported 720 of his own men killed, wounded, or captured.[114]

Among the Union stricken was an unidentified officer, shot multiple times, including "one ragged Minie ball that had torn its way directly through his body." Col. George T. Rogers of the Sixth Virginia summoned an ambulance crew to remove the suffering Federal, who, although almost too weak to talk, managed to request that he be sent to some hospital where he would not die utterly alone. The litter bearers carefully carried him toward a Confederate aid station not 200 yards distant, but they soon returned, reporting that their patient had expired. "A few days after I saw in our camp the sword, boots, and spurs of that dead man," wrote Rogers. "It was all very sad."[115]

six

THE WHOLE FACE OF THE COUNTRY UTTERLY CHANGED

Late-Summer Interlude

The victorious Confederates conducted a parade through Petersburg on August 26, leading the legions of Federal prisoners along the streets in "a kind of triumphal entry." The Twenty-Sixth North Carolina band rendered jaunty tunes as Cooke's, Lane's, and MacRae's Brigades marched "with the captured colors borne at the head of their column," an officer on General Bratton's staff commenting that he had "never seen North Carolinians walk so proudly." A surgeon in the Forty-Second North Carolina recalled, "When the prisoners were marched through Petersburg they made quite a show and considerable excitement and rejoicing among our people," who lined the city sidewalks to witness the spectacle. "The rebels jeered and jibed at our boys as we passed through Petersburg but we answered them back," wrote a defiant William Endicott of Sleeper's Tenth Massachusetts Battery. "I actually heard the chorus of 'Rally round the Flag Boys' sung as we marched through the lower part of town. I was happy to see it was torn to pieces."[1]

Most Confederates viewed the Second Battle of Reams' Station as an unqualified success. "Since I last wrote, another signal victory has, by the blessing of God, been achieved by Confederate armies," rejoiced Alva Spencer of the Third Georgia, who located the battle at "Peanis Station." A semiliterate South Carolinian informed his parents: "Thave bin a nother fight on the Petersburg and Welddon railroad. . . . Our men whip them badly." He repeated a rumor that as a result of the battle, Lincoln had sent emissaries to Richmond seeking an armistice. "I hop and trust to god they may git it." A soldier correspondent to the *Richmond Daily Examiner* called the action at Reams' Station "a glorious victory. The invincibility of Southern valour has never, in any battle of the war, been more signally displayed, and never has the superiority of the Southern soldier over the Yankee been more apparent." He considered the engagement "a masterpiece, finished and perfected in the highest style of the military art."[2]

Robert E. Lee expressed his approbation in several ways. He wrote Hampton the day after the fight, calling the performance of the cavalry "worthy of all praise." The Confederate commander singled out the service of the North Carolinians at Reams' Station in an unusually effusive letter to Governor Zebulon Vance. "I have frequently been called upon to mention the services of North Carolina soldiers in this army, but their gallantry and conduct were never more deserving of admiration than in the engagement at Reams' Station, on the 25th instant," he praised, naming Cooke's, MacRae's, Lane's, and Barringer's Brigades as deserving of "the warm commendation of their corps and division commanders and the admiration of the army." Lee's acclaim, while no doubt sincere, masked an ulterior motive. Fearing that Wilmington would be an early target of a Federal amphibious attack, the general sought to spur the governor to rally his reserves and militia to defend that vital port city and its rail connections to Virginia. With less calculation, he expressed similar sentiments in an August 26 telegram to the secretary of war, crediting not only the North Carolina infantry and Hampton's cavalry but also "the giver of all victory." Maj. Joseph A. Englehard, Wilcox's assistant adjutant general, either read or was informed of Lee's message to Secretary Seddon because he wrote to a friend on August 28: "We had a brilliant little fight. . . . It was a 'Tar Heel' Fight . . . and we get Genl Lee to thanking God, which you know means something brilliant."[3]

Brigadier General Conner also commented on Lee's "high spirits" as a result of the victory and considered the outcome "worth to us all the men we lost. It was the first time in this campaign that we have taken breastworks, and our troops had begun to believe that they could not take them. . . . Their success has given them great confidence in themselves, and the next time they are put at works they will take them at the first rush." Samuel F. Harper, a clerk assigned to A. P. Hill's headquarters, summarized the opinion of most Confederates regarding Reams' Station: "Everything was accomplished that was intended & it is considered a brilliant thing." A commissary officer in Hill's corps viewed the recent victory as a harbinger of better days. "I think our cause looks bright and brightening," he wrote, "and if it were not that I have proved a false prophet heretofore I would predict a speedy peace."[4]

Some Confederates bristled at Yankee accounts that distorted the conduct and outcome of the battle. "I was considerably surprised at Meade's lying dispatches," wrote Willie Pegram, "as he has always been so truthful . . . but I suppose it is impossible for a man to keep such bad company without being corrupted." An Alabama gunner protested Hancock's claim that rain-soaked roads explained his inability to remove the nine cannons that fell into Confederate hands. "I'll tell you what sort of rain it was that caused him to lose those guns and their equipment," he informed the editor of the *Columbus Daily Sun*, "it was the rain of iron which the rebels poured upon them." Lt. Col. Allen S. Cutts requested that five of the captured pieces be assigned to his battalion to compensate for five of his Parrott rifles that had become unserviceable.[5]

Lt. Hugh Randolph Crichton of the Forty-Seventh North Carolina sought to reassure his correspondents that the failure to reclaim control of the entire Weldon Railroad was irrelevant. He explained, without benefit of actual knowledge, that the Confederates had stockpiled three months' provisions and that the Richmond & Danville Railroad would continue to transport supplies to the army, as would General Early's forces in the fertile Shenandoah Valley. "Don't be alarmed about the situation," he counseled, "all is well. There is more peace sentiment in the north that we can possibly think of, a radical peace man will be the next president of the United States."[6]

A pair of internal Confederate squabbles marred the battle's otherwise ebullient aftermath. General Wilcox resented reports that Heth's brigades alone bore responsibility for the victory. "It was my fight," he protested. "I gave the orders . . . had my horse killed, one of my aides had his killed, two couriers had theirs killed & my Adjutant General wounded." Similarly, General Lane would take offense at General Mahone's claim that he had captured the guns actually seized by North Carolinians. Still, rare were sour sentiments from Confederates, such as the one expressed by North Carolina private William Martin, who considered Reams' Station "the hardest fight in which I have participated yet. . . . They are trying men's souls now on quarter rations and fighting so much the men are getting very tired of such work."[7]

Despair, recrimination, and excuse making were the standard reactions to Reams' Station among Union voices. Capt. Henry S. Joy of the Third New York Cavalry agreed with Private Martin, as he wrote in an August 26 letter, that the fighting had been "hard . . . but yesterday oh my! Did they just give it to us." Lieutenant Dauchy, the New York battery commander, considered the battle "the most humiliating event in the history of the Second Corps," while Cyrus Comstock of Grant's staff deemed the outcome "disgusting. Warren lost 3,000 [prisoners] the other day—& now Hancock 2,000. I had much rather they were killed or wounded—that would look like they fought."[8]

The guns had hardly cooled when Union participants began offering explanations and rationalizations for the defeat. Theodore Lyman condemned the fighting caliber of the Second Corps and the leadership qualities of John Gibbon. "This disgraceful affair was the weak effort of the dregs of what had been two splendid divisions, now worn to a shadow by fighting, privation, climate, and marching," he confided to his diary the day after the battle. "Gibbon's had greatly depreciated through the want of confidence that many officers & men had in its commander." A Richmond newspaper reprinted an article from the *Washington Chronicle* that blamed the defeat on inexperienced "substitutes, aliens, and drafted men" who so heavily populated Hancock's regiments.[9]

General Hancock agreed with these assessments. "I attribute the bad conduct of some of my troops to their great fatigue, owing to the heavy labor exacted of them and to their enormous losses during the campaign, especially in officers." He hastened to add that many of his regiments contained large numbers of new recruits, including some officers not fluent in English, and that this "material compares very unfavorably with the veterans absent." The corps commander admitted before dawn on the twenty-sixth: "It will be a long time before . . . my command [is] organized so as to be serviceable. . . . If the Second Corps, after its great losses, is to be relied upon as a power this fall it can only fulfill expectations by giving it its best officers." Some years after the war, he criticized Meade for failing to utilize the field telegraph that ran between army headquarters and Reams' Station and for not sending the dispatched reinforcements straight down the railroad. "The whole fault of Reams Station . . . was in reference to these two points and it was not my fault that the battle was not a success," he wrote his former adjutant, Francis Walker. "General Meade was certainly responsible for it." Hancock would also claim that the Confederates outnumbered him two or three to one.[10]

Walker was among the captured Federals marched into Petersburg. In his history of the Second Corps written well after the war, Walker identified five proximate causes for the Union defeat. He argued that Meade should have either strongly reinforced Hancock on the night of the twenty-fourth, when it became apparent that a large body of Confederates was on the move, or ordered him to fall back out of harm's way. The reinforcements Meade finally sent took the long way to Reams' Station via Jerusalem Plank Road, arriving too late to change the tactical calculus, and army headquarters grossly overestimated Hancock's strength by a factor of three. Walker also condemned the poorly located and constructed works that Hancock defended and agreed that the new soldiers performed badly.[11]

George Meade anticipated that he would receive a lion's share of the blame. "I expect the papers will howl and I shall catch it for not having sent more rein- forcements and earlier," he confessed to his wife, "because it is *now* seen that if we could have got reinforcements on the field before the breaking of his lines, Hancock would have secured a most brilliant victory." Meade sought to justify his decisions by explaining, "Hancock expressed himself as confident of main- taining his position, and did not call for reinforcements, which I nevertheless sent as soon as I found how heavily he was engaged."[12]

Many Federals expressed dismay at the carnage inflicted on the Second Corps. Cpl. John Welsh of the Thirty-Sixth Wisconsin described Reams' Station as "the hardest battle that was ever fought since this war has ben in effect. It was a hard site to see so many lay dead." While this relatively inexperienced soldier might be forgiven his hyperbole, a veteran, Washington Roebling, reflected a similar degree of fatalistic shock. "Last night the old 2nd Corps was pretty smashed up," he informed his wife. "Brownson was killed. Francis A. Walker is missing, and in case you ever get tired of me and count upon [James] Beaver as my successor it will be of no avail as the poor fellow was shot . . . and may not get over it. This business of getting killed is a mere question of time, it will happen to all of us sooner or later if the war keeps on."[13]

Not every Unionist painted such a dark picture. A number of Northerners believed, albeit erroneously, that Confederate casualties vastly exceeded their own, mitigating their defeat. Capt. William W. Folwell of the Fiftieth New York Engineers informed his mother that "the Rebs can of course claim a victory but it would not take many such to wipe out their army." Lyman quoted an officer on Hancock's staff as observing that "the Rebels licked us but a dozen more such lickings and there will be nothing left of the Rebel army." He reported that Meade remained in "good spirits and said he hoped Bob Lee would go ahead with these attacks and he would soon get used up." The army commander in- formed General Grant early on the afternoon of the twenty-sixth that witnesses reported they "had never seen such a collection of dead and wounded that covered the field, almost all Confederates."[14]

Other Federals admitted being beaten but boasted that they still controlled the vital railroad. "The rebels suffered terribly in the battle, much worse than we did," wrote Fifth Corps hospital steward Elmer Wallace of the Twenty-Fourth Michigan, "and gained no material advantage, for our corps occupies the road, so that it is useless to them, and we are strongly fortified so that the johnies will dare not attack us." Lyman agreed. "Thus all strategic results lie with us and we hold the Weldon road."[15]

The battle exacerbated the testy relations between Hancock and Gibbon that had existed since July. Gibbon approached his superior shortly after the engagement and "urged that steps should at once be taken to reorganize the corps, which in its present shape could never again do efficient service." The sting of defeat was too raw for Hancock to entertain such a suggestion, and he responded by criticizing the battlefield performance of Gibbon's division. Gibbon blamed any poor conduct on his new recruits and took leave of his angry superior, only to write Hancock that night offering, disingenuously, to forsake his command if the reorganization he recommended entailed disbanding the Second Division. Hancock quickly replied that perhaps it would be best if he did relinquish command of his division. Highly insulted, Gibbon submitted a formal request to be relieved. This unpleasant exchange ended when Hancock agreed to withdraw the inflammatory letter and Gibbon retracted his request for reassignment. "We parted on tolerably good terms," wrote Gibbon, "but there was a soreness of feeling remaining probably on both sides that never entirely disappeared." It was no coincidence that shortly after this unpleasant affair, Grant chose Gibbon to take command of the Eighteenth Corps while General Ord was absent on disability leave.[16]

Before he left for Butler's army, Gibbon initiated another controversy. On August 30 he issued General Orders No. 63, depriving three of his regiments of the honor of carrying their flags "until by their conduct in battle they show themselves competent to protect them." Gibbon accused the 8th New York Heavy Artillery, the 164th New York, and the 36th Wisconsin of disgracing themselves by losing their banners at Reams' Station. He also intended to so punish the 20th Massachusetts, but because all of that regiment's officers had been captured, no report had been filed on which to base an official action.[17]

The members of the affected regiments, as might be imagined, reacted poorly to such humiliation. "Why are we particularly pointed out . . . as being . . . deprived of holding up the stars and stripes, our emblem of liberty for which we have enlisted to defend & maintain," inquired Capt. Norton Cook of the Eighth New York Heavy Artillery, who in a letter home, documented the regiment's honorable service record. Pvt. Guy Taylor of the Thirty-Sixth Wisconsin wrote his wife that the regimental color-bearer was "shot ded and the rebs was rite on him . . . and no man in the world cood get them. . . . The Boys all say if they do not give up the collors . . . they will not do any more then they are ablidge to and if the boys set out to shurk they wont be good for nothing for it is the greatist plais in the armey for shurk that ever was."[18]

This acrimony eventually reached army headquarters, and on September 23 Meade issued General Orders No. 37, endorsing Gibbon's action, and ordered that it applied in the future to any "regiment or battery that loses its colors in action . . . through misconduct in battle." Five days later Hancock formally challenged Gibbon's action and submitted a lengthy request to Grant to restore the colors to all three regiments. He cited the outstanding combat record compiled by the Second Corps and the heroic behavior of the three units in previous battles as well as observing that other regiments lost their flags at Globe Tavern and Reams' Station without suffering equal punishment. Hancock argued: "I respectfully request that their colors may be returned. . . . They are entitled to the same privileges as other regiments—that is, the right to strive to avoid the penalties of General Orders No. 37."[19]

Lt. George Albee of the Thirty-Sixth Wisconsin was among the prisoners taken at Reams' Station. He was soon paroled and made his way to Washington, where he gained an audience with Assistant Postmaster General Alexander W. Randall, a former two-term Wisconsin governor. Randall arranged for Albee to meet with the president, and the lieutenant made his case for the return of the regimental banners. Lincoln referred him to Secretary Stanton, who passed Albee's written petition down the chain of command, where it finally landed at brigade headquarters.[20]

In the meantime, Gibbon experienced a change of heart and wrote Meade seeking to reverse his action. "The three regiments mentioned in my order ought not to be made to suffer the disgrace alone when others in other corps, in this corps, and even in this division have also lost their colors," he argued. Because Meade's directive applied to future failures, Gibbon felt that his three regiments should no longer suffer the consequences retroactively. A few weeks later he responded to Meade's request for an explanation of the rationale behind depriving the three regiments of their flags. Despite his recent appeal, Gibbon replied that he based his decision on "an old established rule, that a regiment which loses its colors without being able to show that their loss was attended with a glorious and persistent effort to defend them should be deprived of the right to bear others." Gibbon also received correspondence from Randall accusing him of perpetrating "a gross act of injustice" to the Wisconsin troops, obviously responding to Albee's appeal. "I respectfully submit that Governor Randall knows nothing authentic upon a subject which he has characterized in such strong terms, and have no doubt he would consider it very much out of place in me, a soldier, to so characterize any act of his, on the one-sided representations of one of his minor clerks in the Post-Office Department," snapped the offended general. On November 7 Meade returned the flags to the three aggrieved regiments, ending this lengthy and contentious episode.[21]

Late-Summer Interlude

The issue of flags aside, the Union performance at Reams' Station left much to be desired. Commanders in the Second Corps who identified the shameful behavior of green recruits as the primary cause of their defeat certainly had a point. General Miles spoke for many when he blamed "a few dutch cowards" for the outcome. But it was not quite that simple. Hancock and his division commanders discounted the possibility of a Confederate attack and did too little to improve the faulty defenses they ultimately lost. David Gregg failed in reconnaissance to locate some 8,000 Confederate infantry within a few miles of the Union position, while Meade erred by leaving Hancock so isolated that reinforcements failed to reach him in time, due in no small part to the round-about route they were ordered to follow.[22]

Although the Confederates earned a lopsided victory, as historian Craig Chapman asserts, they were fortunate that some 1,750 men were able to rout the Federals in a final attack devoid of tactics beyond a headlong frontal charge. "Had the Union troops held a little longer," observes Chapman, "the Confederates would have suffered a bloody repulse."[23]

As it was, Hill and Hampton lost about 800 men at Reams' Station. To what purpose was the sacrifice of these soldiers? Clearly, Lee harbored no illusions that an attack at Reams' Station would force the Army of the Potomac off the Weldon Railroad. The Fifth Corps had solidified its hold on that key artery, Warren was not targeted by the Confederate offensive, and Hill's men quickly returned to their established lines after the engagement, risking no further assaults. The most that can be said operationally for the Confederate victory is that it forestalled a potential Union push toward Boydton Plank Road and Dinwiddie Court House while limiting the distance Lee's wagons would travel to supply his army from the south; Stony Creek Depot became the Rebel railhead on the Weldon line. Nevertheless, such an impressive tactical achievement buoyed Southern morale and embarrassed Union arms, critical factors as Northern citizens contemplated their votes in the upcoming elections.[24]

On August 26 Grant was uncertain that the Confederate attacks had run their course. "I think the chances are that Warren will be attacked in rear this afternoon by the same force that attacked Hancock yesterday," he advised Meade. "If Warren can prepare for both a front and rear attack the enemy will be most severely handled." Meade assured the general-in-chief that he had made the necessary arrangements to meet a renewed Confederate offensive. But at 9:15 that evening, he informed Grant that "the usual quiet has prevailed along the lines to-day." The time had come to consolidate the gains earned by the bloody combat of the previous week.[25]

The Federals continued to fortify their position along the railroad while connecting the western end of their permanent defenses near Jerusalem Plank Road with their expanded left flank. Maj. Nathaniel Michler, soon to be acting chief engineer of the Army of the Potomac, received orders after the fighting at Reams' Station to "select positions for large works on or near [the Weldon Railroad] for the protection of the left flank of the army, and also to connect them, by a system of redoubts, with Fort Sedgwick." General Warren took a personal interest in the construction of two large, four-bastioned forts that would solidify his hard-earned hold on the railroad. One arose just west of the tracks, where the Blick house once stood, and the other about a mile south on the east side of the right-of-way. The engineers also laid out the connecting works to create a continuous line of fortifications along the entire Union front.[26]

"It is a very fine thing to witness the immense operations of this army," wrote Capt. William Rawle. "All the engineering skill known is brought into play. . . . From the distance, you would see a plain all cut up by earthworks . . . but going close up to it, the work that has been done and is doing is marvelous." Pvt. John M. Spear of the Twenty-Fourth Massachusetts agreed. "The whole surface of the ground in front of us, as far as ones eyes can see in all directions, has been dug over," he wrote. "There are lines of forts, batteries, and rifle-pits, seemingly in utter confusion, but upon closely inspecting them some appearance of regularity can be seen."[27]

Union fortifications at Petersburg followed the standard practice employed by Civil War armies. The most important locations hosted enclosed works called redoubts or forts, sufficiently large to contain a garrison strong enough to hold its own against an attack and mounting from four to as many as eighteen cannon. At intermediate points along the line, artillery positions open at the rear—redans or lunettes—would, in conjunction with the forts, provide enfilading fire in either direction. A continuous line of infantry works several feet thick and ten or twelve feet high, usually fronted by a ditch four or six feet wide and deep, connected these strongpoints. The bronze, loamy clay found in this part of Virginia, interspersed with sandy soil, was easily removed and stood up well when formed into slopes. Soldiers stabilized the interior of these works with logs laid horizontally and parallel with the parapet, supports called revetments.[28]

Covered ways provided secure communication along the line and to the rear. These roofless excavations, twelve feet wide and at least six feet deep, protected soldiers and vehicles from enemy rifle fire, although exploding shells, particularly those fired from mortars, which lobbed projectiles at high trajectories, still presented a danger. These subterranean corridors stayed busy as

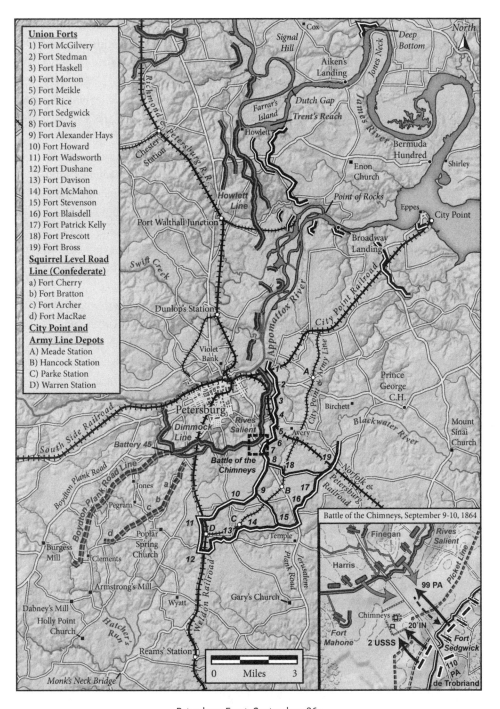

Union Forts
1) Fort McGilvery
2) Fort Stedman
3) Fort Haskell
4) Fort Morton
5) Fort Meikle
6) Fort Rice
7) Fort Sedgwick
8) Fort Davis
9) Fort Alexander Hays
10) Fort Howard
11) Fort Wadsworth
12) Fort Dushane
13) Fort Davison
14) Fort McMahon
15) Fort Stevenson
16) Fort Blaisdell
17) Fort Patrick Kelly
18) Fort Prescott
19) Fort Bross

Squirrel Level Road Line (Confederate)
a) Fort Cherry
b) Fort Bratton
c) Fort Archer
d) Fort MacRae

City Point and Army Line Depots
A) Meade Station
B) Hancock Station
C) Parke Station
D) Warren Station

North

Cox
Signal Hill
Aiken's Landing
Jones Neck
Deep Bottom

Richmond & Petersburg R.R.
Chester Station

Farrar's Island
Dutch Gap
Trent's Reach
Howlett

James River

Bermuda Hundred
Shirley

Howlett Line
Enon Church

Point of Rocks
Eppes
City Point

Port Walthall Junction
Broadway Landing

Swift Creek
Dunlop's Station

Appomattox River
City Point & Army Line

City Point Railroad

Prince George C.H.

Violet Bank

Petersburg
Dimmock Line
Rives Salient
Battery 45

Avery
Birchett
Blackwater River
Mount Sinai Church

South Side Railroad

Battle of the Chimneys

Boydton Plank Road Line
Jones
Pegram

Norfolk & Petersburg Railroad

Burgess Mill
Clements
Poplar Spring Church

Weldon Railroad

Temple
Jerusalem Plank Road

Armstrong's Mill
Wyatt
Gary's Church

Dabney's Mill
Holly Point Church
Hatcher's Run

Reams' Station

0   Miles   3

Monk's Neck Bridge

Battle of the Chimneys, September 9–10, 1864

Finegan
Rives Salient
Harris
99 PA
Chimneys
Picket Line
20 IN
Fort Mahone
2 USSS
Fort Sedgwick
110 PA
de Trobriand

Petersburg Front, September 1864

troops, ammunition wagons, and artillery pieces traversed the space to, from, and behind the front. Covered ways also connected the main line with advanced positions manned by pickets and vedettes. Abatis—obstructions consisting of fallen trees, limbs, and branches—fronted the length of the works. Fraise—the sharpened stakes placed in a deep trench and pointed toward the enemy that the soldiers called "gut rippers"—complemented the abatis. Tripwires anchored to stumps or stakes a few inches from the ground added yet another hazard for attacking troops. Impediments called chevaux-de-frise appeared in some places. Soldiers cut small logs, about eight inches in diameter and sixteen feet long, and bored two-inch holes though them every twelve or sixteen inches, through which they drove sharpened stakes some seven feet long. "These bristling affairs were then placed by night about 100 or 150 feet in front of the works, and the ends locked up together with wire, so that they could not be cut apart easily," wrote one admiring Federal. "The thing looked like the head of a revolving horse-rake with two sets of teeth."[29]

Bombproof shelters—long trenches cut into the ground, often located just behind the parapet walls of forts and entrenchments and parallel with them—provided protection for soldiers stationed on the front lines. Rough wooden slabs lined the interior of these shelters, whose roofs were supported by uprights across which planks were laid and covered with a thickness of earth. "It is in such places . . . that we sleep," wrote Private Spear. "The building of them is slow and hard work . . . but it is the only way in which we can live."[30]

Although engineer officers from the regular army or the volunteers of the Fifteenth and Fiftieth New York Engineers directed construction, soldiers performed the actual labor. "All night long the division was hard at work building pits to connect the 3d Division of our corps at the Jones house with the 9th Corps & slashing the woods in front of the very extended line," wrote Captain Noyes. "All day long the division was at work. . . . After three or four hours of digging, would come then four more of chopping & so on. An immense amount of work was done. The men had no time to cook & eat even." Surgeon Charles G. Merrill of the Twenty-Second USCT considered the "amount of labor which has been done on this portion of the line . . . perfectly astounding; covered ways running zigzag for protection to passing troops—forts, ditches, abattis, mines, countermines—all attest to the terrible labor which has been imposed on our already exhausted army." Corporal Bechtel explained, "We have been at work either day or night for some time, and scarcely time to wash our clothing."[31]

Some troops resented the back-breaking labor required to fortify their newly won real estate. "Instead of getting on clean shirts and acting like Christians, this beautiful Sabbath day, we were sent out to work making 'dead falls,' pit holes, infernal traps for cavalry, and a network of telegraph wire fixed about four inches from the ground in such a way that it would be sure to trip up and stop a charge of infantry," groused a Fifth Corps soldier. "Since my last writing the regiment have built about 1 ½ miles of breastworks or rifle pits," reported Sergeant Monks of the 155th Pennsylvania, "and as soon as they were about strong enough to fight behind, they moved us off to the left to build others. The men were greatly enraged and I haven't heard so much growling for a long time as was done yesterday afternoon."[32]

The Fourth Division of the Ninth Corps, comprising Black regiments, shouldered their portion of the work, much to the fascination of Lt. Col. Byron Cutcheon of the Twentieth Michigan. "They were genuine 'down south negroes' mostly former slaves, who had come within our lines, chiefly in Virginia and North Carolina," recalled Cutcheon. "They exhibited the usual good nature and light heartedness of the negro combined with their strong religious ... tendencies. ... While they worked they sang ... melodies. Those who were not at work held religious meetings similar to the 'down home camp meeting.'" Cutcheon was amazed when some of the participants "become wildly excited and 'get the power' so that they would fall down in a trance and be carried off by their comrades as if dead. ... I have seen as many as a dozen in a single evening laid out on the grass in a comatose condition."[33]

The behavior of these African Americans notwithstanding, the result by the first week of September impressed most observers. "I think if General Lee could see these works he would bid goodbye to any hopes ... of ever taking this line," wrote Lt. Thomas J. Owen of the Fiftieth New York Engineers. "We have got a line of brest works here that the hole Southern army Can't take from us," agreed Pvt. Mack Ewing of the Second Michigan. "It would be perfectly astonishing to any citizen, or any person outside of the army to come here, and see the immense amount of earth we have dug since we have been here," wrote another Michigander. "We thought we done a great deal of work at Yorktown, but it was very small compared with our immense work here."[34]

Isolated voices found this emphasis on engineering misplaced. Charles Griffin, for example, informed a correspondent: "The 5th Corps is squatted on the Weldon railroad building horrible mud forts. ... The engineers of this army have a mania for piling dirt wherever they find a good place for a fort imagining that some day they might meet you there and then it would be a handy thing to have about. If this army fails it is because it has always been controlled by staff influences. ... We stop to build forts when we ought to be fighting the enemy." Yet most Federals placed such confidence in their new fortifications that they hoped the Confederates would resume the offensive after Reams' Station. "We are all expecting the Rebels to attack us every day and our boys are all anxious for them to come for we are certain of whipping them," wrote Pvt. Henry Clay Heisler of the Forty-Eighth Pennsylvania. "Never were our boys more anxious for the enemy to attack us or ever more certain of whipping them."[35]

General Grant feared that such an attack might come from the south and took steps to thwart it. "A line should be selected at once in rear of our present line, and facing from it, which can be taken at any time if the enemy should come in from the rear," he wrote acting army commander John Parke on September 4. Grant credited a spy's report that a large portion of Jubal Early's force in the Shenandoah Valley was seen moving from the Piedmont town of Gordonsville toward Richmond. "My own impression is that if the enemy attack, and I expect it, he will hold his present lines from the James River to the Weldon road with a force not exceeding three divisions," explained the general-in-chief. "With the balance they will likely march entirely around our left and attack in the rear near the Jerusalem plank road."[36]

Orders from army headquarters reached all corps commanders instructing them how to respond should such an assault occur, while the engineers promptly began describing a new line of defense facing south and running eastward from the Weldon Railroad to Jerusalem Plank Road and beyond, eventually reaching to the edge of the swampy Blackwater River. "Works were constructed, heavy guns planted and streets were cut from the forts on the main line to the rear, so every organization would have a road to facilitate rapid movements," recalled a soldier from the Nineteenth Maine. The troops worked with a will, most of them believing that Early was about to pounce on them from the south. "We have been laboring with great diligence for the last week in throwing up fortifications in our rear and on our left flank so we can arrest any assault the Johnnies may try to make," wrote an officer in the Nineteenth USCT. "Early has returned and is now trying to get on our flank and rear," echoed brigade commander Robert McAllister. "We are ready for him and are expecting a battle every day—I may say every hour."[37]

Although the army "worked night and day for four days" without rest to complete the new line, Early's failure to appear eased tensions. Colonel Wainwright harbored doubts from the outset about the rumors of an impending attack from the Valley Confederates. Referencing Grant's warning and its source, the artillery commander confided to his diary that, "as the general is so minute, he has strong grounds to form an opinion on; more than what he gives at the head of his dispatch." Lt. Col. Steve Clark of the Thirteenth Ohio Cavalry began to think that Early would not dare test the new Union line because the Confederates "are by no means fond of butting their heads against our fortifications."[38]

Late-Summer Interlude

Within forty-eight hours of Grant's orders, the rear line had progressed sufficiently that Cpl. William Boston declared on September 6, "Our rear is now about as well fortified as our front." The lieutenant general had evinced the same concern for an attack from behind during his siege of Vicksburg in the summer of 1863, so it was unsurprising that he spared no labor in preparing to meet such an eventuality at Petersburg. The engineering mirrored that practiced in creating the main line of works. Six large forts and nine batteries composed the rear line, which ran for about four miles. By September 11, both new lines were essentially complete. Some sixteen miles of works now faced north and south, comprising nineteen forts and redoubts and forty-one artillery batteries, all connected by an unbroken infantry curtain.[39]

The addition of so much new engineering promised confusion, as a formal identification system had not been adopted for the forts and batteries along both lines. Ben Butler anticipated such a problem and on July 15 issued General Orders No. 80, providing names for all the forts and batteries in his department "in honor of the memory of some of the gallant dead of this army, who have fallen in this campaign." Warren adopted Butler's idea on September 5, recommending the "naming of our forts and redoubts so that they can be designated in orders." He selflessly suggested renaming the large fort along Jerusalem Plank Road, then known as Fort Warren, in honor of Col. P. Stearns Davis of the Thirty-Ninth Massachusetts, who was mortally wounded there on July 11. He also proposed names for the two forts being constructed along the Weldon Railroad under his close observation. A week later Meade's headquarters issued Special Orders No. 247, calling on corps commanders to suggest names for the "redoubts of the line of entrenchments . . . after officers who have fallen during the present campaign."[40]

Hancock, Parke, Birney, and Gibbon all submitted names of officers from their respective corps, as did division commander Robert Potter. Most, though not all, of the suggestions were adopted. On September 21 army headquarters circulated a list of the official names for the forts, while the batteries were given consecutive Roman numerals, moving east to west. The huge fort east of Jerusalem Plank Road that had been known as Redoubt G but widely referred to as "Fort Hell," officially became Fort Sedgwick in honor of the Sixth Corps commander killed at Spotsylvania Court House in May, although the soldiers continued to employ the more colorful designation. Major Michler ordered the erection of painted sign boards at the entrances to all the forts and batteries designating the new names. This protocol would be continued throughout the campaign.[41]

The completion of both lines did not halt Federal engineering initiatives. The soldiers continued to construct gabions and fascines; wooden elements used to strengthen fortifications. The Fiftieth New York Engineers had already constructed more than 20,000 gabions and 5,000 fascines in June alone. These skilled volunteers also built magazines and bombproofs in the forts, while improving the drainage along the entire line. They finished nearly 2,000 yards of roads, "corduroyed" one-third of the covered ways, and completed 6,700 square feet of substantial bridging. Both sides continued mining activities. "Rebel deserters say that the Rebels are mining under one of our forts," reported Lt. George Barnum of the 100th New York. "We have countermined and can see not a trace of their work. We have a man stationed in our mine all the time and by placing a drum on the sides of the mine you can hear the sound of either pick or shovel at a distance of 10 rods so we can tell when they get anywhere near us." Sgt. Edward Schilling of the 4th Maryland reported that "bomb proofs are everywhere," including in the sides of some covered ways, "like bank swallows' nests. . . . So are the soldiers' graves. . . . The brave fellows are buried where they fell."[42]

An anecdote recorded by Sgt. John P. Brogan of the Sixth-Fifth New York illustrates the extent to which Union engineering altered the landscape. An old farmer approached Brogan one day inquiring about the location of his obliterated house because the man and his wife had buried a supply of meat outside one of its walls. He told Brogan, "I believe to the Lord that big pile of dirt out thar, pointing to a newly erected fort, is whar my house used to be, but I'm not certain of anything . . . for you can beat all creation for digging." "The whole face of the country utterly changed," concluded Brogan, "all evidences of previous settlements vanished."[43]

Perhaps the most spectacular Union engineering achievement arrived by rail. The City Point & Army Line found its origin in the prewar City Point Branch of the South Side Railroad. This short line, finished in 1838, connected Petersburg with City Point, whose deep water at the confluence of the James and Appomattox Rivers avoided the periodic need to dredge the Appomattox near its head of navigation at Petersburg. From the outset of the campaign, City Point served as the supply base for Grant's operations, and shortly thereafter work began converting the civilian tracks to military use. Charles L. McAlpine, engineer of construction and repairs with the army's Military Railroads of Virginia, replaced rotten ties, improved bridges, and changed the gauge to match the army's standard. By July 7, trains began to roll from the wharves at City Point to Grant's front lines. That month six locomotives logged more than 6,000 miles and carried 35,370 passengers. Soldiers such as the cavalry's Nathan Webb greeted this transportation innovation enthusiastically. "The railroad is fast progressing," he wrote in his diary. "It is highly encouraging to the intelligent rank and file to see such vigor infused into the conduct of the campaigns after having participated in the effete administration of McClellan. We know now that every day that Grant is doing something." Capt. James Nichols agreed after traveling on the railroad from City Point to the Eighteenth Corps hospital on July 31. "I could not get over the singularity of my position riding on a railroad almost entirely constructed for the use of the army and the piles of stones along the road gave me the best idea of the extent of the army that I have ever enjoyed."[44]

On July 22 Grant ordered McAlpine to connect his existing tracks to the Federal lines near the Norfolk & Petersburg Railroad. Work was deferred in anticipation of the attack that crossed the Norfolk line on July 30 and resulted in the Battle of the Crater. But following the engagements along the Weldon Railroad in August, revised orders arrived to extend construction all the way to Fifth Corps headquarters at Globe Tavern in response to Meade's concerns about supplying Warren's troops. Swampy ground east of the Weldon Railroad, particularly intractable after a heavy rain, severely impeded wagon transportation. Grant sent instructions on August 29 to the army's chief quartermaster, Rufus Ingalls, to "extend the City Point Railroad, with the least practicable delay to the Weldon railroad, the extension to pass in rear of our present lines, and at points giving the greatest accommodation to our troops." General Ingalls responded immediately, contacting Meade's chief engineer and offering to begin work without delay, action the army commander embraced. Ingalls then wired the Quartermaster General Montgomery Meigs, who assigned Maj. Erasmus L. Wentz to superintend construction.[45]

The engineers estimated that the work would require four weeks, but Ingalls thought that he could do better. Meade volunteered to provide whatever additional labor the construction crews required and suggested that rails and ties could be scavenged from the Norfolk Railroad. Major Wentz commenced construction promptly, and his progress astonished everyone. "It was built on top of the ground, without grading," remembered a Pennsylvanian. "Where it crossed the Norfolk road, it was necessary to build a trestle work three hundred yards long and ten feet high." Cpl. Gilbert Thompson of the U.S. Engineers thought the railroad ignored "all the rules of engineering in its construction not being leveled at all following the curves of the ground." Remarkably, the line reached Warren's command post on September 12, barely a fortnight after Grant authorized its construction. "It will be a vast convenience to us, and a great saving of mule flesh and oaths," thought Wainwright.[46]

The first engine to reach Warren's headquarters blew its whistle for five consecutive minutes, "probably as a note of defiance or challenge to the rebs," wrote Elmer Wallace. The Confederates rose to that challenge. "Yesterday the Yankees were discovered to have constructed a railroad running from City Point to some point to the right of this city," wrote a member of the Hardaway Artillery. "The Whitworth gun of the battery was immediately placed in position to command it, and opened fire on the first train that passed up." That shot missed, but it "had the effect of increasing the speed of the train from ten to thirty miles an hour." The vulnerable spot was near the Avery house, and as the trains passed this point, the shrill whistle of Whitworth bolts could be heard along the tracks. The Confederates rarely hit their target—"for every shot they fire we give them at least a dozen"—although one projectile did manage to strike a keg of spikes carried on a flatcar, "knocking smithereens out of them."[47]

General Meade, understandably, was upset that his trains were compelled to face repeated danger and sent a pointed message to Grant, complaining that had Major Wentz consulted with Maj. James C. Duane, his chief engineer, or himself, "the very serious mistake which has been made in the location of the road could have been avoided, as the only condition I had to make was that the road should be laid out of sight and beyond the range of the enemy's batteries." Grant replied that Wentz planned to "sink the road five feet where it is in view of the rebel batteries, throwing all the earth toward the enemy," making an embankment of eleven feet and a cut of five. This expedient would eventually serve its purpose, but for about two weeks the trains ran mostly at night to minimize the risk.[48]

Meade ordered depots of supplies established to serve the Second, Ninth, and Fifth Corps, named Hancock, Parke, and Warren respectively. "Our railroad is now in full operation," Wainwright recorded, "the depot for this corps is in rear of the tavern & had been officially christened Warren Station; that for the 9th Corps at the Aiken house about a mile east of this Parke.... Hancock station for the 2d Corps & the cavalry... is where the RR crosses the [Jerusalem] plank road." Most of the freight wagons upon which the Fifth Corps had previously relied eventually rumbled east beyond Jerusalem Plank Road, as the railroad made their employment unnecessary. Meade assigned his provost-marshal authority to enforce the rules for soldier use of the railroad, all enlisted men and officers wishing to ride requiring a pass. The army modified some of the passenger cars to accommodate the sick and wounded by replacing seats with long rows of stretchers fixed to the walls by large india-rubber straps. Nine trains ran daily in each direction, providing adequate supplies to every corps on the line, although those engines pulling particularly heavy loads occasionally had to make multiple runs to negotiate uphill grades. "There were methods in all the arrangements of the Quartermasters' and Commissaries' departments," observed a war correspondent. "Every regiment could count upon receiving its supplies promptly whenever needed."[49]

Late-Summer Interlude

Naturally, Federals of all ranks welcomed this new addition to their military infrastructure. "The cars run from City Point right past our camp," wrote musician Ransom F. Sargent of the Eleventh New Hampshire. "I tell you it sounds good to hear the whistle and [it] must strike terror to the rebels." Capt. Charles F. Stinson of the Nineteenth USCT wrote his sister: "This is getting to seem really like a civilized land and why? Because I am today standing in my cabin and see the iron horse winding his way around the curve on its way to Weldon."[50]

The engineers completed their work so rapidly that the arrival of the trains caught some soldiers by surprise. "Scarcely had we learned such a road was planned, before one evening the whistle of a locomotive was heard down the line," recalled a Pennsylvania drummer boy. Observers used various metaphors to describe the unusual appearance of the ungraded tracks. "It looked like a fly crawling over a corrugated washboard," wrote Lt. Col. Horace Porter of Grant's staff. Another Federal thought the tracks were "as crooked as a dog's hind leg." Despite its odd appearance, the City Point & Army Line provided an unbroken stream of food and munitions to man and beast for as long as the Federals remained in their hard-won positions. Lt. Dayton E. Flint of the Fifteenth New Jersey spoke for many Union soldiers when he called the railroad "another evidence of the enterprise of the universal Yankee."[51]

The setback along the Weldon Railroad did not stimulate railroad construction in the Confederate camps, but Southern engineers and their labor sources were far from idle. To keep supplies flowing from the south, Lee relied on horse- or mule-drawn vehicles from his new railhead, some eighteen miles below Petersburg. The Confederates built a military wagon road that connected Flat Foot Road to Quaker Road, which, in turn, led to Boydton Plank Road and thence into the Cockade City. This new artery also provided access to the plank road via a route farther east, connecting to Vaughan and Duncan Roads.[52]

Several country byways offered the Federals opportunity to interdict this new Rebel supply route, so Confederate engineers began planning a pair of defensive lines to protect their wagon trains. When he arrived in Petersburg, Lee inherited an elaborate complex of artillery redans and infantry works along the Dimmock Line, named after the young engineer, Charles Dimmock, who had overseen its construction in 1862 and 1863. These works rested on the Appomattox River both below and above Petersburg, with fifty-five batteries numbered sequentially from east to west circling the city along a nearly ten-mile front. Battery 45 guarded Boydton Plank Road two miles west of Petersburg, and the first of the new lines began there, coursing southwest in front of and parallel to Boydton Plank Road. As early as September 11, Wade Hampton recognized the defensive necessity for such a line, sparking an order from Lee to Maj. Samuel

R. Johnston, an engineer on the headquarters staff, to investigate its feasibility. Work commenced on September 16. Two brigades from Heth's Division and three from Field's, returned from the north side of the James River, provided the labor. The soldiers scratched out the mere outline of these new earthworks, extending a mile below Duncan Road, before new orders arrived.[53]

On September 20 Lee reassigned these five brigades to build a line of works that paralleled Squirrel Level Road, angling southwest to cross Church Road and terminating at an unnamed rural byway that connected Squirrel Level Road with Duncan Road. The line extended for about three miles and featured several strongpoints, named Forts Cherry and Bratton on the northern end, Fort Archer where the line intersected Church Road, and Fort MacRae anchoring the line's southern extremity. By September 28, these works, albeit modest by Union standards, were essentially complete.[54]

While the soldiers constructed the Boydton Plank and Squirrel Level lines, troops farther east created a reserve position behind their main fortifications. The Federals had captured the original Dimmock Line between Batteries 2 and 15 during Grant's initial offensive in June. Beauregard's troops had created a new defensive perimeter closer to Petersburg to compensate for this loss, those works reconnecting with the intact portion of the Dimmock Line. As early as September 9, the soldiers stationed east of Jerusalem Plank Road labored on a reserve position behind the main works, consisting of artillery lunettes and infantry breastworks. "The rear line is a very strong one," thought Pvt. John M. Brice of the Sixth South Carolina, "the strongest I ever saw and I suppose is intended for our troops to fall back in case of emergency." Only artillery resided in these new fortifications, including the Whitworth rifle that fired on the City Point & Army Line.[55]

As with the Federals, the common soldiers performed most of this labor. "I have been busy as a bee for several days past," explained Sgt. Robert Henry Maury, "doing what? With pick and shovel digging out to strengthen our fortifications. . . . For six hours every day during the past week I have been in the trenches working like a ditcher." A Tennessee private assigned to what he called the "Pioneer Corps" admitted: "We have to work pretty hard. . . . My hands are a little sore and I feel somewhat tired . . . after I have quit work." Hampton contributed as many of his troopers as he could spare, but slaves conscripted from farms and plantations throughout southern Virginia provided the largest supplement to the infantry's labor. Ordnance lieutenant James A. W. Bryan of Lane's Brigade reported on September 11 seeing a "large force of negroes" employed on the fortifications. Lane's North Carolinians considered the African Americans as "a great relief, as the laborious work of throwing up such

Late-Summer Interlude

heavy batteries was telling on the energies of the men." Nevertheless, Capt. A. B. Mulligan of the Fifth South Carolina Cavalry approved assigning troops to such taxing manual labor. "At the beginning of this war many of our officers considered it rather cowardly to do this but now all sensible men & good officers agree as to the importance of using every means in their power to protect their men from unnecessary danger & exposure."[56]

Much of this work had to be done at night in order to avoid pinpoint shelling and industrious sharpshooters. This was particularly true when placing chevaux-de-frise in front of the works. "The ticklish thing . . . was putting them together in front of our line in 'No-Man's-Land,'" wrote Cpl. Mathews W. Venable of the First Confederate Engineers. "This had to be done on dark nights, without noise, as both sides were on 'double-trigger' all the time, and the least noise at night . . . would raise 'a hell of shot and shell' from both sides." Like the Federals, the graycoats built fascines and gabions by the hundreds, but the First Corps artillery commander, Brig. Gen. Edward Porter Alexander, contributed several more novel innovations to improve the security of the line. For example, Alexander furnished the artillery with "bullet-proof oak shields, which were fastened to the axles at the trunnions, and were as wide as the spread of the wheels," according to a cannoneer in the Washington Artillery. "They had a slit cut in them, cross-shaped, through which the gunners could safely aim."[57]

As Lee's lines lengthened westward, his thinned battalions struggled to cover the extended front. The engineers provided some relief by building dams across waterways to flood the ground in front of their positions, creating what they called inundations. Work details from Brig. Gen. Matt Ransom's and Gracie's Brigades built a dam near Gracie's Salient, just north of the Crater. An even larger structure impounded Rohoic Creek near Boydton Plank Road west of Battery 45. This dam stretched some 300 feet across, was 100 feet thick at the base, and 30 feet thick at the top. During rainy periods, its impounded water covered the ground for more than half a mile behind the dam, creating a watery obstacle that eliminated the need to deploy troops in that sector.[58]

With the memory of the Crater explosion never far from consciousness, Lee's engineers dug countermines in an effort to avoid another unpleasant surprise. "We now have a good system of countermines at the only places favorable for such attempts," wrote General Alexander. These shafts covered the front from Colquitt's Salient to Rives Salient, where the opposing lines rested sufficiently close to threaten a reprise of the July 30 blast. "In many places our mines or galleries are extensive," boasted Colonel Trimmier of the Forty-First Alabama. The most remarkable Confederate countermine emanated from the Squirrel Level Line just west of that roadway. Scales's North Carolinians dug a gallery that eventually stretched 323 yards, ending near an abandoned house that sat forty feet higher than the nearby Confederate works. Fearing that the Federals might locate a battery there to their great advantage, the Tar Heels created a mine just ten feet below the surface and prepared magazines for powder charges should the Yankees attempt to occupy that key terrain. They started the work on September 15 but did not complete it until November.[59]

Lt. William Alexander Gordon of the First Confederate Engineers described the product of this accumulated labor: "Our first line of defence consisted of salients or forts on commanding positions connected each with the other by deep and strong trenches. In front were protecting abattis, at first of branches of trees sharpened at the ends, and later made of heavy hewed timber in which sharpened spikes were inserted and which were connected by iron chains. . . . When finished the main line of defense was very strong and could probably have resisted successfully any direct attack the Yankees might have made."[60]

Of course, both sides augmented their engineering prowess with human capital in the form of pickets and vedettes. "Now that the enemy were constantly in our immediate presence, the importance of an active, vigilant and spirited picket line . . . became more and more vital and indispensable to the safety of our lines," wrote one Confederate. The pickets were generally several hundred yards in front of the main line of works, although distances varied depending on the local terrain and the proximity of antagonists. A picket post consisted of a small excavation that could accommodate from two to eight soldiers. The displaced earth would be heaped in front of the trench or hole as a barrier, sometimes augmented by logs or gabions. Twenty to fifty feet often separated the posts from one another, although as the campaign progressed, these became connected into an unbroken line. A short distance in advance of the picket line appeared even smaller entrenchments protecting the vedettes, usually two men per post. The vedette lines were sometimes so close to the enemy that they were only occupied at night.[61]

Regimental officers assigned picket duty to their men on a rotating basis, the frequency of such duty dependent on the strength of the regiment and the number of posts to be manned. Each shift lasted twenty-four hours, during which time no assigned soldier could go to sleep. "We do duty 2 days and are off 1," explained Capt. George D. Bowen of the Twelfth New Jersey. "First, we go on duty on the Main Line, here we must be awake all day. At night we have to be awake half the time one half keeping watch half the night, the other half the balance. From here we go to the Skirmish line; here we stay 24 hours, not allowed to sleep at all. . . . It is at least 11 P.M. when we get in from there. . . . So it goes day after day, 2 days out of camp one day in." The Tenth Corps issued elaborate orders specifying the protocol for picket duty, dividing each picket guard into four reliefs and rotating them in and out of the posts to a picket reserve for their twenty-four hour obligation. "As a general rule, there should be in each relief one corporal for every three sentinels' posts, one sergeant for every six posts, one subaltern for every ten posts, and a captain or field officer commanding," read these instructions. Not every unit followed such rigid guidelines, but men on both sides agreed that standing picket "was the hardest duty a soldier has. It fatigues both body and mind," wrote Sgt. Daniel W. Sawtelle of the Eighth Maine. "All his senses are acutely alive to the danger which he is every moment expecting. . . . You may have marched all the day before in the hot sun and nearly ready to die for the want of sleep. Yet to do so and be caught by your officer, would be death if the enemy did not surprise you and take the job out of their hands."[62]

Picket duty became particularly onerous during inclement weather. "Picture old Confed with slouch hat on & a splendid Yankee oil cloth wrapped around him sitting sailor fashion flat on the grass in an old field a few hundred yards from the enemy the wind & rain beating mercilessly against him, and peal after peal of heaven's artillery in quick succession startling all nature while the lurid glare of the lightning lit the darkness. . . . Old Confed looking at his watch by the lightning blaze to see if the hour had come to change the vidette," read an entry in the diary of Sgt. Edward Crockett. "Old Confed receiving his portion of the glory of war." Rain usually ruined whatever rations a picket might have carried with him. "Our hardtack was often in the same condition as our bodies on account of the wet, as also our coffee, sugar, pepper, salt & pork," wrote Maine's John W. Haley. "Sweet pork and salt coffee were combinations which we should have never selected if we had been consulted but the weather so frequently put this beyond our control and when we got them mixed together we had a mess which we think would have puzzled a French cook . . . and would have proved too sticky for the stomach of a Dutchman. This was generally the condition of our haversacks when on picket in a storm."[63]

Other hazards included losing one's way in the darkness and stumbling into the enemy's picket posts or risking being mistaken for the foe and coming under friendly fire. Pvt. William J. Miller of the Twelfth South Carolina encountered shallow graves, exposed by the rain, in making his way back from his picket duty, a gruesome discovery in the gloom. Of course, enemy fire often kept pickets under threat of instant death. "It is not at all agreeable to have the balls constantly whistling over one's head," admitted Captain Bowen.[64]

Occasionally, pickets would turn the deadly exchange of fire into a game. A New Yorker remembered when a comrade put his hat and shirt on a ramrod and raised them above the picket post, eliciting a shout from the Rebel opposite him. "It won't do, Yank. Your neck is too skinny! Place your head under the hat and we'll accommodate you!" A Pennsylvania regiment expanded on this ruse, manufacturing a mannequin dressed in full uniform and standing it up by a post. They attached wires to the head and hands of the dummy to provide the faux soldier with animation, much to the consternation of the Confederates, who riddled it with bullets to no apparent effect. During one quiet interlude along the picket lines north of the James, the Confederates "engaged in a variety of fancy and other dances opposite our outposts," wrote an amazed correspondent. "The dancing would scarcely have been noticed, but having ladies . . . for partners within speaking distance of our videttes attracted some attention, and afforded no little amusement."[65]

While fandangoes along the picket lines may have been rare, fraternization between the pickets grew commonplace. "Our pickets and the yankey's pickets is friendly and don't fire at each other," wrote Lt. Henry M. Talley of the 14th Virginia. "If they did I could kill one every time." Cpl. Theodore W. Skinner of the 112th New York agreed that "there is no shooting on the picket lines at this front and it is a good plan too for there is no use of pickets popping at one another all of the time." These informal truces were matters of mutual agreement. "We are very clost to the rebs but we don't shoot at on a nother for we made a bargan not to," explained Pvt. William Webb of the 94th New York, "and so we can walk war [where] we ar." Lieutenant Lockley reported: "The pickets on both sides holding amicable intercourse. Our men . . . report that the rebel soldiers declare that if they had their own way they would never fire another gun at a Union soldier. It seems grievous that we should continue this murderous war, while such a feeling animates the combatants." "It was a singular sight," remembered a Pennsylvanian, "to see the soldiers of two great hostile armies walking about unconcernedly within a few yards of each other, with their bayonets sticking in the ground, bantering and joking together, exchanging the compliments of the day and even saluting officers of the opposing forces with as much ceremony, decorum and respect, as they did their own."[66]

Not every officer looked so benignly on cordial relations between pickets. No less an authority than Robert E. Lee published Special Orders No. 167 on July 18, admonishing First Corps commander Richard Anderson: "The practice of permitting communication between our pickets and skirmishers and those of the enemy, is highly injurious to the service and subversive of discipline. No intercourse or conversation with the enemy shall be allowed, and no officers or man will be permitted to go outside of our picket lines except by authority of the Corps commander." The men broadly ignored such proscriptions unless a dutiful authority was present to enforce them. "The soldiers on picket would occasionally make private arrangements for a truce or armistice, to enable them to stand up and walk around," recalled a soldier from Maine, "but the rebel officer would invariably give orders to commence firing. At such times, the 'Johnnies' would always give timely warning to our men, to get into their pits. The common expression was 'Hunt your holes, Yanks, we have got to fire' and they would never commence until the 'Yanks' had all retired to their pits." Even then the troops often simply fired in the air "to make a show of vigilance." Sometimes strict officers would separate the friendly enemies "by threats and persuasion," which often translated into harsh punishments. Hard labor, fines, and public humiliation were all levied against pickets caught consorting with their opponents.[67]

Such penalties did little to curb illicit interaction between sentries. The men in blue and gray shared water sources, picked corn from the same fields, and even bathed together in the same streams. "At one point there was a brook which was used by both sides by mutual agreement," remembered Pvt. Jerome Jennings of the Eighty-Fifth Pennsylvania. "The holding up of a canteen was the safety guarantee, and the men walked down coolly for water, often meeting their foes at the creek." Addison S. Boyce of the Twentieth Michigan informed a correspondent that the pickets "both washed themselves in the same brooks that runs between our lines." In one instance the opposing pickets gathered at a spring and cooked their meals together, entertained by a Federal who played an accordion for "quite a knot" of Confederates. Cornfields occasionally remained in no-man's-land, and these drew interest from both armies. "Sometimes when we were peaceable, both sides would go in and pick as much corn as they wished," recalled an Alabaman. Eighteenth Corps staff officer Solon Carter agreed. "Our men go into a corn field and pick corn with the rebs without being troubled." Cpl. Imri Spencer of the Fourteenth Connecticut explained in a letter: "We are on quite intimate terms with the Rebs . . . and agreed to not fire on one another. Consequently we went outside our lines and got corn and maters [tomatoes], they did the same."[68]

Playing cards provided a favorite pastime for friendly pickets. "It was no uncommon sight, when visiting the picket posts, to see an equal number of 'graybacks and bluebellies' . . . enjoying a social game of euchre or seven-up and sometimes the great national game of draw poker, with army rations and sutler's delicacies as the stakes," wrote a Pennsylvanian. "Grub is trumps with hungry men every time." On at least one occasion, the enemy pickets played with the two presidents as the imaginary stakes—the Lincolnite lost. "There, says the winner, Old Abe belongs to me." "I'll send him over by the Petersburgh Express," joked the Federal, referencing the nom de guerre of a long-range Union weapon that mimicked the masthead of a popular city newspaper.[69]

It was not unusual for pickets to sneak a visit to their enemy's posts. "Today I was out on the line and there was a lot of Rebs there and one of them invited me to go with him back [and] told me he would insure me a safe trip," wrote Tilton Reynolds of the 105th Pennsylvania. "So another fellow of our Regt and myself went over inside their picket line and stayed about ½ an hour and had a great chat." In early September two New York soldiers, at the invitation of their Rebel hosts, donned Confederate uniforms and attended a ball in Petersburg. Private Haley testified that on pleasant evenings the Rebel pickets would come over to Union pits and complain about the continuation of the war. "We generally treated them to a cup of coffee and a few sutler's cakes, which had a mollifying effect on them and impressed them with our goodness."[70]

Such trust motivated some Confederates to pass letters to their Federal counterparts to be mailed to recipients residing behind Union lines. One Southerner transmitted a sealed envelope directed to a person in Pennsylvania, written by a wounded Union soldier in a Confederate hospital. Most such transactions were honorable, but Sgt. John F. Sale of the Twelfth Virginia harbored doubts. "Many of our boys have sent letters home by the pickets, but I was afraid to trust them," he wrote his aunt. "I have heard of one instance where a letter was given a Yankee to send and he opened it, read it, and then wrote another, giving a most deplorable account of the man's condition thereby causing the man's friends a great deal of uneasiness."[71]

Few days passed without the sentries exchanging simple banter. "The pickets would jump over the breastwork and meet halfway between the lines . . . swap jokes and grind each other over their past battles, each party sure to stand up in support of his own army," wrote Wyman White of the Second U.S. Sharpshooters. "I never heard of anyone losing his temper in these wordy battles." True enough, but often the repartee would assume a biting nature, the soldiers taunting one another with references to the armies' victories or defeats. Lt. Joseph Prime of the Seventh USCT met a Tennessee counterpart between the lines one August day. "He was a pleasant sort of fellow but one of the most inveterate secessionists I ever saw," wrote Prime. "He said that there had never been a battle . . . but what they (the Rebels) have got the best of it. I just reminded him of the battles of Antietam and Gettysburg, Malvern Hill and a few others that upon consideration he thought the 'Johnnies' got the worst of it." At least one Confederate believed the constant conversation between the pickets went too far. "They were talking all along the line . . . so much untill they go to using sharp language to each other," wrote Sgt. William Russell of the Twenty-Sixth

Virginia. "They were talking from 3 o'clock untill they were relieved . . . walking our respective posts, all on both sides were gay & merry singing, talking, and laughing all night. . . . They were all very sociable (too much for my use)."[72]

Trading often dominated picket intercourse, verbal and otherwise. The articles most often exchanged included newspapers and Yankee coffee for Rebel tobacco. Of course, like all manner of fraternization, officers usually frowned on such swaps, so the practitioners of this forbidden commerce employed stealth to consummate their bargains. "Johnny Reb watches an opportunity, when his officer is otherwise engaged, steals cautiously out to a point equidistant from the two lines, sticks a note on a twig or bush, expressing his wishes, lays down a package of tobacco, a southern paper, or whatever commodity he may have to dispose of, and returns to his post," explained a soldier from Maine. "Immediately a 'Yank' glides cautiously out, brings in the package or the note, which is, for instance, to the effect that 'Johnny' would like cheese, sugar, coffee, a 'nife,' or 'ennythink' else for his 'terbakker.' 'Yank' computes the value of the tobacco, and makes up a package of its equivalent worth . . . carries it out, and returns to his post, when 'Johnny' again emerges from his pit, and receives his merchandise. Not a word is spoken; and this trading is continued day after day."[73]

The soldiers would usually signal one another of their wish to trade, then crawl out between the picket lines where brush or tall grass would conceal them from disapproving officers. Where such stealth was not required, the pickets would saunter out between the lines holding a newspaper, indicating their desire to trade. The exchange would occur midway between the posts at what the soldiers called trading stations, sometimes without benefit of conversation. Remarkably, large numbers of soldiers engaged in such negotiations simultaneously. Pvt. Jesse R. Bowles of the Fifty-Fifth Virginia wrote his sister in September: "Our men and the Yankees exchanged papers. . . . I reckon one hundred of our men went out there and got some knives from them." Bowles added that no one from his regiment participated, as "Capt. Davis commanding the regiment would not let any have anything to do with them."[74]

Obtaining enemy papers not only provided the soldiers with news from the other side but also offered their best gauge of enemy public opinion. As satisfying as this was to the mind, pleasures of the palate provided the most prized articles of this illicit commerce. "The good understanding between the pickets went so far that during the evenings there was a regular trading of the tobacco of the Confederates for the coffee of the Federals . . . and often they drank their coffee together while making the barter," recalled General de Trobriand. When more discretion was required, the pickets would sneak out and place a plug of tobacco or a bag of coffee on a convenient stump, then return to find the desired article at the same place deposited by an unseen partner. If the picket lines were particularly proximate, the traders would carefully toss the items into the opposing posts, thus avoiding detection by their officers, not to mention the risk of being shot by an overzealous enemy.[75]

Occasionally, the traders found themselves under arrest for violating orders prohibiting such transactions. Yet at other times commanders tendered their approval, such as when Eighteenth Corps headquarters suspended the proscription against trading newspapers "with a view of encouraging desertions from the enemy." More frequently, however, swapping was done with the complicity of officers who simply looked the other way.[76]

Most soldiers conducted their trading with honesty. A soldier from Rhode Island, for example, hurled a large jackknife, a much-valued article, into his opposing picket post, attaching a note requesting three heads of tobacco in return. Soon a bundle came flying back containing the knife and a tobacco plug. "Friend Yank," read the note. "The knife is a good one, but we are not allowed to trade. However, you are welcome to this piece of tobacco. Signed, 'soldier.'" Still, some swapping ended badly. Lt. Charles Buckingham of the 146th New York went out to exchange a paper when he was shot by a Rebel picket. A New York artilleryman crossed the lines to exchange coffee for tobacco but neglected to bring the coffee. When he returned with the desired item, some Confederate officers seized him and eventually consigned him to a Richmond prison. On rare occasions pickets would lure would-be traders into their lines only to make them prisoners, "the standing offer of a furlough for fifteen days for the capture of a Yankee is too great a temptation for their good faith and honor," a correspondent to the *Utica Weekly Herald* informed his readers. Sometimes, the Confederates would send money into the Union picket line, requesting to purchase some delicacy or article of clothing. "One Johnny gave one of our men a 20 dollar greenback and told him to get a hat and bring it back to him," wrote Capt. Walter Wallace Smith of the Second U.S. Sharpshooters. The faithless Federal kept the money, "& poor Johnny is without a hat."[77]

These demonstrations of amity notwithstanding, just as often the picket lines erupted in deadly volleys. "The picket firing has been incessant ever since I reached here," wrote Pvt. Luther N. Ralls of the Thirty-Fourth Virginia. "It sounds more like some ten or fifteen hands chopping in a new ground than anything I can compare it to, but this is of daily occurrence." The volume of such fire beggared description. Private Haley reported that each soldier was required to carry 150 rounds of ammunition on picket duty and was expected to fire them all before morning. "This firing off cartridges served two purposes," wrote the acerbic Haley. "It helped to break the monotony of sitting all night . . . and also served to enrich some one who had a contract for cartridges or for powder and lead." According to another Federal: "Sometimes the firing of a single picket would quickly develop into an engagement extending for a mile along the line. . . . [B]rigades would fire twenty or thirty thousand rounds of ammunition during a single night." Pvt. Jacob M. Roberts of the Fourteenth New York Heavy Artillery wrote his sister: "As usual the Pickets are firing to night like smack sometimes a hole volley of musketry. . . . Oh it was a bad plase for a fighting man to display his collers for he would shure to get them riddled." General Ord reported that "every day from 20 to 30 of my men and about the same number of Rebels in my front are carried groaning—maimed or dying to the hospital."[78]

Black soldiers on the Union picket line often drew the particular ire of their grayclad counterparts. "The Rebs seem to have a spite at them," wrote a soldier in the 155th Pennsylvania. A correspondent to the *New York Times* reported in early September that "two of the colored pickets on our right were brought in on stretchers. The firing between them and the enemy is almost constant." Cpl. Edgar Ashton of the 3rd Virginia explained to his aunt: "Neither side are allowed to fire at each other. We do not wait for orders if the negroes are put on the picket line."[79]

Yet there is abundant evidence to suggest that enmity between Confederate soldiers and U.S. Colored Troops sometimes disappeared. "The pickets in our front . . . are on very good terms with us; a fact which is quite remarkable as all our troops are colored," wrote Capt. James H. Wickes of the Fourth USCT. The African American war correspondent Thomas M. Chester reported in early September that "the rebels and our colored soldiers now converse together on apparently very friendly terms, and exchange such luxuries as apples, tobacco, and hard tack." Capt. John Owen of the Thirty-Sixth USCT informed his mother, with no little surprise, that "the rebels are very friendly . . . and one tried to buy a piece of hardtack from one of my darkies with $2 worth of tobacco."[80]

Officers sometimes levied formal discipline on those who violated proscriptions against fraternization, but both sides also meted out informal penalties to men who failed to honor those truces. "The other day one of the 'Johnnies' discharged his piece on the picket line & his officer made him walk a beat in front of the pickets on both sides four hours & carry a log of wood on his back," wrote the Ninth New Hampshire's Lt. Oscar D. Robinson. "This morning one of our men carelessly discharged his piece and is being punished in the same way." A similar episode unfolded in front of the Ninth New Jersey after a single Rebel shot broke the sanctity of a ceasefire among the pickets. "Airy one hurt by that shot?" rang out a Confederate voice. "No, it hit this rail," came the Yankee reply. "Throw the rail this way and I'll make the —— fool who fired the shot carry it till dark." The offending Confederate then paraded in plain view of both picket lines, carrying his burden of shame the balance of the day. When a soldier from Joseph Davis's Brigade shot a Federal during a ceasefire, John H. Walters of the Norfolk Artillery Blues wrote, "While I believe in the abstract principle of killing a Yankee where even one is found on our soil, yet in such a case as this, it was not only brutal, but dishonorable in the extreme."[81]

Conflicts along the picket lines sometimes assumed a more organized form beyond mere random firing. These engagements found their origin in a range of motives. Sometimes the object was to secure a batch of prisoners to obtain information. In other cases some commanding officer would deem it necessary to adjust his own picket line and in the process dislodge the enemy's. These forays often amounted to elaborate raids, such as the "seine-haulings" conducted by Maj. Thomas J. Wooten of the Eighteenth North Carolina. On September 7, for example, Wooten captured eleven Federal pickets near the Davis house, killed two others, and wounded another. Three days later he conducted another raid, this time capturing a beef cow, with which his men escaped unharmed.[82]

The largest of these conflicts unfolded on the night of September 9 along Jerusalem Plank Road. Fort Sedgwick, on the east side of the road, faced a complex of Confederate fortifications at Rives Salient, the largest of which, Fort Mahone, carried the nickname "Fort Damnation." On the west side of the highway and between the lines stood two stark brick chimneys, the remains of a burned dwelling that would give this engagement its name. The Rebels established their picket line in front of these chimneys along a ridge and in such proximity to the Federal works that the grayclad sentries could almost look down into the enemy's trenches. Federals standing atop Fort Sedgwick could easily carry on a conversation with the Confederate pickets.[83]

General de Trobriand, whose brigade manned the works around the fort, considered the enemy picket line a serious inconvenience and thought it posed "real dangers" should the informal truce that existed along the opposing lines fracture. The diminutive Frenchman believed he could rectify the situation by attacking the Rebel sentries with a coup de main and obtained the approval of his division commander, Gershom Mott. General Mott, in turn, consulted corps commander Hancock, who examined the proposed point of attack on September 8 and authorized the action for the night of September 9–10.[84]

Mott selected three of his regiments—the 20th Indiana, 99th Pennsylvania, and 2nd U.S. Sharpshooters—to execute the assault. Lt. Col. George Meikel of the 20th would advance to the left of Fort Sedgwick, with the sharpshooters, also under Meikel's command, on his left. The Pennsylvanians, led by Col. Edwin R. Biles, would go forward to the right of the fort using a lone tree as their guide. The troops would advance at midnight, some armed with entrenching tools, and instructed not to fire a shot. De Trobriand issued these orders to Meikel and Biles at 10:00 P.M. The troops on other portions of the picket line and in the fortifications were alerted to be ready to support the attackers and to repulse any attempt by the graycoats to regain their lost posts. The Second Corps artillery also prepared to open on the Confederates if necessary. The 110th Pennsylvania drew the unique assignment of rolling dozens of gabions forward from the fort to help establish the new picket line that would result from the attack.[85]

The Federals waited anxiously for the moon to go down. At 1:00 A.M., when "the darkness was profound," a lone bugle sounded, and the three regiments moved out silently. A sergeant in the sharpshooters recalled that the distance to be covered was short, "and before the Rebels had time to catch their breath, we were in their pits and right among them." Some of the Confederates were asleep; one said that when a Yankee hit him over the head with a shovel, "I got real waked up." A Virginian admitted that the first thing he knew, a Yankee had him by the hair hauling him out of his pit; he "didn't have time to get the stopper out of the end of his gun." A brief hand-to-hand struggle ensued, but within fifteen minutes the unsuspecting Confederates had either fled or fallen captive.[86]

Floridians from Finegan's Brigade, along with a few of Brig. Gen. Nathaniel Harris's Mississippians, occupied the captured posts. The flawed reputation of Finegan's command caused some Confederates to blame them for the surprise. "We lost a few days ago 150 men who were picked off the piquet line *asleep*," wrote Col. Fitz William McMaster. "They were Floridians under Finegan." Brigade commander Joseph Davis wrote his uncle, the president, "I have but little confidence in Finegan's Brigade." Reports varied widely regarding the number of captured Floridians, but all counted significantly fewer of them than the estimate of the indignant McMaster. Some Confederates even exonerated the unfortunate Floridians completely, ascribing the miniature disaster to "a mean Yankee trick," accusing the Federals of posing as deserters to gain access to the Confederate position.[87]

De Trobriand lost relatively few men in his attack, the most prominent of whom was Colonel Meikel, "a young man of great bravery and merit"—perhaps too much of the former. Attired in a bright red shirt and a pair of white pants, Meikel mounted the captured Rebel picket line, refusing the pleas of his men to take cover. In the words of Private Haley, "he who would not heed the entreaties of his friends or the dictates of his own reason listened to the persuasive eloquence of a minie ball, which tore its way through a vital part." Stretcher-bearers, one of whom was killed, removed the stricken Hoosier, who died a few hours later. "His loss was keenly felt in the brigade, and all who had been brought in contact with him," lamented de Trobriand. "It seems as if some evil power drives some folks to their own destruction," concluded Haley, who called the slain officer "a general favorite on account of his fine soldierly bearing." A Union fort near where he fell would soon bear his name.[88]

The Federal attack, styled the "Battle of the Chimneys," fell short of perfection. Colonel Biles had been instructed to "take his regiment in front of that part of our line which extends from Fort Hell to a point on the right opposite to a single tree, where a new line of pickets will be advanced during the evening." But "being deceived by the darkness, and carried on by the success," Biles advanced the Ninety-Ninth Pennsylvania beyond its designated position. When daylight arrived, the Confederates recognized Biles's vulnerability and counterattacked, capturing two of his officers and fifty-two men. The Rebels tried to drive the rest of the interlopers back, but Biles's mistake, "arising from the darkness of the night, as well as from a generous impulse to pursue a retreating foe," reported Mott, "did not otherwise impair the complete success of the operation." Georgia artillerist Francis Marion Coker rationalized the setback in a letter to his wife. "We allowed them to keep the portion of the line we didn't want."[89]

Federal soldiers thereafter completed their new picket positions, including refacing some of the captured Rebel pits. That day the firing from both sides became intense. "After this affair the picket firing was incessant and most desperate for over a week," recalled a New Yorker. "If a man raised his head, on either side, a score of bullets were fired at it." The quartermaster of the Twentieth Indiana likened the atmosphere along the new picket line to "a hornet's nest . . . when the hornets have been stirred up with a sharp stick. You can scarcely imagine how spiteful they [the Confederates] are. They fire at every man they see within range." Colonel McAllister reported that his brigade expended 60,000 rounds in a single day.[90]

The historian of the Second Corps considered the Battle of the Chimneys "one of the most creditable operations" of the campaign. General Hancock, no doubt relieved to be able to report something positive after the recent debacle at Reams' Station, issued General Orders No. 30, praising the three regiments that made the attack as well as other units that played a supporting role. "To General Mott, who directed the whole operation, and to General de Trobriand, who was particularly charged with its execution, and to the officers and men of the regiments mentioned, the thanks of the major-general are accorded," he declared.[91]

A larger Federal operation with more modest ambitions began on September 15. Meade ordered Warren to probe westward from his position along the Weldon Railroad to ascertain the location of the Confederate right and to pave the way for a possible extension of his lines. Warren selected Crawford's division for the task, and Crawford, in turn, chose Brig. Gen. Henry Baxter's brigade—1,200 strong—to carry it out, supplemented by some 800 troopers from the Sixteenth Pennsylvania Cavalry and the First Battalion of Pennsylvania Cavalry, led respectively by Lt. Col. John K. Robison and Maj. Richard J. Falls. Baxter, a prewar resident of Jonesville, Michigan, where he engaged in the milling business, had just celebrated his forty-third birthday. Early in the war he served as a captain in the Seventh Michigan and had worked his way up to brigadier general by 1863, his promotion largely due to his leadership during the amphibious attack on Fredericksburg the previous December. During that operation, Baxter received the second of his three battle wounds during the war.[92]

The bluecoats moved out shortly after 4:00 A.M., using a woodland road to reach the intersection of Vaughan Road and the byway leading to Poplar Spring Church. The cavalry dispersed a small body of enemy horsemen at the crossroads, Robison's troopers heading west toward the little sanctuary, while Fall's men pushed south on Vaughan Road. Robison's contingent reached the intersection with Squirrel Level Road, where most of the opposing cavalry fled north, taking refuge in the newly constructed Squirrel Level Line a little less than a mile away. Here, the Pennsylvanians encountered a thin line of Rebel infantry, which prompted Baxter to summon most of his brigade in relief of the troopers. The Confederates showed no inclination either to retreat or to attack, and the Federals remained content to unleash a relatively harmless skirmish fire. At 11:00 A.M. orders arrived to withdraw, the desired information having been ascertained. Both sides sustained only light casualties.[93]

Minor clashes such as these would occasionally erupt along the lines in September, but General Grant remained content to bide his time. "Although I feel myself strong enough for offensive actions, I am holding on quietly to get advantage of recruits and convalescents, who are coming forward very rapidly," he wrote General Sherman on September 12. "My lines are necessarily very long, extending from Deep Bottom, north of the James, across the peninsula formed by the Appomattox and the James, and south of the Appomattox to the Weldon [Rail]road. This line is very strongly fortified and can be held with comparatively few men." Grant explained that when he felt ready to resume the offensive, he would target the South Side Railroad, cut the Richmond & Danville Railroad, and detach a force of 6,000–10,000 men to attack Wilmington, North Carolina.[94]

A Massachusetts soldier echoed Grant's assessment of the expanding Union army. "Reinforcements are arriving daily in large numbers," he wrote his parents, "and we are gaining strength very fast." Capt. George W. Whitman of the

Fifty-First New York, younger brother of the famous poet and essayist, agreed. "Recruits have been coming to the Army pretty fast lately and I think Grant will soon have force enough for another movement." Both of these men reflected the consensus in the Army of the Potomac that their works were simply too strong for Lee to risk attacking them. In the meantime, field, line, and noncommissioned officers spent much of their time training the newly arrived troops. "This place has become a camp of instruction," wrote Musician David Lane of the Seventeenth Michigan. "Barely enough men are left in the rifle pits to watch the enemy; the rest are drilling—drilling in squads, by companies, battalions, brigades, and, twice a week, an entire division at a time."[95]

A special celebration on September 13 broke the monotony of training and camp life. Congress had recently authorized the presentation of medals for acts of bravery, and General Meade issued the first of these awards to two privates and a sergeant who had captured flags on August 21. Warren collected a number of festive banners with which he decorated Globe Tavern, making "the rotten tumble-down old house look quite respectable." A regimental band took its place on the balcony, "which discoursed (not) eloquent music," and most of Crawford's division assembled before a makeshift platform. Introductory ceremonies kicked off the festivities, "in which our old friend 'Spiritus Frumenti,' bore a conspicuous part." Warren then delivered a speech that "did not present anything of note, except a good deal of hesitation and an almost complete breakdown, but which, I do not doubt, under the pruning knife of the reporter or editor, will appear well enough in print," observed a critical New Yorker. Meade then presented the medals and made a few remarks with classical references, after which "three cheers were given, the bands tooted and all hands who could get seats went in and ate and drank," reported Washington Roebling. "This matter of giving medals to privates for capturing battle flags is a very good thing and ought to have been introduced long ago, but better late than never as it is with a great many other things except getting married."[96]

The day did not go so well for General Cutler. Grant officially abolished his Fifth Corps division and consolidated it with the remaining units of Warren's command, recommending that the ailing and slightly wounded brigadier be assigned to recruiting duty. Meade requested that one of the remaining divisions comprise only regiments that had previously served in the abolished First Corps; Crawford assumed command of this reconstituted organization. But Wainwright thought poorly of its leader. "It would almost seem as if they were determined not to give the old 1st a chance, putting it under a man such as Crawford," he confided to his diary. "He is certainly no better than Cutler & not so good as the old man was a year ago." Opinions regarding Crawford's competence aside, the soldiers of the defunct First Corps heartily approved of their new organization. "This order puts all the original 1st Corps regiments still left in the field in one Division which gives great satisfaction to the round badges," wrote the quartermaster of the Seventy-Sixth New York.[97]

A similar consolidation reordered the Ninth Corps. Julius White, commander of the First Division, also suffered from ill health and, perhaps more relevantly, limited competence, so he was sent home and his division abolished. White's command had been severely depleted by casualties and disability, a circumstance that justified its organizational demise. "I must say I think it was too bad to break up such a fine division as ours, which has fought so splendidly," thought Capt. Charles Mills. "But we were so reduced that I have feared it for some time." White's regiments were divided between Willcox's and Potter's divisions, with Willcox's command now designated as the First Division, while Ferrero's U.S. Colored Troops became the new Third Division.[98]

Lee's table of organization remained relatively stable. Several brigades, however, received new commanders in August and September. Brig. Gen. George Steuart, captured in the Mule Shoe at Spotsylvania in May, took over a Virginia brigade in Pickett's Division following his exchange. Similarly, Brig. Gen. James J. Archer left Johnson's Island prison after a lengthy internment and assumed command of a brigade that combined his old unit with that of Brig. Gen. Henry H. Walker. General Kirkland had sufficiently recovered in mid-August to retake the field, but by then MacRae had performed so well that there was no impetus to replace him. Beauregard requested that Kirkland take over James G. Martin's North Carolina brigade, its former commander having been transferred out of Beauregard's department due to ill health. "Gen. Kirkland is much chagrined at losing his brigade," wrote an officer in the Forty-Seventh North Carolina. "This part of it he does not like as every man who has ever served in Lee's army is proud of it & unwilling to pass into any other."[99]

Amid the reordering of brigades and divisions in late summer, soldiers and officers of both armies maintained a keen interest in military affairs farther south, particularly events on the Gulf Coast and around Atlanta. On August 5 Rear Admiral David Farragut vanquished a small Confederate fleet in Mobile Bay, led by the formidable ironclad ram *Tennessee*, setting the stage for the capture of the forts protecting the entrance to the harbor. Fort Gaines on Dauphin Island surrendered on August 7, while Fort Morgan, on the eastern shore, fell sixteen days later. "Last night the report reached us that Mobile had fallen and the boys throwed their caps, and cheered the whole length of the line, much to the chagrin of the Johnnies who opened a rapid musketry fire," wrote Pvt. Edward Griswold of the First Connecticut Light Artillery, although in reality the city itself remained in Confederate hands. Many Rebels put an optimistic spin on their defeat in Alabama, ignoring the fact that Farragut's victory all but eliminated the port of Mobile. "The falls of Forts Morgan and Gaines are not necessarily fatal to our success in Mobile," wrote Lt. Thomas Jewett Goree. "Confidence is generally felt in our ability to hold the place." Catherine Ann Deveraux Edmonston, a diligent North Carolina diarist, was equally optimistic. "[Maj.] Gen [Dabney] Maury . . . claims that he will make [Mobile] a second Charleston. God grant it."[100]

Concern about affairs around Atlanta dwarfed interest in Mobile Bay. Soldiers and civilians of every stripe around Petersburg followed events in Georgia with intense interest, especially Lee's soldiers from the Peach State. General Sherman had commenced his campaign in North Georgia at the same time that Grant and Meade began the Overland Campaign. By late August, Sherman and his opponents—first Gen. Joseph E. Johnston and then Gen. John Bell Hood— had shed blood over a corridor more than 120 miles long from the outskirts of Chattanooga to the gates of Atlanta. Grant, of course, kept close tabs on his most trusted subordinate, although he exercised little direct influence on Sherman's operations.[101]

The final battle for Atlanta took place at Jonesborough, south of the city, on August 31. Confederate defeat there prompted Hood to order the evacuation of the city the next day. On September 2, Union forces entered the town. Almost immediately the good news reached the Federal forces around Petersburg. "We heard yesterday before dark of the capture of Atlanta," wrote General Paine on September 3. "The telegram was dated Marietta Sep. 2. . . . My regts know of it same day & before dark." "The different regiments in camp were soon electrified with the news, and . . . the . . . cheers from headquarters made the welkin ring with rejoicings and congratulations, until the spirt of enthusiasm reached the outermost pickets," wrote a war correspondent. "The rebels in the woods opposite to our pickets rushed out inquiring what was the matter with the Yankees, and when informed that it was owing to the fall of Atlanta they forgot to return thanks for a courteous reply to their question."[102]

On the evening of September 4, the Union lines offered more than cheers to celebrate the occasion. "I have received your dispatch announcing the capture of Atlanta," Grant wrote Sherman at 9:00 P.M. "In honor of your great victory I have ordered a salute to be fired with shotted guns from every battery bearing upon the enemy. The salute will be fired within an hour amidst great rejoicing." Sometime around midnight, the thirteen-inch mortar dubbed the "Petersburg Express" fired a shell that arced through the night sky, the signal for as many as 120 mortars and cannons to follow suit. "The way Grant celebrated the fall of

Atlanta was a caution," wrote James D. Benton, the surgeon of the 111th New York. "It was ahead of all the pyrotechnic displays I ever witnessed and more grandly terrible than the whole Revolutionary War and all the independence days from that time to this." Hospital clerk Edward Brooks was equally impressed. "The flashes of cannon illuminated the horizon and the burning fuzes of bombs marked their course from side to side in rapid succession through the celestial vault."[103]

This bombardment surprised many Confederates and even some Federals. "Not a soldier . . . knew the cause of such an unprecedented fusillade," wrote Sergeant White. A man in the Tenth Connecticut considered the bombardment "impressive pyrotechny" but admitted that "what it all meant we were at a loss to understand. There were no signs of an attack by either party; and when after half an hour or so, the exhibition closed without any apparent results, we went back to our blankets more mystified than ever." These Nutmeggers learned the next day the reason for such a fulsome demonstration, although elsewhere staff officers circulated along the lines announcing Sherman's triumph. Most Confederates were equally confused. "Last night we had a most terrific cannonade along the lines," wrote Capt. John McLure of the Palmetto Sharpshooters. "I have not heard . . . the cause, beyond that it was begun by the Yankees with shouts of 'Atlanta.' I suppose it was a kind of jollification."[104]

"The rebels for a short time seemed dumfounded," thought Lt. Joshua Dearborn. "I guess the 'Johnnies' thought something had busted," explained Lieutenant Reynolds. "They remained quiet for a few moments." A soldier in the Seventeenth Maine assumed that the Confederates expected a massive assault to follow the bombardment, as did Hospital Steward Charles W. Hamlin. "So sudden was the firing commenced that I imagine the enemy supposed we were about to make an attack, for they opened fire on us immediately." A trooper in the Sixth Ohio Cavalry admitted that the Confederate gunners "responded quite handsomely," an assessment Cpl. Joseph A. Griner of the Eighth Pennsylvania Cavalry shared: "The Rebs replied very lively, and I have very seldom heard a more furious cannonade than was kept up for an hour or more." But the sardonic Private Haley judged the Confederate response "feeble," and although Lieutenant Barnum considered the return fire "anything but pleasant," he allowed that the Federals' sturdy bombproofs meant that "no one was hurt."[105]

Amid this cacophony of ordnance, Union regimental bands appeared behind the lines to serenade the gunners. "During the cannonade the bands in the rear were playing National airs," wrote Lt. Benjamin Wright of the Tenth Connecticut. Apparently, this makeshift symphony continued even after the firing ceased, robbing Captain Rawle of his sleep. "All the bands commenced playing and the men cheering, which succeeded perfectly in keeping us awake," he grumbled in a letter to his mother.[106]

Pvt. Orrin Sweet Allen of the 112th New York reported that he "achered meself, as my stomick is sore after the cheering." Although a few soldiers lodged similar complaints, many Federals viewed the victory at Atlanta as momentous. A soldier-correspondent to the *Easton Gazette* opined, "The capture of Atlanta . . . and the almost total demoralization of Hood's forces is a death blow to all rebel hopes in the Southwest, and while its discouraging effects must be seriously felt in the rebel army here, it adds vigor, energy and determination to our troops, such as I never witnessed before." Some Federals considered the capture of Atlanta to be of equal or greater importance than the fall of Richmond. The most optimistic bluecoats foresaw in Atlanta's demise a quick end to the entire Confederate war effort, while others worried that Hood's defeated army would move north to reinforce Lee. "The fall of Atlanta has done our troops more good than anything that has happened since the war [began]," thought Musician John L. Houck of the Forty-Fourth New York. Sgt. Oliver C. Benton of the Seventeenth New York Battery hoped that Sherman's success would rub off on Grant. "Sherman is the only one that has done what was asked of him to do in the commencement of this spring's work," he wrote his sweetheart, "but I still have hopes that Grant will do something more this fall, if nothing more than to take Petersburg."[107]

Naturally, reaction among the Confederates took a different tone. At first some were loath to believe such unwelcome tidings. "Last night the Yanks had quite a lively time and such Huzzas I never heard," wrote Pvt. John D. McGeachy of the Fifty-First North Carolina. "They halloed that Atlanta had fallen but I don't think there is any such good news for them." Soon enough, however, the truth circulated throughout Lee's army, and many voices quickly located the setback's cause. "I'm fully convinced . . . of the incompetency of Hood," wrote the Third Georgia's Alva Spencer. "Hood is a nice fellow," echoed Capt. William E. Bird of the Fifteenth Georgia, "but isn't owner of sufficient mental calibre for the crisis."[108]

Men such as Lt. Henry D. Wells of the Twenty-Third South Carolina admitted that Hood did not have "the ability of managing as large an army" as he commanded but blamed Jefferson Davis for removing Johnston from command of the Army of Tennessee. Lieutenant Goree believed that Johnston's policy of "wishing to keep his army intact even at the sacrifice of Atlanta" was preferable to Hood's bloody and unsuccessful attacks. "I fear Hood was outgeneraled by Sherman," thought General Beauregard. "When will Mr. Davis learn wisdom from experience?" One Georgian saddled Gen. Braxton Bragg, serving as a military advisor to the president, with responsibility for Confederate defeat. "Had not the evil genius of Missionary Ridge presided over the counsels at Atlanta," he wrote, "peace would have come this winter."[109]

While Maj. Henry DeShields, a quartermaster in Field's Division, admitted that "Hood was outgeneraled by Sherman," he believed that "the taking of Atlanta is no great loss to the Confed." Even General Lee declared that the capture of Atlanta "is not very grievous & . . . I hope we will soon recover from [it]." Lt. James B. Manson of the Forty-Fifth Georgia admitted that the "fall of Atlanta is an event to be deplored it is true, but . . . I can't see that Sherman has gained any military advantage by its occupation." Capt. Thomas J. Norman of the Seventeenth North Carolina allowed that he was "not one of those who always 'look on the bright side of a picture' [but] I see no cause to despair." Private Spencer went so far as to predict that "in six months, Genl Hood's army will be feasting on the Yankee rations now in Atlanta."[110]

Not every Southern soldier shared such optimism. "We feel quite gloomy about the fall of Atlanta," wrote Sgt. Jessie W. Stribling of the Palmetto Sharpshooters. "If something is not done to redeem Georgia very soon the fate is sealed." Pvt. Franklin L. Riley of the Sixteenth Mississippi wondered, "how we can possibly win the war if we lose Atlanta and remain cooped up here in Petersburg?" "The fall of Atlanta has done us much injury," admitted Col. John Marshall Martin of the Ninth Florida. "I fear the sorrow of that disaster will be increased before many weeks by the evacuation of the little town we have been defending for the last two months."[111]

These and other soldiers saw military calamity in Georgia, but even more Confederates viewed the defeat in political terms. "The peace element at the North seems for the moment obscured & darkened by the great victory of the capture of Atlanta," wrote artillerist Francis Marion Coker. "While the possession of Atlanta, as a military question, is or was of but little moment to us as long as the army remains there . . . yet I fear it will have a great effect on the November election in the North, and that not all to our benefit," agreed Private Walters. Coker, Walters, and many other Rebel soldiers hoped that the peace movement in the North would bring the war to a close. "This unfortunate affair is rather a serious one for our cause just at this time," Sgt. Hugh Denson of the Tenth Alabama recorded in his diary, "while the peace element at the north was gaining ground so rapidly." Lieutenant Wells predicted that the loss of Atlanta would prolong the war for at least a year, as did Henry Chambers. "This calamity lengthens the duration of this cruel war which we were beginning to think was rapidly drawing to a close." Pvt. John W. Stott of the Nineteenth Virginia Battalion of Heavy Artillery minced no words. "Atlanta has fallen! The prospect of peace a few days ago so bright is overshadowed by the dark cloud of disaster."[112]

But in just a few days, Wade Hampton and the Confederate cavalry would give these despairing Confederates something to celebrate.

seven

SEPTEMBER 1864

"And this brings us to the question of bread and meat, and I tell you it was at this time a very serious matter." So wrote Pvt. David Cardwell of the Confederate horse artillery, describing the state of his army's rations in the late summer of 1864. General Lee reported on August 22 that the army's supply of corn was exhausted, and a few weeks later the Confederate commissary of subsistence, Maj. S. Bassett French, admitted that the government had less than fifteen days of meat available to feed Lee's troops and the government dependents around Richmond and Petersburg. "The collection of meat from all sources during the past thirty days would not subsist the Army of Northern Virginia for one week," wrote French. Such desperate times demanded equally bold solutions.[1]

Major General Hampton had developed a group of talented coon hunters and deer stalkers from his command into a collection of military spies known informally as the "Iron Scouts." Sgt. George D. Shadburne of the Jeff Davis Legion cavalry, a regiment in Pierce M. B. Young's Brigade of Butler's Division, led these intrepid irregulars. Shadburne, a twenty-two-year-old Texan, earned a reputation as a daring soldier who was "tall, active and resolute." He and the rest of the Iron Scouts spent much of their time exploring enemy dispositions by night and hiding in outbuildings or in the homes of friendly citizens during daylight hours. These men sometimes dressed in civilian disguise or Union uniforms, risking capital punishment should they be apprehended so attired.[2]

On September 3 Lee wrote Hampton suggesting that he investigate the feasibility of a foray behind Union lines "at City Point and other points where his [the enemy's] wagons are parked in his rear." Based on reports from Hampton's scouts, Lee thought that the Federals were "very open to attack," although he also harbored concerns that the Yankees might be planning a raid of their own. "Keep your cavalry as much together as possible, your pickets on the alert, and your scouts out and watchful," Lee advised. "You must keep on hand three days' rations and forage so as to start without delay." Lee's reference to Yankee wagons suggests that he hoped Hampton could secure the contents of those vehicles to alleviate his supply emergency.[3]

Two days later Shadburne sent Hampton a remarkably detailed message—one historian has called it "a textbook model of what such reports should be"—outlining Union dispositions, troop strength, and military assets. Buried in his report was mention of a herd of 3,000 cattle, "attended by 120 men and 30 citizens, without arms," at Coggins Point on the James, eight miles downriver from City Point. Shadburne had no authority to recommend operational decisions, of course, but tellingly, he did not neglect to mention that "the greatest danger I think would be on the Jerusalem plank road in returning." He also painstakingly described the road network leading to the herd and the relatively weak Federal troop presence blocking the way. Hampton could not miss Shadburne's implication that those beeves seemed ripe for the taking.[4]

The livestock Shadburne had seen embodied the Federals' ongoing practice of providing fresh meat to their troops. Cattle from the North arrived by ship at City Point, then nourished themselves in rich pastures near the Federal logistical hub until slaughtered, when a replacement supply would appear. The need to safeguard these herds did not escape Union authorities. On August 8, for example, General Meade ordered an increase in the cavalry guard around Coggins Point. Five days later he recommended to Grant that the herd be moved nearer City Point while the cavalry was engaged in operations north of the James, an expedient endorsed by General Kautz, whose small division from the Army of the James shouldered responsibility for the cattles' security. While most of David Gregg's division was engaged around Reams' Station, Meade again advised against moving the beeves back to the lush grazing land at Coggins Point. Once Grant's August offensive had run its course, the army commander reported that Kautz's division had returned to picket duty, guarding the Union rear from Jerusalem Plank Road to the James and thus in position to protect the cattle. As late as September 13, General Gregg reported nothing more serious on Kautz's front than "dismounted guerrillas" who "lurk in the thickets for the purpose of stealing horses" after dark.[5]

Something more serious—much more serious—was by then in the final planning stages. Hampton grasped Shadburne's subtle suggestion and composed a letter to Lee on the evening of September 8 outlining his idea for a raid targeting the Federal cattle herd. The commanding general conveyed his approval the next day but expressed concern about how the raiders would affect their escape "embarrassed with cattle or wagons." Lee offered a few suggestions, or rather admonitions, about the enterprise and requested a meeting with his cavalry chief to discuss the details. It is not clear that such a meeting occurred, but by the thirteenth Hampton had selected the force he would take and the routes he would follow.[6]

Hampton drew on the two cavalry divisions remaining with the Army of Northern Virginia, as Fitzhugh Lee's brigades were still with Jubal Early in the Shenandoah Valley. He turned first to Rooney Lee's Division. Now recovered from his bout with poison oak, Lee led the North Carolinians of Barringer's Brigade and his old Virginia regiments now under Col. J. Lucius Davis. Hampton then selected Tom Rosser's Laurel Brigade of Butler's Division and added about 100 additional troopers from Butler's other two brigades, Young's and Dunovant's; Lt. Col. Lovick Miller of the Sixth South Carolina Cavalry took charge of this small contingent. Hampton then solicited the cavalry brigade in Beauregard's command under James Dearing to add more firepower to the expedition. Two sections of guns, one each from Capt. Edward Graham's Petersburg Battery and Captain McGregor's Stuart Horse Artillery, under the general direction of Maj. R. Preston Chew, would go along, as would a detachment of eighty makeshift pioneers drawn from Butler's and Lee's Divisions, directed by Lt. John F. Lanneau, an engineer assigned to Hampton's staff. Thus, somewhere between 3,500 and 4,000 soldiers composed Hampton's strike force. Shadburne worked his magic and obtained some herding dogs to join the expedition.[7]

Hampton faced three obvious challenges. First, what route would he follow to skirt the expanded Union lines now facing both north and south while avoiding detection by mounted Federal pickets? Second, how could he wrangle some 3,000 head of cattle sufficiently quickly to evade the inevitable Union response? Lastly, and as Lee had suggested the thorniest question, could he effectively select a path back to Confederate lines without being intercepted while burdened with the beeves?

The cavalry chief addressed the first question when he informed his immediate subordinates that they would follow Boydton Plank Road southwest, away from the intended target, then cut southeast on a country road leading to a crossing of the formidable Rowanty Creek at Wilkinson's Bridge, just north of Stony Creek Depot on the Weldon Railroad. The troopers would then head northeast and cross Jerusalem Plank Road and the Norfolk & Petersburg Railroad before reaching the site of Cook's Bridge over the swampy Blackwater

River. Hampton knew that bridge had been destroyed, so Lanneau's detachment would have to repair it. Once across the Blackwater, the troopers would split into three distinct columns, one each to protect the flanks and the third to capture the cattle.

On the night of September 13, the men received extra rations, indicating to the otherwise uninformed troopers that something big was brewing. The column would depart at 1:00 A.M., September 14. As luck would have it, the movement would coincide with the departure of General Grant, who planned to meet with Phil Sheridan to discuss affairs in the Shenandoah Valley. "Tomorrow morning . . . we are going to leave this camp on a raid and will not return for five or six days," Rosser informed his wife. "The expedition is not a very important one but the distance is great. We are going down on the James River after some cattle that are reported there." Rosser may have underestimated the significance of the operation, but he was right about the distance. His route to the cattle corral would span fifty miles.[8]

Capt. Nathaniel A. Richardson, the Federal volunteer commissary of subsistence, unwittingly shortened Hampton's journey. Richardson moved the herd to Coggins Point on August 29 and held it there for more than two weeks. He pronounced the grazing "abundant and good" until September 15, when he shifted the animals two miles southwest to the Harrison farm, where they could fatten on fresher pastures. Richardson carefully reported that 2,486 head had been moved under the care of a chief herder, five assistant herders, and sixty drovers. One of Shadburne's scouts described these beeves as "a fine lot of cattle and all about the same color, a milk and cider, broad horns and would weigh about 900 lbs. each," adding that they were all steers. In addition to the unarmed herders, a cavalry guard of about 150 troopers from the Thirteenth Pennsylvania Cavalry protected the cattle.[9]

In the hour after midnight, September 14, Hampton's rank and file knew as little about the impending raid as the cattle guards. Some of the Confederates speculated that they were going to surprise and capture a brigade of Black troops. Others thought they were en route to join Fitz Lee's Division in the Valley. "We had no intention or idea that beeves had any place in the picture at all," wrote one of Chew's gunners. The column moved out in the darkness, heading southwest on Boydton Plank Road, with Lee's Division in the lead, followed by the artillery, Miller's small battalion, the Laurel Brigade, and Dearing's troopers. The engineers brought up the rear, while Hampton and Shadburne rode at the front. The column turned southeast on a byway west of Rowanty Creek, eventually crossing the Weldon Railroad and halting just short of Wilkinson's

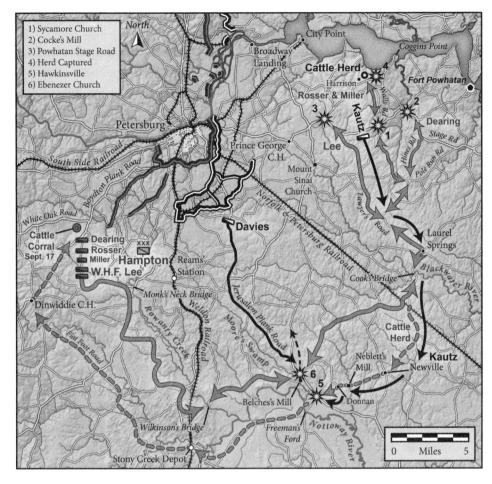

Key:
1) Sycamore Church
2) Cocke's Mill
3) Powhatan Stage Road
4) Herd Captured
5) Hawkinsville
6) Ebenezer Church

Beefsteak Raid, September 14–17, 1864

Bridge, where, after a brisk ride covering nearly twenty miles, they halted for what remained of the night.[10]

The troopers arose before 4:00 A.M. on September 15, saddled their horses, and resumed the march within an hour. Their route took them northeast across Jerusalem Plank Road and the Norfolk & Petersburg Railroad, traversing flat, marshy terrain through pine forests and an occasional small farmstead. Scouts preceded the column and covered the flanks, on the lookout for Yankee patrols and detaining any civilians who might reveal their presence. Just before crossing the plank road, Hampton reached the site of Belches's Mill on Moore's Swamp, a tributary of the Nottoway River. Here, Benjamin W. Belches, the forty-seven-year-old owner of the destroyed mill, emerged from his home and joined the cavalcade, supplementing Shadburne's knowledge of the local geography. About midafternoon the column halted on the banks of the Blackwater River, where only naked pilings of what was once Cook's Bridge appeared out of the murky water. Hampton specifically chose this route, counting on the ruined bridge to convince the Federals that no threat could emanate from its direction and thus provide them no reason to watch it. Now it was Lanneau's turn to go to work. His ersatz engineers cut trees and fashioned planking to provide a new surface for the span. Some of the tired troopers used this delay to rest themselves and their mounts, while others foraged for edibles in the surrounding woods.[11]

Lanneau had selected only men "accustomed to the use of the ax." These eighty soldier-woodsmen wielded their tools with a vengeance, and around dusk a rude platform 100 feet long connected each bank of the Blackwater by spanning the piers of the old bridge. It took until after midnight for the entire column to negotiate Lanneau's rickety but serviceable structure by the light of burning pine knots. There would be no bivouac this night. Hampton's troopers rode silently ahead—"several times the musical men of the column were cut short in attempted songs, which they thoughtlessly began"—preparing to execute the maneuvers that the South Carolinian had explained to his brigade commanders while awaiting the bridge repairs.[12]

Rosser and Miller drew the most important assignment. They would target the Union detachment near Sycamore Church, the point at which the Federal picket line ran closest to the herd. After vanquishing these bluecoats, Rosser and Miller would drive directly for the cattle, overwhelm the small body of guards around the corral, and begin rounding up the bullocks. Lee's two brigades would ride north on Lawyer's Road and assume a blocking position near Prince George Court House, site of the largest Federal encampment. Their job would be to prevent those Yankees from breaking through to rescue the herd. Similarly, Dearing's regiments would guard Rosser's right, east of the corral. They would eliminate the small picket post thought to be near Cocke's Mill, then block the road leading from Fort Powhatan and its garrison, downriver on the James. Once Rosser and Miller had the beeves on the move toward Confederate lines, couriers would inform Lee and Dearing to withdraw toward Cook's Bridge, where the reunited column would recross the Blackwater. Hampton would accompany Rosser and Miller.[13]

The Confederates quietly advanced north to a crossroads hamlet called Laurel Springs, turning northwest there onto Lawyer's Road. Lee's Division led the way, covering some three miles to the intersection with Hines Road. There, Rosser, Miller, and Dearing turned northeast, while Lee's two brigades continued north on Lawyer's Road heading for Powhatan Stage Road and their assigned position blocking the route from the Union bivouac at Prince George Court House. Dearing and Rosser rode together another three miles, at which point Hampton and Shadburne led Rosser and Miller west on Pole Run Road and then north on Walls Road toward Sycamore Church, while Dearing continued on Hines Road. "It was evident that General Hampton was not unmindful of the danger to which his command was exposed," remembered one of Rosser's men. "There were times when our line of march led through dense forests which obscured the moonlight and left us in comparative darkness." Rosser's column halted at 3:30 A.M., September 16, at a ford over a small stream about half a mile south of Powhatan Stage Road and Sycamore Church.[14]

Ahead in the moonlight rested some 250 men of the First District of Columbia Cavalry under Maj. J. Stannard Baker. This regiment, comprising volunteers primarily from Maine and armed with sixteen-shot Henry rifles, began the Petersburg Campaign with no experience in horsemanship. During the intervening three months, the unit had largely shed its poor reputation and had drawn the important mission of picketing a line from Sycamore Church two miles east to Cocke's Mill, where Capt. William S. Howe led about 150 men of the regiment. A contingent from the Eleventh Pennsylvania Cavalry was encamped some distance behind Baker's troopers, but the Third New York Cavalry, several miles west at Prince George Court House, provided Baker his nearest significant support. Baker had obstructed the roads leading to his camp, leaving only a narrow gap on the byway where Rosser quietly waited in anticipation of dawn and the commencement of his attack.[15]

Hampton used the time before sunrise to discuss with Shadburne and Rosser the tactics required to overwhelm Baker's slumbering soldiers. The sergeant volunteered to take his scouts and 200 dismounted troopers through a ravine and into the Union camp, subduing the Federals before they awoke. Rosser objected. "Shadburne will fail," he told Hampton with characteristic bluntness. "The enemy will be awakened before he can reach them." Rosser preferred a traditional mounted charge. "I will take them quickly," he assured the South Carolinian. Hampton agreed, consoling a disappointed Shadburne that he would have other opportunities to further distinguish himself. He then turned to Rosser, warning the Virginian, "let the blood and the mistake, if such it be, be yours."[16]

Rosser selected the Bath Squadron, Companies F and G of his Eleventh Virginia Cavalry under Lt. Andrew Gatewood, to ride quietly in advance of the command and eliminate the lone vedette and the small picket reserve on duty in front of Baker's bivouac. The brigade commander instructed Gatewood that if this sentry fired at his men to charge full tilt through the reserve and into the camp, the Seventh Virginia Cavalry would be right behind him in support. As it turned out, when the surprised sentry spotted the approaching gray column, he wasted no time in firing but instead hightailed it through the reserves toward his sleeping comrades. Gatewood's men unloaded random shots at the fleeing figure just as the first rays of light penetrated the surrounding forest. Of course, the firing alerted Baker's men, and they roused themselves to meet the unknown threat.

Gatewood dashed ahead, encountering the obstructions that blocked the road, the cramped opening only sufficient to accommodate a single rider. The Virginians halted and began to take casualties as the Federals of the picket reserve emptied their Henry rifles at these shadowy targets. Rosser, as promised, called up the Seventh Virginia Cavalry, which dismounted and began to remove the barriers, opening the roadway for the Twelfth Virginia Cavalry, which then dashed into the Federal camp. "The enemy, covered by darkness and from behind trees, kept up a rapid fusillade with repeating rifles upon the front and flanks of the charging column," recalled one of Rosser's troopers, "the streaks of flame from their guns now and then revealing their forms to the aim of the assailants." Yet the suddenness of the attack in near darkness precluded any organized resistance by the plucky Federals. Joined by the Seventh Virginia Cavalry, the men of the Twelfth Virginia Cavalry, who had dismounted at Shadburne's suggestion and Rosser's order, began rounding up the groggy bluecoats, including Major Baker, who had been turned out of his tent so quickly that he surrendered en déshabillé. Most of Baker's contingent became prisoners, along with four of his troopers killed and three others wounded. Of the roughly 250 men in camp that morning, 219 became casualties, along with the seizure of 300 horses, two ordnance wagons loaded with ammunition, two four-mule teams, assorted camp paraphernalia, and "oranges, lemons, cigars, crackers, and good things and useful." "We divided the sixteen-shooters and had plenty of ammunition," boasted Sgt. George W. Watson of the Twelfth Virginia Cavalry. As a Pennsylvanian phrased it, Rosser had "knock[ed] the mischief out of the 1st Dist of Columbia Cavy." The Confederates suffered as well, the Seventh Virginia Cavalry losing three men killed and fifteen wounded, the rest of Rosser's brigade suffering proportionately.[17]

This action at Sycamore Church lasted only thirty minutes, but by its conclusion, the warm sun had begun to reveal the landscape that stood between the Confederates and the cattle herd two miles distant. Capt. Henry H. Gregg of the Thirteenth Pennsylvania Cavalry, David Gregg's brother, listened intently to the sound of combat to the south. He commanded the small contingent of troopers that guarded the herd, which had spent the night quietly contained in its corral. Soon, the mystery of the firing revealed itself in the form of a few fugitives from the First District Cavalry, who streamed into Gregg's camp with panicked tales of the Rebel attack. Gregg had barely enough time to organize his troops before Rosser's lead element, the Thirty-Fifth Virginia Battalion— known as the "Comanches"—appeared on the horizon. Col. Thomas Massies's Twelfth Virginia Cavalry and Col. Oliver Funsten's Eleventh Virginia Cavalry soon galloped up. Hampton had tarried at Sycamore Church, where he could easily communicate with Lee and Dearing, while the Seventh Virginia Cavalry hurriedly organized the prisoners and secured the captured booty.[18]

Rosser, at the head of his command, spotted Gregg's thin blue line deployed in his front. The Federal captain had responded with alacrity and steeled his outnumbered men for whatever was coming their way. Wishing to avoid further combat, which could only cause a delay in rounding up the cattle and returning to Confederate lines, Rosser ordered Pvt. Cary Seldon of the Twelfth Virginia Cavalry to ride forward bearing a white handkerchief at the point of his saber. Sgt. Alfred Kenyon from Gregg's command rode out to meet Seldon, who point-edly stated, "General Rosser demands your surrender." Kenyon declined, using colorful language to express his response, sending Seldon back to convey the Yankee refusal. Rosser turned to Lt. Col. Elijah White at the head of the Co-manches and intoned, "Come down on them, White."[19]

These Virginians immediately charged with howls and shrieks. Captain Richardson, who had prepared for just such an emergency, ordered his drovers to open the corral and drive out the cattle. "The enemy came up shouting and firing with great vehemence," he reported, sending Gregg's outgunned troopers in hasty flight and, according to Richardson, exhibiting "their usual barbarity by shooting down the unarmed herders, stabbing them after they lay helpless on the ground, stripping and robbing them." Federal resistance crumbled in five minutes. "The herders had thrown down the fence of the corral, and by firing pistols and yelling Indian fashion, had stampeded the cattle, and they were running like mad," remembered Rosser. He sent the Seventh Virginia Cavalry, which had just arrived from Sycamore Church, to gallop ahead of the herd and arrest its progress. "This was not easily obeyed, for the young steers ran like buffalo, and it was requiring too much of a jaded cavalry to force it into a race like this," the commander admitted. Fortunately, the steers eventually expended their energy, and the Virginians managed to get them under control with the help of Shadburne's herding dogs. "In our brigade were quite a number of cowboys, not of the Texas or Western sort, but real Virginia cowboys, who knew the habits and dispositions of cattle," explained a member of the Twelfth

Virginia Cavalry. Captain Gregg was among the many captured defenders. By 8:00 A.M. and without further incident, the beeves were on the road heading for Cook's Bridge.[20]

Meanwhile, the engagement at Sycamore Church coincided with the advance of the flanking columns, Lee to the west and Dearing to the east. Dearing's men rode immediately toward Cocke's Mill, which rested along Powell's Creek on Powhatan Stage Road. West of the mill, the highway climbed a steep hill, on the brow of which the Federals had constructed light works. At Dearing's approach Captain Howe rushed as many of his battalion as he could muster into these modest fortifications. The Confederates launched a mounted charge, but the Federals' Henry repeaters drove them back. Dearing rallied his troopers for another assault, but this also failed. The Confederates then advanced on the flanks of the stubborn Yankees while maintaining pressure against their front. This compelled the outnumbered Howe to order a retreat, directing his men to make for Sycamore Church and Baker's camp, unaware of Rosser's victory there. Some of the Virginia troopers at the church replaced their worn-out jackets with captured Union uniforms, so when Howe's unsuspecting men approached what they thought were friendly forces, they quickly became captives.[21]

Dearing considered his combat "pretty severe," but Howe's departure allowed him to adopt a blocking position across the road leading from Fort Powhatan. He also cut the telegraph line connecting the fort with City Point, forestalling communications that might have facilitated a timely and unified Federal response. "Rosser's brigade & mine made all of the captures and did the fighting," Dearing informed his wife. A newspaper account credited Dearing with capturing thirty-five prisoners in addition to five or six teams and Howe's camp equipment. Once the cattle were organized and placed on the road, a messenger appeared with instructions for Dearing to depart as well.[22]

In the meantime, the western arm of Hampton's raiders, Lee's Division, with Davis's brigade in the van, rode north on Lawyer's Road. As dawn broke, they, too, heard Rosser's engagement and proceeded toward Powhatan Stage Road, where they encountered an outpost of eighty-five men of Companies B and D, Eleventh Pennsylvania Cavalry, under Capt. James E. McFarlan. According to Maj. Samuel Wetherill, commander of Kautz's Second Brigade, McFarlan offered some resistance and "fell back in good order, losing a few men and horses of the advanced posts." Lieutenant Beale of the Ninth Virginia Cavalry reported the situation differently. "These unsuspecting creatures, tho' warned of our approach . . . had hardly time to escape, and that without waiting to put on their clothing," he wrote. Whatever the case, McFarlan's troopers withdrew west to within sight of Prince George Court House, where the Third New York

Cavalry, under Lt. Col. Ferris Jacobs, rallied the retreating Pennsylvanians. The Federals countercharged, driving back Davis, joined now by Barringer's Tar Heels, who had originally trotted south on the road to Mount Sinai Church. Some of Lee's troopers built a fieldwork near the junction of the stage road with Lawyer's Road and unlimbered McGregor's section of Chew's Horse Artillery. "You know we worked with a will building breastworks," testified a soldier from the Tenth Virginia Cavalry. According to General Kautz, these hasty works extended more than half a mile and consisted of "earth and trees newly felled." The Federals skirmished here until word reached Lee of Rosser's success, prompting the Virginian to retire and eventually rejoin Dearing and the Laurel Brigade. Hampton summarized the situation in his official report: "As soon as the attack was made at the church, General Lee, on the left, and General Dearing, on the right, attacked the enemy most successfully, and established themselves rapidly and firmly at the points they were ordered to secure."[23]

The Confederate column, led by Rosser and followed by Dearing, with Lee assuming the rear guard, briefly came under annoying but nonlethal fire from Union gunboats in the James as they started south on the trot. The herd reached the Blackwater about 10:00 A.M. in advance of the cavalry. Hampton placed two of his staff officers, Maj. Andrew R. Venable and Maj. Garland M. Ryals, in charge of commanding the escort managing the captured beeves. They received valuable assistance from some of Richardson's experienced herders who, in the words of one Confederate, "served their new masters as well and apparently as readily as if these had been their original employers," although watchful troopers "always rode alongside with a handy weapon to insure loyalty." The drovers wisely divided the huge herd into smaller groups, separated by short intervals, rendering them easier to control.[24]

When the animals started crossing Lanneau's rudimentary structure over the Blackwater, Venable, Shadburne, and an assistant quartermaster on Hampton's staff identified only as Captain Henry carefully counted the cattle. They tallied 2,486 head, exactly the number Richardson had reported the previous day. Once the beeves and the troopers crossed the bridge, Lanneau's workmen dismantled it, while the Second North Carolina Cavalry kept a careful watch from the southwest bank for Yankee pursuers. In order to put extra distance between the bullocks and the bluecoats, Hampton directed the drovers to lead the cattle south then west through the crossroads hamlets of Newville and Hawkinsville, about two miles south of the general line of retreat. The herd then crossed the Nottoway River at Freeman's Ford. Hampton recognized that with Cook's Bridge once again out of service, the Federals would most likely use Jerusalem Plank Road to interdict his return. He ordered the Laurel Brigade to assume a blocking position across this highway. Rosser, in turn, sent White's Comanches ahead to carry out that task until the rest of the brigade and Chew's artillery could join them.[25]

The Union cavalry would eventually challenge Rosser on Jerusalem Plank Road, but it took hours for them to do so. General Kautz first notified cavalry headquarters at 6:00 A.M. that his pickets had been driven in between Mount Sinai Church and Powhatan Stage Road. He did not know it, but this had been the handiwork of Lee's Division guarding Hampton's left flank. Kautz dismissed the skirmishing as "not yet . . . serious," deeming it merely a minor retaliation for a previous cavalry encounter. An hour later, however, the general reported that the Confederates in question had made a stand on Powhatan Stage Road and that he feared for the safety of the First District of Columbia Cavalry at Sycamore Church. At 7:30 A.M. he sent yet another message, this time to army headquarters, expressing concern that the Confederates had successfully targeted his First District troopers and lamenting, "I have no force to resist a serious attack."[26]

Not until 8:30 A.M., some thirty minutes after Hampton had the cattle heading south, did Kautz finally comprehend the grand Rebel mission, explaining to cavalry headquarters, "I did not know that the cattle were there until this morning." To his credit, the general pledged to pursue the rustlers with his available force—the Third New York Cavalry and the Eleventh Pennsylvania Cavalry—leaving the brigade of infantry, then en route by Meade's orders, to guard Prince George Court House. Cavalry headquarters confirmed the raid and ordered Kautz to strengthen his picket line and "send a strong party to Cocke's Mill to obtain information, and follow to that point with the rest of your command and attack the enemy, and delay their movements if practicable." Brig. Gen. Henry Davies, acting cavalry commander in Gregg's temporary absence, would saddle up his available men and assist in the chase. Clearly, the Federal high command grasped neither the strength nor the whereabouts of Hampton's raiders, as Kautz's two understrength regiments would be no match for the Confederates' four brigades.[27]

Several diversionary attacks further complicated the Union response. Cadmus Wilcox advanced skirmishers from three of his brigades near the Davis house on the Weldon Railroad, seizing between 90 and 100 prisoners from Warren's Maryland Brigade. Warren's attention, consequently, focused on his front and not the cavalry and cattle coming around his rear. Young's and Dunovant's brigades also pestered the Fifth Corps picket line. Warren would be of no help as Kautz and Davies set out to recapture the purloined livestock before it reached safety behind Confederate lines.[28]

The Third New York Cavalry proceeded to Sycamore Church, where a remnant of the First District of Columbia Cavalry under Capt. Thomas C. Speers, which had escaped from Rosser's attack, now reappeared. These troops, along with a section of artillery, began following the Rebel return shortly after 12:30 P.M., a portion of the Eleventh Pennsylvania Cavalry trotting behind. Kautz personally commanded this aggregation, numbering 500–700 troopers. The general informed army headquarters that a secondhand report numbered Hampton's force at 14,000 cavalry and infantry (a ruse perpetrated by Mr. Belches), adding that another civilian had counted about 3,000 Rebel troopers on Powhatan Stage Road. It is doubtful that Kautz credited these exaggerated numbers, elsewise his pursuit with a fraction of the alleged Confederate strength would have been prohibitively foolish. As it was, his modest cohort could only hope to delay the Confederates and provide Davies time to cut them off.[29]

Kautz reached Cook's Bridge just after Lanneau's engineers destroyed it. The North Carolinians on the far bank delighted in taunting the tardy Federals by bellowing like cattle and facetiously inviting the bluecoats to come over the river and retrieve their bullocks. It would take hours for Kautz to repair the bridge and resume the chase. The Federals eventually replaced the planking and caught up to Hampton's rear guard near Hawkinsville on Jerusalem Plank Road at 10:00 P.M. The Third New York Cavalry engaged in a sharp skirmish with the dismounted Rebels, but Kautz decided that numbers were not in his favor and thus "fell back a short distance and waited for daylight." His jaded troopers had covered thirty miles in their fruitless pursuit.[30]

George Meade, who in Grant's absence commanded all the Federal forces, learned of the raid by 7:40 A.M. He immediately instructed Davies to "get together all your available force and attack the parties and endeavor to recover the cattle." Meade dutifully notified Grant of the situation. It would take time, but Davies managed to assemble about 2,100 men from his two scattered brigades. He led them south on Jerusalem Plank Road, hoping to arrest the Rebel withdrawal. By 2:00 P.M., the Federals began to engage the advanced positions held by the Comanches, gradually forcing the Virginians back to the ground White had selected to make his stand.[31]

White had chosen well. He deployed his men on a slight ridge near Ebenezer Church and Belches's ruined mill, facing north. The Belches's millpond secured his left flank while swampy ground, difficult of passage, protected his right. A small stream, flanked by wetlands on its margins, ran across his front, spanned on the plank road by a flimsy corduroy bridge made of poles, the only practical way of reaching the Confederate line. White dismounted his men, who took position behind a breastwork of fence rails and logs. Chew's guns unlimbered to control access to the bridge.[32]

Rosser now arrived with the remainder of the Laurel Brigade, dismounting a portion of his men to extend White's flanks while maintaining a mounted force along the road. Davies brought some artillery of his own, and soon a spirited duel developed between Chew and the Union guns, even as Miller's small battalion further reinforced Rosser. Some of the Federal shells soared over the Confederate battle line and into the horse-holders in the rear, although they caused little damage to Rosser's defenders. The Virginian, however, called for additional reinforcements. Dearing's Brigade galloped up first, followed by a portion of Lee's Division. "We made haste to reach [Rosser]," wrote Lieutenant Beale, "sometimes at a trot, sometimes at a gallop . . . and at full speed came into line of battle just as the sun went down." One Federal remembered that "General Davies and his troopers got their blood up and charged the works most gallantly, surprising the enemy and capturing prisoners." The blue tide receded, only to rise again when Rosser and his aides withdrew from the hilltop to avoid the whizzing projectiles that made their position uncomfortable. Mistaking this small adjustment as the portents of a wholesale retreat, the bluecoats rushed forward again, meeting a devastating volley at a range of less than 100 yards. Saddles emptied, and the Federals fell back quickly, their enemies bellowing like bovines to add insult to injury.[33]

Davies renewed his bombardment, Lt. Robert Clarke's Battery A, Second U.S. Artillery rendering good service. Chew's guns replied as Davies prepared another assault. Dismounting elements of both of his brigades, the general deployed the Eighth Pennsylvania Cavalry, the First Maine Cavalry, and the Sixteenth Pennsylvania Cavalry on the east side of the road and the Sixth Ohio Cavalry and First Massachusetts Cavalry on the west side. Once again the Federals closed on the Rebel battle line, the Massachusetts troopers engaging in a brief hand-to-hand struggle before withdrawing out of range. "Who that was there can ever forget the wild grandeur of the scene?" asked one Southerner. "The sun shedding its parting beams upon the battling hosts, the heavy plunging of the shot and shell through the ranks of men and horses, the waving of battle flags, the galloping of staff officers and couriers over the field, the defiant shouts of our men calling to the Yankees to 'come and get some beef for supper,' all made up a scene strangely mingling the sublime and the ridiculous."[34]

By 8:00 P.M., as the gathering darkness cast long shadows on the battlefield, Davies decided that this particular nut was simply too hard to crack. "The enemy were in large force, and occupied a position too strong to be taken by the force under my command," he explained, "being protected by earth-works, and having in their front a stream and mill-pond impassable except by the road, and the road bridge over the stream was destroyed." Davies now opted to pin the Rebels down in hopes that Kautz would appear in their rear. But Kautz was miles away, busy repairing Cook's Bridge, and in any case, his force was much too small to cause Hampton any serious trouble. Hearing nothing from Kautz, at 10:00 P.M. Davies decided to break contact and withdraw north on the plank road. Hampton considered sending Lee to outflank the Federals, but once the sun disappeared, the diminished visibility recommended against such a delicate maneuver. Except for Kautz's brief skirmish with the Confederate rear guard, the wide-ranging fighting of September 16 had ended. "Gregg, the Yankee general, acted badly considering we had his brother . . . a prisoner in our hands," wrote Beale, ascribing the Federal futility to the absent division commander. "He became silent & withdrew as much to say 'Hampton, I'll have nothing to do with any such man; you steal my cattle and then beat me when I come to take them back.'"[35]

Hampton left a small rear guard at Ebenezer Church and remounted the bulk of his command. The troopers crossed Rowanty Creek at Wilkinson's Bridge and bivouacked around midnight near the same ground they had used two days earlier. "Horse & man tired alike we threw ourselves upon the ground & reposed in safety until morning," wrote an officer in the Eleventh Virginia Cavalry. Earlier, Major Venable halted the herd on the far side of the Nottoway River to provide men and beasts a well-deserved rest. En route just beyond Neblett's millpond between Newville and Hawkinsville, the herders passed a modest home where a young girl watched in amazement as the hundreds of cattle bellowed past. Venable dismounted to chat with the young lady, Margaret Donnan, and her father, John. Spotting the only cow in the herd, Margaret asked the kindly Venable if she could have her. As the story goes, the cow had been reserved for General Mahone, whose quirky dietary habits demanded fresh milk, but the child's request touched a soft spot in Venable's heart. He picked out instead a particularly exhausted steer and presented it to Margaret as a gift.[36]

Kautz's command spent an uncomfortable night in its makeshift camp east of the Ebenezer Church battlefield. "We had no blankets and nothing to eat," the general wrote. "We were entirely unprovided for a chase." At daylight his enervated riders probed forward to Jerusalem Plank Road and discovered both Davies and the Confederates gone. "The command, having been hastily turned out to repel an attack, was not prepared for so long a march, and I thought it prudent to return," Kautz reported. His men were back in their original camps by 1:00 P.M. Meade communicated with Davies before dawn on the seventeenth, advising that "no effort should be spared to recapture the cattle so long as there is any chance left to do so," adding that "when in your judgment nothing further can be done, you can return." Davies promptly dispatched a brigade westward that reached the Weldon Railroad at 5:00 A.M. Here, the blueclad troopers learned that the cattle herd had progressed beyond their reach and that reports credited Hampton with 6,000 men. Davies, too, withdrew to his original lines.[37]

While the Federals retreated, Hampton and his men proceeded, now in safety, back to friendly venues via Boydton Plank Road. The cattle halted at a corral at that highway's intersection with White Oak Road eight miles south-west of Petersburg. The next day the beeves completed their trek into the city, where, due to the lack of feed for such a large herd, they all eventually met their intended fate. Enough cattle immediately entered the slaughter pen to provide nourishment for the soldiers as early as September 18. "We are enjoying the luxury of fresh beef which Gen. Hampton transferred from Grant's Commissary to ours," Pvt. Joseph Shank of Cutts's artillery battalion informed a friend that day.[38]

The butchering took place in a large field. A soldier in the First Confederate Engineers passed the location on his way back to camp. "I asked if they would sell me some of the 'trimmings' which usually are the butcher's share when a beef is killed." The bloodshedders offered to sell him a head for five dollars. "Dirt cheap was my thought," remembered the hungry engineer. "It was a pretty bloody and ill-shaped load, but I tackled it in order to take the mess some fresh meat. I took the head by the long horns and placed it face down on my head." When he and his unorthodox millinery arrived in camp, the men of his mess expressed great elation and proposed "to make a night of it."[39]

The Commissary Department directed the beef to be issued every other day. A Richmond editor estimated that the steers averaged 800 pounds each, and by multiplying that by 2,486 head, he arrived at an aggregate weight of 1,988,800 pounds, enough to feed 50,000 men a pound each for forty days. Confederates were unanimous in praising the animals' condition. "A prettier lot of beef I never saw," ran the typical appraisal. "They are certainly the greatest sight in the way of cattle I ever saw," echoed a South Carolinian.[40]

Beef rations had all but disappeared in Lee's army, a steady diet of bacon providing most of the protein. "Have been eating pork so long that I am really ashamed to look a hog in the face," wrote Pvt. John R. Zimmerman of the Seventeenth Virginia. "At the sight of such fine beef my appetite became as keen as a razor," a Georgia soldier informed his sister, "and you can imagine me with a long rib in one hand & hoecake in the other face almost greased from ear to ear. I tell you, I have never enjoyed a piece of beef so much." The supply lasted at least through the middle of October. "We are still enjoying the delicious beef captured by Gen. Hampton," recorded Zimmerman on October 5. "Hampton steaks as the men call it." By October 16, at least one Confederate had eaten enough. "Yankee beef for breakfast and dinner," recorded Lt. Col. Joseph Frederick Waring of the Jeff Davis Legion. "Really we have eaten so much beef that I am getting tired of it."[41]

Estimates of the actual number of cattle that arrived in Petersburg vary. Hampton reported that of the 2,486 purloined beeves, 2,468 arrived behind Confederate lines. The 18 missing head may have been "the few broken-down cattle" Kautz claimed to secure during his pursuit. Davies estimated Kautz's recovery at "some fifty head," although nowhere in the written record does Kautz mention that number. In addition to the meat, whatever its quantity, the herd provided hides for leather to produce much-needed shoes. The raiders also captured a large number of blankets, wagons, all manner of camp equipment, and 304 prisoners, primarily from the First District Cavalry and the Thirteenth Pennsylvania Cavalry. The Rebels hustled along these captives, most of them on foot, as Hampton's horsemen made their way to safety.[42]

The Confederate cavalry accomplished all this at a cost of ten men killed, forty-seven wounded, and four missing. The army unanimously agreed with a commissary in Hill's corps, who pronounced the raid "a brilliant affair." The *Richmond Examiner* called Hampton's achievement "one of the boldest and most brilliant things of the war." A South Carolina quartermaster thought, "Genl. Hampton has displayed himself ever since the command of the cavalry devolved on him as a splendid leader." "Don't you suppose Hampton's boys felt very proud," a Georgian asked in a letter home. "They certainly deserve great credit, both officers and men." General Lee thought so as well. On September 17 he proffered Hampton his "high appreciation of the skill and boldness you displayed, and my gratification at your handsome and valuable success." Lee requested that his cavalry chief "convey to the officers and men of your command my thanks for the courage and energy with which they have executed your orders, by which they have added another to the list of important services rendered by the cavalry during the present campaign." Hampton did so the following day. He circulated General Orders No. 11, in which he added his own "appreciation of the gallantry of his officers and men, whose conduct in battle is all that he could desire, and inspires him with pride and perfect confidence in such a command."[43]

As would be expected, Union reaction to the raid assumed a markedly different tone. "The rebels captured from us the other day nearly 3,000 head of beef cattle," a New Yorker informed his family. "It was a very discreditable affair for us." Ben Butler estimated the value of the herd at "almost two million dollars" and considered its loss "an enormous blunder. It has almost paid the enemy in supplies for cutting off the Weldon road." Grant's new military secretary, Col. Ely S. Parker, thought that the raid "had a very bad look against us & cannot be easily explained." Capt. John Noyes wrote his mother that he knew how the rebels accomplished such an unlikely capture. "It is said that the officer in charge of the cattle was playing the piano at the home of a fair secesh dame when the cattle were taken & escaped," he explained. There were some Federals who credited, if grudgingly, the audacious venture. "It was a bold and clever trick of the Rebel Cavalry," admitted a New Jersey volunteer, "and there is not a man here, but what says, they deserve [the cattle] after such a daring raid." Lt. Col. Michael R. Morgan, chief commissary of subsistence for Grant's armies, recalled that when the general-in-chief returned to City Point and learned the particulars of Hampton's exploit—soon widely known as the Beefsteak Raid—"it was one of the three times when I saw from his face that he was troubled, that things had not gone to his satisfaction." But, wrote Morgan, "he got over it . . . and would say facetiously in this connection, 'I have the best commissary of any of these armies; he not only feeds my troops, but feeds the enemy as well.'"[44]

While the raid's salubrious effect on Confederate diets is indisputable, the loss of the cattle in this regard generated mixed reviews from the Federals. There were certainly those, such as Private Haley, who, in speaking of the raid, observed, "We don't relish this, for we have yet to see the time when we had too much beef." The men of his regiment, the 17th Maine, for several weeks received salt codfish to substitute for their beef ration. "After being carried in a filthy haversack and wet a few times, the codfish became too ripe to endure," remembered one of these soldiers. After the war, whenever this veteran would become unhappy with the fare served at home, he would think of "that stinking salt codfish we had to eat in the early fall of 1864, and a spirit of sweet contentment sweeps over my soul." But Cpl. James Coburn of the 141st Pennsylvania informed his parents that the loss of the herd made no "difference with our rations as there are enough cattle in the Corps herds & division herds to last until another lot can be got from the north." A correspondent for the *New York Times* dismissed the loss of the steers as "only a trifle to us. . . . Physicians tell us of patients being so reduced as to get literally drunk after eating a beefsteak. It is to be hoped that these marauders will get so intoxicated upon the beef they have just stolen, as to attempt such a march upon us again." Pvt. Charles Biddlecom of the 147th New York adopted an entirely different perspective on the loss of the cattle. "We shall be short our beef ration," he admitted, "and that would be terrible very! The beef is so good, so fat, so tender. That is, if you call nail rods and India rubber tender."

Biddlecom speculated: "The beef will kill more Rebs than we shall with bullets. If it don't, their stomachs are capable of digesting even pig lead and tin scraps."[45]

An embarrassment of this magnitude demanded an explanation and many were the voices that either assigned responsibility or scrambled to avoid it. General Kautz believed: "The blame will fall on Genl Meade. He knows the cattle were there and I did not, even if I had I could not have protected them for I am holding a line fifteen miles in length with about four hundred men." Meade, as had been the case after Reams' Station, understood that he would be held accountable. On the day of the raid, he sarcastically wrote his wife that "Grant's absence, and the usual friendly spirit of the press, will undoubtedly attribute this loss to my negligence," adding, "I really had as much to do with it as you had, except that I had called attention to the danger of having cattle there." Colonel Wainwright had learned of the general's warnings and blamed Grant for doing nothing to heed them. An officer on Meade's staff confirmed that his boss had no control over the cattle herd and observed that "Grant has never been accustomed to deal with an adversary such as he has now before him." Some, such as Pvt. Charles E. Field of the 108th New York, looked lower down the chain of command. Field thought the Union pickets "must have been caught napping" and that "such carelessness is to be regretted, together with intoxicated officers, [as] the cause of many defeats." Colonel Morgan alluded to Meade's concern about the safety of the herd but allowed that no one in particular was responsible. He called for an investigation and expected that Captain Richardson would request a court of inquiry.[46]

Although the Federals had unquestionably grown complacent about the security of their cattle and the Union cavalry numbered too few and were too dispersed to mount a strong defense or a timely pursuit, Confederate skill more than Yankee neglect explains the raid's success. Sergeant Shadburne and his scouts provided all the information required to attempt such a risky undertaking. Hampton moved quickly and stealthily, ensuring that his troopers would surprise their adversaries. The diversionary attacks persuaded Warren to remain far to the north of the Rebels' return route. And despite the occasional tactical hiccup, the grayclad troopers acquitted themselves well in combat at Sycamore Church, at Cocke's Mill, along Powhatan Stage Road, and at Ebenezer Church. All this more than validated Lee's decision to elevate Hampton to command the Cavalry Corps. As a North Carolinian observed after the raid, the South Carolinian was "fast proving himself equal, if not superior to Stewart."[47]

The Rebel soldiers on the picket line spent less time debating credit or blame for the raid than they did taunting their blueclad opponents. Periodically, they broke into loud "moos" to remind the Yankees who had their cattle. At other times they would simply shout "beef beef beef" or ask the pickets opposite them, "have you seen anything of our cow?" Other Southerners sardonically inquired if the Northerners "would not like to trade this and that for beef." For the first two days after the raid, the Union boys would reply with shouts of "Atlanta Atlanta," but after September 19, as a soldier in the 121st New York phrased it, "the joke was on the other side for our men could offer to trade Early's battle flags and guns."[48]

This retort referenced General Sheridan's recent victories over the Confederate army in the Shenandoah Valley. Jubal Early's twin defeats at Winchester on September 19 and Fisher's Hill three days later marked the first true Rebel setbacks in a campaign that began three months earlier and had taken the graycoats to the outskirts of Washington. Sheridan's August 7 ascension to command in the Valley paid few dividends during the first five weeks of his tenure. Grant had given his young subordinate orders to drive Early up the Valley perhaps as far as Staunton, where the Virginia Central Railroad connected the Valley to Richmond. Sheridan, as commander of the new Middle Military Division, was to "put himself south of the enemy and follow him to the death." Grant also wanted him to destroy the agricultural bounty of the Valley by ravaging crops, seizing livestock, and depriving the local farmers of the means to produce food and fodder for Lee's army. But throughout August and early September, Early and Sheridan conducted what one Federal officer called a "mimic war." The two forces maneuvered as far up the Valley as Strasburg without coming to serious blows. When "Marse Robert" sent Fitz Lee's cavalry division, Maj. Wilfred E. Cutshaw's battalion of artillery, and Maj. Gen. Joseph B. Kershaw's infantry division toward the Valley, Sheridan fell back to his defensive lines near Harpers Ferry. "The reports we get say matters are very badly mismanaged" in the Valley, wrote Colonel Wainwright. "There can be no doubt that Sheridan has at the least three men to Early's one . . . yet nothing has been done there for a month past."[49]

Remembering President Lincoln's admonition that little would be done in the Valley unless Grant would "force it," the general-in-chief decided to visit Sheridan and compel decisive action. This journey, which began on September 15, explains the lieutenant general's absence during the Beefsteak Raid. Grant traveled straight to the Valley, bypassing Washington and the potential complications of entrusting his chief of staff, Henry Halleck, as an intermediary. At Charles Town near Harpers Ferry, Grant sent a courier to summon Sheridan, who promptly arrived from his nearby headquarters. The two officers met under

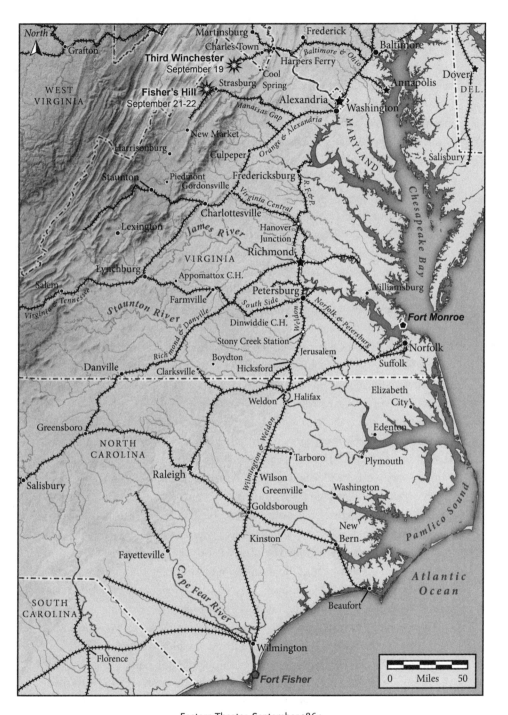

Eastern Theater, September 1864

a large oak tree at the Rutherford house. Grant asked Sheridan if he had a map showing the position of his army and that of Early, fully prepared to use it to explain his own plan for an offensive. Sheridan promptly produced a detailed map and began outlining his idea for whipping the Confederates. "Seeing that he was so clear and so positive in his views and so confident of success, I said nothing," remembered Grant, assigning his own operational scheme to his pocket.[50]

Sheridan proved as good as his word. He attacked Early's infantry east of Winchester and deployed his cavalry north of town. These twin thrusts sent the Confederates "whirling through Winchester" and dashing south to the "Gibraltar of the Valley," a range of ridges and knobs collectively known as Fisher's Hill. The Shenandoah Valley here narrowed to barely four miles in width between the North Fork of the Shenandoah River and an arm of Massanutten Mountain to the southeast and Little North Mountain to the northwest. Early arrayed his infantry on this elevated terrain behind works on his right and center, unwisely trusting his left flank on lower ground to his cavalry. His mounted troops had earned few plaudits, and the fighting on September 22 would do nothing to enhance their reputation. Sheridan maneuvered an infantry force under George Crook around Early's left, routing the hapless horsemen and spreading panic down the line. With the bulk of Sheridan's army attacking Early in front, the Confederate line collapsed. The defeated Rebels retreated some sixty miles to Brown's Gap in the Blue Ridge.[51]

These twin reversals shattered the hopeful predictions of many Confederates at Petersburg. "Early is certainly on the wing again & is said to be thundering at Washington," Major DeShields had written in early August. "The light of our campfires will soon be reflected in the waters of the Potomac," concurred an artillery private. Soldiers such as Lieutenant Crichton, writing from his camp near Petersburg, believed that Early's campaign would "necessitate the withdrawal of Genl. Grant from this place." The Petersburg firebrand Edmund Ruffin believed that "the seat of active war & field fighting will be transferred to the Valley" and affairs around Petersburg and Richmond would be limited to "a mere blockade by gunboats & by fortified camps & garrisons of the enemy at Bermuda Hundred, City Point, & on James River above these points."[52]

Therefore, it came as a shock to most of the Rebels when on the morning of September 21, the Federals opened with a "shotted salute" celebrating Sheridan's triumph at Winchester. Orders circulated through Union ranks on the night of the twentieth that "a salute of 100 guns is to be fired at sunrise to-morrow from the guns bearing on the enemy on General Butler's line, on General Birney's line, and on the portion of the line occupied by General Hancock's troops in honor of General Sheridan's victory in the Shenandoah Valley." Solon Carter delighted that night in the prospect that "the Rebs will think the Devil is after them tomorrow morning." The news of Sheridan's battle reached Union lines at Petersburg via telegraph and circulated quickly to the rank and file. "The troops . . . as [news of the battle] is finished . . . give vent to their feelings in three rousing, prolonged cheers," wrote Private Field. "The bands are all in full blast one of them is performing the 'Star Spangled Banner.'" A soldier in the Fifth New York believed that he had "never heard such cheering since the early days of the war . . . peal upon peal went up, hour after hour. Bands played in all directions, and if the rebels had not obtained the news they must have supposed us all gone mad."[53]

At 5:00 A.M. on the twenty-first, that huge thirteen-inch mortar, the Petersburg Express, fired several times in quick succession, unleashing the bombardment ordered by Grant. The celebratory firing lasted an hour, "making the hills echo," thought one impressed Unionist. Confederate cannoneers, surprised by this unexpected salvo, replied vigorously until Lt. Andrew Knox of the First Connecticut Heavy Artillery, who oversaw the large mortar, ordered another shot to signal the end of the exercise. When reports of Sheridan's follow-up victory at Fisher's Hill arrived, Grant ordered a second shotted salute. Once again the Petersburg Express started the show. This time, however, the Confederates replied with much less spirit. "Guess they got tired of saluting our victories," quipped Luther A. Rose of the Telegraph Service. "After the salute was over we sent out an officer to exchange papers," explained Captain Carter. "The rebs were pretty sullen and didn't seem to care to hear the news from Gen. Early."[54]

Some Confederate correspondents and diarists downplayed the Yankee "hullabulloo," dismissing it as "nothing of importance." A North Carolinian wrote his father that when the enemy "open all their batteries" and "call out to us the 'news' we give them an invitation to take Petersburg." Despite such bravado, many Rebels expressed profound disappointment or outright grief upon learning of Early's fate. "Everything is looking pretty blue about now," admitted staff officer Giles Cooke. "Let us hope and pray for better times." A chaplain in Hill's corps reckoned that "God is now trying us in a fiery furnace. . . . I believe he is bringing us a sense of our own dependence on His aid." Others thought, "our affairs approach a crisis," or that "our prospects look gloomy," the first such strongly pessimistic opinions widely expressed by Lee's men since they arrived at Petersburg.[55]

Still, not every Confederate viewed Early's setbacks so bleakly. Captain Norman of the Seventeenth North Carolina admitted, "The fall of Atlanta and the defeat of Early in the Valley have spread much gloom and despondency throughout the Confederacy," but he saw "no cause to despair and doubt the ultimate success of our cause." Artilleryman Charles Baughman confessed to his mother that the news of Early's defeats "depressed me very much but I soon recovered my spirits and I am now . . . as confident as I was before. If Early is whipped never mind we will make it all right when Mr. Grant brings his boys against us." Men such as Sgt. James W. Biddle of the First North Carolina Cavalry minimized the results in the Valley, claiming they bore little importance, a viewpoint emphatically shared by Private Stott, who sneered at the reports of great demonstrations in Northern cities celebrating Sheridan's triumphs. "Oh! Deluded people! What if they have gained an insignificant victory? Have they yet accomplished the mighty purpose, they have been vainly struggling for during the last three years? The people of the South are as determined and resolute and strong as ever and such a people would bid defiance to a world in arms."[56]

Few Confederates dismissed the reverses in the Valley more forcefully than a correspondent from the Troup Artillery to the *Southern Watchman* of Athens, Georgia. Citing editorials in Northern newspapers that predicted Sheridan's victories promised imminent calamity for the Confederate cause, this soldier responded, "if we could only make ourselves believe these flaming editorials, representing our weakness and demoralization . . . we couldn't have the audacity to resist them any longer." But, he added, "we don't believe a word of it. We have seen these braggarts beaten back too often, to imagine for a moment that they can crush us." He concluded with a plea that more men enlist in the army or return from furlough. "There are men enough, if brought forward in the South, to whip every man the enemy can bring against us, including every Yankee who deals in wooden nutmegs and peddles cheap calico."[57]

Early manfully reported his situation to Lee, who responded with an encouraging letter on September 27. "I very much regret the reverses that have occurred to the army in the Valley," he confessed, "but trust they can be remedied." Lee directed Kershaw's veteran division, which he had earlier recalled, to again reinforce the Army of the Valley District, along with Cutshaw's Artillery Battalion. A few days later he authorized the Laurel Brigade, fresh from the Beefsteak Raid, to go west as well and augment Early's demoralized "buttermilk rangers." Only Richard Anderson and his staff would return to the Richmond-Petersburg front from the Valley. With words of support, Lee wished Early "every prosperity and success." False rumors circulated among the Confederates in late September that Early had redeemed his defeats. "I hope this is true as it is time he was doing something," thought a critical Virginia trooper. Pvt. John Walters believed that such good news was "not impossible, yet it is so improbable that it would be folly to build a hope upon." South Carolina colonel Fitz William McMaster rejected any such report out of hand, believing that Early was "not general enough to gain any signal advantage" in the Valley. Sgt. Berkeley Minor of the Confederate Engineers employed an analogy from American history to illustrate his feelings toward the defeated lieutenant general. "I feel towards Early as Gov. Peter Stuyvesant towards his general Von Poffenburg. He may be a most talented general, but I never wish to see his ill-starred face again."[58]

The mood in the Union camps around Petersburg stood in stark contrast to the sudden gloom prevailing among so many Confederates. "The troops were never in better spirit than they are at the present time," reported New York musician John Houck. "The soldiers are all very much elated at the continued successes we have been having lately," wrote Elmer Wallace, "and I do not think I can see the army more confident of success than now." Officers arranged orchestrated demonstrations of these sentiments. "On receipt of the dispatch [announcing Sheridan's victories] we cautioned the men not to cheer until a bugle should be sounded from Hd Qrs so that while other troops cheered by regiments our brigade cheered together," explained Henry Gawthrop. "The cheering commenced early in this morning on the right," wrote Sgt. Stephen Rogers on September 23, "and passed down the line and it was nearly noon before it had passed the length of the line." Captain Gawthrop guessed that "the Johnnies thought peace was declared for they yelled and halloed."[59]

Private Haley wielded his caustic pen at the expense of General Early. "Jubal was not a shining example of Christianity," Haley scribbled in his diary. "He could crowd as many profane expletives in a given space and time as any man known in the Rebel army, such being the case it would be a fair inference that he exercised his peculiar talent to its full extent, this being the only branch of military science in which he was a success except in running away and bragging." A few days later Haley pronounced Early to be "the most thoroughly thrashed general in the Confederacy." Sgt. John E. Irwin of the Twentieth Michigan delighted in writing his sister, "I guess Early will wish Washington was in Patagonia and *he* in Spitzbergen."[60]

A number of Unionists noted that Sheridan had achieved something few other Federal commanders had done: win a victory west of the Blue Ridge. "It is the first good news we have been able to get out of the Valley," wrote Brigadier General Bragg. "It has always seemed as if the Rebs had a special license to come & go through that section of country without let or hindrance." Captain Mills pronounced Sheridan "great and glorious. He has done two things hitherto unattainable to all appearances—gained a victory in the 'valley of humiliation,' and *followed it up*, a feat hitherto never attempted, or at any rate accomplished, in the history of the war."[61]

Some Federals saw in Sheridan's victories something even greater than the tactical defeat of Early's army. "I have never seen the time when the army thought the war so near its close," wrote Colonel Wainwright. "Sheridan has cut them all to pieces in the Shenandoah Valley," thought Lt. Amory K. Allen of the Twentieth Indiana. "A good fight or two more will make a finish of the Rebellion and I don't think it will be long till we have it." Even George Meade, who harbored a deep, if muted, resentment that Sheridan reaped the glory in the Valley that he thought should have been his, told his wife that the "defeat of Early will prove a severe blow to the rebs. . . . There have been rumors they were going to evacuate Petersburg, and I should not be surprised if they did contract their lines and draw in nearer Richmond." Grant shared this belief and warned Butler and Meade to be on the lookout for evidence that Lee "may be induced to detach from here."[62]

Grant would soon initiate his own response to Sheridan's accomplishments, but in the meantime, other issues occupied Union leaders around Petersburg and Richmond. Benjamin Butler's two corps enjoyed a quiet September in terms of combat, but each experienced command changes that reordered their organizations. General Ord returned from sick leave on September 22 to resume command of the Eighteenth Corps, sending Gibbon back to his Second Corps division, a circumstance Gibbon found deflating. But Gibbon learned that his nemesis, General Hancock, intended to depart on a prolonged leave of absence and that he would assume temporary control of the Second Corps. Then, much to Gibbon's further disappointment, Hancock decided to remain in the field, leaving the division commander in his subordinate role. "Here I am back again once more at my old post," Gibbon wrote his wife, "but not in command of the 2nd Corps as I expected, Genl Hancock having decided not to go on leave just at this time. Had I known this sooner I think I should have asked for a few days leave. . . . I have been here only 24 hours," added the ambitious officer. "I feel rather stupid playing second fiddle after playing first."[63]

During Gibbon's tenure at the Eighteenth Corps, Brig. Gen. George J. Stannard returned on September 15 at the head of the First Division, replacing Joseph Carr, who had been unpopular with some of the troops. Hiram Burnham supplanted Col. Edgar M. Cullen in command of Stannard's Second Brigade. On September 19 Brig. Gen. Charles A. Heckman assumed command of the Second Division when Adelbert Ames went on leave. Col. Edward H. Ripley of the Ninth Vermont arrived from New Bern, North Carolina, to take temporary command of Heckman's First and Second Brigades. The Third Division, comprising U.S. Colored Troops, was reorganized under General Paine, with brigades commanded by Col. John H. Holman, Col. Alonzo G. Draper, and Col. Samuel A. Duncan.[64]

The Tenth Corps received a shock when the temporary head of its Third Division died in a most unusual way. Joshua Blackwood Howell was among the oldest of the active commanders in Butler's army, having turned fifty-eight on September 11. This New Jersey native came from a long line of military officers and rose to the rank of general in the Pennsylvania Militia before the war. He entered Federal service as colonel of the Eighty-Fifth Pennsylvania and saw action along the southern Atlantic coast before his regiment became part of the Army of the James. Howell visited corps headquarters on the night of September 12, and while riding back to camp, his horse, "taking a divergent road, was suddenly checked, reared and fell back on his rider." Howell perished on the fourteenth from injuries sustained in this fall.[65]

Less exalted members of the Army of the James also died during September while working on Butler's Dutch Gap Canal. The enthusiasm and progress experienced at the outset of this endeavor had waned, due in no small part to the dangerous and unhealthy conditions that afflicted those assigned to the project. The Black troops of Butler's army, along with African American civilian workers, now provided the labor that extended and deepened the excavation. These men used hand tools to scour the ditch, sweltering under a hot sun or drenched by summer thunderstorms. The walls of the canal blocked any refreshing breezes, and the sick list expanded to the point that, at any given time, half the workers were ill.[66]

The Confederates continued to lob mortar shells into the excavation, which proved nearly as lethal as disease. "The workmen are constantly harassed by the explosion of rebel shells in their midst, which sometimes occasions fearful destruction among them," recalled the chaplain of the First USCT. Surgeon Charles G. Merrill wrote home, "We send three hundred men a day to work on the canal; a dangerous duty; some are killed or wounded daily." A soldier in the Sixth USCT recalled that a small boat remained anchored on the river "ready to convey the wounded across the river to the hospital, and it usually made two or three trips or more daily for that purpose." Lt. William McKnight of the Seventeenth Virginia wrote his sister, "Our battery opens on them occasionally causing them to drop the 'shovel and the hoe and dig out.'" He admitted that the substantial distance to the canal from the mortar batteries across the river greatly reduced their accuracy, but a new position on an eminence called Signal Hill, a mile up the left bank of the James from Dutch Gap, promised much deadlier results when completed. Butler had officers stationed as watchmen to warn of incoming fire. When these observers judged that one of the high-arching missiles was likely to land in the canal, they would call out "Holes," and the workers would take shelter in "cellar-like" depressions dug into the excavation's sides until the danger passed. Work on the canal slowed, and although some Federals thought that it had almost reached its goal, it would be several more months before the labor concluded.[67]

Rebel artillerists also targeted another of Butler's innovations. The general had erected a huge observation tower near Point of Rocks along the left bank of the Appomattox River, just upstream from its confluence with the James, and two others along the James itself. By all accounts, Confederate gunners achieved less success here than they did in harassing construction of the canal. "They have erected an observatory about two miles off," wrote Lieutenant McKnight. "We sometimes give it a shot but have not yet succeeded in striking it." Sgt. Seth Plumb of the Eighth Connecticut informed his family that "the rebels tried to destroy one of our lookouts . . . and wasted a large quantity of ammunition but all to no effect." An Alabama newspaper described the largest of these observatories as "a mere framework of wooden beams, superimposed one upon another in a conical form and ascended by means of a rough ladder." A soldier in the Ninth New York Heavy Artillery considered the structure "a remarkably tall affair and I shouldn't wonder if the Gulf of Mexico could have been seen from its summit." Although Pensacola remained invisible from this perch, men armed with a telescope could make out the streets of Richmond and Petersburg from its platform.[68]

Federal naval presence on the James not only helped defend Butler's various engineering endeavors but also facilitated prosecution of the campaign by protecting Grant's bustling supply base at City Point. Acting Rear Admiral Samuel Phillips Lee led the North Atlantic Blockading Squadron, a command that included the vessels prowling the James River. Lee, known as "Old Triplicate" for his devotion to paperwork and detail, received his assignment in September 1862, replacing Rear Admiral Louis M. Goldsborough. A native Virginian and third cousin of Robert E. Lee, who he physically resembled, Admiral Lee had political connections in addition to a distinguished war record earned on the Mississippi River. He married the daughter of Francis Blair, a prominent Missouri and Washington politico, and thus was the brother-in-law of Lincoln's postmaster general, Montgomery Blair.[69]

Lee commanded the largest fleet in the U.S. Navy, at one time numbering 114 ships. He bore responsibility for blockading the Atlantic coast from the mouth of the Cape Fear River northward, but in mid-September some 30 of his vessels dropped anchor either in Hampton Roads or upriver on the James. This portion of the fleet, styled the Second Division, was under the direct leadership of Capt. Melancton Smith, another veteran of the brown-water operations in the West. Despite his superiority over the outclassed James River Squadron of the Confederate Navy—his fleet included several powerful ironclads of the *Monitor* class—Smith presided over a stalemate along the river through the summer and early autumn. Both sides obstructed the James to impede navigation and prevent potential attack, so the navies were reduced to supplementing the numerous land batteries that lined both banks of the river. Admiral Lee's subordinates spent part of their time trolling for torpedoes—"mines" in modern parlance—while dealing with a rash of illness among them caused by the area's malarial nature and close confinement on board the ships.[70]

Lee's Confederate counterpart, Capt. John Kirkwood Mitchell, had spent thirty-five of his fifty-three years in the U.S. Navy. At the outbreak of the war, Mitchell resigned his commission and offered his sword to the Confederacy. He inherited the hopeless task of defending New Orleans against the overwhelming firepower of a Union fleet in the spring of 1862 and fell captive to the Federals. Once exchanged, Mitchell came to Richmond and helmed a desk in the capital before receiving command of the James River Squadron in May 1864. His fleet numbered about a dozen vessels, including several ironclads. In combination with the heavy guns along the shore, torpedoes, and obstructions, Mitchell oversaw a formidable defensive complex. An officer in the Confederate Marines at Drewry's Bluff believed that if the Union navy attempted to steam up the James, "they would never get back. What with the guns from here and below, the rams with 'infernal machines' at their bows to explode when running into the enemy—-and the torpedoes on the bottom of the river &c &c they will think the gates of the 'infernal regions' have opened." Mitchell's offensive abilities, however, were limited to exchanging fire with Union shore batteries and harassing the workmen at the Dutch Gap Canal.[71]

With affairs on the James at an impasse, the Navy Department in Washington looked to the capture of Wilmington, North Carolina, as the priority for Admiral Lee's command. Wilmington, via the Cape Fear River, had become the major Confederate port once Admiral Farragut conquered Mobile Bay in August and was, because of its railroad connections, the port of entry for Richmond and Petersburg. "The importance of closing Wilmington and cutting off Rebel communication is paramount to all other questions," wrote Navy Secretary Gideon Welles, "more important, practically, than the capture of Richmond." Admiral Lee had proposed several schemes for closing Wilmington's docks by subduing the forts that guarded the mouth of the river, but the army never seemed to have the available manpower required for a combined operation. Secretary of War Stanton notified Grant on September 1 that "the Navy Department appears very anxious that the army should take Wilmington," with the influential assistant secretary of the navy, Gustavus V. Fox, on his way to City Point to meet with the general-in-chief to discuss the matter. "Whether any operations there be possible, and if possible, whether expedient to be undertaken now, is left wholly to your judgment," Stanton reassured Grant. The lieutenant general, in fact, mentioned to "Cump" Sherman his wish to send 6,000–10,000 men against Wilmington if the navy could gather a fleet strong enough to support them.[72]

Welles harbored hopes that Grant would provide the troops necessary to attack Wilmington's defenses, but he thought it necessary to find a new admiral to lead the naval portion of any such operation. "Admiral Lee is true and loyal, careful, and circumspect almost to a fault," wrote the secretary, "but, while vigilant, he has not the dash and impetuous daring" required for the job. Who better to replace him than the hero of Mobile Bay? On September 17 Welles ordered Lee to replace Farragut in command of the Western Gulf Blockading Squadron, allowing Farragut to come north and succeed Lee.[73]

Farragut, however, declined the appointment. "After having completed seven months of blockade duty . . . and nearly three years of duty in this Gulf and its tributaries, and nearly five years out of six in the Gulf of Mexico, Central America, and the Mississippi River . . . I require rest, as my health [is] beginning to fail," he explained. Welles then turned to Rear Admiral David Dixon Porter. He did so with some hesitation, however, as this selection was liable to "cut Lee to the quick." Porter was younger than Admiral Lee, who had ranked him during his entire career. Moreover, Porter had received rapid promotion based on his sterling accomplishments on the Mississippi River, particularly in cooperation with Grant during the Vicksburg Campaign. His selection would strike an old salt like Lee rather harshly. But when Welles evaluated other potential commanders, none equaled the fifty-one-year-old Porter. Several weeks would pass, but Porter formally assumed command of the North Atlantic Blockading Squadron on October 12.[74]

Robert E. Lee understood full well the importance of protecting Wilmington and the railroads that connected that port to his army, now via Stony Creek and the wagon haul into Petersburg. On August 29 his effusive letter to Governor Vance praising the valor of North Carolina soldiers at Reams' Station also urged Vance to make "every effort" to defend Wilmington. The governor replied a week later, suggesting swapping the garrison troops on the coast for veterans from Lee's army, along with the possibility that "General Beauregard be sent there . . . not only because of the great confidence felt in him, but also because of the very little reposed in General [W. H. C.] Whiting," the current ranking officer in the city. Beauregard had chafed at his virtual demotion to corps command throughout the Petersburg Campaign, although he served Lee loyally in his nominal role as a department head. General Lee understood and appreciated the Louisianan's desire for an independent assignment, and the opportunity presented by Vance's letter seemed too good to ignore. Perhaps the War Department could find a permanent home for Beauregard in North Carolina. "I leave tomorrow for Wilmington," Beauregard informed a correspondent on September 7, "to prepare for Farragut next October. I am here [at Petersburg] performing the play of Hamlet with that character left out 'by special request.'"[75]

Beauregard briefly returned to the Cockade City after his visit to Wilmington, but in the meantime, President Davis asked Lee discreetly if he thought Beauregard would accept an assignment to the western theater. Lee thought the president sought to substitute Beauregard for General Hood, whose standing had suffered after the loss of Atlanta. He informed Davis on September 19 that after consulting with Beauregard on the matter, the general had indicated that although he was "fearful of not being equal to the present emergency but being anxious to do all in my power to serve the cause, I will obey with alacrity any order of the War Department which may put me in command of that army," meaning the Army of Tennessee. Davis then ordered Beauregard to Charleston, South Carolina, and later arranged to meet him in Augusta, Georgia, on October 2, during the president's return to Richmond from visiting Hood and Lt. Gen. Richard Taylor, the commander of the forces operating in Alabama and east Mississippi. Having obtained the acquiescence of these two officers, Davis stunned Beauregard with an offer to take command of a new administrative entity, the Military Division of the West, with authority over both Hood and Taylor. Davis's distrust of the Louisianan had not diminished, but in this assignment he found a way to provide the troubled general with a welcome escape from Lee's supervision, trade on Beauregard's high reputation to inspire sagging Confederate morale, and place him in a position of authority more apparent than real. Beauregard accepted and thus bowed out of the Petersburg Campaign, where despite his subordinate status, he had achieved so much.[76]

rant remained interested in capturing Wilmington, but several events in late September would put that objective on hold. Sources continued to suggest that Lee might be preparing to evacuate Petersburg, providing an opportunity to strike the Confederates while they were in motion. Grant notified Meade to be on the lookout for such an eventuality. In the meantime, General Butler paid a visit to the general-in-chief with an audacious proposal. Utilizing a map of the Confederate defenses north of the James that had been snatched from the body of General Chambliss in August, and benefiting from the intelligence provided by his network of "secret service men," Butler proposed to launch a surprise assault on the Rebel lines southeast of Richmond. He had gone so far as to compose an order for Grant's approval, which, according to Butler, the lieutenant general complimented "in high terms and yielded his assent."[77]

Ben Butler had always championed African American troops and felt they had enjoyed few opportunities "to show their valor or staying qualities in action." Furthermore, he believed that the Black soldiers had been unfairly blamed for the calamity at the Crater and wanted to prove that these men would fight—and fight well. Thus, he proposed to make a key portion of the attack with the U.S. Colored Troops in the Army of the James. Grant and Butler made a reconnaissance together on September 26 as far upriver as Dutch Gap, traveling on board the *Greyhound*, Butler's headquarters steamer, gaily decked with flags. The officers discussed Butler's plan, but in truth, Grant had already decided to authorize the offensive. On the day before his ride up the river, he wrote his wife Julia that "in a few days more I [s]hall make another stir here."[78]

Thus, a combination of events precipitated the "stir" Grant had in mind. The rumors of Lee's evacuation of Petersburg might mask his actual intention to further reinforce Early at Sheridan's peril. Butler's proposal, although conceived as a reputation builder for the U.S. Colored Troops, promised larger rewards. And if previous ventures across the James provided any insight, such an offensive would draw troops from the Petersburg front as well as prevent detachments to Early's command. If Lee weakened the Rebel forces south of the Appomattox by sending troops to the Valley or across the James, then the possibility opened that a strike toward Boydton Plank Road and the South Side Railroad might succeed. Grant saw in Butler's suggestion an opportunity to aid Sheridan, threaten Lee's two remaining lines of communication at Petersburg, or even capture the Confederate capital.

On September 27 Grant reduced to writing his verbal approval of Butler's plan. He specified that the Bermuda Hundred line could be held by artillery and new soldiers then arriving at the front. The attack itself would take place on the twenty-ninth, the troops moving into position across the James under cover of darkness. Butler's divisions would make their crossing at Deep Bottom and at some additional point upriver where the two columns would remain within mutual supporting distance. "The object of this movement is to surprise and capture Richmond," Grant boldly advised. The lieutenant general emphasized the need for celerity if the gambit was to succeed. He promised that Meade's

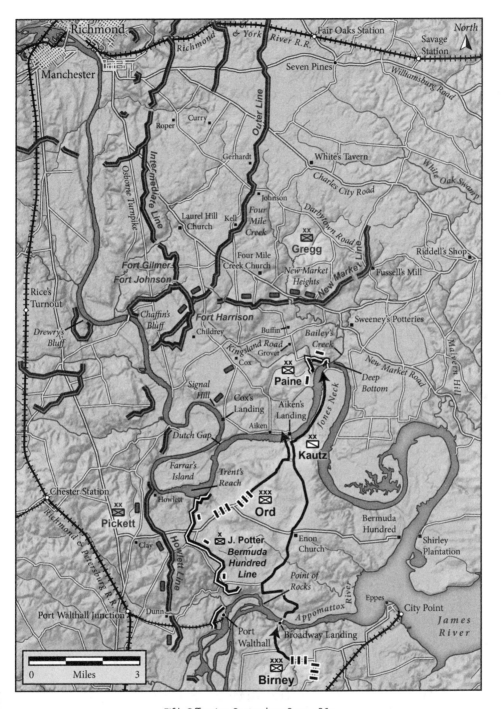

Fifth Offensive, September 28–29, 1864

army would undertake a simultaneous movement to the west. "The prize sought is either Richmond or Petersburg, or a position which will secure the fall of the latter," Grant concluded.[79]

The general-in-chief gave Meade his marching orders the same day. Clearly, Butler's attack held primacy in Grant's thinking, much as it had in July and, to a lesser extent, in August. He described Meade's role as "a co-operative movement" and suggested that the Army of the Potomac make a show of massing on the left to "convince the enemy that the South Side road and Petersburg are the objects of our efforts." But if Lee detached enough troops to the Richmond defenses to justify an attempt to move toward Petersburg or the South Side Railroad, Grant wanted Meade to do so, "and in your own way."[80]

Butler went to work assembling his strike force. His army's two corps, the Tenth and Eighteenth, would provide his infantry power, and Kautz's cavalry would contribute the mounted arm. David Birney's Tenth Corps included two White divisions led by Alfred Terry and Robert Foster. A third division, once again under command of the corps commander's older brother William, consisted of two brigades of Black troops. The Tenth Corps had been ensconced in the Petersburg trenches since late August and had to be relieved without alerting the Confederates. In the predawn hours of September 25, elements of Hancock's corps quietly replaced Birney's soldiers, who now encamped well behind the lines, out of sight of the enemy. The White troops enjoyed their leisure away from the perils of the front, while some of William Birney's Black soldiers received new shoes and underwent additional drill. The Tenth Corps was to cross the Appomattox to Bermuda Hundred on the night of the twenty-seventh, but Birney misconstrued his orders and did not start until 3:00 P.M. the following day. "There was much . . . speculation as to the nature and direction of the new move," wrote a soldier in the Tenth Connecticut. "The opinion prevailed that it was to be North Carolina or the Shenandoah."[81]

The Eighteenth Corps was dispersed on both sides of the James. Like Birney, forty-five-year-old Edward Ord commanded two White divisions and one Black one. Described by one historian as a "bluff, irascible, impetuous, willful Regular," Ord enjoyed a strong friendship with Grant that, more than anything else, earned him his corps command. Theodore Lyman, Meade's expressive aide, framed Ord as "a tall man, with bushy eyebrows and a nervous manner, who looked like an eccentric Irishman who was about to tell a funny story." The soldiers' nickname for E. O. C. Ord was "Old Alphabet."[82]

Stannard's First Division defended the line guarding Bermuda Hundred. Two of Heckman's Second Division brigades, under the temporary command of Colonel Ripley, had been detached to support the cavalry in its pursuit of

Hampton and the cattle, then assigned to dig works around City Point to improve security for the vital depot in light of the Confederates' brazen raid. On the night of September 27–28, Ripley responded to orders to return to the lines at Bermuda Hundred. "It was a most cruel forced march," remembered Ripley, "and it was long after daylight when we re-entered our old Camp."[83]

Paine's Third Division of Black troops provided the garrison at Deep Bottom and much of the labor force toiling on the Dutch Gap Canal. Some of his men were well downriver, serving under Brig. Gen. Gilman Marston, but Butler ordered them to rejoin the division. Thus, Paine's troops were the only ones not required to cross the James to participate in this operation. The division commander made a good first impression. A Bostonian from a prominent family, the thirty-one-year-old Paine had graduated from Harvard and joined the Massachusetts bar. Chaplain Henry M. Turner of the First USCT made Paine's acquaintance shortly after the general assumed command of the division. "I . . . found him to be very approachable, affable, and mannerly," observed the reverend. Captain Carter, serving on Paine's staff, informed his wife on August 11 that "Gen. Paine appears like a very nice man." That opinion soon changed, however, as Paine showed himself to be lazy and a petty tyrant. "He lies in bed till 11 or 12 o'clock and then wants all the business done in ten minutes," complained the captain. "I want to get clear of the shit ass and don't care much how it is done." In a letter written just before orders for the offensive reached division headquarters, Carter wrote his wife: "You asked where Gen. Paine is from and if he is married. He is a Boston lawyer and I think not married and I advise every woman to keep clear of the ugly cuss if they want to be happy."[84]

Butler replaced Ord's veterans at Bermuda Hundred with a new provisional brigade led by Col. Joseph H. Potter. Potter's command consisted of green regiments from Pennsylvania recently recruited for one year's service. Butler permitted Ord the discretion to assign as many experienced units as he thought necessary to bolster these rookies. The corps commander designated the Eleventh Connecticut, Fifth Maryland, and Fortieth Massachusetts, along with a strong collection of guns, to supplement Potter's neophytes. Of the roughly 7,000 men left to man the trenches at Bermuda Hundred, only 800 were combat tested. Butler also instructed his acting chief engineer, Peter S. Michie, to prepare the bridges necessary to execute his plan. Michie coated the pontoon bridge over the Appomattox River at Broadway Landing with manure to deaden the noise of Birney's passing troops. He similarly treated the bridges crossing the James from Jones Neck to Deep Bottom. This industrious young engineer— Michie was only twenty-five—also surveyed the banks of the river between Dutch Gap and Deep Bottom for a suitable place to construct another crossing.

He found just the right spot 600 yards below the Albert M. Aiken house at a point where the river was 1,320 feet across. Capt. James W. Lyon, the army's chief pontonier, gathered sixty-seven pontoon boats from Broadway Landing and Deep Bottom and assembled a crew of 100 soldiers from Butler's specialists and the Fifteenth New York Engineers to build the bridge. Work began after dark on September 28 and was expected to be finished before midnight. But the tide receded so much that evening that "the last nine boats had to be dragged over the soft mud and placed in position by hand." The engineers finally finished their labor at 2:00 the following morning.[85]

Not until the evening of September 28 did Butler brief his key subordinates. Birney, Ord, and Kautz arrived at his command post near Point of Rocks, where they received copies of Butler's instructions for the offensive. "The orders covered sixteen pages of letter paper," Kautz recalled. "They had been copied by a manifold letter writer, and we each received a copy, upon which we followed the reading of Genl. Butler who was desirous that we should fully understand the instructions and gave us the opportunity to ask explanation on any obscure points."[86]

These orders, among the most detailed ever written during the Civil War, essentially articulated what Grant had previously approved. They invoked Grant's primary goal of capturing Richmond or, in failing that, to at least "draw re-enforcements from the right of the enemy's line in sufficient numbers so as to enable the Army of the Potomac to move upon the enemy's communication near Petersburg." Butler would send Ord's two White divisions to the new bridge at Aiken's Landing, while Birney would cross at Deep Bottom and join Paine's division there. Kautz's troopers would follow the Tenth Corps. The plan depended upon speed, stealth, and cooperation between the two wings of the offensive, which were to attack in tandem. Kautz would attempt to turn the Rebels' left flank, and all three components, if successful, would press on into Richmond. Once in the capital, Butler's men were to burn the bridges across the James while the engineer contingent accompanying the infantry prepared earthworks to hold the bridgeheads. The soldiers would travel light, leaving all their equipment behind save for "a single blanket rolled up and slung over their shoulders, a haversack with three days' cooked rations, and sixty rounds of cartridges in their cartridge-boxes and on their persons." Both artillery and supply wagons would be kept on the right bank of the river until the initial lines of Confederate defense had been breached. As an extra incentive Butler promised to promote by one grade every officer and man of the first division, brigade, and regiment to enter Richmond, along with a bonus of six months' extra pay.[87]

Benjamin Butler is usually rated among the least competent of the Union army's senior commanders, yet his preparations for this operation were worthy of the finest military planners. Grant approved his scheme without modification. Butler committed some 26,600 soldiers to his offensive and had them all in motion on the evening of September 28.[88]

Stannard started about 9:00 P.M., Burnham's brigade in the lead and the 118th New York at the head of the column. The troops plodded relatively noiselessly through the darkness, many wondering about their ultimate destination. "Not a clattering canteen was allowed to swing, nor a word of boisterous mirth to escape from any reckless lips," recalled Capt. William S. Hubbell of the 21st Connecticut. "For several hours we divided the time between short marches and naps on the ground during the corresponding halts," remembered Capt. Cecil Clay of the 58th Pennsylvania. When the 118th New York and 10th New Hampshire had traveled about two miles, they received orders to halt and exchange their Enfield rifles for seven-shot Spencer repeaters. Hustling to catch up with the rest of their brigade, they reached the bridge site as the engineers put the finishing touches on the new span. These two regiments would act as division skirmishers and be the first to cross the bridge. Some troops received breakfast before the division started across the pontoons, which had been covered in "hay and earth to deaden the sounds of tramping men and horses."[89]

Heckman's division followed Stannard, departing their Bermuda Hundred camps around 1:00 A.M. "The night was very dark and cloudy and it was with the utmost difficulty that the ponderous columns . . . surging toward the pontoons at Aikens Landing could be kept from fusing into one fluid mass in the inky gloom," wrote Colonel Ripley. Heckman's men arrived at the bridge around daybreak. Pvt. Joseph M. Alexander of the Second Pennsylvania Heavy Artillery in Col. Harrison Fairchild's brigade remembered that men were poised at each end of the bridge, holding ropes to keep the span taut, but it swayed nonetheless, tumbling a handful of unfortunates into the river.[90]

Terry's Tenth Corps division left its camps east of Petersburg around 3:00 P.M. on the twenty-eighth, crossing the Appomattox at Broadway Landing and arriving at Deep Bottom at 2:00 the next morning. The men at first thought they would be boarding transports at City Point, but when the column turned left to cross the Appomattox, they realized that Deep Bottom would be their likely destination. A soldier in the Twenty-Fourth Massachusetts called this a "very tedious tramp," while another man in that regiment declared it "by far the hardest march that I have had."[91]

Foster's division followed Terry's, but the First Division's wagon train impeded Foster's progress. "It seemed to us that every wagon in the whole army were blocking the roads ahead of us," complained Lt. Nicholas De Graff. The head of Foster's column reached the bridge at Broadway Landing at 8:35 P.M.

Once across the Appomattox, they trudged through Bermuda Hundred and up Jones Neck toward Deep Bottom. "We marched all night and you better believe some of the boys were pretty near played out and I among them," admitted Pvt. Bayard Cooper of the 203rd Pennsylvania. Cooper may have understated the situation. A surgeon in Terry's division declared that he had never seen so many men collapse from fatigue during a march. As many as a third of Foster's division broke down en route, and even those who reached Deep Bottom were enervated by their ordeal. It remained to be seen how much this debilitation would affect Butler's plans.[92]

William Birney's Black division brought up the rear of the Tenth Corps. These men did not reach the Appomattox until after dark, around 9:00 P.M. "A tedious night march" brought the division to the Deep Bottom bridges between 1:00 and 4:00 A.M., with some of the men halting exhausted along the way and others discarding their equipment to lighten their loads.[93]

Paine's troops at Dutch Gap enjoyed the easiest journey to their destination. Before dark they boarded transports for the short trek downriver to Deep Bottom, joining their comrades who garrisoned that position. About midnight they disembarked and grabbed whatever sleep they could. They were joined there by the two regiments Marston dispatched from his command below City Point. Kautz's cavalry had no journey at all. His division was already positioned on Jones Neck and had orders not to cross the river until all the infantry had cleared the way. Two battalions of the First New York Engineers trailed behind Heckman's division with three wagons filled with tools to be used if and when the infantry required them.[94]

All things considered, Butler felt pleased with the course of events that night. The head of both Ord's and Birney's columns began crossing their respective bridges more or less on schedule. The army commander had spent the early evening prowling the south bank of the James from opposite Aiken's Landing to Jones Neck and then returned to Aiken's Landing to oversee the completion of the new bridge. Satisfied that the span would be completed on time, he returned to his headquarters to snatch a couple hours of sleep. Up again at 3:00 A.M. and fortified with a strong cup of coffee, the general trotted toward Deep Bottom, where the African American troops in which he had placed so much confidence were poised for the order to advance. After the war Butler was asked why he put his Black soldiers in such a responsible role. "The negro had no sufficient opportunity to demonstrate his valor and his staying qualities as a soldier," he replied. "Therefore, I determined to put them in position to demonstrate the fact of the value of the negro as a soldier . . . in behalf of their race and in behalf of the Union."[95]

One hundred miles to the north, Abraham Lincoln dictated a message to his general-in-chief on this fateful morning. The president shared Butler's hopes for the elevation of America's Black population and had gradually shifted the Union war effort to include a new birth of freedom throughout the fractured country. But this day Lincoln's thoughts focused on less lofty concerns, specifically the possibility that Lee would detach troops from the Richmond-Petersburg front to reinforce Early and enable him "to turn upon Sheridan." Grant replied a few hours later from Deep Bottom. "Your dispatch just received," wrote the general. "I am taking steps to prevent Lee sending re-enforcements to Early by attacking him here."[96]

eight

I DID NOT EXPECT TO CARRY RICHMOND

North of the James, September 29

Pvt. William S. Neel of the Fifteenth Georgia, a regiment in Henry "Rock" Benning's Brigade, exulted in his camp life north of the James River. "What a glorious rest it was . . . after five months of constant and hard campaigning from the Wilderness . . . till September." He described his bivouac as "a most delightful place . . . with plenty of shade to shelter us, good springs close by to get drinking and cooking water and a large clear creek close by to bathe in. It was a treat to see how the boys reveled in these matchless luxuries . . . writing to their 'best girl' back in Georgia, or to their precious loved ones at home." A Texas soldier shared these sentiments. "Just now we are on the north side of the James, about eight miles below Richmond, taking our ease something in the manner of the old planter's darkies down in Alabama." He described his unit's mission as keeping tabs on "Beast Butler's negroes" at Deep Bottom, and "that is what we are doing, and not grumbling at the task," as the "darkies, so far, appearing devoid of belligerent propensities, and picket duty, consequently, being very light." Like his Georgia comrade, this Texan believed that his brigade, John Bell Hood's old command (now led by John Gregg), had earned this stressless assignment, for they had been "marching, fighting, and what is infinitely worse, lying in the trenches under a broiling sun, and starving." A Rebel gunner simply told his brother, "we have been having as good a time as a soldier can have."[1]

These three men were part of the relatively small Confederate force positioned south and east of Richmond on the left bank of the James River. Some

7,700 soldiers directly manned the defenses that guarded the many roads leading north and west into the Confederate capital. Many of these troops reported to Richard S. Ewell, formerly head of Lee's Second Corps but now commander of the Department of Richmond. Ewell's personnel included a large number of Virginia Reserves, Local Defense troops, and heavy artillerists stationed in and around Richmond. Most of these men possessed little or no combat experience and would almost certainly falter in an open fight. The only veteran infantry under Ewell's control was the severely depleted Tennessee brigade that had come east under Bushrod Johnson in the spring. These regiments had fought well under Col. John S. Fulton earlier in the campaign. Johnson had risen to division command, and Fulton had died of wounds on July 4, so John M. Hughs of the Twenty-Fifth Tennessee now led the brigade. The thirty-year-old Hughs had been a hotel keeper on East Tennessee's Cumberland Plateau before the war and gained field experience in the western theater. Hughs's ascension, however, unsettled General Johnson. Writing to Ewell on September 22, Johnson called for Hughs to be relieved of a command "for which he is entirely disqualified," adding that "he should be brought to trial." Under the colonel's lax leadership, desertion ran rampant and discipline suffered. By late September, barely 400 soldiers remained in the brigade, divided among five tiny Volunteer State regiments.[2]

Ewell's best unit reported to Martin Gary. This thirty-three-year-old South Carolinian, called the "Bald Eagle" for his receding hairline and distinguished combat record, graduated from Harvard, then returned to his native state to practice law. Gary was among the most ardent of South Carolina's secessionists and parlayed his state-militia commission into service with the Hampton Legion at the outbreak of the war, rising steadily from captain to brigadier general. His mounted brigade comprised the Seventh South Carolina Cavalry, the Twenty-Fourth Virginia Cavalry, and the horsemen of the Hampton Legion. Gary's three regiments averaged a bit more than 400 men apiece.[3]

The rest of Ewell's soldiers instilled little confidence in their ability to meet an attack. The Twenty-Fifth Virginia Battalion and another small reserve battalion, altogether numbering 643 rifles, rounded out the lieutenant general's infantry arm. John Pemberton still directed Ewell's cannoneers. His battalions of heavy artillery, crewed by men who had rarely fired a shot in anger, suffered from a lack of ammunition and generally inadequate ordnance. Pemberton's field artillerymen, however, had seen action earlier in the war and could be counted on to acquit themselves with honor, although many of their battery horses were too feeble to provide the guns much mobility. These cannoneers numbered roughly 2,500 men.[4]

The most experienced and combat-tested troops north of the river belonged not to Ewell's command, but to Charles Field's Division of Lee's First Corps. Gregg's Texas Brigade—which included the often-overlooked Third Arkansas—had been reduced to around 500 hardened veterans. It had gone north of the James in late July, and along with Benning's Brigade, were the only elements of Lee's army still on that side of the river. Col. Dudley DuBose had commanded the Georgians since early May, following Benning's wounding in the Wilderness. They, too, had been depleted so badly that the entire brigade counted less than half the regulation strength of a single regiment. Gregg and DuBose combined numbered fewer than 1,000 men.[5]

Fractured command authority exacerbated the handicaps of this understrength force. Although Ewell's department geographically included that portion of Henrico County where all these troops deployed, the Texans and Georgians reported not to Ewell, but to General Gregg, Field's ranking officer north of the James. Lee recognized the organizational hazard of this split authority and on September 28 ordered Lt. Gen. Richard Anderson, his First Corps commander recently returned from the Shenandoah Valley, to cross the river and assume overall control. He also instructed the general to implement improvements to the fortifications in this sector. Anderson would leave for the north side early the next morning.[6]

The fortifications in question guarded the road network approaching the Confederate capital. An inner line of pentagonal forts surrounded the city, defended by detachments from the heavy artillery battalions. The Intermediate Line, anchored on the James both above and below the city, coursed roughly five miles out from town. An extension of this line ran south to a large enclosed work called Fort Gilmer, crossed Mill Road, and then turned west to form the northern rampart of a fortified camp surrounding Chaffin's Bluff on the James. At intervals along these unbroken trenches, battery positions provided interlocking fire, although most of this line remained unmanned and was only partially fronted by obstructions. The Outer, or Exterior, Line anchored on the James and in part forming the lower arm of the fortified camp, ran north, intersecting the extension of the Intermediate Line at Fort Harrison, a large open battery on a broad plateau. The Outer Line then continued north, east of and parallel to the Intermediate Line, all the way to the Chickahominy River, covering the five roads that ran in to Richmond like the digits of a hand. But the portion of this line north of New Market Road had deteriorated and lacked positions for artillery. A pontoon bridge at Chaffin's Bluff provided the closest connection between the troops north of the James and the rest of Lee's army. Most of the work on these fortifications had been completed in 1862. The newest defenses—still unfinished in late September—started at Camp Holly on New Market Heights, ran south to New Market Road, then westward along the south side of that highway to tie into the Outer Line below Fort Harrison. This so-called New Market Line was, on its right, little more than a chest-high breastwork—one Confederate called it "a shallow, straggling ditch"—but in front of the Texas Brigade and up onto New Market Heights, it was more fully developed, including two lines of abatis and a field of fire hundreds of yards wide.[7]

Such an extensive labyrinth of earthworks required many more troops than were available to Ewell and Gregg. Thus, successful resistance to any serious assault would depend on the ability of the outgunned Confederates to rally to the danger points long enough for reinforcements to arrive from across the James.[8]

Logically, the best troops on the north side defended the New Market Line, the landscape closest to the Union toehold at Deep Bottom. Gary's cavalry held the left of these works, some of his Seventh South Carolina Cavalry supporting four ten-pounder Parrott rifles of the First Rockbridge Artillery on New Market Heights. The bulk of Gary's men occupied the trenches below the high ground, serving as infantry. The Texans formed on Gary's right under the immediate command of Frederick Bass of the First Texas. Bass's regiment connected with Gary's Twenty-Fourth Virginia Cavalry near the point where Four Mile Creek penetrated the Confederate works. The Fourth and Fifth Texas extended the line westward, and the Third Arkansas formed the brigade's right. Colonel Bass established headquarters at the large, white-painted Phillips house directly on the line of fortifications, scene of several parties and dances, including one on the night of September 28. To the Arkansans' right, a portion of DuBose's Georgians, the Twenty-Fifth Virginia Battalion, under Lt. Col. Wyatt M. Elliott, and Lt. Col. John Guy's Second Virginia Reserve Battalion, extended westward. Two Napoleon smoothbores from the Third Richmond Howitzers anchored the far-right flank. General Gregg established his command post at Fort Harrison and bore overall responsibility for this front line, perhaps 2,800 men in all. Another 1,400 soldiers manned the artillery along portions of the Intermediate and Outer Lines, particularly at strongpoints such as Fort Harrison.[9]

Hughs's brigade occupied the line southwest of Gregg's forces, including the high ground at Signal Hill, where the Confederates hoped to position mortars and other ordnance to pummel the Dutch Gap Canal. On September 28 seven companies of the Seventeenth Georgia of DuBose's brigade joined 200 convicts and 300 impressed Black slaves to work on Fort Harrison. About 500 gunners under Lt. Col. John M. Maury manned the ordnance in the fortified camp at Chaffin's Bluff and also drilled as infantry. Other artillery units, including Maj. Alexander W. Stark's Battalion, immediately north of Chaffin's Bluff, and Lt. Col.

Charles E. Lightfoot's Battalion, in position along the Intermediate Line, were supported by 1,500 of Ewell's second-tier soldiers. Some 2,700 reserves, militia, and Local Defense troops also reported to Ewell in the city and would be, for what they were worth, available in an emergency. This polyglot force reporting to multiple commanders (until Anderson arrived) would be adequate to deal with any mischief that Paine's bridgehead garrison at Deep Bottom might manufacture. Their ability to resist a larger force thrown across the James would be a different matter.[10]

Intimations of just such an initiative circulated among some Confederates on the night of September 28–29. A picket stationed in front of the Texas Brigade reported that "some movement was on foot among the Yankees." The officer who commanded the picket line that night, Lt. James D. Pickens of the Third Arkansas, sent a courier to report these suspicions to General Gregg and later visited the general personally to express his concern. Similarly, one of Gary's vedettes told a comrade in the Seventh South Carolina Cavalry that he heard the Federals moving artillery and marching during the night. Pvt. George McRae of DuBose's Twentieth Georgia detected the sounds of the enemy crossing the pontoon bridge at Deep Bottom. "They seemed to be travelling rapidly," thought the soldier, "footmen, horsemen and artillery; and the length of time they were crossing indicated a large force." McRae, however, could not be certain which direction these mysterious marchers were heading. Perhaps they were the Deep Bottom garrison crossing to the south side to participate in some offensive there. A cannoneer felt certain that the noise indicated a movement to the north side. Regardless, these many warnings met with skepticism. A Texan discounted such a report from a comrade he considered to be "fond of looking on the gloomy side of everything," laughing at the prospect of such dire news. He would soon regret his skepticism.[11]

As the sky lightened after 5:00 A.M. on Thursday, September 29, any Rebels along the New Market Line still doubting a Federal approach quickly became believers. Confederate pickets spotted two blue divisions advancing astride the road leading north from Deep Bottom—Paine's African Americans on the left and Terry's three brigades on the right. These columns reached Kingsland Road and engaged the grayclad pickets, who offered token resistance before rapidly falling back on their reserves. Colonel Duncan's small brigade led Paine's advance, hurrying to keep up with its skirmishers, as Col. Joseph C. Abbott's brigade of Terry's division, led by the Seventh Connecticut, crossed Kingsland Road on Duncan's right.[12]

Duncan left his rookie outfit, the Tenth USCT, at City Point, so only two regiments, the Fourth and Sixth USCT, accompanied him this morning. Paine

North of the James, September 29

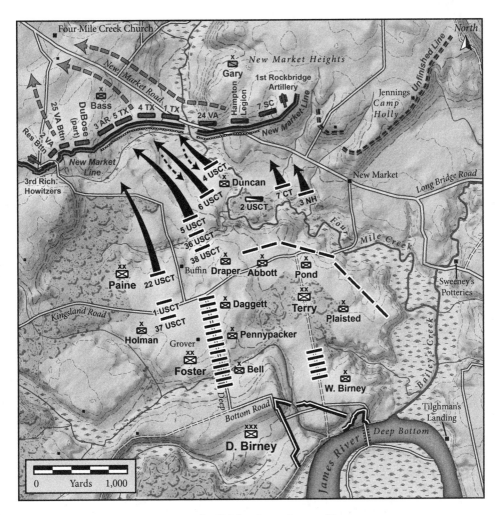

New Market Heights, September 29, 1864

committed the dismounted men of the Second USCT Cavalry to extend Duncan's right and serve strictly as skirmishers. Duncan's command numbered around 1,100 officers and men. He positioned the Fourth USCT in his front and the Sixth USCT en echelon to its left and rear along Kingsland Road. Paine then shifted all of these troops eastward to narrow the growing gap between his division and Terry's. Doing so, however, increased the difficulties Duncan's brigade would face in reaching the main Confederate defenses just south of New Market Road. His men now fronted a small feeder stream of Four Mile Creek that coursed through a deep ravine. Once across this obstacle, the Black troops would enter an open field, on the far side of which lay a solid line of felled trees, and beyond that another row of abatis in advance of the main branch of Four Mile Creek and the strong earthworks behind which the Texas Brigade waited.[13]

Capt. John McMurray, commanding Company D, Sixth USCT, led his men across the swampy ravine and into the field beyond. Officers re-formed their units "with as much care and accuracy as though we had been on parade," thought the captain. The Confederate skirmishers vanished in their front, although in the dim light of dawn, made more opaque by dense fog, the main Rebel defenders were not yet visible. The Federals arranged their lines in peace, the Confederates limiting their fire to a few scattered shots from the retreating pickets. McMurray and the rest of Duncan's troops understood, however, that as soon as they received the order to advance, they would face the full fury of their enemies. "Would it be death, or wounds, or capture," wondered the captain. "Would it be victory or death?"[14]

General Paine explained in a letter home that he "waited a good while to hear Terry begin because I wanted him to draw some of the enemy away from me if he could, but after waiting . . . & not hearing from Terry I started my column." The division commander revealed his lack of combat experience, not to mention basic military sense, by failing to provide Duncan with additional support, retaining the balance of his division—Draper's and Holman's brigades—well to the rear. Paine would make his attack with Duncan's men alone, and even then ordering these two regiments to advance individually. The Fourth USCT charged first. The only field officer with the regiment that morning, Maj. Augustus S. Boernstein, led the 400 men of his unit, with his White adjutant in charge on the right and his ranking Black soldier, Sgt. Maj. Christian A. Fleetwood, on the regiment's left. About 5:40 A.M. Boernstein, mounted and in front, started his unit forward. The Confederates immediately opened a rattling fire on the advancing troops. Captain Wickes wrote his father several days later that the battle was "a perfectly terrible encounter. . . . We were all cut to pieces. We got up to the second line of abatis within three or four yards of the ditch, but by that time the line was so cut up that it was impossible to keep the men in their places." The regimental color guard lost eleven of its twelve men in this assault. The attackers charged with uncapped rifles, a tactic intended to prevent them from halting in the open to return fire. This, of course, left them defenseless until they could breach the enemy line and close with the bayonet. Many became entangled in the abatis or bogged down in the marshy ground along Four Mile Creek, becoming easy targets.[15]

By then, the Sixth USCT arrived on the left of the beleaguered Fourth, two of its companies detached as skirmishers and thus not part of the main assault. They, too, absorbed casualties as they crossed the open field. Colonel Duncan was among the fallen, disabled by a minié ball to the ankle, one of four bullets that struck him in a matter of minutes. Col. John W. Ames of the Sixth now assumed command of the brigade, or at least what remained of it. "It was slow work, and every step of our advance exposed us to the murderous fire of the enemy," explained McMurray. Not only did they face resistance from their immediate front, but enemy riflemen also gained positions on either flank to level deadly enfilade fire into their ranks. The powder smoke became so dense that the Federals could see only a few feet ahead of them, as many now desperately attempted to load their rifles.[16]

A portion of the Fourth USCT reached the main branch of Four Mile Creek opposite the First Texas, while the Sixth USCT confronted the Fourth and Fifth Texas head on. At first the Confederates saw through the fog only "what appeared to be a moving black wall a hundred feet away." But as the Federals reached the final line of obstructions only a few yards shy of the Texans—one defender every five or six feet—the Confederates made each shot count. "Our trusty rifles wielded by willing hands & brave hearts pour swift destruction into their ranks," recorded a member of the Fourth Texas. "They reel & fall by scores." There can be little doubt that those hands became especially willing because they were facing Black men. "Here for the first time we met negro troops," explained a private in the Fifth Texas. "No man in our old Brigade would have retreated from, or surrendered to Niggers," wrote Sgt. D. H. Hamilton of the First Texas. "When they charged up within good range the fun began. . . . Only a few of them escaped. We killed about a million dollars worth of niggers, at current prices." Some of the Texans demeaned the bravery of their opponents by testifying that they charged only because Whites drove them forward at the point of the bayonet. Others recalled that the African Americans yelled "Remember Fort Pillow & give them no quarter," battle cries that further raised Rebel bloodlust. "It was like flaunting a red flag before a mad bull," wrote Hamilton.[17]

The Third Arkansas, on the right end of Bass's line, received orders to mount their works and fire down on the left flank of Duncan's survivors, which the men did, "slaughtering them like sheep." On the left of the Texans, the Twenty-Fourth Virginia Cavalry blasted the exposed right of the Fourth USCT. Casualties in Duncan's brigade were staggering. "It was very evident that there was too much work cut out for our regiments," admitted Fleetwood. Colonel Ames grasped the truth in Fleetwood's assessment. He asked McMurray, who stood nearby: "Captain, don't you think we had better fall back? We haven't force enough to take this line, and if we remain here we will probably all be killed." McMurray agreed, prompting Ames to give the order. "We must have more help, boys," he cried. "Fall back."[18]

Retreating proved almost as hazardous as attacking. The Confederates continued to pour in their fire, disabling so many of the brigade's White officers that the Black sergeants largely directed the survivors off the field. When the two bloodied regiments finally withdrew out of range, more than one-third of their number failed to answer roll call. The Fourth USCT suffered 178 casualties, including 27 officers and men killed. The Sixth USCT lost 209 men during the brief time the brigade was in action—less than forty minutes. Writing from the Chesapeake General Hospital at Fort Monroe, Colonel Duncan assured his future wife that he was "flat as a flounder and merry as a cricket. . . . I have been thinking the matter over," he continued, "& have come to the conclusion that on Sept. 29 the Johnnies *meant me*, and if they were firing at my ankle joint, they had at least one mighty fine marksman among them." Others in the brigade, such as Captain McMurray, emerged less cheery. "When we had gathered up all our men, and ascertained in one way and another who were killed and who were wounded, we found the regimental loss to be . . . nearly sixty percent." Only three of McMurray's own company escaped unhurt.[19]

Now that Duncan's Third Brigade had been used up, General Paine committed Colonel Draper's Second Brigade. Alonzo Draper, who had just turned twenty-nine, hailed from Vermont but had moved to Lynn, Massachusetts, where he joined the bar and devoted his legal energies to supporting the local industrial workers. He entered service with the First Massachusetts Heavy Artillery and in August 1863 took command of what would become the Thirty-Sixth USCT. Elevated to brigade command in 1864, Draper led a unit numbering around 1,300 men and comprising the Fifth USCT and Thirty-Eighth USCT in addition to his old regiment.[20]

While Duncan's brigade executed its fateful charge, Draper's men had been instructed to "lie down and wait for further orders" near the abandoned home of Alfred R. Buffin, just north of Kingsland Road. When orders to advance arrived, Draper moved ahead to the ravine through which ran the small tributary of Four Mile Creek. The Twenty-Second USCT of the First Brigade accompanied Draper, serving as skirmishers on his left. The colonel's own three regiments remained at the ravine under orders, subjected to an annoying shelling from the Rockbridge Artillery on New Market Heights. Finally, with the pitiful remains of Duncan's brigade having escaped the field, Draper received instructions to attack. He formed his men into columns six companies wide and ten ranks deep. The bluecoats emerged into the open field 800 yards from the Confederate line and, with a shout, charged ahead, losing men at every step. The swampy margins of Four Mile Creek just shy of the Confederate line arrested their momentum; according to Draper, "Our men were falling by scores." The Fifth USCT lost its commander, Lt. Col. Giles W. Shurtleff, along with a number of line officers. It appeared that Draper would suffer the same disastrous fate as Duncan's brigade preceding him.[21]

At this point the Confederates had sustained few casualties. The Third Arkansas and Fourth Texas had each captured a battle flag, along with a number of Duncan's men. Some of these prisoners readily agreed to become body servants for their captors to avoid incarceration, while others were taken behind the lines and murdered. The Confederates also killed some of the wounded Black soldiers lying on the ground before them. There were soon so many dead and disabled Federals in front of the Confederate works that the bodies impeded the flow of Four Mile Creek. "The boys nearly covered the ground with dead nigs," boasted Musician Samuel S. Watson of the First Texas. A New York soldier testified that after the fight, "we could have walked on their dead bodies from the outer to the inner side of the abatis without touching soil, so thick were they strewn in that deadly charge." "It was a sight which I never wish again to behold," wrote another New Yorker. Lt. Col. Clinton M. Winkler of the Fourth Texas found the sight of so many dead African Americans and their White officers "sickening in the extreme."[22]

Amid this carnage, some of Draper's soldiers began returning fire while a few others wielded axes against the stubborn abatis to facilitate better access to the Rebel works. After nearly thirty minutes of bloody stalemate, Colonel Draper, now dismounted, ordered his valiant troops to restart their charge, encouraging them by personal example, sword in hand and waving his men ahead. Casualties made company commanders of several Black sergeants, who rose to the challenge. Up and over the works went Draper's men. The entire Confederate line suddenly melted in front of them, the Rebels streaming up New Market Heights or northwest along New Market Road. "On we went through the double line of abatis and over their works like a whirlwind," exulted Lt. Joseph J. Scroggs. The victorious Federals pursued up the heights but secured few prisoners among the fleet-footed graycoats. "Twas a glorious day for colrd troops," wrote the wounded Shurtleff from his hospital bed at Fort Monroe. "I never saw a regt fight as the 5th did."[23]

Draper's soldiers and officers had ample reason to be proud. Their attack cost them some 400 casualties, including 66 officers and men killed—indisputable evidence of their fortitude under the fiercest of combat conditions. But their conquest of the Confederate line was as much a product of a voluntary Rebel withdrawal as it was of an irresistible Union attack. Capt. Alexander C. Jones of the Third Arkansas recalled the arrival of a "swift messenger" who brought news of a threat to Fort Harrison, more than a mile to the northwest of the New

Market Line, and delivered General Gregg's orders for the Texas Brigade to fall back and assist with the defense of that imperiled position. These orders arrived about 8:00 A.M. Some of the Texans, unaware of Gregg's instructions, blamed their retreat on the collapse of either the militia and Georgians on their right or Gary's dismounted cavalry on their left. In any case, despite Paine's piecemeal tactics and his division's loss of nearly 900 officers and men, the Rebels had yielded the New Market Line. Later, fourteen of Paine's African American soldiers would receive the Medal of Honor for this accomplishment.[24]

Ben Butler rode through the battlefield after the guns had cooled, gazing upon the "sable faces made by death a ghastly, tawny blue, with their expression of determination, which never died out of brave men's faces who die instantly in a charge." He considered that charge "the most gallant and dashing of the war." The army commander felt more emotion on this battlefield than on any other as he reflected on the sacrifice made by his Black troops. "To us there is patriotism, fame, love of country, pride, ambition, all to spur us on," he wrote his wife, "but to the negro, none of all these for his guerdon of honor. But there is one boon they love to fight for, freedom for themselves and their race forever." Butler's African American soldiers reciprocated these warm feelings. "They rarely fail to salute Butler with both hand and smile, seeming to recognize him as a friend," wrote an observer.[25]

Of the nine brigades available to General Birney, only Duncan's and Draper's saw serious action below New Market Heights. Paine's First Brigade—Colonel Holman's—remained in reserve save for the Twenty-Second USCT, which sustained modest losses during Draper's assault. On Paine's right, Abbott's brigade advanced across Kingsland Road, the Seventh Connecticut joined by the Third New Hampshire on the skirmish line as the Confederate defenses came into view. Abbott gave the order to attack, but by the time his soldiers reached the enemy line, the Rebels had fled, although Gary's cavalry lost a few troopers while covering the retreat. Daniel Eldredge of the Third New Hampshire remembered negotiating "thick undergrowth and a mill stream" when he "finally advanced onto the turnpike but the Johnnies left and we were glad." Lt. William Hinson of the Seventh South Carolina Cavalry ascribed Gary's withdrawal to the Texans' departure. "We retreated hastily," admitted Sgt. Robert A. Turner of the Hampton Legion Cavalry, "being much exposed to the enemy's fire." Pvt. Charles Crosland, a courier on Gary's staff, recalled an even less ceremonious skedaddle. "We . . . were as chaff before the wind. We ran in panic for the line of works farther back commanded by Ft. Harrison." Gary's withdrawal precipitated the retreat of the Rockbridge Artillery from its position on the heights. "The break through our lines was on our right, which placed the Federals almost in our rear," wrote one of the cannoneers. "On the principle that the chased dog is generally the fleetest, we succeeded in reaching the breastworks" along the Intermediate Line. Similarly, the two guns of the Richmond Howitzers on the Confederate right also limbered to safety, halting on New Market Road near Laurel Hill Church.[26]

The other two brigades of Terry's division—Francis Pond's First and Harris Plaisted's Third—played no role against the New Market Line. The Tenth Connecticut of Colonel Plaisted's brigade advanced far enough to watch a few Rebel shells soar over their heads before hearing the cheers of Draper's troops and watching "with pride and joy" as "the old flag flung to the breeze in the light of the rising sun" over the captured works. William Birney's brigade remained in reserve along Deep Bottom Road, while Foster's division languished behind Paine south of Kingsland Road along the lane leading to the Widow Grover's home, west of Deep Bottom Road.[27]

While Paine's division dealt with the New Market Line, the remainder of the Eighteenth Corps began its advance from Aiken's Landing. They would follow Varina Road, which coursed northwest parallel to and south of New Market Road before bending almost due north to merge with New Market Road at a point between the Confederate Outer and Intermediate Lines. The 10th New Hampshire and 118th New York of Burnham's brigade, armed with their newly acquired Spencer rifles, led the march that began before dawn. The balance of Burnham's troops, trailed by the rest of Stannard's division, followed behind. "The night was dark, and our movement difficult and slow," admitted a soldier in the 118th New York. Cpl. Heman E. Baker of that regiment harbored some reservations about their new firearms. "We then had the long Springfield rifles, which were changed for the Spencer repeating rifles," he recalled. "We did not know how this change would work, whether for the better or worse." Col. Michael T. Donohoe, the twenty-five-year-old commander of the 10th New Hampshire—a former textile worker and clothing-store clerk—directed the skirmishers from horseback. Butler had placed Donohoe under arrest for some petty transgression, but the colonel requested to join the expedition, albeit without his dress sword, signifying his compromised status. Dressed in a dark-blue cape with light-blue lining, Donohoe made an impression on the skirmishers as they advanced slowly through the gloom astride Varina Road, shaking off the fatigue caused by their overnight march. Word passed through the ranks that Rebel skirmishers waited about a mile ahead.[28]

About 4:00 A.M. shots rang out from the darkness. The fire came from pickets of Hughs's Seventeenth and Twenty-Third Tennessee, who were deployed on high ground about a mile inland from the James. "It seemed as if some of their guns must have been loaded for a month, for when they would shoot, we could see a streak of fire for about ten rods long," thought Pvt. Thomas Moore of the Ninety-Sixth New York, which moved up to support Donohoe's skirmishers. One Federal cried out in pain after being hit, but it did not take long for the Yankees to send these few graycoats streaming back to their reserve picket line. "Heave after them—double quick!" shouted General Burnham, a former Maine lumbermen, and up the road dashed his brigade.[29]

The pursuit pushed through the camps of the picket reserve, who joined the vedettes on their mad scramble for safety in the main Confederate defenses. "The chase through the woods was exciting and continued at a more than 'double-quick' pace," according to a New Yorker. "We passed through an outpost camp where food was still cooking and everything tokened hasty abandonment before breakfast." Private Moore could not resist snatching a steaming cup of coffee from a campfire, yelling in mock exasperation as a Confederate disappeared in the trees. "Here, you d——d Johnny, come back and blow this coffee; it's too hot to drink." The Tennesseans continued to withdraw, stopping occasionally to fire at their pursuers and claiming a few victims by doing so. Undaunted, Burnham's troops followed for more than a mile through the forest before halting at the edge of a large field. Across the open ground less than a mile distant rose the scarred earth of the Confederate defenses, now visible in the early dawn and crowned on the highest terrain by Fort Harrison. "When we took a view of the situation, it looked as if we couldn't make it," recalled Moore. But General Burnham thought otherwise. "You can take it, boys," he intoned. "There is nothing there but school boys and pickups."[30]

Of course, that was not literally true, but the Confederate defenders facing Stannard's division more closely resembled an amateur force than an experienced contingent of Lee's veterans. Moreover, Stannard's three brigades outnumbered them almost four to one.[31]

The works confronting the Federals appeared well developed but lacked abatis or other obstructions to slow the attackers. To the Yankees' right, a portion of the Outer Line ran from Battery 11, where the works crossed Varina Road, south to Fort Harrison, also called Battery 9. The southern portion of the Camp Wall ran south from Fort Harrison to Battery 5. Those works then bent back to the west-northwest toward the river, terminating at Fort Hoke, where the Camp Wall met an interior stretch of works called the Diagonal Line. These entrenchments, which were occupied and defended instead of Batteries 3–8 of the Camp Wall, then crossed Osborne Turnpike at Fort Maury and ended above the river on Chaffin's Bluff with Jones's Salient. From Fort Hoke the Diagonal

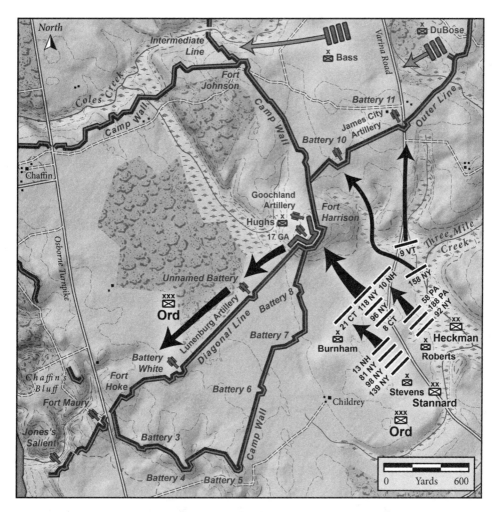

Fort Harrison, September 29, 1864

Line ran northeast to Battery White, then to an unnamed battery, and terminated at another small work adjacent to the southwest corner of Fort Harrison.
The distance from Fort Harrison to Chaffin's Bluff was about a mile and a half.

The men defending this line, no more than 800 in all, reported to Dick Ewell.
In addition to Hugh's understrength Tennessee brigade and the battalion of
the Seventeenth Georgia from DuBose's command that had been detailed to
work on Fort Harrison, Ewell could count on only two threadbare battalions of
Virginia Reserves for his infantry force. The rest of his defenders consisted of
Maury's artillery battalion of five batteries. The Lunenburg Artillery, the Goochland Artillery, the James City Artillery, the Pamunkey Artillery, and the Halifax

Light Artillery—all Virginians—deployed at various forts and batteries along the line. Lieutenant Colonel Maury was absent in Richmond this morning, so Maj. Richard Cornelius Taylor was in command of the guns. The Confederates concentrated the bulk of their strength in the strongpoints along Osborne Turnpike, where they expected the most trouble, leaving the area in and around Fort Harrison pitifully undermanned.[32]

Major Taylor dispersed his batteries along the defenses from Jones's Salient on the far Rebel right to Batteries 10 and 11 on the left. Lt. John Guerrant's Goochland Artillery took position in Fort Harrison, although the company counted only thirty-five gunners. A total of nine cannon, including those in the adjacent fortification, filled the embrasures of Fort Harrison. This ample ordnance included powerful siege artillery, such as a 100-pounder Parrott rifle and two eight-inch Columbiads. But only four of the weapons were functional, the rest suffering from clogged or spiked vents that had somehow remained unrepaired. Northeast of the fort, Lt. Lemuel Davis positioned the four guns of his James City Artillery in Batteries 10 and 11. But there, much to his disgust, the available ammunition was too large to fit the bores of two of his cannon. This accumulated negligence reflected badly on Maury, Ewell, and especially Pemberton.[33]

Fort Harrison's infantry contingent included five of the seven Seventeenth Georgia companies—seventy-three men—that had been working with the convicts and impressed slaves strengthening the fortifications as well as portions of the two battalions of Virginia Reserves. Some of Hughs's Tennesseans, who had fled their picket posts or migrated up the line from Signal Hill, also drifted into the fort. "The force to defend Ft. Harrison was very small, a mere handful," according to Capt. Cornelius Tacitus Allen of the Lunenburg Artillery, as Stannard prepared his assault. General Gregg, now fully cognizant of the threat, sent couriers to the defenders of the New Market Line, ordering their withdrawal and directing them to reinforce the threatened sector centered on Fort Harrison—this directive precipitated their sudden departure during Draper's final thrust. But they would be too late to save Fort Harrison. Capt. George W. Breckinridge of the Second Battalion of Virginia Reserves was among those second-class soldiers who entered Fort Harrison that morning. "As we came in sight of Fort Harrison and filed right to reach the line of fortifications, I had to stop for a moment to gaze spellbound on the grandest spectacle I had ever imagined," he remembered. "The mile or more of open country in front of the fort was blue with Yankees advancing in column. . . . What a sight it was!"[34]

Stannard's three brigades were the troops that so impressed Breckinridge. General Ord seemed equally awed by the prospect of attacking such an apparently strong position and called for the engineers to move up and prepare fortifications for the left of his corps. Stannard protested that waiting to entrench would cost precious time. Ord agreed to forego building works, but gazing at the distant Rebel fortifications, "which seemed to loom up like a mountain of red sand against the sky," he turned to his subordinate and said: "It is too strong for us to risk an attack. . . . We must wait for the other division [Heckman's] before we assault." Stannard objected to this suggestion as well. "Oh, hell, General! My division can take that fort!" he replied. Persuaded by Stannard's confident enthusiasm, Ord relented, instructing him to "advance across the open at quick time directly to the attack, and at double-quick" once his men reached the up-slope leading to Fort Harrison.[35]

While their superiors debated, Stannard's three brigade commanders began arranging their troops for an assault. Burnham's men remained in front, with Donohoe's two regiments still acting as skirmishers. Burnham's other two regiments, the Ninety-Sixth New York and Eighth Connecticut, lined up directly behind the skirmishers along Varina Road, massed in column for maximum drive and momentum. The Third Brigade, under Col. Samuel H. Roberts, moved behind Burnham on the right of Varina Road. Colonel Roberts, an antebellum salesman and bookkeeper who celebrated his forty-fourth birthday the previous day, was described by one of his men as "a tall, oldish looking man . . . with a thin, dyspeptic looking face." He advanced the Twenty-First Connecticut to extend the left of Donohoe's skirmish line and placed his Fifty-Eighth Pennsylvania in his front line, their left on Varina Road, with the other two regiments behind in close column. Stannard's First Brigade lined up left of the highway. Its commander, Col. Aaron F. Stevens, a New Hampshire lawyer, placed his old regiment, the Thirteenth New Hampshire, in his front line, their right flank on the road, followed by the remainder of his brigade. Stannard's columns rarely exceeded four companies in width and stretched back as many as fifty ranks deep. Such an attack formation would present a narrow target as it crossed about 1,400 yards of open ground before reaching the fort. The course of the attack would be northwest, first sloping downhill and then rising abruptly to Fort Harrison at the crown of the ridgeline. "To capture this tremendous battery we now prepared to advance," wrote a New England officer, "most of us, no doubt, with many misgivings, and with little expectation of seeing old Connecticut again."[36]

The attack commenced at 6:00 A.M. on "a beautiful, bright, clear morning." "As we stepped out into that open field the sight was enough to whiten the lips of the bravest," wrote Capt. Merlin C. Harris of the Ninety-Sixth New York. "About three-fourths of a mile before us, and stretching out of sight to the left and right, was a line of the heaviest works we had ever faced." Almost immediately, two shots rang out from Fort Harrison. The first shell overshot the emerging blue columns, but the second crashed close to Harris's men, adding extra urgency to their desire to navigate the killing ground between them and the Rebel works as quickly as possible. As the distance between Burnham's leading brigade and the rest of the division widened, Ord and Stannard worried that Roberts and Stevens were moving too slowly. Those commanders maintained a measured pace, fearful that if their men broke into a run, they would be too exhausted to overwhelm the defenders once they reached the works.[37]

The grayclad cannoneers limited their rate of fire until Burnham's men reached about halfway across the field, so much so that some of the Federal skirmishers believed that the fort had been abandoned. Then the Rebels erupted with all their available firepower, including the artillery on either side of Fort Harrison. "The heavy guns . . . opened on us . . . and from every point, right and left, along their line," recalled Captain Clay. Most of the shots continued to go long, sparing Burnham's men but doing serious harm to the supporting brigades. Donohoe's skirmish line pressed ahead, driving away the few Confederates who had ventured in front of their works. Stannard's attackers advanced with uncapped rifles—except for the skirmish line—just as had the Black troops who were attacking the New Market Line at this very moment. As the Federals approached the fort, the Confederate infantry opened fire, as did Rebel gunboats on the James. "The shot and shell of the enemy tore through our ranks, and their musketry told on our men and officers at every step," wrote Sgt. Edwin Ware of the Thirteenth New Hampshire. "But the gaps were instantly closed—the advance unchecked—officers and men vying with each other, in this march of death, to maintain the firmness and integrity of the column." Ware's comrades halted to dismantle "a heavy zig-zag rail fence leading from the left side of the Varina road along the lane leading to Mr. Childrey's house."[38]

Despite suffering serious losses, Burnham's troops managed to reach a point about 100 yards short of Fort Harrison, where sheltering defilade allowed them to catch their breath and re-form for the final push into the works. Stevens's brigade arrived shortly after Burnham's, though without its commander. Just before the brigade reached a northward bend in Varina Road, Stevens took a bullet in the thigh, a wound that would send him home for the rest of the war. Lt. Col. John B. Raulston of the Eighty-First New York assumed command of the brigade. Soon enough, Roberts's men also joined the huddled mass of bluecoats gasping for breath. Roberts had been sick with "bilious colic" and had no business taking the field that day. But as one of his officers wrote, "nothing would keep him on his back when his command was to be in action." Roberts, his neck stock twisted so the bow was facing backward and wildly brandishing his revolver by the muzzle, shouted, "Now men, just two minutes to take that fort! Just two minutes, men!"[39]

Maj. James B. Moore, the officer commanding the battalion from the Seventeenth Georgia at Fort Harrison, absorbed a quick artillery lesson from an ailing cannoneer and helped direct the fire of a thirty-two pounder that had pummeled the Federals as they approached. The enfilading blasts from the position just south of the fort had also taken its toll as Stannard's men methodically crossed the open field, preserving their energy for the final contest. The Rebel engineers' failure to construct a glacis to eliminate the defilade now providing the attackers their welcome respite from this deadly maelstrom of lead and iron, along with the absence of abatis in front of the fort, were just two keys to Fort Harrison's imminent demise. Ammunition for both cannons and rifles began to run low, persuading some of the Virginia Reserves to abandon their posts. "We would have held the fort if the newish had not run," thought an overly sanguine Tennessee captain. All these circumstances allowed the Federals to reach the deep moat in front of the fort with enough manpower to challenge the remaining defenders.[40]

General Stannard had remained at the far end of the field, along with Ord, observing as his men reached the shelter beneath the fort. Looking to the right of his temporarily immobile troops, he could see Confederates entering the works north of Fort Harrison, prompting him to send Capt. William L. Kent, his acting assistant adjutant general, "to move the column at once to the assault." Stannard credited the captain, along with Colonel Donohoe, for putting the entire division into motion. No doubt these two brave officers contributed to the final push, but a degree of spontaneity also played a role. Some of the regimental commanders spied the approaching enemy reinforcements themselves, while others simply resumed the attack when they saw their comrades forge ahead.[41]

Whatever the stimulus, all three brigades headed for the deep ditch guarding the front of Fort Harrison. The short distance between their defilade and the moat was exposed to fire. "That ditch was our only haven," recalled Captain Harris, "and the regiment seemed to have but two thoughts—to get there quick, and to take our flag along." Their comrades in the 118th New York shared similar instincts. "The charging troops advance, mount the ridge, pass over the murderous space before the fort, [and go] into the ditch." Stevens's brigade received specific orders to attack, and "the column suddenly sprang forward as one man, charged up the hill in a solid body, and rushed straight over ditch and parapet of the long southeast face of the main fort. . . . All the regiments in the assaulting force being more or less mixed up until the fort was captured."[42]

Most of the Federals scaled the fort's steep walls, while a few dashed around the moat and into Fort Harrison's open rear, or gorge. The defenders fired until the bluecoats entered the ditch, then rolled lighted shells into the moat and flung various blunt objects down on their assailants. A fuse mallet struck the head of a sergeant in the Fifty-Eighth Pennsylvania, leaving him more irate than injured. "Damn a man who'll hit a man in the head with a thing like that at a time like this," he fumed. The Federals plunged their bayonets into the fort's earthen walls and used the gunstocks as steps to ascend some twenty feet from the base of the moat to the parapet. Others leapt onto the shoulders of comrades who boosted them up, while some simply scrambled upward on hands and knees.[43]

As the first attackers reached the top of the fort, they met a handful of determined defenders. These opponents waged a brief, if bitter and deadly, close-quarters struggle. "When we climb up on one side of the walls, the enemy's men are in their places on the other side," reported a soldier in the Thirteenth New Hampshire. "We look down upon the points of their bayonets, and upon their sallow, savage faces—and a fierce hand-to-hand conflict ensues." Some of Moore's Georgians wielded their rifles like clubs, while Colonel Hughs rode up to the fort's banquet and emptied his revolver into the blue masses. But this contest was as one sided as it was short lived. The Yankees' appearance atop the fort's walls prompted most of the remaining garrison to retreat. "Seeing the hopelessness of further efforts to save the fort . . . I gave the orders to get out in the best manner possible and re-form on the next line of works, about one mile in our rear," wrote Moore. Most of the Reserves scattered before the Federals reached the parapet, and the gunners also took to their heels. A few of the Confederates halted among the dozens of log huts used as quarters near the rear of the fort. For the first time all day, many of the Federals loaded their rifles and exchanged fire with these valiant diehards. "The firing is at such short range, that some of our men's faces are actually burned and blackened by the flashes of fire from the muzzles of the enemy's rifles," wrote a New Hampshire man. But soon enough these Rebels either skedaddled or joined those seized along the parapet as prisoners of war.[44]

Several Federal regiments jammed their colors into the top of the captured works, triggering the usual postbattle debate as to which unit deserved the honor of being first to conquer Fort Harrison. General Stannard simply credited members of his division with replacing the Confederate flag with one of his own, a verity to be sure. Three of Burnham's regiments claimed the distinction—the 8th Connecticut, 96th New York, and 118th New York. Other claimants included the 13th New Hampshire, 81st New York, and 21st Connecticut. Cpl. Charles Blucher of the 188th Pennsylvania in Roberts's brigade would receive a Medal of Honor for allegedly planting the first national colors atop Fort Harrison, but perhaps one Federal hit closer to the truth when he wrote: "Gen. Burnham's brigade did not capture Fort Harrison; any more than Col. Stevens' brigade or Col. Roberts' brigade did. These three brigades were all mixed together."[45]

In any event, Fort Harrison had fallen, and so had some 600 of Stannard's men. Chief among them was General Burnham, fatally shot in the bowels as he led his brigade into the fort. Clutching his stomach, Burnham cried out, "Oh! Oh! Oh! and spun around a moment and then fell." He survived only a few moments, Colonel Donohoe assuming brigade command. By this time, Colonel Cullen of the Ninety-Sixth New York had relieved Roberts, whose illness finally drove him from the field, leaving all three of Stannard's brigade commanders hors de combat. The Federals' reward, in addition to control of the fort, included fifty prisoners and nine pieces of artillery, though some of them beyond salvage. Major Taylor, who had been wounded in the final stages of the attack, fell captive to Donohoe. The colonel treated Taylor with particular kindness when he discovered they had common friends in Norfolk. Lieutenant Colonel Maury arrived from Richmond just in time to join the other prisoners. The number of Confederate dead and wounded are unknown, but some no doubt fell when the Federals reversed the remaining functional artillery and fired at their fleeing enemies.[46]

Ord moved into the conquered fort—it was now 8:00 A.M.—intent on exploiting the advantage he had won so early in the day. Stannard's division had certainly done its job, so Ord turned his attention to his other division, that of Charles Heckman. The forty-one-year-old Heckman had served as a sergeant in the Mexican War, and upon his discharge had worked as a conductor for the Central Railroad of New Jersey. A native of the Delaware Valley, Heckman joined the Ninth New Jersey as its lieutenant colonel in October 1861 and eventually rose to regimental and brigade command, earning his star in November 1862. Described by an admirer as retaining "all the elasticity and buoyancy of youth," Heckman possessed a sonorous voice and struck a bold and dashing figure when mounted. He often carried a flute, which he played during slack times on campaign. Heckman gained combat experience in 1862 on the North Carolina coast under Ambrose Burnside and again in May 1864 at Drewry's Bluff, where Beauregard's forces overwhelmed his brigade and captured him, a setback many ascribed to Heckman's poor generalship. After Heckman's exchange in September, Butler elevated the released general to command of Ord's Second Division when General Ames took a leave of absence on September 19. Heckman's staff found him "a very pleasant man and very easy to get along with," an assessment Ord would question on September 29.[47]

Ord ordered Heckman to follow Stannard's attackers along the woods on the right of Varina Road, keeping his men under cover until opposite Fort Harrison, and "then attack it on the . . . east front as rapidly as possible." Heckman initially did as he was instructed. But when he entered the woods east of the road, he discovered that instead of an open forest fostering easy marching, he encountered a swampy woodland along the margins of Three Mile Creek. Most of his division became mired in this unfriendly terrain—no one had apparently reconnoitered—but the Ninth Vermont, a part of Edward Ripley's Second Brigade, stayed close enough to the road to avoid the muck. Heckman approached Ripley and ordered the colonel "to charge the curtain and redoubt, extending to the enemy's left of Fort Harrison." These orders would carry the Vermonters well northwest of where Ord wanted them. Instead of advancing against the eastern face of Fort Harrison, the Vermonters would march directly north on Varina Road, where Battery 11 on the Outer Line stood defiantly in their path. Had Heckman managed to avoid the swampy woods and obeyed Ord's instructions, his three brigades could have moved either directly west toward Richmond or ranged along the rear of the Confederate Intermediate Line, placing those works and their defenders in jeopardy.[48]

Ripley, just twenty-four years old and with youthful looks to match his age, led his large regiment, including many new recruits, up the highway, only to encounter the shattered remains of a Rhode Island battery that had been the target of Fort Harrison's ordnance. Dead and dying horses blocked the road. As the cannoneers labored to roll their animals out of the way, more rounds ploughed into the assemblage, hitting horses and men, one clipping Colonel Ripley in the side of his head. Knocked off his horse and momentarily stunned to insensibility, he recovered sufficiently to ask one of his officers a singular question: "Is not my head gone?" When assured that his cranium remained properly attached, Ripley realized that the shell had merely grazed his hair and cap, but the windage of the passing projectile "had seemed as harsh and cruel as iron."[49]

The Ninth Vermont passed the bottleneck of suffering animals and advanced to a cut in the road, taking musketry fire the entire way. Two of its companies halted in that depression, staring directly at Battery 11 and expecting at any moment to receive a mortal round of canister from its guns. Lieutenant Davis's James City Artillery manned those cannon and the guns in adjacent Battery 10. But faulty ammunition kept two of the four pieces silent, and by the time the Vermonters reached the cut, the gunners had abandoned the other two, as had their infantry supports from the Virginia Reserves.[50]

Ripley, anticipating imminent mayhem, screamed at his men to get away from the cut, but in their excitement the troops seemed beyond orders, intent only on placing their flag on the works. Led by the regimental color-bearer, six-foot-two-inch Sgt. Felix Quinn, the Vermonters charged ahead, Ripley among the first twenty attackers to gain the parapet. Some of the retreating Confederates halted long enough to fire one parting volley that felled a number of Federals. Still, the portion of the Outer Line immediately northeast of Fort Harrison was now firmly in Union hands. The 158th New York, a part of Col. James Jourdan's First Brigade, managed to extricate itself from the swampy woods and charge Battery 10. Absorbing "a fearful fire of grape, canister and musketry," these men from Brooklyn charged over the battery, capturing its ordnance and scattering the supporting infantry. To the northwest, Confederate forces remained in the Intermediate Line, soon bolstered by the troops arriving from the New Market Line. Similarly, the Rebels held the fortifications south of Fort Harrison, including almost the entire fortified camp at Chaffin's Bluff. It was now about 8:30 A.M., and Butler's goal of entering the Confederate capital still seemed within reach.[51]

Ewell learned of Butler's crossing of the James before dawn and passed this information to both General Lee and General Braxton Bragg, President Davis's military advisor in Richmond. "Affairs look serious," Ewell later wrote Bragg, with no little overstatement. "The enemy have possession of Fort Harrison." Lee took immediate action. He asked Bragg to marshal the local reserve troops in Richmond, a request echoed by Ewell. Lee also advised General Pickett, whose division guarded the Howlett Line at Bermuda Hundred, to prepare a brigade to cross the river and assist with Ewell's defense, then ordered Field with the rest of his division—the brigades of "Tige" Anderson, Bratton, and Col. Pinckney D. Bowles—to move to the north side, along with a substantial number of guns. Lee even requested help from the Confederate Navy to guard the bridge connecting Chaffin's Bluff to the right bank. Dick Anderson had started for the north side as earlier instructed, but he would not arrive until 11:00 A.M., leaving Ewell and Gregg to coordinate something like an integrated response to the emergency. Lee decided his own presence would be required on the north side as well, but he would wait to evaluate the Federals' intentions around Petersburg before departing.[52]

If the situation along the threatened Confederate defenses seemed chaotic, it was nothing compared to conditions in Richmond. The sound of combat immediately reached the city, and rumors spread that the Union army threatened to enter the capital. "You never saw such a scene as this city presented," wrote one resident. "The bells were tolling, stores closed and every man from sixteen to sixty-five wherever found in the street or in his house without regard to any papers of release, or anything else was placed in prison bounds until enrolled in a company (even paroled men were taken) and then armed and sent to Chaffin's Bluff." Prisoners from Castle Thunder, a notorious Richmond jail, also received arms and instruction to join the heterogeneous aggregation heading for the front lines. Cpl. John William Ford Hatton, a Marylander assigned to Chimborazo Hospital, a huge facility perched high on Richmond's East End, joined other patients who rushed from their beds to watch the unfolding spectacle. "This unexpected renewal [of combat] fanned the flames of excitement into frenzy," he recorded. "Those who had not entirely lost their heads—or probably those who had not heads at all ran from the wards and clustered upon the southern declivity of the Chimborazo Hill to see what was going on." Hatton watched as this motley militia marched past Rocketts Landing, with "a promiscuous crowd following in the wake of the troops." Authorities continued to arrest every White man they could find, while many women hastily packed bags, preparing to evacuate. "Some I suppose are thinking of their sins and some upon their clothes," wrote one disapproving lady.[53]

It would take time for any of these questionable reinforcements to mobilize and trek to Ewell's collapsing perimeter. The one-legged lieutenant general, now that the center of his line had been compromised, faced two responsibilities. He must hold the right end of his defenses along Osborne Turnpike to protect his vital connection with the manpower en route from Lee's army while simultaneously ensuring that the Intermediate Line remained intact, lest the Federals rush unimpeded directly for Richmond.[54]

Fortunately for Ewell, his opponents required time to organize their next moves. Stannard's men in Fort Harrison were now a disordered, if victorious, rabble, so he and Ord worked diligently to restore unit cohesion. Only two of Heckman's regiments had advanced into the Outer Line, while the bulk of his division gradually extricated itself from the swampy forest. The Tenth Corps troops involved in the occupation of the New Market Line, like Stannard's division, worked to regain command and control, while the rest of Birney's force—Foster's division and William Birney's brigade—remained along Kingsland Road, preparing to march up New Market Road toward the Confederate works. After the New Market Line collapsed, Kautz's cavalry, supplemented by the First New York Mounted Rifles, eight pieces of horse artillery, and the Fourth Wisconsin Battery—some 2,200 men—crossed the bridge at Deep Bottom and started for Darbytown Road, aiming for what they hoped would be the far left flank of Confederate resistance.[55]

Cyrus Comstock of Grant's staff crossed the James at Aiken's Landing around 4:00 that morning to serve as liaison for the general-in-chief. Grant remained at City Point, coordinating both wings of his offensive until after the New Market

Line and Fort Harrison had fallen. Then, leaving Col. Ely Parker in charge at headquarters, he steamed upriver to Deep Bottom, disembarking around 9:30 A.M. Lt. Henry Brown of William Birney's Twenty-Ninth Connecticut informed his home folks that "as soon as Grant was known to be approaching every man was on his feet & quiet breathless quiet prevailed[;] a cheer could never express what we felt." He added that the entire army would follow Grant wherever he led. "I have never heard even a doubt expressed of his ability to completely subdue the rebellion. . . . I am his completely." David Birney then sent the Tenth Corps up New Market Road, heading for the Confederate lines.[56]

After leaving Birney's command, Grant and his accompanying staff members rode rapidly to Fort Harrison, arriving about 10:00 A.M. He entered a scene of destruction, the ground covered with blood, shells, and the dead and dying of both sides. Moreover, the Confederates lobbed the occasional projectile into the fort, prompting Grant's aide, Lt. Col. Adam Badeau, to reflection: "'Twas quite like old times for us once more. I didn't like it any better than I used to." The general-in-chief remained in the captured fort about an hour, gazing at the spires of Richmond in the distance and assessing the remaining Confederate defenses. Badeau watched as Grant sat cross-legged, his back to the parapet, drafting orders as a shell burst over his head, causing those around him to duck for cover. The general never flinched as he completed instructions to both the Tenth and Eighteenth Corps to resume the offensive.[57]

Grant hoped to consult directly with Ord, but by the time he arrived at Fort Harrison, Ord had been wounded and removed from the field. The Eighteenth Corps commander had understood full well the importance of exploiting the advantage won thus far. Once he had reassembled a sufficient number of men from Stannard's division, he began moving north up the Camp Wall toward a small installation called Fort Johnson, which anchored the northeast corner of the Camp Wall. Dubose had arrived there with a portion of his exhausted men from the New Market Line, along with some of Moore's Seventeenth Georgia and a handful of the most intrepid from the Virginia Reserves. Although Pvt. Henry J. Ellis of the Second Georgia made an invidious comparison of Colonel DuBose to General Benning, who he was sure would have retaken Fort Harrison had he been in command, DuBose stood long enough to permit the Texas Brigade to arrive and take position up the Intermediate Line near a strongpoint called Fort Gilmer.[58]

Ord's brief attempt to move north up the Intermediate Line had been discouraged by this new show of strength, so he had turned to his other objective, the pontoon bridge at Chaffin's Bluff. Gathering a hodgepodge of men from Burnham's and Roberts's brigades, now under the leadership of Donohoe and

Cullen respectively, Ord personally led the advance down the Diagonal Line toward the unnamed battery and Battery White. They drove Captain Allen and his Lunenburg Artillery out of both positions and sent them fleeing down the line toward Forts Hoke and Maury near Osborne Turnpike, where they joined the defenders there to make a stand. The front line was no place for a corps commander, and Ord paid the price for his impetuosity. A Rebel bullet struck him in the fleshy part of the upper leg, fortunately missing the bone. Ord attempted to remain in the field by applying an improvised tourniquet, but a surgeon arrived and persuaded him to retire. The wounded commander summoned Heckman, his senior subordinate, and turned control of the corps over to him. Ord then left the field, in the words of Theodore Lyman, on "an ordinary stretcher of commerce." He attempted to contact Grant to request reinforcements, ammunition, and a replacement other than Heckman, but the general-in-chief was then somewhere between Deep Bottom and Fort Harrison, and Ord's couriers could not find him or General Butler. Colonel Donohoe also fell wounded during the advance, adding to the attrition experienced in the Eighteenth Corps leadership that morning.[59]

Heckman's original mission was to follow Stannard and assail the northeast side of Fort Harrison. Once that bastion had been reduced, he was to move north along the inside of the Camp Wall and the Intermediate Line, taking those positions from the rear, while Birney's corps along New Market Road threatened the Confederate left flank on Heckman's right. Fort Johnson met the Intermediate Line about half a mile northwest of Fort Harrison. Lt. Col. Robert Hardaway commanded the artillery from Lee's army assigned to assist Ewell. He had positioned the Richmond Howitzers and Rockbridge Artillery along the New Market Line, and these batteries had joined the Texas Brigade and the rest of the Confederate defenders there in retreat. Hardaway deployed Capt. Willis J. Dance's Powhatan Artillery, with its four three-inch rifles, in Fort Johnson and Capt. Charles B. Griffin's Salem Flying Artillery, with four twelve-pounder Napoleons, in Fort Gregg, the next battery to the north. The Second Georgia's refugees from captured Battery 11, about 100 strong under Lt. Col. William S. Shepherd, who had risen from a private to the command of his regiment, fled into Fort Johnson. A few of Major Moore's Seventeenth Georgia also drifted into the fort, joined there by the regimental commander, Lt. Col. William A. Barden.[60]

Ripley's brigade remained the only intact component of Heckman's division to escape the swamp completely. Rather than order it to pass through Fort Harrison and approach Fort Johnson from the rear as Ord intended, Heckman instructed Ripley to advance directly from his position around captured Battery

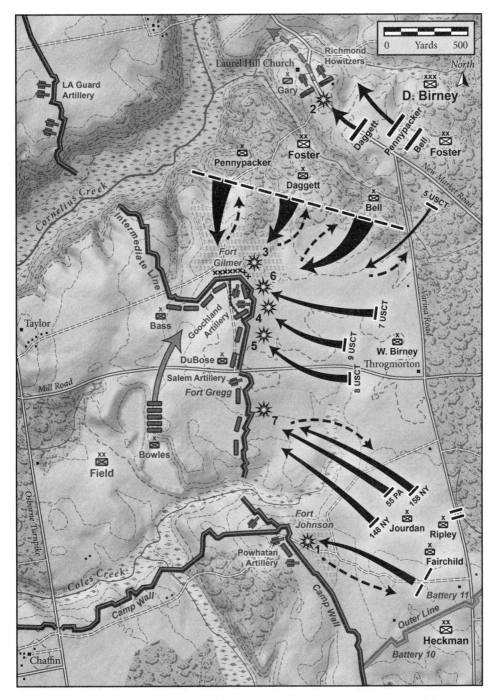

LA Guard Artillery

Cornelius Creek

Laurel Hill Church

Richmond Howitzers

x
⊠
Gary

xxx
⊠
D. Birney

2

Daggett

Pennypacker

Bell

xx
⊠
Foster

x
⊠
Pennypacker

xx
⊠
Foster

x
⊠
Daggett

x
⊠
Bell

New Market Road

North

0   Yards   500

5 USCT

Intermediate Line

Fort Gilmer

3

xxxxxxx

6

4

5

Varina Road

7 USCT

9 USCT

8 USCT

x
⊠
W. Birney
Throgmorton

Taylor

x
⊠
Bass

Goochland Artillery

DuBose ⊠

Salem Artillery

Fort Gregg

Mill Road

7

x
⊠
Bowles

xx
⊠
Field

55 PA

158 NY

148 NY

x
⊠
Jourdan

x
⊠
Ripley

Osborne Turnpike

Fort Johnson

Powhatan Artillery

1

x
⊠
Fairchild

Battery 11

Coles Creek

Camp Wall

Camp Wall

Outer Line

xx
⊠
Heckman

Chaffin

Battery 10

Attacks on Fort Johnson, Laurel Hill Church, and Fort Gilmer, September 29, 1864

11. This would put Ripley's troops on a collision course with Fort Gilmer, a distinctive strongpoint north of Mill Road and about 1,300 yards north of Fort Johnson. Doing so would require Ripley to pass directly beneath the combined fire of Forts Johnson and Gregg. The brigade commander quickly realized that those positions' "formidable strength and heavy garrisons" would expose his men to "a wicked waste of life." He sent a staff officer to summon Heckman to "come himself and to see what he had ordered me into." But the general failed to appear. Ripley reluctantly advanced his brigade, members of the Eighth Maine serving as skirmishers. Almost immediately the New Englanders encountered heavy slashings impeding their progress, as the guns in the forts played havoc on the struggling troops. The brigade commander had seen enough and ordered his units to fall back and take cover in the folds of Varina Road.[61]

Heckman now realized that to conquer Fort Gilmer, he must first suppress Fort Johnson. He called on his Third Brigade commander, Colonel Fairchild, to make the assault now that Fairchild's men had at last emerged from the morass east of Varina Road. The forty-four-year-old Fairchild, a western New York banker before the war, led his old regiment, the Eighty-Ninth New York, along with the huge Second Pennsylvania Heavy Artillery (now serving as infantry). Learning nothing from Ripley's futile advance, Heckman ordered Fairchild to move straight from Battery 11 toward Fort Johnson. Maj. James L. Anderson, in command of the Pennsylvanians, asked the colonel for the honor of leading this attack, a request quickly granted. Anderson formed the regiment into three battalions in a wedge-shaped formation, one battalion in front and the other two 100 yards behind on either flank. The Eighty-Ninth New York would follow in a third line. Between the Federals and their target, 1,200 yards distant, coursed a small stream, beyond which arose a plateau and then a cornfield. A deep moat and a line of abatis fronted Fort Johnson.[62]

As soon as the Pennsylvanians appeared beyond the Outer Line, Dance's gunners opened on them. The Federals forged ahead, and in crossing the little brook, their formation disintegrated, one of the battalions drifting away and out of the fight. The rest of the regiment moved up the slope and through the cornfield under a punishing fire. Anderson, near the head of his men, had his head "shot clear off his shoulders by a solid shot or shell." His next in command, Maj. David Sadler, assumed control, but he soon fell wounded. With the Virginia artillerists now firing canister and the Georgians blazing away with their rifles, the Pennsylvanians plunged into the moat, suffering terrible casualties en route. "Bullets, grape, and canister were flying so fast that it reminded one of a swarm of bees buzzing around," remembered one attacking soldier. A few of the bravest bluecoats scaled the wall and reached the parapet, only to be shot down or hauled in and made prisoner. The Eighty-Ninth New York witnessed this slaughter and kept its distance, stranding the Pennsylvania survivors in the moat or just in front of the fort. Some of the Georgians snuck around south of Fort Johnson, then jumped out to fire at the left flank of the trapped Federals. More of the Yankees fell captive, while the rest fled in panic back to Battery 11. Fairchild's attack cost him 279 casualties, including 150 men captured. Lieutenant Colonel Shepherd and Captain Dance were both wounded during the fight, along with 22 additional dead or wounded in the Powhatan Artillery. The Georgians' losses in Fort Johnson were not reported.[63]

The sight of the Pennsylvanians' captured battle flags flying in mock celebration from the parapet of Fort Johnson evidently persuaded Heckman to spare Jourdan's brigade from a duplicate mission of death. The battlefield fell quiet, save for an exchange of artillery between fourteen guns brought up by Maj, George Cook, commanding the Eighteenth Corps artillery, and the cannon at Forts Johnson and Gregg. For several hours, the Federals reorganized themselves, the war's most promising opportunity to capture Richmond fading away. The Confederates, too, welcomed the respite, which allowed the balance of the fugitives from the New Market Line to arrive, and spent the lull redeploying their forces along the Intermediate Line.[64]

General Gregg positioned the Texas Brigade from Fort Gregg southward to a little stream called Coles Creek. DuBose placed the Twentieth Georgia between the creek and Fort Johnson and divided the Fifteenth Georgia between Fort Gregg and Fort Gilmer. A handful of gunners and a few of the Virginia Reserves joined the Georgians in Fort Gilmer. The Twenty-Fifth Virginia Battalion deployed along the Intermediate Line north of Fort Gilmer. Farther north still, the Louisiana Guard Artillery unlimbered its four twelve-pounder Napoleons, and on their left the Rockbridge Artillery arrived from New Market Heights with its four Parrott rifles. The last of the New Market Line defenders, Gary's cavalry and the Richmond Howitzers, halted along New Market Road near Laurel Hill Church. General Anderson arrived at 11:00 A.M. but exercised no discernible influence on this revised Confederate configuration. South of the James, Pickett responded to his orders to rush reinforcements across the river. Instead of dispatching one of his four organic brigades, he selected a single regiment from each of them and placed this provisional unit under Col. Edgar B. Montague, a Tidewater lawyer and merchant and the commander of the Thirty-Second Virginia. This cobbled brigade arrived at Chaffin's Bluff around 1:00 P.M.[65]

With the Eighteenth Corps combat depleted and hampered by the loss of so many of its senior commanders, Union fortunes now depended on the Tenth Corps. Foster's division had remained idle throughout the early morning while the USCT regiments attacked the New Market Line. At 8:30 A.M., however, Foster put his three brigades in motion, marching northwest up New Market Road toward Richmond, with Col. Rufus Daggett's First Brigade in the van. Daggett, a twenty-six-year-old New York tinsmith and hardware merchant, placed the 142nd New York at the head of his column to serve as skirmishers. Sgt. Edward King Wightman of the 3rd New York remembered passing by "the slaughtered negroes [who] lay piled in heaps" along the road.[66]

Daggett's four regiments, reduced to fewer than 1,000 men due to straggling during their long trek to Deep Bottom, marched without incident until Grant and his entourage rode by. "The men sprang to their feet and cheered till they fairly caused the old fellow, cigar and all to fall from his saddle," wrote Wightman. In about an hour the Federals reached the point where New Market Road crossed the Outer Line, near its intersection with Mill Road. A handful of Gary's cavalrymen fired a few shots, but the 142nd New York, followed by the rest of the brigade, charged ahead, "the enemy falling back rapidly, leaving their works in our possession," reported Foster. The division commander halted here for a brief rest, allowing his other two brigades to catch up.[67]

In due course Foster resumed the march. New Market Road at this point entered a thick forest, reducing visibility so significantly that the Federals could not see Gary's dismounted troops supporting four twelve-pounder Napoleons of the Third Richmond Howitzers on the high ground ahead near Laurel Hill Methodist Church. Foster became acutely aware of their presence, however, when the ordnance belched shells down the open road corridor. He tried to deploy his troops from column of march into three brigade-sized lines of battle, but the formation of the ground left Daggett's men in front, with Col. Galusha Pennypacker's Second Brigade behind and to their right, while Col. Louis Bell's Third Brigade organized behind Pennypacker. The Confederate fire, according to Lt. Col. Albert M. Barney, commanding the 142nd New York, created "considerable confusion" among the men. Sergeant Wightman wrote that the "shells tore through our ranks with awful effect," blaming the officers for advancing the skirmish line only twenty paces beyond the head of the column. Casualties mounted, particularly in the ranks behind the 142nd New York. "We being in the front of the column," wrote the regiment's Lt. William H. Richmond, "were better off than those further back for as it nearly always happened, their range was high so the shells went over our heads, but those in rear of us suffered terribly. . . . Those cussed shells mowed terrible swaths among us."[68]

Foster realized that something had to be done because not only was he taking fire from his front, but the guns off to his left in Fort Gilmer pounded him as well. He decided to mount an attack, ordering all three of his brigades to charge, with Bell's and Pennypacker's aiming for the left flank of the Confederate position ahead. Because the Hampton Legion Cavalry was absent, retreating up Darbytown Road, Gary could support the guns with troopers from only the Seventh South Carolina Cavalry and the Twenty-Fourth Virginia Cavalry, who had managed to make it to Laurel Hill Church. Seeing an entire Union division screaming up the slope toward their position, Gary and the Howitzers knew their stand must come to an end. "We had to limber up and get away from there as best we could," explained one of the gunners, "which was by running nearly to Richmond." By the time the Federals reached the high ground, their quarry had fled, "retiring in such haste as to leave their killed and wounded on the field and the road strewn with artillery ammunition and implements," wrote Foster. Maj. Ephraim A. Ludwick, leading the 112th New York, was among Daggett's casualties, suffering a serious arm wound.[69]

Foster now rested his exhausted division, while the third element of the Federal offensive, General Kautz's cavalry, pursued its mission of reaching Richmond. Kautz cleared New Market Road, once the Tenth Corps moved out of his way, leading his troopers north to Darbytown Road, where they turned northwest, hoping to dash unimpeded into the capital. All went well until they approached the Intermediate Line between 10:00 and 11:00 A.M. Here, a small collection of heavy artillerists posed the lone impediment barring Kautz's access to Richmond. The gunners opened fire on his lead regiment, the Fifth Pennsylvania Cavalry, inflicting nearly two dozen casualties on these dismounted troopers. Mindful that he had been instructed to avoid a prolonged fight, Kautz drew back and rode north cross-country to the next highway leading to Richmond, Charles City Road. Once again Rebel artillery disputed his passage. Kautz ordered an attack, but the Confederate heavy guns drove him back. By midafternoon, the Federals withdrew once again, riding nearly as far north as the Chickahominy River until after dark. One last attempt to push into Richmond faltered in confusion, as might be expected after sunset, and the bluecoats retreated. Kautz accomplished nothing on September 29, beyond wearing out man and beast, when a bolder commander might have achieved a marked success.[70]

For ninety minutes after Foster's victory at Laurel Hill Church, Kautz's futile probing constituted the only Federal movement of any significance. Terry's and Paine's divisions along with William Birney's brigade did move up from the battlefield below New Market Heights, halting along New Market Road southeast of Mill Road and the Outer Line. Only Birney's USCT regiments advanced far enough to be in position to support Foster, who remained idle while reorganizing his units and hoping that his many stragglers would appear.

The exhausted Eighteenth Corps milled around Fort Harrison, their ability to renew the offensive all but drained.[71]

The Federals' inactivity allowed their opponents to direct reinforcements toward Fort Gilmer, which, after the loss of Fort Harrison, represented the primary obstacle preventing a breakthrough to Richmond. Fort Gilmer formed a pronounced salient along the Intermediate Line. "The front parapet was very thick and substantially constructed with a wide and deep moat in front making the wall from top to bottom of the ditch too high to be scaled without machinery," wrote one Confederate. "The rear was secured with large posts well fixed in the ground and cut smooth and regular at the top." A double line of abatis protected the fort's northern face—the one facing Foster's position around Laurel Hill Church—but no such obstructions fronted the portion of the fort facing east. Two heavy guns manned by a detachment from the Goochland Artillery frowned out from embrasures, supported by portions of the Fifteenth and Twentieth Georgia, along with a few of the Virginia Reserves. While Foster prepared his attack, General Gregg rushed the Texas Brigade toward the works northwest of Fort Gilmer. "We had supposed that our powers of physical endurance had already reached their limit," remembered the well-traveled Captain Jones of the Third Arkansas, "yet I venture to say that we made that half mile in about as short time as men ever passed over the same distance. Panting for breath, we took position in the entrenchments on the left of the fort." DuBose hurried most of the rest of his brigade northward to the works on Fort Gilmer's right. The Alabama brigade of Field's Division was en route but had not yet reached the threatened portion of the Confederate defenses.[72]

By this time, General Butler had joined David Birney near the intersection of New Market and Varina Roads. Grant had not seen Butler but did send a message at noon informing the army commander that he was returning to Deep Bottom in order to resume communication with Meade. He advised Butler that if the Army of the James could not reach Richmond that afternoon, it should fall back below Chaffin's Bluff to prevent being attacked from the rear by Confederates crossing the river there. Butler replied less than an hour later, assuring Grant that Birney had started his attack and confirming that, indeed, grayclad reinforcements from Petersburg had started for the Confederate lines on the left bank.[73]

Butler's assurance proved a bit premature. Not until 1:25 P.M. did Foster receive orders from Birney to begin his assault within ten minutes. His target would be Fort Gilmer, which he would attack by moving southwest and then almost due south against its north face. The orders specified that William Birney's Black troops would attack simultaneously from the east and that Paine's division would provide support, if necessary. Foster aligned his division, with Pennypacker's brigade on the right, Daggett's in the center, and Bell's on the left. Rather than forming his men into narrow, deep columns, his attack formation presented a long, thin line with no immediate reserves to exploit a breakthrough. Even worse, the division counted only some 1,400 men, a reduction in strength due mostly to straggling, which Pennypacker called "unnecessary and disgraceful," in addition to skulking and a few casualties. Foster's men would have to travel three-fourths of a mile to reach their goal, crossing a landscape featuring multiple ravines, tangled brush, and the abatis fronting their approach. The division stepped out as ordered at 1:35 P.M.[74]

Many of the Federals recognized the difficulty in reaching Fort Gilmer. "Not a man or officer who participated in the charge had any idea the work could be carried," recalled a soldier in the 112th New York. Colonel Bell expressed pessimism about the assault, a view shared by Nicholas De Graff of his 115th New York. "To us it looked like suicide to attempt it." Despite such reservations, Foster's troops stepped out unflinchingly, the general near the front. The battle line reached the first ravine, drained by a small tributary of Cornelius Creek, without serious loss, ploughed through the marshy ground, and toiled up the opposite slope. At this point the artillery at Fort Gilmer, along with the Louisiana Guard Artillery on Foster's right, leveled a telling fire on the attackers. Foster's men sustained heavy casualties until they reached a second ravine, 350 yards beyond the first, that provided temporary shelter.[75]

The Federals struggled through what Lieutenant Richmond considered "the worst old slashing of timber I ever saw men try to get through." A soldier in the 117th New York reported in a letter home, "As we advanced they poured into us from right & left grape & canister, creating death & destruction in our ranks." With casualties mounting, "cheers and cries of agony and horror strangely mingled" as the survivors forged ahead through the brush and down into a third miry ravine, "the din and roar of the enemy's fire increasing every moment and disasters multiplying at every step."[76]

Now, only a cornfield stood between the attackers and the twin rows of abatis fronting the fort. "Such a time I never saw," admitted Sgt. Hermon Clarke of the 117th New York. "The only thing I can compare it with is as grass falls before a mowing machine, so that corn fell before the balls." Wightman considered the incoming fire "the most murderous, pitiless storm of musketry, shrapnel, and grape and cannister that I ever conceived of. The ripping, howling, and screaming of the missiles, mingled with the shouts of the attacking party, the yells of the rebels [and] the groans of the wounded were horrible beyond description."[77]

Despite being grossly outnumbered—the norm that day—the Georgians, Texans, and their stalwart artillery comrades stopped Foster's attack at the abatis. Many of Gregg's men shuffled up and down the works, responding to any particular Federal advance. "Those Arkansas men did good shooting," boasted Captain Jones, "and with every shot there went up a Confederate yell to emphasize their aim. No doubt those Yankees thought ... that they were facing thousands instead of about one hundred Arkansas ragamuffins." At least one Confederate remembered seeing Dick Ewell "mounted on an old gray horse, as mad as he could be, shouting to the men, and seeming to be everywhere at once."[78]

By this time, attrition in Foster's three brigades had robbed the division of further progress. The general called on Paine for help, and that division commander ordered the Fifth USCT of Draper's brigade to move up from reserve and reinforce Bell on the left. These troops charged forward, encountering the same geographic and manmade obstacles that had thwarted their predecessors. "A battery to our right raked these ravines from end to end and our progress through them being necessarily slow we lost a great many men before gaining solid ground," wrote the regiment's Lieutenant Scroggs. In concert with a New York outfit, the Fifth USCT forged ahead "with a blind desperation." The result was predictable. Only ten of Scroggs's company of fifty men returned to the Union lines. Capt. Elliott F. Grabill considered this attack "a mad enterprise" and confessed that the Fifth USCT faced "the hottest musketry fire I was ever in. Our regiment melted under it. . . . Ah, it was a sad sight to see the remnant return."[79]

Foster's men retreated, some under orders and others spontaneously. Casualties in his division testified to the futility of his assault. Bell suffered 143 losses. All but one officer fell killed or wounded in the 115th New York. Pennypacker reported 40 casualties, including his own slight wound, but Daggett's brigade in the center of the attack formation paid the highest price. Daggett was shot, and 271 additional members of his brigade fell killed or wounded or were taken prisoner. The 117th New York lost 132 out of the 275 men who made the assault, the worst regimental loss in the division. Sgt. James Beard of the 142nd New York went in with twelve other soldiers in his squad; only two emerged unscathed. "It was an awful sight to see the ground," he wrote his family. "All over with dead and wounded and in many places one will fall [a]cross the other and lay until they are buried." Foster would report a grand total of 463 casualties—about a third of the men who made the attack—knocking his division out of action for the remainder of the day.[80]

The effort to take Fort Gilmer, however, would continue. Now, William Birney's brigade received orders to reduce the position. Like his younger brother, the forty-five-year-old Birney possessed no prewar military training.

He practiced law and established a newspaper in Philadelphia before entering service as a captain in a New Jersey regiment. He earned combat experience in the early years of the war and rose to command the Fourth New Jersey before accepting the command of a USCT regiment and brigade in the spring of 1863. He spent considerable time recruiting former slaves in Maryland, his abolitionist credentials nearly as solid as his famous father's. Capt. Henry Grimes Marshall of the Twenty-Ninth Connecticut, a regiment in Birney's brigade, observed, "Brig. Gen. Birney is anxious to achieve fame & glory & will," adding that he was not "afraid to send men in to get it while he sleeps well to the rear tho they say he is brave."[81]

Birney brought five regiments up New Market Road, halting them at the Outer Line. At around 2:00 p.m. he responded to his brother's orders to move forward, although the plan had been for Birney to advance simultaneously with Foster. The failure to coordinate their attacks rests with the corps commander. Birney decided to leave the inexperienced Forty-Fifth USCT behind and designated the Twenty-Ninth Connecticut as brigade reserve, sending the Ninth, Eighth, and Seventh USCT northwest on New Market Road. These commands then turned left into the woods, crossed Varina Road, and deployed facing west astride Mill Road. By this time, Foster's division had commenced its retreat, so Birney's three regiments would go in alone. To make matters worse, the brigadier committed his units one at a time—Paine had done the same with Duncan's brigade that morning—diluting the chances of what was already a doubtful endeavor.[82]

The Ninth USCT, led by Capt. Edwin S. Babcock, advanced west on the north side of Mill Road to a ravine about 1,500 yards from Fort Gilmer. Babcock designated four companies under Capt. Douglas G. Risley as skirmishers and formed the rest of the regiment in line of battle. Facing more than half a mile of "rough cleared land with stumps and brush," the Black soldiers began their attack. They immediately encountered severe artillery fire that enfiladed both of their flanks. The regiment reached a point about half the distance to the fort, the men tired and bleeding. Babcock ordered them to halt, re-form, and lie down while he returned to Birney's command post to seek further instructions. The brigade commander told him to shift to the right to eliminate the enfilading fire from that direction. By the time Babcock returned to the front, however, his senior officer, Capt. Hugh S. Thompson, had already ordered the regiment to resume the assault, only to have it battered so badly that it was forced to retreat. About one-third of the regiment had fallen.[83]

The Eighth USCT would be next to challenge the metallic hell in front of Fort Gilmer. Maj. George E. Wagner moved out of the forest south of Mill Road immediately opposite Fort Gregg, a smaller battery a few hundred yards south of Fort Gilmer. His eight available companies numbered only 250 men, and his orders were to send only half of them forward. Led by Capt. John S. Cooper, these determined soldiers braved a deluge of fire, reaching within 200 yards of the Confederate works when "like a prudent officer he halted his men and made them lie down." Wagner then advanced the remainder of his regiment, joining Cooper's battalion. The major reconnoitered the Rebel position and "soon became convinced" that resuming the attack "could arrive at no other result . . . than to have [his regiment] slaughtered and still make no impression on the enemy's position." Wagner offered to renew the assault, but Birney wisely ordered him to simply halt and maintain his ground. The Eighth USCT suffered fifty-three officers and men killed or wounded.[84]

It was now the Seventh USCT's turn. Birney instructed Col. James Shaw, the regimental commander, to move his men north of Mill Road and take Fort Gilmer with a direct assault. At this point conflicting stories regarding Shaw's orders emerge, a controversy that is beyond resolution. According to Shaw, Capt. Marcellus Bailey, Birney's assistant adjutant general, arrived with revised orders to send only four companies forward to "attack and take the work that is firing." Shaw replied that he understood that he was to employ his entire regiment, but Bailey reiterated that Birney now wanted him to use only four companies. The general stoutly denied issuing any such order and blamed Shaw for misconstruing his intent. It mattered little in the event, as no single regiment at this point could hope to conquer Fort Gilmer and its adjacent works.[85]

The first of Field's reinforcements, Alabamans under Colonel Bowles, raced into Fort Gilmer about the time that Shaw readied his attack. Lt. George Reese of the Forty-Fourth Alabama marched near the rear of Bowles's brigade and all at once "heard a yell in front, and . . . saw our boys running pellmell without any order for the breastworks, and on the other side saw an innumerable host of negro troops marching in regular double-quick step for the same works." The Alabamans poured into the fort and joined the artillerists, Texans, and Georgians who had already repulsed Foster and the first two of Birney's assaults. "We ran into, and on the flanks of the redoubt, and the old 4th Alabama never in all its existence received such a royal welcome," wrote the regimental adjutant, Robert T. Coles. "Cheer after cheer went up . . . from our hard-pressed comrades . . . fearing our works would be stormed and taken before re-enforcements would reach them."[86]

Shaw chose Capt. Julius A. Weiss to take Companies C, D, G, and K of the Seventh USCT and make the charge. "What, capture a fort with a skirmish line?" the captain cried incredulously. "We'll try, but it can't be done." Weiss dutifully arranged his battalion, consisting of nine officers and 189 men, and led them out of a shallow ravine and onto the open field in front of Fort Gilmer. They rushed forward without firing a shot, as many as 77 of their number falling dead or wounded after covering most of the distance to the fort. The Confederates unleashed shell, then canister, and finally musketry as the survivors dove into the deep moat fronting Fort Gilmer, where they found temporary shelter. "The way those negroes fell . . . was very gratifying to the people on our side of the works," remembered Cpl. Charles Johnston of the Salem Flying Artillery.[87]

The moat proved to be a false refuge for the 120 officers and men who reached it. Confederates above them fired down into the ditch, almost certain to make a hit. "We would run to different angles in the fort and take aim, rise up, and fire at the same time," recalled a soldier in the Fifth Texas. Confederate guns swept the field behind the pinned men, so retreat would be equally deadly. The Federals saw that storming the fort offered their only hope, but its steep walls presented an almost insurmountable obstacle. Some mounted the shoulders of a pair of comrades, who at a signal heaved the armed men up and onto the parapet. But as soon as these intrepid fellows reached the top, the Confederates greeted them with rifle shots at point-blank range. "Not a head appeared but that it was quickly perforated with one or more balls," testified a Georgian.[88]

One of these brave men became an enduring icon of Confederate disdain for African American soldiers. Known only as "Corporal Dick" and considered the best man in his regiment, his comrades boosted the determined corporal up to the parapet. "Corporal Dick, did not have a hair on his head; it was so slick it reminded me of a Virginia onion," recalled Pvt. John Francis Methvin of the Salem Flying Artillery. "He was one of those who got upon the shoulders of another negro and made an effort to come over into the fort; he was shot between the eyes and fell into the ditch." Joseph B. Polley of the Fourth Texas gleefully remembered one of the Black soldiers crying out, "Cawpul Dick done dead!" "There was great lamentation" when this "conspicuous leader, jet black, and bald as a badger," met his reward, recalled another cannoneer. This struck the Confederates as highly humorous, and "Cawpul Dick" became a running joke and derogative placeholder for every Black soldier for years after the war. "Yes, Dick was a game kind of nigger and his boldness was worthy of a better cause than his efforts to murder Southern people," conceded a member of the Richmond Howitzers.[89]

The surviving cohort of Weiss's forlorn hope now faced a new hazard. The Confederates began lighting artillery shells and tossing them over the works into the ditch, now packed with the dead as well as the living. "After we had killed a number of them they appeared to get tired of that kind of exercise and gave us a breathing spell," recalled a Texan, "when one of our artillery fellows found time to cut and light the fuse to a shell, which he threw over amongst them. It exploded, evidently doing much damage." This act was repeated several times, eliciting entreaties to "stop frowing dem tings over har! We giv up!" Lt. Robert M. Spinney at last displayed a white handkerchief at the end of his sword, signifying the desire to capitulate. Seven White officers and between seventy and eighty Black soldiers surrendered.[90]

The balance of Weiss's battalion was, in the words of Colonel Shaw, "lost . . . almost entire." Only one of the men who made the charge escaped unhurt or uncaptured, although nineteen who fell wounded prior to reaching the moat managed to crawl to safety. The vengeful Confederates dispatched some of the captured and wounded Blacks until word of this shameful behavior reached Ewell, who ordered it stopped. But surviving as a captive was no guarantee of a reprieve. Lt. George R. Sherman would later report that of the seventy-nine men of the regiment he knew to be imprisoned, fifty-five perished within six months.[91]

William Birney's attack at Fort Gilmer generated a number of Confederate canards, often repeated in other contexts. Among the most frequently employed claimed that the Union soldiers, whether Black or White, were drunk and that gunpowder mixed with liquor filled their canteens. Some Rebels testified that the White officers had to force their Black comrades to go forward at the point of a sword or by threat of being shot if they hesitated. Cpl. John Lokey reported that one of the captured Black soldiers offered to serve him "for the balance of my days" rather than go to prison. In another example of Confederate hatred for U.S. Colored Troops, several Rebels swore that a well in front of Fort Gilmer provided a common grave for many of the slain. "Our boys . . . filled the well with dead negroes, putting Corporal Dick at the bottom," bragged Private Methvin. "This well was a common grave for those unfortunate bands of enemies of ours," averred Pvt. Andrew Jackson Andrews of the Richmond Howitzers, "and it would have paid them much better to have been employed on some good farm than to stand in front of the ranks of Confederate game chickens to be slain as common fiends and their remains to be scattered as chaff before a wind."[92]

A captain in the Seventeenth Georgia summarized the sentiments of most Confederates regarding the battle for Fort Gilmer: "The brilliant achievements of this small Confederate force, holding at bay the hordes of the enemy . . . until the reenforcements could arrive from Petersburg and fighting all day long against such tremendous odds, were unsurpassed during the war." In contrast stands the diary entry of the Seventh USCT's Joshua Dearborn, who wrote that the conduct of the battle "looks as though the object to be obtained was to sacrifice colored troops that the great loss might prove their bravery and furnish capital wherewith their general might manufacture material for another star. . . . If this rushing troops by detail to destruction proves anything it is the unfitness of officers to command."[93]

One additional offensive spasm marked the culmination of the serious combat north of the James this bloody day. All of Colonel Jourdan's brigade of Heckman's division eventually emerged from the swampy ground east of Varina Road and joined the 158th New York around Battery 10 on the Outer Line. Heckman ordered Jourdan to charge ahead against Fort Gregg, with the understanding that Stannard's division would provide support on his left while the Tenth Corps attacked simultaneously on his right. By this time, Birney had already failed and Stannard's men were preoccupied with the situation around Fort Harrison, so Jourdan's three regiments would advance alone, continuing the day's pattern of piecemeal Federal assaults.[94]

Jourdan placed the 55th Pennsylvania in the front of his attack formation, with the 158th New York in echelon to its right and the 148th New York deployed as skirmishers on the Pennsylvanians' left. Shortly before 4:00 P.M. the Federals lurched ahead, drawing immediate fire from Fort Johnson on their left to Fort Gilmer on their right. "The 55th charged for more than a quarter of a mile through an open 'slashing' in the face of a terrific fire of cannon and deadly musketry from three redoubts well supported by a heavy body of infantry," recalled Capt. Josiah Hissong. "We reached a point within 20 yards of the battery, when[,] our ranks almost annihilated, we discovered that our supports had failed to come up." The Federals approached Fort Gregg so closely "that the features of the men at the guns could be distinctly seen, every charge could be heard rammed home, and the word 'fire' heard at every discharge."[95]

The 15th and 20th Georgia provided the bulk of the infantry in Fort Gregg, having dashed into those works as Jourdan started across the field. As the Pennsylvanians neared the Confederate line, Sgt. Augustine Flanagan, the regimental color-bearer, enthusiastically waved his banner urging the regiment onward when a Rebel bullet laid him low. Sgt. Hezekiah Hammer then picked up the fallen flag while the fire of a handful of men from the 148th New York managed to drive the gunners away from their pieces. A corporal from the 158th New York actually pierced the Confederate works and made off with the flag of the 20th Georgia, marking the high-water point of Jourdan's assault. "No troops could stand the terrible fire to which they were subjected," however, and the blue wave receded back to the Outer Line, leaving twenty dead, 113 wounded, and fifty-one missing.[96]

Earlier in the afternoon, Grant had instructed Butler that if Birney's attacks proved unsuccessful, "I think it will be advisable to move out to the Central road," another name for Darbytown Road. Foster's and Birney's disasters certainly met Grant's criteria for failure, so Butler ordered Terry to shift his division northward in hopes of linking with Kautz's cavalry for a combined push into Richmond. Terry led his three brigades north from New Market Road about 3:00 P.M., reaching Darbytown Road just west of the unoccupied Outer Line. The Federals then turned northwest and tramped to within three miles of Richmond, "the city being distinctly visible from the head of the column." Terry looked in vain for Kautz, who by this time had ridden well north in search of an unopposed route into the Confederate capital. Resting in place for about an hour and, unbeknown to him, facing only light resistance behind the looming Intermediate Line, Terry withdrew under orders to the intersection of Mill and New Market Roads, arriving just before dark after having marched ten fruitless miles.[97]

By this time, the Federal high command had all but decided to pause the offensive that had shown so much promise that morning. Heeding Grant's admonition to create a defensive line south of Chaffin's Bluff, Chief Engineer John Barnard, assisted by Colonel Comstock, laid out a new perimeter. The line ran from Cox's Ferry on the James up to Fort Harrison and then along the Outer Line as far as New Market Road. From there the line curved away from the old Confederate works to Darbytown Road, where it was refused facing north. The Federals reversed the works along the captured Outer Line, and Stannard's men worked furiously to close the open gorge of Fort Harrison, a task left uncompleted that night. Grant returned to City Point late that afternoon, telling Butler to hold the ground already captured and probe around the Confederate left in the morning, although he did not foreclose the option of resuming the attack before dark if Butler saw a promising opportunity to do so. In a message to Halleck in Washington, the general-in-chief rationalized the day's disappointing results by expressing low expectations. "I did not expect to carry Richmond," temporized Grant, couching Butler's offensive as a diversion in favor of Meade. "The great object, however, is to prevent the enemy sending re-enforcements to Early."[98]

In this, at least, Grant spoke truthfully, but Confederate reinforcements, if not heading west, were on the move across the James that afternoon. In addition to Montague's provisional brigade, Bratton's South Carolinians arrived, while "Tige" Anderson's Georgians, the last element of Field's Division, were en route. Perhaps most importantly, General Lee was across the James by midafternoon. Ewell expressed his intent to counterattack "as soon as the troops come up." Montague did retake Fort Hoke, which a portion of Cullen's brigade had driven a small body of heavy artillerists out of those works late in the day. The Virginians, aided by elements of Hughs's Tennesseans, also regained most of the Diagonal Line but fell well short of recapturing Fort Harrison. The Rebels made no attempt to drive the Yankees away from their positions farther north.[99]

Thus ended a momentous day north of the James. Federal forces came closer to entering the Confederate capital than ever before, only to see a lack of coordination between Butler's two corps and his cavalry arm squander a possible turning point in the Civil War. Butler bears much responsibility for this failure. He allocated three of his five divisions to attack the thin line of Confederate defenders at the base of New Market Heights when a smaller force would have sufficed, leaving only Stannard's and Heckman's divisions to move directly against the Richmond defenses. Moreover, once Stannard's men captured Fort Harrison, Heckman disobeyed his orders to advance behind the fort and take the Intermediate Line in reverse, further weakening Union firepower where it was most needed. "Had General Heckman obeyed my orders many valuable lives would have been saved, and his division, reaching the work after Stannard's had taken it, would have been available to have attacked the only other work which intervened between us and Richmond," wrote Ord. Ord's wounding left the overmatched Heckman in charge of the Eighteenth Corps, while Butler disappeared from the front when decisive leadership was most required. Edward Porter Alexander, chief of artillery in Lee's First Corps, believed that if Butler had not "made the mistake of striking upon both flanks at the same time," then "Richmond would have been his immediate prize." The attacks against Fort Gilmer by the Tenth Corps never achieved concentration of force, allowing the small number of Rebel defenders to parry each blow sequentially.[100]

The common soldier, as always, paid the price for faulty leadership. Individual acts of bravery abounded in the Federal ranks on September 29, none more so than in the USCT regiments. At New Market Heights and in front of Fort Gilmer, the Black soldiers displayed courage and resilience while absorbing catastrophic casualties. Their performance went far to erase doubts about their ability and willingness to fight, unfairly raised following the Battle of the Crater in July. "Their praises," Butler informed the secretary of war, "are in the mouth of every officer in this Army. Treated fairly and disciplined they have fought most heroically." Ben Butler, whatever his shortcomings, deserves credit for providing African American soldiers with a canvas that they would paint with fortitude and pride.[101]

Such combat prowess was on full display among the Confederate defenders this day. Gregg's Texans, DuBose's Georgians, Gary's troopers, and even Ewell's inexperienced gunners and reserves punched well above their weight in the face of overwhelming odds during every encounter. Brigade and regimental commanders positioned their forces just where they were most needed following the loss of the New Market Line and Fort Harrison. Both Ewell's judicious biographer and the battle's most careful student give that peculiar general great credit for staving off disaster. The one-legged Ewell certainly provided active encouragement during the crisis and perhaps put an end to the shameful massacre of Black prisoners at Fort Gilmer, but his tactical influence on events remained somewhat muted.[102]

Robert E. Lee had to contend with threats to both Richmond and Petersburg on September 29, not unlike the situation he faced when Grant crossed the James in mid-June. As he had earlier, the army commander reacted judiciously, committing forces to the north side of the James in proportion to the perceived threat while mindful of the necessity of defending his Petersburg lines of communication.

The fighting on September 29 left both sides searching for resolution. Butler and Grant agreed to meet early the next morning at Deep Bottom to discuss battle plans for the thirtieth. On the Confederate side, Lee redoubled his desire to repair the damage sustained that Thursday. In addition to Montague and Field's fresh brigades, he summoned to the north side Robert Hoke's Division, Alfred Scales's Brigade from the Third Corps, a division of cavalry, and "as many batteries as could be spared" under the command of Brigadier General Alexander. Lee considered trying to regain Fort Harrison that night using Field's troops. But by the time Field marshaled his brigades opposite the captured stronghold, Richard Anderson, whose influence on events had been minimal, deemed it inadvisable to assault just then. The next contest for control of Fort Harrison would commence in the morning.[103]

nine

THE FEARFUL DESTRUCTION OF LIFE IN OUR RANKS

The Fifth Offensive Continues, September 29–30

The military situation north of the James River on the evening of Thursday, September 29, posed a legitimate threat to the Confederacy's quest for independence. Robert E. Lee's defense of Petersburg was at its root a means of defending Richmond, and the loss of that city would likely deal a death blow to the nascent nation. Therefore, any direct menace to the Confederate capital became Lee's priority. Ben Butler's latest offensive most certainly represented the greatest such danger in more than two years.

Meeting this crisis required shifting troops from the Petersburg front across the James while at the same time marshaling all of Richmond's available manpower. By the night of the twenty-ninth, at least 4,000 emergency troops mustered for duty in the city, many reporting without weapons or uniforms. "Officers and men on furlough, citizens visiting the city on business, exempts and detailed men, clerks in the Departments, printers, newspaper men, Express men—all were required to take up arms for the defense of the capital," wrote war correspondent Peter Wellington Alexander. Civilian prisoners, walking wounded from army hospitals, and virtually any White male thought to be between the ages of sixteen and fifty-five suddenly found themselves impressed for emergency military duty. "Houses were searched by the provost guard for citizens of retiring disposition," observed Pvt. Eugene Levy of Louisiana's Donaldsonville Artillery, "'tis strange how many of these suddenly became 60 years old in order to claim exemption from service."[1]

These tyros, while at best qualified only to man fortifications, would be of little use in realizing Lee's intention to regain Fort Harrison. For that, the Confederate commander required experienced troops, and they could only be found along the lines at Petersburg. Tige Anderson's Georgians filed in after dark, completing the shift of Field's Division to the north side of the James, but two factors—logistics and the Yankees—delayed Lee's efforts to amass an even more powerful strike force.[2]

Shifting Maj. Gen. Robert Hoke's four brigades along with Brig. Gen. Alfred Scales's Tar Heel regiments, temporarily assigned to Hoke, posed the first problem. Hoke's troops had just relieved Bushrod Johnson's Division along the front lines east of Petersburg when the orders arrived to rush to the north side. Late on the morning of the twenty-ninth, Johnson's men once again swapped places with Hoke's. "The order urged us to use all haste," reported John Elmore Hall of Johnson's Fifty-Ninth Alabama. "It did not take the brigade long to move back into our old position." Although Hoke's brigades now stood ready to move north, unusual activity in the Federal lines froze them in place until they could be sure that the Unionists intended no serious mischief. Not until midafternoon were Hoke's and Scales's 6,700 men on the march. They crossed the Appomattox River and continued north several miles to Dunlop's Station, the new railhead for the single-track Richmond & Petersburg line; Union artillery controlled the railroad's Petersburg depot near the river. Sufficient transportation existed for only one brigade at a time, and Field's troops occupied the cars until 6:00 P.M. Not until then did Clingman's Brigade, still led by Colonel Hector McKethan, climb on board. They disembarked at Rice's Turnout near Drewry's Bluff and trooped across the James on a pontoon bridge, arriving at Chaffin's Bluff around 10:00 P.M., about the same time the Georgians of Colquitt's Brigade started their journey at Dunlop's. Kirkland's and Hagood's brigades followed at one-hour intervals, Hagood's South Carolinians reaching Ewell's fortified camp north of the James at nine the next morning.[3]

Seven additional batteries made their way across the James during the night, adding some thirty guns to Lee's inventory. The Confederate commander hoped to transfer more ordnance to the north side, along with Rooney Lee's cavalry division, but Union activity south and southwest of Petersburg convinced him to leave those units in place. Still, the Confederates shifted about 11,700 fresh troops across the James between the afternoon of September 29 and the morning of September 30. This provided Richard Anderson, Dick Ewell, and artillery commander Porter Alexander some 16,000 men to redeem the ground lost the previous day and perhaps drive the Yankees back to their Deep Bottom bridgehead.[4]

The Rebels were not the only ones thinking offensively on September 30. Butler was fully aware that apart from the capture of the New Market Line and Fort Harrison, his attacks on the twenty-ninth had failed, and the unrealized goal of reaching Richmond remained a priority. But before he could resume the initiative, he thought it necessary to prepare for the anticipated Confederate counterattack. Shortly after 9:00 P.M. Butler apprised Grant of his dispositions and requested that a corps be sent him from the Army of the Potomac, if Meade could spare one, to guard against a Confederate force crossing the James in his rear. Grant replied a couple of hours later with his agreement to meet with Butler early the next morning but explaining that, because Meade intended to initiate an attack of his own on the thirtieth with the hope of capturing Petersburg, none of his forces could be spared.[5]

Meanwhile, Butler's weary troops continued to strengthen their newly won positions. The open gorge at Fort Harrison posed the most urgent problem. "Every available man is at work all day and night without rest or sleep," recalled a soldier in the Thirteenth New Hampshire. "The enemy had a quantity of baled hay for his horses stored in the fort, and this is rolled out and placed in line as a breast-work; timber and logs are used also, and barrels and boxes are set up and shoveled full of earth." Most of Stannard's and Paine's divisions spent the night laboring on the fortifications as engineer troops helped fabricate abatis. But while the rank and file sacrificed a night's sleep preparing a defense, Grant and Butler remained committed to resuming the offensive. "If the enemy do not re-enforce by more than a division we will give them another trial in the morning," Grant advised Butler.[6]

The two officers met at Deep Bottom as planned early on Friday. But for some reason, they decided to defer offensive action that day. Grant returned to City Point around 8:00 A.M. and informed Meade: "General Butler's forces will remain where they are for the present." Perhaps Grant thought better of launching simultaneous attacks on both his flanks, as Meade had orders to advance that morning. Maybe Butler now considered his battered army, weakened by the previous day's casualties and exhausted from a sleepless night of digging, ill prepared to risk another assault so soon. The generals are silent on the issue.[7]

In any event, apart from adding a few of the previous day's stragglers, Butler would face September 30 with the survivors who marched and fought on September 29 with one important exception. General Ord's wound proved sufficiently serious to warrant a thirty-day leave of absence, and his temporary replacement, Charles Heckman, had demonstrated little capacity to command a corps. Fortuitously, Brig. Gen. Godfrey Weitzel, the army's chief engineer, returned from a reconnaissance mission in North Carolina late on the twenty-ninth. If Butler had a pet subordinate, it had to be Weitzel. Beginning early in 1862, when Weitzel joined Butler's Gulf Coast army as a lieutenant of engineers, Butler continually promoted the young German. Weitzel possessed impressive credentials to be sure. He graduated second in the West Point class of 1855 and had shown promise as a field officer in Louisiana. So, when the twenty-eight-year-old appeared at Bermuda Hundred, Butler summoned him to the north side and, by 10:00 A.M. on September 30, placed him in command of the Eighteenth Corps. Weitzel would later express doubt about his ability to manage such a large responsibility. "I often, very often (I tell you frankly) mistrust my own abilities," he wrote his superior. "I think you are over-rating me." Nevertheless, Weitzel represented an improvement over Heckman, who returned to command of his division.[8]

As the morning wore on, Butler positioned his infantry between New Market and Kingsland Roads. Weitzel bore responsibility for Butler's left, with Stannard's division defending Fort Harrison and Heckman's brigades extending south as far as the Varina-Kingsland intersection. The Tenth Corps occupied the line from Fort Harrison north to New Market Road. Kautz guarded the army's right as far north as Darbytown Road. Butler became convinced that he now faced all of Lee's infantry save Johnson's and Mahone's Divisions. He was wrong, of course, as General Heth's troops remained in their trenches southwest of Petersburg and only Scales's Brigade from Wilcox's Division had made the trek across the James. Still, the Federal commander braced for what he thought would be an imminent and powerful attack that must be repulsed first before he could possibly resume his offensive.[9]

Lee remained committed to just such a course of action, but the question remained where to launch his assault. The army commander, accompanied by Richard Anderson and Dick Ewell, conducted a reconnaissance before dawn and evaluated intelligence provided by other observers. At some point during their ride, Ewell's horse stumbled, throwing the one-legged general painfully to the ground. Lt. Col. Moxley Sorrel, a First Corps staff officer, checked the fallen officer for broken bones, relieved to find only severe cuts and bruises around his head. Lee ordered the injured Ewell to seek medical treatment in Richmond. When he returned to the field later in the day, wrapped in bandages from his head to his neck, Ewell "resembled a mummy more than a lieutenant general," in the words of his biographer.[10]

In truth, Lee depended little on Ewell and his ill-trained troops to execute the day's offensive, so he and "Fighting Dick" Anderson continued to discuss their options. A successful blow against the exposed Union left might well isolate Butler from his connection to the river but would come to grief if Grant had

The Fifth Offensive Continues, September 29–30

dispatched reinforcements using the bridges at Aiken's Landing, a contingency Lee could not know. Attacking the right flank would entail a long march across the Union front and hazard a thrust by the bluecoats into the weakened Confederate center, opening a clear path to Richmond. This left the salient at Fort Harrison as the most attractive target. If successful there, the Confederates would regain most of their lost real estate but probably sacrifice the chance to inflict a more crippling blow. In point of fact, Union control of Fort Harrison posed little danger to Confederate fortunes, as subsequent events would demonstrate. The fort's advanced position from the rest of the new Union line left it vulnerable to enfilading fire, and the Rebels could (and would) construct a new line around Fort Harrison to connect with their intact fortifications on either end. "Why General Lee wanted to retake it has always seemed to me a puzzle," wrote Sgt. Joseph William Eggleston of the Nelson Artillery, "unless it be that his invariable rule was to fight on all possible opportunities." Perhaps at an earlier time, Marse Robert the gambler would have risked executing a flank attack for the possible reward of driving his enemy completely away from Richmond—but not now. Shortly after sunrise, orders circulated to assemble a force opposite Fort Harrison. Lee was not willing to go for broke but was equally unwilling to allow the Union gains of the previous day to go unchallenged.[11]

The gray chieftain developed his plan in consultation with Anderson, Alexander, Field, Hoke, and Colquitt. A vigorous shelling from Alexander's guns, augmented by fire from the navy's gunboats on the James, would precede the attack. After a bombardment of thirty minutes, the infantry assault would commence precisely at 2:00 P.M. Field would commit three brigades to attack from a position behind Fort Johnson, 400–500 yards northwest of Fort Harrison. Hoke would advance two of his brigades to a deep ravine, invisible to the enemy, not more than 200 yards from the fort. Field's troops would begin the charge, and Hoke would go forward when Field gained an adjacent position, meaning that both wings of attackers would crash into Fort Harrison simultaneously and from different directions.[12]

Field selected for the assault the three brigades that had recently crossed the river, leaving DuBose's and Gregg's commands to confront the Tenth Corps. Accordingly, Bowles, Bratton, and Tige Anderson left the area around Fort Gilmer between 6:00 and 8:00 A.M. and took position along the northern face of the Camp Wall west of Fort Johnson. The Georgians, in the center, were flanked on the right by Bratton's Carolinians and on their left by Bowles's Alabamans. These men left their knapsacks and accoutrements behind as ordered, carrying only their "guns, forty rounds of cartridges, and [a] canteen of water." Between nine and ten o'clock, Bratton gathered his regimental commanders and

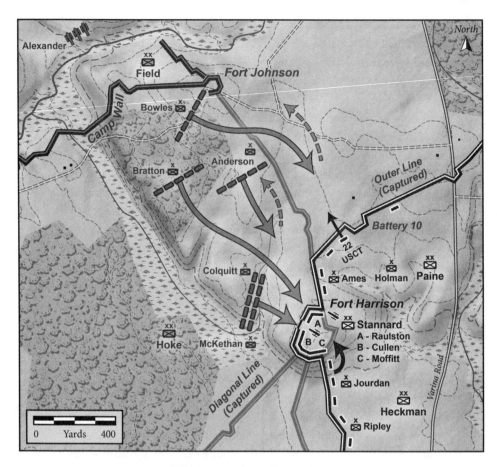

Fort Harrison, September 30, 1864

"gave full and explicit instructions," emphasizing the need to coordinate the assault with Hoke. Anderson would lead Field's attack against Fort Harrison, and Bratton would follow, while Bowles assaulted a position just northwest of the fort. Once the victorious troops reached their targets, regimental commanders would employ discretion either to pursue the defeated Yankees or to remain in the fort, depending "altogether upon the degree of disorganization which their regiments had suffered in the assault."[13]

Hoke's brigades moved up from their brief bivouacs along Osborne Pike—McKethan's Tar Heels followed by Colquitt's Georgians, the two brigades designated to assist Field. Sgt. Maj. William Henry von Eberstein of the Sixty-First North Carolina of McKethan's command overheard two naval officers chatting just before his regiment departed for their jump-off point. "What a pity to have such men cut and shot to pieces as they are going to be," one of the officers

The Fifth Offensive Continues, September 29–30

lamented. "If the General knew the ground as well as I did, which they had to charge over, he would never order it," replied the other. These remarks set von Eberstein to thinking. "We are going to catch the devil and many of us will be lost." Hoke worried that the artillery bombardment would threaten his own men more than the Federals, as so many of the Confederates' explosive charges were faulty, causing the shells to detonate prematurely. Colonel McKethan considered the entire enterprise a mistake in light of the improvements made by the Federals overnight. But these protests, whether forcefully conveyed to Lee or not, failed to dissuade the Confederate commander, and the Carolinians and Georgians filed down ready to enter the sheltering ravine close to Fort Harrison.[14]

Several idle hours passed as the anxious Rebels endured an increasingly sweltering day. The skies clouded and humidity levels rose with a promise of rain. By 11:00 A.M., Alexander had posted some thirty guns and mortars in good position to bombard Fort Harrison. Shortly thereafter the guns on board the Confederate vessels opened, aided by spotters on shore who signaled adjustments to the range. Many of these shells fell short, however, endangering the waiting Rebel infantry more than the enemy, just as Hoke had feared. Alexander's guns roared into action around noon, and although they avoided imperiling friendly troops, most of their shots went long, sparing the Union defenders, who continued to strengthen their works with renewed urgency, convinced more than ever that an attack was imminent.[15]

Stannard's division reoccupied Fort Harrison about 8:00 A.M., relieving Paine's African Americans, who had spent the night working on the fortifications with particular emphasis on closing the gorge. Stannard's men took up where the Black troops left off, creating a "sort of horseshoe line of rifle pits to protect our flanks," according to Sgt. John C. Ladd of the Twenty-First Connecticut. The soldiers concentrated on the left and center portions of the gorge, assuming that the assaults would come from the southwest. About a third of the gorge remained virtually unprotected—the precise position targeted by Field.[16]

Not long before the Confederates began their shelling, orders came for Lieutenant Colonel Raulston's brigade to move right to this vulnerable portion of the fort. "We have here no cover whatever," observed a worried New Hampshire man. Immediately, the brigade began using "dippers, bayonets and sticks, each man for himself, throwing up little mounds of earth for protection." They managed to move a few small logs into place, cannibalized from abandoned soldier huts, creating a shelter "about a foot high, with a few shovelfuls of earth thrown up to keep them in place." Before they could improve on this feeble foundation, the Rebel guns reopened, and engineering work gave way to a search for shelter from the incoming rounds. Cullen's brigade formed on Raulston's left. On Cullen's left Burnham's brigade, now led by Lt. Col. Stephen Moffitt of the 96th New York, anchored Stannard's left flank. Moffitt positioned the 118th New York, its men armed with Spencer repeaters, at the front, opposite the ravine that McKethan and Colquitt would soon populate. Paine's men occupied the reversed Outer Line directly north of Fort Harrison, while Jourdan's brigade of Heckman's division stretched south from the fort's southeastern corner.[17]

Shortly before 1:00 P.M., Hoke advanced McKethan and Colquitt to the sheltering depression a short distance from the fort. Field ordered Anderson's and Bratton's brigades to glide through the woods south of Fort Johnson, halting them a good deal farther from Fort Harrison to keep them concealed. He then, at 1:45 P.M., told Anderson to move ahead to a shallow swale short of the fort and lay down, with Bratton to follow. Assuming this maneuver would consume fifteen minutes, both wings of the attack force would begin their assault at 2:00 P.M. as ordered. If Lee's plan was to succeed, it was imperative that all four brigades charge simultaneously.[18]

Alexander's guns, joined again by the navy, began their scheduled bombardment at 1:30 P.M., right on time. "The scene now baffles any description of my pen," recorded Pvt. John H. Westervelt of the First New York Engineers. "The shot and shell poured in on the hill and fort faster than you could count them by tens. The hill was torn up like a tornado and the roar was deafening." Alexander, fully aware of the infantry's role, made certain that his cannonade would not impede the assault that would begin immediately after his guns fell silent. Capt. William Burgwyn of McKethan's command watched in awe as "the ground shook with the mighty concussion" of Alexander's fusillade, while "smoke enveloped the field," lingering in the humid air. The thin line of Union pickets that had advanced in front of Fort Harrison sought cover, although the Confederate shells inflicted few casualties. The Union guns positioned along the line replied in what proved to be a most spirited exchange of iron. Then, as quickly as it started, the Rebel fire ceased.[19]

This was the signal for Anderson and Bratton to advance to a point parallel with Hoke's two crouching brigades. Field explained: "I directed General Anderson, commanding my leading brigade, to move up as close as possible to the work and let his men lay down, so as at the proper moment spring up and reach the work simultaneously with Hoke, who had much less distance to charge than I. General Anderson, failing to inform his men of his intention, they mistook the advance for an assault and instead of halting and laying down, rushed forward to attack." The Georgians advanced with a yell and "were soon past control."[20]

The Fifth Offensive Continues, September 29–30

Bratton, who had carefully explained the battle plan to his obedient regimental commanders, watched in dismay as Anderson's premature attack drew Federal fire. "To give my promised support and carry out my part in the arrangement it was necessary for my brigade to file out at the double-quick, and, without halting, or even moderating to quick time, to move . . . in line against the enemy," Bratton reported. "I deplored this and felt that my men were not having a fair chance, but it was too late to give new orders and instructions." The South Carolinians arose and began their charge. They faced a dash of at least 500 yards across ground only thinly studded with trees and in perfect range of the waiting defenders. At first Bratton and Anderson met only shelling, but as they drew closer to the fort, the Union cannoneers switched to canister. Then, as the surviving Confederates closed to within 200 yards, "there issued forth from the frowning parapet a furious storm of bullets such as would appall the stoutest heart." Nineteen-year-old Col. James Hagood, commander of the First South Carolina and younger brother of Brig. Gen. Johnson Hagood, thought the battle noise "sounded like the magnified roar of a thousand kettle drums."[21]

Fortunately for the Rebels, the cannoneers in Fort Harrison soon exhausted their ammunition. Now all that stood between Field and the fort was Stannard's infantry, Raulston's troops standing shoulder to shoulder behind their pitiful excuse for a breastwork. What Bratton knew to be a disjointed advance appeared to the waiting Federals as a "long line of gray" advancing "as steadily as if on a gala day parade" and emerging "from the woods with flags flying, and the swords of his officers waving and flashing." The men of the Thirteenth New Hampshire, seeing this large force running resolutely toward them, planted their regimental flag in the center of their formation and began singing "The Battle Cry of Freedom" as both a tonic for taut nerves and an expression of determination equal to that of their approaching foes.[22]

When the Confederates reached within easy rifle range, a tremendous volley felled many of the Georgians and Carolinians, whose ranks had begun to meld. This proved too much for Anderson's troops. They halted, absorbed the rain of minié balls and Spencer rounds, then turned, panic-stricken, making for the shelter of the woods from whence they came. This, of course, further disordered Bratton's men as the Georgians streamed through them. "Our regimental organizations were so broken up that it was impossible to proceed any longer with the harmony so essential in giving momentum to bodies of men," explained Colonel Hagood, "and the fearful destruction of life in our ranks, by the enemy's rapidly succeeding vollies, would not suffer us to pause in order to reform." Some of the Carolinians retreated, albeit with a bit less haste than their Georgia comrades. A portion of Bratton's men, primarily from the 1st and

6th South Carolina and the 2nd South Carolina Rifles, managed to maintain their momentum. They ran the gauntlet toward defilade in the low ground immediately below Fort Harrison, enduring blizzards of rifle fire. "It seemed impossible for a flea to crawl unhurt across the deadly space we had traversed," wrote Hagood. The 118th New York along with the 10th New Hampshire, armed with their Spencers, contributed much of this mayhem from their position to Bratton's right. "Our boys were working their self-shooters for all they were worth," boasted Corporal Baker. "They were surprised at the terrible hail of lead that was being hurled among them by the small number of men they saw on our low line of earthworks we had hastily constructed the night before." Not forty yards short of the fort, these determined Carolinians implored the men behind them, who were still braving the fire, to join in a final push through the defenders. But that was too much to ask of the beleaguered Rebels. Those in advance joined their less valorous mates in retreating across the killing ground. Field's attack, launched in contravention to orders, had failed.[23]

Its only notable achievement was the wounding of General Stannard. The forty-three-year-old Vermonter had operated a foundry in Saint Albans and earned a colonelcy in the state militia before the war. After service in two Vermont regiments, his capture at Harpers Ferry in 1862, and his subsequent exchange, Stannard gained promotion to brigadier general. His brigade played a key role in the repulse of Pickett's Charge at Gettysburg, where he received the first of several battle wounds. During Field's attack, Stannard mounted a huge traverse in Fort Harrison from which he could observe his three brigades, "pacing up and down like an angry lion." A bullet hit him just above his right elbow, whirling him around and knocking him to the ground. His devoted troops, relieved that the wound had not been fatal, removed their general to safety, and later, doctors amputated his arm, terminating his military career. "He was every inch a soldier," wrote one admiring subordinate, "brave, fearless and as firm as a rock." Colonel Cullen moved up to division command, but Butler requested a more qualified replacement, and Grant promised to send him William Humphrey from the Ninth Corps.[24]

The unwavering Union defense primarily explains Field's failure, but the Confederates contributed to their own futility. The third element of Field's strike force, Bowles's brigade, moved left according to orders and engaged a portion of the Twenty-Second USCT that occupied a minor bulge in the line north of Fort Harrison. Here the Alabamans remained until expelled by a countercharge, offering no relief to the rest of their division. More importantly, neither of Hoke's units attacked in concert with Field.[25]

The Fifth Offensive Continues, September 29–30

It is easy to explain, but difficult to justify, Hoke's decision to wait until 2:00 P.M. to begin his attack. To be sure, that was the hour designated for the coordinated Rebel assault, but Anderson and then Bratton went forward some fifteen minutes earlier and were slaughtered while McKethan and Colquitt waited idly a few hundred yards from the fort. This was not the only time in the campaign that Hoke failed to cooperate, but why he waited to launch his assault until Field's men had been vanquished defies logic. But wait he did. Furthermore, neither Dick Anderson, the ostensive overall commander of the offensive, nor General Lee, who watched Field's tragedy unfold, intervened to halt what had obviously become a botched operation. Promptly at 2:00 P.M., McKethan emerged from his sheltering ravine and made for Fort Harrison.[26]

"As we started the whole Yankee line opened on us in plain view," wrote Captain Burgwyn, "and I suppose they were three lines deep behind their works and as they were all armed with seven shooters the fire was awful." McKethan's regiments maintained their alignment until they reached the base of the fort, where their momentum ceased. Not unlike Field's men, McKethan's sought refuge among the few remaining soldier huts or whatever depression or vegetation they could find. "We had to charge through a ravine grown up with bryers close to the battery," recalled von Eberstein. "There were few of us who got there. The Yankees had complete control of us."[27]

Colquitt's Georgians also emerged from the gully, only to witness the deadly fate of the North Carolinians. "The fort was nearly a semi-circle with the convex side next to the attacking party so constructed as to allow two lines of battle to face at the same time which brought an enfilading fire from each flank converging in the center," explained Lt. George Warthen of the Twenty-Eighth Georgia. "I had 13 guns in the fight had two killed and five wounded." Captain Washington Dunn of the Twenty-Seventh Georgia considered the brigade's position "as bad a place as I was ever in." Bratton sought out Hoke and promised to advance again in conjunction with Colquitt and McKethan, but in the end the South Carolinians failed to launch a second assault. Hoke withheld Kirkland, Hagood, and Scales as well, ensuring the profitless sacrifice of his other two brigades.[28]

Just prior to Hoke's advance, Colonel Jourdan, accompanied by his two New York regiments, shifted north into Fort Harrison and, by virtue of his seniority, replaced Cullen in command of its defenders. Some of the division's troops had exhausted their ammunition but were resupplied when Stannard's acting ordnance officer, Capt. John Brydon, courageously led an ammunition wagon into the fort. The Federals perceived three or four separate assaults, but every witness agreed that the Rebel attacks wilted as they approached the ramparts. "Give them hell boys,—sock it to them fellows," screamed a captain to his contingent of the Ninety-Sixth New York. "The most invincible courage could not stand such a fire as our brave boys poured into them," wrote a soldier in the Twenty-First Connecticut. "And the next tremendous volley caused them . . . to 'change their minds' and more quickly than I can write it, a portion of the column faced about and engaged in the 'pursuit of happiness' at a much higher velocity than the illustrious seeker of the same."[29]

Not all of the attackers risked fleeing. Some of McKethan's men remained huddled beneath the fort in a small ravine covered with scraggy underbrush, hoping for a rescuing attack or, failing that, waiting for darkness to conceal their escape. "From the time we lay down about 3:00 P.M. till dusk there we lay about seventy yards from the enemy line, some entirely exposed and some shielded from view by some weeds and grass," wrote Burgwyn, "but all entirely at the mercy of the enemy." As night approached and rain poured down, some of the Confederates waved a white handkerchief or similar token of surrender and leapt up toward the fort, a few of them falling victim to Confederate sharpshooters, who shot their own men by error in the gloom. Capt. Enoch Goss of the Thirteenth New Hampshire led a small body of the First Division sharpshooters over the works just before dark, rounding up the remainder of McKethan's men who had neither surrendered nor skulked away in the shadows. "Nearly two hundred were thus secured, while the ground in our front was thickly strewn with killed and wounded," remembered one Unionist. "It was a sad day's work for the Johnnies." A Tennessee soldier agreed. "It was horrible to see the sufferings the federals inflicted in this action."[30]

Casualty figures bear this out. Bratton engaged 1,294 men and lost 377 in killed and wounded, including those of the wounded who became prisoners. Only estimates for Anderson's and Bowle's losses exist, raising Field's total casualties to about 472. McKethan's brigade numbered 857, of whom 455 were either killed, wounded, or captured, including nearly 300 of his Tar Heels who surrendered or were otherwise made prisoners. "The brigade felt the losses sustained in this assault the balance of the war," noted Captain Burgwyn. "It could never recruit up its depleted ranks." Lt. Edmund J. Jones, the only officer left unscathed in the Thirty-First North Carolina, told his mother, "the Brigade is literally cut to pieces." Colquitt suffered some 222 losses of all categories. Thus, about 1,150 Confederate soldiers were sacrificed in the poorly executed assaults. "The attack came off as we expected and half of our Regiment has gone to their eternal home," mourned Pvt. John Kennedy Coleman of the Sixth South Carolina. "Never again will they answer to their names, never again will they fight for their country that was more dear to them than life itself. They fill a soldier's grave—may they rest in peace."[31]

No one regretted the failure more than the army commander. Lee watched the tragedy unfold from near Fort Gilmer and had ridden forward to encourage Hoke's survivors as they staggered back to their jump-off points. "I had always thought General Lee was a very cold and unemotional man, but he showed lots of feeling and excitement on that occasion," thought one Confederate. When the attacks concluded, Lee once again rode up and down the lines comforting his defeated men by asserting that Fort Harrison was not all that important anyway. "This talk cheered the men, and they, although worn out with fatigue, replied by cheering their beloved general." That evening at the Chaffin house, Lee reviewed the day's events with his staff and several other officers, including John Pemberton. When the former lieutenant general commented that he supposed Lee would try to take the fort the next day, Lee demurred. "General Pemberton," he replied, using the officer's previous title, "I made my effort this morning and failed, losing many killed and wounded. I . . . shall have no more blood shed at the fort unless you can show me a practical plan of capture; perhaps you can. I shall be glad to have it." Pemberton remained silent.[32]

Lee informed the Richmond authorities of the day's events in a brief telegram, conveyed in the passive voice. "An attempt was made this afternoon to retake Battery Harrison," he wrote Secretary Seddon, "which, though partly successful, failed." Other Confederates demonstrated less reluctance to locate the blame for this tactical disaster, although the alleged culprits were many. Tige Anderson and Robert Hoke provided the most obvious targets. "It is not hard to discover the causes of failure," wrote Colonel Hagood of the First South Carolina, "they obtrude themselves in almost every point of the narrative." "General Anderson failing to inform his men of his intention, they mistook the advance for an assault and instead of halting and laying down rushed forward to the attack," wrote Field. "Hoke, though aware I was attacking prematurely, waited for the moment agreed upon, and thus the concentrated fire of the fort was poured upon my troops." An officer on Field's staff wrote home: "Genl Lee's plans, perfectly simple, failed through the tardiness of a Maj. Genl who wouldn't act in concert with Genl Field. This is the second time that Genl Hoke has failed to support our movements." Captain Burgwyn, in turn, blamed Field for not succeeding in his attack, as well as holding Kirkland and Johnson Hagood culpable for failing to support the rest of the division. Colonel McKethan pointed to Colquitt for his lackluster effort, while Colquitt criticized his own troops. "You deceived me," he is supposed to have cried. "You have sacrificed this North

Carolina Brigade." At least two of the participants blamed the army commander himself. "Genl Lee had selected the most exposed and dangerous position for our Brigade to charge," wrote Lt. Amos. W. Murray of the Sixth Georgia. Sergeant Eggleston thought that once Field's attacks failed, Lee should have halted Hoke's assault. "Why he did not forbid their charge and re-arrange the attack I never knew," he lamented.[33]

Many Southern analysts found the dedication and stamina of the fighting men themselves unequal to an otherwise achievable venture. "Our troops have fought so long behind breastworks that they have lost all spirit in attacking or they would have carried it easily," thought artillery commander Alexander. A Richmond newspaper reported that Lee's men "did not attack with their usual impetuosity," and the commanding general's aide, Lt. Col. Walter H. Taylor, blamed the setback on a lack of energy. But in hindsight General Alexander would conclude that regardless of the mistakes, "it was . . . almost a hopeless task," and General Bratton agreed that the mission of retaking Fort Harrison was "too much for human valor."[34]

The capture and successful defense of Fort Harrison was a debt paid in blood by the Army of the James. The fighting on September 29 and 30 cost Butler 3,327 casualties, including 383 killed and 645 captured or missing. The Eighteenth Corps accounted for 70 percent of the losses, including a number of high-ranking officers such as Ord, Stannard, and Burnham, whose name would now adorn the captured bastion. Paine's African American troops sustained an outsized portion of these casualties during their attacks at New Market Heights and Fort Gilmer.[35]

As would be expected, the Federal participants exulted over their relatively easy triumph on September 30. "Night fell on a bloody field; but Fort Harrison and the intrenchments had been held and saved, and a brilliant victory perched upon the Union banners," wrote a New Yorker. A New Hampshire man thought that the defense of Fort Harrison was "the coolest, sharpest, most deliberate, and most 'business-like' battle" his regiment had ever witnessed. Sgt. Simeon Gallup of the First Rhode Island Light Artillery spoke for a number of bluecoats who considered the victory that day "quite a step nearer Richmond than ever before."[36]

Pvt. Lyman Bell Sperry of the Ninety-Eighth New York joined other members of his regiment the next morning "going over the battlefield & picking up trophies," including a battle flag and several officers' swords. But the vast majority of Union witnesses felt too much revulsion to traverse the horrible, if by now familiar, postcombat scene that greeted them with the morning light. "Our front was littered with dead and wounded," wrote a New Yorker. "In little

The Fifth Offensive Continues, September 29–30

gullies and slightly protected places where wounded had crawled, we could see bodies in heaps." Capt. George Tobey Anthony of a New York battery admitted to his brother: "Language cannot describe the scene of a Battle field. I doubt if any form of mutilation can be inflicted upon the human body that I have not witnessed, or any measure of suffering that can be picturd out to man that has not been Expeencd." General Stannard would tell Colonel Ripley that never in his whole army career, including the famous Confederate charge on July 3 at Gettysburg, had he ever seen "such sickening slaughter as those breechloaders made of those Rebel columns." As many as fifty Union ambulances worked through the night and into the next morning transporting Confederate and Union wounded to hospitals in the rear. Some of the dead remained on the field for several days before the antagonists agreed on a truce. Lt. Thomas Porterfield of the Second Pennsylvania Heavy Artillery took charge of a burial squad. "Its memories are with me yet," he admitted after the war. "The sight and stench was something awful; they lay in all sorts of positions—sitting, laying and kneeling, piled together and separate." Capt. George Naylor Julian of the Thirteenth New Hampshire called the rotting Confederate dead "most disgusting objects."[37]

Rain continued to pour through the night and into the next morning. "Almost everybody is drenched and mud is redundant," groused a member of Butler's staff. Yet the army commander had stumbled upon an abandoned Confederate camp, complete with a number of creature comforts, which his entourage incorporated into a snug assemblage of tents. "Forgetful of native fastidiousness, everybody benefitted . . . by the protection which this stained, mildewed, vermin-suggestive camp equipage of the rebels affords." The Eighteenth Corps provost marshal delivered nearly 300 prisoners to Butler's headquarters, assuming that there would be an adequate guard posted nearby. But only Butler's staff and a handful of orderlies were present at this makeshift bivouac, and the orderlies, "changing their clothes, appeared amongst [the prisoners] quite often," until several companies from the Tenth Corps arrived to provide adequate security.[38]

At 7:50 on the evening of the thirtieth, Butler informed Grant that the attacks of the day "appear to be directed to the recapture of the big fort. It is evident that that capture troubles the enemy much; indeed, the prisoners say they are told it shall be taken if it costs every man they have got and all we have got." Once again he appealed for reinforcements. "We are much weaker than you suppose," he explained. But no reinforcements would be coming from Meade's army. "Be well on your guard to act defensively," Grant replied. "If the enemy are forced from Petersburg they may push to oppose you." His attention was now focused on the complementary offensive southwest of Petersburg that had already achieved some success.[39]

Grant assigned the Army of the Potomac a contingent mission at the outset of his Fifth Petersburg Offensive. Meade's initial responsibility was simply to persuade the Confederates that he intended to launch a new thrust westward toward Lee's remaining lines of communication—Boydton Plank Road and the South Side Railroad. This ruse, hoped Grant, would prevent the Rebels from detaching troops to counter Butler's push for Richmond or reinforce Early in the Shenandoah Valley. Meade quietly moved a portion of the Second Corps into the trenches vacated by the Tenth Corps and paraded a division of the Ninth Corps "at places within view of the enemy," from the Avery house westward to the Gurley house, in accordance with Grant's wishes. Trains on the military railroad ran hourly, festooned with soldiers atop the cars and hanging from the open doorways so the Rebels would see them, only to secrete themselves on the inside during the return trip. On September 27 Grant informed Meade of Butler's impending offensive and outlined Meade's role, although as was his habit, the general-in-chief granted the Pennsylvanian extensive latitude to execute his responsibilities. The Army of the Potomac would be under arms at dawn on September 29, with sixty rounds of ammunition and three- or four-days' rations. Meade would still do his best to freeze Rebel reinforcements from moving across the James, Butler's offensive still holding primacy in Grant's mind. Yet should Butler's gambit stall and a significant volume of Confederates depart for Chaffin's Bluff, Meade was to turn his demonstration into an actual attempt to reach the railroad or capture Petersburg. Grant also reminded him to defend his existing lines by retaining, at a minimum, sufficient garrisons in the forts to repel any Confederate assault.[40]

Meade issued the requisite instructions to defend all the enclosed works between the Appomattox River and the Weldon Railroad. "Division commanders will impress upon the commanders of inclosed works the necessity of holding these works under every contingency," read General Orders No. 36, "no matter what may occur in the connecting lines, the forts are to be held." On September 28 he circulated orders for the demonstration Grant desired. Warren would provide two of his divisions and Parke would contribute his two White divisions to the mission, the remainder of these corps to garrison the forts west of Jerusalem Plank Road. Hancock would retain responsibility for the line between the Appomattox and Jerusalem Plank Road, while Gregg's cavalry division screened the infantry and helped gauge Confederate strength. Artillery from both the Fifth and Ninth Corps would accompany the infantry, along with sufficient transportation to resupply the troops with ammunition and forage for the battery animals. "Our destination is doubtless once more to the left,"

Colonel Wainwright recorded in his diary, "& we are alive with anticipations of what may be the result."[41]

On September 28 General Hancock detected the unusual commotion incident to Hoke's departure from the works east of Petersburg and Johnson's return. The Federals made enough of a fuss to put the Rebels on alert, Johnson having received orders to anticipate enemy aggression in his sector. "Every preparation was made for an attack," wrote Pvt. George J. Johnston of Gracie's Sixtieth Alabama. "Men counted off and disposed, hand Grenades & ammunition issued and the morning sun rose brilliant upon our firm & undaunted line." At the other end of their defenses, the Confederates were busy constructing the Squirrel Level Line. Lee had ordered the construction of these fortifications on September 20, and by the twenty-eighth, they were complete, if modest in scale. The left of these breastworks rested just east of its namesake road, about half a mile south of the unfinished Confederate works that lay a few hundred yards in front of and parallel to Boydton Plank Road. From there the Squirrel Level Line ran southwest almost three miles, ending along an unnamed farm road. A number of small forts along its length provided platforms for artillery. Fort Cherry guarded the left, where the works crossed Squirrel Level Road. About 1,000 yards southwest stood Fort Bratton, and another half mile beyond that stood Fort Archer, an enclosed, five-sided bastion adjacent to Church Road on William Peebles's farm. The line then ran more west than south, terminating at a partially completed work styled Fort MacRae.[42]

General Warren endeavored to ascertain what resistance he could expect as his men marched west. Confederate deserters reported the existence of the Squirrel Level Line as well as the primary defenses south of Boydton Plank Road, swearing these were defended by "considerable infantry." That may have been true on the morning of September 29, but Lee's decision to strip his right flank in favor of reinforcing the north side of the James left the Squirrel Level Line in the hands of James Dearing's small cavalry brigade. Dearing had proven himself a reliable fighter during the Beefsteak Raid and elsewhere, but he had fallen ill after his return from Cocke's Mill—"I was in bed and unable to ride," he informed his wife—leaving the brigade under the command of Col. Joel R. Griffin of the Eighth Georgia Cavalry. This young officer, a lawyer in Macon before the war, was ill suited for the enhanced responsibility of leading a brigade of around 1,500 men. He placed the Fourth North Carolina Cavalry on his far left, with the Seventh Confederate Cavalry joining his Georgians to defend the line on either side of Fort Archer, where the four guns of Captain Graham's Petersburg Artillery unlimbered. This skeleton force would soon confront four full infantry divisions and their associated ordnance.[43]

That force included Charles Griffin's and Romeyn B. Ayres's divisions of Warren's corps, supplemented by J. William Hofmann's brigade of Samuel Crawford's division. General Parke contributed Orlando Willcox's and Robert Potter's divisions. The remainder of the infantry—Hancock's corps, Ferrero's division, and the rest of Crawford's brigades—garrisoned the line from the Appomattox to the Weldon Railroad. All but one of Gregg's cavalry regiments would aid Meade's mobile forces, whose mission on the morning of September 29 remained entirely dependent on Lee's reaction to Butler's offensive. When the Confederate commander ordered Hoke and Scales to join Field's men north of the James, that left only two brigades of Wilcox's Division, along with Johnson's, Heth's, and Mahone's commands, to protect the entire Petersburg front. The Petersburg Militia, under Lt. Col. Fletcher Archer, turned out, along with all the detailed men and noncombatant troops the Rebels could muster to supplement the veterans. "We have ordered all the militia out of Petersburg and all the cooks and pioneers are ordered in the ditches," wrote Surgeon William J. Mosely of the Tenth Georgia Battalion. "All the convalescents from the Hospital," too. Once Lee departed for the north side, A. P. Hill assumed command at Petersburg.[44]

Because Meade's license to attack depended upon evidence that the Confederate defenses around Petersburg had been weakened, he dispatched his cavalry to discover what they could about the Rebels' dispositions. Until such information became available, he would spend the morning of September 29 biding his time. At 1:30 that afternoon Grant informed the general, from his temporary command post at Deep Bottom, "re-enforcements are beginning to come from Petersburg. I doubt whether it will be advisable for you to make any advance this evening," although characteristically, he left that decision up to Meade. The army commander replied two hours later that Gregg had "found the enemy in force," and his signal officers suggested that the Confederates remained strongly entrenched in his front. Meade concluded that the reinforcements Grant discerned were probably only Hoke's reserve division. "I shall not therefore make a movement to the left to-day," he agreed, but "shall be prepared to advance at daylight to-morrow." Orders circulated to Warren and Parke to be ready to move at dawn, but late that night Meade temporized. "My signal officer reports that not over 7,000 infantry have been observed moving toward Richmond, and that nearly 5,000 have moved to our left," he wrote Grant. "I do not see indications sufficient to justify my making an attempt on the South Side Railroad." He claimed, with significant underestimation, that the four full divisions designated for his offensive numbered only 16,000 troops, far fewer than the force available to him in August when he seized the Weldon Railroad. Grant continued to provide his subordinate with leeway, telling Meade that he need not prepare to advance until 8:00 the next morning, and then only if "you find the enemy still further reduced, or if ordered." He also abandoned any notion of targeting the South Side Railroad but still hoped that if Meade found reason to risk an assault, he would follow up all the way to Petersburg.[45]

Meade's troopers were the only element of his army that saw action on September 29. Gregg committed almost his entire division to this reconnaissance, leaving only the Sixteenth Pennsylvania Cavalry behind to patrol the ground east of the Weldon Railroad. Gregg assembled the rest of Charles Smith's Second Brigade and the entirety of General Davies's First Brigade, riding west and then south on Halifax Road. His ten regiments and two batteries, numbering more than 4,300 soldiers, sought both to ascertain the location and strength of the enemy south and west of Warren's flank and to contribute to the goal of freezing Confederate troops at Petersburg.[46]

The Federal horsemen made an early start, and by 7:00 A.M., Gregg reached a westbound byway styled Wyatt, or Lower Church, Road just north of Reams' Station. Gregg hoped to effect a crossing of several tributaries of Rowanty Creek and reach Vaughan Road, a more substantial thoroughfare that led northeast and perhaps around the Confederate right. Gregg sent the First New Jersey Cavalry south toward Reams' Station and directed Smith's brigade to ride west. The Jerseymen charged through Reams' Station "with a shout, such as has become characteristic" of the regiment, driving away a few Rebel pickets and capturing a handful of men. Davies then probed ahead with the balance of his brigade and established picket lines at Reams' Station and westward out Depot Road, where they remained for the balance of the day.[47]

Smith's troopers, with Gregg at their head, forged west across Arthur's Swamp and reached Vaughan Road by 10:45 A.M., encountering sporadic, light resistance from Confederate cavalry. The Federals pushed on southwest, crossing Hatcher's Run and reaching Armstrong's Mill, where they destroyed the telegraph line that connected the Confederate railhead at Stony Creek with Petersburg and scattered a camp of dismounted cavalry. Three hours later Gregg had advanced north on Duncan Road within half a mile of the Squirrel Level Line, where the presence of Confederate troops halted further progress. Gregg now determined to return to the McDowell farm, just west of the Wyatt house, and from there probe north on Vaughan Road toward a country meetinghouse called Poplar Spring Church.[48]

Wade Hampton's two divisions had camps along the route leading from Stony Creek to Petersburg. Rooney Lee's two brigades—Barringer's and Davis's—bivouacked west of Rowanty Creek on the Confederates' military

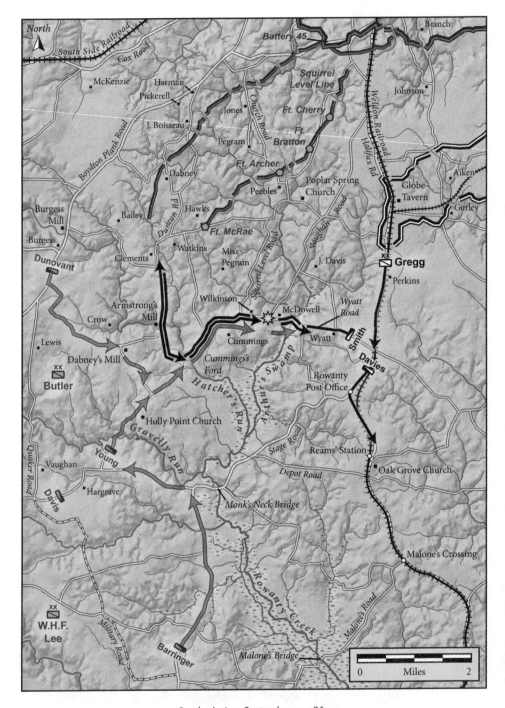

Cavalry Action, September 29, 1864

road, with Davis at the military road's intersection with Quaker Road and Barringer to the south, west of Malone's Bridge. Young's Brigade of Butler's Division camped northeast of Davis along Vaughan Road, and Dunovant's South Carolinians rested near Burgess Mill on Boydton Plank Road. General Lee had summoned his son's division to the north side of the James, squelching Hampton's plan for a grand divisional review that morning. Rooney's troopers had started for the north side when Gregg's reconnaissance prompted Hampton to recall them.[49]

Once Gregg surrendered the initiative and started back the way he had come, Hampton called on Dunovant and Young, supported by Barringer, to pursue the retiring Yankees. About 4:00 P.M. Butler's troopers assailed Smith's skirmish line, which withdrew to the main Federal defensive position around the McDowell house. Barringer promptly dismounted the two regiments with him, the Second and Fifth North Carolina Cavalry. Capt. James F. Hart's Battery of horse artillery unlimbered two of its guns. These cannoneers had been recuperating along the Rapidan River in central Virginia and had just returned to the front when they were called into action. Preston Chew, Hampton's chief of artillery, ordered the guns to open and challenged his cannoneers to knock the Union artillery opposite them "into a cocked hat." Cpl. William J. Verdier, in charge of gun number 1, launched three shots, the third one exploding a caisson loaded with ammunition, avenging the loss of one of their own ammunition vehicles several months earlier.[50]

Hampton now dismounted all of his available troopers and sent them forward in a charge. Young and Dunovant aimed for the Union center and right, while the Tar Heels, under the direct leadership of Col. William P. Roberts, assaulted the Yankee left held by the Fourth and Thirteenth Pennsylvania Cavalry. The North Carolinians drove the Pennsylvanians back, only to have the First Maine Cavalry arrive to limit the damage. Gregg appealed to Warren for help, and the Fifth Corps commander dispatched Edgar M. Gregory's brigade from Griffin's division. The Federals withdrew to a line of hasty works near the Wyatt house, where the contest continued until the gathering darkness finally silenced the guns. Gregory arrived after the fighting had run its course. The Confederates certainly had the best of this little fight, called the Battle of Wyatt's Farm. Butler restored his picket line protecting Lee's communications from Stony Creek, while Barringer withdrew to reunite with Davis along Boydton Plank Road. Gregg recalled Davies's men and had them develop a picket line from Wyatt's down to Reams' Station, while Smith withdrew to regroup. The Federals lost several dozen men in this sharp cavalry engagement, while Hampton's casualties were minimal.[51]

espite Hampton's success in thwarting Gregg's probe, the Confederates faced a critical situation on the night of September 29–30. Lee had stripped the Petersburg front of nine infantry brigades—three-eighths of his available strength—to counter Butler's offensive north of the James. This left only fifteen infantry brigades to defend the extended Petersburg lines, along with Pickett's diminished force on the Howlett Line at Bermuda Hundred. Powell Hill now faced a possible Union attack—it might come at any place along the line or around his right flank—with just three divisions and Lane's and McGowan's Brigades of Wilcox's command. Hill counted only 20,200 infantry and artillery at Petersburg in addition to Hampton's cavalry, a fraction of the three full Federal corps that opposed him.[52]

Hill opted to hold Heth's Division near Battery 45 on Boydton Plank Road as a mobile reserve to respond to any Yankee initiative, including the possibility of joining forces with Lee across the James. He left Johnson to man the works from the Appomattox River around to the Crater. From there Mahone's Division stretched west all the way to the Weldon Railroad, while Griffin's cavalry held the Squirrel Level Line. These dispositions, the best that Hill could devise, reflected the Rebels' desperate situation. Clearly, Richmond must be defended and the Federal thrust north of the James at least contained, if not repulsed. This left the Petersburg lines thinly held and subject to collapse in the event of any determined attack. More likely than frontal assaults, thought the Confederate high command, the Federals would swing west to reach Lee's communications along Boydton Plank Road and the South Side Railroad. If Dearing's men folded before Heth or other infantry arrived, or if these reinforcements proved inadequate to protect the Rebel supply lines, Petersburg would be in peril, cut off from outside succor. Grant had employed the same strategy in July and August, failing utterly in July and achieving only partial success the following month. But this, his Fifth Petersburg Offensive, seemed different. Butler's initial victories had sputtered out, but hope remained that his limited gains had created an opportunity for Meade's army to change the campaign's calculus in the most decisive manner to date.[53]

Lee fully appreciated this crisis. Even if Petersburg should fall, either through a coup de main or by the severance of its supply corridors, the Confederate chieftain must preserve his army. He ordered the removal of some of the military stockpiles in Petersburg and had a new pontoon bridge constructed upstream from town, near Battersea plantation, to expedite the possible retreat of his troops on the right. Doctor John Herbert Claiborne, the medical director in Petersburg, began removing patients from the military hospitals to safer facilities farther west. "The evacuation of the city is growing less improbable every day," wrote one soldier. The Petersburg firebrand Edmund Ruffin agreed: "The residents of Petersburg think that the town is to be evacuated."[54]

Fortunately for the Confederates, General Meade failed to fully appreciate the Rebels' tenuous situation. The reports he received suggested that Lee had not sufficiently diminished his Petersburg manpower to warrant a bold advance, and Gregg's experience on the twenty-ninth seemed to confirm that the Confederates remained in considerable strength. "I can throw a force out to Poplar Spring Church and engage the enemy, if you deem advisable," Meade wrote Grant late on the night of the twenty-ninth, "but this will only be extending our lines without a commensurate object, unless . . . engaging the enemy is so deemed." Grant so deemed. At 8:15 the following morning, the general-in-chief ordered Meade to "move out now and see if an advantage can be gained. It seems to me the enemy must be weak enough at one or the other place to let us in." Here, Grant demonstrated the tenacity, although sometimes misplaced, that marked his generalship throughout the campaign, and Meade—loyal if more risk averse than his superior—promptly obeyed. "In accordance with your dispatch . . . I have sent orders to Warren to move out to the Poplar Spring Church, and to Parke to endeavor to get around and come up on Warren's left, and, if practicable, outflank the enemy," he replied. Before 9:00 A.M. Meade sent instructions to the Fifth Corps commander to advance to the little church "and endeavor to secure the intersection of the Squirrel Level road, so as to enable us to gain a position on the right of the enemy." Meade told Parke to "try to open a route across the swamp to vicinity of Miss Pegram's, below Poplar Spring Church, and take post on Warren's left." Gregg received orders to ride west toward Wilkinson's house on Squirrel Level Road south of the infantry. Meade's erroneous maps underestimated the mile and a half between Miss Pegram's and Poplar Spring Church.[55]

Warren promptly put his two divisions and its associated artillery on the march south on Halifax Road, then west on the narrow byway leading to Poplar Spring Church. Griffin's three brigades led the column, followed by a single artillery battery. Ayres's troops moved next, and the remaining five batteries under Wainwright brought up the rear of the corps. It took an hour for this cavalcade to clear the road leading from the Aiken and Gurley houses so Parke could join the advance, with Potter's division in the van. Two Ninth Corps batteries followed Potter, then came Willcox's three brigades, accompanied by the other two batteries under the corps artillery chief, Lt. Col. John A. Monroe. It took fully three hours for these 24,000 soldiers to embark on their trek to the church, about a mile and a half west of Halifax Road.[56]

As historian Richard Sommers notes, these twelve brigades and forty-two guns could pack a powerful punch, but Meade retained significantly more men in Petersburg's permanent fortifications. At first blush this appears to be another example of the overcaution that so frequently plagued the Army of the Potomac. Could the Union high command really believe that Lee posed such an offensive menace that so many troops were necessary to defend the most sophisticated field fortifications of the war? Many of those troops, however, had only recently joined the army and lacked basic combat skills. Moreover, the route to the Confederate target was so constricted that even these four divisions needed hours to traverse the landscape. Meade's decision to limit his venture to four divisions, all led by competent subordinates, reflected geographic and readiness realities, despite his evident skepticism about his mission's prospects.[57]

Meade intended that Parke move to Warren's left, forge a crossing of the miry watershed of Arthur's Swamp, and advance up Duncan Road toward Boydton Plank Road. Warren would press west and north through the Peebles farm, a large clearing west of Squirrel Level Road and in front of the Squirrel Level Line, then turn north. Gregg would cover the infantry's left and rear. Once they reached Boydton Plank Road, the two corps would, presumably, march northeast toward Petersburg in conformity with Grant's instructions to capture the city. Yet Meade's map underestimated the intervening real estate between Warren and Parke. Should Parke follow his orders explicitly, a substantial gap would open between the left of the Fifth Corps and his own right, offering the Confederates two vulnerable flanks. Moreover, neither Warren nor Parke had tactical control over more than their own troops. Without Meade, who remained behind—first at army headquarters and then in conference with Hancock and Ferrero—the two corps would operate independently, their coordination only a matter of mutual agreement.[58]

The road leading west to Poplar Spring Church was narrow and, once west of Vaughan Road, traversed thick woods with scrubby pine on either side. Both factors slowed the march, although according to Wainwright, "Warren had got all the pioneers of the Fifth Corps in a body . . . in rear of his advance; and as soon as we entered the wood he set them to work widening the road, and cutting a second one alongside of it." The general also deployed several regiments as skirmishers to warn of a possible ambush. These circumstances caused the column to progress at a snail's pace. Warren admitted in a letter to his wife that he felt "the anxiety of responsibility," which no doubt exacerbated his innate caution. The New Yorker frequently displayed a distressing reluctance to assume the offensive throughout his tenure in corps command, so it was unsurprising that plunging into a dense forest with an unknown enemy lurking in his front, and possibly on his flanks, caused him concern.[59]

The Fifth Offensive Continues, September 29–30

"It was a beautiful day and the troops were in high spirits," testified Cpl. Charles W. Owen of Griffin's First Michigan. "We knew that trouble was ahead and that we could not go far without running into the 'Johnnies.'" James Gwyn's seven regiments, at the head of Griffin's column, began the march "with drums beating and colors flying to the breeze," a gala atmosphere abetted by "the soul cheering strains of music" from the division's brass band. The jaunty airs dissipated as the bluecoats reached the confining forest along Poplar Spring Church Road.[60]

Parke's soldiers also commented on a day of "perfect autumnal beauty," with its "balmy air, fragrant with the scent of pines [and] the clear sunlight and cloudless sky." Despite such ideal conditions, Warren's languid pace made their progress glacial. Lieutenant Colonel Cutcheon of Willcox's Twentieth Michigan also cited the accompanying artillery and ambulances as the cause of their delay. Potter designated the Seventh Rhode Island to serve as divisional pioneers. Armed with axes, picks, and shovels, the Rhode Islanders, recorded Cpl. Peleg G. Jones, "went through the woods & bushes throwing fence rails & all obstructions down as we went along expecting to come on the Johnnys every minute but found the coast all clear." Sgt. Maj. Leander O. Merriam of the Thirty-First Maine expressed the anticipation felt by Parke's anxious troops. "A march in that direction by a strong force . . . was well understood to mean trouble ahead, and we all had a pretty clear idea of what was to come. The fact that the Johnnies . . . would fight desperately for the last Railroad which was their only source of supply, didn't make the outlook more of a holiday kind to the men of the division which had been selected for the picnic."[61]

When Warren's vanguard reached Poplar Spring Church about 11:00 A.M., Merriam's prediction seemed prescient. Graham's four guns in Fort Archer opened on the Federals, lobbing shells over the woods that intervened between themselves and the church. The captain's efforts caused little damage beyond driving Pastor Job Talmage, a Unionist from New Jersey, and his family to seek cover and unnerving the new recruits of the 198th Pennsylvania. But the shelling did convince the already wary Warren to proceed deliberately. He directed Ayres to move north on Vaughan Road to provide flank protection for Griffin. He then easily routed a thin veneer of Rebel vedettes, who withdrew to their main picket line around the Peebles house. These Rebel sharpshooters, concealed in the abandoned dwelling and its outbuildings, managed to kill Lt. John Conahey of the 118th Pennsylvania as he was conferring with General Griffin. Shortly thereafter, Warren finally began deploying Griffin's division for an assault.[62]

It took time for Griffin to uncoil his line of battle, concealing it in the drainage of Arthur's Swamp just west of the church. With Ayres already out of the way along Vaughan Road, Parke now arrived at the head of his two divisions. The Seventh Rhode Island began hacking a military road to the south consistent with Meade's orders—a process that, if allowed to run its course, would delay Warren's assault for hours. The corps commanders conferred and decided to modify Meade's plan. Instead of attempting to move south around Warren's left, Potter and Willcox would shift right, between Vaughan Road and the church, and provide direct support for Griffin, who would still bear responsibility for dispatching the unknown Confederate force before them. The officers of Griffin's Forty-Fourth New York knew, as did their comrades, that "there was serious business ahead." They exchanged addresses of their relatives, who they promised to notify if any of their number failed to survive the impending contest.[63]

Griffin completed his deployment about 1:00 P.M. Col. Horatio G. Sickel, a forty-seven-year-old businessman from Bucks County, Pennsylvania, positioned his brigade on the left of the division's line. One of the oldest senior commanders in the army at age sixty-one, Colonel Gregory placed his Second Brigade on Sickel's right. Gwyn's troops held the far right of Griffin's line. All three brigades were concealed in the ravine north of Poplar Spring Church Road. Fort Archer and the adjacent Squirrel Level Line lay some 800 yards across Squirrel Level Road and beyond the broad field of the Peebles farm. To reach their goal, the attackers would move slightly down, then up to William Peebles's abandoned buildings and across open ground, where the Petersburg Artillery and the dismounted troopers from the Seventh Confederate Cavalry under Maj. Jesse H. Sikes awaited.[64]

Griffin envisioned three neat lines of battle, one brigade after the other, but that is not what unfolded. In fact, the assault proved to be almost spontaneous, occasioned by the advance of Griffin's skirmishers. The Federal pickets had been stymied by the sharp fire emanating from around the Peebles farm, so the Twentieth Maine received orders to "push our skirmish line to the house, develop the enemy's line, go as far as we could, take all we could, and hold all we got." "I believe I am safe in saying that the Twentieth Maine was not clamoring for that job," admitted Maj. Ellis Spear, who exchanged brief salutations with the colonel of the Sixteenth Michigan, Norval E. Welch. "Goodbye" chirped Welch. "I will meet you on the other side of the water," he promised, with unconscious irony.[65]

The order to advance "came ringing out in loud tones," recorded Sgt. Nathan S. Clark. "Attention Battalion Forward Double Quick March." The Maine men dutifully reached their stalled picket line, but they, too, halted as Graham's four guns "had a clean sweep across the field." Seeing their skirmishers stymied,

The Fifth Offensive Continues, September 29–30

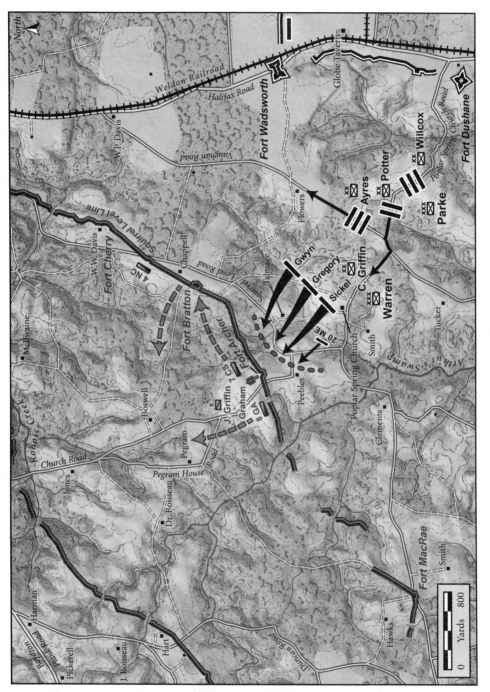

Fort Archer, September 30, 1864

Colonel Gwyn and Major Spear rode out among them, waving their hats and swords and shouting "Come on!" The men of the Twentieth Maine arose and began to charge across the field, triggering the advance of most of the division, some as ordered and the rest of their own volition. Forgotten was any notion of a picture-book attack. Each regiment moved ahead, everyone aiming more or less at the relentless cannon and carbine fire that now erupted from Fort Archer and its adjacent works. "We heard a devil of a yelling and, on looking around, saw troops running towards the enemy's works whooping like so many demons," recalled a soldier from the Eighty-Third Pennsylvania. "The Eighty-Third followed suit."[66]

"As we advanced on the double-quick, their infantry opened a fearful fire upon us, and their artillery poured in grape and canister at a close range," wrote a soldier from the 20th Maine. The 16th Michigan and 118th Pennsylvania charged side by side, absorbing what the 16th's Pvt. Alfred A. Apted called "the cusidest fire of musketry and canon ever. . . . It was the worst fire a mortal ever endured." The Federals withstood the "awful" musketry and artillery for several hundred yards before reaching a line of abatis fronting the fort. Soldiers from both regiments quickly cleared a space wide enough for eight men to pass, then poured through the opening. Once the Federals reached the abatis, Graham's guns ceased firing and began to limber up.[67]

The Confederate fusillade had certainly taken its toll, but now the overwhelming blue mass surged into the moat and around the sides of little Fort Archer. Sikes's defenders began to bleed to the rear or up the line toward Fort Bratton as Graham's gunners tried to escape with their pieces. Lt. John Scott raised the banner of the Eighty-Third Pennsylvania on the parapet, giving rise to the boast that theirs was the first flag to wave over the enemy's defenses, even as elements of the regiment rushed around to the fort's rear. These men blocked the escape of some fifty Rebels, including Sikes, who surrendered to Capt. Chauncey P. Rogers. Sikes had just fired at Captain Salter of the Sixteenth Michigan, who prepared to dispatch his antagonist, when Rogers intervened in response to a Masonic sign flashed by the Rebel major.[68]

Colonel Welch, a law graduate of the University of Michigan and a prominent citizen of Ann Arbor, led his regiment to the works just to the right of Fort Archer. Gaining the parapet, he called on his men to go forward, promising an officer's commission to the first of his soldiers to join him. Just then, two balls pierced his skull, and his lifeless body collapsed into the moat. "Welch was always brave, on this occasion he was reckless," thought a comrade. Colonel Gwyn provided Griffin with another significant casualty. The brigade commander, who was reportedly sick that morning, tried to ride up the steep exterior face

The Fifth Offensive Continues, September 29–30

of Fort Archer, but his horse stumbled, tossing its rider aside and falling on him. The impact injured Gwyn's leg and tore open an old wound, forcing him to relinquish brigade command to Major Spear.[69]

The capture of one of Graham's guns somewhat compensated for the carnage Griffin's division sustained. The Rebel gunners managed to extricate three of their four pieces and were in the process of removing the fourth when Lt. Albert E. Fernald of the Twentieth Maine appeared behind the works and leveled his revolver at the head of the driver atop the limber. A few nearby Confederates fired at Fernald but only succeeded in wounding the battery horses, rendering the gun immobile. The cannon, a three-inch ordnance rifle, turned out to be one that had belonged to the Tenth Massachusetts Battery, lost at Reams' Station a few weeks earlier. It was the first piece captured by the Fifth Corps since the campaign began in May and thus a particular point of pride.[70]

Two of Graham's guns made a brief stand at a little lunette a few hundred yards up Church Road. Griffin's men swarmed toward this diminutive fortification, driving the last of the Confederate defenders in hasty retreat. Based on reports received in his sick bed, Dearing informed his wife: "My men fought very well. We probably have lost one piece of arty & many men killed and wounded," although later he would admit that his presence was necessary to "make these men fight." General Young witnessed the panicked retreat of Dearing's Brigade. "Hold your ground down there, you damned scoundrels," he shouted to no avail.[71]

"General Griffin has just carried the intrenchments on Peebles' farm in splendid style," Warren informed army headquarters at 1:30 P.M. "Our loss is not very great . . . and we have taken a number of prisoners." Griffin's victory, though stirring, was merely a means to an end. Seizure of the supply line via Boydton Plank Road remained Meade's goal. An hour later Warren promised to do just that. "I will push up as fast as I can get my troops in order toward Petersburg on the Squirrel Level Road," he wrote Meade. Yet progress continued at the deliberate pace that characterized the Union offensive all day. It took until 3:00 P.M., for example, for the Eighty-Third Pennsylvania to occupy Fort Cherry. Meanwhile, the Ninth Corps troops moved up to Peebles farm and extended Griffin's perimeter to the west and south, including occupying the empty works at Fort MacRae.[72]

Instead of immediately sending his fresh brigades north toward Boydton Plank Road, Parke had his men fortify, the notion of cutting a road to Miss Pegram's and moving around the Confederate flank now obsolete. "We dawdled till the middle of the afternoon," observed the colonel of the Thirty-Sixth Massachusetts. Some of Potter's troops expected to advance once they reached the captured works and were stunned when "a halt was ordered, and the movement came to a complete stand-still. . . . This fatal and inexplicable delay continued, although it was evident that the advantage of a surprise was being thrown away." Griffin's division, to be sure, needed time to regroup after its ragged assault, but the Ninth Corps troops then on the scene might easily have formed lines of battle and advanced toward Boydton Plank Road. Warren and Parke decided instead to consolidate their conquest of the Squirrel Level Line and pause the offensive, another example of the conservative generalship that frustrated Grant, who remained at City Point to stay in touch with affairs on both his fronts. Meade might have compelled the offensive to continue, but he opted to stay at Globe Tavern, where he was in no position to enforce his will on his reluctant subordinates. Once again the Army of the Potomac achieved tactical success but failed to exploit it.[73]

This irresolute mindset extended to Gregg's cavalry, which rode as far west as Armstrong's Mill and halted, content to guard Parke's left flank. At 2:25 P.M. Meade sent a message to City Point, apprising the general-in-chief of Griffin's victory, explaining Warren's and Parke's efforts to widen the breach, and reporting Gregg's unchallenged progress. Tellingly, he also told Grant that he had ordered Gregg and Hancock to be alert for a cavalry attack along Jerusalem Plank Road, exhibiting the defensive thinking that also animated Warren and Parke. Grant, no doubt vexed by Meade's lack of aggressiveness, responded by urging his subordinate to resume the advance. "If the enemy can be broken and started, follow him up closely," Grant advised, "I can't help believing that the enemy are prepared to leave Petersburg if forced a little."[74]

By the time Grant sent this response, Meade had finally joined Warren and Parke at the front. He was pleased to note that Parke by then had advanced Potter's division with Willcox in support, prepared to move north toward Boydton Plank Road via the clearing at the Pegram farm west of Church Road. Readily approving Parke's revised mission, Meade told Warren to move Griffin's division up to extend Parke's right. Also, at Grant's behest, he ordered Gregg to send one of his brigades beyond Armstrong's Mill and form the left of this coordinated advance. Perhaps against his instincts, Meade now presided over an impending attempt to threaten Petersburg with three infantry divisions and a single cavalry brigade.[75]

These preparations commenced around 3:00 P.M. Simon Goodell Griffin's brigade of Potter's division would lead the way. Griffin, a forty-year-old from New Hampshire, gained a wealth of combat experience serving under Burnside. Like others in the Ninth Corps, he served in Virginia, North Carolina, Kentucky, and at Vicksburg. He moved his brigade through the trees and into the large clearing shared by the Oscar Pegram, Joseph C. Boswell, and Doctor

The Fifth Offensive Continues, September 29–30

Alfred Boisseau homesteads. On the northern end of this wide expanse, a fringe of trees blocked sight of the large house and farm owned by Robert H. Jones and, beyond that, Boydton Plank Road. Thick vegetation bordered the clearing both east and west.[76]

Potter then called on his other brigade, led by Col. John I. Curtin, the twenty-seven-year-old nephew of Pennsylvania's governor and a prewar civil engineer, to "move on in support" of Griffin. Curtin marched his brigade from near Fort Bratton on Squirrel Level Road to Griffin's left, with his own left resting on the farm lane that ran from the Pegram house to Doctor Boisseau's residence. All was quiet, save for a few rounds fired from unseen Rebel batteries, hidden by the distant forest.[77]

Parke assigned Willcox a supporting role, guarding both of Potter's flanks. General John Hartranft's brigade drew the most important job. His seven regiments deployed on Curtin's left, his right connecting with Curtin near Doctor Boisseau's and his left "strongly refused" near the banks of marshy Arthur's Swamp. Lieutenant Colonel Cutcheon claimed that he could see Boydton Plank Road in the distance and, no doubt, the scarred earth marking the unfinished line of Confederate works that fronted it. Willcox sent his Third Brigade east of Church Road as support for Potter's right. Col. Napoleon Bonaparte McLaughlen—who, consistent with his name, had made the army his career—commanded the six regiments in this brigade. He advanced the 100th Pennsylvania as skirmishers, with the rest of his men well behind in line of battle. But then a divisional staff officer reached McLaughlen with orders to fall back to the left of the Pegram house in general support of Potter and Hartranft. Willcox left his First Brigade, under young Col. Samuel Harriman, near the Pegram house in general corps reserve. The Ninth Corps artillery dropped trail back at the Peebles farm, out of position to support Potter and Hartranft or to bolster Willcox's reserves.[78]

Parke would not receive the support from Charles Griffin that he expected. Rather than advance east of Church Road on Potter's right—the assumption that led Parke to withdraw McLaughlen—Griffin's brigades settled in around the Peebles farm along with the Ninth Corps artillery. Ayres remained on Vaughan Road out of the tactical picture as well, so the impending Union advance was now reduced to just three of the twelve brigades that had marched west. Perhaps Parke sensed this weakness. He also fretted about reports of Rebel cavalry threatening his left and rear. Whatever the cause, the Ninth Corps commander let two hours pass without ordering his troops forward. Warren encouraged his counterpart to begin the assault but to no avail, having no authority to compel an advance. Meade, who did have such authority, only encouraged Parke to attack, then retired to the Peebles house to, in the words of Lieutenant Colonel Lyman, "wait developments." Not until about 5:00 P.M. did Parke finally set his troops in motion.[79]

The Confederates took full advantage of these four hours between Griffin's attack on Fort Archer and Parke's advance. Hampton had been apprised of Dearing's collapse and the capture of the Squirrel Level Line shortly after it occurred. The cavalry commander consulted with General Heth, and together they determined to launch a counterattack, the infantry to assault the Federal front and the cavalry to move against their left flank. Hampton directed Rooney Lee's two brigades, along with a section of Captain McGregor's horse artillery, to ride down Duncan Road and occupy the unfinished works opposite the Pegram-Boisseau clearing.[80]

Hampton also sent a courier to Cadmus Wilcox to report the loss of Fort Archer. Wilcox's two brigades, Lane's and McGowan's, had only recently returned from their aborted march to the north side of the James and had assembled—along with Heth's men—near Battery 45. Acting on his own authority, Wilcox put Lane and McGowan on the road, sending a member of his staff to inform A. P. Hill of his decision. From his headquarters on Dunn's Hill, across the Appomattox from Petersburg, Hill lodged no objection and ordered Heth to send MacRae's and Archer's Brigades to follow Wilcox. The Confederate infantry dashed southwest on Boydton Plank Road and then turned south on Church Road, making for the works that they had begun constructing several weeks earlier but had not finished. A few hundred yards beyond lay the clearing around the Jones house, and through the woods beyond that lay the Pegram-Boisseau field, across which Potter's men were now cautiously marching.[81]

Simon Griffin shook out his Second New York Mounted Rifles (dismounted) as skirmishers, with the Eleventh and Sixth New Hampshire leading a methodical advance. The brigade covered about a quarter mile beyond the Pegram house to a slight ravine, beyond which a thin line of Confederates—Joel Griffin's fugitives from the Squirrel Level Line—blocked their progress. The Yankee Griffin formed two lines of battle and easily scattered the Rebels, advancing across a fence and into the clearing dominated by the elegant Jones home and its many outbuildings.[82]

The sharpshooter battalions of Wilcox's brigades were first to arrive. Major Wooten moved up at the double-quick and deployed his Tar Heel marksmen on the west side of Church Road opposite the Jones house, now swarming with Federals. The South Carolinians appeared next, forming on the east side of the road and coming under random fire. Moving forward from the cover of the unfinished works, both sets of sharpshooters headed for the Jones clearing.

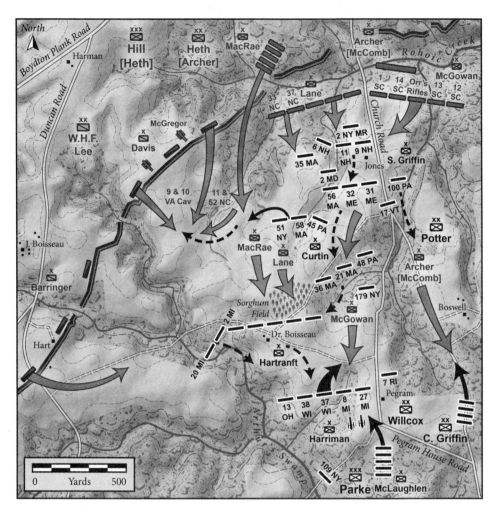

Pegram's Farm, September 30, 1864

"When everything was ready, with arms at a trail and bodies well stooped, the beautiful line slipped across and up the sloping side of the inclining basin, until our movements could no longer be concealed," wrote a South Carolinian. "Up guards, and at 'em! Fire and charge!" Wooten's men maneuvered behind and then around the house, "thus isolating the enemy." When the screaming Carolinians arrived, they took possession of the home and with it some forty prisoners. Griffin's men looked around for help and found themselves alone. Only Parke's corps had advanced beyond Fort Archer, only three brigades had gone north of the Pegram house, and only Griffin's 1,200 men had reached the Jones farm. Gathering in their front were some 5,500 veteran Confederate infantry.[83]

Of course, neither Simon Griffin nor Potter knew the odds against them at this moment. Potter may have been surprised at the appearance of the Rebel sharpshooters, as "up to this time the indications were that the enemy had mostly withdrawn." Mindful of his orders to press ahead, he told General Griffin to resume the advance, but the brigade commander fretted about his flanks. One regiment of Curtin's brigade moved up on his left, and he saw the 100th Pennsylvania across Church Road on his right in skirmish formation, but no line of battle behind them. Betraying his uncertainty, Griffin advanced only the four regiments of his first line toward the Jones house, leaving the rest of the brigade in reserve back at the little ravine. The 6th New Hampshire rushed into the Jones house clearing, slightly ahead of the rest of Griffin's diminutive cohort. "There was a high board fence around the house and out-buildings," remembered Capt. Lyman Jackman, "so compactly built that the men could not climb over it." Another officer found a gate and two or three companies rushed into the yard, scattering the Rebel sharpshooters. "But neither the men within this enclosure nor those without saw a strong line of the enemy which was advancing upon" their position.[84]

That battle line consisted of the balance of Wilcox's two brigades. They arrived at the unfinished works shortly after their sharpshooter battalions commenced their advance. Seeing the Federals' relatively weak response and sensing an opportunity to redeem the day's reversals, Wilcox positioned Lane's Brigade west of Church Road and McGowan's to the east. Heth now appeared and assumed overall command as both Archer and MacRae rushed into position behind McGowan and Lane, respectively, forming en echelon and thus extending both of Wilcox's flanks. Heth ceded control of his two brigades to Archer, who, in turn, delegated authority over his brigade to Col. William McComb of the Fourteenth Tennessee. Heth asked Wilcox to oversee the tactical operation of all four brigades while he coordinated with Hampton opposite the Federal left.[85]

As Lane's men advanced a short distance prior to their assault, a stray bullet found Colonel Barbour of the Thirty-Seventh North Carolina, inflicting a mortal wound—a loss "felt deeply" by the regiment. Col. Robert V. Cowan commanded Lane's right-most regiment, the Thirty-Third North Carolina. He saw a "good opportunity" to hit Griffin's vulnerable left around the Jones house and, in concert with the Thirty-Seventh North Carolina, advanced "and delivered several volleys into their flank." Although Cowan acted without orders, in a matter of moments the rest of Lane's Brigade went forward. The Tar Heels, shrieking the Rebel Yell, bore down on Griffin's startled warriors.[86]

At the opposite end of Griffin's deteriorating position, McGowan's regiments charged "in a style which elicited universal admiration," claimed Adj. James Fitz

James Caldwell. That depended, of course, on one's perspective. Sergeant Major Merriam, from his position in Griffin's reserve line, watched as "three heavy lines of battle, with full ranks, colors flying as straight as if on parade," came bearing down on the Jones house. "I had never before seen a full rebel line of battle in the open," he admitted. "In all of our previous battles they had either been behind their intrenchments or partially covered by the timber. But there was no attempt at covering themselves here, and my heart went rapidly downward as I saw their strength and knowing how thin and light was the line formed by the Second Brigade." "I have heard of Ma Parlington trying to sweep back the Atlantic Ocean with her mop," wrote a soldier in the Eleventh New Hampshire, employing an ob-scure analogy. "We were engaged in similar work." Some of Griffin's men sought shelter in the brick basement of the Jones house and were captured. The rest of the Federals ran for their lives, with Wilcox's men hot on their heels. "We all soon advanced with a real old Confederate yell, easily driving the enemy before us & leaving the ground over which we moved strewn with Yankee dead & wounded, while the prisoners went pouring to the rear," explained General Lane.[87]

Griffin's rout had been exacerbated by his lack of flank support. The 100th Pennsylvania skirmishers, the only element of McLaughlen's brigade to advance on his right, had withdrawn prior to Wilcox's attack, meaning that McGowan enjoyed clear sailing during his assault across Church Road. The situation was not much better on Griffin's left. Only one of Curtin's regiments, the 35th Mas-sachusetts, advanced parallel with Griffin, the rest of the First Brigade remaining in the rear. Thus, when the 33rd North Carolina, now reinforced by a part of MacRae's Brigade, bore down on Lane's right, Curtin's men were caught by surprise. "I discovered that there was a force of the enemy on my right in a large open field," reported Colonel Cowan. "Having been ordered by Brigadier-General Lane to look out for my right flank, I wheeled a part of my regiment to the right and attacked this part of the enemy."[88]

Curtin, like Griffin, had deployed the rest of his command in two lines, four regiments in front and three back. The brigade commander then conducted a personal reconnaissance off to the left even as the sounds of Griffin's battle reverberated to the northeast. When he returned, Curtin discovered that the Confederate juggernaut had passed by the right of both of his lines. "Such was the pressure upon the flank of the second line that it was compelled to fall back to a position at right angles with the first line," he wrote. Lt. Col. William F. Draper, in command of the Thirty-Sixth Massachusetts, one of Curtin's sec-ond-line regiments, sensed "disaster in the air" so that, "if the 36th was to be saved from capture, it must depend upon itself." He changed front and "opened fire, temporarily checking the enemy's advance."[89]

Potter hoped to adjust his lines to impede the Rebel onslaught, but "the enemy pressing vigorously, and having got nearly behind my right, and penetrating also between the two brigades, the lines commenced falling back in considerable confusion." Failing to rally Griffin's men and seeing Curtin's second line in such evident peril, the division commander ordered Curtin to retreat. Potter also called on the Seventh Rhode Island to abandon its tools and establish a position near the Pegram house around which the fugitives could rally. The three regiments in Curtin's second line withdrew "in good order," the colonel reported. Other accounts tell a different story. Capt. Henry S. Burrage of the Thirty-Sixth Massachusetts recalled "a lively scattering over the fences and through the grounds of the Boisseau house . . . each man doing his level best to preserve a life for future usefulness to his country." Pvt. John Dentzer of the Forty-Eighth Pennsylvania admitted, "Most of our boys had to throw there knapsacks away so they would not be captchered by the rebols."[90]

Curtin's first line was not so lucky. When Lane's and MacRae's attackers swept past these three regiments, the Federals spotted an opportunity to assail MacRae's exposed flank and rear. The Fifty-First New York, Fifty-Eighth Massachusetts, and Forty-Fifth Pennsylvania wheeled right and charged—a bold move motivated, at least in part, by the desperate fate of their comrades in the collapsing second line. The unexpected blow fell on MacRae's Eleventh North Carolina, led by Lt. Col. William J. Martin, and Fifty-Second North Carolina. "The situation was critical," remembered Martin. "There was no time to ask for orders." He managed to turn the two regiments ninety degrees, ordered the men to lower their bayonets, and told them to charge. The Federal line shuddered and fell back firing, heading west, as retreat to the south seemed impossible due to the collapse of the rest of the brigade. Each time the Yankees stopped to level a volley, the North Carolinians absorbed the fire and kept coming.[91]

Matters now went from bad to worse for the beleaguered bluecoats. Their escape route led directly toward Duncan Road, behind which waited Rooney Lee's troopers and two pieces of horse artillery. As the Federals drew closer, Captain McGregor opened with one of his guns, which advanced near enough for some of the Federals to turn as if to capture it. At this juncture Hampton unleashed the Ninth and Tenth Virginia Cavalry, and the other half of McGregor's section joined in. "These regiments went in line of battle, dismounted, and reserved their fire until very near the enemy," the general reported. "McGregor kept his guns on the line of battle, charging with the troops, and keeping up a steady and accurate fire." Hampton pronounced this attack "one of the handsomest I have seen, and it reflects the highest credit on the troops engaged in it."[92]

Curtin now found himself with this portion of his brigade hemmed in on the south by MacRae and Lane, on the east by two regiments of aggressive Tar Heels, and on the west by the approaching dismounted cavalry. "The troops of my first line were completely cut off by this rapid movement of the enemy, so that all efforts to extricate them were of no avail," he lamented. Recognizing the hopelessness of his position, the colonel turned to his men and shouted: "It's no use, boys. Let every man look to himself"—good advice, which he would personally follow. Mounted upon his prized horse Burnside, a gift from his soldiers when they were stationed in Kentucky, Curtin whirled around only to have the splendid animal shot in the head, tumbling the colonel violently to the ground. Unhurt and highly motivated, Curtin was one of the few Federals in that predicament to escape. The better part of all three regiments surrendered. "The 58th Regiment was a bout all taken prisoners," confessed Pvt. William Henry Lewin in a letter to his wife, "and I am one of them." Capt. William T. Ackerson of the Fifty-First New York recorded in his diary, "We found ourselves cut off and surrounded and as we were in a trap we had to surrender and I'm sorry to say nearly the whole regiment is here in Petersburg." The Forty-Fifth Pennsylvania went into the fight with about 200 enlisted men, 170 of whom became prisoners along with eight of their officers. "These regiments were lost by holding on too long to their positions," explained a distraught General Potter. "The order for their withdrawal could not be got them in season." Curtin fumed that if he had been informed of the brewing disaster in a timely fashion, "I could have easily changed the position of my first line so as to have met the assault which was made by the enemy on the right of my second line"—an impossibility, given the staggered alignment of Potter's division.[93]

General Hartranft knew nothing about the collapse of Potter's two brigades until Curtin's fugitives came streaming past his position near the Boisseau house. A sorghum field blocked his view of Potter's disaster, but now, apprised of the developing emergency, Hartranft rallied a few of Curtin's men and resisted the entreaties to retreat delivered by a staff officer from Meade's command post. He slowly withdrew his brigade about 100 yards, deploying it a bit beyond the Boisseau house and facing north, with two of his Michigan regiments facing west, thus refusing his left flank. Portions of the three regiments that had formed Curtin's second line, along with the Thirty-Fifth Massachusetts, took position on Hartranft's right, the brigadier not yet admitting "the necessity of retiring."[94]

That need soon became apparent. The rest of MacRae's Carolinians, along with Lane's Brigade, now appeared out of the sorghum, bearing down on Hartranft's right. These soldiers viewed their attack as one continuous advance, not discerning their sequential triumphs over Griffin, Curtin, and now Hartranft.

As Hartranft's right crumbled, Confederate cavalry erupted from the works to the west, endangering Hartranft's vulnerable left, anchored on the morass of Arthur's Swamp. "The boys seeing that they were likely to be captured a panic set in," wrote Lewis Crater of Hartranft's Fiftieth Pennsylvania, "and a grand rush was made for shelter." Pvt. George Parks of the Twenty-Fourth New York Cavalry (dismounted) reported: "The bullets was as thick as flies. . . . We was ordered to run . . . but the rebs was within 20 yards. Our curnal taken prisoner." That officer, Col. William C. Raulston, had been in front of the line with the brigade skirmishers when the Confederate attack struck. He stood by a large persimmon tree, waving his sword and encouraging his men to rally when the Rebels scooped him up, along with most of the skirmishers.[95]

Hartranft's two left regiments—the Second and Twentieth Michigan—faced the full fury of the charging Rebel cavalry. As the Tar Heel infantry enfiladed Hartranft's line from the northeast, Lieutenant Colonel Cutcheon noticed the cavalry threatening the brigade's left, of which his regiment was the anchor. "There was nothing to do but to fall back," he reported. "Immediately on our left was a tangled swamp and having been run out to the left farther than any other regiment, in falling back I found myself and my little regiment cut off from the rest by the swamp. Here we all came near being captured." Cutcheon managed to struggle through the boggy wetland, leaving two dozen of his men behind as prisoners. Maj. Gen. Andrew A. Humphreys, Meade's chief of staff, now arrived to deliver positive, if by then unnecessary, orders to Hartranft to retreat, as the Confederate attack reached its peak fury. "The rebs began to yell like demonds & advance upon us flanking us right and left," recorded Pvt. Joseph H. Harper of the Forty-Sixth New York, a new recruit experiencing his first battle. "They were double our number but we stood as long as possible & then fell back somewhat disordered to the [Pegram] house."[96]

McGowan joined Lane and MacRae in pursuing the three routed Federal brigades. In addition to the scattered corpses and many wounded, the Pegram-Boisseau field was now littered with small arms and Yankee accoutrements, including oilcloths, blankets, canteens, overcoats, knapsacks, and even pants. Some of the knapsacks had been cut at the shoulder straps, indicating that their owners had abandoned them in an effort to speed their getaway. "There was literally no end to the plunder of all description that we brought off after the action," asserted Lt. Thomas L. Norwood of the Thirty-Seventh North Carolina.[97]

By this time, the grayclad pursuers had lost much of their unit cohesion, although McGowan thought it unwise to "dampen the ardor of victorious pursuit by stopping to reform." The Rebels progressed to within a few hundred yards of the Pegram house, where they encountered a strong Federal line, complete with artillery, just in rear of the residence and along the ridge upon which it stood. Earlier, Willcox had moved Harriman's brigade forward as Potter's lines collapsed, supported by the Thirty-Fourth New York Battery. This force made a brief stand before retreating in the face of the increasingly disorganized but undiminished Confederate momentum. They fled back to the latitude of the Pegram house, where the Seventh Rhode Island served as a bulwark around which the fugitives could form. Many of Hartranft's soldiers rallied here, as did Harriman's troops and even some of Potter's men. Now, Charles Griffin's division at last appeared on Parke's right. "We double quicked it all the way out to the line of battle and I never heard so many bullets in all my life go a past me," wrote Pvt. Frederick Rees of Gregory's Ninety-First Pennsylvania. "As we was going out I heard General Warren say their goes Griffins first division to save the army of the Potomac." Griffin's men succeeded in blocking Archer's Brigade, on the left of the Confederate assault, from turning the Union right flank. "Our little Division of 3,000 muskets stood like a wall of iron," boasted Lt. George P. McClelland, an aide to Colonel Gregory. "Many say that the fight in the evening was the fiercest of the whole campaign," wrote Capt. Howard L. Prince of the Twentieth Maine. "The 1st Division and the 3rd Brigade in particular has covered itself with glory." Griffin's stalwart defense, abetted by a bold use of artillery along the firing line, repulsed the Rebels and completed a last stand that ended the Confederate counteroffensive, earning praise from General Warren.[98]

"We had now driven them near a mile, in confusion and rout, and there was considerable disorder in our ranks," admitted McGowan. "The impulse of the first charge had spent itself; we had no supports; both flanks were uncovered, night was approaching; and, therefore, it was impossible to make a fresh charge and carry the position of the Pegram house, which was a strong one, defended . . . by overwhelming numbers of fresh troops." "Night put an end to the flagitious or grossly wicked and bloody days work," wrote a soldier in the Thirty-Seventh North Carolina, as torrents of rain now drenched the blood-soaked landscape.[99]

After darkness enveloped the sodden battlefield, Meade took steps to create a solid defensive line. "I have directed General Warren to intrench himself in his position and extend if practicable to the Weldon railroad, and General Parke to intrench on Warren's left," he informed Grant. Harriman's brigade covered the left, extending to near Fort MacRae. Hartranft formed on his right up to Fort Archer, with McLaughlen's brigade on Hartranft's right. Potter's battered division provided the link between Willcox and Warren, both busily refacing the works along the Squirrel Level Line to guard against a renewal of the Confederate assaults via Church Road or across the Pegram-Boisseau field. Warren also began digging works running eastward to connect with Crawford's division west of Globe Tavern. Ayres's division would bear responsibility for this portion of the developing perimeter.[100]

Although the final Union position that evening proved too much for Wilcox, Heth, and Hampton, the Federals paid a stiff price for retaining the day's modest gains. Warren suffered 626 casualties, primarily in Griffin's division. Gwyn's brigade lost the most men, and the Twentieth Maine absorbed more than any Fifth Corps regiment. But Parke's grim numbers dwarfed Warren's. Willcox lost 354 soldiers, the vast majority, as would be expected, in Hartranft's brigade. Potter's division counted 1,650 in killed, wounded, and missing—710 in Simon Griffin's command and 939 in Curtin's. Eighty-six percent of Curtin's casualties were prisoners of war, and two-thirds of Griffin's casualties were men captured or missing. Including a handful of killed and wounded in the artillery, Meade's two corps lost 2,636 men on September 30. Of that number, 1,736 officers and men were missing and presumed captured, meaning that almost two out of three Union casualties this day became prisoners of war.[101]

After dark Colonel Davies led his cavalry past Armstrong's Mill in an effort to take position on Parke's left. The First New Jersey Cavalry followed a squadron of dismounted men from the Sixth Ohio Cavalry up Duncan Road, feeling their way slowly in the rainy gloom. But soon the Federals heard sounds of jingling sabers and moving cavalry. The captain of the advance squadron shouted, "Who goes there?" "Butler's South Carolina Brigade," came the reply. The Union officer summoned the responder to "advance and give the countersign." As the unsuspecting Rebel—Capt. Andrew Pickens Butler, cousin of Brig. Gen. M. C. Butler—approached, the Federals seized him and then shouted "Fire!" "The rapid and continuing rattle of hoofs on the gravel road . . . gave notice that we had driven them from the field," reported Maj. Myron H. Beaumont of the Jersey regiment. But this encounter terminated the Union advance, and Davies's men withdrew to Vaughan Road.[102]

At 9:00 P.M. Meade summarized the day's events for his superior, informing the lieutenant general that he did "not think it judicious to make another advance to-morrow unless re-enforced or some evidence can be obtained of the weakening of the enemy." Grant promptly replied that he need not attack the next day "unless in your judgment an advantage can be gained," advising him, however, to "hold on to what you have, and be ready to advance. We must be greatly superior to the enemy in numbers on one flank or the other, and by working around each end, we will find where the enemy's weak point is." He added that he would order Ben Butler to probe up Darbytown Road in the morning. Two hours later Meade sent orders to both Parke and Warren to

The Fifth Offensive Continues, September 29–30

"send out a strong reconnaissance at daylight to-morrow to ascertain the position of the enemy," and he so informed Grant. This exchange neatly illustrates the relationship that had developed between these senior Union commanders. Grant, from his position at City Point, delegated almost complete operational discretion to Meade while at the same time suggesting bolder endeavors than Meade would otherwise prefer. Meade, the obedient subordinate, understood Grant's wishes—expressed but not ordered—and complied, perhaps against his own better judgment.[103]

Confederate losses on September 30, though not insignificant, were but a mere shadow of their opponents' casualties. Lane and McGowan sacrificed some 273 men, MacRae and Archer 217, and Hampton 106, for a total of around 600 men. One death struck a particular chord with General Lane. As he was moving through the field in pursuit of the fleeing Federals, he came upon a soldier from the Seventh North Carolina kneeling over a severely wounded man. "General may I stay with my brother," beseeched the grief-stricken private. "I am no straggler. See he has been shot." Lane quickly recognized that the wound was mortal but recalled his own feelings when his brother and aide-de-camp, Rooker, was killed at Chancellorsville. The general allowed the distraught soldier to stay with his dying brother but reminded him of his duty, observing that his brother was beyond saving. Lane then moved on but moments later watched with pride as the soldier he had addressed ran by him, rifle in hand, toward the enemy. "Here I am general," he shouted, "I have thought over what you said & I am going to the front."[104]

Both Lane and McGowan withdrew their weary troops to the Jones house by 9:00 P.M., leaving the sharpshooters of both brigades "along Pegram's fence" as a picket line. That night Wilcox's men "slept upon our arms, victors of the field." MacRae and Archer also gathered at the Jones farm, and by then, General Hill had joined them. He ordered Heth's two brigades to march back to the vicinity of Battery 45 along Boydton Plank Road, where they reunited with the rest of their division. "Having rested but a few minutes," recalled a member of the Second Maryland Battalion, "the Battalion was marched off toward Petersburg. . . . On roads crowded with troops, ambulances, wounded &c., marching by night . . . scarcely more than a mile an hour was accomplished."[105]

Opinions on the conduct and results of the fighting on September 30 varied. General Humphreys pronounced it "a pretty little fight" and called the day "a great success." Enlisted men, such as the musician John L. Houck, held a more muted view. Houck admitted to his wife: "We have had another awful battle last Friday," but "we drove the Johnnies two miles and a half and we hold the ground and their line of breastworks but it was an awful time." Captain Salter claimed that Griffin's stand at the end of the battle saved the army, no thanks to Parke's corps. "Their generals seem to be the most utterly incapable men, and their troops the most cowardly of any in our army," he wrote. "They do not seem to be good for anything since they have not Gen. Burnside to drive them. . . . Our men hate them about as much as the rebels."[106]

Meade's offensive on the Peebles and Pegram farms shared elements of all these analyses. There can be no doubt that the men of both corps fought well, Salter's libel of the Ninth Corps notwithstanding. Charles Griffin's men bravely faced deadly fire in their capture of Fort Archer and battled with distinction along Church Road. Hartranft's brigade acquitted itself under difficult circumstances, while Potter's disaster was born of an untenable position. At the end of the day, the Federals had complete control of the Squirrel Level Line and retained their position on the Pegram farm. Whether bolder generalship would have earned them a lodgment on Boydton Plank Road cannot be known. It certainly took Warren inordinately long to start his attack at Fort Archer, and Parke delayed in advancing against the Jones farm and the final Confederate line, employing but a fraction of his available firepower in the advance. The lack of a single guiding hand hampered the Union effort until Meade arrived, and even then the army commander exercised little direct control, ceding conduct of the final attack to his corps commanders. General Grant envisioned no less than the capture of Petersburg, while Meade, Warren, and Parke sought much more modest achievements.

Assessments on the Confederate side were decidedly less ambiguous. "The Yankees were whipped on an open field," wrote the Thirty-Seventh North Carolina's William Alexander, "everything worked well—the wounded men speak in the highest terms of the Genls commanding; the old light division again covered herself with glory." A Maryland soldier averred that "the odds against the Confederates were fearful, and nothing but their patriotism and old habit of conquering carried them through it to victory." "We punished the enemy severely," wrote Adjutant John Crawford Anderson of the Thirteenth South Carolina, but he admitted they "gained very little advantage." It is hard to gainsay the performance of any of the Rebels engaged this day. All four infantry brigades, particularly Lane's and MacRae's, enjoyed almost complete tactical dominance, aided by the timely participation of Hampton's dismounted troopers. Wilcox was master of the field, while Heth saw that the infantry and cavalry coordinated their efforts. General Hill had almost nothing to do with events on September 30, but that was about to change. As one Confederate predicted, "Tomorrow will tell a mighty tale in the history of this war."[107]

ten

A MOVE IN THE RIGHT DIRECTION

The Fifth Offensive Concludes, October 1–2

A slow, drizzling rain greeted the chilly dawn on October 1, a day that the Second Maryland Battalion's Pvt. Samuel Ammen called ugly and raw. The dim morning light revealed Powell Hill's plan for regaining the ground that his counterattack on September 30 failed to redeem. In truth, the lieutenant general hoped for even more. If all went well, he would isolate the four divisions that had ventured west of the permanent Union defenses and cut them off, destroying a portion of the Federal army in detail. At the very least, he intended to drive the Yankees back to the Weldon Railroad and in the process safeguard the security of the remaining lines of supply and communication to Petersburg and Richmond.[1]

Hill premised his strategy on the assumption that Warren and Parke would concentrate the bulk of their strength on their exposed left. Doing so would render their right vulnerable, as the Pegram farm lay two and a half miles west of the refused Federal line at Halifax Road and the Weldon Railroad. Intelligence from Mahone's Division suggested that, in fact, the Federal position along Squirrel Level Road was weak, so Hill determined to use that corridor through the Dinwiddie woods to guide his offensive. All four of Heth's brigades would provide the firepower, supported by two of Willie Pegram's batteries, the Purcell Artillery and the Crenshaw Artillery.

Perhaps Hill reflected on how much the situation mirrored events six weeks earlier. Then, a Union force sallied west from their fortifications to make a lodgment on the Weldon Railroad. Heth's counterattack limited their progress on August 18, and the next day Mahone sliced around the lightly held Union right

369

in a spectacular attack, handicapped only by a lack of sufficient force to exploit their initial advantage. Heth complemented Mahone's gambit with a diversionary assault against the Federal front. This time, his division would have the starring role, while Wilcox, whose two brigades had endured a soggy night near the Jones farm, would provide the diversion.[2]

Heth's infantry and Pegram's artillery numbered 4,750 men, as strong a strike force as the Confederates could muster, while Mahone's and Johnson's Divisions continued to defend the Petersburg fortifications. Wilcox, supported by Thomas Brander's Letcher Artillery, counted 2,400 troops poised to discharge their portion of the counteroffensive. Although the Fifth and Ninth Corps infantry and artillery still substantially outnumbered Hill's forces, the Confederate commander hoped that a vulnerable flank and the element of surprise would compensate for the deficit.[3]

Meanwhile, back in Petersburg, the Confederate provost guard dealt with the hundreds of Union prisoners seized on September 30. Most of the captives spent a miserable night on Merchant's Island, a spit of land in the Appomattox River. Next morning they relocated to a tobacco warehouse, where they gobbled a meager meal, then marched across the river and onto trains that took them to their new lodgings at Richmond's Libby Prison. "We are searched by the Provost and have everything taken from us but our clothes and our memorandum books," wrote Captain Ackerson. "They do not even leave us our pocket knives or our forks and spoons."[4]

Hill's was not the only headquarters busy that night. Meade took to heart Grant's suggestion that the Confederates in his front must have been diminished by transfers north of the James. The orders for a morning reconnaissance he sent to Parke, Warren, and Gregg at midnight had hardly arrived before he dispatched a follow-up message. Grant had shared Butler's identification of the forces he had faced that day, news that compelled Meade to add more teeth to his previous directive. "General Butler has Field's and Hoke's divisions and a part of Pickett's before him," he informed his two corps commanders. "If your reconnaissance show the enemy to have left your front, and the indications are that he has sent more troops against Butler, it is advisable that you get onto the Boydton plank road." Meade, however, made such an advance contingent on his subordinates' belief that it would be "practicable," a determination that was by no means certain given the cautious instincts of Warren and Parke.[5]

Meade also took the important step of ordering one of Hancock's divisions to prepare to move west. He wanted these men relieved from the fortifications and held in reserve, pending the outcome of the morning's reconnaissance. The Second Corps commander selected Gershom Mott's division, shifting his other

The Fifth Offensive Concludes, October 1–2

two divisions—Nelson Miles's and John Gibbon's—to cover Mott's section of the line. Hancock began the process of relieving the Third Division during the night, placing the troops out of sight between Second Corps headquarters and the Avery house. "Oh these night operations what a bore they are!" wrote Gibbon. "The staff had to be roused at once and sent out to start off & post the troops and it was long after daylight before the operation was ended in a cold drenching rain with the trenches all flooded with water."[6]

While the telegraph lines hummed between the various Federal headquarters, grimmer events unfolded at the field hospitals treating the wounded. Union surgeons had been busy since the afternoon attacks against Fort Archer, and as the casualties poured in from the fight on the Pegram, Boisseau, and Jones farms, the medical facilities quickly became overwhelmed. Wounded men lay all around the hospital tents, some finding shelter from the rain, others enduring the elements. Sergeant Major Merriam was among the fortunate waiting their turn, although he shuddered as those with the worst injuries cried and groaned in pain, while others bore up with "white face and shut teeth. . . . There was to be seen almost every imaginable kind of mutilation with blood stains everywhere, while at an operating table under an open fly and in plain view of all, the surgeons worked silently and rapidly."[7]

As the generals plotted and the surgeons sawed, the soldiers of the Fifth and Ninth Corps dug. Such preparations were prudent, to be sure, but they also betrayed the defensive mindset that prevailed at those corps headquarters, as would become apparent in the morning. Parke occupied the left of Meade's lines, Harriman's brigade extending to the junction of Squirrel Level Road and the farm lane running past the Clements house, less than a mile south of the Peebles farm. Hartranft withdrew from the vicinity of the Pegram house between midnight and 2:00 A.M. and formed on Harriman's right. "We had thrown up a good breast-work, with pickets well out in front," reported Colonel Cutcheon. McLaughlen prepared works that connected Harriman's and Hartranft's positions.[8]

Potter's division continued the line on Willcox's right and somewhat in advance, his own right terminating around Fort Archer. Parke left several regiments on the Pegram farm, both to cover the realignment of his corps and to provide a picket line for the developing fortifications. Charles Griffin's men worked hard to reface the captured Squirrel Level Line from Fort Archer to the southern end of a clearing associated with the Chappell farm. Sickel's brigade adjoined Potter, then Gwyn's command, with Gregory on Griffin's right. Brig. Gen. Joseph Bartlett, who had arrived the previous day from sick leave, assumed command of Gwyn's brigade. Artillery unlimbered to bolster the infantry. "We

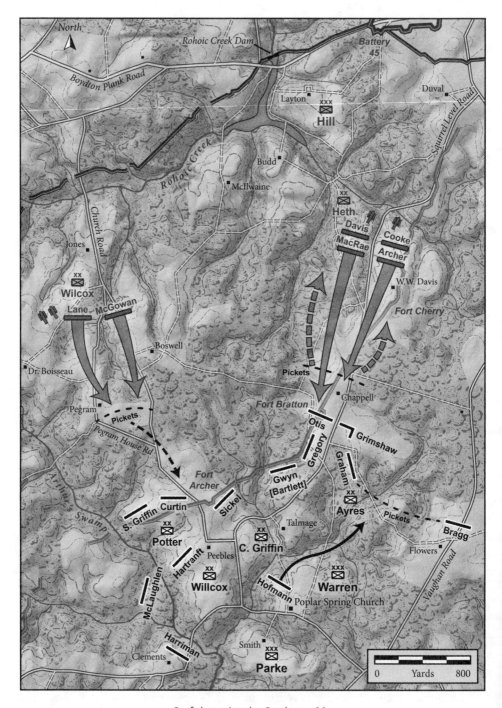

Confederate Attacks, October 1, 1864

. . . moved along the line we had taken, which was soon converted from rebel to Yankee works and their forts filled with our guns," wrote a soldier in the 155th Pennsylvania. Willcox, Potter, and Griffin were now in position to contest any renewal of the Confederate attacks across Pegram's fields or down Church Road.[9]

Ayres's division, which had been spared combat on September 30, now began describing a line that began on Griffin's right, incorporated the abandoned Fort Bratton, and continued east in an attempt to connect with Crawford and the established fortifications west of the Weldon Railroad. While Ayres stretched east, Crawford expanded west. Lt. Col. Elwell S. Otis, commander of Ayres's First Brigade, occupied Fort Bratton and its adjacent works, with the 12th and 14th U.S. Infantry on the right, the 146th New York and 15th New York Heavy Artillery on the left, and the rest of the brigade in reserve. Their deployment directly blocked Squirrel Level Road. Ayres's other two brigades bent back south, then east, creating a salient along Squirrel Level Road. Warren ordered the Iron Brigade of Crawford's division to move from their reserve position to the Flowers farm along Vaughan Road, where they arrived a few hours before dawn. They immediately entrenched while sending skirmishers to create, if not an unbroken ribbon of fortifications, at least a continuous picket line on Ayres's right. Although the connection between Ayres and Crawford remained imperfect, the Federal redeployment that night denied Hill the unguarded flank along Squirrel Level Road upon which he predicated his plans. The near disaster on August 19 had taught the Unionists a lesson. Following every Federal tactical advance, the Rebels had responded with a counterattack. This time the graycoats would mount a frontal assault in order to reverse the losses of September 30.[10]

The rain that started on the evening of the thirtieth continued through the night, at times falling in torrents and, in the words of Colonel Cutcheon, "making our position in the flats a decidedly moist and uncomfortable one." Captain Jackman agreed that it was "a rainy, dismal night" that made most Union soldiers miserable. "We came up then and were moved to the right and threw up works during the night the rain pouring down," wrote Captain Gawthrop. "Hd Qrs wagons were not allowed up and Oh! didn't we get wet." The downpours also complicated the otherwise familiar process of preparing fortifications. "The work was very difficult, as the constant rain gave the freshly turned earth the consistency of mud," remembered a soldier from the Thirty-Sixth Massachusetts. "The aspect of the men, as they painfully prodded the moist ground with sticky shovels or crouched around smoky and sputtering fires, was lugubrious in the extreme, and their feelings corresponded with their looks."[11]

For some reason, Meade's late-night instructions to conduct a dawn recon-naissance failed to reach Parke until 5:15 the following morning. The Ninth Corps commander proved none too eager to obey. "I much fear that my loss is much heavier than I supposed it to be at the time you left yesterday," he explained. "Before sending out a reconnaissance from my corps, I would much prefer making ourselves secure in our present position, which I cannot fully ascertain and realize until after daylight." Meade's directives did reach Warren in a timely manner, but he, too, hesitated to undertake a forward movement. This reluctance to employ their approximately 17,000 men, combined with Meade's absence miles away at army headquarters, ceded the initiative to Hill, who even at this moment prepared the final arrangements for his morning attack.[12]

In the predawn gloom Heth gathered all four of his brigades at the intersection of Squirrel Level and Boydton Plank Roads. The troops marched south under lowering skies and deployed between 6:45 and 7:00 A.M. Shielded by the woods that separated the William W. Davis farm from Chappell's, MacRae's Brigade aligned west of the road and Archer formed his soldiers across the road on the left. Joseph Davis and John R. Cooke moved their brigades up in support. A strip of felled timber about fifty yards deep fronting some thick woods faced Archer's men. Across the road the woods gave way to the open fields and scattered buildings of the Chappell property. A fringe of trees hid Otis's picket line and fortifications from clear view in the muted light. Heth paused here to allow Wilcox to arrange his force for the diversionary assault.[13]

Wilcox advanced from his soggy bivouac around 7:00 A.M., and within an hour both of his brigades were in position. "We advanced down the Church Road and deployed to the right," wrote Adjutant Caldwell, "connecting with Gen. Lane's brigade, which had advanced down the road leading to the Pe-gram house." McGowan's men halted in the woods astride Church Road, but the North Carolinians advanced to a point overlooking the Pegram-Boisseau fields, where "a good view was had of Pegram's house and the enemy at work" building fortifications. The Tar Heels formed a line of battle and began tearing down a fence to create a temporary breastwork. Brander's battery arrived and unlimbered on Lane's right, in position to enfilade the Federal works. Both brigades advanced their skirmishers to the front of their formations. Wilcox understood his mission and would await the sound of Heth's guns before he unleashed his troops.[14]

Hampton's cavalry would not be idle this day. While Butler's Division remained near the Armstrong house on Duncan Road, Rooney Lee's troopers were roused from their slumber and sent back down that narrow byway and into the incomplete earthworks from which they attacked the previous day. Here,

The Fifth Offensive Concludes, October 1–2

Lucius Davis's brigade dismounted while Rufus Barringer's men rode all the way to Fort MacRae, which Parke's troops had abandoned during the night. By 8:00 A.M., all of Hill's units were poised to launch their attacks.[15]

The Federals suspected something was brewing. Ayres's pickets spotted Heth's buildup along Squirrel Level Road, and Federal signal stations reported the Rebels moving into place. If Warren and Parke needed any more reason to ignore Meade's orders to undertake a strong reconnaissance of their own, this news provided it. The Fifth and Ninth Corps would hold tight and await the Confederates' next move. They did not wait long.

Both MacRae and Archer advanced astride Squirrel Level Road shortly after 8:00 A.M. As they emerged into the clearing of the Chappell farm, they encountered the Federal pickets. Otis's 17th U.S. Infantry and 140th New York had just relieved the 10th and 12th U.S. Infantry when the Southerners struck. The adjutant of the 140th New York reported that the regiment had "hardly enough time to form before the Rebel column came down upon them." The blueclad pickets gave way, some of the Federals falling with wounds and others scooped up as prisoners. Lieutenant Colonel Otis, a twenty-six-year-old Harvard-educated lawyer, ordered the 10th U.S. Infantry to reinforce the collapsing line, personally leading them forward. A Confederate minié ball found Otis, inflicting "an ugly wound thro his nose & cheek." Maj. James Grindlay of the 146th New York assumed command of the brigade. While stretcher-bearers removed Otis from the field, the remaining Yankee skirmishers hastily retreated to the main line around Fort Bratton.[16]

The Confederates rushed ahead and caught sight of the strong Federal works, generously manned and full of fight. Instead of a flank ripe for the taking, Heth now confronted an entrenched enemy blocking his path. Surprised by this unwelcome discovery, the division commander pulled back and called on his two supporting batteries to pound the Federal position. Pegram's fire elicited a reply from the Federal ordnance, and for thirty minutes the two sides exchanged salvos. When the guns fell silent, around 9:00 A.M., Heth decided to probe forward with MacRae's Brigade to gauge the result of Pegram's work. But the Forty-Fourth and Fifty-Second North Carolina either misunderstood their assignment or decided that a cautious approach was unnecessary. The two veteran regiments broke ranks and launched a spirited attack. Not unlike Tige Anderson's mistaken assault at Fort Harrison the previous day, the overeager Tar Heels prompted the rest of MacRae's troops to rush ahead as well, unwilling to allow their comrades to face Yankee bullets alone. The North Carolinians encountered "such a shower of lead that they went back like sheep," limiting their casualties but leaving General MacRae seething at their lack of discipline.

General Ayres witnessed this action and was later overheard remarking, "We have walloped them four times."[17]

But Heth was not quite finished. Now Archer, east of the road, and Joseph Davis's Mississippians and Carolinians, aligned behind MacRae's shattered regiments on the west side, started forward. Perhaps this was a part of the "close and careful reconnaissance" that Heth would report conducting, but if so, MacRae's futile experience made any such probe unnecessary. Even worse, the two brigades failed to cooperate. The Second Maryland Battalion led Archer's advance. That unit veered to the right and crossed Squirrel Level Road, perhaps in an effort to support MacRae. This maneuver, however, placed them directly in Davis's path, which, according to a Confederate, "threw the command into the utmost confusion." As the Marylanders attempted to restore order, the Fortieth Virginia lost its commander, Capt. Robert Beale Davis—his corpse would be abandoned on the field—while a cannonball decapitated an officer in the Forty-Seventh Virginia. This was enough mayhem for the Fifty-Fifth North Carolina, Davis's Tar Heel regiment, which unceremoniously fled. Yet they performed better than Archer's Twenty-Second Virginia, which simply refused to make the attack. Davis predictably made little progress. "Oh, it was an awful time Saturday charging the Yankees in the rain through the woods and swamps and thickets," wrote Pvt. James King Wilkerson of the Fifty-Fifth North Carolina, "and the balls flying thick and fast in every direction, and men getting killed, and wounded hollering all over the woods."[18]

Cooke's Brigade hardly budged. "Heath's Division crossed our main line, passed around the rear and intended to charge a fort that the enemy had taken from us but Archer's Brigade failed to come up," recorded a tactically confused Cpl. Isaac F. Caveness of Cooke's Forty-Sixth North Carolina. "We were halted and we thought it prudent to give it up." Joseph Mullen of Cooke's Twenty-Seventh North Carolina reported that his regiment "laid there in the rain about two hours. Genl Heth reconnoitered their position in person and found it would be too great a sacrifice to attack them and ordered us to fall back." Heth explained that he "concluded not to make a determined assault, which, if successful, would have been with such heavy loss that no further attack could have been made successfully on these series of enclosed forts." The Rebels withdrew to the far left end of their Squirrel Level Line near the W. W. Davis house. Heth's efforts may not have strictly qualified as "a determined assault," but some 400 of his men lay dead or wounded as a result of his piecemeal and poorly coordinated thrusts. Ayres's losses were a fraction of those. Theodore Lyman summarized the action in his usual pithy fashion. "They concluded that Ayres, who was in the woods, was the soft man, and charged him and caught a right smart of volleys,

The Fifth Offensive Concludes, October 1–2

from which they all cleared out, except the dead men, for your reb has a clear eye for a hot posish, and won't stay in one if he knows himself."[19]

Wilcox's diversion achieved somewhat more success. Once again he turned to his reliable sharpshooter battalions to lead his advance, Major Dunlop's South Carolinians along Church Road and Wooten's Tar Heels on the lane leading to the Pegram house. The Letcher Artillery sat poised to open fire upon hearing Heth's guns, while the bulk of Lane's and McGowan's men waited expectantly, their actions dependent on events. Once Heth's skirmishers engaged the Federals on Squirrel Level Road, Brander's guns commenced an effective enfilade fire on the Federal picket line along the Pegram house ridge, "making the rail fence into kindling-wood in a manner more lively than agreeable," according to Captain Jackman. General Lane characterized this bombardment as "both destructive and demoralizing," as he witnessed the Federal pickets scrambling for the rear.[20]

The sharpshooters then dashed over the intervening ground before all the disorganized bluecoats could either defend themselves or make a clean getaway. Dunlop gleefully reported, "We charged and routed the skirmishers without firing a gun, and pursued them up the sloping ridge, yelling and firing at every jump; stormed over their fortifications, crushed their line of battle into fragments, and sent them swarming through the woods in complete route." Wooten's men enjoyed similar success. The Carolinians between them corralled between 200 and 300 prisoners, "at least two men to every *one* engaged," estimated Dunlop. "There were a good many [prisoners] for only a few cared to take the risk of retreating across a field raked with deadly precision by canister and grape shot," recalled one New Hampshire man. Lane reported no casualties in Wooten's battalion, and Dunlop suffered perhaps a dozen men wounded. As some Confederates led this sizable aggregation of captured bluecoats to the rear, Brander's gunners mistook such a large body of Federals as evidence of an attack and fired a few rounds before Wooten sent runners back to halt this friendly fire.[21]

Those Union skirmishers who managed to make their escape joined the main Federal position back at the Peebles farm. Some of Lane's troops, along with Brander's guns, moved up and joined the sharpshooters at the Pegram farm, exchanging fire with the entrenched Federals. Skirmishing continued through the day as the skies continued to dump rain on the already soaked soldiers. Wilcox, who had barely avoided one of Brander's errant projectiles, risked no further effort to penetrate the Federal line, a decision consistent with his mission. The entire Confederate counterattack upon which Hill had counted had now run its course.[22]

Warren informed Meade at 8:00 A.M. of the developing Confederate assaults, predicting "a hard time" for the Fifth Corps. Shortly thereafter he reported that Ayres had repulsed the Rebel attacks; he also mistakenly assumed that Otis's wound was mortal. Warren shifted Hofmann's brigade from reserve into the line on his right, helping bridge the gap between Ayres's division and Crawford's, but warned Meade, "We are not strong enough to act offensively." Parke also dutifully reported his withdrawal from the Pegram farm back to the Peebles area, assuring the army commander, "We now hold the intrenchments strong." Both Union corps continued to improve their fortifications, although the rain returned with a vengeance, "making everything very disagreeable." Both sides engaged in "a sharp picket fire," and Grindlay's troops made a minor advance in the afternoon to drive away some annoying Rebel marksmen concealed in the Chappell buildings.[23]

By then, Mott's division began to arrive around the Peebles farm. At 8:00 that morning Hancock wrote Meade that the Third Division's three brigades had been completely relieved from their positions along the fortifications between Fort Morton, opposite the Crater, to Fort Alexander Hays, between Jerusalem Plank Road and the Weldon Railroad. Mott massed his troops behind the Avery house and near the Chieves house along Jerusalem Plank Road, later shifting most of them to the military railroad's "trestle bridge" that spanned a deep ravine formed by Blackwater Swamp. At 9:30 A.M. Meade ordered Hancock to send Mott to the Peebles house and report to General Parke. "He will not need any artillery," Meade elaborated. "Trains of cars will take his troops to the Weldon railroad close to Warren's headquarters, where they will give him some one to show him the road to Peebles." Mott's brigades would board the military railroad at either Hancock Station or near the trestle bridge. Meade added in a subsequent message that ammunition and supply wagons should be sent to the Weldon Railroad. The army commander clearly intended that Mott's fresh brigades would spur Warren and Parke to assume the offensive.[24]

It would take time to transport Mott's 5,000 officers and men, a situation exacerbated by a lack of logistical coordination between the responsible officers. Never before in military history had an army used, in the words of historian Richard Sommers, "a railroad to facilitate grand-tactical movement in the midst of battle." Hancock relayed Meade's orders to Mott at 10:30 A.M., promising sixty railroad cars and instructing him to load his brigades "at the station near the trestle bridge and at the Jones house." Mott received these orders around noon. His Third Brigade, under Col. Robert McAllister, had commenced moving before dawn and soon after daylight arrived at the trestle bridge, where it waited in the rain until 3:00 P.M. for its transportation. Byron Pierce's Second Brigade arrived at Hancock Station at 12:30 P.M. and, along with Mott, boarded the cars thirty minutes later. General de Trobriand's First Brigade began boarding with Pierce. Three trains made three round trips in order to ferry all of Mott's men to Parke.[25]

Once the trains finally started rolling, they made good time, the first cars arriving at Globe Tavern about 2:00 P.M. Meade, who had once again ridden forward that morning, greeted Mott and urged him to take the road to Poplar Springs Church and the Peebles house as quickly as possible. A staff officer from Crawford's headquarters guided Pierce's brigade, which arrived at the Peebles house between 2:30 and 2:40 P.M., a rapid march indeed. The division continued to arrive in relays, the last of its units, McAllister's brigade, reporting to Parke between 5:00 and 6:30 P.M. De Trobriand pronounced the journey as extremely unpleasant. "Horrible time all day long," he wrote; "incessant rain."[26]

Meade kept Grant apprised of the situation around the Peebles house, informing the general-in-chief that once Mott's division arrived, "I will assume the offensive," a promise he reiterated later that morning. He, of course, also informed Parke and Warren of Mott's impending arrival and his expectation that once that division appeared, the entire force would "endeavor to envelop [Hill's] right flank." Tellingly, Meade specified that both Mott and Gregg would report to Parke, reflecting the army commander's distrust of Warren's offensive inclinations.[27]

Just before Mott's appearance at the Peebles house, Parke sent a discouraging message to Meade. "Any advance that we may be able to make this evening may result in the taking of the Pegram house, but I think nothing further." He promised to use Potter and Willcox to do so and to direct Mott to extend the line to the left. This was, of course, much less than Meade had expected, but just as on the previous day, the army commander was not personally present to enforce his will. Instead, he lingered both at Hancock's headquarters and then at Globe Tavern, waiting until 3:00 P.M. before heading for the Peebles farm. When he finally arrived, there was, as Lyman phrased it, "a power of generals" present, including Parke, Warren, Gregg, Willcox, and Potter, the latter, according to Lyman, "looked very dismal."[28]

Meade had promised Grant just prior to departing for Peebles's that he would "see Warren and Parke and then determine what I will do, being most desirous to attack," adding conditionally, "unless I should not deem it judicious to do so." His next message to Grant came from Globe Tavern at 7:00 P.M. Explaining that Mott's division experienced "considerable delay" in transit and arrived late "in connection to the weather, no movement was made. . . . I have given orders to Parke and Warren to advance at daylight tomorrow and endeavor to effect a lodgment on the Boydton plank road." Meade, indeed, sent orders to

Parke at 6:45 that evening to "move forward as soon after daylight to-morrow as practicable and attack the enemy . . . the object being finally to effect a lodgment upon Boydton plank road, within reach of the South Side Railroad, or, if we prove to be strong enough, to follow the enemy closer to Petersburg." Similar orders went to Warren, admonishing him to "use your whole force in attacking" except the troops detailed to the permanent forts.[29]

Thus, another day elapsed without venturing an offensive. Meade, who returned to Globe Tavern by 5:30 P.M., had been unwilling to compel Warren, Parke, and Mott to hazard an attack until all reinforcements were on the scene, and the logistical challenges of transporting those soldiers resulted in their delayed appearance. The Federals were no nearer their stated goal of reaching Boydton Plank Road than they had been in the morning, but Meade was determined to rectify this disappointment on October 2.[30]

Although the Federal infantry enjoyed a relatively quiet day following Hill's morning attacks, General Gregg and his cavalry remained busy. Meade envisioned his mounted arm as an integral part of the planned offensive on October 1. At midnight army headquarters instructed Gregg to advance at daylight, ascertain the location of the enemy, and then cooperate with Parke's "reconnaissance" by riding north on Duncan Road, guarding Parke's left. The abysmal weather combined with darkness delayed the transmission of this order. Like Meade's tardy communication with Parke, it did not reach Gregg at his command post near the McDowell house until about 5:00 A.M. The cavalry commander had anticipated remaining on the defensive this day, consistent with his previous instructions to guard Vaughan Road, so Meade's new directive to participate in an offensive caught him by surprise. But that dependable officer promised to begin as soon as possible, noting that he had not yet issued forage and rations for the day.[31]

Quickly enough, Gregg led his troopers north on Vaughan Road and then west on Poplar Spring Church Road to gain a position on Parke's left. They encountered Barringer's men around Fort MacRae and halted. By then, however, Parke had informed Gregg that Heth's and Wilcox's impending assaults had obviated the need to locate the Rebel infantry and that he should instead ensure the security of the infantry's rear. "The best position to do this," Gregg informed Meade, "is on the Vaughan Road" at its intersection with Wyatt Road at McDowell's house and slightly north around yet another Davis residence. But before he could return the bulk of his division to these points, Pierce Young's Rebel troopers surprised the First Maine Cavalry near McDowell's, the only unit Gregg had left behind. The Yankee horsemen fled north on Vaughan Road, ceding

The Fifth Offensive Concludes, October 1–2

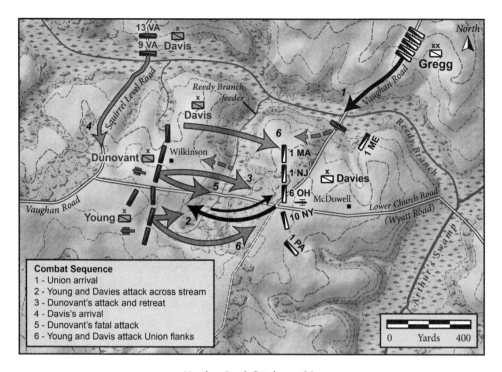

Vaughan Road, October 1, 1864

the important intersection to the Confederates, who halted and fortified the crossroads, wisely unwilling to risk a further probe without reinforcements.[32]

The rest of Gregg's regiments remained with the infantry until Heth's and Wilcox's attacks had run their course, then returned down Vaughan Road, intent on reclaiming the ground lost by the First Maine. The Federals engaged Young's outnumbered horsemen at 10:45 A.M., and two hours later Gregg reported that he had regained the intersection of Vaughan and Wyatt Roads, the Rebels retreating westward, crossing a tributary of Reedy Branch, a tentacle of Arthur's Swamp, and halting on high ground near the Wilkinson house. The Confederate position, supported by horse artillery, seemed to Gregg a bit too daunting to hazard a further advance. Still cherishing hopes of launching a coordinated counteroffensive spearheaded by Mott, at 2:00 P.M. army headquarters ordered Gregg to test the Rebel position at Wilkinson's. "If you can occupy an equal or greater force of the enemy than your own, and keep them from joining those we attack, it will be equivalent to joining the attack here, particularly if you beat them," Meade advised.[33]

As matters then stood, the opposing cavalry faced one another only 500 yards apart. The Confederate position centered on high ground around the

Wilkinson house, just east of where Squirrel Level Road terminated at its intersection with Vaughan Road. The blueclad troopers deployed on equally elevated terrain surrounding the McDowell home, just east of where Wyatt, or Lower Church, Road merged into Vaughan Road and where the latter began its short east–west stretch. The swampy streamlet crossed by a narrow causeway on Vaughan Road flowed between the two houses. Thick woods along the waterway would pose an obstacle to attacking troops from either side. This small slice of Dinwiddie County would witness the most sustained fighting south of Petersburg on October 1.[34]

General Davies would comply with Meade's desire for action, as his brigade and Young's pulsed back and forth across the intervening terrain, the Federals eventually confining their opponents to the ground west of the branch. General Young was not pleased. The twenty-seven-year-old South Carolinian had moved with his family to Georgia as a youth and resigned his cadetship at West Point when his adopted state left the Union. Promoted steadily to brigadier general, he commanded a mixture of units from the Deep South. Young sat astride his horse on an elevation that provided him a clear view of the action and was "cursing and storming in that stentorian voice of his," recalled a trooper, "which could be heard for half a mile. 'Hold your ground down there, you damned scoundrels' was one of his mildest expressions." Just then, M. C. Butler's other brigade, Dunovant's South Carolinians, appeared at Wilkinson's, and the division commander ordered them to join Young in a counterattack. General Dunovant dismounted the Fourth and Fifth South Carolina Cavalry and led the troopers down the slope and through the swampy rivulet north of Vaughan Road. A gap opened between his right and Young's left, through which a Federal regiment penetrated, while more Union cavalry threatened Dunovant's left. The South Carolinians promptly retreated, along with the remaining men from Young's Brigade, taking position in the hasty works on Wilkinson's hill. From here they repulsed a spirited Yankee charge. Relative quiet then prevailed.[35]

Gregg instructed the Tenth New York Cavalry and the Sixth Ohio Cavalry to prepare slight works above the west bank of the creek, while the First Massachusetts Cavalry dug in on the east side. Should the Confederates threaten these lines with yet another assault, the advanced men were to retire to the main Federal position back on the McDowell house hill, which they had fortified the previous day. Each side unlimbered artillery and exchanged a desultory fire. Between rounds, Dunovant's veterans of the Beefsteak Raid taunted the nearby bluecoats by "bellowing like bulls, and shouting over to the Yankees, 'Good, fat beef over here; come over and get some.'" This invariably elicited a volley from the forward Union line, the bullets "rattling on the rail piles" of the Confederate works.[36]

This relatively harmless exchange of epithets and ammunition would continue until around 3:00 that afternoon. Wade Hampton used the intervening time to arrange an attack that promised to crush the Federals on the west side of the stream at the very least and perhaps drive the main body completely away from their stronghold at McDowell's. To do so, he summoned the Ninth and Thirteenth Virginia Cavalry of Davis's brigade to ride to Squirrel Level Road from their position on Duncan Road and then south, using a farm lane to gain a position beyond the Union right flank. When ready, they would descend on the Federals while Butler's Division charged directly from the west. In the event, however, Davis advanced directly down Squirrel Level Road, threatening not the Union right, but Butler's left. "We . . . discovered the mistake just in time to prevent them firing into us & we into them," wrote one of Davis's men. The excitement did at least persuade the two Federal regiments west of the creek to fall back, but a handful of the Ohio boys were captured before they could escape.[37]

The Yankees regrouped to the east, and the action paused as Confederate commanders contemplated their next move. Butler thought that a flanking maneuver around the Federal left offered the best opportunity to gain the high ground around McDowell's and open Vaughan Road to the north. He ordered Dunovant to execute that effort, to which the South Carolinian saluted and, betraying his dissatisfaction, replied, "General, let me charge 'em, we've got 'em going and let us keep 'em going." The thirty-year-old Dunovant had been court-martialed and dismissed from Confederate service in 1862 for drunkenness and frequent unexcused absences. The governor of South Carolina later reinstated him as colonel of the Fifth South Carolina Cavalry, and the chastened Carolinian did his best from that point forward to restore his reputation. Arriving in Virginia in 1864, Dunovant generally performed well and assumed command of Butler's Brigade when that officer took over Hampton's Division. Butler described Dunovant as "the beau ideal of a soldier, a knightly, chivalric gentlemen, thorough in the details of discipline and order, exacting, but always just, guarding with care and solicitude the interests of his soldiers." But on the night of September 30, it was his unwillingness to believe that Federal cavalry confronted him on Duncan Road that led to the capture of Andrew Pickens Butler. Historian Richard Sommers speculates that Dunovant's eagerness to launch a frontal attack stemmed, at least in part, from his desire to compensate for this embarrassing error and further erase his 1862 disgrace. Be that as it may, Butler initially rejected Dunovant's appeal, expressing the fear that a head-on, old-fashioned cavalry charge would cost too many lives. But Dunovant persisted. "My men are perfectly enthusiastic and ready to charge, an' we've got the Yankees demoralized, one more charge will finish 'em. Let me charge them." Butler relented. "Charge them, sir, if you wish."[38]

The South Carolinians dashed down the slope toward the creek on foot, with Dunovant still mounted near the head of his advancing brigade. "Suddenly the dense woods in our front became alive with rebels, who came on at a double-quick, shouting and yelling like so many fiends, firing as they advanced," wrote Major Beaumont, whose First New Jersey Cavalry had joined the front line. The Federals east of the stream unleashed a vicious volley. Sgt. James T. Clancy of the Jersey regiment fired his carbine at the mounted officer, then storming across the little corduroy bridge. Clancy's bullet struck Dunovant squarely in the skull. The general reeled in the saddle and toppled, but his foot hung up in a stirrup, dragging his now-lifeless body a short distance as his crazed horse ran madly into the Federal line and disappeared into the woods.[39]

Word soon reached Hampton that Dunovant had been mortally wounded. Doctor John B. Fontaine, the corps medical director, heard this report and, calling to a courier to join him, immediately "dashed at gallop in the direction of Gen. D.," hoping that the wound was not fatal. The doctor rode past the horse artillery, which had advanced down the slope and was receiving counterbattery fire from the Federals. Just as Fontaine approached the bridge, a shell exploded above him, "a piece of which—a very small fragment, struck him upon the chin and glancing downward entered the left side of the throat near the socket." The accompanying aide lifted the doctor from the saddle and laid him upon the ground until litter bearers bore him to the rear. Taken to a nearby house, another physician examined Fontaine, who pronounced his case hopeless. Fontaine lingered until 7:30 that evening before joining Dunovant in death. "Each of these officers, in his own sphere, was an admirable one," reported Hampton, "both were zealous in the performance of their duties and both were a loss to the service and to the country."[40]

Dunovant's demise and the stiff Federal resistance thwarted the South Carolinians' attack, and they retreated across the stream. Hampton now positioned his forces for the flank movement he had originally conceived, but this time he would strike the Federals from two directions. Davis's Virginians deployed north of Vaughan Road in position to assail Davies's right, while Butler moved to the left with both of his brigades. Hampton also called on Rooney Lee to bring forward the Tenth Virginia Cavalry and one of Barringer's North Carolina regiments to support Davis, but these reinforcements would not arrive before Hampton, concerned with the dwindling daylight that rainy afternoon, ordered his available forces forward. This time the advanced Union line gradually fell

The Fifth Offensive Concludes, October 1–2

back, halting on the high ground at McDowell's, where the rest of Davies's men, along with Smith's First Maine Cavalry, made their stand.

The Confederates crossed the stream and charged against both Federal flanks as well as straight east on Vaughan Road. The graycoats closed to within fifty yards of the Union line when the Federals opened with every available gun. For a few desperate moments, the outcome hinged in the balance, but ultimately the determined bluecoats proved too tough to crack. The gray tide receded, and after a very brief Union counterattack, Gregg's troopers returned to their lines, content to have held their position.[41]

At 6:30 P.M., Gregg reported that he had repulsed repeated Confederate assaults "in front and on both flanks." He later passed along the intelligence gleaned from a captured officer that four brigades of Hampton's cavalry were present, and although Union forces there numbered only six regiments, along with a single battery, "these will make a strong resistance if we are attacked again in the morning." Later that night Meade authorized Gregg to call on Parke if he needed support, predicting that the Rebels would undoubtedly try again.[42]

The cavalry fight along Vaughan Road on October 1, more fierce than sanguinary, cost Hampton some 130 casualties. Gregg lost fewer than 100 men, nearly half of whom were snatched up during the last retreat across the stream. The fighting, as had the earlier cavalry conflicts, bore little relationship to the larger Federal objectives. Meade's quest to interdict the Confederate supply lines had thus far been fruitless, although he would try one more time the following day.[43]

eade's latest orders to Parke and Warren reached their respective headquarters not long after the guns fell silent along Vaughan Road. Parke dutifully passed along Meade's instructions to Gregg, but Warren took the opportunity to compose a lengthy response, detailing an alternative course of action. His suggestion was technically logical, but it stood in contrast to the strategy pursued by Grant and Meade. To express his ideas in writing amid active operations and in contravention to the commanding general's own operational plan violated proper protocol—given Warren's shaky relationship with his superior, it defied common sense. The Fifth Corps commander had the unfortunate habit of offering unsolicited advice that sometimes bordered on insubordination. Apparently, Meade considered it as such because he made no reply nor modification to his issued orders. Nail by nail, Warren was sealing his own professional coffin.[44]

Unlike Warren, Meade would not challenge the wishes of his superior. General Grant sent Meade orders that night to advance both Crawford and Hancock to test the Confederates in their front. He based this directive upon the mistaken belief that either Mahone or Johnson had moved west and reinforced Hill. Meade obediently told Crawford to watch for an opportunity to attack in the morning but informed the general-in-chief that, contrary to his assumption, the Confederates remained entrenched in front of Crawford. Grant quickly admitted his error, demonstrating yet again his respect for Meade's judgment. He also asked about the outcome on Gregg's front, and Meade forwarded the cavalry commander's report expressing both his ability to hold his position and the continuing presence of a large body of enemy horsemen. Meade and Parke would allow Gregg to remain in position guarding access to the Federal rear via Vaughan Road, removing the cavalry from the offensive that was to commence at daybreak.[45]

Meade anticipated resuming the fight that had concluded the previous day along Squirrel Level Road and the Pegram-Boisseau field. A. P. Hill, however, had other plans. Shortly after nightfall, the Virginian began to withdraw his brigades from the positions they occupied at the close of combat. His rationale is a matter of speculation. Perhaps he had given up hope of reversing the Yankee incursion and felt that holding the primary defenses along Boydton Plank Road offered him the best chance of protecting his communications. Moreover, moving his infantry closer to Petersburg would shorten the march to Chaffin's Bluff should Lee call for further reinforcements north of the James River. And finally, the lack of offensive inclinations by the Federals on October 1 may have convinced him that the Yankees had abandoned further aggressive intentions.[46]

Whatever his thinking, Hill reduced the forces confronting Meade's five infantry divisions from nearly 14,000 men to merely the brigades of Archer and Davis, along with some of Hampton's and Joel Griffin's cavalry, no more than 4,300 soldiers of all arms. Archer took position in the works spanning Church Road, while Davis ranged southwest on Archer's right. Joel Griffin's dismounted troopers took position north of Doctor Boisseau's. All the Rebel units had quietly withdrawn from their advanced positions at the Chappell and Pegram farms, Cooke, MacRae, Lane, and McGowan halting near the familiar bivouac around Battery 45. Only a thin line of pickets at the Jones and W. W. Davis properties remained to contest the impending Federal attacks.[47]

Sunday, October 2, dawned with the promise of a dry day, as the incessant rain finally ceased about daylight, creating conditions more conducive to movement on Dinwiddie County's unimproved road network. Parke instructed Mott to prepare his division for such movement by 5:30 A.M. and to report to him personally at 6:00. But since the Ninth Corps commander directed Willcox and Potter to report for orders at 6:30 A.M., Mott's anxious troops cooled their heels until orders arrived. Once Willcox and Potter joined the gathering, Parke led

The Fifth Offensive Concludes, October 1–2

the assembled generals to Warren's headquarters, where he revealed his plan for the morning offensive.[48]

Parke envisioned an advance of Potter, Willcox, and Mott—from right to left—for the purpose, he later wrote, of "developing the force of the enemy and position of his works." Whether this explanation was simply an ex post facto justification for day's meager results or a reflection of the tentative generalship that characterized his and Warren's decisions throughout the entire Fifth Offensive, that language was inconsistent with Meade's expressed purpose of reaching Boydton Plank Road and threatening Petersburg. Warren received no specific mission other than a vague understanding that he was to support the right of the Ninth Corps. Before the first Union soldier took a step toward the Confederates, the operation's potential had already diminished.[49]

While Potter and Willcox had the straightforward assignment of advancing directly toward the Pegram farm, where they expected to encounter the Rebel line, Mott's 4,500 men bore responsibility for finding the Confederate right. To do so, they would march west on the farm road that ran past Fort MacRae, reach Duncan Road, and then, if all went well, move north toward Boydton Plank Road. Mott started his men about 7:00 A.M., Pierce's brigade in the lead, followed by McAllister's and de Trobriand's. They encountered some resistance from Barringer's Third North Carolina Cavalry around Fort MacRae and the lower end of the Squirrel Level works, but they easily dispersed the gray troopers. Still, this little skirmish and the still-muddy condition of the byway slowed the Union approach. Barringer's Carolinians continued to snipe at the Yankees' ponderous progress. Not until almost noon did Mott's troops reach Duncan Road, having taken five hours to cover about two miles.[50]

Although Mott's languid pace may be excused by the condition of the roads, the annoying Rebel opposition, and the uncertainty inherent in a flank march devoid of immediate support, the Ninth Corps possessed no such alibi. Parke simply indulged the cautious mindset that characterized his generalship throughout the entire operation. About 8:00 A.M. he advanced only a robust skirmish contingent borrowed from all five of his brigades, expecting to develop the formidable Rebel forces that had occupied the Pegram farm the previous day. Instead, when his skirmishers reached the Pegram house ridge, they discovered that the Confederates had disappeared. Surprised and perplexed, the Ninth Corps commander halted for more than an hour, gingerly probing ahead to ensure that the graycoats were not lurking in ambush. The only soldiers they found were dead. "We passed over some of the ground that we fought on the 30th and I saw some 8 or 9 of our men laying there stripped stark naked laying on top of the ground and never buried," wrote Pvt. Samuel E. Wilson of the

100th Pennsylvania. "I tell you it looked hard." Some of the corpses had already decayed, blackened and bloated caricatures of the human beings they once were. After more than an hour, Parke finally advanced his main line to the Pegram farm. He halted there, Potter stretching east to cover Church Road and Willcox extending westward toward Arthur's Swamp, where Harriman's brigade refused the left flank of the corps, waiting for Mott to appear. A bolder commander might have forged ahead, consistent with the goal of reaching Boydton Plank Road, but that was not John Parke this day. Instead, he awaited Meade's arrival to obtain further instructions.[51]

Meanwhile, Warren advanced along Squirrel Level Road in conjunction with Parke and was equally astonished to encounter only minor skirmish fire from around the W. W. Davis house. Warren assigned Col. Arthur Grimshaw's Third Brigade of Ayres's command to probe ahead and locate the main Confederate deployment. Leaving the 3rd Delaware behind, the rest of Grimshaw's men formed in the woods on the east side of the road and advanced obliquely toward the Davis house. "As soon as we came out of the cover of the woods they gave it to us," explained Captain Gawthrop. "I expected to go down every minute." The color corporal of the 157th Pennsylvania fell wounded, but the Federals raised a yell, and the few Confederates opposite them retired. Like the Ninth Corps to their left, Warren pushed no farther. We "certainly expected to have a fight today but were agreeably disappointed," admitted Captain Prince. Later that morning Warren received a report from his signal station at Globe Tavern confirming that the Confederates had abandoned their advanced lines in favor of a position farther north.[52]

As Parke and Warren tiptoed ahead, Meade confidently apprised Grant that his offensive was underway and then rode to Globe Tavern, arriving about 10:15 A.M. After instructing Lieutenant Colonel Lyman to locate a venue for new army headquarters, Meade learned that neither Warren nor Parke had engaged the Confederates that he—and everyone else—had assumed were holding their previous positions. This news changed the entire calculus of the army commander's plans. At 11:00 A.M. Meade notified Grant that the Confederates had withdrawn: "The inference is the enemy refuse battle outside their works, to which they have retired awaiting attack. Without your orders I shall not attack their intrenchments, but on being satisfied they are not outside of them I will take up the best position I can, connecting with the Weldon railroad and extending as far to the left as practicable, having in view the protection of my left flank, and then intrench." He solicited Grant's opinion of this course of action, to which the general-in-chief responded immediately. "Carry out what you propose," Grant agreed, "and hold what you can, but make no attack

The Fifth Offensive Concludes, October 1–2

against defended fortifications." Later, when Grant arrived at City Point from Deep Bottom, he told Meade to hold only what he could defend and granted the Pennsylvanian permission to abandon, if necessary, any of his captured ground to protect Union positions from the Weldon Railroad eastward. Meade immediately suspended the attack orders to both Warren and Parke and told them instead to entrench and make certain they secured their left flank. For seventy-two hours, Grant and Meade had cherished the possibility of interdicting Lee's supply routes from the southwest. Now, even the territorial gains achieved the preceding two days had become expendable.[53]

Grant's acquiescence may be explained by events on the north side of the James and his usual willingness to defer to his subordinate's judgment. But Meade's decision to terminate his attack plans is more difficult to fathom. Perhaps the circumspection exercised by his two corps commanders had convinced him that they would not hazard the sort of assault that now seemed necessary to reach their goal. Maybe Meade had eschewed attacking earthworks under any circumstances, anticipating Grant's admonition. Or possibly his innate conservatism—a trait well established in the Army of the Potomac—provided sufficient rationale to cancel the offensive.[54]

Warren and Parke did indulge brief spasms of aggressiveness late that morning, although they no doubt felt relief that they were no longer expected to hazard a full-scale assault. Shortly before noon Ayres again advanced Grimshaw's brigade, supported by the 5th and 140th New York from Major Grindlay's command, targeting the Rebel marksmen from Davis's Brigade, who still pestered them with sharpshooting from around the W. W. Davis house. The bluecoats easily rousted these annoying riflemen. "The rebs left the house as quickly as the breastworks before," remarked Gawthrop gleefully. Later, when the Confederates ventured forward to outflank their victorious foe, the remnants of the old Pennsylvania Reserves opened on them with Spencer repeaters and, again in the words of Captain Gawthrop, "gave them notice to quit." Ayres then fell back to his starting point and resumed fortifying.[55]

On Warren's left the Ninth Corps ventured forward from the Pegram farm as far as Doctor Boisseau's property. The Federals easily dislodged the Confederate pickets there, and Willcox followed about 300 yards north with McLaughlen's brigade. But the orders to entrench and the appearance of a stronger Confederate line accompanied by some shelling, leaving one man killed and eight wounded, caused Willcox to recall his troops. During these maneuvers, General Hartranft had assigned Lieutenant Colonel Cutcheon command of the Forty-Sixth New York in addition to his own regiment. This caused a problem for Cutcheon, who referred to the Forty-Sixth as "a German regiment ... [that]

I found had never been drilled in English and when they got into confusion, I found it difficult to make them understand [orders]." Despite this challenge, the regiment and the rest of the brigade emerged unharmed.[56]

Having heard nothing from Lee to indicate that more troops were needed north of the James, combined with the delayed, then tepid, probes executed by Warren and Parke, Hill decided to release Heth's two reserve brigades to reinforce Archer, Davis, and Barringer. Cooke's Tar Heels were the first to depart Battery 45. "We left our place of repose quite early," recorded Corporal Mullen, "and moved down the Plank Road about 2 miles, then turned down the Squirrel Level road." They began to improve the unfinished fortifications there when the sound of Parke's skirmishing prompted them to move to the right, halting just west of Church Road. MacRae's troops were the next to arrive. They took position east of Duncan Road, near the Hart house, filing in behind the shallow works there. Three batteries of Pegram's artillery followed quickly behind. They arrived just in time, as Mott's division had finally started north after their deliberate march to Duncan Road.[57]

Pierce and McAllister moved up Duncan Road, skirmishing with Barringer's pesky troopers, until they came in sight of the Rebel breastworks on the ridge dominated by the Hart house. Pegram's guns opened fire, as did the arriving Carolinians. "As no orders were given to press the attack, we lay down and held our position," reported a soldier in the Eleventh New Jersey.[58]

This respite allowed Heth to perfect his defensive deployment. Barringer's dismounted troopers withdrew to positions on the far right of the Confederate works west of Duncan Road. MacRae straddled that byway, and Davis shifted over to MacRae's left. Cooke continued the line to the northeast, followed by Griffin's cavalry and finally Archer, who remained on Heth's far left beyond Church Road. Pegram placed the Crenshaw Battery west of Duncan Road, where it could enfilade any movement up that byway. His other two batteries, the Purcell Artillery and Capt. Thomas Gregg's Battery C, Eighteenth South Carolina Heavy Artillery Battalion, took position on MacRae's left, where they could rain fire either down Duncan Road or toward the Pegram-Boisseau field. Once in place, the soldiers worked feverishly to improve the half-finished works.[59]

Both armies now contented themselves with engineering, the Federals vigorously creating a new line marking their advanced positions, and the Confederates equally busy enlarging their existing fortifications. Hill retained Wilcox's two brigades in the works between Battery 45 and the Weldon Railroad, and neither Gregg nor Hampton ventured aggressive action along Vaughan Road.

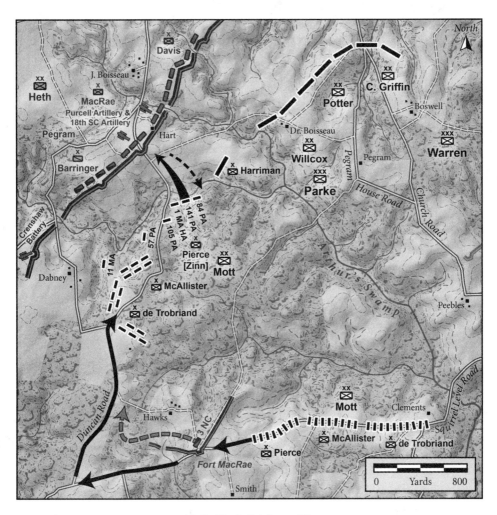

Mott's Attack, October 2, 1864

Pegram did remain active, his guns targeting both Mott and Parke. One of his shots elicited particular attention.[60]

Meade and his staff had gathered around the Pegram house about 1:00 P.M., halting behind Company F, 155th Pennsylvania. Naturally, the army commander drew a crowd of subordinates, eager to consult with him. Charles Griffin and Joseph Bartlett stood nearby along with two dozen other Fifth Corps officers, while some enlisted men in the vicinity indulged in a midday meal. Pegram maintained his fire on Parke's position, some of his shots soaring over their intended targets and into the rear. One of the errant projectiles passed directly between Griffin and Bartlett, ripping a piece off the tail of Andrew Humphreys's horse, grazing Meade's leg and boot, and burying itself in the ground without exploding, instead cascading mud over the entire assemblage. "It was one of those rebel Parrott's, with raised rings," explained Lyman. "It came butt-end foremost and did not explode." Had it done so "or gone six inches to the right or left, some or all might have been killed," thought Captain Prince, an opinion shared by Lyman. "Had I been there, I should have been the odd man that would have been hit. . . . The staff could not well have been arranged again so that there would have been room for a three-inch shell to pass without hitting somebody." Meade informed his wife of this battlefield serendipity, concluding that "a more wonderful escape I never saw. At first, I thought my leg was gone, as I felt and heard the blow plainly, but it only rubbed the leather of my riding-boot, without even bruising the skin." In a subsequent letter he called the episode "a pretty close shave," assuring his spouse that he would not "commit the folly of foolish and unnecessary exposure" but reminding her that "there are times when it is my duty and it is proper I should take my chances."[61]

Meade retired to the Peebles house as the stalemate across the entire battle-field persisted into midafternoon. Parke, now feeling sufficiently comfortable about his defensive preparations, took it upon himself to order a reconnaissance "to develop the position and force of the enemy." Willcox and Mott would exe-cute these orders. Harriman's brigade, on Willcox's left, and Pierce's command, on Mott's right, would cooperate in the probe. In hindsight, this action had little to recommend it. Meade and Grant now considered their offensive at an end, and no reconnaissance was required to ascertain that the Confederates manned the trenches extending from Warren's right to and beyond Mott's position along Duncan Road. True, the Federals could not know just how strongly the Rebels were deployed or that Hill was rushing reinforcements to his right, but even if the probe revealed a weakness, there was nothing to suggest that Parke or Meade would exploit such a discovery.[62]

At this moment, Pierce's skirmishers from the 84th Pennsylvania occupied a ravine formed by a small branch of Arthur's Swamp east of Duncan Road and about 300 yards south of the Confederate works. Pierce then advanced the remainder of these Pennsylvanians, along with three additional regiments from his brigade—the 141st Pennsylvania, 105th Pennsylvania, and 1st Massachusetts Heavy Artillery. He placed Lt. Col. George Zinn of the 84th in direct com-mand of this demi-brigade, the rest of Pierce's troops serving as supports and reserves. Mott ordered McAllister to deploy a regiment to the left to suppress the fire coming from the Crenshaw Artillery, which was in position to enfilade Zinn's approach. McAllister assigned the 11th Massachusetts to discharge this responsibility. Harriman shifted to the left, understanding that he was to advance only if Pierce asked him to do so.[63]

At 3:00 P.M. Zinn's four regiments boiled out of their sheltering ravine, heading for MacRae's position around the Hart house and Davis's Brigade on the Tar Heels' left. The Federals charged "most gallantly" and had covered about half the distance to the Rebel works when the Crenshaw Battery opened on their left "with canister and spherical case and raked us fiercely," remembered a Bay State soldier. The Carolinians and Mississippians poured lead into the charging bluecoats as the artillery continued to exact its toll. Zinn's men advanced as far as a few rods from the Rebel line before they reached the limit of their endurance. Zinn gave the order to retreat, and as he fell back, a Confederate ball struck his right leg, causing a serious wound. His men removed him from the field. The assault lasted all of ten minutes, and in that time the Yankees suffered sixty-eight casualties.[64]

Meanwhile, the Eleventh Massachusetts maintained an unequal contest with the Rebel infantry and artillery, losing fourteen men while managing only to shoot Pegram's horse. Harriman's brigade did not budge. The brigade commander heard accusations that Zinn's repulse was "attributed in part to the failure of my brigade to properly support the advancing column." Harriman protested that at no time did he receive orders to do more than hold his position, an assertion confirmed by General Willcox. Many of Willcox's troops could plainly see Zinn's effort, eliciting some harsh criticism. "The charge was decidedly feeble," wrote Cutcheon, and it "'petered out' before it reached the enemy's works. . . . If it was a faint, I do not understand why it was made. If it was a real attack, I cannot conceive why it was not pushed with more vigor." In fact, Meade did not order or desire Mott to venture this assault. At 3:10 P.M., as Zinn had reached the apogee of his attack, Mott received word from Parke that he had just seen Meade, who wished the division to "take up a line and intrench." Thus, the battle along Duncan Road—the final serious action on October 2—was forlorn, fruitless, unnecessary, and against the wishes of the commanding general.[65]

The Confederates who resisted Mott's assault proved more than adequate for the task. But Hill could not know that this would be the Federals' last offensive thrust of the day. Hancock and Crawford had shown little inclination to threaten the left and center of the Rebels' Petersburg defenses, Grant's wishes notwithstanding, so Hill ordered both Johnson and Mahone to send a brigade to reinforce Heth. Johnson selected Wise's Brigade, Virginians under the command of Col. John T. Goode, while Mahone picked Nathaniel Harris's battle-tested Mississippians. Mahone led both units as far west as the Weldon Railroad before the corps commander learned of the Federals' repulse and the absence of further signs of aggression. Consequently, he halted Mahone but directed him to remain around Battery 45 in case the situation changed.[66]

Relative quiet now prevailed southwest of Petersburg as both armies concentrated on adjusting their defensive positions and stiffening their fortifications. "Our men have been at work all night constructing a new breastworks in rear of the one they made before," read a typical Union diary entry. At noon on October 3, Meade apprised Grant of the previous day's actions: "We now hold securely the Pegram house, with our left refused and the cavalry to the rear on the Vaughan and Ducking [Duncan] roads. . . . Generals Parke and Warren are busily . . . intrenching in this position." The army commander continued to encourage his subordinates to protect the ground they occupied, telling Parke, for example, "to have the intrenchments, slashing, &c., pushed forward as rapidly as possible, working all the men you can." By 10:00 P.M., Meade assured Grant that his left was so well protected that he would send Mott's division back to the Second Corps. "I do not think the enemy will attempt to disturb us now," he predicted.[67]

The Federal works may have been made strong, but some of the Union commanders harbored reservations about the quality of the troops defending them. Colonel McAllister complained: "One half of my Brigade are raw recruits, some of whom have never been in battle nor even fired off a gun. Some of them do not understand the English language. We have a great number of Dutch, some French—all nations but the Hottentots." General de Trobriand agreed, griping that the new levies in his brigade lacked "even knowledge of how to load a gun. . . . What's the use of such reinforcements except to furnish arms and uniforms to the enemy if one puts them in line of battle. The best thing [to do] is to put them in the dustpan or in the pocket."[68]

Confederates, though thankful they had prevented the enemy from interdicting their remaining lines of communication, voiced concern about the future. "Old Grant has been trying to get possession of the South Side R.R. which if he could get and hold would force us into abandoning Petersburg and probably Richmond," wrote Surgeon William J. Mosely. "But he has not got it yet and he has got to fight for it [but] if he does get it he may . . . hold it for I did not believe he could hold the Weldon RR and he has done it." Sgt. Abram G. Jones of Barringer's Brigade wrote his father, "I don't think the quiet that now prevails will last long."[69]

Not every Confederate soldier engaged in engineering labor around the clock. Some found time to earn a little extra money in a fashion unique to 1864. "I was amused yesterday during the shelling," wrote General Lane, "to see some of our artillerists running out and picking up fragments of shells. They collect large quantities of these and dispose of them to the foundries, getting eight cents a pound for the iron and ten for the lead. Five or six passed me during the day loaded down with fragments." Unexploded shells attracted even more attention. "You will see a half dozen confederate soldiers running at a fearful rate to claim the prize," wrote an Alabaman. Lane also admitted that all the Yankee dead "that had on passable clothes were stripped," but he denied the accusation that his men otherwise abused the corpses.[70]

And corpses there were—many of them. Federal casualties during the Fifth Offensive on the Petersburg front alone numbered nearly 3,000 men. Confederate losses are estimated at slightly more than 1,300 soldiers. The Ninth Corps suffered the most, the majority of their casualties being prisoners of war. The scenes at the numerous field hospitals left a ghastly impression at odds with Victorian sensibilities. "Oh, what a sight," remembered Pvt. Henry F. Charles of the Twenty-First Pennsylvania Cavalry. "The dead and wounded had all been removed, but the arms and legs that had been amputated still lay there on a pile. Some with boots and shoes still on, parts of pants and underwear, and arms with white hands sticking out of tattered shirt sleeves. You get sick looking at all the blood and dirt and could almost feel the pain that was suffered there. It was," he thought, "the most disgusting scene I ever saw and I hoped it would be the last."[71]

Connecticut's Andrew Knox considered his army's campaign southwest of Petersburg "the most important movements that has ever taken place during the war." A correspondent for the *New York Times* was more circumspect in his praise, writing, "All things considered, I think that the recent movement may safely be set down as a move in the right direction." Colonel Wainwright, noting the expansion of his army's lines westward, felt that "we have gained a position which may be of value to us in future operations." Lieutenant Colonel LaMotte was confident that "the Johnnies won't attack," citing the powerful fortifications the army was building to create a seamless connection from the Pegram farm and Church Road to the existing works along the Weldon Railroad.[72]

To be sure, Meade's army had captured much of the Squirrel Level Line, a position that in Confederate hands threatened to keep them pinned down at Globe Tavern. This compelled the Rebels to extend their own fortifications as far as five miles to the southwest, eventually anchoring on Hatcher's Run. On the other hand, Lee's forces had retained their two remaining lines of communication to the south via Boydton Plank Road and the South Side Railroad, the avowed objective of Meade's initiative, and inflicted losses more than twice their own. Some Federals, such as Capt. Josiah Jones, bemoaned the massive casualties sustained by his army, calling it "a perfect slaughter," and confided to his diary: "We cannot take the South Side R.R. any more than we can take Petersburg.... We can hold our own and that is about all." Certainly, that would be the case should the senior Federal commanders there continue to shrink from taking the bold steps necessary to defeat Lee's defenders.[73]

Many Confederates celebrated what they saw as a triumph between September 30 and October 2. "In this fight our troops gained a most decided victory with small loss but most heavy to the enemy," wrote General Scales. "If we can gain such victories with what troops we have & against such odds what will we do when we get in all the detailed men." Artillery colonel William T. Poague admitted to his mother that the Federals "got a little more of Va. soil under [their] control, but we killed and captured a considerable number of Yankees and the account balances in our favor." A Richmond newspaper (over)estimated that Grant had suffered 5,000 casualties for every mile he advanced. "If our readers will take the trouble to count his losses in taking the Weldon road, thence to the Vaughan and now to the Squirrel Level road, they will find this a correct estimate. At this rate it will cost him thirty thousand more men to reach the Southside. More than that, we reckon."[74]

Lieutenant Colonel Pegram expressed supreme confidence in his army's prowess in a letter to his sister. "Our position here is so strong that Grant might mass his whole army against it and I do not think we would have anything to fear." He considered the campaign thus far "the most remarkable in the annals of history," one for which "it would be impossible for the best writer in the world to do justice to this noble army." Noting that "our troops are in remarkably fine spirits," he qualified his praise and optimism by admitting that "nearly every man & officer feels the want of physical strength." Francis Marion Coker, the Georgia cannoneer, felt that they could "hold them at bay at all points.... The only difficulty we labour under is *inferiority of numbers.*" He admitted that "our lines being very long, they are necessarily weak at some point," offering Grant the chance to break them. General Lee perceived the same issue. "If the enemy cannot be prevented from extending his left, he will eventually reach the Appomattox and cut us off from the south side altogether," he advised cavalry chief Hampton. This possibility unsettled men such as Capt. Samuel S. Brooke of the Forty-Seventh Virginia. "We did not succeed in dislodging them and had to retire to our second line of earthworks where we are now confronted by a heavy force of the Yankees & hourly expecting an attack," he informed a correspondent. "This month will be a month of suffering & trial for our little army & if we are not assisted by those who are now staying at home shirking duty I don't know what may not happen to us."[75]

A Confederate staff officer, Maj. Thomas Claybrook Elder, neatly summarized the strategic situation in a letter to his wife. Grant, he wrote, "moves a heavy body of troops to the north side of James river and pretends that he is going to advance on Richmond from that direction. Genl Lee is obliged to move a force over there too because if Grant should find the way imperfectly guarded, he would actually dart into Richmond. This being done, Grant casts his eye around Petersburg and finding a weak point he assaults." On September 29 and 30, Grant certainly tried to capture Richmond, and on October 1 his forces on the north side of the James were not quite finished.[76]

hortly before midnight on September 30, Grant advised Butler of events on Meade's side of the river, which led him to believe that "no heavy force had been sent north of the James. I think it would be advisable for you to reconnoiter up the Darbytown road, and if there appears to be any chance for an advance make it." Butler's comparatively easy repulse of the day's attacks at Fort Harrison had left him ebullient, but now intelligence gleaned from a Confederate officer gave him pause. This informer—it is unclear whether he was a prisoner or a deserter—told him that Heth's and Wilcox's Divisions were north of the James, along with Field's and Hoke's. "We shall be attacked in the morning and we shall make the best fight we can," wrote Butler, his optimism extinguished. Once again he begged Grant to send him "a division or two" as reinforcements. And once again Grant declined, although he did promise to send a corps north of the James "if the enemy continues to hold his present force at Petersburg." When Butler persisted, the general-in-chief's patience finally expired. At 3:00 A.M. Grant forwarded Meade's earlier report that he faced Heth, Wilcox, Mahone, and Johnson, telling Butler, "Under existing circumstances you must discard the idea of receiving reenforcements, and if attacked make the best defense you can with the troops with you."[77]

Whether chastened or not, Butler proceeded to do just that. He ordered Weitzel to shift Paine's division from north of Fort Harrison to the army's left, blocking access to the Union rear via Osborne Turnpike, and told David Birney to shift leftward to cover the gap created by the Third Division's departure. These adjustments left the Eighteenth Corps holding the line from the James to Fort Harrison and the Tenth Corps in position along the old Outer Line from Fort Harrison to New Market Road. Kautz and his cavalry remained on the Federal right along Darbytown Road. All through that rainy night, Union fatigue parties labored to improve the fortifications, reverse the captured Confederate works, and strengthen the makeshift barriers across Fort Harrison's gorge. "Here we are in the trenches of an earthwork which used to be a reb work & faced this way now we have reversed it & it faces the Rebs," wrote an officer in the Twenty-Ninth Connecticut, "and [it] is fringed with a regular brush of sharpened stakes which Johnny would find it rather difficult to get through let alone the destructive fire he would meet." By dawn of October 1, the Army of the James was well protected.[78]

Butler may have been deluded regarding the Confederate troops opposing him, but he was right about Lee's desire to test him that morning. The Confederate commander moved Field's Division back to Fort Johnson during the night, while Hoke retired to the entrenched camp immediately around Chaffin's Bluff. Lee met with his commanders on the morning of October 1, and although details of that council are elusive, it may be inferred that the officers discussed plans to renew the effort to reclaim Fort Harrison. General Alexander's guns reopened on the Federals, and Lee called on the navy to resume its bombardment as well. "Our attempt to retake Fort Harrison on yesterday having failed, I respectfully request that you will direct your guns to fire upon it and also in its rear, that as much injury as possible may be inflicted upon the force occupying the fort," Lee wrote to Commodore John K. Mitchell. The navy began its bombardment at 10:00 A.M., but no infantry assault followed. For whatever reason, Lee declined to make another run at Fort Harrison and contented himself with ordering the construction of a new line behind the captured fort, connecting Forts Johnson and Hoke. If combat was to reoccur north of the James on October 1, the bluecoats would have to initiate it.[79]

When, by 8:30 that morning, no Confederate infantry had ventured forward, Butler decided to act on Grant's suggestion, albeit in a most conservative fashion. He instructed Birney to "take two brigades of Terry's division and make a reconnaissance in force up the Darbytown Road toward Richmond. You may be able to get through." He enclosed instructions to Kautz to cooperate with the infantry probe but left the operation contingent on Birney's perception that the Rebels were not forming for an attack of their own. Birney selected Pond's First and Abbott's Second Brigades of Terry's division for the reconnaissance and ordered General Foster to "select one good regiment and send it as a line of skirmishers to drive in the enemy's pickets on New Market Road" as a feint in favor of the advance on Darbytown Road. These measures complied with Grant's specifications for a reconnaissance but nothing more. Terry's two brigades numbered between 4,300 and 4,400 men, hardly enough to exploit any weakness they might discover. Not unlike Warren and Parke beyond the south side of the James, Butler now took counsel of his fears and no longer entertained visions of entering the Confederate capital. Most of the Army of the James would remain stationary and on the defensive October 1.[80]

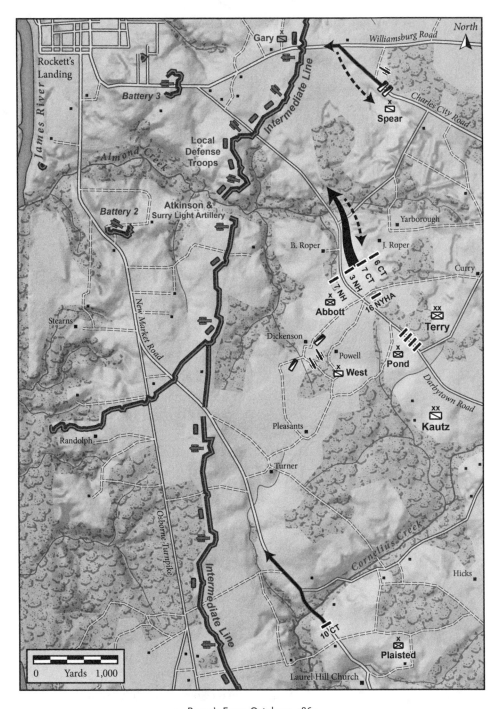

Roper's Farm, October 1, 1864

Consistent with this mentality, Birney seemed in no hurry to begin his reconnaissance. It would take him nearly three hours to begin shifting Pond and Abbott northward to Darbytown Road, and not until 1:25 P.M., nearly five hours after Butler issued his orders, did the two brigades reach that highway. Birney promised to lead the advance personally but then failed to do so. General Terry assumed direct command instead, Abbott's New Englanders in the lead followed by Pond's four regiments. They joined Kautz and, after a brief consultation, decided to send Sam Spear's cavalry brigade, along with two guns, north to Charles City Road to look after Terry's right. Col. Robert M. West's troopers would lead the infantry up Darbytown Road, accompanied by eight pieces of horse artillery. The column started marching at 2:00 P.M. in what New Hampshire's Daniel Eldredge noted was "a very nasty day . . . wet and muddy and a nasty drissle."[81]

Colonel Abbott aligned his brigade in skirmish formation astride the road, with the Sixth Connecticut on the right and on their left, in order, the Seventh Connecticut, Third New Hampshire, and Seventh New Hampshire. His battalion of the Sixteenth New York Heavy Artillery remained in reserve. "In this manner we advanced to within 1,000 yards of the outer works of Richmond," wrote Eldredge, "nearer than any infantry had been during the war." As the infantry sloshed across rain-soaked fields and waded swollen streamlets, West's troopers diverted off to the south to provide flank protection, joined by two sections of artillery. Only a few grayclad skirmishers annoyed Terry's advance, the elements posing a more formidable obstacle.[82]

The Federals emerged into the fields owned, south of the road, by Benjamin Roper and north of the highway by his kinsman James. The "heavy works of the enemy was in plain sight, distance apparently about 1,400 yards," reported Col. Alfred P. Rockwell of the Sixth Connecticut. Because the Intermediate Line here ran almost due north–south and Darbytown Road angled northwest, the regiments on Abbott's left approached closer than those on the right. In any event, all the Federals soon fell under artillery fire emanating from the works. These guns belonged to Lt. Col. John W. Atkinson's First Division of heavy artillery, abetted by the Surry Light Artillery of Lightfoot's Battalion, all of Pemberton's command. Only Local Defense troops and Gary's cavalry supported these guns, but they would prove enough to halt Abbott, West, and Pond. "The enemy evidently had every foot of ground measured for ranges of their guns, for their fire came accurate and heavy," reported Maj. Fredrick W. Prince of the Sixteenth New York Heavy Artillery. West's light ordnance responded, but despite losing one of the Surry Light Artillery's pieces to a Federal round, the Rebel gunners dominated the exchange.[83]

Lt. Charles August Henninghausen of the Second Virginia Reserves was among the second-class troops defending the line south of Darbytown Road. "The falling fine rain and the fog had softened the clay of the breastworks so that our men couldn't get good footing to look over the works but kept sliding back again," he wrote. As the artillery duel grew more intense, the lieutenant noticed women and children rushing toward them, seeking to escape the fusillade. One of the young women, pressing an infant against her chest and dragging a four-year-old girl behind her, managed with assistance to clamber over the works and flee to the rear. When the call came for his unit to assist the defenders on their left, Henninghausen and his men ran along the ditch behind the works "through mud and mire and often in water up to their knees" that had turned the ground behind the works into "a lake of mud."[84]

Terry had certainly found the Confederate line he was seeking, and beyond a doubt, the relentless fire from his front and both flanks made it obvious that the Rebels intended to defend that position. He wisely withdrew his troops into the sheltering woods, hoping to hear good news from Spear.

Samuel Perkins Spear was a tough customer. He made the U.S. Army a career before the war, reaching the rank of sergeant major, then rising to command the Eleventh Pennsylvania Cavalry in the volunteer service before gaining brigade command in January 1864. He now dismounted his troopers and easily scattered Gary's skirmishers. But when he approached closer to the Confederate line, just west of where Charles City Road blended into Williamsburg Road, more Rebel artillery opened fire. Spear responded with his two guns, but they were no match for the heavier and more numerous Confederate ordnance. Like Terry, Spear knew an impossible task when he saw one and retired.[85]

The third prong of Birney's offensive, the diversionary attack along New Market Road, would enjoy only limited success. Foster decided against using one of his own Second Division regiments and instead turned to his former brigade, now under Colonel Plaisted, in Terry's First Division. The Tenth Connecticut, led by Col. John L. Otis, a thirty-seven-year-old textile manufacturer from Lyme, received the assignment. It was an odd choice, as only 153 men answered the roll call that morning, "a thinned regiment with hardly more rifles than were borne by one of its ten companies three years ago," according to the regimental chaplain. Like Abbott and Spear, the Nutmeggers easily dispersed the Confederate skirmishers they encountered, but unlike their comrades farther north, once they confronted the main Rebel line, the Tenth Connecticut held its ground. "When the enemy brought a force upon our left flank our boys met that . . . and silenced its fire," boasted Chaplain Henry Clay Trumbull. "The rebels sent an entire regiment to reinforce their skirmish line. That was also held in check. For fully two hours our men stood there audaciously, pouring in a fire upon the enemy's line as though we had a brigade with us instead of a squad." The Connecticut boys continued exchanging shots with the Confederates (probably DuBose's Georgians) and only retired under orders at dusk. No Union unit this day fought better than the Tenth Connecticut, but ultimately their brave performance achieved no tangible advantage. The Confederates accumulated plenty of firepower to stymie Terry and Kautz, so as a diversion, their gambit failed.[86]

Likewise, Terry began withdrawing shortly before sunset, slowly trudging back along Darbytown Road through the drenching rain. Spear returned down Charles City Road. By 9:00 P.M., the Federals had regained their old lines. "This period of time is recalled by all interested as one of extreme discomfort," wrote a Massachusetts soldier, "since the day before, rain had begun, and both officers and men were without shelter except for the blankets they carried. All night long the men suffered from the driving rain." The Confederates remained on high alert into the evening hours despite the weather, not knowing that Butler had already done his worst this day. Yet had they read Birney's correspondence late that afternoon, they would have had even more reason to remain vigilant. The Tenth Corps commander sent celebratory messages to Butler, boasting that the Rebel pickets had been driven "in confusion" and had run "without much fight." At 4:35 that afternoon, he informed army headquarters: "I see no reason for recalling General Terry. . . . I have ordered him to attack any force outside [the] main works." But this was so much idle talk. The fighting on October 1 had ended, and so too had Butler's portion of the Fifth Offensive.[87]

Casualties on October 1 mirrored the Federals' modest efforts. Abbott reported one man killed, sixteen wounded, and eighteen missing. Spear added three wounded and one missing. Including the losses sustained by the Tenth Connecticut, the Army of the James suffered a grand total of forty-two casualties. Confederate losses went unreported but were undoubtedly fewer. The combat north of the James on October 1 proved anticlimactic to the profound potential promised by events on the morning of September 29.[88]

Butler sent Grant an incomplete but rather cheery summary of the day's results that night. His earlier assertion that he faced all but two of Lee's divisions reached Meade's headquarters, where it engendered a derisive reception, reflecting the latent rivalry between the two armies. "Ben Butler had quite a stampede last night," Lieutenant Colonel Lyman informed his wife, "having got so far away from home he conceived the whole southern host was massed to crush him and communicated the same with much eloquence by the instrumentality of the magnetic telegraph; whereat Maj. Gen. Humphreys, Chief of

The Fifth Offensive Concludes, October 1–2

Staff, had the brutality to laugh." Grant responded with the same operational mindset that had prompted him to permit Meade the option of surrendering the ground he had captured if necessary to protect his existing works. "I think it will be advisable to select a line which can be held with one of your corps as now composed, giving you an outlet at Deep Bottom or Aiken's," he advised Butler. "The other corps could be kept on the north side as well as elsewhere, but held ready for any emergency." Grant worried that Butler's advanced position either could be turned by a flank attack or "would cause the enemy to so prepare that no surprise on that side could again be made." Clearly, the general-in-chief had given up on his Fifth Offensive north of the James as he had in Meade's sector, Mott's ill-advised probe on Duncan Road notwithstanding.[89]

Butler complied and asked for Major General Barnard and Colonel Comstock from Grant's staff to help lay out the new line. Grant promised to send those men in the morning. But despite his obvious belief that opportunity for more meaningful achievements had passed, he gave Butler latitude to act as he wished, noting that Meade intended to make a reconnaissance the next day. Butler consulted with his corps commanders and wrote Grant at 9:45 A.M. on October 2 that his army's senior commanders believed that if they advanced en masse on Darbytown and Charles City Road, they could break the lightly held Confederate lines. All that was required was an additional corps to hold the Union lines while the Army of the James executed its triumphal assault. "I am very strongly of the opinion that this plan would succeed," wrote a once-again-undaunted Butler, "and I trust the lieutenant general has confidence enough in my means of obtaining information that I am not deceived as to the facts."[90]

Grant met with his subordinate that morning while Comstock and Barnard identified the new defensive position he had requested. Whether reacting to Butler's written suggestion or deciding during their conference, Grant rejected the proposal. The lieutenant general also overruled Butler's preference for a longer line, endorsing his engineers' recommendation for a more compact position. The line would start on Four Mile Creek above Deep Bottom, then go west to where the captured Confederate New Market Line intersected the old Outer Line just south of the junction of New Market and Mill Roads. From there, the works would trace the reversed Confederate trenches to Fort Harrison, then bend back to the left flank at Cox's Hill. The Tenth and Eighteenth Corps joined near Fort Harrison. The Federals refused their line at New Market Road, but Kautz patrolled farther north along Darbytown and Charles City Roads.[91]

Lee also spent early October perfecting the new fortifications that connected Forts Hoke and Johnson, thereby emasculating the Fort Harrison salient and leaving the Rebels as relatively strong as they had been prior to the Union offensive. The Confederate commander still worried about the security of his left flank, despite the feeble effort rendered there by Terry and Kautz on the first. Two grayclad brigades, Bowles's and Montague's, probed down New Market Road on October 2, while Gary's troopers explored Darbytown and Charles City Roads. Minor skirmishing ensued, although Birney considered it a concerted attack and warned of an even larger impending assault. Lee ventured no such action, nor did he intend to do so. The reconnaissance satisfied him that Butler had not positioned his army for another immediate attempt to turn the Confederate left, and as a bonus it had kept the Yankees focused on their own security. Lee felt satisfied that Richmond remained unthreatened for the present, though he still coveted the notion of driving the Federals back to their bridgehead at Deep Bottom, if not completely across the James. Grant and Butler were now equally convinced that their efforts on the north side were at a temporary end, content to have captured significant Confederate acreage, including many Rebel fortifications. The fighting north of the James between September 29 and October 2 cost Butler 3,350 casualties, while Lee lost about 1,700 men. Thus, the Fifth Petersburg Offensive tallied roughly 6,300 Union losses and some 3,000 for their opponents.[92]

Grant foreclosed any immediate initiatives in this sector on October 4. In a message to Butler, the general-in-chief recognized that the "difficulty of holding more than we now have . . . should keep us from further offensive operations until we get more men," adding that he expected to accumulate "30,000 additional veteran troops in the next ten days, besides all the new troops that may come." Those experienced soldiers would come from Sheridan's command in the Shenandoah Valley, as that general's recent victories there and his ongoing effort to sterilize the Valley as a source of Confederate supply portended the end of active operations west of the Blue Ridge. Grant left for Washington on October 6 to discuss the transfer, leaving Butler in command.[93]

General Lee offered Grant another source of Union reinforcements on October 1. "With a view of alleviating the sufferings of our soldiers, I have the honor to propose an exchange of prisoners of war belonging to the armies operating in Virginia, man for man, or upon the basis established by the cartel," he wrote. Grant replied the following day inquiring if the "colored troops" captured in Butler's recent battles would be returned "the same as white soldiers." Lee responded on October 3 assuring Grant that he "intended to include all captured soldiers of the United States of whatever nation and color under my control." He added, importantly: "Deserters from our service and negroes belonging to our citizens are not considered subjects of exchange and were not included in my proposition. If there are any such among those stated by you to have been captured

The Fifth Offensive Concludes, October 1–2

around Richmond, they cannot be returned." Grant terminated this dialogue by informing Lee: "The Government is bound to secure to all persons received into her armies the rights due to soldiers. This being denied by you in the persons of such men as have escaped from Southern masters induces me to decline making the exchanges you ask." He did promise to refer the matter to the secretary of war and to adhere to any contrary decision the government might render.[94]

Ben Butler exceeded even Grant in his attention to the dignity, rights, and recognition of Black soldiers. He addressed a dispatch to Secretary Stanton boasting about the performance of his African American troops. "Their praises are in the mouth of every officer in this army," he beamed. "Treated fairly and disciplined, they have fought most heroically." When Butler learned that the Confederates employed captured Black soldiers on the fortifications around Fort Gilmer, "a practice justified by no rule of war," he dispatched a protest to the Confederate commissioner of exchange, Robert Ould, along with notification of a countermeasure. "I have ordered a like number of officers and soldiers captured by us . . . into the canal at Dutch Gap and put them at hard labor, and shall continue to add to their number until this practice is stopped," he snarled. Eventually, Lee agreed to halt the obnoxious practice, and in return Grant, who had been supportive of Butler's retaliation, "directed the withdrawal of the Confederate prisoners employed in Dutch Gap Canal." The participation and sacrifice of Black soldiers in Butler's late-September operations north of the James significantly elevated the perception, status, and treatment of these men.[95]

These negotiations did nothing to diminish the physical exertion undertaken by Butler's soldiers. Work continued on strengthening Fort Harrison, which the Federals would soon rename Fort Burnham. Butler assigned his acting chief engineer, Peter Michie, to superintend the construction of the line recommended by Barnard and Comstock. He obtained work parties from various infantry regiments and the experienced men of the 1st New York Volunteer Engineers to perform the labor, supplemented by the 127th USCT. The left of that line would be anchored on a powerful work named Fort Brady, built on what the Confederates called Signal Hill. Within a week Michie reported that this line was "secure and in good condition" but that the portion of the works held by the Tenth Corps was "very weak and not well laid out." Birney had simply reversed the Confederate's Outer Line, leaving poor fields of fire in places, among other deficiencies. "I have urged a new line, with appropriate works, to protect our right flank and make it secure, but an unwillingness has been manifested to have this carried out," Michie complained.[96]

Perhaps the corps commander's physical condition explained the failure. On October 4 Butler informed General Birney that he was about to shift his headquarters "outside of everybody's pickets, if I get gobbled you will have command." The army commander did not realize that, just then, Birney was confined to his tent and under the care of the corps medical director. The Philadelphian had complained as early as September 6, "My health is really poor, and . . . between the ague & diarrhea I feel like asking for a leave." Birney's condition had not improved, and Butler now ordered him home to recuperate. He would never return to the army.

On the evening of October 18, David Birney died, a victim of malaria. Butler issued General Orders No. 135 announcing Birney's demise, calling the departed general a "patriot—the hero—the soldier. By no death has the country sustained a greater loss." Meade deemed Birney's demise "undoubtedly a loss to the army," a sentiment shared by many of his former subordinates. The highly capable Alfred Terry now assumed command of the Tenth Corps.[97]

The deaths of the many soldiers killed in front of Fort Harrison on September 30—unlike Birney, perishing far from home—lay where they fell for several days in the no-man's-land between the lines. Although some effort was made to bury these poor souls, not until October 8 did an informal truce allow the pickets from both armies to inter the decaying corpses. A New York officer instigated the arrangement after he could no longer endure the horrible stench emitting from the unburied dead. Waving a newspaper as if to trade, he approached the Rebel pickets and proposed a joint burial detail. With the unspoken acquiescence of ranking officers on both sides, Billy Yank and Johnny Reb wielded shovels and interred, by one account, more than 500 Confederates. "The bodies are scattered here through the dense brush, and but for the stench would be difficult to find," wrote one of the Federals.[98]

Conditions and affairs were not much different south of the James. "A gentle southern breeze raised the pulverized 'sacred soil' in wavy clouds as if to shut from view the sickening sight of myriads of new made graves, scarce deep enough to cover the garments of the rebel dead," wrote William H. Hagar, a new recruit of the Forty-Fifth Pennsylvania. Meade's soldiers, like Butler's, spent most of the next few days laboring on fortifications. They laid out redoubts that soon adopted the names of slain officers in the recent offensive. Fort Welch, for example, arose near the Pegram house, while Fort Fisher guarded Church Road. The engineers concentrated on building the forts, while the infantry threw up the connecting trenches. The Federals spaced their redoubts such that they enjoyed mutually supporting fire, while artillery batteries, open at the rear and located between the forts, ensured that no ground in front of the line was immune from enfilade as well as frontal fire. Infantry curtains connected the forts and batteries. Large details cut wood for abatis, which the soldiers positioned in front of their works at night. "I wish you could take a look round here some day and see the grounds," wrote Hagar. "As far as the eye can see is dotted with white tents, in front of the lines is a breastwork running along like a fence." Meade specified that the fortifications encompass all the ground captured in his recent operations as well as a parallel line facing south to connect with Fort Dushane on the Weldon Rail Road. By October 5, General de Trobriand pronounced the work "well advanced." "The Army of the Potomac have now about 28 miles of works thus built and thus defended," explained Colonel McAllister. "Then add Butler's lines and we have about 40 miles—and are now extending them. Can it be possible the Rebels can stretch much more?"[99]

That night Mott's division moved east, allowing the rest of the Second Corps to close up between Fort Sedgwick on Jerusalem Plank Road and the Appomattox River. Ayres manned the line between Vaughan and Squirrel Level Roads, his right stretching to connect with Crawford's position at Globe Tavern and Fort Wadsworth. Griffin held the works between Squirrel Level and Church Roads, while Parke refused the army's far left flank, anchored near the Clements house, where a bastion named Fort Cummings was under construction.[100]

A. P. Hill was able to answer McAllister's rhetorical question in the affirmative, but only just barely. He continued to hold the ever-more-formidable works in front of Boydton Plank Road, extending from Battery 45 southwest to beyond Duncan Road. Barringer's troopers manned the trenches on the far Confederate right, with three of Heth's brigades strung out to their left. Hill brought Lane and McGowan into line covering Church Road, where they joined Archer's Brigade, blocking that likely artery of Federal advance. Mahone and Johnson still defended the Rebel center and left, nestling up against the Appomattox River. A gap existed between Archer and Mahone, plugged precariously by the Petersburg militia. Barringer's right was unprotected, although the rest of Hampton's cavalry roamed the countryside to the south, on the alert for any threatening Federal moves.[101]

The Confederates could accept these shortcomings, at least for the time being, because Meade evinced nothing to suggest he intended to renew his offensive. Now, both ranking commanders focused on adding manpower to replace the thousands of men each had lost on both sides of the James. Grant's intention to transfer the bulk of Sheridan's Valley force to the Petersburg front would be delayed by two months, thanks to a surprise Confederate attack at Cedar Creek on October 19, reigniting active operations west of the Blue Ridge. New levies did join the army, only compensating in part for the departure of veteran units whose terms of enlistment had expired.[102]

In the South, however, the manpower reservoir had run dry. On October 4 Lee addressed a letter to Secretary Seddon wondering "whether there is any prospect of my obtaining any increase to this army. If not," Lee warned, "it will be very difficult for us to maintain ourselves." The gray commander explained that in the wake of Grant's Fifth Offensive, the enemy's superior strength allowed him to "extend on each flank with numbers so much greater than ours that we can only meet his corps, increased by recent recruits, with a division reduced by long and arduous service." He warned Seddon, "We cannot fight to advantage with such odds, and there is the gravest reason to apprehend the result of every encounter." For starters, Lee recommended that Black workers replace laborers, teamsters, and other noncombatants, who would return to the ranks. More importantly, White men exempted from service must be mustered for active duty. Otherwise, Lee expressed doubt that he could hold the Richmond-Petersburg lines until winter inhibited active campaigning.[103]

The harried cabinet officer responded promptly to Lee's urgent message, assuring the general that he had done and would do everything in his power to accommodate his requests. That day the army's adjutant general, Samuel Cooper, issued General Orders No. 76 revoking all military details except for men involved with munitions or other supplies indispensable to the army. He also ordered that every man exempted due to physical disabilities be reexamined; those found fit should be mustered in to service. Only time would tell if these expedients would prove sufficient.[104]

Lee was undoubtedly sincere when he painted such a dire picture of the operational situation at the conclusion of the Fifth Petersburg Offensive. But the Confederates enjoyed one important advantage. They held interior lines and used them to shift forces to where they were most needed at any given time. As Grant's aide Adam Badeau would observe after the war, "holding the chord of the circle [Lee] could transfer troops in a few hours, while Grant, on the arc, required a day to move his men from Petersburg to the Richmond front, or from Fort Harrison to Peeble's farm. The superiority in numbers possessed by one was more than equalized by the position the other enjoyed." And that superiority was not as great as some believed. "The enemy have allowed us to retain the ground acquired by our recent movement, and seem to be busy fortifying against another advance," Meade informed his wife on October 7. "We have been reinforced, but not to the extent imagined by the sanguine public; neither is Richmond so near its fall as you tell me people believe."[105]

Of course, Lee maintained the opposite view. He wrote his wife: "The enemy is very numerous. Still increasing & is able by his superiority of numbers to move at pleasure. Still I trust he may not be permitted to have everything his own way." On October 7 he would test that hypothesis.[106]

eleven

THE GUNS OF OCTOBER

The loss of Fort Harrison on September 29 still rankled. Robert E. Lee's attempt to regain the position misfired, and for the next several days, the Confederate commander concentrated on establishing a new defensive line behind the captured bastion as well as strengthening his existing works to deter another Federal effort to seize the Rebel capital. By Thursday, October 6, "Marse Robert" was ready to try again, not only to reclaim Fort Harrison but also to drive the Yankees back to their fortified bridgehead at Deep Bottom and perhaps across the James.

Lee summoned all the ranking officers on the north side of that river to a council of war at his headquarters near the Chaffin farm. Never had such an assemblage gathered in this sector. Attendees included the head of the Department of Richmond, Richard Ewell; the First Corps acting chieftain, Richard H. Anderson; division commanders Robert Hoke and Charles Field; Martin Gary, head of the local cavalry brigade; E. P. Alexander, the senior artilleryman; and an unexpected guest in the person of the Confederate president. Jefferson Davis had just returned from one of his visits to the troubled western theater and arrived at Lee's command post to consult regarding recent events and to learn about his generals' plans.[1]

The course of this conference remains obscure, if not its outcome. Some sources speculate that Gary responded to Lee's request for suggestions and that Lee adopted the cavalryman's ideas. More likely, Lee had already considered his options and determined upon a preferred course of action. If true, he used this

409

council of war to explain his proposed operation to all the relevant commanders and solicit their input. Lee understood that conditions around Petersburg argued against transferring any more of A. P. Hill's troops across the James. In fact, he had already returned Scales's Brigade to the south side. This meant that Field, Hoke, Gary, and Alexander would execute his offensive, as Ewell's second-tier soldiers were unfit for combat outside their fortifications. The matter of where to attack seems, in hindsight, equally obvious. The Union lines now extended from Fort Harrison to the James, eliminating the Federal left as a potential target. The experience of September 30 militated against another frontal attack. But the Union right offered a vulnerable flank. Butler's works ended at New Market Road, beyond which only Kautz's small cavalry division patrolled the corridors along Darbytown and Charles City Roads. Defeat Kautz, and the Confederates might turn the Federal right, roll it up toward Fort Harrison, and perhaps compel the Yankees to execute a wholesale retreat.[2]

Lee ordered Field, Hoke, and Alexander to move out of the defenses that night under Anderson's direction, their places filled by Ewell's amateur infantry and the makeshift brigade from Pickett's Division under Colonel Montague. Anderson's troops would march to Darbytown Road and halt some two miles west of the old Outer Line. At the same time, Gary, joined by Bowles's Alabamans of Field's Division and a battalion of artillery under Lieutenant Colonel Lightfoot of Ewell's department, would gather in supporting distance on Charles City Road. At daybreak these 9,000 soldiers would attack Kautz and, after dispersing the Federal cavalry, wheel right and overwhelm the exposed Union flank. If all went well, the contagion would spread to Fort Harrison and persuade the Yankees to retire to their fortified bridgehead above Deep Bottom. "This offered an unexpected opportunity for a *coup de main* on the part of the Confederates," thought Colonel Hagood of the First South Carolina, "which ... might end in the destruction of Butler's force north of the James River."[3]

Kautz's troopers, 1,700 strong and supported by two batteries of artillery, occupied a perilous position. The bulk of his force concentrated on Doctor Jesse L. Johnson's farm, called Plainfield, along Darbytown Road. The general also maintained a picket line fifteen miles long extending up Darbytown Road, over to White's Tavern on Charles City Road, and then back down Darbytown Road, watching the Union right as far as Deep Bottom. Samuel Spear's brigade deployed north of Darbytown Road and Robert West's brigade covered the fields west of the Johnson house, Kautz's headquarters. The Fourth Wisconsin Battery unlimbered its four guns on either side of Darbytown Road, while Battery B, First U.S. Artillery deployed "in a very commanding position, between the right and center of the line." The First New York Mounted Rifles, operating independently from Kautz, extended the picket line to a point about halfway between Darbytown and New Market Roads. Kautz's nearest support—Pond's brigade of Terry's division—lay more than a mile to the south.[4]

The terrain contributed to the cavalry's vulnerability. Woods extended west and north of the Johnson farm, and branches of Four Mile Creek coursed on either side of Kautz's deployment, obstructing his tenuous connection to Terry's infantry. "I very soon realized that I was in a very dangerous position," remembered the cavalry commander. "There was but one narrow country road that crossed the north branch and the main stream near their junction. This road was our only route to the main force . . . and being badly cut up and leading through woods, was difficult to get over in a hurry with artillery." Kautz had only completed rudimentary fortifications across his position and requested implements to expedite that work. Butler responded that the infantry needed all such tools, cavalierly advising Kautz that if he was threatened, "the cavalry had legs and could run away."[5]

Sometime on the evening of October 6, two refugees from Richmond entered Kautz's lines. They reported seeing three of Field's brigades and "a good supply of artillery" heading toward the cavalry's position. Although one of these witnesses had been "drinking a little," casting some doubt on his reliability, Kautz sent the informants to Tenth Corps headquarters with a request to pass them along to Butler. "I made my preparations accordingly and notified my superiors," wrote Kautz, "from which however I received neither orders nor instructions, and I had nothing to do but to fight until I was driven." Those "preparations" seemed to be limited to informing West and Spear to have their men ready for action at 4:00 A.M.[6]

Word of the potential Confederate attack filtered down to Terry's division in due time. "Shortly after we got to bed . . . we received orders from Div Head Qrs to have every man turned out at 4 the next morning," wrote Lt. Benjamin Wright, a staff officer in Plaisted's brigade, "as they had information from pretty reliable sources that the enemy would attack or attempt to make a reconnaissance." For the soldiers of the Eleventh Maine, "the night was an anxious one," but others in Terry's camps were skeptical. "So many announcements of the kind had proved incorrect, that few anticipated trouble," wrote Chaplain Trumbull, "even while they faithfully obeyed the orders received."[7]

While the Federals slept in anticipation of an early reveille, Dick Anderson led Field's and Hoke's Divisions and Alexander's two battalions of artillery on their trek to Darbytown Road. These nine brigades and nineteen guns started on Osborne Turnpike between 9:00 and 10:00 P.M., heading for Curry's plantation, about two miles northwest of Kautz's headquarters at Johnson's house.

Lee intended to accompany the troops and told Alexander to meet him at 2:00 A.M. for the march to the jump-off point. The artillerist was shocked when Lt. Col. Charles Venable of Lee's staff arrived at Alexander's headquarters at 1:30 A.M. imploring the brigadier to hurry up as "the Old Man is out here waiting for you & mad enough to bite nails." Alexander immediately mounted and rode to where Lee waited. The gray commander coldly (and inaccurately) insisted that he had specified a 1:00 A.M. start and further scolded Alexander for failing to obtain a guide. "It was the one time, in all the war, when I saw him apparently harsh & cross," thought the chastened Georgian.[8]

Gary's troopers spent a short night in their bivouacs near Charles City Road. They had been issued forty rounds of ammunition and two days' cooked rations before they retired. Strangely, the cavalrymen also received new sabers, a weapon that the war's evolving tactics had rendered nearly obsolete. They roused between 2:00 and 3:00 A.M. Col. Alexander Cheves Haskell, commander of Gary's Seventh South Carolina Cavalry, made a short speech to his unit, promising "some hard fighting" and vowing to lead the regiment into combat. "Col. Haskell informed the men that Genl Lee expected a great deal from Gary's Brigade that day, for if they failed the whole object of the attack would be frustrated," wrote Lt. William Hinson. The colonel's words inspired this officer. "I would have charged them against such odds as [they faced] at Balaclava," he vowed. The South Carolinians trotted out of camp well before dawn and joined the brigade's other two regiments, the Twenty-Fourth Virginia Cavalry and the Hampton Legion Cavalry, on Charles City Road.[9]

Anderson had his two divisions back on the road before dawn as well, Field's units in front. The Kentuckian chose John Bratton's and Tige Anderson's brigades to lead the column, while the Texas Brigade and DuBose's Georgians followed. Hoke brought up the rear with his four brigades. Gary and Bowles were to strike first on Charles City Road, routing the small Federal force there, then Field would hit Kautz in a charge straight down Darbytown Road.[10]

Colonel Haskell, in temporary command of the cavalry brigade while Gary controlled the demi-division along Charles City Road, encountered Spear's blueclad pickets about 6:00 A.M., the day dawning "as fair as a laughing girl," as a New Yorker remembered. The Federal sentries, bolstered by a reconnaissance force sent by Spear, drove back the Rebel advance guard, prompting Haskell to mount a charge of his own. The Confederates sent the reinforced Unionists scurrying back down Charles City Road and off to the south via a farm path. Spear rallied his men, no more than 200 strong, and made a brave stand as the rest of the Confederate cavalry arrived. But the Yankees, now badly outnumbered, eventually retreated toward Kautz's main body at the Johnson farm.[11]

The Confederate infantry and artillery began their push down Darbytown Road in concert with Haskell's attack to the north. General Bratton advanced his Fifth South Carolina north of the highway to drive away enemy pickets belonging to West's brigade. "With bugle calls, I soon had my men in groups twenty paces apart deployed as skirmishers and [we advanced] firing," wrote Col. Asbury Coward, commanding those Carolinians. Plucky Federals from the Third New York Cavalry "harassed the advance of the enemy, fighting on foot in the woods and . . . deceived them as to the kind of troops they would encounter," reported Colonel West. Eventually, however, the Union skirmishers withdrew after mirroring Spear's stubborn stand on Charles City Road.[12]

These twin delaying actions necessitated a pause in the Rebel offensive. Bowles's brigade moved up on Haskell's right, along with a battery of artillery. At the same time, Bratton advanced the balance of his regiments, stretching northeast toward Bowles's right flank. The Carolinians formed in line of battle north of Darbytown Road some 600–800 yards from Kautz's unfinished works. Tige Anderson's Georgians then moved across from Bratton on the south side of the highway. Not until at least 7:30 A.M. were the Confederates in position to resume their attacks.[13]

This hiatus, broken only by an occasional exchange of artillery and musketry fire, lulled Kautz into a sense of security, or at least indecision, regarding the strength and intent of his enemy. "As no great force had been reported, it was uncertain whether a serious attack was contemplated or only a reconnaissance similar to others on one or two previous occasions," wrote Kautz. He recalled that his nocturnal informants had characterized the developing Confederate movements as "a reconnaissance in some force," adding that "from all I had heard up to this time I believed the division would be able to hold its position." He placed West's two regiments astride Darbytown Road, buttressed by the Fourth Wisconsin Battery, which deployed a section on each side of the highway. Spear's two regiments guarded Kautz's right, with Lt. Robert Hall's Battery B supporting Spear from two lunettes on high ground north of Darbytown Road. Kautz dismounted his troopers while, in accordance with custom, one-fourth of his men remained in the rear as horse-holders. This left fewer than 1,300 bluecoats now facing some 3,700 Confederates, with another 5,300 in immediate support. Kautz's confidence was about to be shattered.[14]

About 8:00 A.M. Tige Anderson and Bratton moved forward to the attack, Bratton still north of Darbytown Road and the Georgians to the south. Bowles's Alabamans moved ahead simultaneously south of Charles City Road, securing the connection with Bratton's left. Gary ordered Haskell to position a portion of the cavalry on Bowles's left while keeping about 100 of his men mounted in

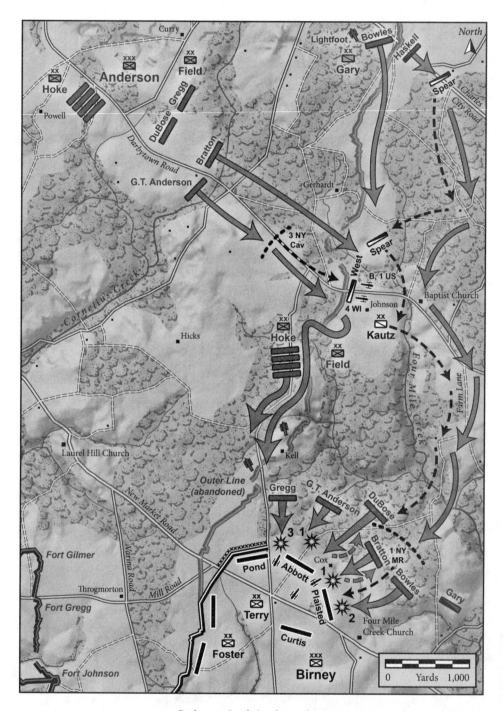

Darbytown Road, October 7, 1864

reserve. "It soon became apparent that the attack was a serious one," recorded a now-enlightened Kautz, illusions of victory fleeting. But rather than ordering a retreat, the general held his ground, hoping that infantry support would arrive to save him.[15]

The Georgians reached the Union line first. Lt. Col. Christopher Kleinz, commanding West's Fifth Pennsylvania Cavalry, reported that the Rebels "attacked my line with great fury, but were promptly repulsed." North of Darbytown Road, two of Bratton's regiments—the First South Carolina and the Second South Carolina Rifles—"double-quicked forward under a brisk fire of musketry for about a hundred paces," driving a handful of troopers from the Third New York Cavalry. Seeing this threat to his right, West repositioned a portion of his brigade to face toward the South Carolinians, while the rest continued to confront Anderson. A gap existed between Spear and West, who now deployed his brigade in an L-shaped formation, facing both west and north. When Bowles advanced in concert with Bratton and Anderson, Spear's outnumbered troopers fled south. "The men shot with precision," wrote a soldier in the Fifteenth Alabama, "and soon we hurled the enemy back."[16]

Bratton now unleashed his entire brigade, arrayed in three lines, against the portion of West's brigade north of Darbytown Road. "They edged down toward us so long as they could find cover in the sinuosities of the line; then swinging around their left they formed in three lines and advanced directly upon our flanks," reported the Union colonel. The Fifth Pennsylvania Cavalry stood its ground with the aid of punishing fire from the Wisconsin cannoneers. "It was not very pleasant for those of us who were out of the breastworks with the Yankees shooting at us," admitted a South Carolinian. The Federal resistance prompted some 200 of Bratton's men to execute a desperate measure. Throwing down their guns, these disheartened Confederates began yelling "Deserters!" while running toward the Federal line. Their attempt to evade Union bullets— not to mention service in the Confederate army—proved short lived. Their comrades began shooting them in the back, prompting the would-be defectors to pick up their rifles and resume their places in line.[17]

Bratton now sent two of his regiments across the road to assist the stalled Georgians, ordered two others to hit West's right flank, and sent one regiment around to the rear of the Federal cavalry. These maneuvers compelled the Wisconsin gunners to fall back, two of their guns having become disabled. Soon thereafter, Kautz's stubborn resistance crumbled. Spear's retreat exposed Battery B, which "was thus hotly engaged with the enemy alone for full ten minutes after the other troops had retired." By this time, Haskell had advanced a portion of the Seventh South Carolina Cavalry behind the Union position, hastening what had by then become a disordered scramble for survival. Anderson's men joined Bratton and Haskell, as did Bowles's Alabamans. "The men went yelling, running and firing right through horses, wagons, cannon and camps, troopers fleeing in every direction," testified the Fourth Alabama's Robert T. Coles.[18]

Although a few of Kautz's panicked soldiers managed to join some of the horse-holders in a mounted retreat, most fled on foot, with the Confederates in hot pursuit. Another of the Wisconsin guns became mired in the boggy lane that provided the Yankees their only avenue of escape, creating a bottleneck that trapped the remaining Union ordnance. The cannoneers abandoned their guns and caissons, some mounted draft horses, while others simply ran away. Haskell's troopers slashed into what had become an undisciplined mob, cutting down some of the fugitives as others chose to surrender. "We attacked the Yankees again yesterday," recorded John Kennedy Coleman in his diary, "and made them 'skedaddle' like fury." Anderson's Georgians arrived at the abandoned Union positions, "cheering like fools," thought Colonel Hagood. "They planted their standards on the parapet no longer held by the enemy and looked as if they would like to be considered as having done something brilliant." Hagood added that the South Carolinians were not "deceived by the bombast of the Georgians." More than 100 prisoners fell into Confederate hands, along with all eight of Kautz's cannon. The rest of the Federals dashed for all they were worth toward New Market Road and Terry's infantry.[19]

With only Union prisoners now north of Four Mile Creek, Haskell rode across the stream and into the fields north of the Cox house to reconnoiter. The First New York Mounted Rifles had disappeared by then, leaving an Irish teamster to drive the regimental headquarters wagon toward New Market Road. The colonel captured this unlucky fellow, then joined Sgt. DuBose Snowden and Pvt. William H. Welch, all heading back toward Darbytown road to report and reorganize for the next phase of the operation.[20]

As these Confederates rounded a curve in the narrow, wood-lined lane, the sound of hoofbeats echoed ahead. Soon a small body of Federals appeared, among them General Kautz. The Federal cavalry commander, commendably, had been among the last to fall back and had joined perhaps a dozen other fugitives in making his way across Four Mile Creek, heading for New Market Road. The two parties, both startled, reached for their weapons, the Federals calling for their outnumbered opponents to surrender. Haskell answered by firing his revolver, hitting two of the bluecoats. "As many of those in the lead of the cavalry as could get a shot at us opened fire," according to Welch. Haskell was in the middle of the road and made the most conspicuous target. The volley struck Snowden, who reeled in the saddle. Haskell also fell from his horse, a bullet fired by Sgt. James G. Keech of the Eleventh Pennsylvania Cavalry entering Haskell's left eye. Keech excitedly approached Kautz, shouting that he had shot a Rebel officer with three stars on his collar. The Federals halted and examined the apparently mortally wounded man.[21]

Keech knelt over his victim, presuming him dead or nearly so, and relieved him of a gold watch, a ring, his sword, and personal papers that identified him, including Gary's orders for the attack. Kautz and his party then left Haskell to his fate, making for the Union lines along New Market Road. Although Kautz reported the colonel killed and turned over his captured effects to army head-quarters, the South Carolinian was very much alive. Haskell would recover and eventually return to active duty despite losing sight in his wounded eye.[22]

Kautz initially reported 18 killed and 54 wounded during the morning's combat, along with 274 men captured or missing. Those figures were later modified to 18 killed, 69 wounded, and 142 missing for a total of 229 casualties. "I have no one to reproach except myself, and only for the reason that I did not retire earlier," admitted Kautz, "and that I did not have the foresight to anticipate the seriousness of the attack. I have, however, the satisfaction of feeling that the loss of my division, and the resistance it opposed to the enemy, gave time to the Tenth Army Corps to deploy and prepare for the attack." Indeed, his division acquitted itself as best it could against overwhelming odds.[23]

The disordered and dismounted troopers who streamed into friendly lines along New Market Road provided Birney's soldiers with their first indisputable proof of a serious Confederate threat. "It was amusing to see them come in," wrote an unsympathetic Lt. George Barnum. "Most all had lost their Hats and Horses and they came in in all ways." The corps commander promptly informed Butler, "General Kautz is routed, and enemy are moving to my rear & right." Butler was stunned. "What has become of Kautz?" he responded. "You say routed; I hope not as bad as that." Birney's infantry began the day relieved that the rumored dawn attack on their position had not materialized. "After a night of vigilance, the morning came with no disturbance [and] there was many a joke cracked over the last needless scare," wrote Chaplain Trumbull. Yet it was now apparent that the danger was real and emanated not from the west, but from the north. General Birney mounted—his terminal ailment not yet sufficiently advanced to prevent him from ignoring his doctor's orders to remain in bed—and began adjusting his defense. Butler also appreciated the crisis. "Let your right fall back and be ready to meet the enemy, who are advancing," he advised Birney, perhaps unnecessarily. "Take good care that the enemy do not get between your right and Deep Bottom."[24]

Earlier, Butler told Birney to "be ready to send assistance to Kautz when he needs it," but a positive order to do so never materialized. For his part, Birney concentrated on defending his own sector, never initiating steps to send succor to his vulnerable comrade. The army's high command remained wedded to a defensive mindset, neither Butler nor Birney willing to strike a Confederate force maneuvering beyond its fortifications.[25]

Unshaken by the "flying groups desperate . . . to get under the wing of our division" and the "broken cavalry . . . riding recklessly through branches and copses," Terry's three brigades remained firm, despite the panicked troopers now among them. Pond's brigade, supported by the Seventh Connecticut of Abbott's command, already faced north in the well-constructed return north of New Market Road that Butler had presciently specified a few days earlier. But this line did not extend far enough east to prevent Pond's right from being turned. Terry tried to rectify that deficiency by shifting Abbott's brigade to Pond's right. Plaisted's brigade then moved from its position south of New Market Road to Abbott's right. Plaisted refused his own right flank, although it was unanchored on any natural or artificial obstacle, leaving Terry's division in a crescent-shaped formation parallel to New Market Road, with Abbott's men some 500 yards north of the highway. "The minutes were few before we were passing quickly down the Newmarket road with the other regiments of our division," confirmed Trumbull.[26]

Pond's men behind their strong breastworks also enjoyed a tangle of recently cut slashing fronting their position. Neither Abbott nor Plaisted shared such advantages. Moreover, Abbott deployed in proximity to thick woods that limited his field of fire, as did the right end of Pond's command. But Pond's position became more formidable once Lt. Col. Richard H. Jackson, corps artillery chief, unlimbered twenty-two guns overlooking the open ground on Terry's left. Birney ordered Foster to expand his division to cover the portion of the line vacated by Abbott and Plaisted, a task rendered more difficult when the corps commander removed Col. N. Martin Curtis's brigade from Foster's control to a reserve position behind Terry's center. William Birney's Black troops, on Foster's left, also broadened their front to help cover the remainder of the Tenth Corps works behind the refaced Outer Line.[27]

Birney's redeployment assuaged Butler's concern that the Rebels might easily sweep southeast and gain the Federal rear. The army commander now advised Weitzel to "be ready to move [the Eighteenth Corps] to the aid of Birney if the attack develops itself on our right." But as the minutes passed without an assault, Butler began to fret that the action along Darbytown Road might merely be a feint in favor of a primary assault against Fort Harrison. When Weitzel reported that no Confederate infantry had appeared in his front and only artillery firing interrupted the quiet along his lines, Butler again focused on Birney.

The Guns of October

The army commander finally found an opportunity to interview the garrulous informants, whose testimony prompted him to conclude that the Confederate initiative that morning was "but a demonstration on the right, and it may be possible to push them." At 10:00 A.M. he informed Grant's headquarters, "If I can learn with a little more certainty about this movement on my right I shall take the offensive with two divisions of Birney's."[28]

Butler's dismissal of Kautz's displacement as the product of a mere demonstration stemmed from the long delay between the cavalry's rout and further Confederate aggression. To be sure, Lee and his generals understood that their victory along Darbytown Road represented little more than a prelude to the decisive attack intended to roll up the Federal infantry and evict them from Fort Harrison. Why it took the Confederates several hours to ready that effort remains uncertain. Colonel Hagood offered the explanation that Field expected Hoke to conduct the follow-up to his dispersal of the cavalry. "Hour after hour passed away and not one sound was heard which indicated that the Confederates pursued the enemy," he wrote with some exaggeration. "Finally General Field determined to continue the movement with his own Division, while he sent to ascertain what had become of Hoke." This indictment reflects the lingering antipathy maintained by Field's men toward Hoke, whose failure to support them on September 30 still stung. More likely, the time required to realign the troops from the morning's combat may explain the delay, and no doubt the swampy, wooded landscape complicated reorganization and deployment. In any case, the intervening time proved valuable to Terry, who used it to create his evolving defensive position.[29]

Eventually, the Confederates untangled themselves and prepared for what they hoped would be a pivotal strike against Butler's right. Field's Division would once again spearhead the assault. The Texas Brigade, under John Gregg, occupied the division's right, its right flank anchoring on the old Outer Line. To Gregg's left, Tige Anderson, Bratton, and Bowles extended the formation, with DuBose's Georgians close by in reserve. Gary, once again in direct command of his brigade, guarded Field's left, while Hoke formed in column to Field's right and rear. Ample artillery poised to support the infantry. Sometime between 9:00 and 9:30 A.M., the Confederate battle line began to advance, a swarm of skirmishers leading the way.[30]

Some of the troopers from the First New York Mounted Rifles were the first to contest their progress. This unit, led by Col. Edwin V. Sumner, son of a former corps commander in the Army of the Potomac, employed its Spencer repeaters with good effect. Taking position in some rifle pits, the New Yorkers maintained their position until their ammunition dwindled and the main

Confederate force appeared at the edge of the woods. A New York newspaper claimed that Sumner's men held off the Rebel attack until Terry could complete a line of works. This inflated the regiment's contribution, but there can be no doubt that these dismounted cavalrymen offered a laudable initial impediment to the Confederate assault.[31]

Now Jackson's Federal artillery opened, including two Requa "machine guns," manned by crews from the Sixteenth New York Heavy Artillery. These unusual pieces featured twenty-five barrels that fired .58-caliber bullets in volleys. With an effective range of 1,300 yards, the Requa Gun was an effective antipersonnel weapon that helped confine the Confederates to the cover of the forest. "The fire was delivered slowly and efficiently," boasted Lieutenant Colonel Jackson, but it drew the inevitable response from Porter Alexander. The Georgian executed "that beautiful manoeuvre in artillery drill of 'Fire advancing by half battery,'" in which "one half of a battery stands & fires, while the second half advances a short distance, when it also halts & opens fire. At its first shot, the first half stops firing, limbers up, & then at a gallop itself passes the second & takes a still more advanced position & opens. So they go, alternately, one half always firing & the other advancing."[32]

As the artillery duel persisted at an ever-decreasing range, Field prepared his brigades for the main assault. His immediate opponents mustered about 4,300 men in their front line, with Curtis's 900 in ready reserve, less than two-thirds of the Confederate force on the field. Lee for once wielded the stronger battalions but only if he employed his brigades simultaneously. Otherwise Terry would enjoy numerical parity, albeit with only Pond's brigade adequately dug in. Most importantly, the Confederate battle plan presumed that once Kautz had been routed, the graycoats would encounter the unprotected right flank of Butler's line. Their delay in forming for the decisive assault—avoidable or otherwise—combined with prompt action by Butler, Birney, and Terry, meant that Lee would instead conduct a standard frontal attack, an echo of Heth's predicament on October 1.[33]

To make matters worse, Field could not coordinate his five brigades to attack in unison. Bratton and DuBose emerged first and received a punishing fire from elements of Abbott's Third New Hampshire and Seventh Connecticut, who advanced from the main line and worked their lever-action Spencers with a vengeance. "Field's men were moving forward handsomely, & still cheering, when this skirmish line opened fire & discharged their seven shots apiece in less than a minute," remembered Alexander. "It made quite a hot volley, & gave the idea of a considerable force." Once the skirmishers fell back, Terry's line opened with a devastating volley at close range, staggering the Rebels. Anderson's Georgians made almost no progress, while Bowles's troops on the Confederate left drifted off, contributing little to the attack. The Federals' fire drove DuBose completely out of the fight, leaving Field with only Bratton and Gregg, on the division's right, to sustain the assault.[34]

The South Carolinians angled to their left and confronted Terry's right and center, defended by Plaisted and Abbott. "We got up within forty yards of the enemy and was ordered to halt[,] our line being cut down so fast it was thought advisable to halt and await reinforcements," explained Pvt. Simon P. Wingard of the Palmetto Sharpshooters. "But the support did not come and we was compelled to fall back. It was the heaviest fire we ever was under and we lost about one-third of our men." Colonel Hagood agreed. "We got within twenty paces of them before we dreamed of their proximity," he wrote. "The most infernal musketry imaginable now greeted us and brought our column to a dead halt, every man throwing himself on the ground to seek protection from the leaden storm which roared through the woods." General Bratton reported that his troops gained a position fifty yards from the Union line, but "the brigade on my right . . . did not come up, and the enemy in its front poured its fire into me. The brigade on my left fell back and retired entirely from the contest." Bratton fell wounded in the left shoulder, and the South Carolinians withdrew to their starting point.[35]

The 16th New York Heavy Artillery, in the center of Abbott's convex position, played a conspicuous role in Bratton's repulse. "Our men never fired a gun till they approached to within fifteen yards, when a Rebel captain, planting his colors in the ground, shouted, 'Now you d——d Yankees, there is our flag: we will fight for it,'" one of the heavies explained to a New York newspaper. "These were his last words on this earth: a ball entering his eye sent him to settle accounts with his maker." The veterans of the 100th New York holding the far right of Plaisted's deployment, many of whose enlistments had expired, did not perform so well. Bratton's first volley sent them "in wild and disgraceful confusion" toward the rear, leaving the stalwart, if diminutive 10th Connecticut alone on the right. Aided by the 24th Massachusetts and 11th Maine on their left, the Nutmeggers held their ground, securing the Federal flank. "I don't know when I have shed tears before but when I saw the 100th run as they did and then to see the little band of not much more than 100 men of the 10th Conn stand as they did, I could not help but shed tears over the noble boys," wrote an officer on Plaisted's staff. Terry's center and right remained safe for the moment.[36]

That moment proved fleeting, for now Bowles's rallied Alabamans moved forward. As the unit farthest east, Bowles enjoyed the best opportunity to turn the Union right. He deployed his brigade in a double line of battle and advanced, like Bratton, without skirmishers. With the 100th New York in retreat, Bowles might have gained New Market Road east of Plaisted's line and rolled it up from right to left. Instead, the Alabamans drove straight ahead. Plaisted managed to rally his shaky New Yorkers, and Bowles's attack faltered. Plaisted called on Terry for help, which promptly arrived in the form of two of Curtis's regiments, the 112th and 142nd New York. The Union right—the most vulnerable sector of the entire Tenth Corps—had held.[37]

The Texas Brigade would be the last of Field's units to attack during this disjointed affair. Perhaps as a product of the absence of overall control by the ranking Confederate commanders—Lee included—or maybe because of the daunting prospect of assaulting fixed fortifications fronted by a tangle of abatis, Gregg balked. He sent a courier to Lieutenant General Anderson suggesting that the Confederates retire safely, content with vanquishing the unfortunate Kautz. Anderson would hear nothing of the sort. "Say to General Gregg, Sir, press the enemy," came his reply.[38]

The thirty-six-year-old Gregg was a native of north Alabama but moved to Texas as a young man and gained a measure of political success, serving as a district judge and a member of the Texas secession convention. He served in the Confederate Congress in Montgomery but resigned his seat and returned to Texas, where he raised the Seventh Texas Infantry. Captured with the garrison at Fort Donelson, Tennessee, in February 1862, he was exchanged in August and promoted to brigadier general. His brigade fought in the Vicksburg Campaign, battling a superior force to a standstill at Raymond, Mississippi, in May 1863. The War Department transferred his brigade to the Army of Tennessee that autumn, and Gregg participated in the Battle of Chickamauga in September, where he sustained a serious wound. Upon his recovery, he reported to Lee and assumed command of Hood's famous Texas Brigade. Gregg had no formal military training, but like other distinguished amateur commanders, he was considered a "born soldier." His pivotal role in the Battle of the Wilderness, where his counterattack helped stave off disaster, cemented Lee's esteem for this adopted Texan.[39]

Press the enemy—Gregg would try. His brigade jumped off, probably around 10:30 A.M., with Anderson's Georgians on their left. Immediately, Jackson's artillery, including the Requa Guns, opened fire, supplemented by Pond's entrenched infantry, spewing out a blanket of iron and lead that punished the Confederates. "All the guns that could be brought to bear on his infantry were used with good effect," reported Jackson. Anderson's Brigade melted away "and as at Fort Harrison disgraced themselves," groused one of the Texans. Undeterred, Gregg's veterans continued ahead "with the old Texas yell," but they quickly became entangled in the fallen tree limbs that trapped many at point-blank range. "As we went down on them our line got very badly scattered from having to charge over that abattis or fallen timber," wrote a soldier in the Fourth Texas. "The enemy held their fire until we were within one hundred and fifty yards of them when two ranks arose and fired, as they went down the other two ranks arose and fired and so on." The brigade went on "by jerks and spurts, . . . climbing logs, pushing our way through brush and fallen timber, but an individual coming the same route 5 minutes afterwards could have walked upon the mangled corpses of our boys," remembered a private in the Fifth Texas.[40]

The brigade suffered catastrophic casualties, including its commander. General Gregg advanced with his troops, directing their movements as best he could under such hellish conditions, when a Federal bullet struck him in the neck, killing him almost instantly. The command devolved upon Frederick Bass, but he, too, fell wounded, leaving Lt. Col. Clinton Winkler of the Fourth Texas in charge. An officer on the brigade staff asked Winkler for permission to take a few men to retrieve Gregg's body. "This was given, and in that rain of shot and shell, where it seemed nothing could live, they ran, rolled his body on the blanket, and safely bore it to the rear, when the brigade was withdrawn from the field." Indeed, by this time, the Texans and their Arkansas comrades had retreated, although a few men ventured out again, only to be captured or shot. Gregg's brigade lost at least 150 of the 600 men they took into battle.[41]

Lee witnessed the Texans' failure, and by then, word had reached him of the equally futile assaults farther east. The gray commander accepted this disappointing outcome and decided to spare Hoke from replicating Field's grim experience. Many of Field's soldiers would ascribe their setback to Hoke's non-participation, but in this instance the North Carolinian was blameless. For whatever reason, General Lee eschewed his costly habit of committing additional troops following an initial failure. Perhaps he distrusted Hoke, based on that officer's previous performances. More likely, his stomach for accepting risk and its consequent drain on the army's diminishing manpower animated his decision. Johnson Hagood, commanding a brigade in Hoke's Division, thought as much. "The chances of success were not deemed sufficient to warrant the shattering of the whole disposable force for the defence of this front of Richmond," he wrote. Whatever the cause, the battles on October 7 had ended.[42]

Alexander's artillery covered Field's withdrawal, although some of the infantry surrendered rather than risk a wound while retreating. At 11:15 A.M. Birney informed Butler, "I have repulsed the attack of the enemy on my right flank with great slaughter." Indeed, E. P. Alexander estimated Confederate losses at 1,000 men, a figure with which Butler agreed, along with 150 prisoners and deserters.

Some Federals, such as Pvt. Harrison Nesbitt of the 203rd Pennsylvania of Foster's command, reported that 1,500 Rebels had fallen in the fight. The actual number of Southern losses probably did not much exceed 600, but they included one brigadier killed and another badly hurt. Alexander Haskell's brother, Maj. John C. Haskell, a battalion commander in Alexander's artillery, joined the list of the wounded, a minié ball creasing his scalp. Terry sustained 208 total casualties, the 16th New York Heavy Artillery losing nearly one-third of that number. Adding Kautz's casualties from the fight along Darbytown Road and a few of the wounded cannoneers, Union losses on October 7 totaled 458 men.[43]

The outcome on New Market Road emboldened the operationally mercurial Butler to advocate an offensive once again. He responded immediately to Birney's note, suggesting that the Tenth Corps advance two of its divisions to slice behind Field's brigades "and get between them and their base," a notion strengthened by Butler's belief that no new Rebel troops had arrived from Petersburg. When Birney failed to act upon these instructions, Butler reiterated them at noon. "I think we must not let them intrench on the Darbytown Road," he admonished. "Please advance upon them in such force as you can spare, and see if we cannot get on their flank." Birney, whose physical condition would soon confine him to an ambulance, responded: "The enemy are not falling back from the Darbytown road, and hold a very strong position vacated by Kautz. I will try them at once, although I think they are preparing to assault me." This intelligence, faulty as it was because Lee had no intention of renewing his attack, prompted Butler to shift gears yet again. "If you can coax the enemy to attack you, do so," he now told Birney.[44]

This directive, along with Birney's deteriorating health, precluded offensive action from the Tenth Corps. Butler and Weitzel now again indulged their fear of a Confederate attack against the Eighteenth Corps, but this, too, was a chimera. Butler did order Birney to advance late that afternoon, but by the time Terry's division arrived at Darbytown Road, the Confederates had disappeared. Lee returned Field and Hoke to defensive positions that once again guarded the Darbytown and New Market Roads toward Richmond, leaving the Federals in control of the ground they occupied that morning. After dark, however, Butler ordered Terry to abandon the position on Darbytown Road and return to New Market Road, apparently concluding that the position on the Johnson farm stretched his defenses too far. Terry led his troops back to their camps between 9:00 and 10:00 that night.[45]

The relatively small-scale fighting on October 7 along Darbytown and New Market Roads bore more significance than its modest size would suggest. Never again would Lee entertain the hope of expelling the Federals from their positions north of the James, a goal he had cherished since August. From this point forward, the Rebels would remain on the defensive in this sector, compelled to maintain a force sufficiently large to protect their capital. That is not to say that all combat would cease on the north side, for in less than a week, the armies would clash again. In the meantime, action resumed on the Petersburg front.

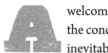 welcome quiet prevailed south of the Appomattox River following the conclusion of the combat on October 2, although minor clashes inevitably occupied those troops nearest the enemy. For example, the Thirty-Sixth Massachusetts burned Doctor Boisseau's house on October 4, losing a handful of men in the process. The Federals continued to lob shells into Petersburg, one mortally wounding a soldier who had left his unit without permission to obtain food from the city market, paying the ultimate price for his disobedience. The bombardment did nothing to interrupt services at Saint Paul's Church, where on October 4 Brig. Gen. Archibald Gracie was among several worshippers formally confirmed in their faith. That same day Grant announced that cavalry general James Wilson, who was serving in the Shenandoah Valley with Sheridan, had been sent to command Sherman's troopers in Georgia. The next day the general-in-chief informed Chief of Staff Halleck of his intention to come to Washington to meet with Admiral Porter and to consult with the administration regarding accumulating reinforcements for his armies. He departed at 10:20 A.M. on the sixth. General Warren took advantage of the martial respite to indulge a short leave of absence, naming Samuel Crawford as acting corps commander "to the indignation . . . of old cocks like Griffin and Ayres," thought Theodore Lyman.[46]

While at the capital, Grant received reports of the October 7 fighting on Butler's front. He telegraphed Meade immediately, ordering him to "make such demonstrations on your left in the morning as to detain the enemy's forces there and prevent any concentration north of the James River." Meade failed to see the threat implicit in these instructions. Butler had not requested his assistance, and to his knowledge no Rebel troops had departed his front to cross the rivers. In fact, a deserter reported that Scales's Brigade of Wilcox's Division had recently returned to Petersburg from Henrico County. Yet Grant's orders must be obeyed, and Meade accordingly notified both Crawford and Parke to "send out reconnaissances . . . to-morrow morning at 7 o'clock and drive in the enemy's pickets, and follow it up with such other movements as will give the impression that we are about advancing in force." Parke and Crawford communicated in the predawn hours to coordinate their movements, hastening with commendable efficiency to commence their demonstration at the appointed hour.[47]

Crawford specified that only his expansive picket line, some 1,500 strong, would threaten the Confederate works. Henry Baxter, now acting Third Division commander while Crawford temporarily led the corps, would advance the Iron Brigade and Colonel Hofmann's New Yorkers and Pennsylvanians east of the Weldon Railroad in support. Ayres's division would provide similar backup as far west as Squirrel Level Road. A brigade from Griffin's division would join with elements of Potter's Ninth Corps troops astride Church Road to press back the Rebel pickets along that corridor. As many as 6,000 troops formed behind these skirmishers, who would be led by Col. Edmund L. Dana of the 143rd Pennsylvania. The most difficult assignment belonged to Willcox's division, which had orders to move west, then turn north on Duncan Road to advance in concert with Potter's left. Meade's limited goal, consistent with Grant's objective, was to force the grayclad pickets back to their main line on a broad, unbroken front but to refrain from assaulting the Confederate works. Doing so, he believed, would forestall any Rebels from shifting across the James, if such was, in fact, the enemy's intention.[48]

October 8 brought with it the season's first taste of autumn. "Oh, how cold it was!" remembered Virginian George Bernard. "The cutting wind . . . would almost freeze us." Baxter's and Ayres's skirmishers moved out in the morning chill around 7:30 and soon encountered spirited resistance from their Confederate counterparts, bringing the movement to a sudden halt. This, in turn, compelled Potter and Griffin to stop, lest they lose contact with the stalled units on their right. Moreover, it would take Willcox some time to march west and then north to connect with Potter's left, so the Federal demonstration experienced a lackluster start. By midmorning, however, Baxter's overwhelming numbers compelled the Rebels along the railroad to withdraw beyond the ruins of the W. P. Davis house. At the same time, Ayres's skirmishers pushed their way up Squirrel Level Road to a point just south of the W. W. Davis house, while Willcox scattered a thin line of dismounted cavalry around Fort MacRae and moved toward Duncan Road. Here, however, more Confederates appeared, and rumors of Rebel reinforcements headed Willcox's way persuaded the Michigander to suspend his march and establish a blocking position west of Fort MacRae. At 12:30 that afternoon, the division commander reported that he could advance no farther, stymied as much by apparitions as by the enemy.[49]

Willcox's overcaution forced Potter to halt just beyond Fort Welch, the northwest salient of the permanent Federal works, to avoid outdistancing his support. Although the Confederates refrained from initiating their own attacks, they were now alert to this unexpected enemy advance and fully manned their skirmish lines as well as their permanent fortifications. When word of the

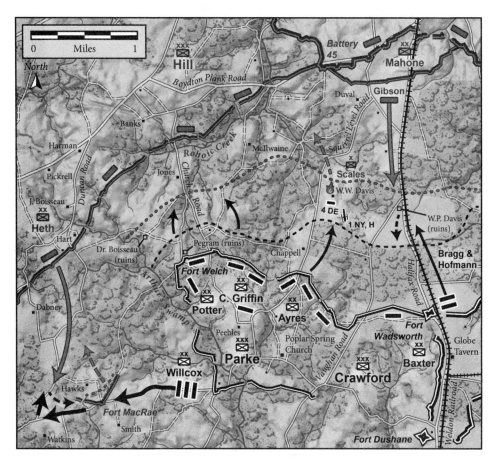

Second Squirrel Level Road, October 8, 1864

undiminished presence of Confederate troops reached Meade, he was more than willing to cancel an operation that he considered pointless. The army commander instructed Crawford and Parke, "When you have advanced your reconnaissance as far as you can with security, and have obtained all the information of the position and force of the enemy that is practicable . . . you will withdraw the force engaged in the movement." Ordering that this be "done in concert between the two corps," Meade told his subordinates to advance their picket lines "as far in front as practicable."[50]

Parke obeyed this directive without hesitation, but Crawford sought to establish his new picket line along Squirrel Level Road as far north as the W. W. Davis house, a notion opposed by both Baxter and Griffin. Crawford acquiesced, but Ayres saw in Crawford's order the opportunity to eliminate an irritant. For more than a week, Confederate sharpshooters, once again concealed in the Davis house and its various dependencies, had harassed Ayres's pickets with annoying and occasionally deadly fire. The division commander ordered a section of Battery H, First New York Light Artillery to pummel the Davis homestead with its Napoleons. This bombardment did violence to the structures but failed to destroy the buildings completely or silence the Confederate riflemen. For that, infantry would be required.[51]

Ayres turned to Arthur Grimshaw, commander of his Third Brigade, who selected fifty soldiers from the 190th Pennsylvania to advance and torch the Davis property. These men, veteran troops from the old Pennsylvania Reserves armed with Spencer repeating rifles, seemed an ideal choice. But the unrelenting Confederate fire dissuaded these experienced men from a charge they saw as doomed. Ayres sent a staff officer, Lt. Eldridge T. Yardley of Grimshaw's brigade, with peremptory orders to venture the attack. Yardley told the colonel that he would personally lead the effort with men from Grimshaw's old regiment, the 4th Delaware. The colonel liked this idea and assigned two companies of the 4th, led by Capt. Daniel H. Kent, to execute the mission.[52]

As Kent and his men went forward, Capt. Charles E. Mink, commanding Battery H, resumed his fire over the heads of the infantry. "It was grand to see these men of the 4th marching steadily up to the house," thought Henry Gawthrop. "Mink was in his glory and sent shots through the house." The gunners ceased firing when the attackers let out a cheer. "I knew the house was doomed when they started," Gawthrop continued. "They did not stop at the ditch like the bucktails but went on and soon the smoke from the house told of their success." Scales's North Carolinians, who had occupied the now-burning dwelling, withdrew northeast into some sheltering woods, leaving the Davis buildings unprotected from the blueclad arsonists. Soon the farm was an inferno that spared only the barn and one smaller outbuilding. A Richmond newspaper referred to the Davis home as "one of the finest country buildings in this section" and reported it "entirely consumed by the devouring element."[53]

The Tar Heels rallied, some of whom advanced toward the conflagration, compelling Kent to withdraw to his jump-off points. Farther west, Heth's division probed toward Willcox's stalled position, forcing these Federals to fall back to Fort MacRae. The Unionists made their stand here, and the Confederates did not challenge them, unwilling to bring on a full-throated engagement and content to protect their right flank. After dark both Crawford and Parke withdrew, Willcox establishing a new picket line west of Arthur's Swamp, while Potter and Griffin returned to their original positions.[54]

The day's final action flared up east of the Weldon Railroad. Late in the day William Mahone ordered Wright's Brigade, once again under Colonel Gibson,

The Guns of October

to assail Colonel Hofmann and the Iron Brigade. Hofmann retreated at the slightest nudge, but the Westerners and Pennsylvanians under Edward Bragg held their ground. The Georgians were satisfied with evicting the Yankees from the previously burned remains of the W. P. Davis home, near the intersection of Vaughan and Halifax Roads, ending the combat on October 8, styled the "Second Battle of Squirrel Level Road," although the action spanned a much wider front. Casualties proved as minimal as the battle's significance: perhaps seventy-five Federals and around twenty Confederates. None of the principal commanders on either side harbored any desire to resume the bloody fighting of the previous week, all content to maintain the status quo, determining that initiating another major battle at Petersburg was not then worth the risk.[55]

The soldiers awoke on Sunday, October 9, to a heavy frost, the precursor of another unseasonably frigid day. The weather did not deter the mourners, including President Davis and the entire Texas Brigade, who attended the funeral of General Gregg. They escorted the body to Hollywood Cemetery, where the fallen leader was buried with full military honors. Louisiana private Eugene Levy was among the throng who visited the capitol and witnessed Gregg lying in state and "the funeral obsequies of the dead hero, and had the pleasure to see our noble president amid the solemn cortege." Gen. Braxton Bragg, Maj. Gen. Charles Field, Brig. Gen. William Nelson Pendleton, and Postmaster General John Reagan were among the pallbearers. At this same time, Grant returned to City Point and David Birney prepared to depart on the sick leave from which he would never return. The quiet that prevailed on both sides of the James allowed division commanders Mott and Ferrero and Meade's chief of staff, Andrew Humphreys, to indulge in furloughs. In Petersburg, army musicians conducted a concert at the Virginia Hospital to benefit refugees who had found shelter in the city after being driven from their homes. Meanwhile, Confederate authorities rounded up African American males to labor on the fortifications surrounding the city.[56]

Historian Richard Sommers calls the next few days around Petersburg, "a season of alarms and adjustments." Those adjustments included reworking the respective fortifications, particularly on the Confederates' side. General Hill ordered the works extended on his right all the way to Hatcher's Run, although he lacked the troops to fully defend them. Modifications along the Federal trench lines were more modest, including closing gaps along the picket lines and completing the forts and batteries west of the Weldon Railroad begun after the fighting between September 30 and October 2. On October 12 Meade sent orders to Crawford and Parke soliciting the names of officers slain during the fighting around the Peebles farm "with a view to the naming of the new redoubts." All five of Crawford's suggestions were adopted, and six of the seven officers proposed by Parke lent their names to forts.[57]

Other adjustments appeared in the tables of organization. Temporary commanders assumed control over units in Meade's army whose permanent leaders had taken leave, including a number of brigadiers. The Confederate cavalry experienced several leadership changes as well. General Dearing returned to duty, relieving the overmatched Joel Griffin. General Young resumed direct command of his brigade, and Col. B. Huger Rutledge of the Fourth South Carolina Cavalry assumed command of Dunovant's Brigade in Butler's Division. Col. Richard L. T. Beale replaced Lucius Davis in charge of Chambliss's Brigade in Rooney Lee's Division; Davis would disappear from the army's rolls. In the infantry, Matt Ransom returned to command of his brigade of North Carolinians.[58]

Union leadership would respond to several perceived threats in mid-October, none of which materialized. Meade fully expected the Confederates to test his new picket lines on the ninth, causing a sleepless night for, as it turned out, no good reason, as the Rebels did nothing that day to disturb the equilibrium. More serious was the report of a Florida deserter on the night of October 11 who revealed that the Confederates intended to explode a mine on Hancock's front. The Second Corps commander guessed that Fort Stedman would be the intended target. A close interrogation of the informant suggested instead that the mine might lie somewhere near Fort Sedgwick. Acting Chief Engineer Nathaniel Michler ordered an investigation and concluded that Battery 21, near Fort Sedgwick, would present the most tempting target but that measures had been taken to prevent a mine from reaching the Union works. When no such shaft was discovered, this particular dread eventually disappeared.[59]

Deserters also provided the grist for another worrisome report. Georgians from Mahone's Division testified on October 11 that as many as 10,000 fresh troops, led by Maj. Gen. W. H. C. Whiting, had arrived from Wilmington at Stony Creek Depot, Lee's advanced supply base on the Weldon Railroad. Such a serious addition to Confederate manpower, if true, would significantly alter the operational calculus around Petersburg. Meade immediately ordered David Gregg to mount "a cavalry reconnaissance . . . as soon as practicable to see if any corroboration of this report can be obtained from citizens, contrabands, or others." Gregg, in turn, ordered Colonel Smith to select one regiment from his brigade for this mission and dispatch it at 6:00 that evening. Smith chose the Thirteenth Pennsylvania Cavalry, led by Maj. George F. McCabe. McCabe's nocturnal investigation determined that "no new force had arrived at Stony Creek Station," and by dawn the next morning, his report made its way up the chain of command. Deserters continued to repeat this tale, suggesting that it might have been intentionally planted to dissuade the Yankees from attempting a fresh offensive.[60]

Grant, of course, remained committed to active operations and had counted on reinforcements from Sheridan's Army of the Shenandoah to assist him. Anticipating such additions, Grant's chief of staff, Brig. Gen. John A. Rawlins, informed his wife: "We will have here before Monday [October 17] some of the old organized and reliable heroes of the war. Then you will hear of battles terrible as any as have yet been fought, and I trust, victories that will move the national heart as did Donelson, Vicksburg, and Chattanooga." But when Early's Confederates moved down the Valley in mid-October, Sheridan suspended the transfer of his veterans to the Army of the Potomac, causing Grant to defer another major offensive.[61]

Affairs north of the James also became quiet following the failed Confederate attack on October 7. "Everything remains about as usual, and the same condition of things exists as upon other portions of our line, where the Rebs regard us as *fixtures*," explained Colonel Ripley of the Eighteenth Corps. "By common consent picket firing and sharpshooting is given up." This allowed Ripley to cease playing "woodchuck" and permitted him to sit "on the edge of my hole to enjoy the sunlight." The Confederates, however, continued to explode mortar shells over the Federal works. "It's no use trying to get behind anything for protection as you do for other shells," Ripley admitted.[62]

This minor aggravation notwithstanding, conditions for some behind Butler's lines assumed an air more relaxed than their proximity to the Rebel lines might suggest. David McKelvy, one of the "election commissioners" sent to the army to help administer the upcoming presidential contest, enjoyed the music from several brass bands, including those from beyond the Confederate lines. "All was peace and harmony," he wrote, "and one was only reminded that he was in the midst of war by the occasional booming of a gun or the bursting of a shell."[63]

Most of Butler's rank and file experienced a much less bucolic respite from active campaigning. "I tell you Sister we are any thing but happy now . . . to be in . . . such a plais as this with nothing but hard tack full of wormes and poor salt pork for to eat and nothing but our over coats to sleep in and a muddy trench to ly in," groused Pvt. George J. Paddock of Colonel Fairchild's Nineteenth Wisconsin. Reflecting on the shattered hope that his regiment would be sent to a rear area far from these unpleasant conditions at the front, Paddock added, "I tell you Ann this aint Norfolk." To make matters worse, orders to improve their fortifications required exhausting labor.[64]

Butler had bombproofs added to the interior of Fort Burnham (formerly Fort Harrison). Tenth Corps soldiers constructed new works on their right, extending their refused flank to discourage the sort of attack that threatened their line on October 7. The troops cleared trees to improve fields of fire and built new military roads to expedite communications. The cavalry corduroyed the primitive path linking its position on Darbytown Road with the infantry deployment farther south that had cost them their artillery on the seventh. The engineers created an improved position along the left of the Tenth Corps line and built a military road behind the entire corps front. The Eighteenth Corps also strengthened its position by adding a number of strongpoints along its fortifications and hardening their defenses near the James. "We have tolerable lines of breastworks finished with occasional redoubts nearly finished [and] hold a very threatening position here & a very annoying one to the enemy," wrote General Paine. "The line we hold now is called the 3d line of defense around Richmond," explained an optimistic Pvt. Henry Pippitt of the Second Pennsylvania Heavy Artillery. "She will soon fall. She can't hold out much longer."[65]

David Birney's departure (and imminent death) and Alfred Terry's temporary appointment as Tenth Corps commander opened a vacancy at the head of the First Division, which was filled by Adelbert Ames. The brigadier general returned from a twenty-day leave on October 9 to find his old Eighteenth Corps division now under the command of General Heckman, his superior by date of commission if not ability. Thus, he was a logical choice to assume control of Terry's three brigades. A twenty-eight-year-old native of Maine, Ames graduated fifth in his class at West Point and had broad experience in both artillery and infantry. Described by one historian as "ruthless and vindictive," Ames nevertheless possessed all the positive attributes necessary for division command. Three days after he assumed his new duties, his senior brigade commander, Colonel Hawley, returned from a month's leave. This competent officer resumed control of Ames's Second Brigade on October 13, sending Colonel Abbott back to his regiment, the Seventh New Hampshire. In William Birney's Third Division, comprising African American troops, Col. Ulysses Doubleday, "a very sociable and agreeable man" and the brother of Maj. Gen. Abner Doubleday, took command of the Second Brigade. Less salutary was the return of Gilman Marston from sick leave. A political general of no particular ability, Marston assumed command of the First Division of the Eighteenth Corps, superseding Joseph Carr, who was sent to command Fort Pocahontas, some twelve miles as the crow flies below City Point, on the left bank of the James.[66]

Brig. Gen. George Washington Custis Lee's appointment as head of the Local Defense Forces marked the only change in the Confederate high command north of the James. This would be the first opportunity for Robert E. Lee's eldest son to lead troops in the field. Montague's makeshift brigade returned to Pickett's command in Bermuda Hundred, while Ewell's forces atrophied from wholesale desertions by reluctant citizens who had been pressed into frontline service from the streets of Richmond. One company of "Snatchups" saw its ranks shrink from ninety to twenty in the days following the October 7 fight. Lee's artillery chieftain, General Pendleton, returned to Lexington on leave following Gregg's funeral, allowing E. P. Alexander to continue to lead the artillery units assigned to the north side. Alexander would further contribute to the Confederate defense by suggesting a way to strengthen the positions guarding the capital.[67]

Such an expedient seemed necessary as the Confederates expected to be attacked at any moment. "Grant seems to be verry uneasy and . . . looks as if he would like to fight in a few days," wrote Joseph Shank, a Georgia cannoneer. "He knows his master Abe wants him to do big things by the first Wednesday in November. . . . As Sherman walked into Atlanta so would Grant like to walk into Richmond." Pvt. James Rawlings of the Rockbridge Artillery admitted in an October 10 letter, "Last night we expected an attack and I never dreaded anything more in my life," his anxiety animated by the unreliability of the emergency troops supporting his guns. He also expressed surprise at the throngs of civilians who continued to visit the lines around Fort Gilmer to gaze upon the still-unburied corpses of the Black troops killed there days earlier. "Even ladies with their babies & young children . . . walk about & look at dead bodies with the most disgusting interest. . . . I had always felt that the callousness of the men was the saddest feature of the war, but when women love to look on death & bloodshed it is disgusting and repulsive."[68]

Fort Gilmer would provide the southern anchor for a new line of works conceived by Alexander. The Georgian reconnoitered the Confederate line as it existed on October 9, then rode into Richmond to consult with Maj. Gen. Jeremy Gilmer, chief of the Engineer Bureau. Alexander suggested creating a line connecting Fort Gilmer with the old Outer Line just below Charles City Road. From there, the Outer Line extended all the way to the Chickahominy River, terminating on that unfordable swampy waterway. Doing this (and reoccupying that portion of the Outer Line) would obstruct New Market, Darbytown, and Charles City Roads at points more easterly than the intact Intermediate Line, thus confining Federal operations farther from the capital. As such, the proposed line would minimize Butler's gains north of New Market Road in the same way that the new line behind Fort Harrison had neutralized the capture of that position, although on a grander scale. With Gilmer's blessing, Alexander drew the proposed plan on a map and presented it to General Lee. The Confederate commander approved the idea, and that night engineers began laying out the new fortifications.[69]

Troops from Hoke's and Field's Divisions, aided by slaves and impressed civilians, went to work, creating fortifications that Alexander pronounced "the most beautiful line of entrenchments which I saw during the whole war." "We work at the ditch till late at night," recorded a Texan, and by the morning of the thirteenth, the line was defensible as far north as Darbytown Road. The two miles from Fort Gilmer to Darbytown Road featured eight mutually supporting redoubts bearing names such as Battery Colquitt, Battery Kirkland, Battery Hagood, and Battery Clingman. The soldiers laid rows of abatis, emplaced mines, and established fortified picket posts in advance of these works, styled the Alexander Line. Hoke's brigades manned the southern portion of the new line, with Colquitt's Georgians on Hoke's right between Fort Gilmer and New Market Road. Field occupied the defenses to and just beyond Darbytown Road. Gary's cavalry ranged up to Charles City Road. Alexander placed the Rockbridge Artillery, the Powhatan Artillery, and the Third Company, Richmond Howitzers in the batteries between Fort Gilmer and Darbytown Road, although not all of his new redans contained ordnance.[70]

At 9:30 on the morning of October 12, General Kautz notified Butler: "The enemy is very busy fortifying on [Darbytown] road, near to our pickets. The officer on picket thinks they are building a fort at a point less than half a mile from the old line of intrenchments." Butler passed this intelligence to Grant, who notified his subordinate, "I think it is advisable to send out a strong reconnaissance of infantry and cavalry to drive the enemy from the work they are doing on the Central [Darbytown] road." He warned, however, that the operation should not advance so far as to risk being cut off, and that the Eighteenth Corps should support the reconnaissance force should it be attacked. Butler responded immediately, sending orders to General Terry at 12:30 P.M. to execute such a probe. Yet he had earlier sent his chief of staff, Lt. Col. George Kensel, into Confederate lines under flag of truce to protest the use of Black prisoners of war as laborers at Fort Gilmer. The Rebels had made no reply by late afternoon, so in accordance with military protocol, Terry could not commence his probe until the truce expired. Thus, Butler essentially placed a priority on the welfare of his Black troops over executing orders from the general-in-chief, although he could not have predicted the Rebels' failure to respond promptly to his appeal.[71]

Butler's instructions directed Terry to take two of his divisions—preferably Ames's First and William Birney's Third—along with Kautz's cavalry to "make a reconnaissance in force and drive away, if practicable, the enemy from the works

The Guns of October

they are now building on the Darbytown (or Central) road. Weitzel has been ordered to support your line if necessary." Consistent with Grant's admonition, he warned Terry against advancing too far and that he was likely to face 6,000 "of the enemy's veteran troops—Early and Hoke's divisions." These orders reflect a strange incongruity—beyond issuing them while Kensel's flag of truce still prevented offensive action. On the one hand, Kautz's intelligence, and Butler's and Grant's understanding of it, implied that the Confederate work on Darbytown Road was isolated and thus susceptible to the limited objective inherent in Grant's instructions. Conversely, Butler informed Terry that he would encounter two full Rebel divisions, even if he confused Early's for Field's, a force fully capable of challenging Terry's strike force. Grant clearly intended this to be a relatively modest undertaking with an equally limited objective, not part of any larger coordinated offensive. Yet Butler instructed Terry to "push the enemy into his old line of fortifications, but not pursue farther unless you see such indications of giving way as will justify it." Did he want Terry simply to drive the enemy from their developing work on Darbytown Road or to force them south toward Fort Gilmer? Did he believe that Terry's two divisions would be more than a match for 6,000 Rebel defenders, or did he assume these Confederates would be too far distant to interfere with his attack? There is no evidence to suggest that Butler understood the scale of the Alexander Line or that Hoke and Field defended it not only to but even beyond Darbytown Road. His confusion would be a recipe for disaster.[72]

In any event, Terry hastened to obey Butler's directives, and by 3:25 P.M., he notified the army commander that Ames and Birney were poised to move forward. Weitzel shifted northward to cover the portion of the line vacated by Birney, while Foster's Tenth Corps division refused Butler's right flank, anchored beyond New Market Road. One brigade from Foster's division—his First under Colonel Curtis—would protect Birney's left, while Kautz's troopers provided support on Ames's right. Terry told Ames to advance along Darbytown Road, with his right on or just beyond that highway, while Birney's USCT division moved on Ames's left, intending to turn what he believed to be the left of the enemy's established defenses south of Darbytown Road. Terry counted about 4,700 men in his two divisions, 3,100 with Ames and 1,600 with Birney. Three batteries of artillery along with what was left of Kautz's horse artillery would join the assault. But Terry's preparations that afternoon would be for naught. Shortly after 5:00 P.M. Butler informed his corps commander that the Confederates had not yet returned his flag of truce, thus, with Grant's concurrence, he suspended the assault. Terry's men trudged back to their camps, as a cold rain added misery to their wasted preparations. New orders circulated that night to make the attack at dawn the next morning.[73]

These directives essentially repeated those for the aborted October 12 attack, although the axis of approach would shift slightly north. Ames was charged with advancing "out to and across the Darbytown road, forming in the open ground beyond," to attack the enemy "and endeavor to find and turn the left of their intrenchments." Birney's division would move simultaneously south of Darbytown Road, while Curtis's brigade advanced south of Birney toward the Kell house. The cavalry would still cover Ames's right but would send another column west on Charles City Road, "dislodge the enemy there, and, if possible, take them in reverse down toward the Darbytown road." The artillery would follow Kautz as far as Darbytown Road, then halt and report to the division commanders to which they were assigned. Terry admonished Ames to "take great care not to extend so far to the right as to leave a dangerous gap between his left and General Birney's right." All the troops would begin promptly at 4:00 A.M.[74]

The Confederates had not detected Terry's preparations on October 12, although the general feeling persisted that at some early date the Yankees would try them again. Field, in particular, worried about the security of his left flank, which dangled unsupported near Darbytown Road. He sought and received approval from Richard Anderson to move Winkler's Texas Brigade from his far right to a point north of the highway. "Late last evening," recorded Edward Crockett of the Fourth Texas, "we move up to the left a half mile or more & are put in position just after dark, during a rain, with orders to throw up a new line of works. We work at the ditch till late at night cutting a ditch three feet wide & three deep." Before dawn on the thirteenth, the Texans had created a defensible line, fronted in places with newly slashed abatis.[75]

Shortly after midnight Lt. Col. Edward Campbell of the Eighty-Fifth Pennsylvania, Terry's officer of the day, reported "the movement of wheels toward our right," noting, "axes could be heard pounding as if in the construction of fortifications." Campbell correctly concluded that "forces of the enemy have been moved to the neighborhood of the Darbytown road from our left." Terry passed Campbell's report to Butler "for what it may be worth," although this important intelligence, which revealed the arrival of the Texans, failed to alter Terry's plans.[76]

Federal officers aroused their troops around 3:00 A.M., October 13. Kautz, who began experiencing malarial symptoms, recalled "a feeling on the part of nearly every officer and soldier in the command that we were only marching out to lose several hundred men and be repulsed." His illness and the residual effects of the cavalry's defeat on October 7 may have colored his perception, as there is little evidence that other elements of Terry's contingent shared such gloomy

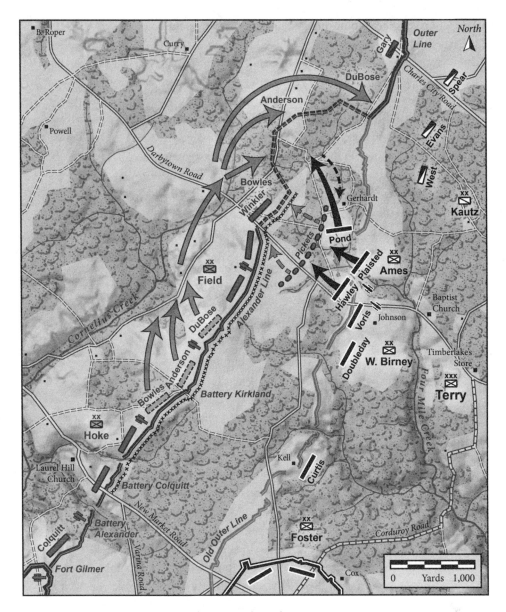

Darbytown Road, October 13, 1864

thoughts. After gulping down their morning coffee, the soldiers were ready to march by 4:00 A.M.[77]

Pond's brigade led Ames's men out of camp, although Ames had to prod his First Brigade commander to get moving. By 4:20 A.M., the entire column was in motion, Plaisted and Hawley following Pond. Birney's two brigades were the last to depart, Col. Alvin Voris's First Brigade leading Doubleday's Second Brigade. The infantry used the new corduroy road leading north to Darbytown Road near Timberlake's Store and Johnson's farm, reaching there before sunrise, around 6:00 A.M. The rain gave way to a clear if bracing morning, and Terry's column presented an "exhilarating and inspiring picture" as it tramped through the fading darkness.[78]

Terry positioned Ames's three brigades north of Darbytown Road. Pond, who reported leading 882 men into action that morning, took position on the division's right about 900 yards north of the highway. He placed the Sixty-Second Ohio and two companies of the Thirty-Ninth Illinois in front as skirmishers, with the Eighty-Fifth Pennsylvania and Sixty-Seventh Ohio in line of battle, the remainder of the Thirty-Ninth Illinois serving as brigade reserve. Plaisted filed in on Pond's left. Four companies of the Tenth Connecticut advanced as skirmishers, the Twenty-Fourth Massachusetts and Eleventh Maine extending Pond's line of battle, and the balance of the Tenth Connecticut in reserve. Hawley's five regiments, 1,100 strong, formed Ames's left. The Seventh Connecticut provided the brigade's skirmish line, with the Sixth Connecticut and the Sixteenth New York Heavy Artillery in line of battle, their left resting on Darbytown Road. The Third and Seventh New Hampshire formed in double column in reserve. Thus, Ames divided his regiments into roughly equal thirds on the skirmish line, in line of battle, and in reserve.[79]

Birney's Black troops extended Ames's formation south of Darbytown Road. Colonel Voris's right flank hugged the highway, and Colonel Doubleday moved up a short time later on the First Brigade's left. The Eighth USCT served as skirmishers for the entire division, whose job it would be to fix the enemy in place while Ames turned their left flank. Curtis moved his brigade behind the existing Union picket line to Birney's left. By sunrise, Terry had his infantry ready to advance on schedule.[80]

The attack would be delayed, however, because the cavalry was not yet in position on the right. It would take Kautz until around 6:35 A.M. to arrive. The cavalry commander offered no explanation for his tardiness, although his deteriorating health may have played a role. Spear's brigade remained mounted and trotted to Charles City Road, while Col. Andrew W. Evans's new brigade and West's two regiments dismounted and extended Pond's line north toward

Charles City Road. The artillery unlimbered behind Terry's infantry in Johnson's field.[81]

Once the entire Union force of some 8,000 officers and men was in position, Terry ordered it to test the Confederate picket line. The Federals entered the dense woods to the west, encountering the Rebel skirmishers, most of whom gave way without a struggle. Only the Texas Brigade's vedettes offered much of a fight, but eventually they, too, retreated to the main Confederate works.[82]

Ames's men pursued deliberately until they could hear Confederate officers shouting orders some distance ahead. "A sharp fire from an unseen enemy" halted the skirmishers about 8:00 A.M. They stopped at the edge of the woods, beyond which lay the abatis and then, 100 yards to the west, the Alexander Line. "Each brigade felt of its own front," wrote Hawley. "I found from 150 to 300 yards of slashed young wood before me then the works with two or three guns and lined with two ranks of rebs. Pretty much the same all along." Colonel Plaisted concluded, "It was altogether an ugly looking chance for a charge." South of Darbytown Road, the Eighth USCT emerged from the woods to find, according to Maj. George Wagner, "a strong line of intrenchments in my front, a battery to my left, and one immediately in front of my right, all strongly manned." Colonel Doubleday determined that the Rebel line extended well beyond his left flank. The Union advance ground to a halt. At 10:30 A.M. Terry informed Butler that his divisions had encountered substantial lines of abatis in front of strong works defended by both artillery and infantry. "At present . . . I think we cannot pierce their works except by massing on some point and attacking in column," he explained. The new corps commander sought Butler's imprimatur before venturing such an assault. More time elapsed.[83]

At noon Butler dutifully consulted Grant, forwarding Terry's report and inquiring if he should "order an attack on the works." The lieutenant general replied promptly, counseling against an assault. "The reconnaissance now serves to locate [the Confederates] for any future operations," wrote Grant. "To attack now we would lose more than the enemy and only gain ground which we are not prepared to hold, nor are we prepared to follow up any advantage we might gain." Butler so informed Terry, instructing him that because his reconnaissance had located the enemy as intended, he should "retire at leisure." Thus, it appeared that the Union initiative on October 13 had reached an inauspicious and nearly bloodless end.[84]

Although Terry could not have known it and is thus blameless, when his troops halted in front of the Rebels' slashings early that morning, the Confederate left did, in fact, remain vulnerable to a turning movement. That window of opportunity, however, soon closed. The scattering of his skirmish line and

Gary's report that Federal cavalry approached on Charles City Road alerted Field to the looming threat. Lee and Dick Anderson arrived on the scene and ordered immediate steps to bolster the Texans' left. Colonel Bowles's brigade leapfrogged from Field's right to deploy in the rudimentary works extending to Winkler's left. The Alabamans immediately began improving the fortifications in their front, which now extended beyond Pond's right. Hoke shifted north to cover the line vacated by Bowles.[85]

The stalemate along Terry's entire front featured only the casual exchange of musketry and artillery. This otherwise almost harmless fire claimed Maj. Willis F. Jones, Field's nephew and adjutant general. Field had dispatched the young Kentuckian with a message for Col. Joseph Walker, now in command of Bratton's Brigade, when a sharpshooter's bullet bored into his brain, knocking him from his horse and killing him instantly. The grieving division commander considered Jones's death "the saddest event of the war." Henry DeShields, the general's quartermaster, escorted Jones's body to the rear, where a metallic coffin was obtained in Richmond. Mourners buried Jones in Hollywood Cemetery. "It is particularly sad when Marylanders & Kentuckians are shot down here after fighting their own neighbors & friends & then to be killed with no hope of ever having a lasting resting place among their own people," thought Deshields, "to be buried and forgotten among strangers."[86]

While the two sides traded their desultory fire and Butler and Grant communicated regarding the inadvisability of further offensive action, Kautz informed Terry that "there was a place beyond Ames's right in front of which there appeared to be no slashing" and that "there appeared to be no works of consequence and that the enemy was still intrenching." Before Butler's orders to cease offensive action reached Terry, the corps commander ordered Ames to "extend his right toward the Charles City road, and attempt to get through the line." In truth, Bowles had by then improved these works and refused the flank of this portion of the line, creating something of a reentrant angle where defenders could deliver an enfilading fire. The woods in front of the Federals obscured these preparations as well as masked the abatis that guarded the Rebel fortifications, explaining (but not excusing) Kautz's faulty intelligence.[87]

The aggressive Ames made an equally flawed examination and agreed that "there was nothing in his front, or if there were works, that no obstacles covered them." Ames opted to shift Pond's brigade northward, then charge against the allegedly vulnerable position. Hawley and Plaisted would demonstrate in their fronts and prepare to exploit any gains achieved by Pond. Terry evidently told Birney to demonstrate in his sector as well. Pond moved north shortly after noon.[88]

Yet it would take the Federals nearly two more hours before they commenced their assault. Upon further examination, Ames discovered that his initial point of attack faced the prepared Confederate works, so a point farther north was required. More reconnaissance followed before the general felt he had located the vulnerable position. Ames's confidence did not extend to his officers. "The circumstances surrounding us at the time were very discouraging indeed," wrote Capt. Homer A. Plympton of the Thirty-Ninth Illinois. "The men all knew before going in the difficulties ahead; all the officers of the Brigade were opposed to the charge, and reported so to the general commanding the Corps; but it made no difference." General Hawley agreed with them. "Every field officer . . . protested against the charge." This pessimism extended to the rank and file, as revealed by Cpl. Elias S. Peck of the Tenth Connecticut. "We knew that a good many would be killed and wounded and each man was telling his comrade where his watch and money was and in case he should fall he wanted the other to take it." Such protests failed to dissuade Ames or Terry, although they undoubtedly delayed the assault even more. Ames was committed to an attack.[89]

Ames provided Pond with additional manpower from the Third New Hampshire and the six reserve companies of the Tenth Connecticut. The colonel placed his Sixty-Seventh Ohio, Thirty-Ninth Illinois, and Sixty-Second Ohio in the front line, left to right, with the battalion of the Tenth Connecticut on his far right. The Eighty-Fifth Pennsylvania and the Third New Hampshire aligned in support thirty yards behind the front ranks. According to Hawley, Ames told him, "The moment the assault commenced my strong skirmish line should move up as far as practicable and vigorously engage the enemy, and that in case Colonel Pond should be successful, and the enemy in my front should show signs of breaking, I should charge with my whole force." Pond's six small regiments numbered not quite 1,000 men. Such a body might have accomplished its goal before the Alabamans arrived and strengthened their works—but after this, their assault was doomed.[90]

The Federals aligned astride a farm lane leading west past the Gerhardt house about one-half mile south of Charles City Road. The narrow byway was bordered by thick undergrowth that promised to slow the attackers. George W. Yates, the color sergeant of the Thirty-Ninth Illinois, waited with the rest of Pond's frontline troops for the order to advance. His comrades saw him remove a group of letters from his pocket, read them over, then tear them into pieces, throwing the fragments into the air. "Boys, I shall in all likelihood fall," he said. "When the order is given to charge, let not one of you desert these colors. Save them, whether I am lost or not."[91]

Pond's attack commenced around 2:00 P.M., minutes before Butler's orders to suspend the offensive reached Terry and thus too late for them to filter down the chain of command. The battle line struggled forward, delayed and somewhat disorganized by the thick undergrowth that shielded it from view, although the Confederates could hear officers' orders as the Federals lurched ahead. Soon enough, the attackers reached the open ground fronting the Alabamans' line, 150 yards distant, and let out a shout. "I could see [the Confederates] plain," wrote Corporal Peck. "They was just as thick as they could stand in two ranks and were loading and firing just as fast as they could and their works run so that they could get a cross fire on us."[92]

Pond's attackers had unknowingly entered the concave portion of Bowles's defenses and instantly paid a heavy price. Enfilading fire from rifles and cannons as well as frontal fire from Bowles's left-most regiments cut swaths in the Union ranks. "The artillery was shooting [as was the] infantry as far up and down the line as could reach them," recalled one Confederate. The Tenth Connecticut, on the formation's right, went forward with a shout, "not of enthusiasm or hope, but of earnest determination," led by all three of its field officers for the first time since early in the war, even though the regiment brought fewer than 100 men into the fight. Maj. Henry Camp positioned himself on the regiment's left and charged ahead, only to fall with a mortal wound. "Our major was worth more than their whole line of works," thought one of his men. The much-lamented officer was among the forty-five Nutmeggers killed, wounded, or captured in the assault. "It was the hottest fire that our reg't ever was under," thought Peck.[93]

The rest of Pond's front line suffered an equally decisive repulse. A sergeant in the Thirty-Ninth Illinois remembered: "As we made the assault through the brush, the air seeming filled with whizzing bullets, the scream of solid shot and shell, the rattle and sweep of grape and canister through our ranks. Comrades fell on our right and our left," including Capt. George T. Heritage, commanding the regiment. Color Sergeant Yates sprang forward at the head of his unit. He made a conspicuous target and soon fell, pierced by four bullets. As his comrades shrank before the unrelenting fire, the wounded Yates clutched his flag, retaining a fragment as a bold Confederate left the works and ripped the prize from his hands. The Rebels eventually retrieved Yates, who still clung to the bloody fragment of his regimental banner, and would parole the wounded hero; he died at a hospital in Annapolis less than two weeks later. The Thirty-Ninth Illinois lost sixty men in the attack.[94]

Most of the Federals failed to even penetrate the abatis. "Human endurance could stand up no longer against this terrific fire of musketry and artillery," admitted Colonel Pond, who ordered his battered brigade to retire. Elias Peck and another soldier had taken cover behind a stump "in hopes that the rebels would slacken their fire a little but they did not." Surrounded by the dead and wounded and watching as Confederate bullets continued to find targets along the ground, Peck decided to risk a run for safety. "I thought it was shure death to lay there and I may as well die getting away as to lay there so I took my gun & started[.] As I was agoing I saw two men helping a wounded man off and all 3 fell dead together." Peck managed to escape unscathed. Colonel Otis of the Tenth Connecticut reported, "My regiment has taken part in more than forty battles and skirmishes" but had never before retreated under fire. "I have not seen a more hopeless task undertaken since I entered the [service]."[95]

Pond's repulse rendered the supporting attacks on his left pointless, and they, too, withdrew amid a shower of fire. "They turned face backward and dragged off their mangled and howling squadrons to their earthen dens," crowed the *Richmond Daily Dispatch*, mischaracterizing the generally disciplined Federal retreat. "The Yanks made an assault on our works in front of Field's Division but were sent back faster than they could come," boasted the Fifty-First North Carolina's John McGeachy, "only some who are left to rot on the field." In fact, the assault lasted all of ten minutes, and in that short time, Pond lost 218 of his men, including 14 killed and 191 wounded. The Confederates suffered between thirty and eighty casualties, among them the mortally wounded commander of the Forty-Seventh Alabama, Lt. Col. Leigh R. Terrell. Texan Edward Crockett summarized the outcome of the attack in a succinct diary entry. "We repulse the Yankees at all points easily. Their loss considerable ours almost none."[96]

The cavalry on Charles City Road, which had become engaged in nothing more than long-distance sniping, were the first to flee the field. "The greater part of the day was spent in pressing in [the] forest to find an enemy that showed himself in nearly equal force all along the line," wrote Kautz. "It was manifest that an attack was doubtful of everything except a severe loss and the orders was received to withdraw." The First Maryland Cavalry counted twenty-one casualties, more than the rest of the division combined. The Federal artillery "belched forth their fiery breath with an almost continuous roar," according to a soldier in the Eleventh Maine, providing covering fire during the infantry's withdrawal.[97]

Shortly after 3:30 P.M., the battlefield grew quiet. Lee, fully aware of his vulnerable flank, had by then ordered Field's two Georgia brigades—Anderson's and DuBose's—to shift north and extend Bowles's left. Anderson filed in next to the Alabamans and DuBose even farther north, but they arrived after the Yankees disengaged. A few of Bowles's men, joined by some Georgians and Texans, ventured out to locate the Union position, picking their way through their abatis. They managed to dislodge a few of Plaisted's skirmishers, but soon, Federal fire compelled the graycoats to return to the safety of their works. Terry, now apprised of Grant's and Butler's orders to suspend further attacks, told Ames and Birney to fall back, first to the abandoned Outer Line and then to their camps. The Second Battle of Darbytown Road had come to an anticlimactic end.[98]

At 7:00 that evening Terry sent Butler a brief status report. "My troops are all in," he wrote his commander. "We were not followed except by a line of skirmishers on the extreme right. These came on but for a short distance, and were soon stopped by the artillery." Terry estimated his loss at between 300 and 400 men; later it would be officially tallied at 396. Adding the 41 casualties in Kautz's division, the fruitless and ill-advised operation cost the Federals 437 soldiers. Hawley spoke for many when he noted that such a high casualty count was "pretty heavy for a mere reconnaissance."[99]

Butler neglected to inform Grant about what had transpired, causing the general-in-chief to inquire twice that evening for details about "the result of General Terry's reconnaissance. Such wild rumors were afloat about Varina this evening that I feel much anxiety to know the facts." Butler finally replied at 9:50 P.M. with a detailed summary of the day's events, confessing that "Ames was unsuccessful, owing to the enemy's lines being retired, which gave the impression that there was a gap in the line." After exaggerating the tepid Confederate pursuit, the army commander assured his superior that "there is not the slightest cause for any anxiety."[100]

Butler's cheery spin on the afternoon's misadventures did little to influence the candid conclusion shared by most Federals that the day had been, in the words of Cpl. Joseph R. Ward of the Thirty-Ninth Illinois, "an awful defeat." Ward blamed the setback on "the mismanagement of our officers who were drunk," although other analyses absolved Union commanders of inebriation. General Ames placed the onus on Colonel Pond, who he accused of chronic tardiness. "He displayed, at least I thought he did, great indifference throughout the entire day, and only did what he was ordered to do when he found it could not be avoided." Nothing in the record, however, suggests that Pond blatantly dragged his feet, although it is entirely plausible that Ames understood, explicitly or otherwise, that the colonel viewed his assignment as a forlorn hope. Ample evidence exists to demonstrate the pessimism that infected many of the attackers. No doubt, the extended time between Terry's initial deployment and the commencement of his assault benefited the Confederates. As Corporal Peck observed, "the idea of our waiting all day for the rebels to bring all the reinforcements there that they wanted and then charge on them" promised disaster. Pond may have contributed to this delay, but if so, he shared responsibility with both Ames and Terry.[101]

At least one participant held Terry solely responsible. "I think it was a wretched piece of business in . . . General Terry and he ought to be made to suffer," wrote Sgt. Maj. Erwin Welsh of the Sixty-Seventh Ohio. "To speak the truth he acted more like a fool than a general and if my boy could not use more judgment after he is three years older I should feel almost like disowning him." Welsh pointed to the poor reconnaissance that led his brigade to enter the reentrant angle that magnified their bloody repulse. Kautz and Ames more directly bear the burden of ordering Pond to charge into a trap without accurate knowledge of the Rebel defenses.[102]

Historian Bryce Suderow locates the failure at the highest levels of command. "Grant was in such a hurry to mount the attack that he had not bothered to determine how complete the Confederate earthworks were or how many Confederates held it." Butler, argues Suderow, suffered from the same dearth of information, and the two leaders between them failed to make clear their intentions: Was the operation a reconnaissance or a full-throated attack? Yet whatever ambiguity existed in Grant's orders should be understood more as contingency than confusion. Hawley lamented the casualty count, but he allowed, "We found out their exact position, though we did not do what Grant hoped, *break up* their operations on the Darbytown Road." Some participants, such as Lieutenant Wright, expressed skepticism regarding the advantage that would have been gained if the attack had been successful. "What profit would it have been to us?" he wondered. "Probably some one would have got some glory but we think it will take a good deal of such glory to pay for such valuable lives." Of course, had Butler's orders to suspend the attack arrived a few minutes sooner, the entire episode would have been moot.[103]

General Lee dispatched a short message to the War Department announcing the victory. "Our loss very slight," he informed Secretary Seddon. Field's four brigades remained in position north of Darbytown Road that night, while Walker's South Carolinians stayed south of the highway, connecting with Hoke's left. Colquitt's Georgians extended the line as far south as New Market Road. The next morning some of Bowles's men ventured out to bury the Federals slain the previous afternoon. Capt. Joseph Banks Lyle soon spotted an officer, Colonel Rockwell of the Sixth Connecticut, bearing a flag of truce seeking to recover the body of Major Camp. Lyle rode to the rear and handed the request to Richard Anderson for his consideration. Shortly thereafter General Lee appeared. Lee and Anderson approved a ceasefire for the stated purpose, and Lyle received orders to return Camp's corpse and "offer an apology for the denuded condition of the body." Meanwhile, other Confederates went onto the battlefield. "It was the usual scene," explained Pvt. William Moultrie Reid of the Palmetto Light

Artillery, "negroes and white men lying promiscuously. There were not more than 30 or 40 in all & all almost naked."[104]

Southern voices united in their analysis of the battle. "We call this one of the most complete and satisfactory, as it was one of the most important, victories of the campaign," puffed the *Richmond Daily Dispatch*, with obvious exaggeration. "The Yankees may call it a 'reconnaissance' or what they please—Whenever they feel in the humor of making another of these reconnaissances, our troops will afford them the usual facilities." The editor joined many Confederate soldiers who viewed Second Darbytown Road as a harbinger of bigger things to come. "From every indication, there will soon be fought the great battle of the campaign, and our hills will tremble with the reverberations of artillery, the dogs of rampant war which guard Richmond, the Carthage of the South." In preparation for such a showdown, the Rebels labored tirelessly to improve their fortifications. "We have been working day and night and scarcely had time to eat what little grub we had to eat," related Pvt. David A. Hampton of the Forty-Second North Carolina. "We are putting up the best works now that I ever seen." Adj. George Moffett was among those who predicted an impending battle north of the James. "Some how I feel that we will win," he wrote, but admitting: "Grant is a tough colt. It is very hard to hold him in one place long enough to strike him, & he moves rapidly to points where we are vulnerable."[105]

Indeed, Grant would initiate another offensive, but not as immediately as these Rebels predicted. In the meantime, the troops on both the Richmond and the Petersburg fronts pursued what had by now become routine: labor with pick and shovel. Hancock concentrated on completing the forts that provided the line of circumvallation facing south. By October 18, the Second Corps had completed Fort Blaisdell, and crews began the finishing touches on Fort Patrick Kelly. Ninth Corps troops finished Fort Fisher, the bastion guarding Church Road on the Pegram farm. The installation measured 120 feet long by 100 feet wide and mounted seven guns. On Butler's front the main line ran from Cox's Hill, overlooking the James, up to Fort Harrison and then along the old Outer Line to Darbytown Road, fronted now in most places by abatis and wire entanglements. Engineers also described a line protecting New Market Heights and Deep Bottom. A huge redoubt, styled Fort Brooks, arose on the western end of New Market Heights. A companion installation on the eastern end of the heights, near old Camp Holly, was named Fort Southard. This elaborate network of earthworks suggested that the Unionists might never be driven out of Henrico County.[106]

Dick Anderson's soldiers completed the Alexander Line to Charles City Road between October 17 and 19, but that lieutenant general would no longer be responsible for its defenders. James Longstreet had written to Walter Taylor of Lee's staff on October 7 seeking permission to return to active duty, being willing to serve anywhere, including in the Trans-Mississippi, if Lee had no place for him in the Army of Northern Virginia. Lee, of course, was delighted to welcome back his "old war horse," despite his paralyzed right arm. Longstreet took command of the troops north of the James and in Bermuda Hundred, officially assuming his new post on October 19. Ewell now reported to Longstreet, as did Field and Hoke as long as they remained in his jurisdiction. Counting Pickett's Division at Bermuda Hundred, Longstreet controlled some 18,000 men. "It was gratifying to the Genl to see the wild enthusiasm manifested by the veterans of his command on his appearance amongst them after such a long absence," wrote Longstreet's aide-de-camp, Thomas Goree. "When the men saw him coming, they mounted the breastworks and while he rode down the lines made the welkin ring with cheers for 'the old bull of the woods' as they love to designate him." The lieutenant acknowledged that his chief was "no favorite with the President & Bragg, yet he has what is much better, the unbounded confidence of Genl Lee and the officers and troops of his command." Anderson now headed a new Fourth Corps—Beauregard's former troops—but in practical terms it was only Bushrod Johnson's Division. Never again would this adequate if undistinguished officer lead a force commensurate with his rank.[107]

In the meantime, "Beast" Butler expelled some forty women and children from the informal village of Darbytown. Some of that community's men had taken the oath of allegiance, and thus the general assigned guards to protect their property. Five of those sentries were killed, and the citizens, guilty or innocent of the murders, fled to Richmond. This prompted Butler to depopulate the entire area. The Union commander ordered these refugees to board his personal steamboat, *Greyhound*, with the choice of being sent north or down the James to Suffolk and beyond Union lines. A correspondent from the *Philadelphia Inquirer* noted the pitiable condition of these destitute women dressed in rags, and "some of the little boys had on Uncle Sam's pants, made up, of course, to fit."[108]

A different kind of rear-area responsibility occupied Grant in mid-October. On the morning of the sixteenth, a steamer docked at City Point and disgorged quite an aggregation of Washington dignitaries, chief of whom were Edwin Stanton and the new secretary of the treasury, William Pitt Fessenden. These officials wished to confer with Grant, Meade, and Butler, hoping to gain firsthand understanding of military affairs. Grant suggested they meet first with Butler, notifying that commander shortly after noon that he and Stanton would steam up to Aiken's Landing and asking him to meet them there with transportation. While touring the Union lines, Stanton spoke frequently, expressing his joy at being away from Washington and heaping praise on Sheridan and the president.[109]

The next morning Grant sent word to Meade that, in the words of Lieutenant Colonel Lyman, "Secretary Stanton, with a long tail," wished to visit the Army of the Potomac and its leader. Meade remarked sullenly, "The devil! I shan't have time to smoke my cigar," as the staff scurried about to arrange a proper reception for the secretary of war. Within an hour or two, the group arrived, "the greatest posse of large bugs," according to the sardonic Lyman. Grant and others rode in, while the two cabinet officers arrived in ambulances. Meade took them to Fort Wadsworth, where Stanton, upon being informed that only a picket line separated him from the Rebels, made an excuse for leaving, "no doubt fully informed as to the state of matters down here," quipped a sarcastic Charles Wainwright. Meade then joined the group back at City Point, where they conferred with Admiral Porter. Stanton and his party returned to Washington on the eighteenth, learning the next day of Sheridan's great victory at Cedar Creek, a battle that all but crippled Early's little army in the Shenandoah Valley.[110]

Stanton's counterpart in Richmond, James Seddon, eschewed personal junkets in favor of responding to Lee's perpetual calls to strengthen his army. "I . . . shall, if possible, with zeal and energy strain the powers and means of the Department to accomplish an efficient recruitment," he promised the general. Seddon hoped to secure fresh levies by reducing the heretofore generous number of exemptions granted to men otherwise fit for active service. He also increased the number of free and enslaved Black men, impressed or otherwise, who served the army as laborers. Reserves would be assigned rear-area duties, such as guarding prisoners, thus freeing regular troops to rejoin their units. The walking wounded left hospital beds to return to the front. "From these measures, I trust an adequate force may be obtained to relieve the gravity of the present situation and avert apprehended consequences," assured Seddon.[111]

The secretary was as good as his word, issuing General Orders No. 76 that canceled all military details except those men involved in the production of war materiel and called for the examination of men previously deemed physically unfit for service. Lee welcomed this expedient. "I have great hope that the operation of General Orders No. 76 . . . will bring much strength to our armies in the field," he wrote to General Cooper, the army's adjutant and inspector general. "The difficulty now will be to get it promptly carried into effect"—prescient words, for within two weeks, Grant would once again test Confederate arms during his Sixth Petersburg Offensive.[112]

twelve

A GREAT CALAMITY WILL BEFALL US

The Sixth Petersburg Offensive, October 27–28

The combat southwest of Petersburg and north of the James River during the second week of October gave way to a period of calm across the entire Richmond-Petersburg front. "Grant keeps persistently quiet," reported the *Richmond Daily Examiner*. "So far as fighting is concerned, the north side is as still as the grave." Similar conditions prevailed around Petersburg. "The quiet of the lines during the past twenty-four hours has been undisturbed except by the usual artillery firing in front of Second Corps," George Meade informed Grant. These relatively tranquil conditions accommodated a variety of activities behind the lines. A Norwegian artist named Ballen made the rounds at Union headquarters, drawing sketches of prominent generals for a large mural and picture book, including likenesses of Meade and Grant. According to Theodore Lyman, "Mr. Ballen made a drawing of the General [Meade], which looked like an old Jew extremely intoxicated upon which the Chief good humoredly remarked: 'Well, he's served Grant worse than he did me; that's one good thing.'" The soldiers in the Union's Iron Brigade built a racetrack behind their works. Watching the horses and wagering on the outcomes proved quite popular with the men. Confederate soldiers continued to spend some of their leisure time collecting shell fragments and minié balls behind their lines to augment their sporadic paydays.[1]

The troops thoroughly embraced their respite from hostilities, but men in both blue and gray assumed that active operations would resume soon enough. "Everything is very quiet but it is the quiet which precedes the storm," Quartermaster Uberto Burnham of the 76th New York confided to his diary on October

25. "Old soldiers who watch the way straws are drifted are sure that an important movement is impending." Although Second Corps commander Hancock fretted that the Confederates might cross the Appomattox River behind his right flank, most speculation focused on the far Confederate right southwest of Petersburg. "We are working for the R.R. that leads to Petersburg called the southside RR," Pvt. William Lamont of the 179th New York informed his sister. "When the whistle blows the Joneys will crow and hollow why don't you get it." Wade Hampton agreed and recommended to General Lee that the works extending southwest toward Hatcher's Run be strengthened and adequately defended to counter just such a turning movement. "We should suppose, from a passage in a late number of the *New York Herald*, that the '*Boydton Plank Road*' on the extreme right of our line, will be Grant's next point of attack," editorialized a Richmond newspaper. "We have found the indications of the Northern newspapers pretty correct."[2]

These prognostications were, at least in part, accurate. Grant reflexively chafed at stalemate. Union grand strategy demanded that Federal armies maintain the initiative, not only to diminish or defeat the Confederates but also to imbue the civilian North with an unshakable belief in ultimate victory, particularly in light of the impending elections. Grant charged his chief engineer, John Barnard, with examining all viable opportunities for achieving a breakthrough, but that officer's October 15 report proved anything but encouraging. "I have studied carefully the whole problem," wrote General Barnard, "and . . . I cannot convince myself that there is any one offering chances . . . of success." Only if Grant could gather a mobile force of 40,000 men while maintaining a sufficient deterrent in his expanded lines might anything worthwhile be accomplished. The general-in-chief's plan to add troops from Phil Sheridan's army in the Shenandoah Valley had been thwarted by Jubal Early's attack at Cedar Creek on October 19, but Sheridan's victory there so encouraged Grant that he decided to challenge Barnard's advice.[3]

Grant summoned Meade on the morning of October 21 to join him in a "ride round the works west of the Weldon road." He remained focused on the two primary supply arteries critical to Lee's survival and that of the two cities he defended: Boydton Plank Road and the South Side Railroad. The generals' reconnaissance suggested that a strong force, albeit perhaps less robust than the one Barnard had specified, could occupy the defenders on Lee's right, while another column marched west, beyond the Rebel works, to sever both the road and the railroad. The general-in-chief expected that with Early's failure to redeem the Valley, most of his troops would come east to reinforce Lee. Any decisive blow, he thought, must be struck before this occurred. Moreover, as

Sgt. Oliver Charles Benton of the Seventeenth New York Battery explained on October 16, "One thing certain, if Grant expects or intends to take Richmond this fall, he must do some big thing before many days or he will get stuck in the mud and will have to lay over until spring." These factors, added to his natural instincts to sustain pressure on his opponent, persuaded Grant to accept the risk inherent in any such offensive. The stakes loomed especially high because a military disaster on the eve of the presidential election might undermine Lincoln's candidacy and perhaps swing the contest to the Democrats, raising the prospect of a negotiated peace.[4]

Grant first sought to determine how many troops he could devote to such an operation. As soon as the two generals returned from their reconnaissance, Meade sent a confidential message to Winfield S. Hancock inquiring about the number of Second Corps men who could participate in such a movement consistent with maintaining an adequate defense of their entrenchments. The next morning the army commander posed the same question to Gouverneur Warren and John Parke. The corps commanders replied promptly. The three reported that, together, they could provide some 36,000 soldiers to an offensive. Combining these troops with David Gregg's 5,000 cavalry, Grant would achieve the manpower Barnard thought necessary for success. The general-in-chief, consistent with his usual custom, left the details of the operation to Meade and his capable chief of staff, A. A. Humphreys.[5]

Grant would also employ his usual tactic of initiating simultaneous maneuvers with Meade and Ben Butler. He met with his two army commanders— probably at City Point on the evening of October 23—to review the role each would play in the upcoming offensive. He issued orders the following day, specifying that the twin operations would begin on October 27. Meade's goal would be "to gain possession of the South Side Railroad, and to hold it and fortify back to your present left," employing all three of his infantry corps and the cavalry division as Meade had suggested. The men would carry three days' rations and sixty rounds of ammunition, indicating Grant's expectation of a prolonged and contentious operation. The Army of the James would simultaneously "demonstrate against the enemy" in its front, avoiding an attack "against intrenched and defended positions, but feel[ing] to the right beyond the front," and if possible "turn[ing] it." Butler's men, too, would carry three days' rations and sixty rounds of ammunition. Grant suggested detaching Butler's cavalry to raid the Virginia Central Railroad but admitted that under August Kautz's leadership, such a raid might not be wise. He left that option to Butler.[6]

Army headquarters notified Hancock, Warren, Parke, and Gregg on October 24 that orders for the offensive would be forthcoming and to prepare their units for active operations. As promised, Meade circulated a complex, twelve-part directive the following day. Those orders rested upon the erroneous assumption that the Confederate works running southwest toward Hatcher's Run terminated about a mile northeast of that stream.[7]

Each of Meade's commanders received distinct assignments. The Ninth Corps, some 11,450 strong, including Edward Ferrero's Black division, would advance "at such hour of the morning of the 27th as will enable him to attack the right of the enemy's infantry, between Hatcher's Run and their new works at Hawks' and Dabney's, at the dawn of day." Parke's mission assumed that "the enemy's line of intrenchments is incomplete at that point" and, by "a secret and sudden movement," the Ninth Corps could surprise the Rebels "and carry their half-formed works." If they captured the line, Parke's troops were to "follow up the enemy closely, turning toward the right." Should his attack fail, the Ninth Corps would "remain confronting them until operations on the left draw off the enemy."[8]

Meade assigned the most difficult job to Warren, despite his enduring distrust of that officer's judgment and aggressiveness. The Fifth Corps would bring about 13,000 men to the operation, and its objectives would be contingent on Parke's fate. Should the Ninth Corps turn the Confederate works, Warren would advance on Parke's left and join him in driving northeast up the Rebel line toward Boydton Plank Road. If, on the other hand, the Ninth Corps failed to breach the Rebel works, Warren would "cross Hatcher's Run and endeavor to turn the enemy's right by recrossing at the first practicable point above Boydton plank road, keeping on the right of Hancock." From there the Fifth Corps would return to the plank road and control the bridge over Hatcher's Run at Burgess Mill, all the while occupying a position between the Second and Ninth Corps. Warren's role would be straightforward if Parke's attack succeeded, but otherwise he would face a daunting march through poorly understood terrain involving two crossings of Hatcher's Run. Although Meade left it unsaid, such a march would be feasible only if Hancock's portion of the operation unfolded as designed.[9]

The Second Corps would contribute 12,000 troops to Meade's plan. Hancock would begin his march at 2:00 A.M. using Vaughan Road, cross Hatcher's Run at Cumming's Ford, and proceed to Boydton Plank Road, a route presumably well beyond the Confederate defenses. Marching cross-country to Claiborne Road, the troops would use that country lane to recross Hatcher's Run and reach the South Side Railroad near Sutherland Station. Gregg's cavalry would advance south of Hancock, using Quaker Road to reach the plank road and then shadow Hancock's left flank, fending off enemy cavalry known to be prowling beyond the Rebel fortifications. All the men involved in this huge and complicated operation would now carry four days' rations along with their extra ammunition, enough to sustain them while consolidating their gains and dealing with the inevitable Confederate response. If successful, this movement would pin the Rebels into the inner ring of Petersburg's works and sever their direct supply lines. Lee must then either risk a counterattack outside of his trenches, abandon Petersburg and withdraw to a tight circle around Richmond, or even evacuate the capital.[10]

This audacious plan contained two serious flaws. First, Meade's assumption that the enemy fortifications were unfinished and vulnerable was simply wrong. The Confederates completed their line by October 24, including rows of abatis and a cleared field of fire. "The new line to Hatcher's Run will be ready for occupation to-morrow," Hampton informed A. P. Hill on the twenty-second; two days later the cavalry chief informed Lee that "a new line of works, which extends to Hatcher's Run . . . is now finished." As this message affirmed, the works extended all the way to commanding ground above Hatcher's Run and were not refused a mile or more to the northeast as the Federals believed. This meant, of course, that Parke would encounter formidable fortifications and that Warren would strike the front of the Rebel defenses, not skirt an exposed flank. Moreover, the terrain along the right bank of Hatcher's run was terra incognita to the Yankees, tangled and difficult of passage. Warren had no idea that in order to recross the stream above Boydton Plank Road, he would have to travel all the way to Claiborne Road, placing the Fifth Corps miles from Parke's left and sharing the route with Hancock. "The country . . . was very imperfectly known to us, and was as densely wooded as the Wilderness," admitted General Humphreys. The Confederate cavalry, combined with the Dinwiddie forest, had done a masterful job of preventing the Federals from conducting the sort of comprehensive reconnaissance such an operation required. Parke and Warren would pay the price for this failure on October 27.[11]

Preparations for the offensive, although its details remained unknown to the rank and file, turned the Union camps into beehives of activity. "Grant is making another one of his curious movements. Folks don't understand it," confessed Musician Charles Lewis Rundlett. "There is going to be a big strike somewhere." "The camp is in great commotion as I write," explained Lt. John T. Andrews of the 179th New York. "All were expecting a fight today here 'on the left' . . . but we don't know what the place is." When Andrews heard the order for the distribution of ammunition and three days' rations, "I thought that meant a fight." Sergeant John Irwin of the 20th Michigan saw Grant, Meade, Warren, and Parke riding along the Ninth Corps lines and watched as corps headquarters packed up. "Indications like these which to a greenhorn might be nothing," Irwin wrote his mother, "to old soldiers look rather ominous." Officers sent surplus baggage to City Point, men led spare horses to the rear, and teamsters parked their wagons in secure places. Meade's orders to the corps commanders were supposed to be confidential, but Lieutenant Colonel Lyman scoffed at this attempt at secrecy. "Confidential! Fiddlesticks!!" he exclaimed in a letter home. "As if in an army of Yankees half the people don't wag their tongues at both ends. Two days . . . ago the rebel pickets wished to know in a sarcastic manner when 'that move' was coming off; adding with reprehensible profanity that they meant to give us something beginning with H on the Boydton road." Grant reviewed the orders and approved them with one minor clarification. If Parke found the Confederates unassailable, he wanted the Ninth Corps to "only confront them until the movement of the other two corps had its effect." Meade responded that this was exactly what his orders implied, admitting that to ascertain the enemy's strength and position, Parke must make at least a partial attack. "Great results are confidently expected," wrote Colonel Wainwright, who would accompany the infantry with ten rifled cannon and twelve smoothbores.[12]

General Butler waited until October 26 to communicate Grant's orders for his portion of the next day's offensive. They were only marginally less complex than Meade's and even more rife with contingency. As was the case with Meade's command, the Army of the James would employ its cavalry division and each of its infantry corps.

Butler instructed Alfred Terry to assign 8,500 men and eight guns of his Tenth Corps to "feel along the enemy's lines to the right as far, at least, as the Charles City road, pushing the enemy's skirmish lines, but not attacking their works." This was to be accomplished by 7:00 A.M. Meanwhile, Godfrey Weitzel would lead 7,500 of his Eighteenth Corps soldiers and two artillery batteries on a long march behind Terry's troops to reach Williamsburg Road. "It is assumed that this march will have flanked the enemy's defended intrenched line," Butler advised. Once in their designated places, both infantry corps would be bound by circumstances. Butler decided against sending his cavalry on a raid and instead assigned the troopers to protect the "the flanks and head of General Weitzel's column" and to scatter the enemy's pickets and scouts. If everything broke his way, Weitzel could outflank the Rebels and advance all the way to Richmond. "The prize is large," Butler added, "and if we are that near[,] the attempt to seize [Richmond] will justify loss." Shortly after noon he shared these orders with Grant for review and approval. "Your orders are recd," the general-in-chief replied. "They meet the case in hand exactly."[13]

Butler then forwarded the approved instructions to his commanders, causing the usual flurry of activity. "Preparations are going forward and in all probability this is the last night we shall remain in our present quarters," reported staff officer Solon Carter. "Many surmises where we are going but none know," confessed the Ninety-Eighth New York's Lyman Sperry. One rumor circulated that the army was on its way to North Carolina. Pvt. Silas Mead, an ambulance attendant assigned to General Ames's headquarters, speculated that the preparations portended "a little bigger reconnaissance than we had two weeks ago. Old squinty Butler is out ... somewhere, so I do not feel in much danger. ... Am at Division Hd Qrs. ... That's where I like to be ... to the rear of the Generals." Many of Butler's Black soldiers prepared for action by singing patriotic songs. "Never was an army in better spirits, or more confident of a victory," wrote African American newspaper correspondent Thomas Morris Chester.[14]

Amid these preparations, the ever-sensitive George Meade found time to worry about "the fiendish and malicious attack" on him written in a New York newspaper, while both Butler and Grant scrawled short letters to their wives on the eve of battle. "In the morning we make a movement both at Petersburg and Richmond," Butler wrote to Sarah. "I have done all I can do. ... The night before a battle—how many thoughts are crowded into it. How many a poor fellow is never to see another night. The chance of us all, but we will do our duty, and the rest is with the Disposer of All." Grant's note to Julia waxed less philosophical. "To-morrow a great battle will probably be fought," he wrote. "I do not like to predict results therefore will say nothing about what I expect to accomplish."[15]

On the Petersburg front, Hampton's cavalry bore responsibility for the southern end of the fortifications down to Hatcher's Run. "My men here think they can whip anybody now, and they are in the finest possible spirits," the general informed his sister. "If a great battle comes off I think they will make their mark." He placed some 700 cavalrymen in the works deployed as infantry, connecting with Cooke's Brigade of Heth's Division on their left. That number could swell to 1,800 by moving his mounted units, which patrolled to the south, behind the trenches. Hampton believed he could defend about a mile of the recently completed line but beseeched Powell Hill to man the rest. The cavalry chief also erected several small dams along Hatcher's Run to impound that narrow stream into more of an obstacle, protecting each of them with earthworks. He and Hill examined the line on October 24. Hampton again lobbied the Third Corps commander to contribute as many as 1,500 men to supplement or replace his troopers. Doing so, he argued, would allow him to cross Hatcher's Run on one of its dams and strike the Yankees on their flank should they venture an advance. In any event, the Rebels were prepared to meet an assault northeast of Hatcher's Run.[16]

Optimism ran high in Confederate camps north of the James as well. Capt. Eugene Burnett, an officer on Colquitt's staff in Hoke's Division, considered the works recently completed in his front the strongest he had ever seen. Robert Hoke's four brigades defended the line between New Market and Darbytown Roads. Ewell's troops, including Custis Lee's reserves, connected with Hoke's right and extended down to the James, while Charles Field's veterans deployed from Hoke's left to and beyond Charles City Road. Mart Gary's cavalry patrolled in Field's front toward White Oak Swamp and on the infantry's left. "Every effort was made to strengthen my works and dispose of the force at my command so as to cover the long line I had to defend as well as possible," reported James Longstreet. "Our troops are in good spirits and feel confident that they can drive back any force the enemy may send against them," wrote Capt. Samuel S. Biddle of the Sixty-First North Carolina. Lt. William Taylor Mason, an aide to Porter Alexander, agreed. "We can hold our line against the whole Yankee nation," he boasted. Hoke and Field, who defended the works targeted by Butler, counted about 8,000 officers and men present for duty.[17]

On the night of Wednesday, October 26, Hoke and his staff crept beyond their works to listen for evidence of enemy movements. "The night was still and frosty, and . . . on such nights you can hear noises an incredible distance," recalled the general. "We heard the rumbling of artillery and all other noises which showed that General Butler was on the move." Indeed, the Army of the James was hours away from commencing its offensive.[18]

Butler's men arose at 4:00 A.M. on October 27, gobbled a quick breakfast, and began their march before dawn. General Terry felt so unwell, caused by "a very painful carbuncle," that he rode in a buggy, thus moving toward the familiar fields surrounding the Johnson house, he quipped, "after the manner of the ancients, in a chariot." His three divisions, led by Adelbert Ames, Robert Foster, and Joseph Hawley, in charge this day of Terry's Black brigades, shifted north to gain their assigned positions along Darbytown Road. None of Terry's units had to travel more than six miles. Foster, an antebellum Indiana tinsmith, reached that highway about 7:00 A.M. He sent skirmishers from Martin Curtis's First Brigade to cover the division front, supplemented by men from Galusha Pennypacker's Second Brigade. Louis Bell's Third Brigade halted in reserve. Soon a sharp picket fire erupted, but the Confederate skirmishers quickly withdrew to their main line.[19]

Ames's division filed in on Foster's right, north of Darbytown Road. Joseph Abbott anchored the left of his Second Brigade on the highway, with Harris

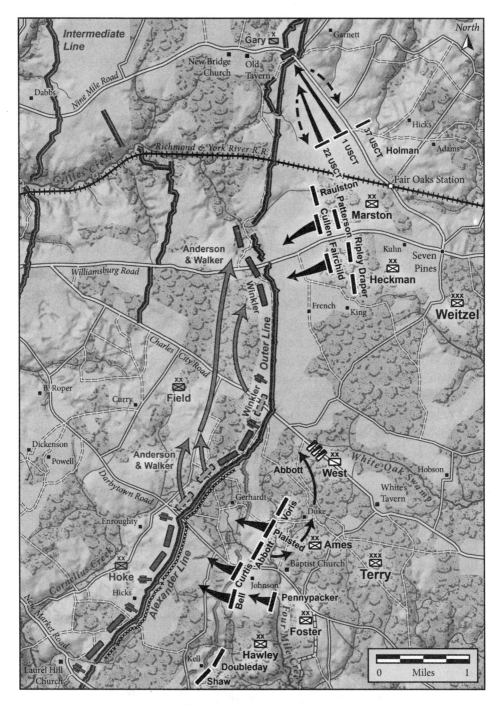

Intermediate Line

North

New Bridge Church

Old Tavern

Garnett

Dabbs

Nine Mile Road

Hicks

Gillies Creek

Richmond & York River R.R.

37 USCT

1 USCT

22 USCT

Fair Oaks Station

Holman

Adams

Raulston

Patterson

Cullen

Marston

XX

Anderson & Walker

Williamsburg Road

Winkler

Ripley

Draper

Fairchild

Kuhn

Seven Pines

Heckman

XX

French

King

Weitzel

XXX

Charles City Road

Outer Line

B. Roper

Curry

Field

XX

Winkler

Dickenson

Powell

Anderson & Walker

Darbytown Road

Abbott

West

XX

White Oak Swamp

Hobson

White's Tavern

Enroughty

Gerhardt

Voris

Duke

Plaisted

Abbott

Ames

XX

Terry

XXX

Cornelius Creek

Hoke

XX

Hicks

Alexander Line

Curtis

Bell

Johnson

Baptist Church

Pennypacker

New Market Road

Four Mile Creek

Foster

XX

Kell

Hawley

XX

Doubleday

Shaw

Laurel Hill Church

0   Miles   1

Williamsburg Road, October 27, 1864

Plaisted's Third Brigade on his right and Alvin Voris's First Brigade Ames's rightmost unit. The Third (USCT) Division deployed south of Darbytown Road, Ulysses Doubleday's Second Brigade on Foster's left and Colonel James Shaw's regiments on Doubleday's left. They halted near the Kell house, with the Twenty-Ninth Connecticut in advance as skirmishers, covering both brigade fronts. As they went forward, the skirmishers encountered a tangle of bushes and trees, making it difficult to maintain a solid line. "The first intimation we had of the Reb pickets was a volley from them behind piles of logs," explained Capt. Charles Griswold. Several of the "smoked Yankees" fell wounded, but the officers straightened their line, which then charged ahead. "The way the boys went after those pickets yelling at the top of their voice, John couldn't stand and see black faces coming, so away goes his gun and everything else he could divest himself of and he leaves very rapidly for home." Some of the Confederates fell captive, and only the intercession of their officers kept vengeful Black soldiers from murdering their prisoners. Once the Federals reached open ground, they could see "not one hundred yards distant . . . heavy breastworks, first a heavy line of slashing . . . and over the whole looked three nasty guns," recalled Lt. Thomas Gray Bennett. The Union skirmishers fell back to the cover of the woods as several rounds of canister wounded two orderlies riding near the lieutenant.[20]

Terry deployed all eight of his brigades on a line three miles in length, facing the impressive works of the Alexander Line. He saw nothing to suggest that he could achieve a breakthrough here. Butler arrived at 9:30 A.M. and, from his Johnson house headquarters, informed Grant that Terry had driven the Confederate pickets and that Weitzel was on the move "where he ought to be." He assured the general-in-chief, "All going well."[21]

That was not entirely true. Weitzel had, indeed, started his march on time, his troops on the road by 5:00 A.M., proceeding at least part of the way at the double-quick, "our blankets rolled and tied at the ends, making a loop over the shoulder," wrote a soldier in the 118th New York. Weitzel had with him all three brigades of his First Division under the mediocre Gilman Marston. Charles Heckman led two of his Second Division brigades, Edward Ripley's and Harrison Fairchild's, while two brigades from the Third (USCT) Division, under John Holman and Alonzo Draper, joined the column. The cavalry, led by Robert West because General Kautz was absent on sick leave, preceded the infantry, clearing the route of any roaming grayclad horsemen. Weitzel made commendable time as his troops followed roads east, then north, to reach Darbytown Road by 8:00 A.M., several miles behind Terry's deployment.[22]

Hearing evidence of Terry's skirmish with the Confederate pickets, Weitzel's pace slowed as he made his way north to White's Tavern on Charles City Road.

John Raulston's brigade of Marston's division, at the head of Weitzel's column, arrived there at 9:50 A.M. Weitzel composed another message to Butler, informing him that West reported the Confederate line extending across Charles City Road and that Terry's troops did not reach that far north. The corps commander acknowledged that his orders specified that he proceed to Williamsburg Road to find the Confederate left flank, but, betraying sudden indecision, Weitzel asked Butler to "send me orders what you wish me now to do."[23]

If Butler responded, that reply has been lost. In any event, Weitzel did shift his corps to Williamsburg Road, crossing White Oak Swamp, scattering a few Rebel cavalry pickets, and filing onto the highway by early to midafternoon, considerably later than expected. The 11th Pennsylvania Cavalry engaged more grayclad troopers along the road, clearing them away with minimal trouble. Weitzel's men found themselves on the Seven Pines battlefield of May–June 1862, as evidenced by eroded fortifications, bleached bones, and numerous soldier graves. Lieutenant Colonel Raulston advanced the 13th New Hampshire as skirmishers, who pushed their Rebel counterparts back to the Confederate-held Outer Line. They were joined by elements of Colonel Cullen's 118th New York and 10th New Hampshire, which approached the works, halting under fire in a shallow depression within 100 yards of the frowning fortifications.[24]

Those trenches were now filling with Confederate infantry. General Longstreet, whose useless arm did nothing to diminish his keen military sense, discerned that Terry's static presence along Darbytown Road presented no imminent threat. "Being convinced the skirmishing between New Market and Charles City roads was but a feint, and the real move was to flank our position by crossing the swamp and taking the unoccupied works on the Williamsburg and Nine Mile roads down which they would sweep, I . . . ordered Field and Hoke to move by the left flank along the works, leaving only strong lines of skirmishers on the fronts they were leaving," wrote Longstreet. The lieutenant general also sent two battalions of artillery with the infantry and told Gary to shift his cavalry to cover Nine Mile Road, north of Williamsburg Road.[25]

Field's Division responded immediately, the Texas Brigade, on the division's left, leading Tige Anderson's Georgians and Joseph Walker's South Carolinians on a dash northward behind the Outer Line. Hoke shifted to cover the works vacated by Field. "We were ordered at double quick time to run, up the old intrenchments to the left," recalled Pvt. Jasper Brightwell of Anderson's Eighth Georgia. "We were hot and much fatigued by our long run, and if many an old soldier's hand trembled as he loaded his musket, it was not from fear, but overexertion." As Field's men approached, they spied a lieutenant and some twenty Virginia Home Guards maintaining a brisk fire toward Weitzel's skirmishers. It appeared the Federals were about to launch a determined attack, prompting the game lieutenant to order his men to stick to their work. "We'll die right here, for it won't do for them to get these works," he allegedly proclaimed. Just then the vaunted Texas Brigade swung into view, and not a moment too soon.[26]

Winkler's panting veterans halted behind their works astride Williamsburg Road as Weitzel readied his attack. Marston placed the balance of Cullen's brigade north of the road, its left flank resting on the highway, with Lt. Col. Joab Patterson's Third Brigade in support 100 yards to the rear. Raulston shifted to Cullen's right. Heckman deployed Ripley's brigade and Draper's USCT brigade, temporarily under Heckman's command, south of Williamsburg Road. Fairchild's three regiments then advanced in front of Ripley and Draper "to act as a charging party, in conjunction with Colonel Cullen's brigade, of the First Division." Holman, with the rest of his USCT division, was still en route. Weitzel informed Butler that, according to Marston, Field's troops occupied the works to his front with some artillery, but he had ordered Marston "to feel them and see if he can get in." Once again betraying his tentative grasp of contingences, Weitzel inquired if, should Marston fail, he should continue north at the risk of being cut off from communications with the rest of the army. "I am entirely lost from Terry," he wrote anxiously.[27]

Weitzel thus committed only two of his seven available brigades to the assault, Cullen's and Fairchild's. He judged that this force would be sufficient to overcome light resistance, but if the Rebels proved to be in greater strength, better to accept the repulse of two brigades than risk his entire corps. His reconnaissance, obviously faulty, left him with the impression that only "a small body of dismounted cavalry" and three guns defended the works in his front. Marston learned from Maj. Levi S. Dominy, commanding the 118th New York, that "there appeared to be a considerable force in his front, and that reinforcements were arriving." Weitzel ignored this intelligence. Between 3:30 and 4:00 P.M., he ordered the assault to begin.[28]

Fairchild brought about 700 men to his task, his own 89th New York on the right of his formation, the 19th Wisconsin on the left, and the 148th New York, temporarily attached to his command, in the center. They moved forward, joined by some of Ripley's 8th Maine, who had advanced with the skirmish line and would participate in the charge. Battery A, 1st Pennsylvania Artillery unlimbered a section on each side of Williamsburg Road to provide covering fire once the infantry commenced its advance. North of the road Cullen readied his five regiments. The twenty-one-year-old native of Brooklyn, a Columbia College graduate, had volunteered his brigade when Colonel Patterson, Weitzel's first choice, expressed reservations. His brigade numbered little more than 1,000 men.[29]

The Sixth Petersburg Offensive, October 27–28

Preceded by a cloud of skirmishers, Cullen advanced north of the highway. "Forward and deploy! Some faces look a little paler than common," recalled Heman Baker of the 118th New York. "Boom came that first cannon shot . . . but we went on right down under their guns within forty or fifty rods of their main line." But the Federals could go no farther. "We entered a ravine close up to the enemy's works and under fire," explained another New Yorker. "We saw that the enemy in our front was in force and being rapidly reinforced, and we sent back for reserves, but none came." Cullen's survivors huddled in the shelter of that depression, pinned down, although the ravine provided lifesaving defilade from the relentless Confederate fire.[30]

Fairchild's advance was equally unsuccessful. He began his assault almost half a mile from the Rebel works, enduring artillery blasts for half that distance before Field's foot soldiers opened fire. "Every man started with a cheer the grape and canister flying around us like hail," Private Paddock of the Nineteenth Wisconsin wrote his father, "but they reserved their infantry untill we got within about 30 rods of their fort when they opened on us and such a deadly fire never was opened on a lot of men as that was. Such crys and groans was then sent up as men fell to the right and left with cryes of mercy. There were gaps cut in the ranks of our Regt the width of six men." Sgt. George Tillotson of the Eighty-Ninth New York agreed. "When we got within musket range of the fort there is no describing the fire we were under. . . . Notwithstanding the havock we kept on til some were within thirty rods of the fort. What there was left fell flat on the ground and lay there as thin as possible. . . . If a man stirred to make an attempt to get away he would get a score at least of bullets at him in an instant."[31]

Although the Texans (and Third Arkansas) had arrived only shortly before Weitzel launched his attack, they formed behind the fortifications in good time and enjoyed what Lieutenant Colonel Winkler called "a perfect frolic," scooping up some of the helpless attackers. Capt. Watson D. Williams of the Fifth Texas conceded that the Yankees fought well but reported that they "were repulsed with great slaughter. Our Div captured 9 stands of colors of which 4 were captured by our brigade. We captured—that is our Brigade . . . more Yankees than the Brigade numbered." "The boys said that they just went out & bagged them like coveys of partridges," echoed Pvt. Benjamin Simms Fitzgerald. No one surpassed Joseph Banks Lyle, an officer on Walker's staff, for corralling the prostrate Federals hunkered down helplessly in front of the Rebel works. Lyle ventured out alone and persuaded several hundred of the trapped soldiers to surrender. He led them inside the Confederate works, bringing three regimental flags "and swords by the armful."[32]

Of course, not every blueclad survivor submitted so willingly. "A good many crawled off like snakes," explained Sergeant Tillotson, "and the wounded except those nearest the fort were taken off." Others, such as Sgt. George M. Englis of the Eighty-Ninth New York, decided to risk running the gauntlet back to the sheltering woods where the attack began. "Says I old boy here tis a chance to go to Libbey but I guess they don't live very well down there so I rather think I will try these old legs. . . . I think I made pretty big time." Fairchild lost 366 in the attack, an attrition rate of more than 50 percent. Cullen fared little better, suffering 344 casualties. "We gave the Yanks a reception they will never forget," wrote a Georgian. Field's entire division lost just forty-five men.[33]

While the issue along Williamsburg Road had not yet been settled, Butler directed Weitzel to send Colonel Holman "across York River Railroad to try and find the enemy's left." Weitzel rushed an order to Holman, instructing him to proceed up the tracks "until he should arrive within sight of the enemy's line, and then to halt and report to corps headquarters." Holman placed the Twenty-Second USCT, under Col. Joseph B. Kiddoo, at the front of his column, followed by the First USCT, with the Thirty-Seventh USCT in the rear. They crossed the railroad and reached Nine Mile Road east of a landmark called Old Tavern, then proceeded northwest along the highway.[34]

Thus far, Holman had encountered only a few Rebel cavalry, but soon he spotted strong fortifications ahead blocking the road. He halted and formed a line of battle, with the First and Twenty-Second USCT south of Nine Mile Road and the Thirty-Seventh USCT to the north. Lt. Col. Abial G. Chamberlain of the Thirty-Seventh USCT warned the brigade commander that a force of 1,500–2,000 Confederates manned the works ahead. Although an exaggeration, this report caused Holman to prepare to meet an assault rather than deliver one.[35]

In fact, only about forty men from the Twenty-Fourth Virginia Cavalry of Gary's Brigade, along with two guns, were on the Nine Mile Road at that moment. "Our brigade having a long line of entrenchments to defend were run from right to left and back again as the threats were made," wrote Lieutenant Hinson of Gary's Seventh South Carolina Cavalry. These few troopers presented no offensive threat, and soon enough, Holman realized it. When the Rebel gunners directed a few shells toward his formation, the colonel decided to charge.[36]

Holman designated the First and Twenty-Second to make the attack. The First USCT deployed with its right flank on Nine Mile Road, and the Twenty-Second filed in left of the First, its left near the railroad. The Thirty-Seventh would remain in reserve. An open field stretched in front of the First USCT, but Kiddoo's regiment, which included a number of new, untrained soldiers, faced a patch of woods between them and the Rebel line. As the Black troops moved

The Sixth Petersburg Offensive, October 27–28

forward, reinforcements from the Hampton Legion Cavalry arrived to bolster the Virginians. "On nearing the road we could hear orders being given in the woods in front," wrote South Carolinian Stephen Welch. "Before leaving the timber, they raised a yell & started for the works, which we had not reached, we then ran & it was a foot race." The new recruits of the Twenty-Second USCT, betraying their lack of experience, "kept firing their muskets while advancing, and in the midst of the excitement broke and ran, causing the worst of confusion." Colonel Kiddoo fell wounded, and although Lt. Col. Ira Terry did his best to rally the disorganized regiment, it failed to reach the Confederate works.[37]

The First USCT had better luck. Persevering under "a severe fire of musketry, grape, and canister, [it] advanced gallantly across the open field and carried a part of the enemy's line, getting possession of the two guns (iron 12-pounders)." Although Colonel Holman was shot, the Federals at last achieved their goal of striking the Confederate left. But one lone regiment would not be enough to exploit the advantage. After ten or fifteen minutes, when no support appeared and "the 24th Va & 7th S.C. came tearing up, yelling like demons," the Federals spiked the two captured cannon and retreated. "They broke and fled as only affrighted cuffees can flee," snarled a South Carolinian. "We drove them like sheep," wrote Cpl. William H. Goodwin of the Twenty-Fourth Virginia Cavalry. "I never saw [our] men so egar to meet the enemy in my life." Capt. Henry Ward of the First USCT remained behind with a few of his men and attempted to bring off the Rebel guns, but he and his soldiers were captured before they could make their escape. "No quarters were given, at least this was the case with a majority of our boys," testified one Rebel trooper. "They were actually clubbed to death with the rifles."[38]

Colonel Chamberlain led the brigade off the field in a pouring rain, bivouacking about midnight. Holman suffered 176 casualties, including 124 in the First USCT. Confederate losses were minimal, although Col. William T. Robins, commanding the Twenty-Fourth Virginia Cavalry, was disabled with a wound to the foot. A few days after the battle, seven of Kiddoo's junior officers petitioned Butler's headquarters for a court of inquiry regarding their colonel's performance, the implication being that Kiddoo was drunk. Weitzel wrote Butler that he thought "all this [was] unwarranted and prompted by malice somewhere. I consider Colonel Kiddoo the finest gentleman and officer in my Third Division."[39]

Butler remained on the Tenth Corps front during the day and at 3:30 P.M. informed Grant that Hoke's Division had shifted to the north. "Shall I make a trial on this outstretched line?" he asked the general-in-chief. Forty minutes later, before Grant responded, Hawley's skirmishers, the Twenty-Ninth Connecticut, reported seeing the Confederates in their front "going from their right to their left at a double-quick." Terry authorized Hawley to "push in" if he thought the works in his front had been stripped.[40]

The Twenty-Ninth Connecticut, one of the best Black regiments in the army, probed ahead, shouting "Remember Fort Pillow" and drawing a sharp response, including from artillery that enfiladed their position. They halted and returned fire, some of the men expending as many as 200 rounds each by raiding the cartridge boxes of the slain. The rain poured down as the two sides exchanged volleys until darkness ended the contest. The Twenty-Ninth Connecticut remained on the field until 3:00 A.M., when the Seventh USCT relieved it.[41]

North of Darbytown Road, Ames advanced to test the Rebels in his front. "At 4 P.M. a bold push was made with the skirmish line to ascertain whether troops had been moved from our front to the enemy's left, to meet Weitzel," reported Colonel Plaisted. The 10th Connecticut, supplemented by portions of the 24th Massachusetts and 100th New York, advanced "with vigor," encountering an impenetrable line of abatis. "We hadn't more than get down when they opened on us from inside of their defenses . . . and the way the grapeshot and shell [came in] was not very comfortable," confessed Cpl. William H. Goff of the 24th Massachusetts. "Our skirmishers found themselves opposed to a full line of battle, posted in a strong earthworks with a firm abattis before it," wrote Chaplain Trumbull. "There they stood and fired at the enemy, hour after hour." The Unionists maintained their position until dusk, when exhausted ammunition supplies prompted their withdrawal. Abbott moved his brigade farther to the right, the 3rd New Hampshire advancing as skirmishers. These troops reached Charles City Road and halted, encountering less musketry than Plaisted but stymied by "heavy artillery fire from their redoubts."[42]

Foster experienced rougher treatment than either of Terry's other divisions. In conjunction with Ames, Terry ordered his Second Division "to make a strong demonstration on the enemy's works, to drive them from their rifle-pits, and if not developing too severe a fire to push forward and take the works, the object being to ascertain the strength of the enemy and his position." Foster selected Curtis's and Bell's brigades to make this probe. Curtis advanced south of Darbytown Road. "It was a terrible place to charge, through thick woods," wrote the 117th New York's Sgt. Hermon Clarke. As they pushed through the forest and into the open field beyond, the men discovered what one described as "the cussedest old time slashing I ever saw. Why they fairly roasted us a live for we could hardly have gotten through it if there wasn't a gun within a mile of us." A severe enfilading artillery fire added to the peril of the motionless Yankees. "Let me tell you [we] fed them but well on grape and canister," wrote Private Hampton of the 42nd North Carolina. "After remaining there for half an hour listening to the shrieking and howling of missiles overhead and losing about one tenth of our men, we retired by order without having had a glimpse of the enemy," explained Edward Wightman of the 3rd New York. This useless attack cost Colonel Curtis, who was struck four times by spent bullets, 204 casualties.[43]

On Curtis's left, Bell's brigade deployed its line of battle, preceded by skirmishers borrowed from Pennypacker's brigade. The 115th New York and 3rd Indiana formed Bell's front, followed by the 9th Maine, a regiment composed largely of new recruits. Bell's advance scattered the grayclad skirmishers from their "gopher holes" and then plunged into a belt of woods in front of the enemy's line, "where it was met by a fire from four pieces of artillery and a sharp musketry fire, which increased in severity as we approached the works," reported the colonel. "The situation we were in cannot be described," wrote Pvt. David S. Libbey of the 9th Maine. "Why they did not kill all of us is a mystery." Some of these rookies fired into the rear of the 115th New York, adding to the confusion and casualty count. When Bell received the order to withdraw, seventy-two of his soldiers had fallen.[44]

Pennypacker moved up to cover the withdrawal of Foster's other brigades. Although skirmishing continued during the remainder of that soggy day, Butler's attacks had ended. "Each division general along the line would have been delighted to have found a weak place on their front, and earned a star by a successful assault," observed a cynical member of the 100th New York. "But no, all that could be done would be to add to hospital numbers with hundreds of wounded." Butler's misadventures on October 27 most certainly provided patients for army hospitals. The Army of the James suffered 787 wounded that day, along with 118 killed and another 698 captured or missing. "We have not been able to turn the enemy's left," Butler admitted to Grant, "although Weitzel has demonstrated to the left of the Williamsburg Road. . . . Terry holds from Darbytown to our intrenched lines on the New Market road. Have you any orders?" Grant told him to avoid further assaults but prepare to repulse a Confederate attack. At that point the lieutenant general's primary concern was the fate of his larger offensive along Hatcher's Run and Boydton Plank Road.[45]

The Ninth Corps camps were astir as early as 2:00 A.M. on October 27. A light rain added to the predawn gloom as the men hastily prepared a cold breakfast (officers prohibited the kindling of fires) and prepared to move out well before sunrise. Willcox's First Division was on the move between 3:00 and 3:30 A.M. His troops passed through the Union lines at Fort Cummings, now the southwestern anchor of the Federal fortifications, heading west on the country road that led toward the Smith, Hawks, and Watkins farms before merging with Duncan Road. Byron Cutcheon's brigade led the march, followed by John Hartranft's and Napoleon McLaughlen's brigades. For some reason—perhaps the misty darkness or maybe uncertainty regarding their orders—the column halted once it reached the Union picket line, resuming the advance at daylight. At least one participant considered this halt problematic. Cpl. George Allen of the Fourth Rhode Island recalled that as soon as it became light, the blueclad soldiers were "in plain view of the rebel lines [and] they crowded on top of their works and watched where we were going."[46]

Allen's recollection may be faulty, for once the advance resumed, a premature shot rather than visible evidence alerted the small Rebel vedette post at Fort MacRae to the approaching Federals. The Fifty-Seventh Massachusetts managed to kill one of the Confederates, but the rest made their escape, doing more to warn their comrades than whatever any other Rebels might have seen. Cutcheon and Hartranft pushed ahead, past the Smith and Hawks houses and into the fields of the Watkins farm. Encountering a larger body of Confederate skirmishers—probably some of Hampton's dismounted cavalry—Willcox deployed Hartranft on his left and Cutcheon on his right and advanced, the Confederates quickly melting westward into a strip of woods. The bluecoats followed, crossing Duncan Road and reaching the clearing surrounding the modest Clements house about 9:00 A.M. In their front lay a tangle of abatis and beyond that, the fresh earth of the main Confederate line. Willcox's advance, which had progressed at a snail's pace, now halted completely.[47]

Warren issued orders to the Fifth Corps to begin its march at 5:30 A.M., but Meade wished him to advance in concert with Parke, telling his querulous subordinate to start at 4:00 A.M. instead. The troops were awake by 3:00 A.M., prepared their breakfasts, and made ready to march, not knowing, wrote Pvt. Henry D. Didcock of the 187th New York, "wether we had to travel 4 miles or 40." Warren dutifully complied with his commander's instructions, maintaining the order of march he originally decreed. Charles Griffin's First Division led. Some 4,707 strong, this command contained 2,803 new recruits who had never fired a rifle, of whom almost half "were ignorant of the manual." Romeyn Ayres followed with his 4,704 men, 812 of whom were similarly ill trained. Samuel Crawford's division brought up the rear with two brigades; his third, Henry Baxter's, was left behind to defend the corps entrenchments. Very few of Crawford's troops suffered from the inexperience that characterized the other divisions, making it curious that Warren selected his least-seasoned division to take the lead.[48]

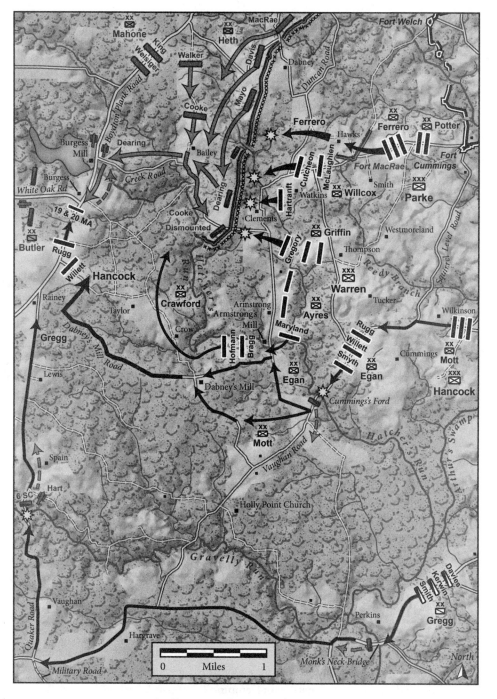

Sixth Offensive, October 27, 1864: Union Advance

The Fifth Corps made a poor start, a predictable consequence in the stygian environment, as Warren churlishly mentioned in his report. While Grant and Meade sat in silent observation, the corps passed through Fort Cummings once Parke's men had cleared the area. When it became light, around 5:30 A.M., Warren untangled his formations and disappeared into the trees, following a narrow forest road that the Confederates had obstructed with various makeshift barricades. "It was a real Virginia forrest of the densest description of small pines and a tangled mass of undergrowth, briars, & weeds," wrote Lt. Henry Matrau of the 6th Wisconsin. Griffin eventually reached the clearing surrounding the Thompson farm, about a mile and a half from Fort Cummings. Warren feared that continuing his current trajectory would take him too far south, so he ordered a crude road cleared westward, which in half a mile reached Duncan Road. An existing woods path led west from there. Griffin advanced and in short order encountered Rebel skirmishers. He ordered Edgar Gregory's brigade to form two lines of battle and press ahead, pushing back the Confederates, then halting under fire when they arrived at the abatis fronting the main enemy fortifications. "We advanced our line to within 50 yards of the Rebel breastworks, driving their skirmishers into them," wrote Capt. George McClelland of the 155th Pennsylvania. "Their sharpshooters then got to work . . . and killed and wounded quite a number of our regiment." Like Parke's men 800 yards to their right, the Fifth Corps halted and began entrenching.[49]

Henry Heth commanded the Confederates opposing Parke and Warren. A thirty-eight-year-old Virginian, Heth graduated dead last in the West Point class of 1847 but remained in the U.S. Army until the outbreak of the war. One observer described him as "a small man, wears only a mustache, dresses plainly, has dark hair and quite a brilliant eye, when excited . . . seems to be quite social & humorous." This fellow, a man of the cloth, feared that the general was "too fond of ardent spirits," although he confessed, "I do not know any thing about his habits." Heth spent the first part of the war in western Virginia, but his friendship with Lee—he was allegedly the only man the army commander addressed by his given name—earned him brigade command in the Army of Northern Virginia. Considered a competent if unspectacular leader, Heth was thought by one critic to betray "a persistent tendency to act on impulse before evaluating his own and the enemy's capabilities." On October 27 the major general commanded not only the five brigades of his own division but also Lane's and McGowan's Brigades of Wilcox's Division, Dearing's Brigade of cavalry, and 700 dismounted troopers from Hampton's command. Between 15,000 and 18,000 soldiers reported to Heth on October 27.[50]

At dawn only the horseless cavalry occupied the right end of the Confederate line down to Hatcher's Run. But once Heth learned of Warren's and Parke's approach, he ordered Joe Davis's Brigade, followed by John Cooke's North Carolinians, to reinforce the outgunned troopers. They arrived, in Heth's words, "in opportune time, checking the enemy's advance." Heth then shifted Archer's Brigade, under Col. Robert Mayo, and Henry H. Walker's Virginians to close on Cooke, and finally ordered MacRae's Brigade to move next to Mayo. "Lane and McGowan were directed to fill up any interval on the left which might be created by the movement" of Heth's Division.[51]

Parke probed ahead, hoping to exploit a weakness in Heth's defenses. Willcox reported that the works in his front were "protected by abatis of rails and slashed timber" that made them unassailable. Parke then ordered Edward Ferrero's USCT division to move up on Willcox's right "and push forward and see what was in their front." Ferrero's First Brigade, under Col. Delevan Bates, led the Third Division through a forest so thick that the brigade frequently halted to realign. Bates emerged into the Clements house clearing on Willcox's right, where they endured deadly volleys from the Confederates barely 100 yards in their front. The African Americans shed casualties before they joined the rest of the Federals in digging their own protective works. Ferrero's Second Brigade made a connection with Potter's division, refusing the right of the stymied Ninth Corps.[52]

Thus, by 9:00 A.M., both the Ninth and Fifth Corps had stalled, Grant's hope to turn the Confederate right a bust. Warren dug in as far south as Hatcher's Run, while Parke's works stretched back to the Hawks farm, a combined line nearly two miles in length. The Ninth Corps would accomplish no more than to occupy the Rebels in their front. Warren, however, prepared to execute his contingent assignment to move north up the right bank of Hatcher's Run, recross the stream, then turn east to slice behind the Confederate right. Shortly after 9:00 A.M. General Humphreys met with Warren and told him to cross Hatcher's Run at Armstrong's Mill with a portion of his corps, then move up Dabney's Mill Road to execute his mission, while simultaneously guarding Hancock's right. Within an hour, Grant and Meade arrived, confirming Humphreys's instructions. Crawford's two brigades—Edward Bragg's and William Hofmann's—reinforced by the Maryland Brigade of Ayres's division, would make the march. Warren was told to anchor Crawford's right on Hatcher's Run and, upon arriving opposite the right of the enemy's intrenchments, cross the stream, attack the Rebels' flank, and drive the enemy from the line, opening the way for the rest of his corps and Parke's to resume their advance. These instructions modified Warren's original orders. Rather than moving sufficiently upstream to get completely around the Confederate works, he would instead assault the enemy flank wherever he found it. After sending Maj. Washington Roebling to reconnoiter the route, Warren ordered Crawford forward. His three brigades began crossing Hatcher's Run at Armstrong's Mill at 11:45 A.M., nearly three hours after the corps had reached the Confederate line.[53]

By this time, the Second Corps and General Gregg's cavalry division had executed their portion of the offensive as planned, reaching Boydton Plank Road. Nelson Miles's First Division remained behind at Petersburg to man the corps entrenchments, so Hancock advanced early that morning with only Brig. Gen. Thomas W. Egan's Second Division and Gershom Mott's Third Division. Hancock ordered the troops to move out at 2:00 A.M., later modified to 3:30 A.M., with Egan in the lead. The column marched south on Halifax Road, then west on Lower Church (or Wyatt) Road, and south again on Vaughan Road to its crossing of Hatcher's Run at Cumming's Ford. From there, the soldiers used Dabney's Mill Road to reach Boydton Plank Road. If all went according to plan, the Federals would then follow White Oak Road westward, turn north on Claiborne Road, recross Hatcher's Run, and reach the South Side Railroad. From the intersection of Dabney's Mill and Boydton Plank Roads, the distance to the railroad measured more than five miles.[54]

Hancock started right on time, Thomas Smyth's Third Brigade at the head of Egan's column, followed by Col. James M. Willett's Second Brigade, with Lt. Col. Horace P. Rugg, in temporary command of Egan's own First Brigade, bringing up the rear. Mott's division followed. A squadron of the Sixth Ohio Cavalry preceded the infantry. Major Michler assigned his aide-de-camp, Capt. William H. Paine, to guide the column as it plunged deep into the back roads of Dinwiddie County. The Federals encountered their first opposition about daylight just after turning onto Vaughan Road, where a few Confederate vedettes fired on Smyth. Egan ordered the Fourth Ohio Battalion and the Seventh West Virginia, all under Lt. Col. Frank J. Spalter, to advance as skirmishers and disperse this minor resistance. Spalter did his job well, driving the Rebels back to their fortified position on the far side of Hatcher's Run at Cumming's Ford. Here, cavalrymen of the Jeff Davis Legion of Young's Brigade had obstructed the ford and deployed behind barricades on the right bank. "Spalter dashed at the enemy, but was killed at the first onset." With the skirmishers stymied, Egan ordered Smyth to form across the road, with Willett and Rugg in support. Smyth promptly obeyed, and led by the Twelfth New Jersey, the Federals waded the waist-deep stream and overwhelmed the grayclad troopers, capturing a few of them and sending the rest galloping off to the west.[55]

It was now 7:30 A.M. Hancock informed Meade that he had forced the crossing "after a little brisk firing" and heard sounds of combat "in the direction of Gregg." The Union cavalry had departed along with Parke and Hancock at 3:30 A.M., riding south with Charles Smith's brigade in the lead, followed by brigades under Michael Kerwin and Henry Davies. Portions of the Sixth Ohio Cavalry and First Maine Cavalry scattered a few Confederate pickets about a mile northeast of Monk's Neck Bridge over Rowanty Creek, pursuing them to Vaughan Road, then north on Quaker Road to its crossing of Gravelly Run. Here, Gregg ran into trouble.[56]

Hampton had dispersed his cavalry divisions under Rooney Lee and M. C. Butler on a wide front, from Burgess Mill on Boydton Plank Road to Malone's Crossing on the Weldon Railroad, two miles below Reams' Station. Small bodies guarded the various stream crossings beyond the Confederate right, such as the troopers who opposed Hancock at Cumming's Ford and those Gregg now confronted along Gravelly Run. The bulk of Butler's Division camped near Quaker Road, while Lee's brigades bivouacked well to the south. The dawn advances of Hancock and Gregg stirred the Rebel cavalry into action.[57]

Hampton sought to trap Gregg's troopers between his two divisions. He told Lee to move to the intersection of Vaughan and Quaker Roads to strike the enemy's rear. In the meantime, a section of Hart's Battery of horse artillery rushed down Quaker Road and unlimbered north of Gravelly Run to block the Federals' progress, in what Gregg characterized as a position "of great natural strength upon a commanding eminence." Supported by a few dismounted cavalry and a company of the Sixth South Carolina Cavalry, Hart's guns barked out, freezing the Federal advance. Colonel Smith rode forward to assess the situation.[58]

A single bridge, fifty yards long, spanned the stream and its boggy margins. The terrain was too marshy for horsemen to navigate easily except at the bridge. Consequently, Smith dismounted the Sixth Ohio Cavalry and First Maine Cavalry with orders to charge, the Twenty-First Pennsylvania Cavalry remaining mounted and ready to follow across the span. The troopers rushed through the mire under spirited canister and carbine fire, slogging through to the opposite shore, as the Pennsylvanians trotted across the bridge, half of the regiment then deploying on each flank of their horseless comrades. Hampton issued urgent orders to the artillery to "hold the bridge at all hazards until I can support you," and soon Young's Brigade arrived in rear of the guns. The cannoneers were now taking casualties, including Captain Hart, whose leg wound would require amputation. The issue remained in doubt when word arrived that Federal infantry had reached Boydton Plank Road heading for White Oak Road in the Confederates' rear. Hampton had little choice but to order the defenders along Quaker Road to withdraw and try to arrest the Yankees' dash toward the South Side Railroad. Rooney Lee's troopers, who had exchanged fire with the rear of Gregg's column and stood ready to make their attack, received similar instructions to disengage. The scene of action now changed to Boydton Plank Road near Burgess Mill.[59]

Egan's division, after brushing aside the roadblock at Cumming's Ford, turned north on Duncan Road and reached Armstrong's Mill on Hatcher's Run at 8:30 A.M., shortly thereafter making connection with the Fifth Corps. Egan then turned west on the country lane leading toward Dabney's portable sawmill. Mott cut across country and joined Egan near the mill—its location was marked by a huge pile of sawdust—having skirmished with Rebel horsemen most of the way. Egan then resumed the march to Boydton Plank Road, emerging less than a mile southwest of where the highway crossed Hatcher's Run at Burgess Mill. Hampton wanted Dearing's Brigade to block Hancock's approach, sending staff officer Andrew Venable to convey the order. But Heth countermanded these instructions, deeming it vital that Dearing remain in the Confederate works on the northeast side of Hatcher's Run. Heth sent Venable back to inform the cavalry chief of his decision. But the Federals seized Venable near Dabney's Mill before he could deliver his message. Thus, Hampton, thinking that Dearing would obstruct the Federals in their march northward, was surprised when scouts reported Hancock's presence in his rear. Now it would be up to the South Carolinian to cobble together enough resistance to stall the Union advance until infantry reserves could arrive.[60]

Those reserves belonged to William Mahone. The thirty-seven-year-old Mahone had risen from colonel of the Sixth Virginia to major general and command of the finest infantry division in Lee's army. Small in stature and weighing around 100 pounds, he spoke with a high, squeaking voice and earned a reputation as an eccentric. "Mahone is a small man talks very fine and is ugly enough to scare any set of men that did not know him," thought a Georgia artillerist. But, the cannoneer admitted, "he is very sociable and will talk with a private as quick as he would with a lt. General. He is much liked by his men." Throughout the Petersburg Campaign, whenever Lee needed to throw a strong punch, most often he called on Mahone.[61]

Such was the present occasion. When word of the Union offensive arrived at Mahone's headquarters in the Petersburg works, he designated three of his five brigades to make the trek westward. His old Virginia brigade, still led by David Weisiger, and the Alabama brigade, under Col. Horace King, left immediately, with Mahone personally leading the march. Nathaniel Harris's Mississippi brigade followed around noon, leaving the trenches in small groups to prevent the

Federals, who were close by, from noticing their departure. Bushrod Johnson's Division then fanned out and, with the help of Mahone's other two brigades, covered the vacated works.[62]

Mahone's orders were to proceed to Battery 45 on Boydton Plank Road, where the Dimmock Line turned north to anchor on the Appomattox River upstream from Petersburg. When he arrived there, Capt. John "Ham" Chamberlayne, an artillery officer, informed him that affairs on Heth's front had grown relatively stable, but the Yankees had appeared near Burgess Mill. Mahone immediately rode southwest and soon encountered Heth, who apprised him of the crisis a few miles ahead.[63]

Egan's division, with Rugg's brigade now in the van, posed the immediate problem. These Federals deployed about one-half mile south of the Burgess farm and the plank road's critical intersection with White Oak Road. At 10:30 A.M. a message from Meade reached Hancock informing him that Parke was stymied, but Warren was "working his way to cross Hatcher's Run on Parke's left," although the Fifth Corps found the going slow. "It would be well for you to keep up a communication with Warren to ascertain his progress," Meade advised. Rugg advanced a swarm of skirmishers from two Massachusetts regiments, the Nineteenth and Twentieth, toward the Burgess farm. Dearing's Brigade, which Heth had now released, was there to meet them, supported by several batteries. The grayclad troopers dashed up from their positions guarding the trenches downstream along Hatcher's Run, deployed around the Burgess farm buildings, and forced the Federal skirmishers to ground. Egan responded by ordering forward the rest of his division, while a Federal battery managed to force the annoying Rebel guns to change positions. Gregg's division, now unimpeded, trotted up Quaker Road and joined the infantry in Hancock's rear on Boydton Plank Road.[64]

Dearing bought time for the rest of the Confederate cavalry to arrive at the scene of danger. Hampton deployed Butler's Division across White Oak Road, its left on the Burgess millpond, which extended upstream from the plank road, and its right stretching off to the south. Hart's Battery made its way from its fight above Gravelly Run to bolster Butler's troopers, who built hasty works to strengthen their defense. At the same time, Lee's Division appeared on the plank road south of Dabney's Mill Road. His two brigades took position across the highway behind Gregg, supported by more of Preston Chew's horse artillery.[65]

Egan determined to dispense with the opposition that had thwarted Rugg's skirmishers. He ordered Willett's brigade to attack, while the skirmishers, led by Capt. A. Henry Embler, made a second attempt to dislodge Dearing. "Our line of battle was formed athwart the Boydton Road," explained Cpl. Nelson

Armstrong of Willett's Eighth New York Heavy Artillery, serving as infantry. "This road was a public highway in time of peace and was protected on each side by an old-fashioned rail fence. . . . We formed in line at the right of the road . . . and about one-quarter mile from the bridge where the Boydton Road crosses the run." Willett and Embler charged, "driving the enemy before us toward and across Hatcher's Creek," reported Willett, "after which I halted the brigade and formed line of battle on the high ground." Dearing's men had erected a barricade where a toll gate once stood, Egan quipping that in passing it "the Virginia highway regulations were not observed." The Confederates, displaced but not beaten, rallied south of Hatcher's Run in some shallow works near the base of the hill.[66]

In the meantime, Mott's division began to emerge from the wooded depths of Dabney's Mill Road between noon and 12:30 P.M. "The farther we advanced [on Dabney's Mill Road] the sharper grew the skirmish firing along Eagan's front, and every few moments a wounded man would be carried past toward the rear," wrote a soldier in the 124th New York. "Some of these wounded men looked very pale and others presented blood-stained faces or garments, suggesting unpleasant thoughts to those who were pressing forward." Regis de Trobriand's brigade arrived first and, crossing the plank road, deployed facing southwest. Byron Pierce's brigade next appeared, moving north on the plank road and halting in a large field surrounded by dense woods, where his soldiers formed a line of battle facing northeast, then stacked arms and rested. Robert McAllister's brigade brought up the rear, following closely on Pierce's heels. His brigade swung onto the plank road and massed east of the highway.[67]

Although Parke and Warren had failed to penetrate the Confederate defenses north of Hatcher's Run, Hancock and Gregg had achieved their initial objective. "I am at the Burgess house, on Boydton Plank," Hancock informed Meade at 12:30 P.M. "Part of the enemy's cavalry retired by Burgess' across Hatcher's Run. . . . I am about moving out on White Oak road." Hancock started Mott's division toward that rude country byway and the railroad beyond, while Egan remained along the plank road facing northeast toward Dearing and the stubborn artillery fire that resumed from north of Hatcher's Run. Hancock called up a brigade of cavalry "to relieve Egan, in order that he might follow Mott." With only Butler's Division of dismounted troopers blocking his path—no match for two divisions of infantry—it appeared that Hancock was poised to complete the last leg of his march to the South Side Railroad. Then word arrived from Meade to halt.[68]

A turning point in the Federal offensive had been reached. Apart from Hancock and Gregg's portions, Meade's battle plan had fizzled. The Union high command now abandoned its original mission of severing the South Side Railroad

The Sixth Petersburg Offensive, October 27–28

and focused instead on the more limited goal of dislodging the Confederates from their positions along the left bank of Hatcher's Run. In order to do this, in Grant's judgment, Hancock should wait for Crawford's brigades to arrive on his right. He believed their combined pressure against Heth's right and rear, with Griffin, Ayers, and Parke still threatening the Rebel front, would compel the graycoats to abandon their entrenched positions and fall back closer to Petersburg. If all went well, the Federals would retain control of Boydton Plank Road, shutting down that avenue of Lee's communications. This accomplished, Union forces would still be in position to make another run, eventually, toward the South Side Railroad. Moreover, the intense artillery fire that continued to rain down on Egan's men from Graham's Battery north of Hatcher's Run and Hart's guns along White Oak Road had to be suppressed. No Union commander was then aware of Mahone's approach—a much greater threat to the Federals on Boydton Plank Road than the pesky artillery.[69]

Hancock obediently suspended Mott's advance to White Oak Road and dispatched Maj. Henry H. Bingham, the corps judge advocate, to locate Crawford. "I found General Crawford without difficulty at a point about one mile from Major-General Hancock's headquarters and . . . a short three-quarters of a mile from the right of the Second Corps line," reported Bingham. He apprised Crawford of the situation on Hancock's front, then returned to inform his commander that Crawford "intended throwing around his left and connecting with the right of the Second Corps."[70]

By then, Meade and Grant, "with a long mounted tail" of staff officers and orderlies, had appeared on the plank road and were in discussion with Hancock under the limbs of a giant oak tree. "They are having gay times, and talk and laugh as though nothing was going to happen; but then their fun comes to a sudden stop," wrote one of the many soldiers who witnessed the gathering. As a steady rain began to fall, so did a storm of Rebel projectiles, fired from the distant artillery. Staff officer Thomas Livermore thought the incoming fire "made it quite hot. I well remember one shot which almost took off several heads, including that of General Rawlins and myself." Meade reported, "Hancock was accordingly authorized to make the attempt to carry the bridge" and in so doing silence the Rebel ordnance on the far side of Hatcher's Run. In this case, the general's use of passive voice was more than mere convention. As he explained to his wife, "General Grant has been on the field all day, sanctioning everything that was done." The lieutenant general usually delegated operational conduct to his army commanders, so his hands-on approach with this offensive indicated its importance to him, despite how he would characterize it postfacto.[71]

Egan deployed all three of his brigades spanning Boydton Plank Road at the Burgess farm, Rugg on the left, Willett in the center, and Smyth on the right, east of the highway. A section of Napoleons from Lt. Butler Beck's Batteries C and I, Fifth U.S. Artillery banged away at the guns north of the mill. Dearing's troopers, thinking they saw an opportunity to capture Beck's pieces, made a bold dash back up the hill from Hatcher's Run. Beck's cannoneers unleashed canister rounds as Egan's men fired volleys, all of which staggered the dismounted cavalry. Col. Valentine H. Taliaferro, commander of Dearing's Seventh Confederate Cavalry, fell wounded. Dearing, who went into the attack mounted, had his horse shot from under him, and a number of his men were killed or wounded. "I lost some twelve or fifteen officers," he told his wife, and his brigade suffered eighty-eight total casualties in this bold but foolish assault. The Confederates retreated as fast as they had attacked, pursued by a portion of Smyth's brigade, some of whom crossed the creek before returning to their lines. Egan was now the undisputed master of the Burgess farm and the intersection of White Oak Road with the plank road.[72]

The Confederate guns, however, continued to pour shells into the gaggle of officers back at the big oak tree, unsettling some of the noncombatants who had ventured forth with Meade and Grant. "There was a civilian friend of Grant's and an aide-de-camp of Gen. Barnard … and sundry other personages all trying to giggle and all wishing themselves at City Point," noted Lyman, who dared not duck or dodge, while Meade sat calmly, showing no fear. Eventually the army commander commented, "This is pretty hot, it will kill some of our horses." "Oh yes, thought I, horses!" wrote a relieved Lyman.[73]

Grant was equally unfazed by the bombardment but grew unsettled by the conflicting reports that reached his informal command post. Summoning his trusted aide, Lt. Col. Orville Babcock, the general rode through Egan's deployment, almost as far as the bridge spanning Hatcher's Run, to ascertain for himself the tactical situation. They were under fire the entire time, a reckless and unnecessary risk by the country's highest-ranking soldier. To make matters worse, the general's horse became tangled in some downed telegraph line; while Grant sat serenely on his immobile mount, Babcock carefully uncoiled the wire, Grant cautioning him not to injure the animal. Having seen the strength of the Rebel position on the high ground north of Hatcher's Run, Grant returned to the oak tree and, red faced, told Hancock that "some damned fool had thrown telegraph wire in the road." Hancock replied, "Yes, yes, great many damned fools in this army," perhaps implicitly including, at least at that moment, the man to whom he spoke.[74]

Grant now not only abandoned the effort to reach the South Side Railroad but also gave up hope of turning the Confederates out of their fortifications by advancing up Boydton Plank Road. He told Hancock merely to remain astride the highway until the following morning, then withdraw by the same route he had used to reach his current position. What prompted Grant's decision? The Confederates along Duncan Road were more firmly entrenched than had been assumed, and it seemed clear that Warren and Parke were neutralized. Dislodging the Rebels from the high ground north of Burgess Mill would be a time-consuming and costly endeavor, and Hancock could not move west on White Oak Road with such a force in his rear, not to mention the need to disperse the cavalry blocking that road. The rain continued to fall, complicating any maneuvers, and on top of these factors, Crawford had not yet arrived to reinforce the Second Corps. In light of all this, Grant's decision to retain Hancock on Boydton Plank Road until the next day is curious. In any case, he and Meade turned their horses south about 3:30 P.M. and, overcoming trouble from the confusing and tangled terrain, picked their way back along the path they had come. Meade halted at the Armstrong house, while Grant continued to City Point, leaving the army commander to tend to the residue of the forsaken offensive.[75]

Crawford's failure to appear in a timely fashion played a significant role in Grant's decision. The thirty-four-year-old physician from Pennsylvania had been tasked with two distinct but concurrent missions. His three brigades were to support Hancock's right while the Second Corps headed for the railroad and at the same time cross Hatcher's Run and dislodge Heth by threatening his rear. Now both offensive endeavors were moot, and the most Crawford could accomplish would be to buttress the stationary Second Corps until Hancock's withdrawal the next morning.[76]

Crawford began his march expeditiously enough. Bragg's Iron Brigade led the column, fronted by a double line of skirmishers from the 7th Wisconsin. Hofmann's brigade followed, the 147th New York guarding the division's left. The Maryland Brigade brought up the rear. Soon, however, the column entered the Virginia version of a trackless jungle. Colonel Hofmann clinically reported that their route "was through a very dense wood. It was with great difficulty that even an approximation to an alignment could be preserved." Musician Henry M. Kieffer provided a more colorful description of that march:

> Away into the woods we plunge, in line of battle, through briers and
> tangled undergrowth, beneath the great trees dripping with rain.
> We lose points of the compass, and halt every now and then to close
> up a gap in the line to the right or left. Then forward we go through

the brush again . . . until I feel certain that officers as well as men are getting pretty well 'into the woods' as to the direction of our advance. It is raining and we have no sun to guide us, and the moss is growing on the wrong side of the trees. I see one of our generals, sitting on his horse, with his pocket compass on the pommel of his saddle, peering around into the interminable tangle . . . with an expression of no little perplexity.

Lieutenant Matrau confessed to his parents, "We got completely lost & bewildered in this jungle."[77]

Bragg's brigade followed a small tributary of Hatcher's Run, mistaking it for the main creek, and lost contact with Hofmann. A forty-year-old Philadelphia hosiery merchant, Hofmann had recently earned a brevet promotion to brigadier general. Finding himself now in the division lead, he dispersed a few stray Rebels and sent a regiment across Hatcher's Run to, in Crawford's words, "feel the enemy's works." At last, Crawford was executing one of his two ordered objectives, albeit quite tentatively and without the knowledge that it was no longer relevant. The incursion behind Heth's line, minimal as it was, elicited a strong response from the Confederates. Davis's Brigade, which upon Dearing's departure guarded the return on Heth's far right, rushed to meet this threat to their flank and rear. According to Adj. Charles M. Cooke of the Fifty-Fifth North Carolina, three of Davis's regiments executed a charge "with great desperation and the enemy were driven in great disorder and confusion across the run, and our lines . . . were reestablished."[78]

General Warren nixed any notion Crawford might have had to renew his attacks. The corps commander located Crawford around 4:00 P.M. and, after evaluating the situation, told his subordinate that he was in just the right position and not to advance or venture another crossing of Hatcher's Run. It is hard to square Warren's pronouncement with Crawford's objectives. He was certainly not in the right location to aid Hancock, who had no idea what had happened to his promised support, nor had he been able to open a path for Griffin and Ayres to penetrate the Confederate defenses on the northeast side of the stream. Warren even wrote later that Crawford's march "had now led him to quite a different position from what had been expected." But the corps commander rightly noted that Crawford's troops were in "a dense forest of great extent" and his men "were getting lost in great numbers, in fact, whole regiments losing all idea of where to find the rest of the division." Sometime later, Major Roebling met with Warren near Dabney's Mill and persuaded him to order Crawford to recross Hatcher's Run and take possession of the Confederate works, which

The Sixth Petersburg Offensive, October 27–28

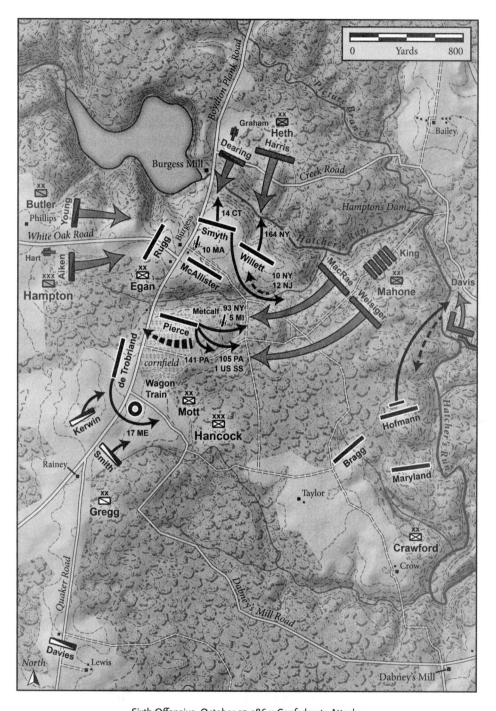

Sixth Offensive, October 27, 1864: Confederate Attacks

the major believed were vulnerable. Roebling returned to Crawford to convey Warren's wishes, when he was "astonished to see rebel stragglers coming in on our left and rear." Those Confederates belonged to Mahone's Division.[79]

Mahone, Heth, and Dearing met around 3:00 P.M. along the plank road some distance northeast of Burgess Mill. The course of their conversation, if not the outcome, is in some doubt. Mahone, who was prone to exaggerate his role in planning operations, asserted that he learned from Dearing and Heth of a hidden road that crossed Hatcher's Run on one of Hampton's dams and led to Hancock's right and rear. "I then said, 'General Dearing, we will cross on General Hampton's dam and get shortly behind whatever force there is in your front, and as soon as you hear our guns, press the enemy in your front and force a crossing.'" Heth, whose account is more contemporary to the event, claimed authorship of the attack plan. "I directed Major-General Mahone . . . to attack the enemy, approaching him by the blind path." He continued, "I piloted General Mahone for some distance on this path." Heth arranged not only for Dearing to charge across the creek at Burgess Mill in concert with Mahone but also for Hampton, with Butler and Lee, to do so from the west and south respectively.[80]

Mahone would employ Weisiger's and King's brigades along with MacRae's North Carolinians borrowed from Heth's Division. Harris was still en route, as was Scales's Brigade from Wilcox's command. Heth hoped these two units would assist Dearing in executing his part of the combined attack. Whichever officer was its architect, the Confederate plan was a bold one. Mahone held the key, as he had during previous counteroffensives. His makeshift division would penetrate the void on Hancock's right created by Crawford's failure to connect with the Second Corps, turning that flank and threatening the Union rear. Dearing, with whatever infantry support would be available from Harris and Scales, would charge across the Burgess Mill bridge in Hancock's front, while Butler assailed the Union left, and Rooney Lee pounded in from the Federal rear. This was exactly the kind of tactical opportunity the outnumbered Confederates always coveted: to strike an isolated Union force outside of its works. Of course, Grant ran this sort of risk in each of his flanking maneuvers. But by this time in this case, Grant had decided the reward was not worth the risk. He erred, however, in leaving Hancock dangling with exposed flanks once he canceled the offensive. Based on experience, he might have expected the Confederates to reprise their preferred mode of counteroffensive: to slice between his flanking force and his established line—here, between Hancock and Crawford.[81]

In fairness to Grant, none of his subordinate commanders harbored suspicions of the impending four-pronged attack. Gregg's horsemen relaxed around the intersection of Boydton Plank and Quaker Roads. Egan remained astride the plank road, Rugg now on his left across the mouth of White Oak Road, Smyth in the center, and Willett east of the highway. Mott positioned McAllister's brigade behind Smyth and Willett, while the rest of his division, Pierce and de Trobriand, lounged along the plank road to the south. Beck's guns required more ammunition, so the Tenth Massachusetts Battery moved up to replace them while Beck replenished his limber chests. The Federals did not fortify, an oversight explained both by Hancock's complacency and his intention to depart the following morning.[82]

Hancock did recognize that until Crawford appeared on his right, it would be prudent to strengthen that flank. He called on Mott, who dispatched the 5th Michigan and 93rd New York of Pierce's command, to support a section of Beck's artillery under Lt. Richard Metcalf, posted in the field east of the plank road, followed shortly thereafter by the balance of Pierce's brigade. The Confederate artillery north of Burgess Mill continued to harass Egan's troops, so Hancock "determined to assault the bridge and gain possession of the high ground beyond" in order to silence those annoying guns. As the 164th New York of Willett's brigade and Smyth's 14th Connecticut led the foray across Hatcher's Run, the corps commander ordered Egan to make a connection with the elusive Crawford. Egan, in turn, told Smyth to execute this move, and the colonel sent the 10th New York and 12th New Jersey into the woods beyond Pierce and Metcalf. "Just at this time," wrote Hancock, "about 4 p.m., a volley of musketry immediately on my right, which was followed by a continuous fire, left no doubt that the enemy were advancing." Mahone's attack was underway.[83]

Accompanied by Heth, who knew the location of the road and dam spanning Hatcher's Run, the diminutive Mahone led his three brigades over Hampton's narrow structure, the men crossing two abreast. Heth then received a note from Dearing "stating that the enemy had driven him from the bridge at Burgess' Mill, that he had fallen back, and that all the roads leading to the rear of my lines were open to his advance." Leaving Mahone in sole command of the flanking force, Heth hastened back across the stream and to the plank road, discovering to his relief that Dearing's warning had been a false alarm. Meanwhile, Mahone shook out a skirmish line in the thick woods and pushed ahead on what one Tar Heel considered "a tortuous and circuitous route" toward what he expected to be Hancock's right flank and rear.[84]

Mahone told his skirmishers, including MacRae's sharpshooter battalion under Capt. Samuel S. Lilly, under no circumstances to fire a gun "but upon coming upon the enemy to engage him in conversation," giving an agreed-upon signal to start the attack. A squad from the Tenth New York, prowling through the forest searching for Crawford, instead spotted "a strong column of the enemy marching quickly along a wood road directly toward the rear of Gen. Egan's position." One of the New Yorkers rushed back to inform Egan and Smyth of the impending danger, but the warning came too late. The Rebel skirmishers gave the signal that they had reached the Union line. Mahone placed MacRae's Brigade on his right, Weisiger's on his left, and the Alabamans in column of regiments behind his center, establishing a skirmish line to cover his left flank. He had everyone fix bayonets and dress on their colors, a force about 3,400 strong. Mahone then passed up and down his line, "giving words of cheer ... and urging that they reserve their fire and rely on the bayonet. I then gave the command to forward, and off the line moved, going forward with an impetuous step." Progress proved difficult through what Lt. James Eldred Phillips of the Twelfth Virginia described as "a thick swampy piece of ground."[85]

The first resistance came from the skirmishers of the 5th Michigan and 93rd New York. These men had penetrated deep into the forest and were quickly overwhelmed. Pierce advanced the 105th Pennsylvania and the 1st U.S. Sharpshooters, who, along with the balance of the Michiganders and New Yorkers, managed to hold the Rebels back for a few moments before Mahone's much longer line wrapped around their flanks. Pierce rushed the 141st Pennsylvania into the fight but to no avail. The Confederates captured both of Metcalf's guns, wounding the lieutenant and taking him prisoner. Pierce's survivors fled through the Burgess cornfield back to and beyond Boydton Plank Road. "There was a scene of confusion and excitement, rarely witnessed upon a battlefield," wrote one Federal. The victorious Confederates pushed all the way to the plank road, reaching the highway south of its intersection with White Oak Road and in the rear of Egan's division. Lt. Lemuel Hoyle of MacRae's 11th North Carolina gleefully described the action for his mother: "Our brigade, notwithstanding there was a line of the enemy on our right flank, charged the enemy in their front in the most gallant style driving them in confusion, capturing several pieces of artillery, and a large number of prisoners and breaking through the Yankee lines."[86]

Mahone had achieved another one of his spectacular breakthroughs. With no artillery support and only a fraction of his enemy's manpower, he had penetrated the heart of the Second Corps, routing one brigade and in essence dividing Hancock's forces in two. Not far to the south lay the Federal supply wagons, carrying the spare ammunition Hancock would need to sustain a fight. With Dearing and now Harris to the north, Hampton with Butler to the west, and Rooney Lee to the south, it is little wonder that some of the Federals referred to the battle as "the Bull Pen, (we playing Taurus)." Yet there was another way of assessing the tactical situation. Mahone's relatively small force was now wedged between four Union brigades to his north and west and a brigade of infantry and Gregg's cavalry to his south. His initial success would become a trap if the other elements of the Confederate counteroffensive failed to achieve similar success.[87]

Harris's Mississippians arrived north of Burgess Mill around 3:00 P.M. When Heth returned from guiding Mahone across Hatcher's Run, he told Harris and Dearing "to advance with all possible speed and prevent the enemy from crossing Hatcher's Run, and hold the bridge at all hazards, also to attack vigorously by crossing the creek as soon as Mahone opened." Both commands charged as ordered, but in Heth's estimation, "the attack was feeble and without result." Dearing's dismounted troopers, who must have been exhausted after fighting since early that morning, did their best but received scant support from Harris. The Mississippian explained why his respected brigade—proud veterans of many a battle—performed so poorly. "I formed on the left of Dearing, but owing to the distance to be covered I was compelled to deploy very nearly the whole of my command as skirmishers," he reported. "I advanced my line in order to make the required demonstration, but my force was too weak to press the enemy to advantage." Harris contended that Heth wished only "a demonstration" and would tell Mahone later that Heth instructed him to hold the north side of the run "at all hazards" and then departed, never again to be seen by him during the fight. The dichotomy between Heth's orders to execute a vigorous attack and Harris's belief he was only to make a demonstration cannot be reconciled. Beyond dispute is the fact that the brigadier brought fewer than 600 soldiers to the field. Thus, Heth believed that even had Dearing and Harris succeeded in capturing the high ground around the Burgess farm, they could not have held the position.[88]

The rattle of musketry and the shrieks of the Rebel Yell signaling Mahone's assault alerted Hampton to order Butler's two brigades to move east from their positions astride White Oak Road, a few hundred yards from a heavy skirmish line held by Rugg's brigade. With Pierce Young's troopers on the left and Butler's old brigade, now under Col. Hugh Aiken, on the right, the division charged ahead on foot, only generals, field officers, and their staffs mounted. Aiken's Fifth South Carolina Cavalry led the attack, but moments after starting, its leader, Lt. Col. Robert J. Jeffords, fell from the saddle, killed instantly. Undaunted, the Confederates dashed across the open fields "with a yell that made the welkin ring," encountering "a most murderous fire." Pvt. John N. Cummings of Jeffords's command considered the fight "a desperate struggle and only for the mercies of God that everyone of our company that was engaged was not killed."[89]

Two of Hampton's sons were the most noteworthy casualties. Thomas Preston Hampton, a twenty-year-old aide-de-camp on his father's staff, rode with the vanguard of the attackers, waving his hat and encouraging the troops. Thus a conspicuous target, a minié ball slammed into his groin, unseating him. Soon, the elder Hampton and some of his attendants reined up, the general recognizing his stricken boy. "My son, my son," Hampton muttered as he cradled the dying youth. Someone summoned an ambulance, and Lieutenant Hampton was taken under the care of surgeon Thomas "Watt" Taylor. As the collection of officers huddled around young Hampton, another shot struck Wade Hampton IV, causing this second of Hampton's sons to fall that day, although he survived his wound. Distraught but still cognizant of his duty, General Hampton retired, halting to oversee the firing of Hart's Battery. Most Confederate accounts describe Hampton's attack as highly successful. In fact, the Federals maintained their position west of Boydton Plank Road, and in the words of General Egan, holding the Rebels "completely in check." As with Dearing and Harris, Butler's portion of the combined Confederate offensive failed.[90]

General Hancock responded immediately to the Confederate assaults. "At the first sound of [Mahone's] attack I sent Major Mitchell, my senior aide, to General Egan, with orders . . . to desist from his assault on the bridge and to face his command to the rear and attack the enemy with his whole command," he reported. Egan needed no such prompting. Recognizing the crisis created by Mahone's incursion, the general immediately dispatched McAllister's brigade to assail the right of the enemy's now somewhat-scattered formation, held by the North Carolinians. "Having a large number of recruits, and but few officers and time precious," wrote McAllister, "I deemed it best to about-face and move on the enemy with my rear rank in front." Four regiments "moved down the hill on the charge over the gulleys and through the thick hazel-brush under a severe flank fire." The Eleventh New Jersey at the head of McAllister's troops reached Metcalf's abandoned guns and reclaimed them while corralling about 100 of MacRae's men.[91]

Mahone, observing the unfolding situation, ordered King's Alabamans up from reserve. MacRae managed to re-form a portion of his brigade and, in combination with King, countercharged, driving McAllister back to the Burgess farm, "capturing from them the same artillery that we took as we went," wrote one Tar Heel.[92]

Meanwhile, after he delivered Hancock's orders to Egan, the intrepid Major Mitchell rode back along the plank road, looking for help for McAllister, Willett, and Smyth. He found the Thirty-Sixth Wisconsin of Rugg's brigade and ordered this small regiment—its men still smarted from having their colors confiscated after Reams' Station—to charge the Rebels. "Seeing the perilous condition," wrote a Wisconsin officer, "Capt. [George] Fisk ordered the Regt to face by the

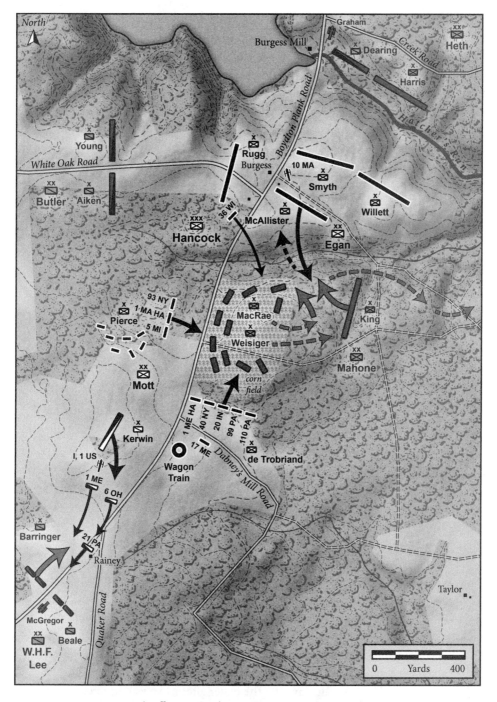

North

Graham

Burgess Mill

Creek Road

xx
Heth

x
Dearing

x
Harris

Hatcher's Run

x
Young

White Oak Road

x
Rugg
Burgess

Boydton Plank Road

10 MA

x
Smyth

xx
Butler

x
Aiken

36 W

x
McAllister

x
Willett

xxx
Hancock

x
Egan

93 NY
1 MA HA
5 MI

x
Pierce

x
MacRae

x
King

x
Weisiger

xx
Mott

xx
Mahone

corn
field

x
Kerwin

1 ME HA
40 NY
20 IN
99 PA
110 PA

I, 1 US

17 ME

x
de Trobriand

1 ME

Wagon
Train

Dabney's Mill Road

6 OH

x
Barringer

21 PA
Rainey

Taylor

Quaker Road

McGregor

xx
Beale

W.H.F.
Lee

0   Yards   400

Sixth Offensive, October 27, 1864: Union Counterattacks

rear fix bayonets & charge." Mitchell then told Colonel Rugg to move his entire brigade against Mahone. The lieutenant colonel declined to do so, citing Egan's orders to maintain his position and emphasizing that a portion of his command was at that very moment confronting Hampton and Butler. These were legitimate reasons to ignore Mitchell's directive, but Rugg's poor reputation and his unwillingness to detach the portion of his brigade not then engaged along White Oak Road would lead to his court-martial and removal from the army. Meanwhile, McAllister rallied his men and, in combination with the gunnery of the Tenth Massachusetts Battery, managed to halt MacRae and King.[93]

Weisiger's Brigade, on Mahone's left, also had its hands full. Mott's First Brigade was in position south of Mahone's breakthrough, and its commander, General de Trobriand, immediately ordered his troops to change front and face the enemy. Philippe Regis Denis de Kereden de Trobriand was one of the Union's better foreign-born commanders. The forty-eight-year-old Frenchman emigrated to the United States after a career in the French army and organized the Fifty-Fifth New York at the outbreak of the war. He obtained his general's star in January 1864 and was popular with his men. "He is always familiar with us and has a good word for our regiment," wrote a soldier from the Seventeenth Maine. "Ze 17th of Maine ees von dam splendid battalions," the burly de Trobriand had intoned. He proved equal to the challenge at hand.[94]

Mott told de Trobriand to form a new line along Dabney's Mill Road in order to protect the nearby wagons. The Frenchman detached the 17th Maine for this duty and aligned the 1st Maine Heavy Artillery along the plank road with the 40th New York, 20th Indiana, 99th Pennsylvania, and part of the 110th Pennsylvania in front of the 17th Maine. Led by Hancock, Mott, de Trobriand, and the ubiquitous Major Mitchell, the brigade advanced, firing as it went and "cheering lustily." Weisiger's Virginians turned to meet this new threat, shooting several mounted officers of de Trobriand's staff. Fifteen of the brigade's officers were killed or wounded, along with 150 of de Trobriand's men. But by then, Pierce had managed to rally a portion of his broken brigade, and the 5th Michigan, 1st Massachusetts Heavy Artillery, and 93rd New York joined de Trobriand's left, bearing down on the Virginians.[95]

This pressure from the south and west, combined with McAllister's and Egan's stand to the north, rendered Mahone's situation untenable. "Our commanding officers did not know what to do," wrote Lieutenant Hoyle. "Some talked of surrendering, some of forming where we were and fighting to the last, others of cutting our way out. The better alternative was adopted." MacRae ordered his troops to "about face and fight their way out." Maj. Charles M. Stedman of the Forty-Fourth North Carolina admitted that "every man of them knew their situation to be critical." General MacRae personally directed his beleaguered veterans back to the shelter of the woods as the Carolinians attempted to spike Metcalf's guns as they passed. Weisiger's soldiers had no chance to resist the juggernaut headed their way. The Virginians joined the rest of Mahone's troops, retreating into the forest. Mahone would claim that "rain and darkness" caused him to abandon his position, but his casualties belied that facile explanation. Weisiger suffered 328 losses and MacRae 516, most of these prisoners of war. "The enemy were driven into the woods in complete confusion," wrote Hancock, "and another brigade advancing against them would have secured many trophies," a veiled reference to Rugg's failure to participate in the counterattack.[96]

The last of the Confederate attacks enjoyed little more success. Rooney Lee positioned two regiments of Barringer's Brigade west of the plank road and two of Beale's to the east, with orders from Hampton to charge in concert with Mahone. The four guns of Captain McGregor's battery rumbled along with the troopers. The Ninth Virginia Cavalry led the advance, the sound of Mahone's clash audible to the north, when a yell startled the Virginians "& in a moment a column of Yankee cavalry came charging down upon us from a body of woods just in our front."[97]

These blueclad troopers belonged to the Twenty-First Pennsylvania Cavalry, the only regiment of Colonel Smith's Third Brigade still south of the infantry. The various attacks against the Second Corps had prompted Gregg to send most of Smith's and Kerwin's brigades to reinforce Hancock. Davies's brigade, deployed south along Quaker Road, was too far away to lend immediate assistance. Maj. Oliver B. Knowles, commanding the Twenty-First Pennsylvania Cavalry, saw the approaching Confederates and boldly charged, hoping to hold the enemy at bay until reinforcements arrived. Lee ordered his men to dismount, but before the order could be executed, the Pennsylvanians closed on the Virginians, "cutting & slashing with their sabers and employing their pistols." Barringer's Brigade then arrived and threatened to overlap Knowles's courageous fighters. The Sixth Ohio Cavalry now appeared, and Gregg, alive to Lee's threat, called for all his available regiments to return from Hancock's front and deal with this latest crisis.[98]

The Spencer-armed First Maine Cavalry was next on the scene. They formed on the right of the Twenty-First Pennsylvania Cavalry and, despite briefly wavering in the face of Lee's carbines and McGregor's shells, stood firm. Their performance was notable in that 200 of these men and fourteen officers had already received their discharge at the expiration of their terms of enlistment. A section of Battery I, First U.S. Artillery roared in support of the blueclad troopers, and in short order the remainder of Kerwin's brigade appeared. The antagonists, fighting at close range and on foot, maintained the contest under continuous downpours until the growing darkness prompted both sides to withdraw. Lee had driven Gregg northward and certainly gave as good as he received, but without sustained success from the other three prongs of the Rebel offensive, his attack could achieve little. As the last of the combatants disengaged, the Battle of Burgess Mill, First Boydton Plank Road or First Hatcher's Run came to an end.[99]

Two more scenes of combat, minor postscripts to the fighting this eventful day, unfolded southeast of Petersburg. Hancock's First Division, led by the capable Nelson Miles, was left to man the fortifications between the Appomattox River and Battery 24, west of Jerusalem Plank Road. As the rest of the Second Corps made its way to Boydton Plank Road, army headquarters ordered Miles to assemble a force of as many as 2,000 men. "Should you discover that the enemy has greatly weakened his forces in your front," Meade instructed, "you may be required to . . . make an attempt to break through the enemy's line."[100]

Although Bushrod Johnson's Division had to expand to cover the trenches vacated by Mahone, the strength of the Confederate fortifications, still bristling with artillery, made it unlikely that any force of 2,000 men could penetrate the defenses. General Miles certainly saw things that way, as he ventured no such attack. But he would initiate two limited forays on the evening of the twenty-seventh "to determine [the enemy's] strength," more along the lines of the occasional trench raids conducted by both armies and unrelated to Hancock's primary offensive.[101]

The first such endeavor began shortly after dark along the portion of the Federal works opposite the Crater and manned by Col. St. Clair Mulholland's Fourth Brigade. According to Mulholland, Miles wished "to deceive the enemy as to the force holding the Union line," a motive entirely inconsistent with Meade's instructions and of questionable necessity. Miles ordered Mulholland to make a demonstration to that effect, and the colonel selected 100 men of the 148th Pennsylvania, armed with Spencer rifles, for the job. The Pennsylvanians passed the Union picket line and crept toward an entrenched artillery position called Davidson's Battery, just west of Baxter Road. Ten of the raiders, wielding axes, chopped a hole in the chevaux-de-frise, allowing their comrades to charge through the gap. The Confederates, who happened at that moment to be rotating the picket details, at first mistook the attackers for friends. This hesitation allowed the Federals to enter the fort and gather a handful of prisoners, including the ranking officers of the Forty-Sixth Virginia.[102]

"It was excitement of the real kind," wrote a private in the Thirty-Fourth Virginia, "but was soon over." A portion of Gracie's Alabama brigade charged toward the fort, dislodging the Pennsylvanians. Lt. Henry D. Price, Mulholland's adjutant general, was the most lamented of the Union fallen. He had galloped up to his commander just before the attack commenced, insisting on participating. Unbuckling his sword belt and handing the empty scabbard to another officer, Price said, "Tom, if I am killed, send these to my mother." Price fell at the head of the assault, his body returned two days later under flag of truce.[103]

Later that evening Miles sent another party across no-man's-land near Rives Salient and the Chimneys, scene of the September battle. Lt. Col. Denis F. Burke of the Eighty-Eighth New York of Col. Clinton MacDougall's Consolidated Brigade led 130 of his men into the Confederate lines, overwhelming the picket line held by the Holcombe Legion, seizing eight prisoners, and controlling about 200 yards of the enemy's position. Brig. Gen. William Wallace quickly assembled a force from the Legion and his Eighteenth South Carolina, expelling the intruders and restoring the line. "The Yankees . . . held a small portion of our picket line for about one hour," wrote Sgt. Drayton S. Pitts of the Holcombe Legion, "and then we charged them and recaptured our picket line and about 25 or 30 of the rascals." Miles reported a total of four officers and sixty-three men killed, wounded, or missing as a result of these two pointless attacks. "This taking of strongholds & then abandoning them should not be encouraged," thought an officer in the Twenty-Eighth Massachusetts. "The effect upon the men is bad. They cannot see the use of butting against barriers for the sake of keeping up the circulation."[104]

From late in the afternoon until well after dark, messages passed between Hancock and army headquarters at the Armstrong house. Grant's orders specified that Hancock withdraw the next morning, but the Second Corps faced several dilemmas. Hancock had heard nothing from Crawford since 4:00 P.M. Meade offered to send Ayres's division to reinforce him, but Hancock was uncertain that these troops would arrive any more expeditiously than the elusive Crawford. Most importantly, the infantry, the artillery, and Gregg's cavalry had all but exhausted their ammunition, and receiving a resupply by morning seemed at least as doubtful as the appearance of more troops. Shortly after Lee and Gregg exchanged their final shots, Hancock dispatched a staff officer to Meade's command post to ask permission to retreat. Two hours later Meade's reply arrived. "The commanding general directs me to say," wrote Humphreys, "that you can withdraw at once if you deem it most judicious, or at any time during the night."[105]

"Reluctant as I was to leave the field, and by so doing lose some of the fruits of my victory, I felt compelled to order a withdrawal rather than risk disaster by awaiting an attack in the morning only partly prepared," Hancock explained with eminent logic. Mott would lead the retreat via Dabney's Mill Road at 10:00 P.M. Egan would follow, halting at the mill in order to cover Crawford's escape. Their destination was the Gurley house, near the Weldon Railroad, but Meade ordered Hancock to halt after recrossing Hatcher's Run to receive fresh ammunition. Warren would see to Crawford's removal and notify Egan when it was safe for him to fall back as well. Gregg would retire down Quaker Road.[106]

Dabney's Mill Road, not much more than a forest path thickly lined with woods, could only accommodate one-way traffic, meaning that ambulances and supply wagons could not reach the battlefield while Hancock's weary men tramped southeast. The corps commander and his officers did their best to collect as many of the wounded as the available transportation could accommodate, but some of the stricken were left behind in the care of detailed surgeons. De Trobriand's brigade would provide a picket line while the rest of the corps began its march. Promptly at 10:00 P.M., the troops headed into the narrow roadway leading to safety behind Union lines.[107]

More miserable conditions for a night march could hardly be imagined. Corporal Armstrong remembered the night as being "one of the darkest of history; nothing could be seen on our road through the forest,—not a star in the heavens nor an opening in the clouds above us." The cold rain not only added to the soldiers' discomfort but also left the roadway a quagmire, badly "cut up by the moving cavalry and artillery that had passed before us." De Trobriand began his withdrawal at 1:00 A.M. on the twenty-eighth, leaving campfires burning to deceive the enemy. Six hours later his brigade arrived at Armstrong's Mill, rejoining the rest of the corps. Less than perfect communications that awful night left a party of the First Minnesota and Seventh Michigan on the field after everyone else had departed. Capt. James C. Farwell of the First Minnesota discovered his predicament after daylight and managed to fend off probing Confederate cavalry while leading his men to safety by way of Reams' Station.[108]

Warren sent Roebling to Dabney's Mill about daylight to inform Egan that Crawford's division had returned and that he could withdraw as well. Warren had informed Crawford at 1:00 A.M. of Hancock's retreat and ordered him to hold his position until morning. Crawford shook out a skirmish line and dug shallow works as his troops huddled in the downpour, "shivering under our India rubber blankets," and prohibited from kindling fires that would reveal their location. Crawford circulated orders around 2:00 A.M. to prepare to move out, and within the hour the division began its retreat. "When we withdrew we did

The Sixth Petersburg Offensive, October 27–28

it under a lively fire from the hillside where the rebs were posted behind trees from which they could take deliberate aim," recorded Pvt. William L. Perry of the 150th Pennsylvania. "Considering the critical condition in which we were . . . we have to say 'we escaped well.'" By midmorning, Hancock, Gregg, and Crawford were all safely within friendly lines. "Sic transit Gloria Mundi," noted artillery chief Henry Hunt.[109]

The elements were just as unkind to the Confederates that night. "Before we got out of the woods a heavy rainstorm came up and literally soaked us, and then marching through the bushes to the Plank Road made things worse," wrote Lt. Col. William H. Stewart of Weisiger's Sixty-First Virginia. "I was thoroughly chilled and had it not been for a drink from a captured canteen, I would have been forced to the hospital." Confederate plans for the following day once again introduced the dichotomy between Heth's report and Mahone's memory. According to Mahone, Hill contacted him about midnight with orders to renew the attack in the morning. Mahone then suggested that fresh brigades from Heth's and Wilcox's commands supplement the units that fought on the twenty-seventh. These reinforcements supposedly appeared, and Mahone marched around the head of the Burgess millpond to form a junction with the cavalry. He met Hampton, informed him of the plan, and the two rode off to "join forces and attack the enemy." In a short time they encountered General Young, who reported that the Yankees had fled. Mahone allegedly urged a pursuit that he claimed did not occur. Heth's more credible account simply noted that he met with Hampton during the night and agreed on a combined attack, but upon discovering the enemy had departed, the attack plan became moot. Hampton, whose version of events agreed with Heth's, did conduct a pursuit with Dearing's Brigade. The graycoats skirmished with the Federal rear guard between Dabney's and Armstrong's Mills, then returned to camp.[110]

The Rebels now ventured onto the battlefield and found the detritus typical of such grim landscapes. One Confederate spied a new red flannel shirt on a dead Federal and bent down to claim it. "As he turned him over on his face he found very little of the Yankee or the shirt either, as his whole back had been torn off by a shell." The scavenger turned the hideous corpse back and "without a word, mounted and rode off." Another graycoat had better luck. Noticing a freshly dug but shallow grave, this scavenger "commenced to grabble." He soon unearthed a leg, attached to a desirable cavalry boot. Warming to his task, he completed enough of the excavation to expose the other leg and delightedly exclaimed, "By golly, boys I've got 'em!" and "cooly pitched his old shoes into the hole, drew the boots onto his own feet [and] after throwing a little dirt back to fill up the hole" departed. The Confederates gathered some 250 Federal wounded whom Hancock could not evacuate and formed details to bury the dead and collect abandoned guns and equipment. Robert E. Lee, from his head-quarters at Chaffin's Bluff, briefed the secretary of war on the previous day's results. "General Hill reports that . . . Mahone captured 400 prisoners, 3 stands of colors, and 6 pieces of artillery. The latter could not be brought off, the enemy having possession of the bridge. . . . On the Williamsburg road yesterday General Field captured upward of 400 prisoners and 7 stands of colors. The enemy left a number of dead in front of our works and returned to his former position today."[111]

Lee's report left the unmistakable impression that Grant's latest gambit had failed, an opinion shared by most Confederates. "I promised to give you a de-tailed account of the fight," wrote Lt. Col. William Stokes of the Fourth South Carolina Cavalry. "From two of their surgeons who were left in charge of about sixty of their wounded . . . we have learned that it is one of their greatest defeats of the war." Pvt. Edward L. Wells, another South Carolina trooper, wrote his mother: "We were completely successful all along the Line, between here & Petersburg, as also on the other side of the James. They have lost many in killed, & wounded, besides more than two thousand prisoners. It is supposed by us to have been the Grand Election battle of Abe Lincoln." Artillerist Willie Pegram also saw things that way. "The results of this victory are the most important we have obtained since we have been here," he wrote his mother, "for it is generally regarded as Grant's grand attempt to get possession of the South Side Railroad before the election."[112]

General Lee acknowledged Hill's report of the battle and expressed his ap-preciation of the results. "You have rendered valuable service and I desire to tender to you, and to the officers and men engaged my thanks for what they have accomplished." He singled out Hampton for specific praise, further validation of his decision to promote the South Carolinian to corps command. There were a few critics of the operation. Colonel McMaster, commander of the Seventeenth South Carolina in Johnson's Division, explained to his wife that "Gen A. P. Hill made a number of blunders in a fight on our right last Thursday," citing the failure to capture more of Hancock's men. "Lee & Hampton are the only Genls we have here whose places could not be easily supplied by Tom Dick or Harry." Mahone blamed Harris for failing to support his breakthrough.[113]

Confederate casualties totaled about 1,360 inclusive of all the units that participated in the combat along Hatcher's Run and Boydton Plank Road. At this stage of the campaign, even such relatively minor losses would be hard to replace. "We whipped them back easily; so much so that I hardly think it was a determined movement," wrote Col. Samuel Melton from his post in the War

Department. In fact, Union reports frequently dismissed the entire effort as a mere reconnaissance. "The absurdity of calling the movement a reconnaissance in force, is so palpable that none will be deceived by it," chortled a Richmond newspaper. War correspondent Peter Wellington Alexander called the Federals "great economists of truth and in many instances . . . set up claims which are as preposterous as they are unfounded."[114]

"In my last I wrote you about the fight we had," wrote Second Corps ambulance driver William A. Leonard. "Well, I see in the Papers they try to make it out as a reconnaissance in force, well I don't want to reconnoiter in force again if that is the way they do it." Capt. Charles Mills, now an officer on Hancock's staff, warned his mother not to believe what she read in the papers "that the movement of the 27th October was merely a reconnaissance. It was intended for a very important move, and as such was a failure." Many in Meade's army viewed the outcome similarly. Musician George W. Fox of the Eighth New Jersey called the operation "one of the great blunders of the War. The move was made to accomplish something so as to help elect Old Abe but it turned out the wrong way." The opinionated Colonel Wainwright thought that the newspaper accounts, echoing Grant's dispatch to Washington that characterized the operation as a reconnaissance, "affords a vast deal of amusement in the army, considering there were greater exertions and preparations made for this expedition than any previous one." Pvt. William Hamilton, serving as a clerk at Fifth Corps headquarters, called the operation "an immense failure," while Lieutenant Colonel Lyman termed it "a well-conducted fizzle."[115]

Those Northerners who declared the offensive a disaster placed the blame on various factors and commanders. Sergeant Crater of the Fiftieth Pennsylvania laid responsibility at Meade's feet, considering the effort motivated by politics and not military advantage. Francis Walker, Hancock's chief of staff, condemned the effort to flank the Confederates with "a comparatively insignificant force," which allowed the enemy to hold their line with small numbers while concentrating a force large enough to cripple the advance. Hancock himself thought that the Second Corps performed well, but "everyone else seemed to quit." Wainwright faulted the Ninth Corps for its tardy start and noted that Crawford's failure to reinforce Hancock, although not his fault, led to the discomfiture of the Second Corps. Grant was not nearly as charitable. "Where was Crawford," he asked Meade, stating that if that division had been in position, it and the Second Corps "could have annihilated all of the enemy south of the run." Meade provided the most apt explanation, blaming the setback on execution of a plan based on faulty intelligence.[116]

Not every soldier in blue embraced such a negative impression. The Fourth Maryland's Sgt. Edward Schilling informed his parents, "All I can say [is] the move was a success as far as damage to the enemy was concerned." General Miles admitted that "certain officers" did not manage the battle particularly well, but "our troops whipped the enemy in the fight." He mentioned the large haul of Confederate prisoners, as did a Union surgeon. "The reconnaissance of a day or two ago was successful in capturing more than one thousand prisoners," wrote the doctor. No less an analyst than Lieutenant General Grant thought the "battle . . . yesterday resulted much in our favor back of Petersburg." Perhaps soldier Alfred B. Thompson arrived at the most judicious analysis: "I guess on the whole it was a draw game."[117]

Union casualties sustain that assessment. Hancock, Warren, and Parke reported a total loss of 1,487 of all causes, the Second Corps suffering the most by far. When Gregg's 271 casualties are included, Meade counted 1,758 men killed, wounded, or missing, proportionately similar to Confederate totals.[118]

Much less ambivalence characterized the postmortem of Butler's portion of the offensive. "We have been accommodating Mr. Grant and I am proud to say that the great Ulysses has been foiled in every effort to break our lines," wrote Col. Robert F. Graham of General Hagood's Twenty-First South Carolina. "The enemy only came within a hundred yards of our lines and were driven back with great slaughter."[119]

Northern newspapers tried to place Butler's offensive in the most positive light. "If we do not herald the results of this movement as a 'grand victory,'" reported the New York Times, "it is impossible to conceive how the rebel papers— and by a very natural process the Copperhead ones among us—can have the impudence to be claiming one on their side." Weitzel admitted that his troops "have had a hard time of it" but defended his performance as being "as lively as possible under the circumstances. If it had been possible to have avoided two hours delay on the march, I think I would have gotten around the enemy's left." Cyrus Comstock disagreed. "Butler thought—he could take Richmond . . . & was perfectly willing to run the risk of losing 2 or 3000 men in an unsuccessful assault. There was not one chance in ten of doing it." Theodore Lyman, as always, couched Butler's failure in unique terms. "You are correct in seeing the late move as a 'slump,'" he wrote his wife. "That is somewhat true, and Butler's was slump-er." John Rawlins evidenced the disdain for Butler that prevailed among Grant's staff. "I am free to say I fear the continuance of General Butler in command will some day work disaster of a serious character to our arms."[120]

Although Grant's Sixth Petersburg Offensive clearly failed to achieve its stated objectives of seizing the South Side Railroad and possibly the Confederate capital, it fell far short of a disaster. Most Union forces, particularly the Second Corps, fought bravely and with determination. Casualties were comparatively light when measured against earlier battles. Butler's occupation of the north side of the James, despite the setbacks of October 27, remained secure. Most importantly, the Confederate defensive perimeter now extended from Nine Mile Road, across the James, through Bermuda Hundred, and southwest of Petersburg to Hatcher's Run, some thirty-five miles. "On last Thursday at Burgess' Mill we had three brigades to oppose six divisions," Lee wrote Jefferson Davis on November 2. "On our left two divisions to oppose two corps." The gray commander warned, "Unless we can obtain a reasonable approximation to [the enemy's] force I fear a great calamity will befall us."[121]

The events between early August and the end of October 1864 resulted in the dire situation now facing the Army of Northern Virginia. Grant, Meade, and Butler had orchestrated three major offensives that captured key portions of Richmond's defenses and threatened the capital, choked off the direct line of rail communications linking Petersburg to Wilmington and its southern source of supplies, and stretched Rebel manpower almost to the breaking point. In the Shenandoah Valley the season began with a Confederate army fresh from an incursion to the outskirts of Washington and ended with that army decisively defeated and wrecked beyond salvation. In Georgia Sherman had conquered Atlanta and prepared to march to the sea, while a combined operation closed Mobile, the South's last significant Gulf Coast port. Hope of foreign intervention had long since fled.

Yet one event remained that might salvage the Confederate cause and erase their grim military prospects. "The election in Yankeedom draws nigh and I hope and believe will result in good to the country," wrote Georgia artillerist Francis Marion Coker. "If McC[lellan] is elected I think other plans for restoring peace will be resorted to beside fighting, which of course is independence for us." As October turned to November, all eyes in the armies of blue and gray around Petersburg, resting in deep trenches overlooking ground stained by the blood of thousands during the previous eighty-nine days, turned to the results of a vote that might determine the outcome not only of the campaign for Petersburg but of the war itself.[122]

ACKNOWLEDGMENTS

I began this project in 2006, and during the intervening generation, the list of friends, colleagues, archivists, librarians, and institutions to which I am indebted would almost demand a volume of its own. The roster of folks who I thanked in volume 1 also deserve hearty recognition for their help with this one. Some, however, warrant special mention, and others assisted in the preparation of this second volume.

The publications of three Petersburg Campaign scholars are implicit in this book. John Horn, Richard Sommers, and Hampton Newsome all provided guidance regarding the complex military maneuvers addressed in these pages through their fine studies and with personal consultation. My frequent reference to their monographs demonstrates how much I respect their understanding of events. I recommend Horn's *The Siege of Petersburg: The Battles for the Weldon Railroad*, Sommers's *Richmond Redeemed: The Siege at Petersburg*, and Newsome's *Richmond Must Fall: The Richmond-Petersburg Campaign, October 1864* to readers interested in more tactical detail than they will find in this volume.

William Marvel of South Conway, New Hampshire, read the entire manuscript and offered many useful comments that improved the clarity of my prose. He is the finest wordsmith and editor I know. George C. Rable, professor emeritus at the University of Alabama and one of my oldest friends, sent me countless suggestions for source material and helped track down a number of obscure journal articles. Jimmy Blankenship, former historian at Petersburg National Battlefield, accompanied me on all my field trips to Petersburg, pointing out the locations of historic homes, roads, and battle scenes. He also generously provided me with a draft of his excellent study of Grant's military railroad. Similarly, Robert E. L. Krick, the outstanding former historian at Richmond National Battlefield Park, escorted me across the historic landscapes of Henrico County as well as fact-checked my accounts of the combat north of the James River. Rick Eiserman of Carlisle, Pennsylvania, shared his extensive collection of material on the Texas Brigade as well as the hospitality of his home.

Current and former National Park Service historians Mike Andrus, Ann Blumenshine, Emmanuel Dabney, John Hennessy, Jim Ogden, David Ruth, and Patrick Schroeder all assisted with generosity and good cheer. Special thanks go to Brett Schulte, administrator of a spectacular website—the Siege of Petersburg Online: A Richmond-Petersburg Campaign Site (www.beyondthecrater. com)—whose collection of material is simply unequaled. Anyone remotely interested in the Petersburg Campaign should avail themselves of Schulte's digital archive.

Several friends deserve particular thanks for forwarding source material that might have otherwise eluded me. Noah "Andy" Trudeau of Washington, D.C., conveyed dozens of relevant newspaper articles. Keith Bohannon, professor of history at the University of West Georgia and the guru of all things Civil War Georgia, helped me with material from his state. Edward "Andy" Altemos shared his important manuscript on the Fifteenth New York Heavy Artillery, which I am happy to say is now in print. Richard Benton, Ted Linton, Scott Maugher, and Bryce Suderow all tracked down source material and offered insights that enhanced my research. Gordon Berg generously squired me around the nation's capital on an extended research trip. And Edward Alexander once again crafted the excellent maps that enhance this narrative.

I visited dozens of archives and libraries in the preparation of this book and enjoyed the privilege of working with skilled and dedicated professionals. They include Carol Bowman of the Prince George Historical Society, Nancy Davis Bray of Georgia College & State University, Desiree Butterfield-Nagy of the University of Maine, Peter Corina of Cornell University, Tom Crew of the Library of Virginia, Kira Dietz of Virginia Tech University, Charles Doran and Ann Lee Pauls of Princeton University, Malia Ebel of the New Hampshire Historical Society, John Fierst of Central Michigan University, Jeff Giambrone of the Mississippi Department of Archives and History, Gideon Goodrich of Penn State University, Linda Hocking of the Litchfield Historical Society, Sarah Kozmo of the Onondaga Historical Association, John McClure of the Virginia Museum of History and Culture, Lisa McCown of Washington & Lee University, Lesley Martin of the Chicago Historical Society, Amanda Nelson of Wesleyan University, Phil Palen of the Gowanda Area Historical Society, Lauren Patton of the Indiana State Library, Alexander Rankin of Boston University, Ed Richi of the Delaware Historical Society, Jay Satterfield of Dartmouth College, Christopher Schnell of the Abraham Lincoln Presidential Library, Anne Shepard and Mickey Devrise of the Cincinnati Historical Society, Jeannie Sherman of the Connecticut State Library, Christopher Shields of the Greenwich Historical Society, Steve Tettamanti of the New Jersey Historical Society, Keeley Tulio of the Union League of Philadelphia, John Versluis of the Texas Heritage Museum, Joe Weber of the American Jewish Archives, and Nichol Westerdahl and Isabell McCullough of Syracuse University.

The editors of the Civil War America Series, Caroline Janney and Aaron Sheehan-Dean, have been unfailingly supportive of this multivolume endeavor, as has Mark Simpson-Vos and the staff at the University of North Carolina Press. Gary W. Gallagher, the editor emeritus of Civil War America and a dear friend, has taken my project under his wing and helped it along immeasurably. His encouragement, insight, and, most of all, suggestions for improvements are deeply appreciated.

Dr. Richard J. Sommers, to whom this volume is dedicated, gave me the most important gift of my historical career. Only a few months before Dick passed away from a hideous cancer, he and his wife Tracy invited me to their home after we had enjoyed a dinner together at Dick's favorite Carlisle restaurant. There he surprised me with boxes of material from his personal archives dealing with aspects of the Petersburg story that he intended to consult in new publications but, as he told me, would not have time to utilize. He wanted me to have them so that I might employ them in my Petersburg project. The trust and respect of that uniquely kind and talented mentor will humble me for the rest of my days.

Last but certainly not least, I thank those with whom I share my domesticity. Ozzie and Mike, four-legged companions, observed much of my writing from various office perches and provided welcome respites from the computer. Most of all, my wonderful wife Margaret has cheerfully permitted the muse of history to embed so deeply in our home. Without Maggie's love and support, my work would not be possible.

A. Wilson Greene
Walden, Tennessee

NOTES

1. Hazard Stevens to "Dear Mother," July 3, 1864, Hazard Stevens Papers, Manuscript Division, Library of Congress, Washington.

2. McLaurin, "Eighteenth Regiment," 59–60.

1. U.S. War Department, *War of the Rebellion*, ser. 1, 40(1):172 (hereafter *OR*; all references are to series 1 unless otherwise noted). The location of Second Corps headquarters at this time is elusive. Francis Walker, author of the corps history, placed it at "the shot-riddled building on the Norfolk Road known as 'The Deserted House'" in mid-July 1864. See Walker, *Second Army Corps*, 557. But sketches by Theodore Lyman place Second Corps headquarters along Jerusalem Plank Road, perhaps at the Jones house, where the court would reconvene in late August. See Lowe, *Meade's Army*, 220, 222, 226.

2. Simon, *Papers of Ulysses S. Grant*, 11:369 (hereafter Simon, *Grant Papers*); *OR*, 40(1):171.

3. *OR*, 40(1):18, 171–72; Forstchen, "28th United States Colored Troops," 153; Marvel, *Burnside*, 410.

4. For Grant's promotion to general in chief and a succinct summary of the development of his strategy, see Simpson, *Ulysses S. Grant*, 256–65.

5. Rhea, *Battle of the Wilderness*, 34; *OR*, 33:1136, 1045, 36(1):284–85; Greene, *Campaign of Giants*, 13.

6. Rhea, *Battle of the Wilderness*, 38; Warner, *Generals in Blue*, 202–4; Theodore Lyman to "Doux Mimilieu," Nov. 12, 1864, Theodore Lyman Letters, Massachusetts Historical Society, Boston; Henry Bingham, "Memoirs of General Hancock," William Palmer Civil War Collection, Western Reserve Historical Society, Cleveland; 314; Chesson, *Journal of a Civil War Surgeon*, 182; Walker, *General Hancock*, 236–37; Jordan, *Winfield Scott Hancock*, 44.

7. Edward P. "Ned" Brownson to "Dear Sal," Aug. 20, 1864, O. A. Brownson Papers, Hesburgh Library, University of Notre Dame, South Bend; Jordan, *Winfield Scott Hancock*, 98, 101–9. Captain Brownson would be mortally wounded at Second Reams' Station in August 1864. See *OR*, 42(2):526.

8. Warner, *Generals in Blue*, 541–42.

9. Charles Bolton Diary, Aug. 5, 1864, Charles Bolton Papers, Massachusetts Historical Society, Boston; Thomas, *Three Years with Grant*, 202. Other sketches of Warren are in Rhea,

Battle of the Wilderness, 39; and Greene, *Campaign of Giants*, 181–82. Both Robinson and Wadsworth were wounded during the Overland Campaign, Wadsworth mortally.

10. Greene, *Campaign of Giants*, 21, 360–61.

11. Marvel, *Burnside*, 215, 342, 372. Meade led a division in the First Corps at Fredericksburg in 1862.

12. Marvel, *Burnside*, 346; Cutcheon, *Twentieth Michigan Infantry*, 148; Jackman, *Sixth New Hampshire*, 331.

13. Greene, *Campaign of Giants*, 257–58; Wood, *Reminiscences of the War*, 69–70; Lowe, *Meade's Army*, 122; Nevins, *Diary of the Civil War*, 165.

14. Wise, *End of an Era*, 342; Claiborne, quoted in Levin, "Earth Seemed to Tremble," 28; John E. Hall to "Dear Father," Nov. 10, 1864, Hall Family Papers, Alabama Department of Archives and History, Montgomery; Guelzo, *Robert E. Lee*, 316.

15. Gallagher, "Our Hearts Are Full of Hope"; Rhea, *Battle of the Wilderness*, 21.

16. Harllee, *Kinfolks*, 666–67. There are several excellent biographies of Longstreet, among them Wert, *General James Longstreet*. Lee preferred an offensive strategy, while Longstreet frequently advocated the defensive.

17. Gordon, *Reminiscences*, 38; Pfanz, *Richard S. Ewell*, 257, 273, 397, 401, 403.

18. Wiatt, *Confederate Chaplain William Edward Wiatt*, 203; Robertson, *General A. P. Hill*, 11–12, 268, 272, 299.

19. Freeman, *Lee's Lieutenants*, 424–25, 436. Stuart was wounded during the Battle of Yellow Tavern and died the next day. There are several good biographies of Stuart. One of the better ones is Wert, *Cavalryman of the Lost Cause*.

20. A good overview of these battles, collectively called the Overland Campaign, is Trudeau, *Bloody Roads South*. Gordon C. Rhea's four volumes covering this same period are among the best campaign studies of our generation. In addition to his work on the Wilderness previously cited, see Rhea, *Battles for Spotsylvania Court House; To the North Anna River*; and *Cold Harbor*.

21. Greene, *Campaign of Giants*, 33–37; William D. Henderson, "Civil War Petersburg: A Statistical View," 6–8, Richard Bland College. For a more comprehensive look at Petersburg on the eve of the Civil War, see Greene, *Civil War Petersburg*, 3–30.

22. Greene, *Civil War Petersburg*, 93–94, 97–104, 108–9. These defenses were named for Capt. Charles H. Dimmock, the engineer who oversaw their construction. Redans are artillery strongpoints open at the rear. This design allowed the Confederates, if necessary, to shift cannons easily from one position to another.

23. Greene, *Campaign of Giants*, 91–93; Greene, *Civil War Petersburg*, 163–72, 176–82. The Bermuda Hundred Campaign of May 1864 is the subject of two worthwhile studies: Robertson, *Back Door to Richmond*, and Schiller, *Bermuda Hundred Campaign*. The best account of the fighting on June 9 is Robertson, *First Battle for Petersburg*.

24. The conduct of Grant's movement to Petersburg and the fighting between June 15 and 18—the First Offensive—is covered in Greene, *Campaign of Giants*, 42–212. The most comprehensive treatment of the movement to the James is Rhea, *On to Petersburg*. Thomas J. Howe treats the First Offensive in detail in *Wasted Valor*. Petersburg allegedly earned the moniker "Cockade City" in reference to its volunteers who served in the War of 1812.

25. *OR*, 40(2):157. The Weldon Railroad was officially named the Petersburg Railroad but was widely known by soldiers and civilians by the name of the North Carolina town where it terminated. Historians generally refer to it by its informal name, as will I.

26. Establishing the Deep Bottom bridgehead is admirably described in Price, *First Deep Bottom*, 35–39. The infantry actions are covered in Greene, *Campaign of Giants*, 213–56. Hancock had been incapacitated by a flare-up of his Gettysburg wound, thus Birney, as senior division commander, led the Second Corps.

27. For the Wilson-Kautz Raid, see Greene, *Campaign of Giants*, 273–310. In addition to the Weldon (Petersburg) and the South Side Railroads, the raiders disrupted the Richmond & Danville Railroad.

28. Harvey A. Marckres to "Dear Brother," July 4, 1864, Harvey A. Marckres Letters, Henry E. Huntington Library, San Marino; Sears, *Lincoln's Lieutenants*, 713; "From the Ninety-Fourth," *Northern New York Times* (Watertown), Aug. 2, 1864.

29. The fighting at First Deep Bottom is covered in Price, *First Deep Bottom*, 59–107; and Greene, *Campaign of Giants*, 399–417.

30. *OR*, 40(1):82. The construction of the mine, its origins, and the Confederate attempt to locate it are capably covered in Hess, *Into the Crater*, 1–24.

31. For the evolution of plans for the mine explosion and subsequent assault, see Greene, *Campaign of Giants*, 419–24.

32. See Greene, *Campaign of Giants*, 394–98, 421–22. Cemetery Hill is the location of Blandford Church and Cemetery, a prominent historic site in modern Petersburg.

33. Gibbon, *Personal Recollections*, 253; Cleveland, *New Hampshire Fights the Civil War*, 112; Greene, *Campaign of Giants*, 164, 167–68, 422–26.

34. Lt. Charles F. Stinson to "Dear Ones at Home," Aug. 1, 1864, Pearce Civil War Collection, Navarro College, Corsicana.

35. *Richmond Daily Examiner*, Aug. 1, 1864; soldier letter, "In the Trenches near Petersburg," Aug. 4, 1864, *Pittsfield (Mass.) Sun*, Aug. 18, 1864; Pvt. William E. Parker to "Dear Father," Aug. 3, 1864, Parker Family Papers; and J. McG. Moseley to "My dear friend," Aug. 8, 1864, Alice Boozer Letters, both in South Caroliniana Library, University of South Carolina, Columbia; Pvt. George Martin to "Mr. Wm Beachum," Aug. 5, 1864, Beachum Family Papers, Mitchell Memorial Library, Mississippi State University, Starkeville; Capt. Waters Whipple Braman to "Friend Maggie," Aug. 3, 1864, Waters Whipple Braman Letters, Manuscripts and Special Collections, New York State Library, Albany; Pvt. Joseph Cross to "Dear Wife," July 31, 1864, Joseph Cross Civil War Letters, American Antiquarian Society, Worcester.

36. Sloan, *Reminiscences of the Guilford Grays*, 103–4; Lt. E. N. Wise to John Warwick Daniel, Nov. 14, 1905, John Warwick Daniel Papers, Albert and Shirley Small Special Collections Library, University of Virginia, Charlottesville. Wise's reference to Indians acknowledged the presence of Ottawa, Delaware, Chippewa, Huron, Oneida, and Potawatomi tribesmen serving with Company K, First Michigan Sharpshooters.

37. Greene, *Campaign of Giants*, 506–7.

38. Pvt. Frank Foote, "Death Grapple at Petersburg," *Jackson (Miss.) Clarion*, Sept. 17, 1884; Stewart, *Pair of Blankets*, 163.

39. Greene, *Campaign of Giants*, 510–12.

40. Fred E. Townsend, "History and Reminiscences of the 17th Maine Volunteer Infantry," Paul Bean Collection, Special Collections Department, Raymond H. Folger Library, University of Maine, Orono; Arden, *Letters from the Storm*, 242; Cavanaugh, *Otey, Ringgold, and Davidson Virginia Artillery*, 62; Lt. Oscar D. Robinson to "Dear Sister," Aug. 3, 1864, Oscar D. Robinson Papers, Rauner Library, Dartmouth College, Hanover; Greene, *Campaign of Giants*, 512–14.

41. Fleet and Fuller, *Green Mount*, 335–36; Fitz William McMaster to "My Dear Wife," Aug. 23, Oct. 19, 1864, Fitz William McMaster Papers, South Caroliniana Library, University of South Carolina, Columbia.

42. Henry Wise to "My beloved wife," Aug. 5, 1864, Wise Family Papers, Virginia Museum of History and Culture, Richmond; *OR*, 40(1):753–55; Walker, *Second Army Corps*, 568; Greene, *Campaign of Giants*, 514–15.

43. Corson, *My Dear Jennie*, 125; Joseph Banks Lyle Diary, July 31, 1864; and Paul M. Higginbotham to his brother Aaron, Aug. 1, 1864, Paul M. Higginbotham Papers, both in, Virginia Museum of History and Culture, Richmond; P. G. T. Beauregard to "Dear General [Thomas Jordan]," Aug. 2, 1864, P. G. T. Beauregard Papers, Manuscripts Division, Library of Congress, Washington.

44. Benjamin F. Butler Notebook, Special Collections, Carol M. Newman Library, Virginia Tech University, Blacksburg; Newsome, Horn, and Selby, *Civil War Talks*, 253; William Mahone to "My dear Sir," Aug. 6, 1864, copy, Petersburg National Battlefield; Crist, *Papers of Jefferson Davis*, 10:577, 583; Folsom, *Heroes and Martyrs of Georgia*, 76.

45. Carter, *Welcome the Hour of Conflict*, 260; Samuel Wickliffe Melton to "My dear wife," Aug. 14, 1864, Samuel Wickliffe Melton Papers, South Caroliniana Library, University of South Carolina, Columbia.

46. "Letter from the Troup Artillery," *Southern Watchman* (Athens, Ga.), Aug. 31, 1864.

47. Jordan and Jordan, *Dear Friend Amelia*, 128; Butler Notebook; Welles, *Diary*, 92; Styple, *Writing and Fighting the Civil War*, 282; Simpson, *Ulysses S. Grant*, 366; Warren S. Gurney to "Dear Folks at Home," Aug. 2, 1864, Warren S. Gurney Papers, John Hay Library, Brown University, Providence.

48. Welles, *Diary*, 92, 94; Woodbury, *Burnside and the Ninth Army Corps*, 446; Sgt. William J. Glackens to "Dear Parents," Aug. 8, 1864, copy in bound vol. 85, Richmond National Battlefield Park; Fisher A. Cleaveland to "Jennie," Aug. 8, 1864, John L. Nau III Civil War Collection, Houston; L[eander] O. Merriam, "Personal Recollections of the War for the Union," copy in bound vol. 190, Fredericksburg & Spotsylvania National Military Park, 59.

49. George F. Towle Diary, July 31, 1864, New Hampshire Historical Society, Concord; Paxton, *Sword and Gown*, 390–91; Gouverneur K. Warren to "My lovely Emmie," July 31, 1864, Gouverneur K. Warren Papers, Manuscripts and Special Collections, New York State Library, Albany; Edward Otho Cresap Ord to "Dearest Molly darling," Aug. 8, 1864, Edward Otho Cresap Ord Letters, C. H. Green Library, Stanford University, Palo Alto; Badeau, *Military History of Ulysses S. Grant*, 2:484; Sumner, *Diary of Cyrus B. Comstock*, 285 (hereafter Sumner, *Comstock Diary*); Meade, *Life and Letters*, 217–18.

50. Coco, *Through Blood and Fire*, 147; Scott, *Forgotten Valor*, 557; Smith et al., *Reminiscences of Major General Zenas R. Bliss*, 379.

51. Wheeler, "Petersburg"; Austin Kendall to "Dear Friends at Home," Aug. 7, 1864, David Walbridge Kendall Papers, Bentley Historical Library, University of Michigan, Ann Arbor; Warren S. Gurney to "Dear Uncle," July 30, 1864, Gurney Papers; "Letter from Co. D," *Cape Ann Light and Gloucester Telegraph* (Gloucester, Mass.), Aug. 13, 1864.

52. Thomas F. Walter Memoir, copy in bound vol. 420, Fredericksburg & Spotsylvania National Military Park; Alfred H. Terry to "Dearest Mammy," Aug. 2, 1864, Alfred Howe Terry Papers, Connecticut Historical Society, Hartford; Benjamin Butler to "My Dearest Little Wife," Aug. 1, 1864, in Marshall, *Private and Official Correspondence of Gen. Benjamin F. Butler*, 4:575 (hereafter Marshall, *Butler's Correspondence*); Lyman A. Barton to "Dear Sister,"

Aug. 12, 1864, Barton Family Papers, Vermont Historical Society, Barre; Harrison Montague to "Friend Mather," Aug. 7, 1864, Harrison Montague Letters, Civil War Documents Collection, Army Heritage and Education Center, Carlisle.

53. Charles Wainwright Diary, Aug. 2, 1864, Henry E. Huntington Library, San Marino; Orville S. Dewey to "My Dear Mollie," July 31, 1864, Orville S. Dewey Letters, Gilder-Lehrman Collection, New-York Historical Society, New York; William F. Smith to "My Dear Mother," Aug. 5, 1864, William F. Smith Letters, Lewis Leigh Collection, Army Heritage and Education Center, Carlisle; A[lonzo] D. Lewis to "Dear Mother," Aug. 7, 1864, copy, Petersburg National Battlefield; Scott, *Forgotten Valor*, 561.

54. Murray, *Ontario County Troops*, 99; Pvt. Newton Spencer to "Dear *Democrat*," Aug. 12, 1864, quoted in Merrill, "Court-Martial of Private Spencer," 38; Charles Kline to "Dear Mother and Sister," Aug. 1, 1864, Charles Kline Civil War Letters, South Carolina Historical Society, Charleston; John A. Bodamer Diary, July 30, 1864, James S. Schoff Civil War Collection, Clements Library, University of Michigan, Ann Arbor.

55. Capt. Charles M. Coit to "Dear All," Aug. 3, 1864, Capt. Charles M. Coit Letters, Gilder-Lehrman Collection, New-York Historical Society, New York; Elisha Clark to "Dear friend Dincey," Aug. 13, 1864, copy in bound vol. 209, Fredericksburg & Spotsylvania National Military Park; Edwin B. Paddock to "Dear Sister," Aug. 3, 1864, George J. and Edwin B. Paddock Letters, 1861–1865, Wisconsin Historical Society, Madison; Alonzo Rich to "Dear Father," July 31, 1864, Alonzo G. Rich Letters, Massachusetts Historical Society, Boston.

56. "Alfred" to "Friend Eddy," Aug. 14, 1864, Eddy Family Papers, Bentley Historical Library, University of Michigan, Ann Arbor; Joseph Barlow to "My dear Wife," Aug. 7, 1864, Joseph Barlow Papers, Army Heritage and Education Center, Carlisle; Styple, *Writing and Fighting the Civil War*, 275.

57. Blackford, *War Years with Jeb Stuart*, 260; Scarborough, *Diary of Edmund Ruffin*, 529 (hereafter Scarborough, *Ruffin Diary*).

58. Samuel H. Putnam to "Dear Brother," Aug. 1, 1864, Samuel H. Putnam Letters, Albert and Shirley Small Special Collections Library, University of Virginia, Charlottesville; Thomas, *Boys in Blue from the Adirondack Foothills*, 216; Charles Mead to "Bro Gil," Aug. 5, 1864, Charles Mead Correspondence, Bentley Historical Library, University of Michigan, Ann Arbor; Nathan Webb Diary, July 31, 1864, James S. Schoff Civil War Collection, Clements Library, University of Michigan, Ann Arbor; *OR*, 42(2):48; Joseph Barlow to "My dear Wife," Aug. 7, 1864, Barlow Papers.

59. Irving, *More Than Conqueror*, 173; Jackman, *Sixth New Hampshire*, 331; Theodore S. Bowers to James H. Wilson, Aug. 2, 1864, in Simon, *Grant Papers*, 11:363; Thomas J. Kessler to "My Dear friends at Home," Aug. 5, 1864, Thomas J. Kessler Letters, Gilder-Lehrman Collection, New-York Historical Society, New York; Henry Snow to "My Dear Mother," Aug. 3, 1864, Henry Snow Letters, Connecticut Historical Society, Hartford.

60. Josiah Jones Diary, Aug. 7, 1864, New Hampshire Historical Society, Concord; Sparks, *Inside Lincoln's Army*, 410; Louis Palma di Cesnola to "My dear Friend," Aug. 1, 1864, Luigi Palma di Cesnola Papers, Rauner Library, Dartmouth College, Hanover.

61. Grant to Halleck, Aug. 1, 1864, in Simon, *Grant Papers*, 11:361; Grant to "Dear Ammen," Aug. 18, 1864, in Simon, *Grant Papers*, 12:36; "Saturday's Assault . . . the Failure and Its Causes," *New York Times*, Aug. 3, 1864; Page, *Letters of a War Correspondent*, 207; Romig, *Phipps' Letters*, 66; Uberto A. Burnham to "Dear Father," Aug. 10, 1864, Uberto A. Burnham Papers, Manuscripts and Special Collections, New York State Library, Albany.

62. Priest, *One Surgeon's Private War*, 118; George S. Youngs to "Dear Sister," Aug. 10, 1864, in "Jeff's Prayers Are as Effective as Abe's," 126th N.Y., Billy Yank & Johnny Reb Letters, https://georgeyoungsblog.wordrpress.com; Acken, *Blue-Blooded Cavalryman*, 177.

63. *OR*, 40(1):172–76; James Cornell Biddle to "My own darling wife," Aug. 11, 1864, James Cornell Biddle Letters, Historical Society of Pennsylvania, Philadelphia; Edward O. C. Ord to "Dearest," Aug. 10, 1864, Ord Letters; Edward P. Brownson to "Dear Sal," Aug. 9, 1864, Brownson Papers; Wainwright Diary, Aug. 14, 1864; Josiah Jones Diary, Aug. 6, 1864.

64. *OR*, 40(1):531–32.

65. *OR*, 40(1):44–54. On the acrimony between Burnside and Meade, see Greene, *Campaign of Giants*, 492–93, 507, 510.

66. *OR*, 40(1):54–74. For a useful comparison of Meade's testimony to Burnside's, see Forstchen, "28th United States Colored Troops," 153–60.

67. Meade, *Life and Letters*, 220; *OR*, 40(1):75–129. Grant's Fourth Offensive explains the interruption in the proceedings. The Jones house exists in 2024 on the west side of Jerusalem Plank Road, albeit a few hundred yards south of its wartime location.

68. *OR*, 42(2):142, 168; Scott, *Forgotten Valor*, 564; George Meade to "Dear Margaret," Aug. 13, 1864, George Meade Papers, Army Heritage and Education Center, Carlisle; Simon, *Grant Papers*, 11:414–15; James Cornell Biddle to "My own darling wife," Aug. 25, 1864, James Cornell Biddle Letters. For a defense of Burnside, see Woodbury, *Burnside and the Ninth Army Corps*, 454–60; and Marvel, *Burnside*, 411–12. The Joint Committee on the Conduct of the War held a subsequent investigation that shifted the blame from Burnside to Meade. As a highly political body, its impartiality was always questionable. See Marvel, *Burnside*, 415–16.

69. Anderson, *Fifty-Seventh Regiment of Massachusetts Volunteers*, 229–30; Woodbury, *Burnside and the Ninth Army Corps*, 464; "The Petersburg Failure," *Irish-American Weekly* (New York), Aug. 20, 1864; Crabtree and Patton, *Journal of a Secesh Lady*, 604–5; Meade, *Life and Letters*, 221.

70. *OR*, 42(2):29–30; General Orders No. 31, Andrew A. Humphreys Papers, Historical Society of Pennsylvania, Philadelphia; General Orders No. 31, Gen. Richard Coulter Papers, Pennsylvania State Archives, Harrisburg; Chesson, *Journal of a Civil War Surgeon*, 187; Mushkat, *A Citizen-Soldier's Civil War*, 205.

71. Blackford, *War Years with Jeb Stuart*, 268–69; Jackson, *First Regiment Engineer Troops*, 85; John Alexander Sloan, "A North Carolinian in the War between the States," Southern Historical Collection, Louis Round Wilson Library, University of North Carolina, Chapel Hill; Pvt. William H. Smith Diary, Aug. 3–4, 1864, Confederate Miscellaneous Collection (microfilm), Georgia State Archives, Morrow.

72. Thomas Strayhorn Letter (extract), n.d., State Archives of North Carolina, Raleigh; Adj. George H. Moffett to "Dear Liz," Aug. 5, 1864, George H. Moffett Family Papers, South Carolina Historical Society, Charleston; John L. G. Wood to "My dear Father," Aug. 5, 1864, United Daughters of the Confederacy Collection, Georgia State Archives, Morrow.

73. *OR*, 42(2):19, 26; Washington Roebling Journal, Aug. 2, 1864, Roebling Family Papers, Archibald Alexander Library, Rutgers University, New Brunswick; Henry H. B. Chamberlain to "Dearest Minnie," Aug. 3, 1864, Henry H. B. Chamberlain Papers, Gail and Stephen Rudin Civil War Collection, Cornell University, Ithaca; Julius Frederic Ramsdell Diary, Aug. 4, 1865, Julius Frederick Ramsdell Papers, Southern Historical Collection, Louis Round Wilson Library, University of North Carolina, Chapel Hill; Cassedy, *Dear Friends at Home*, 554–56; Plumb, *Your Brother in Arms*, 214. For information on Fort Sedgwick, see Greene,

Campaign of Giants, 357–58. Fort Sedgwick no longer exists, having given way to commercial development in the 1960s.

74. *OR*, 42(2):1155, 1158–60; Jackson, *First Regiment Engineer Troops*, 74–75. Officials at Petersburg National Battlefield have identified what they believe to be evidence of Confederate mining in this area, although the exact configuration of the galleries remains in doubt. Portions of the works at Gracie's and Colquitt's Salients are preserved in Petersburg National Battlefield. Both were named after brigadiers in Beauregard's command.

75. Jackson, *First Regiment Engineer Troops*, 81–82; W. W. Blackford, "Memoirs: First and Last Battles in Virginia," Library of Virginia, Richmond.

76. *OR*, 42(2):24–25, 50–51; Drake, *9th New Jersey*, 238–39; Derby, *Bearing Arms in the 27th Massachusetts*, 363; Emmerton, *Twenty-Third Regiment Massachusetts Volunteer Infantry*, 225.

77. James Parley Coburn to "Ever Dear Parents," Aug. 6, 1864, James Parley Coburn Letters, Thomas Clemens Collection, Army Heritage and Education Center, Carlisle; Henry C. Metzger to his brother, Aug. 6, 1864, Henry C. Metzger Letters and Diary, John L. Nau III Civil War Collection, Houston; Charles Hamlin to "Dear Sister," Aug. 10, 1864, Charles Hamlin Letters, Manuscripts and Special Collections, New York State Library, Albany; John L. Smith to "My Dear Mother," Aug. 7, 1864, John L. Smith Letters, Historical Society of Pennsylvania, Philadelphia; John L. Houck to "Dear Wife," Aug. 7, 1864, John L. Houck Papers, Manuscripts and Special Collections, New York State Library, Albany; William F. Smith to "My Dear Mother," Aug. 7, 1864, William F. Smith Letters; Henry Clay Heisler to "Dear Sister," Aug. 15, 1864, Henry Clay Heisler Papers, Manuscripts Division, Library of Congress, Washington.

78. Henry S. Graves to "Dear Wife," Aug. 7, 1864, Henry S. Graves Letters, Norton Pearl Collection, Western Michigan University, Kalamazoo; Henry F. Young to "Dear Father," Aug. 6, 1864, in Larson and Smith, *Dear Delia*, 256. Neither of these soldiers, nor others like them, were personally in position to witness such an operation, so their reports were likely the product of camp rumor.

79. George H. Moffett to "Dear Liz," Aug. 6, 1864, Moffett Family Papers; Hephner, "Where Youth and Laughter Go," 23–24; Thomas A. McParlin to "Wife," Aug. 7, 1864, Thomas A. McParlin Papers, Richard Sommers Papers, Author's Collection, Walden; "Letter from the 23rd Mass Reg't," *Cape Ann Light and Gloucester Telegraph* (Gloucester, Mass.), Aug. 13, 1864; Robert McAllister to "My dear Ellen," Aug. 6, 1864, in Robertson, *Civil War Letters of General Robert McAllister*, 476 (hereafter Robertson, *McAllister Letters*); *OR*, 42(1):885; Philip McKay to "Dear Brother," Aug. 6, 1864, Philip McKay Papers, Kenan Research Center, Atlanta History Center.

80. Thomas W. G. Inglet to "My Dear Wife," Aug. 12, 1864, T. W. G. Inglet Letters, Library of Virginia, Richmond; James J. Kirkpatrick Diary, Aug. 6, 1864, Briscoe Center for American History, University of Texas, Austin; James Thomas Petty Diary, Virginia Museum of History and Culture, Richmond; Rufus A. Barrier to "Dear Father," Aug. 6, 1864, Barrier Family Letters, Hesburgh Library, University of Notre Dame, South Bend. Some of these men had not been in position to witness the aftermath of the explosion, suggesting that their testimony was derived from camp chatter.

81. *OR*, 42(2):1162–63; Fred Harris to "My dear Aunt," Aug. 8, 1864, David Bullock Harris Papers, Rubenstein Special Collections Library, Duke University, Durham, N.C.; "Special Correspondence, August 10, 1864," *Montgomery (Ala.) Daily Mail*, Aug. 23, 1864; R. Lee Barfield to "My Own Dear Maggie," Aug. 9, 1864, in "Confederate Letters Written by Mr. Lee Barfield of Dooly County, Georgia, 1861–1865," Georgia State Archives, Morrow; Wiley,

Norfolk Blues, 141; Scarborough, *Ruffin Diary*, 527–28. It is likely that the Confederates, realizing that their mine had not damaged the Federals' main works, rationalized the explosion as merely a demonstration of their engineering capabilities.

82. Theodore Lyman to "My Dear Little Woman," Lyman Family Papers, Massachusetts Historical Society, Boston; Chaplain Robert Dickson Diary, Aug. 5, 1864, Historical Society of Pennsylvania, Philadelphia.

83. E. O. C. Ord to "Dearest," Aug. 10, 1864, Ord Letters; *OR*, 42(1):807, 42(2):68–69. Butler, as the senior officer at Petersburg, communicated with Washington because Grant was absent on August 5.

84. Joseph Barlow to "My dear Wife," Aug. 7, 1864, Barlow Papers; Emmerton, *Twenty-Third Regiment Massachusetts Volunteer Infantry*, 225; "Letter from the 23rd Mass Reg't"; Harrison Montague to "Friend Mather," Aug. 7, 1864, Montague Letters; Frank L. Smith to "Dear Father," Aug. 8, 1864, Frank L. Smith Letters, Massachusetts Historical Society, Boston.

85. William Boston to "Dear Aunt," Aug. 7, 1864, William Boston Diary and Letters, Bentley Historical Library, University of Michigan, Ann Arbor; Addison S. Boyce to "Dear Mary," Aug. 5, 1864, copy, Petersburg National Battlefield; Lane, *Soldier's Diary*, 187; William F. Smith to "My Dear Mother," Aug. 7, 1864, William F. Smith Letters; Samuel Ripley to "Dear Mary," Aug. 8, 1864, Samuel Ripley Papers, James S. Schoff Civil War Collection, Clements Library, University of Michigan, Ann Arbor; John D. Timmerman to "Dear Wife," Aug. 7, 1864, John D. Timmerman Papers, Ronald Boyer Collection, Army Heritage and Education Center, Carlisle; Irwin, *Quaker Soldier*, 134; Perry, *Letters from a Surgeon*, 220.

86. *OR*, 42(1):793; Charles M. Coit to "Dear All," July 19, 1864, Capt. Charles M. Coit Papers, Sterling Library, Yale University, New Haven; "From the 11th Regiment," *Connecticut War Record* (New Haven), January 1865.

87. *OR* 42(1):793, 42(2) 65, 69, 71, 82; Tapert, *Brothers' War*, 216–20. The largest Union work in the Hare's Hill area would be named for the slain colonel. Fort Stedman remains in excellent condition and is a primary tour stop at Petersburg National Battlefield.

88. John L. Stuart to "Dear Mother," Aug. 10, 1864, John Lane Stuart Papers, Rubenstein Special Collections Library, Duke University, Durham, N.C.; Dr. Oze Robert Broyles to "My dear Mother," Aug. 6, 1864, copy in bound vol. 88, Richmond National Battlefield Park; Wiley, *Norfolk Blues*, 141.

89. *OR*, 42(2):114; Thomas and Sauers, *Never Want to Witness Such Sights*, 225; Leigh, *J. J. Scroggs's Diary and Letters*, 334; Jordan and Jordan, *Dear Friend Amelia*, 127.

90. Giles Buckner Cooke Diary, Aug. 17, 1864, Virginia Museum of History and Culture, Richmond; Jackson, *First Regiment Engineer Troops*, 90; Cutchins, *A Famous Command—Richmond Light Infantry Blues*, 156; James McHenry Howard, "Biographical Sketch of Walter H. Stevens," Virginia Museum of History and Culture, Richmond.

91. Joseph H. Rogers Diary, Aug. 14–22, Henry E. Huntington Library, Palo Alto; Turtle, "History of the Engineer Battalion," 8–9; Charles Francis Adams Jr. to his mother, Aug. 12, 1864, in Ford, *Cycle of Adams Letters*, 176; McFadden, *Aunt and the Soldier Boys*, 144.

92. Rayburn, "Sabotage at City Point," 31–32.

93. Rice, "Act of Great Daring," 63.

94. Rice, "Act of Great Daring," 63; *OR*, 42(1):954.

95. *OR*, 42(1):955; Rice, "Act of Great Daring," 63–64; Rayburn, "Sabotage at City Point," 31–32. It is unclear whether the African American was a member of the crew or a dockside laborer.

96. B. H. Hibbard to "My Dear Bro George," Aug. 10, 1864, B. H. Hibbard Letters, Albert and Shirley Small Special Collections Library, University of Virginia, Charlottesville; Samuel F. Jayne to "My beloved Charlie," Aug. 9, 1864, Samuel Ferguson Jayne Papers, James S. Schoff Civil War Collection, Clements Library, University of Michigan, Ann Arbor; Theodore Bowers to "My Dear Rowley," Aug. 9, 1864, William R. Rowley Papers, Abraham Lincoln Presidential Library, Springfield; Scarborough, *Ruffin Diary*, 531; Marion Hill Fitzpatrick to "Dear Amanda," Aug. 13, 1864, in Lowe and Hodges, *Letters to Amanda*, 166; and in McCrea, *Red Dirt and Isinglass*, 508; Benjamin Wesley Justice to "My Sweet Darling Wife," Aug. 10, 1864, Benjamin Wesley Justice Letters, Confederate Miscellaneous Collection, Woodruff Library, Emory University, Atlanta. Although some of these descriptions may be embellished, there is no doubt about the explosion's great effect.

97. Styple, *Writing and Fighting the Civil War*, 281; Thompson, *13th Regiment New Hampshire Volunteer Infantry*, 438 (hereafter Thompson, *13th New Hampshire*); Sparks, *Inside Lincoln's Army*, 412; William Foster to "Dear Kate," Aug. 10, 1864, William Foster Papers, Western Reserve Historical Society, Cleveland; Schaff, "Explosion at City Point," 480; Freeman, *Letters from Two Brothers*, 139; Porter, "Explosion at City Point"; Rice, "Act of Great Daring," 63; *OR*, 42(1):955.

98. Blackett, *Thomas Morris Chester*, 95–96; *Richmond Daily Examiner*, Aug. 23, 1864; James Otis Moore to "Dearest Lizzie," Aug. 10, 1864, James Otis Moore Letters, Rubenstein Special Collections Library, Duke University, Durham, N.C. Moore's letter is published in O'Donnell, "'Accidental' Explosion at City Point," 357–58.

99. Solon Carter to "My own darling Em," Aug. 9, 1864, Solon Carter Letters, Army Heritage and Education Center, Carlisle; Thomas, *Three Years with Grant*, 246; Miller, *Drum Taps in Dixie*, 137; Thomas James Owen to "Dear Friends at Home," Aug. 10, 1864, in Floyd, *"Dear Friends at Home,"* 49; Chesson, *Journal of a Civil War Surgeon*, 188; Parker, *Henry Wilson's Regiment*, 485.

100. Rutan, *If I Have Got to Go and Fight*, 118; Schaff, "Explosion at City Point," 481.

101. Holstein, *Three Years in Field Hospitals*, 85; Theodore Bowers to "My Dear Rowley," Aug. 9, 1864, Rowley Papers; *OR*, 42(1):17; Morgan, "From City Point to Appomattox," 236; Theodore Lyman to "My Dear Minnette," Aug. 14, 1864, Lyman Family Papers. Some reports list only one of the orderlies fatally wounded.

102. *OR*, 42(2):102, 112.

103. Pvt. Thomas Reed to "Dear Gal," Aug. 13, 1864, in Spies, *Yours Only*, 170–71; Palladino, *Diary of a Yankee Engineer*, 157; Pvt. Edward Griswold to "Dear Sister," Aug. 12, 1864, Griswold Family Papers, Rubenstein Special Collections Library, Duke University, Durham, N.C.; Joseph Hawley to "My Darling," Aug. 9, 1864, Joseph Hawley Correspondence and Papers, Manuscripts Division, Library of Congress, Washington.

104. Reed, *War Papers of Frank B. Fay*, 127; *Philadelphia Weekly Press*, Aug. 12, 1864; William Foster to "Dear Kate," Aug. 10, 1864, Foster Papers; Styple, *Writing and Fighting the Civil War*, 281.

105. *OR*, 42(2):96; Lane, *Soldier's Diary*, 188; Cole, *Freedom's Witness*, 137; Robertson, *McAllister Letters*, 480.

106. Joseph Barlow to "My dear Wife," Aug. 10, 1864, Barlow Papers; "Letter from the 23d Mass Regt," *Cape Ann Light and Gloucester Telegraph* (Gloucester, Mass.), Aug. 20, 1864; George Naylor Julian to "My Dear Parents," Aug. 10, 1864, George Naylor Julian Papers, University of New Hampshire, Durham, N.H.; Marion Hill Fitzpatrick to "Dear Amanda," Aug.

13, 1864, in McCrea, *Red Dirt and Isinglass*, 508; "From Petersburg," *Richmond Daily Dispatch*, Aug. 12, 1864; Henry S. Graves to "Dear Wife," Aug. 10, 1864, Graves Letters.

107. John Daniel Follmer, "Three Years in the Army," entry of Aug. 9, 1864, Civil War Collection of Personal Papers, Clarke Historical Library, Central Michigan University, Mount Pleasant; "A War Echo: Diary of an Old Fourteenth Regiment Soldier," *Brooklyn (N.Y.) Daily Standard-Union*, June 4, 1892; Carter, *Four Brothers in Blue*, 474; Blackford, *Letters from Lee's Army*, 272.

108. *OR*, 42(2):197; Porter, *Campaigning with Grant*, 274–75.

109. There are a number of monographs that deal with events in the Shenandoah Valley in June and July 1864. One good option is B. F. Cooling, *Jubal Early's Raid on Washington*.

110. *OR*, 37(2):223; Greene, "Union Generalship in the 1864 Valley Campaign," 41–42. For an excellent description of these battles and the entire campaign in July and early August, see Patchan, *Shenandoah Summer*.

111. Glatthaar, *Partners in Command*, 212–14; Simon, *Grant Papers*, 11:308–10; *OR*, 37(2):444; Basler, *Collected Works of Abraham Lincoln*, 7:469–70. The burning of Chambersburg, Pennsylvania, is covered in Haselberger, *Confederate Retaliation*, 75–101.

112. *OR*, 37(2):558, 582; Basler, *Collected Works of Abraham Lincoln*, 7:476. For discussions of the July 31 meeting between Lincoln and Grant, see McPherson, *Tried by War*, 227–29; and Rafuse, "Wherever Lee Goes," 73.

113. *OR*, 37(2):572, 582; Rauscher, *Music on the March*, 200; Porter, *Campaigning with Grant*, 272.

114. Agassiz, *Meade's Headquarters*, 210; Wert, *From Winchester to Cedar Creek*, 12; Theodore Lyman to "My Dearest," Aug. 15, 1864, Lyman Family Papers; Walter Wallace Smith to "Dear Parents," Aug. 11, 1864, Walter Wallace Smith Papers, Rubenstein Special Collections Library, Duke University, Durham, N.C.; Rafuse, *Meade and the War in the East*, 146; Meade, *Life and Letters*, 218–19. Halleck retained reservations about Sheridan in independent command despite his critical role in advancing Sheridan's early wartime career. See Nash, "In the Right Place and at the Right Time," 156–57, 160.

115. *OR*, 42(2):48; Sparks, *Inside Lincoln's Army*, 409; Theodore Bowers to William R. Rowley, Aug. 9, 1864, Rowley Papers; George Meade to Dear Margaret, Aug. 9, 10, 1864, Meade Papers. Meade's original letters differ from the edited versions published in Meade, *Life and Letters*. The best summary of Meade's relationship with Grant is Rafuse, "Wherever Lee Goes."

116. *OR*, 40(3):714. The composition of Sheridan's force is described in Greene, "Union Generalship in the 1864 Valley Campaign," 45–47.

117. *OR*, 37(2):559, 42(2):39, 46–47, 53; Henry Halleck to Ulysses S. Grant, Aug. 2, 1864, Philip H. Sheridan Papers, Manuscripts Division, Library of Congress, Washington; Frederick Augustus Buhl Diary, Aug. 1, 4, 1864, King Family Papers, Bentley Historical Library, University of Michigan, Ann Arbor; Beaudry, ed., *War Journals of Louis N. Beaudry*, 153–54.

118. Wert, "Jubal A. Early and Confederate Leadership," 21, 24; Gallagher, "Two Generals and a Valley," 9.

119. *OR*, 42(2):1161; R. E. Lee to R. H. Anderson, Aug. 10, 1864, Civil War Letters Collection, Manuscripts and Special Collections, New-York Historical Society, New York; Hugh Randolph Crichton to "Dear Jennie," Aug. 11, 1864, Lucy Tunstall Alston Williams Papers, Southern Historical Collection, Louis Round Wilson Library, University of North Carolina, Chapel Hill; Scarborough, *Ruffin Diary*, 531–32.

120. Grimsley, "Lack of Confidence," 105; Twain quoted in Newsome, *Richmond Must Fall*, 23; Horowitz, "Benjamin Butler," 193; Joseph Hawley to his wife, June 20, 1864, Hawley Correspondence and Papers.

121. Butler, *Butler's Book*, 744; Ames, "Dutch Gap Canal," 30–31; Longacre, *Regiment of Slaves*, 110; *OR*, 40(3):570–71. Dutch Gap may have received its name in memory of a German immigrant who had tried unsuccessfully to create a canal there many years previously, or it may reference "Dale's Dutch Gap," a defensive ditch around Thomas Dale's settlement at Henricus town.

122. *OR*, 42(1):657–58, 42(2):70; Daniel Eldredge Journal, 2:247, New Hampshire Historical Society, Concord; Brady, *Story of One Regiment*, 232; Charles Kline to "Dear Mother and Sister," Aug. 7, 1864, Kline Civil War Letters; Theodore Lyman to "My Dear Little Woman," Aug. 17, 1864, Lyman Family Papers; Longacre, *Army of Amateurs*, 192–95. Michie held the brevet rank of major.

123. Trudeau, *Like Men of War*, 283–84; R. E. Lee to "My Dear Mary," Aug. 14, 1864, in Dowdey and Manarin, *Wartime Papers of R. E. Lee*, 836–37; Gustavus S. Dana to Capt. Lemuel Norton, Aug. 13, 1864, Benjamin F. Butler Papers, Manuscripts Division, Library of Congress, Washington; *OR*, 42(2):1168; Coski, *Capital Navy*, 166–67.

CHAPTER TWO

1. Field, "Campaign of 1864 and 1865," 551; Manarin, *Henrico County—Field of Honor*, 446 (hereafter Manarin, *Field of Honor*).

2. James I. Robertson Jr., "Charles W. Field," in Current, *Encyclopedia of the Confederacy*, 571; McArthur and Burton, *Gentleman and an Officer*, 98–99. Hood had been sent west in September 1863 and ten months later took command of the Army of Tennessee.

3. Powell, "Memory of Our Great War," 88. The Confederate order of battle is listed in Suderow, "Nothing but a Miracle," 20. For the three best modern accounts of the action at Second Deep Bottom, see Suderow, "Nothing but a Miracle"; Manarin, *Field of Honor*; and Horn, *Siege of Petersburg*. Their collective wisdom is inherent in my account.

4. Price, *First Deep Bottom*, 115; Greene, *Campaign of Giants*, 401; Suderow, "Nothing but a Miracle," 12; Manarin, *Field of Honor*, 452; U.S. War Department, *War of the Rebellion*, ser. 1, 40(3):761–62 (hereafter *OR*; all references are to series 1 unless otherwise noted). Field's five brigades numbered 5,952 present for duty in mid-July, while Lane's and McGowan's Brigades represented perhaps half of Wilcox's 5,581 men. Both Lane and McGowan were brigadier generals. Colonel Barbour sometimes spelled his name "Barber."

5. Pfanz, *Richard S. Ewell*, 402–5; Jones, *Campbell Brown's Civil War*, 266–67; *OR*, 40(3):822, 42(2):1164–65.

6. Stowits, *One-Hundredth Regiment of New York Volunteers*, 328 (hereafter Stowits, *100th New York*); Greene, *Campaign of Giants*, 234. For a description of the operations at First Deep Bottom, see Price, *First Deep Bottom*; and Greene, *Campaign of Giants*, 399–418.

7. McCabe, *Life and Campaigns of General Robert E. Lee*, 522; William E. Endicott to "Dear Mother," Aug. 18, 1864, William E. Endicott Papers, Special Collections, Auburn University.

8. Simon, *Grant Papers*, 11:401, 403; Grant, *Personal Memoirs*, 321; Porter, *Campaigning with Grant*, 276; Walker, *Second Army Corps*, 568–69, 612; Humphreys, *Virginia Campaign of '64 and '65*, 268; Manarin, *Field of Honor*, 452, 457; *OR*, 42(2):136, 162. Lee did detach Hampton's cavalry division on August 11 with orders to go as far west as Culpeper. See *OR*,

42(2):1170–71. The strength of Hancock's force is only speculative. Official returns for the Second Corps counted 14,857 present for duty. Birney's strength is generally estimated at 9,000, while Gregg's cavalry numbered 4,215, yielding a total of 28,072. See *OR*, 40(3):728, 737. The closest students of the operation offer conflicting numbers: Manarin, *Field of Honor*, 457 (over 27,000); Suderow, "Nothing but a Miracle," 12 (29,000); and Horn, *Siege of Petersburg*, 18 (as many as 38,000).

9. *OR*, 42(2):124, 131–33, 135–36; Longacre, *Army of Amateurs*, 195–96. For Grant's orders at First Deep Bottom, see *OR*, 40(3):437–38.

10. *OR*, 42(2):131–33, 42(1):339; James C. Hamilton, "History of the 110th Pennsylvania," Union League of Philadelphia, 192; Houghton, *17th Maine*, 222; Jacob Lyons Diary, Aug. 12, 1864, Southern Historical Collection, Louis Round Wilson Library, University of North Carolina, Chapel Hill; Matthews, *Soldiers in Green*, 250; Meier, *Memoirs of a Swiss Officer*, 177; Pomfret, "Letters of Frederick Lockley," 87; Frederick Lockley Journal, 344, Frederick Lockley Papers, Henry E. Huntington Library, San Marino; Samuel B. Pierce to "Dear Brother," Aug. 21, 1864, Samuel B. Pierce Letters, Manuscripts and Special Collections, New York State Library, Albany; Crotty, *Four Years Campaigning*, 151; Baker, *Letters Home*, 202–3; Welch, *Boy General*, 184; Powelson, *Company K of the 140th Pa*, 39. Smyth temporarily replaced the ailing John Gibbon in command of Hancock's Second Division. See Gibbon, *Personal Recollections*, 254.

11. Washburn, *Military History and Record of the 108th Regiment N.Y. Volunteers*, 84 (hereafter Washburn, *108th New York*); Weygant, *124th New York*, 362; John Buttrick Noyes to "Dear Mother," Aug. 16, 1864, John Buttrick Noyes Civil War Letters, Houghton Library, Harvard University, Cambridge; Pomfret, "Letters of Frederick Lockley," 87; Meier, *Memoirs of a Swiss Officer*, 177.

12. Paxton, *Sword and Gown*, 392; Robertson, *McAllister Letters*, 480; Hoisington, *My Heart toward Home*, 364; Ripley, *Vermont Riflemen*, 193; Hamilton, "110th Pennsylvania," 193.

13. Houghton, *17th Maine*, 223; Carter, *Four Brothers in Blue*, 476; Marbaker, *11th New Jersey*, 207; Waitt, *19th Regiment Massachusetts Volunteer Infantry*, 345 (hereafter Waitt, *19th Massachusetts*); Smith, *19th Maine*, 224; George B. Smith Reminiscences, 1864–1865, Minnesota Historical Society, Saint Paul, 31; Myers, *We Might as Well Die Here*, 222; George C. Hand Diary, Aug. 12, 1864, copy, Petersburg National Battlefield; *OR*, 42(1):292; Kirk, *Heavy Guns and Light*, 327; Pomfret, "Letters of Frederick Lockley," 87; White, *Civil War Diary of Wyman S. White*, 277; Miller, *Harvard's Civil War*, 404.

14. *OR*, 42(2):136, 140–41, 42(1):216–17; Manarin, *Field of Honor*, 457; Suderow, "Nothing but a Miracle," 12–13.

15. *OR*, 42(1):217; Walker, *Second Army Corps*, 569–70.

16. *OR*, 42(2):149, 42(1):217.

17. Benjamin M. Peck Diary, Aug. 13, 1864, Special Collections, Carol M. Newman Library, Virginia Tech University, Blacksburg; Keating, *Carnival of Blood*, 242; Matthews, *Soldiers in Green*, 250; Silliker, *Rebel Yell & the Yankee Hurrah*, 189; Weygant, *124th New York*, 363; Stewart, *140th Pennsylvania*, 229; Hoisington, *My Heart Toward Home*, 364; Samuel Ripley to "Dear Mary," Aug. 15, 1864, Ripley Papers, Clements Library, University of Michigan, Ann Arbor; Walker, *Second Army Corps*, 569.

18. Weygant, *124th New York*, 363; *OR*, 42(1):241; Stewart, *140th Pennsylvania*, 229; Miller, *Harvard's Civil War*, 404; Myers, *We Might as Well Die Here*, 222; Mulholland, *116th Pa Volunteer Infantry*, 252 (hereafter Mulholland, *116th Pennsylvania*); Boyle, *Party of Mad Fellows*, 371;

Lafayette Church to "My dear Susie," Aug. 15, 1864, Lafayette and Nathan Church Letters, Clarke Historical Library, Central Michigan University, Mount Pleasant.

19. Ripley, *Vermont Riflemen*, 193; Gibbs, King, and Northrup, *Ninety-Third New York*, 81; Hamilton, "110th Pennsylvania," 193; Hand Diary, Aug. 13, 1864; Myers, *We Might as Well Die Here*, 222; Jordan, *Winfield Scott Hancock*, 156; Carter, *Four Brothers in Blue*, 476; Smith, *19th Maine*, 224; Miller, *Harvard's Civil War*, 404; Paxton, *Sword and Gown*, 392; Meier, *Memoirs of a Swiss Officer*, 177–78; Silliker, *Rebel Yell & the Yankee Hurrah*, 189–90; Houghton, *17th Maine*, 223.

20. Mulholland, *116th Pennsylvania*, 252–53; Lafayette Church to "My dear Susie," Aug. 15, 1864, Church Letters.

21. Lockley Journal, 346; George C. Walters Diary, Aug. 14, 1864, Walters Diary and Letters, bound vol. 261, Fredericksburg & Spotsylvania National Military Park; *OR*, 42(1):217; Weygant, *124th New York*, 363–64; Townsend, "Reminiscences of the 17th Maine," University of Maine, Orono. This last source is the journal of John W. Haley, which differs substantially from the published version, Silliker, *Rebel Yell & the Yankee Hurrah*.

22. *OR*, 42(1):340, 217, 247, 241; Marbaker, *11th New Jersey*, 207; Miller, *Harvard's Civil War*, 403–4; Smith, *19th Maine*, 224–25; Kirk, *Heavy Guns and Light*, 327–28. Multiple sources provide timing for the arrival on shore, ranging from 4:00 to 9:00 A.M., but it seems reasonable that most of Hancock's troops were on the ground between 7:30 and 8:00 A.M., save for the units of Broady's brigade, whose vessel had grounded downriver, and the Fifty-Third Pennsylvania, which assisted with the construction of the landing facilities.

23. Briscoe, "Visit to General Butler," 439; Keyes, *Lewis Atterbury Stimson, M.D.*, 40; Silas Edward Mead to "My Dear Friend," Oct. 5, 1864, Silas Edward Mead Papers, William E. Finch Jr. Archives, Greenwich Historical Society; Theodore Lyman to "Dove Mimileiu," Nov. 12, 1864, Lyman Letters, Massachusetts Historical Society, Boston.

24. *OR*, 42(2):163–64. Two of Birney's four regiments served previously in north Florida and two at Hilton Head, South Carolina. They arrived in Virginia on August 12 and the next day formed a brigade.

25. *OR*, 42(2):162–63.

26. Towle Diary, Aug. 13, 1864, New Hampshire Historical Society, Concord; *OR*, 42(1):687, 724; Clark, *Thirty-Ninth Regiment Illinois Volunteer Veteran Infantry*, 162 (hereafter Clark, *Thirty-Ninth Illinois*); Little, *Seventh Regiment New Hampshire Volunteers*, 290–91 (hereafter Little, *Seventh New Hampshire*); Nicholas De Graff Diary, Aug. 14, 1864, *Civil War Times Illustrated* Collection, Army Heritage and Education Center, Carlisle; James M. Nichols Diary, Aug. 13, 1864, New York Military Museum, Saratoga Springs; Price, *Ninety-Seventh Regiment, Pennsylvania Volunteer Infantry*, 314; Beecher, *First Light Battery*, 539–40. The batteries included the First Connecticut; Fourth New Jersey; Battery C, Third Rhode Island; and Batteries C and D, First U.S. Artillery.

27. Weigley, "David McMurtrie Gregg," 10; Wilson, *Under the Old Flag*, 364.

28. *OR*, 42(1):39, 80, 42(2):135; Lloyd, *1st Regiment Pa Reserve Cavalry*, 110–11; Capt. John W. Haseltine Diary, Aug. 13, 1864, typescript in bound vol. 146, Richmond National Battlefield Park; Wells A. Bushnell Memoir, Western Reserve Historical Society, Cleveland, 305–6. The July returns counted 182 officers and 4,033 enlisted men present for duty in Gregg's division. See *OR*, 40(3):728.

29. *OR*, 42(2):149–50. William Jennings died in 1853, manumitting his slaves to Liberia, and his widow moved to Richmond. The house may have been abandoned or in ruins by 1864. My thanks to Edward Alexander for providing information on the Jennings house.

30. Maxfield and Brady, *Roster & Statistical Record of Company D of the Eleventh Regiment Maine Infantry*, 41 (hereafter Maxfield and Brady, *Company D, Eleventh Maine*); "From the Tenth Connecticut," *Hartford (CT) Daily Courant*, Aug. 24, 1864; *OR*, 42(1):745; "Field's Division," *Richmond Daily Enquirer*, Aug. 31, 1864; Manarin, *Field of Honor*, 456.

31. *OR*, 42(2):172, 42(1):738, 745, 751, 754; Suderow, "Nothing but a Miracle," 16; Maxfield and Brady, *Company D, Eleventh Maine*, 41; "From the Tenth Connecticut," Aug. 24, 1864; Trumbull, *Knightly Soldier*, 257–58; Bratton, "Report of Operations," 552. One Federal claimed that Colonel Pond "got behind a tree and laughed idiotically." See Clendaniel, *Such Hard & Severe Service*, 71. A detailed account of this action, illustrated with several maps, is in Manarin, *Field of Honor*, 462–70.

32. *OR*, 42(1):217, 241, 340, 357–58; Hamilton, "110th Pennsylvania," 193; Houghton, *17th Maine*, 223–24; Hays, *Under the Red Patch*, 268–69; Erasmus C. Gilbreath Reminiscences, Indiana Division, Indiana State Library, Indianapolis; Suderow, "Nothing but a Miracle," 17; Manarin, *Field of Honor*, 470–71. Bailey's Creek flows into Four Mile Creek before emptying into the James. Some of Conner's men apparently supplemented Bratton's troops along the Confederate picket lines.

33. Walker, *Second Army Corps*, 572; Roback, *Veteran Volunteers of Herkimer and Otsego Counties in the War of the Rebellion, Being a History of the 152nd N.Y.V.*, 114 (hereafter Roback, *152nd New York*); John Buttrick Noyes to "Dear Mother," Aug. 16, 1864, Noyes Civil War Letters.

34. Manarin, *Field of Honor*, 471–72; *OR*, 42(1):292. Walker thought that Hancock assigned Barlow responsibility for Smyth's division in part to pave the way for Barlow's promotion to major general. See Walker, *Second Army Corps*, 572.

35. For a brilliant synopsis of Barlow's civilian background and military record, see Waugh, "Francis Channing Barlow's Civil War," 138–75. For a full biography of Barlow, with emphasis on the Civil War years, see Welch, *Boy General*. Diarrhea, combined with the effects of Barlow's previous wounds, compromised his health.

36. George Emerson Albee Diary, Aug. 15, 1864, Library of Virginia, Richmond; Bruce, *Twentieth Regiment of Massachusetts Volunteer Infantry*, 416 (hereafter Bruce, *Twentieth Massachusetts*); *OR*, 42(1):241, 292; Manarin, *Field of Honor*, 472–73. The Consolidated Brigade, created on June 27, 1864, combined the Second and Third Brigades of Barlow's division.

37. *OR*, 42(1):727–28, 758; Nichols Diary, Aug. 14, 1864; John Lafayette Oxford Diary, Aug. 14, 1864, Confederate Miscellaneous Collection, Woodruff Library, Emory University, Atlanta; Manarin, *Field of Honor*, 473; Horn, *Siege of Petersburg*, 35. Pemberton had positioned these guns close enough to Deep Bottom to reach the Union pontoon bridge there, but because of their short range, they lay outside the Confederate fortifications at New Market Heights. See Horn, *Siege of Petersburg*, 7.

38. Field, "Campaign of 1864 and 1865," 551–52; Manarin, *Field of Honor*, 473; Horn, *Siege of Petersburg*, 32.

39. *OR*, 42(1):248, 267, 291, 42(2):173; Manarin, *Field of Honor*, 475–76; Suderow, "Nothing but a Miracle," 19, 21. Bryce Suderow times Hogg's attack as commencing before 1:00 P.M.

40. *OR*, 42(1):248; Myers, *We Might as Well Die Here*, 223; Keating, *Carnival of Blood*, 244; Manarin, *Field of Honor*, 476–77; Suderow, "Nothing but a Miracle," 21; Horn, *Siege of Petersburg*, 33.

41. *OR*, 42(1):248, 292; Suderow, "Nothing but a Miracle," 21; Miller, *Harvard's Civil War*, 407. For information on Colonel Macy, see Macy, *Genealogy of the Macy Family*.

42. Miller, *Harvard's Civil War*, 406–7; Smith, *19th Maine*, 227; Suderow, "Nothing but a Miracle," 21.

43. "To the Editor of the *Examiner*," *Richmond Daily Examiner*, Sept. 2, 1864; Suderow, "Nothing but a Miracle," 21.

44. *OR*, 42(1):292; Samuel Ripley to "Dear Mary," Aug. 15, 1864, Ripley Papers; Miller, *Harvard's Civil War*, 407–8; Smith, *19th Maine*, 227; John Buttrick Noyes to "Dear Father," Aug. 14, 1864, Noyes Civil War Letters. Lt. Col. Horace P. Rugg of the Fifty-Ninth New York assumed command of Macy's brigade.

45. Sturkey, *Hampton Legion Infantry*, 87; W. A. Kelly Diary, Aug. 14, 1864, Kelly Papers, College of Charleston; "Field's Division"; *OR*, 42(1):316; E. B. Quiner manuscript regimental history, Clement E. Warner Papers, Wisconsin Historical Society, Madison; Aubery, *Thirty-Sixth Wisconsin*, 116; Suderow, "Nothing but a Miracle," 21.

46. *OR*, 42(1):248, 292; David Coon to "Dear Wife," Aug. 15, 1864, David Coon Civil War Letters, Wisconsin Historical Society, Madison. Casualty figures are provided in many of the after-action reports in *OR*, 42(1). For a summary, see Manarin *Field of Honor*, 479–80. Bryce Suderow numbers Confederate casualties at thirty-seven but provides no documentation for this figure. Suderow, "Nothing but a Miracle," 22.

47. *OR*, 42(1):81; Manarin, *Field of Honor*, 471–72; Lloyd, *1st Regiment Pa Reserve Cavalry*, 111; Tobie, *First Maine Cavalry*, 307.

48. *OR*, 42(1):637, 42(2):179; Manarin, *Field of Honor*, 481–82; Tobie, *First Maine Cavalry*, 307–8; Haseltine Diary, Aug. 14, 1864; Webb Diary, Aug. 14, 1864, Clements Library, University of Michigan, Ann Arbor.

49. Blackett, *Thomas Morris Chester*, 102–3; Joseph H. Prime to "Dear Wife," Aug. 20, 1864, Joseph H. Prime Papers, Hesburgh Library, University of Notre Dame, South Bend; Califf, *Seventh Regiment, U.S. Colored Troops*, 34–35 (hereafter Califf, *Seventh U.S. Colored Troops*); Dobak, *Freedom by the Sword*, 370; Samuel Armstrong to "Dear Mother," Aug. 18, 1864, typescript in bound vol. 112, Richmond National Battlefield Park.

50. Walker, *Second Army Corps*, 574–75; Field, "Campaign of 1864 and 1865," 552; Horn, *Siege of Petersburg*, 45–46.

51. *OR*, 42(2):167–69. In fact, Lee had ordered Field's Division to go to the Shenandoah Valley, but Grant's offensive canceled this departure.

52. Dowdey and Manarin, *Wartime Papers of R. E. Lee*, 835–38; Field, "Campaign of 1864 and 1865," 552; Caldwell, *History of a Brigade of South Carolinians First Known as "Gregg's" and Subsequently as "McGowan's Brigade,"* 229 (hereafter Caldwell, *McGowan's Brigade*); Manarin, *Field of Honor*, 483–84; Suderow, "Nothing but a Miracle," 22.

53. *OR*, 42(2):174–75. These orders refer to Darbytown Road as "Central Road."

54. Califf, *Seventh U.S. Colored Troops*, 35; *OR*, 42(1):688, 724, 728; Little, *Seventh New Hampshire*, 291; Towle Diary, Aug. 14, 1864; Beecher, *First Light Battery*, 542; Clark, *Thirty-Ninth Illinois*, 162; Dickey, *85th Regiment, Pennsylvania Volunteer Infantry*, 366 (hereafter Dickey, *85th Pennsylvania*); Waite, *New Hampshire in the Great Rebellion*, 207; Alfred Howe Terry to "Dear Hatty," Sept. 3, 1864, Terry Papers, Connecticut Historical Society, Hartford; Nichols Diary, Aug. 15, 1864; "Knapsack," *The Traveler*, Aug. 29, 1864, letters, https://civilwarletters.com; Manarin, *Field of Honor*, 483; Horn, *Siege of Petersburg*, 49. The Twenty-Ninth Connecticut was an African American unit.

55. *OR*, 42(1):710, 746; Alfred Howe Terry to "Dear Hatty," Sept. 3, 1864, Terry Papers; Manarin, *Field of Honor*, 487; Eldredge, *Third New Hampshire*, 519.

56. Leo, "Forty-Eighth Regiment," quoted in Styple, *Writing and Fighting the Civil War*, 283; Stowits, *100th New York*, 287; *OR*, 42(1):710; Eldredge, *Third New Hampshire*, 520.

57. *OR*, 42(2):174, 42(1):340, 358; Houghton, *17th Maine*, 224; de Trobriand, *Four Years with the Army*, 629; Townsend, "Reminiscences of the 17th Maine"; Weygant, *124th New York*, 365.

58. *OR*, 42(1):218, 340, 42(2):204; Preston, *Tenth Regiment of New York Cavalry*, 224 (hereafter Preston, *Tenth New York Cavalry*).

59. William A. Curtis, "Reminiscences of the War," Confederate Veteran Collection, Rubenstein Special Collections Library, Duke University, Durham, N.C.; Manarin, *Field of Honor*, 483–84.

60. *OR*, 42(1):637; Harrell, *2nd North Carolina Cavalry*, 311–12; George W. Flack Diary, Aug. 15, 1864, copy in bound vol. 260, Fredericksburg & Spotsylvania National Military Park.

61. *OR*, 42(1):241–42, 249, 362–63; Curtis, "Reminiscences"; Gibbs, King, and Northrup, *Ninety-Third New York*, 81; Carter, *Four Brothers in Blue*, 476–77; Meier, *Memoirs of a Swiss Officer*, 178–79; Harrell, *2nd North Carolina Cavalry*, 312–13; Peck Diary, Aug. 15, 1864; Manarin, *Field of Honor*, 489–92, 494. John Horn estimates that the Unionists lost about 100 men on August 15 and the Confederates half as many. See Horn, *Siege of Petersburg*, 57.

62. *OR*, 42(2):200, 207–8, 42(1):218.

63. William Andrew Mauney Diary, Aug. 15, 1864, Eleanor S. Brockenbrough Library, Museum of the Confederacy, Richmond; Harris, *Historical Sketches of the Seventh Regiment North Carolina Troops*, 54 (hereafter Harris, *Seventh North Carolina*); Hardy, *General Lee's Immortals*, 322; Caldwell, *McGowan's Brigade*, 230; Axford, *Fielding's Diary*, 127; Williams, *Rebel Brothers*, 105–6, 110–11.

64. *OR*, 42(2):1177; Andrew, *Wade Hampton*, 231; Tower, *Lee's Adjutant*, 181; Freeman, *R. E. Lee*, 482; John William McLure to "My Dearest Kate," Aug. 17, 1864, McLure Family Papers, South Caroliniana Library, University of South Carolina, Columbia. It is uncertain why Lee chose to ride in an ambulance that afternoon.

65. Robert E. Simms Diary, Aug. 15, 1864, Army Heritage and Education Center, Carlisle; Edward Richardson Crockett Diary, Aug. 15, 1864, Edward Richardson Crockett Diary and Papers, Martin L. Crimmins Collection, Briscoe Center for American History, University of Texas, Austin; Bratton, "Report of Operations," 552; Schmutz, *Bloody Fifth*, 225; "Field's Division"; Field, "Campaign of 1864 and 1865," 552.

66. Doster, *Fourth Pennsylvania Cavalry*, 95; Holmes, *Horse Soldiers in Blue*, 177; Tobie, *First Maine Cavalry*, 309; Mohr and Winslow, *Cormany Diaries*, 464; Child, *5th Regiment, New Hampshire Volunteers*, 286 (hereafter Child, *5th New Hampshire*); *OR*, 42(1):250; Manarin, *Field of Honor*, 497–98; Horn, *Siege of Petersburg*, 61.

67. Mohr and Winslow, *Cormany Diaries*, 465; Tobie, *First Maine Cavalry*, 309; Doster, *Fourth Pennsylvania Cavalry*, 95; Romig, *Phipps' Letters*, 67; Webb Diary, Aug. 16, 1864; *OR*, 42(1):637.

68. *OR*, 42(1):637; Holmes, *Horse Soldiers in Blue*, 177; Mohr and Winslow, *Cormany Diaries*, 465; Doster, *Fourth Pennsylvania Cavalry*, 95–96. Gregg would return to duty in the fall.

69. Barringer, *Fighting for General Lee*, 164; Mohr and Winslow, *Cormany Diaries*, 465–66; Romig, *Phipps' Letters*, 67; Theodore Lyman to "My Dearest Little Wife," Aug. 20, 1864, Lyman Family Papers, Massachusetts Historical Society, Boston; Harrell, *2nd North Carolina Cavalry*, 314; "Late Cavalry Fighting on the Charles City Road," *Richmond Semi-Weekly Enquirer*, Aug. 23, 1864; Beale, *Ninth Virginia Cavalry*, 137.

70. *OR*, 42(2):228, 253–54, 1189; Balfour, *13th Virginia Cavalry*, 36–37; Horn, *Siege of Petersburg*, 63.

71. Krick, *9th Virginia Cavalry*, 29; Beale, *Ninth Virginia Cavalry*, 137–38; Daughtry, *Gray Cavalier*, 202; Byrd C. Willis Diary, Aug. 16, 1864, Library of Virginia, Richmond; Horn, *Siege of Petersburg*, 63; Manarin, *Field of Honor*, 499–500.

72. *Hillsborough (N.C.) Recorder*, Aug. 24, 1864; Roberts, "Additional Sketch Nineteenth Regiment," 104; Rufus Barringer, "The First North Carolina: A Famous Cavalry Regiment," *Charlotte (N.C.) Democrat*, Feb. 15, 1895; Trout, *Galloping Thunder*, 562; Wade Hampton Connected Narrative, Hampton Family Papers, South Caroliniana Library, University of South Carolina, Columbia, 66; Longacre, *Gentleman and Soldier*, 207; Crockett Diary, Aug. 16, 1864; Schmutz, *Bloody Fifth*, 225; Joe Joskins [Robert Campbell], "A Sketch of Hood's Texas Brigade of the Virginia Army," Historical Research Center, Texas Heritage Museum, Hill College, Hillsboro, 182–84; Manarin, *Field of Honor*, 500–501.

73. *OR*, 42(1):616, 639, 42(2):223–24, 229; Manarin, *Field of Honor*, 501; Horn, *Siege of Petersburg*, 64.

74. Edmond A. Hatcher to "My own Dear Florence," Aug. 17, 1864, copy in bound vol. 292, Fredericksburg & Spotsylvania National Military Park; "Late Cavalry Fighting on the Charles City Road"; Curtis, "Reminiscences"; Tobie, *First Maine Cavalry*, 311.

75. *OR*, 42(1):242; Doster, *Fourth Pennsylvania Cavalry*, 96; Follmer, "Three Years in the Army," entry of Aug. 16, 1864, Civil War Collection of Personal Papers, Clarke Historical Library, Central Michigan University, Mount Pleasant; Haseltine Diary, Aug. 16, 1864; Holmes, *Horse Soldiers in Blue*, 178; Polley, *Hood's Texas Brigade*, 250; Robert E. Fitzgerald Diary, Aug. 16, 1864, Eiserman (Private) Collection, Carlisle.

76. *OR*, 42(2):229–30, 42(1):640, 116, 121; Crockett Diary, Aug. 16, 1864; Curtis, "Reminiscences"; Polley, *Hood's Texas Brigade*, 251; *Richmond Semi-Weekly Enquirer*, Aug. 23, 1864. "D.B.R." was probably Pvt. David B. Rea of the Fifth North Carolina Cavalry. Thanks to Robert E. L. Krick for identifying this soldier correspondent.

77. Roe, *Twenty-Fourth Massachusetts*, 340.

78. Alfred Howe Terry to "Dear Hatty," Sept. 3, 1864, Terry Papers; Towle Diary, Aug. 16, 1864. Evidently, Birney failed to conduct a reconnaissance prior to ordering Terry's assault, and with equal culpability, neither Barlow nor Hancock, who knew of the millpond's existence, communicated its presence to Birney.

79. Croffut and Morris, *Connecticut during the War*, 651; Eldredge Journal, vols. 3 and 6, New Hampshire Historical Society, Concord; Eldredge, *Third New Hampshire*, 520; Beecher, *First Light Battery*, 543; Brady, *Eleventh Maine*, 243; "From the Tenth Connecticut," Aug. 24, 1864; *OR*, 46(1):746.

80. Marino, "General Alfred Howe Terry," 324; Maxfield and Brady, *Company D, Eleventh Maine*, 43.

81. Samuel H. Root Diary, Aug. 16, 1864, Civil War Documents Collection, Army Heritage and Education Center, Carlisle; Beecher, *First Light Battery*, 543; *OR*, 42(1):728, 363, 688; Little, *Seventh New Hampshire*, 292; Maxfield and Brady, *Company D, Eleventh Maine*, 43.

82. Caldwell, *McGowan's Brigade*, 230; Harris, *Seventh North Carolina*, 54; Dunlop, *Lee's Sharpshooters*, 147; Axford, *Fielding's Diary*, 127–28; Thomson, "John C. C. Sanders," 105; *Richmond Daily Enquirer*, Aug. 31, 1864; Manarin, *Field of Honor*, 494; Horn, *Siege of Petersburg*, 73. It is possible that the Ninth and Eleventh Georgia were not in position until after the Union attack.

83. Field, "Campaign of 1864 and 1865," 552; *OR*, 42(1):746; Manarin, *Field of Honor*, 503.

84. Wiggins, *My Dear Friend*, 146; Allardice, *Confederate Colonels*, 52–53. For biographical information on Girardey and his performance at the Crater, see Greene, *Campaign of Giants*, 469–75. Brig. Gen. Ambrose "Rans" Wright had been the Georgia brigade's commander but remained on sick leave.

85. *OR*, 42(2):235; Towle Diary, Aug. 16, 1864; "From the Tenth Connecticut," Aug. 24, 1864; Maxfield and Brady, *Company D, Eleventh Maine*, 43.

86. *OR*, 42(1):739, 746–47; Trumbull, *Knightly Soldier*, 259; Maxfield and Brady, *Company D, Eleventh Maine*, 43; "From the Tenth Connecticut," Aug. 24, 1864.

87. *OR*, 42(2):236, 42(1):688, 696; Dickey, *85th Pennsylvania*, 366; Eldredge, *Third New Hampshire*, 520; Walkey, *Seventh Connecticut*, 161; Horn, *Siege of Petersburg*, 70–71; Manarin, *Field of Honor*, 506–8.

88. Field, "Campaign of 1864 and 1865," 552; *OR*, 42(2):1180; Corbin, *Letters of a Confederate Officer*, 57; Freeman, *R. E. Lee*, 483; Rafuse, *Lee and the Fall of the Confederacy*, 194; Manarin, *Field of Honor*, 513.

89. Manarin, *Field of Honor*, 514; *OR*, 42(1):696; J[ames] A. Swearer, "A Feint before Petersburg Attended by a Useless Sacrifice of Life," *Philadelphia Weekly Times*, July 28, 1883; Root Diary, Aug. 16, 1864; Clark, *Thirty-Ninth Illinois*, 163–64. For the batteries involved in the bombardment, see Horn, *Siege of Petersburg*, 71–72.

90. Ransom Bedell to "Dear Cousin," Ransom Bedell Letters, Abraham Lincoln Presidential Library, Springfield; *OR*, 42(1):688; Alvin C. Voris to "My dear wife," Aug. 19, 1864, Albert Voris Letters, Virginia Museum of History and Culture, Richmond; Woodruff, *Fifteen Years Ago*, 175; Swearer, "Feint before Petersburg."

91. Field, "Campaign of 1864 and 1865," 553.

92. Field, "Campaign of 1864 and 1865," 553; Corbin, *Letters of a Confederate Officer*, 57; "North of the James," *Richmond Daily Enquirer*, Aug. 18, 1864; "Company B, Sixty-Fourth Georgia," *Macon (Ga.) Daily Telegraph*, Sept. 1, 1864. The Confederates retrieved Girardey's body and sent it first to Richmond, then to Augusta, Georgia, for burial. Col. William Gibson, the officer who had performed poorly at the Crater, assumed command of the brigade. He would resign his commission later that fall.

93. Harris, *Seventh North Carolina*, 54; Hardy, *General Lee's Immortals*, 322; Mauney Diary, Aug. 16, 1864; Field, "Campaign of 1864 and 1865," 553; *OR*, 42(2):218, 42(1):696.

94. Field, "Campaign of 1864 and 1865," 553; Caldwell, *McGowan's Brigade*, 230; Corbin, *Letters of a Confederate Officer*, 58; "Letter from Anderson's Brigade," *Augusta (Ga.) Constitutionalist*, Aug. 26, 1864; John E. Davis, "Federal Soldier's Incident," 242; *OR*, 42(1):747; *Richmond Daily Enquirer*, Aug. 18, 31, 1864.

95. Walkey, *Seventh Connecticut*, 161; *OR*, 42(1):711; Cadwell, *Old Sixth Regiment*, 100; Eldredge, *Third New Hampshire*, 521; Ferdinand Davis Reminiscences, Bentley Historical Library, University of Michigan, Ann Arbor; Scott, *105th Pennsylvania*, 117–18; Manarin, *Field of Honor*, 524–26; Horn, *Siege of Petersburg*, 84.

96. *OR*, 42(1):700; Manarin, *Field of Honor*, 526. Mason is routinely referred to as a captain, but the authoritative roster of the army's staff officers lists him as a lieutenant. See Krick, *Staff Officers in Gray*, 217.

97. Alfred Howe Terry to "Dear Hatty," Sept. 3, 1864, Terry Papers; *OR*, 42(1):765–66; De Graff Diary, Aug. 16, 1864; Manarin, *Field of Honor*, 526, 536; Horn, *Siege of Petersburg*, 89–90; Styple, *Writing and Fighting the Civil War*, 283.

98. *OR*, 42(2):229; Lockley Journal, Aug. 16, 1864; Horn, *Siege of Petersburg*, 90, 93; Manarin, *Field of Honor*, 526; Armstrong to "Dear Mother," Aug. 18, 1864.

99. *OR*, 42(1):701; Caldwell, *McGowan's Brigade*, 231; Hardy, *Thirty-Seventh North Carolina*, 206. For detailed tactical descriptions of the Confederate counterattack that are implicit in the summary that follows, see Horn, *Siege of Petersburg*, 84–100, Manarin, *Field of Honor*, 529–43, and Suderow, "Nothing but a Miracle," 26–29. Readers will notice a number of inconsistencies between these accounts that stem from contradictions in the available source materials.

100. Joseph Reid Journal, Alabama Department of Archives and History, Montgomery, 135–36; Laine and Penny, *Law's Alabama Brigade*, 294; Oates, *War between the Union and the Confederacy*, 374. The remainder of the Fifteenth Alabama was on picket duty near Deep Bottom.

101. Laine and Penny, *Law's Alabama Brigade*, 294–95; "Special Correspondence," *Montgomery (Ala.) Daily Mail*, Sept. [?], 1864; Scott, *105th Pennsylvania*, 117; *OR*, 42(1):364; Tilton C. Reynolds to "Dear Mother," Aug. 17, 1864, Tilton C. Reynolds Papers, Manuscripts Division, Library of Congress, Washington.

102. John Daniel McDonnell, "Recollections," copy in bound vol. 113, Fredericksburg & Spotsylvania National Military Park; Silo, *115th New York*, 141–43; John Reardon, "Memories of the Civil War," *St. Johnsville (N.Y.) News*, May 13, 1908; Clendaniel, *Such Hard & Severe Service*, 71; *OR*, 42(1):688, 724–25; Davis Reminiscences; Cadwell, *Old Sixth Regiment*, 101; Lyle Diary, Aug. 16, 1864, Virginia Museum of History and Culture, Richmond; Bratton, "Report of Operations," 552; John Kennedy Coleman Diary, Aug. 16, 1864, South Caroliniana Library, University of South Carolina, Columbia.

103. Price, *Ninety-Seventh Regiment, Pennsylvania Volunteer Infantry*, 315; Augustus A. Dean, "Recollections of Army Life during the Civil War 1861–1865," copy, Petersburg National Battlefield.

104. *OR*, 42(1):766; Styple, *Writing and Fighting the Civil War*, 283; Blackett, *Thomas Morris Chester*, 104; Armstrong to "Dear Mother," Aug. 18, 1864.

105. *OR*, 42(2):235; Lockley Journal, Aug. 16, 1864; Myers, *We Might as Well Die Here*, 224; Keating, *Carnival of Blood*, 246; Manarin, *Field of Honor*, 543–44.

106. Horn, *Siege of Petersburg*, 103; Alvin Voris to "My dear wife," Aug. 19, 1864, Voris Letters; Jordan, *Some Events and Incidents*, 91; De Graff Diary, Aug. 16, 1864; *Richmond Daily Enquirer*, Aug. 31, 1864. Hancock reported to Grant that his total casualties on the sixteenth numbered at least 1,500 men. See *OR*, 42(2):222. Private Jordan called the battle "Hazel Mills," having misheard Fussell. Bryce Suderow tallied 1,583 Federal casualties and 726 Confederate losses. See Suderow, "Nothing but a Miracle," 30.

107. Kelly Diary, Aug. 16, 1864, Kelly Papers; D. G. Fleming to "Dear Sister," Sept. 1, 1864, Franklin M. Fleming Letters, Hargrett Rare Book and Manuscripts Library, University of Georgia, Athens; Hamil, *Memories and Recollections*, 29–30.

108. Oxford Diary, Aug. 16, 1864; Mauney Diary, Aug. 16, 1864; Samuel L. Dorroh to "Dear Mag," Sept. 1, 1864, Samuel Lewis Dorroh Papers, South Caroliniana Library, University of South Carolina, Columbia; Styple, *Writing & Fighting from the Army of Northern Virginia*, 296; Martin D. Hood to "Dear Bro," Aug. 17, 1864, Hood Family Papers, Hargrett Rare Book and Manuscripts Library, University of Georgia, Athens; Blesser, *Hammonds of Redcliffe*, 125; John W. Lokey, "My Experience in the War between the States," Confederate Miscellaneous Collection (microfilm), Georgia State Archives, Morrow; Power, *Lee's Miserables*, 186–87.

Although the evidence is persuasive that some of the Black troops were murdered, the number of such victims must have been small, given the relatively few African Americans involved in the battle and the absence of outrage usually expressed by Union participants after any such massacre.

109. *OR*, 42(1):219, 292, 341, 390; Robertson, *McAllister Letters*, 482; Marbaker, *11th New Jersey*, 208–9; Thomas A. Smyth Diaries, Aug. 16, 1864, Delaware Public Archives, Dover.

110. Bratton, "Report of Operations," 552–53; Austin, *General John Bratton*, 232; Lyle Diary, Aug. 16, 1864; *OR*, 42(1):878–79, 42(2):231–33; Manarin, *Field of Honor*, 546; Silliker, *Rebel Yell & the Yankee Hurrah*, 191.

111. Hewitt, Trudeau, and Suderow, *Supplement to the Official Records of the Union and Confederate Armies* (hereafter *OR Supp.*), 318; Harris, *Movements of the Confederate Army in Virginia*, 33; Ott, "Civil War Diary of James J. Kirkpatrick," 216; Evans, *16th Mississippi*, 285–86; Riley, *Grandfather's Journal*, 209; Loehr, *First Virginia Infantry*, 53; Manarin, *Field of Honor*, 546. One regiment from Scales's Brigade also joined the Confederate forces across the James. See Alfred M. Scales to "My own darling wife," Aug. 18, 1864, Alfred Moore Scales Papers, East Carolina University, Greenville.

112. *OR*, 42(2):222, 247–48; Manarin, *Field of Honor*, 547; Coski, *Capital Navy*, 167; *Richmond Daily Dispatch*, Aug. 19, 1864.

113. De Trobriand, *Four Years with the Army*, 632; Shaw and House, *First Maine Heavy Artillery*, 139–40; *OR*, 42(1):249, 42(2):250; Walker, *Second Army Corps*, 578; Samito, *"Fear Was Not in Him,"* 213; DeMontravel, *Hero to His Fighting Men*, 33. For an account of the First Maine's fatal attack on June 18, see Greene, *Campaign of Giants*, 200–205. Barlow would briefly return to duty in August.

114. *OR*, 42(1):220, 243, 42(2):250; Manarin, *Field of Honor*, 547; Copp, *Reminiscences*, 463; Malcolm, *Civil War Journal of Private Heyward Emmell*, 118 (hereafter Malcolm, *Emmell Journal*); Hamilton, "110th Pennsylvania," 197.

115. *OR*, 42(1):701; Talbot, *Samuel Chapman Armstrong*, 116–17. Armstrong, like all officers in Black units, was White.

116. *OR*, 42(2):250, 255, 43(1):822.

117. Robert E. Lee to "Gen" [Charles Field], Aug. 17, 1864, Frederick Dearborn Collection, Houghton Library, Harvard University, Cambridge; Wells, *Hampton and His Cavalry*, 273; *OR*, 51(2):1035; Halliburton, *Saddle Soldiers*, 164; Washington, *Laurel Brigade*, 268; Caldwell, *McGowan's Brigade*, 234; Flack Diary, Aug. 18, 1864; Preston, *Tenth New York Cavalry*, 225; Manarin, *Field of Honor*, 550–51; Horn, *Siege of Petersburg*, 107–8; Suderow, "Nothing but a Miracle," 30. Lee officially moved his headquarters to Chaffin's Bluff on the eighteenth. See *OR*, 42(2):1186.

118. Hardy, *Thirty-Seventh North Carolina*, 206; Caldwell, *McGowan's Brigade*, 234; Mauney Diary, Aug. 18, 1864; Hewitt, Trudeau, and Suderow, *OR Supp.*, 318, 493–94, 499–500, 503–4.

119. Towle Diary, Aug. 18, 1864; *OR*, 42(1):701, 728, 753; Root Diary, Aug. 18, 1864; William W. Willoughby Diary, Aug. 18, 1864, American Antiquarian Society, Worcester; Maxfield and Brady, *Company D, Eleventh Maine*, 45–46; "Knapsack," *The Traveler*, Aug. 29, 1864; Trumbull, *Knightly Soldier*, 266–67; Pettingill Memoir, Siege of Petersburg online.

120. Hewitt, Trudeau, and Suderow, *OR Supp.*, 318; Dowdey and Manarin, *Wartime Papers of R. E. Lee*, 839–40; *OR*, 42(1):220, 341, 42(2):265, 268–71, 286, 1185.

121. George Phillip Clark Diary, Aug. 19, 1864, Library of Virginia, Richmond; Hardy, *Thirty-Seventh North Carolina*, 206–7; Kirkpatrick Diary, Aug. 19, 1864, University of Texas,

Austin; *OR*, 42(1):220, 42(2):299–303; Robert E. Lee to Richard S. Ewell, Aug. 19, 1864, Telegrams Received by the Confederate Secretary of War, Microcopy M618, Roll 18, National Archives and Records Service, Washington; Brady, *Story of One Regiment*, 254–55. Bryce Suderow takes Grant to task for seeking to make an attack with little possible benefit. See Suderow, "Nothing but a Miracle," 30.

122. *OR*, 42(2):325.

123. *OR*, 42(2):332–37, 352; Diary of Lt. Joshua H. Dearborn, Aug. 20, 1864, Guilford Free Public Library; David Coon to "My dear Wife and Children," Aug. 22, 1864, Coon Civil War Letters; Joseph H. Prime to "Dear Wife," Aug. 21, 1864, Prime Papers; Nichols Diary, Aug. 21, 1864.

124. *OR*, 42(2):1192–93, 42(1):879; Austin, *General John Bratton*, 232; D. G. Fleming to "My Dear Sister," Sept. 1, 1864, Fleming Letters; Halliburton, *Saddle Soldiers*, 165; Harris, *Seventh North Carolina*, 55; Manarin, *Field of Honor*, 554; Horn, *Siege of Petersburg*, 112.

125. *OR*, 42(1):116–21.

126. Horn, *Siege of Petersburg*, 113–14. Louis Manarin estimates 1,170 Rebel losses and Bryce Suderow 1,500. See Manarin, *Field of Honor*, 556; and Suderow, "Nothing but a Miracle," 31.

127. Corbin, *Letters of a Confederate Officer*, 60; "Field's Division"; Ruffin Thomson to "Dear Pa," Aug. 18, 1864, Ruffin Thomson Papers, Southern Historical Collection, Louis Round Wilson Library, University of North Carolina, Chapel Hill.

128. Towle Diary, Aug. 20, 1864; Meade, *Life and Letters*, 222; Ansell L. White to "Dear Mother," Aug. 22, 1864, Capt. Ansell L. White Letters, Lewis Leigh Collection, Army Heritage and Education Center, Carlisle. For a critical analysis of Union generalship at Second Deep Bottom, see Suderow, "Nothing but a Miracle," 31.

CHAPTER THREE

1. Greene, *Civil War Petersburg*, 4.

2. U.S. War Department, *War of the Rebellion*, ser. 1, 42(2):152–53 (hereafter *OR*; all references are to series 1 unless otherwise noted); Warren to Emily Warren, Aug. 17, 1864, Warren Papers, New York State Library, Albany.

3. *OR*, 42(2):153, 176, 168–69, 180, 194; Lyman Bell Sperry Diary, Aug. 15, 1864, Gilder-Lehrman Collection, New-York Historical Society, New York; Charles H. Salter to "My dear friend," Aug. 17, 1864, Divie Bethune Duffield Papers, Charles M. Burton Historical Collection, Detroit Public Library.

4. *OR*, 40(2):671, 689–90; Freeman, *R. E. Lee*, 453; Rowland, *Jefferson Davis, Constitutionalist*, 313; *OR*, 42(2):1169. Davis ascribed the information to Robert Ould, the government's chief agent of prisoner exchange.

5. *OR*, 42(2):211–12, 226. For the shift of Confederate troops north of the James, see chapter 2.

6. *OR*, 42(2):244. The strategic link between events around Richmond and Petersburg and the course of the 1864 Valley Campaign should never be ignored. It is clear that Sheridan's success loomed at least as large in Grant's mind as any achievement around Richmond or Petersburg.

7. *OR*, 42(2):245, 251. The Third New York Cavalry and the First District of Columbia Cavalry were assigned to support Warren.

8. *OR*, 42(2):245, 271; Flanagan, "Life of General Gouverneur Kemble Warren," 289. Mahone sent only three of his five brigades across the James. Grant also told Meade that "Johnson's old brigade" had crossed the James, thus conveying that six additional Rebel brigades had vacated the area.

9. Editor, *Cape Ann Light and Gloucester Telegraph* (Gloucester, Mass.), Sept. 3, 1864; Corydon O. Warner to "Dear Sister," Aug. 21, 1864, Corydon O. Warner Collection, New York State Military History Museum, Saratoga Springs; *OR*, 42(2):271, 42(1):458, 460; Pullen, *Twentieth Maine*, 221; Powell, *Fifth Army Corps*, 710–11; Smith, *Corn Exchange Regiment*, 498; William Stowell Tilton Diary, Aug. 18, 1864, Massachusetts Historical Society, Boston; Gerrish, *Army Life*, 211. Fort Warren would be renamed Fort Davis in early September. It remains well preserved and publicly accessible in 2024.

10. Powell, *Fifth Army Corps*, 711; *OR*, 42(1):428, 464; Porter, "Operations against the Weldon Railroad," 247; Maj. Charles K. Winne, "A Medical Inspector's Journal of the Wilderness Campaign and the End of the Civil War," Aug. 18, 1864, Josiah Trent Collection, Rubenstein Special Collections Library, Duke University, Durham, N.C.; Jordan, *Happiness Is Not My Companion*, 181; Gibbs, *First Battalion Pennsylvania Six Months Volunteers and the 187th Regiment Pennsylvania*, 115 (hereafter Gibbs, *187th Pennsylvania*); George K. Leet to William R. Rowley, Aug. 20, 1864, Rowley Papers, Abraham Lincoln Presidential Library, Springfield; Horn, *Siege of Petersburg*, 122; Bearss, *Petersburg Campaign: The Eastern Front Battles*, 244–45 (hereafter Bearss, *Eastern Front Battles*). The Gurley house was "a large, square, white house, with very red brick chimneys at each gable." A contemporary drawing depicts a two-story dwelling with a small front porch, four windows across the first floor, and seven others across the second. The family had abandoned their home in June at the approach of the Federals, and graffiti now adorned the walls, which were accented by sea-green wainscoting. See Bearss, *Eastern Front Battles*, 245; Francis W. Knowles Journal and Diary, East Carolina University, Greenville; *History of the 5th Massachusetts Battery*, 921–22.

11. *OR*, 42(1):428–29, 458, 460, 42(2):272; Charles Wainwright Diary, Aug. 18, 1864, Henry E. Huntington Library, San Marino; Bearss, *Eastern Front Battles*, 245.

12. *OR*, 42(1):857; Theodore Lyman to "My Honey Love," Aug. 23, 1864, Lyman Family Papers, Massachusetts Historical Society, Boston; Beauregard to A. P. Hill, Aug. 18, 1864, Beauregard Papers, Library of Congress, Washington. Nothing remains of Globe Tavern, although I remember seeing some remnants of its foundation in 1974. In 2024, the relative positions of Halifax Road and the railroad are reversed in this vicinity.

13. *OR*, 42(1):458, 461; Tilton Diary, Aug. 18, 1864; Gibbs, *187th Pennsylvania*, 115–16; Zerah Coston Monks to "Dear Hattie," Aug. 25, 1864, Zerah Coston Monks Family Papers, Western Reserve Historical Society, Cleveland; Smith, *Corn Exchange Regiment*, 499.

14. William T. Sherman to Ulysses S. Grant, Sept. 23, 1864, David M. Gregg Papers, Manuscripts Division, Library of Congress, Washington; Charles E. LaMotte to "My dear Mother," Nov. 3, 1864, Charles E. LaMotte Letters, Delaware Public Archives, Dover.

15. Letter, Aug. 26, 1864, in "1862–65: Charles Clarence Miller to Parents," 140th N.Y., Billy Yank & Johnny Reb Letters; *OR*, 42(1):474; Augustus C. Golding Diary, Aug. 18, 1864, copy in bound vol. 48, Richmond National Battlefield Park; "A War Echo: Diary of an Old Fourteenth Regiment Soldier," *Brooklyn (N.Y.) Daily Standard-Union*, June 4, 1892.

16. *History of the 121st Regiment Pennsylvania Volunteers*, 90; *OR*, 42(1):461.

17. *OR*, 42(2):272, 42(1):471, 474, 480; Brainard, *Campaigns of the 146th Regiment, New York State Volunteers*, 238 (hereafter Brainard, *146th New York*); Horn, *Siege of Petersburg*,

124. For a contemporary map showing the Blick house and its surroundings, see *OR*, 42(1):433.

18. *OR*, 42(2):273.

19. *OR*, 42(1):471, 474, 540; Raiford, *4th North Carolina Cavalry*, 77; "Extracts from the Journal of Col. Robert Hayes," Joshua Chamberlain Papers, Manuscripts Division, Library of Congress, Washington; Hewitt, Trudeau, and Suderow, *Supplement to the Official Records of the Union and Confederate Armies* (hereafter *OR Supp.*), 432. According to John Horn, the section of guns supporting Dearing's cavalry came from the Petersburg Artillery. Horn, *Siege of Petersburg*, 128. The Federal guns may have been the Third Massachusetts Battery. The Davis house was owned at the time by Petersburg businessman Reuben Ragland. It would burn on September 11, 1864.

20. *OR*, 42(1):474; Brainard, *146th New York*, 238; "Extracts from the Journal of Col. Robert Hayes"; "Report of Capt. P. W. Stanhope, 12th US Infantry," Aug. 24, 1864, William H. Noble Papers, Rubenstein Special Collections Library, Duke University, Durham, N.C.

21. *OR*, 42(1):491, 502; Greenleaf, *Letters to Eliza*, 126 (Aug. 22, 1864); Small, *Road to Richmond*, 154; Ramsdell Diary, Aug. 18, 1864 Ramsdell Papers, University of North Carolina, Chapel Hill; Horn, *Siege of Petersburg*, 121.

22. *OR*, 42(1):857–58, 42(2):1186; Carmichael, *Lee's Young Artillerist*, 133; Wise, *Long Arm of Lee*, 896; Henry Heth, "Report of Operations of Heth's Division May 4th to December 7th, 1864," Henry Heth Papers, Eleanor S. Brockenbrough Library, Museum of the Confederacy, Richmond; William H. Smith Diary, Aug. 18, 1864, copy in bound vol. 15, Richmond National Battlefield Park; Washington L. Dunn Diary, Aug. 18, 1864, United Daughters of the Confederacy Collection, Georgia State Archives, Morrow; Cooke, "Fifty-Fifth Regiment," 3:309. Mayo's command was the result of the consolidation of Archer's and Walker's Brigades. See *OR*, 42(2):1273–74. Beauregard's orders to Hill and Hoke specified that the operation would be under the direction of Mahone, but there is no evidence that Mahone exercised any direct influence over the impending combat. See Beauregard to A. P. Hill and Beauregard to Robert F. Hoke, both Aug. 18, 1864, Beauregard Papers.

23. Heth, "Report of Operations"; Joseph R. Davis to "My dear Uncle [Jefferson Davis]," Aug. 19, 1864, Confederate Military Leaders Collection, Eleanor S. Brockenbrough Library, Museum of the Confederacy, Richmond; Stubbs, *Duty, Honor, Valor*, 591; Samuel Z. Ammen, "Maryland Troops in the Confederate Army," Thomas Clemens Collection, Army Heritage and Education Center, Carlisle, 153; William H. Smith Diary, Aug. 18, 1864, copy in bound vol. 15, Richmond National Battlefield Park; Carmichael, *Lee's Young Artillerist*, 135; Horn, *Siege of Petersburg*, 128–29; George K. Leet to William R. Rowley, Aug. 20, 1864, Rowley Papers; Roebling Journal, Aug. 18, 1864, Roebling Family Papers, Rutgers University, New Brunswick; *OR*, 42(1):509; Bowerman, "Cutting off Lee."

24. Horn, *Siege of Petersburg*, 129; Bearss, *Eastern Front Battles*, 252; Cooke, "Fifty-Fifth Regiment," 309; Roebling Journal, Aug. 18, 1864; *OR*, 42(1):471, 480; Schroeder, *We Came to Fight*, 177; Bowerman, "Cutting off Lee"; Camper and Kirkley, *First Maryland Infantry*, 167–68.

25. *OR*, 42(1):491, 508; Small, *Road to Richmond*, 154.

26. Ammen, "Maryland Troops in the Confederate Army," 156–57; *OR*, 42(1):508; Small, *Road to Richmond*, 155; Thomas and Sauers, *Never Want to Witness Such Sights*, 229; Horn, *Siege of Petersburg*, 130–31. It is, of course, doubtful that "almost everyone" of the Marylanders purloined a melon, although some, no doubt, did.

27. *OR*, 42(1):509; Rhea, *To the North Anna River*, 160.

28. Horn, *Siege of Petersburg*, 132; *OR*, 42(1):471, 534; Bearss, *Eastern Front Battles*, 255.

29. *OR*, 42(1):483–84; Charles E. LaMotte to "Dear Father," Aug. 22, 1864, LaMotte Letters.

30. Charles E. LaMotte to "Dear Mother," Sept. 8, 1864 and to "Dear Father," Aug. 22, 1864, LaMotte Letters; *OR*, 42(1):484, 540; Cooke, "Fifty-Fifth Regiment," 310; Pvt. William Henry Bachman Memoir, Mississippi Department of Archives and History, Jackson, 82; Bearss, *Eastern Front Battles*, 256.

31. *OR*, 42(2):274, 42(1):471, 474, 484; Heth, "Report of Operations"; Smith, *Seventy-Sixth Regiment New York Volunteers*, 308; Porter, "Operations against the Weldon Railroad," 252.

32. *OR*, 42(1):488, 534–35; Horn, *Siege of Petersburg*, 133–35; Corydon O. Warner to "Dear Sister," Aug. 21, 1864, Warner Collection; Nathan S. Clark Diary, Aug. 19, 1864, Maine State Archives, Augusta.

33. *OR*, 42(1):488, 492, 510, 535; Dutton, "Weldon Railroad"; Driver, *First and Second Maryland Infantry*, 282; Bearss, *Eastern Front Battles*, 257; Taylor, *Gouverneur Kemble Warren*, 192. Almost all of the August 18 battlefield is unpreserved, much of it covered with industrial buildings in 2024.

34. William H. Smith Diary, Aug. 18, 1864, copy in bound vol. 15, Richmond National Battlefield Park; *OR*, 42(2):274.

35. *OR*, 42(1):429, 480; Schroeder, *We Came to Fight*, 173, 180; Bennett, *Sons of Old Monroe*, 467.

36. Cooke, "Fifty-Fifth Regiment," 310; Horn, *Siege of Petersburg*, 138; Joseph R. Davis to "My dear Uncle [Jefferson Davis]," Aug. 19, 1864.

37. *OR*, 42(2):275; Bearss, *Eastern Front Battles*, 258–59.

38. Ramsdell Diary, Aug. 18, 1864; Memoir of John F. Huntingdon, William Orland Bourne Papers, Manuscripts Division, Library of Congress, Washington.

39. *OR*, 42(2):276, 281–84; Horn, *Siege of Petersburg*, 136–37.

40. *OR*, 42(2):1187; *Athens (Ga.) Southern Banner*, Aug. 31, 1864; Hewitt, Trudeau, and Suderow, *OR Supp.*, 319; Curtis, "Reminiscences," Duke University, Durham, N.C.; Horn, *Siege of Petersburg*, 137; Bearss, *Eastern Front Battles*, 264.

41. *OR*, 42(2):266.

42. *OR*, 42(2):277; Dawes, *Service with the Sixth Wisconsin*, 12, 20.

43. Wainwright Diary, Aug. 19, 1864; *OR*, 42(1):535, 538. Warren stated that he sent Bragg to Crawford at 4:00 A.M., Crawford reported that Bragg appeared at his headquarters at 3:00 A.M., while Bragg recorded his arrival on Crawford's front at 2:00 A.M. See *OR*, 42(1):429, 492, 534.

44. *OR*, 42(1):429, 492, 536–37; Herdegen and Murphy, *Four Years with the Iron Brigade*, 306; Roebling Journal, Aug. 19, 1864.

45. *OR*, 42(1):492, 535–36; Venner, *Hoosier's Honor*, 272; Roebling Journal, Aug. 19, 1864; Gustrowsky, "UPR: Report of Lieutenant Colonel Mark Finnicum, 7th WI, August 18–21, 1864," Siege of Petersburg online.

46. *OR*, 42(1):429, 537–40, 42(2):314.

47. Lewis Crater Diary, Aug. 19, 1864, Special Collections, University of Iowa, Iowa City; Boston Diary, Aug. 19, 1864; *OR*, 42(1):589, 593, 42(2):293; Scott, *Forgotten Valor*, 567; Horn, *Siege of Petersburg*, 143–44.

48. *OR*, 42(2):305; Bearss, *Eastern Front Battles*, 268.

49. Memoir of John F. Huntingdon; *OR*, 42(1):474; Frederick Winthrop to "My Dear Frank," Aug. 23, 1864, Frederick Winthrop Papers, Massachusetts Historical Society, Boston; Golding Diary, Aug. 19, 1864; letter, Aug. 26, 1864, in "1862–65: Charles Clarence Miller to Parents," Billy Yank & Johnny Reb Letters; Reese, *Sykes' Regular Infantry Division*, 328.

50. Andrew R. Linscott to "Dear Mary," Aug. 24, 1864, Andrew R. Linscott Papers, Massachusetts Historical Society, Boston; Ramsdell Diary, Aug. 19, 1864; Thomas and Sauers, *Never Want to Witness Such Sights*, 230; *OR*, 42(1):504, 510; John Vautier Diary, Aug. 19, 1864, copy in bound vol. 371, Fredericksburg & Spotsylvania National Military Park.

51. *OR*, 42(1):341; Robertson, *McAllister Letters*, 484; Silliker, *Rebel Yell & the Yankee Hurrah*, 192.

52. *OR*, 42(2):293, 315. White replaced James Ledlie in command of the First Division.

53. *OR*, 42(2):306, 316; Lowe, *Meade's Army*, 251; Pvt. Frank Lobrano Diary, Aug. 19, 1864, Louisiana Historical Collection, Special Collections, Tulane University, New Orleans; Horn, *Siege of Petersburg*, 143.

54. *OR*, 42(2):294; Lowe, *Meade's Army*, 251; Agassiz, *Meade's Headquarters*, 219.

55. Newsome, Horn, and Selby, *Civil War Talks*, 263–64; Morrison, *Memoirs of Henry Heth*, 190.

56. Hewitt, Trudeau, and Suderow, *OR Supp.*, 318; Newsome, Horn, and Selby, *Civil War Talks*, 263.

57. *OR*, 42(2):1190; Beauregard to Hagood, Aug. 18, 1864, and Beauregard to A. P. Hill, Aug. 19, 1864, Beauregard Papers; Cooke Diary, Aug. 19, 1864, Virginia Museum of History and Culture, Richmond.

58. *OR*, 42(2):1190.

59. Beauregard to A. P. Hill, Aug. 19, 1864, Beauregard Papers; Newsome, Horn, and Selby, *Civil War Talks*, 264; Heth, "Report of Operations"; Morrison, *Memoirs of Henry Heth*, 190; *OR*, 42(1):858; Horn, *Siege of Petersburg*, 149.

60. Stewart, *Pair of Blankets*, 170. Lt. George Warthen of Colquitt's Twenty-Eighth Georgia numbered the brigade as "less than 1200." See Warthen to "Hon James Thomas," Aug. 28, 1864, George Warthen Letters, Rubenstein Special Collections Library, Duke University, Durham, N.C. The inspection report of August 15 for Weisiger's brigade tallied 1,086 officers and men present for duty, armed with Enfield rifles. See Confederate Inspection Report 4-P-17, Aug. 15, 1864, War Department Collection of Confederate Records, RG 109, Microfilm M935, Roll 10, National Archives and Records Service, Washington. Mahone recalled that his troops and those of Heth numbered fewer than 6,000. See Newsome, Horn, and Selby, *Civil War Talks*, 267.

61. Bearss, *Eastern Front Battles*, 272; Dunn Diary, Aug. 19, 1864; William H. Smith Diary, Aug. 19, 1864, copy in bound vol. 15, Richmond National Battlefield Park; Ammen, "Maryland Troops in the Confederate Army," 153; Newsome, Horn, and Selby, *Civil War Talks*, 268, 273, 277; Folkes, *Confederate Grays*, 5; Horn, *Petersburg Regiment*, 309; Horn, *Siege of Petersburg*, 150; Stewart, *Pair of Blankets*, 171. Whortleberries are juicy edibles with a nutlike flavor.

62. Ammen, "Maryland Troops in the Confederate Army," 153; Goldsborough, *Maryland Line*, 136; Porter, "Operations against the Weldon Railroad," 254–55; Carmichael, *Lee's Young Artillerist*, 135. It is probable, in the absence of references to additional Confederate artillery, that Pegram drew only these eight guns from three of his batteries.

63. Morrison, *Memoirs of Henry Heth*, 191–92.

64. Roebling Journal, Aug. 19, 1864; *OR*, 42(1):535; Curtis, *Twenty-Fourth Michigan*, 271; and Herdegen and Murphy, *Four Years with the Iron Brigade*, 306. Bragg's headquarters were near the future site of Union Fort Howard, which is no longer extant. There were several small homesteads in that area, two of which were owned by Vaughan and Wright. The sources do not indicate which of these places provided Bragg his command post. Newsome, Horn, and Selby, *Civil War Talks*, 287.

65. *OR*, 42(1):535, 539, 42(2):307; Humphreys, *Virginia Campaign of '64 and '65*, 275; Curtis, *Twenty-Fourth Michigan*, 271; Gustrowsky, "UPR: Report of Lieutenant Colonel Mark Finnicum."

66. Curtis, *Twenty-Fourth Michigan*, 271; Dunn, *Iron Men, Iron Will*, 295; Humphreys, *Virginia Campaign of '64 and '65*, 275; Powell, *Fifth Army Corps*, 713; *OR*, 42(1):493, 539; Smith, *Twenty-Fourth Michigan*, 222.

67. *OR*, 42(1):535, 539–40; Elmer D. Wallace to "My Dear Parents," Aug. 20, 1864, Elmer D. Wallace Papers, Bentley Historical Library, University of Michigan, Ann Arbor; Bearss, *Eastern Front Battles*, 274.

68. *OR*, 42(1):535, 538; Bearss, *Eastern Front Battles*, 274–75. The mill referenced by Bragg was probably Risden's sawmill, located about 250–300 yards west of the Wright and Vaughan houses. See Newsome, Horn, and Selby, *Civil War Talks*, 287.

69. *OR*, 42(1):539; Beaudot and Herdegen, *Irishman in the Iron Brigade*, 125–26. Sullivan's account first appeared as "The Fight for the Weldon Road," *Milwaukee Sunday Telegraph*. June 28, 1885.

70. Jordan, *Happiness Is Not My Companion*, 182; Agassiz, *Meade's Headquarters*, 220; *OR*, 42(1):125. The table presented in the *Official Records* represents the brigade losses for the entire battle, but Bragg reported that his casualties on the other days of combat were nominal.

71. Horn, *Siege of Petersburg*, 150–51; Newsome, Horn, and Selby, *Civil War Talks*, 277.

72. Hewitt, Trudeau, and Suderow, *OR Supp.*, 433; *OR*, 42(2):312; Wainwright Diary, Aug. 19, 1864.

73. *OR*, 42(1):471, 504, 510, 522, 42(2):313–14; Hall, *97th Regiment New York Volunteers*, 218 (hereafter Hall, *97th New York*); Wainwright Diary, Aug. 19, 1864.

74. Bearss, *Eastern Front Battles*, 276, 278; *OR*, 42(1):479, 504, 510, 522, 42(2):313; Hewitt, Trudeau, and Suderow, *OR Supp.*, 433; Reese, *Sykes' Regular Infantry Division*, 328–29.

75. *OR*, 42(2):313; Horn, *Siege of Petersburg*, 153; Roebling Journal, Aug. 19, 1864; Porter, "Operations against the Weldon Railroad," 255; *Richmond Daily Dispatch*, Aug. 22, 1864. Heth's postbattle report suggested that he began his assault once he heard Mahone's guns.

76. Horn, *Siege of Petersburg*, 154; Bearss, *Eastern Front Battles*, 276; Cooke, "Fifty-Fifth Regiment," 310; Henry Gawthrop Diary, Aug. 19, 1864, Delaware Historical Society, Wilmington; Charles E. LaMotte to "Dear Mother," Aug. 21, 1864; and LaMotte to "Dear Father," Aug. 22, 1864, LaMotte Letters; *OR*, 42(1):471, 484.

77. Ammen, "Maryland Troops in the Confederate Army," 154; Driver, *First and Second Maryland*, 283.

78. Ramsdell Diary, Aug. 19, 1864; *OR*, 42(1):493; Horn, *Siege of Petersburg*, 154; Bearss, *Eastern Front Battles*, 278.

79. Newsome, Horn, and Selby, *Civil War Talks*, 265–66.

80. Crocker, "Dread Days in Dixie"; Eberly, *Bouquets from the Cannon's Mouth*, 202; *OR*, 42(1):429, 493–94; Newsome, Horn, and Selby, *Civil War Talks*, 266–67.

81. Porter, "Operations against the Weldon Railroad," 256; Bearss, *Eastern Front Battles*, 279; Wainwright Diary, Aug. 19, 1864; *OR*, 42(1):541.

82. *OR*, 42(1):510, 517; Hall, *97th New York*, 219–20; Thomas, *Boys in Blue from the Adirondack Foothills*, 242; Vautier Diary, Aug. 19, 1864.

83. Charles McKnight Diary, Aug. 19, 1864, Historical Society of Pennsylvania, Philadelphia; Locke, *Story of the Regiment*, 359.

84. Dusseault, *Company E, 39th Infantry*, 33; Horn, *Siege of Petersburg*, 156; "The 104th N.Y. Vols: A Short History of the Wadsworth Guards," *Warsaw–Wyoming County Times* (Warsaw, N.Y.), June 21, 1894; John Barry to "Dear friend, Sir," Aug. 25, 1864, Daniel Musser Collection, Pennsylvania State Archives, Harrisburg; Thomas and Sauers, *Never Want to Witness Such Sights*, 231.

85. "Report of Capt. P. W. Stanhope."

86. *OR*, 42(1):479, 494.

87. Hewitt, Trudeau, and Suderow, *OR Supp.*, 434; *OR*, 42(1):472, 474; Powell, *Fifth Army Corps*, 714; Bearss, *Eastern Front Battles*, 282. Brady was wounded before his surrender. See Reese, *Sykes' Regular Infantry Division*, 329.

88. *OR*, 42(1):474; Frederick Winthrop to "My Dear Frank," Aug. 23, 1864, Winthrop Papers; Golding Diary, Aug. 19, 1864; Schroeder, *We Came to Fight*, 181. The soldiers involved in rescuing the colors were Lt. August Thieman and Sgt. Ovila Cayer. See Horn, *Siege of Petersburg*, 158.

89. Ludwig, "Eighth Regiment," 407; McKethan, "Fifty-First Regiment," 213; Thomas and Sauers, *Never Want to Witness Such Sights*, 231; Dusseault, *Company E, 39th Infantry*, 33.

90. Horn, *Petersburg Regiment*, 311; *Richmond Daily Dispatch*, Aug. 22, 1864; Morrison, *Memoirs of Henry Heth*, 191; Porter, "Operations against the Weldon Railroad," 258. Heth's ungenerous accusation, combined with his effort to deny Mahone any role in conceiving the attack plan, reveals his postwar antipathy toward Mahone, whose politics clashed with Heth's.

91. Newsome, Horn, and Selby, *Civil War Talks*, 266; McKeithan, "Fifty-First Regiment," 213.

92. Stewart, *Pair of Blankets*, 172.

93. Crater Diary, Aug. 19, 1864.

94. Roebling Journal, Aug. 19, 1864; Theodore Lyman to "My Little Wife," Nov. 9, 1864, Lyman Family Papers; Coco, *Through Blood and Fire*, 155. Hartranft's Fifty-First Pennsylvania was one of the two regiments that successfully stormed "Burnside's Bridge" at the Battle of Antietam in September 1862.

95. Scott, *Forgotten Valor*, 567, 570; *OR*, 42(1):589, 593.

96. Goldsborough, *Maryland Line*, 136; Ammen, "Maryland Troops in the Confederate Army," 154; Alexander S. Patten Diary, Aug. 19, 1864, copy in bound vol. 94, Fredericksburg & Spotsylvania National Military Park.

97. Byron M. Cutcheon Autobiography, Bentley Historical Library, University of Michigan, Ann Arbor, 341–42; Cpl. Benjamin F. Marsh to "Dear Mother," Aug. 21, 1864, Marsh Family Papers, Michigan State University, East Lansing.

98. *OR*, 42(1):589, 595; Cutcheon Autobiography, 343; Crater Diary, Aug. 19, 1864; David S. Munroe to "Dear Mother," Aug. 21, 1864, David Smalley Munroe Papers, Bentley Historical Library, University of Michigan, Ann Arbor.

99. *OR*, 42(1):550; Elbert Corbin Diary, Aug. 19, 1864, Schuylkill County Historical Society, Pottsville; Lowe, *Meade's Army*, 252. White would soon afterward report himself ill and submit his resignation.

100. *OR*, 42(1):550, 557, 564; Gavin, *Campaigning with the Roundheads*, 542; Wilkinson, *May You Never See the Sights*, 272; Scott, *Forgotten Valor*, 567; Horn, *Siege of Petersburg*, 162.

101. Newsome, Horn, and Selby, *Civil War Talks*, 266–67, 274; *OR*, 42(1):589.

102. Newsome, Horn, and Selby, *Civil War Talks*, 271–76; Folkes, *Confederate Grays*, 5–6; *OR*, 42(1):550.

103. *OR*, 42(1):474–75; Frederick Winthrop to "My Dear Frank," Aug. 23, 1864, Winthrop Papers.

104. Bearss, *Eastern Front Battles*, 287; Schroeder, *We Came to Fight*, 183; *OR*, 42(1):475.

105. *OR*, 42(1):458, 467, 475; Powell, *Fifth Army Corps*, 714–15.

106. Burrage, *36th Regiment, Massachusetts Volunteers*, 248–49 (hereafter Burrage, *36th Massachusetts*); Roebling Journal, Aug. 19, 1864; Hall, *97th New York*, 220; Bearss, *Eastern Front Battles*, 289; *OR*, 42(1):594, 42(2):315. Only small sections of Mahone's August 19 battlefield remain undeveloped and have public access. They remain unmarked in 2024.

107. *OR*, 42(2):294–95, 307–9.

108. Curtis, "Reminiscences"; George William Beale to "Dear Mother," Aug. 20, 1864, Beale Family Papers, Albert and Shirley Small Special Collections Library, University of Virginia, Charlottesville; Beauregard to A. P. Hill, Aug. 19, 1864, Beauregard Papers.

109. *OR*, 42(1):430, 596; Daniel A. Lowber Diary, Aug. 19, 1864, Special Collections, Carol M. Newman Library, Virginia Tech University, Blacksburg.

110. Horn, *Siege of Petersburg*, 172–73n49; "From Petersburg Express," *Athens (Ga.) Southern Banner*, Aug. 31, 1864; *OR*, 42(1):858; William H. Smith Diary, Aug. 20, 1864, copy in bound vol. 15, Richmond National Battlefield Park; George William Beale to "Dear Mother," Aug. 20, 1864, Beale Family Papers.

111. Francis Marion Coker to "My darling wife," Aug. 19, 1864, Capt. Francis Marion Coker Papers, Francis Hodgson Heidler Collection, Hargrett Rare Book and Manuscripts Library, University of Georgia, Athens.

112. William C. Weidner, "After the Reserves: An Unofficial History of the 190th and 191st Pennsylvania Volunteer Infantry Regiments, June 1, 1864, through June 28, 1865," Bill Weidner Papers, Army Heritage and Education Center, Carlisle; Crocker, "Dread Days in Dixie." The island is called Merchant's Island and sits just upstream from Campbell's Bridge.

CHAPTER FOUR

1. U.S. War Department, *War of the Rebellion*, ser. 1, 42(2):307–9, 292, 294 (hereafter *OR*; all references are to series 1 unless otherwise noted).

2. "Grant's Army," *New York Times*, Aug. 23, 1864; Walcott, *Twenty-First Regiment Massachusetts Volunteers*, 353–54; Scott, *Forgotten Valor*, 571.

3. McCoy, "At the Weldon Railroad"; Sumner, *Comstock Diary*, 286.

4. Warren to "My Sweet Emmie," Aug. 20, 1864, Warren Papers, New York State Library, Albany; Lowe, *Meade's Army*, 253; Hall, *97th New York*, 220; Thomas, *Boys in Blue from the Adirondack Foothills*, 242.

5. *Richmond Daily Dispatch*, Aug. 22, 1864; *Athens (Ga.) Southern Banner*, Aug. 31, 1864; Folkes, *Confederate Grays*, 6.

6. Stewart, *Pair of Blankets*, 175; letter, Apr. 14, 1920, John Calvin Metcalf Papers, Albert and Shirley Small Special Collections Library, University of Virginia, Charlottesville; Newsome, Horn, and Selby, *Civil War Talks*, 275; Burnett letter, Aug. 24, 1864, Jordan-Burnett Papers, Hargrett Rare Book and Manuscripts Library, University of Georgia, Athens.

7. Humphreys, *Virginia Campaign of '64 and '65*, 276. The thirteen Union brigades came from Crawford's three, Ayres's three, Cutler's two, Willcox's two, White's two, and Griffin's one (Tilton). Potter's brigades and Griffin's other two (Gwyn and Gregory) made no meaningful contribution to the fighting.

8. Newsome, Horn, and Selby, *Civil War Talks*, 280. For an excellent analysis of the fighting on August 19, see Horn, *Siege of Petersburg*, 174–76.

9. Porter, "Operations against the Weldon Railroad," 260.

10. *OR*, 42(2):301, 326, 338. This was yet another source of Meade's displeasure with the Fifth Corps commander.

11. *OR*, 42(2):301–3, 327.

12. *OR*, 42(2):1191. Lee's reply to Beauregard is missing, but his intent can be inferred from Beauregard's response. See *OR*, 42(2):1192. See also Freeman, *R. E. Lee*, 486.

13. Hagood, *Memoirs*, 288–89.

14. *OR*, 42(1):940, 42(2):1192; Cooke Diary, Aug. 20, 1864, Virginia Museum of History and Culture, Richmond. Brig. Gen. Matt Ransom had been wounded in May and had yet to return to active duty.

15. *OR*, 42(2):1192; Bearss, *Eastern Front Battles*, 299–300; Horn, *Siege of Petersburg*, 182–83. On August 19 Kirkland assumed command of the North Carolina brigade previously led by Brig. Gen. James Martin in Hoke's Division. See *OR*, 42(2):1190. Kirkland had been wounded at Cold Harbor, and MacRae had so ably led his brigade since then that when Kirkland recovered, he was reassigned to command Martin's Brigade rather than returning to his old command (renamed MacRae's Brigade) in Heth's Division.

16. Bearss, *Eastern Front Battles*, 300–301; Hewitt, Trudeau, and Suderow, *Supplement to the Official Records of the Union and Confederate Armies* (hereafter *OR Supp.*), 474. Mahone's courier, Robert R. Henry, stated that Col. Theodore Brevard of the Eleventh Florida led Finegan's Brigade, but I found no corroborating evidence of that. See Newsome, Horn, and Selby, *Civil War Talks*, 290.

17. Hagood, *Memoirs*, 289; George H. Moffett, "With Hagood's Brigade in Virginia," Moffett Family Papers, South Carolina Historical Society, Charleston, 53–54; Riley, *Grandfather's Journal*, 209; Cockrell and Ballard, *Mississippi Rebel*, 307; Hillhouse, *Heavy Artillery and Light Infantry*, n.p. Battery 45, also known as Fort Lee, is overgrown but well preserved in 2024 and protected by the National Park Service.

18. Hess, *Lee's Tar Heels*, 243; Chapman, *More Terrible Than Victory*, 215; Day, "Life among the Bullets," 216; Bearss, *Eastern Front Battles*, 301.

19. *OR*, 42(2):1192; Horn, *Siege of Petersburg*, 184.

20. Porter, "Operations against the Weldon Railroad," 261–62; Bearss, *Eastern Front Battles*, 301; Horn, *Siege of Petersburg*, 184. For information on Roger Pryor, see, in addition to the usual biographical compendiums, Greene, *Civil War Petersburg*, 359. Some sources describe Pryor as a private. His wife Sara authored a valuable memoir that sheds light on wartime Petersburg.

21. Crater Diary, Aug. 20, 1864, University of Iowa, Iowa City; "A War Echo: Diary of an old Fourteenth Regiment Soldier," *Brooklyn (N.Y.) Standard-Union*, June 4, 1892.

22. Camper and Kirkley, *First Maryland Infantry*, 171; Horn, *Siege of Petersburg*, 181; Gibbs, *187th Pennsylvania*, 119; *OR*, 42(2):328, 340.

23. *OR*, 42(1):544, 552, 590, 594, 596; Cutcheon Autobiography, Bentley Historical Library, University of Michigan, Ann Arbor, 343–44.

24. *OR*, 42(2):338; Bearss, *Eastern Front Battles*, 294; Porter, "Operations against the Weldon Railroad," 261; Horn, *Siege of Petersburg*, 182.

25. *OR*, 42(1):544, 552, 590, 594; Carruth et al., *35th Massachusetts*, 287; Scott, *Forgotten Valor*, 568; Stephen Rogers to "Dear Father and Mother," Aug. 20, 1864, Stephen Rogers Letters, Abraham Lincoln Presidential Library, Springfield; Cutcheon, *Twentieth Michigan Infantry*, 150.

26. Roe, *Thirty-Ninth Massachusetts*, 253; *OR*, 42(1):505.

27. *OR*, 42(1):475, 481; Schroeder, *We Came to Fight*, 185.

28. *OR*, 42(1):536; Curtis, *Twenty-Four Michigan*, 272; Gaff, *On Many a Bloody Field*, 378; Dunn, *Iron Men, Iron Will*, 295–96.

29. *OR*, 42(1):461; Gibbs, *187th Pennsylvania*, 119; *History of the 121st Regiment Pennsylvania Volunteers*, 90; Tilton Diary, Aug. 20, 1864, Massachusetts Historical Society, Boston.

30. *OR*, 42(1):472, 475, 541, 590, 594, 596; Hall, *97th New York*, 220–21; Schroeder, *We Came to Fight*, 185; Coco, *Through Blood and Fire*, 151; Camper and Kirkley, *First Maryland Infantry*, 171; Frey, "Recollections of Army Life"; McCoy, "At the Weldon Railroad."

31. Hall, *97th New York*, 221; Tilton Diary, Aug. 20, 1864; Locke, *Story of the Regiment*, 361; Herdegen and Murphy, *Four Years with the Iron Brigade*, 307.

32. Roman, *General Beauregard*, 272; Freeman, *R. E. Lee*, 487; Cooke Diary, Aug. 21, 1864. Cooke located Beauregard's headquarters at the "Powder Mills," but it is probable that he referred to the Lead Works. Freeman states that Lee arrived in the afternoon and observed the battle, but the fighting unfolded in the morning, suggesting that the Confederate commander was present well before noon.

33. Hagood, *Memoirs*, 290; Moffett, "With Hagood's Brigade in Virginia," 54–55; Porter, "Operations against the Weldon Railroad," 262; Clark, *A Glance Backward*, 63; Fortin, "Herbert's History of the 8th Alabama," 174; Hewitt, Trudeau, and Suderow, *OR Supp.*, 319; Riley, *Grandfather's Journal*, 209; Cockrell and Ballard, *Mississippi Rebel*, 307. There is some uncertainty about the route taken by Mahone's brigades other than Hagood's. Edwin C. Bearss states that all of Mahone's force used Squirrel Level and Poplar Spring Roads to reach Vaughan Road, relying on Hagood's statement that he halted his brigade at the church "while the column passed on." Bearss, *Eastern Front Battles*, 301–2. Hagood's statement is ambiguous and could mean that the "column passed on" along Vaughan Road in their front, not past them on Poplar Springs Road. The evidence cited above persuades me that Mahone's troops—except for Hagood, whose brigade Hill had promised to use only in an emergency—used only Vaughan Road to reach their deployment, which put them closer to the enemy and thus in keeping with the idea of retaining Hagood in reserve.

34. Cockrell and Ballard, *Mississippi Rebel*, 307; *OR*, 42(1):939.

35. Roche, "Fighting for Petersburg," 528. It is certainly plausible that Pryor accompanied Mahone's column, although no other source specifically mentions his presence.

36. John Lane Stuart to "Dear Mother," Aug. 22, 1864, Stuart Papers, Duke University, Durham, N.C.; G[arland] S. Ferguson to "Dear Brother," Aug. 23, 1864, Evelyn McIntosh Hyatt Collection, State Archives of North Carolina, Raleigh; Thomas Stryhorn to "Dear

Sister," Aug. 22, 1864, in Wagstaff, "Letters of Thomas Jackson Strayhorn," 332; Joseph Mullen Diary, Aug. 21, 1864, Eleanor Brockenbrough Library, Museum of the Confederacy, Richmond; Chapman, *More Terrible Than Victory*, 216; Bearss, *Eastern Front Battles*, 301.

37. Rufus Barringer Memoirs, Rufus Barringer Papers, Southern Historical Collection, Louis Round Wilson Library, University of North Carolina, Chapel Hill; Curtis, "Reminiscences," Duke University, Durham, N.C.; Wiley, *Norfolk Blues*, 144; Carmichael, *Lee's Young Artillerist*, 135–36.

38. *OR*, 42(2):366–67; Roebling Journal, Aug. 21, 1864, Roebling Family Papers, Rutgers University, New Brunswick.

39. Porter, "Operations against the Weldon Railroad," 262–63; Wiley, *Norfolk Blues*, 144–45; Bearss, *Eastern Front Battles*, 302; Carmichael, *Lee's Young Artillerist*, 136–37.

40. *OR*, 42(1):472, 541; Nevins, *Diary of Battle*, 454; Horn, *Siege of Petersburg*, 188; Carruth et al., *35th Massachusetts*, 288; Roebling Journal, Aug. 21, 1864; Campbell, *Grand Terrible Dramma*, 262.

41. George Breck, "From Battery L," *Rochester (N.Y.) Union & Advertiser*, Sept. 10, 1864; *OR*, 42(1):481; Horn, *Siege of Petersburg*, 188.

42. Parker, *Henry Wilson's Regiment*, 521; *OR*, 42(2):354, 367.

43. Newsome, Horn, and Selby, *Civil War Talks*, 291; Waters, *Small but Spartan Brigade*, 159–60; Hewitt, Trudeau, and Suderow, *OR Supp.*, 319; Evans, *16th Mississippi*, 287; Kirkpatrick Diary, Aug. 21, 1864, University of Texas, Austin; Horn, *Siege of Petersburg*, 189–90. I found no source that mentions the whereabouts of Wright's, Scales's, or Thomas's troops, all of whom must have been in reserve and would not be engaged.

44. Waters, *Small but Spartan Brigade*, 161; Horn, *Siege of Petersburg*, 191–92; Newsome, Horn, and Selby, *Civil War Talks*, 291; Roebling Journal, Aug. 21, 1864; *OR*, 42(1):484; Roche, "Fighting for Petersburg," 528.

45. Manuscript biography, n.d., William Henry Sanders Papers, Alabama Department of Archives and History, Montgomery. Perrin had been killed on May 12 at Spotsylvania Court House.

46. Manuscript biography, William Henry Sanders Papers; Fortin, "Herbert's History of the 8th Alabama," 174; *OR*, 42(1):488; Clark, *A Glance Backward*, 63.

47. Clark, *A Glance Backward*, 63; Dr. William Sanders to "Dear Father & Mother," Aug. 25, 1864, John C. C. Sanders Papers, University of Alabama, Tuscaloosa.

48. Griffin, *11th Alabama*, 206–7; Theodore G. Trimmier to "Dear Mary," Aug. 22, 1864, Lt. Col. Theodore G. Trimmier Collection, Tennessee State Library and Archives, Nashville; Waters, *Small but Spartan Brigade*, 161.

49. *OR*, 42(1):536, 939; Roche, "Fighting for Petersburg," 529–30; Hewitt, Trudeau, and Suderow, *OR Supp.*, 319; Cockrell and Ballard, *Mississippi Rebel*, 308–9.

50. Charles E. LaMotte to "Dear Father," Aug. 22, 1864, LaMotte Letters, Delaware Public Archives, Dover; Herdegen and Murphy, *Four Years with the Iron Brigade*, 308; Bowerman, "Cutting off Lee."

51. Roche, "Fighting for Petersburg," 529; Fowler, *Memorials of William Fowler*, 110–11.

52. Hewitt, Trudeau, and Suderow, *OR Supp.*, 474; *Athens (Ga.) Southern Banner*, Aug. 31, 1864; Martin and Outlaw, "Eleventh Regiment," 599; Chapman, *More Terrible Than Victory*, 216. Kirkland's brigade evidently remained in reserve unengaged.

53. Robinson, "Fifty-Second Regiment," 248; Chapman, *More Terrible Than Victory*, 218; *OR*, 42(1):481; Brainerd, *146th New York*, 241.

54. Chapman, *More Terrible Than Victory*, 218; Young, "Pettigrew-Kirkland-MacRae Brigade," 564; *OR*, 42(1):475; Hess, *Lee's Tar Heels*, 244.

55. Pearce, *Diary of Captain Henry A. Chambers*, 213 (hereafter Pearce, *Chambers Diary*); Graham, "Fifty-Sixth Regiment," 377; Day, "Life among the Bullets," 216.

56. Garland S. Ferguson to "Dear Brother," Aug. 23, 1864, Hyatt Collection; Burgwyn, "Thirty-Fifth Regiment," 625; Day, "Life among the Bullets," 216. I include Lee's observation with the caveat that the anecdote may well be apocryphal.

57. Burgwyn, "Thirty-Fifth Regiment," 265; John Lane Stuart to "Dear Mother," Aug. 22, 1864, Stuart Papers; Graham, "Fifty-Sixth Regiment," 377; Day, "Life among the Bullets," 216.

58. Thomas Stryhorn to "Dear Sister," Aug. 22, 1864, in Wagstaff, "Letters of Thomas Jackson Strayhorn," 314; Ignatius Wadsworth Brock to "My Dear Sister," Aug. 23, 1864, Rubenstein Special Collections Library, Duke University, Durham, N.C.; Huckaby and Simpson, *Tulip Evermore*, 46.

59. Andrew Linscott to "Dear Mary," Aug. 24, 1864, Linscott Papers, Massachusetts Historical Society, Boston; Greenleaf, *Letters to Eliza*, 131 (Aug. 22, 1864); *OR*, 42(1):505; Freeman, *Letters from Two Brothers*, 140; Thomas and Sauers, *Never Want to Witness Such Sights*, 233.

60. J. Edward Peterson to "Dear Brother," Aug. 22, 1864, J. Edward Peterson Papers, Moravian Music Foundation, Winston-Salem; Pearce, *Chambers Diary*, 213; John Lane Stuart to "Dear Mother," Aug. 22, 1864, Stuart Papers; Hess, *Lee's Tar Heels*, 245.

61. Hagood, *Memoirs*, 290, 298; *OR*, 42(1):936; George H. Moffett to "Dear Liz," Oct. 5, 1864, Moffett Family Papers; Edwin C. Bearss, "General Hagood Meets Captain Dailey: Petersburg National Battlefield Background to Event Depicted," n.d., Petersburg National Battlefield.

62. Cooke Diary, Aug. 27, 1864. For Hagood's role in the First Petersburg Offensive, see Greene, *Campaign of Giants*, 120–21. Hagood would be elected governor of South Carolina in 1880. The Citadel plays football in Johnson Hagood Stadium.

63. Baxley, *No Prouder Fate*, 138; Izlar, *Edisto Rifles*, 81–82; Hagood, *Memoirs*, 291; Moffett, "With Hagood's Brigade in Virginia," 53–57.

64. Hagood, *Memoirs*, 292; *OR*, 42(2):1196; "Bloodiest Charge of the War," in Wolfe, *Private F.W.D.*, 35–38; John Neil, "Hagood's Brigade at Globe Tavern, August 21, 1864," *Winnsboro (S.C.) News and Herald*, May 3, 1905. Some published maps depict Gwyn's brigade on the right of Griffin's division, but the evidence suggests that Tilton's brigade was on Griffin's right, with Gwyn and Gregory, in that order, to their left. See Horn, *Siege of Petersburg*, 189; and Bearss, *Eastern Front Battles*, 309.

65. *OR*, 42(1):482–83; Frey, "Recollections."

66. Hagood, *Memoirs*, 292, 294; *OR*, 42(2):1196. Maloney is listed as "P. K. Malony" in the brigade muster roll. I have used the spelling employed in Hagood's memoir.

67. Izlar, *Edisto Rifles*, 84; Hagood, *Memoirs*, 294; Moffett, "With Hagood's Brigade in Virginia," 53–57.

68. Beaudot, "Bravest Act of the War," 8; Hagood, *Memoirs*, 294; *OR* 42(2):1196.

69. Hagood, *Memoirs*, 294–95; Beaudot, "Bravest Act of the War," 8; DuBose, *B Company, 21st South Carolina*, 109; Moffett, "With Hagood's Brigade in Virginia," 57; Young, "In Petersburg during the Siege," 426. There is controversy regarding the identity of the flag Dailey captured. General Hagood, in his August 22 report to General Beauregard, identified the flag as belonging to the Twenty-Seventh South Carolina, and he repeated this identification

in 1879 correspondence with Dailey. *OR*, 42(2):1196. But in the after-action report of the Eighteenth Massachusetts, written on August 27, 1864, Capt. Luther Bent announced the capture of the Twenty-Seventh's flag. *OR*, 42(1):468. Edwin C. Bearss, a careful student of the battle, identifies the flag as belonging to the Twenty-Seventh, while John Horn, in a more recent study, argues that the flag in question belonged to the Eleventh South Carolina. Bearss, *Eastern Front Battles*, 313; Horn, *Siege of Petersburg*, 199–200. Other sources are equally ambiguous. My conclusion is that the flag probably belonged to the Eleventh South Carolina. One authoritative source lists the Twenty-Seventh's flag as being returned and the Eleventh's flag bearing a battle honor for Weldon Railroad and not captured until 1865. See *Flags of the Confederate Armies*. This strongly suggests (although does not definitively prove) that the Twenty-Seventh's flag remained in Federal hands, while the Eleventh retained its flag long enough to obtain a battle honor for the action on August 21.

70. Hagood, *Memoirs*, 295.

71. Beaudot, "Bravest Act of the War," 12. It is puzzling that the celebrated Dailey would require validation of his wound from Hagood. This suggests that the reconciliation atmosphere after Reconstruction may have animated this tale.

72. Young, "In Petersburg during the Siege," 425; Henry Gawthrop to "Dear Father," Aug. 21, 1864, Gawthrop Letters and Diary, Delaware Historical Society, Wilmington; *OR*, 42(1):484, 542.

73. Hagood, *Memoirs*, 298; Porter, "Operations against the Weldon Railroad," 265; Uberto A. Burnham to "Remembered Parents," Sept. 8, 1864, Burnham Papers, New York State Library, Albany; Charles H. Salter to "My dear Friend," Aug. 23, 1864, Duffield Papers, Burton Historical Collection, Detroit Public Library.

74. Cooke Diary, Aug. 21, 1864; Freeman, *R. E. Lee*, 487; Porter, "Operations against the Weldon Railroad," 265. Mahone had not committed his Georgia brigade, reflecting, perhaps, his lack of confidence in Colonel Gibson. Trains from the north stopped at Dunlop's Station because Union artillery fire could reach the Richmond & Petersburg Railroad farther south.

75. *OR*, 42(2):389; Memoirs, Barringer Papers, 8; Means, "Sixty-Third Regiment," 620; Horn, *Siege of Petersburg*, 202.

76. Tilton Diary, Aug. 21, 1864; *OR*, 42(1):461; Gibbs, *187th Pennsylvania*, 122, 125; *History of the 121st Regiment Pennsylvania Volunteers*, 91; Memoirs, Barringer Papers, 8; Means, "Sixty-Third Regiment," 620.

77. *OR*, 42(2):354–55, 368–69; Hand Diary, Aug. 21, 1864, copy, Petersburg National Battlefield.

78. *OR*, 42(2):355.

79. *OR*, 42(2):355, 369.

80. Simon, *Grant Papers*, 12:56.

81. Vautier Diary, Aug. 21, 1864, copy in bound volume 371, Fredericksburg & Spotsylvania National Military Park; Vautier, *88th Pennsylvania*, 199; Smith, *Corn Exchange Regiment*, 508.

82. Newsome, Horn, and Selby, *Civil War Talks*, 288; Hewitt, Trudeau, and Suderow, *OR Supp.*, 474, Nevins, *Diary of Battle*, 455.

83. Dowdey and Manarin, *Wartime Papers of R. E. Lee*, 842; John Lane Stuart to "Dear Mother," Aug. 22, 1864, Stuart Papers; *OR*, 42(1):431, 595, 939. John Horn consulted a number of sources in calculating Confederate casualties on August 21. See Horn, *Siege of Petersburg*, 204–5n34.

84. "The Fight at Petersburg," *Richmond Daily Dispatch*, Aug. 23, 1864.

85. "Letter from Petersburg, Aug. 24, 1864," *Montgomery (Ala.) Daily Advertiser*, Sept. 2, 1864.

86. George H. Moffett to "Dear Liz," Sept. 14, 1864, Moffett Family Papers; Moffett, "With Hagood's Brigade in Virginia," 57; Hagood, *Memoirs*, 296; *OR*, 42(2):1196. Hagood was not promoted. He and his brigade are memorialized by a monument maintained by the National Park Service several hundred yards north of where their attack occurred. Sgt. William Izlar of the Twenty-Fifth South Carolina raised the funds after the war to erect this stone marker.

87. Hall T. McGee Diary, Aug. 21, 1864, South Carolina Historical Society, Charleston; J. Edward Peterson to "Dear Brother," Aug. 22, 1864, Peterson Papers; Fortin, "Herbert's History of the 8th Alabama," 174; Robert C. Mabry to "My Dear Wife," Aug. 24, 27, 1864, Robert C. Mabry Papers, State Archives of North Carolina, Raleigh; Rude, *Tas*, 14.

88. John Elmore Hall to "My Dear Father," Aug. 27, 1864, Hall Family Papers, Alabama Department of Archives and History, Montgomery; Thomas Jewett Goree to "My dearest Mother," Aug. 26, 1864, in Goree, *Thomas Jewett Goree Letters*, 228; Francis W. Smith to "My Darling Wife," Aug. 22, 1864, Smith Family Papers, Virginia Museum of History and Culture, Richmond; "Fight at Petersburg."

89. Ignatius Wadsworth Brock to "My Dear Sister," Aug. 23, 1864; Thomas Strayhorn to "Dear Sister," Aug. 22, 1864, in Wagstaff, "Letters of Thomas Jackson Strayhorn," 333; Dowdey and Manarin, *Wartime Papers of R. E. Lee*, 842.

90. Nevins, *Diary of Battle*, 453; New York soldier quoted in Bennett, *Sons of Old Monroe*, 471; Peleg G. Jones Diary, Aug. 21, 1864, Gilbert Family Papers, Rhode Island Historical Society, Providence.

91. *OR*, 42(1):122–28. The engagement is frequently called the Battle of Globe Tavern.

92. "Reams Station Cultural Landscape Study," sec. 2, p. 37; Horn, *Siege of Petersburg*, 205. The Confederate infantry engaged were three brigades on August 18, five on August 19, and seven on August 21—Cooke's, Ransom's, MacRae's, Finegan's, Sanders's, Harris's, and Hagood's. Union brigades engaged throughout the battle numbered eleven in the Fifth Corps and four in White's and Willcox's Ninth Corps divisions. I am not including Kirkland's, Scales's, or Thomas's brigades on the Confederate side, whose participation on August 21 is all but invisible, nor Potter's division of the Ninth Corps, which was never significantly engaged.

93. *OR*, 42(2):377, 391–92.

94. Dowdey and Manarin, *Wartime Papers of R. E. Lee*, 843; *OR*, 42(2):1194–95.

95. *OR*, 42(2):1194.

96. Wert, *From Winchester to Cedar Creek*, 29–41; Greene, "Union Generalship in the 1864 Valley Campaign," 47–50.

97. *OR*, 42(2):1194.

98. *OR*, 42(2):1199–1200.

99. Zerah Coston Monks to "Dear Hattie," Aug. 25, 1864, Monks Family Papers, Western Reserve Historical Society, Cleveland; *OR*, 42(2):442.

CHAPTER FIVE

1. U.S. War Department, *War of the Rebellion*, ser. 1, 42(2):376–79, 384–85, 390 (hereafter *OR*; all references are to series 1 unless otherwise noted).

2. *OR*, 42(1):221, 42(2):357–58; Stewart, *140th Pennsylvania*, 233; Keating, *Carnival of Blood*, 251.

3. Dowdey and Manarin, *Wartime Papers of R. E. Lee*, 813; *OR*, 42(2):1171; Andrew, *Wade Hampton*, 226–27. Butler would receive promotion to major general on September 19 and Dunovant elevation to brigadier general on August 22.

4. Wellman, *Giant in Gray*, 154. There are several modern biographies of Hampton, the best of which is Andrew, *Wade Hampton*. Others include Longacre, *Gentlemen and Soldier*, and Cisco, *Wade Hampton*.

5. Daughtry, *Gray Cavalier*, 209; Barringer, *Fighting for General Lee*, 167–68; Wells, *Hampton and His Cavalry*, 278; Vogtsberger, *Dulanys of Welbourne*, 197; "To the Editor of the Examiner," *Richmond Daily Examiner*, Sept. 7, 1864.

6. *OR*, 42(1):606, 643; Lt. Col. Joseph Frederick Waring Diary, Aug. 22, 1864, Southern Historical Collection, Louis Round Wilson Library, University of North Carolina, Chapel Hill; Jesse R. Sparkman Diary, Aug. 22, 1864, copy in bound vol. 373, Fredericksburg & Spotsylvania National Military Park.

7. *OR*, 42(1):833–34, 606, 208, 42(2):393, 408; Bearss, *Eastern Front Battles*, 328; Vogtsberger, *Dulanys of Welbourne*, 209; Trout, *Galloping Thunder*, 564.

8. *OR*, 42(1):221, 250–51, 261, 269; Keating, *Carnival of Blood*, 251–52; Walters Diary, Aug. 22, 1864, copy in bound volume 261, Fredericksburg & Spotsylvania National Military Park; Poriss and Poriss, *While My Country Is in Danger*, 126–27; Walker, *Second Army Corps*, 581. The division's commander, Francis Barlow, remained on the sick leave he began on August 17 caused by chronic diarrhea.

9. *OR*, 42(2):392, 42(1):261; John Buttrick Noyes to "Dear Mother," Aug. 27, 1864, Noyes Civil War Letters, Harvard University, Cambridge; Martin Sigman Memoirs, copy in bound vol. 320, Fredericksburg & Spotsylvania National Military Park; Charles Hamlin to "Dear Sister Louise," Aug. 26, 1864, Hamlin Letters, New York State Library, Albany; Husk, *111th New York*, 154; Keating, *Carnival of Blood*, 252; Barnard, *Irish Brigade*, 129–30.

10. Mulholland, *116th Pennsylvania*, 256; *OR*, 42(1):222, 251, 42(2); 393; Husk, *111th New York*, 154; Barnard, *Irish Brigade*, 129; John Buttrick Noyes to "Dear Mother," Aug. 27, 1864, Noyes Civil War Letters; Pomfret, "Letters of Frederick Lockley," 89.

11. *OR*, 42(2):418–19.

12. *OR*, 42(2):419–20, 436–37; Simon, *Grant Papers*, 12:75. Although Grant's message to Meade is marked 2:15 P.M. in the *Official Records*, the entry in the Grant Papers suggests that it was received at that time and sent an hour earlier.

13. *OR*, 42(1):251, 261.

14. *OR*, 42(2):435–36.

15. "Reams Station Cultural Landscape Study," sec. 2, pp. 38–39; *OR*, 42(1):269, 835, (2):427; Horn, *Siege of Petersburg*, 214. Edwin C. Bearss, in *Eastern Front Battles*, misnames Depot Road as Dinwiddie Stage Road. Monk's Neck is the Anglicized version of the Native American word *Moccoseneck*, which means "big stones" and was the original name of Rowanty Creek.

16. For a more detailed description of this encounter, see Horn, *Siege of Petersburg*, 214–17.

17. *OR*, 42(2):427.

18. *OR*, 42(1):606–7; Halliburton, *Saddle Soldiers*, 165; Hand, *One Good Regiment*, 146; Mohr and Winslow, *Cormany Diaries*, 472; Bearss, *Eastern Front Battles*, 336–39; Horn, *Siege of Petersburg*, 217–19.

19. *OR*, 42(1):269, 42(2):427, 436; Wade Hampton Connected Narrative, Hampton Family Papers, South Caroliniana Library, University of South Carolina, Columbia, 71; Wells,

Hampton and His Cavalry, 277; Wade Hampton to "My Dear Sir," Francis A. Walker Papers, Union League of Philadelphia.

20. *OR*, 42(2):425–26, 42(1):322.

21. *OR*, 42(1):222, 322; Billings, *Tenth Massachusetts Battery*, 303; Page, *Fourteenth Regiment Connecticut Volunteer Infantry*, 294 (hereafter Page, *Fourteenth Connecticut*).

22. *OR*, 42(1):406, 410; Aldrich, *Battery A, First Regiment Rhode Island Light Artillery*, 375.

23. Hart, *Plodding and Thinking*, 28; *OR*, 42(1):222, 293, 317, 322, 406–7, 420; Maull, *Thomas A. Smyth*, 34; Albee Diary, Aug. 24, 1864, Library of Virginia, Richmond.

24. Poriss and Poriss, *While My Country Is in Danger*, 123n17. The Porisses located this account in the Library of Virginia. For the fighting at First Reams' Station, see Greene, *Campaign of Giants*, 296–303.

25. *OR*, 42(1):222, 250, 261, 42(2):447; Mulholland, *116th Pennsylvania*, 257; Welch, *Boy General*, 195–97.

26. *OR*, 42(1):250, 278–79, 282, 302, 323; Bearss, *Eastern Front Battles*, 343; Page, *Fourteenth Connecticut*, 294, 302; Kirk, *Heavy Guns and Light*, 336–37; "From the 14th Regiment, C.V.," *Waterbury (Conn.) American*, Sept. 16, 1864.

27. Page, *Fourteenth Connecticut*, 294; Metzger Diary, Aug. 24, 1864, Metzger Letters and Diary, Nau Civil War Collection, Houston; Child, *5th New Hampshire*, 287; Kirk, *Heavy Guns and Light*, 337; Stewart, *140th Pennsylvania*, 233–34; Mulholland, *116th Pennsylvania*, 257.

28. *OR*, 42(1):221–22, 250, 607; Harrell, *2nd North Carolina Cavalry*, 324; Horn, *Siege of Petersburg*, 222; "Reams Station Cultural Landscape Study," sec. 2, p. 39; Walters Diary, Aug. 24, 1864. Malone's Crossing marked the place where a country road leading to the home of one D. Malone intersected the tracks about three miles south of Reams' Station.

29. Horn, *Siege of Petersburg*, 220–21; Billings, *Tenth Massachusetts Battery*, 311; Miller, *Harvard's Civil War*, 412; Smith, *19th Maine*, 233–34; Walker, *Second Army Corps*, 582–83; Bruce, *Twentieth Massachusetts*, 419.

30. Bruce, *Twentieth Massachusetts*, 419; Walker, *Second Army Corps*, 582–83; Horn, *Siege of Petersburg*, 220–21; soldier quoted in Guelzo, "As Plain as a Deep Scar," 29. Earl J. Hess has likened Hancock's men in their constricted works to "settlers cowering in a circled wagon train." Hess, *Lee's Tar Heels*, 248. In 2024 Halifax Road runs on the alignment of the wartime Weldon Railroad at Reams' Station.

31. *OR*, 42(1):244–45, 322–23; Bearss, *Eastern Front Battles*, 344.

32. *OR*, 42(1):407, 420; Bearss, *Eastern Front Battles*, 345; Dauchy, "Battle of Ream's Station," 131; Billings, *Tenth Massachusetts Battery*, 312.

33. *OR*, 42(1):222, 250, 261; Mahood, *Written in Blood*, 304; Stewart, *140th Pennsylvania*, 233–34; Husk, *111th New York*, 154; Mulholland, *116th Pennsylvania*, 257; Keating, *Carnival of Blood*, 253; Page, *Fourteenth Connecticut*, 294; Waitt, *19th Massachusetts*, 347; Aldrich, *Battery A, First Regiment Rhode Island Light Artillery*, 376; Billings, *Tenth Massachusetts Battery*, 312; "Spectator," correspondent of the *Petersburg Express*, quoted in *Raleigh (N.C.) Weekly Confederate*, Sept. 7, 1864.

34. *OR*, 42(2):448, 42(1):222.

35. *OR*, 42(1):19–20, 42(2):441–42, 455. For a cogent argument that Ord should have relieved Hancock of the responsibility of destroying the railroad south of Reams' Station, see Horn, *Siege of Petersburg*, 219.

36. *OR*, 42(2):448–49, 42(1):222–23; Bearss, *Eastern Front Battles*, 346.

37. *OR*, 42(1):223, 42(2):452; Metzger Diary, Aug. 24, 1864. Either Warren or Hancock mistimed Warren's reply as 9:00 A.M. on the twenty-fourth.

38. Hampton to "My Dear Sir," Mar. 29, 1884, Walker Papers; Wells, *Hampton and His Cavalry*, 277; Walker, "Reams' Station," 278–79; Horn, *Siege of Petersburg*, 233.

39. Hampton to "My Dear Sir," Mar. 29, 1884; *OR*, 42(2):1202.

40. Freeman, *R. E. Lee*, 488; Horn, *Siege of Petersburg*, 223–24.

41. Wilcox, "Battle of Reams Station," 63; William D. Alexander Diary, Aug. 24, 1864, Southern Historical Collection, Louis Round Wilson Library, University of North Carolina, Chapel Hill; Edward J. Hale, "From Lane's Brigade," *Fayetteville (N.C.) Observer*, Sept. 8, 1864; Hewitt, Trudeau, and Suderow, *Supplement to the Official Records of the Union and Confederate Armies* (hereafter *OR Supp.*), 469, 507; Kelly Diary, Aug. 24, 1864, Kelly Papers, College of Charleston; Caldwell, *McGowan's Brigade*, 234.

42. Lemuel J. Hoyle to "My Dear Mother," Aug. 29, 1864, Lemuel J. Hoyle Papers, Southern Historical Collection, Louis Round Wilson Library, University of North Carolina, Chapel Hill; Benjamin Wesley Justice to "My Sweet Darling Wife," Aug. 30, 1864, Justice Letters, Emory University, Atlanta; Hess, *Lee's Tar Heels*, 248; Newsome, Horn, and Selby, *Civil War Talks*, 289; Horn, *Petersburg Regiment*, 319; Bearss, *Eastern Front Battles*, 349.

43. *OR*, 42(1):858; Carmichael, *Lee's Young Artillerist*, 138; Trout, *Galloping Thunder*, 564–65. All of Pegram's guns belonged to the Third Corps. Ross's Battery came from Allen Cutts's Battalion. Clutter's guns and the Hardaway Artillery were part of David McIntosh's Battalion. "Hurt's Battery near Petersburg," *Columbus (Ga.) Daily Sun*, Sept. 10, 1864. Written by a member of Hurt's Battery, this article includes Grandy's Norfolk Light Artillery among the batteries accompanying Hill, although I have found no other source that documents its presence.

44. Hoyle to "My Dear Mother," Aug. 29, 1864, Hoyle Papers; Newsome, Horn, and Selby, *Civil War Talks*, 289; Robert Powel Page to "My darling little wife," Aug. 24, 1864, Robert Powel Page Papers, Virginia Museum of History and Culture, Richmond. A portion of the Thirty-Fifth Virginia Cavalry Battalion, the Comanches, escorted a wagon train to Stony Creek on the morning of the twenty-fourth. See Myers, *The Comanches*, 324.

45. Wilcox, "Battle of Reams Station," 63; Alexander Diary, Aug. 24, 1864; Hardy, *Thirty-Seventh North Carolina*, 207; Dunlop, *Lee's Sharpshooters*, 189–90.

46. Benjamin Wesley Justice to "My Sweet Darling Wife," Aug. 30, 1864, Justice Letters; Mullen Diary, Aug. 24, 1864, Museum of the Confederacy, Richmond; Stedman, "Forty-Fourth N.C. Infantry," 342; Hoyle to "My Dear Mother," Aug. 29, 1864, Hoyle Papers; Hess, *Lee's Tar Heels*, 248; George Bernard Diary, Albert and Shirley Small Special Collections Library, University of Virginia, Charlottesville. As of 2024, the Joseph Boisseau house, Tudor Hall, is preserved by Pamplin Historical Park.

47. Andrew, *Wade Hampton*, 233; Hampton to "My Dear Sir [Walker]," Mar. 29, 1884; Brooks, *Butler and His Cavalry*, 303; *OR Supp.*, 469; Horn, *Petersburg Regiment*, 320.

48. *OR*, 42(2):498, 502. John Horn suggests that Pickett's foray paid "rich dividends by drawing the attention of the Unionist high command to the right while Lee's blow neared from the left" but neglects to define such an advantage. Horn, *Siege of Petersburg*, 227–28.

49. *OR*, 42(1):942–43; Harrell, *2nd North Carolina Cavalry*, 325; Beale, *Lieutenant of Cavalry*, 181. Beale's account was reprinted as "Rooney Lee's Men at Reams' Station," *Richmond Times-Dispatch*, Mar. 19, 1905.

50. Wilcox, "Battle of Reams Station," 63; Hardy, *General Lee's Immortals*, 325; Caldwell, *McGowan's Brigade*, 235; Dunlop, *Lee's Sharpshooters*, 190; Horn, *Siege of Petersburg*, 229; Bearss, *Eastern Front Battles*, 355.

51. *OR*, 42(2):481, 497; Walker, *Second Army Corps*, 585.

52. *OR*, 42(1):223, 607, 42(2):481.

53. *OR*, 42(1):302, 323; Washburn, *108th New York*, 84; Lt. Frank M. Riley Diary, Aug. 25, 1864, copy in bound vol. 97, Richmond National Battlefield Park; George D. Bowen Diary, Aug. 25, 1864, copy in bound vol. 228, Fredericksburg & Spotsylvania National Military Park; Page, *Fourteenth Connecticut*, 309; "From the 14th Regiment, C.V.," *Waterbury (Conn.) American*, Sept. 16, 1864; Longacre, *To Gettysburg and Beyond*, 243; Cowtan, *Tenth New York*, 310; Roback, *152nd New York*, 117; Smith, *19th Maine*, 234; Aubery, *Thirty-Sixth Wisconsin*, 154; Hart, *Plodding and Thinking*, 29.

54. *OR*, 42(1):251, 261–62, 288; Bacarella, *Lincoln's Foreign Legion*, 180; Husk, *111th New York*, 155; Pellicano, *Conquer or Die*, 154; Keating, *Carnival of Blood*, 254–55; Billings, *Tenth Massachusetts Battery*, 312; Mulholland, *116th Pennsylvania*, 258; Gayley, *148th Pennsylvania*, 39; Sigman Memoirs, 41; John Buttrick Noyes to "Dear Father," Sept. 10, 1864, Noyes Civil War Letters; Child, *5th New Hampshire*, 287; Bearss, *Eastern Front Battles*, 355; Horn, *Siege of Petersburg*, 228.

55. Beale, *Lieutenant of Cavalry*, 181–82; Willis Diary, Aug. 25, 1864, Library of Virginia, Richmond; Harrell, *2nd North Carolina Cavalry*, 324; Barringer, *Fighting for General Lee*, 168; Washington, *Laurel Brigade*, 271; Wells, *Hampton and His Cavalry*, 279; Romig, *Phipps' Letters*, 68; *OR* 42(1):834–35, 943; Bearss, *Eastern Front Battles*, 356–57; Horn, *Siege of Petersburg*, 229–30.

56. *OR*, 42(1):835, (2):482; Horn, *Siege of Petersburg*, 231; Bearss, *Eastern Front Battles*, 357.

57. *OR*, 42(1):223, 245, 293, 323–24; John Gibbon to "My dearest Maria," John Gibbon Papers, Historical Society of Pennsylvania, Philadelphia; Gibbon, *Personal Recollections*, 261; Maull, *Thomas A. Smyth*, 34; William F. Smith to "Dear Mother," Aug. 27, 1864, William F. Smith Letters, Army Heritage and Education Center, Carlisle; Haines, *Co. F 12th New Jersey*, 79–80; Longacre, *To Gettysburg and Beyond*, 244; Page, *Fourteenth Connecticut*, 309; Cowtan, *Tenth New York*, 310–11.

58. *OR*, 42(1):302, 407, 414; Jacob Bechtel to "Miss Cannie," Aug. 28, 1864, Jacob Bechtel Letters, Gettysburg National Military Park; Smith, *19th Maine*, 234; Aubery, *Thirty-Sixth Wisconsin*, 154; Billings, *Tenth Massachusetts Battery*, 313; Henry Sleeper to "My dear General," Mar. 3, 1884, Walker Papers; Alex Ward, "Employment of Artillery during the Battles of the Siege of Petersburg," Petersburg National Battlefield; *OR Supp.*, 521, 524.

59. *OR*, 42(1):607, 943; Bearss, *Eastern Front Battles*, 362; Horn, *Siege of Petersburg*, 233.

60. *OR*, 42(1):223, 245, 293, 324; Bearss, *Eastern Front Battles*, 362–63.

61. *OR*, 42(1):302, 317–18, 407, 414; Bearss, *Eastern Front Battles*, 363; Horn, *Siege of Petersburg*, 234–35.

62. Mohr and Winslow, *Cormany Diaries*, 472–73; *OR*, 42(1):607; Hand, *One Good Regiment*, 147; John Daniel Follmer Diary, Aug. 25, 1864, Historical Society of Pennsylvania, Philadelphia.

63. Cadmus Wilcox, "Reams Station," R. E. Lee's Headquarters Papers, Virginia Museum of History and Culture, Richmond; Harris, *Seventh North Carolina*, 55; Caldwell, *McGowan's Brigade*, 235; *OR Supp.*, 469. The Federal gunners opened a sporadic fire after Rebel

skirmishers picked off several of their men and horses. See Rhodes, *Battery B, First Regiment Rhode Island Light Artillery*, 328.

64. Wilcox, "Battle of Reams Station," 63; Dunlop, *Lee's Sharpshooters*, 190–92; Sigman Memoirs, 41; Horn, *Siege of Petersburg*, 235–37; Bearss, *Eastern Front Battles*, 366–67.

65. *OR*, 42(1):224, 251–52, 287–88; Mahood, *Written in Blood*, 305; Mulholland, *116th Pennsylvania*, 259; Gayley, *148th Pennsylvania*, 39; Warner Journal, Aug. 25, 1864, Warner Papers, Wisconsin Historical Society, Madison; Horn, *Siege of Petersburg*, 237–38.

66. *OR*, 42(2):481–82, 485, 487–88, 42(1):391–92; Robertson, *McAllister Letters*, 488; Humphreys, *Virginia Campaign of '64 and '65*, 280; Hancock to "My dear General," Feb. 22, 1884, Walker Papers.

67. Wilcox, "Battle of Reams Station," 64; Wilcox, "Notes on the Richmond Campaign, 1864–1865," Cadmus Marcellus Wilcox Papers, Virginia Museum of History and Culture, Richmond; Wilcox, "Reams Station," Lee Headquarters Papers. The two regiments from Conner's brigade may have been the Twenty-Eighth and Thirty-Third North Carolina. *OR*, 42(1):288.

68. *OR*, 42(1):288; Serff, "Life of James A. Beaver," 47–48; Burr, *Life and Achievements of James Addams Beaver*, 164–65; James A. Beaver to "My Dear Mother," Aug. 24, 1864, James A. Beaver Collection, Pennsylvania State Archives, Harrisburg; Dr. A. W. Acheson, *Beaver (Pa.) Radical*, Nov. 3, 1869; Kohler, *Ready, Always Ready*, 178–79. For an account of Beaver's June 16 wounding, see Greene, *Campaign of Giants*, 143. Surgeons amputated the colonel's leg, ending his military career. He recovered and would be elected governor of Pennsylvania. Beaver Stadium at Penn State University bears his name.

69. Wilcox, "Reams Station," Lee Headquarters Papers; Wilcox, "Battle of Reams Station," 64–65; Wilcox, "Notes on the Richmond Campaign"; Rogers, "Retaking the Railroad at Reams Station," 581.

70. Frederick Lockley to "*Ma tres chere Femme*," Aug. 27, 1864, Lockley Papers, Huntington Library, San Marino; Keating, *Carnival of Blood*, 257; Wilcox, "Reams Station," Lee Headquarters Papers.

71. Walker, "Reams' Station," 280–81; Robertson, *General A. P. Hill*, 299.

72. *OR*, 42(1):224, 245; Wilcox, "Battle of Reams Station," 64–65; "Notes on the Richmond Campaign." Edwin C. Bearss describes a distinct second assault, without identifying the attackers. Bearss, *Eastern Front Battles*, 369. A number of sources refer vaguely to a second attack, while many others fail to acknowledge such an occurrence. Some Federals accounts mention a third attack an hour or more later.

73. *OR*, 42(2):482–83, (1):224; Humphreys, *Virginia Campaign of '64 and '65*, 280; Dauchy, "Battle of Ream's Station," 132. Francis Walker writes that despite the telegraph line being extended to Reams' Station, Meade continued to communicate with Hancock via courier. Walker, "Reams' Station," 278. John Horn argues that Meade's concern for the army's rear stemmed from his belief in the imminent arrival of Confederate troops from the Shenandoah Valley, which explained his decision to send Mott's forces and Willcox's division down Jerusalem Plank Road. Horn, *Siege of Petersburg*, 243–45. The evidence for this is conjectural, and Meade would offer a different rationale later that evening.

74. Dunlop, *Lee's Sharpshooters*, 192–94; *OR*, 42(1):407, 415; Billings, *Tenth Massachusetts Battery*, 314–16; Rhodes, *Battery B, First Regiment Rhode Island Light Artillery*, 328; Aldrich, *Battery A, First Regiment Rhode Island Light Artillery*, 377; DeMontravel, *Hero to His Fighting Men*, 35.

75. Billings, *Tenth Massachusetts Battery*, 317; Aldrich, *Battery A, First Regiment Rhode Island Light Artillery*, 377; Dunlop, *Lee's Sharpshooters*, 193; Hess, *Rifle Musket in Civil War Combat*, 168.

76. *OR*, 42(1):225–26, 391–93, 42(2):484; Robertson, *McAllister Letters*, 488; Marbaker, *11th New Jersey*, 210–11. General Mott remained with the balance of his division along the Petersburg fortifications.

77. Carmichael, *Lee's Young Artillerist*, 138; "Hurt's Battery near Petersburg," *Columbus (Ga.) Daily Sun*, Sept. 9, 1864; *OR Supp.*, 474; Ethelbert Fairfax to "Dear Jennie," Sept. 7, 1864, Ethelbert Fairfax Letters, Eleanor Brockenbrough Library, Museum of the Confederacy, Richmond; Wilcox, "Battle of Reams Station," 65; Hess, *Lee's Tar Heels*, 249; Horn, *Siege of Petersburg*, 246; Bearss, *Eastern Front Battles*, 379–80.

78. Wilcox, "Notes on the Richmond Campaign"; Wilcox, "Battle of Reams Station," 65; *OR Supp.*, 475, 492; Horn, *Siege of Petersburg*, 247.

79. "Hurt's Battery near Petersburg" *Columbus (Ga.) Daily Sun*, Sept. 10, 1864; Westwood Todd, "Reminiscences of the War between the States, April 1861–July 1865," Southern Historical Collection, Louis Round Wilson Library, University of North Carolina, Chapel Hill; "To the Editor of the *Examiner*," *Richmond Daily Examiner*, Sept. 5, 1864; Miller, *Harvard's Civil War*, 415; Roback, *152nd New York*, 119; Jacob Bechtel to "Miss Cannie," Aug. 28, 1864, Bechtel Letters; *OR*, 42(1):226, 293; Bearss, *Eastern Front Battles*, 380–81; Horn, *Siege of Petersburg*, 250–51.

80. Edward J. Hale, "From Lane's Brigade," *Fayetteville (N.C.) Observer*, Sept. 8, 1864; Kearney, "Fifteenth Regiment," 747; Lawhon, "Forty-Eighth Regiment," 121; Mullen Diary, Aug. 25, 1864; Stedman, "Battle at Reams' Station," 115; Chapman, *More Terrible Than Victory*, 225–26; Underwood, *26th North Carolina*, 388–89.

81. *OR Supp.*, 469, 499; McDaid, "Four Years of Arduous Service," 307–8; Hardy, *General Lee's Immortals*, 326. Speer died four days later.

82. "From Lane's Brigade, Extracts from Letters dated August 28," *Fayetteville (N.C.) Observer*, Sept. 8, 1864; Hardy, *Thirty-Seventh North Carolina*, 208–9.

83. Mullen Diary, Aug. 25, 1864; Hess, *Lee's Tar Heels*, 252.

84. *OR*, 42(1):253, 408.

85. Underwood, *26th North Carolina*, 83. MacRae received command of Kirkland's Brigade on June 27.

86. Young, "Pettigrew-Kirkland-MacRae Brigade," 565; Hess, *Lee's Tar Heels*, 252; Chapman, *More Terrible Than Victory*, 228.

87. Stedman, "Forty-Fourth Regiment," 30; John Alexander Sloan, "North Carolinian in the War between the States," 73:6, Southern Historical Collection, Louis Round Wilson Library, University of North Carolina, Chapel Hill.

88. Nelson A. Miles to "Dear Uncle," Sept. 12, 1864, Nelson A. Miles Papers, Army Heritage and Education Center, Carlisle; Keating, *Carnival of Blood*, 262–66; Frederick, *Story of a Regiment*, 263–64; Bacarella, *Lincoln's Foreign Legion*, 181; Charles Lee Diary, Aug. 25, 1864, Henry E. Huntington Library, San Marino.

89. *OR*, 42(1):253, 289; Simons, *125th New York*, 242–43; Husk, *111th New York*, 258–59.

90. Smith Reminiscences, Minnesota Historical Society, Saint Paul; John Buttrick Noyes to "Dear Father," Sept. 10, 1864, Noyes Civil War Letters; Mulholland, *116th Pennsylvania*, 261; Keating, *Carnival of Blood*, 265–66; Billings, *Tenth Massachusetts Battery*, 321–22.

91. Wilcox, "Battle of Reams Station," 65; *OR Supp.*, 475; Sloan, "North Carolinian in the War between the States," 73:6; John Wright to "Dear Father and Fanny," John Wright Family Papers, State Archives of North Carolina, Raleigh; Lemuel J. Hoyle to "My Dear Mother," Aug. 29, 1864, Hoyle Papers; Benjamin Wesley Justice to "My Sweet Darling Wife," Aug. 30, 1864, Justice Letters; Stedman, "Forty-Fourth Regiment," 30–31; William J. Baker to "My Dearest Wife," Aug. 29, 1864, Blanche Baker Papers, Southern Historical Collection, Louis Round Wilson Library, University of North Carolina, Chapel Hill.

92. *OR*, 42(1):226, 245, 253, 302; *OR Supp.*, 427–28.

93. Hart, *Plodding and Thinking*, 29; Aubery, *Thirty-Sixth Wisconsin*, 154; Miller, *Harvard's Civil War*, 416–17.

94. *OR*, 42, (1):262, 407–8, 421; Barnard, *Irish Brigade*, 132; George Cove to Julia Parsons, Aug. 28, 1864, Parsons Family Papers, University of New Hampshire, Durham, N.H.; *OR Supp.*, 492; Sloan, "North Carolinian in the War between the States," 73:8; Dauchy, "Battle of Ream's Station," 131–32, 134; Naisawald, *Grape and Canister*, 415.

95. *OR*, 42(1):226, 253, 262, 591; Scott, *Forgotten Valor*, 270; Riddell, "Ream's Station Again"; *Santa Cruz (Calif.) Evening News*, July 20, 1909.

96. *OR Supp.*, 507–8; Rhodes, *Battery B, First Regiment Rhode Island Light Artillery*, 330–31; *OR*, 42(1):270, 408; Horn, *Siege of Petersburg*, 262; Aldrich, *Battery A, First Regiment Rhode Island Light Artillery*, 378; Billings, *Tenth Massachusetts Battery*, 319; Kirk, *Heavy Guns and Light*, 348–49; William E. Endicott to "Dear Mother," Oct. 13, 1864, Endicott Papers, Auburn University; William A. Templeton to "Diear brother," Sept. 3, 1864, Templeton Family Papers, South Caroliniana Library, University of South Carolina, Columbia. It is probable that the Twelfth South Carolina and Orr's Rifles accompanied Haskell.

97. Walker, "Reams' Station," 291; *OR*, 42(1):226, 293.

98. *OR*, 42(1):293; *Portland (Maine) Evening News*, Jan. 8, 1887; Smith, *19th Maine*, 236–37.

99. *OR*, 42(1):293, 306, 308, 318, 324; Maull, *Thomas A. Smyth*, 35; Bearss, *Eastern Front Battles*, 392; Horn, *Siege of Petersburg*, 266.

100. Maull, *Thomas A. Smyth*, 35; Page, *Fourteenth Connecticut*, 310; Cowtan, *Tenth New York*, 312; Haines, *Co F 12th New Jersey*, 81; George Hopper to "Dear Brother & Sister," Sept. 5, 1864, George Hopper Letters, Army Heritage and Education Center, Carlisle; Horn, *Siege of Petersburg*, 267.

101. *OR*, 42(1):311, 943; Cheek, "Addenda to Ninth Regiment," 776; Harrell, *2nd North Carolina Cavalry*, 326; Jacob Bechtel to "Miss Cannie," Aug. 28, 1864, Bechtel Letters; Horn, *Siege of Petersburg*, 270; Bearss, *Eastern Front Battles*, 393.

102. *OR*, 42(1):943; Wade Hampton to "My Dear Sir," Mar. 29, 1884, Walker Papers; Trout, *Galloping Thunder*, 566. Both John Horn and Edwin C. Bearss credit Hampton with two batteries—eight guns—of horse artillery, but McGregor had only two pieces, one of which had been disabled earlier in the day, and Hart's Battery was absent on August 25. Horn, *Siege of Petersburg*, 271; Bearss, *Eastern Front Battles*, 393. The Seventh Virginia Cavalry had been assigned to cover the infantry, and Dunovant's Brigade had ridden to Hampton's right to guard his right flank.

103. Washington, *Laurel Brigade*, 273; Wade Hampton to "My Dear Sir," Mar. 29, 1884; Mesic, *Cobb's Legion Cavalry*, 138; *OR*, 42(1):943; Wells, *Hampton and His Cavalry*, 281.

104. Beale, *Lieutenant of Cavalry*, 184; Harrell, *2nd North Carolina Cavalry*, 321; Mesic, *Cobb's Legion Cavalry*, 138; Washington, *Laurel Brigade*, 274.

105. Washington, *Laurel Brigade*, 274; Chiswell Dabney to "Dear Bettie," Aug. 29, 1864; and Dabney to "Dear Mother," Aug. 29, 1864, Saunders Family Papers, Virginia Museum of History and Culture, Richmond; Howard, *Sketch of Cobb Legion Cavalry*. I have found no other source that mentions Pryor's presence.

106. *OR*, 42(1):294, 318; George Hopper to "Dear Brother & Sister," Sept. 5, 1864, Hopper Letters; Maull, *Thomas A. Smyth*, 35; Townshend, *Seventh Michigan*, 187; Waitt, *19th Massachusetts*, 347.

107. *OR*, 42(1):607; Follmer Diary, Aug. 25, 1864; Thomas J. Gregg to "Dear Ben," Aug. 26, 1864, Library of Virginia, Richmond; James Mitchell to "Dear Brother David," Sept. 2, 1864, James Mitchell Letters, Petersburg National Battlefield.

108. *OR*, 42(1):227, 254; Nelson A. Miles to "Dear Uncle," Sept. 12, 1864, Miles Papers. For Hancock's alleged inconsolable humiliation, see Tucker, *Hancock the Superb*, 254–55; and Jordan, *Winfield Scott Hancock*, 162.

109. Winfield S. Hancock to "My dear General," Feb. 27, 1884, Walker Papers; *OR*, 42(1):227, 263, 591; Cutcheon, *Twentieth Michigan Infantry*, 151.

110. Samuel Fessenden to "My Dear Father," Sept. 4, 1864, Samuel Fessenden Letters, Library of Virginia, Richmond; Houston, *Thirty-Second Maine*, 379; Dr. William Child, *Letters from a Civil War Surgeon*, 257; Keating, *Carnival of Blood*, 271; *OR*, 42(1):227, 283, 302, 318; Aubery, *Thirty-Sixth Wisconsin*, 154; Child, *5th New Hampshire*, 278.

111. *OR*, 42(2):484–86.

112. *OR*, 42(1):607; T. C. Evans, "Thirteenth North Carolina," *Raleigh (N.C.) Daily Confederate*, Sept. 8, 1864; letter from *Tout Le Monde*, in Styple, *Writing & Fighting from the Army of Northern Virginia*, 298; Vogtsberger, *Dulanys of Welbourne*, 217; "Hurt's Battery near Petersburg," *Columbus (Ga.) Daily Sun*, Sept. 10, 1864; "Spectator," correspondent of the *Petersburg Express*, quoted in *Raleigh (N.C.) Weekly Confederate*, Sept. 7, 1864.

113. Washington, *Laurel Brigade*, 276; Vogtsberger, *Dulanys of Welbourne*, 199; Willis Diary, Aug. 26, 1864; Beale, *Lieutenant of Cavalry*, 187; Mesic, *Cobb's Legion Cavalry*, 138; Newsome, Horn, and Selby, *Civil War Talks*, 294; *OR Supp.*, 469, 476, 508; Caldwell, *McGowan's Brigade*, 236; Mullen Diary, Aug. 25–26, 1864; Alexander Diary, Aug. 25, 1864; Dunlop, *Lee's Sharpshooters*, 200; *OR*, 42(1):944.

114. *OR*, 42(1):129–32, 940. For a detailed summary of casualties, see Horn, *Siege of Petersburg*, 276–77.

115. Rogers, "Retaking the Railroad at Reams Station," 581.

CHAPTER SIX

1. Julius Leinbach Diary, Aug. 26, 1864, Southern Historical Collection, Louis Round Wilson Library, University of North Carolina, Chapel Hill; Lyle Diary, Aug. 26, 1864, Virginia Museum of History and Culture, Richmond; Wilson, *Confederate Soldier*, 183; William E. Endicott to "Dear Mary," Oct. 21, 1864, Endicott Papers, Auburn University. Two months of Union shelling had inflicted significant damage to buildings in the eastern half of Petersburg.

2. Wiggins, *My Dear Friend*, 146; John Thomas Vassey to "Dear Father and Mother," Aug. 27, 1864, John Thomas Vassey Letters, Tennessee State Library and Archives, Nashville; "Avis" to the editor of the *Examiner*, *Richmond Daily Examiner*, Sept. 7, 1864.

3. U.S. War Department, *War of the Rebellion*, ser. 1, 42(2):1204–1207 (hereafter *OR*; all references are to series 1 unless otherwise noted); Englehard letter, Aug. 28, 1864, North Carolina Digital Collections.

4. Conner, *Letters*, 149; Samuel F. Harper to "My Dear Sister," Aug. 26, 1864, Samuel Finley Harper Letters, State Archives of North Carolina, Raleigh; John R. Turner Letter (no salutation), Sept. 4, 1864, John R. Turner Papers, Rubenstein Special Collections Library, Duke University, Durham, N.C.

5. Willie Pegram to "My dear Sister," Sept. 1, 1864, Pegram-Johnston-McIntosh Family Papers, Virginia Museum of History and Culture, Richmond; "Letter from Petersburg," *Columbus (Ga.) Daily Sun*, Sept. 15, 1864; *OR*, 42(2):1205.

6. Hugh Randolph Crichton to "Dear Phil & Jennie," Aug. 28, 1864, Lucy Tunstall Alston Williams Papers, Southern Historical Collection, Louis Round Wilson Library, University of North Carolina, Chapel Hill.

7. Wilcox quoted in Patterson, *From Blue to Gray*, 83; Levin, "William Mahone, the Lost Cause, and Civil War History," 407; William Martin to Miss H. R. McIntosh, Aug. 28, 1864, Harriet R. McIntosh Papers, Southern Historical Collection, Louis Round Wilson Library, University of North Carolina, Chapel Hill.

8. Henry S. Joy to "Dear Harry," Aug. 26, 1864, Henry S. Joy Papers, Civil War Documents Collection, Army Heritage and Education Center, Carlisle; Dauchy, "Battle of Ream's Station," 139; Sumner, *Comstock Diary*, 287.

9. Lowe, *Meade's Army*, 258; *Richmond Daily Dispatch*, Sept. 7, 1864.

10. *OR*, 42(1):227, 42(2):517, 524, 886; Meade to "My dear General," Feb. 21, 22, 1884, Walker Papers, Union League of Philadelphia.

11. Walker, *Second Army Corps*, 602–6.

12. George Meade to his wife, Aug. 26, 1864, Meade Papers, Army Heritage and Education Center, Carlisle.

13. John Welsh to "Mr. Burk Sir," Sept. 17, 1864, William Burke Papers, Kenan Research Center, Atlanta History Center; Washington Roebling to "My dear Emily," n.d. [Aug. 26, 1864], Roebling Family Papers, Rutgers University, New Brunswick. Lt. Col. Caleb B. Hobson of the Fifty-First North Carolina claimed credit for capturing Walker.

14. William Watts Folwell to "Dear Mother," Aug. 26, 1864, William Watts Folwell Diary and Correspondence, Minnesota Historical Society, Saint Paul; Lyman to his wife (no salutation), Aug. 26, 1864, Lyman Family Papers, Massachusetts Historical Society, Boston; *OR*, 42(2):518.

15. Elmer D. Wallace to "Dear Mother," Sept. 2, 1864, Wallace Papers, Bentley Historical Library, University of Michigan, Ann Arbor; Lyman to his wife (no salutation), Aug. 26, 1864, Lyman Family Papers.

16. Gibbon, *Personal Recollections*, 259–62; Jordan, *Winfield Scott Hancock*, 163–64; *OR*, 42(2):691. For the origin of the damaged relationship between Hancock and Gibbon, see Gibbon, *Personal Recollections*, 251; and Greene, *Campaign of Giants*, 416–17.

17. *OR*, 42(2):595, 42(3):496; Miller, *Harvard's Civil War*, 419. The surgeon of the Twentieth Massachusetts reported that out of 150 men of his unit on the line at Reams' Station, only "14 men bearing rifles escaped." Nathan Hayward to "Dear Father," Aug. 29, 1864, Nathan Hayward Letters, Massachusetts Historical Society, Boston.

18. Dunn, *Full Measure of Devotion*, 1:416; Guy Taylor to "My dear Wife," Sept. 3, 1864, quoted in Alderson and Alderson, *Letters Home to Sarah*, 102.

19. *OR*, 42(2):981, 1071–72.

20. *OR*, 42(3):494–95; Lavery and Jordan, *Iron Brigade General*, 121–22. As governor, Randall recruited thousands more soldiers than the state's quota and was thus a powerful figure, despite his relatively minor position in Lincoln's administration. Camp Randall Stadium on the campus of the University of Wisconsin at Madison is on the site of the military encampment named for the governor.

21. *OR*, 42(3):40, 495–96, 544.

22. Nelson Miles to "Dear Uncle," Sept. 12, 1864, Miles Papers, Army Heritage and Education Center, Carlisle.

23. Chapman, *More Terrible Than Victory*, 233.

24. *OR*, 42(1):940, 942.

25. *OR*, 42(2):518–19.

26. *OR*, ser. 3, 5:173; Nevins, *Diary of Battle*, 459. Maj. James C. Duane, Meade's chief engineer, became ill and formally went on leave September 7. Grant requested that Michler be sent to Sheridan in the Shenandoah Valley, but on August 29 Meade protested that he could not spare him as he was "the only officer of experience I have to act as chief engineer." *OR*, 42(2):564–65.

27. Acken, *Blue-Blooded Cavalryman*, 179; Spear, *Army Life*, 259–60.

28. Badeau, *Military History of Ulysses S. Grant*, 3:7–9.

29. William Boston to "Dear Aunt," Sept. 8, 1864, Boston Diary and Letters, Bentley Historical Library, University of Michigan, Ann Arbor; Buell, *Cannoneer*, 241; letter from Lt. H.H.S., Sept. 2, 1864, *Rochester (N.Y.) Daily Union & Advertiser*, Sept. 7, 1864. Lt. H.H.S. belonged to the Fiftieth New York Engineers, although the regimental muster roll contains no officer with those initials.

30. Badeau, *Military History of Ulysses S. Grant*, 3:9; Spear, *Army Life*, 264.

31. John Buttrick Noyes to "Dear Father," Sept. 8, 1864, Noyes Civil War Letters, Harvard University, Cambridge; Charles G. Merrill letter (no salutation), Aug. 28, 1864, Charles G. Merrill Papers, Sterling Library, Yale University, New Haven; Jacob Bechtel to "Miss Candis," Sept. 11, 1864, Bechtel Letters, Gettysburg National Military Park.

32. Letter, Aug. 28, 1864, *Brooklyn (N.Y.) Daily Standard-Union*, June 4, 1892; Zerah Coston Monks to "My dear Hattie," Aug. 27, 1864, Monks Family Papers, Western Reserve Historical Society, Cleveland.

33. Cutcheon Autobiography, Bentley Historical Library, University of Michigan, Ann Arbor, 356–58.

34. Thomas J. Owen to "Dear Father and Friends at Home," Sept. 15, 1864, in Floyd, *"Dear Friends at Home,"* 57; Ewing, *From Home to Trench*, 71; Poremba, *If I Am Found Dead*, 195. The Union army had built extensive fortifications near Yorktown, Virginia, in the spring of 1862.

35. Charles Griffin to "My dear Barnard," Sept. 3, 1864, George Middleton Barnard Papers, Massachusetts Historical Society, Boston; Henry Clay Heisler to "Dear Sister," Sept. 2, 1864, Heisler Papers, Library of Congress, Washington.

36. *OR*, 42(2):682. Meade was absent on leave at this time, and Parke, commander of the Ninth Corps, served temporarily in his place.

37. *OR*, 42(2):691, 719; *OR*, ser. 3, 5:174; Smith, *19th Maine*, 243; Charles F. Stinson to "My Dear Sis Sarah," Sept. 11, 1864, Charles F. Stinson Letters, Lewis Leigh Collection, Army Heritage and Education Center, Carlisle; Robertson, *McAllister Letters*, 494.

38. Paxton, *Sword and Gown*, 394; Wainwright Diary, Sept. 4, 1864, Henry E. Huntington Library, San Marino; Steve Clark to "Dear Del," Sept. 10, 1864, Steve Clark Papers, Jay Luvaas Collection, Army Heritage and Education Center, Carlisle.

39. Boston Diary, Sept. 6, 1864, Boston Diary and Letters; Nathaniel Michler Map 4, George Meade Collection, Historical Society of Pennsylvania, Philadelphia; Buell, *Cannoneer*, 257; *OR*, 51(1):274–76. For Grant's creation of a line of countervallation at Vicksburg, see Smith, *Siege of Vicksburg*. A large Confederate force threatened Grant's rear at Vicksburg, but Early had no plans to target Petersburg, the scout's report from Gordonsville notwithstanding.

40. *OR*, 40(3):270–71, 40(2):706, 798.

41. *OR*, 42(2):822, 827, 846, 871–73, 954–56, 968–69, 51(1):276. For a detailed description of the location of all Union forts and batteries, the size of the garrisons, and the number of guns mounted, see "List of Field Works, the Armaments and Garrisons," Card 3297, Henry Hunt Military Papers, Manuscripts Division, Library of Congress, Washington.

42. Letter from Lt. H.H.S., Sept. 2, 1864, *Rochester (N.Y.) Daily Union & Advertiser*, Sept. 7, 1864; *OR*, ser. 3, 5:174; George Barnum to "Dear Father," Aug. 29, 1864, George Barnum Letters, copy, Petersburg National Battlefield; Everstine, *Three Years in the Volunteer Army*, 78–79. Schilling's account was originally published in *Skaneateles (N.Y.) Democrat*, Sept. 22, 1864. A corduroy road consisted of wooden planks laid perpendicularly on the surface in order to provide a firm roadbed. The ridged appearance of the planks resembled corduroy fabric.

43. John P. Brogan, "The Beginning of the End," 3–4, William Palmer Civil War Collection, Western Reserve Historical Society, Cleveland.

44. Bennett, "Grant's Railroad," 14–15; *OR*, ser. 3, 5:81; Webb Diary, July 19, 1864, Clements Library, University of Michigan, Ann Arbor; Nichols Diary, July 31, 1864, New York Military Museum, Saratoga Springs; James Blankenship, "As Smooth as a Greased Wheel: The History of the United States Military Railroad during the Petersburg Campaign," unpublished manuscript. Blankenship's work is the most thorough treatment of the Union's military railroads yet produced. Maj. Gen. George B. McClellan commanded the Army of the Potomac in 1861 and 1862.

45. *OR*, 40(3):388, 40(2):564–67; *OR*, ser. 3, 5:70.

46. *OR*, 42(2):566; Dr. A. W. Acheson, serialized history of the 140th Pennsylvania, *Beaver (Pa.) Radical*, Oct. 27, 1869; Gilbert Thompson Memoir, Sept. 6, 1864, Manuscripts Division, Library of Congress, Washington; Johnston, *Virginia Railroads in the Civil War*, 220–21; Nevins, *Diary of Battle*, 459.

47. Elmer D. Wallace to "My Dear Parents," Sept. 13, 1864, Wallace Papers; *OR*, 42(2):795; Styple, *Writing & Fighting from the Army of Northern Virginia*, 298; Nevins, *Diary of Battle*, 459; William E. Potter to "Dear Thompson," Sept. 11, 1864, William E. Potter Letters, copy, Petersburg National Battlefield; George Barnum to "Dear Father," Sept. 10, 1864, Barnum Letters; William M. Read Diary, Sept. 25, 1864, William M. Read Letters and Diary, copy, Petersburg National Battlefield. The Confederates greatly exaggerated the speed of the train, which averaged about six miles per hour.

48. *OR*, 42(2):805; Austin Kendall to "My Dear Mother and All," Sept. 23, 1864, Austin Kendall Papers, Civil War Documents Collection, Army Heritage and Education Center, Carlisle; McFadden, *Aunt and the Soldier Boys*, 147–48.

49. *OR*, 42(2):798, 1032; Wainwright Diary, Sept. 14, 1864; Rosenblatt and Rosenblatt, *Hard Marching Every Day*, 315; Blankenship, "As Smooth as a Greased Wheel"; Parker, *51st Pennsylvania*, 585; Coffin, *Freedom Triumphant*, 182.

50. Ransom F. Sargent to "My own sweet Wife," Sept. 11, 1864, Ransom F. Sargent Civil War Papers, Rauner Library, Dartmouth College, Hanover; Charles F. Stinson to "My Dear Sis Sarah," Sept. 11, 1864, Stinson Letters. Of course, the railroad did not run to Weldon; Stinson meant the Weldon Railroad.

51. Kieffer, *Recollections of a Drummer Boy*, 233; Porter, *Campaigning with Grant*, 212; Bilby, *Three Rousing Cheers*, 229.

52. Sommers, *Richmond Redeemed*, 179.

53. Sommers, *Richmond Redeemed*, 179–80; Greene, *Campaign of Giants*, 39–40; Wade Hampton to Robert E. Lee, Sept. 11, 1864, Samuel R. Johnston Papers, Virginia Museum of History and Culture, Richmond; James R. Hagood, "Memoirs of the First South Carolina Regiment of Volunteer Infantry in the Confederate War for Independence, from 12 April 1861 to 10 April 1865," South Caroliniana Library, University of South Carolina, Columbia, 177–78; Hess, *In the Trenches at Petersburg*, 151; Hess, *Lee's Tar Heels*, 258.

54. Sommers, *Richmond Redeemed*, 180; Hess, *In the Trenches at Petersburg*, 151–52; Hess, *Lee's Tar Heels*, 258; Lyle Diary, Sept. 23, 1864.

55. Henry Calvin Conner to "My dear Ellen," Sept. 9, 1864, Henry Calvin Conner Papers, South Caroliniana Library, University of South Carolina, Columbia; John M. Brice to "Dear Father," Sept. 19, 1864, in *Recollections and Reminiscences, 1861–1865 through World War 1*, 5:161; E. P. Alexander to "Dear Father," Sept. 22, 1864, Alexander-Hillhouse Family Papers, Southern Historical Collection, Louis Round Wilson Library, University of North Carolina, Chapel Hill.

56. Robert Henry Maury to "My dear Puss," Oct. 1, 1864, in "1864: Robert Henry Maury, Jr. Letters," Cabell's Artillery (Va.); Johnston, "Vinson Confederate Letters," 109–10; James A. W. Bryan Diary, Sept. 11, 1864, Bryan Family Papers, Southern Historical Collection, Louis Round Wilson Library, University of North Carolina, Chapel Hill; Harris, *Seventh North Carolina*, 56; Hutchinson, *My Dear Mother & Sisters*, 163; Hess, *In the Trenches at Petersburg*, 153–54.

57. Henry Calvin Conner to "My dear Ellen," Sept. 9, 1864, Conner Papers; Venable, "In the Trenches at Petersburg," 61; Owen, *In Camp and Battle with the Washington Artillery*, 334.

58. Archibald Gracie IV to "My Dear Friend [Col. H. M. Rutledge]," June 30, 1908, Archibald Gracie Papers, Alabama Department of Archives and History, Montgomery; James Eldred Phillips Memoir, James Eldred Phillips Papers, Virginia Museum of History and Culture, Richmond, 62; Dunlop, *Lee's Sharpshooters*, 219–20. A monument in 2024 marks the location of the dam on Rohoic Creek. The site of the Gracie's Salient dam is preserved in Petersburg National Battlefield.

59. E. P. Alexander to "Dear Father," Sept. 22, 1864, Alexander-Hillhouse Papers; Theodore Trimmier to "My Dear Wife," Sept. 17, 1864, Trimmier Collection, Tennessee State Library and Archives, Nashville; Eugene Levy, "Donaldsonville Cannoneers at the Siege of Petersburg," *New Orleans Times-Picayune*, Aug. 4, 1902; Jackson, *First Regiment Engineer Troops*, 92; Hess, *In the Trenches at Petersburg*, 154. National Park Service historians recently discovered evidence of this mine.

60. William Alexander Gordon Memoirs, Washington and Lee University, Lexington, 149.

61. Dunlop, *Lee's Sharpshooters*, 155; Allen, "Civil War Letters," 381; Longacre, "Roughest Kind of Campaigning," 340; John J. Owen to "Dearest Mother," Sept. 10, 1864, John J. Owen Jr. Papers, Massachusetts Historical Society, Boston; Little, *Seventh New Hampshire*, 280–81; Acken, *Blue-Blooded Cavalryman*, 187; George Barnum to "Dear Father," Aug. 29, 1864, Barnum Letters. Excellent examples of such picket posts are preserved in Pamplin Historical Park.

62. "Diary of Captain George D. Bowen," *Valley Forge Journal*, 210; George Stearns to "Dear Brother," June 21, 1864, George Stearns Papers, New Hampshire Historical Society, Concord; A. H. Sanger to "Dear Parents," Sept. 8, 1864, A. H. Sanger Papers, Gregory Coco Collection, Army Heritage and Education Center, Carlisle; George S. Hupman to "Dear Parents," Sept. 11, 1864, George S. Hupman Letters, Library of Virginia, Richmond; *OR*, 40(3):542; Buckingham, *All's for the Best*, 303–4.

63. Crockett Diary, Sept. 8, 1864, Crockett Diary and Papers, University of Texas, Austin; John W. Haley Diary, Sept. 8, 1864, Paul Bean Collection, Special Collections Department, Raymond H. Folger Library, University of Maine, Orono.

64. Botkin, *Civil War Treasury*, 437–38; William Joseph Miller, "Recollections," in *Recollections and Reminiscences, 1861–1865 through World War 1*, 5:222–23; George Bowen Diary, Sept. 27, 1864, copy in bound volume 228, Fredericksburg & Spotsylvania National Military Park.

65. Thomas, *Boys in Blue from the Adirondack Foothills*, 221; Acken, *Blue-Blooded Cavalryman*, 186; Blackett, *Thomas Morris Chester*, 122.

66. Henry M. Talley to "My Dear Mother," July 7, 1864, Henry C. Brown Papers, State Archives of North Carolina, Raleigh; Theodore W. Skinner to "Dear folks at home," Aug. 22, 1864, Theodore W. Skinner Letters, Civil War Documents Collection, Army Heritage and Education Center, Carlisle; Pomret, "Letters of Fred Lockley," 88; Hays, *Under the Red Patch*, 270–71.

67. Special Orders No. 167, Lee Headquarters Papers, Virginia Museum of History and Culture, Richmond; Houghton, *17th Maine*, 236; Crocker, "Dread Days in Dixie"; Jennings, "Crawford's Narrow Escape"; Thompson, *Friendly Enemies*, 77–78.

68. Jennings, "Crawford's Narrow Escape"; Addison S. Boyce to "Dear Mary," Aug. 12, 1864, Boyce Letters, Petersburg National Battlefield; Joseph N. Haynes to "Dear Father," Sept. 4, 1864, Joseph N. Haynes Papers, Rubenstein Special Collections Library, Duke University, Durham, N.C.; Thompson Memoir; Jordan, *Some Events and Incidents*, 89; Solon Carter to "My own darling wife," Aug. 29, 1864, Carter Letters, Army Heritage and Education Center, Carlisle; Imri Spencer (no salutation), Aug. 23, 1864, Imri Spencer Letters, Library of Virginia, Richmond.

69. Hays, *Under the Red Patch*, 271; Silliker, *Rebel Yell & the Yankee Hurrah*, 194; Sallada, *Silver Sheaves*, 101–2.

70. Tilton C. Reynolds to "Dear Mother," Sept. 21, 1864, Reynolds Papers, Library of Congress, Washington; Malcolm, *Emmell Journal*, 119; Haley Diary, Sept. 1, 1864.

71. Roger Hannaford Memoir, Aug. 3, 1864, Roger Hannaford Papers, Cincinnati Historical Society; Spear et al., *Recollections of General Ellis Spear*, 138; John F. Sale to "Dear Auntie," Sept. 17, 1864, John F. Sale Papers and Diaries, Library of Virginia, Richmond.

72. White, *Civil War Diary of Wyman S. White*, 282–83; Joseph H. Prime to "Dear Wife," Aug. 27, 31, 1864, Prime Papers, University of Notre Dame, South Bend; William Russell Diary, Sept. 16, 1864, Rubenstein Special Collections Library, Duke University, Durham, N.C.

73. Houghton, *17th Maine*, 228–29.

74. Ritchie, *Four Years in the First New York Light Artillery*, 184; Charles W. Smith to "Dear Emma," Aug. 29, 1864, Capt. Charles W. Smith Letters, Lewis Leigh Collection; and Henry F. Charles Civil War Record, 21, Ronald Boyer Collection, both in Army Heritage and Education Center, Carlisle; Hilton A. Parker to "Dear Father," July 17, 1864, Hilton A. Parker Letters, James S. Schoff Civil War Collection, Clements Library, University of Michigan, Ann Arbor; Jesse R. Bowles to "Dear Sister Lucie," Sept. 15, 1864, Bowles Family Papers, Earl Gregg Swem Library, College of William and Mary, Williamsburg.

75. De Trobriand, *Four Years with the Army*, 640; Morgan, *Recollections of a Rebel Reefer*, 214; Malcolm, *Emmell Journal*, 119.

76. George Tillotson to "My Dear Wife," Aug. 28, 1864, George Tillotson Letters, Gilder-Lehrman Collection, New-York Historical Society, New York; *OR*, 40(2):445–46, 42(2):1000.

77. Allen, *Fourth Rhode Island*, 297; Thomas, *Boys in Blue from the Adirondack Foothills*, 220; Brainard, *146th New York*, 242–43; "On the Picket Line with Gen. Grant's Army," *Utica (N.Y.) Weekly Herald*, Sept. 6, 1864; Walter Wallace Smith to "Dear Parents," Sept. 1, 1864, Walter Smith Papers.

78. Luther N. Ralls to "My very dear wife," Sept. 29, 1864, Luther N. Ralls Letters, Albert and Shirley Small Special Collections Library, University of Virginia, Charlottesville; Silliker, *Rebel Yell & the Yankee Hurrah*, 200; Haley Diary, Sept. 14, 1864; Keating, *Carnival of Blood*, 298; Jacob M. Roberts to "Dear Sister," Sept. 25, 1864, Jacob M. Roberts Letters, Manuscripts and Special Collections, New York State Library, Albany; Edward Ord to "Dearest," Aug. 17, 1864, Ord Letters, Stanford University, Palo Alto.

79. George P. McClelland to "Dear Lizzie," Aug. 5, 1864, George P. McClelland Papers, Senator John Heinz History Center, Pittsburgh; "From the Trenches," *New York Times*, Sept. 18, 1864; Edgar Ashton to "Dear Aunt," Sept. 9, 1864, Edgar Ashton Letters, James I. Robertson Jr. Civil War Sesquicentennial Legacy Project, Library of Virginia, Richmond.

80. James H. Wickes to "Dear Judge," Aug. 26, 1864, McCullough Family Papers, Hugh Lennox Bond Collection, Maryland Historical Society, Baltimore; Blackett, *Thomas Morris Chester*, 115; John Owen Jr. to "My Dear Mother," Sept. 10, 1864, Owen Papers.

81. Oscar D. Robinson to "Dear Mother," Aug. 17, 1864, Robinson Papers, Dartmouth College, Hanover; Drake, *9th New Jersey*, 231–32; Howell, "Keeping Their Bargain"; Wiley, *Norfolk Blues*, 155.

82. Bryan Diary, Sept. 7, 10, 1864. For additional information on Wooten and his operations, see Ray, *Shock Troops of the Confederacy*, 212–15; and McLaurin, "Eighteenth Regiment," 59.

83. Hamilton, "110th Pennsylvania," Union League of Philadelphia, 201. Fort Damnation complemented the informal name by which Fort Sedgwick was known, Fort Hell.

84. De Trobriand, *Four Years with the Army*, 640–41.

85. *OR*, 42(1):342–43, 392, 776, 42(2):761–62; de Trobriand, *Four Years with the Army*, 641; Weygant, *124th New York*, 374; Marbaker, *11th New Jersey*, 220; Robertson, *McAllister Letters*, 498–99; Hamilton, "110th Pennsylvania," 202.

86. De Trobriand, *Four Years with the Army*, 642; White, *Civil War Diary of Wyman S. White*, 285–86; Matthews, *Soldiers in Green*, 255; Paxton, *Sword and Gown*, 395.

87. Bernard Diary, Sept. 10, 1864, University of Virginia, Charlottesville; Wiley, *Norfolk Blues*, 152; Fitz William McMaster to "My dear Pollie," Sept. 16, 1864, McMaster Papers, University of South Carolina, Columbia; Crist, *Papers of Jefferson Davis*, 11:22; Halliburton,

Saddle Soldiers, 169; Luther A. Rose Diary, Sept. 10, 1864, Manuscripts Division, Library of Congress, Washington; *OR*, 42(2):777. Union and Confederate sources counted between forty and ninety-five Confederate prisoners captured during the raid. See "Letter from Hurt's Battery," *Columbus (Ga.) Daily Sun*, Sept. 17, 1864; John Lane Stuart to "Dear Mother," Sept. 17, 1864, Stuart Papers, Duke University, Durham, N.C.; Francis Marion Coker to "My Precious Wife," Sept. 10, 1864, Coker Papers, University of Georgia, Athens; A. L. P. Vairin Diary, Sept. 10, 1864, Mississippi Department of Archives and History, Jackson; Marsena Patrick Diary, Sept. 10, 1864, Manuscripts Division, Library of Congress, Washington; and Stevens, *Berdan's United States Sharpshooters*, 493. Many Confederates had blamed the Florida Brigade for the defeat at Weldon Railroad (Globe Tavern) on August 21.

88. Hamilton, "110th Pennsylvania," 203; William H. Gilder to "Dear Ma," Sept. 12, 1864, William H. Gilder Letters, Manuscripts and Special Collections, New York State Library, Albany; Weygant, *124th New York*, 375; Silliker, *Rebel Yell & the Yankee Hurrah*, 198–99; Gilbreath Reminiscences, Indiana State Library, Indianapolis; de Trobriand, *Four Years with the Army*, 642. Fort Meikel, previously called Redoubt E, sat between Forts Morton and Rice—specifically between Batteries 18 and 19—just west of the Norfolk & Petersburg Railroad. It could mount six guns and accommodate a garrison of 100 men. It is no longer extant.

89. *OR*, 42(2):761, 42(1):343; Marbaker, *11th New Jersey*, 221; Wiley, *Norfolk Blues*, 152; Francis Marion Coker to "My precious wife," Sept. 10, 1864, Coker Papers.

90. Weygant, *124th New York*, 375; Dennis Tuttle to "My Dear Annie," Sept. 15, 1864, Dennis Tuttle Correspondence, Manuscripts Division, Library of Congress, Washington; Robertson, *McAllister Letters*, 500.

91. Walker, *Second Army Corps*, 607; *OR*, 42(2):888.

92. Powell, *Fifth Army Corps*, 728; *OR*, 42(1):511; Thomas and Sauers, *Never Want to Witness Such Sights*, 246. Baxter, who was also wounded during the Wilderness fight, took command of the brigade earlier led by Coulter and Wheelock at Weldon Railroad.

93. *OR*, 42(1):511–12, 42(2):839–42; Powell, *Fifth Army Corps*, 728.

94. *OR*, 39(2):364.

95. Stephen O. Rogers to "Dear Father and Mother," Sept. 18, 1864, Rogers Letters, Abraham Lincoln Presidential Library, Springfield; Loving, *Civil War Letters of George Washington Whitman*, 131; Lane, *Soldier's Diary*, 203.

96. "Petersburg: Presentation of United States Medals for Bravery," *New York Herald*, Sept. 16, 1864; Tilney, *My Life in the Army*, 134–35; McKelvey, *Rochester in the Civil War*; Miers, *Wash Roebling's War*, 30; Meade, *Life and Letters*, 228. Meade's speech is reproduced in the *Herald* article. The three recipients were Sgt. John H. Schilling, Third Delaware; Pvt. S. C. Anderson, Eighteenth Massachusetts; and Pvt. George W. Reed, Eleventh Pennsylvania.

97. *OR*, 42(2):636–37, 750–54, 789, 800–801, 804–5; General Orders No. 35, Sept. 12, 1864, Coulter Papers, Pennsylvania State Archives, Harrisburg; Wainwright Diary, Sept. 14, 1864; Herdegen and Murphy, *Four Years with the Iron Brigade*, 309; Uberto A. Burnham Diary, Sept. 12, 1864, Burnham Papers, New York State Library, Albany. "Old man" Cutler was fifty-seven years old and had been slightly wounded on August 21. The complete reorganization of the Fifth Corps is beyond the scope of this work. For a detailed breakdown, see Welcher, *Union Army*, 385–87. The First Corps's badge was a circle.

98. *OR*, 42(2):642–43; Coco, *Through Blood and Fire*, 160–61; Stevenson Diary, Sept. 14, 1864. Potter's command remained the Second Division. For a detailed breakdown of the new Ninth Corps organization, see Welcher, *Union Army*, 436–37.

99. *OR*, 42(2):1189–90; Telegrams Received by the Confederate Secretary of War 1861–1865, Microcopy M618, Roll 17, National Archives and Records Service, Washington; McBrien, *Tennessee Brigade*, 103; Benjamin Wesley Justice to "My Sweet Darling Wife," Sept. 1, 1864, Justice Letters, Emory University, Atlanta; Hess, *Lee's Tar Heels*, 242. Steuart took command of Barton's Brigade, which had been temporarily led by Col. William Aylett.

100. Edward Griswold to "Dear Sister," Sept. 10, 1864, Griswold Family Papers, Duke University, Durham, N.C.; Thomas Jewett Goree to "My dearest Mother," Aug. 26, 1864, in Goree, *Thomas Jewett Goree Letters*, 229; Crabtree and Parton, *Journal of a Secesh Lady*, 605. For a comprehensive account of Mobile's role in the Civil War, see Bergeron, *Confederate Mobile*.

101. There is a vast literature dealing with the 1864 Atlanta Campaign. Two of the best treatments are Castel, *Decision in the West*, and McMurry, *Atlanta 1864*. For an example of the sort of advice Grant offered Sherman, see *OR*, 38(5):569.

102. Charles J. Paine to "Dear Father," Sept. 3, 1864, Charles Jackson Paine Papers, Virginia Museum of History and Culture, Richmond; Blackett, *Thomas Morris Chester*, 118.

103. Simon, *Grant Papers*, 12:127; Califf, *Seventh U.S. Colored Troops*, 40; Capt. Charles W. Smith to "Dear Emma," Sept. 8, 1864, Charles W. Smith Letters; David B. Birney to "My Dear Gross," Sept. 6, 1864, David B. Birney Papers, Army Heritage and Education Center, Carlisle; Loperfido, *Death, Disease, and Life*, 69; Edward Brooks Diary, Sept. 5, 1864, Pearce Civil War Collection, Navarro College, Corsicana. The large mortar, also called the "Dictator," was mounted on a railroad car behind the captured Confederate Battery 5 on the Dimmock Line. A similar piece is on display in 2024 at Petersburg National Battlefield.

104. White, *Civil War Diary of Wyman S. White*, 283; Trumbull, *Knightly Soldier*, 292; John W. McLure to "My Dearest Kate," Sept. 5, 1864, McLure Family Papers, University of South Carolina, Columbia.

105. Diary of Lt. Joshua H. Dearborn, Sept. 5, 1864, Guilford Free Public Library; Tilton C. Reynolds to "Dear Mother," Sept. 6, 1864, Reynolds Papers; Houghton, *17th Maine*, 233; Charles Hamlin to "Dear Sister Louise," Sept. 10, 1864, Hamlin Letters, New York State Library, Albany; Alcinus Ward Fenton to "Dear Mother," Sept. 4, 1864, Alcinus Ward Fenton Papers, Western Reserve Historical Society, Cleveland; Woodward, "Civil War of a Pennsylvania Trooper," 56; Haley Diary, Sept. 4, 1864; George Barnum to "Dear Father," Sept. 10, 1864, Barnum Letters.

106. Benjamin Wright to "My Dear Abbie," Sept. 5, 1864, Benjamin Wright Papers, Wisconsin Historical Society, Madison; Acken, *Blue-Blooded Cavalryman*, 184.

107. Orrin Sweet Allen to "Dear Frank," Sept. 10, 1864, Orrin Sweet Allen Letters, Virginia Museum of History and Culture, Richmond; "Army Correspondence," *Easton (Md.) Gazette*, Oct. 1, 1864; Irving, *More Than Conqueror*, 163; Ritchie, *Four Years in the First New York Light Artillery*, 186; Spear, *Army Life*, 261; Samuel P. Glass to "Dear Wife," Sept. 7, 1864, Samuel P. Glass Collection, Pennsylvania State Archives, Harrisburg; John B. Foote to "My Dear Mother," Sept. 12, 1864, John B. Foote Papers, Rubenstein Special Collections Library, Duke University, Durham, N.C.; Oscar D. Robinson to "Dear Sister," Sept. 13, 1864, Robinson Papers; John L. Houck to "Dear Wife," Sept. 10, 1864, Houck Papers, New York State Library, Albany; O. Charles Benton to "My Darling Cora," Sept. 10, 1864, Benton-Beach Family Correspondence, Hesburgh Library, University of Notre Dame, South Bend.

108. John D. McGeachy to "Dear Sister," Sept. 3, 1864, Catherine Buie Letters, Rubenstein Special Collections Library, Duke University, Durham, N.C.; Wiggins, *My Dear Friend*, 151; Rozier, *Granite Farm Letters*, 185.

109. Henry Duplessis Wells to "Dear Carrie," Sept. 5, 1864, Henry Duplessis Wells Papers, Southern Historical Collection, Louis Round Wilson Library, University of North Carolina, Chapel Hill; Goree, *Thomas Jewett Goree Letters*, 228; P. G. T. Beauregard to "Dear General," Sept. 7, 1864, Beauregard Papers, Library of Congress, Washington; Ezekiel D. Graham to "Miss Laura," Sept. 14, 1864, Ezekiel D. Graham Letters, United Daughters of the Confederacy Collection, Georgia State Archives, Morrow, typescript. Soon after taking command of the army, Hood launched successive attacks that failed to dislodge Sherman and cost the Confederates serious casualties.

110. Henry DeShields to "My darling Sweetness," Sept. 15, 1864, Henry C. DeShields Letters, James I. Robertson Jr. Civil War Sesquicentennial Legacy Project, Library of Virginia, Richmond; Dowdey and Manarin, *Wartime Papers of R. E. Lee*, 851; James B. Manson to "My Dear Friend," Sept. 24, 1864, Fannie B. Tompkins Childress Papers, Albert and Shirley Small Special Collections Library, University of Virginia, Charlottesville; William Coleman to "My Dear Sister," Sept. 6, 1864, William Coleman Letters, Pearce Civil War Collection, Navarro College, Corsicana; Thomas J. Norman to "My Dear Sister," Sept. 24, 1864, William Henry Wills Papers, Southern Historical Collection, Louis Round Wilson Library, University of North Carolina, Chapel Hill; Wiggins, *My Dear Friend*, 155.

111. Jessie W. Stribling to "Uncle Warren," Sept. 7, 1864, *Recollections of the South Carolina United Daughters of the Confederacy*, 2:430; Riley, *Grandfather's Journal*, 211; John Marshall Martin to "My Dear Sallie," Sept. 17, 1864, John Marshall Martin Papers, Virginia Museum of History and Culture, Richmond.

112. Francis Marion Coker to "My precious wife," Sept. 10, 1864, Coker Papers; Wiley, *Norfolk Blues*, 150; Hugh Denson Diary, Sept. 4, 1864, Emily Smith York Papers and Diary, Special Collections, Auburn University; Henry Calvin Conner to "My dear Ellen," Sept. 9, 1864, Conner Papers; Henry Duplessis Wells to "Dear Carrie," Sept. 5, 1864, Wells Papers; Pearce, *Chambers Diary*, 216; John W. Stott Diary, Sept. 5, 1864, *Civil War Times Illustrated* Collection, Army Heritage and Education Center, Carlisle.

CHAPTER SEVEN

1. Cardwell, "Brilliant Cavalry Coup," 474; U.S. War Department, *War of the Rebellion*, ser. 1, 42(2):1195 (hereafter *OR*; all references are to series 1 unless otherwise noted); *OR*, ser. 4, 3:653.

2. "Great Cattle Raid of 1864," 166; Bushong, *Fightin' Tom Rosser*, 104–5; Lykes, "Hampton's Cattle Raid," 2; Mewborn, "Herding Yankee Cattle," 10. Richard Lykes's and Horace Mewborn's articles are the best secondary sources on the raid, and their scholarship is implicit in my account. The only book-length treatment of the raid is Boykin, *Beefsteak Raid*, which is undocumented, dated, and more noted for colorful anecdotes than impeccable verity.

3. *OR*, 42(2):1233–34.

4. *OR*, 42(2):1235–36; Starr, *Union Cavalry*, 402. Coggins is sometimes rendered possessive (Coggins').

5. *OR*, 42(2):88, 143, 166, 467, 565, 810.

6. *OR*, 42(2):1242.

7. *OR*, 42(1):944; Mewborn, "Herding Yankee Cattle," 12; Lykes, "Hampton's Cattle Raid," 4, 6; McDonald, "Hampton's Cattle Raid," 94; Trout, *Galloping Thunder*, 567.

Lt. James Johnson and Lt. John Bauskett took command of the engineer detachment from Butler's Division, while Lt. Francis Smith Robertson, the engineer officer on Rooney Lee's staff,
commanded the men from his division. Colonel Davis now led the brigade previously commanded by General Chambliss, who was killed during the Second Deep Bottom operations.

8. Lykes, "Hampton's Cattle Raid," 5–6; Daughtry, *Gray Cavalier*, 216; Thomas Rosser to
"My darling wife," Sept. 13, 1864, Thomas L. Rosser Papers, Albert and Shirley Small Special
Collections Library, University of Virginia, Charlottesville. The sources disagree on the
volume of rations Hampton distributed, varying from three to five days' supply.

9. *OR*, 42(1):26–28; Augustus Avant Memoir, 18, Augustus Avant Papers, Georgia State
Archives, Morrow. One of Edmund Ruffin's grandsons described the location of the cat-
tle as "the Shellbanks Mr. Winfield and Col. Dick Harrison's farms." Letter to "My Dear
Grandfather," Oct. 10, 1864, Ruffin Family Papers, Virginia Museum of History and Culture,
Richmond.

10. Brooks, *Butler and His Cavalry*, 316; Calhoun, *Liberty Dethroned*, 141; Divine, *35th Battalion Virginia Cavalry*, 56–57; *OR*, 42(1):944; Lykes, "Hampton's Cattle Raid," 7; Mewborn,
"Herding Yankee Cattle," 12. Most secondary sources, including Lykes, have the Confederates
turning onto Flat Foot Road at Dinwiddie Court House. Horace Mewborn states that the
column turned south at Quaker Road. I have not seen a primary source that clarifies this
issue but am inclined to trust Mewborn's account.

11. Alfred Moore Diary, Sept. 15, 1864, Hesburgh Library, University of Notre Dame,
South Bend; Washington, *Laurel Brigade*, 285–86; *OR*, 42(1):945; Curtis, "Reminiscences,"
Duke University, Durham, N.C.; John W. Gordon Diary, Sept. 15, 1864, Eleanor Brocken-
brough Library, Museum of the Confederacy, Richmond; Rev. L. H. Davis, "Famous Cattle
Raid," 440; Mewborn, "Herding Yankee Cattle," 13–14; Lykes, "Hampton's Cattle Raid," 7–8.

12. *OR*, 42(2):1247; Moore, *Graham's Petersburg, Jackson's Kanawha, and Lurtry's Roanoke
Horse Artillery*, 28 (hereafter Moore, *Graham's Battery*); Raiford, *4th North Carolina Cavalry*,
79; Staats, *Grassroots History*, 248; Wells, *Hampton and His Cavalry*, 289; Brooks, *Butler and
His Cavalry*, 317.

13. *OR*, 42(1):945; Dr. William B. Conway, "Gen. Wade Hampton's Cattle Raid near City
Point in 1864," *The State* (Columbia, S.C.), Oct. 5, 1902; Andrew, *Wade Hampton*, 235; Mewborn, "Herding Yankee Cattle," 14; Lykes, "Hampton's Cattle Raid," 8.

14. Mewborn, "Herding Yankee Cattle," 14; Lykes, "Hampton's Cattle Raid," 9; Divine,
35th Battalion Virginia Cavalry, 57; Rev. L. H. Davis, "Famous Cattle Raid," 440.

15. Tobie, *First Maine Cavalry*, 348; Mewborn, "Herding Yankee Cattle," 14–15; Lykes,
"Hampton's Cattle Raid," 9. For background on the First District of Columbia Cavalry, see
Greene, *Campaign of Giants*, 274.

16. "Great Cattle Raid of 1864," 166.

17. Washington, *Laurel Brigade*, 287; Bushong, *Fightin' Tom Rosser*, 107; Rev. L. H. Davis,
"Famous Cattle Raid," 440–41; *OR*, 42(1):822–23; *Under the Maltese Cross*, 319; Tobie, *First
Maine Cavalry*, 349–53; "Great Cattle Raid of 1864," 166; "General Hampton's Raid around
Grant," *Richmond Daily Dispatch*, Sept. 20, 1864; Kesterson, *Last Survivor*, 30; Divine, *35th
Battalion Virginia Cavalry*, 57; Acken, *Blue-Blooded Cavalryman*, 188; Mewborn, "Herding
Yankee Cattle," 15–16. One source claims that Hampton received one of the Henry rifles,
carved his name into the stock, and carried the weapon for the remainder of the war. See
Mesic, *Cobb's Legion Cavalry*, 141.

18. *OR*, 42(1):26, 28; Mewborn, "Herding Yankee Cattle," 44; Lykes, "Hampton's Cattle Raid," 10.

19. Washington, *Laurel Brigade*, 288–90; Hand, *One Good Regiment*, 152; Myers, *The Comanches*, 330–31; Lykes, "Hampton's Cattle Raid," 10–11; Mewborn, "Herding Yankee Cattle," 44.

20. Divine, *35th Battalion Virginia Cavalry*, 57–58; *OR*, 42(1):28–29; Hand, *One Good Regiment*, 152; Myers, *The Comanches*, 331; Washington, *Laurel Brigade*, 291; Baylor, *Bull Run to Bull Run*, 243; Wellman, *Giant in Gray*, 158.

21. Merrill, *First Maine and First District of Columbia Cavalry*, 282–84; Fletcher, "Fighting Them Over"; Parker, *General James Dearing*, 80; Mewborn, "Herding Yankee Cattle," 16–17. Cocke's Mill is no longer extant. It was located near the modern community of Garysville.

22. James Dearing to "My Own dear darling wife," Sept. 18, 1864, Dearing Family Papers, Virginia Museum of History and Culture, Richmond; Lykes, "Hampton's Cattle Raid," 12; Mewborn, "Herding Yankee Cattle," 17.

23. *OR*, 42(1):842–43, 836, 821–22, 829, 945, 42(2):874; Beale, *Lieutenant of Cavalry*, 195; Thomas Ruffin to "My Dear Father," Sept. 22, 1864, Ruffin Family Papers; Brooks, *Butler and His Cavalry*, 319; Mewborn, "Herding Yankee Cattle," 17, 44, 46.

24. Brooks, *Butler and His Cavalry*, 319; *OR*, 42(1):945; Wells, *Hampton and His Cavalry*, 292–93; McCabe, "Major Andrew Reid Venable," 69–70; Mesic, *Cobb's Legion Cavalry*, 141; Mewborn, "Herding Yankee Cattle," 46.

25. *OR*, 42(1):27, 946; Washington, *Laurel Brigade*, 295; Harrell, *2nd North Carolina Cavalry*, 331; Divine, *35th Battalion Virginia Cavalry*, 58; Rev. L. H. Davis, "Famous Cattle Raid," 441; Lykes, "Hampton's Cattle Raid," 13; Mewborn, "Herding Yankee Cattle," 46. Note that the tour map accompanying the Mewborn article on page 53 marks the modern location of Newville, not to be confused with its historic location, as marked on the map on page 55 (and on the map of the raid in this book). I have not been able to identify Captain Henry.

26. *OR*, 42(2):873–74.

27. *OR*, 42(2):875–76. The infantry would come from Smyth's Second Corps brigade.

28. Smith, "Executions at Petersburg"; Wilcox, "Notes on the Richmond Campaign," Wilcox Papers, Virginia Museum of History and Culture, Richmond; Bryan Diary, Sept. 16, 1864, Bryan Family Papers, University of North Carolina, Chapel Hill; W. A. Templeton to "Dear Sister," Sept. 19, 1864, Templeton Family Papers, University of South Carolina, Columbia; T. W. G. Inglet to "My Dear Mattie," Sept. 18, 1864, Inglet Letters, Library of Virginia, Richmond; *OR*, 42(1):852, 42(2):852; Gilbert J. Wright to "Dear Dorothy," Sept. 17, 1864, Wright Letters, United Daughters of the Confederacy Collection, Georgia State Archives, Morrow.

29. *OR*, 42(1):35, 615, 830, 837, 42(2):877–78.

30. *OR*, 42(1):33, 822, 830, 837; Harrell, *2nd North Carolina Cavalry*, 332; Gordon Diary, Sept. 16, 1864; Andrew, *Wade Hampton*, 237; Starr, *Union Cavalry*, 405. Kautz noted that this skirmish occurred at 2:00 A.M. August V. Kautz Diary, Sept. 17, 1864, August V. Kautz Papers, Manuscripts Division, Library of Congress, Washington. Hawkinsville was located at what is now the intersection of Virginia Routes 35 and 626. There is nothing left of this hamlet in 2024.

31. *OR*, 42(2):852, 867, 42(1):35, 614–15.

32. Kesterson, *Last Survivor*, 30; Trout, *Galloping Thunder*, 568; Mewborn, "Herding Yankee Cattle," 46.

33. Washington, *Laurel Brigade*, 295; Rev. L. H. Davis, "Famous Cattle Raid," 441; Beale, *Lieutenant of Cavalry*, 195; Harrell, *2nd North Carolina Cavalry*, 331; Mewborn, "Herding Yankee Cattle," 47; "Great Cattle Raid of 1864," 167.

34. Mewborn, "Herding Yankee Cattle," 47; Lykes, "Hampton's Cattle Raid," 17 (quote).

35. *OR*, 42(1):614, 946; Staats, *Grassroots History*, 251; George William Beale to "My Dear Mother," Sept. 19, 1864, Beale Family Papers, University of Virginia, Charlottesville.

36. Washington, *Laurel Brigade*, 296; Moore Diary, Sept. 16, 1864; *OR*, 42(1):946; "Great Cattle Raid of 1864," 167; Rev. L. H. Davis, "Famous Cattle Raid," 441; George William Beale to "My Dear Mother," Sept. 19, 1864, Beale Family Papers; Mewborn, "Herding Yankee Cattle," 47–48; Lykes, "Hampton's Cattle Raid," 18. The tale of Margaret's steer is widely repeated in the literature and is included here with the caveat that it is suspiciously precious.

37. August V. Kautz, "Reminiscences of the Civil War," 86, Kautz Papers, Library of Congress, Washington, 86; Kautz Diary, Sept. 17, 1864; *OR*, 42(1):614, 822, 837, 42(2):891, 896–98.

38. Lyle Diary, Sept. 18, 1864, Virginia Museum of History and Culture, Richmond; Joseph Shank to "My dear friend," Sept. 18, 1864, Shank Collection, Georgia State Archives, Morrow; Pearce, *Chambers Diary*, 218.

39. Venable, *Eighty Years After*, 45.

40. Mackintosh, *Dear Martha*, 137; Moore, *Graham's Battery*, 29; Wellman, *Giant in Gray*, 158; Fleet and Fuller, *Green Mount*, 340; South Carolina soldier quoted in Glatthaar, *General Lee's Army*, 384.

41. Charles Baughman to "Dear Ma," Sept. 18, 1864, Baughman Family Papers, Virginia Museum of History and Culture, Richmond; John R. Zimmerman Diary, Sept. 19, Oct. 5, 1864, The Lloyd House, Alexandria; James Paul Verdery to "Dear Sister," Sept. 23, 1864, Eugene and James Verdery Letters, Rubenstein Special Collections Library, Duke University, Durham, N.C.; Waring Diary, Oct. 16, 1864, University of North Carolina, Chapel Hill.

42. *OR*, 42(1):615, 946, 42(2):898; Glatthaar, *General Lee's Army*, 384; Curtis, "Reminiscences"; Baylor, *Bull Run to Bull Run*, 244; Fletcher, "Fighting Them Over"; Lykes, "Hampton's Cattle Raid," 18–19.

43. *OR*, 42(1):946, 952; John R. Turner to "My Dear Mother," Sept. 22, 1864, Turner Papers, Duke University, Durham, N.C.; *Richmond Examiner* quoted in Cisco, *Wade Hampton*, 144; Capt. John William McLure to "My dearest Kate," Sept. 18, 1864, McLure Family Papers, University of South Carolina, Columbia; Wiggins, *My Dear Friend*, 158; Hampton, "Extract from Gen. Wade Hampton's Report of Cavalry Operations," 76 (hereafter Hampton, "Extract from Report of Cavalry Operations").

44. Uberto A. Burnham to "Remembered Parents," Sept. 21, 1864, Burnham Papers, New York State Library, Albany; Marshall, *Butler's Correspondence*, 5:144; Ely S. Parker to "Friend Charles," Sept. 23, 1864, Library of Virginia, Richmond; John Buttrick Noyes to "Dear Mother," Sept. 19, 1864, Noyes Civil War Letters, Harvard University, Cambridge; James Mitchell to "Dear Brother," Oct. 22, 1864, copy, Mitchell Letters, Petersburg National Battlefield; Morgan, "From City Point to Appomattox," 237.

45. Silliker, *Rebel Yell & the Yankee Hurrah*, 200; Jordan, *Red Diamond Regiment*, 203; James Parley Coburn to "Dear Parents," Sept. 28, 1864, Coburn Letters, Army Heritage and Education Center, Carlisle; J. R. Hamilton, "The Rebels Luxuriating on Fresh Beef," *New York Times*, Sept. 23, 1864; Aldridge, *No Freedom Shrieker*, 215.

46. August V. Kautz to "My Dear Mrs. Savage," Sept. 22, 1864, August V. Kautz Papers, Abraham Lincoln Presidential Library, Springfield; Meade, *Life and Letters*, 228; Wainwright

Diary, Sept. 18, 1864, Henry E. Huntington Library, San Marino; James Cornell Biddle to "My own darling wife," Sept. 16, 1864, James Cornell Biddle Letters, Historical Society of Pennsylvania, Philadelphia; Charles E. Field to "My Friend Hattie," Sept. 16, 1864, Hattie Burleigh Papers, Army Heritage and Education Center, Carlisle; *OR*, 42(1):25–26.

47. Williams, *Papers of William Alexander Graham*, 177; Lykes, "Hampton's Cattle Raid," 19–20. Of course, the reference was to Jeb Stuart.

48. Huyette, "Reminiscences of a Private," 94; Hamilton R. Dunlap letter (recipient unknown), n.d., Dunlap Diary and Letters, Mary Gyla McDowell Collection, Eberly Family Special Collections Library, Penn State University, State College; Child, *5th New Hampshire*, 283; George K. Leet to "My Dear Colonel," Sept. 18, 1864, Rowley Papers, Abraham Lincoln Presidential Library, Springfield; Washburn, *108th New York*, 86; Zeller, *Ninth Vermont*, 163; Isaac O. Best, "The Siege and Capture of Petersburg," James S. Schoff Civil War Collection, Clements Library, University of Michigan, Ann Arbor.

49. *OR*, 43(1):719, 721, 43(2):815–16; Simon, *Grant Papers*, 11:358–59; "Mimic War" quoted in Wert, *From Winchester to Cedar Creek*, 38; Wainwright Diary, Sept. 18, 1864.

50. *OR*, 37(2):582, 43(2):83; Grant, *Personal Memoirs*, 327–28; Sheridan, *Personal Memoirs*, 9; Wert, *From Winchester to Cedar Creek*, 43. Grant feared that Halleck would modify his orders to Sheridan.

51. Wert, *From Winchester to Cedar Creek*, 99. For the Third Battle of Winchester, see Patchan, *Last Battle of Winchester*. The best published treatment of Fisher's Hill is Krick, "Stampeede of Stampeeds," 161–99. My thanks to Richard B. Kleese of Strasburg, Virginia, for sharing the draft of a manuscript on Fisher's Hill that he coauthored, which is by far the most detailed description of the battle yet written. Both battlefields are substantially preserved and interpreted with exhibits and walking trails in 2024.

52. Henry DeShields to "My Darling," Aug. 2, 1864, DeShields Letters, Library of Virginia, Richmond; Adam Stephen Dandridge to "Dear Lem," Aug. 8, 1864, Bedinger and Dandridge Family Papers, Rubenstein Special Collections Library, Duke University, Durham, N.C.; Hugh Randolph Crichton to "Dear Jennie," Aug. 11, 1864, Lucy Tunstall Alston Williams Papers, University of North Carolina, Chapel Hill; Scarborough, *Ruffin Diary*, 531.

53. Moore, *Story of a Cannoneer*, 266; *OR*, 42(2):939; Solon Carter to "My own precious Em," Sept. 20, 1864, Carter Letters, Army Heritage and Education Center, Carlisle; Charles E. Field to "My Friend Hattie," Sept. 20, 1864, Burleigh Papers; Tilney, *My Life in the Army*, 137.

54. Little, *Seventh New Hampshire*, 304; Beecher, *First Light Battery*, 571; De Graff Diary, Sept. 21, 1864, Army Heritage and Education Center, Carlisle; John R. Mitchell Diary, Sept. 21, 1864, Army Heritage and Education Center, Carlisle; Uberto A. Burnham to "Remembered Parents," Sept. 21, 1864, Burnham Papers; Andrew Knox to "My Dear Wife," Andrew Knox Letters, Gilder-Lehrman Collection, New-York Historical Society, New York; William Woodlin Diary, Sept. 23, 1864, Gilder-Lehrman Collection; Sperry Diary, Sept. 24, 1864, Gilder-Lehrman Collection; Rose Diary, Sept. 24, 1864, Library of Congress, Washington; Solon Carter to "My darling Em," Sept. 24, 1864, Carter Letters. The Petersburg Express, also called the Dictator, was removed to Broadway Landing on September 28, ending its deployment on the Union front lines after firing 45 rounds in July and 173 rounds in August and September.

55. Crockett Diary, Sept. 25, 1864, Crockett Diary and Papers, University of Texas, Austin; Benjamin H. Sims Journal, Sept. 24, 1864, State Archives of North Carolina, Raleigh; Williams, *Papers of William Alexander Graham*, 182; Cooke Diary, Sept. 23, 1864, Virginia

Museum of History and Culture, Richmond; John Cowper Granbery to his wife, Sept. 24, 1864, John Cowper Granbery Letters, Albert and Shirley Small Special Collections Library, University of Virginia, Charlottesville; Francis W. Smith to "My Own Wife," Sept. 25, 1864, Smith Family Papers, Virginia Museum of History and Culture, Richmond; Bernard Diary, Sept. 22, 1864, University of Virginia, Charlottesville.

56. Thomas J. Norman to "My Dear Sister," Sept. 24, 1864, Wills Papers, University of North Carolina, Chapel Hill; Charles Baughman to "Dear Mother," Sept. 28, 1864, Baughman Family Papers; J. W. Biddle to "My dear Pa," Sept. 25, 1864, Samuel Simpson Biddle Letters, Rubenstein Special Collections Library, Duke University, Durham, N.C.; Stott Diary, Sept. 25, 1864, Army Heritage and Education Center, Carlisle.

57. "Letter from the Troup Artillery," *Southern Watchman* (Athens, Ga.), Oct. 19, 1864.

58. Jones, *Life and Letters of General Robert Edward Lee*, 340–41; Sommers, *Richmond Redeemed*, 4; Julius A. Summers to "My dear Wife," Sept. 28, 1864, Julius A. Summers Letters, Rubenstein Special Collections Library, Duke University, Durham, N.C.; Wiley, *Norfolk Blues*, 158; Fitz William McMaster to "My Dear Wife," Aug. 18, 1864, McMaster Papers, University of South Carolina, Columbia; Journal of Charles Norborne Berkeley Minor, Roller Family Papers, Virginia Museum of History and Culture, Richmond.

59. John L. Houck to "Dear Wife," Sept. 24, 1864, Houck Papers, New York State Library, Albany; Elmer D. Wallace to "My Dear Parents," Sept. 27, 1864, Wallace Papers, Bentley Historical Library, University of Michigan, Ann Arbor; Henry Gawthrop letter, Sept. 24, 1864, Gawthrop Letters and Diary, Delaware Historical Society, Wilmington; Stephen O. Rogers to "Dear Emma," Sept. 23, 1864, Rogers Letters, Abraham Lincoln Presidential Library, Springfield.

60. Haley Diary, Sept. 21, 1864, University of Maine, Orono; Silliker, *Rebel Yell & the Yankee Hurrah*, 202; John E. Irwin to "Dear Sister," Sept. 22, 1864, James and Sybil Irwin Family Papers, Bentley Historical Library, University of Michigan, Ann Arbor.

61. Edward S. Bragg to "My Dear Wife," Sept. 27, 1864, Edward S. Bragg Letters, Wisconsin Historical Society, Madison; Coco, *Through Blood and Fire*, 173. Union forces won the First Battle of Kernstown in March 1862, a victory that would lead, however, to a series of defeats at the hands of Stonewall Jackson.

62. Nevins, *Diary of Battle*, 465–66; Allen, "Civil War Letters," 381–82; Meade, *Life and Letters*, 229–31; *OR*, 42(2):960, 1010. This once again demonstrates the importance Grant placed in Sheridan's success. One might argue that in August and September, the Petersburg Campaign served, at least in part, as a holding action in favor of Sheridan's operations in the Shenandoah Valley.

63. Gibbon, *Personal Recollections*, 263–66; John Gibbon to "My dearest Maria," Sept. 24, 26,1864, Gibbon Papers, Historical Society of Pennsylvania, Philadelphia.

64. Herbert Valentine Journal, Sept. 16, 1864, Herbert E. Valentine Papers, Phillips Library, Peabody-Essex Museum, Salem; Eisenschiml, *Vermont General*, 237–42; Jerimiah Bishop to "Friend Cargill," Sept. 18, 1864, Cargill Family Papers, Bailey-Howe Library, University of Vermont, Burlington; Leigh, *J. J. Scroggs's Diary and Letters*, 352.

65. Dickey, *85th Pennsylvania*, 377–81; Mushkat, *A Citizen-Soldier's Civil War*, 220; Clark, *Thirty-Ninth Illinois*, 139; *OR*, 42(2):650, 811. Howell had assumed command of the division on September 1 due to the illness of William Birney. A brief biographical sketch of Howell is in Warner, *Generals in Blue*, 240.

66. Paradis, *Blow for Freedom*, 66.

67. Cole, *Freedom's Witness*, 149; Charles G. Merrill to "Dear Father," Sept. 25, 1864, Merrill Papers, Yale University, New Haven; McMurray, *Recollections of a Colored Troop*, 45–46; Longacre, *Regiment of Slaves*, 110–12; Allen W. Robbins, ed., "The American Civil War Letters of William and Charles McKnight," Alexandria Public Library, 47–48; Sommers, *Richmond Redeemed*, 12; Butler, *Butler's Book*, 747–48; Paradis, *Blow for Freedom*, 66; William F. Smith to "Dear Mother," Sept. 9, 1864, William F. Smith Letters, Army Heritage and Education Center, Carlisle; O. Charles Benton to "My Darling Cora," Sept. 10, 1864, Benton-Beach Family Correspondence, University of Notre Dame, South Bend. Work on the battery at Signal Hill began as early as September 19. See a letter from a soldier of the Lunenburg Artillery in *Richmond Sentinel*, Oct. 12, 1864.

68. Partridge, "With the Signal Corps," 91; William McKnight to "Dear Sister," Sept. 22, 1864, in Robbins, "Civil War Letters of William and Charles McKnight"; Seth F. Plumb to "Dear Sister and friends at home," Sept. 19, 1864, Plumb Family Correspondence, Litchfield Historical Society; "From the James River," *Boston Evening Transcript*, Sept. 17, 1864; "Our Richmond Correspondence," *Mobile Daily Advertiser & Register*, Sept. 25, 1864; Alfred S. Roe, "Narrative of Service," Alfred S. Roe Papers, Special Collections and Archives, Wesleyan University, Middleton, 22–23; Robert Nelson Verplanck to "Dear Mary," Sept. 13, 1864, Robert Nelson Verplanck Letters, Adriance Memorial Library, Poughkeepsie; Henry Pippitt to "Dear Mother," Sept. 28, 1864, Henry Pippitt Letters, James S. Schoff Civil War Collection, Clements Library, University of Michigan, Ann Arbor. Photographs of this tower have been frequently published. See, for example, William C. Davis, *Image of War*, 1:439. It is surprising that Lee's skilled artillerists did not hit this target.

69. *Official Records of the Union and Confederate Navies in the War of the Rebellion*, 7:695 (hereafter *ORN*); Musicant, *Divided Waters*, 230; Symonds, *Lincoln and His Admirals*, 306; McPherson, *War on the Waters*, 111.

70. Symonds, *Lincoln and His Admirals*, 306; *ORN*, 10:406–7, 462–63; Zatt, "Joint Operations in the James River Basin," 77.

71. Coski, *Capital Navy*, 154–56, 166–67; Ruffin Thomson to "Dear Pa," Sept. 11, 1864, Thomson Papers, University of North Carolina, Chapel Hill; William H. Wall to John Mitchell, Aug. 14, 1864; Robert Baker Pegram to Mitchell, Aug. 15, 1864; and Stephen Mallory to Mitchell, Sept. 15, 1864, John Kirkwood Mitchell Papers, Virginia Museum of History and Culture, Richmond. For a description of the Confederate defenses on and along the James below Richmond, see *ORN*, 10:466–67.

72. *OR*, 42(2):624, 39, 42(2):364; Welles, *Diary*, 146. The port of Galveston, Texas, remained open to Confederate commerce, but it paled in significance to Wilmington.

73. Welles, *Diary*, 127; *ORN*, 10:467.

74. *ORN*, 21:655, 10:473–74, 557; Welles, *Diary*, 146–47. Porter enjoyed a robust military heritage. His father was a distinguished naval officer, his older brother William a ranking naval officer in his own right, his cousin Fitz John Porter a Union general, and his foster brother was Farragut. Admiral Lee assumed command of the Mississippi River Squadron.

75. *OR*, 42(2):1206–1207, 1235; Williams, *P. G. T. Beauregard*, 236, 239–40; Roman, *General Beauregard*, 274; Beauregard to Thomas Jordan, Sept. 7, 1864, Beauregard Papers, Library of Congress, Washington.

76. Williams, *P. G. T. Beauregard*, 240–41; Roman, *General Beauregard*, 274–79; *OR*, 39(2):846; Cooper, *Jefferson Davis, American*, 490–92; Confidential Memorandum,

Beauregard to Lee, Sept. 19, 1864, Lee Headquarters Papers, Virginia Museum of History and Culture, Richmond.

77. *OR*, 42(2):881–82, 1010; Butler, *Butler's Book*, 721. The rumors that Petersburg would be evacuated circulated among civilians in Richmond as well. See Emma Mordecai Diary, Sept. 12, 1864, Mordecai Family Papers, Southern Historical Collection, Louis Round Wilson Library, University of North Carolina, Chapel Hill.

78. Butler, *Butler's Book*, 721–22; Manarin, *Field of Honor*, 571–72; Elliott F. Grabill to "My Own Anna," Sept. 27, 1864, Elliott F. Grabill Papers, Oberlin College Archives; Simon, *Grant Papers*, 12:206. The *Greyhound* had been a Confederate blockade runner before its capture by the blockading fleet in May 1864. It was then transferred to the James River for Butler's use.

79. *OR*, 42(2):1058–59.

80. *OR*, 42(2):1046–48. Grant mistakenly assured Sheridan that Lee had sent no troops to Early since the Union victory at Winchester, missing the detachment of Kershaw, Cutler, and Rosser. Simon, *Grant Papers*, 12:208.

81. *OR*, 42(2):1080–81, 42(1):729, 760, 769; Henry H. Brown to "Dear Friends at Home," Oct. 5, 1864, Henry H. Brown Papers, Connecticut Historical Society, Hartford; Dobak, *Freedom by the Sword*, 373; Henry Clay Trumbull, "From the Tenth Connecticut," *Hartford (Conn.) Daily Courant*, Oct. 10, 1864.

82. Sommers, *Richmond Redeemed*, 18–19; Lowe, *Meade's Army*, 230; Huntington, *Searching for George Gordon Meade*, 307.

83. *OR*, 42(1):798; Eisenschiml, *Vermont General*, 247.

84. Price, *New Market Heights*, 32–33; *OR*, 42(2):1088–89; Cole, *Freedom's Witness*, 137; Solon Carter to "My own Precious Wife," Aug. 11, 22, 1864; and Carter to "My own precious Em," Sept. 20, 1864, Carter Letters.

85. *OR*, 42(2):1088, 42(1):661–62; Longacre, *Army of Amateurs*, 243; Sommers, *Richmond Redeemed*, 7–8, 22–23; Manarin, *Field of Honor*, 582.

86. Sommers, *Richmond Redeemed*, 18; Kautz, "Reminiscences of the Civil War," 88.

87. *OR*, 42(2):1082–88; Bruce, "Petersburg June 15—Fort Harrison, September 29," 89. It is unclear how Butler proposed to have such vast emoluments approved.

88. Sommers, *Richmond Redeemed*, 21. Richard Sommers is an impeccable source on this operation, and his figure is used here. Yet Ord reported 4,000 men in his two White divisions and 10,000 in Birney's corps plus Paine's division. See *OR*, 42(1):793. Kautz reported committing 1,700 horsemen. See *OR*, 42(1):823.

89. *OR*, 42(1):798; Henry Snow to "My Dear Mother," Oct. 3, 1864, Snow Letters, Connecticut Historical Society, Hartford; Hubbell, "Battle of Fort Harrison," 288; David F. Dobie to "My dear friend Hattie," Oct. 3, 1864, David F. Dobie Papers, Albert and Shirley Small Special Collections Library, University of Virginia, Charlottesville; Clay, "Personal Narrative of the Capture of Fort Harrison," 76; Cunningham, *Adirondack Regiment*, 147; Head, *Report of the Adjutant-General*, 726; Thompson, *13th New Hampshire*, 459.

90. Edward H. Ripley, "Gives First Hand Account of Battle of Fort Harrison," *Richmond News-Leader*, Apr. 27, 1939; Alexander, "Fighting and Suffering around Bermuda Hundred."

91. Roe, *Twenty-Fourth Massachusetts*, 360; Spear, *Army Life*, 267; Daniel Eldredge Manuscript Notebook, MOLLUS of Massachusetts Civil War Collection, Houghton Library, Harvard University, Cambridge; *OR*, 42(1):702, 726.

92. *OR*, 42(1):760, 769; De Graff Diary, Sept. 28, 29, 1864; Bayard Taylor Cooper to "Dear Parents," Sept. 30, 1864, Bayard Taylor Cooper Papers, Civil War Documents Collection, Army Heritage and Education Center, Carlisle; Sommers, *Richmond Redeemed*, 27–28.

93. Henry Grimes Marshall to "Dear Folks at Home," Oct. 2, 1864, Henry Grimes Marshall Letters, James S. Schoff Civil War Collection, Clements Library, University of Michigan, Ann Arbor; Diary of Lt. Joshua H. Dearborn, Sept. 28, 1864, Guilford Free Public Library; Wilson, *Black Phalanx*, 434; Califf, *Seventh U.S. Colored Troops*, 41; Henry H. Brown to "Dear Friends at Home," Oct. 5, 1864, Henry H. Brown Papers; *OR*, 42(1):772; Woodlin Diary, Sept. 28, 1864; Trudeau, *Like Men of War*, 284.

94. Montgomery, "Union Officer's Recollections of the Negro as a Soldier," 175; Longacre, *Regiment of Slaves*, 116; Elliott Grabill to "My own dearest Anna," Sept. 28, 1864, Grabill Papers; Sommers, *Richmond Redeemed*, 22, 26; *OR*, 42(1):674–75.

95. Butler, *Butler's Book*, 730–31; Bryant, "Model Regiment," 124–25.

96. *OR*, 42(2):1090; Basler, *Collected Works of Abraham Lincoln*, 8:29.

CHAPTER EIGHT

1. W. S. Neel, "One of 'Old Rock's' Brigade," *Atlanta Journal*, Apr. 19, 1902; Polley, *Letters to Charming Nellie*, 249; W. S. Burwell to "Dear Ed," Oct. 5, 1864, Edmund Studwick Burwell Papers, Southern Historical Collection, Louis Round Wilson Library, University of North Carolina, Chapel Hill.

2. Sommers, *Richmond Redeemed*, 10, 15; Siburt, "Colonel John M. Hughs," 92–93; U.S. War Department, *War of the Rebellion*, ser. 1, 42(2):1266 (hereafter *OR*; all references are to series 1 unless otherwise noted). A brief biographical sketch of Hughs, whose name is sometimes spelled "Hughes," is in Allardice, *Confederate Colonels*, 204. After the war Hughs became a whiskey distiller in Lynchburg, Tennessee, where he mentored Jack Daniels.

3. Doyle, "Ride with Kautz"; Charles J. Calrow, "Fort Harrison. A Study," 1932, Douglas Southall Freeman Papers, Manuscripts Division, Library of Congress, Washington, 13. The returns for Ewell's department on September 20 credited Gary with 1,245 effectives. See *OR*, 42(2):1266.

4. Sommers, *Richmond Redeemed*, 16–17; Calrow, "Fort Harrison," 13–14; Manarin, *Field of Honor*, 577; *OR*, 42(2):1266.

5. Jones, "Texas and Arkansas at Fort Harrison," 24; Moore, "Attack of Fort Harrison," 418; Manarin, *Field of Honor*, 576. Field remained on the Petersburg front in direct command of the remainder of his division.

6. *OR*, 42(2):1298–99, 42(1):875; Hewitt, Trudeau, and Suderow, *Supplement to the Official Records of the Union and Confederate Armies* (hereafter *OR Supp.*; all references are to vol. 7, pt. 1), 258; Dawson, *Reminiscences of Confederate Service*, 125.

7. Sommers, *Richmond Redeemed*, 14–15; Manarin, *Field of Honor*, 570; Price, *New Market Heights*, 23–24; Jones, "Texas and Arkansas at Fort Harrison," 24; Gallagher, *Fighting for the Confederacy*, 474; Schmutz, *Bloody Fifth*, 233; McCarty postwar lecture, Thomas L. McCarty Diary and Papers, Briscoe Center for American History, University of Texas, Austin. The five major highways, north to south, were Nine Mile Road, Williamsburg Road, Charles City Road, Darbytown Road, and New Market Road, sometimes called River Road. Osborne Pike also entered Richmond on an almost due north trajectory. My thanks to Robert E. L. Krick,

historian at Richmond National Battlefield Park, for helping me understand these complex fortifications, both conceptually and on the ground. Many of these works are preserved by the National Park Service, although almost nothing is protected of the fields across which the various Union assaults took place.

8. Sommers, *Richmond Redeemed*, 15. There were other bridges over the James upstream from the one at Chaffin's Bluff.

9. Sommers, *Richmond Redeemed*, 17; Carter, *Two Stars in the Southern Sky*, 246; McCarty postwar lecture; Price, *New Market Heights*, 25–26; Manarin, *Field of Honor*, 570, 576–78. These sources offer varying estimates of Confederate strength here. Louis Manarin counts 3,500; Richard Sommers says 2,900; and James Price estimates fewer than 1,800 men. Butler's scouts put the number at just shy of 3,000 defenders, counting Hughs's brigade. See *OR*, 42(2):1083–84. My estimate credits Gary with 1,200; Bass with 500; the two Virginia battalions with 600; DuBose with 400; and 100 men manning the guns on each end of the New Market Line.

10. Siburt, "Colonel John M. Hughs," 92–93; Moore, "Attack on Fort Harrison," 418–19; Clifford Dickinson, "Union and Confederate Engineering Operations at Chaffin's Bluff/Chaffin's Farm, June 1862–April 3, 1865," 71–73, Richmond National Battlefield Park; Richard Cornelius Taylor, "Personal Experiences of Major Richard Taylor," copy in bound vol. 51, Richmond National Battlefield Park; Jones, *Campbell Brown's Civil War*, 269; Manarin, *Field of Honor*, 576; Sommers, *Richmond Redeemed*, 16–17. Deserters provided the Federals an accurate idea of Confederate dispositions as early as September 9. See *OR*, 42(2):766.

11. Polley, "Polley Lost a Foot," 569; Pickens, "Fort Harrison," 484; West, *Found among the Privates*, 88; George McRae, "The Tragic Death of a Brave Picket," *Atlanta Journal*, Mar. 15, 1902; Moore, *Story of a Cannoneer*, 263.

12. Manarin, *Field of Honor*, 586; Price, *New Market Heights*, 59; Mulholland, *Military Order*, 516. Civil twilight began at 5:38 A.M. on September 29, and the sun rose twenty-six minutes later.

13. Sommers, *Richmond Redeemed*, 31–33; Robertson, "From the Crater to New Market Heights," 190; Manarin, *Field of Honor*, 588–89; Paradis, *Blow for Freedom*, 70. The American Battlefield Trust preserves a portion of this battlefield in 2024.

14. McMurray, *Recollections of a Colored Troop*, 52; Montgomery, "Union Officer's Recollections of the Negro as a Soldier," 176.

15. Charles Paine to "Dear Father," Oct. 3, 1864, Paine Papers, Virginia Museum of History and Culture, Richmond; James H. Wickes to "Dear Judge," Oct. 7, 1864; and Wickes to "My dear Father," Oct. 4, 1864, McCullough Family Papers, Bond Collection, Maryland Historical Society, Baltimore; Beyer and Keydel, *Deeds of Valor*, 434–35; Longacre, *Regiment of Slaves*, 118–19; Field, *Union Infantryman versus Confederate Infantryman*, 65; Blackett, *Thomas Morris Chester*, 139–40. The second line of obstructions may have included chevaux-de-frise.

16. McMurray, *Recollections of a Colored Troop*, 51–53; Samuel Duncan to "Well Miss Julia," Oct. 22, 1864, Duncan-Jones Correspondence, New Hampshire Historical Society, Concord; Mulholland, *Military Order*, 517; Paradis, *Blow for Freedom*, 71–73.

17. Manarin, *Field of Honor*, 592; Polley, "Polley Lost a Foot," 570; Crockett Diary, Sept. 29, 1864, Crockett Diary and Papers, University of Texas, Austin; Polley, *Hood's Texas Brigade*, 253; Schmutz, *Bloody Fifth*, 233; Thomas L. McCarty Diary, Sept. 29, 1864, McCarty Diary and Papers; Nabours, "Active Service of a Texas Command," 70; Hamilton, *Company M, 1st Texas*, 61.

18. Emerson, *War of the Confederacy*, 76; Ramsey, *7th South Carolina Cavalry*, 105–6; Sturkey, *Hampton Legion Infantry*, 91; Beyer and Keydel, *Deeds of Valor*, 434–35; McMurray, *Recollections of a Colored Troop*, 54; Mulholland, *Military Order*, 517.

19. Paradis, *Blow for Freedom*, 74, 77; Bryant, "Model Regiment," 118; Field, *Union Infantryman versus Confederate Infantryman*, 60; *OR*, 42(1):136; Samuel A. Duncan to "Well Miss Julia," Oct. 22, 1864, Duncan-Jones Correspondence; McMurray, *Recollections of a Colored Troop*, 55.

20. Price, *New Market Heights*, 36–37; Bryant, "Model Regiment," 119.

21. Manarin, *Field of Honor*, 569; *OR*, 42(1):819; Sommers, *Richmond Redeemed*, 36; Leigh, *J. J. Scroggs's Diary and Letters*, 367–68.

22. Emerson, *War of the Confederacy*, 76; Pickens, "Fort Harrison," 484; Schmutz, *Bloody Fifth*, 235; Joskins, "Hood's Texas Brigade," Hill College, Hillsboro, 192; Polley, *Hood's Texas Brigade*, 253; Polley, *Letters to Charming Nellie*, 260; Burkhardt, *Confederate Rage, Yankee Wrath*, 178; Jones, "Texas and Arkansas at Fort Harrison," 24; Samuel Watson to "Dear Friend Harriet," Oct. 21, 1864, Samuel Watson Letters, Eiserman (Private) Collection, Carlisle; Stowits, *100th New York*, 306; George Barnum to "My Dear Mother," Oct. 2, 1864, Barnum Letters, copy, Petersburg National Battlefield; Winkler, *Confederate Capital and Hood's Texas Brigade*, 94; Ural, *Hood's Texas Brigade*, 225.

23. Bryant, "Model Regiment," 120–21; Aliyetti, "Gallantry under Fire," 33; Blackett, *Thomas Morris Chester*, 151; Joseph J. Scroggs Diary, Sept. 29, 1864, *Civil War Times Illustrated* Collection, Army Heritage and Education Center, Carlisle; Giles W. Shurtleff to "My dear Edward," Oct. 2, 1864, Reverend Edward H. and Ada Clark Merrell Correspondence, University of Wisconsin at Oshkosh.

24. *OR*, 42(1):136; Jones, "Texas and Arkansas at Fort Harrison," 24; Ural, *Hood's Texas Brigade*, 225; McCarty Diary, Sept. 29, 1864; Nabours, "Active Service of a Texas Command," 70; Joskins, "Hood's Texas Brigade," 193; Polley, *Hood's Texas Brigade*, 254; Hamilton, *Company M, 1st Texas*, 62; Price, *New Market Heights*, 86. Unsurprisingly, casualty figures vary from those provided in the *Official Records*. Solon Carter, an officer on Paine's staff, cited losses of 587. See Carter, "Fourteen Months' Service with Colored Troops," 172. My figure includes casualties reported by the Twenty-Second USCT and the Second USCT Cavalry. The Fifth USCT reported the largest regimental loss in the division, but some of its casualties occurred later in the day. Twelve of the fourteen Medals of Honor were awarded on April 6, 1865. See Robertson, "From the Crater to New Market Heights," 192. Confederate casualties at New Market Heights were not reported.

25. Marshall, *Butler's Correspondence*, 5:191–92; Butler, *Butler's Book*, 733; Briscoe, "Visit to General Butler," 438.

26. *OR*, 42(1):702, 719, 726, 817–18; Eldridge Manuscript Notebook, Sept. 29, 1864, Harvard University, Cambridge; Crosland, *Reminiscences of the Sixties*, 33; Robert A. Turner Diary, Sept. 29, 1864; and William Godber Hinson Diary, Sept. 29, 1864, William Godber Hinson Papers, both in South Caroliniana Library, University of South Carolina, Columbia; Moore, *Story of a Cannoneer*, 263; McCarthy, *Richmond Howitzer Battalion*, 273.

27. "From the Tenth Connecticut," *Hartford (Conn.) Daily Courant*, Oct. 10, 1864; Sommers, *Richmond Redeemed*, 29.

28. Cunningham, *Adirondack Regiment*, 148; H[eman] E. Baker, "In Front of Richmond," *Adirondack Record* (Au Sable, N.Y.), July 25, 1919; Head, *Report of the Adjutant-General*, 726; David F. Dobie to "My dear friend Hattie," Oct. 3, 1864, Dobie Papers, University of Virginia, Charlottesville; Hubbell, "Battle of Fort Harrison," 299.

29. Siburt, "Colonel John M. Hughs," 93; Thomas Moore, "Memories of a Civil War Veteran," *Sandy Creek (N.Y.) Evening News*, Feb. 26, 1953; Harris, "Fort Harrison"; Cunningham, *Adirondack Regiment*, 148. Burnham was a large man who had experienced a childhood tragedy when his drunken father murdered his mother.

30. Cunningham, *Adirondack Regiment*, 148; Harris, "Fort Harrison"; Baker, "Incidents"; David F. Dobie to "My dear friend Hattie," Oct. 3, 1864, Dobie Papers; Moore, "Memories." Burnham's reference to "pickups" pertained to the emergency militia rounded up for service.

31. Sommers, *Richmond Redeemed*, 42. Stannard's division numbered approximately 3,000 men.

32. Linden Kent to "My Dear Ma," Oct. 2, 1864, Eleanor Brockenbrough Library, Museum of the Confederacy, Richmond; Taylor, "Personal Experiences"; Sommers, *Richmond Redeemed*, 39–41; Manarin, *Field of Honor*, 600–601. Taylor's brother, Walter, served on General Lee's staff. Richard Sommers refers to the unnamed battery as Battery X, a convention to describe a position whose wartime identity is unknown.

33. Rosser S. Rock to "My own sweet Sister," Nov. 25, 1864, Rosser S. Rock Letters, Eleanor Brockenbrough Library, Museum of the Confederacy, Richmond; Sommers, *Richmond Redeemed*, 41–42; Allen, "Fight at Chaffin's Farm," 418; *Richmond Sentinel*, Oct. 12, 13, 1864; Taylor, "Personal Experiences."

34. C. Tacitus Allen Memoirs, Rubenstein Special Collections Library, Duke University, Durham, N.C.; Sommers, *Richmond Redeemed*, 42; Manarin, *Field of Honor*, 601, 603; Crenshaw, *Fort Harrison*, 37; Moore, "Attack on Fort Harrison," 419; Siburt, "Colonel John M. Hughs," 93; Breckinridge, "Story of a Boy Captain," 415.

35. Hubbell, "Battle of Fort Harrison," 299–300; *OR*, 42(1):794; Sommers, *Richmond Redeemed*, 43.

36. Charles Coit to "Dear All," Oct. 4, 1864, Coit Letters, New-York Historical Society, New York; Clay, "Personal Narrative of the Capture of Fort Harrison," 77; *OR*, 42(1):798; Ware, "Battery Harrison"; Thompson, *13th New Hampshire*, 477–78; Hubbell, "Battle of Fort Harrison," 291; Sommers, *Richmond Redeemed*, 43.

37. Harris, "Fort Harrison"; Clay, "Personal Narrative of the Capture of Fort Harrison," 77–78; Thompson, *13th New Hampshire*, 478; Sommers, *Richmond Redeemed*, 45. The fog that lingered near the river did not extend this far inland, explaining the clarity of the morning at Fort Harrison.

38. Cunningham, *Adirondack Regiment*, 148–49; *Story of the Twenty-First Regiment, Connecticut Volunteer Infantry*, 300 (hereafter *Story of the Twenty-First Connecticut*); Ware, "Battery Harrison"; Head, *Report of the Adjutant-General*, 798; Thompson, *13th New Hampshire*, 477.

39. Head, *Report of the Adjutant-General*, 726; Croffut and Morris, *Connecticut during the War*, 665; Cunningham, *Adirondack Regiment*, 149; *OR*, 42(1):805; Thompson, *13th New Hampshire*, 461, 478; Clay, "Personal Narrative of the Capture of Fort Harrison," 79; Hubbell, "Battle of Fort Harrison," 292.

40. Houghton and Houghton, *Two Boys*, 113; Allen, "Fort Harrison," 300; Siburt, "Colonel John M. Hughs," 93; Rosser S. Rock to "My own sweet Sister," Nov. 25, 1864, Rock Letters; Moore, "Attack on Fort Harrison," 418; W. Dwight Reinhardt to "Dear Aunt," Oct. 4, 1864, Mary Hunter Kennedy Papers, Southern Historical Collection, Louis Round Wilson Library, University of North Carolina, Chapel Hill.

41. *OR*, 42(1):798; Clay, "Personal Narrative of the Capture of Fort Harrison," 79; Bruce, "Petersburg June 15—Fort Harrison, September 29," 92. Ord claimed that he sent his entire staff to urge the men to resume the attack, while the historian of the 118th New York gave credit to Burnham, who dispatched an aide on the brigade staff to order the men ahead. See *OR*, 42(1):794; and Cunningham, *Adirondack Regiment*, 149.

42. Harris, "Fort Harrison"; Cunningham, *Adirondack Regiment*, 149; Thompson, *13th New Hampshire*, 478–79.

43. *Richmond Sentinel*, Oct. 13, 1864; Clay, "Personal Narrative of the Capture of Fort Harrison," 80; Thompson, *13th New Hampshire*, 479; Ware, "Battery Harrison"; *OR*, 42(1):794; Hubbell, "Battle of Fort Harrison," 292.

44. Thompson, *13th New Hampshire*, 462; Houghton and Houghton, *Two Boys*, 114; Siburt, "Colonel John M. Hughs," 93; Moore, "Attack on Fort Harrison," 418–19; Rosser S. Rock to "My own sweet Sister," Nov. 25, 1864, Rock Letters; *Story of the Twenty-First Connecticut*, 301; Cunningham, *Adirondack Regiment*, 150; Ware, "Battery Harrison."

45. *OR*, 42(1):798, 805, 848; Cunningham, *Adirondack Regiment*, 149; Croffut and Morris, *Connecticut during the War*, 666; Hubbell, "Battle of Fort Harrison," 293; Thompson, *13th New Hampshire*, 479; E. T. Peters, "The Advance," *Philadelphia Inquirer*, Oct. 3, 1864; Sommers, *Richmond Redeemed*, 48.

46. Thompson, *13th New Hampshire*, 471; *OR*, 42(1):794, 799; Sommers, *Richmond Redeemed*, 48–49; Taylor, "Personal Experiences." Stannard reported 92 officers and men killed and 502 wounded during the day, with 330 others missing, many of whom he expected to turn up later. For a lengthy treatment of the Donohoe-Taylor episode, see "Our Stories," *Norfolk Virginian-Pilot*, Nov. 7, 2010.

47. Thompson, *13th New Hampshire*, 462; Everts, *9th New Jersey*, 132–33; *OR*, 42(2):892; Solon Carter to "My own darling," Oct. 17, 1864, Carter Letters, Army Heritage and Education Center, Carlisle; Sommers, *Richmond Redeemed*, 64. Richard Sommers states that the Federals captured Fort Harrison at 7:00 A.M., but Ord times the arrival of Stannard's men at the defilade in front of the fort at 7:30, and it seems reasonable that about thirty minutes transpired between their final assault and the complete expulsion of the Confederate defenders.

48. *OR*, 42(1):793; Edward H. Ripley, "Gives First Hand Account of Battle of Fort Harrison," *Richmond News-Leader*, Apr. 27, 1939; Sommers, *Richmond Redeemed*, 54–55.

49. Ripley, "First Hand Account"; Sommers, *Richmond Redeemed*, 54. The unlucky unit was Battery F, First Rhode Island Light Artillery.

50. *Richmond Sentinel*, Oct. 13, 1864; Ripley, "First Hand Account"; Sommers, *Richmond Redeemed*, 55. Some accounts place elements of the Twentieth Georgia and the Sixty-Third Tennessee in Battery 11 as well. Some of the Vermonters referred to Battery 11 as Battery Morris.

51. Ripley, "First Hand Account"; Zeller, *Ninth Vermont*, 167, 169; Benedict, *Vermont in the Civil War*, 242; "The 158th Brooklyn Regiment," *Brooklyn (N.Y.) Daily Eagle*, Oct. 10, 1864.

52. *OR*, 42(2):1302–3; Pfanz, *Richard S. Ewell*, 416; *OR Supp.*, 258; Crenshaw, *Fort Harrison*, 53; Sommers, *Richmond Redeemed*, 50. Bowles commanded Law's Brigade.

53. "Sarah" to A. L. Washington, Sept. 29, 1864, Alexander-Hillhouse Papers, University of North Carolina, Chapel Hill; John Rison to "Dear Friend," Sept. 30, 1864, James I. Robertson Jr. Civil War Sesquicentennial Legacy Project, Library of Virginia, Richmond; Cpl. John

William Ford Hatton Memoir, Manuscripts Division, Library of Congress, Washington; Jones, *Rebel War Clerk's Diary*, 295.

54. Sommers, *Richmond Redeemed*, 51. Ewell lost a leg in combat in August 1862 at the Brawner Farm, a part of the Second Manassas Campaign.

55. Kautz, "Reminiscences," Library of Congress, Washington, 89; Kautz, *August Valentine Kautz*, 152; Kautz Diary, Sept. 29, 1864, Kautz Papers, Library of Congress, Washington.

56. Sumner, *Comstock Diary*, 290; Sommers, *Richmond Redeemed*, 75; Henry H. Brown to "Dear Friends at Home," Oct. 5, 1864, Henry H. Brown Papers, Connecticut Historical Society, Hartford; Oliver W. Davis, *Life of David Bell Birney*, 259.

57. Sumner, *Comstock Diary*, 290; Badeau, *Military History of Ulysses S. Grant*, 3:71–72; Adam Badeau to "Dear Wilson," Oct. 1, 1864, Civil War Letters of Adam Badeau, Firestone Library Special Collections, Princeton University; Porter, *Campaigning with Grant*, 301; Chernow, *Grant*, 446.

58. Henry J. Ellis to "Dear Sister," Oct. 2, 1864, Bell Wiley Collection, Woodruff Library, Emory University, Atlanta; *OR Supp.*, 463–64; Houghton and Houghton, *Two Boys*, 114–15; Moore, "Attack on Fort Harrison," 419; Sommers, *Richmond Redeemed*, 53–54.

59. *OR*, 42(1):794–95; Allen, "Fight at Chaffin's Farm," 418; Cresap, *Appomattox Commander*, 134; Smith, "Perfectly Terrible Encounter," 31; Bruce, "Petersburg June 15–Fort Harrison, September 29," 95; Theodore Lyman to "My Dear Frank," Nov. 11, 1864, Lyman Letters, Massachusetts Historical Society, Boston; Sommers, *Richmond Redeemed*, 74.

60. *OR*, 42(1):935; Manarin, *Field of Honor*, 632; *OR Supp.*, 463; Moore, "Attack on Fort Harrison."

61. Ripley, "First Hand Account"; Benedict, *Vermont in the Civil War*, 243; Buckingham, *All's for the Best*, 305; Zeller, *Ninth Vermont*, 173; Houghton and Houghton, *Two Boys*, 115; Sommers, *Richmond Redeemed*, 64–65.

62. Ward, *Second Pennsylvania Veteran Heavy Artillery*, 107–8; Manarin, *Field of Honor*, 633; Sommers, *Richmond Redeemed*, 66.

63. Ward, *Second Pennsylvania Veteran Heavy Artillery*, 108–10; Pippitt, "Before Richmond"; Wells, "Forts Harrison and Gilmer," 32; Henry J. Ellis to "Dear Sister," Oct. 2, 1864, Bell Wiley Collection, Woodruff Library, Emory University, Atlanta; Moore, "Attack on Fort Harrison," 419; Sommers, *Richmond Redeemed*, 66–69; Manarin, *Field of Honor*, 632–36.

64. Hissong, "55th Pa."; Sommers, *Richmond Redeemed*, 73; Manarin, *Field of Honor*, 637.

65. Manarin, *Field of Honor*, 637; Sommers, *Richmond Redeemed*, 69, 71–72.

66. *OR*, 42(1):760, 764; William H. Richmond Reminiscence, Civil War Collection of Personal Papers, Clarke Historical Library, Central Michigan University, Mount Pleasant; Longacre, *From Antietam to Fort Fisher*, 209.

67. Longacre, *From Antietam to Fort Fisher*, 209; Jackson and O'Donnell, *Back Home in Oneida*, 164–65; Smith, *Jerimiah Smith*, 107; *OR*, 42(1):760, 764.

68. Manarin, *Field of Honor*, 640; *OR*, 42(1):760, 765; Longacre, *From Antietam to Fort Fisher*, 209; Richmond Reminiscence.

69. *OR*, 42(1):760, 935; W. S. Burwell to "Dear Ed," Oct. 5, 1864, Burwell Papers; John J. Reardon, "Memories of the Civil War," *St. Johnsville (N.Y.) News*, May 27, 1908; Smith, *Jerimiah Smith*, 107; Hyde, *One Hundred and Twelfth Regiment New York Volunteers*, 103; William L. Hyde to "My Dear Wife," Oct. 1, 1864, www.soldierstudies.org, accessed July 28, 2017 (site discontinued); Manarin, *Field of Honor*, 640.

70. Kautz, *August Valentine Kautz*, 152; Kautz Diary, Sept. 29, 1864; Kautz, "Reminiscences," 89–90; *OR*, 42(2):1149; Sommers, *Richmond Redeemed*, 100–105; Manarin, *Field of Honor*, 659–62.

71. Manarin, *Field of Honor*, 642–43; Sommers, *Richmond Redeemed*, 80–81.

72. Sommers, *Richmond Redeemed*, 83–84; Hatton Memoir; Jones, "Texas and Arkansas at Fort Harrison," 24; Granberry, "That Fort Gilmer Fight," 413; Linden Kent to "My Dear Ma," Oct. 2, 1864; W. I. Thomas to "My Dear Cousin," Nov. 4, 1864, Bryant Family Papers, Library of Virginia, Richmond; Timberlake, "Last Days in Front of Richmond," 303; *Richmond Sentinel*, Oct. 13, 1864.

73. *OR*, 42(2):1109–10; Manarin, *Field of Honor*, 644.

74. *OR*, 42(1):760–61, 765, 767; Silo, *115th New York*, 153; Sommers, *Richmond Redeemed*, 80–81; Manarin, *Field of Honor*, 645. A number of Foster's men timed their advance at 3:00 P.M.

75. Hyde, *One Hundred and Twelfth Regiment New York Volunteers*, 103; Mowris, *One Hundred and Seventeenth Regiment New York Volunteers*, 136; Bouton, *Memoir of General Louis Bell*, 24; De Graff Diary, Sept. 29, 1864, Army Heritage and Education Center, Carlisle; Longacre, *From Antietam to Fort Fisher*, 210 (letter also published in *New York Times*, Oct. 23, 1864); *OR*, 42(1):765.

76. Richmond Reminiscence; John B. Foote to "Dear Father," Oct. 2, 1864, Foote Papers, Duke University, Durham, N.C.; Longacre, *From Antietam to Fort Fisher*, 210.

77. Sommers, *Richmond Redeemed*, 85; Jackson and O'Donnell, *Back Home in Oneida*, 165; Longacre, *From Antietam to Fort Fisher*, 210–11.

78. Polley, *Letters to Charming Nellie*, 261; Jones, "Texas and Arkansas at Fort Harrison," 25; Johnston, "Attack on Fort Gilmer," 440.

79. Leigh, *J. J. Scroggs's Diary and Letters*, 368–69; Elliott F. Grabill to "Dearly Beloved," Sept. 30, 1864, Grabill Papers, Oberlin College Archives; *OR*, 42(1):769. It is not clear why Paine designated just one of his regiments to assist Foster, although his decision may simply be an example of his inexperience in command. See Trudeau, *Like Men of War*, 296.

80. *OR*, 42(1):133–34, 765, 767, 769; Silo, *115th New York*, 154; Jackson and O'Donnell, *Back Home in Oneida*, 165; John B. Foote to "Dear Father," Oct. 2, 1864, Foote Papers; James Beard to "Dear Brother and Sister," Oct. 3, 1864, James Beard Letters, Tennessee State Library and Archives, Nashville.

81. Warner, *Generals in Blue*, 35; Henry Grimes Marshall to "My loved Brother," Sept. 20, 1864, Marshall Letters, Clements Library, University of Michigan, Ann Arbor.

82. Sommers, *Richmond Redeemed*, 88; Trudeau, *Like Men of War*, 297.

83. *OR*, 42(1):774–75; Henry H. Brown to "Dear Friends at Home," Oct. 5, 1864, Henry H. Brown Papers; Talbot, *Samuel Chapman Armstrong*, 118.

84. *OR*, 42(1):780–81; Joseph C. Califf to "Dear General," Aug. 10, 1878, in Califf, *To the Ex-Members and Friends of the 7th U.S.C.T.*, 6.

85. *OR*, 42(1):772, 42(3):253–54; Califf, *Seventh U.S. Colored Troops*, 41–42; Birney, *General William Birney's Answer*, 14–22; Sommers, *Richmond Redeemed*, 90.

86. *OR*, 42(2):1303, 42(1):875; *OR Supp.*, 258; Jones, "Texas and Arkansas at Fort Harrison," 24–25; Reese, "What Five Confederates Did at Petersburg," 286; Stocker, *From Huntsville to Appomattox*, 184.

87. Sherman, *Assault on Fort Gilmer*, 7; *OR*, 42(1):772; Crenshaw, *Fort Harrison*, 76; Manarin, *Field of Honor*, 654; Trudeau, *Like Men of War*, 298; Califf, *Seventh U.S. Colored Troops*, 42–43; Johnston, "Attack on Fort Gilmer," 441.

88. Sherman, *Assault on Fort Gilmer*, 9; Califf, *Seventh U.S. Colored Troops*, 43; Lott, "Two Boys of the Fifth Texas," 417; Burkhardt, *Confederate Rage, Yankee Wrath*, 180; Trudeau, *Like Men of War*, 299; Granberry, "That Fort Gilmer Fight," 413.

89. John Francis Methvin Memoir, copy in bound vol. 91, Richmond National Battlefield Park; Polley, *Letters to Charming Nellie*, 262; McCarty postwar lecture; *OR Supp.*, 464; Moore, *Story of a Cannoneer*, 264; Andrews, *Sketch of the Boyhood Days*, 49.

90. May, "Fight at Fort Gilmer," 588; Martin, "Assault upon Fort Gilmer," 269–70; Hatton Memoir; Trudeau, *Like Men of War*, 299; Califf, *Seventh U.S. Colored Troops*, 43.

91. *OR*, 42(1):773; Burkhardt, *Confederate Rage, Yankee Wrath*, 181; Pfanz, *Richard S. Ewell*, 417; Sherman, *Assault on Fort Gilmer*, 11–12. I include Ewell's role in ending the murder of Black captives in deference to the general's fine biographer, who chose to credit it. But R. E. L. Krick, the impeccable historian at Richmond National Battlefield Park, doubts that the news of an episode of such probable brevity would have had time to reach Ewell and his reply get back to the perpetrators before the killing had ceased of its own accord.

92. Martin, "Assault upon Fort Gilmer," 270; Perry, "Assault on Fort Gilmer," 415; Lokey, "My Experience," Georgia State Archives, Morrow, 22–23; Methvin Memoir; Andrews, *Sketch of Boyhood Days*, 49.

93. Martin, "Assault upon Fort Gilmer," 270; Diary of Lt. Joshua H. Dearborn, Sept. 29, 1864, Guilford Free Public Library. This was, of course, an indictment of William Birney.

94. Manarin, *Field of Honor*, 658; Sommers, *Richmond Redeemed*, 92; *Brooklyn (N.Y.) Daily Eagle*, Oct. 10, 1864.

95. Hissong, "55th Pa."; *OR*, 42(2):1116; "Army Correspondence," *Bedford (Pa.) Inquirer*, Dec. 9, 1864.

96. Flanigan, "That Fight at Fort Gilmer," 23; *OR*, 42(3):166–67, 42(1):135; Manarin, *Field of Honor*, 659; Sommers, *Richmond Redeemed*, 92–93.

97. *OR*, 42(2):1110, 42(1):703, 726; *Hartford (Conn.) Daily Courant*, Oct. 10, 1864; Roe, *Twenty-Fourth Massachusetts*, 360; Sommers, *Richmond Redeemed*, 93–94; Manarin, *Field of Honor*, 659–60.

98. *OR*, 42(2):1091, 1110–11; *Story of the Twenty-First Connecticut*, 294, 307; Manarin, *Field of Honor*, 662; Sommers, *Richmond Redeemed*, 94. Cox's Ferry was an alternative name for Cox's Landing.

99. *OR*, 42(2):1304; Sommers, *Richmond Redeemed*, 97–98; Manarin, *Field of Honor*, 662–63. Lee's decision to take personal command of the situation in Henrico County may be an indication that he lacked confidence in Dick Anderson.

100. *OR*, 42(1):794; Gallagher, *Fighting for the Confederacy*, 475.

101. *OR*, 42(3):65. Butler would later have a special medal struck and presented to several hundred of his Black troops who attacked New Market Heights. See Trudeau, *Like Men of War*, 300.

102. Pfanz, *Richard S. Ewell*, 417–18; Sommers, *Richmond Redeemed*, 62–63.

103. *OR*, 42(2):1111; Barefoot, *General Robert F. Hoke*, 222; Sommers, *Richmond Redeemed*, 110–12; Freeman, *Lee's Lieutenants*, 590–91; Gallagher, *Fighting for the Confederacy*, 477; Hagood, *Memoirs*, 305; Field, "Campaign of 1864 and 1865," 555–56.

CHAPTER NINE

1. Styple, *Writing & Fighting the Confederate War*, 249–51; Eugene Levy, "Donaldsonville Cannoneers at the Siege of Petersburg," *New Orleans Times-Picayune*, Aug. 4, 1902; Sommers,

Richmond Redeemed, 108–9. Sgt. Charles N. B. Minor of the Confederate Engineers estimated that "upwards of 7000 men" were conscripted on September 29, including couriers belonging to Lee and Early—doubtless an exaggeration. Journal of Charles Norborne Berkeley Minor, Oct. 11, 1864, Virginia Museum of History and Culture, Richmond.

2. Sommers, *Richmond Redeemed*, 111.

3. John Hall to "Dear Father," Sept. 29, 1864, Hall Family Papers, Alabama Department of Archives and History, Montgomery; Hagood, *Memoirs*, 305; Dunn Diary, Sept. 29–30, 1864, Georgia State Archives, Morrow; Schiller, *A Captain's War*, 151; Barefoot, *General Robert F. Hoke*, 222; Hewitt, Trudeau, and Suderow, *Supplement to the Official Records of the Union and Confederate Armies* (hereafter *OR Supp.*), 258–59; Morgan, *Recollections of a Rebel Reefer*, 208; Manarin, *Field of Honor*, 679–80; Sommers, *Richmond Redeemed*, 111–12. Hoke's four brigades numbered 5,538 and Scales's regiments 1,210. See U.S. War Department, *War of the Rebellion*, ser. 1, 42(2):1244, 1307 (hereafter *OR*; all references are to series 1 unless otherwise noted). It is curious that Lee chose to accept the extra time necessary to swap Johnson's Division for Hoke's. Perhaps he felt that Johnson's long service in the trenches left his troops unfit for combat in the field.

4. Wise, *Long Arm of Lee*, 897; E. Porter Alexander to his wife, Oct. 3, 1864, E. Porter Alexander Papers, Southern Historical Collection, Louis Round Wilson Library, University of North Carolina, Chapel Hill; Sommers, *Richmond Redeemed*, 113–14. The batteries that crossed the James were the Fredericksburg Artillery; Clutter's Richmond Battery; the Richmond Fayette Artillery; Battery E, First North Carolina Artillery; the Second Palmetto Artillery; Battery F, Thirteenth North Carolina Light Artillery; and the Nelson Artillery.

5. *OR*, 42(2):1111.

6. Thompson, *13th New Hampshire*, 463; *OR*, 42(1):662, 800, 42(2):1111.

7. *OR*, 42(2):1118. For an informed speculation regarding Grant's decision to remain on the defensive north of the James, see Sommers, *Richmond Redeemed*, 129–30.

8. *OR*, 42(2):1146, 1148; Marshall, *Butler's Correspondence*, 5:298–99. Most biographical sketches list Cincinnati as Weitzel's birthplace, but his biographer asserts that he was born in Winzeln, Germany. See Quatman, *Young General*, 2.

9. *OR*, 42(2):1142, 1144–45. McGowan's and Lane's Brigades of Wilcox's Division started for the pontoon bridges about 9:00 that morning. See Caldwell, *McGowan's Brigade*, 236–37; Harris, *Seventh North Carolina*, 56; James Lane letter, Oct. 2, 1864, James Henry Lane Papers, Special Collections, Auburn University.

10. Sorrel, *Confederate Staff Officer*, 256; Pfanz, *Richard S. Ewell*, 418; Sommers, *Richmond Redeemed*, 133.

11. Joseph William Eggleston Autobiography, Virginia Museum of History and Culture, Richmond, 49–50. For a cogent analysis of Lee's options, see Sommers, *Richmond Redeemed*, 133–34.

12. Dean, "Recollections of Army Life," copy, Petersburg National Battlefield; Field, "Campaign of 1864 and 1865," 556–57.

13. Rufus Hollis, "Confederate Veteran," *Scottsboro Citizen*, Alabama Department of Archives and History, Montgomery; *OR*, 42(1):880; Hagood, "Memoirs of the First SC Regiment," University of South Carolina, Columbia, 180; Manarin, *Field of Honor*, 681; Sommers, *Richmond Redeemed*, 134.

14. William Henry von Eberstein Memoir, William Henry von Eberstein Papers, East Carolina University, Greenville; Burgwyn, "Clingman's Brigade," 495–96; McKethan, "Fifty-First Regiment," 213.

15. E. Porter Alexander to his wife, Oct. 3, 1864, Alexander Papers; *Official Records of the Union and Confederate Navies in the War of the Rebellion*, 10:755, 757; Sommers, *Richmond Redeemed*, 135–36.

16. *OR*, 42(1):800; Manarin, *Field of Honor*, 682; Ladd, "Fort Harrison"; *Story of the Twenty-First Connecticut*, 307.

17. Thompson, *13th New Hampshire*, 480; Sperry Diary, Sept. 30, 1864, New-York Historical Society, New York; Ware, "Battery Harrison"; *OR*, 42(1):800, 805; Cunningham, *Adirondack Regiment*, 151.

18. Sommers, *Richmond Redeemed*, 137.

19. Palladino, *Diary of a Yankee Engineer*, 171–72; Gallagher, *Fighting for the Confederacy*, 478; Burgwyn, "Clingman's Brigade," 496; Barefoot, *General Robert F. Hoke*, 224; Oliver W. Davis, *Life of David Bell Birney*, 263.

20. Field, "Campaign of 1864 and 1865," 557; Baldwin, *Struck Eagle*, 327; Austin, *General John Bratton*, 236; *OR*, 42(1):880; E. Porter Alexander to his wife, Oct. 3, 1864, Alexander Papers; Coffin, *Freedom Triumphant*, 191; Pollard, *Southern History of the War*, 101; Hewitt, "Lee's Most Maligned General," 100.

21. *OR*, 42(1):880; Hagood, "Memoirs of the First SC Regiment," 180–82.

22. Thompson, *13th New Hampshire*, 481; *Story of the Twenty-First Connecticut*, 282.

23. Hagood, "Memoirs of the First SC Regiment," 182–84; H[eman] E. Baker, "In Front of Richmond," *Adirondack Record* (Au Sable, N.Y.), July 25, 1919.

24. Zeller, *Ninth Vermont*, 182; Denny, *25th Massachusetts Volunteer Infantry*, 357; *OR*, 42(2):1143, 42(1):801; Edward H. Ripley, "Gives First Hand Account of Battle of Fort Harrison," *Richmond News-Leader*, Apr. 27, 1939; Sommers, *Richmond Redeemed*, 143. Grant's selection of Humphrey is curious since that officer mustered out of service on September 30. "The loss of Colonel Humphrey was quite unexpected to most of the brigade, and it was with great regret that they took leave of this gallant and able officer." Cutcheon Autobiography, Bentley Historical Library, University of Michigan, Ann Arbor, 358; Cutcheon, *Twentieth Michigan Infantry*, 154–55; *OR*, 42(2):1137; Simon, *Grant Papers*, 12:244. The division's First Brigade commander, Col. Benjamin C. Christ, also mustered out that day, thus elevating two new officers, John F. Hartranft and Samuel Harriman, to brigade command on the very day of battle. See *OR*, 42(1):558.

25. Laine and Penny, *Law's Alabama Brigade*, 304; *OR*, 42(1):818; Sommers, *Richmond Redeemed*, 142.

26. It is possible that McKethan and Colquitt, hidden in their ravine, did not have a clear view of Field's premature assault, but surely the sounds of such fierce combat reached their ears. See Manarin, *Field of Honor*, 689. Even so, the Confederate high command witnessed Field's repulse. Field earlier blamed Hoke for a failure to cooperate in an offensive on June 24. See Greene, *Campaign of Giants*, 268–72.

27. Schiller, *A Captain's War*, 151, 153; McKethan, "Fifty-First Regiment," 214; von Eberstein Memoir.

28. George Warthen to "Dear Uncle," Oct. 6, 1864, Warthen Letters, Duke University, Durham, N.C.; Dunn Diary, Sept. 30, 1864; Sommers, *Richmond Redeemed*, 144–45.

29. *Story of the Twenty-First Connecticut*, 285; Cunningham, *Adirondack Regiment*, 152; Thomas Moore, "Memories of a Civil War Veteran," *Sandy Creek (N.Y.) Evening News*, Feb. 26, 1953; Thompson, *13th New Hampshire*, 481; Ware, "Battery Harrison"; "From the 21st

Regiment," *Connecticut War Record* (New Haven), May 1865. Brydon's name was sometimes spelled "Bryden."

30. Schiller, *A Captain's War*, 153; Ward, *Second Pennsylvania Veteran Heavy Artillery*, 114; *OR*, 42(1):806; Head, *Report of the Adjutant-General*, 800; *Story of the Twenty-First Connecticut*, 309; Ware, "Battery Harrison"; Croffut and Morris, *Connecticut during the War*, 669; Capt. William Henry Harder Memoir, Tennessee State Library and Archives, Nashville.

31. *OR*, 42(1):880; Burgwyn, "Clingman's Brigade," 496; Edmund Jones Williams to "Dear Ma," Oct. 2, 1864, Edmund Jones Williams Papers, Southern Historical Collection, Louis Round Wilson Library, University of North Carolina, Chapel Hill; Manarin, *Field of Honor*, 692–93; Sommers, *Richmond Redeemed*, 146, 148; Coleman Diary, Oct. 1, 1864, University of South Carolina, Columbia.

32. Granberry, "That Fort Gilmer Fight," 413; Freeman, *R. E. Lee*, 503–4; Morgan, *Recollections of a Rebel Reefer*, 211; Sorrel, *Confederate Staff Officer*, 253.

33. Dowdey and Manarin, *Wartime Papers of R. E. Lee*, 860; Hagood, "Memoirs of the First SC Regiment," 186; Field, "Campaign of 1864 and 1865," 557; Henry DeShields to "My Darling," Oct. 11, 1864, DeShields Letters, Library of Virginia, Richmond; Schiller, *A Captain's War*, 153; *OR Supp.*, 466; von Eberstein Memoir; A. W. Murray to "Miss Sophronia Thompson Dear Cousin," Oct. 8, 1864, Gurr Family Papers, Hargrett Rare Book and Manuscript Library, University of Georgia, Athens; Eggleston Autobiography, 50.

34. E. Porter Alexander to his wife, Oct. 3, 1864, Alexander Papers; newspaper quoted in Laine and Penny, *Law's Alabama Brigade*, 304; Lockwood, *Lee's Adjutant*, 195; Gallagher, *Fighting for the Confederacy*, 478; *OR*, 42(1):880.

35. *OR*, 42(1):137; Marvel, *Tarnished Victory*, 190.

36. Hall and Hall, *Cayuga in the Field*, 259; Thompson, *13th New Hampshire*, 482; Simeon Gallup to "Dear Sister," Oct. 6, 1864, Simeon Gallup Letters, James S. Schoff Civil War Collection, Clements Library, University of Michigan, Ann Arbor.

37. Sperry Diary, Oct. 1, 1864; Cunningham, *Adirondack Regiment*, 152; George Tobey Anthony to "Dear Brother," Oct. 1, 1864, George Tobey Anthony Letters, James S. Schoff Civil War Collection, Clements Library, University of Michigan, Ann Arbor; Ripley, "First Hand Account"; Paul Fay to "Friend Antis," Nov. 5, 1864, Paul Fay Letters, Manuscripts and Special Collections, New York State Library, Albany; Ward, *Second Pennsylvania Veteran Heavy Artillery*, 114; George Naylor Julian to "My dear Parents & Sister," Oct. 5, 1864, Julian Papers, University of New Hampshire, Durham.

38. "Grant's Operations," *New York Times*, Oct. 4, 1864; Butler, *Butler's Book*, 738. Butler quickly had log huts built for himself and his staff.

39. *OR*, 42(2):1143–44.

40. *OR*, 42(2):1008, 1046–47, 1064; Charles Cummings to "My Dear Wife," Sept. 30, 1864, Charles Cummings Papers, Vermont Historical Society, Barre.

41. *OR*, 42(2):1054, 1069, 1073–75; Wainwright Diary, Sept. 28, 1864, Henry E. Huntington Library, San Marino.

42. George Johnston Diary, Sept. 28, 1864, Kenan Research Center, Atlanta History Center; Robinson, "Fifty-Second Regiment," 249; Sommers, *Richmond Redeemed*, 245–46. Fort Cherry was located just south of the William Wyatt Davis house and named for Capt. Macon G. Cherry of Company C, Forty-Fourth North Carolina. It could accommodate as many as seven guns but never held that many. It is no longer extant. Forts Bratton, Archer, and

MacRae were named after brigade commanders. Nothing remains of Fort Bratton. The Federals would modify Fort Archer and rename it Fort Wheaton. It is preserved as an isolated unit of Petersburg National Battlefield. A small remnant of Fort MacRae exists on private property in 2024. The Confederate line parallel to Boydton Plank Road, extending from the original Confederate defenses at Battery 45, was intended to protect Lee's new wagon supply line coming up from Stony Creek. Much of it is well preserved, including a section in Pamplin Historical Park. For the origin of these fortifications, see chapter 6.

43. *OR*, 42(2):1074; Parker, *General James Dearing*, 83; James Dearing to "My own precious wife," Oct. 2, 1864, Dearing Family Papers, Virginia Museum of History and Culture, Richmond; Sommers, *Richmond Redeemed*, 218, 246–47. General Dearing suffered from chills, fever, and severe headaches, experiencing a particularly bad bout on September 29. Colonel Griffin was in his late twenties.

44. William J. Mosely to "My Dear Parents," Sept. 30, 1864, William J. Mosely Collection, Georgia State Archives, Morrow; Bearss, *Petersburg Campaign: The Western Front Battles*, 7, 10 (hereafter Bearss, *Western Front Battles*); Sommers, *Richmond Redeemed*, 185–87.

45. *OR*, 42(2):1091–94, 1103–4. The term of service for two regiments, the Fourth Rhode Island and the Fiftieth Pennsylvania, expired on September 30, although some members of both units remained in the ranks during this operation.

46. Sommers, *Richmond Redeemed*, 191; *OR*, 42(1):619.

47. *OR*, 42(2):1106, 42(1):634; Longacre, *Jersey Cavaliers*, 227. The confluence of Hatcher's Run and Gravelly Run form Rowanty Creek, which was crossed just below the confluence at Monk's Neck Bridge on a road leading from Reams' Station toward Dinwiddie Court House. Another marshy stream, Arthur's Swamp, joins Hatcher's Run just before its confluence with Gravelly Run. All of these waterways provided something of a challenge for troops intending to cross them.

48. *OR*, 42(2):1107; Bearss, *Western Front Battles*, 12–13. Poplar Spring Church was destroyed during the war, but a modern sanctuary called Sharon Baptist Church sits near its wartime location in 2024.

49. Sommers, *Richmond Redeemed*, 198; Harrell, *2nd North Carolina Cavalry*, 333; Hampton, "Extract from Report of Cavalry Operations," 78; *OR*, 42(1):947; John Nathaniel Peed to "Dear Mother," Oct. 5, 1864, Peed Family Letters, Hesburgh Library, University of Notre Dame, South Bend; Daughtry, *Gray Cavalier*, 220.

50. Harrell, *2nd North Carolina Cavalry*, 335; "Hart's Horse Artillery," *Charleston (S.C.) Daily Courier*, Oct. 15, 1864; Louis Sherfesse Memoir, South Caroliniana Library, University of South Carolina, Columbia; Trout, *Galloping Thunder*, 569.

51. Hopkins, *Little Jeff*, 236–37; Harrell, *2nd North Carolina Cavalry*, 336; Gordon Diary, Sept. 29, 1864, Museum of the Confederacy, Richmond; Waring Diary, Sept. 29, 1864, University of North Carolina, Chapel Hill; Robert Saussy to "Dear Rad," Oct. 23, 1864, Joachim Saussy Papers, Rubenstein Special Collections Library, Duke University, Durham, N.C.; A. F. Coon to "Dr Sir," Oct. 1, 1864, John Covode Papers, Manuscripts Division, Library of Congress, Washington; Tobie, *First Maine Cavalry*, 359; Holmes, *Horse Soldiers in Blue*, 184; Hand, *One Good Regiment*, 158–59; Bearss, *Western Front Battles*, 14–15; Sommers, *Richmond Redeemed*, 202–5.

52. Sommers, "Petersburg Autumn," 34. To reiterate, Lee ordered Hoke's four brigades, the remaining three brigades from Field's Division, Scales's Brigade from Wilcox's command, and the makeshift brigade deducted from Pickett. Thomas's Brigade of Wilcox's Division was north of the Appomattox along Swift Creek. Richard Sommers estimates that 27,000

Confederates of all arms remained on the Petersburg lines. Meade's mobile force numbered about 24,000 men, and some 39,000 Federals remained behind to man the works. See Sommers, *Richmond Redeemed*, 228.

53. For an insightful evaluation of the Confederate commands and their commanders and a cogent summary of the strategic situation on the night of September 29–30, see Sommers, *Richmond Redeemed*, 206–18. Lane and McGowan were on the move for the north side by 9:00 A.M. on September 30.

54. *OR*, 42(3):38; Henry Bird to "My dear Maggie," Sept. 20, 1864, Bird Family Papers, Virginia Museum of History and Culture, Richmond; Scarborough, *Ruffin Diary*, 599; Sommers, *Richmond Redeemed*, 208.

55. *OR*, 42(2):1094, 1118, 1131, 1137; Sommers, *Richmond Redeemed*, 238. Miss Pegram's was also known as the Westmoreland house and stood due south of Fort MacRae between Squirrel Level and Duncan Roads. It allegedly burned on October 8, 1864. The Federals sometimes incorrectly referred to the nearby Watkins house as Miss Pegram's.

56. Sommers, *Richmond Redeemed*, 230–41; Gavin, *Campaigning with the Roundheads*, 566. Willcox's order of march by brigade was Hartranft, McLaughlen, and Harriman. The Aiken house, Willcox's headquarters, was inhabited, according to the opinionated Theodore Lyman, by five women: "one over 50 years old, the others 35 and younger, four are ugly, one is merely homely but suffers from fits." Lyman Letters, Massachusetts Historical Society, Boston. Neither dwelling is extant.

57. For a fuller analysis of this issue, see Sommers, *Richmond Redeemed*, 223–34; and Sommers, "Petersburg Autumn," 36. It should be noted that a large number of new recruits also populated the regiments selected for the offensive.

58. Sommers, *Richmond Redeemed*, 238, 243; Jordan, *Happiness Is Not My Companion*, 191. Richard Sommers, the unparalleled student of this action, refers to the upper portion of Duncan Road as Harman Road. The Harman house sat in the southwest corner of this country byway and Boydton Plank Road, ground preserved by Pamplin Historical Park in 2024. For simplicity's sake, I will refer to the road's entire length as Duncan Road, conforming with its modern nomenclature.

59. Sommers, *Richmond Redeemed*, 241–42, 248; Sommers, "Petersburg Autumn," 36; *OR*, 42(1):477; Smith, *Corn Exchange Regiment*, 513; Nevins, *Diary of Battle*, 466; Warren to "My Sugar Plum," Oct. 1, 1864, Warren Papers, New York State Library, Albany. The Eighteenth Massachusetts, supported by three more of Gwyn's regiments, provided the skirmishers. Warren's hesitation on the offensive, revealed at Spotsylvania in early May and repeated during the First Petersburg Offensive, the Battle of the Crater, and at the Weldon Railroad, had tarnished his standing with Grant and Meade.

60. Owen, *First Michigan*; William M. Read Diary, Oct. 4, 1864, William M. Read Letters and Diary, copy, Petersburg National Battlefield; Spear et al., *Recollections of General Ellis Spear*, 149; Marshall, *Company "K" 155th Pa.*, 202; Judson, *Eighty-Third Regiment Pennsylvania Volunteers*, 232 (hereafter Judson, *Eighty-Third Pennsylvania*).

61. Burrage, *36th Massachusetts*, 258–59; *OR*, 42(1):581; Cutcheon Autobiography, 358; Peleg Jones Diary, Sept. 30, 1864, Gilbert Family Papers, Rhode Island Historical Society, Providence; Merriam, "Personal Recollections of the War for the Union," copy in bound vol. 190 Fredericksburg & Spotsylvania National Military Park, 67.

62. Sommers, *Richmond Redeemed*, 247; Bearss, *Western Front Battles*, 19; Smith, *Corn Exchange Regiment*, 513–14; Woodward, *198th Pennsylvania*, 14; Aunt Lib to "Dear one," Feb.

21, n.d., typescript, Sanderson-Talmage Letters, Petersburg National Battlefield; Howard L. Prince, "Peebles Farm," Richard J. Sommers Papers, Author's Collection, Walden. A Union fort located at the intersection of Squirrel Level Road and modern Flank Road would be named after Lieutenant Conahey and is preserved within Petersburg National Battlefield. The 198th Pennsylvania had left Philadelphia only eleven days earlier. The Talmages' residence was destroyed later in the fighting, and the family returned to New Jersey.

63. Sommers, *Richmond Redeemed*, 249; *OR*, 42(2):1131, 42(1):581; Nash, *Forty-Fourth Regiment New York Volunteer Infantry*, 209 (hereafter Nash, *Forty-Fourth New York*).

64. Sommers, *Richmond Redeemed*, 251.

65. Prince, "Peebles Farm"; Spear et al., *Recollections of General Ellis Spear*, 150; *Under the Maltese Cross*, 321.

66. Nathan S. Clark Diary, Sept. 30, 1864, Maine State Archives, Augusta; Prince, "Peebles Farm"; Judson, *Eighty-Third Pennsylvania*, 232.

67. Gerrish, *Army Life*, 215; Alfred A. Apted Diary, copy in bound vol. 195, Fredericksburg & Spotsylvania National Military Park; John L. Smith to "My Dear Mother," Oct. 4, 1864, John L. Smith Letters, Historical Society of Pennsylvania, Philadelphia; Smith, *Corn Exchange Regiment*, 514; Nash, *Forty-Fourth New York*, 210.

68. Sommers, *Richmond Redeemed*, 253; Judson, *Eighty-Third Pennsylvania*, 233; Nash, *Forty-Fourth New York*, 210; Read Diary, Oct. 4, 1864; Prince, "Peebles Farm."

69. Crawford, *16th Michigan*, 479; Nash, *Forty-Fourth New York*, 210; Owen, *First Michigan*; Charles Salter to "My Dear Friend," Oct. 5, 1864, in Poremba, *If I Am Found Dead*, 213; Cutcheon Autobiography, 358; Sommers, *Richmond Redeemed*, 253–54; Prince, "Peebles Farm"; Bearss, *Western Front Battles*, 21.

70. Gerrish, *Army Life*, 216; Pullen, *Twentieth Maine*, 226; Moore, *Graham's Battery*, 29; Trout, *Galloping Thunder*, 569–70; Bearss, *Western Front Battles*, 21; Sommers, *Richmond Redeemed*, 254.

71. James Dearing to "My own precious wife," Oct. 2, 1864, Dearing Family Papers; Parker, *General James Dearing*, 83.

72. *OR*, 42(2):1131–32; Sommers, *Richmond Redeemed*, 255–56.

73. *OR*, 42(1):578; Draper, *Recollections*, 172; Burrage, *36th Massachusetts*, 259; Carruth et al., *35th Massachusetts*, 297; Bearss, *Western Front Battles*, 24; Sommers, "Petersburg Autumn," 38; Sommers, *Richmond Redeemed*, 258–60.

74. *OR*, 42(2):1119; Sommers, *Richmond Redeemed*, 260–64.

75. *OR*, 42(1):546, 578, 581; Lowe, *Meade's Army*, 273; Albert A. Pope Diary, Sept. 30, 1864, *Civil War Times Illustrated* Collection, Army Heritage and Education Center, Carlisle; Houston, *Thirty-Second Maine*, 391; Sommers, *Richmond Redeemed*, 266–67. Ayres's division was still on Vaughan Road and not directly involved in the advance.

76. *OR*, 42(1):587; Sommers, *Richmond Redeemed*, 268–69; Jackman, *Sixth New Hampshire*, 335; unknown soldier, Eleventh New Hampshire, to "Dear Aunt Louisa," Oct. 7, 1864, Grant Family of Lyme Civil War Letters, copy in bound vol. 401, Fredericksburg & Spotsylvania National Military Park; Merriam, "Personal Recollections." The Boswell house stood east of Church Road and, like the Boisseau and Pegram homes, does not survive; it burned in 1953. Part of the Jones farm is preserved by the American Battlefield Trust in 2024, although the house burned in 1865.

77. *OR*, 42(1):581; Carruth et al., *35th Massachusetts*, 297.

78. *OR*, 42(1):552, 558, 565, 570, 574; Sommers, *Richmond Redeemed*, 270–71; Cutcheon *Autobiography*, 360; Gavin, *Campaigning with the Roundheads*, 568; Lowber Diary, Sept. 30, 1864, Virginia Tech University, Blacksburg; Knowles Journal and Diary, East Carolina University, Greenville.

79. *OR*, 42(1):579; Chapman, *More Terrible Than Victory*, 241; Sommers, *Richmond Redeemed*, 271–72; Lowe, *Meade's Army*, 274.

80. Hampton, "Extract from Report of Cavalry Operations," 78; *OR*, 42(1):947; Trout, *Galloping Thunder*, 571.

81. Wilcox, "Battle of Jones's Farm," 67; Sommers, *Richmond Redeemed*, 211, 273–74. Much of this land is preserved in 2024 by the American Battlefield Trust and Pamplin Historical Park.

82. *OR*, 42(1):587; Jackman, *Sixth New Hampshire*, 335–36; Lord, *Ninth Regiment New Hampshire Volunteers*, 527 (hereafter Lord, *Ninth New Hampshire*); Trout, *Galloping Thunder*, 571; Wilcox, "Battle of Jones's Farm," 68.

83. Hardy, *General Lee's Immortals*, 330; McDaid, "Four Years of Arduous Service," 309–10; Lane, "Lane's Corps of Sharpshooters," 5; *OR Supp.*, 496; Caldwell, *McGowan's Brigade*, 237; Dunlop, *Lee's Sharpshooters*, 210–11; *OR*, 42(1):587; Jackman, *Sixth New Hampshire*, 336; Chapman, *More Terrible Than Victory*, 241; Sommers, *Richmond Redeemed*, 276; Sommers, "Petersburg Autumn," 40.

84. *OR*, 42(1):579, 587; Rutan, *If I Have Got to Go and Fight*, 144–45; Jackman, *Sixth New Hampshire*, 336; Lord, *Ninth New Hampshire*, 527; Marvel, *Race of the Soil*, 298; Sommers, *Richmond Redeemed*, 277. The four regiments Griffin advanced were the Sixth, Ninth, and Eleventh New Hampshire and the Second Maryland. The dismounted New Yorkers again served as skirmishers.

85. Wilcox, "Battle of Jones's Farm," 68–69; Wilcox, "Notes on the Richmond Campaign," Wilcox Papers, Virginia Museum of History and Culture, Richmond; Sommers, *Richmond Redeemed*, 275–76.

86. Hardy, *Thirty-Seventh North Carolina*, 211; Thomas L. Norwood to "Dear Uncle," Oct. 22, 1864, Lenoir Family Papers, Southern Historical Collection, Louis Round Wilson Library, University of North Carolina, Chapel Hill; *OR Supp.*, 502; McDaid, "Four Years of Arduous Service," 311–12.

87. Caldwell, *McGowan's Brigade*, 237; Merriam, "Personal Recollections," 69; Unknown soldier to "Dear Aunt Louisa," Oct. 7, 1864, Grant Family of Lyme Civil War Letters; Lord, *Ninth New Hampshire*, 527; Otis Bosworth Diary, Sept. 30, 1864, Hesburgh Library, University of Notre Dame, South Bend; James Henry Lane letter, Oct. 2, 1864, Lane Papers.

88. *OR*, 42(1):582; Sommers, *Richmond Redeemed*, 277, 279, 282; *OR Supp.*, 502–3.

89. *OR*, 42(1):581–82; Draper, *Recollections*, 173.

90. *OR*, 42(1):579, 582; Burrage, *36th Massachusetts*, 262; John Dentzer to "Dear Mother," Oct. 6, 1864, Dentzer Family Papers, Rubenstein Special Collections Library, Duke University, Durham, N.C.

91. Chapman, *More Terrible Than Victory*, 243–44; Sommers, *Richmond Redeemed*, 288; Hess, *Lee's Tar Heels*, 262–63; Martin and Outlaw, "Eleventh Regiment," 600.

92. *OR*, 42(1):948; Sommers, *Richmond Redeemed*, 288–89; Trout, *Galloping Thunder*, 571.

93. *OR*, 42(1):582; Roberts, *As They Remembered*, 156; William Henry Lewin to "My dear wife," Oct. 1, 1864, William Henry Lewin Papers, Virginia Museum of History and Culture,

Richmond; William T. Ackerson Diary, Sept. 30, 1864, William T. Ackerson Papers, Monmouth County Historical Association Library and Archives, Freehold; Albert, *Forty-Fifth Regiment Pennsylvania Veteran Volunteer Infantry*, 164, 166.

94. *OR*, 42(1):565; Herek, *These Men Have Seen Hard Service*, 257; Sommers, *Richmond Redeemed*, 283–84.

95. Crater Diary, Sept. 30, 1864, University of Iowa, Iowa City; Sommers, *Richmond Redeemed*, 284–88; Hess, *Lee's Tar Heels*, 262–63; Overfield, *Civil War Letters of Private George Parks*, 40; Bullock, "Col. W. C. Raulston." Three officers and forty-two enlisted men in the Twenty-Fourth New York Cavalry were captured. Raulston was taken to Petersburg and then transferred to the Confederate prison in Danville, Virginia, where he was mortally wounded during an escape attempt. Lt. Col. John B. Raulston was his brother.

96. Cutcheon Autobiography, 360–62; *OR*, 42(1):570–71; Joseph H. Harper Diary, Sept. 30, 1864, Civil War Documents Collection, Army Heritage and Education Center, Carlisle. Richard Sommers speculates that the Confederate cavalry was from the Second and Third North Carolina of Barringer's Brigade and the Thirteenth Virginia from Davis's. See *Richmond Redeemed*, 285.

97. Mauney Diary, Sept. 30, 1864, Museum of the Confederacy, Richmond; Hardy, *Thirty-Seventh North Carolina*, 331; Thomas L. Norwood to "Dear Uncle," Oct. 22, 1864, Lenoir Family Papers.

98. *OR*, 42(2):1133; Powell, *Fifth Army Corps*, 732; Frederick Rees to "Dear Father," Oct. 6, 1864, Rees Family Letters, copy, Petersburg National Battlefield; Plumb, *Your Brother in Arms*, 233; Prince, "Peebles Farm"; Sommers, *Richmond Redeemed*, 288–305.

99. Caldwell, *McGowan's Brigade*, 239–40; Collins quoted in Hardy, *Thirty-Seventh North Carolina*, 212.

100. *OR*, 42(2):1121, 1132, 1137; Sommers, *Richmond Redeemed*, 314–16.

101. *OR*, 42(1):139–42.

102. *OR*, 42(1):635; Pyne, *First New Jersey Cavalry*, 247; Sommers, *Richmond Redeemed*, 322–23.

103. *OR*, 42(2):1121–22, 1133, 1138. Lee and Beauregard enjoyed a similar partnership, although tactical rather than operational discretion prevailed between the two.

104. Sommers, *Richmond Redeemed*, 306; James Lane letter, Oct. 6, 1864, Lane Papers; "Incidents of Gallantry, Men of Lane's Brigade," Military Collection, State Archives of North Carolina, Raleigh; Lane, "Glimpses of Army Life," 413. Lane reported 111 casualties, including nine killed and 97 wounded. McGowan counted 162 total casualties, with twenty-six killed and 129 wounded. See casualty table, n.d., Lane Papers; and Caldwell, *McGowan's Brigade*, 241. Lane's story might be too dramatic to be literally factual.

105. Wilcox, "Battle of Jones's Farm," 69; *OR Supp.*, 497, 501, 503; Bryan Diary, Sept. 28–Oct. 1, Bryan Family Papers, University of North Carolina, Chapel Hill; Dunlop, *Lee's Sharpshooters*, 213; Caldwell, *McGowan's Brigade*, 240; Hess, *Lee's Tar Heels*, 264; Krick, *40th Virginia*, 55; Driver, *First and Second Maryland*, 292; Sommers, *Richmond Redeemed*, 307–9.

106. Agassiz, *Meade's Headquarters*, 237; John L. Houck to "Dear Wife," Oct. 7, 1864, Houck Papers, New York State Library, Albany; Charles Salter to "My Dear Friend," Oct. 5, 1864, in Poremba, *If I Am Found Dead*, 214; Walker and Girardi, "What the Good Law Says," 424; Crawford, *16th Michigan*, 486. I am grateful to Robert I. Girardi for lending me his and Paula C. Walker's unpublished manuscript. Salter's disdain for the Ninth Corps reflected that organization's enduring status as outsiders in the Army of the Potomac.

107. Alexander Diary, Sept. 30, 1864, University of North Carolina, Chapel Hill; Driver, *First and Second Maryland*, 290; John Crawford Anderson to "Dear Mother," Oct. 2, 1864, Anderson Family Papers, South Caroliniana Library, University of South Carolina, Columbia.

CHAPTER TEN

1. Ammen, "Maryland Troops in the Confederate Army," Army Heritage and Education Center, Carlisle; U.S. War Department, *War of the Rebellion*, ser. 1, 42(1):635 (hereafter *OR*; all references are to series 1 unless otherwise noted); Bushnell Memoir, Western Reserve Historical Society, Cleveland, 313; Sommers, *Richmond Redeemed*, 309.

2. Heth, "Report of Operations," Museum of the Confederacy, Richmond; Hewitt, Trudeau, and Suderow, *Supplement to the Official Records of the Union and Confederate Armies* (hereafter *OR Supp.*), 477; Sommers, *Richmond Redeemed*, 308–9.

3. Sommers, *Richmond Redeemed*, 309.

4. Ackerson Diary, Sept. 30–Oct. 1, 1864, Ackerson Papers, Monmouth County Historical Association Library and Archives, Freehold.

5. *OR*, 42(2):1133, 1138, 1141–42, 42(3):17; Sommers, *Richmond Redeemed*, 312–13.

6. *OR*, 42(2):1128–29, 42(3):14, 42(1):344; John Gibbon to "My dearest Maria," Oct. 1, 1864, Gibbon Papers, Historical Society of Pennsylvania, Philadelphia.

7. Merriam, "Personal Recollections of the War for the Union," copy in bound vol. 190 Fredericksburg & Spotsylvania National Military Park.

8. *OR*, 42(1):558, 566, 571, 575; Sommers, *Richmond Redeemed*, 314–15. That farm lane ran east–west, connecting Squirrel Level Road with Duncan Road. No wartime name is associated with this road, which Sommers refers to by its modern appellation, Route 673.

9. Jackman, *Sixth New Hampshire*, 337; Josiah Jones Diary, Oct. 1, 1864, New Hampshire Historical Society, Concord; *OR*, 42(1):588; Rutan, *If I Have Got to Go and Fight*, 146; Marshall, *Company "K" 155th Pa.*, 204; *Under the Maltese Cross*, 323; Sommers, *Richmond Redeemed*, 315. Robert W. Chappell acquired this property in the 1830s or 1840s. He died in 1855; his widow, Harriett, lived in the house during the war.

10. Brainard, *146th New York*, 245; *OR*, 42(1):478; *History of the 121st Regiment Pennsylvania Volunteers*, 92; Sommers, *Richmond Redeemed*, 315–16.

11. Cutcheon, *Twentieth Michigan Infantry*, 157; Jackman, *Sixth New Hampshire*, 337; Henry Gawthrop letter, Oct. 6, 1864, Gawthrop Letters and Diary, Delaware Historical Society, Wilmington; Burrage, *36th Massachusetts*, 264–65.

12. *OR*, 42(3):25; Sommers, *Richmond Redeemed*, 318–19; Sommers, "Petersburg Autumn," 44. In an untimed message to Crawford dated October 1, Parke stated that the telegraph line had just been opened to the Peebles house. This suggests that Meade's orders transited via couriers, who apparently had trouble locating Parke in the sodden darkness that night. See *OR*, 42(3):23. Meade's headquarters were at the Birchett house, the site of which is on the Fort Gregg-Adams military base, formerly Fort Lee.

13. Chapman, *More Terrible Than Victory*, 246; Hess, *Lee's Tar Heels*, 264–65; Sommers, *Richmond Redeemed*, 326; Bearss, *Western Front Battles*, 55–56; *OR Supp.*, 477; Mullen Diary, Oct. 1, 1864, Museum of the Confederacy, Richmond; Musselman, *47th Virginia*, 81; Krick, *40th Virginia*, 55; Driver, *First and Second Maryland*, 292. The William Wyatt Davis residence, a large and elegant home, is usually designated as the W. W. Davis house. See Fletcher Archer

to "My dear wife," Oct. 9, 1864, Fletcher Archer Letters, Petersburg Museums Collection. The home was the seat of a 300-acre farm called Rohoic.

14. Caldwell, *McGowan's Brigade*, 241; *OR Supp.*, 491, 495; Hardy, *General Lee's Immortals*, 332; Harris, *Seventh North Carolina*, 57; Cadmus Wilcox's Report, Lee Headquarters Papers, Virginia Museum of History and Culture, Richmond, 10–11; Lane, "Lane's North Carolina Brigade," 356; Sommers, *Richmond Redeemed*, 326–27.

15. Daughtry, *Gray Cavalier*, 222; Trout, *Galloping Thunder*, 572; Sommers, *Richmond Redeemed*, 324, 327.

16. Sommers, *Richmond Redeemed*, 327–28; *OR*, 42(1):478; Brainard, *146th New York*, 245; S[hedrick] J. Jackson Diary, Oct. 1, 1864, copy in bound vol. 231, Fredericksburg & Spotsylvania National Military Park; adjutant, 140th New York, quoted in Bennett, *Sons of Old Monroe*, 480; Frederick Winthrop to "My Dear Frank," Oct. 10, 1864, Winthrop Papers, Massachusetts Historical Society, Boston; Bearss, *Western Front Battles*, 56. Otis received a brevet to brigadier general as a result of his action. He recovered from his wound, served in the Spanish-American War, and was military governor of the Philippines from 1898 to 1900.

17. Carmichael, *Lee's Young Artillerist*, 145; Willie Pegram to "My Dear Sister," Oct. 5, 1864, Pegram-Johnston-McIntosh Family Papers, Virginia Museum of History and Culture, Richmond; Chapman, *More Terrible Than Victory*, 246–47; Hess, *Lee's Tar Heels*, 266; *OR*, 42(1):478; Gawthrop letter, Oct. 6, 1864; Sommers, *Richmond Redeemed*, 333–34.

18. *OR Supp.*, 477; Krick, *40th Virginia*, 55; Driver, *First and Second Maryland*, 292; Goldsborough, *Maryland Line*, 141; Musselman, *47th Virginia*, 81; James King Wilkerson to "Dear Father," Oct. 6, 1864, James King Wilkerson Papers, Rubenstein Special Collections Library, Duke University, Durham, N.C.; Sommers, *Richmond Redeemed*, 334–35.

19. I[saac] F. Caveness Diary, Oct. 1, 1864, Briscoe Center for American History, University of Texas, Austin; Mullen Diary, Oct. 1, 1864; *OR Supp.*, 477; Theodore Lyman to "My Dear Frank" [Francis Palfrey], Nov. 11, 1864, Theodore Lyman Letters, Papers of the Military Historical Society of Massachusetts, Boston University; Sommers, *Richmond Redeemed*, 335–36. Ayres reported 150 casualties for the Fifth Offensive, almost one-third of whom were prisoners from Otis's brigade and taken along the picket line. See *OR*, 42(1):140.

20. Wilcox's Report, 10–11; *OR Supp.*, 501; Lane, "Lane's North Carolina Brigade," 356.

21. Dunlop, *Lee's Sharpshooters*, 213–14; *OR Supp.*, 497; Lane, "Lane's North Carolina Brigade," 356; James Lane letters, Oct. 2, 4, 1864, Lane Papers, Auburn University; Mauney Diary, Oct. 1, 1864, Museum of the Confederacy, Richmond; Lord, *Ninth New Hampshire*, 528; Josiah Jones Diary, Oct. 1, 1864; Jackman, *Sixth New Hampshire*, 337; Sommers, *Richmond Redeemed*, 336; Evans, *Random Acts of Kindness*, 243; Hardy, *General Lee's Immortals*, 332. A handful of Union prisoners and a few of Wooten's sharpshooters were struck by this errant fire.

22. *OR Supp.*, 501; James Lane letter, Oct. 4, 1864, Lane Papers; Harris, *Seventh North Carolina*, 57; Hardy, *Thirty-Seventh North Carolina*, 212; Sommers, *Richmond Redeemed*, 330.

23. *OR*, 42(3):18, 25; Pope Diary, Oct. 1, 1864, Army Heritage and Education Center, Carlisle; Brainard, *146th New York*, 246; Bennett, *Sons of Old Monroe*, 480.

24. Bearss, *Western Front Battles*, 61; *OR*, 42(3):11–13, 42(1):344; Sommers, *Richmond Redeemed*, 364.

25. *OR*, 42(3):13, (1):344, 366, 393; Sommers, *Richmond Redeemed*, 365–66. Richard Sommers estimates Mott's strength at 5,800 men. See Sommers, *Richmond Redeemed*, 369. Hancock provided this number in a message at 11:00 A.M. but modified it to "about 5,000" two hours later.

26. Sommers, *Richmond Redeemed*, 360–61, 366; Regis de Trobriand Diary, Oct. 1, 1864, U.S. Military Academy, West Point; *OR*, 42(1):344, 366, 393; *OR Supp.*, 439.

27. *OR*, 42(3):4–5, 18, 25.

28. *OR*, 42(3):26; Theodore Lyman to "My Sweetness," Oct. 5, 1864, Lyman Letters, Massachusetts Historical Society, Boston.

29. *OR*, 42(3):5–7, 19, 26–27.

30. Sommers, *Richmond Redeemed*, 368–69; Bearss, *Western Front Battles*, 70–71.

31. *OR*, 42(2):1141–42, 42(3):27.

32. *OR*, 42(3):27–28; Bushnell Memoir, 313; Daughtry, *Gray Cavalier*, 221; Sommers, *Richmond Redeemed*, 331–32; Trout, *Galloping Thunder*, 572.

33. *OR*, 42(1):635, 42(3):28; Sommers, *Richmond Redeemed*, 337; Bearss, *Western Front Battles*, 63–64.

34. Sommers, *Richmond Redeemed*, 337. Richard Sommers calls the impending engagement the "Battle of the Vaughan Road."

35. Brooks, *Butler and His Cavalry*, 327; Sommers, *Richmond Redeemed*, 338–39; Preston, *Tenth New York Cavalry*, 229. Dunovant had been promoted to brigadier general on August 22.

36. Sommers, *Richmond Redeemed*, 339–40; Brooks, *Butler and His Cavalry*, 330; Trout, *Galloping Thunder*, 572.

37. Quoted in Daughtry, *Gray Cavalier*, 222; *OR*, 42(1):635, 948; Sommers, *Richmond Redeemed*, 342–43; Preston, *Tenth New York Cavalry*, 230–31; Trout, *Galloping Thunder*, 573; Brooks, *Butler and His Cavalry*, 330–31; Bushnell Memoir, 313.

38. Sommers, *Richmond Redeemed*, 322–23, 344; Dunovant, "Gen. John Dunovant," 183–84; Brooks, *Butler and His Cavalry*, 331.

39. Sawyer, "Death of Colonel John Dunovant," 127; *OR*, 42(1):635–36; Waring Diary, Oct. 1, 1864, University of North Carolina, Chapel Hill; Bearss, *Western Front Battles*, 67; Calhoun, *Liberty Dethroned*, 143–44; Preston, *Tenth New York Cavalry*, 231. Richard Sommers states that Dunovant was shot through the chest, but the bulk of the contemporary evidence suggests a head wound. Sommers, *Richmond Redeemed*, 344. Clancy received the Medal of Honor in recognition of his feat.

40. George Freaner to "My Dear Madam," Oct. 6, 1864, Virginia Museum of History and Culture, Richmond; *OR*, 42(1):948. The house to which Doctor Fontaine was carried is not identified but most likely was the Wilkinson residence.

41. Sommers, *Richmond Redeemed*, 345–49; Bearss, *Western Front Battles*, 67–68. The rest of Smith's brigade guarded the ground between the Wyatt house and the Weldon Railroad.

42. *OR*, 42(3):29.

43. *OR*, 42(1):948; Sommers, *Richmond Redeemed*, 351.

44. *OR*, 42(3):19–20, 29–30; Sommers, *Richmond Redeemed*, 370–71. The coffin for Warren's military career would close on April 1, 1865.

45. *OR*, 42(3):6–7, 29; Sommers, *Richmond Redeemed*, 373.

46. For more fulsome analyses of Hill's decision, see Sommers, "Petersburg Autumn," 46; and Sommers, *Richmond Redeemed*, 375–77.

47. Sommers, *Richmond Redeemed*, 377; Hardy, *General Lee's Immortals*, 333; *OR Supp.*, 510–11; Hess, *Lee's Tar Heels*, 268; Driver, *First and Second Maryland*, 293; Musselman, *47th Virginia*, 82. Archer and Davis together numbered 1,900 infantry, and the troopers left behind accounted for the remainder of the Confederate defending forces.

48. *OR*, 42(1):344; Peck Diary, Oct. 2, 1864, Virginia Tech University, Blacksburg; Sommers, *Richmond Redeemed*, 378.

49. *OR*, 42(1):546–47; Sommers, *Richmond Redeemed*, 378–79; Bearss, *Western Front Battles*, 72.

50. *OR*, 42(1):344, 366, 393, 42(3):36; *OR Supp.*, 439–40; de Trobriand Diary, Oct. 2, 1864; de Trobriand, *Four Years with the Army*, 652; *History of the Fifty-Seventh Regiment Pennsylvania Veteran Volunteer Infantry*, 127; Peck Diary, Oct. 2, 1864; Bearss, *Western Front Battles*, 72–73; Sommers, *Richmond Redeemed*, 379–83.

51. *OR*, 42(3):44, 42(1):554, 558–59, 567, 571, 580, 588; Samuel E. Wilson to "Dear Parents," Oct. 5, 1864, copy in bound vol. 210, Fredericksburg & Spotsylvania National Military Park; Drake, *Remember Me to All the Friends*, 269; Pope Diary, Oct. 2, 1864; Lowber Diary, Oct. 2, 1864, Virginia Tech University, Blacksburg; Gavin, *Campaigning with the Roundheads*, 575; Herek, *These Men Have Seen Hard Service*, 260; Cutcheon Autobiography, Bentley Historical Library, University of Michigan, Ann Arbor, 363; Sommers, *Richmond Redeemed*, 383–84; Bearss, *Western Front Battles*, 73–74.

52. Gawthrop letter, Oct. 6, 1864, Gawthrop Letters and Diary; Prince, "Peebles Farm," Oct. 2, 1864, Author's Collection, Walden; Nathan S. Clark Diary, Oct. 2, 1864, Maine State Archives, Augusta; *OR*, 42(1):478, 42(3):41; Bearss, *Western Front Battles*, 75–76; Sommers, *Richmond Redeemed*, 384–85.

53. *OR*, 42(3):36, 41, 43; Lowe, *Meade's Army*, 275; Sommers, *Richmond Redeemed*, 388–89.

54. For a fuller contemplation of Meade's motives, see Sommers, *Richmond Redeemed*, 387–90. For a more explicitly critical evaluation of Meade, see Sommers, "Petersburg Autumn," 47–48.

55. Gawthrop letter, Oct. 6, 1864; *OR*, 42(1):478; Sommers, *Richmond Redeemed*, 390–91. Grindlay's report states that the Maryland Brigade made this advance, but the evidence supports Grimshaw.

56. Knowles Journal and Diary, East Carolina University, Greenville; Bosworth Diary, Oct. 2, 1864, University of Notre Dame, South Bend; *OR*, 42(1):554, 559–60, 567, 575; Diary of Sgt. George L. Preston, Oct. 2, 1864, Eberly Family Special Collections Library, Penn State University, State College; Gavin, *Campaigning with the Roundheads*, 575; Cutcheon Autobiography, 363; Sommers, *Richmond Redeemed*, 392.

57. Mullen Diary, Oct. 2, 1864; Hess, *Lee's Tar Heels*, 268; Chapman, *More Terrible Than Victory*, 248; Heth, "Report of Operations"; Sommers, *Richmond Redeemed*, 392–93. The Hart house in 2024 is preserved in Pamplin Historical Park, as is a good portion of Mott's and MacRae's battlefield.

58. *OR*, 42(1):366, 393; *OR Supp.*, 439; Tilton C. Reynolds to "Dear Mother," Oct. 4, 1864, Reynolds Papers, Library of Congress, Washington; Marbaker, *11th New Jersey*, 224; Sommers, *Richmond Redeemed*, 393–94.

59. Sommers, *Richmond Redeemed*, 394; Heth, "Report of Operations"; Hess, *Lee's Tar Heels*, 268; Musselman, *47th Virginia*, 82; Mullen Diary, Oct. 2, 1864; Caveness Diary, Oct. 2, 1864; *OR Supp.*, 511.

60. Sommers, *Richmond Redeemed*, 396, 399.

61. Sommers, *Richmond Redeemed*, 394–98; Allen, "More about Mink"; Humphreys, *Andrew Atkinson Humphreys*, 250–51; William M. Read Diary, Oct. 2, 1864, Read Letters and Diary, copy, Petersburg National Battlefield; Lowe, *Meade's Army*, 275–76; Theodore Lyman to "Sweetest Minnette," Oct. 2, 1864, Lyman Family Papers, Massachusetts Historical Society,

Boston; Prince, "Peebles Farm," Oct. 2, 1864; Marshall, *Company "K" 155th Pa.*, 204; Agassiz, *Meade's Headquarters*, 238; Meade, *Life and Letters*, 231–32.

62. *OR*, 42(3):45, 42(1):344, 554, 575; Sommers, *Richmond Redeemed*, 401–2.

63. *OR*, 42(1):344, 366, 393, 559; Bearss, *Western Front Battles*, 74; Sommers, *Richmond Redeemed*, 403–4.

64. *OR*, 42(1):344, 366–67; *OR Supp.*, 440; Carter, *Four Brothers in Blue*, 490; Roe and Nutt, *First Regiment of Massachusetts Heavy Artillery*, 192; Hess, *Lee's Tar Heels*, 268–69; Chapman, *More Terrible Than Victory*, 249; Bearss, *Western Front Battles*, 75; Sommers, *Richmond Redeemed*, 404–5.

65. *OR*, 42(1):344–45, 393–94, 554, 559; Robertson, *McAllister Letters*, 512; Cutcheon Autobiography, 363; Sommers, *Richmond Redeemed*, 405. Richard Sommers calls this little engagement the "Battle of Harman Road."

66. Sommers, *Richmond Redeemed*, 406–8. Federal signal stations informed Meade of Mahone's movements. See *OR*, 42(3):37.

67. Pope Diary, Oct. 3, 1864; *OR*, 42(3):50–51, 63.

68. Robertson, *McAllister Letters*, 512; de Trobriand Diary, Oct. 3, 1864. McAllister used the familiar pejorative "Dutch" to refer to German immigrants.

69. William J. Mosely to "My Dear Parents," Oct. 3, 1864, Mosely Collection, Georgia State Archives, Morrow; A[bram] G. Jones to "Dear Father," Oct. 6, 1864, Jones Family Papers, Southern Historical Collection, Louis Round Wilson Library, University of North Carolina, Chapel Hill.

70. Lane, "Glimpses of Army Life," 413–14; Carter, *Welcome the Hour of Conflict*, 270.

71. Sommers, *Richmond Redeemed*, 416. Counting Meade's casualties earlier in September, the Army of the Potomac lost 242 men killed, 1,159 wounded, and 1,983 captured or missing. See *OR*, 42(1):144. As for Confederate forces, specific casualty figures were reported for McGowan's Brigade (162) and MacRae's Brigade (137). See Dunlop, *Lee's Sharpshooters*, 214, Caldwell, *McGowan's Brigade*, 241, and Hess, *Lee's Tar Heels*, 269. A number of Federal officers killed during these actions would be remembered in the names of Union forts, to wit: Capt. Weston H. Keene, Twentieth Maine; Capt. Orange S. Sampson, Twenty-First Massachusetts; Capt. James H. Wheaton, First Michigan; Lt. Jacob E. Siebert, Twentieth Michigan; Lt. George W. Emery, Ninth New Hampshire (the fort was spelled "Emory"); Lt. William D. Rice, Ninth New Hampshire; Lt. James P. Gregg, Forty-Fifth Pennsylvania; Lt. Otis Fisher, Eighth U.S. Infantry; Lt. Thomas D. Urmston, Twelfth U.S. Infantry; and Lt. Col. Charles Cummings, Seventeenth Vermont (along with Lt. John Conahey and Col. Norval E. Welch as previously mentioned). See *OR*, 42(3):207; Powell, *Fifth Army Corps*, 733; and "Union Officers Lost at Battle of Peebles Farm," Petersburg National Battlefield. For a brilliant discussion of how soldiers perceived death and burial, see Faust, *This Republic of Suffering*.

72. Andrew Knox to "My dear wife," Sept. 30, 1864, Knox Letters, New-York Historical Society, New York; "The Army of the Potomac," *New York Times*, Oct. 8, 1864; Wainwright Diary, Oct. 5, 1864, Henry E. Huntington Library, San Marino; Charles E. LaMotte to "My dear Mother," Oct. 3, 1864, LaMotte Letters, Delaware Public Archives, Dover.

73. Josiah Jones Diary, Oct. 2, 1864.

74. Alfred M. Scales to his wife, Oct. 9, 1864, copy in bound vol. 15-01, Fredericksburg & Spotsylvania National Military Park; Cockrell, *Gunner with Stonewall*, 139; "The Situation at Petersburg," *Richmond Daily Dispatch*, Oct. 5, 1864; Power, *Lee's Miserables*, 207–10.

75. Willie Pegram to "My Dear Sister," Oct. 5, 1864, Pegram-Johnston-McIntosh Family Papers; Francis Marion Coker to "My dear wife," Oct. 5, 1864, Coker Papers, University of Georgia, Athens; *OR*, 42(3):1133; Samuel S. Brooke to "My dear Sister," Oct. 4, 1864, John Milton Binckley Papers, Manuscripts Division, Library of Congress, Washington.

76. Thomas Claybrook Elder to "My Dear Wife," Oct. 6, 1864, Thomas Claybrook Elder Papers, Virginia Museum of History and Culture, Richmond.

77. *OR*, 42(2):1144–45, 42(3):30.

78. *OR*, 42(2):1147–48; Henry Grimes Marshall to "My Dear Hattie," Oct. 5, 1864, Marshall Letters, Clements Library, University of Michigan, Ann Arbor; Manarin, *Field of Honor*, 695.

79. Sommers, *Richmond Redeemed*, 148–50, 156–57; *Official Records of the Union and Confederate Navies in the War of the Rebellion*, 10:762–65. Perhaps Lee decided against another assault because he realized the Federals had improved their defenses overnight. Without additional troops, he may have concluded that he did not have sufficient manpower to recapture the fort—even more likely, he did not wish to accept the casualties that would accrue even if successful. Lee was keenly aware of the growing numerical disparity between his army and Grant's. See, for example, *OR*, 42(3):1134. But perhaps something as simple as the miserable weather dissuaded him.

80. *OR*, 42(3):32–33, 35; Sommers, *Richmond Redeemed*, 159; Manarin, *Field of Honor*, 697.

81. *OR*, 42(3):33, 42(1):703; Kautz, *August Valentine Kautz*, 152; Eldredge Manuscript Notebook, Oct. 1, 1864, Harvard University, Cambridge; Manarin, *Field of Honor*, 697–99; Sommers, *Richmond Redeemed*, 158.

82. *OR*, 42(1):703, 726, 848; Eldredge, *Third New Hampshire*, 542; William G. Hinson Diary, Charleston Library Society; Sommers, *Richmond Redeemed*, 161; Manarin, *Field of Honor*, 699–700. The 206th Pennsylvania remained behind to provide labor for constructing Fort Brady on Signal Hill. See Daniel Fair to "Dear Mother," Oct. 7, 1864, Daniel McClure Fair Papers, Senator John Heinz History Center, Pittsburgh.

83. *OR*, 42(1):708, 713, 716; Sommers, *Richmond Redeemed*, 160–61; Manarin, *Field of Honor*, 701. This fight would be known as the Battle of Roper's Farm.

84. Charles August Henninghausen Papers, Virginia Museum of History and Culture, Richmond.

85. Sommers, *Richmond Redeemed*, 163; Manarin, *Field of Honor*, 703. Spear must have possessed other talents, as three women claimed a widow's pension when he died after the war.

86. "From the Tenth Connecticut," Oct. 10, 1864; *OR Supp.*, 441; *OR*, 42(1):730; Sommers, *Richmond Redeemed*, 167. The Tenth Connecticut suffered only three casualties during this action.

87. Roe, *Twenty-Fourth Massachusetts*, 361–62; *OR*, 42(3):33, 42(1):679; Sommers, *Richmond Redeemed*, 164–66, Manarin, *Field of Honor*, 705.

88. *OR*, 42(1):703, 42(3):35; Manarin, *Field of Honor*, 705.

89. *OR*, 42(3):31; Sommers, *Richmond Redeemed*, 170–71; Theodore Lyman to "My Sweet Minette," Oct. 6, 1864, Lyman Letters, Massachusetts Historical Society. Lyman dated the cited reference as "Sund Oct 2nd."

90. *OR*, 42(3):32, 48; Sommers, *Richmond Redeemed*, 171–72.

91. Sumner, *Comstock Diary*, 291; *OR*, 42(1):662; Dickinson, "Union and Confederate Engineering Operations at Chaffin's Bluff/Chaffin's Farm," Richmond National Battlefield Park, 106–7; Manarin, *Field of Honor*, 706–7. Comstock probably influenced Grant's decision

by pointing out the hazards of Butler's proposal. Grant fully understood that the immediate transfer of one of Meade's corps to the north side was impractical.

92. *OR*, 42(3):49, 65, 42(1):680; Sommers, *Richmond Redeemed*, 174–76.

93. *OR*, 42(3):78, 51, 66, 91; Grant, *Personal Memoirs*, 335–36; Simon, *Grant Papers*, 12:263. Grant proposed to recall the Sixth and Nineteenth Corps from the Shenandoah Valley. Starting late in September and continuing for nearly two weeks, Sheridan's cavalry left a fiery trail of destruction in the Valley that came to be known as "the Burning." For a comprehensive treatment of this episode, see Heatwole, *The Burning*.

94. *OR*, ser. 2, 7:906–7, 909, 914. The Dix-Hill Cartel, signed in July 1862, established a table of equivalents for the exchange of prisoners and outlined the mechanics of such exchanges. For the background behind and the implementation of the cartel, see Sanders, *While in the Hands of the Enemy*. The government sustained the general-in-chief, and prisoner exchange on Grant's terms would not occur until January 1865. For a succinct summary of this issue, see McPherson, *Battle Cry of Freedom*, 798–800.

95. *OR*, 42(3):65, 286; *OR*, ser. 2, 7:967–69, 1018–19; Trudeau, *Like Men of War*, 300.

96. *OR*, 42(1):662–63, 42(3):163.

97. *OR*, 42(3):78–79, 150, 157, 275–76, 298; David Birney to "My Dear Gross," Sept. 6, 1864, Birney Papers, Army Heritage and Education Center, Carlisle; Oliver W. Davis, *Life of David Bell Birney*, 275–79; Meade, *Life and Letters*, 235; Robertson, *McAllister Letters*, 523; de Trobriand, *Four Years with the Army*, 654–55; Thomas and Sauers, *Never Want to Witness Such Sights*, 254; Waters Braman to "Dear Cousin Em," Oct. 21, 1864, Braman Letters, New York State Library, Albany. Birney's last words were (allegedly), "Keep your eyes on that flag, boys!" Adelbert Ames assumed command of Terry's division.

98. Thompson, *13th New Hampshire*, 492. Some accounts date this episode on October 5. The number of soldiers buried is speculative, and 500 probably reaches the upper limit.

99. William Henry Hagar to "My Dear Sister Mary," Oct. 9, 1864, William Henry Hagar Letters, Henry E. Huntington Library, San Marino; Sommers, "Grant's Fifth Offensive," 229; Herek, *These Men Have Seen Hard Service*, 261; *OR*, 42(1):394, 575; de Trobriand, *Four Years with the Army*, 652; Robertson, *McAllister Letters*, 512–13. An excellent example of Federal engineering during this phase of the campaign is preserved between Fort Fisher and Fort Welch in Petersburg National Battlefield. The Federals also began construction on two observation towers near Squirrel Level Road and Church Road as well as a series of fortifications around City Point. See *OR*, 42(1):213.

100. *OR*, 42(3):84, 42(1):367; Sommers, *Richmond Redeemed*, 409–11.

101. Sommers, *Richmond Redeemed*, 412–15. During the next few weeks, the Confederates would extend their right to rest on the high ground above Hatcher's Run. This ground, where the works remain impressive, is preserved by the American Battlefield Trust in 2024.

102. Richard Sommers estimates that Grant's total losses numbered some 7,300 during his Fifth Offensive, while Lee suffered 3,700 casualties. See Sommers, *Richmond Redeemed*, 446.

103. *OR*, 42(3):1134.

104. *OR*, 42(3):1135–36; Gilchrist, *General Orders from the Adjutant and Inspector-General's Office, Confederate States Army*, 107–8.

105. Badeau, *Military History of Ulysses S. Grant*, 3:78; Meade, *Life and Letters*, 232.

106. Robert E. Lee to his wife, Oct. 9, 1864, Lee Family Papers, Virginia Museum of History and Culture, Richmond.

CHAPTER ELEVEN

1. Sommers, "Grant's Fifth Offensive," 339; Manarin, *Field of Honor*, 710; Newsome, *Richmond Must Fall*, 29–30. Lee's headquarters was at the Taylor farm, east of Osborne Turnpike and near Cornelius Creek, about one mile north of the upper wall of the entrenched camp at Chaffin's Bluff. See Sommers, "Grant's Fifth Offensive," 366; and U.S. War Department, *War of the Rebellion*, ser. 1, 42(3):226 (hereafter *OR*; all references are to series 1 unless otherwise noted).

2. Louella Pauline Gary, "Life of Martin Witherspoon Gary," Virginia Museum of History and Culture, Richmond, 22; Newsome, *Richmond Must Fall*, 29–30; Manarin, *Field of Honor*, 710. Both Hampton Newsome and Louis Manarin accept the assertion that Gary presented the plan that Lee adopted at the conference. Richard Sommers is skeptical, based on the conjecture that it would have been out of character for Lee to call a council just to obtain suggestions as well as that he would not have ordered its execution so quickly without adequate planning. See Sommers, "Grant's Fifth Offensive," 367–68. Despite the absence of commentary from the other participants, Louella Gary's narrative should be treated with caution.

3. Sommers, "Grant's Fifth Offensive," 340–41; Newsome, *Richmond Must Fall*, 30; Manarin, *Field of Honor*, 710–11; Sturkey, *Hampton Legion Infantry*, 95; Trudeau, "Darbytown Road Debacle," 33; Gallagher, *Fighting for the Confederacy*, 479; Hagood, "Memoirs of the First SC Regiment," University of South Carolina, Columbia, 188; Schmutz, *Bloody Fifth*, 241.

4. *OR*, 42(1):823, 845, 848; Manarin, *Field of Honor*, 715; Kautz, "How I Won My First Brevet," 374–75; Newsome, *Richmond Must Fall*, 32. Jacob S. Atlee owned Plainfield, but his son-in-law, Doctor Johnson, was in residence there.

5. Sommers, "Grant's Fifth Offensive," 318–19; Newsome, *Richmond Must Fall*, 31–32; Kautz, "How I Won My First Brevet," 375–76.

6. *OR*, 42(1):826, 42(3):98–99; Kautz to Butler, Oct. 6, 1864, Kautz Papers, Library of Congress, Washington; Roper, Archibald, and Coles, *Eleventh Pennsylvania Volunteer Cavalry*, 142–43; Kautz, "Reminiscences," and Kautz Diary, Oct. 6, 1864, Kautz Papers, Library of Congress, Washington, 91. Kautz timed the arrival of these refugees at either 9:00 or 10:00 P.M. in his postwar accounts. Yet he sent a message forwarding "four deserters and two Refugees" to Butler at 7:00 P.M. See Kautz, "How I Won My First Brevet," 376; Kautz to "Colonel," Aug. 17, 1866, Alexander C. Haskell Papers, Southern Historical Collection, Louis Round Wilson Library, University of North Carolina, Chapel Hill; and Marshall, *Butler's Correspondence*, 5:227. Kautz must have been skeptical of the refugees' testimony because of his limited reaction to it.

7. Benjamin Wright to "My Dear Abbie," Oct. 8, 1864, Benjamin Wright Papers, Wisconsin Historical Society, Madison; Brady, *Story of One Regiment*, 274; Trumbull, *Knightly Soldier*, 292; Roe, *Twenty-Fourth Massachusetts*, 362.

8. Sommers, "Grant's Fifth Offensive," 344, 371–72; Gallagher, *Fighting for the Confederacy*, 481–82. Alexander's artillery included Maj. John C. Haskell's Battalion of Flanner's Battery, the Rowan Artillery, and the Palmetto Battery, and Maj. Marmaduke Johnson's Battalion of Clutter's Richmond Battery and the Fredericksburg Artillery. For a breakdown of the guns in each of these batteries, see Manarin, *Field of Honor*, 710.

9. Hewitt, Trudeau, and Suderow, *Supplement to the Official Records of the Union and Confederate Armies* (hereafter *OR Supp.*), 445; Daly, *Alexander Cheves Haskell*, 155–56; Hinson Diary, Oct. 7, 1864, Charleston Library Society; Smith, *Jerimiah Smith*, 110.

10. Field, "Campaign of 1864 and 1865," 557; Sommers, "Grant's Fifth Offensive," 352; Manarin, *Field of Honor*, 714; Smith, *Jerimiah Smith*, 110; Gallagher, *Fighting for the Confederacy*, 482–83. Civil twilight was at 5:45 that morning and sunrise at 6:11. It is curious that Field chose to lead with the two brigades that had suffered in the failed attack on September 30.

11. *OR*, 42(3):113, 42(1):823; Stahler, *Enoch Stahler*, 2; Kautz Diary, Oct. 7, 1864; Roper, Archibald, and Coles, *Eleventh Pennsylvania Volunteer Cavalry*, 143; *OR Supp.*, 446; Daly, *Alexander Cheves Haskell*, 156; Sommers, "Grant's Fifth Offensive," 352–54; Newsome, *Richmond Must Fall*, 37; Manarin, *Field of Honor*, 717.

12. *OR*, 42(1):826, 881; Stahler, *Enoch Stahler*, 2; Austin, *General John Bratton*, 239; Lyle Diary, Oct. 7, 1864, Virginia Museum of History and Culture, Richmond; Hagood, "Report of Colonel J. R. Hagood," 437; Hagood, "Memoirs of the First SC Regiment," 189–90; Baldwin, *Struck Eagle*, 330; Bratton, "Report of Operations," 556.

13. Hagood, "Memoirs of the First SC Regiment," 189; *OR*, 42(1):881; Lyle Diary, Oct. 7, 1864; Daly, *Alexander Cheves Haskell*, 155; Sturkey, *Hampton Legion Infantry*, 97. The battery that accompanied Bowles and Gary may have been the Surry Light Artillery. Bratton's deployment, from left to right, was the Second South Carolina Rifles, First South Carolina, Sixth South Carolina, and the Palmetto Sharpshooters.

14. *OR*, 42(1):823, 827, 831, 845, 848; Roper, Archibald, and Coles, *Eleventh Pennsylvania Volunteer Cavalry*, 143; Sommers, "Grant's Fifth Offensive," 356.

15. Kautz Diary, Oct. 7, 1864; Newsome, *Richmond Must Fall*, 38–39; Sommers, "Grant's Fifth Offensive," 357.

16. *OR*, 42(1):832–33, 881; Hagood, "Memoirs of the First SC Regiment," 190; Dean, "Recollections of Army Life," copy, Petersburg National Battlefield; Baldwin, *Struck Eagle*, 331; Jordan, *Some Events and Incidents*, 97; Sommers, "Grant's Fifth Offensive," 358.

17. *OR*, 42(1):827, 831, 881; Dean, "Recollections of Army Life"; Sommers, "Grant's Fifth Offensive," 393.

18. *OR*, 42(1):846, 848, 881; Stocker, *From Huntsville to Appomattox*, 186; Newsome, *Richmond Must Fall*, 42–45.

19. *OR*, 42(1):824, 833, 846, 848; Coleman Diary, Oct. 8, 1864, University of South Carolina, Columbia; Sommers, "Grant's Fifth Offensive," 365–66; Hagood, "Memoirs of the First SC Regiment," 191; Lyle Diary, Oct. 7, 1864; Marshall, *Butler's Correspondence*, 5:236. Many Confederate sources mention capturing nine or ten guns, but it is clear the Federals had only eight guns and lost them all during the retreat.

20. Sommers, "Grant's Fifth Offensive," 369; Newsome, *Richmond Must Fall*, 46. For a colorful and embellished account of this episode, see Daly, *Alexander Cheves Haskell*, 149.

21. *OR Supp.*, 447; *OR*, 42(1):824; Kautz to "Colonel," Aug. 17, 1866, Haskell Papers; Kautz, "How I Won My First Brevet," 383; Kautz Diary, Oct. 7, 1864; Hinson Diary, Oct. 7, 1864, Charleston Library Society; Kautz, "Reminiscences," 91–92; Sommers, "Grant's Fifth Offensive," 370; Manarin, *Field of Honor*, 725; Newsome, *Richmond Must Fall*, 47.

22. Kautz, "How I Won My First Brevet," 383; West, *Found among the Privates*, 82; Sturkey, *Hampton Legion Infantry*, 98; Crosland, *Reminiscences of the Sixties*, 32; Newsome, *Richmond Must Fall*, 47.

23. *OR*, 42(1):824–25, 145–46. As usual, Confederate casualty figures are elusive and not isolated for this phase of the battle.

24. Marshall, *Butler's Correspondence*, 5:231; George Barnum to "Dear Father," Oct. 10, 1864, Barnum Letters, Petersburg National Battlefield; *OR*, 42(3):109; Sommers, "Grant's Fifth Offensive," 372.

25. *OR*, 42(3):109; Trumbull, *Knightly Soldier*, 292. For a more expansive exploration of Butler's and Birney's mindsets, see Sommers, "Grant's Fifth Offensive," 374–77.

26. Brady, *Story of One Regiment*, 274; *OR*, 42(3):49, 42(1):703, 716, 721, 730–31; *OR Supp.*, 442; Sommers, "Grant's Fifth Offensive," 377; Trumbull, *Knightly Soldier*, 294; Roe, *Twenty-Fourth Massachusetts*, 362; Henry Clay Trumbull, "From the Tenth Connecticut," *Hartford (Conn.) Daily Courant*, Oct. 14, 1864; Robert E. L. Krick to "Dear Prof. Sommers," Aug. 29, 2003, Sommers Papers, Author's Collection, Walden.

27. "The Army of the James," *New York Times*, Oct. 11, 1864; *OR*, 42(1):783, 788; Sommers, "Grant's Fifth Offensive," 380, 417; Newsome, *Richmond Must Fall*, 51–52; Manarin, *Field of Honor*, 727–29.

28. *OR*, 42(3):107, 109–10, 113–14; Sommers, "Grant's Fifth Offensive," 381–82.

29. Hagood, "Memoirs of the First SC Regiment," 191–92.

30. Lyle Diary, Oct. 7, 1864; *OR*, 42(1):881; Robert E. Fitzgerald Diary, Oct. 7, 1864, Eiserman (Private) Collection, Carlisle; Sommers, "Grant's Fifth Offensive," 385–87, 424. The timing of Field's attack is speculative, as conflicting sources leave the matter in doubt.

31. *OR*, 42(1):844–45; Cronin, *Evolution of a Life*, 248–49; David Cronin to A. J. Wall, May 5, 1925, Civil War Letters Collection, New-York Historical Society, New York; Sommers, "Grant's Fifth Offensive," 385–87; Newsome, *Richmond Must Fall*, 53–54. Maj. Gen. Edwin Vose Sumner commanded the Second Corps at Antietam and the Right Grand Division at Fredericksburg in 1862. He died in March 1863 en route to his new assignment in the Department of the Missouri.

32. *OR*, 42(1):783–84; Gallagher, *Fighting for the Confederacy*, 483; Newsome, *Richmond Must Fall*, 55.

33. Sommers, "Grant's Fifth Offensive," 390.

34. *OR*, 42(1):721; Gallagher, *Fighting for the Confederacy*, 483; Sommers, "Grant's Fifth Offensive," 392–94; Newsome, *Richmond Must Fall*, 58–59.

35. Simon P. Wingard to "My dear Brother," Oct. 8, 1864, Simon P. Wingard Letters, Rubenstein Special Collections Library, Duke University, Durham, N.C.; Hagood, "Memoirs of the First SC Regiment," 193; *OR*, 42(1):881; Austin, *General John Bratton*, 240; Lyle Diary, Oct. 7, 1864.

36. Styple, *Writing and Fighting the Civil War*, 300; Benjamin Wright to "My Dear Abbie," Oct. 8, 1864, Wright Papers; *OR*, 42(1):731, 759; Croffut and Morris, *Connecticut during the War*, 671; *OR Supp.*, 443; Trumbull, "From the Tenth Connecticut"; Brady, *Story of One Regiment*, 275–76; Roe, *Twenty-Fourth Massachusetts*, 363.

37. *OR*, 42(1):731; Sommers, "Grant's Fifth Offensive," 396–99; Manarin, *Field of Honor*, 736–38; Newsome, *Richmond Must Fall*, 62–63. Some sources conflate the attacks of Bratton and Bowles, making it difficult to discern a clear sequence of events. For example, some accounts suggest that many of the men of the 100th New York, believing that their enlistment terms had expired, fled upon Bowles's appearance rather than during Bratton's attack.

38. Quoted in Sommers, "Grant's Fifth Offensive," 403.

39. Freeman, *Lee's Lieutenants*, 343; Winkler, *Confederate Capital and Hood's Texas Brigade*, 196–97; Carter, *Two Stars in the Southern Sky*. Gregg and his brigade were the protagonists

in the famous "Lee to the Rear" episode on May 6, 1864, at the Widow Tapp field in the Wilderness. That landscape is preserved by the National Park Service.

40. *OR*, 42(1):784; Joskins, "Hood's Texas Brigade," Hill College, Hillsboro, 215; Basil Crow Brashear Memoir, Historical Research Center, Texas Heritage Museum, Hill College, Hillsboro; Smith, *Reminiscences*, 58; Polley, *Hood's Texas Brigade*, 257.

41. Winkler, *Confederate Capital and Hood's Texas Brigade*, 195; Sommers, "Grant's Fifth Offensive," 405.

42. Hagood, *Memoirs*, 308. Lee's motives are only speculative. For a thought-provoking discussion of why Lee declined to commit half of his infantry, see Sommers, "Grant's Fifth Offensive," 406–8. Examples of Lee reinforcing failure are his attacks at Malvern Hill on July 1, 1862, and at Gettysburg on July 3, 1863. The engagements on October 7 are variously known as "First Darbytown Road," "Darbytown and New Market Roads," or "Johnson's Farm and Four Mile Creek."

43. *OR*, 42(3):110, 119, 42(1):144–46, 881; Gallagher, *Fighting for the Confederacy*, 484; Harrison Nesbitt to "Dear Wife," Oct. 9, 1864, Harrison Nesbitt Letters, Civil War Documents Collection, Army Heritage and Education Center, Carlisle; Newsome, *Richmond Must Fall*, 65; Sommers, "Grant's Fifth Offensive," 424, 1223. Johnson Hagood states that Hoke's Division lost 200 men, but this figure seems excessive because Hoke's brigades were subject only to artillery fire. See Hagood, *Memoirs*, 308.

44. *OR*, 42(3):110–11.

45. *OR*, 42(3):112, 116–17, 42(1):704, 709, 717. Curtis's brigade joined Terry's division in this advance.

46. *OR*, 42(3):79, 87, 91, 96, 107, 43(2):249; Porter, *Campaigning with Grant*, 316–17; Stephen Rogers to "Dear Father & Mother," Oct. 9, 1864, Rogers Letters, Abraham Lincoln Presidential Library, Springfield; Journal of Charles Norborne Berkeley Minor, Oct. 4, 1864, Virginia Museum of History and Culture, Richmond; Agassiz, *Meade's Headquarters*, 242. Lieutenant Colonel Draper of the Thirty-Sixth Massachusetts misidentified Doctor Boisseau's house as the Sanborn house.

47. *OR*, 42(3):102, 106, 127; Wainwright Diary, Oct. 9, 1864, Henry E. Huntington Library, San Marino; Theodore Lyman to "My Birdness," Oct. 11, 1864, Lyman Letters, Massachusetts Historical Society; Sommers, "Battle No One Wanted," 11.

48. *OR*, 42(3):141–42, 42(1):559, 566, 575; Wilkinson, *May You Never See the Sights*, 303; Sommers, "Grant's Fifth Offensive," 430–32; Sommers, "Battle No One Wanted," 11. Richard Sommers speculates that Gregory's brigade was the unit selected by Griffin. Ferrero's division of U.S. Colored Troops was in the best position to make the movement to Duncan Road, but prejudice toward Black troops deemed them unqualified for such a risky maneuver, therefore Willcox received the assignment.

49. Newsome, Horn, and Selby, *Civil War Talks*, 299; Sommers, "Grant's Fifth Offensive," 437–43; Sommers, "Battle No One Wanted," 12–13; *OR*, 42(3):135, 137, 139, 42(1):554–55, 566–67, 575; Ewing, *From Home to Trench*, 79–80; Cutcheon Autobiography, Bentley Historical Library, University of Michigan, Ann Arbor, 365. The W. P. Davis house burned on September 11.

50. *OR*, 42(3):125–26; Sommers, "Grant's Fifth Offensive," 441–53.

51. *OR*, 42(3):131–33; Sommers, "Battle No One Wanted," 14–15; Sommers, "Grant's Fifth Offensive," 453–60.

52. Sommers, "Battle No One Wanted," 15; Sommers, "Grant's Fifth Offensive," 460–61; Carisio, *Quaker Officer*, 91.

53. Carisio, *Quaker Officer*, 91; "From Petersburg," *Richmond Daily Dispatch*, Oct. 11, 1864; Sommers, "Grant's Fifth Offensive," 461–62. Lyman thought the owner of the W. W. Davis house was a Confederate officer, killed on his property during the Fifth Offensive. I have found no such officer. See Lyman to "My Birdness," Oct. 11, 1864, Lyman Letters, Massachusetts Historical Society.

54. Sommers, "Battle No One Wanted," 16–17; Sommers, "Grant's Fifth Offensive," 462–71.

55. Sommers, "Battle No One Wanted," 17–18; Sommers, "Grant's Fifth Offensive," 471–73; *OR*, 42(1):555, 560, 567, 575, 580; Wilkinson, *May You Never See the Sights*, 304.

56. Ural, *Hood's Texas Brigade*, 230; Crockett Diary, Oct. 9, 1864, Crockett Diary and Papers, University of Texas, Austin; "Donaldson Cannoneers at the Siege of Petersburg," *New Orleans Times-Picayune*, Aug. 4, 1902; *Richmond Daily Dispatch*, Oct. 10, 1864; Newsome, *Richmond Must Fall*, 73; *OR*, 42(3):143, 147, 150, 157; Sommers, "Grant's Fifth Offensive," 497–98; Agassiz, *Meade's Headquarters*, 243; Pearce, *Chambers Diary*, 233. General Pendleton was Lee's chief of artillery.

57. Sommers, "Grant's Fifth Offensive," 473, 490, 505–6; *OR*, 42(3):180, 207. For the names of these forts, see chapter 10, note 71. Lt. John W. Fiske of the Fifty-Eighth Massachusetts was the only nominated officer whose name was not chosen.

58. Sommers, "Grant's Fifth Offensive," 497–99.

59. Sommers, "Grant's Fifth Offensive," 476–77, 484–85; *OR*, 42(3):176–77,179, 42(1):169–70. Both armies indulged an enduring fear of mining.

60. *OR*, 42(3):158, 160–61, 176, 182, 42(1):642; Sommers, "Grant's Fifth Offensive," 488–89.

61. John Rawlins to his wife, Oct. 10, 1864, James H. Wilson Collection, Manuscripts Division, Library of Congress, Washington. For Sheridan's proposed transfer of the Sixth Corps to Petersburg and Early's movement down the Valley that resulted in the Battle of Cedar Creek on October 19, see Mahr, *Battle of Cedar Creek*.

62. Eisenschiml, *Vermont General*, 244, 256–57.

63. Bird and Crofts, "Soldier Voting in 1864," 402.

64. George J. Paddock to "Dear Sister," Oct. 13, 1864, Paddock Letters, Wisconsin Historical Society, Madison.

65. Newsome, *Richmond Must Fall*, 74; *OR*, 42(3):150; Sommers, "Grant's Fifth Offensive," 513–16, 520–21; Charles J. Paine to "Dear Father," Oct. 11, 1864, Paine Papers, Virginia Museum of History and Culture, Richmond; Henry Pippitt letter, Oct. 13, 1864, Pippitt Letters.

66. *OR*, 42(3):150, 157; Henry Grimes Marshall to "Dear Folks at Home," Oct. 10, 1864, Marshall Letters, Clements Library, University of Michigan, Ann Arbor; Sommers, "Grant's Fifth Offensive," 527–29. Heckman's commission as brigadier general was dated November 29, 1862; Ames's, May 20, 1863. Ames married Ben Butler's daughter, Blanche, in 1870 and become embroiled in Mississippi Reconstruction politics. In 1893 he received the Medal of Honor for bravery at First Manassas. He died in 1933, the last Civil War general to perish. Fort Pocahontas is preserved as private property in 2024 and is open to the public on occasion. Carr had been in command of the First Division for only a few days. See *OR*, 42(3):89.

67. *OR*, 42(3):1141; Joseph Hilton letter, Oct. 14, 1864, Joseph Hilton Letters, Confederate Miscellaneous Collection, Woodruff Library, Emory University, Atlanta; Sommers, "Grant's Fifth Offensive," 533–35.

68. Joseph A. Shank to "Dear Friend," Oct. 9, 1864, Shank Collection, Georgia State Archives, Morrow; James Rawlings to "Dear Nannie," Oct. 10, 1864, Rawlings Family Papers, Albert and Shirley Small Special Collections Library, University of Virginia, Charlottesville. Shank's date reference was, of course, to the impending U.S. presidential election.

69. Gallagher, *Fighting for the Confederacy*, 486; Trudeau, "Costly Union Reconnaissance," 44.

70. Gallagher, *Fighting for the Confederacy*, 486; Trudeau, "Costly Union Reconnaissance," 44; Crockett Diary, Oct. 12–13, 1864; *OR Supp.*, 260; Hagood, "Memoirs of the First SC Regiment," 193–94; Laine and Penny, *Law's Alabama Brigade*, 308; Field, "Campaign of 1864 and 1865," 558; Manarin, *Field of Honor*, 748; Sommers, "Grant's Fifth Offensive," 542–45. South to north, Hoke's deployment was Colquitt, Kirkland, Hagood, and McKethan (Clingman's Brigade). Field had the Texas Brigade on his right, followed by Bowles, Anderson, DuBose, and Bratton, the South Carolinians now commanded by Col. Joseph Walker of the Palmetto Sharpshooters following Bratton's wounding on October 7. In 2024 the portion of the Alexander Line between Fort Gilmer and Virginia Highway 5 is preserved in Richmond National Battlefield Park.

71. *OR*, 42(3):182–84; Newsome, *Richmond Must Fall*, 77–78; Manarin, *Field of Honor*, 745–46; "The Army of the James," *New York Times*, Oct. 18, 1864. Kensel withdrew the flag at 4:55 P.M.

72. *OR*, 42(3):186, 191. On these same issues, see Sommers, "Grant's Fifth Offensive," 551–53. Another oddity is that Terry's men had orders to carry three days' rations with blankets, a directive wholly at odds with a mission of disrupting construction of an earthwork. See Lt. Benjamin Wright to "My Dear Abbie," Oct. 12, 1864, Wright Papers.

73. *OR*, 42(3):183–84, 186–88, 190; Brady, *Story of One Regiment*, 277–78; Elias S. Peck to "Dear Mother," Oct. 14, 1864, Peck Letters, Siege of Petersburg online; Califf, *Seventh U.S. Colored Troops*, 47; Alonzo West Diary, Oct. 12, 1864, Bryce Suderow (Private Collection), Washington; Beecher, *First Light Battery*, 596; Sommers, "Grant's Fifth Offensive," 556–58, 564. The First Connecticut Light Artillery definitely accompanied Terry. The identity of the other two batteries is speculative. They were, perhaps, the Fourth New Jersey Battery and either Battery E or Battery D, First U.S. Artillery.

74. *OR*, 42(3):190; Sommers, "Grant's Fifth Offensive," 570.

75. William Moultrie Reid to "Dear Parents," Oct. 14, 1864, William Moultrie Reid Collection, South Caroliniana Library, University of South Carolina, Columbia; Sommers, "Grant's Fifth Offensive," 565–66; Field, "Campaign of 1864 and 1865," 558; *OR*, 42(1):876; Robert E. Fitzgerald Diary, Oct. 13, 1864; Crockett Diary, Oct. 12, 1864; Laine and Penny, *Law's Alabama Brigade*, 308. Field's memoirs suggest that he moved the Texans without authorization from Lieutenant General Anderson, but Richard Sommers demonstrates that Anderson did, in fact, approve the movement. See Sommers, "Grant's Fifth Offensive," 667nn103–4.

76. *OR*, 42(3):217–18.

77. Kautz, "Reminiscences," 92–93; Brady, *Story of One Regiment*, 278; Putnam, *Joseph R. Hawley*, 61; Clark, *Thirty-Ninth Illinois*, 173; Dickey, *85th Pennsylvania*, 400; Blackett, *Thomas Morris Chester*, 148; *OR*, 42(1):681, 685, 690, 706, 722, 725, 732, 740, 776; "From the Tenth Connecticut," *Hartford (Conn.) Daily Courant*, Oct. 22, 1864; Peck to "Dear Mother," Oct. 14, 1864; Roe, *Twenty-Fourth Massachusetts*, 371; Wilson, *Black Phalanx*, 442; Beecher, *First Light Battery*, 596; West Diary, Oct. 13, 1864.

78. *OR*, 42(1):681, 685–86, 690, 732–33, 776; Brady, *Story of One Regiment*, 278; Dickey, *85th Pennsylvania*, 400; Marino, "General Alfred Howe Terry," 364.

79. *OR*, 42(1):685, 690, 706, 722, 726, 733, 740, 42(3):218; Peck to "Dear Mother," Oct. 14, 1864; Roe, *Twenty-Fourth Massachusetts*, 371; Joseph Hawley to "Dear Sir," Oct. 25, 1864, William Conant Church Papers, Manuscripts Division, Library of Congress, Washington.

80. *OR*, 42(1):776; Califf, *Seventh U.S. Colored Troops*, 47; Sommers, "Grant's Fifth Offensive," 574–75.

81. *OR*, 42(1):681, 42(3):218; Beecher, *First Light Battery*, 596; Bryce Suderow, "'An Ugly Looking Chance for a Charge': The Battle of Darbytown Road, October 13, 1864," News and Notes, Siege of Petersburg Online, www.beyondthecrater.com; Sommers, "Grant's Fifth Offensive," 575. Colonel Evans, commander of the First Maryland Cavalry, would officially assume command of a brigade consisting of his regiment and the First New York Mounted Rifles on October 14. The First Maryland Cavalry had been serving with the Tenth Corps, and the New Yorkers had been unbrigaded. See *OR*, 42(3):67, 233.

82. In addition to Terry's 3,100 and Birney's 1,600 soldiers, Curtis added around 1,050 men, Kautz some 1,800 cavalry, and there were between 400 and 500 artillerists. See Sommers, "Grant's Fifth Offensive," 670–71nn14–15; and *OR*, 42(1):681, 714, 733, 756, 776–77.

83. *OR*, 42(1):706–7, 714, 726, 733, 777, 781, 42(3):218–19; Putnam, *Joseph R. Hawley*, 61.

84. *OR*, 42(3):213, 219. It is unclear why ninety minutes elapsed between Terry's inquiry and Butler's message to Grant. Whatever the cause, the delay allowed the Confederates to improve their defenses.

85. Field, "Campaign of 1864 and 1865," 558; *OR*, 42(1):876; *OR Supp.*, 260; Laine and Penny, *Law's Alabama Brigade*, 309; Sommers, "Grant's Fifth Offensive," 579–80; Trudeau, "Costly Union Reconnaissance," 47. James Longstreet was also present, although he had not yet been assigned to command troops. See Newsome, *Richmond Must Fall*, 85.

86. Lyle Diary, Oct. 13, 1864; Field, "Campaign of 1864 and 1865," 559; Henry DeShields to "My Sweetness," Oct. 16, 1864, DeShields Letters, Library of Virginia, Richmond; "From below Richmond," *Richmond Daily Dispatch*, Oct. 14, 1864.

87. *OR*, 42(3):219, 42(1):682, 690, 707, 722, 741, 750; "Campaign in Virginia," Oct. 22, 1864; Putnam, *Joseph R. Hawley*, 61; Blackett, *Thomas Morris Chester*, 148; "From the Tenth Connecticut," Oct. 22, 1864; Dickey, *85th Pennsylvania*, 400; Clark, *Thirty-Ninth Illinois*, 173; Beecher, *First Light Battery*, 597; Sommers, "Grant's Fifth Offensive," 589–90.

88. *OR*, 42(1):682; Sommers, "Grant's Fifth Offensive," 590; Trudeau, "Costly Union Reconnaissance," 47. An abandoned section of the Outer Line ran parallel to Charles City Road, then turned north to cross it. Ames may have mistaken these works for the main Confederate fortifications. See Manarin, *Field of Honor*, 757.

89. Clark, *Thirty-Ninth Illinois*, 174; Hawley to "Dear Sir," Oct. 25, 1864, Church Papers; Peck to "Dear Mother," Oct. 14, 1864; Sommers, "Grant's Fifth Offensive," 591–92.

90. *OR*, 42(1):682, 690, 707, 722, 741; Dickey, *85th Pennsylvania*, 401; Newsome, *Richmond Must Fall*, 85–86.

91. Sommers, "Schematic Design of the Second Battle of the Darbytown Road, Oct. 13, 1864," in "Grant's Fifth Offensive"; Suderow, "Ugly Looking Chance for a Charge"; Trumbull, *Knightly Soldier*, 302; Clark, *Thirty-Ninth Illinois*, 174–75.

92. Trudeau, "Costly Union Reconnaissance," 47; Hawley to "Dear Sir," Oct. 25, 1864; *OR*, 42(1):707, 42(3):213; Osmun Latrobe Diary, Oct. 13, 1864, Virginia Museum of History and Culture, Richmond; Peck to "Dear Mother," Oct. 14, 1864. Butler's order to Terry to "reconnoiter the ground thoroughly and to return to his old position" went out before 1:20

P.M. That it failed to reach him prior to the attack does little credit to the efficiency of Federal communications that day.

93. Dean, "Recollections"; Laine and Penny, *Law's Alabama Brigade*, 310; "From the Tenth Connecticut," Oct. 22, 1864; *OR*, 42(1):147, 741; Peck to "Dear Mother," Oct. 14, 1864.

94. Clark, *Thirty-Ninth Illinois*, 174–76; *OR*, 42(1):146, 690–91. The commanding officer of the Sixty-Second Ohio, Lt. Col. Samuel B. Taylor, was also mortally wounded.

95. *OR*, 42(1):690, 741; Peck to "Dear Mother," Oct. 14, 1864.

96. "From below Richmond," *Richmond Daily Dispatch*, Oct. 14, 1864; John D. McGeachy to "Dear Sister," Oct. 14, 1864, Buie Letters, Duke University, Durham, N.C.; *OR*, 42(1):690, 853; Field, "Campaign of 1864 and 1865," 559; "The Battle Last Thursday," *Richmond Daily Dispatch*, Oct. 21, 1864; Crockett Diary, Oct. 13, 1864. Birney's two brigades lost eighty-one men during the day. Some Confederates exaggerated both the role and casualties of these Black troops. See, for example, Jessie W. Stribling to "Uncle Warren," Sept. 7, 1864, in *Recollections and Reminiscences, 1861–1865 through World War I*, 2:438; and George H. Moffett to "Dear John," Oct. 14, 1864, Moffett Family Papers, South Carolina Historical Society, Charleston. Confederate casualties are obviously estimates. Newspaper accounts reported between thirty and fifty. See Trudeau, "Costly Union Reconnaissance," 48; Suderow, "Ugly Looking Chance for a Charge"; and Sommers, "Grant's Fifth Offensive," 606. Terrell would die of his wounds in a Richmond hospital nine days later.

97. Sommers, "Grant's Fifth Offensive," 597–99; Kautz Diary, Oct. 13, 1864; Kautz, "Reminiscences," 93; West Diary, Oct. 13, 1864; *OR*, 42(1):147; Brady, *Story of One Regiment*, 279. Sgt. Robert A. Turner of the Hampton Legion Cavalry recorded in his diary that General Lee was "standing not far from the line with all the dignity of a grave and dauntless warrior—his eagle eye flashing and kindling with patriotic ardor. We felt all was well with us." Turner Diary, Oct. 15, 1864, University of South Carolina, Columbia.

98. Sommers, "Grant's Fifth Offensive," 598–600; Califf, *Seventh U.S. Colored Troops*, 47; Spear, *Army Life*, 269; Roe, *Twenty-Fourth Massachusetts*, 372; Peck to "Dear Mother," Oct. 14, 1864; Dickey, *85th Pennsylvania*, 401; *OR*, 42(1):682, 690, 707, 714, 717, 722, 726, 733–34, 756–57, 777, 782, 876; Beecher, *First Light Battery*, 599; Sturkey, *Hampton Legion Infantry*, 100; Trudeau, "Costly Union Reconnaissance," 48.

99. *OR*, 42(3):220, 42(1):148; Hawley to "Dear Sir," Oct. 25, 1864. Richard Sommers counts 442 Federal casualties. See Sommers, "Grant's Fifth Offensive," 1230.

100. *OR*, 42(3):214–15. Varina is the name of the general area of eastern Henrico County where the fighting occurred.

101. Cummins and Hohweiler, *An Enlisted Man's View*, 171; *OR*, 42(1):686; Peck to "Dear Mother," Oct. 14, 1864. Pond would lose his brigade command and return to command of his regiment. He resigned his commission on November 6 and received an honorable discharge. See *OR*, 42(3):465, 539.

102. Erwin Welsh to "Dear Wife," Oct. 16, 1864, Erwin Welsh Collection, Michigan History Center, Lansing; Marino, "General Alfred Howe Terry," 368–69; Newsome, *Richmond Must Fall*, 90.

103. Suderow, "Ugly Looking Chance for a Charge"; Hawley to "Dear Sir," Oct. 25, 1864; Benjamin Wright to "My Dear Abbie," Oct. 13, 1864, Wright Papers.

104. *OR*, 42(1):853, 876, 42(3):1148; Lyle Diary, Oct. 14, 1864; William Moultrie Reid to "Dear Parents," Oct. 14, 1864, Reid Collection. The condition of the Federal bodies suggests

that the Confederates stripped them overnight to enhance their own wardrobes, an urgent imperative given the change in the weather.

105. *Richmond Daily Dispatch*, Oct. 14, 21, 1864; David Hampton to "Dear Uncel and Family," Oct. 14, 1864, Caleb Hampton Papers, Rubenstein Special Collections Library, Duke University, Durham, N.C.; George Moffett to "Dear John," Oct. 14, 1864, Moffett Family Papers.

106. *OR*, 42(3):264–65; Hopkins, *Seventh Rhode Island*, 222; Manarin, *Field of Honor*, 763–65. Fort Fisher would be expanded later. In 2024 it is well preserved in Petersburg National Battlefield.

107. Sommers, "Grant's Fifth Offensive," 1231; *OR*, 42(3):1140, 42(1):2, 871; Manarin, *Field of Honor*, 768; Longstreet, *From Manassas to Appomattox*, 594; Freeman, *Lee's Lieutenants*, 613; Thomas Jewett Goree to "My dear Sister," Oct. 21, 1864, in Goree, *Thomas Jewett Goree Letters*, 232–33; Elliott, *Richard Heron Anderson*, 121.

108. Manarin, *Field of Honor*, 767–68; *Philadelphia Inquirer*, Oct. 24, 1864.

109. Porter, *Campaigning with Grant*, 304–6; Marshall, *Butler's Correspondence*, 5:266. Other members of Stanton's entourage included Montgomery Meigs, the army's chief quartermaster; Amos B. Eaton, commissary general of the army; Joseph K. Barnes, the army's surgeon general; Congressman Samuel Hooper of Massachusetts; and the current and former collectors of the Port of New York, Simeon Draper and Hiram Barney. Brig. Gen. Francis Fessenden, the secretary's son—he recently lost a leg during the Red River Campaign in Louisiana—joined his father on the trip. The elder Fessenden had reluctantly assumed his new post in early July.

110. Porter, *Campaigning with Grant*, 306; Agassiz, *Meade's Headquarters*, 248–49; Lowe, *Meade's Army*, 281; Nevins, *Diary of Battle*, 474; Simpson, *Ulysses S. Grant*, 385. Lyman, as usual, offered candid descriptions of each of the Washington visitors. See Lowe, *Meade's Army*, 281.

111. *OR*, 42(3):1135; Newsome, *Richmond Must Fall*, 110.

112. Newsome, *Richmond Must Fall*, 110; *OR*, 42(3):1144.

CHAPTER TWELVE

1. "The North Side," *Richmond Daily Examiner*, Oct. 19, 1864; U.S. War Department, *War of the Rebellion*, ser. 1, 42(3):280 (hereafter *OR*; all references are to series 1 unless otherwise noted); Theodore Lyman to "Dear Small Woman," Oct. 14, 1864, Lyman Letters, Massachusetts Historical Society, Boston; Jordan, *Happiness Is Not My Companion*, 198; James Lane letter, Oct. 11, 1864, Lane Papers, Auburn University. Some officers complained that the horseracing interfered with good discipline, and General Warren ordered it halted.

2. Burnham Diary, Oct. 25, 1864, Burnham Papers, New York State Library, Albany; Oscar Robinson to "Mr. Bragg, Dear Sir," Oct. 26, 1864, Elmer Bragg Letters and Diary, Rauner Library, Dartmouth College, Hanover; Oscar Robinson to "Dear Mother," Oct. 26, 1864, Robinson Papers, Dartmouth College, Hanover; William Lamont to "Dear Sister," Oct. 24, 1864, William Lamont Letters, Wisconsin Historical Society, Madison; *OR*, 42(3):245, 1146; "North Side."

3. *OR*, 42(3):233–34; Porter, *Campaigning with Grant*, 309; Newsome, *Richmond Must Fall*, 117. The unexpected Confederate offensive that resulted in the Battle of Cedar Creek compelled Sheridan to retain his army in the Shenandoah Valley.

4. *OR*, 42(3):290; O. Charles Benton to "Dear Cora," Oct. 16, 1864, Benton-Beach Family Correspondence, University of Notre Dame, South Bend; Woodbury, *Burnside and the Ninth Army Corps*, 469; Newsome, *Richmond Must Fall*, 121.

5. *OR*, 42(3):294, 305, 307; Humphreys, *Andrew Atkinson Humphreys*, 255; Newsome, *Richmond Must Fall*, 124–25.

6. *OR*, 42(3):317–18, 331–32. Hampton Newsome states that Grant met separately that evening with Butler and Meade. Newsome, *Richmond Must Fall*, 129. Louis Manarin contends that the three officers met together at City Point. Manarin, *Field of Honor*, 769. Neither of these fine accounts cite evidence of where Butler met with Grant. Lyman notes only that Meade "rode to City Point, to consult, probably, on the coming move" but says nothing about who attended that meeting. Lowe, *Meade's Army*, 284.

7. Humphreys, *Virginia Campaign of '64 and '65*, 294; Newsome, *Richmond Must Fall*, 132–33; *OR*, 42(3):323–26, 328–31.

8. *OR*, 42(3):313, 340–41.

9. Newsome, *Richmond Must Fall*, 125; *OR*, 42(3):341.

10. Newsome, *Richmond Must Fall*, 124–25, 132–35; *OR*, 42(3):340–42. Hampton Newsome, the offensive's premier scholar, calls this plan "conservative" because it did not entail disassociation from the army's base of supplies at City Point. Although this is certainly true, Meade and Grant, in my view, undertook a bold and risky operation whose goal was nothing less than terminating Lee's months-long defense of Petersburg.

11. *OR*, 42(3):1159; 1162; Humphreys, *Andrew Atkinson Humphreys*, 255; Badeau, *Military History of Ulysses S. Grant*, 3:116, 118; Newsome, *Richmond Must Fall*, 135–37. Faulty information provided by Confederate deserters added to the Federals' misunderstanding of the situation. See *OR*, 42(3):318–19.

12. Charles Lewis Rundlett to "Dear Father & Mother," Oct. 26, 1864, Charles Lewis Rundlett Letters, Library of Virginia, Richmond; John T. Andrews to "Dear Homer," Oct. 25, 1864, John T. Andrews Letters, Library of Virginia, Richmond; John E. Irwin to "Dear Mother," Oct. 26, 1864, Irwin Family Papers, Bentley Historical Library, University of Michigan, Ann Arbor; Houston, *Thirty-Second Maine*, 407; Theodore Lyman to "My golden-feathered chick-a-biddy," Oct. 26, 1864, Lyman Letters, Massachusetts Historical Society; *OR*, 42(3):355; Nevins, *Diary of Battle*, 476.

13. *OR*, 42(3):366–68; Simon, *Grant Papers*, 12:348. Weitzel took the Sixteenth New York Battery and Battery A, First Pennsylvania Light Artillery with him.

14. *OR*, 42(3):354, 371–72; Solon Carter to "My own darling Em," Oct. 25, 1864, Carter Letters, Army Heritage and Education Center, Carlisle; Sperry Diary, Oct. 26, 1864, New-York Historical Society, New York; Wickman, *We Are Coming Father Abra'am*, 375; Silas Edward Mead to "My Dear Tillie," Oct. 27, 1864, Silas Mead Papers, Greenwich Historical Society; Blackett, *Thomas Morris Chester*, 177.

15. Meade, *Life and Letters*, 236–37; Marshall, *Butler's Correspondence*, 5:287; Simon, *Grant Papers*, 12:50–51.

16. Cauthen, *Family Letters of the Three Wade Hamptons*, 110; *OR*, 42(3):1159–60, 1162; Newsome, *Richmond Must Fall*, 139–40.

17. Eugene Burnett letter, Oct. 21, 1864, Jordan-Burnett Papers, University of Georgia, Athens; *OR*, 42(1):871, 42(3):1156; Gallagher, *Fighting for the Confederacy*, 492; Samuel S. Biddle to "My Dear Pa," Oct. 20, 1864, Samuel Biddle Letters, Duke University, Durham,

N.C.; Willie Mason to "My Dear Sister," Oct. 23, 1864, Alexander Papers, University of North Carolina, Chapel Hill.

18. Quoted in Barefoot, *General Robert F. Hoke*, 233–34.

19. Alfred Howe Terry to "My Dearest Mammy," Nov. 10, 1864, Terry Papers, Connecticut Historical Society, Hartford; James Beard to "Dear Brother & Sister," Oct. 30, 1864, Beard Letters, Tennessee State Library and Archives, Nashville; Jackson and O'Donnell, *Back Home in Oneida*, 174; Mowris, *One Hundred and Seventeenth Regiment New York Volunteers*, 141; Longacre, *From Antietam to Fort Fisher*, 213; OR, 42(1):762, 767, 769; Bayard Cooper to "Dear Parents & Sisters," Nov. 1, 1864, Cooper Papers, Army Heritage and Education Center, Carlisle; David S. Libbey to "Dear May," Oct. 31, 1864, Libbey Papers, Rubenstein Special Collections Library, Duke University, Durham, N.C.; Manarin, *Field of Honor*, 775, 777; Newsome, *Richmond Must Fall*, 148. Terry also complained of malarial symptoms—"my system is saturated with it," he wrote his mother.

20. OR, 42(1):704, 734, 771, 777, 779; William Hunt Goff to "Dear Mother," Oct. 28, 1864, in "Civil War Letters of William Hunt Goff" (online); Diary of Lt. Joshua H. Dearborn, Oct. 27, 1864, Guilford Free Public Library; Trudeau, *Like Men of War*, 305; Croffut and Morris, *Connecticut during the War*, 675; Charles Griswold to "Dear Sister," Oct. 30, 1864, Griswold Family Letters, New York Public Library; Dobak, *Freedom by the Sword*, 396; *Norwich (Conn.) Morning Bulletin*, Nov. 7, 1864; Thomas Gray Bennett Papers, Civil War Documents Collection, Army Heritage and Education Center, Carlisle, 64; Newsome, *Richmond Must Fall*, 149–50; Manarin, *Field of Honor*, 777. Louis Manarin asserts that Ames preceded Foster, which is possible. The commander of the Third New Hampshire in Abbott's brigade reported reaching Darbytown Road at 5:30 A.M. See OR, 42(1):722. Voris assumed command of the First Brigade, First Division the day before the battle.

21. OR, 42(3):390; Newsome, *Richmond Must Fall*, 151, 153.

22. OR, 42(3):397, 42(1):795, 802, 804, 806–7; George J. Paddock to "Dear Father," Oct. 31, 1864, Paddock Letters, Wisconsin Historical Society, Madison; H[eman] E. Baker, "In Front of Richmond," *Adirondack Record* (Au Sable, N.Y.), July 25, 1919; Thompson, *13th New Hampshire*, 499; Valentine Barney to "My dear Maria," Oct. 29, 1864, Valentine Barney Papers, Vermont Historical Society, Barre; Solon Carter to "My own precious wife," Oct. 29, 1864, Carter Letters; Scroggs Diary, Oct. 27, 1864, Army Heritage and Education Center, Carlisle; George Tillotson to "My Dear Wife," Oct. 30, 1864, Tillotson Letters, New-York Historical Society, New York; Patch, *This from George*, 167; Newsome, *Richmond Must Fall*, 155; Manarin, *Field of Honor*, 778. Colonel Holman was the nominal commander of the Third Division units, although he exercised authority over only his own brigade.

23. OR, 42(1):804, 42(3):397; Newsome, *Richmond Must Fall*, 156–57. Earlier Weitzel had confessed to a lack of self-confidence. Here, perhaps, was an example of that flaw.

24. OR, 42(1):796, 802, 806, 871–72; Thompson, *13th New Hampshire*, 499; Baker, "In Front of Richmond"; Estes, "Second Fair Oaks"; George J. Paddock to "Dear Father," Oct. 31, 1864, Paddock Letters; Patch, *This from George*, 167; George Tillotson to "My Dear Wife," Oct. 30, 1864, Tillotson Letters; Washington, *Eagles on their Buttons*, 63; Scroggs Diary, Oct. 27, 1864; James Otis Moore to "My Dearest Lissie," Oct. 30, 1864, Moore Letters, Duke University, Durham; Blackett, *Thomas Morris Chester*, 172; Newsome, *Richmond Must Fall*, 157–58. Various accounts time Weitzel's arrival between 1:00 and 3:00 P.M. This is not surprising given the length of a column forced to march on one narrow road.

25. OR, 42(1):872; Longstreet, *From Manassas to Appomattox*, 577.

26. Simpson, *Hood's Texas Brigade*, 443; Polley, *Hood's Texas Brigade*, 259; Jasper H. Brightwell, "A Great Achievement by Private Soldiers," *Atlanta Constitution*, May 28, 1887; Trowbridge, "Conspicuous Feats of Valor," 25; Parker, "Captain Lyle," 165. Dramatic quotes such as the one credited to the brave Virginia lieutenant are often manufactured or embellished, even while the essence of the sentiment rings true.

27. *OR*, 42(1):802, 804, 806–8, 812, 814, 42(3):398; Newsome, *Richmond Must Fall*, 158–59; Manarin, *Field of Honor*, 786. Weitzel once again displayed his self-professed lack of confidence.

28. *OR*, 42(1):796, 802, 808; Cunningham, *Adirondack Regiment*, 158; George Tillotson to "My Dear Wife," Oct. 30, 1864, Tillotson Letters.

29. *OR*, 42(1):151, 812; Patch, *This from George*, 167; Buckingham, *All's for the Best*, 310; Newsome, *Richmond Must Fall*, 159–60. Marston claimed that he selected Cullen to make the assault. The twenty-nine-year-old Patterson, a graduate of Dartmouth College, had no prewar military experience.

30. Baker, "In Front of Richmond"; Cunningham, *Adirondack Regiment*, 157–58; Newsome, *Richmond Must Fall*, 162; Manarin, *Field of Honor*, 792–93.

31. George J. Paddock to "Dear Father," Oct. 31, 1864, Paddock Letters; George Tillotson to "My Dear Wife," Oct. 30, 1864, Tillotson Letters.

32. Winkler, *Confederate Capital and Hood's Texas Brigade*, 198; Watson D. Williams to "My Dear Laura," Nov. 1, 1864, Capt. Watson D. Williams Papers, Historical Research Center, Texas Heritage Museum, Hill College, Hillsboro; Benjamin Simms Fitzgerald Diary, Oct. 27, 1864, Southern Historical Collection, Louis Round Wilson Library, University of North Carolina, Chapel Hill; "One Man Captures Six Hundred," *Newberry (S.C.) Herald and News*, Oct. 6, 1905; Manarin, "Over 500 Yankees Captured Singlehandedly," 1; Robert Knox Sneden Memoir, 362, Virginia Museum of History and Culture; Newsome, *Richmond Must Fall*, 166–67. Lyle's accomplishment seems exaggerated, yet Cullen lost 246 men captured and Fairchild 258, so perhaps "several hundred" is a plausible number.

33. George Tillotson to "My Dear Wife," Oct. 30, 1864, Tillotson Letters; Patch, *This from George*, 170; *OR*, 42(1):150–51, 877; Newsome, *Richmond Must Fall*, 167; R. Lee Barfield to "My Dear Sister," Oct. 30, 1864, Fleming Letters, University of Georgia, Athens.

34. *OR*, 42(1):796, 814–15; Blackett, *Thomas Morris Chester*, 178; Newsome, *Richmond Must Fall*, 168–69; Manarin, *Field of Honor*, 799.

35. *OR*, 42(1):815, 818; Blackett, *Thomas Morris Chester*, 176. The fort was called Battery Ewell. See Newsome, *Richmond Must Fall*, 375n11.

36. Newsome, *Richmond Must Fall*, 171; Manarin, *Field of Honor*, 800; Hinson quoted in Ramsey, *7th South Carolina Cavalry*, 125.

37. *OR*, 42(1):815, 818–19; Priest, *Stephen Elliott Welch*, 64; Manarin, *Field of Honor*, 801.

38. *OR*, 42(1):815–16; Priest, *Stephen Elliott Welch*, 64–65; "Gary's Cavalry Brigade," *Daily South Carolinian* (Columbia), Nov. 22, 1864; Goodwin, "Letters of William Hiten Goodwin," 76; West, *Found among the Privates*, 91–93. The murder of wounded and captured Black soldiers was, by this time, shamefully routine. For a more detailed tactical account of this action, see Manarin, *Field of Honor*, 800–803.

39. Carter, "Fourteen Months' Service with Colored Troops," 174; *OR*, 42(1):816, 151, 42(3):442–43; Manarin, *Field of Honor*, 803; Newsome, *Richmond Must Fall*, 173. Kiddoo avoided punishment for his performance and in 1865 received a brevet promotion to brigadier general for his service on June 15, 1864. See Greene, *Campaign of Giants*, 106–9.

40. *OR*, 42(3):390–91, 396.

41. Charles Griswold to "Dear Sister," Oct. 30, 1864, Griswold Family Letters; Croffut and Morris, *Connecticut during the War*, 675; Burkhardt, *Double Duty*, 129–30; *Norwich (Conn.) Morning Bulletin*, Nov. 7, 1864; Bennett Papers, 65–66; *OR*, 42(1):771, 777. The Twenty-Ninth Connecticut went into battle with thirteen officers and 571 men, suffering eighty casualties. See "From the Twenty-Ninth Regiment," *Windham County Transcript* (West Killingly, Conn.), Nov. 17, 1864; and *OR*, 42(1):150.

42. *OR*, 42(1):705, 723, 734; William Hunt Goff to "Dear Mother," Oct. 28, 1864, in "Civil War Letters of William Hunt Goff"; "From the Tenth Connecticut," *Hartford (Conn.) Daily Courant*, Nov. 5, 1864.

43. *OR*, 42(1):149, 763; Jackson and O'Donnell, *Back Home in Oneida*, 174; Richmond Reminiscence, Central Michigan University, Mount Pleasant; David Hampton to "Dear Uncle & family," Nov. 1, 1864, Caleb Hampton Papers, Duke University, Durham, N.C.; Longacre, *From Antietam to Fort Fisher*, 213; Newsome, *Richmond Must Fall*, 174. The Forty-Second North Carolina was in Kirkland's Brigade.

44. *OR*, 42(1):149, 768, 770; David S. Libbey to "Dear May," Oct. 31, 1864, Libbey Papers; Silo, *115th New York*, 158.

45. *OR*, 42(1):152, 768, 42(3):391; Stowits, *100th New York*, 316. Longstreet reported a grand total of sixty-four casualties in Field's Division, Gary's Brigade, and the artillery. See *OR*, 42(1):877; Longstreet, *From Manassas to Appomattox*, 578; and Longstreet, "Report of Affair of October 27," 543.

46. *OR*, 42(1):556, 560, 568, 576; Harper Diary, Oct. 27, 1864, Army Heritage and Education Center, Carlisle; Wilkinson, *May You Never See the Sights*, 307; Allen, *Fourth Rhode Island*, 313; Allen, "Hatcher's Run as Told in a Comrade's Diary"; Lord, *Ninth New Hampshire*, 534; Albert B. Stearns to "Dear Sister," Oct. 30, 1864, Albert B. Stearns Papers, New Hampshire Historical Society, Concord; Bosworth Diary, Oct. 27, 1864, University of Notre Dame, South Bend; Gavin, *Campaigning with the Roundheads*, 581; Ewing, *From Home to Trench*, 84.

47. *OR*, 42(1):548, 556, 560, 568, 576, 949, 1159; Gavin, *Campaigning with the Roundheads*, 581–82; Hewitt, Trudeau, and Suderow, *Supplement to the Official Records of the Union and Confederate Armies* (hereafter *OR Supp.*), 479–80; James King Wilkerson to "My dearest Parents," Oct. 30, 1864, Wilkerson Papers, Duke University, Durham, N.C.; Wellman, *Giant in Gray*, 160; Newsome, *Richmond Must Fall*, 179–80. Only two miles separated Fort Cummings from the Clements house. The American Battlefield Trust preserves the Clements house and the nearby Confederate earthworks, both of which are accessible in 2024 via an interpretive trail. Nothing remains of Fort Cummings.

48. *OR*, 42(3):361–63, 42(1):434, 507; Smith, *Seventy-Sixth Regiment New York*, 313. Warren had confidence in Griffin and rightly so. Perhaps this explains his decision.

49. *OR*, 42(1):437, 459, 42(3):385; Curtis, *Twenty-Fourth Michigan*, 278; Matthews, *149th Pennsylvania*, 195; Reid-Green, *Letters from Home*, 98; William M. Read to "My Dear Mother," Oct. 30, 1864, Read Letters and Diary, copy, Petersburg National Battlefield; Judson, *Eighty-Third Pennsylvania*, 234; Woodward, *198th Pennsylvania*, 19; "Incident at Hatcher's Run"; Henry D. Didcock to "Dear Father Mother & Brother," Nov. 21, 1864, Henry D. Didcock Letters, Gowanda Area Historical Society; Marshall, *Company "K" 155th Pa.*, 208; Plumb, *Your Brother in Arms*, 235. McClelland was promoted to captain on September 30.

50. Wiatt, *Confederate Chaplain William Edward Wiatt*, 203; Morrison, *Memoirs of Henry Heth*, lvii; *OR Supp.*, 480; Newsome, *Richmond Must Fall*, 184.

51. *OR Supp.*, 480–81. Heth's headquarters that morning were at the Pickerell house on Boydton Plank Road. This home is still extant in 2024, though much modified and privately owned. The Second Maryland Battalion was also in Walker's Brigade, which was consolidated with Archer's.

52. *OR*, 42(1):548–49, 580; Robert Gordon Dill, "Personal Reminiscences of the War of the Rebellion," 259–60, Denver Public Library; Smith, "Civil War Letters of Quartermaster Sergeant John C. Brock," 159–60; Pope Diary, Oct. 27, 1864, Army Heritage and Education Center, Carlisle; Houston, *Thirty-Second Maine*, 408.

53. *OR*, 42(1):437; Humphreys, *Virginia Campaign of '64 and '65*, 296–97; Newsome, *Richmond Must Fall*, 192, 195.

54. *OR*, 42(3):340, 359–60, 42(1):230–31. Egan commanded the division vice John Gibbon, who took leave on October 8 to escort his sister from North Carolina to his home in Philadelphia. Gibbon would return on October 29. See *OR*, 42(3):121, 429.

55. *OR*, 42(1):175, 231, 295, 319, 325, 332–33, 338–39; William H. Paine Diary, Oct. 27, 1864, Abraham Lincoln Presidential Library, Springfield; Smyth Diaries, Oct. 27, 1864, Delaware Public Archives, Dover; Haines, *Co. F 12th New Jersey*, 85–86; Washburn, *108th New York*, 87; Page, *Fourteenth Connecticut*, 317; Hopkins, *Little Jeff*, 239–40; Waring Diary, Oct. 27, 1864, University of North Carolina, Chapel Hill; Bearss, *Western Front Battles*, 96–97.

56. *OR*, 42(3):379, 42(1):608–9, 648; Holmes, *Horse Soldiers in Blue*, 186; Merrill, *First Maine and First District of Columbia Cavalry*, 287–88; Tobie, *First Maine Cavalry*, 363; Gray, "Echoes," 281; Bearss, *Western Front Battles*, 100–101; Newsome, *Richmond Must Fall*, 202.

57. Hampton Connected Narrative, Hampton Family Papers, South Caroliniana Library, University of South Carolina, Columbia, 95–96; Newsome, *Richmond Must Fall*, 202–3; Bearss, *Western Front Battles*, 101–2; *OR*, 42(3):1162, 42(1):949, 952.

58. *OR*, 42(1):608; Trout, *Memoirs of the Stuart Horse Artillery*, 238; Sherfesse Memoir, University of South Carolina, Columbia; U. R. Brooks, "War History: Maj. U. R. Brooks Gives Some Interesting Incidents Which Came under His Own Observation, and Which Should Be Preserved for the Future Historian," *Anderson (S.C.) Intelligencer*, Sept. 15, 1897; Trout, *Galloping Thunder*, 574; Holmes, *Horse Soldiers in Blue*, 186.

59. *OR*, 42(1):629, 648; Gray, "Echoes," 282; Tobie, *First Maine Cavalry*, 363–64; Trout, *Galloping Thunder*, 575; Wells, *Hampton and His Cavalry*, 333; Harrell, *2nd North Carolina Cavalry*, 339; Fred C. Foard Papers, 7, State Archives of North Carolina, Raleigh; Daughtry, *Gray Cavalier*, 226.

60. Newsome, *Richmond Must Fall*, 204–7, 212; Bearss, *Western Front Battles*, 103; *OR*, 42(1):231; McCabe, "Major Andrew Reid Venable," 70–71. Elements of the Nineteenth Maine captured Venable. See *OR*, 42(1):306.

61. Isaac McQueen Auld to "Dear Mother," July 13, 1864, Isaac McQueen Auld Papers, Civil War Documents Collection, Army Heritage and Education Center, Carlisle; J. A. Shank to "Dear Friend," July 2, 1864, Shank Collection, Georgia State Archives, Morrow. Moxley Sorrel recounted the oft-cited anecdote that when Mahone's wife learned that her husband had suffered a slight flesh wound, she commented, "now I know it is serious, for William has no flesh whatever." See Sorrel, *Confederate Staff Officer*, 264.

62. Newsome, *Richmond Must Fall*, 213–14; Bearss, *Western Front Battles*, 118; Wiley, *Norfolk Blues*, 168; Axford, *Fielding's Diary*, 131; *OR Supp.*, 471; Harris, *Movements of the Confederate Army in Virginia*, 35; Evans, *16th Mississippi*, 291.

63. Newsome, Horn, and Selby, *Civil War Talks*, 310–11; E. N. Thurston to Mahone, Sept. 26, 1889, Mahone Family Papers, Library of Virginia, Richmond.

64. *OR*, 42(3):379, 42(1) 296, 303, 310, 609, 641, 648; Waitt, *19th Massachusetts*, 351; Tobie, *First Maine Cavalry*, 364; Holmes, *Horse Soldiers in Blue*, 187; Romig, *Phipps' Letters*, 75; Hand, *One Good Regiment*, 166; Styple, *Writing & Fighting from the Army of Northern Virginia*, 306; "Gen. James Dearing," 216.

65. *OR*, 42(1):949, 953; Longacre, *Gentleman and Soldier*, 218; Cisco, *Wade Hampton*, 145; Mesic, *Cobb's Legion Cavalry*, 145–47; Calhoun, *Liberty Dethroned*, 147; Hopkins, *Little Jeff*, 240–41; "Letter from Virginia," *Charleston (S.C.) Daily Courier*, Nov. 4, 1864; Wells, *Hampton and His Cavalry*, 333; Dick Beale to "Dear Mother," Oct. 29, 1864, Beale Family Papers, University of Virginia, Charlottesville; Gordon Diary, Oct. 27, 1864, Museum of the Confederacy, Richmond; Newsome, *Richmond Must Fall*, 218–19.

66. *OR*, 42(1):296, 319; Armstrong, *Nuggets of Experience*, 67; Newsome, *Richmond Must Fall*, 223. Captain Embler was acting chief of staff in Gibbon's division and fulfilled that function while Egan was in command. The time of this attack is uncertain. Egan placed it shortly after 11:30 A.M., while Willett had it at 2:00 P.M., which is certainly too late, as determined in context with other events.

67. *OR*, 42(1):346, 359, 367, 394; Weygant, *124th New York*, 381; Jordan, *Red Diamond Regiment*, 207; Floyd, *40th (Mozart) Regiment New York Volunteers*, 235; de Trobriand, *Four Years with the Army*, 661; Hamilton, "110th Pennsylvania," Union League of Philadelphia, 210; *History of the Fifty-Seventh Regiment Pennsylvania Veteran Volunteer Infantry*, 131–32; Carter, *Four Brothers in Blue*, 491; Van Santvoord, *One Hundred and Twentieth Regiment New York State Volunteers*, 156; Marbaker, *11th New Jersey*, 230.

68. *OR*, 42(3):380, 42(1):231, 296; Lowe, *Meade's Army*, 286; Humphreys, *Virginia Campaign of '64 and '65*, 298–99.

69. Badeau, *Military History of Ulysses S. Grant*, 3:120; de Trobriand, *Four Years with the Army*, 661; Rutan, *If I Have Got to Go and Fight*, 172; Theodore Lyman to "My honey-heart Cherry," Oct. 31, 1864, Lyman Letters, Massachusetts Historical Society; Shaw and House, *First Maine Heavy Artillery*, 148; Craft, *141st Pa*, 231; *OR*, 42(1):36, 231; Newsome, *Richmond Must Fall*, 223. Edwin C. Bearss argues that this modification in Union objectives was foreordained by the undersized force committed to the offensive. See Bearss, *Western Front Battles*, 122–23.

70. *OR*, 42(1):238–39.

71. Theodore Lyman to "My Dear Frank," Nov. 11, 1864, Lyman Letters, Massachusetts Historical Society; Theodore Lyman to "My honey-heart Cherry," Oct. 31, 1864, Lyman Letters; Rose Diary, Oct. 27, 1864, Library of Congress, Washington; Coco, *Through Blood and Fire*, 211; Lowe, *Meade's Army*, 286; Crotty, *Four Years Campaigning*, 159; Livermore, *Days and Events*, 402; *OR*, 42(1):36; Meade, *Life and Letters*, 237.

72. *OR*, 42(1):296, 303, 310, 319, 326, 427; "Campaign in Virginia," Nov. 5, 1864; Humphreys, *Virginia Campaign of '64 and '65*, 290; James C. Farwell, "Report of 1st Minn Battalion of the Battle of Boydton Plank Road," Nov. 15, 1864, Minnesota Historical Society, Saint Paul; Rodenbaugh, *Army of the United States*, 393; Alex Ward, "Employment of Artillery during the Battles of the Siege of Petersburg," Petersburg National Battlefield, 21–23; Cowtan, *Tenth New York*, 324–25; Roback, *152nd New York*, 128–29; Bruce, *Twentieth Massachusetts*, 426; Styple, *Writing & Fighting from the Army of Northern Virginia*, 306; James Dearing to "My darling precious wife," Oct. 29, 1864, Dearing Family Papers, Virginia Museum of History and Culture, Richmond; Newsome, *Richmond Must Fall*, 223–25, 389n83. It was widely reported that Dearing had been killed in this attack. See, for example, Moses Barker to "My Very Dear

Wife," Oct. 27, 1864, Moses Barker Letters, Library of Virginia, Richmond; and Jones, *Rebel War Clerk's Diary*, 317.

73. Theodore Lyman to "My honey-hearted Cherry," Oct. 31, 1864, Lyman Letters, Massachusetts Historical Society.

74. Porter, *Campaigning with Grant*, 310–11; Badeau, *Military History of Ulysses S. Grant*, 3:120–21; Livermore, *Days and Events*, 403; Lowe, *Meade's Army*, 286–87.

75. Badeau, *Military History of Ulysses S. Grant*, 3:121–22; *OR*, 42(1):232; Lowe, *Meade's Army*, 287; Paine Diary, Oct. 27, 1864; Newsome, *Richmond Must Fall*, 227. Perhaps Grant wished to avoid withdrawing Hancock in the presence of the enemy until Crawford arrived. Still, it is more difficult to explain Grant's thinking in this regard than it is his decision to cancel the offensive.

76. *OR*, 42(1):36, 437, 496.

77. *OR*, 42(1):496, 507, 525; Smith, *Twenty-Fourth Michigan*, 229; Aldridge, *No Freedom Shrieker*, 231; Reid-Green, *Letters from Home*, 98; Kieffer, *Recollections of a Drummer Boy*, 227. Kieffer's account also appeared as "An Incident at 'Hatcher's Run,'" *National Tribune*, Apr. 15, 1882.

78. *OR*, 42(1):496; Cooke, "Fifty-Fifth Regiment," 311.

79. *OR*, 42(1):438, 442, 496; Newsome, *Richmond Must Fall*, 234–35.

80. Newsome, Horn, and Selby, *Civil War Talks*, 311; *OR Supp.*, 481–82; Newsome, *Richmond Must Fall*, 239–40. To make the authorship of the attack plan even more contentious, Hampton claimed to have advised Heth "to attack by throwing a force across the dam at my works." *OR*, 42(1):953.

81. *OR Supp.*, 482; Newsome, *Richmond Must Fall*, 240–41. Neither Meade, Hancock, nor Warren anticipated Mahone's flank attack. Earl J. Hess asserts that Grant ordered Hancock to remain until the following morning, "hoping he might lure the Confederates into attacking across the open ground north of the run where Federal artillery could punish them." Hess, *Lee's Tar Heels*, 271. This explanation is plausible but speculative and unconvincing.

82. Robertson, *McAllister Letters*, 527; *OR*, 42(1):395; Newsome, *Richmond Must Fall*, 241–42.

83. *OR*, 42(1):232, 297, 326, 333, 346, 367; Cowtan, *Tenth New York*, 325; Gibbs, King, and Northrup, *Ninety-Third New York*, 84; Carter, *Four Brothers in Blue*, 491; Craft, *141st Pa*, 230.

84. Newsome, Horn, and Selby, *Civil War Talks*, 311–12; *OR Supp.*, 482; Lemuel J. Hoyle to "My Dear Mother," Nov. 5, 1864, Hoyle Papers, University of North Carolina, Chapel Hill. Mahone claimed that he suggested that Heth coordinate Dearing's attack with his own, causing the general to depart. The location of the dam is in question. Perhaps it spanned Hatcher's Run near where a postwar (and now abandoned) railroad crossed the stream.

85. Newsome, Horn, and Selby, *Civil War Talks*, 312–13; *OR Supp.*, 484; Robinson, "Fifty-Second Regiment," 250; Cowtan, *Tenth New York*, 325; "Gen. Weisiger's Reply to Gen. Mahone," unidentified newspaper clipping, 1880, Jedidiah C. Hotchkiss Papers, Manuscripts Division, Library of Congress, Washington; James Eldred Phillips Memoir, Phillips Papers, Virginia Museum of History and Culture, Richmond, 64–65. MacRae brought about 1,400 troops to the action, Weisiger and King about 1,000 each. See Newsome, *Richmond Must Fall*, 395n76. Mahone's battle line stretched for one-quarter mile. Francis Walker quotes Heth as saying that Mahone's strength was "probably not less than 4500; certainly not exceeding 5000," but this estimate is too high. Walker, "Expedition to the Boydton Plank Road," 335.

86. *OR*, 42(1):367–68, 374–75, 412; Craft, *141st Pa*, 231; *History of the Fifty-Seventh Regiment Pennsylvania Veteran Volunteer Infantry*, 132–33; Carter, *Four Brothers in Blue*, 492; Bloodgood, *Personal Reminiscences*, 297; Gibbs, King, and Northrup, *Ninety-Third New York*, 85; Scott, *105th Pennsylvania*, 122–23; Newsome, Horn, and Selby, *Civil War Talks*, 304; Chapman, *More Terrible Than Victory*, 258–59; Lemuel J. Hoyle to "My Dear Mother," Nov. 5, 1864, Hoyle Papers.

87. Haines, *Co. F 12th New Jersey*, 86; Newsome, *Richmond Must Fall*, 253–54; Chapman, *More Terrible Than Victory*, 259; Hess, *Lee's Tar Heels*, 273; Bearss, *Western Front Battles*, 136. Egan's three brigades and McAllister's brigade were to Mahone's north and west, and de Trobriand's brigade was to his south. Other Federals called the engagement "the Bull Ring Fight." See, for example, Hyndman, *History of a Cavalry Company*, 247.

88. *OR Supp.*, 471–72, 482–83; William Mahone to Nathaniel Harris, Sept. 16, 1889, Mahone Family Papers; Newsome, *Richmond Must Fall*, 254–55.

89. Calhoun, *Liberty Dethroned*, 148; Elmore, "Incidents of Service," 543; Cisco, *Wade Hampton*, 145; *OR*, 42(1):298, 949; Brooks, "War History," *Anderson (S.C.) Intelligencer*, Sept. 15, 1897; "Letter from Virginia," *Charleston (S.C.) Daily Courier*, Nov. 4, 1864; John N. Cummings to "My Dear Carrie," Oct. 29, 1864, John N. Cummings Letters, South Caroliniana Library, University of South Carolina, Columbia. The four units holding Rugg's position were the Sixty-Ninth Pennsylvania, Seventh Michigan, Nineteenth Massachusetts, and First Minnesota Battalion.

90. Andrew, *Wade Hampton*, 243–44; Zimmerman Davis, "A Cavalry Chronicle," *Anderson (S.C.) Intelligencer*, June 8, 1882; Taylor, "Battle of Burgess' Mill," 115–16; Wellman, *Giant in Gray*, 161; Wells, *Hampton and His Cavalry*, 335. R. E. Lee wrote a comforting note to General Hampton: "I grieve with you at the death of your gallant son—so young, so brave, so true. I know how much you must suffer. . . . He is now safe from all harm & all evil & nobly died in the defense of the rights of his country." Robert E. Lee to "My dear Genl," Oct. 29, 1865, Confederate Military Leaders Collection, Museum of the Confederacy, Richmond. Wade Hampton IV had joined his father's staff after departing the Army of Tennessee, where he had served on Gen. Joseph Johnston's staff until that officer was relieved in July.

91. *OR*, 42(1):234, 303, 395–96; Marbaker, *11th New Jersey*, 232; Robertson, *McAllister Letters*, 528; Van Santvoord, *One Hundred and Twentieth Regiment New York State Volunteers*, 156. The four regiments were the 120th New York, Eleventh Massachusetts, Eighth New Jersey, and Eleventh New Jersey.

92. Newsome, Horn, and Selby, *Civil War Talks*, 313; Stedman, "Forty-Fourth N.C. Infantry," 343; Lemuel J. Hoyle to "My Dear Mother," Nov. 5, 1864, Hoyle Papers.

93. Warner Papers, Wisconsin Historical Society, Madison; *OR*, 42(1):303, 316; Walker, "Expedition to the Boydton Plank Road," 337–38; Newsome, *Richmond Must Fall*, 262–63. Rugg's conviction would be overturned, but he would not return to the army.

94. *OR*, 42(1):359; Silliker, *Rebel Yell & the Yankee Hurrah*, 220; Newsome, *Richmond Must Fall*, 263.

95. *OR*, 42(1):359–60, 368; Houghton, *17th Maine*, 241; de Trobriand, *Four Years with the Army*, 662–63; Hamilton, "110th Pennsylvania," 211–12; Styple, *Our Noble Blood*, 165; Gaff, *On Many a Bloody Field*, 388; Carter, *Four Brothers in Blue*, 492; Roe and Nutt, *First Regiment of Massachusetts Heavy Artillery*, 193; Newsome, *Richmond Must Fall*, 400n54.

96. Lemuel J. Hoyle to "My Dear Mother," Nov. 5, 1864, Hoyle Papers; Lawing and Lawing, *My Dearest Friend*, 187; Stedman, "Forty-Fourth Regiment," 32; Hess, *Lee's Tar Heels*,

273–74; Newsome, Horn, and Selby, *Civil War Talks*, 314; Newsome, *Richmond Must Fall*, 268; *OR*, 42(1):234.

97. *OR*, 42(1):949; *OR Supp.*, 525; Willis Diary, Oct. 27, 1864, Library of Virginia, Richmond; Daughtry, *Gray Cavalier*, 226.

98. *OR*, 42(1):609, 629; Willis Diary, Oct. 27, 1864; Newsome, *Richmond Must Fall*, 270; Bearss, *Western Front Battles*, 146–47.

99. Merrill, *First Maine and First District of Columbia Cavalry*, 290; Hand, *One Good Regiment*, 168–69; Follmer, "Three Years in the Army," entry of Oct. 27, 1864, Central Michigan University, Mount Pleasant; *OR*, 42(1):609, 641, 648, 950; Newsome, *Richmond Must Fall*, 271; Bearss, *Western Front Battles*, 148.

100. *OR*, 42(3):325–26, 383; Mulholland, *116th Pennsylvania*, 288.

101. *OR*, 42(1):254, 906. Miles would claim privately that if he had another "division or strong brigade I could have taken Petersburg." Nelson Miles to "Dear Brother," Nov. 9, 1864, Miles Papers, Army Heritage and Education Center, Carlisle.

102. Mulholland, *116th Pennsylvania*, 288–91; Lewis Fairchild to "Dear Sophron," Oct. 30, 1864, Lewis Fairchild Letters, Gilder-Lehrman Collection, New-York Historical Society, New York; Pomfret, "Letters of Frederick Lockley," 100; Smith Reminiscences, Minnesota Historical Society, Saint Paul; Brightman, "Glory Enough," 144–49; Charles Baughman to "Dear Mother," Oct. 29, 1864, Baughman Family Papers, Virginia Museum of History and Culture, Richmond; *OR*, 42(1):906; Collins, *46th Virginia*, 65–66; Freeman, *Memoirs*, 45; William Russell Diary, Oct. 28, 1864, Rubenstein Special Collections Library, Duke University, Durham, N.C. The officers captured were Col. Randolph Harrison and Lt. Col. Peyton Wise.

103. Freeman, *Memoirs*, 45; *OR*, 42(1):906; L. Robert Moore to "Dear Ma," Oct. 28, 1864, L. Robert Moore Papers, Virginia Museum of History and Culture, Richmond; Mulholland, *116th Pennsylvania*, 290–91, 294–95.

104. *OR*, 42(1):254–55, 906, 933; Lt. Donald Fleming Diary, Oct. 27, 1864, Confederate Miscellaneous Collection (microfilm), Georgia State Archives, Morrow; Wiley, *Norfolk Blues*, 168; Drayton S. Pitts to "Dear Miss," Oct. 30, 1864, Drayton S. Pitts Letters, James I. Robertson Jr. Civil War Sesquicentennial Legacy Project, Library of Virginia, Richmond; John Buttrick Noyes to "Dear Charles," Oct. 28, 1864, Noyes Civil War Letters, Harvard University, Cambridge.

105. *OR*, 42(1):235–36, 42(3):381–82. One of Hancock's messengers, Major Bingham, was captured en route to army headquarters, although he escaped later that evening.

106. *OR*, 42(1):236, 609, 42(3):382.

107. De Trobriand, *Four Years with the Army*, 664–65; *OR*, 42(1):236; Robertson, *McAllister Letters*, 529–30.

108. Armstrong, *Nuggets of Experience*, 74; *OR*, 42(1):236, 298; de Trobriand, *Four Years with the Army*, 667–68; Newsome, *Richmond Must Fall*, 285–86.

109. *OR*, 42(1):439, 497, 507, 525; "Incident at Hatcher's Run"; Croner, *A Sergeant's Story*, 140; William L. Perry Diary, Oct. 28, 1864, Save the Flags Collection, Army Heritage and Education Center, Carlisle; Journal of the Petersburg Siege Operations, Oct. 28, 1864, Hunt Military Papers, Library of Congress, Washington. The Latin phrase translates "thus passes the glory of the world."

110. Stewart, *Pair of Blankets*, 184; Newsome, Horn, and Selby, *Civil War Talks*, 315–16; *OR Supp.*, 483–84; *OR*, 42(1):950.

111. Calhoun, *Liberty Dethroned*, 149; Elmore, "Incidents of Service," 593; Phillips Memoir, 65; Gallagher, *Fighting for the Confederacy*, 492; *OR*, 42(1):853–54.

112. Halliburton, *Saddle Soldiers*, 178–79; Smith, Smith, and Childs, *Mason Smith Family Letters*, 147; Willie Pegram to "My dear Mother," Oct. 28, 1864, Pegram-Johnston-McIntosh Family Papers, Virginia Museum of History and Culture, Richmond.

113. R. E. Lee to "General," Oct. 31, 1864, Lee Headquarters Papers, Virginia Museum of History and Culture, Richmond; Fitz William McMaster to "My Dear Wife," Oct. 31, 1864, McMaster Papers, University of South Carolina, Columbia; E. N. Thurston to William Mahone, Sept. 26, 1864, Mahone Family Papers.

114. "The Real Object and Complete Failure of Grant's Late Movement," *Richmond Whig*, Nov. 9, 1864; Styple, *Writing & Fighting the Confederate War*, 256–58. This estimate of Confederate casualties comes from careful calculation by Alfred Young and Bryce Suderow. My thanks to Mr. Suderow for sharing this research.

115. William A. Leonard to "Dear Parents," Nov. 1, 1864, William A. Leonard Papers, Special Collections, Carol M. Newman Library, Virginia Tech University, Blacksburg; Coco, *Through Blood and Fire*, 218–19; George W. Fox to "Dear Brother," Nov. 3, 1864, Civil War Letters of the Fox Brothers, Ohio State University E-History; Nevins, *Diary of Battle*, 478–79; *OR*, 42(3):373; William Hamilton to "Dear Mother," Nov. 1, 1864, William Hamilton Letters, Manuscripts Division, Library of Congress, Washington; Theodore Lyman to "My Love Minette," Oct. 28, 1864, Lyman Letters, Massachusetts Historical Society.

116. Crater Diary, Oct. 28, 1864, University of Iowa, Iowa City; Walker, *Second Army Corps*, 635–36; Hancock to "My dear Genl," Nov. 3, 1864, Francis C. Barlow Letters, Massachusetts Historical Society, Boston; Nevins, *Diary of Battle*, 478–79; *OR*, 42(3):402–3, 405.

117. Everstine, *Three Years in the Volunteer Army*, 92; Nelson Miles to "Dear Brother," Nov. 9, 1864, Miles Papers; Edw. B. to "My Dear Eckert," Oct. 30, 1864, George B. Eckert Correspondence, Albert and Shirley Small Special Collections Library, University of Virginia, Charlottesville; Simon, *Grant Papers*, 12:362; Alfred B. Thompson to "Sister Fanny," Oct. 30, 1864, Alfred B. Thompson Letters, Bailey-Howe Library, University of Vermont, Burlington.

118. *OR*, 42(1):153–60.

119. Harllee, *Kinfolks*, 607–8.

120. *New York Times*, Nov. 5, 1864; *OR*, 42(3):399; Sumner, *Comstock Diary*, 293; Theodore Lyman to "Love, Minette," Nov. 4, 1864, Lyman Letters, Massachusetts Historical Society; Wilson, *John A. Rawlins*, 270.

121. Dowdey and Manarin, *Wartime Papers of R. E. Lee*, 868. Lee obviously overstated Federal strength around Burgess Mill.

122. Francis Marion Coker to "My darling wife," Nov. 4, 1864, Coker Papers, University of Georgia, Athens.

BIBLIOGRAPHY

MANUSCRIPTS AND ARCHIVAL SOURCES

Albany, N.Y.
    Manuscripts and Special Collections, New York State Library
        Waters Whipple Braman Letters
        Uberto A. Burnham Papers
        Civil War Letters Collection
        Paul Fay Letters
        William H. Gilder Letters
        Charles Hamlin Letters
        John L. Houck Papers
        Samuel B. Pierce Letters
        Jacob M. Roberts Letters
        Gouverneur K. Warren Papers
Alexandria, Va.
    Alexandria Public Library
        Allen W. Robbins, ed., "The American Civil War Letters of
            William and Charles McKnight"
    The Lloyd House
        John R. Zimmerman Diary
Ann Arbor, Mich.
    Bentley Historical Library, University of Michigan
        William Boston Diary and Letters
        Byron M. Cutcheon Autobiography
        Ferdinand Davis Reminiscences
        Eddy Family Papers
        James and Sybil Irwin Family Papers
        David Smalley Munroe Papers
        David Walbridge Kendall Papers
        King Family Papers
        Charles Mead Correspondence
        Elmer D. Wallace Papers
    Clements Library, University of Michigan
        James S. Schoff Civil War Collection

George Tobey Anthony Letters
Isaac O. Best, "The Siege and Capture of Petersburg"
John A. Bodamer Diary
Simeon Gallup Letters
Samuel Ferguson Jayne Papers
Henry Grimes Marshall Letters
Hilton A. Parker Letters
Henry Pippitt Letters
Samuel Ripley Papers
Nathan Webb Diary

Athens, Ga.
Hargrett Rare Book and Manuscripts Library, University of Georgia
Franklin M. Fleming Letters
Gurr Family Papers
Francis Hodgson Heidler Collection
Capt. Francis Marion Coker Papers
Hood Family Papers
Jordan-Burnett Papers

Atlanta, Ga.
Kenan Research Center, Atlanta History Center
William Burke Papers
George Johnston Diary
Philip McKay Papers
Woodruff Library, Emory University
Confederate Miscellaneous Collection
Joseph Hilton Letters
Benjamin Wesley Justice Letters
John Lafayette Oxford Diary
Bell Wiley Collection
Henry J. Ellis Letter

Auburn, Ala.
Special Collections, Auburn University
William E. Endicott Papers
James Henry Lane Papers
Emily Smith York Papers and Diary
Hugh Denson Diary

Augusta, Maine
Maine State Archives
Nathan S. Clark Diary

Austin, Tex.
Briscoe Center for American History, University of Texas
I[saac] F. Caveness Diary
Martin L. Crimmins Collection
Edward Richardson Crockett Diary and Papers, 1864–65
James J. Kirkpatrick Diary
Thomas L. McCarty Diary and Papers

Baltimore, Md.
> Maryland Historical Society
>> Hugh Lennox Bond Collection
>> McCullough Family Papers

Barre, Vt.
> Vermont Historical Society
>> Valentine Barney Papers
>> Barton Family Papers
>> Charles Cummings Papers

Blacksburg, Va.
> Special Collections, Carol M. Newman Library, Virginia Tech University
>> Benjamin F. Butler Notebook
>> William A. Leonard Papers
>> Daniel A. Lowber Diary
>> Benjamin M. Peck Diary

Boston, Mass.
> Boston University
>> Papers of the Military Historical Society of Massachusetts
>>> Theodore Lyman Letters
> Massachusetts Historical Society
>> Francis C. Barlow Letters
>> George Middleton Barnard Papers
>> Charles Bolton Papers
>> Nathan Hayward Letters
>> Andrew R. Linscott Papers
>> Lyman Family Papers
>> Theodore Lyman Letters
>> John J. Owen Jr. Papers
>> Alonzo G. Rich Letters
>> Frank L. Smith Letters
>> William Stowell Tilton Diary
>> Frederick Winthrop Papers

Burlington, Vt.
> Bailey-Howe Library, University of Vermont
>> Cargill Family Papers
>> Alfred B. Thompson Letters

Cambridge, Mass.
> Houghton Library, Harvard University
>> John Buttrick Noyes Civil War Letters
>> Frederick Dearborn Collection
>>> Robert E. Lee to Charles Field, August 17, 1864
>> MOLLUS of Massachusetts Civil War Collection
>> Daniel Eldredge Manuscript Notebook

Carlisle, Pa.
> Army Heritage and Education Center
>> Joseph Barlow Papers

David B. Birney Papers
Ronald Boyer Collection
    Henry F. Charles Civil War Record
    John D. Timmerman Papers
Hattie Burleigh Papers
Solon Carter Letters, 1862–65
Civil War Documents Collection
    Isaac McQueen Auld Papers
    Thomas Gray Bennett Papers
    Bayard Taylor Cooper Papers
    Joseph H. Harper Diary
    Henry S. Joy Papers
    Austin Kendall Papers
    Harrison Montague Letters
    Harrison Nesbitt Letters
    Samuel H. Root Diary
    Theodore W. Skinner Letters
Civil War Times Illustrated Collection
    Nicholas De Graff Memoir and Diary
    Albert A. Pope Diary
    Joseph J. Scroggs Diary
    John W. Stott Diary
Thomas Clemens Collection
    Samuel Z. Ammen, "Maryland Troops in the Confederate Army"
James Parley Coburn Letters, 1862–65
Gregory Coco Collection
    A. H. Sanger Papers
George Hopper Letters
Lewis Leigh Collection
    Elias S. Buterbaugh Letters
    Capt. Charles W. Smith Letters
    William F. Smith Letters
    Charles F. Stinson Letters
    Capt. Ansell L. White Letters
Jay Luvaas Collection
    Steve Clark Papers
George Meade Papers
Nelson A. Miles Papers
John R. Mitchell Diary
Save the Flags Collection
    William L. Perry Diary
Robert E. Simms Diary
Bill Weidner Papers
Eiserman (Private) Collection
    Robert E. Fitzgerald Diary
    Samuel Watson Letters

Chapel Hill, N.C.
    Louis Round Wilson Library, University of North Carolina
        Southern Historical Collection
            E. Porter Alexander Papers
            William D. Alexander Diary
            Alexander-Hillhouse Family Papers
            Charles Haynes Andrews Papers
            Blanche Baker Papers
            Rufus Barringer Papers
            Bryan Family Papers
            Edmund Studwick Burwell Papers
            Benjamin Simms Fitzgerald Diary
            Alexander C. Haskell Papers
            Wiley C. Howard, *Sketch of Cobb Legion Cavalry and Some Incidents and Scenes Remembered* (1901) (Suffolk, Va.: N.p, 1986)
            Lemuel J. Hoyle Papers
            Jones Family Papers
            Mary Hunter Kennedy Papers
            Julius Leinbach Papers and Diary
            Lenoir Family Papers
            Jacob Lyons Diary
            Harriet R. McIntosh Papers
            Mordecai Family Papers
            Julius Frederic Ramsdell Papers
            John Alexander Sloan, "A North Carolinian in the War between the States"
            Ruffin Thomson Papers
            Westwood Todd, "Reminiscences of the War between the States, April 1861–July 1865"
            Lt. Col. Joseph Frederick Waring Diary
            Henry Duplessis Wells Papers
            Edmund Jones Williams Papers
            Lucy Tunstall Alston Williams Papers
            William Henry Wills Papers
Charleston, S.C.
    Charleston Library Society
        William G. Hinson Diary
    College of Charleston
        Kelly Papers
    South Carolina Historical Society
        Charles Kline Civil War Letters
        Hall T. McGee Diary
        George H. Moffett Family Papers
Charlottesville, Va.
    Albert and Shirley Small Special Collections Library, University of Virginia
        Beale Family Papers
        George Bernard Diary

Fannie B. Tompkins Childress Papers
John Warwick Daniel Papers
David F. Dobie Papers
George B. Eckert Correspondence
John Cowper Granbery Letters
B. H. Hibbard Letters
John Calvin Metcalf Papers
Samuel H. Putnam Letters
Luther N. Ralls Letters
Rawlings Family Papers
Thomas L. Rosser Papers

Cincinnati, Ohio
    Cincinnati Historical Society
        Roger Hannaford Papers
Cleveland, Ohio
    Western Reserve Historical Society
        Wells A. Bushnell Memoir
        Alcinus Ward Fenton Papers
        William Foster Papers
        Zerah Coston Monks Family Papers
        William Palmer Civil War Collection
            Henry Bingham, "Memoirs of General Hancock"
            John P. Brogan, "The Beginning of the End"
Columbia, S.C.
    South Caroliniana Library, University of South Carolina
        Anderson Family Papers
        Alice Boozer Letters
        John Kennedy Coleman Diary
        Henry Calvin Conner Papers
        John N. Cummings Letters
        Samuel Lewis Dorroh Papers
        James R. Hagood, "Memoirs of the First SC Regiment of Volunteers
                in the Confederate War for Independence,
                from 12 April 1861 to 10 April 1865"
        Hampton Family Papers
            Wade Hampton Connected Narrative
        William Godber Hinson Papers
        McLure Family Papers
        Fitz William McMaster Papers
        Samuel Wickliffe Melton Papers
        Parker Family Papers
        Louis Sherfesse Memoir
        Templeton Family Papers
        Robert A. Turner Diary
Concord, N.H.
    New Hampshire Historical Society

Duncan-Jones Correspondence
Daniel Eldredge Journal
Josiah Jones Diary
Albert B. Stearns Papers
George Stearns Papers
George F. Towle Diary

Corsicana, Tex.

Pearce Civil War Collection, Navarro College
Edward Brooks Diary
William Coleman Letters
Charles F. Stinson Letter

Denver, Colo.

Denver Public Library
Robert Gordon Dill, "Personal Reminiscences of the War of the Rebellion"

Detroit, Mich.

Detroit Public Library
Charles M. Burton Historical Collection
Divie Bethune Duffield Papers

Dover, Del.

Delaware Public Archives
Charles E. LaMotte Letters
Thomas A. Smyth Diaries

Durham, N.H.

University of New Hampshire
George Naylor Julian Papers
Parsons Family Papers

Durham, N.C.

Rubenstein Special Collections Library, Duke University
C. Tacitus Allen Memoirs
Bedinger and Dandridge Family Papers
Samuel Simpson Biddle Letters
Ignatius Wadsworth Brock Letter
Catherine Buie Letters
Confederate Veteran Collection
William A. Curtis, "Reminiscences of the War"
Dentzer Family Papers
John B. Foote Papers
Griswold Family Papers
Caleb Hampton Papers
David Bullock Harris Papers
Joseph N. Haynes Papers
Libbey Papers
James Otis Moore Letters
William H. Noble Papers
"Report of Capt. P. W. Stanhope, 12th U.S. Infantry," August 24, 1864
William Russell Diary (typescript)

Joachim Saussy Papers
Walter Wallace Smith Papers
John Lane Stuart Papers
Julius A. Summers Letters
Josiah Trent Collection
 Maj. Charles K. Winne, "A Medical Inspector's Journal of the
 Wilderness Campaign and the End of the Civil War"
John R. Turner Papers
Eugene and James Verdery Letters
George Warthen Letters
James King Wilkerson Papers
Simon P. Wingard Letters
East Lansing, Mich.
 Michigan State University
 Marsh Family Papers
Fredericksburg, Va.
 Fredericksburg & Spotsylvania National Military Park
 Alfred A. Apted Diary, Bound Volume 195
 George D. Bowen Diary, Bound Volume 228
 Elisha Clark Letter, Bound Volume 209
 George W. Flack Diary, Bound Volume 260
 The Grant Family of Lyme Civil War Letters, Bound Volume 401
 Edmond A. Hatcher Letter, Bound Volume 292
 S[hedrick] J. Jackson Diary, Bound Volume 231
 John Daniel McDonnell, "Recollections," Bound Volume 113
 L[eander] O. Merriam, "Personal Recollections of the War
 for the Union," Bound Volume 190
 Alexander S. Patten Diary, Bound Volume 94
 Alfred M. Scales Letters, Bound Volume 15-01
 Martin Sigman Memoirs, Bound Volume 320
 Jesse R. Sparkman Diary, Bound Volume 373
 John Vautier Diary, Bound Volume 371
 Thomas F. Walter Memoir, Bound Volume 420
 George C. Walters Diary and Letters, Bound Volume 261
 Samuel E. Wilson Letter, Bound Volume 210
Freehold, N.J.
 Monmouth County Historical Association Library and Archives
 William T. Ackerson Papers
Gettysburg, Pa.
 Gettysburg National Military Park
 Jacob Bechtel Letters
Gowanda, N.Y.
 Gowanda Area Historical Society
 Henry D. Didcock Letters
Greenville, N.C.
 East Carolina University
 Francis W. Knowles Journal and Diary

            Alfred Moore Scales Papers
            William Henry von Eberstein Papers
Greenwich, Conn.
        William E. Finch Jr. Archives, Greenwich Historical Society
            Silas Edward Mead Papers
Guilford, Conn.
        Guilford Free Public Library
            Diary of Lt. Joshua H. Dearborn
Hanover, N.H.
        Rauner Library, Dartmouth College
            Elmer Bragg Letters and Diary
            Luigi Palma di Cesnola Papers
            Oscar D. Robinson Papers
            Ransom F. Sargent Civil War Papers
Harrisburg, Pa.
        Pennsylvania State Archives
            James A. Beaver Collection
            General Richard Coulter Papers
            Samuel P. Glass Collection
            Daniel S. Hopkins Reminiscences
            Daniel Musser Collection
Hartford, Conn.
        Connecticut Historical Society
            Henry H. Brown Papers
            Henry Snow Letters
            Alfred Howe Terry Papers
Hillsboro, Tex.
        Historical Research Center, Texas Heritage Museum, Hill College
            Basil Crow Brashear Memoir
            Joe Joskins [Robert Campbell], "A Sketch of Hood's Texas
                    Brigade of the Virginia Army"
            Capt. Watson D. Williams Papers
Houston, Tex.
        John L. Nau III Civil War Collection (now housed at the University
                of Virginia)
            Fisher A. Cleaveland Letter
            Henry C. Metzger Letters and Diary
Indianapolis, Ind.
        Indiana State Library, Indiana Division
            Erasmus C. Gilbreath Reminiscences
Iowa City, Iowa
        Special Collections, University of Iowa
            Lewis Crater Diary
Ithaca, N.Y.
        Cornell University
            Gail and Stephen Rudin Civil War Collection, 1861–65
                Henry H. B. Chamberlain Papers

Jackson, Miss.
    Mississippi Department of Archives and History
        Pvt. William Henry Bachman Memoir
        A. L. P. Vairin Diary
Kalamazoo, Mich.
    Western Michigan University
        Norton Pearl Collection
            Henry S. Graves Letters
Lansing, Mich.
    Michigan History Center
        Erwin Welsh Collection
Lexington, Va.
    Washington and Lee University
        William Alexander Gordon Memoirs
Litchfield, Conn.
    Litchfield Historical Society
        Plumb Family Correspondence
Madison, Wis.
    Wisconsin Historical Society
        Edward S. Bragg Letters
        David Coon Civil War Letters
        William Lamont Letters
        George J. and Edwin B. Paddock Letters, 1861–65
        Clement E. Warner Papers
        Benjamin Wright Papers
Middleton, Conn.
    Special Collections and Archives, Wesleyan University
        Alfred S. Roe Papers
Montgomery, Ala.
    Alabama Department of Archives and History
        Archibald Gracie Papers
        Hall Family Papers
        Rufus Hollis, "Confederate Veteran," *Scottsboro Citizen*
        Joseph Reid Journal
        Willian Henry Sanders Papers
Morrow, Ga.
    Georgia State Archives
        Augustus Avant Papers
        "Confederate Letters Written by Mr. Lee Barfield of Dooly
            County, Georgia, 1861–1865"
        Confederate Miscellaneous Collection (microfilm)
            John W. Lokey, "My Experience in the War between the States"
            Lt. Donald Fleming Diary
            Pvt. William H. Smith Diary
        William J. Mosely Collection

J. A. Shank Collection
United Daughters of the Confederacy Collection
Washington L. Dunn Diary
Ezekiel D. Graham Letters (typescript)
John L. G. Wood Letter
Gilbert J. Wright Letters
Mount Pleasant, Mich.
Clarke Historical Library, Central Michigan University
Lafayette and Nathan Church Letters
Civil War Collection of Personal Papers
John Daniel Follmer, "Three Years in the Army"
William H. Richmond Reminiscence
Nashville, Tenn.
Tennessee State Library and Archives
James Beard Letters
Capt. William Henry Harder Memoir
Lt. Col. Theodore G. Trimmier Collection
John Thomas Vassey Letters
New Brunswick, N.J.
Archibald Alexander Library, Rutgers University
Roebling Family Papers
New Haven, Conn.
Sterling Library, Yale University
Capt. Charles M. Coit Papers
Charles G. Merrill Papers
New Orleans, La.
Special Collections, Tulane University
Louisiana Historical Association Collection
Pvt. Frank Lobrano Diary
New York, N.Y.
New-York Historical Society
Civil War Letters Collection
R. E. Lee to R. H. Anderson
David Cronin to A. J. Wall, May 5, 1925
Gilder-Lehrman Collection
Capt. Charles M. Coit Letters
Orville S. Dewey Letters
Lewis Fairchild Letters
Thomas J. Kessler Letters
Andrew Knox Letters
Lyman Bell Sperry Diary
George Tillotson Letters
William Woodlin Diary
New York Public Library
Griswold Family Letters, 1862–79

Oberlin, Ohio
    Oberlin College Archives
        Elliott F. Grabill Papers
Orono, Maine
    Special Collections Department, Raymond H. Folger Library, University of Maine
        Paul Bean Collection
            John W. Haley Diary
            Fred E. Townsend, "History and Reminiscences of
                the 17th Maine Volunteer Infantry"
Oshkosh, Wis.
    University of Wisconsin at Oshkosh
        Reverend Edward H. and Ada Clark Merrell Correspondence
Palo Alto, Calif.
    C. H. Green Library, Stanford University
        Edward Otho Cresap Ord Letters
Petersburg, Va.
    Petersburg Museums Collection
        Fletcher Archer Letters
    Petersburg National Battlefield
        George Barnum Letters
        Edwin C. Bearss "General Hagood Meets Captain Dailey: Petersburg
            National Battlefield Background to Event Depicted"
        Addison S. Boyce Letters
        Augustus A. Dean, "Recollections of Army Life during the Civil War 1861–1865"
        George C. Hand Diary
        A[lonzo] D. Lewis Letter
        William Mahone Letter
        James Mitchell Letters
        William E. Potter Letters
        William M. Read Letters and Diary
        "Reams Station Cultural Landscape Study" (draft), January 29, 1999
        Rees Family Letters
        Sanderson-Talmage Letters
        "Union Officers Lost at Battle of Peebles Farm"
        Alex Ward, "Employment of Artillery during the Battles
            of the Siege of Petersburg"
    Richard Bland College
        William D. Henderson, "Civil War Petersburg: A Statistical View"
Philadelphia, Pa.
    Historical Society of Pennsylvania
        James Cornell Biddle Letters
        Chaplain Robert Dickson Diary
        John Daniel Follmer Diary
        John Gibbon Papers
        Andrew A. Humphreys Papers
        Charles McKnight Diary

George Meade Collection
Nathaniel Michler Map
John L. Smith Letters, 1864
Union League of Philadelphia
James C. Hamilton,
"History of the 110th Pennsylvania"
Francis A. Walker Papers
Pittsburgh, Pa.
Senator John Heinz History Center
Daniel McClure Fair Papers
George P. McClelland Papers
Pottsville, Pa.
Schuylkill County Historical Society
Elbert Corbin Diary
Poughkeepsie, N.Y.
Adriance Memorial Library
Robert Nelson Verplanck Letters
Princeton, N.J.
Firestone Library Special Collections, Princeton University
Civil War Letters of Adam Badeau
Providence, R.I.
John Hay Library, Brown University
Warren S. Gurney Papers
Rhode Island Historical Society
Gilbert Family Papers
Raleigh, N.C.
State Archives of North Carolina
Henry C. Brown Papers
Fred C. Foard Papers
Samuel Finley Harper Letters
Evelyn McIntosh Hyatt Collection
G[arland] S. Ferguson Letter
Robert C. Mabry Papers
Military Collection
"Incidents of Gallantry, Men of Lane's Brigade"
Benjamin H. Sims Journal
Thomas Strayhorn Letter (extract)
John Wright Family Papers
Richmond, Va.
Library of Virginia
George Emerson Albee Diary
John T. Andrews Letters
Moses Barker Letters
W. W. Blackford, "Memoirs: First and Last Battles in Virginia"
Bryant Family Papers
George Phillip Clark Diary

Samuel Fessenden Letters

Thomas J. Gregg Letter

George S. Hupman Letters

T. W. G. Inglet Letters

Mahone Family Papers

Ely S. Parker Letter

James I. Robertson Jr. Civil War Sesquicentennial Legacy Project

    Edgar Ashton Letters

    Henry C. DeShields Letters

    Drayton S. Pitts Letters

    John Rison Letter

Charles Lewis Rundlett Letters

John F. Sale Papers and Diaries

Imri Spencer Letters

Byrd C. Willis Diary

Eleanor S. Brockenbrough Library, Museum of the Confederacy (now housed at
        the Virginia Museum and Natural History and Culture)

    Confederate Military Leaders Collection

        Joseph R. Davis Letter

        R. E. Lee Letter

    Ethelbert Fairfax Letters

    John W. Gordon Diary

    Henry Heth Papers

    Linden Kent Letter

    William Andrew Mauney Diary

    Joseph Mullen Diary

    Rosser S. Rock Letters

Richmond National Battlefield Park

    Samuel Armstrong Letter, Bound Volume 112

    Dr. Oze Robert Broyles Letter, Bound Volume 88

    Clifford Dickinson, "Union and Confederate Engineering Operations at
        Chaffin's Bluff/Chaffin's Farm, June 1862–April 3, 1865"

    William J. Glackens Letter, Bound Volume 85

    Augustus C. Golding Diary, Bound Volume 48

    Capt. John W. Haseltine Diary, Bound Volume 146

    John Francis Methvin Memoir, Bound Volume 91

    Lt. Frank M. Riley Diary, Bound Volume 97

    William H. Smith Diary, Bound Volume 15

    Richard Cornelius Taylor, "Personal Experiences of Major
        Richard Taylor," Bound Volume 51

Virginia Museum of History and Culture

    Orrin Sweet Allen Letters

    Baughman Family Papers

    Bird Family Papers

    Giles Buckner Cooke Diary

Dearing Family Papers
Joseph William Eggleston Autobiography
Thomas Claybrook Elder Papers
George Freaner Letter
Louella Pauline Gary, "Biography of General Martin Witherspoon Gary"
Charles August Henninghausen Papers
Paul M. Higginbotham Papers
James McHenry Howard, "Biographical Sketch of Walter H. Stevens"
Samuel R. Johnston Papers
Osmun Latrobe Diary
Lee Family Papers
R. E. Lee Headquarters Papers
William Henry Lewin Papers
Joseph Banks Lyle Diary
John Marshall Martin Papers
John Kirkwood Mitchell Papers
L. Robert Moore Papers
Robert Powel Page Papers
Charles Jackson Paine Papers
Pegram-Johnston-McIntosh Family Papers
James Thomas Petty Diary
James Eldred Phillips Papers
Roller Family Papers
        Journal of Charles Norborne Berkeley Minor
Ruffin Family Papers
Saunders Family Papers
Smith Family Papers
Robert Knox Sneden Memoir
Alvin C. Voris Letters
Cadmus Marcellus Wilcox Papers
Wise Family Papers

Saint Paul, Minn.
Minnesota Historical Society
James C. Farwell, "Report of 1st Minn Battalion, of the Battle of
        Boydton Plank Road," November 15, 1864
William Watts Folwell Diary and Correspondence
George B. Smith Reminiscences, 1864–65

Salem, Mass.
Phillips Library, Peabody-Essex Museum
Herbert Valentine Papers

San Marino, Calif.
Henry E. Huntington Library
William Henry Hagar Letters
Charles Lee Diary
Frederick Lockley Papers

Harvey A. Marckres Letters

Joseph H. Rogers Diary

Charles Wainwright Diary

Saratoga Springs, N.Y.

New York State Military History Museum

James M. Nichols Diary

Corydon O. Warner Collection

South Bend, Ind.

Hesburgh Library, University of Notre Dame

Barrier Family Letters

Benton-Beach Family Correspondence

Otis Bosworth Diary

O. A. Brownson Papers

Alfred Moore Diary

Peed Family Letters

Joseph H. Prime Papers

Springfield, Ill.

Abraham Lincoln Presidential Library

Ransom Bedell Letters

August V. Kautz Papers

William H. Paine Diary

Stephen Rogers Letters

William R. Rowley Papers

Starkville, Miss.

Mitchell Memorial Library, Mississippi State University

Beachum Family Papers

State College, Pa.

Eberly Family Special Collections Library, Penn State University

Mary Gyla McDowell Collection

Hamilton R. Dunlap Diary and Letters

Diary of Sgt. George L. Preston

Diary of Doctor Silas Stevenson

Tuscaloosa, Ala.

University of Alabama

John C. C. Sanders Papers

Walden, Tenn.

Author's Collection

Richard Sommers Papers

Thomas A. McParlin Papers

Howard L. Prince, "Peebles Farm"

Washington, D.C.

Manuscripts Division, Library of Congress

P. G. T. Beauregard Papers

John Milton Binckley Papers

William Orland Bourne Papers

Memoir of John F. Huntingdon
Benjamin F. Butler Papers
Joshua Chamberlain Papers
    "Extracts from the Journal of Col. Robert Hayes"
William Conant Church Papers
John Covode Papers
Douglas Southall Freeman Papers
    Charles J. Calrow, "Fort Harrison. A Study," 1932
David M. Gregg Papers
William Hamilton Letters, 1864–65
Cpl. John William Ford Hatton Memoir
Joseph Hawley Correspondence and Papers
Henry Clay Heisler Papers
Jedidiah C. Hotchkiss Papers
Henry Hunt Military Papers
August V. Kautz Papers
Marsena Patrick Diary
Tilton C. Reynolds Papers
Luther A. Rose Diary
Philip H. Sheridan Papers
Gilbert Thompson Memoir
Dennis Tuttle Correspondence
James H. Wilson Collection
National Archives and Records Service
    Telegrams Received by the Confederate Secretary of War, Microcopy M618
    War Department Collection of Confederate Records,
        Record Group 109, Microfilm M935
Bryce Suderow Private Collection
    Alonzo West Diary
West Point, N.Y.
U.S. Military Academy
    Regis de Trobriand Diary
Williamsburg, Va.
Earl Gregg Swem Library, College of William and Mary
    Bowles Family Papers
Wilmington, Del.
Delaware Historical Society
    Henry Gawthrop Letters and Diary
Winston-Salem, N.C.
Moravian Music Foundation
    J. Edward Peterson Papers
Worcester, Mass.
American Antiquarian Society
    Joseph Cross Civil War Letters
    William W. Willoughby Diary

Acken, J. Gregory, ed. *Blue-Blooded Cavalryman: Captain William Brooke Rawle in the Army of the Potomac, May 1863–August 1865*. Kent, Ohio: Kent State University Press, 2019.

Agassiz, George R., ed. *Meade's Headquarters, 1863–1865: Letters of Colonel Theodore Lyman from the Wilderness to Appomattox*. Boston: Atlantic Monthly Press, 1922.

Alderson, Kevin, and Patsy Alderson, eds. *Letters Home to Sarah: The Civil War Letters of Guy C. Taylor, Thirty-Sixth Wisconsin Volunteers*. Madison: University of Wisconsin Press, 2011.

Aldridge, Katherine M., ed. *No Freedom Shrieker: The Civil War Letters of Union Soldier Charles Biddlecom*. Ithaca, N.Y.: Paramount Marketing, 2012.

Andrews, Andrew Jackson. *A Sketch of the Boyhood Days of Andrew Jackson Andrews*. Richmond, Va.: Hermitage, 1905.

Arden, Linda Foster, ed. *Letters from the Storm: The Intimate Civil War Letters of Lt. J. A. H. Foster, 155th Pennsylvania Volunteers*. Chicora, Pa.: Firefly, 2010.

Armstrong, Nelson. *Nuggets of Experience*. San Bernadino, Calif.: Times-Mirror, 1904.

Axford, Faye Axton, ed. *William Eppa Fielding's Diary, 9th Alabama. "To Lochaber Na Mair": Southerners View the Civil War*. Athens, Ala.: Athens Publishing, 1987.

Badeau, Adam. *Military History of Ulysses S. Grant, from April 1861, to April, 1865*. Vols. 2–3. New York: D. Appleton, 1881.

Baker, Joel B. *Letters Home*. Delevan, N.Y.: N.p., 1996.

Barnard, Sandy, ed. *Campaigning with the Irish Brigade*. Terre Haute, Ind.: AST, 2001.

Basler, Roy P., ed. *The Collected Works of Abraham Lincoln*. Vols. 7–8. New Brunswick, N.J.: Rutgers University Press, 1953.

Baylor, George. *Bull Run to Bull Run: Four Years in the Army of Northern Virginia*. Richmond, Va.: H. F. Johnson, 1900.

Beale, George William. *A Lieutenant of Cavalry in Lee's Army*. Boston: Gorham, 1918.

Beaudot, William J. K., and Lance J. Herdegen, eds. *An Irishman in the Iron Brigade: The Civil War Memoirs of James P. Sullivan, 6th Wis. Volunteers*. New York: Fordham University Press, 1993.

Beaudry, Richard E., ed. *War Journals of Louis N. Beaudry, Fifth New York Cavalry*. Jefferson, N.C.: McFarland, 1996.

Beyer, Walter F., and Oscar F. Keydel, eds. *Deeds of Valor: How American Heroes Won the Medal of Honor*. Vol. 1. Detroit: Perrien Keydel, 1901.

Birney, William. *General William Birney's Answer to Libels Clandestinely Circulated by James Shaw, Jr*. Washington, D.C., 1878.

Blackett, R. J. M., ed. *Thomas Morris Chester: Black Civil War Correspondent*. Baton Rouge: Louisiana State University Press, 1989.

Blackford, Susan Leigh, comp. *Letters from Lee's Army: Memoirs of Life in and out of the Army in Virginia during the War between the States*. New York: Charles Scribner's Sons, 1947.

Blackford, W. W. *War Years with Jeb Stuart*. New York: Charles Scribner's Sons, 1945.

Blesser, Carol, ed. *The Hammonds of Redcliffe*. New York: Oxford University Press, 1981.

Bloodgood, John D. *Personal Reminiscences of the War*. New York: Hunt & Eaton, 1893.

Botkin, B. A., ed. *A Civil War Treasury of Tales, Legends, and Folklore*. New York: Random House, 1960.

Bouton, John Bell. *A Memoir of General Louis Bell*. New York: Privately printed, 1865.

Brooks, Ulysses R. *Butler and His Cavalry in the War of Secession*. Columbia, S.C.: State Company, 1909.

Buckingham, Peter, ed., *All's for the Best: The Civil War Reminiscences and Letters of Daniel W. Sawtelle*. Knoxville: University of Tennessee Press, 2001.

Buell, Augustus C. *The Cannoneer: Recollections of Service in the Army of the Potomac*. Washington, D.C.: National Tribune, 1890.

Burkhardt, George S., ed. *Double Duty in the Civil War: The Letters of Sailor and Soldier Edward W. Bacon*. Carbondale: Southern Illinois University Press, 2009.

Butler, Benjamin F. *Butler's Book*. Boston: A. M. Thayer, 1892.

Calhoun, Charles M. *Liberty Dethroned*. Greenwood, S.C., 1903.

Califf, Joseph C. *To the Ex-Members and Friends of the 7th U.S.C.T.* Fort Hamilton, N.Y., 1878.

Campbell, Eric A., ed. *"A Grand Terrible Dramma," from Gettysburg to Petersburg: The Civil War Letters of Charles Wellington Reed*. New York: Fordham University Press, 2000.

Carter, John C., ed. *Welcome the Hour of Conflict: William Cowan McClellan and the 9th Alabama*. Tuscaloosa: University of Alabama Press, 2007.

Carter, Robert Goldthwaite. *Four Brothers in Blue; or, Sunshine and Shadows of the War of the Rebellion: A Story of the Great Civil War from Bull Run to Appomattox*. Austin: University of Texas Press, 1978.

Cassedy, Edward K., ed. *Dear Friends at Home: The Civil War Letters and Diary of Sergeant Charles T. Bowen, Twelfth United States Infantry, 1861–1864*. Baltimore: Butternut & Blue, 2001.

Cauthen, Charles E., ed. *Family Letters of the Three Wade Hamptons, 1872–1901*. Columbia: University of South Carolina Press, 1953.

Chesson, Michael B., ed. *The Journal of a Civil War Surgeon*. Lincoln: University of Nebraska Press, 2003.

Child, Dr. William. *Letters from a Civil War Surgeon*. Solon, Maine: Polar Bear & Co., 2001.

Clark, George. *A Glance Backward*. Houston: Press of Rein & Sons, 1914.

Cockrell, Monroe F., ed. *Gunner with Stonewall: Reminiscences of William Thomas Poague*. Wilmington, N.C.: Broadfoot, 1987.

Cockrell, Thomas D., and Michael B. Ballard, eds. *A Mississippi Rebel in the Army of Northern Virginia: The Civil War Memoirs of Private David Holt*. Baton Rouge: Louisiana State University Press, 1995.

Coco, Gregory A., ed. *Through Blood and Fire: The Civil War Letters of Major Charles J. Mills, 1862–1865*. Gettysburg, Pa.: By the author, 1982.

Coffin, Charles C. *Freedom Triumphant: The Fourth Period of the War of the Rebellion from September, 1864 to Its Close*. New York: Harper & Brothers, 1891.

Cole, Jean Lee, ed. *Freedom's Witness: The Civil War Correspondence of Henry McNeal Turner*. Morgantown: West Virginia University Press, 2013.

Conner, James. *Letters of General James Conner, CSA*. Columbia, S.C.: R. L. Bryan, 1933.

Copp, Elbridge J. *Reminiscences of the War of the Rebellion*. Nashua, N.H.: Telegraph, 1911.

Corbin, Richard Washington. *Letters of a Confederate Officer to His Family in Europe during the Last Year of the War of Secession*. Paris: Neal's English Library, 1902. Reprint, New York, 1913.

Corson, Blake W., ed. *My Dear Jennie*. Richmond, Va.: Dietz, 1982.

Crabtree, Beth G., and James W. Patton, eds. *Journal of a Secesh Lady: The Diary of Catherine Ann Devereaux Edmondston*. Raleigh: North Carolina Division of Archives and History, 1979.

Crist, Lynda Laswell, ed. *The Papers of Jefferson Davis*. Vol. 10, *October 1863–August 1864;* . Baton Rouge: Louisiana State University Press, 1999.

———. *The Papers of Jefferson Davis*. Vol. 11, *September 1864–May 1865*. Baton Rouge: Louisiana State University Press, 2003.

Croner, Barbara M., ed. *A Sergeant's Story: Civil War Diary of Jacob J. Zorn, 1862–65*. Apollo, Pa.: Closson, 1999.

Cronin, David Edward. *The Evolution of a Life Described in the Memoirs of Major Seth Eyland*. New York: Charles M. Green, 1884.

Crosland, Charles. *Reminiscences of the Sixties*. Columbia, S.C.: State Company, 1910.

Crotty, Daniel G. *Four Years Campaigning in the Army of the Potomac*. Grand Rapids, Mich.: Dygert Brothers, 1874.

Cummins, D. Duane, and Daryl Hohweiler, eds. *An Enlisted Soldier's View of the Civil War: The Wartime Papers of Joseph Richardson Ward, Jr.* West Lafayette, Ind.: Belle, 1989.

Dawson, Francis W. *Reminiscences of Confederate Service*. Reprint, Baton Rouge: Louisiana State University Press, 1980.

De Trobriand, Regis. *Four Years with the Army of the Potomac*. Boston: Ticknor, 1889.

Dowdey, Clifford, and Louis H. Manarin, eds. *The Wartime Papers of R. E. Lee*. Boston: Little, Brown, 1961.

Drake, Janet M., ed. *Remember Me to All the Friends: Civil War Letters from George W. Harwood, Massachusetts 36th Regiment*. Framingham, Mass.: Damianos, 2022.

Draper, William Franklin. *Recollections of a Varied Career*. Boston: Little, Brown, 1908.

Eisenschiml, Otto, ed. *Vermont General: The Unusual War Experience of Edward Hastings Ripley, 1862–1865*. New York: Devin-Adair, 1960.

Emerson, Samuel H. *History of the War of the Confederacy, 1861–1865*. Malvern, Ark., 1918.

Evans, Robert, ed. *The 16th Mississippi Infantry: Civil War Letters and Reminiscences*. Jackson: University Press of Mississippi, 2002.

Everstine, Barbara Schilling, ed. *My Three Years in the Volunteer Army of the United States of America, from August 12th, 1862, to June 10th, 1865: Edw. Schilling, Co. F, Fourth Md. Vol. Infty*. Frostburg, Md.: Council of the Alleghenies, 1985.

Ewing, Wallace K. ed. *From Home to Trench: The Civil War Letters of Mack and Nan Ewing*. Grand Haven, Mich.: W. K. Ewing, 2000.

Fleet, Betsy, and John D. P. Fuller, eds. *Green Mount: A Virginia Plantation Family during the Civil War: Being the Journal of Benjamin Robert Fleet and Letters of his Family*. Lexington: University of Kentucky Press, 1962.

Floyd, Dale E., ed. *"Dear Friends at Home . . .": The Letters and Diary of Thomas James Owen, Fiftieth New York Volunteer Engineer Regiment during the Civil War*. Washington, D.C.: Office of the Chief of Engineers, 1985.

Folkes, Joseph E. *The Confederate Grays*. Richmond, Va.: Kate Folkes Minor, 1947.

Ford, Worthington Chauncey, ed. *A Cycle of Adams Letters, 1861–1865*. Vol. 2. Boston: Houghton Mifflin, 1920.

Fowler, Philemon H. *Memorials of William Fowler*. New York: Anson D. F. Randolph, 1875.

Freeman, Walker Burford. *Memoirs of Walker Burford Freeman*. Richmond, Va.: N.p., 1925.

Freeman, Warren Hapgood, ed. *Letters from Two Brothers Serving in the War for the Union* to *Their Family at Home in West Cambridge, Mass.* Cambridge, Mass.: H. O. Houghton, 1871.

Gallagher, Gary W., ed. *Fighting for the Confederacy: The Personal Recollections of General Edward Porter Alexander.* Chapel Hill: University of North Carolina Press, 1989.

Gerrish, Theodore. *Army Life: A Private's Reminiscences of the Civil War.* Portland, Maine: Hoyt, Fogg, & Donham, 1882.

Gibbon, John. *Personal Recollections of the Civil War.* New York: G. P. Putnam's Sons, 1928.

Gilchrist, Robert C., ed. *General Orders from the Adjutant and Inspector-General's Office, Confederate States Army, from July 1, 1864, to December 31, 1864.* Columbia, S.C.: Evans and Cogswell, 1865.

Gordon, John B. *Reminiscences of the Civil War.* New York: Charles Scribner's Sons, 1903.

Goree, Langston James, V., ed. *The Thomas Jewett Goree Letters: The Civil War Correspondence.* Bryan, Tex.: Family History Foundation, 1981.

Grant, Ulysses S. *Personal Memoirs of Ulysses S. Grant.* 1885. Reprint, 2 vols. in 1, New York: Bonanza Books, 1974.

Greenleaf, Margery, ed. *Letters to Eliza from a Union Soldier.* Chicago: Follett, 1970.

Hagood, Johnson. *Memoirs of the War of Secession.* Germantown, Tenn.: Guild Bindery, 1994.

Halliburton, Lloyd. *Saddle Soldiers: The Civil War Correspondence of General William Stokes of the 4th South Carolina Cavalry.* Orangeburg, S.C.: Sandlapper, 1993.

Hamil, John W. *Memories and Recollections of John W. Hamil.* Cragford, Ala.: N.p., 1915.

Harllee, William Curry, ed. *Kinfolks: A Genealogical and Biographical Record.* New Orleans: Searcy & Pfaff, 1934.

Hart, Walter Osgood. *Plodding and Thinking.* N.p, n.d.

Head, Natt. *Report of the Adjutant-General of the State of New Hampshire.* Concord, N.H.: George E. Jenks, State Printer, 1866.

Herdegen, Lance, and Sherry Murphy, eds. *Four Years with the Iron Brigade: The Civil War Journals of William Ray, Company F, Seventh Wisconsin Volunteers.* Cambridge, Mass.: Da Capo, 2002.

Hewitt, Janet B., Noah Andre Trudeau, and Bryce A. Suderow, eds. *Supplement to the Official Records of the Union and Confederate Armies.* Pt. 1, vol. 7. Wilmington, N.C.: Broadfoot, 1997.

Hoisington, Daniel John, ed. *My Heart toward Home: Letters of a Family during the Civil War.* Roseville, Minn.: Edinborough, 2001.

Holstein, Anna Morris. *Three Years in Field Hospitals of the Army of the Potomac.* Philadelphia: J. B. Lippincott, 1867.

Houghton, William R., and M. B. Houghton. *Two Boys in the Civil War and After.* Montgomery, Ala.: Paragon, 1912.

Howard, Wiley C. *Sketch of Cobb Legion Cavalry and Some Incidents and Scenes Remembered.* Suffolk, Va.: N.p., 1986.

Huckaby, Elizabeth Paisley, and Ethel C. Simpson, eds. *Tulip Evermore: Emma Butler and William Paisley, Their Lives in Letters, 1857–1887.* Fayetteville: University of Arkansas Press, 1985.

Humphreys, Andrew Atkinson. *The Virginia Campaign of '64 and '65: The Army of the Potomac and the Army of the James.* New York: Charles Scribner's Sons, 1883. Reprint, Wilmington, N.C.: Broadfoot, 1989.

Hutchinson, Olin Fulmer, ed. *"My Dear Mother & Sisters": Civil War Letters of Capt. A. B. Mulligan, Co. B, Fifth South Carolina Cavalry.* Spartanburg, S.C.: Reprint Co., 1992.

Irving, Theodore. *"More Than Conqueror"; or, Memorials of Col. J. Howard Kitching.* New York: Hurd and Houghton, 1873.

Irwin, John P. *A Quaker Soldier in the Civil War: Letters from the Front.* Philadelphia: Xlibris, 2008.

Jackson, Harry F., and Thomas F. O'Donnell, eds. *Back Home in Oneida: Hermon Clarke and His Letters.* Syracuse, N.Y.: Syracuse University Press, 1965.

Jones, J. William. *Life and Letters of General Robert Edward Lee: Soldier and Man.* New York: Neale, 1906.

Jones, John B. *A Rebel War Clerk's Diary at the Confederate States Capital.* Vol. 2. Philadelphia: J. B. Lippincott, 1866.

Jones, Terry L., ed. *Campbell Brown's Civil War: With Ewell and the Army of Northern Virginia.* Baton Rouge: Louisiana State University Press, 2001.

Jordan, Mary, and Joyce Hatch, eds. *Dear Friend Amelia: The Civil War Letters of Private John Tidd.* Ithaca, N.Y.: Six Mile Creek, 2011.

Jordan, William C. *Some Events and Incidents during the Civil War.* Montgomery, Ala.: Paragon, 1909.

Kesterson, Brian Stuart, ed. *The Last Survivor: The Memoirs of George William Watson, a Horse Soldier in the 12th Virginia Cavalry.* Parsons, W.V.: McClain Printing, 1993.

Kieffer, Harry M. *The Recollections of a Drummer Boy.* Boston, 1883.

Lane, David. *A Soldier's Diary: The Story of a Volunteer.* Jackson, Mich., 1905.

Larson, Michael J., and John David Smith, eds. *Dear Delia: The Civil War Letters of Captain Henry F. Young, Seventh Wisconsin Infantry.* Madison: University of Wisconsin Press, 2019.

Lawing, Mike, and Carolyn Lawing, eds. *My Dearest Friend: The Civil War Correspondence of Cornelia McGimsey and Lewis Warlick.* Durham, N.C.: Carolina Academic, 2000.

Leigh, Larry, comp. *J. J. Scroggs's Diary and Letters.* Thomaston, Ga.: Privately printed, 1996.

Livermore, Thomas L. *Days and Events, 1860–1866.* Boston: Houghton Mifflin, 1920.

Longacre, Edward G., ed. *From Antietam to Fort Fisher: The Civil War Letters of Edward King Wightman, 1862–1865.* Rutherford, N.J.: Associated University Presses, 1985.

Longstreet, James. *From Manassas to Appomattox.* 1896. Reprint, Secaucus, N.J.: Blue and Grey, 1988.

Loperfido, Christopher E., ed. *Death, Disease, and Life at War: The Civil War Letters of Surgeon James D. Benton, 111th and 98th New York Infantry Regiments, 1862–1865.* Eldorado Hills, Calif.: Savas Beattie, 2017.

Loving, Jerome M., ed. *Civil War Letters of George Washington Whitman.* Durham, N.C.: Duke University Press, 1975.

Lowe, David W., ed. *Meade's Army: The Private Notebooks of Lt. Col. Theodore Lyman.* Kent, Ohio: Kent State University Press, 2007.

Lowe, Jeffrey C., and Sam Hodges, eds. *Letters to Amanda: The Civil War Letters of Marion Hill Fitzpatrick, Army of Northern Virginia.* Macon, Ga.: Mercer University Press, 1998.

Mackintosh, Robert Harley, Jr. *"Dear Martha": The Confederate Letters of a South Carolina Soldier, Alexander Faulkner Fewell.* Columbia, S.C.: R. L. Bryan, 1976.

Malcolm, Jim, ed. *The Civil War Journal of Private Heyward Emmell, Ambulance and Infantry Corps: A Very Disagreeable War.* Madison, N.J.: Fairleigh Dickinson University Press, 2011.

Marshall, Jessie Ames, comp. *Private and Official Correspondence of Gen. Benjamin F. Butler during the Period of the Civil War*. Vols. 4–5. Norwood, Mass.: Plimpton, 1917.

Matthews, James M. *Soldiers in Green: The Civil War Diaries of James Mero Matthews 2nd U.S. Sharpshooters*. Sandy Pointe, Maine: Civil War Round Table, 2002.

McCarthy, Carlton, ed. *Contributions to a History of the Richmond Howitzer Battalion*. Richmond, Va.: Carlton McCarthy, 1883–86.

McFadden, Janice Bartlett Reeder, ed. *Aunt and the Soldier Boys from Cross Creek Village, Pa*. Santa Cruz, Calif.: Moore's Graphic Arts, 1970.

McKelvey, Blake, ed. *Rochester in the Civil War: George Breck's Civil War Letters from the "Reynolds Battery."* Rochester, N.Y.: Rochester Historical Society, 1944.

McMurray, John. *Recollections of a Colored Troop*. Brookville, Pa.: McMurray, 1994.

Meade, George Gordon, ed. *The Life and Letters of George Gordon Meade*. Vol. 2. New York: Charles Scribner's Sons, 1913.

Meier, Heinz K. ed. *Memoirs of a Swiss Officer in the American Civil War*. Bern, Switz.: Herbert Land, 1972.

Miers, Earl Schenck, ed. *Wash Roebling's War: Being a Selection from the Unpublished Civil War Letters of Washington Augustus Roebling*. Newark, Del.: Curtis Paper, 1961.

Miller, Delavan. *Drum Taps in Dixie*. Watertown, N.Y.: Hungerford-Holbrook, 1905.

Mohr, James C., and Richard E. Winslow, eds. *The Cormany Diaries*. Pittsburgh: University of Pittsburgh Press, 1982.

Moore, Edward A. *The Story of a Cannoneer under Stonewall Jackson*. New York: Neale, 1907.

Morgan, James D. *Recollections of a Rebel Reefer*. Boston: Houghton Mifflin, 1917.

Morrison, James L., ed. *The Memoirs of Henry Heth*. Westport, Conn.: Greenwood, 1974.

Mulholland, St. Clair. *Military Order: Congress Medal of Honor Legion of the United States*. Philadelphia: Town Printing, 1905.

Murray, R. L. *Ontario County Troops in the Civil War*. Vol. 2. Wolcott, N.Y.: Benedum Books, 2003.

Mushkat, Jerome, ed. *A Citizen-Soldier's Civil War: The Letters of Brevet Major General Alvin C. Voris*. De Kalb: Northern Illinois University Press, 2002.

Nevins, Allan, ed. *A Diary of Battle: The Personal Journals of Colonel Charles S. Wainwright, 1861–1865*. New York: Harcourt, Brace, and World, 1962.

———, ed. *Diary of the Civil War, 1860–1865: George Templeton Strong*. Vol. 4. New York: Macmillan, 1962.

Newsome, Hampton, John Horn, and John G. Selby, eds. *Civil War Talks: Further Reminiscences of George S. Bernard & His Fellow Veterans*. Charlottesville: University of Virginia Press, 2012.

Oates, William C. *The War between the Union and the Confederacy*. New York, 1905. Reprint, Dayton, Ohio: Morningside Bookshop, 1974.

Overfield, Joseph M., ed. *The Civil War Letters of Private George Parks, Company C, 24th New York Cavalry*. Buffalo, N.Y.: Gallagher Printing, 1992.

Page, Charles A. *Letters of a War Correspondent*. Boston: L. C. Page, 1899.

Palladino, Anita, ed. *Diary of a Yankee Engineer: The Civil War Story of John H. Westervelt, Engineer, 1st New York Volunteer Engineer Corps*. New York: Fordham University Press, 1997.

Patch, Eileen Mae Knapp, ed. *This from George: The Civil War Letters of Sergeant George Magusta Englis, 1861–1865, Company K, 89th New York Regiment of Volunteer Infantry Known as the Dickinson Guard.* Binghamton, N.Y.: Broome County Historical Society, 2001.

Paxton, John Randolph. *Sword and Gown.* New York: Knickerbocker, 1926.

Pearce, T. H., ed. *Diary of Captain Henry A. Chambers.* Wendell, N.C.: Broadfoot's Bookmark, 1983.

Perry, Martha Derby, comp. *Letters from a Surgeon of the Civil War.* Boston: Little, Brown, 1906.

Plumb, Robert C., ed. *Your Brother in Arms: A Union Soldier's Odyssey.* Columbia: University of Missouri Press, 2012.

Polley, Joseph B. *A Soldier's Letters to Charming Nellie.* New York: Neale, 1908.

Poremba, David Lee, ed. *If I Am Found Dead: Michigan Voices from the Civil War.* Ann Arbor, Mich.: Ann Arbor Media Group, 2006.

Poriss, Gerry Harder, and Ralph G. Poriss, eds. *While My Country Is in Danger: The Life and Letters of Lt. Col. Richard S. Thompson, Twelfth New Jersey Volunteers.* Hamilton, N.Y.: Edmonston, 1994.

Porter, Horace. *Campaigning with Grant.* New York: Century, 1897.

Priest, John Michael, ed. *One Surgeon's Private War: Doctor William W. Potter of the 57th New York.* Shippensburg, Pa.: White Mane, 1996.

———. *Stephen Elliott Welch of the Hampton Legion.* Shippensburg, Pa.: Burd Street, 1994.

Rauscher, Frank. *Music on the March.* Philadelphia: Wm. F. Fell, 1892.

Recollections and Reminiscences, 1861–1865 through World War 1. 7 vols. N.p.: South Carolina Division, United Daughters of the Confederacy, 1990–[97].

Reed, William Howell, ed. *War Papers of Frank B. Fay, with Reminiscences of Service in the Camps and Hospitals of the Army of the Potomac, 1861–1865.* Boston: George H. Ellis, 1911.

Reid-Green, Marcia, ed. *Letters from Home: Henry Matrau of the Iron Brigade.* Lincoln: University of Nebraska Press, 1993.

Riley, Franklin Lafayette. *Grandfather's Journal: Company B, Sixteenth Mississippi Infantry Volunteers, Harris's Brigade, Mahone's Division, Hill's Corps, ANV, May 27, 1861–July 15, 1865.* Dayton, Ohio: Morningside, 1988.

Ripley, William Y. *Vermont Riflemen in the War for the Union.* Rutland, Vt.: Tuttle, 1883.

Ritchie, Norman L., ed. *Four Years in the First New York Light Artillery: The Papers of David F. Ritchie.* Hamilton, N.Y.: Edmonston, 1997.

Robertson, James I., Jr., ed. *The Civil War Letters of General Robert McAllister.* New Brunswick, N.J.: Rutgers University Press, 1965.

Rodenbaugh, Theophilus F. *The Army of the United States: Historical Sketches of Staff and Line with Portraits of Generals in Chief.* New York: Mayard, Merrill, 1896.

Roman, Alfred. *The Military Operations of General Beauregard in the War between the States, 1861 to 1865.* Vol. 2. New York: Harper and Brothers, 1884.

Romig, Nancy Byers, ed. *Porter Phipps' Letters Home from the Civil War.* Export, Pa., 1994.

Rosenblatt, Emil, and Ruth Rosenblatt, eds. *Hard Marching Every Day: The Civil War Letters of Private Wilbur Fisk 1861–1865.* Lawrence: University Press of Kansas, 1992.

Rowland, Dunbar, ed. *Jefferson Davis, Constitutionalist: His Letters, Papers, and Speeches.* Vol. 6. Jackson, Miss., 1923.

Rozier, John, ed. *The Granite Farm Letters: The Civil War Correspondence of Edgeworth and Sallie Bird*. Athens: University of Georgia Press, 1988.

Rude, Beverly A. *Tas: The Civil War Experiences of Captain Tacitus T. Clay*. St. Paul, Minn.: Edit Write, 1992.

Sallada, William H. *Silver Sheaves Gathered through Clouds and Sunshine*. Des Moines, Iowa: Mills and Co., Printers, 1879.

Samito, Christian G., ed. *"Fear Was Not in Him:" The Civil War Letters of Major General Francis C. Barlow, U.S.A.* New York: Fordham University Press, 2004.

Scarborough, William Kauffman, ed. *The Diary of Edmund Ruffin*. Vol 3. Baton Rouge: Louisiana State University Press, 1989.

Schiller, Herbert M., ed. *A Captain's War: The Letters and Diaries of William H. S. Burgwyn*. Shippensburg, Pa.: White Mane, 1994.

Scott, Robert Garth, ed. *Forgotten Valor: The Memoirs, Journals, & Civil War Letters of Orlando B. Willcox*. Kent, Ohio: Kent State University Press, 1999.

Sheridan, Philip H. *Personal Memoirs of P. H. Sheridan*. Vol. 2. New York: Charles L. Webster, 1888.

Silliker, Ruth, ed. *The Rebel Yell & the Yankee Hurrah: The Civil War Journal of a Maine Volunteer*. Camden, Maine: Down East Books, 1985.

Simon, John Y., ed. *The Papers of Ulysses S. Grant*. Vol. 11, *June 1–August 15, 1864*; Vol. 12, *August 16–November 15, 1864*. Carbondale: Southern Illinois University Press, 1984.

Sloan, John A. *Reminiscences of the Guilford Grays*. Washington, D.C.: R. O. Polkinhorn, Printer, 1883. Reprint, Wendell, N.C.: Broadfoot's Bookmark, 1978.

Small, Harold Adams, ed. *The Road to Richmond: The Civil War Memoirs of Major Abner R. Small of the 16th Maine*. Berkeley, Calif., 1939. Reprint, New York: Fordham University Press, 1957.

Smith, Daniel E., Alice R. Huger Smith, and Arney R. Childs, eds. *Mason Smith Family Letters, 1860–1868*. Columbia: University of South Carolina Press, 1950.

Smith, M. V. *Reminiscences of the Civil War*. N.p., n.d.

Smith, Thomas T., et al., eds. *The Reminiscences of Major General Zenas R. Bliss, 1854–1876*. Austin: Texas State Historical Association, 2007.

Sorrel, G. Moxley. *Recollections of a Confederate Staff Officer*. Edited by Bell Irvin Wiley. Jackson, Tenn.: McCowat-Mercer, 1959. Reprint, Wilmington, N.C.: Broadfoot, 1987.

Sparks, David S., ed. *Inside Lincoln's Army: The Diary of General Marsena Rudolph Patrick, Provost Marshal General, Army of the Potomac*. New York: Thomas Yoseloff, 1964.

Spear, Abbott, et al., eds. *The Civil War Recollections of General Ellis Spear*. Orono: University of Maine Press, 1997.

Spear, John M. *Army Life in the Twenty-Fourth Regiment, Massachusetts Volunteer Infantry, Dec. 1861 to Dec. 1864*. Boston, 1892.

Spies, Mary-Joy, ed. *Yours Only, Thomas: Letters from a Union Soldier*. Valhalla, N.Y.: Mile High Books, 1999.

Stahler, Enoch. *Enoch Stahler: Miller and Soldier*. Washington, D.C.: Hayworth, 1909.

Stewart, William H. *A Pair of Blankets: War-Time History in Letters to the Young People of the South*. New York, 1911. Reprint, Wilmington, N.C.: Broadfoot, 1990.

Stocker, Jeffrey D., ed. *From Huntsville to Appomattox: R. T. Cole's History of 4th Regiment, Alabama Volunteer Infantry, C.S.A., Army of Northern Virginia*. Knoxville: University of Tennessee Press, 1996.

Styple, William B., ed. *Our Noble Blood: The Civil War Letters of Regis de Trobriand*. Kearny, N.J.: Belle Grove, 1997.

——, ed. *Writing & Fighting from the Army of Northern Virginia: A Collection of Confederate Soldier Correspondence*. Kearny, N.J.: Belle Grove, 2003.

——, ed. *Writing & Fighting the Confederate War: The Letters of Peter Wellington Alexander, Confederate War Correspondent*. Kearny, N.J.: Belle Grove, 2002.

——, ed. *Writing and Fighting the Civil War: Soldier Correspondence to the* New York Sunday Mercury. Kearny, N.J.: Belle Grove, 2000.

Sumner, Merlin E., ed. *The Diary of Cyrus B. Comstock*. Dayton, Ohio: Morningside, 1987.

Tapert, Annette, ed. *The Brothers' War: Civil War Letters to Their Loved Ones from the Blue and Gray*. New York: Vintage Books, 1989.

Thomas, Benjamin P., ed. *Three Years with Grant as Recalled by War Correspondent Sylvanus Cadwallader*. New York: Alfred A. Knopf, 1955.

Thomas, Mary Warner, and Richard A. Sauers, eds. *"I Never Want to Witness Such Sights": The Civil War Letters of James B. Thomas, 107th Pennsylvania*. Baltimore: Butternut & Blue, 1995.

Tilney, Robert. *My Life in the Army: Three Years and a Half in the Fifth Army Corp Army of the Potomac 1862–1865*. Philadelphia: Ferris and Leach, 1912.

Tower, R. Lockwood, ed. *Lee's Adjutant: The Wartime Letters of Colonel Walter Herron Taylor, 1862–1865*. Columbia: University of South Carolina Press, 1995.

Trout, Robert J., ed. *Memoirs of the Stuart Horse Artillery Battalion: Moorman's and Hart's Batteries*. Knoxville: University of Tennessee Press, 2008.

Vogtsberger, Margaret Ann, ed. *The Dulanys of Welbourne: A Family in Mosby's Confederacy*. Berryville, Va.: Rockbridge, 1995.

Walton, Matthew Venable. *Eighty Years After; or, Grandpa's Story*. Charleston, W.V.: Hood-Hiserman-Brodhag, 1929.

Welles, Gideon. *Diary of Gideon Welles*. Vol. 2, *April 1, 1864–December 31, 1866*. Boston: Houghton Mifflin, 1911.

Wells, Edward L. *Hampton and His Cavalry in '64*. Richmond, Va.: B. F. Johnson, 1899.

West, Robert Jerald L., trans. *Found among the Privates: Recollections of Holcomb's Legion 1861–64, by James L. Strain & Adolphus E. Fant, Correspondents to the* Union County News, *Union County, South Carolina*. Sharon, S.C., 1977.

White, Russell C., ed. *The Civil War Diary of Wyman S. White, First Sergeant, Company F 2nd United States Sharpshooters*. Baltimore: Butternut & Blue, 1993.

Wiatt, Alex L., ed. *Confederate Chaplain William Edward Wiatt. An Annotated Diary*. Lynchburg, Va.: H. E. Howard, 1994.

Wiggins, Clyde G., III, ed. *My Dear Friend: The Civil War Letters of Alva Benjamin Spencer, 3rd Georgia Regiment, Company C*. Macon, Ga.: Mercer University Press, 2007.

Wiley, Kenneth, ed., *Norfolk Blues: The Civil War Diary of the Norfolk Light Artillery Blues*. Shippensburg, Pa.: Burd Street, 1997.

Williams, Edward B., ed. *Rebel Brothers: The Civil War Letters of the Truehearts*. College Station: Texas A&M University Press, 1995.

Williams, Max R., ed. *The Papers of William Alexander Graham*. Vol. 6, *1864–1865*. Raleigh: North Carolina Department of Cultural Resources, 1976.

Wilson, James Harrison. *Under the Old Flag*. Vol. 1. New York: D. Appleton, 1912.

Wilson, LeGrand James. *The Confederate Soldier*. Fayetteville, Ark., 1902. Reprint,
 Memphis: Memphis State University Press, 1973.

Winkler, Mrs. Angelina Virginia. *The Confederate Capital and Hood's Texas Brigade*. Austin,
 Tex.: Eugene Von Boeckmann, 1894.

Wise, John Sergeant. *The End of an Era*. Boston: Houghton, Mifflin, 1902.

Wolfe, Ruth Dantzler, comp. *Private F.W.D., 1861–1865: Experiences of Private F. W. Dantzler
 during the War between the States*. N.p.: privately printed, 1936.

Wood, C. J. *Reminiscences of the War: Biography and Personal Sketches of All the
 Commanding Officers of the Union Army*. N.p.: published by the author, 1880.

UNIT HISTORIES

Albert, Allen D., ed. *History of the Forty-Fifth Regiment Pennsylvania Veteran Volunteer
 Infantry, 1861–1865*. Williamsport, Pa.: Grit, 1912.

Aldrich, Thomas M. *The History of Battery A, First Regiment Rhode Island Light Artillery in
 the War to Preserve the Union, 1861–1865*. Providence, R.I.: Snow & Farnham, Printers,
 1904.

Allen, George H. *Forty-Six Months with the Fourth Rhode Island Volunteers*. Providence,
 R.I.: J. A. & R. A. Reid, Printers, 1887.

Altemos, Edward A. *From the Wilderness to Appomattox: The Fifteenth New York Heavy
 Artillery in the Civil War*. Kent, Ohio: Kent State University Press, 2023.

Anderson, John. *The Fifty-Seventh Regiment of Massachusetts Volunteers in the War of the
 Rebellion*. Boston: E. B. Stillings, 1896.

Aubery, James M. *The Thirty-Sixth Wisconsin Volunteer Infantry*. Milwaukee: Evening
 Wisconsin, 1900.

Bacarella, Michael. *Lincoln's Foreign Legion: The 39th New York Infantry, Garibaldi Guard*.
 Shippensburg, Pa.: White Mane, 1996.

Baldwin, James J., III. *The Struck Eagle: A Biography of Brigadier General Micah Jenkins,
 and a History of the Fifth South Carolina Volunteers and the Palmetto Sharpshooters*.
 Shippensburg, Pa.: Burd Street, 1996.

Balfour, Daniel T. *13th Virginia Cavalry*. Lynchburg, Va.: H. E. Howard, 1986.

Barringer, Sheridan R. *Fighting for General Lee: General Rufus Barringer and the North
 Carolina Cavalry Brigade*. El Dorado Hills, Calif.: Savas Beattie, 2016.

Baxley, Neil. *No Prouder Fate: The Story of the 11th South Carolina Volunteer Infantry*.
 Wilmington, N.C.: Broadfoot, 2009.

Beale, Richard Lee Tuberville. *History of the Ninth Virginia Cavalry in the War between the
 States*. Richmond, Va.: B. F. Johnson, 1899.

Beecher, Herbert W. *History of the First Light Battery, Connecticut Volunteers*. New York: A.
 T. De La Mare, 1901.

Benedict, George G. *Vermont in the Civil War*. Vol. 2. Burlington, Vt.: Free Press, 1886–88.

Bennett, Brian A. *Sons of Old Monroe: A Regimental History of Patrick O'Rourke's 140th NY*.
 Dayton, Ohio: Morningside, 1992.

Bilby, Joseph G. *Three Rousing Cheers: A History of the Fifteenth New Jersey from Flemington
 to Appomattox*. Hightstown, N.J.: Longstreet House, 1993.

Billings, John D. *The History of the Tenth Massachusetts Battery of Light Artillery in the War of the Rebellion, 1862–1865*. Boston: Arakelyan, 1909.

Brady, Robert. *The Story of One Regiment: The Eleventh Maine Infantry Volunteers in the War of the Rebellion*. New York: J. J. Little, 1896.

Brainard, Mary G. *Campaigns of the 146th Regiment, New York State Volunteers*. New York: 1915.

Bruce, George A. *The Twentieth Regiment of Massachusetts Volunteer Infantry, 1861–1865*. Boston: Houghton Mifflin, 1906.

Burrage, Henry S. *History of the 36th Regiment, Massachusetts Volunteers*. Boston: Rockwell and Churchill, 1884.

Cadwell, Charles K. *The Old Sixth Regiment, Its War Record, 1861–65*. New Haven, Conn.: Tuttle, Morehouse, & Taylor, 1875.

Caldwell, J. F. J. *The History of a Brigade of South Carolinians First Known as "Gregg's" and Subsequently as "McGowan's Brigade."* Reprint, Dayton, Ohio: Morningside, 1984.

Califf, Joseph C. *Record of the Services of the Seventh Regiment, U.S. Colored Troops from September 1863 to November 1866*. Providence, R.I.: E. L. Freeman & Co., Printers, 1878.

Camper, Charles, and J. W. Kirkley, comps. *Historical Record of the First Maryland Infantry*. Washington, D.C.: Gibson Brothers, 1871.

Carruth, Sumner, et al. *History of the 35th Massachusetts Volunteers*. Boston: Mills, Knight, 1884.

Cavanaugh, Michael A. *The Otey, Ringgold, and Davidson Virginia Artillery*. Lynchburg, Va.: H. E. Howard, 1993.

Chapman, Craig S. *More Terrible Than Victory: North Carolina's Bloody Bethel Regiment, 1861–65*. Washington, D.C.: Brassey's, 1998.

Child, William. *A History of the 5th Regiment, New Hampshire Volunteers in the American Civil War, 1861–1865*. Bristol, N.H.: 1893. Reprint, Gaithersburg, Md.: Ron Van Sickle Military Books, 1988.

Clark, Charles M. *The History of the Thirty-Ninth Regiment Illinois Volunteer Veteran Infantry*. Chicago: Veteran Association of the Regiment, 1889.

Clark, Walter, ed. *Histories of the Several Regiments and Battalions from North Carolina in the Great War 1861–'65*. 5 vols. Raleigh, N.C.: E. M. Uzzell, Printer and Binder, 1901.

Clendaniel, Dan. *Such Hard & Severe Service: The 85th Pennsylvania in the Civil War*. Vol. 2, 1864–1865. Morgantown, W.V.: Monongahela Books, 2021.

Collins, Darrel L. *46th Virginia Infantry*. Lynchburg, Va.: H. E. Howard, 1992.

Cowtan, Charles W. *Services of the Tenth New York Volunteers (National Zouaves) in the War of the Rebellion*. New York: Charles H. Ludwig, 1882.

Craft, David. *History of the 141st Pa Volunteers*. Towanda, Pa.: Reporter-Journal Printing, 1885.

Crawford, Kim. *The 16th Michigan Infantry*. Dayton, Ohio: Morningside House, 2002.

Croffut, W. A., and John M. Morris. *The Military and Civil History of Connecticut During the War of 1861–1865*. New York: Ledyard Bill, 1868.

Cunningham, John L. *Three Years with the Adirondack Regiment: 118th New York Volunteer Infantry*. Norwood, Mass.: Plimpton, 1920.

Curtis, Orson Blair. *History of the Twenty-Fourth Michigan, of the Iron Brigade, Known as the Detroit and Wayne County Regiment*. Detroit: Winn & Hammond, 1891.

Cutcheon, Byron Mac. *The Story of the Twentieth Michigan Infantry*. Lansing, Mich.: Robert Smith Printing, 1904.

Cutchins, John A. *A Famous Command—Richmond Light Infantry Blues*. Richmond, Va.: Garrett & Massie, 1934.

Dawes, Rufus R. *Service with the Sixth Wisconsin Volunteers*. Dayton, Ohio: Morningside Bookshop, 1984.

Denny, Joseph Waldo. *Wearing of the Blue in the 25th Massachusetts Volunteer Infantry*. Worcester, Mass.: Putnam & Davis, 1879.

Derby, William P. *Bearing Arms in the 27th Massachusetts Regiment*. Boston: Wright & Potter, 1883.

Dickey, Luther S. *History of the 85th Regiment, Pennsylvania Volunteer Infantry*. New York: J. C. & W. E. Powers, 1915.

Divine, John E. *35th Battalion Virginia Cavalry*. Lynchburg, Va.: H. E. Howard, 1985.

Dobak, William A. *Freedom by the Sword: The U.S. Colored Troops, 1862–1867*. Washington, D.C.: Center of Military History, U.S. Army, 2011.

Doster, William E. *A Brief History of the Fourth Pennsylvania Cavalry*. Pittsburgh, 1891. Reprint, Hightstown, NJ: Longstreet House, 1997.

Drake, James Madison. *History of the 9th New Jersey*. Elizabeth, N.J.: Journal Printing House, 1889.

Driver, Robert, Jr. *First and Second Maryland Infantry, CSA*. Charlottesville, Va.: Rockbridge, 1999.

DuBose, Henry Kershaw. *History of B Company, 21st South Carolina*. Columbia, S.C.: R. L. Bryan, 1909.

Dunlop, William S. *Lee's Sharpshooters; or, The Forefront of Battle*. Little Rock, Ark.: Tunnah & Pittard, 1899.

Dunn, Craig L. *Iron Men, Iron Will. The Nineteenth Indiana Regiment of the Iron Brigade*. Indianapolis: Guild Press of Indiana, 1995.

Dunn, Wilbur R. *Full Measure of Devotion: The 8th NY Heavy Artillery*. 2 vols. Kearney, Neb.: Morris, 1997.

Dusseault, John H. *Company E, 39th Infantry in the Civil War*. Somerville, Mass.: Somerville Journal, 1908.

Eberly, Robert E., Jr. *Bouquets from the Cannon's Mouth: Soldiering with the Eighth Regiment of the Pennsylvania Reserves*. Shippensburg, Pa.: White Mane Books, 2005.

Eldredge, Daniel. *The Third New Hampshire and All about It*. Boston: E. B. Stillings, 1893.

Emmerton, James. *Record of the Twenty-Third Regiment Massachusetts Volunteer Infantry in the War of the Rebellion, 1861–1865*. Boston: William Ware, 1886.

Everts, Hermann. *Complete and Comprehensive History of the 9th New Jersey*. Newark, N.J.: A. S. Holbrook, 1865.

Floyd, Frederick C. *History of the 40th (Mozart) Regiment New York Volunteers*. Boston: F. H. Gilson, 1909.

Frederick, Gilbert. *The Story of a Regiment*. Chicago: C. H. Morgan, 1895.

Gaff, Alan D. *On Many a Bloody Field: Four Years in the Iron Brigade*. Bloomington: Indiana University Press, 1996.

Gavin, William G. *Campaigning with the Roundheads: The History of the 100th Pennsylvania Regiment*. Dayton, Ohio: Morningside, 1989.

Gayley, Alice Jane. *The 148th Pennsylvania Volunteers: The Story of Company I.* Butler, Pa.: Mechling Bookbindery, 1998.

Gibbs, A. Judson, David A. King, and Jay H. Northrup. *History of the Ninety-Third New York Infantry.* Milwaukee: Swain & Tate, 1895.

Gibbs, James M. *History of the First Battalion Pennsylvania Six Months Volunteers and the 187th Regiment Pennsylvania Volunteer Infantry.* Harrisburg, Pa.: Central Printing and Publishing House, 1905.

Goldsborough, William W. *The Maryland Line in the Confederate States Army.* Baltimore: Guggenheimer, Weil, 1900.

Griffin, Ronald C. *The 11th Alabama Volunteer Infantry in the Civil War.* Jefferson, N.C.: McFarland, 2008.

Haines, William P. *History of the Men of Co. F 12th New Jersey Volunteers.* Mickelton, N.J., 1897.

Hall, Henry, and James Hall. *Cayuga in the Field: A Record of the 19th New York Volunteers . . . and the 75th New York Volunteers.* Auburn, N.Y.: Truair, Smith, 1873.

Hall, Isaac. *History of the 97th Regiment New York Volunteers.* Utica, N.Y.: L. C. Childs & Son, 1890.

Hamilton, D. H. *History of Company M, 1st Texas Volunteer Infantry Hood's Brigade.* Waco, Tex.: W. M. Morrison, 1962.

Hand, Harold, Jr. *One Good Regiment: The 13th Pennsylvania Cavalry in the Civil War, 1861–1865.* Victoria, BC: Trafford, 2000.

Hardy, Michael C. *General Lee's Immortals: The Battles and Campaigns of the Branch-Lane Brigade in the Army of Northern Virginia, 1861–1865.* El Dorado Hills, Calif.: Savas Beattie, 2018.

———. *The Thirty-Seventh North Carolina Troops.* Jefferson, N.C.: McFarland, 2003.

Harrell, Roger H. *The 2nd North Carolina Cavalry.* Jefferson, N.C.: McFarland, 2004.

Harris, James S. *Historical Sketches of the Seventh Regiment North Carolina Troops, 1861–'65.* Mooresville, N.C.: Mooresville Printing, 1893.,

Harris, W. M., comp. *Movements of the Confederate Army in Virginia and the Part Taken by the 19th Mississippi Regiment, from the Diary of Gen. Nat. H. Harris.* Duncansby, Miss.: William M. Harris, 1901.

Hays, Gilbert Adams. *Under the Red Patch: Story of the Sixty-Third Regiment Pennsylvania Volunteers, 1861–1864.* Pittsburgh: Market Review, 1908.

Herek, Raymond J. *These Men Have Seen Hard Service: The First Michigan Sharpshooters in the Civil War.* Detroit: Wayne State University Press, 1998.

Hess, Earl J. *Lee's Tar Heels: The Pettigrew-Kirkland-MacRae Brigade.* Chapel Hill: University of North Carolina Press, 2002.

Hillhouse, Don. *Heavy Artillery and Light Infantry: A History of the 1st Florida Special Battalion and 10th Infantry Regiment.* Rome, Ga.: Don Hillhouse, 1992.

History of the Fifty-Seventh Regiment Pennsylvania Veteran Volunteer Infantry. Meadville, Pa.: McCoy & Calvin, Printers, 1904.

History of the 5th Massachusetts Battery. Boston: Luther E. Cowles, 1902.

History of the 121st Regiment Pennsylvania Volunteers. Philadelphia: Burk & McFetridge, 1893.

Holmes, Torlief S. *Horse Soldiers in Blue: First Maine Cavalry.* Gaithersburg, Md.: Butternut, 1985.

Bibliography

Hopkins, Donald A. *The Little Jeff: The Jeff Davis Legion Cavalry, Army of Northern Virginia.* Shippensburg, Pa.: White Mane Books, 1999.

Hopkins, William P. *The Seventh Rhode Island Volunteers in the Civil War, 1862–1865.* Providence, R.I.: Providence Press, Snow and Farnham, 1903.

Horn, John. *The Petersburg Regiment in the Civil War: A History of the 12th Virginia Infantry from John Brown's Hanging to Appomattox, 1859–1865.* El Dorado Hills, Calif.: Savas Beattie, 2019.

Houghton, Edwin B. *The Campaigns of the 17th Maine.* Portland, Maine: Short & Loring, 1866.

Houston, Henry C. *The Thirty-Second Maine Regiment of Infantry Volunteers.* Portland, Maine: Southworth Brothers, 1903.

Husk, Martin W. *The 111th New York Infantry: A Civil War History.* Jefferson, N.C.: McFarland, 2009.

Hyde, William L. *History of the One Hundred and Twelfth Regiment New York Volunteers.* Fredonia, N.Y.: W. McKinstry, 1866.

Hyndman, William. *History of a Cavalry Company.* Philadelphia: James B. Rodgers, 1872.

Izlar, William V. *A Sketch of the War Record of the Edisto Rifles, 1861–1865.* Columbia, S.C.: State Company, 1914.

Jackman, Lyman. *History of the Sixth New Hampshire Regiment in the War for the Union.* Concord, N.H.: Republican Press Association, 1891.

Jackson, Harry L. *First Regiment Engineer Troops, P.A.C.S.: Robert E. Lee's Combat Engineers.* Louisa, Va.: R.A.E. Design, 1998.

Jordan, William B. *Red Diamond Regiment: The 17th Maine Infantry, 1862–1865.* Shippensburg, Pa.: White Mane, 1996.

Judson, Amos M. *History of the Eighty-Third Regiment Pennsylvania Volunteers, 1861–1865.* Erie, Pa.: B. F. H. Lynn, 1865.

Keating, Robert. *Carnival of Blood: History of the 7th NY Heavy Artillery.* Baltimore: Butternut & Blue, 1998.

Kirk, Hyland C. *Heavy Guns and Light: A History of the 4th New York Heavy Artillery.* New York: C. T. Dillingham, 1890.

Kohler, David. *"Ready, Always Ready": The Story of the 148th Pennsylvania Volunteer Infantry.* Hoosick Falls, N.Y.: Merriam, 2017.

Krick, Robert E. L. *40th Virginia Infantry.* Lynchburg, Va.: H. E. Howard, 1985.

Krick, Robert K. *9th Virginia Cavalry.* Lynchburg, Va.: H. E. Howard, 1982.

Laine, J. Gary, and Morris M. Penny. *Law's Alabama Brigade in the War between the Union and the Confederacy.* Shippensburg, Pa.: White Mane, 1996.

Little, Henry F. W. *The Seventh Regiment New Hampshire Volunteers in the War of the Rebellion.* Concord, N.H.: Ira C. Evans, Printer, 1896.

Lloyd, William Penn. *History of the 1st Regiment Pa Reserve Cavalry.* Philadelphia: King & Baird, 1864.

Locke, William H. *The Story of the Regiment.* Philadelphia: J. P. Lippincott, 1868.

Loehr, Charles T. *War History of the Old First Virginia Infantry Regiment, Army of Northern Virginia.* Richmond, Va.: Wm. Ellis Jones, 1884. Reprint, Dayton, Ohio: Morningside Bookshop, 1978.

Longacre, Edward G. *Jersey Cavaliers: A History of the First New Jersey Volunteer Cavalry, 1861–1865.* Hightstown, N.J.: Longstreet House, 1992.

———. *A Regiment of Slaves: The 4th United States Colored Infantry*. Mechanicsburg, Pa.: Stackpole Books, 2003.

———. *To Gettysburg and Beyond: The 12th New Jersey Infantry*. Hightstown, N.J.: Longstreet House, 1988.

Lord, Edward O., ed. *History of the Ninth Regiment New Hampshire Volunteers in the War of the Rebellion*. Concord, N.H.: Republican Press Association, 1895.

Mahood, Wayne. *Written in Blood: History of the 126th New York Infantry in the Civil War*. Hightstown, N.J.: Longstreet House, 1997.

Marbaker, Thomas D. *History of the 11th New Jersey Volunteers*. Trenton, N.J., 1898. Reprint, Hightstown, NJ: Longstreet House, 1990.

Marshall, D. Porter. *Company "K" 155th Pa. Volunteer Zouaves*. N.p., 1888.

Marvel, William. *Race of the Soil: The Ninth New Hampshire Regiment in the Civil War*. Wilmington, N.C.: Broadfoot, 1988.

Matthews, Richard E. *The 149th Pennsylvania Volunteer Infantry Unit in the Civil War*. Jefferson, N.C.: McFarland, 1994.

Maxfield, Albert, and Robert Brady Jr. *Roster & Statistical Record of Company D of the Eleventh Regiment Maine Infantry Volunteers*. New York: T. Humphrey, 1890.

McBrien, Joe Bennett. *The Tennessee Brigade*. Chattanooga, Tenn.: Hudson Printing, 1977.

Merrill, Samuel H. *The Campaigns of the First Maine and First District of Columbia Cavalry*. Portland, Maine: Bailey & Noyes, 1866.

Mesic, Harriet Bey. *Cobb's Legion Cavalry: A History and Roster of the Ninth Georgia Volunteers in the Civil War*. Jefferson, N.C.: McFarland, 2009.

Miller, Richard F. *Harvard's Civil War: A History of the Twentieth Massachusetts Volunteer Infantry*. Hanover, N.H.: University Press of New England, 2005.

Moore, Robert H. *Graham's Petersburg, Jackson's Kanawha, and Lurtry's Roanoke Horse Artillery*. Lynchburg, Va.: H. E. Howard, 1996.

Mowris, James A. *A History of the One Hundred and Seventeenth Regiment New York Volunteers*. Hartford, Conn.: Case, Lockwood, 1866.

Mulholland, St. Clair A. *The Story of the 116th Pa Volunteer Infantry*. Philadelphia, 1899.

Musselman, Homer D. *The 47th Virginia Infantry*. Lynchburg, Va.: H. E. Howard, 1991.

Myers, Frank M. *The Comanches: A History of White's Battalion, Virginia Cavalry*. Baltimore: Kelly, Piet, 1871.

Myers, Irvin G. *We Might as Well Die Here: The 53d Pennsylvania Veteran Volunteer Infantry*. Shippensburg, Pa.: White Mane, 2004.

Nash, Eugene A. *A History of the Forty-Fourth Regiment New York Volunteer Infantry in the Civil War, 1861–1865*. Chicago: R. R. Donnelley and Sons, 1911.

Owen, Charles W. *The First Michigan: Three Months and Three Years*. Quincy, Mass.: Quincy Herald Print, 1903.

Owen, William Miller. *In Camp and Battle with the Washington Artillery*. Boston: Ticknor, 1885.

Page, Charles D. *History of the Fourteenth Regiment Connecticut Volunteer Infantry*. Meriden, Conn.: Horton Printing, 1906.

Paradis, James M. *The Blow for Freedom: The 6th United States Colored Infantry in the Civil War*. Shippensburg, Pa.: White Mane, 2000.

Parker, John Lord. *Henry Wilson's Regiment: History of the Twenty-Second Massachusetts Infantry, the Second Company Sharpshooters, and the Third Battery in the War of the Rebellion.* Boston: Rand Avery, 1887.

Parker, Thomas H. *History of the 51st Pennsylvania Infantry.* Philadelphia: King & Baird, Printers, 1869.

Pellicano, John M. *Conquer or Die: The 39th New York Volunteer Infantry, Garibaldi Guard, a Military History.* Flushing, N.Y.: Pellicano, 1996.

Polley, J. B. *Hood's Texas Brigade.* New York, 1910. Reprint, Dayton, Ohio: Morningside Bookshop, 1976.

Powell, William H. *The Fifth Army Corps: A Record of Operations during the Civil War in the United States of America, 1861–1865.* New York: G. P. Putnam's Sons, 1896.

Powelson, Benjamin. *History of Company K of the 140th Pa Volunteers.* Steubenville, Ohio: Carnahan Printing, 1906.

Preston, Noble D. *History of the Tenth Regiment of New York Cavalry.* New York: D. Appleton, 1892.

Price, Isaiah. *History of the Ninety-Seventh Regiment, Pennsylvania Volunteer Infantry, during the War of the Rebellion, 1861–1865.* Philadelphia: B & P Printers, 1875.

Pullen, John J. *The Twentieth Maine.* Philadelphia: J. B. Lippincott, 1957.

Pyne, Henry R. *History of the First New Jersey Cavalry.* Trenton, N.J., 1871. Reprint, New Brunswick, NJ: Rutgers University Press, 1961.

Raiford, Neil Hunter. *The 4th North Carolina Cavalry in the Civil War.* Jefferson, N.C.: McFarland, 2003.

Ramsey, Marc F. *The 7th South Carolina Cavalry: To the Defense of Richmond.* Wilmington, N.C.: Broadfoot, 2011.

Ray, Fred L. *Shock Troops of the Confederacy: The Sharpshooter Battalions of the Army of Northern Virginia.* Asheville, N.C.: CFS, 2006.

Reese, Timothy J. *Sykes' Regular Infantry Division, 1861–1864.* Jefferson, N.C.: McFarland, 1990.

Rhodes, John H. *History of Battery B, First Regiment Rhode Island Light Artillery.* Providence, R.I.: Snow & Farnham, Printers, 1894.

Roback, Henry, ed. *The Veteran Volunteers of Herkimer and Otsego Counties in the War of the Rebellion, Being a History of the 152nd N.Y.V.* Utica, N.Y.: L. C. Childs & Son, 1888.

Roe, Alfred S. *The Thirty-Ninth Massachusetts Volunteers.* Worcester, Mass.: Commonwealth, 1914.

———. *Twenty-Fourth Massachusetts Infantry.* Worcester, Mass.: Twenty-Fourth Veteran Association, 1907.

Roe, Alfred S., and Charles Nutt. *The History of the First Regiment of Massachusetts Heavy Artillery.* Worcester, Mass.: Commonwealth, 1917.

Roper, John L., Henry C. Archibald, and George W. Coles. *History of the Eleventh Pennsylvania Volunteer Cavalry.* Philadelphia: Franklin Printing, 1902.

Rutan, Edwin P., II. *"If I Have Got to Go and Fight, I Am Willing": A Union Regiment Forged in the Petersburg Campaign, the 179th New York Volunteer Infantry, 1864–1865.* Park City, Utah: RTD, 2015.

Schmutz, John F. *The Bloody Fifth: The Fifth Texas Infantry Regiment, Hood's Texas Brigade, Army of Northern Virginia.* El Dorado Hills, Calif.: Savas Beattie, 2016.

Schroeder, Patrick. *We Came to Fight: History of the 5th New York Veteran Volunteers*. Brookneal, Va.: Patrick A. Schroeder, 1998.

Scott, Kate M. *History of the 105th Pennsylvania Volunteers*. Philadelphia: Collins Printing, 1877.

Shaw, Horace H., and Charles J. House. *The First Maine Heavy Artillery, 1862–1865*. Portland, Maine: N.p., 1903.

Silo, Mark. *The 115th New York in the Civil War*. Jefferson, N.C.: McFarland, 2007.

Simons, Ezra D. *A Regimental History of the 125th New York Volunteers*. New York: Ezra D. Simons, 1888.

Simpson, Harold B. *Hood's Texas Brigade: Lee's Grenadier Guard*. Waco, Tex.: Texian, 1970.

Smith, Abram P. *History of the Seventy-Sixth Regiment New York Volunteers*. Cortland, N.Y.: Truair, Smith, & Miles, Printers, 1867.

Smith, Donald L. *Twenty-Fourth Michigan of the Iron Brigade*. Harrisburg, Pa.: Stackpole, 1962.

Smith, John D. *History of the 19th Maine*. Minneapolis: Great Western Printing, 1909.

Smith, John L. *History of the Corn Exchange Regiment, the 118th Pennsylvania Volunteers*. Philadelphia: J. L. Smith, 1888.

Stevens, Charles A. *Berdan's United States Sharpshooters in the Army of the Potomac*. St. Paul, Minn.: Price-McGill, 1892.

Stewart, Robert L. *History of the 140th Pennsylvania Regiment*. Philadelphia, 1912.

The Story of the Twenty-First Regiment, Connecticut Volunteer Infantry during the Civil War, 1861–1865. Middletown, Conn.: Stewart Printing, 1900.

Stowits, George H. *History of the One-Hundredth Regiment of New York Volunteers*. Buffalo, N.Y.: Printing House of Matthew & Warren, 1870.

Stubbs, Steven. *Duty, Honor, Valor: Story of the 11th Mississippi Infantry*. Philadelphia, Miss.: Dancing Rabbit, 2000.

Sturkey, O. Lee. *The Hampton Legion Infantry, CSA*. Wilmington, N.C.: Broadfoot, 2008.

Thomas, Howard. *Boys in Blue from the Adirondack Foothills*. Prospect, N.Y.: Prospect Books, 1960.

Thompson, S. Millett. *13th Regiment New Hampshire Volunteer Infantry*. Boston: Houghton, Mifflin, 1888.

Tobie, Edward P. *History of the First Maine Cavalry, 1861–1865*. Boston: Emery & Hughes, 1887.

Townshend, David G. *The Seventh Michigan Volunteer Infantry: The Gallant Men and Flag in the Civil War, 1861–1865*. Fort Lauderdale, Fla.: Southeast, 1993.

Trout, Robert J. *Galloping Thunder: The Stuart Horse Artillery Battalion*. Mechanicsburg, Pa.: Stackpole Books, 2002.

Under the Maltese Cross: Antietam to Appomattox: The 155th Pennsylvania Infantry. Pittsburgh: 155th Regimental Association, 1908.

Underwood, George C. *History of the 26th North Carolina*. Goldsboro, N.C.: 1901. Reprint, Wendell, N.C.: Broadfoot's Bookmark, 1978.

Van Santvoord, Cornelius. *The One Hundred and Twentieth Regiment, New York State Volunteers*. Rondout, N.Y.: Kingston Freeman, 1894.

Vautier, John D. *History of the 88th Pennsylvania Volunteers in the War for the Union*. Philadelphia: J. B. Lippincott, 1894.

Venner, William Thomas. *Hoosier's Honor: The Iron Brigade's 19th Indiana Regiment*. Shippensburg, Pa.: Burd Street, 1998.

Waitt, Ernest L., comp. *History of 19th Regiment Massachusetts Volunteer Infantry*. Salem, Mass.: Salem, 1906.

Walcott, Charles F. *History of the Twenty-First Regiment Massachusetts Volunteers*. Boston: Houghton, Mifflin, 1882.

Walker, Francis A. *History of the Second Army Corps in the Army of the Potomac*. New York: Charles Scribner's Sons, 1887.

Walkey, Stephen W., comp. *History of the Seventh Connecticut Volunteer Infantry*. Hartford, Conn., 1905.

Ward, George Washington. *History of the Second Pennsylvania Veteran Heavy Artillery*. Philadelphia: G. W. Ward, 1904.

Washburn, George H. *A Complete Military History and Record of the 108th Regiment N.Y. Volunteers from 1862 to 1864*. Rochester, N.Y.: E. R. Andrews, 1894.

Washington, Bushrod C., ed. *A History of the Laurel Brigade by Capt. William N. McDonald*. Baltimore: Sun Job Printing Office, 1907.

Washington, Versalle F. *Eagles on Their Buttons: A Black Infantry Regiment in the Civil War*. Columbia: University of Missouri Press, 1999.

Waters, Zack C. *A Small but Spartan Brigade: The Florida Brigade in Lee's Army of Northern Virginia*. Tuscaloosa: University of Alabama Press, 2010.

Weygant, Charles. *History of the 124th New York Regiment*. Newburgh, N.Y., 1877.

Wickman, Don. *We Are Coming Father Abra'am: The History of the 9th Vermont Volunteer Infantry, 1862–1865*. Lynchburg, Va.: Schroeder, 2005.

Wilkinson, Warren. *Mother, May You Never See the Sights I Have Seen: The 57th Massachusetts in the Last Year of the Civil War*. New York: Harper Collins, 1990.

Wise, Jennings Cropper. *The Long Arm of Lee; or, the History of the Artillery of the Army of Northern Virginia*. Vol. 2. New York: Oxford University Press, 1959.

Woodruff, George H. *Fifteen Years Ago; or, The Patriotism of Will County, Designed to Preserve the Memory of Will County Soldiers*. Joliet, Ill.: James Goodspeed, 1876.

Woodward, Evan M. *History of the 198th Pennsylvania Volunteers*. Trenton, N.J.: MacCrellsh & Quigley, 1884.

Zeller, Paul G. *The Ninth Vermont Infantry: A History and Roster*. Jefferson, N.C.: McFarland, 2008.

ONLINE PRIMARY SOURCES

Billy Yank & Johnny Reb Letters, transcribed by Will Griffing. https://billyyankjohnnyreb.wordpress.com/2015/12/05/list-of-soldiers-letters/.

The Civil War Letters of the Fox Brothers, transcribed by David H. Fox. Ohio State University E-History, 1999. https://ehistory.osu.edu/exhibitions/civil-war-letters-fox-brothers.

"The Civil War Letters of William Hunt Goff, Company H, 24th Massachusetts." https://williamhuntgoff.wordpress.com.

"1862–65: Charles Clarence Miller to Parents." *Spared & Shared 21* (blog), April 21, 2020. https://sparedcreative21.art.blog/2020/04/21/1862-65-charles-clarence-miller-to-parents/.

"1864: Robert Henry Maury, Jr. Letters." *Spared & Shared 10* (blog), September 8, 2015. https://sparedshared10.wordpress.com/2015/09/08/1864-robert-henry -maury-jr-letters/.

Englehard, Joseph Adolphus. Letter, August 28, 1864. North Carolina Digital Collections. https://digital.ncdcr.gov/Documents/Detail/letter-from-joseph-adolphus -engelhard-august-28-1864/411500.

Frey, Charles A. "Recollections of Army Life," 1886. https://charlesfrey.wordpress.com.

Gustrowsky, Roy, trans. "UPR: Report of Lieutenant Colonel Mark Finnicum, 7th WI, August 18–21, 1864." The Siege of Petersburg Online: A Richmond-Petersburg Campaign Site. www.beyondthecrater.com.

Hyde, William L. Letter. soldierstudies.org (site discontinued).

"Jeff's Prayers Are as Effective as Abe's: The Civil War Letters of George S. Youngs, 126th New York Vols." https://georgeyoungsblog.wordpress.com.

Letters from an Iowa Soldier in the Civil War. https://civilwarletters.com.

Peck, Elias S. Letters. The Siege of Petersburg Online: A Richmond-Petersburg Campaign Site. www.beyondthecrater.com.

Pettingill, Pvt. Sewall. Memoir. The Siege of Petersburg Online: A Richmond-Petersburg Campaign Site. www.beyondthecrater.com.

The Siege of Petersburg Online: A Richmond-Petersburg Campaign Site. www.beyondthecrater.com.

Suderow, Bryce. "'An Ugly Looking Chance for a Charge': The Battle of Darbytown Road, October 13, 1864." The Siege of Petersburg Online: A Richmond-Petersburg Campaign Site. www.beyondthecrater.com.

Wright, Benjamin. Letter. soldierstudies.org (site discontinued).

ADDRESSES, ARTICLES, AND ESSAYS

Alexander, Joseph M. "Fighting and Suffering around Bermuda Hundred." *National Tribune*, July 31, 1890.

Aliyetti, John E. "Gallantry under Fire." *Civil War Times Illustrated* 35, no. 5 (October 1996): 30–35.

Allen, Amory K. "Civil War Letters of Amory K. Allen." *Indiana Magazine of History*, 31, no. 4 (December 1935): 338–86.

Allen, C[ornelius] T. "Fight at Chaffin's Farm, or Fort Harrison." *Confederate Veteran* 13, no. 9 (September 1905): 418.

———. "Fort Harrison: The Most Destructive Single Shot, September 29, 1864." In Newsome, Horn, and Selby, *Civil War Talks*, 299–301.

Allen, David. "More about Mink." *National Tribune*, July 11, 1895.

Allen, George H. "Hatcher's Run as Told in a Comrade's Diary." *National Tribune*, March 11, 1886.

Ames, John. "Dutch Gap Canal." *Overland Monthly* 4, no. 1 (January 1870): 30–38.

Beaudot, William J. K. "The Bravest Act of the War." *Virginia Country's Civil War Quarterly* 6 (1986): 6–13.

Bennett, Gordon C. "Grant's Railroad: Route through Danger." *Civil War Times Illustrated* 22, no. 6 (October 1983): 14–20.

Bird, Margaret McKelvy, and Daniel W. Crofts, eds. "Soldier Voting in 1864: The David McKelvy Diary." *Pennsylvania Magazine of History & Biography* 115, no. 3 (July 1991): 371–413.

Bowerman, Richard N. "Cutting off Lee." *National Tribune*, June 26, 1902.

Bratton, John. "Report of Operations of Bratton's Brigade from May 7th, 1864, to January, 1865." *Southern Historical Society Papers* 8 (1880): 547–59.

Breckinridge, G[eorge] W. "Story of a Boy Captain." *Confederate Veteran* 13, no. 9 (September 1905): 415–16.

Brightman, Austin C. "Glory Enough: The 148th Pennsylvania Volunteers at Fort Crater." *Civil War Regiments* 2, no. 2 (1992): 141–55.

Briscoe, E. "A Visit to General Butler and the Army of the James." *Fraser's Magazine of Town and Country* 71 (April 1865): 434–48.

Bruce, George A. "Petersburg June 15—Fort Harrison September 29: A Comparison." In *Papers of the Military Historical Society of Massachusetts*, 14:83–115.

Bullock, Seymour. "Col. W. C. Raulston." *National Tribune*, January 15, 1891.

Burgwyn, William H. S. "Thirty-Fifth Regiment." In Clark, *Histories of the Several Regiments and Battalions from North Carolina*, 2:591–628.

———. "Clingman's Brigade." In Clark, *Histories of the Several Regiments and Battalions from North Carolina*, 4:480–500.

"The Campaign in Virginia," *Army and Navy Journal*, November 5, 1864.

"The Campaign in Virginia." *Army and Navy Journal*, October 22, 1864.

Cardwell, David. "A Brilliant Cavalry Coup." *Confederate Veteran* 26, no. 11 (November 1918): 474–76.

Carter, Solon A. "Fourteen Months' Service with Colored Troops." In *Civil War Papers Read before the Commandery of the State of Massachusetts Military Order of the Loyal Legion of the United States*, 1:155–79. Boston: Published by the Commandery, 1900.

Cheek, Col W. H. "Addenda to Ninth Regiment." In Clark, *Histories of the Several Regiments and Battalions from North Carolina*, 1:775–83.

Clay, Cecil. "A Personal Narrative of the Capture of Fort Harrison." In *War Papers Being Papers Read before the Commandery of the District of Columbia Military Order of the Loyal Legion of the United States*, 1:73–84. 1903. Reprint. Wilmington, N.C.: Broadfoot, 1993.

Conway, Dr. William B. "Gen. Hampton's Cattle Raid near City Point in 1864." *The State*, October 5, 1902.

Cooke, Charles M. "Fifty-Fifth Regiment." In Clark, *Histories of the Several Regiments and Battalions from North Carolina*, 3:287–312.

Crocker, Pvt. Silas. "Dread Days in Dixie." *National Tribune*, August 9, 1900.

Dauchy, George K. "The Battle of Ream's Station." In *Military Essays and Recollections: Papers Read before the Commandery of the State of Illinois, Military Order of the Loyal Legion of the United States*, 3:125–40. Chicago: Dial, 1899.

Day, W. A. "Life among the Bullets—In the Rifle Pits." *Confederate Veteran* 29, no. 6 (June 1921): 216–19.

Davis, John E. "A Federal Solder's Incident." *Southern Historical Society Papers* 17 (1889): 241–42.

Davis, Rev. L. H. "Famous Cattle Raid." *Confederate Veteran* 26, no. 10 (October 1918): 440–42.

"The Diary of Captain George D. Bowen." *Valley Forge Journal* 2 (June 1985): 176–231.

Doyle, W. E. "A Ride with Kautz." *National Tribune*, July 6, 1899.

Dunovant, Adelia A. "Gen. John Dunovant, Houston, Tex." *Confederate Veteran* 16, no. 4 (April 1908): 183–84.

Dutton, Grove H. "Weldon Railroad." *National Tribune*, April 15, 1886.

Elmore, Albert Rhett. "Incidents of Service with the Charleston Light Dragoons." *Confederate Veteran* 24, no. 12 (December 1916): 538–43.

Estes, James. "Second Fair Oaks." *National Tribune*, August 5, 1909.

Field, C. W. "Campaign of 1864 and 1865." *Southern Historical Society Papers* 14 (1886): 542–63.

Flanigan, W[illiam] A. "That Fight at Fort Gilmer." *Confederate Veteran* 13, no. 3 (March 1905): 123.

Fletcher, J. "Fighting Them Over." *National Tribune*, November 30, 1899.

Fortin, Maurice S., ed. "Colonel Hilary A. Herbert's History of the 8th Alabama Volunteer Regiment, CSA." *Alabama Historical Quarterly* 39, no. 1–4 (1977): 5–321.

Gallagher, Gary W. "Our Hearts Are Full of Hope: The Army of Northern Virginia in the Spring of 1864." In *The Wilderness Campaign*, edited by Gary W. Gallagher, 36–65. Chapel Hill: University of North Carolina Press, 1997.

———. "Two Generals and a Valley: Philip H. Sheridan and Jubal A. Early in the Shenandoah." In *The Shenandoah Valley Campaign of 1864*, edited by Gary W. Gallagher, 3–33. Chapel Hill: University of North Carolina Press, 2006.

"Gen. James Dearing." *Confederate Veteran* 9, no. 5 (May 1901): 215–16.

Goodwin, William H. "Letters of William Hiten Goodwin." *Louisa County Historical Magazine* 17, no. 2 (Winter/Spring 1985–86): 74–77.

Graham, Robert D. "Fifty-Sixth Regiment." In Clark, *Histories of the Several Regiments and Battalions from North Carolina*, 3:313–404.

Granberry, J. A. H. "That Fort Gilmer Fight." *Confederate Veteran* 13, no. 9 (September 1905): 413.

Gray, Stephen. "Echoes: On the Boydton Plank Road." *Maine Bugle* 3, no. 3 (July 1896): 281–83.

"Great Cattle Raid of 1864 in Virginia." *Confederate Veteran* 22, no. 4 (April 1914): 166–67.

Greene, A. Wilson. "Union Generalship in the 1864 Valley Campaign." In *Struggle for the Shenandoah: Essays on the 1864 Valley Campaign*, edited by Gary W. Gallagher, 41–76. Kent, Ohio: Kent State University Press, 1991.

Grimsley, Mark. "A Lack of Confidence: Benjamin F. Butler." In *Grant's Lieutenants from Chattanooga to Appomattox*, edited by Steven E. Woodworth, 105–31. Lawrence: University Press of Kansas, 2008.

Guelzo, Allen C. "As Plain as a Deep Scar: The Disaster at Reams Station, August 25, 1864." *North & South* 9, no. 2 (May 2006): 26–36.

Hagood, James R. "Report of Colonel J. R. Hagood, First S.C. Volunteers, of Campaign of 1864." *Southern Historical Society Papers* 13 (1885): 434–38.

Hampton, Wade. "Extract from Gen. Wade Hampton's Report of Cavalry Operations in Fall of 1864." *Transactions of the Southern Historical Society* (1874): 72–80.

Harris, Merlin C. "Fort Harrison: How It Was Stormed Early in That September Day." *National Tribune*, May 12, 1887.

Hewitt, Lawrence Lee. "Lee's Most Maligned General." In *Lee and His Generals: Essays in Honor of T. Harry Williams*, edited by Lawrence Lee Hewitt and Thomas E. Schott, 81–113. Knoxville: University of Tennessee Press, 2012.

Hissong, Josiah. "The 55th Pa.: What It Did and Suffered at Fort Harrison." *National Tribune*, July 21, 1887.

Horowitz, Murray M. "Benjamin Butler: Seventeenth President?" *Lincoln Herald* 77 (Winter 1975): 191–203.

Howell, Marshall. "Keeping Their Bargain." *National Tribune*, March 22, 1923.

Hubbell, W[illiam] S. "Battle of Fort Harrison." In *Story of the Twenty-First Regiment Connecticut Volunteer Infantry*, 287–311.

Huyette, Miles C. "Reminiscences of a Private." In *National Tribune Scrapbook*, 1:83–102. Washington, D.C.: National Tribune, 1909.

"An Incident at Hatcher's Run." *National Tribune*, April 15, 1882.

Jennings, Jerome. "Crawford's Narrow Escape." *National Tribune*, May 24, 1923.

Johnston, Charles. "Attack on Fort Gilmer, September 29, 1864." *Southern Historical Society Papers* 1 (1876): 438–42.

Johnston, Hugh Buckner, ed. "The Vinson Confederate Letters." *North Carolina Historical Review* 25, no. 1 (January 1948): 100–110.

Jones, A[lexander] C. "Texas and Arkansas at Fort Harrison." *Confederate Veteran* 25, no. 1 (January 1917): 24–25.

Kautz, A[ugust] V. "How I Won My First Brevet." In *Sketches of War History, 1861–1865: Papers Prepared for the Ohio Commandery of the Military Order of the Loyal Legion of the United States*, edited by W. H. Chamberlin, 4:363–87. Cincinnati: Robert Clarke, 1896.

Kearney, H[enry] C. "Fifteenth Regiment." In Clark, *Histories of the Several Regiments and Battalions from North Carolina*, 1:733–49.

Krick, Robert E. L. "A Stampeede of Stampeeds: The Confederate Disaster at Fisher's Hill." In *The Shenandoah Valley Campaign of 1864*, edited by Gary W. Gallagher, 161–99. Chapel Hill: University of North Carolina Press, 2006.

Ladd, John C. "Fort Harrison." *National Tribune*, April 10, 1919.

Lane, James H. "Glimpses of Army Life in 1864." *Southern Historical Society Papers* 18 (1890): 406–22.

———. "History of Lane's North Carolina Brigade." *Southern Historical Society Papers* 9 (1891): 353–61.

———. "Lane's Corps of Sharpshooters: The Career of This Famous Body." *Southern Historical Society Papers* 28 (1900): 1–8.

Lawhon, W[illiam] H. H. "Forty-Eighth Regiment." In Clark, *Histories of the Several Regiments and Battalions from North Carolina*, 3:113–24.

Levin, Kevin M. "The Earth Seemed to Tremble." *America's Civil War* 19, no. 2 (May 2006): 22–28.

———. "William Mahone, the Lost Cause, and Civil War History." *Virginia Magazine of History and Biography* 113, no. 4 (2005): 379–412.

Longacre, Edward G., ed. "The Roughest Kind of Campaigning: Letters of Sergeant Edward Wightman, Third New York Volunteers, May–July 1864." *Civil War History* 28, no. 4 (December 1982): 324–50.

Longstreet, James. "General Longstreet's Report of Affair of October 27, 1864." *Southern Historical Society Papers* 7, no. 11 (1879): 541–43.

Lott, Jess B. "Two Boys of the Fifth Texas Regiment." *Confederate Veteran* 13, no. 9 (September 1905): 417.

Ludwig, H. T. J. "Eighth Regiment." In Clark, *Histories of the Several Regiments and Battalions from North Carolina*, 1:389–415.

Lykes, Richard. "Hampton's Cattle Raid, September 14–17, 1864." *Military Affairs* 21, no. 1 (Spring 1957): 1–20.

Manarin, Louis H. "Over 500 Yankees Captured Singlehandedly." *Henrico County Historical Society Magazine* 18 (1994): 1–7.

Martin, Judge. "The Assault upon Fort Gilmer." *Confederate Veteran* 13, no. 6 (June 1905): 269–70.

Martin, W. J., and E. R. Outlaw, "Eleventh Regiment." In Clark, *Histories of the Several Regiments and Battalions from North Carolina*, 1:583–604.

May, T. J. "The Fight at Fort Gilmer." *Confederate Veteran* 12, no. 12 (December 1904): 587–88.

McCabe, W[illiam] Gordon. "Major Andrew Reid Venable, Jr." *Southern Historical Society Papers* 37 (1909): 61–73.

McCoy, Thomas F. "At the Weldon Railroad." *National Tribune*, March 13, 1890.

McDonald, W. N. "Hampton's Cattle Raid." *Confederate Veteran* 31, no. 3 (March 1923): 94–96.

McKethan, A[ugustus] A. "Fifty-First Regiment." In Clark, *Histories of the Several Regiments and Battalions from North Carolina*, 3:205–21.

McLaurin, William H. "Eighteenth Regiment." In Clark, *Histories of the Several Regiments and Battalions from North Carolina*, 2:14–78.

Means, Paul B. "Additional Sketch of the Sixty-Third Regiment (Fifth Cavalry)." In Clark, *Histories of the Several Regiments and Battalions from North Carolina*, 3:545–657.

Merrill, R. G., ed. "The Court-Martial of Private Spencer." *Civil War Times Illustrated* 27, no. 10 (February 1989): 34–40.

Mewborn, Horace. "Herding Yankee Cattle: The Beefsteak Raid, September 14–17, 1864." *Blue & Gray* 22, no. 3 (Summer 2005):11, 8–20, 44–48.

Montgomery, Horace. "A Union Officer's Recollections of the Negro as a Soldier." *Pennsylvania History* 28, no. 2 (April 1961): 156–86.

Moore, James B. "The Attack of Fort Harrison." *Confederate Veteran* 13, no. 9 (September 1905): 418–20.

Morgan, Michael. "From City Point to Appomattox with General Grant." *Journal of Military Science Institution* 149 (September–October 1907): 227–55.

Nabours, W[illiam] A. "Active Service of a Texas Command." *Confederate Veteran* 24, no. 2 (February 1916): 69–72.

Nash, Steven E. "In the Right Place and at the Right Time: Philip H. Sheridan." In *Grant's Lieutenants from Chattanooga to Appomattox*, edited by Steven E. Woodworth, 155–71. Lawrence: University Press of Kansas, 2008.

O'Donnell, J. H. "The 'Accidental' Explosion at City Point." *Virginia Magazine of History and Biography* 72, no. 3 (July 1964): 356–60.

Parker, Elmer Otis. "Captain Lyle: Forgotten Hero of the Confederacy." *Prologue* 4, no. 3 (Fall 1972): 165–72.

Partridge, Sylvester B. "With the Signal Corps from Fortress Monroe to Richmond, May 1864–April 1865." In *War Papers Read before the Commandery of the State of Maine*,

Military Order of the Loyal Legion of the United States, 3:83–98. Portland, Maine: Lefavor-Tower, 1908.

Perry, H. H. "Assault on Fort Gilmer." *Confederate Veteran* 13, no. 9 (September 1905): 413–15.

Pickens, J[ames] D. "Fort Harrison." *Confederate Veteran* 21, no. 10 (October 1913): 484.

Pippitt, T. Henry. "Before Richmond: Battle of Chaffin's Farm—Capture of Fort Harrison." *National Tribune,* October 10, 1918.

Polley, Joseph B. "Polley Lost a Foot—A Furlough." *Confederate Veteran* 5, no. 11 (November 1897): 569–71.

Pomfret, John E., ed., "Letters of Frederick Lockley, Union Soldier." *Huntington Library Quarterly* 16, no. 1 (November 1952): 75–112.

Porter, Charles H. "Explosion at City Point." *National Tribune,* December 4, 1913.

——. "Operations against the Weldon Railroad, August 18, 19, 21, 1864." In *Papers of the Military Historical Society of Massachusetts,* 5:241–66.

Powell, Junius L. "A Memory of Our Great War." *Journal of the Military Service Institution of the United States* 48 (1911): 87–99.

Rafuse, Ethan S. "Wherever Lee Goes . . . George G. Meade." In *Grant's Lieutenants from Chattanooga to Appomattox,* edited by Steven E. Woodworth, 47–83. Lawrence: University Press of Kansas, 2008.

Rayburn, Ella S. "Sabotage at City Point." *Civil War Times Illustrated* 22, no. 2 (1983): 28–33.

Reese, George. "What Five Confederates Did at Petersburg." *Confederate Veteran* 12, no. 6 (June 1904): 286.

Rice, Charles. "Act of Great Daring." *Military History* 6, no. 3 (August 1989): 8, 63–66.

Riddell, Rudolph R. "Ream's Station Again." *National Tribune,* October 20, 1910.

Roberts, William P. "Additional Sketch Nineteenth Regiment." In Clark, *Histories of the Several Regiments and Battalions from North Carolina,* 2:104.

Robertson, William Glenn. "From the Crater to New Market Heights: A Tale of Two Divisions." In *Black Soldiers in Blue: African American Troops in the Civil War Era,* edited by John David Smith, 66–69. Chapel Hill: University of North Carolina Press, 2002.

Robinson, John H. "Fifty-Second Regiment." In Clark, *Histories of the Several Regiments and Battalions from North Carolina,* 3:223–53.

Roche, Thomas T. "Fighting for Petersburg." In *Battles and Leaders of the Civil War, Volume 5,* edited by Peter Cozzens, 525–43. Urbanna: University of Illinois Press, 2002.

Rogers, Col. George T. "Retaking the Railroad at Reams Station." *Confederate Veteran* 5: 580–81.

Sawyer, John. "The Death of Colonel John Dunovant as Witnessed by Veteran John Sawyer." In *Recollections and Reminiscences,* 1:127.

Schaff, Morris. "The Explosion at City Point." In *Civil War Papers Read before the Commandery of the State of Massachusetts Military Order of the Loyal Legion of the United States,* 2:477–85. Boston: Published by the Commandery, 1900.

Sherman, George R. *Assault on Fort Gilmer and Reminiscences of Prison Life. Personal Narratives of Events in the War of the Rebellion, Being Papers Read before the Rhode Island Soldiers and Sailors Historical Society.* Ser. 5, no. 7. Providence, R.I.: Published by the Society, 1897.

Siburt, James T. "Colonel John M. Hughs: Brigade Commander and Confederate Guerilla." *Tennessee Historical Quarterly* 51 (Summer 1992): 87–95.

Smith, Donald W. "Perfectly Terrible Encounter." *Military History* 5, no. 3 (April 1987): 26–33.

Smith, Eric Ledell, ed. "The Civil War Letters of Quartermaster Sergeant John C. Brock, 43rd Regiment, United States Colored Troops." In *Making and Remaking Pennsylvania's Civil War*, edited by William Blair and William Pencak, 141–64. University Park: Pennsylvania State University Press, 2001.

Smith, Frank M. "Executions at Petersburg." *National Tribune*, May 18, 1916.

Sommers, Richard J. "The Battle No One Wanted." *Civil War Times Illustrated* 14, no. 5 (August 1975): 10–18.

———. "Petersburg Autumn: The Battle of Poplar Spring Church." In *The Confederate High Command & Related Topics*, edited by Roman J. Heleniak and Lawrence L. Hewitt, 30–52. Shippensburg, Pa.: White Mane, 1990.

Stedman, Charles M. "Battle at Reams' Station. Extract from the 'Memorial Address Delivered May 10, 1890, at Wilmington, N.C., by Hon. Charles M. Stedman.'" *Southern Historical Society Papers* 19 (1891): 113–20.

———. "The Forty-Fourth N.C. Infantry." *Southern Historical Society Papers* 25 (1897): 334–45.

———. "Forty-Fourth Regiment." In Clark, *Histories of the Several Regiments and Battalions from North Carolina*, 3:21–34.

Suderow, Bryce A. "Nothing but a Miracle Could Save Us." *North & South* 4, no. 2 (January 2001): 12–32.

Swearer, J[ames] A. "A Feint before Petersburg Attended by a Useless Sacrifice of Life." *Philadelphia Weekly Times*, July 28, 1883.

Taylor, Thomas. "The Battle of Burgess' Mill—Oct. 1864." *Recollections and Reminiscences*, 6:115–16.

Thomson, Bailey. "John C. C. Sanders: Lee's 'Boy Brigadier.'" *Alabama Review* 30, no. 2 (April 1979): 83–107.

Timberlake, W. L. "The Last Days in Front of Richmond." *Confederate Veteran* 22, no. 7 (July 1914): 303.

Trowbridge, J. W. "Conspicuous Feats of Valor." *Confederate Veteran* 24, no. 1 (January 1916): 25.

Trudeau, Noah Andre. "Costly Union Reconnaissance." *America's Civil War* (July 1994): 42–48, 82.

———. "Darbytown Road Debacle." *America's Civil War* (May 1992): 30–36.

Turtle, Thomas. "History of the Engineer Battalion." *Printed Papers of the Essayons Club of the Corps of Engineers* 1 (1868–72): 1–9.

Venable, M[atthew] W[alton]. "In the Trenches at Petersburg." *Confederate Veteran* 34, no. 2 (February 1926): 59–61.

Wagstaff, Henry McGilbert, ed. "Letters of Thomas Jackson Strayhorn." *North Carolina Historical Review* 13, no. 4 (October 1936): 311–34.

Walker, Francis A. "The Expedition to the Boydton Plank Road, October, 1864." In *Papers of the Military Historical Society of Massachusetts*, 5:319–50.

———. "Reams' Station." In *Papers of the Military Historical Society of Massachusetts*, 5:269–305.

Ware, Edwin. "Battery Harrison." *National Tribune*, November 20, 1887.

Waugh, Joan. "Francis Channing Barlow's Civil War." In *Cold Harbor to the Crater: The End of the Overland Campaign,* edited by Gary W. Gallagher and Caroline E. Janney, 138–75. Chapel Hill: University of North Carolina Press, 2015.

Weigley, Russell F. "David McMurtrie Gregg—A Profile." *Civil War Times Illustrated* 1, no. 7 (November 1962): 10–13, 26–30.

Wells, Stephen F. "Forts Harrison and Gilmer." *National Tribune Scrapbook,* 3:32. Washington, D.C.: National Tribune, 1909.

Wert, Jeffry D. "Jubal A. Early and Confederate Leadership." In *Struggle for the Shenandoah: Essays on the 1864 Valley Campaign,* edited by Gary W. Gallagher, 19–40. Kent, Ohio: Kent State University Press, 1991.

Wheeler, E. C. "Petersburg: Baldy Smith's Corps in the Works at That Place." *National Tribune,* July 18, 1889.

Wilcox, Cadmus M. "Battle of Jones's Farm, Sept. 30, 1864." *Transactions of the Southern Historical Society* 2 (1875): 67–71.

———. "Battle of Reams Station." *Transactions of the Southern Historical Society* 2 (1875): 63–67, 99.

Woodward, Daniel H., ed. "The Civil War of a Pennsylvania Trooper." *Pennsylvania Magazine of History and Biography* 87, no. 1 (January 1963): 39–62.

Young, John D. "In Petersburg during the Siege." In *The New Annals of the Civil War,* edited by Peter Cozzens and Robert I. Girardi, 415–34. Mechanicsburg, Pa.: Stackpole Books, 2004.

Young, Louis G. "The Pettigrew-Kirkland-MacRae Brigade." In Clark, *Histories of the Several Regiments and Battalions from North Carolina,* 4:555–68.

NEWSPAPERS

Adirondack Record (Au Sable, N.Y.)
Anderson (S.C.) Intelligencer
Athens (Ga.) Southern Banner
Atlanta Constitution
Atlanta Journal
Augusta (Ga.) Constitutionalist
Beaver (Pa.) Radical
Bedford (Pa.) Inquirer
Brooklyn (N.Y.) Daily Eagle
Brooklyn (N.Y.) Daily Standard-Union
Boston Evening Transcript
Cape Ann Light and Gloucester Telegraph (Gloucester, Mass.)
Charleston (S.C.) Daily Courier
Charlotte (N.C.) Democrat
Connecticut War Record (New Haven)
Columbus (Ga.) Daily Sun
Daily South Carolinian (Columbia)
Easton (Md.) Gazette

Fayetteville (N.C.) Observer
Hartford (Conn.) Daily Courant
Hillsborough (N.C.) Recorder
Irish-American Weekly (New York)
Jackson (Miss.) Clarion
Macon (Ga.) Daily Telegraph
Montgomery (Ala.) Daily Advertiser & Register
Montgomery (Ala.) Daily Mail
Newberry (S.C.) Herald and News
New Orleans Times-Picayune
New York Herald
New York Times
Norfolk Virginian-Pilot
Northern New York Times (Watertown)
Norwich (Conn.) Morning Bulletin
Petersburg Express
Philadelphia Inquirer
Philadelphia Weekly Press
Pittsfield (Mass.) Sun
Portland (Maine) Evening News
Raleigh (N.C.) Daily Confederate
Raleigh (N.C.) Weekly Confederate
Richmond Daily Dispatch
Richmond Daily Enquirer
Richmond Daily Examiner
Richmond News-Leader
Richmond Semi-Weekly Enquirer
Richmond Sentinel
Richmond Whig
Rochester (N.Y.) Union & Advertiser
St. Johnsville (N.Y.) News
Sandy Creek (N.Y.) Evening News
Santa Cruz (Calif.) Evening News
Southern Watchman (Athens, Ga.)
The State (Columbia, S.C.)
Utica (N.Y.) Weekly Herald
Warsaw–Wyoming County Times (Warsaw, N.Y.)
Waterbury (Conn.) American
Windham County Transcript (West Killingly, Conn.)
Winnsboro (S.C.) News and Herald

GOVERNMENT DOCUMENTS

Official Records of the Union and Confederate Navies in the War of the Rebellion. 30 vols. Washington, D.C.: Government Printing Office, 1894–1922.

U.S. War Department. *The War of the Rebellion: A Compilation of the Official Records of the Union and Confederate Armies.* 128 vols. Washington, D.C.: Government Printing Office, 1880–1901.

REFERENCE WORKS

Allardice, Bruce S. *Confederate Colonels: A Biographical Register.* Columbia: University of Missouri Press, 2008.

Current, Richard N., ed. *Encyclopedia of the Confederacy.* Vol. 2. New York: Simon & Schuster, 1993.

Krick, Robert E. L. *Staff Officers in Gray: A Biographical Register of the Staff Officers in the Army of Northern Virginia.* Chapel Hill: University of North Carolina Press, 2003.

Warner, Ezra J. *Generals in Blue: Lives of the Union Commanders.* Baton Rouge: Louisiana State University Press, 1964.

Welcher, Frank J. *The Union Army, 1861–1865: Organization and Operations.* Vol. 1, *The Eastern Theater.* Bloomington: Indiana University Press, 1989.

SECONDARY SOURCES

Andrew, Rod, Jr. *Wade Hampton: Confederate Warrior to Southern Redeemer.* Chapel Hill: University of North Carolina Press, 2008.

Austin, J. Luke, ed. *General John Bratton: Sumter to Appomattox in Letters to His Wife.* Sewanee, Tenn: Proctor's Hall, 2003.

Barefoot, Daniel W. *General Robert F. Hoke: Lee's Modest Warrior.* Winston-Salem, N.C.: John F. Blair, 1996.

Bearss, Edwin C. *The Petersburg Campaign: The Eastern Front Battles, June–August 1864.* El Dorado Hills, Calif.: Savas Beattie, 2012.

———. *The Petersburg Campaign: The Western Front Battles, September 1864–April 1865.* El Dorado Hills, Calif.: Savas Beattie, 2014.

Bergeron, Arthur W., Jr. *Confederate Mobile.* Jackson: University Press of Mississippi, 1991.

Boykin, Edward. *Beefsteak Raid.* New York: Funk & Wagnalls, 1960.

Boyle, Frank A. *A Party of Mad Fellows: The Story of the Irish Regiments in the Army of the Potomac.* Dayton, Ohio: Morningside, 1996.

Burkhardt, George S. *Confederate Rage, Yankee Wrath: No Quarter in the Civil War.* Carbondale: Southern Illinois University Press, 2007.

Burr, Frank A. *Life and Achievements of James Addams Beaver.* Philadelphia: Ferguson Bros., 1882.

Bushong, Millard K. *Fightin' Tom Rosser, C.S.A.* Shippensburg, Pa.: Beidel Printing House, 1983.

Carisio, Justin. *A Quaker Officer in the Civil War: Henry Gawthrop of the 4th Delaware.* Charleston, S.C.: History Press, 2013.

Carmichael, Peter S. *Lee's Young Artillerist: William R. J. Pegram.* Charlottesville: University Press of Virginia, 1995.

Carter, Davis Blake. *Two Stars in the Southern Sky: General John Gregg, C.S.A., and Mollie.* Spartanburg, S.C.: Reprint Co., 2001.

Castel, Albert. *Decision in the West: The Atlanta Campaign of 1864.* Lawrence: University Press of Kansas, 1992.

Chernow, Ron. *Grant.* New York: Penguin, 2017.

Cisco, Walter Brian. *Wade Hampton: Confederate Warrior, Conservative Statesman.* Washington, D.C.: Brassey's, 2004.

Cleveland, Mather. *New Hampshire Fights the Civil War.* London, N.H.: University Press of New England, 1969.

Cooling, Benjamin Franklin. *Jubal Early's Raid on Washington, 1864.* Baltimore: Nautical & Aviation Publishing Company of America, 1989.

———. *Monocacy: The Battle That Saved Washington.* Shippensburg, Pa.: White Mane, 1997.

Cooper, William J., Jr. *Jefferson Davis, American.* New York: Alfred A. Knopf, 2000.

Coski, John M. *Capital Navy: The Men, Ships, and Operations of the James River Squadron.* Campbell, Calif.: Savas, 1996.

Crenshaw, Douglas. *Fort Harrison and the Battle of Chaffin's Farm.* Charleston, S.C.: History Press, 2013.

Cresap, Bernarr. *Appomattox Commander: The Story of General E. O. C. Ord.* South Brunswick, N.J.: A. S. Barnes, 1981.

Daly, Louise Haskell. *Alexander Cheves Haskell: The Portrait of a Man.* Norwood, Mass.: Plimpton, 1934.

Daughtry, Mary Bandy. *Gray Cavalier: The Life and Wars of General W. H. F. "Rooney" Lee.* Cambridge, Mass.: Da Capo, 2002.

Davis, Oliver W. *Life of David Bell Birney, Major-General, United States Volunteers.* Philadelphia: King & Baird, 1867.

Davis, William C., ed. *The Image of War.* 6 vols. New York: Doubleday, 1981.

DeMontravel, Peter D. *A Hero to His Fighting Men: Nelson A. Miles, 1839–1925.* Kent, Ohio: Kent State University Press, 1998.

Elliott, Joseph Cantey. *Lieutenant General Richard Heron Anderson: Lee's Noble Soldier.* Dayton, Ohio: Morningside, 1985.

Evans, David, ed. *Random Acts of Kindness: True Stories of America's Civil War.* Wilmington, N.C.: Broadfoot, 2001.

Faust, Drew Gilpin. *This Republic of Suffering: Death and the American Civil War.* New York: Alfred A. Knopf, 2008.

Field, Ron. *Union Infantryman versus Confederate Infantryman: Eastern Theater, 1861–1865.* Combat 2. Oxford, Eng.: Osprey, 2013.

The Flags of the Confederate Armies. Returned to the Men Who Bore Them by the United States Government. St. Louis: Bruxton and Skinner, 1905.

Folsom, James Madison. *Heroes and Martyrs of Georgia: Georgia's Record in the Revolution of 1861.* Macon, Ga.: Burke, Boykin, 1864. Reprint, Baltimore: Butternut & Blue, 1995.

Freeman, Douglas Southall. *Lee's Lieutenants: A Study in Command.* Vol. 3. New York: Charles Scribner's Sons, 1944.

———. *R. E. Lee: A Biography* Vol. 3. New York: Charles Scribner's Sons, 1935.

Glatthaar, Joseph T. *General Lee's Army: From Victory to Collapse.* New York: Free Press, 2008.

———. *Partners in Command: The Relationships between Leaders in the Civil War.* New York: Free Press, 1994.

Greene, A. Wilson. *A Campaign of Giants: The Battle for Petersburg.* Vol. 1, *From the Crossing of the James to the Crater.* Chapel Hill: University of North Carolina Press, 2018.

———. *Civil War Petersburg: Confederate City in the Crucible of War.* Charlottesville: University of Virginia Press, 2006.

Guelzo, Allen C. *Robert E. Lee: A Life.* New York: Alfred A. Knopf, 2021.

Haselberger, Fritz. *Confederate Retaliation: McCausland's 1864 Raid.* Shippensburg, Pa.: Burd Street, 2000.

Heatwole, John L. *The Burning: Sheridan in the Shenandoah Valley.* Charlottesville, Va.: Rockbridge, 1998.

Hess, Earl J. *In the Trenches at Petersburg: Field Fortifications & Confederate Defeat.* Chapel Hill: University of North Carolina Press, 2009.

———. *Into the Crater: The Mine Attack at Petersburg.* Columbia: University of South Carolina Press, 2010.

———. *The Rifle Musket in Civil War Combat.* Lawrence: University Press of Kansas, 2008.

Horn, John. *The Siege of Petersburg: The Battles for the Weldon Railroad, August 1864.* El Dorado Hills, Calif.: Savas Beattie, 2015.

Howe, Thomas J. *Wasted Valor, June 15–18, 1864.* Lynchburg, Va.: H. E. Howard, 1988.

Humphreys, Henry H. *Andrew Atkinson Humphreys: A Biography.* Philadelphia: John Winston, 1924.

Huntington, Tom. *Searching for George Gordon Meade.* Mechanicsburg, Pa.: Stackpole Books, 2013.

Johnston, Angus J. *Virginia Railroads in the Civil War.* Chapel Hill: University of North Carolina Press, 1961.

Jordan, David M. *"Happiness Is Not My Companion": The Life of General G. K. Warren.* Bloomington: Indiana University Press, 2001.

———. *Winfield Scott Hancock: A Soldier's Life.* Bloomington: Indiana University Press, 1988.

Kautz, Lawrence G. *August Valentine Kautz, USA: Biography of a Civil War General.* Jefferson, N.C.: McFarland, 2008.

Keyes, Edward Lawrence. *Lewis Atterbury Stimson, M.D.* New York: Knickerbocker, 1918.

Lavery, Dennis S., and Mark H. Jordan. *Iron Brigade General: John Gibbon, a Rebel in Blue.* Westport, Conn: Greenwood, 1993.

Longacre, Edward G. *Army of Amateurs: General Benjamin F. Butler and the Army of the James, 1863–1865.* Mechanicsburg, Pa.: Stackpole Books, 1997.

———. *Gentleman and Soldier: The Extraordinary Life of General Wade Hampton.* Nashville: Rutledge Hill, 2003.

Macy, Silvanus. *Genealogy of the Macy Family from 1635 to 1868.* Albany, N.Y., 1868.

Mahr, Theodore C. *The Battle of Cedar Creek: Showdown in the Shenandoah, October 1–30, 1864.* Lynchburg, Va.: H. E. Howard, 1992.

Manarin, Louis H. *Henrico County—Field of Honor.* Vol. 2. Richmond, Va.: Henrico County, 2004.

Marvel, William. *Burnside.* Chapel Hill: University of North Carolina Press, 1991.

———. *Tarnished Victory: Finishing Lincoln's War.* Boston: Houghton, Mifflin, Harcourt, 2011.

Maull, D[avid] W. *The Life and Military Services of the Late Brigadier General Thomas A. Smyth.* Wilmington, Del: H. & E. F. James, 1870.

McArthur, Judith N., and Orville Vernon Burton. *A Gentleman and an Officer: A Military and Social History of James B. Griffin's Civil War*. New York: Oxford University Press, 1996.

McCabe, James D. *Life and Campaigns of General Robert E. Lee*. New York: Blelock, 1867.

McCrea, Henry Vaughan. *Red Dirt and Isinglass*. Marianna, Fla: Chipola, 1992.

McMurry, Richard M. *Atlanta 1864: Last Chance for the Confederacy*. Lincoln: University of Nebraska Press, 2000.

McPherson, James M. *Battle Cry of Freedom: The Civil War Era*. New York: Oxford University Press, 1988.

———. *Tried by War: Abraham Lincoln as Commander in Chief*. New York: Penguin, 2008.

———. *War on the Waters: The Union & Confederate Navies, 1861–1865*. Chapel Hill: University of North Carolina Press, 2012.

Musicant, Ivan. *Divided Waters: The Naval History of the Civil War*. Edison, NJ: Castle Books, 2000.

Naisawald, L. VanLoan. *The Battle of Lynchburg: Seize Lynchburg If Only for a Single Day*. Lynchburg, Va.: Warwick House, 2004.

———. *Grape and Canister: The Story of the Field Artillery of the Army of the Potomac, 1861–1865*. New York: Oxford University Press, 1960.

Newsome, Hampton. *Richmond Must Fall: The Richmond-Petersburg Campaign, October 1864*. Kent, Ohio: Kent State University Press, 2013.

Parker, William L. *General James Dearing*. Lynchburg, Va.: H. E. Howard, 1990.

Patchan, Scott C. *The Last Battle of Winchester: Phil Sheridan, Jubal Early, and the Shenandoah Valley Campaign, August 7–September 19, 1864*. El Dorado Hills, Calif.: Savas Beattie, 2013.

———. *Shenandoah Summer: The 1864 Valley Campaign*. Lincoln: University of Nebraska Press, 2007.

Patterson, Gerard A. *From Blue to Gray: The Life of Confederate General Cadmus M. Wilcox*. Mechanicsburg, Pa.: Stackpole Books, 2001.

Pfanz, Donald C. *Richard S. Ewell: A Soldier's Life*. Chapel Hill: University of North Carolina Press, 1998.

Pollard, Edward A. *Southern History of the War*. New York, 1866. Reprint, New York: Fairfax, 1977.

Price, James S. *The Battle of First Deep Bottom*. Charleston, S.C.: History Press, 2014.

———. *The Battle of New Market Heights*. Charleston, S.C.: History Press, 2011.

Power, J. Tracy. *Lee's Miserables: Life in the Army of Northern Virginia from the Wilderness to Appomattox*. Chapel Hill: University of North Carolina Press, 1998.

Putnam, Albert D., ed. *Major General Joseph R. Hawley, Soldier and Editor (1826–1905)*. Hartford: Connecticut Civil War Centennial Commission, 1964.

Quatman, G. William. *A Young General and the Fall of Richmond: The Life and Career of Godfrey Weitzel*. Athens: Ohio University Press, 2015.

Rafuse, Ethan S. *George Gordon Meade and the War in the East*. Abilene, Tex.: McWhiney Foundation, 2003.

———. *Robert E. Lee and the Fall of the Confederacy, 1863–1865*. Lanham, Md.: Rowman & Littlefield, 2008.

Rhea, Gordon C. *The Battle of the Wilderness, May 5–6, 1864*. Baton Rouge: Louisiana State University Press, 1994.

————. *The Battles for Spotsylvania Court House and the Road to Yellow Tavern, May 7–12, 1864.* Baton Rouge: Louisiana State University Press, 1997.

————. *Cold Harbor: Grant and Lee, May 26–June 3, 1864.* Baton Rouge: Louisiana State University Press, 2002.

————. *On to Petersburg: Grant and Lee, June 4–15, 1864.* Baton Rouge: Louisiana State University Press, 2017.

————. *To the North Anna River: Grant and Lee, May 13–25, 1864.* Baton Rouge: Louisiana State University Press, 2000.

Roberts, Agatha. *As They Remembered.* New York: William-Frederick, 1964.

Robertson, James I., Jr. *General A. P. Hill: The Story of a Confederate Warrior.* New York: Random House, 1987.

Robertson, William Glenn. *Back Door to Richmond: The Bermuda Hundred Campaign, April–June 1864.* Newark: University of Delaware Press, 1987.

————. *The First Battle for Petersburg: The Attack and Defense of the Cockade City, June 9, 1864.* El Dorado Hills, Calif.: Savas Beattie, 2015.

Sanders, Charles W., Jr. *While in the Hands of the Enemy: Military Prisons of the Civil War.* Baton Rouge: Louisiana State University Press, 2005.

Schiller, Herbert M. *The Bermuda Hundred Campaign.* Dayton, Ohio: Morningside House, 1988.

Sears, Stephen W. *Lincoln's Lieutenants: The High Command of the Army of the Potomac.* Boston: Houghton Mifflin Harcourt, 2017.

Simpson, Brooks D. *Ulysses S. Grant: Triumph over Adversity, 1822–1665.* Boston: Houghton Mifflin, 2000.

Smith, C. Foster. *Jerimiah Smith and the Confederate War.* Spartanburg, S.C.: Reprint Co., 1993.

Smith, Timothy B. *The Siege of Vicksburg: Climax of the Campaign to Open the Mississippi River, May 23–July 4, 1863.* Lawrence: University Press of Kansas, 2021.

Sommers, Richard J. *Richmond Redeemed: The Siege at Petersburg.* Garden City, N.Y.: Doubleday, 1981. Reprint, El Dorado Hills, Calif.: Savas Beattie, 2014.

Staats, Richard J. *A Grassroots History of the American Civil War: The Life and Times of Colonel William Stedman of the 6th Ohio Cavalry.* Bowie, Md.: Heritage Books, 2003.

Starr, Stephen Z. *The Union Cavalry in the Civil War.* Vol. 2, *The War in the East from Gettysburg to Appomattox, 1863–1865.* Baton Rouge: Louisiana State University Press, 1981.

Symonds, Craig L. *Lincoln and His Admirals.* New York: Oxford University Press, 2008.

Talbot, Edith. *Samuel Chapman Armstrong: A Biographical Study.* New York: Doubleday, Page, 1904.

Taylor, Emerson Gifford. *Gouverneur Kemble Warren: Life and Letters of an American Soldier.* Boston: Houghton Mifflin, 1932.

Thompson, Lauren K. *Friendly Enemies: Soldier Fraternization throughout the American Civil War.* Lincoln: University of Nebraska Press, 2020.

Trudeau, Noah Andre. *Bloody Roads South: The Wilderness to Cold Harbor, May–June 1864.* Boston: Little, Brown, 1989.

————. *Like Men of War: Black Troops in the Civil War, 1863–1865.* Boston: Little, Brown, 1998.

Trumbull, Henry Clay. *The Knightly Soldier: A Biography of Major Henry Ward Camp.* Boston: Noyes, Holmes, 1871.

Tucker, Glenn. *Hancock the Superb.* Indianapolis: Bobbs-Merrill, 1960.

Ural, Susannah J. *Hood's Texas Brigade: The Soldiers and Families of the Confederacy's Most Celebrated Unit.* Baton Rouge: Louisiana State University Press, 2017.

Waite, Otis F. R. *New Hampshire in the Great Rebellion.* Claremont, N.H.: Tracy, Chase, 1870.

Walker, Francis A. *General Hancock.* New York: D. Appleton, 1894.

Welch, Richard F. *The Boy General: The Life and Careers of Francis Channing Barlow.* Kent, Ohio: Kent State University Press, 2003.

Wellman, Manly Wade. *Giant in Gray: A Biography of Wade Hampton of South Carolina.* Dayton, Ohio: Morningside Bookshop, 1988.

Wert, Jeffry D. *Cavalryman of the Lost Cause: A Biography of J. E. B. Stuart.* New York: Simon & Schuster, 2008.

———. *From Winchester to Cedar Creek: The Shenandoah Campaign of 1864.* Carlisle, Pa.: South Mountain, 1987.

———. *General James Longstreet: The Confederacy's Most Controversial Soldier.* New York: Simon & Schuster, 1993.

Williams, T. Harry. *P. G. T. Beauregard: Napoleon in Gray.* Baton Rouge: Louisiana State University Press, 1955.

Wilson, James H. *The Life of John A. Rawlins.* New York: Neale, 1916.

Wilson, Joseph T. *The Black Phalanx: History of the Negro Soldiers of the United States.* New York: Arno, 1968.

Woodbury, Augustus. *Major General Ambrose E. Burnside and the Ninth Army Corps.* Providence, R.I.: Sidney S. Rider and Brother, 1867.

DISSERTATIONS, THESES, AND UNPUBLISHED RESEARCH PAPERS

Blankenship, James. "As Smooth as a Greased Wheel: The History of the United States Military Railroad during the Petersburg Campaign." Unpublished manuscript.

Bryant, James Kenneth, II. "A Model Regiment: The 36th U.S. Colored Infantry in the Civil War." Master's thesis, University of Vermont, 1996.

Flanagan, Vincent J. "The Life of General Gouverneur Kemble Warren." Ph.D. dissertation, City University of New York, 1969.

Forstchen, William Robert. "The 28th United States Colored Troops: Indiana's African Americans Go to War, 1863–1865." Ph.D. dissertation, Purdue University, 1994.

Hephner, Richard H. "Where Youth and Laughter Go: The Experience of Trench Warfare from Petersburg to the Western Front." Master's thesis, Virginia Tech University, 1997.

Marino, Carl W. "General Alfred Howe Terry: Soldier from Connecticut." Ph.D. dissertation, New York University, 1968.

McDaid, William Kelsey. "Four Years of Arduous Service: The History of the Branch-Lane Brigade in the Civil War." Ph.D. dissertation, Michigan State University, 1987.

Ott, Eugene Matthew, Jr. "The Civil War Diary of James J. Kirkpatrick, Sixteenth Mississippi Infantry, CSA." Master's thesis, Texas A&M University, 1984.

Serff, John Jonas. "The Life of James A. Beaver." Ph.D. dissertation, Penn State University, 1955.

Sommers, Richard J. "Grant's Fifth Offensive at Petersburg." Ph.D. dissertation, Rice University, 1967.

Walker, Paula C., and Robert I. Girardi. "What the Good Law Says: A Military Biography of Major General Gouverneur Kemble Warren." Unpublished manuscript.

Zatt, David K. "Joint Operations in the James River Basin, 1862–1865." Master's thesis, U.S. Army Command and General Staff College, 1993.

INDEX

Andrews, Pvt. Andrew Jackson, 322

Andrews, Lt. John T., 453

Anthony, Capt. George Tobey, 341

Antietam (Sharpsburg), Battle of, 4, 55, 146, 151, 232, 527n94

Appomattox River, 8, 46, 48, 52, 222, 473

Apted, Pvt. Alfred A., 354

Archer, Lt. Col. Fletcher, 344

Archer, Brig. Gen. James J.: resumes brigade command, 241, 360

Archer's Brigade, 469, 595n51; and Battle of Pegram's Farm, 358, 360, 365, 367; on October 1, 374–76; on October 2, 386, 390, 577n47

Armstrong, Cpl. Nelson, 473–74, 490

Armstrong, Col. Samuel, 84

Armstrong house, 374, 477; as Meade's headquarters, 489

Armstrong's Mill, 181, 183, 345, 356, 366, 469–70, 472, 490–91

Army of the James, 2, 10; and Second Offensive, 11; fails to move after Battle of Weldon Railroad, 166; deployment of, September 30, 330; deployment of, October 1, 397; defense line after October 1, 403; and goals of Sixth Offensive, 451

Army of Northern Virginia, 2, 43; optimism of, 6; strength of, 6; and First Offensive, 10; deployment of at Petersburg, early October, 407; advantage of interior lines, 408; measures to obtain reinforcements, 408

Army of Tennessee, 277, 422

Army of the Potomac, 2–3, 5; strength of, 3; casualties May–June, 11; discouragement of, 21–22; and role in Fifth Offensive, 280, 342, 356; deployment of, October 6, 407; and goals of Sixth Offensive, 451

Army of the Shenandoah, 431; composition of, 39; strength of, 40

Arthur's Swamp, 152, 169, 345, 350, 352, 357, 364, 381, 388, 392, 428, 570n47

Ashton, Cpl. Edgar, 235

Atkinson, Lt. Col. John W., 400

Atkinson's First Division (heavy artillery), 400

Atlanta, Georgia, 2; soldier interest in, 241–42; soldier reaction to its capture, 242–46, 266, 269

Augusta, Georgia, 277

Averell, Maj. Gen. William Woods, 40

Avery house, 224, 342, 371, 378

Aylett, Col. William, 550n99

Ayres, Brig. Gen. Romeyn B., 1; description of, 97; and Battle of Weldon Railroad, 101–2, 116, 118, 131; on October 1, 376; and Second Squirrel Level Road, 427–28

Ayers's division: and Battle of Weldon Railroad, 94, 97–98, 103, 105, 108, 125, 144, 149, 159, 162; and Fifth Offensive, 344, 349, 351–52, 357, 572n75, 576n19; deployment of, October 1, 373, 376; and Second Squirrel Level Road, 426; and Sixth Offensive, 466, strength of, 466

Babcock, Capt. Edwin S., 319

Babcock, Lt. Col. Orville, 35, 476

Bachman, Pvt. William Henry, 101

Badeau, Lt. Col. Adam, 18, 309, 408

Bailey, Capt. Marcellus, 320

Bailey's Creek, 43, 52–54, 57, 61, 514n32

Baker, Cpl. Heman E., 297, 336, 461

Baker, Maj. J. Stanard, 253–54

Baker, Maj. Joel B., 46

Baker, Maj. William J., 199

Ballen (artist), 449

Ball's Bluff, Battle of, 57

Barbour, Col. William M., 44; description of, 73; and Second Deep Bottom, 76–78; mortally wounded, 360, 511n4

Barbour's brigade, 72–73, 76, 78–79

Barden, Lt. Col. William A., 310

Barfield, Lt. R. Lee, 28

Barlow, Brig. Gen. Francis C., 3; and Second Deep Bottom, 46, 52, 55–56, 58, 60, 514n34, 517n78; description of, 55, 175; goes on sick leave, 84, 175, 514n35, 535n8; returns to active duty, 172; and "Fight by Moonlight," 173

Barlow, Sgt. Joseph, 20–21, 29, 36

Barlow's division: and Second Deep Bottom, 46, 48, 54–55

Barnard, Brig. Gen. John G., 42, 83, 324, 403, 405, 450–51

Barnes, Lt. Col. Joseph H., 126

Barnes, Joseph K., 590n109

Barney, Lt. Col. Albert M., 314

Barney, Hiram, 590n109

Barnum, Lt. George, 222, 243, 417

Barrier, Lt. Col. Rufus A., 28

Barringer, Brig. Gen. Rufus, 63, 157, 168, 192

Barringer's (Cheek's) Brigade, 168, 176; and Second Deep Bottom, 63, 68; and Battle of Weldon Railroad, 143, 156; and "Fight by Moonlight," 172; and Second Reams' Station, 182, 184, 186, 202–3, 209; and Beefsteak Raid, 249, 257; and Fifth Offensive, 345, 347, 375, 380, 384; and combat on October 2, 390; and Sixth Offensive, 487

Barringer's division: and Second Deep Bottom, 202

Bartlett, Sgt. Jacob, 137

Bartlett, Brig. Gen. Joseph, 391–92; assumes command of Gwyn's brigade, 371

Barton, Pvt. Lyman A., 19

Barton's (Seth) Brigade, 550n99

Bass, Col. Frederick S., 44, 68, 289; wounded, 423

Bates, Col. Delevan, 469

Bath Squadron, Eleventh Virginia Cavalry, 253–54

Batteries 3–8 (Confederate), 298

Battersea plantation, pontoon bridge at, 348

Battery 5 (Confederate), 298, 550n103

Battery 10 (Confederate), 300, 306–7, 323

Battery 11 (Confederate), 298, 300, 306, 310, 312–13, 563n50

Battery 18 (Union), 549n88

Battery 19 (Union), 549n88

Battery 21 (Union), 430

Battery 24 (Union), 488

Battery 45 (Confederate), 137, 225, 348, 367, 390, 394, 473, 529n17

Battery A, First Pennsylvania Artillery, 460, 591n13

Battery A, First Rhode Island Artillery: and march to Reams' Station, 174; at Reams' Station, 177, 200–201

Battery A, Second U.S. Artillery, 260

Battery A, Sumter (Georgia) Artillery, 180

Battery B, First Rhode Island Artillery: and march to Reams' Station, 174; at Reams' Station, 177, 198, 200–201

Battery B, First U.S. Artillery, 410, 413, 415

Battery C, Eighteenth South Carolina Heavy Artillery Battalion, 390

Battery C, Fifth U.S. Artillery, 476

Battery C, First U.S. Artillery, 513n26

Battery C, Third New Jersey Artillery: and march to Reams' Station, 174; at Reams' Station, 177, 204

Battery C, Third Rhode Island Artillery, 513n26

Battery Clingman, 434

Battery Colquitt, 434

Battery D, First U.S. Artillery, 513n26, 587n73

Battery E, First North Carolina Artillery, 567n4

Battery E, First U.S. Artillery, 587n73

Battery Ewell, 593n35

Battery F, First Rhode Island Light Artillery, 563n49

Battery F, Thirteenth North Carolina Artillery, 567n4

Battery H, First New York Light Artillery (Mink's Battery), 428

Battery Hagood, 434

Battery I, Fifth U.S. Artillery, 476

Battery I, First U.S. Artillery, 487

Battery Kirkland, 434

Battery L, First New York Light Artillery, 145

Battery White, 299, 310

Baughman, Charles, 270

Bauskett, Lt. John, 552n7

Blood, Capt. Henry B., 36

Blucher, Cpl. Charles, 304

Boernstein, Maj. Augustus S., 292

Boisseau, Alfred, house and farm of, 357, 362–63, 386; burned on October 4, 425, 585n46

Boisseau, Joseph, 181; house of, 537n46

Bolton, Charles, 4

Boston, Cpl. William, 29, 221

Boswell, Joseph C., house and farm of, 356, 572n76

Bowen, Sgt. Charles T., 26

Bowen, Capt. George D., 228–29

Bowerman, Lt. Col. Richard N., 148

Bowers, Lt. Col. Theodore, 21, 33, 35, 158

Bowles, Pvt. Jesse R., 233

Bowles, Col. Pinckney D., 307, 320

Bowles's brigade: ordered to north side, 307; at Fort Gilmer, 316, 320; on September 30, 331–32, 336; probes on October 2, 404; and First Darbytown Road, 410, 412–13, 415–16, 419, 421–22, 584n37; and Second Darbytown Road, 440, 442–43, 587n70

Boyce, Addison S., 30, 231

Boydton Plank Road, 180–81, 215, 225, 227, 249–50, 262, 278, 347, 350, 357–58, 387, 395, 470, 472–73, 476, 482, 484

Boydton Plank Line, 226, 343, 386, 570n42

Brady, Lt. George K., 122, 527n87

Bragg, Gen. Braxton, 245, 307, 429

Bragg, Brig. Gen. Edward S., 271, 429; description of, 105; and Battle of Weldon Railroad, 102, 105–7, 113, 115–16, 524n43

Branch house, 110

Brander, Capt. Thomas A., 99, 370

Brandy Station, Virginia, 2; Battle of, 67

Bratton, Brig. Gen. John, 44, 82, 87; on September 30, 331–32, 335, 340; wounded on October 7, 421

Bratton's Brigade: and Second Deep Bottom, 53–54, 61, 65, 78; returns to south side, 87; ordered to recross the James, 307, 324; on September 30, 331; and attack on Fort Harrison, 334–35, 338; and

First Darbytown Road, 412–13, 415–16, 419–22, 584n37; commanded by Col. Joseph Walker, 440, 587n70

Breck, Capt. George, 145

Breckinridge, Capt. George W., 300

Breckinridge, Maj. Gen. John C., 40

Brevard, Col. Theodore W., 146, 529n16

Brice, Pvt. John M., 226

Brightwell, Pvt. Jasper, 459

Broadway Landing, 281–83, 555n54

Broady, Lt. Col. Oscar K., 49, 188–89; wounded, 198

Broady's brigade: and Second Deep Bottom, 49, 55–56, 78, 80, 82; and destruction of Weldon Railroad, 175; and Second Reams' Station, 184, 187, 189, 196–98

Brock, Lt. Ignatius W., 150, 162

Brogan, Sgt. John P., 222

Brooke, Capt. Samuel S., 396

Brooks, Edward, 243

Brower, Lt. Henry D., 200

Brown, Pvt. Charles, 145

Brown, Sgt. Charles E., 125

Brown, Lt. Henry, 309

Brownson, Capt. Edward P. "Ned," 3, 23; killed, 202, 212

Bryan, Lt. James A.W., 226

Brydon, Capt. John, 337

Buckingham, Lt. Charles, 234

Buffin, Alfred R., house of, 294

Burgess farm, 473, 476, 483–84

Burgess Mill, 347, 452, 471–73, 477, 480–81, 483

Burgwyn, Capt. William H. S., 150, 334, 337–39

burial of dead, 406

Burke, Lt. Col. Denis F., 489

Burnett, Capt. Eugene, 133, 456

Burnham, Brig. Gen. Hiram, 27, 272, 298, 562n29, 563n41; killed at Fort Harrison, 305

Burnham, Q. M. Uberto A., 22, 449

Burnham's brigade: and Fifth Offensive, 283, 297–98; and Battle of Fort Harrison, 301–2, 309, 334

Charles, Pvt. Henry F., 395

Charles City Road, 57, 59, 63–70, 75, 78, 80, 85, 315, 400–402, 410, 412–13, 433, 438, 441, 443, 559n7

Charleston, South Carolina, 277

Charles Town, West Virginia, 266

Chattanooga, Tennessee, 2, 5, 242, 431

Cheek, Col. William H., 168, 182

Cherry, Capt. Macon G., 569n42

Chester, Thomas Morris, 34, 235, 455

Chester, Capt. Walter T., 105–7, 115

Chew, Capt. Henry F., 202

Chew, Capt. R. Preston, 249, 260, 347, 473

Chickahominy River, 288, 315, 433

Chickamauga, Battle of, 5, 422

Chieves house, 94, 378

Childrey house, 302

Chimborazo Hospital, 308

Chimneys, Battle of the, 236–38, 489, 549n87

Christ, Col. Benjamin C., 568n24

Christian, Col. William S., 118

Christian Commission, U.S., 4, 33

Church, Chaplain Lafayette, 49

Church Road, 226, 343, 356–58, 360–61, 365, 373–74, 377, 388, 395, 406, 426, 446

City Point, Virginia, 9, 47, 222, 247–48, 283; explosion at, 32–37; Union headquarters at, 45, 128, 145, 222, 256, 274, 281, 308

City Point & Army Line Railroad, 222–25, 545n47; Confederates fire at, 224, 226

Claiborne, John Herbert, 348

Claiborne Road, 452–53, 470

Clancy, Sgt. James T.: shoots Dunovant, 384, 577n39

Clark, Capt. A. Judson, 177

Clark, Pvt. Elisha, 20

Clark, Capt. George, 147

Clark, Sgt. Nathan S., 352

Clark, Lt. Col. Steve, 220

Clarke, Sgt. Hermon, 317, 464

Clarke, Lt. Luke, 113, 115

Clarke, Lt. Robert, 260

Clay, Capt. Cecil, 283, 302

Clay, Capt. Tacitus T., 161

Clements house, 371, 407

Clements house (near Duncan Road), 466, 469, 594n47

Clingman, Brig. Gen. Thomas L., 111, 119, 123

Clingman's Brigade, 587n70; and Battle of Weldon Railroad, 111–12, 115, 119–20, 123, 127, 133, 136; and Fifth Offensive, 328; and attack on Fort Harrison, 332, 334, 337–38

Cluseret, Gen. Gustave Paul, 17

Clutter's (Virginia) Battery, 180, 567n4, 582n8

Coan's brigade: and Second Deep Bottom, 55, 77–80

Coan, Lt. Col. William B., 51

Cobb's Georgia Legion, 168, 203–4

Coburn, Cpl. James Parley, 27, 264

Cocke's Mill, 252–53, 258, 553n21; fighting at, 256, 265

Coggins Point, 248, 250

Coker, Capt. Francis Marion, 130, 238, 245, 396, 495

Coleman, Pvt. John Kennedy, 338, 416

Coles, Adj. Robert T., 320, 416

Coles Creek, 313

Colquitt, Brig. Gen. Alfred H., 99, 331; and failure to recapture Fort Harrison, 339–40, 568n26

Colquitt's Brigade: and Battle of Weldon Railroad, 99, 102, 111–12, 115, 119–21, 123–24, 126–27, 136; crosses the James, 328; and attack on Fort Harrison, 332, 334, 337–38; deployment of, 434, 445, 587n70

Colquitt's Salient, 26, 31, 227, 507n74

Comstock, Lt. Col. Cyrus, 18, 83, 132, 210, 308, 324, 403, 405, 494, 580–81n91

Conahey, Lt. John, 351, 579n71

Conner, Brig. Gen. James, 44, 65, 72, 76, 78–80, 82, 85; and Second Reams' Station, 180, 209

Conner's brigade: and Second Reams' Station, 187, 189, 193, 195–97

Dunlop house, 119, 139

Dunlop's Station, 65, 156, 328, 533n74

Dunn, Capt. Washington L., 112, 337

Dunovant, Col./Brig. Gen. John: assumes command of Butler's Brigade, 167, 383, 535n3, 577n35; and Battle of Vaughan Road, 383–84; description of, 383; killed, 384, 577n39

Dunovant's Brigade: and "Fight by Moonlight," 172–73; and Second Reams' Station, 182, 187, 541n102; and Beefsteak Raid, 249, 258; and Fifth Offensive, 347; and Battle of Vaughan Road, 382, 384

Dushane, Col. Nathan T., 98, 100; killed, 145

Dusseault, Lt. John H., 123

Dutch Gap Canal: construction of, 42, 273–74; Confederate bombardment of, 42, 45, 273–75, 289; labor force of, 281; prisoners employed for construction of, 405; origin of name, 511n121

Dutton, Sgt. Grove H., 102

Dyer, Surgeon J. Franklin, 25

Early, Lt. Gen. Jubal A., 8, 37; composition and strength of his force in the Shenandoah Valley, 40; defeats in Shenandoah Valley, 268; criticism of, 271

Eaton, Amos B., 590n109

Ebenezer Church, fighting at, 259–61, 265

Edmonston, Catherine Ann Deveraux, 242

Edwards, Lt. Col. Albert M., 115

Egan, Brig. Gen. Thomas W., 470, 474, 476, 481, 484

Egan's division: and Sixth Offensive, 470, 472–73, 475, 480–82, 490, 598n87

Eggleston, Sgt. Joseph William, 331, 340

Eighteen-Gun Battery, 26

Eighteenth Corps (Smith/Ord/Weitzel), 26, 29, 60, 171, 223, 234; and First Offensive, 10; and Battle of Weldon Railroad, 91, 105, 107, 109, 129; and Fifth Offensive, 280, 316; deployment on September 30, 330; on October 13, 435; plans for Sixth Offensive, 454; strength of, 454; and Battle of Williamsburg Road, 458, 592n24

Eighteenth Massachusetts, 533n69, 549n96, 571n59

Eighteenth North Carolina, 196, 200, 236

Eighteenth South Carolina, 489

Eighth Alabama, 65, 146

Eighth Connecticut, 19, 274, 301, 304

Eighth Corps (Army of West Virginia), 39

Eighth Florida, 146

Eighth Georgia, 57, 79, 81, 459

Eighth Georgia Cavalry, 28, 343

Eighth Maine, 229, 312, 460

Eighth Michigan, 124–25

Eighth New Jersey, 82, 493, 598n91

Eighth New York Heavy Artillery, 46, 201, 213, 474

Eighth North Carolina, 28, 122

Eighth Pennsylvania Cavalry, 52, 59, 63, 243, 260

Eighth U.S. Colored Troops (USCT), 62, 319–20, 438–39

Eighth U.S. Infantry, 579n71

Eighty-Eighth New York, 56, 184, 489

Eighty-Eighth Pennsylvania, 101, 106, 108, 120–21

Eighty-Fifth Pennsylvania, 62, 75, 77–78, 231, 273, 436, 438, 441

Eighty-First New York, 302, 304

Eighty-First Pennsylvania, 172, 184

Eighty-Fourth Pennsylvania, 392

Eighty-Ninth New York, 312–13, 460–62

Eighty-Third Pennsylvania, 354–55

Elder, Maj. Thomas Claybrook, 397

Eldredge, Lt. Daniel, 70, 74, 77, 296, 400

Eleventh Alabama, 146–47

Eleventh Connecticut, 30, 281

Eleventh Florida, 146, 529n16

Eleventh Georgia, 72, 76, 78, 190, 517n82

Eleventh Maine, 45, 53, 62, 72–76, 86, 411, 421, 438, 443

Eleventh Massachusetts, 82, 392–93, 598n91

Eleventh New Hampshire, 14, 225, 358, 361, 573n84

Eleventh New Jersey, 390, 484, 598n91

Eleventh North Carolina, 137, 181, 362, 482

Eleventh Pennsylvania, 100, 121, 549n96

Gary, Brig. Gen. Martin W., 44; and Second Deep Bottom, 58, 84; description of, 287; attends council of war, 409; and First Darbytown Road, 413; and Second Darbytown Road, 440

Gary's Brigade: and Second Deep Bottom, 54, 61, 68; on north side after Second Deep Bottom, 87; strength of, 559n3; defends New Market Line, 289, 296; defends Laurel Hill Church, 313–15; performance on September 29, 325–26; and Battle of Roper's Farm, 400; probes on October 2, 404; and First Darbytown Road, 410, 412, 419; deployment of, 434, 456

Garysville, Virginia, 553n21

Gatewood, Lt. Andrew, 253

Gawthrop, Capt. Henry, 155, 271, 373, 388–89, 428

General Meade (ship), 34

Gerhardt house, 441

Gettysburg, Battle of, 3, 55, 57, 146, 151, 232, 336, 341

Gibbon, Brig. Gen. John, 3, 171, 205, 221, 371; criticized, 211; and relationship with Hancock, 213, 272; selected to command Eighteenth Corps, 213; and General Orders 63, 213–14; returns to Second Corps, 272; on leave, 595n54

Gibbon's division, 171–72; and destruction of Weldon Railroad, 174; strength of, 174; and Second Reams' Station, 185–86, 201, 203–4; and Fifth Offensive, 371

Gibson, Col. William, 136, 428, 518n92, 533n74

Gilbreath, Capt. Erasmus C., 54

Gilmer, Maj. Gen. Jeremy, 433

Girardey, Brig. Gen. Victor, 60; description of, 73; killed, 76, 518n92

Girardey's brigade, 60, 65, 72–73, 75–76, 83, 92, 110

Glendale crossroads, 59, 85

Globe Tavern (Yellow House), 95, 101, 108, 110, 116, 119, 123, 125–26, 139–41, 152, 156,

168–69, 171, 188, 191, 206, 366, 379, 388, 395, 522n12; Fifth Corps headquarters at, 223, 240; Battle of, 534n91

Goff, Cpl. William H., 464

Golden, Pvt. Charles B., 130

Goldsborough, Rear Admiral Louis M., 274

Goochland Artillery, 299–300, 316

Goode, Col. John T., 393

Goodwin, Cpl. William H., 463

Gordon, Maj. Gen. John B., 40

Gordon, Lt. William Alexander, 228

Gordonsville, Virginia, 220

Goree, Lt. Thomas Jewett, 161, 242, 244, 447

Goss, Capt. Enoch, 338

Grabill, Capt. Elliott F., 318

Gracie, Brig. Gen. Archibald, 425

Gracie's Brigade, 28, 227, 489

Gracie's Salient, 26, 227, 507n74; dam at, 546n58

Graham, Capt. Edward, 249, 343

Graham, Capt. Robert, 150

Graham, Col. Robert F., 494

Graham, Col. Samuel A., 100, 145

Graham's (Petersburg) Artillery, 523n19; and Beefsteak Raid, 249; and Sixth Offensive, 475

Grandy's (Virginia) Battery, 144

Granger, Lt. Henry H., 186–87, 191

Grant, Lt. Gen. Ulysses S., 1–2, 4, 22, 24, 31, 171; and Lincoln, 2; and Meade, 2, 92, 129, 164, 344–45, 367, 386; and First Offensive, 10; and Second Offensive, 10–11; and First Deep Bottom, 12; and Battle of the Crater, 13, 15, 17–18; ridiculed by Confederates, 17; and Burnside, 24; and City Point explosion, 35–37; meets with Lincoln at Fort Monroe, 38; and Sheridan's command in Shenandoah Valley, 38–39, 250, 266, 268, 555n50, 558n80; and Benjamin Butler, 41; and Dutch Gap Canal, 42; and concern for Shenandoah Valley, 45, 60, 92, 109, 134, 164, 278, 324, 342, 521n6, 556n62; and Second Deep Bottom, 60, 70, 82–83; and Battle of

Griffin's (Charles) division: and Battle of Weldon Railroad, 94–95, 97, 103, 141, 148, 153, 159, 162; and Fifth Offensive, 344, 349; attacks and captures Fort Archer, 351–52, 354–55; and Battle of Pegram's Farm, 357, 365; refaces Squirrel Level Line, 371; and Second Squirrel Level Road, 426; strength of, 466; and Sixth Offensive, 466, 468

Grimshaw, Col. Arthur, 388, 428

Grimshaw's brigade, 388–89

Grimsley, Mark, 41

Grindlay, Maj. James, 375

Grindlay's brigade, 378, 389

Griner, Cpl. Joseph A., 243

Griswold, Capt. Charles, 458

Griswold, Pvt. Edward, 241

Grover house, 53, 297

Guerrant, Lt. John, 300

Gurley house, 95, 167, 342, 349, 490, 522n10

Gurney, Pvt. Warren S., 18–19

Guy, Lt. Col. John, 289

Gwyn, Col. James, 102, 354; injured, 354–55

Gwyn's brigade: and Battle of Weldon Railroad, 102, 127, 532n64; and Fifth Offensive, 351; attacks Fort Archer, 352; casualties on September 30, 366; on October 1, 371

Hagar, William H., 406–7

Hagood, Col. James, 335–36, 339, 410, 416, 419, 421

Hagood, Brig. Gen. Johnson, 423, 532n62; and Battle of Weldon Railroad, 111, 135–36, 152–56; description of, 152, 160; as brother of James, 335

Hagood's (Johnson) Brigade, 337, 587n70; and Battle of Weldon Railroad, 136–37, 141, 146, 152, 154–56, 159; crosses the James, 328

Hale, Capt. Edward J., 196

Haley, Pvt. John W., 63, 82, 108, 229, 232, 234, 238, 243, 264, 271

Halifax Light Artillery, 299–300

Halifax Road, 95, 98, 123, 141, 143, 149, 174, 176–77, 182–84, 191–92, 345, 349, 369, 470, 522n12, 536n30

Hall, Capt. Delos E., 120

Hall, Cpl. Isaac, 132

Hall, Lt. John Elmore, 161, 328

Hall, Lt. Robert, 413

Halleck, Maj. Gen. Henry W., 2, 35, 37–39, 60, 131, 266, 425, 510n114

Hamil, Pvt. John, 81

Hamilton, Sgt. D. H., 293

Hamilton, Pvt. William, 493

Hamlin, Charles W., 243

Hammer, Sgt. Hezikiah, 323

Hammond, James Henry, 82

Hampton, Pvt. David A., 446, 464

Hampton, Thomas Preston, 483–84

Hampton, Maj. Gen. Wade, 8, 65, 68, 85; assumes command of Cavalry Corps, 167; description of, 167–68; and "Fight by Moonlight," 173; and Second Reams' Station, 179, 181–82, 186, 191, 202–3, 207; recommends new defensive line, 225; and Beefsteak Raid, 246–50, 252–53, 255, 257, 261, 263, 265; and fighting on September 29, 347; and Battle of Pegram's Farm, 358, 362; and Battle of Vaughan Road, 383–84; recommends strengthening line to Hatcher's Run, 450; informs Lee that line is completed, 453; confidence of troops, 455; builds dams on Hatcher's Run, 455, 480; asks Hill for help defending line, 455; and Sixth Offensive, 471–72, 484, 491, 597n80–81

Hampton, Wade, IV, 484, 598n90

Hampton Legion, 168, 287

Hampton Legion Cavalry, 44, 57, 59, 287, 296, 315, 412, 463, 589n97

Hampton Roads, 2, 274

Hampton's Division, 60, 511n8

Hancock, Maj. Gen. Winfield S., 1, 3, 221; description of, 3; and First Deep Bottom, 12; and court of inquiry, 23, 46; and Second Deep Bottom, 46–48, 52, 56, 60, 64, 67–68, 70, 76, 78, 82–84, 517n78; and destruction of Weldon Railroad, 174, 178; and Second Reams' Station, 179, 183, 185–86, 188–92, 198, 200–201, 205, 210–11; and relationship with Gibbon, 213–14; and Battle of the Chimneys, 236, 238; fears Confederate attack across Appomattox, 450; and Sixth Offensive, 470, 474–76, 481, 484, 486–87, 489–90, 493; and Gettysburg wound, 503n26

Hancock Station, 224, 378–79

Hanna, Pvt. Thomas M., 196

Hardaway, Lt. Col. Robert, 310

Hardaway (Alabama) Battery, 180, 224

Hare's Hill, 26–27, 31

Harman house and road, 571n58; Battle of, 579n65

Harney, Lt. Col. George, 102, 147

Harper, Pvt. Joseph H., 364

Harper, Samuel F., 209

Harpers Ferry, West Virginia, 266

Harriman, Col. Samuel, 357, 568n24

Harriman's brigade, 365, 371; on October 2, 388, 392–93

Harris, Engineer Fred, 28

Harris, Capt. James G., 195

Harris, Lt. Col. John L., 136, 143, 150

Harris, Capt. Merlin C., 301, 303

Harris, Brig. Gen. Nathaniel, 83, 85–86, 136, 393, 483

Harrison, Col. Randolph, 599n102

Harrison farm, 250, 552n9

Harris's Brigade, 83, 85, 110, 393; and Battle of the Chimneys, 237; and Sixth Offensive, 472, 480, 482–83

Hart, Capt. James F., 347, 471

Hart, Capt. Patrick, 146

Hart, Pvt. Walter Osgood, 199

Hartford, Connecticut, 304

Hart house, 390, 393, 578n57

Hartranft, Brig. Gen. John Frederick, 108, 389, 568n24; description of, 124; and Battle of Pegram's Farm, 363–64

Hartranft's brigade: and Battle of Weldon Railroad, 108, 124–29, 139–40, 159; and Battle of Pegram's Farm, 357, 363–66;

on October 1, 371; and Sixth Offensive, 466–67

Hart's Battery, 347, 471, 473, 475, 484, 541n102

Hartshorne, Col. William R., 98, 119

Hartshorne's brigade: and Battle of Weldon Railroad, 98, 113, 117, 119, 130, 140

Haseltine, Capt. John W., 59, 69

Haskell, Col. Alexander Cheves, 412–13, 416; wounded, 416–17

Haskell, Maj. John C., 424, 582n8

Haskell, Capt. Langdon Cheves, 200

Hatcher, Pvt. Edmond A., 68

Hatcher's Run, 181, 183, 345, 395, 429, 452–53, 455, 469–70, 474, 476, 481, 570n47

Hatton, Cpl. John William, 308

Hawkinsville, Virginia, 257, 259, 261, 553n30

Hawks farm, 466, 469

Hawley, Col. Joseph R., 35, 41, 79, 432; and Second Darbytown Road, 439, 441, 445

Hawley, Capt. William H., 186

Hawley's (Joseph) brigade: and Second Deep Bottom, 51, 53, 55, 70, 72, 74, 77–79; and Second Darbytown Road, 438, 440

Hawley's (Joseph) division: and Battle of Williamsburg Road, 456

Hayes, Brig. Gen. Joseph, 97–98, 116–17, 122, 131

Hayes's brigade: and Battle of Weldon Railroad, 97–102, 117–18, 127, 162

Heckman, Brig. Gen. Charles A., 272, 432, 586n66; description of, 305; and Battle of Fort Harrison, 306; assumes command of Eighteenth Corps, 310; orders Ripley to attack Fort Gilmer, 310, 312; orders Fairchild to attack Fort Johnson, 312; failures on September 29, 325; returns to command of his division, 329–30; and Battle of Williamsburg Road, 458

Heckman's division: and Fifth Offensive, 280, 283–84; and Battle of Fort Harrison, 306, 308, 310; and Battle of Fort Gilmer, 312

Heisler, Pvt. Henry Clay, 220

Henninghausen, Lt. Charles August, 401

Joy, Capt. Henry S., 210

Julian, Capt. George Naylor, 36, 341

Justice, Capt. Benjamin Wesley, 181, 199

Kautz, Brig. Gen. August V., 451; and Second Offensive, 11; and Beefsteak Raid, 248, 257–59, 261, 263, 265; and Fifth Offensive, 282; and First Darbytown Road, 411, 413, 415–17, 582n6; reports construction of Alexander Line, 434–35; and Second Darbytown Road, 436, 440, 443, 445; on sick leave, 458

Kautz's division, 40; and Battle of Weldon Railroad, 92; and Beefsteak Raid, 248; and Fifth Offensive, 280, 284, 308; attempts to find Confederate left flank on September 29, 315, 324; deployment of, September 30, 330; deployment of, October 1, 397; and Battle of Roper's Farm, 398, 401; and First Darbytown Road, 410; loses all eight cannons, 416, 583n19; casualties at Darbytown Road, 417; and Second Darbytown Road, 435, 438, 444; and plans for Sixth Offensive, 454

Keech, Sgt. James, 417

Keene, Capt. Weston H., 579n71

Kell house, 458

Kelly, Pvt. Dave, 47

Kelly, Capt. William Aiken, 81

Kendall, Pvt. Austin J., 19

Kensel, Lt. Col. George, 434–35, 587n71

Kent, Capt. Daniel H., 428

Kent, Capt. William L., 303

Kenyon, Sgt. Alfred, 255

Kernstown, battles of, 38, 556n61

Kershaw, Maj. Gen. Joseph B., 40

Kershaw's Division: and Shenandoah Valley, 266, 270

Kerwin, Col. Michael, 66, 69, 471

Kerwin's brigade: and Sixth Offensive, 471, 487–88

Kessler, Pvt. Thomas J., 22

Kiddoo, Col. Joseph B., 462–63, 593n39

Kieffer, Henry M., 477

King, Col. J. Horace, 147, 472

King's brigade: and Sixth Offensive, 472, 480, 482, 484, 597n85

Kingsland Road, 53, 60, 290–91, 294, 296–97, 308, 330

Kirkland, Brig. Gen. William, 136, 197; assumes command of Martin's Brigade, 241, 529n15

Kirkland's brigade, 137, 143, 337, 531n52, 587n70; crosses the James, 328

Kirkpatrick, Sgt. James J., 28

Kitching, Col. J. Howard, 21

Kleinz, Lt. Col. Christopher, 415

Kline, Lt. Charles, 20

Knowles, Maj. Oliver B., 487

Knox, Lt. Andrew, 269, 395

Ladd, Sgt. John C., 333

Lamont, Pvt. William, 450

LaMotte, Lt. Col. Charles E., 101, 148, 395

Lane, David, 240

Lane, Brig. Gen. James, 44, 73, 210, 361, 367; on soldiers collecting shell fragments, 394–95; on stripping Union corpses, 395

Lane, Rooker, 367

Lane's Brigade, 44, 85, 226, 468–69, 567n9, 571n53; returns to south side, 87, 138; and Second Reams' Station, 180, 208–9; and Battle of Pegram's Farm, 358, 360, 362–64, 367, 574n104; on October 1, 374, 377; withdraws to Battery 45, 386

Lang, Col. David, 146

Langley, Lt. Col. Francis, 83

Lanier house, 139

Lanneau, Lt. John F., 249–50, 252, 259

Larkin, Maj. James E., 200

Laurel (Rosser's) Brigade, 169; and "Fight by Moonlight," 172; and Second Reams' Station, 182, 202; and Beefsteak Raid, 249–50, 252–54, 257, 260; sent to Shenandoah Valley, 270

Laurel Hill Methodist Church, 297, 313; battle at, 314–15

Laurel Springs, 252

Law, Brig. Gen. Evander M., 44

Lawyer's Road, 252–53, 256–57

Longstreet, Lt. Gen. James, 161; description and wounding of, 6; present at Second Darbytown Road, 588n85; resumes command of First Corps, 447; deployment of his forces, 456; shifts Field and Hoke to cover Williamsburg Road, 459; orders Gary to cover Nine Mile Road, 459

Louisiana Guard Artillery, 313, 317

Lower Church (Wyatt) Road, 168, 345, 380–81, 470

Lowther, Col. Alexander A., 79

Ludwick, Maj. Ephraim A., 315

Lunenburg Artillery, 299–300, 310

Lyle, Capt. Joseph Banks, 445, 461, 593n32

Lyle, Col. Peter, 98

Lyle's (Peter) brigade: and Battle of Weldon Railroad, 98–102, 108, 117–18, 121, 140, 162

Lyman, Lt. Col. Theodore, 5, 28, 35, 109–10, 212, 310, 358, 392; on Sheridan, 39; on Dutch Gap Canal, 42; on David Birney, 51; on Francis Barlow, 55; on Globe Tavern, 95; on Julius White, 125; on events of August 19, 116, 132; on Hancock's corps, 144, 211; on Ord, 280; on fighting on October 1, 376–77, 379, 402; on Potter, 379; on Crawford, 425; and visit of dignitaries, 448; on painting of Meade, 449; and secrecy in army, 454; under fire, 476; on Sixth Offensive, 493–94; on residents of Aiken house, 571n56

Lynch, Col. James C., 172, 199; resumes command of Miles's brigade, 175

Lynch's brigade: and Second Reams' Station, 183–84, 196, 199

Lyon, Capt. James W., 282

Mabry, Pvt. Robert C., 161

MacDougall, Col. Clinton, 489

MacRae, Brig. Gen. William, 136; description of, 180, 197; and Second Reams' Station, 196–97; on October 1, 375; and Sixth Offensive, 486–87

MacRae's Brigade, 241, 469; and Battle of Weldon Railroad, 137, 143, 149–51; and Second Reams' Station, 180–81, 193, 195–98, 200, 208–9; and Battle of Pegram's

Farm, 358, 360–64, 367; on October 1, 374–76; withdraws to Battery 45, 386; combat on October 2, 390, 393; and Sixth Offensive, 480–82, 484, 597n85

Macy, Col. George N., 47; description of, 57; brevetted, 58; injured, 58; replaced by Lt. Col. Horace P. Rugg, 515n44

Macy's brigade: and Second Deep Bottom, 55, 57–58, 60

Mahone, Brig./Maj. Gen. William, 73, 261, 393–94; and Second Offensive, 11; and Battle of the Crater, 14, 17; promoted to major general, 17; and Battle of Weldon Railroad, 110–12, 126, 133–34, 137–38, 141, 145–46, 152–53, 156, 165, 523n22, 525n60; and Second Reams' Station, 210; description of, 472, 595n61; and Sixth Offensive, 472–73, 480–82, 487, 491–92, 597n84

Mahone's Division, 60, 83, 91, 330; at Battle of the Crater, 14; and Battle of Weldon Railroad, 95, 105, 118–19, 137; and Second Reams' Station, 181, 183; and Fifth Offensive, 344, 348, 369–70; and Sixth Offensive, 472, 480, 482–83

Maitland, Maj. John B., 66

Malone's Bridge, 182–83, 347

Malone's Crossing, 176–78, 182, 184, 188, 202, 471, 536n28

Malone's Road, 182

Maloney, Capt. P. K., 154, 532n66

Malvern Hill, 59, 232

Manson, Lt. James B., 245

Marckres, Pvt. Harvey A., 11

Marshall, Capt. Henry Grimes, 319

Marston, Brig. Gen. Gilman, 281, 284, 432; and Battle of Williamsburg Road, 458, 460, 593n29

Martin, Lt. Ben, 154

Martin, Col. John Marshall, 245

Martin, Pvt. William, 210

Martin, Lt. Col. William J., 362

Martin's Brigade, 529n15

Maryland Brigade, 258, 578n55; and Battle of Weldon Railroad, 98–103, 117, 139–40, 145–46; and Sixth Offensive, 468, 477

Mason, Lt. Wiley, Jr., 77–78, 518n96

Meade, Maj. Gen. George G.,(*continued*)
summarizes events on September 30,
366; orders Warren and Parke to recon-
noiter on October 1, 366–67, 370; orders
Second Corps to reinforce Warren and
Parke, October 1, 370, 374, 379; wants to
attack on October 1, 379; distrust of Warren, 379, 529n10, 571n59; whereabouts on
October 1, 379; orders attack on
October 2, 379–80; and Battle of
Vaughan Road, 385; attack plans for
October 2, 386; cancels attack plans on
October 2, 388–89; struck by an artillery
round, 391–92; reports action on October 2, 394; orders a reconnaissance on
October 8, 425, 427; entertains Stanton
and other dignitaries, 448; reports quiet
conditions at Petersburg, 449; develops
plans for Sixth Offensive, 451; issues
orders for Sixth Offensive, 451–52; and
newspaper reports, 455; and Sixth Of-
fensive, 469, 473, 475–77, 489–90, 493;
orders Miles to attack on October 27, 488
Medal of Honor, 118, 296, 304–5, 561n24,
577n39, 586n66
Meigs, Q. M. General Montgomery, 223,
590n109
Meikel, Lt. Col. George: and Battle of the
Chimneys, 236–38
Melton, Lt. Col. Samuel W., 17, 492
Merchant's Island, 370, 528n112
Merriam, Sgt. Maj. Leander O., 18, 351,
361, 371
Merrill, Surgeon Charles G., 218, 273
Metcalf, Lt. Richard, 481–82, 484
Methvin, Pvt. John Francis, 321–22
Metzger, Cpl. Henry C., 175, 179
Michie, Lt. Peter S., 42, 281, 405
Michler, Maj. Nathaniel, 216, 221, 430, 470,
544n26
Middle Military Division, 39, 266
Miles, Brig. Gen. Nelson A., 1, 68, 169;
and "Fight by Moonlight," 173; resumes
command of Barlow's division, 175; and
Second Reams' Station, 196, 198–200,

205, 215; and attacks on October 27, 489;
and Sixth Offensive, 494
Miles's brigade: and Second Deep Bottom,
55–56, 64, 67–69, 78, 80, 82, 85; and
Second Reams' Station, 172
Miles's (Barlow's) division, 470; and de-
struction of Weldon Railroad, 171–72,
175; and Second Reams' Station, 193; and
Fifth Offensive, 371; attacks on October
27, 488–89
military (Confederate) road, 225, 345–47
Miller, Lt. Col. Lovick, 249–50, 252–53, 260
Miller, Pvt. William J., 229
Mill Road, 52, 288, 312, 314, 319–20, 324, 403
Mills, Capt. Charles J., 19, 241, 271, 493
Milton, Lt. Richard, 120
mining operations, 25–32, 430, 507n74,
508n81, 546n59, 586n59
Mink, Capt. Charles E., 428
Minor, Sgt. Charles N. B., 271, 567n1
Minton, Pvt. Thomas M., 195
Missionary Ridge, Battle of, 5, 245
Miss Pegram's, 349, 355, 571n55
Mitchell, Pvt. James, 204
Mitchell, Capt./Commodore John Kirk-
wood, 398; description of, 275
Mitchell, Maj. William G., 48–49, 69, 84,
190, 484, 486
Mobile, Alabama, 2, 47
Mobile Bay, Battle of, 241–42, 275, 495
Moffett, Adj. George H., 160, 446
Moffitt, Lt. Col. Stephen: commands Burn-
ham's brigade, 334
Monks, Sgt. Zerah Coston, 165, 219
Monk's Neck Bridge, 172, 179, 181–82, 187,
471, 535n15, 570n47
Monocacy Junction, Maryland, 39
Monroe, Lt. Col. John A., 349
Montague, Col. Edgar B., 313, 324; recap-
tures Fort Hoke and Diagonal Line, 325;
probes on October 2, 404; and First Dar-
bytown Road, 410; returns to Bermuda
Hundred, 433
Montague, Lt. Harrison, 19
Moore, Maj. James B., 303–4

Moore, Surgeon James Otis, 34
Moore, Pvt. Thomas, 298
Moore's Swamp, 251
Morgan, Lt. Col. Michael R., 35, 263, 265
Mosely, Surgeon William J., 344, 394
Mott, Brig. Gen. Gershom, 3, 540n76; and
    Second Deep Bottom, 46, 49, 82; and
    Battle of the Chimneys, 236, 238; on
    leave, 429; and Sixth Offensive, 481, 486
Mott's division: and Second Deep Bottom,
    48, 52, 54, 60; departs north side, 86, 104,
    108; relieves Ninth Corps, 109; and Battle
    of Weldon Railroad, 115, 139; moves to
    reinforce Warren and Parke, October
    1, 370–71, 378–79, 576n25; on October
    2, 387; and Sixth Offensive, 470, 472,
    474–75, 490
Mount Sinai Church, 257–58
Mount Washington (steamer), 82
Mulholland, Col. St. Clair A., 198, 488
Mulholland's brigade, 488
Mullen, Cpl. Joseph, 195–96, 376, 390
Mulligan, Capt. A.B., 227
Munroe, Sgt. David S., 125
Murfreesboro, Battle of, 5
Murphy, Col. Mathew, 55, 204
Murphy's brigade, 55, 57; and march to
    Reams' Station, 174; at Reams' Station,
    177; and Second Reams' Station, 183, 187,
    199, 201, 204
Murray, Lt. Amos W., 340

Nashville, Tennessee, 2
Neblett's millpond, 261
Neel, Pvt. William S., 286
Nelson (Virginia) Artillery, 331, 567n4
Nesbitt, Pvt. Harrison, 424
New Bern, North Carolina, 272
New Market, Battle of, 37
New Market Heights, 43, 65, 78, 82, 289;
    Battle of, 290–97, 302, 446, 560n12,
    560n15, 561n24
New Market Line, 289, 295–96, 300, 307–8,
    403; strength of defenders of, 560n9
New Market Road, 288–89, 297, 308–9, 314,
324, 330, 398, 401, 403, 416–18, 433, 559n7;
    and First Deep Bottom, 12; and Second
    Deep Bottom, 52, 54, 59, 61–62, 67; and
    Battle of New Market Heights, 291, 295,
    297
New Orleans, Louisiana, 275
Newville, Virginia, 257, 261, 553n25
Nichols, Capt. James M., 87, 223
Nine Mile Road, 459, 462, 559n7
Nineteenth Corps, 39–40
Nineteenth Indiana, 113, 115
Nineteenth Maine, 57, 201, 220, 595n60
Nineteenth Massachusetts, 177, 201, 204,
    473, 598n89
Nineteenth Pennsylvania, 100
Nineteenth U.S. Colored Troops (USCT),
    14, 220, 225
Nineteenth Virginia, 16, 83
Nineteenth Virginia Battalion of Heavy
    Artillery, 246
Nineteenth Wisconsin, 20, 431, 460–61
Ninety-Eighth New York, 340, 455
Ninety-First Pennsylvania, 19, 365
Ninety-Fourth New York, 230
Ninety-Ninth Pennsylvania, 486; and Battle
    of the Chimneys, 236–38
Ninety-Seventh New York, 101, 120–21, 128,
    132
Ninety-Seventh Pennsylvania, 80
Ninety-Sixth New York, 298, 301, 304–5, 338
Ninety-Third New York, 481–82, 486
Ninth Alabama, 65, 147
Ninth Corps (Burnside/Parke), 2, 4; as
    outsiders to the Army of the Potomac,
    574n106; and Battle of the Crater, 12–14;
    criticized, 19, 368; and Battle of Weldon
    Railroad, 91, 103–4, 109, 123, 131, 140, 164;
    and Fifth Offensive, 342, 350, 355–56, 370;
    strength of, 452; and Sixth Offensive,
    452, 469, 477
Ninth Florida, 245
Ninth Georgia, 72, 76, 78, 81, 517n82
Ninth Maine, 465
Ninth Massachusetts Battery, 120, 145
Ninth New Hampshire, 235, 573n84, 579n71

Randall, Alexander W., 214, 544n20

Ransom, Brig. Gen. Matt, 529n14; resumes command of his brigade, 430

Ransom's (Harris's) Brigade, 136–37, 143, 149–51, 159, 227

Raulston, Lt. Col. John B., 302, 459, 574n95

Raulston, Col. William C., 364, 574n95

Raulston's (John B.) brigade, 333; and battle at Fort Harrison, 335; and Battle of Williamsburg Road, 459–60

Rawle, Capt. William Brooke, 23, 216, 243

Rawlings, Pvt. James, 433

Rawlins, Brig. Gen. John A., 431, 475; criticizes Benjamin Butler, 494

Ray, Sgt. William R., 141, 148

Reagan, Postmaster General John, 429

Reams' Station, 108, 156, 169, 171, 345; First Battle of, 11, 175; occupation of August 23, 172; origin of name, 175; fortifications at, 176–77; destruction of, 177–78; Second Battle of, casualties, 207, 215, 543n17; aftermath, 208; analysis of, 208–12, 215

Reardon, Sgt. John, 79

Reed, Pvt. George W., 549n96

Reedy Branch, 381

Redoubt E, 549n88

Redoubt G, 26, 221

Rees, Pvt. Frederick, 365

Reese, Lt. George, 320

Reid, Pvt. William Moultrie, 445

Requa Guns, 420, 422

Reynolds, Lt. Tilton C., 79, 232, 243

Rice, Lt. William D., 579n71

Rice's Turnout, 328

Rich, Cpl. Alonzo, 20

Richards, Capt. William V., 124, 132

Richardson, Sgt. Brinkly J., 151

Richardson, Pvt. Elbert R., 151

Richardson, Capt. Nathaniel A., 250, 255, 265

Richmond, Virginia, 2, 8, 83; reaction to Fifth Offensive, 307–8, 327

Richmond, Lt. William H., 314, 317

Richmond & Danville Railroad, 91, 163, 210, 239, 503n27

Richmond & Petersburg Railroad, 65, 90, 156, 328

Richmond Fayette Artillery, 567n4

Riley, Pvt. Franklin L., 245

Ripley, Col. Edward H., 272, 280–81, 283, 307, 431; description of, 306; wounded, 306

Ripley, Sgt. Samuel, 57

Ripley's brigade, 306, 310, 312; attacks Fort Johnson, 312–13; and Battle of Williamsburg Road, 458, 460

Risden's sawmill, 526n68

Risley, Capt. Douglas G., 319

Rives Salient, 31, 110, 227, 236, 489

Roberts, Pvt. Jacob M., 235

Roberts, Col. Samuel H.: description of, 301; and Battle of Fort Harrison, 302–3, 305

Roberts, Col. William P., 68, 202, 347

Robertson, Lt. Francis Smith, 552n7

Roberts's brigade, 302, 309

Robins, Col. William T., 463

Robinson, Lt. Col. Gilbert P., 126

Robinson, Brig. Gen. John C., 4, 502n9

Robinson, Lt. Oscar D., 235

Robison, Lt. Col. John K., 239

Robuck, Pvt. William P., 147

Roche, Pvt. Thomas T., 143, 147–48

Rockett's Landing, 308

Rockwell, Col. Alfred P., 400, 445

Rodes, Maj. Gen. Robert E., 40

Roebling, Maj. Washington A., 106–7, 113, 118, 124, 128, 144–45, 159, 212; on ceremony of September 13, 240; and Sixth Offensive, 470, 478, 480, 490

Rogers, Capt. Chauncey P., 354

Rogers, Col. George T., 207

Rogers, Sgt. Stephen, 140, 271

Rohoic Creek, 227; dam at, 546n58

Root, Sgt. Samuel H., 85

Roper, Benjamin, 400

Roper, James, 400

Roper's Farm, Battle of, 400–402

Rose, Luther A., 269

Ross, Capt. Hugh M., 180

Second Virginia Reserve Battalion, 289, 300, 401

Second Wisconsin, 154

Seddon, James A., 163, 165, 209, 407–8, 445; efforts to increase army, 448

Sedgwick, Maj. Gen. John, 4

Seldon, Pvt. Cary, 255

Seven Pines Battlefield, 459

Seventeenth Georgia, 289, 299–300, 303, 309–10, 322

Seventeenth Maine, 63, 108, 243, 264, 486

Seventeenth Michigan, 30, 35, 240

Seventeenth New York Battery, 244, 451

Seventeenth North Carolina, 245, 269

Seventeenth South Carolina, 16, 492

Seventeenth Tennessee, 297

Seventeenth U.S. Infantry, 20, 375

Seventeenth Vermont, 579n71

Seventeenth Virginia, 273

Seventh Confederate Cavalry, 95, 343, 352, 354, 476

Seventh Connecticut, 62, 74, 290, 296, 400, 418, 420, 438

Seventh Georgia, 80

Seventh Indiana, 106, 113, 115–16, 140

Seventh Michigan, 82, 186–87, 202, 239, 490, 598n89

Seventh New Hampshire, 77–78, 400, 432, 438

Seventh New York, 184, 197–98

Seventh New York Heavy Artillery, 171, 177, 190, 197

Seventh North Carolina, 195, 367

Seventh Rhode Island, 162, 351–52, 362, 365

Seventh South Carolina Battalion, 152–53, 155

Seventh South Carolina Cavalry, 44, 56–57, 287, 289–90, 296, 315, 412, 415, 462–63

Seventh Texas, 422

Seventh U.S. Colored Troops (USCT), 87, 232, 464; and Second Deep Bottom, 59–60, 62, 64; and attack at Fort Gilmer, 319–22

Seventh Virginia Cavalry, 182, 206, 254–55, 541n102

Seventh West Virginia, 470

Seventh Wisconsin, 27, 113, 115, 140–41, 477

Seventy-Sixth New York, 22, 156, 241, 449

Shadburne, Sgt. George D.: description of, 247; and Beefsteak Raid, 248–50, 252–55, 257, 265

Shank, Pvt. Joseph, 262, 433

Sharon Baptist Church, 570n48

Shaw, Col. James, 320, 322, 458

Shaw's brigade: and Battle of Williamsburg Road, 458

Shay's Tavern, 192, 205

Shay's Tavern Road, 174, 176, 192

Shenandoah Valley, 2, 4, 495; and Third Offensive, 12; campaign in, 37–41; as a source of supply, 210; battles in, 266, 268; Union reaction to victories in, 268–69, 271–72; Confederate reaction to losses in, 268–70; importance of, 556n62; burning of, 581n93

Shepherd, Col. William S., 310, 313

Sheridan, Maj. Gen. Philip H., 8; description of, 5; and First Deep Bottom, 12; takes command in Shenandoah Valley, 38–39; victories in Shenandoah Valley, 266, 268; praise of, 271–72

Sherman, Lt. George R., 322

Sherman, Pvt. Henry W., 145

Sherman, Maj. Gen. William T., 2, 97; and Atlanta Campaign, 242, 495

Shurtleff, Lt. Col. Giles W., 295

Sickel, Col. Horatio G.: description of, 352

Sickel's brigade, 352, 371

Siebert, Lt. Jacob E., 579n71

Sigel, Maj. Gen. Franz, 2, 37

Signal Hill, 82–83, 273, 289, 300, 405, 557n67

Sikes, Maj. Jesse H., 352, 354

Sixteenth Maine, 98, 100

Sixteenth Michigan, 156, 352, 354

Sixteenth Mississippi. 28, 137, 143, 148, 245

Sixteenth New York Battery, 591n13

Sixteenth New York Heavy Artillery, 400, 420–21, 424, 438

Sixteenth Pennsylvania Cavalry, 36, 66–67, 173, 186–87, 204, 206, 239, 260, 345

Tenth Georgia Battalion, 344

Tenth Massachusetts (Sleeper's) Battery, 174, 355; at Reams' Station, 177; and Second Reams' Station, 186–87, 192, 198, 200–201, 208; and Sixth Offensive, 481, 486

Tenth New Hampshire, 283, 297, 336, 459

Tenth New York, 186, 201–2, 481

Tenth New York Cavalry, 382

Tenth New York Heavy Artillery, 19

Tenth U.S. Colored Troops (USCT), 290

Tenth U.S. Infantry, 375

Tenth Virginia Cavalry, 66–67, 257, 362, 384

Terrell, Lt. Col. Leigh R., 443, 589n96

Terry, Brig. Gen. Alfred H., 19; and Second Deep Bottom, 53, 70, 73–75, 77; and Battle of Roper's Farm, 400–401; assumes command of Tenth Corps, 405; and First Darbytown Road, 417; and Second Darbytown Road, 435–36, 439–40, 444–45; and Battle of Williamsburg Road, 456, 592n19

Terry, Lt. Col. Ira, 463

Terry's (Alfred H.) division: at Second Deep Bottom, 51, 70; and Fifth Offensive, 280, 283, 290, 315, 324; and Battle of Roper's Farm, 398, 400–402; and First Darbytown Road, 424; and Battle of Williamsburg Road, 458; and Second Darbytown Road, 587n72

Texas (Gregg's) Brigade, 44, 584–85n39; strength of, 288; and Second Deep Bottom, 61, 65, 68; after Second Deep Bottom, 87; defends New Market Line, 289–90, 292; abandons New Market Line, 296, 310; defends Intermediate Line, 309, 316; performance on September 29, 325–26; on September 30, 331; and First Darbytown Road, 412, 419, 421–23; and Gregg's funeral, 429; and Second Darbytown Road, 436, 439, 587n70, 587n75; and Battle of Williamsburg Road, 459–61

Thieman, Lt. August, 527n88

Third Arkansas, 288–90, 293, 295, 316, 461

Third Corps (Confederate, Hill), 8, 43

Third Delaware, 153, 388, 549n96

Third Georgia, 73, 208, 244

Third Indiana, 465

Third Massachusetts Battery, 523n19

Third Michigan, 46

Third New Hampshire, 62, 70, 296, 400, 420, 438, 441, 464, 592n20

Third New York, 314, 465

Third New York Cavalry, 95, 210, 253, 256–59, 413, 415, 521n7

Third North Carolina Cavalry, 156, 387, 574n96

Third Pennsylvania Cavalry, 23

Third Petersburg Offensive, 12

Third (Company) Richmond Howitzers, 54, 56, 289, 297, 310, 313–15, 322, 434

Third Virginia, 138, 235

Thirteenth New Hampshire, 33, 36, 301–2, 304, 329, 335, 338, 341, 459

Thirteenth Ohio Cavalry, 220

Thirteenth Pennsylvania Cavalry, 59, 63, 66, 184, 250, 254, 263, 347, 430

Thirteenth South Carolina, 368

Thirteenth Virginia Cavalry, 66–67, 574n96; and Battle of Vaughan Road, 383

Thirty-Eighth U.S. Colored Troops (USCT), 294

Thirty-Fifth Massachusetts, 16, 18, 144, 361, 363

Thirty-Fifth North Carolina, 150

Thirty-Fifth Virginia (Cavalry) Battalion (the Comanches), 255, 257, 259, 537n44

Thirty-First Maine, 18, 351

Thirty-First North Carolina, 338

Thirty-Fourth New York Battery, 365

Thirty-Fourth Virginia, 234, 489

Thirty-Ninth Illinois, 62, 75, 438, 441–42, 444

Thirty-Ninth Massachusetts, 98–100, 118, 121, 123, 134, 140, 151, 221

Thirty-Ninth New York, 198

Thirty-Second Massachusetts, 19, 94–95

Thirty-Second Virginia, 313

Walter, Sgt. Thomas F., 19

Walters, Pvt. John H., 31, 144, 236, 245, 270

Ward, Capt. Henry, 463

Ward, Cpl. Joseph R., 444

Ware, Sgt. Edwin, 302

Ware Bottom Church, 182

Waring, Lt. Col. Joseph Frederick, 263

Warner, Lt. Col. Clement E., 199

Warren, Maj. Gen. Gouverneur K. 18, 26, 168–69; description of, 3–4; relationship with Meade, 4, 385; and Battle of Weldon Railroad, 91, 94, 97–98, 101–3, 106–9, 119, 125, 128, 131–33, 135, 139, 143–45, 157–58, 164; command tendencies of, 158, 385; praised, 158–59; and "Fight by Moonlight," 173; and Second Reams' Station, 178–79; orders forts named, 221; and ceremony, September 13, 240; and Beefsteak Raid, 258, 265; and march on September 30, 350; reports capture of Fort Archer, 355; delays in follow-up to capture of Fort Archer, 356–57; prepares works September 30, 365–66; on October 1, 374, 378; tentative generalship of, 387–88, 571n59; takes leave, 425; and Sixth Offensive, 468, 478, 490; orders horseracing stopped, 590n1; confidence in Charles Griffin, 594n48

Warren Station, 224

Warthen, Lt. George, 337

Washington Artillery, 227

Watkins farm, 466

Watson, Sgt. George W., 254

Watson, Samuel S., 295

Weaver, Capt. James F., 188

Webb, Sgt. Nathan, 59, 66, 222

Webb, Pvt. William, 230

Weisiger, Brig. Gen. David A., 110, 126–27, 133

Weisiger's Brigade, 110–12, 119, 123, 126–27, 134, 136; and Second Reams' Station, 180, 193, 203; and Sixth Offensive, 472, 480, 482, 486–87, 597n85

Weiss, Capt. Julius A., 320–22

Weitzel, Brig. Gen. Godfrey: assumes command of Eighteenth Corps, 329–30; description of, 330, 567n8; on October 7, 418; and Battle of Williamsburg Road, 459–60, 494, 592n23, 593n27; praises Kiddoo, 463

Welch, Col. Norval E., 352, 579n71; description of, 354; killed, 354

Welch, Stephen, 463

Welch, Pvt. William, 416

Weld, Capt. Lewis L., 59

Weldon, North Carolina, 90

Weldon Railroad, 11, 45, 60, 85, 90; destruction of, 97, 169, 171

Weldon Railroad, Battle of: analysis of, 131–34, 159–64; casualties, 159, 162–63; as turning point, 163

Welles, Gideon, 18, 275–76

Wells, Pvt. Edward L., 492

Wells, Lt. Henry D., 244–45

Welsh, Sgt. Maj. Erwin, 445

Welsh, Cpl. John, 212

Wentz, Maj. Erasmus, 223–24

West, Col. Robert M., 400; and First Darbytown Road, 411, 413, 415; leads Kautz's division at Battle of Williamsburg Road, 458

Western Gulf Blockading Squadron, 276

Westervelt, Pvt. John H., 334

West's brigade, 400; and First Darbytown Road, 410, 413, 415, 438

Wetherill, Maj. Samuel, 256

Weygant, Capt. Charles, 63

Wheaton, Capt. James H., 579n71

Wheelock, Col. Charles, 101–2, 120, 549n92

Wheelock's (Coulter's) brigade: and Battle of Weldon Railroad, 101, 117–18, 120–21, 140

White, Capt. Ansell, 89

White, Lt. Col. Elijah, 255, 259

White, Lt. J. Chester, 122

White, Brig. Gen. Julius, 109, 126, 131, 525n52, 528n99; description of, 125; relieved of duty, 241

White, Sgt. Wyman S., 47, 232, 243

White Oak Road, 262, 470–71, 473, 475–77, 481–83, 486

White Oak Swamp, 59, 69, 456, 459

White's division, 109, 125–26, 134, 139–40, 144, 206; abolished, 241

White's farm, 157

White's Tavern, 67–68, 410, 458

Whiting, Maj. Gen. W. H. C., 277, 430

Whitman, Capt. George W., 239

Wickes, Capt. James H., 235, 292

Wiedrich, Lt. Col. Michael, 101

Wightman, Sgt. Edward King, 314, 317, 465

Wilcox, Maj. Gen. Cadmus M., 44; and Second Reams' Station, 182, 189–90, 192–93, 196, 210, 258; and Battle of Pegram's Farm, 358; on October 1, 370, 374, 377

Wilcox's Division, 138, 330; and Second Deep Bottom, 54; and Second Reams' Station, 180–81, 187, 191; and Fifth Offensive, 344; and Battle of Pegram's Farm, 360; on October 1, 377; strength of, 511n4

Wilderness, Battle of the, 57, 422

Wiley, Capt. Daniel D., 36

Wilkerson, Pvt. James King, 376

Wilkinson house, 349, 381–82, 577n40

Wilkinson's Bridge, 249–51, 261

Willcox, Brig. Gen. Orlando B., 5, 19–20, 24, 379, 393; in temporary command of Ninth Corps, 91; and Battle of Weldon Railroad, 124, 126, 134; and Second Reams' Station, 205

Willcox's division, 13; and Battle of Weldon Railroad, 105, 107–8, 123–24, 132, 140, 144, 151, 162–63; and Second Reams' Station, 191, 205; reorganized, 241; and Fifth Offensive, 344, 349, 352, 387–89, 571n56; casualties at Pegram's Farm, 366; and Second Squirrel Level Road, 426, 428; and Sixth Offensive, 465–66, 469

Williams, Capt. Watson D., 461

Williamsburg Road, 401, 454, 559n7; casualties at Battle of, 465, 594n45

Williamsburg, Virginia, 3

Williams house, 106, 110, 125, 205

Willett, Col. James M., 470, 474

Willett's brigade: and Sixth Offensive, 470, 473–74, 476, 481

Wilmington, North Carolina, 90, 209, 239, 275–76, 430, 557n72

Wilmington & Weldon Railroad, 90

Willoughby, Pvt. William, 85

Wilson, Brig. Gen. James H., 5, 52; and Second Offensive, 11; sent to command Sherman's cavalry, 425

Wilson, Pvt. Samuel E., 387

Wilson's brigade, 40

Winchester, Third Battle of, 266, 268

Windmill Point, 48

Wingard, Pvt. Simon P., 421

Winkler, Lt. Col. Clinton M., 295, 461; assumes command of Texas Brigade, 423

Winthrop, Col. Frederick, 103, 122, 127, 140

Wisconsin Independent Battalion, 154

Wise, Brig. Gen. Henry A., 16

Wise, Lt. Col. Peyton, 599n102

Wise's Brigade, 393

Wood, Pvt. Alfred, 145

Wood, John L.G., 25

Woodbury, Augustus, 25

Wooten, Maj. Thomas J., 236, 358–59, 377

Wright, Brig. Gen. Ambrose "Rans," 518n84

Wright, Lt. Benjamin, 243, 411, 445

Wright, Col. Gilbert J., 168, 203–4

Wright, Maj. Gen. Horatio G.; description of, 4; and Second Offensive, 11

Wright, John, home of, 113

Wright's (Gibson's) Brigade, 73, 136–37, 428, 531n43

Wright's (Gilbert) Brigade, 182, 202–3

Wyatt's (house), 156, 169, 345, 347

Wyatt's Farm, Battle of, 347

Yardley, Lt. Eldridge T., 428

Yates, Sgt. George W., 441–42

Yorktown, Virginia, 544n34

Young, Capt. Henry Falls, 27

Young, Maj. John D., 187

Young, Capt. Louis G., 149, 197

Young, Brig. Gen. Pierce M. B., 168, 355, 491; description of, 382; and Battle of Vaughan Road, 382; returns to brigade command, 430

Young's Brigade, 168, 247; and Beefsteak Raid, 249, 258; and Fifth Offensive, 347, 380–81; and Battle of Vaughan Road, 382; and Sixth Offensive, 471, 483

Youngs, Cpl. George S., 23

Zimmerman, Pvt. John R., 262–63

Zinn, Lt. Col. George, 392–93